M000249412

WEST ACADEMIC PUBLISHING'S
EMERITUS ADVISORY BOARD

JESSE H. CHOPER
Professor of Law and Dean Emeritus
University of California, Berkeley

LARRY D. KRAMER
President, William and Flora Hewlett Foundation

JAMES J. WHITE
Robert A. Sullivan Emeritus Professor of Law
University of Michigan

WEST ACADEMIC PUBLISHING'S
LAW SCHOOL ADVISORY BOARD

MARK C. ALEXANDER
Arthur J. Kania Dean and Professor of Law
Villanova University Charles Widger School of Law

JOSHUA DRESSLER
Distinguished University Professor Emeritus
Michael E. Moritz College of Law, The Ohio State University

MEREDITH J. DUNCAN
Professor of Law
University of Houston Law Center

RENÉE McDONALD HUTCHINS
Dean & Professor of Law
University of Maryland Carey School of Law

RENEE KNAKE JEFFERSON
Joanne and Larry Doherty Chair in Legal Ethics &
Professor of Law, University of Houston Law Center

ORIN S. KERR
William G. Simon Professor of Law
University of California, Berkeley

JONATHAN R. MACEY
Professor of Law,
Yale Law School

DEBORAH JONES MERRITT
Distinguished University Professor,
John Deaver Drinko/Baker & Hostetler Chair in Law Emerita
Michael E. Moritz College of Law, The Ohio State University

ARTHUR R. MILLER
University Professor and Chief Justice Warren E. Burger Professor of
Constitutional Law and the Courts, New York University

GRANT S. NELSON
Professor of Law Emeritus, Pepperdine University
Professor of Law Emeritus, University of California, Los Angeles

A. BENJAMIN SPENCER
Dean & Trustee Professor of Law
William & Mary Law School

INTRODUCTION TO AMERICAN CONSTITUTIONAL LAW

STRUCTURE AND RIGHTS

Third Edition

■ ■ ■

William Funk

Lewis & Clark Distinguished Professor of Law Emeritus
Lewis & Clark Law School

AMERICAN CASEBOOK SERIES®

WEST
ACADEMIC
PUBLISHING

The publisher is not engaged in rendering legal or other professional advice, and this publication is not a substitute for the advice of an attorney. If you require legal or other expert advice, you should seek the services of a competent attorney or other professional.

American Casebook Series is a trademark registered in the U.S. Patent and Trademark Office.

© 2014, 2020 LEG, Inc. d/b/a West Academic
© 2023 LEG, Inc. d/b/a West Academic
      860 Blue Gentian Road, Suite 350
      Eagan, MN 55121
      1-877-888-1330

West, West Academic Publishing, and West Academic are trademarks of West Publishing Corporation, used under license.

Printed in the United States of America

ISBN: 978-1-68561-563-5

For Renate, because she has to put up with me;

For my children and grandchildren, because I love them;

And for my ConLaw classes that were the guinea pigs for this book.

PREFACE

This is a third edition of my second Constitutional Law casebook. The first casebook was limited to the constitutional structure of the United States, but while its coverage—Judicial Review, Legislative Authority, Federalism limitations, and Separation of Powers—and methodology—cases followed by notes and questions—were traditional, there was a novelty involved as well. Unlike virtually all other Constitutional Law case books, it did not assume that the students were knowledgeable concerning American history or government. Today, the last time many entering law students were exposed to any American history or government was in high school. Foreign students are even less likely to have a background in American history or government. As a result, Constitutional Law courses are unnecessarily difficult and confusing for a large number of students. My first book tried to address that problem. I received enthusiastic responses from students and professors because of my approach, and I hoped that the second book, which continued that approach but which expanded the coverage to include rights expressly or implicitly provided in the Constitution, would receive the same response.

Like the earlier editions, this new edition addresses the lack of background students may bring to a constitutional law course in at least three ways. First, the book begins, not with *Marbury v. Madison*, but with the entire Constitution, from Article I to the Twenty Seventh Amendment, accompanied by comments and questions to expose students to the "forest" of the Constitution as a prologue to the particular "trees" that the book will focus on. Second, it supplies a rich historical narrative both for the original Constitution and for many of the cases that follow, thereby furnishing a context and story for the students. In addition, to further bring the cases alive, pictures and short biographies of current and famous former justices are provided when they first appear in cases. Third, the book consciously strives to anticipate and answer the questions that law students are likely to have and which make legal study more intimidating than necessary. For example, what is a "plaintiff in error" or a "writ"? What is the difference between a "concurring opinion" and an "opinion concurring in the judgment"? What is the difference between a "concurrent resolution" and a "joint resolution," and how is the latter different from a normal "bill"?

This new edition continues this approach to Constitutional Law, but it brings up to date the issues and decisions recently and currently before the Supreme Court and the nation. In addition, like the previous edition, it provides specific problems at the end of most of the distinct subject areas which may be used to facilitate discussion.

Whether student or professor I welcome your comments or questions.

WILLIAM FUNK
Lewis & Clark Distinguished
Professor of Law Emeritus
Lewis & Clark Law School
funk@lclark.edu

February, 2023

SUMMARY OF CONTENTS

TABLE OF CONTENTS

TABLE OF CASES

The principal cases are in bold type.

INTRODUCTION TO AMERICAN CONSTITUTIONAL LAW

STRUCTURE AND RIGHTS

Third Edition

The Justices of the United States Supreme Court

Seated: Associate Justice Sonia Sotomayor, Associate Justice Clarence Thomas, Chief Justice John G. Roberts, Jr., Associate Justice Samuel A. Alito, Associate Justice Elena Kagan.

Standing: Associate Justice Amy Barrett, Associate Justice Neil M. Gorsuch, Associate Justice Brett M. Kavanaugh, Associate Justice Ketanji Jackson.

CHAPTER 1

INTRODUCTION

■ ■ ■

A. THE CONSTITUTION

A constitution is the law that establishes the government of a nation, a subdivision of a nation, or even a supra-national organization. Constitutions are usually called constitutions, but not always. For example, the constitution of the United Nations is called a charter, the constitution of Germany is called the Basic Law, and the first constitution of the United States was called the Articles of Confederation. Constitutions are usually texts, but not always. For example, the United Kingdom is famous for having an "unwritten constitution," which is the body of law that establishes its system of government. A constitution usually contains not just the positive authorities of government—what the government is authorized or required to do—but also restrictions on the government— what the government is forbidden from doing. These restrictions are often what in the United States we call constitutional rights. Under many constitutions, however, the constitutional rights of citizens are not just the protections from what government might do to them. In addition, they are also granted certain positive rights—rights that entitle them to receive certain things from the government, such as, for example, a free public education. The United States Constitution does not contain such provisions, although some state constitutions and several foreign constitutions do. Thus, the United States Constitution does not ensure that persons receive an adequate education, housing, health care, clothing, or nutrition. Our constitutional rights are all negative rights—rights that the government *not* do something, like abridge our freedom of speech.

The United States Constitution is the oldest written national constitution in continuous use. Proposed on September 17, 1787, to the thirteen original states, it was ratified on June 21, 1788, when the ninth state ratified it. Government under the Constitution began on March 4, 1789, when the House of Representatives and the Senate met in New York City. George Washington, elected the first President in February, 1789, was inaugurated in New York City on April 30, 1789, at the Federal Hall on Wall Street, at which point there were only 11 states in the union. North Carolina and Rhode Island were deliberately refraining from joining the United States.

Congress proposed twelve amendments to the states in September, 1789, ten of which, popularly known as the Bill of Rights, were ratified in

1

December 1791. With the proposal of the Bill of Rights, North Carolina was convinced to ratify the Constitution, becoming a state in November. Since the ratification of the Bill of Rights, the United States has ratified 17 other amendments, the most recent in 1992, although that amendment was one of the original 12 proposed in 1789.

This constitutional law book, like virtually all constitutional law books, does not attempt to cover the entire Constitution. It begins with the structural elements of our governmental system as contained in the Constitution (often the subject of a one semester Constitutional Law course). It then turns to the "rights" contained in several of the amendments—specifically, the First Amendment's Free Speech and Religion clauses, the Second Amendment's Right to Bear Arms, the Due Process Clause of the Fifth Amendment, and the Due Process and Equal Protection Clauses of the Fourteenth Amendment (often the subject of another one semester Constitutional Law course). These obviously are not all the rights provisions. For example, the Fourth Amendment's protection against unreasonable searches and the Fifth and Sixth Amendments' protections for criminal defendants are not covered in this book. Those amendments are covered in other courses. Still other provisions of the Constitution are rarely considered in any law school course for various reasons.

That said, we begin with an outline of the entire Constitution. One should have a view of the forest before delving into particular trees in depth.

This summary is not a substitute for reading the actual Constitution, which is found in Appendix A. Rather it is an outline to assist in reading it, with some comments and questions to focus attention on certain aspects.

The Preamble

The preamble is not "law," as the rest of the Constitution is. Like statements of purposes that often introduce statutes passed by legislatures, however, one may look to the preamble to inform the meaning of the constitutional text. For example, the language of the preamble, "we the people," was used to counter the southern states' position prior to the Civil War that the United States was created by the states coming together, suggesting that they could leave if they wished. The preamble, their opponents argued, stood for the proposition that the United States was created by the people, not by the states. Whatever the merits of this argument, it took the Civil War to resolve the issue. The preamble's broad statement of purposes is often used by those who want to counter others' claims that the federal government's powers are strictly limited.

Article I

Article I relates to Congress and the legislative powers of the United States. Section 1 states that all legislative powers "herein granted" are vested in Congress. Thus, we must look to the rest of this article and the Constitution to find what legislative powers are indeed granted. Any legislative powers not listed in the Constitution cannot be exercised by Congress and are retained by the states. This is the source of the common understanding that the federal government is a government of limited powers.

Section 2 addresses matters pertaining to the House of Representatives, including the election of its members. Note that it uses the term "electors"; that is the term used at the time for those who would vote to elect a person. Today we would call them voters. The requirement for a decennial census comes from Section 2's demand that representatives (and direct taxes) be apportioned among the states on the basis of population. Note also that it is the House of Representatives that impeaches someone.

Section 3 is limited to matters pertaining to the Senate, including the selection of Senators. Under the original Constitution, Senators were not elected by voters, but instead were chosen by the state legislature. This reflected the concept that Senators represented the state as a sovereign entity, whereas Representatives represented the people. The Senate is the court that tries an impeachment case after the House has impeached someone. Note that this section describes the only duty identified in the Constitution for the Vice President, and it is unclear what else the Constitution allows the Vice President to do.

Section 4 begins by prescribing that state legislatures determine the times, places, and manners of holding elections for Senators and Representatives in the state, but it allows for Congress to alter what the state legislature establishes, except for the place for choosing Senators. The power to determine the time, place, and manner of an election for representatives has been interpreted to include decisions by the state as to the boundaries of the districts for representatives. Because state legislatures usually are controlled by one political party, there is the possibility, if not likelihood, that the legislature will draw representative boundary lines designed to favor that party. To avoid such favoritism, in modern times some states have provided in their constitutions that an independent commission shall draw the boundary lines instead of the state legislature. This practice was challenged as unconstitutional. In *Arizona State Legislature v. Arizona Independent Redistricting Commission*, 576 U.S. 787 (2015), the Court by a 5–4 vote upheld that practice. The Court concluded that the word "legislature" did not mean only the legislature of the state but also could mean any other means by which a state makes laws, including the adoption of constitutional provisions through ballot initiatives. In reaching this conclusion, the Court relied upon the definition of legislature in 18th century dictionaries as "the power that makes laws" and earlier Court decisions treating the term "legislature" in the Constitution to encompass however a state made laws. The dissent generally argued that "legislature" means the state legislative body elected by the people and that no other Court case had upheld a system of drawing district boundaries that completely excluded that legislative body. More recently, a similar issue has arisen: whether the Constitution allows a state Supreme Court to overturn a legislature's districting decision as unconstitutional under either the United States or state constitutions.

The second sentence in Section 4 was replaced by language in Section 2 of the 20th Amendment.

Section 5 relates to the internal workings of the House and Senate. It is important that each house is the judge of the elections, returns, and qualifications of its own members. Thus, disputed House and Senate elections are decided by each house, not by the courts. Moreover, each house has the power to establish standards and maintain discipline with respect to its members and, therefore, may punish or even expel a member.

Section 6 contains the congressional privilege against arrest when going to or returning from Congress except for "treason, felony and breach of the peace," and against being questioned "in any other place" regarding their speech in either house. The former privilege is effectively meaningless today, inasmuch as the Supreme Court has interpreted "treason, felony and breach of the peace" to refer to all criminal law, *see Williamson v. United States*, 207 U.S. 425 (1908), limiting the privilege to arrest in civil suits, something that was common in 1789 but does not exist today. The "Speech and Debate Clause," however, remains alive and well and will be considered in Chapter 5.

Section 6 also prohibits a member of Congress from being appointed to a federal office whose pay was increased during that member's term in office. Moreover, it absolutely prohibits a person from being both a member of Congress and a federal officer at the same time. This is an important element in separating the executive and legislative powers. Compare this with the United Kingdom where the Prime Minister and other cabinet members *must* be members of the House of Commons.

Section 7 provides the procedural rules for making laws, including provision for Presidential veto and "pocket veto" (when the President neither signs nor returns a bill to Congress within ten days and Congress is not in session). Note that the ten days does not include Sundays.

Section 8 is a major section that will be considered in this book. It contains the list of almost all the things about which Congress can make laws.* Later in this book we will deal with some of them, notably the Commerce Clause, the Taxing and Spending Clause, and the Necessary and Proper Clause. What is important to realize is that if something is not within the specified powers about which Congress is authorized to make laws, then Congress (that is, the United States) cannot make that law.

Section 9 contains a list of laws that Congress is specifically prohibited from making. The first clause, albeit indirectly, prohibited Congress from restricting the importation of slaves for twenty years. The second clause prohibits Congress from suspending the privilege of the writ of habeas corpus (Latin for "you have the body"), except in cases of rebellion or invasion where the public safety requires it. A "writ" is a formal written order issued by a body with administrative or judicial jurisdiction. The writ of habeas corpus is an order issued by a court to an official holding a person in custody, demanding the official to justify why the person is being held. Thus, the writ of habeas corpus is the ultimate safety net for a person held by the federal government for whatever reason. Alleged terrorists held prisoner at the U.S. Naval Base at Guantanamo, Cuba, were able to file habeas petitions challenging their imprisonment. The third clause prohibits Congress from passing bills of attainder or ex post facto (Latin for "after the fact") laws. A bill of attainder is a law in which the legislature finds a person to be a criminal and punishes that person in some way. An ex post facto law is a law that criminalizes action after the fact, so that a person could be prosecuted for something that was lawful when done.

Clause four refers to a "capitation" or other direct tax. In the 18th century, governments obtained their revenues from customs duties (fees paid for the privilege of importing goods), excise taxes (a tax on some transaction—today, gasoline or cigarette taxes are examples), property taxes (a tax paid on real property—e.g., land—or personal property—e.g., an automobile), or a capitation or head tax (a fixed tax levied on each person). The former two were the principal sources of revenue and were known as indirect taxes; the latter two were known as direct taxes and were viewed with some skepticism at the time. These latter taxes were required to be levied in proportion to the population of each state. This meant that the total direct tax from each state would have the same proportion to the total direct taxes in the whole nation as each state's population would have to the nation's population. If population were a good proxy for the income and value of property in a state, such an apportionment might work, but it never was a good proxy, and this limitation created significant problems. The Supreme Court responded by interpreting very narrowly what constituted a direct tax, which solved most of these problems, until the Court reversed itself in 1895 and declared a federal income tax unconstitutional as a direct tax not levied in

---

* Article II, Section 1, clauses 4 and 6, Section 2, clause 2; Article III; Article IV, Sections 1 and 3, clause 2 also authorize Congress to make laws dealing with particular matters.

proportion to population. *Pollock v. Farmers' Loan & Trust Co.*, 157 U.S. 429 (1895). The 16th Amendment in 1913 in effect overruled that case and authorized a federal income tax.

Clause eight prohibits the federal government from granting titles of nobility, and it prohibits any person holding a federal "office of profit or trust" from accepting, without the consent of Congress, any gift, emolument, office, or title from a foreign government. This prohibition received popular attention with respect to President Donald Trump, because some of his businesses, which he retained while President, earned revenue from foreign governments, in particular rates paid by foreign diplomats for staying in his hotels. Whether such revenue would constitute an "emolument" and whether the President holds an office of profit or trust under the United States were questions the issue raised.

Section 10 goes further and specifies what laws *states* may not make. Note that sandwiched between the prohibition on passing bills of attainder and ex post facto laws and the prohibition on granting titles of nobility, both of which Section 9 also prohibited to Congress, is a prohibition on impairing the obligation of contracts, which is not prohibited to Congress.

QUESTIONS

1. "Legislative powers" may be vested in Congress, but what are "legislative powers"? Congress often demands information from executive officials, and sometimes issues subpoenas (a particular form of legal demand) to executive officials and other persons to appear or bring certain documents. Is demanding such testimony or information a "legislative power"? Did you see anything in Article I that would authorize such action?

2. What benefit did slave states receive in terms of their representation in the House of Representatives?

3. Why do you think Senators were to be chosen in a different manner than members of the House of Representatives?

4. If a person believes he has been wrongfully convicted by the Senate after impeachment, wrongfully declared the loser of an election by the House or Senate, or wrongfully expelled from the House or Senate after being elected, what sort of relief might that person seek?

5. On what basis may the House or Senate expel a member?

6. What do you think the exception of Sundays in counting the ten days for a pocket veto says about the Founders' religious views and their reflection in law?

7. In light of Section 8's authorizations to Congress, what kind of role do you think the Founders had in mind for Congress to play in matters of foreign affairs and war making?

8.   Where in Article I do you see the authorization for federal environmental laws, federal laws criminalizing the possession of heroin, or federal laws providing health care for the poor (Medicaid) or elderly (Medicare)?

9.   Article I, Section 8, authorizes Congress to provide for an Army and a Navy and refers to them as the "land and naval forces." There is, of course, no mention of an Air Force, much less a Space Force. Where does Congress get the authority to create an Air Force? Doesn't there need to be a constitutional amendment?

Article II

Article II relates to the President of the United States. Section 1 begins by vesting the "executive power" in the President and then provides the means by which the President and Vice President are elected. This section is the source of what we call the Electoral College, although that term is not used in the Constitution, the entity that actually elects the President and Vice President. Note that it does not provide for a general election to determine who the "electors" are but leaves to the state legislatures to determine the method of appointing the "electors." In the 2016 Presidential election, despite a state law requiring electors to cast their votes for the candidate receiving the most votes in the state, a few electors did not cast their ballot for the candidate that received the most votes in the state. The state of Washington, in accordance with state law, fined those electors, and the electors challenged the constitutionality of such fines, asserting that the Constitution allows electors to choose for themselves for whom they will vote. In *Chiafalo v. Washington*, 140 S.Ct. 2316 (2020), the Supreme Court upheld the fines, concluding that Article II, by providing for a state to "appoint in such manner as the legislature thereof may direct," authorizes states both to impose requirements on how electors may vote and to enforce those requirements. After the 2020 Presidential election, some supporters of President Trump argued that state legislatures could, after the general election, change the manner by which the electors would be selected, allowing the legislature, if it did not like the outcome of the popular vote in the state, to provide a method of appointing electors more to its liking, and thereby change the outcome of the election in that state.

Clause 3 provided how the electors would vote for the President, with the person coming in second being elected Vice President. This was changed by the 12th Amendment. Clause 6, relating to what happens if the President or Vice President leaves office, dies, or is disabled, has been largely supplanted by the 25th Amendment, but it is still Congress that by law determines the order of succession in case of a vacancy in the offices of both the President and Vice President. *See* 3 U.S.C. § 19. Note also that during the period for which he was elected, the President's pay cannot be increased or decreased, and he is prohibited from receiving any other financial benefit from the federal or state governments. Finally, note that the President's oath of office is to protect the Constitution of the United States, not to protect the United States.

Sections 2 and 3 contain a list of powers and duties of the President. Note that there is a specific authorization to the President to require principal officers in the executive departments to provide an opinion in writing on any matter relating to their offices, but there is no specific authorization to the President to be able to direct them to do anything else. Moreover, there is specific authorization for the President to appoint ambassadors, other public ministers and consuls (the term "public ministers and consuls" refers to officers involved in foreign affairs below the rank of ambassador), and all other principal officers of the United States (with the advice and consent of the Senate), but there is no specific authority for the President to fire an officer once appointed.

Section 4 specifies that the President, Vice President, and all civil officers of the United States may be removed from office by impeachment for and conviction of treason, bribery, or other "high crimes and misdemeanors." While treason and bribery are well understood, the phrase "high crimes and misdemeanors" is not. There is some historical basis for interpreting "high" to refer to crimes and misdemeanors against the government, which would be consistent with treason and bribery. Some commentators have suggested that abuses of office that do not rise to the level of a criminal offense may still be "high crimes and misdemeanors." Others, however, have argued that only serious crimes can be "high crimes and misdemeanors." The impeachment of President Andrew Johnson charged him with removing the Secretary of War in violation of the Tenure in Office Act, which required any removal of a cabinet member to be approved by the Senate. No one suggested, however, that this was a criminal offense. Of course, Johnson was not convicted, but whether what motivated the nineteen Senators who voted "Not Guilty" was the fact that the alleged act was not a criminal offense or some other reason is not known. The two articles of impeachment passed by the House with respect to President Clinton both involved criminal offenses, perjury before a grand jury and obstruction of justice. He too was acquitted in the Senate. President Trump is the only person to be was impeached twice: once charged with abuse of power and obstruction of Congress regarding his communications with the President of Ukraine to obtain dirt on his election opponent Joe Biden, and once charged with inciting an insurrection. He was not convicted in either case. Only eight persons have ever been removed from office by impeachment, all of them judges, one of whom was elected to Congress three years later and served as a representative from a Florida district until his death twenty-eight years later.

QUESTIONS

1.   Under the Constitution, could a state legislature provide that the governor of the state should appoint the state's electors of the President without any state election?

2.   In light of Sections 2 and 3's authorities and duties of the President, what kind of role do you think the Founders had in mind for the President to play in matters of foreign affairs and war making?

3.   Section 3 states that the President "shall take care that the laws be faithfully executed." How do you suppose the President is to do that? And what does it mean?

4.   If the President believes that a bill presented to him by Congress for his signature would be unconstitutional, is he required to veto it?

5.   If there is a law that the President believes is unconstitutional, may he decide not to enforce it? Is he prohibited from enforcing it? Or, is he required to enforce it?

Article III

Article III relates to the federal judiciary. Section 1 vests the judicial power of the United States* in a Supreme Court, but it leaves to Congress the determination of whether or to what extent there should be lower federal courts. The Framers were not sure that lower federal courts would be necessary; they believed that state courts might be able to decide most, if not all, the cases that would arise under federal laws. Section 1 of Article III also provides that federal judges shall hold their positions "during good behavior" and shall not have their pay diminished. Both the removal and pay provisions were clearly designed to provide a measure of insulation to judges from retribution from the political branches for unpopular decisions. It is often said that federal judges are appointed for life, but the removal provision clearly allows them to be removed. What the provision leaves unclear is both the meaning of "good behavior" and who (and under what procedure) may remove a judge. As noted above, a few judges have been removed by impeachment, and that is the only way judges have been removed historically.

Section 2 then describes what the federal judicial power extends to, that is, what matters can possibly be brought before federal courts. There are two general categories—cases** and controversies. Scholars disagree

---

*   When the Constitution refers to the "United States," it refers to the national government, not the several states. Thus, the judicial power "of the United States" refers to the judicial power of the federal government. Also, when the Constitution refers to the "laws of the United States," it refers to federal laws, not state laws. Similarly, in Article II, Section 2, where the Constitution gives the President the power to grant pardons for offences "against the United States," it means the President can grant pardons for federal crimes, not state crimes.

**   Section 2 refers to "cases, in law and equity." In English law at the time, court cases could be either cases in equity or cases at law. Cases at law were brought in "common law" courts,

over the purpose in the Constitution of distinguishing between cases and controversies, but it is an issue for scholars only, as no one has ever found that, whatever the distinction, it makes any legal or constitutional difference. Within these two categories the Constitution lists a number of different types of cases and controversies, for each of which there is a reason why a federal court, rather than a state court, might be a better forum. In this book we will see cases almost exclusively brought under the authority to hear cases "arising under" the Constitution or "laws of the United States."

Article III, Section 2, Clause 3 is one of the few "rights" provisions in the original Constitution, requiring a jury trial for all crimes and requiring the trial to be in the state in which the crime was committed. This provision applies only to federal trials, not state trials.

Section 3 is a response to British actions against the colonies, where treason could be charged fairly easily. "Attainder of treason" related to an old British practice of punishing not just the traitor but all his heirs as well.

QUESTIONS

1. May the President remove a Supreme Court Justice he believes is not acting in "good behavior"? May Congress impeach and convict (and thereby remove) a Supreme Court Justice it does not believe is acting in "good behavior"? What is "good behavior" anyway?

2. Article III refers to Congress being able to make exceptions to the Supreme Court's appellate jurisdiction, but it does not specifically provide for exceptions to lower federal courts' jurisdiction over the types of cases and controversies within the judicial power of the United States. Nevertheless, federal courts have *never* been authorized to hear all the cases within the judicial power of the United States. What authority in Article III would justify withholding some of that power from federal courts?

3. Why do you suppose the Framers would want to enable federal courts to hear controversies between citizens of different states, controversies to which the United States might be a party, or controversies between states?

Article IV

Sections 1 and 2 of Article IV relate to the relationship between states. The Full Faith and Credit Clause assures that court judgments and other

---

presided over by judges but whose decisions were made by juries. Cases at equity were brought in the courts of chancery, whose decisions were made not by juries but by judges, who derived their authority from the king. Typically, in civil cases, courts of law would provide money damages as a remedy, whereas courts of equity would enter injunctions. After becoming independent of Great Britain, most states retained this dual system of courts, but some used the same courts to hear both kinds of cases. When Congress created the lower federal courts, it followed this latter model. Subsequently in the mid-nineteenth century most states abolished the distinction between cases in law and equity, as did the United States in 1938. Thus, today, cases in law and equity mean all cases.

public acts by one state will be recognized by other states. Thus, for example, if a person is found liable in one state for breach of a contract and ordered to pay damages to the plaintiff, the plaintiff could use that court judgment in another state to collect upon the defendant's assets without having to bring another lawsuit against the defendant. Added to the Full Faith and Credit Clause is a provision authorizing Congress to prescribe both the way one would have to prove the existence of the public acts, records, or judicial proceedings of the other state in order to have faith and credit given to them and the effect such public acts, etc., would have.

Section 2 begins with the Privileges and Immunities Clause. It assures that when a citizen of one state travels to another state that citizen does not lose the "privileges and immunities" of citizenship. The clause does not, however, specify what are "privileges and immunities" of citizenship. This issue will be addressed in Chapter 4. The extradition clause requires a state to return escaped criminals to the state from which they escaped. Finally, section 2 concludes with what is known as the Fugitive Slave Clause, which likewise requires a state to return to the rightful owner a slave who escaped to that state. This was a provision required by the southern states as a condition to ratification.

Section 3 allows for the admission of new states into the union. In addition, this section contains the Property Clause (Section 3, Clause 2), which specifically authorizes Congress to dispose of property belonging to the United States and to make all rules regarding the territory and property of the United States. This effectively grants Congress plenary power to make rules and regulations regarding what happens to or on federal property. Thus, for example, under this clause Congress can allow for grazing on federal lands or prohibit it, authorize mining on federal lands or prohibit it, create federal parks or give the land away. Note that there is no specific provision for Congress to acquire property for the United States.

Section 4 is called the Guarantee Clause. By its terms the "United States" guarantees "a republican form of government" to every state. How that is to be done is not specified. Nor is it clear what is meant by a "republican" form of government. We know the Framers wished to preclude a state from instituting a monarchical form of government, but many scholars believe that they equally wished to preclude a state from adopting a pure form of democracy, wherein the people would make their own laws, as opposed to electing representatives who would make laws on their behalf.

QUESTIONS

1.   In 1803 the United States concluded a treaty with France for the purchase of the Louisiana Territory for $15 million. This purchase doubled the territory of the United States at the time and included all of what is now

Arkansas, Missouri, Iowa, Oklahoma, Kansas, Nebraska, Minnesota south of the Mississippi River, much of North Dakota, nearly all of South Dakota, northeastern New Mexico, northern Texas, the portions of Montana, Wyoming, and Colorado east of the Continental Divide, and Louisiana. President Jefferson doubted the constitutionality of his purchase, but he did it anyway, letting pragmatic concerns overcome his principles of limited federal power. Can you think of a way this purchase may be justified constitutionally?

2.   If the Guarantee Clause is intended to prohibit direct democracy by the people without a legislature, are state constitutional provisions allowing for laws to be adopted by initiative (the people voting for them rather than the legislature) constitutional?

Article V

This article relates to amendments to the Constitution. It specifies two different methods by which an amendment may be proposed. First, and the way that every amendment has in fact been proposed, Congress by a two-thirds vote can propose new amendments to the states. Congress has only proposed six amendments that were not ratified. Interestingly, the very first amendment proposed by Congress is one of those. What we refer to as the First Amendment was actually the third amendment proposed by Congress. Another of the failed amendments was a proposed Thirteenth Amendment passed by Congress on March 2, 1861. It was an attempt to keep the southern states from seceding by banning any amendment to the Constitution that would interfere with slavery within any state. President Lincoln, in his inaugural address two days later, stated he had no opposition to the proposed amendment. The South seceded anyway, and only two states ratified the proposed amendment. It is ironic that it is the actual Thirteenth Amendment that in fact abolished slavery. A proposed amendment stating that "equality of rights under the law shall not be denied or abridged by the United States or by any State on account of sex" failed to achieve ratification by the necessary three-fourths of the states by 1982.

The other method for proposing an amendment is if the legislatures of two-thirds of the states call for a constitutional convention, which convention can then propose amendments. There have been numerous attempts by states to trigger this method of proposing amendments, usually with respect to a particular issue. None have yet been successful, although an attempt to call a convention to overturn the Supreme Court's decision requiring one person/one vote in elections was only one state short. Currently there is an effort spearheaded by the Citizens for Self Governance to call a convention "for the purpose of stopping the runaway power of the federal government." So far, nineteen states have called for such a convention. Fifteen more would be required.

However the amendments are proposed, Congress can specify whether states can ratify the proposals through legislative action or through state conventions. In either case, it takes three-quarters of the states to ratify an amendment.

Note the two limitations on amendments, only one of which is still applicable: that no state shall without its consent be deprived of equal representation in the Senate. This assures that Wyoming, with a population of less than 600,000 (less than the District of Columbia, which has no Senator), has the same power in the Senate as California, with a population over 39 million. Is this democratic?

QUESTIONS

1.   What if a state legislature ratifies a proposed amendment, but before the amendment receives approval from three-fourths of the state, a new legislature is elected and repeals its ratification? What should be the effect of the repeal? This is no idle question; this has occurred on more than one occasion.

2.   Could an amendment amend Article V to rescind the limitation on amendments, thereby allowing an amendment to provide representation in the Senate to be apportioned on the basis of the states' populations?

Article VI

Clause 2 of Article VI is the Supremacy Clause. It states that the Constitution, laws, and treaties of the United States are the supreme law of the land. Note that this clause does not establish a hierarchy among the Constitution, laws, and treaties. This is because this clause is aimed at the states; it is to establish that federal "law," whether part of the Constitution, laws, or treaties, is supreme over state law. It also requires state judges to follow these federal laws rather than conflicting state laws. Note also that only laws "made in pursuance" of the Constitution are supreme, but that treaties made before the Constitution, because they were made under the authority of the United States under the Articles of Confederation, are also supreme.

The third clause of Article VI requires all federal and state officers and all federal and state legislators personally to swear (or affirm)* to support the Constitution. Finally, this clause also contains a "rights" provision, forbidding any religious qualification for holding any office under the United States. Note that this does not prohibit a state from requiring its state officers to be members of a particular religion.

---

*   The alternative of "affirmation" in place of an "oath" was an accommodation to those religious groups, like the Quakers, who for religious reasons could not swear an oath.

QUESTIONS

1.   Could a state require candidates for the House of Representatives from that state to be members of a particular religion? If not, why not?

2.   If the Supremacy Clause does not establish a hierarchy among the Constitution, the laws, and the treaties of the United States, how do we know that the Constitution is supreme over federal laws? And which is the higher authority between treaties and laws?

Article VII

Article VII governs the ratification of the original Constitution. When nine states ratified the Constitution, it would go into effect. Of course, it would only be in effect in those states that actually ratified it.

First Amendment (1791)

The First Amendment contains the two Religion Clauses—the Establishment Clause and the Free Exercise Clause—as well as the Free Speech Clause and the Free Press Clause. It also addresses the right to peaceably assemble and the right to petition the government. Note that the limitation of the First Amendment is on laws passed by Congress; it says nothing about what states can do. At the time, all the states, except Connecticut and Rhode Island, already had their own bills of rights, so that there was no felt need to protect people from their own states in the new Constitution; the federal Bill of Rights was to protect persons (and states) from the new national government. Also, the Establishment Clause forbids laws "respecting an establishment of religion," not laws "establishing a religion." This phrasing was intended to ensure that the new national government could neither establish a national religion nor disestablish the established religions in the then three states (Connecticut, Massachusetts, and New Hampshire) that had established religions.* Those three states disestablished their religions on their own well before the Civil War.

As you probably know, today the First Amendment does apply to the states, so that states also cannot abridge the freedoms of this amendment or make laws respecting the establishment of religion. How that change occurred will be described later.

Second Amendment (1791)

Written in the passive voice, this amendment by its terms is not limited to protecting against actions by the federal government, but it, like

---

*   An "established religion" refers to an official connection between a particular religion and the government. For example, in all of the three states that had an established religion, the government taxed on behalf of the official state religion. Great Britain then and now has an established religion—the Anglican Church—so that the head of the church, the Archbishop of Canterbury, is appointed by the monarch and serves in the House of Lords.

the rest of the Bill of Rights, was not intended to restrict state governments. Again, like the First Amendment, however, today the Second Amendment also protects a right to keep and bear arms from state infringement. *See McDonald v. City of Chicago*, 561 U.S. 742 (2010).

Third Amendment (1791)

This amendment was a reaction to the British practice of quartering troops in persons' homes without their permission. It has never been interpreted by the Supreme Court and almost never has come up in practice.

Fourth Amendment (1791)

This amendment is particularly important in the investigation of crimes. It too was a reaction to British practice in the colonies where general warrants were used to search for customs violations. A major question is obviously: what is an "unreasonable" search? And should this be interpreted only to reject a search that would have been deemed unreasonable in 1791, or one that "we" would deem unreasonable today? If the National Security Agency intercepts all domestic cell phone traffic and then screens it by computer to find key words indicating terrorist intentions, is this a "search" within the meaning of the Fourth Amendment? These issues are usually dealt with in a course entitled Criminal Procedure rather than Constitutional Law. This amendment, like the first and second, now applies to the states as well the federal government.

Fifth Amendment (1791)

This amendment covers both criminal and non-criminal issues. It requires a grand jury indictment for what we generally today would call felonies. The grand jury at the time was considered a safeguard of citizens' rights, because the grand jury was made up of citizens. Thus, a person could not be charged with a major offense unless the person's peers believed he should be charged. This was a protection against government tyranny. Today, grand juries themselves are often thought to exert excessive government force, and while still made up of ordinary citizens, as a practical matter almost always do what the government attorney asks them to do.

This amendment also contains the Double Jeopardy Clause. Because the Bill of Rights was only intended to apply to the federal government, the double jeopardy prohibited is double jeopardy before federal courts. For example, a person could be tried and found not guilty by a state court, and the federal government could still prosecute the person for the same alleged act. And this does occur.

This amendment also contains the Self Incrimination Clause, which has been interpreted to protect a person from being forced by the government to incriminate himself with respect to a criminal offense as a witness in any proceeding.

Probably the most important part of the Fifth Amendment is the Due Process Clause, prohibiting the federal government from depriving any person of life, liberty, or property without due process of law. Here the major question is: what is "due process of law." Some have suggested that it is the required procedure government must use before depriving someone of life, liberty, or property, such as a hearing before a neutral judge. This type of due process is a topic in an Administrative Law course. Others, including the Supreme Court, have said that in addition the due process of law can encompass certain unenumerated substantive rights, such as a right to use contraceptives or marry someone of the same sex or different race. Chapter 7 of this book treats this form of due process.

Finally, the Fifth Amendment contains the Takings Clause or Just Compensation Clause. This clause is rife with ambiguities. What is private property? What does it mean to "take" it? For example, does government regulation of property that reduces the value of the property constitute a "taking"? What is a "public use"? For example, does it suffice that the property is taken for public purposes, even if the "public" does not get to use the property, as, for example, a government office building? Imagine that property is taken by the government in order to give (or sell) it to a private party. Could this be considered taking for a public use if the general public benefits from the taking? Finally, what is "just compensation"? For example, is the fair market value of the property "just compensation," or should "just compensation" include reimbursing the property owner for the transaction costs necessarily imposed on him by the taking?

Except for the grand jury requirement and the due process clause, the rest of this amendment today applies to states as well. States are subject to the requirements of due process, but through the Fourteenth Amendment's due process clause, rather than this amendment's, although functionally they are the same.

Sixth Amendment (1791)

This amendment is also dealt with in criminal procedure courses and provides federal criminal defendants with various rights designed to better assure a fair trial. It too applies to the states today.

Seventh Amendment (1791)

This amendment preserves the right to a jury trial in federal civil cases "at common law" when the amount involved exceeds $20 and prohibits judges from second-guessing jury determinations except "according to the rules of the common law." As mentioned earlier, at the time of this amendment, cases in court could be either cases at common law or at equity. Cases at equity did not require juries, while common law cases did. This amendment prohibited the federal government from dispensing with juries in federal common law cases. Today, however, we no longer have separate "common law" and equity cases, having merged the two separate types of cases. Nevertheless, this constitutional requirement remains, so that courts have had to assess whether a given modern case would have been a "common law" case back in the day. If so, there must be an opportunity for a jury trial. This makes for some very technical legal history determinations. This amendment does not apply to the states.

Eighth Amendment (1791)

This ban on "cruel and unusual punishments" (or excessive bail and fines) has often been litigated with regard to the death penalty. Clearly, the death penalty was not cruel and unusual in 1791. Indeed, the Constitution mentions the possibility of the death penalty in two places in the Fifth Amendment—once in the requirement for a grand jury indictment in *capital* cases and second in the requirement for due process of law before one is deprived of *life*. But, did the Framers intend that only those punishments deemed cruel and unusual in their day would be prohibited? Or did they intend that a punishment would be prohibited if, at the time it was to be inflicted, it was deemed cruel and unusual? In other words, was the original meaning intended to vary with the changing morals of society? One member of the original Congress objected to this proposed amendment, declaring that if it were adopted, one day whipping would be prohibited. This amendment today applies to the states as well as the federal government.

Ninth Amendment (1791)

This amendment was designed to rebut an argument made against having any bill of rights, that a list of specific rights would suggest that these were all the rights that persons had. At the time, the dominant enlightenment philosophy was that persons enjoyed certain natural rights, even if the philosophers could not agree on exactly what those rights were. Others believed that persons had God-given rights, but again there was no agreement as to what they were. The Ninth Amendment was to make clear that the first eight amendments did not mean that there were not other rights "retained by the people." Nevertheless, the Ninth Amendment poses two difficulties. First, we do not know what those other rights are or how to ascertain them. Second, even if we knew what they were, would they have any legal effect—would they be "constitutional" rights able to be enforced in courts against the government or only a recognition of rights that the government *should* respect? This difficulty has resulted in courts not affording the Ninth Amendment much substantive authority. Indeed, there is no Supreme Court decision finding a "Ninth Amendment right" that would prohibit federal or state action.

Tenth Amendment (1791)

This amendment was to make explicit what was implicit in the Constitution itself—that the new national government only had those powers granted to it and that these powers were limited powers. The powers inherent in government that were not delegated to the new federal government were retained by the states (or the people). At the same time, it is not clear what the legal effect of the Tenth Amendment is, because if a power was not delegated to the new federal government, then it would necessarily have remained with the states, and an attempt by the federal government to exercise that power would be unconstitutional even in the absence of the Tenth Amendment. On the other hand, if the power was delegated to the federal government, then the Tenth Amendment would not apply at all.

Eleventh Amendment (1798)

In *Chisholm v. Georgia*, 2 Dall. (2 U.S.) 419 (1793), the Supreme Court held that Article III authorized federal jurisdiction over a suit against a state by a citizen of another state despite the objections of the state of Georgia that it had sovereign immunity* from any lawsuit. In response to that case, Congress immediately proposed and the states quickly ratified the Eleventh Amendment to overrule that case. Thus, the language of the amendment limits the judicial power of the United States, which had been set out in Article III, so that it does not extend to suits against a state by a citizen of another state or citizens of a foreign state. As will be seen later, however, this amendment has been interpreted to extend well beyond its language, in essence to constitutionalize both state and federal sovereign immunity generally.

Twelfth Amendment (1804)

In the election of 1800, the Federalists, who had controlled the presidency and the Congress since adoption of the Constitution, were swept from office by the Democratic-Republican party, which was led in the south by Thomas Jefferson and in the north by Aaron Burr, the governor of New York. Jefferson was slated by the party to be the candidate for President and Burr for Vice President, and one of the Republican electors was

---

*   Sovereign immunity was a British legal doctrine that the monarch could not be sued in his courts without his consent, because he was the very source of their authority. The expression, "the king can do no wrong," reflects this notion of sovereign immunity. With the elimination of a monarch in the United States, sovereignty now resided in the people. Nevertheless, states continued to believe that sovereign immunity existed so that they could not be sued in any court.

supposed to vote for Jefferson and not for Burr, which would give Jefferson one more vote for President than Burr, making Jefferson the President and, under the original system in Article II, Burr the Vice President. That elector, however, messed up, and Jefferson and Burr both received the same number of votes. Because no one had received a majority of the votes for President, the election, then as now, would be decided by the House of Representatives. Ironically, because the newly elected members of the House (overwhelmingly Democratic-Republican) had not yet been seated, it was the Federalist controlled House that would choose the new President. After seven days and 35 ballots, Hamilton, as a Federalist leader, swung his influence in favor of Jefferson, and Jefferson was elected President with Burr as Vice President.*

The problems evidenced by this election led to the adoption of the Twelfth Amendment, which still governs how we conduct Presidential elections. The Electoral College and its method of selection remains unchanged from Article II, but now the electors cast one ballot for President and one for Vice President. If there is no majority for a choice for President, the House of Representatives, as it originally did under Article II, chooses the President from the top three finishers. Note that, again as originally under Article II, each state gets one vote—California and Wyoming have the same power—as determined by the state's representatives. Similarly, if there is no majority choice for Vice President, the Senate, as it did under Article II, chooses the Vice President from the two highest finishers. Since the election of 1800, however, only one election has been decided in the House or Senate. In 1824 Andrew Jackson received the most popular votes and the most electoral college votes, but he lacked a majority of the electoral college votes because there had been four serious candidates. The House then had to choose between the top three finishers. Each state having one vote, the House chose the second-place finisher, John Quincy Adams, by a 13–7–4 vote. Four years later, Jackson routed Adams to become President. But for the Supreme Court's decision in *Bush v. Gore*, 531 U.S. 98 (2000), that election might have been decided in the House and Senate if the electors from Florida, who were necessary to President George W. Bush's majority, had not been deemed to have been determined in time. In the election of 2020, if Vice President Pence had acceded to President Trump's wish that he not allow the count of votes from several states won by Joe Biden, the election might have gone to the House as well. At the time, although Democrats outnumbered Republicans in the House 222–213, Republicans had a majority in 27 states and therefore could have re-elected Trump 27–23.

---

* Less than four years later, while still Vice President, Burr would kill Hamilton in an illegal duel. Still later he was tried for treason, but acquitted, in a trial presided over by John Marshall.

Thirteenth Amendment (1865)

The first of the three so-called Civil War Amendments, this amendment abolished slavery within the United States and any place subject to its jurisdiction. It also provides authority to Congress to adopt legislation to enforce the prohibition. The scope of this enforcement power has been subject to some question.

Fourteenth Amendment (1868)

The Fourteenth Amendment contains a number of provisions, some more important than others. Section 1 begins with a sentence designed to overrule the notorious pre-Civil War *Dred Scott* case, *Scott v. Sandford*, 19 How. (60 U.S.) 393 (1857), in which the Supreme Court held that a black person, even a free person, could not be a citizen of the United States. In recent years the birthright citizenship right granted by this sentence has become somewhat controversial, because it means that if a person not legally in the United States has a child born in the United States, that child is automatically a United States citizen.

The first clause of the next sentence is known as the Privileges and Immunities Clause of the Fourteenth Amendment (to distinguish it from the Privileges and Immunities Clause of Article IV). The difficulty with this clause (which is also suffered by the Article IV Privileges and Immunities Clause) is determining what are the "privileges and immunities of citizens of the United States" that are protected from state abridgement.

The second clause of the second sentence is called the Due Process Clause of the Fourteenth Amendment. Its effect is to extend the same limitations to states that apply to the federal government under the Fifth Amendment's Due Process Clause. In addition, Supreme Court cases have interpreted it to "incorporate" most of the Bill of Rights to the states; that is, it is what makes most of the Bill of Rights applicable to the states, not just to the federal government as originally intended.

The third clause of the second sentence is known as the Equal Protection Clause. While the Equal Protection Clause was clearly passed to protect the newly freed slaves, its language is general. Exactly what is meant by "equal protection of the laws" is not clear. Laws invariably make distinctions between persons. In order to be a lawyer, one must have graduated from law school and passed the bar exam. Those who have not cannot practice law. Thus, these two groups are treated differently. In one sense, we could say the Equal Protection Clause prohibits wrongful discrimination, but that still leaves the question: what is wrongful discrimination? Should it be only what people thought was wrongful discrimination in 1868 or should it include what people think is wrongful discrimination when the discrimination is taking place? For example, there is no question that people in 1868 did not believe discrimination against women in a wide variety of contexts was wrongful. It was not until 1971 that the Supreme Court recognized discrimination against women as wrongful discrimination.

Section 2 of the amendment eliminated the apportionment of representatives on the basis of the free population and three-fifths of "all other persons" provided for in Article I, Section 2. Now apportionment was to be made solely on the basis of population, but in recognition that the former slave states were likely to deny the right to vote to the former slaves, this section reduced the representation in the House of any such states proportionately.

Section 3 punished those who had sworn an oath to protect the Constitution but then took up arms against the Union, or supported those who did, by banning them from holding any state or federal office. Clearly, this provision was aimed at excluding those who fought or supported those who did in the Civil War, but the language is general. Some have suggested that it prohibits Donald Trump from becoming President again.

Section 4 made clear that the federal government would honor its debts, including those arising out of the Civil War, but that neither the United States nor any state would pay the debts incurred by the Confederacy, thereby punishing those who had supported the Confederacy financially. Moreover, it prohibited the paying of any claim arising from the loss of slaves. Recall the Just Compensation Clause; it might otherwise have been read to require compensation for the government taking away that "private property."

Section 5, like Section 2 of the Thirteenth Amendment, grants Congress authority to enforce this Amendment by appropriate legislation. The extent of this enforcement provision has also been subject to some question. For example, inasmuch as this amendment only places restrictions on states, could Congress pass a law "to enforce" the amendment that banned private discrimination based on race?

Fifteenth Amendment (1870)

The inadequacy of the remedy in the Fourteenth Amendment for states denying newly freed slaves the ability to vote was quickly apparent, and the response was this amendment, prohibiting denial of the right to vote on the basis of race, color, or previous condition of servitude. This amendment as well gives Congress the power to enforce its provisions by law.

Sixteenth Amendment (1913)

This amendment was the direct result of the Supreme Court's decision in *Pollock v. Farmers' Loan & Trust Co.*, 158 U.S. 601 (1895), in which the

Court held that an income tax was a direct tax and therefore prohibited unless apportioned among the states according to Article I. This case in effect had prohibited federal income taxes. The purpose of this amendment was to overrule that case.

Seventeenth Amendment (1913)

The Progressive Era in American history lasted from about 1890 to 1920. One of its features was an attempt to further democratize American government. It was during this period that many state constitutions were amended to enable citizens to make law directly through state initiatives and referenda. This amendment, providing for a popular vote for Senators, rather than their selection by the state legislature, was a product of that era and movement, although a number of states had already so provided.

Eighteenth Amendment (1919)

Also a product of the Progressive Era with its propensity for reform, this amendment instituted Prohibition. This was the first proposed amendment with a time limitation on the period for ratification. It is also one of the few constitutional provisions to act directly on individuals. Normally, only a governmental entity can violate the Constitution, but under this Amendment any person who manufactures, sells, transports, imports, or exports liquor would violate the Constitution. It is the only amendment to have been repealed.

Nineteenth Amendment (1920)

The final amendment from the Progressive Era, this amendment prohibited denying the right to vote on account of sex.

Twentieth Amendment (1933)

Although the original Constitution did not specify a date for either the beginning of a new Congress or the inauguration of the President, the Continental Congress, having declared the new Constitution ratified on September 13, 1788, stated that the new government would begin on the following March 4. Thus, March 4 became the date upon which new Presidents and new Congresses would begin. While the long period from a November election to March might have been acceptable when methods of communication and transportation were still horse and buggy, by the Twentieth Century the long "lame duck" period was both unnecessary and problematical. First, the government was left in a form of partial paralysis for an extended period, and second, because before the days of air conditioners Congress had to adjourn for the summer, it left only a short period of time for legislative work. Finally, even after the Twelfth

Amendment changed the method of electing the President, if the Electoral College did not cast a majority of votes for one person to be President and one person to be Vice President, the decision as to the President and Vice President would be made by the "old" House and Senate, not the newly elected one. The Twentieth Amendment solved these problems by advancing the date of the beginning of the new Congress to January 3 and the date of the inauguration to January 20.

Section 3 addressed an issue that had never arisen before and has not arisen since—who is President if on January 20 for some reason no living person has been elected President.

Twenty-First Amendment (1933)

This amendment repealed Prohibition; it is the only amendment to rescind an earlier amendment. Section 2, like Prohibition itself, is one of the few provisions in the Constitution that acts directly on persons. That is, it prohibits anyone from transporting or importing alcoholic beverages into a state for use or delivery therein, if such use or delivery would violate the laws of the state. This prohibition was written into the Constitution to assure that states could forbid the sale and use of alcoholic beverages in their states if they wished, and the federal government would not be able to override such a state law.

Twenty-Second Amendment (1951)

George Washington refused to run for a third term as President, stating that having escaped a monarchy, the American people should not in effect create a new one. This precedent was maintained, although there were few Presidents who realistically could have hoped to be elected to a third term, until Franklin Roosevelt, who was elected to a third term in 1940 and a fourth term in 1944. This amendment, proposed by a solidly Republican Congress, was to constitutionalize Washington's precedent.

Twenty-Third Amendment (1961)

This amendment provided the means by which persons who live in the District of Columbia may vote in Presidential elections. Technically, it provided to the District the same number of electors in the Electoral College as it would have if it were a state. Because the District was predictably a solid Democratic stronghold, this amendment was a highly political amendment. A later proposed amendment that would give the District actual representation in the House and Senate, like a state, failed to achieve the necessary three-quarters states' ratifications even though its population is greater than Wyoming and Vermont. Again, this failure stemmed from the recognition that such representation would increase Democratic votes in the House and Senate.

Twenty-Fourth Amendment (1964)

This amendment was proposed in the midst of the modern Civil Rights era. Poll taxes, among other things, had been used to discourage African-Americans from voting in the south. This amendment, while not prohibiting poll taxes, prohibited their non-payment from barring someone from voting *in federal elections*. Why did the amendment not also cover state and local elections? Probably for fear that it then would not pass three-fourths of the states. In any case, in 1966 the Supreme Court held that a poll tax in state elections was unconstitutional under the Fourteenth Amendment. *See Harper v. Virginia State Board of Elections*, 383 U.S. 663 (1966).

Twenty-Fifth Amendment (1967)

The absence of a Vice President after Lyndon Johnson became President upon President Kennedy's assassination created an incentive for addressing the question of succession again and, imagining that President Kennedy had survived but been irreparably brain damaged, also the question of how to deal with the disability of the President.

Section 2, recognizing that today a party's nominee for Vice President is usually hand picked as a running mate by the party's nominee for President, provides for the President to fill a vacancy in the Vice Presidency by nominating a person who must be confirmed by a majority of both houses. This change was fortuitous because in 1973 Vice President Agnew resigned, leaving the Vice Presidency vacant. President Nixon nominated Gerald Ford, a congressman from Michigan, who was confirmed as Vice President. Subsequently, Nixon himself resigned, thereby making Gerald Ford President, the only President never elected in any national election.

Section 3 defines the procedure whereby a President may declare himself unable to discharge the duties of the office, so that the Vice President becomes Acting President for a period of time. In 1983, President Reagan sent a letter to the Speaker of the House and the President pro tem of the Senate informing them that Vice President George H.W. Bush would assume the duties and responsibilities of the President while he, President Reagan, was under anesthesia for cancer surgery.

Section 4 establishes the procedure for declaring the President unable to discharge his powers and duties, in which case the Vice President becomes Acting President. It has never been utilized, although there were occasions in American history before this amendment in which it might have been. For example, President Garfield lived for more than two months after he was shot, but he was in no condition to discharge his duties during that time. Inasmuch as this provision contains the potential for a coup d'état, there is a difficult burden to be met to divest the President of his powers and duties when he claims that he is able to perform them. In essence, unless Congress by a two-thirds vote within three weeks of the dispute agrees that the President is unable to perform the functions of the office, the President resumes the powers and duties of the office. Note, however, that during the interim the Vice President acts as President.

Twenty-Sixth Amendment (1971)

The Vietnam War, resulting in the draft of hundreds of thousands of young men under the age of 21, none of whom were entitled to vote under existing law, provided the impetus for this amendment. This amendment was ratified in only 107 days, the shortest period of ratification for any amendment.

Twenty-Seventh Amendment (1992)

This most recent amendment had the longest period of ratification of any amendment. It was in fact the second amendment proposed by Congress in 1789. [The first amendment proposed by Congress in 1789 still has not been ratified. It would cap at 50,000 the number of people a member of the House of Representatives could represent. Currently, a member of the House of Representatives represents approximately 770,000 persons. Were the "first amendment" ratified, instead of 435 members of the House of Representatives, there would be 6700. Probably not a good idea.] This amendment contains a simple idea: one Congress should not be able to raise its own salary; it should only be able to raise it for a subsequent Congress. Not quite the same level of importance as Freedom of Speech, Press, and Religion. By 1791 six states, not the then required ten, had ratified the amendment. Ohio ratified it in 1873 as a protest against a retroactive pay raise Congress had granted itself. Wyoming did the same in 1978. In 1982, a student at the University of Texas, Gregory Watson, discovered this unratified amendment and wrote a paper about it, suggesting that it could and should be ratified. He received a "C" on the paper. Nevertheless, Watson set out to have the amendment ratified. His crusade was picked up by conservative causes,* and in 1992 it had received ratification in thirty-eight states, three-fourths of fifty, if you included the original six from 1791. The question then was whether this amendment had been validly ratified, inasmuch as there had passed over 200 years since its proposal. Congress called for hearings at which law professors opined that the amendment was not valid. However, before Congress did anything, the Archivist of the United States, who by statute has been entrusted with receiving and recording state ratifications of proposed amendments, announced that, the requisite ratifications having been

---

* Mr. Watson did not limit his historical interest to conservative causes, however. He also discovered that Mississippi had never ratified, and in fact had rejected, the Thirteenth Amendment banning slavery. He undertook a campaign to have Mississippi ratify the amendment, which was successful in 1995.

received, the amendment was now in effect. Congress, faced with the option of overruling the Archivist, which would look like it wanted to vote itself pay raises, jumped on the bandwagon and passed resolutions agreeing with the Archivist. But who knows? Maybe the Twenty-Seventh Amendment isn't an amendment at all.

B. READING CONSTITUTIONAL LAW CASES

By now you should have read the entire Constitution and have discovered that for many, if not most, important questions, the text does not provide clear answers. For over 200 years federal and state courts have been interpreting the document, and the decisions of the Supreme Court, because it is the highest court in the land with respect to the meaning of the Constitution, provide answers to many of the questions. Supreme Court decisions, as well as appellate court decisions generally, have two parts: a judgment and an opinion or opinions. A court's judgment is its resolution of the case. For example, the judgment in the case brought to challenge the constitutionality of a state law restricting marriage to a man and a woman was that the law was unconstitutional. But why was it unconstitutional? That is what the opinion is for—to explain how the court arrived at that judgment. Nothing in the Constitution or statutes requires courts to give explanations for their judgments, but it has been the historical practice since well before the existence of the United States and is virtually the universal practice of appellate courts around the world today. Compare this to jury verdicts, which never give reasons explaining why the jury reached the decision it did.

Probably the major reason why courts write opinions is to give notice as to how the court interprets the law. In this way, people can know how a previously ambiguous constitutional or statutory provision will be interpreted by the court in the future. When the Supreme Court interprets the Constitution, lower courts, both state and federal, must follow that interpretation under the doctrine of vertical *stare decisis*. Thus, as a practical matter, the Court's interpretation becomes the law; it is in effect like writing a clarification of the ambiguous text. Of course, the Supreme Court may overrule a prior decision, resulting in a new interpretation, because horizontal *stare decisis*, unlike vertical *stare decisis*, is not mandatory, but prudential. The Court does not often overrule past decisions, but when it does, it can be dramatic. For example, the recent overruling of *Roe v. Wade* in *Dobbs v. Jackson Women's Health Org.*, 142 S.Ct. 2228 (2022), had major consequences.

The remainder of this book after this chapter consists of opinions of the Supreme Court explaining their decisions. Indeed, when one speaks of "constitutional law," one is usually referring to what the Supreme Court has said about the meaning of constitutional provisions, rather than the text of the Constitution itself. How to read court opinions is one of the things that law students learn early in their studies. You usually cannot read court opinions as you would read ordinary descriptive text, much less literature; they must be studied. First, try to discover what the legal issue in the case is. At the Supreme Court level, the issue is almost never about a disputed fact. The facts have already been decided either by the jury or a judge below. The legal issue is the meaning of the law (or constitutional provision) or how it should apply to those facts. Second, look for what the Court actually decides and who wins and who loses; what is the judgment of the Court. Third, what is the Court's reasoning? Often there are layers to the reasoning. For example, in the same-sex marriage case, the Court said that the law forbidding same-sex marriage was unconstitutional because it violated the due process rights of the plaintiffs (the people who brought the case), but the Court then went to some lengths to explain how that was. You need to be able to decipher that reasoning. Fourth, look for "tests" that the Court establishes or utilizes in reaching its decisions. In many areas of the law, the Court has created a heuristic to help decide cases. For instance, if a law discriminates on the basis of race, the Court has said the law is unconstitutional unless such discrimination is necessary to achieve a compelling government interest. Fifth, focus on how the Court relies on or distinguishes cases that are similar to the case before it. Because our concept of justice and the rule of law requires that we treat like cases alike, much of legal reasoning is by analogy. Is this case like previous cases or not like them? For example, is banning marriages between persons of the same sex like banning marriages between persons of opposite races?

C. BACKGROUND AND HISTORY

1. WHY STUDY HISTORY?

From the foregoing sections and several of the questions, it is apparent that the text of the Constitution does not answer many of the most fundamental questions that can arise under it, much less more detailed questions that arise from its administration. How should the Constitution then be interpreted to answer those questions? It is a common, if not universal, approach to interpreting statutes passed by legislatures to look to the legislative intent behind the statute. What did the legislators intend when they adopted the statute? This would be one way of interpreting the Constitution. After all, it is a legal text and in that way is like a statute. What did the drafters in Philadelphia intend when they wrote the original Constitution, and what did members of Congress intend when they drafted constitutional amendments to be submitted to the states for ratification? Of course, unlike normal legislation, the adoption of the Constitution and its amendments involves more than just the drafters; the states had to ratify the Constitution and its amendments, so perhaps we should also consider the intent of the ratifiers (the state constitutional conventions for the original Constitution and usually state legislatures for the amendments). Nevertheless, most commentators and judicial decisions interpreting the Constitution and its amendments generally only look to the intent of the framers, not the ratifiers, if only because they are a more finite group.

How would one determine their intent? In the best case, as is the case with statutes, one could look to reports of congressional committees and statements made by legislators with regard to a proposed amendment. This is not an option with regard to the original Constitution, because it did not emanate from a congressional committee, and the actual proceedings in Philadelphia were not public. Indeed, there was a strict requirement of secrecy enforced on the delegates to the Constitutional Convention. Nevertheless, James Madison, one of the delegates from Virginia and today called "the father of the Constitution," kept a journal that has become the primary source of what little knowledge we have of what transpired in the Convention in Philadelphia. Partially because even Madison's journal is sketchy and also because it was not made public until after his death in 1836, probably the most important source for discerning the intent of the framers is the collection of essays published in New York newspapers prior to the ratification convention in New York and known today as The Federalist Papers. These 85 essays, authored pseudonymously by Madison, Alexander Hamilton (the only delegate from New York to vote for the Constitution), and John Jay (a prominent New York lawyer and former chief justice of the highest New York court), were written as an attempt to convince the people of New York to support the adoption of the Constitution, and in so doing they explained its intents and purposes at some length. It is a fair criticism to note that The Federalist Papers were not written as a dispassionate exposition of the Constitution, but rather they present a one-sided view of the meaning of the Constitution. The "Anti-Federalists" had a different view that was expressed in essays printed in different New York newspapers, but history, they say, is written by the victors, and those supporting the adoption of the Constitution were the victors, so it is The Federalist Papers that today are most often relied upon to gauge the original intent.

The attempt to find the original intent of the Constitution as a means of interpreting the Constitution is often called "**Originalism.**" However, there is another form of originalism that has been articulated by, among others, Justice Antonin Scalia. *See, e.g.,* A Matter of Interpretation: Federal Courts and the Law (1997). Justice Scalia, who did not believe in looking for legislative intent generally, argued in favor of finding the original *meaning*, rather than the original intent. In his theory, the text that was adopted is the law, not what the drafters may have intended it to mean. Only the text itself went through the necessary procedures to become law, not the unarticulated intent of the drafters. To discover the original meaning, Justice Scalia would look to then contemporary dictionaries to assess the meaning of words, but he could also look to contemporary documents, such as the Federalist Papers, to discern what was the context at the time for the law. His search is for how persons at the time would have reasonably read the constitutional or statutory text; his focus is on how the reader would have read the text, rather than on what the drafter intended.

Originalism as a theory of constitutional interpretation arose in reaction to what during the Nineteen Sixties and Seventies was called the Living Constitution. Those espousing a Living Constitution preferred that the ambiguous phrases and concepts in the Constitution should be interpreted in light of modern concerns and experiences, rather than by looking backward to what was thought or intended one or two hundred years ago. Some would even argue that it was the intent or understanding of the Founders themselves that the Constitution would be interpreted to adapt with the times. However, this method of interpretation leaves much discretion to the unelected, undemocratic legal elite that makes up the Supreme Court.

And then there is the attempt to synthesize originalism with a living Constitution. This attempt has been articulated by Professor Jack Balkin at the University of Texas. *See* Living Originalism (2011). While it pays lip service to the original text, it also stresses fidelity to the "principles that underlie the text." Where the text is unclear, one would look to the underlying principles of the original Constitution to discern the correct meaning. But how does one find the "underlying principles" of the Constitution? Having read the Constitution, what do you think the Constitution's underlying principles are that bear on whether a state can criminalize abortion? Professor Balkin finds the underlying principles of the Fourteenth Amendment to create a constitutional right of women to obtain abortions. Critics of this method of interpretation believe that it suffers the same problems as the concept of a Living Constitution, because it allows personal preferences to influence what one says are underlying principles of the Constitution. In other words, the determination of "constitutional law" would become subjective, rather than objective, allowing judges to "make up" constitutional law, rather than just apply constitutional law. Of course, critics of "original intent" and "original meaning" jurisprudence reply that these methodologies are equally prone to subjective manipulation, because history is rarely clear on the issue.

Originalism, whether styled as original intent, original meaning, or original principles, is not the only methodology of interpreting the Constitution. Nevertheless, it is a methodology utilized by a growing number of Supreme Court justices, so this focus on the history and context underlying the adoption of constitutional provisions makes the history and background of the Constitution relevant to its interpretation and hence important to us.

2. HISTORY

a. Pre-Constitution History

As you know, the original 13 states began as colonies of Great Britain. Virginia was the first colony, followed closely by Massachusetts in the early 17th century, but Massachusetts differed greatly from Virginia in that Massachusetts was settled by religious dissenters (Pilgrims and Puritans) who came to America to be able to practice their religion freely, while Virginia was settled by fortune seekers, both rich and poor, rather than by religious dissenters. Several other colonies were founded by persons seeking a place to practice their particular religion—Rhode Island by followers of Roger Williams, Pennsylvania by Quakers, Maryland by Catholics. Others, like Virginia, had their origins more in economic considerations. New York and New Jersey had been Dutch colonies until Great Britain seized them during the Second Dutch-Anglo War in 1664. Georgia, founded in 1732, was the last colony to be established. Substantial immigration followed the establishment of the colonies, so that, while in 1700 the population of the colonies barely reached a quarter million, by 1780 the population was more than 2.75 million. Moreover, the nature of the colonies had changed. Over 30% of the new white immigrants were from Germany, Scotland, and Ireland. The religious orientation of some of the colonies, such as Maryland, had ended. Only the New England colonies retained their homogenous English character. By far the largest state was Virginia, followed by Pennsylvania, Massachusetts, and North Carolina. Slavery was practiced in virtually all the colonies.

The colonies, although clearly subject to Great Britain, as a practical matter governed themselves on a day-to-day basis. Each colony had a lower house whose members were elected by free white male property owners, as well as an upper house and a governor. While the upper house and governor were chosen by different means in different colonies, depending upon the manner in which they were created, the lower house or assembly had the power to make most laws governing daily life. These assemblies became in effect the training grounds for those who became the political leaders of the United States.

Prior to the French and Indian War between 1754 and 1760, which despite the name was the American portion of the Seven Years War between Great Britain and France, Great Britain had not demanded much of the colonies, in part because trade with them was profitable to Great Britain. One result of the war was Great Britain obtaining all of Canada from France. However, the French and Indian War resulted in a number of changes in Great Britain's relations with the colonies. First, as a way to avoid creating difficulties with the native Americans, the King placed restrictions on the settlement of western lands, but the expanding population of the colonies, plus the expectations of those who came to

America in search of new property, created a great pressure for westward expansion. Second, the Quartering Act of 1765 required the colonies to provide housing and supplies to British troops. Third, because the war and administration of the colonies were expensive for Great Britain and the colonies were viewed as prosperous and a good source of revenue, Great Britain began a series of taxing measures, including the Sugar Tax, the Stamp Tax (which required all legal documents, newspapers, books, and playing cards to display a stamp purchased from the British government), and the Townshend Acts (placing import taxes on lead, glass, paint, paper, and tea). The Americans thought they were being taxed too much (Imagine that!) and, of course, had no opportunity to say anything in the matter. Taxation without representation! Accustomed to a benign neglect, the colonists viewed these numerous changes as threatening and the presence of British troops as an affront.

The Boston Massacre in 1770 in which British troops fired on an unarmed mob, killing five, elevated tensions. The colonies engaged in public protests, petitions, and a boycott of British goods, resulting in a repeal of most of these taxes, but the tea tax remained. This was widely evaded by American merchants, such as John Hancock, smuggling tea from Holland. Parliament retaliated in several ways. It increased British enforcement powers by bringing smuggling cases before admiralty courts, with judges appointed by the Crown and no juries, and by authorizing Writs of Assistance—general warrants allowing British customs officials to search for contraband anywhere they wished. In addition, parliament passed a law enabling the British East India Company, the British tea monopoly, to avoid the tax by selling direct to consumers. This, it was hoped, would bankrupt the smugglers. Americans, rather than viewing this as a way to obtain tea at a lower cost, correctly saw that this was an attempt to cut off and punish the American merchants, as well as increase British control over American affairs.

An attempt by the British East India Company to import tea to Boston in 1773 resulted in the famed Boston Tea Party, where the "Sons of Liberty," including noted revolutionary Samuel Adams, dumped tons of tea into Boston Harbor before a cheering crowd. The British Government responded by attempting to punish the Massachusetts Colony by closing the port of Boston until reimbursement was made for the tea destroyed, banning all town meetings without prior government permission, eliminating the elected council, and providing for trials of offenders to be held in England or other colonies rather than in Massachusetts. These laws, called the Coercive Acts by the British and the Intolerable Acts by the Americans, succeeded in uniting the colonies to provide assistance to Massachusetts and against Britain.

In 1774, representatives of all the colonies except Georgia met in Philadelphia in the First Continental Congress* to devise a unified strategy to deal with the British government. Some wished to compromise with Britain; others wanted full independence; the largest number, but short of a majority, sought a "Plan of Union" that would have a Grand Council elected by the colonies as the legislative arm of government and a President General appointed by the King. Unable to agree on any of these approaches, Congress adopted a Declaration and Resolves, which it sent to King George. *See* http://avalon.law.yale.edu/18th_century/resolves.asp. While professing loyalty to the Crown, it demanded the repeal of the Intolerable Acts and asserted various rights of the colonies and colonists. To put pressure on the Crown, the Congress agreed to boycott British goods and to invite Canada to join with the colonies. Finally, the Congress agreed to meet again the following year to consider what action to take in light of King George's response.

The British response was not to be conciliatory, and the British were intent on putting down the incipient rebellion in Massachusetts, sending 12,000 troops to Boston. Meanwhile, the colonists were arming and training in militias, citizens organized and armed for military purposes. In April 1775, the British learned that the colonists were gathering weapons and ammunition in Concord, a town outside Boston, and troops were sent from Boston to find and seize that materiel. Paul Revere and two other patriots** rode out ahead to warn the militias. In Lexington, a town on the way to Concord, 77 militiamen gathered on the town common to meet the 700 British regulars. Neither the British nor the American commander wished to initiate hostilities, but from somewhere a shot was fired, and the American Revolution had begun. The British routed the militiamen and continued to Concord, from which most of the munitions had already been evacuated. Here the Concord Minutemen*** were supported by militia from other nearby towns, and more reinforcements continued to arrive, ultimately reaching more than 1000. An initial skirmish was won by the Americans, and the British began a retreat towards Boston. Repeatedly the Americans ambushed the retreating columns, inflicting serious damage, until British reinforcements from Boston joined the retreating troops. Word of the battles had spread, however, and more militia continued to arrive and join the fray until the British troops finally returned to Boston. The next day Boston was surrounded by some 20,000 militiamen.

In May the already scheduled Second Continental Congress met in Philadelphia to determine a course of action. It quickly decided to create a

---

* Today, the word "Congress" to Americans suggests the national legislature in Washington, D.C., made up of the Senate and the House of Representatives, but in the 18th century the word meant simply a formal assembly of representatives, as of various nations, to discuss problems.

** The term "patriot" was a contemporary term to describe a supporter of the revolution. Those opposed to the revolution were called "tories" (or worse) by patriots and "loyalists" by others.

*** The civilian volunteers were called Minutemen, because they would be ready to fight with a minute's notice.

unified Continental Army under the leadership of General George Washington, who was dispatched to take leadership of the various militias laying siege to Boston. Nevertheless, Congress still held hopes of achieving its previous goal of autonomy within the British empire, rather than actual independence. The Congress adopted a Declaration of the Causes and Necessity of Taking Up Arms, *see* http://avalon.law.yale.edu/18th_century/ arms.asp, in which it declared that the colonies did not intend to dissolve its union with Great Britain and that it had not raised armies with the design of separating from Great Britain. This was quickly followed by a letter to the King expressing a desire to end hostilities and seeking a reconciliation. Moreover, the legislatures of Maryland, New Jersey, New York, North Carolina, and Pennsylvania voted against independence into late 1775. But the war was proceeding apace, with the Battle of Bunker Hill in Boston, the capture of Fort Ticonderoga in New York by Ethan Allen and the Green Mountain Boys, and most importantly the invasion of Canada in late 1775 led by General Benedict Arnold. Congress authorized this expedition in the hope that French-Canadians, only recently subject to British rule, would rise up and join the colonies in the fight. This was not to be, and Arnold's mission was a failure.

The British government, although itself split on the wisdom of a war with the colonies, did not take the proffered olive branch letter seriously. Establishing sovereignty over the colonies became as much a matter of principle for them as autonomy from the government in London was for the Americans. And, in January 1776, Thomas Paine published his pamphlet *Common Sense* in which he rallied Americans to throw off the tyrannical rule of Britain and establish their own independent republic. This pamphlet, reflecting a natural rights philosophy also expressed in the later Declaration of Independence, is said to have been read by virtually every free American and had a dramatic effect on public and political opinion. Or maybe it just gave voice to what was rapidly becoming a foregone conclusion. In any case, on July 4, 1776, Congress adopted the Declaration of Independence irrevocably deciding on independence. *See* http://avalon. law.yale.edu/18th_century/declare.asp. Largely written by Thomas Jefferson with some assistance from Benjamin Franklin, the Declaration provided a justification for what had already taken place and an appeal to the international community for recognition of the thirteen states as new nations, united for purposes of securing their independence from Great Britain. The "United Colonies" in earlier declarations were now the "United States."*

At the same time, the Continental Congress began to act like a national government: appointing ambassadors, signing treaties, raising armies, appointing generals, obtaining loans from foreign states, issuing

---

* Today we think of states as being governmental bodies within a nation, but at the time the term "state" meant a nation state. Thus, the "United States of America" in the Declaration meant 13 separate nation states but united for their joint interests, like the United Nations today.

paper money (called "Continentals"), and disbursing funds. It did not, however, have the power to tax, and it had to rely on requests to the various colonies for support, which was often not forthcoming. At the same time, the states adopted their own constitutions, creating their own governments. These constitutions usually began with a declaration or bill of rights, also reflecting the natural rights philosophy expressed in *Common Sense* and the Declaration of Independence. Thus, they prohibited cruel and inhuman punishment, general warrants, ex post facto laws, taking property without just compensation, and forced self incrimination, and they required freedom of the press, the availability of habeas corpus, the right to bear arms, and the right to a speedy and local trial by jury. These, of course, would later find their reiteration either in the Constitution or in its first ten amendments.

Immediately after the adoption of the Declaration of Independence, the first draft of the Articles of Confederation was presented to the Congress. The unanimity over establishing an army and finally declaring independence, however, did not extend to how the now united states should interact beyond the prosecution of war. It was not until a year later, in 1777, that a final draft of the Articles was completed and approved by the Congress for submission to each of the newly-declared independent states for ratification. Delaware was the first state to ratify, but Maryland held out until 1781 due to land disputes with Virginia and New York. Nevertheless, as a practical matter, the Articles established the government of the United States from 1777 until the ratification of the Constitution in 1789. The Articles are truly the first American constitution and deserve close attention, because they contain the first legal framework governing the "United States." *See* http://avalon.law.yale.edu/18th_century/artconf.asp.

The Articles have some similarities and some differences with the Constitution. Most fundamentally, the Articles did not unequivocally create one nation. Elements of the Articles look more like a league among nations, much like the European Union today. First, Article I styled the new entity a "confederacy," a term described at that time in international law as several sovereign and independent states uniting themselves together by a perpetual confederacy, without ceasing to be, each individually, a perfect state. In addition, Article III expressly provided that the states were entering "a firm league of friendship with each other, for their common defense, the security of their liberties, and their mutual and general welfare, binding themselves to assist each other, against all . . . attacks. . . ." Article II stated that each state "retain[ed] its sovereignty, freedom, and independence, and every power, jurisdiction, and right" not "expressly delegated to the United States, in Congress assembled." Article V provided that each state would have one vote in Congress, just as today each nation has one vote in the United Nations' General Assembly. Nowhere did the Articles provide the United States with the power to exercise sovereign authority over individuals within the several states. Again, just as the United Nations today cannot make a law governing individuals but only laws governing nations, the Congress of the United States could only make laws binding the states within it. Finally, nowhere in the Articles is there a mention of citizenship in the United States; individuals were citizens of their states under such laws as those states might make.

On the other hand, there are elements in the Articles that reflect some sense of nationhood in the United States. For example, Article IV established a freedom of travel among the states and prohibited states from denying citizens of other states the same "privileges and immunities of free citizens" enjoyed by their own citizens. In addition, it provided that each state should give "full faith and credit . . . to the records, acts, and judicial proceedings of the courts and magistrates" in other states. The Constitution largely repeats these provisions in its Article IV. Moreover, Article VI of the Articles of Confederation denies to states a number of powers that sovereign states would normally possess, such as the plenary power to send ambassadors to and receive ambassadors from foreign nations, to enter into treaties with other states or nations, to maintain a standing army or navy, to engage in war, and to grant letters of marque and reprisal. These restrictions, with little change, appear again in Article I, Section 10, of the Constitution. Finally, the Articles did expressly delegate certain traditional sovereign powers to the United States. For example, Congress is given the power to establish a national currency, a national standard of weights and measures, a national post office system, the power to borrow money, and the power to build and equip a navy. These and more are authorities later provided to Congress in the Constitution.

Whatever the legal status of the United States as a nation, as a practical matter, the United States was subordinate to the states. While Article XIII required every state to abide by determinations made by Congress, there was no enforcement mechanism. There was neither a President of the United States* nor a federal court system. Congress could not itself levy taxes; it could only tell states what they should provide to the United States, but states ignored with impunity demands made by Congress to pay their required taxes to the United States. Congress could not even raise its own army but was limited to requisitioning land forces from the states, which they were required to supply, but for which there was also no enforcement mechanism. Again, much like the United Nations today, the United States was beholden to its member states, not as a practical matter sovereign over them. The weakness of Congress quickly became apparent, and fixing the problems was made nearly impossible by

---

*   There was a President of Congress, but just as the Vice President under the Constitution is the President of the Senate, this kind of "president" is merely one who presides over the deliberations of the body; he is not an executive officer.

a requirement that any amendment to the Articles be unanimous among all the states.

After victory in Boston, forcing the British out, Washington and the Continental forces suffered a series of serious losses—the failed invasion of Quebec, the Battle of Long Island resulting in the British occupation of New York, and the New Jersey campaign resulting in the British occupation of Philadelphia, requiring the Continental Congress to flee. The winter of 1776–77 spent at Valley Forge, lacking adequate supplies, nearly did the Continental Army in. Only Washington's surprise attack on the British base in Trenton, New Jersey, on a snowy Christmas night, capturing 1000 Hessian mercenaries, lifted the spirits of his troops enough that they extended their enlistments that otherwise would have expired six days later. Salvation came in the fall of 1777, when a British plan to lead an entire army south from Canada to New York City, effectively to sever the New England colonies from the rest, went awry. Under General Benedict Arnold the American forces surrounded the British army and forced it to surrender at the Battle of Saratoga. While a great triumph in itself, the real significance of the victory was that it convinced France to join the war on America's side. There is an irony in King Louis XVI supporting a revolution against a monarchy, a revolution that undoubtedly helped initiate the French Revolution twelve years later wherein he literally lost his head. One must remember, however, that the French and the British had been warring with one another for centuries and the adage that my enemy's enemy is my friend.

With more French money, French troops, and French ships, the tide turned dramatically. The *coup de grace* was dealt at Yorktown, Virginia, where the French fleet and American and French troops forced the surrender of a British army of 7000 under Lord Cornwallis in 1781. The peace negotiations dragged on and were finally concluded with the Peace of Paris in 1783. Great Britain accepted American independence, ceded lands east of the Mississippi and south of Canada, and granted American access to the Newfoundland fisheries. Congress was to recommend to the states that American loyalists be treated fairly and their confiscated property restored, and both parties agreed that creditors of neither country were to be impeded in the collection of their pre-war debts. This last requirement proved difficult to enforce under the Articles and again proved the weakness of the United States in attempting to control the states.

The one area in which the Articles proved sufficient was dealing with the western lands that were not within any state. Here the Congress could play the honest broker between states vying for the lands, and two laws were passed that helped shape the future of American westward expansion—the Land Ordinance of 1785, governing the disposition of public lands, and the Northwest Ordinance of 1787, providing territorial government of the western lands.

The inability of Congress under the Articles to deal with the economic depression following the War caused the greatest problem for the new governments. Farmers, who made up the bulk of the population of the states, purchased land, goods, and supplies on credit. The depression following the War, however, resulted in reduced income for farmers, and they were unable to pay their debts. States reacted in different ways depending upon their political makeup. States where the control of the government was in the hands of the debtor class either issued paper money and required creditors to accept it in payment of debts or simply passed laws delaying or excusing debts. This upset the merchant and professional classes, but there was nothing Congress could do. It had no power to make laws regarding commerce. States like Massachusetts, where the political establishment represented the merchant class, held fast and provided no breaks to the farmer/debtors. This led to the Shays Rebellion, in which farmers in the western part of the state took up arms against the state. This rebellion was quickly put down by the local militia, but it too demonstrated the weakness of Congress, which had been unable to respond to an appeal for help from the state. At the same time, there were several ongoing disputes between states regarding commerce in the waters adjoining them, and Congress was powerless to act. For example, Virginia, Maryland, Delaware, and Pennsylvania were all involved in a dispute over commerce in and around the Chesapeake Bay.

In 1786, Virginia invited all the states to send delegates to a meeting in Annapolis, Maryland, to consider possible amendments to the Articles. Only five states sent delegates, although these included Alexander Hamilton and James Madison, and the upshot of the Annapolis Convention was to request Congress to call for a convention of the states.

b. The Drafting and Ratification

Congress responded by inviting the states to send delegates to a convention in Philadelphia "for the sole and express purpose of revising the Articles of Confederation." Fifty-five delegates from twelve states* arrived in May 1787. These delegates included most of the leading lights of the day, including Madison, Hamilton, Washington, and Franklin. Some, however, were notably absent, including Thomas Jefferson and John Adams, who were abroad on foreign missions, and Samuel Adams, Patrick Henry, and George Clinton (the Governor of New York), who were adamantly opposed to giving any greater powers to the national government. There was general agreement among those who attended that changes to the Articles were necessary, but there was no consensus yet on the nature of those changes.

A group of nationalists, who favored scrapping the Articles altogether and starting over, met together ahead of the convention to devise a plan to

---

*   Rhode Island was not interested in any changes and boycotted the convention.

present at the beginning of the convention. This plan, dubbed the Virginia Plan, because the Virginia delegates were the primary instigators, provided for a national legislature with an upper and lower house, a national executive, and a national judiciary. While this sounds like what emerged as the Constitution, there were a number of fundamental differences. Both the upper and lower houses of the legislature would be apportioned according to population, so that large states would have greater representation in both houses. Recall that Virginia was by far the largest state at the time, so this proposal would be to its benefit. The legislature would have all the powers to legislate as under the Articles, as well as additional powers to legislate "in all cases to which the separate states are incompetent" and to overrule any state law deemed by the legislature to be inconsistent with the constitution or any treaties. The national executive would be chosen by the national legislature. The national judiciary would consist of a Supreme Tribunal whose members would be appointed by the upper house of the legislature and such inferior tribunals as the legislature might appoint.

This plan was debated for the first two weeks of the Convention and had general support from the more populous states. Opposition to the plan arose from two different sources. First, New Jersey and Delaware opposed it because it deprived them of equal suffrage in the legislature, apportioning both houses on the basis of population and thus both seriously eroding their influence and striking at the principle of their equal sovereignty with the other states. New York and Connecticut (6th and 7th in population at the time) opposed alteration of the structure of the Articles and wished only to add some new legislative powers to Congress. Accordingly, together they presented a counter-proposal, known as the New Jersey Plan. The New Jersey Plan did not generally reject the Articles, although it did extend the authority of Congress beyond what was already in the Articles, authorizing Congress to make laws to raise revenue and regulate trade and commerce between the states and foreign nations. In addition, somewhat like the Virginia Plan, it also allowed Congress to create an Executive, but in this plan it would consist of a Council of several persons chosen by Congress who would execute federal acts, appoint inferior officers, and direct military operations. Also somewhat like the Virginia Plan, Congress could create a Supreme Tribunal, but whose judges would be appointed by the Executive. This Supreme Tribunal would hear in the first instance impeachments of federal officers, and it would have appellate jurisdiction over cases involving ambassadors, captures from an enemy, piracies and felonies on the high seas, foreigners, the construction of any treaty, and any of the acts for the regulation of trade or the collection of the federal revenue. All of these cases in the first instance, however, would be heard in state courts. Finally, and unlike the Virginia Plan, the New Jersey Plan contained a provision that is almost exactly the same as the Supremacy Clause in the Constitution.

The merits and demerits of the two plans were debated for several weeks, but neither side would give way on the basic issue of the makeup of Congress. A special committee was formed, which brought back a new plan, known as the Great Compromise, that provided for proportional representation in a House of Representatives, giving more power to the populous states, but equal representation in a Senate and a requirement that both would have to agree before a law could be made, thereby retaining an equality of power among the states. This broke the deadlock, and as a practical matter decided that the Articles would be jettisoned and that a national government would be created. Nevertheless, there were still many other issues to resolve. For example, while all were agreed that Congress needed the additional authority to make laws regulating commerce, the southern states, reflecting the Articles' requirement that all important laws must be agreed to by at least nine states, wanted to require a two-thirds majority to pass any law under this new authority. This was a sticking point for some time, but ultimately the southern states conceded on this point when the northern states agreed to prohibit Congress from passing export taxes (which would have fallen on the southern states' export of rice, tobacco, and cotton) and to prohibit any law regulating the importation of slaves until 1808. Another example was how to choose the President. There were supporters of a direct popular election, election by state representatives, election by state governors, and election by the Congress. The result, the electoral vote, was another grand compromise. Large states obtained generally proportional strength in the apportionment of electors, but the state legislatures retained the power to determine how the electors would be selected, and if the electors failed to choose a President by a majority vote, then the President would be chosen by a means in which each state would get one vote. As may be seen, much of what is in the Constitution is a product of political compromise rather than grand philosophy.

On September 17, 1787, the final text of the Constitution was adopted "by the unanimous consent of the States present." Of course, Rhode Island was not there. In addition, two of New York's delegates had left the convention because they were opposed to the direction it took in favor of creating a national government, leaving only supra-nationalist Hamilton to vote on behalf of New York. Indeed, of the 55 delegates who attended the convention, only 39 signed the Constitution. For example, George Mason, a delegate from Virginia and the author of Virginia's Declaration of Rights, refused to sign the Constitution because it did not contain a bill of rights, and the Governor of Virginia, Edmund Randolph, also a delegate, had left the convention when the Virginia Plan was not adopted.

Drafting the Constitution was hard enough, but it was only the first step. There still remained the need to have the states ratify it, and ratification was not a foregone conclusion. Today the Constitution may seem to have been inevitable, and in some states at the time ratification was simple. Delaware, again the first state to ratify, did so unanimously, as did Georgia and New Jersey. In Maryland and Connecticut the vote was over 75% in favor of ratification. Elsewhere, however, the Constitution was highly controversial. As noted, Rhode Island did not participate in the convention and did not recognize the call for state conventions to ratify the Constitution. In Massachusetts there was bitter debate, and ratification barely succeeded by a margin of 5%. In Pennsylvania, although the final margin was 17%, the struggle had been much closer than the numbers suggest. The outcome was the same in South Carolina. In North Carolina, the convention met but voted "neither to ratify nor reject the Constitution." When New Hampshire finally ratified the Constitution on June 21, 1788, by a narrow 5% margin, the requisite nine states had ratified the Constitution, but debates in Virginia, the largest state by far, and New York, a centrally important state, were ongoing. It was unthinkable that a new form of government could go into effect absent these states. In Virginia, several leading politicians, such as Patrick Henry and George Mason, were opposed to the Constitution. In New York, two thirds of the members of the convention were from the Anti-Federalist party, and ratification seemed doomed.

A major bone of contention in all the states where there was opposition to the Constitution was the absence of a bill of rights in the Constitution. The delegates in Philadelphia were not necessarily opposed to a bill of rights, but after the 16 weeks of daily work to finish the structural constitution to replace the Articles of Confederation, they were exhausted. Each of the states, however, already had their own bill of rights, and the absence of one in the Constitution for the new national government was viewed as gravely threatening to both individual and state rights. What finally enabled Massachusetts to garner enough votes to ratify the Constitution was the inclusion in its ratification of a recommendation to the new Congress that a bill of rights should be immediately proposed as amendments. This technique also worked in New Hampshire and Virginia to sway enough votes to ratify. Later, in New York, fearing that the new government might actually go forward without New York, the Anti-Federalists used such a letter to justify switching their support to ratification. Two days after New York ratified the Constitution, the Congress sitting under the Articles of Confederation declared that there was a new government that would go into effect the following March. North Carolina held out until after the Bill of Rights had actually been proposed to the states by the new Congress of the United States. Rhode Island held out even longer, actually voting ratification down in its convention's first session. Later, after the United States imposed a tariff on goods from Rhode Island (treating it like a foreign nation), it ratified the Constitution by a vote of 34–32 in 1790.

c. Slavery

No history of the United States prior to the Constitution, or after for that matter, would be sufficient without a discussion of slavery. Scholars are divided on the importance of slavery as an issue in the constitutional convention itself, but there can be no doubt that it was an important issue in 18th century America, and that it greatly affected the culture of at least the southern states, if not the entire country.

The first African slaves in British North America arrived in Jamestown in 1619. These and many others in the early years were treated in the European tradition of slavery—servitude for life or a term of years, more like a performance contract than as being property. As a result, many of these early slaves and their offspring became free persons with full citizenship rights. Indeed, some even became successful enough to have their own slaves. In the 1660s–70s, however, chattel slavery, perhaps imported from the British West Indies, became the virtually exclusive mode of slavery in the southern states and extended into the northern states as well. In chattel slavery, the slave is the property of the owner and the slaves' children likewise the property of the mother's owner. Slaves in the south were used largely on plantations, while slaves in the north tended to be domestics. South Carolina was the most notorious slave state, responsible for approximately 40% of all the slaves imported into the thirteen colonies, with a population of African slaves that by the early 18th century outnumbered whites by two-to-one, and the first colony to adopt a slave code. Slave codes were adopted by all the southern states in order to legalize not only the institution of slavery but also the repressive regime necessary to keep a majority or near-majority of the population in perpetual bondage and degradation. The southern economy, based on the production on large plantations of agricultural products largely for export, such as rice, cotton, tobacco, and indigo, relied upon large numbers of slaves to produce these goods at low cost. The mercantile and small farm economy of the north did not have the same needs.

In the mid-18th century, a movement for abolition began in the north, and laws providing for a gradual end to slavery began to be passed in 1780. Gradual abolition usually took the form of declaring that children of slaves would be born free, or setting a term of years by which time slaves would become free. Gradual abolition was a compromise between the principle of freedom and the economic concerns of the slave owners, who would be deprived of their property without compensation. Moreover, the northern states and even Virginia had banned further importation of slaves during the 1780s. Nevertheless, at the time of the Constitution there continued to be slaves in virtually all of the states, and in the south the institution was thriving with no end in sight.

Several provisions of the Constitution relate to slavery. First, in Article I, Section 2, Clause 3, the apportionment among the states of representatives in the House of Representatives and of direct taxes is made according to the number of free persons (including indentured servants but not Indians not subject to taxation) and three-fifths of all other persons. "All other persons," of course, refers to African slaves. Thus, the southern states would have significantly more representation in the House of Representatives than if only free persons were counted. At the same time, the same states would be liable for a greater proportion of taxation of property than if only free persons were counted. Thus, the "three-fifths" formula was both a benefit and a detriment at the same time.

Second, Article I, Section 9, Clause 1, prohibited Congress until at least 1808 from restricting the importation of "such persons as any of the states now existing shall think proper to admit." "Such persons" are again slaves. Thus, this provision prohibited Congress from abolishing the importation of slaves under its new power to regulate commerce until 1808. This enabled the southern states to continue that importation for at least twenty more years. This provision was viewed as so important by the southern states that they insisted on the inclusion in Article VII, governing amendments to the Constitution, a prohibition on amending this provision of the Constitution before 1808. Interestingly, however, South Carolina itself had banned the importation of slaves in 1787, although it reopened the trade in 1804. The ban on importation probably was not due to moral concerns but rather to the fact that additional supply from new importations would lower the value of the slaves owned and generated by South Carolina plantation owners.

Third, Article IV, Section 2, Clause 3, provides that if a "person held to service or labour" escapes to another state, that state was obliged to return the person to "the party to whom such service or labour may be due." Again, we see that the sensibilities of the Framers led them to avoid the use of the term slave. Nevertheless, this clause is known as the Fugitive Slave Clause.

D. CONSTITUTIONAL INTERPRETATION

The media often portrays judges and justices as "liberal," "conservative," or "activist." These terms, however, are often misused or misunderstood, or have no real meaning. For example, Justice Scalia was usually portrayed as a "conservative" justice. This was due to his appointment by a "conservative" President—Ronald Reagan—and his opinions that are applauded by "conservative" politicians. At the same time, Justice Scalia was sometimes labeled an "activist" justice, because he demonstrated a willingness to challenge accepted constitutional norms as well as a lack of reluctance to declare federal laws unconstitutional. Nevertheless, usually when persons call judges "activist," they use the term as a shorthand way of characterizing judges who are willing to find constitutional rights not expressly enumerated in the Constitution.

Typically, these judges are also branded as "liberal" judges, because "liberal" political groups approve of their decisions. Historically, however, judges appointed by "liberal" Presidents and who were political "liberals" before donning the robe often were "conservative" jurists. That is, they viewed the role of the judiciary to be minimalist, and they were reluctant to interfere with majoritarian decisions. This is particularly true of Justices Hugo Black and Felix Frankfurter, appointed by President Franklin Roosevelt.

The current political debates over appointments to the Supreme Court began with Republican President Richard Nixon, who promised to appoint only "strict constructionists" to the Court, by which he meant judges who would strictly construe, as opposed to liberally construe, the rights provisions of the Constitution. This was in reaction primarily to decisions rendered by the Court under Chief Justice Earl Warren, such as *Brown v. Board of Education* ending legalized school segregation; *Miranda v. Arizona*, *Gideon v. Wainwright*, and *Mapp v. Ohio* recognizing rights of the criminally accused; and *Reynolds v. Sims* imposing the requirement of one person/one vote. Virtually every Republican President since Nixon has reiterated the pledge to appoint "strict constructionists" or their equivalent, and for twenty-five years, until President Bill Clinton, there was no opportunity for a Democratic President to appoint a Supreme Court justice. Nevertheless, sometimes persons expected to be "conservative" by their Republican nominators were not, such as Justice David Souter, while others evolved from a relatively "conservative" position to a more "liberal" position, such as Justice Harry Blackmun, who authored *Roe v. Wade*, and Justice John Paul Stevens, considered the most "liberal" member of the Court by the time of his retirement in 2010. Still others, while usually identified as "conservative," occasionally issued opinions aligned with the "liberals," such as Justice Anthony Kennedy, whose opinions declared laws prohibiting sodomy and banning same-sex marriage unconstitutional. Today, pundits identify Chief Justice John Roberts and Justices Clarence Thomas, Samuel Alito, Neil Gorsuch, Brett Kavanaugh, and Amy Coney Barrett as the "right" wing of the Court. On the "left" there are Justices Sonia Sotomayor, Elena Kagan, and Ketanji Brown Jackson. As you progress through this book, see if you can discern why these justices are perceived in this way.[*]

The vetting of potential Supreme Court nominees by administration officials has improved significantly since Ronald Reagan. They have been aided in this regard by two national organizations, one representing "conservative" judicial principles, the Federalist Society, and one representing "liberal" judicial principles, the American Constitution Society. Lower court judges who have been members of one of these

---

[*] When this edition went to press, Justice Jackson had not yet authored any opinions on the Supreme Court, but her background and her appointment by a Democratic President suggest that she is likely to agree more often with Justices Kagan and Sotomayor than the other justices.

organizations before their elevation to the Supreme Court have so far acted generally as one would have predicted in light of their membership.

A more important question is why justices reach the decisions they do, and in particular why they so often disagree with one another. An idealized view of the Court might imagine that the justices would agree about what the Constitution requires, prohibits, or allows. After 200-plus years shouldn't we know what it says?

Cynics and some political scientists ascribe critical importance to the justices' political orientation, pointing out that there is some correspondence between how particular justices rule in cases and the political party that appointed them. That is, in the simplest sense, Chief Justice Roberts and Justices Thomas, Alito, Gorsuch, Kavanaugh, and Barrett would tend to decide cases in ways that would please the Presidents who appointed them. Similarly, Justices Sotomayor, Kagan, and Jackson would tend to rule in ways that would please the Presidents who appointed them. At the same time, this way of explaining how justices rule is highly imperfect. Not only do justices sometimes rule in ways that would disappoint the Presidents that appointed them, but as mentioned earlier this is not a new phenomenon. Justice Blackmun did not follow the path Richard Nixon would have liked, and perhaps most dramatically Chief Justice Earl Warren, the former conservative Republican Attorney General and Governor of California, appointed Chief Justice by Republican President Dwight Eisenhower, became the symbol of the liberal, activist Court against which all subsequent Republican Presidents have railed. In other words, explaining the split on the Court on the basis of political orientation is not descriptively accurate as a historical matter.

Nevertheless, it is not a coincidence that some justices appointed by a President from one party are likely to disagree with some justices appointed by a President from a different party. There are fundamental ideological differences between the current Republican and Democratic parties. For example, they disagree about the proper relationship between government and the marketplace, government and morals, and the federal government and the states.

President Ronald Reagan in his first inaugural address expressed the Republican view of the relation of government and the marketplace: "government is not the solution to our problem; government is the problem." Democrats, on the other hand, believe that "problems" in the marketplace, from health care and the environment to unaffordable housing and extravagant executive compensation, are problems appropriately dealt with by the government. Republicans, therefore, want the courts to be critical of government regulation of the marketplace, whereas Democrats want courts to be supportive of such regulation.

With respect to the relation between morals and the government, here Republicans tend to be supportive of government regulation designed to preserve majoritarian senses of what is moral, while Democrats tend to believe that morals are a matter for the individual, not the government. Thus, Republicans tend to support laws against abortion, homosexuality, same-sex marriage, drug use, and pornography, whereas Democrats are more likely to view these issues as a matter reserved for individual choice. As a consequence, Republicans view judicial intervention to overturn laws adopted through democratic processes dealing with these issues as improper, while Democrats view courts as appropriate safeguards against majoritarian restrictions on individual choice in these areas.

Contemporary Republicans tend to be more concerned with protecting states' interests against federal incursions. As a result, they want the courts to construe strictly the powers of the federal government that might impinge on state powers. Although when Republicans control the national government, they are less enthusiastic about protecting the rights and powers of states controlled by Democrats. And similarly, when Democrats are not in control of the national government, they tend to glorify the rights and powers of states that are in the Democratic fold.

There are philosophical underpinnings for the parties' different approaches to the relationships between government and the marketplace, government and morals, and the respective powers of the federal and state governments, but the differences at the political level relating to the role of the courts appears to be more pragmatic. That is, Democrats want judges who will decide cases so that the outcomes favor the Democratic position, while Republicans want judges who will decide cases so that the outcomes favor their position. When they are in a position to affect who is appointed to the judiciary, the different parties attempt to bolster their positions by finding persons who they believe will rule in their favor. This is understandable, if not admirable. At the same time, the politicians cannot admit this in so many words, so they create labels or catchwords that supposedly reflect a judicial philosophy that is likely to result in decisions they favor.

There are, however, real judicial philosophies relating to how one should interpret the Constitution. Earlier we discussed "originalism," which is one of them. Closely related is "textualism," meaning that one must interpret the text on its own basis. There are various interpretive canons on how to interpret texts, often with Latin names, such as *noscitur a sociis* (the meaning of a word can be determined by its association with other words in the same phrase or document). For instance, the Second Amendment's right to bear arms follows the phrase "a well regulated militia being necessary to the security of a free state." A textualist might read the right to be somehow connected to the need for a militia, rather than, for example, the need to hunt or even for self-defense. Naturally, there are limits to textualism. For example, a different textualist might note that the Second Amendment's declarative statement of the people's right to bear arms does not grammatically rely on the phrase "a well regulated militia being necessary to a free state," as it would if the introductory phrase had been: "in order to assure a well regulated militia." So, even where the text is relatively precise, textualists might still reach different conclusions, but the Constitution is full of open-ended phrases such as "due process," "equal protection," and "cruel and unusual." What is a textualist to make of them?

Both originalism and textualism anchor constitutional interpretation to a fixed idea. That is, the meaning of the Constitution does not change over time absent constitutional amendment. However, there is a tension between this concept and the judicial rule of *stare decisis*.* That rule provides that prior judicial interpretations should be followed except in extraordinary circumstances. Scholars argue whether the rule of *stare decisis* is constitutionally required, but it is largely an academic argument, because Congress has shown no interest in legislating on the subject, and the Court has never questioned its applicability. *Stare decisis* is in tension with concepts of a fixed constitution, because each decision of the Court in some way alters the prior meaning of the Constitution, if only by making it more specific by deciding a particular case. As you will see, the repeated interpretation of particular parts of the Constitution has resulted in a significant change over time in what the Constitution "says." Thus, the Constitution becomes something of a moving target rather than a static instrument. Originalists and textualists have to deal with *stare decisis*, but for them it is a problem to be overcome in some way.

Those who believe in a "living constitution," however, embrace the idea that the Constitution changes over time. For them change is not a problem; it is what keeps the Constitution alive and meaningful. Indeed, not to interpret the Constitution, and previous interpretations of it, in light of changes in the nation and the world would make the Constitution increasingly either counterproductive or irrelevant. At the same time, any interpretation must be faithful to the principles embedded in the Constitution in order for the interpretation to be deemed valid. Thus, any interpretation must explain how it is faithful to the Constitution, through its text, its history, prior interpretations of the Constitution, or Constitutional principles. Thus, those who believe in a "living constitution" also anchor their interpretation of the Constitution to something immutable, but for these interpreters the immutability is the principles or purposes contained within the language of the Constitution.

---

* *Stare decisis* has two forms—vertical and horizontal. Vertical *stare decisis* requires lower courts to follow the decisions of courts over them; horizontal *stare decisis* generally requires the same court to follow its own precedents. The difference is that the former is an absolute requirement, whereas the latter is a softer requirement that the later court can avoid by overruling its prior decision. When the Supreme Court interprets the Constitution or federal laws, its opinions are binding on all lower courts, state and federal, but the *stare decisis* effect on the Supreme Court itself in later cases is the horizontal, or softer, sort.

Take the death penalty and the Eighth Amendment. That amendment prohibits the infliction of "cruel and unusual punishments." We know for a fact that the death penalty was not considered cruel and unusual in 1791, so for an originalist that would decide the question. On the other hand, we also know that whipping was a common form of punishment in 1791, but it is generally accepted that it would be a cruel and unusual punishment today.* A textualist not aligned with originalists could read the Eighth Amendment and interpret its terms to prohibit a punishment that is considered cruel and unusual at the time that it is administered, as opposed to what was considered cruel and unusual at the time of the amendment. Thus, the text itself could enable the Constitutional prohibition to change over time. But what about a form of punishment unknown at the time of the Eighth Amendment? A person who looks to the purpose or principle of the Eighth Amendment might ask what the underlying principle is of the Amendment. Indeed, the Court has done that. For example, it has said that the amendment "must draw its meaning from the evolving standards of decency that mark the progress of a maturing society." *Trop v. Dulles*, 356 U.S. 86, 100–101 (1958)(plurality opinion). This reflects a "living Constitution" approach. Alternatively, the Court has said that a punishment can be cruel and unusual because it is disproportionate to the offense involved. *See Weems v. United States*, 217 U.S. 349 (1910). This reflects an interpretation of the principle deemed to be encapsulated in the words involved.

Even if one accepts the idea that the Constitution must be interpreted in the context of its time, there can still be a dispute about how the underlying principles apply in the case, because many of the underlying principles of the Constitution are in tension with themselves. For example, the Constitution was a compromise between those who wished a strong central government and those who wished to protect the sovereignty of the states. The structure of the government was created to give effect to both of these principles, but to neither in an absolute sense. Thus, where the text of the Constitution is not clear and consequently how to mediate between these two principles is also not clear, a court has little to guide it. A judge with a skeptical view of federal power is likely to give greater credence to the underlying principle of retained state sovereignty, whereas a judge sympathetic to a strong national government is likely to give less weight to the importance of retained state sovereignty.

Books and articles have been written about different approaches to constitutional interpretation, so here we have only scratched the surface by raising some of the issues. See if you discern yourself developing an interpretive philosophy as you go through this book.

---

* Justice Scalia, reflecting his originalist perspective, opined that he believed flogging as punishment is constitutional, but stupid. *See* http://nymag.com/news/features/antonin-scalia-2013-10/.

E. WHAT COMES NEXT?

The above has been a general introduction to the text and background of the Constitution as a whole. However, as mentioned earlier, this book focuses only on particular parts of the Constitution. We start with the structural aspects of the Constitution because they form the basis for how our governmental system works. This involves an exploration of the powers of the different branches of the federal government: the legislative, executive, and judicial. In this exploration, we consider the extent of the power of each of these branches as well as how these powers can be both separated and overlapping, giving rise to the complementary concepts of **Separation of Powers** and **Checks and Balances**. In addition, we will address the limits of federal power under the Constitution. It is often said that the United States is a government of limited powers, but to most people it is not clear how that is so. This focuses our attention on the concept of **Federalism**, or the vertical separation of powers—the assignment of powers between the states and the federal government. Then, having considered the extent of the powers of the federal government, we study how the Constitution limits the powers of the states in certain ways.

The book then turns to the amendments. This part of a constitutional law course is often called the "rights" portion, as opposed to the structural portion, but one should remember that the structure itself was intended to provide protection of rights, if somewhat indirectly, by separating powers and imposing checks and balances. Moreover, even the original Constitution contains various "rights" provisions, such as protecting the right of habeas corpus, prohibiting both the states and federal government from enacting bills of attainder or ex post facto laws, prohibiting the states from impairing the obligation of contracts, assuring the right to a jury trial in federal criminal cases, and assuring that the privileges and immunities enjoyed by the citizen of a state must also be available to citizens of other states in that state.

CHAPTER 2

THE JUDICIAL POWER

■ ■ ■

A. THE JUDICIARY

The Constitution begins with the legislative power, which it vests in Congress, and continues with the executive power, which it vests in the President, and only then addresses the judicial power of the United States,* which it vests in the Supreme Court and in such lower courts as Congress may create. There is, however, a reason why we begin this book with the judicial power. The reason is that from here on we will be studying the decisions of the Supreme Court interpreting and applying the Constitution in different situations. To help understand these decisions it may help to know something about how the Supreme Court operates and relates to other courts.

Today the Supreme Court consists of nine Justices—eight Associate Justices and one Chief Justice.** Originally, it consisted of six justices, then after about twenty years it was expanded to seven, and then after another twenty years to nine in 1837. Except for a five year period in the 1860s, when it was expanded to ten justices, it has remained at nine justices ever since. The first Jewish Justice was Justice Louis Brandeis, appointed with some controversy in 1916 by President Woodrow Wilson. The first African-American Justice was Justice Thurgood Marshall, appointed in 1967 by President Lyndon Johnson. Marshall had been the lead litigator for the NAACP Legal Defense Fund for years and had been the lead counsel in *Brown v. Board of Education*, the case that declared segregated public education unconstitutional. The first woman Justice was Justice Sandra Day O'Connor, appointed by President Ronald Reagan in 1981. Until 1994, a majority of the members of the Court had always been Protestants. Currently, however, the Court has six Catholics, one Jew, and two Protestants. It has two African-Americans, four women, and one Hispanic. As of this writing the youngest is 51; the oldest is 75. The oldest is Justice Clarence Thomas; the youngest, Justice Amy Coney Barrett. The longest serving justice is Justice Clarence Thomas, appointed in 1991. Six of the

---

* It bears repeating that when the Constitution refers to the "United States," it is referring to the federal government, not to the states. Thus, the "judicial power of the United States" refers to the judicial power of the federal courts, not the state courts. Just as there are legislatures and executives (governors) for states separate from the federal Congress and President, there are separate judicial systems as well.

** The title is Chief Justice of the United States, not Chief Justice of the Supreme Court.

justices were appointed by a Republican President; three by a Democratic President.

Originally, the Supreme Court justices not only sat on the Supreme Court, they also "rode circuit," meaning they also sat as judges on a circuit court. The Judiciary Act of 1789, one of the first acts passed by Congress and which first created federal courts, established a federal district court and a federal circuit court in every state. The district court had jurisdiction over the less important civil and criminal cases, while the circuit court had jurisdiction over the more important civil and criminal cases, as well as over appeals from the district court.* While a single district judge would preside over trials in district courts, a district judge and two Supreme Court justices,** called respectively a circuit judge and circuit justices, would preside over trials in the circuit court as well as hear appeals from district courts. Cases would be appealed to the Supreme Court from the circuit courts. This changed in 1891, when a new judiciary act eliminated circuit riding by justices and created circuit courts of appeals with their own judges to hear appeals from both district courts and circuit courts (which lost their appellate jurisdiction over district courts). In 1911 the trial level circuit courts were abolished, with their jurisdiction being placed in the district courts.

Today, all the federal trial courts of general jurisdiction*** are district courts. Each state has at least one federal district court, and many have more than one; California, New York, and Texas have four, each with jurisdiction over a portion of the state. Do you know what district you are in? While a case in a district court is presided over by one judge, there are usually a number of judges in a particular district court, all of whom may be hearing cases at the same time. For example, the Federal District Court for the Eastern District of New York, which is Long Island, has 28 judges.

The federal circuit courts are all courts of appeal. There are twelve circuit courts of appeal with jurisdiction over the district courts in their geographic region, and one circuit court with nationwide jurisdiction over specialized courts. Do you know what circuit you are in? Three judges sit as a panel to hear a case in the court of appeals, but again the number of judges in a circuit varies from a low of five in the First Circuit to a high of 29 in the Ninth Circuit. Indeed, as a practical matter, the numbers of judges available in a circuit is larger than the number authorized for that

---

    * Many states continue to have both district and circuit state courts as trial courts with different jurisdiction based on the importance of the case.

    ** The Judiciary Act of 1802 reduced the number of circuit justices on a circuit court to one, and authorized the circuit justice and circuit judge to certify cases to the Supreme Court.

    *** A court of general jurisdiction hears both civil and criminal cases, and the civil cases may be of any nature. There are federal courts of specialized jurisdiction, such as the Tax Court, that only hears federal tax cases, and the Court of Federal Claims, which generally hears cases in which people claim the federal government owes them money under a contract, from a tort, or for a "taking" under the Fifth Amendment. These latter courts, however, are not Article III courts, which means that their judges serve for a term of years rather than indefinitely.

circuit, because judges, rather than retire, are able to take senior status. By taking senior status, which opens their position for a new appointment, judges can still maintain an office and sit on cases.

Geographic Boundaries
of United States Courts of Appeals and United States District Courts

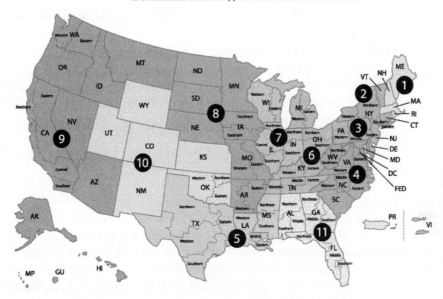

Before the Constitution, there were no federal courts, but of course each of the states had its own court system to apply its own state's law. Nothing in the Constitution changed the state court systems. Today, while state court systems differ somewhat from state to state, most mirror the federal system in having a trial level court, an intermediate court of appeals, and a supreme court.

Recall that the Constitution left to Congress the decision whether to have federal courts below the Supreme Court. The reason was the expectation that state courts would hear cases within the "judicial power" of the United States, so it was unclear what need there would be for lower federal courts. Recall also that Article VI requires that state judges are bound to accept the Constitution and federal laws as the "law of the land." The state court decisions that were within the "judicial power of the United States" could ultimately be appealed to the Supreme Court in order to assure a federal and uniform determination of cases. Lower federal courts have never in our history had jurisdiction over all the cases listed in Article III. Today, for example, diversity jurisdiction cases where the amount in controversy is not more than $75,000 may not be brought in lower federal courts even though they are within the "judicial power of the United States." Moreover, there are a number of situations in which cases that implicate federal law may be brought in either state or federal courts. In addition, a purely state case may raise federal constitutional issues; for example, a state criminal prosecution might arguably violate the defendant's constitutional rights, or a state punishment might arguably be "cruel and unusual." The state courts would then apply the federal law as they best interpret it. Ultimately, however, those cases could be reviewed by the United States Supreme Court with respect to the federal law issues. Reviewing such cases from state courts remains a significant part of the Supreme Court's workload.

The Judiciary Act of 1891, besides creating the circuit courts of appeal, contained another important innovation. Under that Act certain decisions of the courts of appeals and certain final decisions from state courts could be "appealed" to the Supreme Court. However, for most types of cases, the Act instituted the writ of certiorari as the means of obtaining Supreme Court review of lower court decisions. Today, virtually all "appellate" cases come to the Court by way of certiorari. Certiorari is a Latin term meaning "to be informed of." It was a common-law writ in Britain before independence, and after independence, when all the states adopted British common law as American common law, it continued to be a writ here in both state and federal courts. The nature of the writ was an order to a lower court to provide the record of a case before it to the higher court for review. If this sounds like an "appeal," you are correct, except that an "appeal" to a higher court is required to be heard by the higher court, whereas whether to grant a writ of certiorari is discretionary with the higher court. A person petitions the Supreme Court for a writ of certiorari, and if the court grants the petition, then the Court hears the case. Notwithstanding the technical distinction between certiorari and appeal, you will often hear people (including lawyers and judges) refer to a case being appealed to the Supreme Court, when actually it was certiorari, rather than appeal.

In a non-public conference, the justices decide which petitions for certiorari should be granted, in other words, which cases will be heard. If four justices (less than a majority) vote to hear a case, then the Court grants the petition for a writ of certiorari. Interestingly, this "rule of four" is not written down anywhere—not in the Constitution, a statute, or even a court rule; it is just a time-honored practice that the Court could change tomorrow without telling anyone. If the Court "denies cert.," no legal status, such as precedent, attends the denial. It is the same as if the lower court decision had never been appealed at all. If the Court "grants cert.," it sets a schedule for briefs*—first, the petitioner; next, the respondent; and finally a reply brief from the petitioner. The Court may also seek an

---

*   A "brief" is the term for the written arguments made by a person to a court.

"amicus"* brief from the "United States"** if it is not a party to the case, and the Court believes that the views of the "United States" are important to the case. In addition, often other interested persons or groups may "seek leave" (seek permission) to file an amicus brief in a case. Today, it is a rare case before the Supreme Court that does not have at least one amicus brief. Whether they ordinarily have any effect is doubtful, but the fact that on occasion they clearly have had a significant effect provides a sufficient incentive to seek to file such briefs.

While cases in lower courts are titled with the plaintiff's name first, such as Jones v. Smith, where Jones is the plaintiff and Smith the defendant, in the Supreme Court the cases are titled with the petitioner's name first and the respondent's name second. For example, in *Brown v. Board of Education*, Brown was the loser in the court below and thus is the person petitioning the Supreme Court to hear its case and the Board of Education, which won in the court below, is the respondent. Consequently, it is possible that the defendant's name comes first and the plaintiff's name second in the Supreme Court title of the case, depending upon who prevailed in the court below.

Generally, an appellate court, including the Supreme Court, decides questions of law *de novo*.*** An appellate court, however, usually reviews questions of fact or judgment decided by the lower court with some degree of deference to the lower court's determination. This is especially true if the question of fact was decided by a jury.

Sometime after receiving written briefs in the case, the Court hears oral argument, where attorneys for the parties, and rarely for amici, appear before the nine justices and plead their case and answer questions from the justices. On the Wednesday or Friday after oral argument, the members of the Court (and no one else) meet in the Supreme Court conference room to discuss the cases argued earlier that week. According to Supreme Court lore, because again this is not written down anywhere, the discussion of the case begins with the Chief Justice and then proceeds in order of seniority—that is, the length of service on the Court. If the Chief Justice is in the majority for how the case should be decided, he assigns the opinion to one of the justices in the majority or takes it on himself. If the Chief Justice is not in the majority, then the senior-most justice (the Associate Justice who has been on the Court the longest) in the majority assigns the opinion or writes it himself. When the justice has finished a draft, it is circulated among all the justices for comments. If a majority of the justices

---

*   "Amicus Curiae," or "friend of the court" in Latin, is a person a court allows to participate in a case by presenting briefs and/or oral argument but who is not a party to the case.

**   The "United States" is always represented by the office of the Solicitor General in the Department of Justice, whether the "United States" is the petitioner, respondent, or amicus in a case.

***   *De novo* is Latin for "from the beginning" or "anew." In other words, the appellate court does not defer at all to the lower court's determination of the law.

agree with the opinion, we call it the Court's opinion, not the opinion of the justice who authored it. When the opinion for the Court is finished, and any concurring and/or dissenting opinions are finished, the decision of the Court is announced and the opinions released. Occasionally, either before or after oral argument, the Court may dismiss a case as improvidently granted ("DIG"), meaning that they have decided that they should not have taken the case after all. The legal effect is the same as if they had never granted certiorari.

If all the justices agree with the opinion written by the justice authoring the opinion, we say the Court's opinion is unanimous. One or more justices might write a "concurring opinion," even though they agree with the Court's opinion. Nevertheless, the Court's opinion would still be unanimous. The purpose of the concurring opinion would be to express the justice's individual views that might expand on or express limits to the Court's opinion, even while not disagreeing with its reasoning. Sometimes a justice may write an "opinion concurring in the judgment of the Court." This means that the justice does *not* agree with the Court's opinion, but he does agree with the outcome of the case decided by the Court. For example, the Court might decide that the plaintiff loses for some reason, and a justice might agree that the plaintiff should lose, but not for the reason given by the Court. The opinion concurring in the judgment would explain why that justice believed the plaintiff should lose. Obviously, if the justice does not agree with the Court's opinion, the Court's opinion is not unanimous, even if all the justices agree on the same outcome. Often, one or more justices will dissent from the Court's opinion. This means they disagree with the opinion and outcome of the case. Sometimes a justice may concur in part and dissent in part. For example, the Court might find that the plaintiff has jurisdiction to bring the case but loses on the merits, while a justice may agree that the plaintiff has jurisdiction but also believes he should win on the merits. Here, the justice would concur in the opinion as to jurisdiction but dissent on the merits.

Sometimes there is no agreement by a majority of the Court on a particular opinion, but there is agreement by a majority on the outcome of the case. For example, three justices may think the plaintiff should win for one reason; two justices believe the plaintiff should win for another reason; and four justices think the plaintiff should lose. The opinion that commands the most votes and supports the outcome of the case is the "plurality opinion," in this example the three-vote opinion. A plurality opinion is not an opinion of the Court, so it does not have precedential effect. Instead, the opinion with the narrowest grounds supporting the outcome is the opinion that binds lower courts. *See Marks v. United States*, 430 U.S. 188 (1977). There are even circumstances where the Court splits 4–1–4. For example, four justices think the plaintiff should lose for one reason, one justice thinks the plaintiff should lose for another, narrower reason, and four justices think the plaintiff should win. In this circumstance, applying the *Marks'* rule, the opinion by the one justice—with whom no one else agreed—becomes binding precedent for lower courts. *See Grutter v. Bollinger*, 539 U.S. 306, 325 (2003)(discussing *Regents of the Univ. of Cal. v. Bakke*, 438 U.S. 265 (1978)). However, it is not always easy to discern which opinion supporting the outcome is the narrowest.

If for some reason there are less than nine justices deciding a case, for example, if a vacancy had not been filled or a justice recuses* himself or herself, a "majority" is a majority of the justices deciding the case. Thus, if there were only seven justices deciding a case, an opinion joined by four justices would be a majority opinion and thus an opinion of the Court. If there is only an even number of justices deciding the case and they split evenly, for example, 4–4, then the case is said to be "affirmed by an equally divided court," and no opinions are written. This Supreme Court affirmation, however, has no precedential effect. For purposes of precedent, it is as if the case had never been heard.

The Supreme Court still hears cases in its original jurisdiction, almost always involving disputes between two states. However, it does not itself sit as a trial court. Instead, the Court appoints a "special master," perhaps a retired judge or even a law professor, who acts like the trial judge in the case and who renders a "report," which appears like a proposed opinion for the Court. Whichever parties are displeased with the report file a bill of exceptions, which looks like an appeal, with the Court. The Court receives briefs and oral argument as in appellate cases and then renders a final decision.

The Supreme Court "sits" (hears oral arguments) from the first Monday in October each year, which begins the "October Term," until sometime in April. It renders its last opinions for the Term usually late in June.

B. JUDICIAL REVIEW

We now begin with the first of our Supreme Court opinions interpreting the Constitution, but one might ask why it is that we look to the Supreme Court for interpretations of the Constitution. Today, it may seem obvious that the Court is where we would look for interpretations of the Constitution, but it is not obvious from the text of the Constitution.

Recall that the President takes an oath to preserve, protect, and defend the Constitution. Perhaps it should be the President's interpretation that we should study. But then members of the House of Representatives and Senators also take an oath to support the

---

* A justice may recuse himself or herself if there is some ethical conflict. For example, a justice may own stock in one of the parties, and the Court's decision may affect the value of that stock, or a relative or personal friend is a party or an attorney in the case.

Constitution. Perhaps the laws they pass, especially if signed by the President, should be taken as definitive interpretations of the Constitution. And what about state executive, legislative, and judicial officers? They too take an oath to support the Constitution. Why should the Supreme Court of the United States be able to overrule all their considered interpretations of the Constitution? Moreover, to the extent that one believes that the United States is a democracy, is there not a problem with letting unelected judges overrule laws passed by the representatives of the people simply because the judges disagree with the Congress and the President as to the constitutionality of the laws?

The case of *Marbury v. Madison* is generally considered the birth of constitutional law, inasmuch as it is the first case decided by the Supreme Court regarding the constitutionality of a federal statute. It is a difficult case, partly because of its language and partly because of the nature of the Court's analysis, but the following background may help to understand the context in which it occurred.

As long as George Washington, the national hero, had been President, the lingering differences between the Federalists and the Anti-Federalists remained relatively dormant. However, when Washington refused to serve a third term in 1796, the United States "enjoyed" its first contested Presidential election. The Federalists nominated the then Vice President, John Adams, and the anti-Federalists, having formed the Democratic-Republican party, nominated Thomas Jefferson. Under the system then in effect, Adams narrowly won the Presidency and his opponent, Jefferson, became Vice President with the next largest number of votes. At the time, revolutionary France and Great Britain were engaged in war, and while the United States remained neutral, the sympathies for the antagonists split along party lines. The Democratic-Republicans favored the radical democracy the French Revolution seemed to embody. The Federalists favored the moderate, socially conservative approach of British parliamentarianism and feared the spread of revolutionary attitudes in the United States. The Federalists responded by passing the Alien and Sedition Acts, which in essence made it a crime to publish "false, scandalous, and malicious writing" against the government or its officials, and enforced it against their opponents.

The next election, in 1800, was viewed by the Federalists as a struggle to save the Constitution from the radicalism threatened by the Democratic-Republicans, while the Democratic-Republicans saw the election as the last opportunity to avoid tyranny. The vote was close but decisive. The Democratic-Republicans won control of the House, the Senate, and the Presidency. To the Federalists, the future of the Constitution seemed to depend upon the third branch, the Judiciary, whose judges were appointed for life. In the Federalists' view, the courts would be the last bastion of a rule of law under the Constitution in opposition to the rule of the mob, so obvious in France. During the "lame duck" period,* therefore, the then still Federalist-controlled Congress passed the Judiciary Act of 1801, providing for broadened jurisdiction for federal courts and increasing the number of courts, which necessitated appointing new judges, which Adams quickly did. In addition, he appointed the then Acting Secretary of State, John Marshall, to be Chief Justice to fill a seat left vacant by resignation. Because the already sitting judges and the newly appointed ones had been appointed by Federalists, long-term Federalist control of the judiciary seemed assured. Moreover, the "lame-duck" Congress also passed an act for the government of the District of Columbia, which was just then first being used as the Nation's capital—both the Capitol and the White House were first occupied in November 1800. This included a provision for the appointment of justices of the

William Marbury

peace, who were in effect the government administrators for the District, responsible for, among other things, maintaining public order. These too Adams appointed from among loyal Federalists. One was William Marbury, a successful Georgetown businessman. Unfortunately for Marbury and several other of the justices of the peace, in the last minute rush, the then Acting Secretary of State, John Marshall, even as he was at

James Madison

the same time Chief Justice, failed to deliver all the commissions. A commission is the document that evidences an officer's authority, and without it Marbury could not exercise the powers and duties of a justice of the peace. When Marbury sought to obtain his commission from James Madison, the new Secretary of State in the Jefferson administration, Madison ignored him. Marbury accordingly sought to force its delivery by filing suit in the Supreme Court for mandamus against Madison. Mandamus, then and now, is a particular type of court order commanding a government officer to perform a particular legal duty. He filed suit in the Supreme Court because the Judiciary Act of 1789, passed by the first Congress of the United States, provided that: "the Supreme Court shall . . . have power to issue . . . writs

---

* A "lame duck" session refers to a session of the House or Senate occurring after election day in early November and before the new members of the House and Senate under the XXth Amendment are seated on the following January 3. Under the original Constitution, however, the new session did not begin until March 5.

of mandamus . . . to any . . . persons holding office, under the authority of the United States."

Before the Court could hear the case, however, Congress took dramatic action, repealing the Judiciary Act of 1801, which had broadened federal jurisdiction and created new courts. The Federalists argued that the removal of the already appointed judges would be unconstitutional, violating their required life tenure and inconsistent with the independence of the judiciary. Expecting these judges to sue, Congress also passed a law canceling the Supreme Court's term, delaying until 1803 the consideration of all the Supreme Court's cases, including Marbury's.

MARBURY V. MADISON
United States Supreme Court, 1803.
1 Cranch (5 U.S.) 137, 2 L.Ed. 60.

MARSHALL, C.J.

[T]he peculiar delicacy of this case, the novelty of some of its circumstances, and the real difficulty attending the points which occur in it, require a complete exposition of the principles, on which the opinion to be given by the court, is founded. . . .

In the order in which the court has viewed this subject, the following questions have been considered and decided.

1st. Has the applicant a right to the commission he demands?

2dly. If he has a right, and that right has been violated, do the laws of his country afford him a remedy?

3dly. If they do afford him a remedy, is it a mandamus issuing from this court?

The first object of inquiry is,

1st. Has the applicant a right to the commission he demands?

[After a long discussion concerning how appointments are made under the Constitution and when they are final, the Court concluded:] It is therefore decidedly the opinion of the court, that when a commission has been signed by the President, the appointment is made; and that the commission is complete, when the seal of the United States has been affixed to it by the secretary of state. . . .

Mr. Marbury, then, since his commission was signed by the President, and sealed by the secretary of state, was appointed; and as the law creating the office, gave the officer a right to hold for five years, independent of the executive, the appointment was not revocable; but vested in the officer legal rights, which are protected by the laws of this country.

To withhold his commission, therefore, is an act deemed by the court not warranted by law, but violative of a vested legal right.

This brings us to the second inquiry; which is,

2dly. If he has a right, and that right has been violated, do the laws of this country afford him a remedy?

The very essence of civil liberty certainly consists in the right of every individual to claim the protection of the laws, whenever he receives an injury. One of the first duties of government is to afford that protection. In Great Britain the king himself is sued in the respectful form of a petition, and he never fails to comply with the judgment of his court.

The government of the United States has been emphatically termed a government of laws, and not of men. It will certainly cease to deserve this high appellation, if the laws furnish no remedy for the violation of a vested legal right.

If this obloquy is to be cast on the jurisprudence of our country, it must arise from the peculiar character of the case.

It behooves us then to enquire whether there be in its composition any ingredient which shall exempt it from legal investigation, or exclude the injured party from legal redress. . . .

Is it in the nature of the transaction? Is the act of delivering or withholding a commission to be considered as a mere political act, belonging to the executive department alone, for the performance of which, entire confidence is placed by our constitution in the supreme executive; and for any misconduct respecting which, the injured individual has no remedy?

John Marshall

John Marshall is widely credited for modernizing a largely inchoate judicial branch, transforming it from a weak judicial body into an important, powerful mainstay of the American political system. Prior to Marshall's appointment, each justice wrote opinions in each case, and the law of the case had to be discerned from the numerous and often conflicting opinions. This process undermined the court's credibility and clout. Marshall instituted a one-opinion system to represent court decisions. This change, together with judicial review developed in *Marbury v. Madison*, cemented the Supreme Court's place in deciding constitutional matters. Marshall, a pragmatic Federalist, bolstered federal supremacy by writing numerous decisions that supported the national government and broad constitutional interpretation during his lengthy tenure as Chief Justice, 1810–1835.

That there may be such cases is not to be questioned; but that every act of duty, to be performed in any of the great departments of government, constitutes such a case, is not to be admitted. . . . Is it to be contended that where the law in precise terms, directs the performance of an act, in which an individual is interested, the law is incapable of securing obedience to its mandate? Is it on account of the character of the person against whom the complaint is made? Is it to be contended that the heads of departments are not amenable to the laws of their country?

Whatever the practice on particular occasions may be, the theory of this principle will certainly never be maintained. No act of the legislature confers so extraordinary a privilege, nor can it derive countenance from the doctrines of the common law. . . .

It follows then that the question, whether the legality of an act of the head of a department be examinable in a court of justice or not, must always depend on the nature of that act.

If some acts be examinable, and others not, there must be some rule of law to guide the court in the exercise of its jurisdiction.

In some instances there may be difficulty in applying the rule to particular cases; but there cannot, it is believed, be much difficulty in laying down the rule.

By the constitution of the United States, the President is invested with certain important political powers, in the exercise of which he is to use his own discretion, and is accountable only to his country in his political character, and to his own conscience. To aid him in the performance of these duties, he is authorized to appoint certain officers, who act by his authority and in conformity with his orders.

In such cases, their acts are his acts; and whatever opinion may be entertained of the manner in which executive discretion may be used, still there exists, and can exist, no power to control that discretion. The subjects are political. They respect the nation, not individual rights, and being entrusted to the executive, the decision of the executive is conclusive. The application of this remark will be perceived by adverting to the act of congress for establishing the department of foreign affairs. This officer, as his duties were prescribed by that act, is to conform precisely to the will of the President. He is the mere organ by whom that will is communicated. The acts of such an officer, as an officer, can never be examinable by the courts.

But when the legislature proceeds to impose on that officer other duties; when he is directed peremptorily to perform certain acts; when the rights of individuals are dependent on the performance of those acts; he is so far the officer of the law; is amenable to the laws for his conduct; and cannot at his discretion sport away the vested rights of others.

The conclusion from this reasoning is, that where the heads of departments are the political or confidential agents of the executive, merely to execute the will of the President, or rather to act in cases in which the executive possesses a constitutional or legal discretion, nothing can be more perfectly clear than that their acts are only politically examinable. But where a specific duty is assigned by law, and individual rights depend upon the performance of that duty, it seems equally clear that the individual who considers himself injured, has a right to resort to the laws of his country for a remedy. . . .

It is then the opinion of the court,

1st. That by signing the commission of Mr. Marbury, the president of the United States appointed him a justice of peace, for the county of Washington in the district of Columbia; and that the seal of the United States, affixed thereto by the secretary of state, is conclusive testimony of the verity of the signature, and of the completion of the appointment; and that the appointment conferred on him a legal right to the office for the space of five years.

2dly. That, having this legal title to the office, he has a consequent right to the commission; a refusal to deliver which, is a plain violation of that right, for which the laws of his country afford him a remedy.

It remains to be inquired whether,

3dly. He is entitled to the remedy for which he applies. This depends on,

1st. The nature of the writ applied for, and,

2dly. The power of this court.

1st. The nature of the writ.

[The Court held that mandamus would normally be the proper form of action.]

Still, to render the mandamus a proper remedy, the officer to whom it is to be directed, must be one to whom, on legal principles, such writ may be directed; and the person applying for it must be without any other specific and legal remedy.

1st. With respect to the officer to whom it would be directed. The intimate political relation, subsisting between the president of the United States and the heads of departments, necessarily renders any legal investigation of the acts of one of those high officers peculiarly irksome, as well as delicate; and excites some hesitation with respect to the propriety of entering into such investigation. Impressions are often received without much reflection or examination, and it is not wonderful that in such a case as this, the assertion, by an individual, of his legal claims in a court of justice; to which claims it is the duty of that court to attend; should at first view be considered by some, as an attempt to intrude into the cabinet, and to intermeddle with the prerogatives of the executive.

It is scarcely necessary for the court to disclaim all pretensions to such a jurisdiction. An extravagance, so absurd and excessive, could not have been entertained for a moment. The province of the court is, solely, to decide on the rights of individuals, not to enquire how the executive, or executive officers, perform duties in which they have a discretion. Questions, in their nature political, or which are, by the constitution and laws, submitted to the executive, can never be made in this court.

But, if this be not such a question; if so far from being an intrusion into the secrets of the cabinet, it respects a paper, which, according to law, is upon record, and to a copy of which the law gives a right, on the payment of ten cents; if it be no intermeddling with a subject, over which the executive can be considered as having exercised any control; what is there in the exalted station of the officer, which shall bar a citizen from asserting, in a court of justice, his legal rights, or shall forbid a court to listen to the claim; or to issue a mandamus, directing the performance of a duty, not depending on executive discretion, but on particular acts of congress and the general principles of law?

If one of the heads of departments commits any illegal act, under color of his office, by which an individual sustains an injury, it cannot be pretended that his office alone exempts him from being sued in the ordinary mode of proceeding, and being compelled to obey the judgment of the law. . . .

This, then, is a plain case for a mandamus, either to deliver the commission, or a copy of it from the record; and it only remains to be inquired,

Whether it can issue from this court.

The act to establish the judicial courts of the United States authorizes the supreme court "to issue writs of mandamus, in cases warranted by the principles and usages of law, to any courts appointed, or persons holding office, under the authority of the United States."

The secretary of state, being a person holding an office under the authority of the United States, is precisely within the letter of the description; and if this court is not authorized to issue a writ of mandamus to such an officer, it must be because the law is unconstitutional, and therefore absolutely incapable of conferring the authority, and assigning the duties which its words purport to confer and assign.

The constitution vests the whole judicial power of the United States in one supreme court, and such inferior courts as congress shall, from time to time, ordain and establish. This power is expressly extended to all cases arising under the laws of the United States; and consequently, in some form, may be exercised over the present case; because the right claimed is given by a law of the United States.

In the distribution of this power it is declared that "the supreme court shall have original jurisdiction in all cases affecting ambassadors, other public ministers and consuls, and those in which a state shall be a party. In all other cases, the supreme court shall have appellate jurisdiction."

It has been insisted, at the bar, that as the original grant of jurisdiction, to the supreme and inferior courts, is general, and the clause, assigning original jurisdiction to the supreme court, contains no negative or restrictive words; the power remains to the legislature, to assign original jurisdiction to that court in other cases than those specified in the article which has been recited; provided those cases belong to the judicial power of the United States.

If it had been intended to leave it in the discretion of the legislature to apportion the judicial power between the supreme and inferior courts according to the will of that body, it would certainly have been useless to have proceeded further than to have defined the judicial power, and the tribunals in which it should be vested. The subsequent part of the section is mere surplusage, is entirely without meaning, if such is to be the construction. If congress remains at liberty to give this court appellate jurisdiction, where the constitution has declared their jurisdiction shall be original; and original jurisdiction where the constitution has declared it shall be appellate; the distribution of jurisdiction, made in the constitution, is form without substance.

Affirmative words are often, in their operation, negative of other objects than those affirmed; and in this case, a negative or exclusive sense must be given to them or they have no operation at all.

It cannot be presumed that any clause in the constitution is intended to be without effect; and therefore such a construction is inadmissible, unless the words require it. . . .

When an instrument organizing fundamentally a judicial system, divides it into one supreme, and so many inferior courts as the legislature may ordain and establish; then enumerates its powers, and proceeds so far to distribute them, as to define the jurisdiction of the supreme court by declaring the cases in which it shall take original jurisdiction, and that in others it shall take appellate jurisdiction; the plain import of the words seems to be, that in one class of cases its jurisdiction is original, and not appellate; in the other it is appellate, and not original. If any other construction would render the clause inoperative, that is an additional reason for rejecting such other construction, and for adhering to their obvious meaning.

To enable this court then to issue a mandamus, it must be shown to be an exercise of appellate jurisdiction, or to be necessary to enable them to exercise appellate jurisdiction. . . .

It is the essential criterion of appellate jurisdiction, that it revises and corrects the proceedings in a cause already instituted, and does not create that cause. Although, therefore, a mandamus may be directed to courts, yet to issue such a writ to an officer for the delivery of a paper, is in effect the same as to sustain an original action for that paper, and therefore seems not to belong to appellate, but to original jurisdiction. Neither is it necessary in such a case as this, to enable the court to exercise its appellate jurisdiction.

The authority, therefore, given to the supreme court, by the act establishing the judicial courts of the United States, to issue writs of mandamus to public officers, appears not to be warranted by the constitution; and it becomes necessary to enquire whether a jurisdiction, so conferred, can be exercised.

The question, whether an act, repugnant to the constitution, can become the law of the land, is a question deeply interesting to the United States; but, happily, not of an intricacy proportioned to its interest. It seems only necessary to recognize certain principles, supposed to have been long and well established, to decide it.

That the people have an original right to establish, for their future government, such principles as, in their opinion, shall most conduce to their own happiness, is the basis, on which the whole American fabric has been erected. The exercise of this original right is a very great exertion; nor can it, nor ought it to be frequently repeated. The principles, therefore, so established, are deemed fundamental. And as the authority, from which they proceed, is supreme, and can seldom act, they are designed to be permanent.

This original and supreme will organizes the government, and assigns, to different departments, their respective powers. It may either stop here; or establish certain limits not to be transcended by those departments.

The government of the United States is of the latter description. The powers of the legislature are defined, and limited; and that those limits may not be mistaken, or forgotten, the constitution is written. To what purpose are powers limited, and to what purpose is that limitation committed to writing, if these limits may, at any time, be passed by those intended to be restrained? The distinction, between a government with limited and unlimited powers, is abolished, if those limits do not confine the persons on whom they are imposed, and if acts prohibited and acts allowed, are of equal obligation. It is a proposition too plain to be contested, that the constitution controls any legislative act repugnant to it; or, that the legislature may alter the constitution by an ordinary act.

Between these alternatives there is no middle ground. The constitution is either a superior, paramount law, unchangeable by ordinary means, or it is on a level with ordinary legislative acts, and like other acts, is alterable when the legislature shall please to alter it.

If the former part of the alternative be true, then a legislative act contrary to the constitution is not law: if the latter part be true, then written constitutions are absurd attempts, on the part of the people, to limit a power, in its own nature illimitable.

Certainly all those who have framed written constitutions contemplate them as forming the fundamental and paramount law of the nation, and consequently the theory of every such government must be, that an act of the legislature, repugnant to the constitution, is void.

This theory is essentially attached to a written constitution, and is consequently to be considered, by this court, as one of the fundamental principles of our society. It is not therefore to be lost sight of in the further consideration of this subject.

If an act of the legislature, repugnant to the constitution, is void, does it, notwithstanding its invalidity, bind the courts, and oblige them to give it effect? Or, in other words, though it be not law, does it constitute a rule as operative as if it was a law? This would be to overthrow in fact what was established in theory; and would seem, at first view, an absurdity too gross to be insisted on. It shall, however, receive a more attentive consideration.

It is emphatically the province and duty of the judicial department to say what the law is. Those who apply the rule to particular cases, must of necessity expound and interpret that rule. If two laws conflict with each other, the courts must decide on the operation of each.

So if a law be in opposition to the constitution; if both the law and the constitution apply to a particular case, so that the court must either decide that case conformably to the law, disregarding the constitution; or conformably to the constitution, disregarding the law; the court must determine which of these conflicting rules governs the case. This is of the very essence of judicial duty.

If then the courts are to regard the constitution; and the constitution is superior to any ordinary act of the legislature; the constitution, and not such ordinary act, must govern the case to which they both apply.

Those then who controvert the principle that the constitution is to be considered, in court, as a paramount law, are reduced to the necessity of maintaining that courts must close their eyes on the constitution, and see only the law.

This doctrine would subvert the very foundation of all written constitutions. It would declare that an act, which, according to the principles and theory of our government, is entirely void, is yet, in practice, completely obligatory. It would declare, that if the legislature shall do what is expressly forbidden, such act, notwithstanding the express prohibition, is in reality effectual. It would be giving to the legislature a practical and real omnipotence, with the same breath which professes to restrict their powers within narrow limits. It is prescribing limits, and declaring that those limits may be passed as pleasure.

That it thus reduces to nothing what we have deemed the greatest improvement on political institutions—a written constitution—would of itself be sufficient, in America, where written constitutions have been viewed with so much reverence, for rejecting the construction. But the peculiar expressions of the constitution of the United States furnish additional arguments in favor of its rejection.

The judicial power of the United States is extended to all cases arising under the constitution.

Could it be the intention of those who gave this power, to say that, in using it, the constitution should not be looked into? That a case arising under the constitution should be decided without examining the instrument under which it arises?

This is too extravagant to be maintained.

In some cases then, the constitution must be looked into by the judges. And if they can open it at all, what part of it are they forbidden to read, or to obey?

There are many other parts of the constitution which serve to illustrate this subject.

It is declared that "no tax or duty shall be laid on articles exported from any state." Suppose a duty on the export of cotton, of tobacco, or of flour; and a suit instituted to recover it. Ought judgment to be rendered in such a case? Ought the judges to close their eyes on the constitution, and only see the law?

The constitution declares that "no bill of attainder or ex post facto law shall be passed."

If, however, such a bill should be passed and a person should be prosecuted under it; must the court condemn to death those victims whom the constitution endeavors to preserve?

"No person," says the constitution, "shall be convicted of treason unless on the testimony of two witnesses to the same overt act, or on confession in open court."

Here the language of the constitution is addressed especially to the courts. It prescribes, directly for them, a rule of evidence not to be departed from. If the legislature should change that rule, and declare one witness, or a confession out of court, sufficient for conviction, must the constitutional principle yield to the legislative act?

From these, and many other selections which might be made, it is apparent, that the framers of the constitution contemplated that instrument, as a rule for the government of courts, as well as of the legislature.

Why otherwise does it direct the judges to take an oath to support it? This oath certainly applies, in an especial manner, to their conduct in their official character. How immoral to impose it on them, if they were to be used as the instruments, and the knowing instruments, for violating what they swear to support? . . .

If such be the real state of things, this is worse than solemn mockery. To prescribe, or to take this oath, becomes equally a crime.

It is also not entirely unworthy of observation, that in declaring what shall be the supreme law of the land, the constitution itself is first mentioned; and not the laws of the United States generally, but those only which shall be made in pursuance of the constitution, have that rank.

Thus, the particular phraseology of the constitution of the United States confirms and strengthens the principle, supposed to be essential to all written constitutions, that a law repugnant to the constitution is void; and that courts, as well as other departments, are bound by that instrument. . . .

COMMENTS AND QUESTIONS

1.   In trying to decipher this case, ask first: who wins, Marbury or Madison? The answer is Madison. Why does Madison win, or stated another way, why does Marbury lose?

2.   *Marbury v. Madison* is widely recognized as the case that established the authority of the Court to hold federal statutes unconstitutional. What statute did the Court find unconstitutional and why?

3.   The Federalist Papers explicitly address judicial review of laws for constitutionality. Why do you suppose the Court never mentions them?

4.   *Marbury v. Madison* is less well known for its language regarding judicial review of executive action. As explained by the Court, when may executive action be reviewed and when not?

5.   As you can see, in *Marbury* the Court announced that it could review not only the laws passed by the now Democratic-Republican Congress to assure they conformed to the dictates of the Constitution but also the acts of the Democratic-Republican President to assure they conformed to both the law and Constitution. This decision infuriated Jefferson and other Democratic-Republicans, even though they in essence won the case. In a further attempt to bring the judiciary under their thumb, Congress initiated impeachment proceedings against a Federalist judge from New Hampshire. Although a drunk and perhaps insane, no one seriously argued he had committed any "high crimes or misdemeanors," but he was impeached, convicted, and removed. Then Congress took on a bigger fish, Supreme Court Justice Samuel Chase, a noted and outspoken Federalist. Again, there was no serious charge of any criminal behavior, although he had undoubtedly breached judicial decorum in statements from the bench attacking the Democratic-Republicans, but the House impeached him anyway. In the Senate, while a strict party-line vote would have convicted him, he narrowly avoided conviction. The vote may in fact have had more to do with politics than principle, but it established a

precedent that Congress's disagreement with a judge's acts was not a sufficient basis for removal.

6.   Although *Marbury* is *the* case establishing the power of courts to find laws unconstitutional, Marshall describes the issue in the marvelous language of the day as "deeply interesting to the United States; but, happily, not of an intricacy proportioned to its interest." In other words, this was not a difficult question. Indeed, not only had the Federalist papers opined that courts had this power, but it had been exercised by lower federal courts prior to *Marbury*, without any great perturbation. Moreover, as much as the Democratic-Republicans fulminated at *Marbury*, they had earlier called for the courts to declare the Alien and Sedition Acts unconstitutional under the prior administration. A more difficult issue, alluded to earlier in *Calder v. Bull*, 3 U.S. 386 (1798), was whether a court could declare a law invalid, not because it violated a constitutional provision, but because it violated principles of natural justice. In *Calder*, Justice Chase (the one later impeached but not convicted) suggested the power of courts to declare laws invalid on such a basis.

> There are certain vital principles in our free Republican governments, which will determine and over-rule an apparent and flagrant abuse of legislative power; as to authorize manifest injustice by positive law; or to take away that security for personal liberty, or private property, for the protection whereof the government was established. An ACT of the Legislature (for I cannot call it a law) contrary to the great first principles of the social compact, cannot be considered a rightful exercise of legislative authority.

Justice Iredell, however, disagreed, saying:

> If, then, a government, composed of Legislative, Executive and Judicial departments, were established, by a Constitution, which imposed no limits on the legislative power, the consequence would inevitably be, that whatever the legislative power chose to enact, would be lawfully enacted, and the judicial power could never interpose to pronounce it void. It is true, that some speculative jurists have held, that a legislative act against natural justice must, in itself, be void; but I cannot think that, under such a government, any Court of Justice would possess a power to declare it so.

Because all the justices agreed that the law in question in that case did not violate fundamental principles, it was not necessary to resolve the issue. Time, however, has effectively decided it. Today, virtually everyone agrees that a court can declare a law invalid only if it violates the Constitution, not if it only violates someone's notion of natural justice. Nevertheless, some constitutional rights provisions are sufficiently unclear, such as the Due Process Clauses, the Ninth Amendment, and the Fourteenth Amendment's Privileges and Immunities Clause, that one might invest their open-ended text with principles of natural justice and therefore anchor those principles in constitutional text.

7.   Another early case of great significance, although not nearly as well known as *Marbury*, is *Martin v. Hunter's Lessee*, 14 U.S. (1 Wheat.) 304 (1816).* During the Revolutionary War, Virginia passed a law authorizing the confiscation of land owned by Loyalists. As part of the Peace Treaty ending the war with Britain, the United States provided that it would protect the property interests of the Loyalists. Martin was the heir of a Loyalist whose property had been confiscated, and Hunter was the person who had received the land as a result of the confiscation. Despite the confiscation, Martin still was in possession of the land, and Hunter's lessee sought to have Martin evicted. Martin defended on the grounds that the Peace Treaty effectively negated the confiscation. The highest Virginia court did not interpret the Peace Treaty to have that effect. Martin then appealed to the United States Supreme Court, and the Court, interpreting the treaty to nullify the confiscation, reversed and remanded the case to the Virginia court, directing it to enter judgment for Martin. The Virginia court refused. Virginia argued that the Supreme Court had no jurisdiction over it, because Virginia was a separate sovereign, and therefore its courts were not subject to appeal to any higher authority. Just as the Supreme Court could not review a British court interpreting the treaty, the argument went, the Supreme Court could not review the Virginia court. Martin again appealed to the Supreme Court, and Justice Joseph Story [who later wrote Commentaries on the Constitution of the United States, a book that had an enormous influence on constitutional law] authored the opinion declaring that state court judgments involving questions of federal law, here the treaty with Britain, were subject to review by the Supreme Court, as provided in Article III and federal statute. The necessity of having one court be able to maintain a national uniformity for federal law, so that the Constitution and laws of the United States would mean the same thing throughout the United States, has never been questioned since.

8.   Does the decision in *Marbury* recognize a power of the Supreme Court to declare laws unconstitutional, or does it recognize a power of courts generally? Can a state trial court declare a federal law unconstitutional?

9.   Despite the significance of *Marbury*, no federal law was declared unconstitutional thereafter until the decision in the *Dred Scott* case in 1857 declaring unconstitutional the Missouri Compromise's prohibition of slavery in certain northern territories. *Scott v. Sandford*, 60 U.S. (19 How.) 393 (1857). However, in the same period almost 30 state laws were declared unconstitutional. What does *Marbury* have to say about reviewing state laws for their constitutionality?

10. Although today *Marbury* is settled law and its principle unquestioned, there continue to be disputes over the theory upon which it proceeds. Why does the Court believe that *its* determination of the constitutionality of the statutory provision is superior to Congress's? Or, that *its* determination of the lawfulness of the withholding of the commission is superior to the President's? Not long after *Marbury* was decided, President Jefferson wrote to Abigail Adams, the former President's wife: "the opinion

---

*   A lessee is a person who leases property from another, who is called the lessor.

which gives to the judges the right to decide what laws are constitutional and what not, not only for themselves in their own sphere of action but for the Legislature and Executive also in their spheres, would make the Judiciary a despotic branch."

11. In *Marbury*, the Court decides that the provision giving original mandamus jurisdiction to the Court is unconstitutional and therefore without effect. Accordingly, the case is dismissed as not within the Court's jurisdiction. However, that particular provision is part of the Judiciary Act of 1789. Does that mean that the whole act is unconstitutional? The answer in *Marbury* is no. We say that the unconstitutional provision is severable from the rest of the act. Courts are often faced with this question, whether the whole act or just the offensive provision is unconstitutional. Sometimes Congress in passing a law includes a severability provision, stating what should occur if a particular provision is found unconstitutional. In those cases, courts should follow what the statute directs. When Congress is silent, there is still a presumption in favor severability. As Justice Kavanaugh wrote in a recent case: "The presumption . . . reflects the confined role of the Judiciary in our system of separated powers—stated otherwise, the presumption manifests the Judiciary's respect for Congress's legislative role by keeping courts from unnecessarily disturbing a law apart from invalidating the provision that is unconstitutional." *Barr v. Am. Assoc. of Political Consultants, Inc.*, 140 S.Ct. 2335 (2020). However, the presumption is rebuttable; it can be overcome if the rest of statute would not be capable of functioning independently.

PROBLEM

Imagine that Congress passes a bill, the Freedom from Unauthorized Surveillance Act (FUSA) that makes it unlawful for the National Security Agency (NSA) to intercept any domestic telecommunications without a prior judicial warrant. FUSA provides that if any person's telecommunication is intercepted without such a warrant, the person may sue in federal court for punitive damages of $1 million per interception. FUSA also provides, however, that if such a case is brought and the government wishes to contest the constitutionality of the law, it may remove the case before decision to the Supreme Court of the United States to rule on the constitutionality of the law. The bill passes both houses of Congress but is vetoed by the President on the basis that he believes it unconstitutionally interferes with his powers as Commander-in-Chief by requiring a warrant before a national security surveillance. Nevertheless, the Congress overrides his veto and the FUSA becomes law. Thereafter, a person discovers that NSA has intercepted his emails without a prior judicial warrant; he sues for the punitive damages; and the Department of Justice seeks to remove the case to the Supreme Court to argue that the law requiring a warrant is

unconstitutional. The plaintiff argues that the Court does not have
jurisdiction to hear the case. How should the Supreme Court rule?

Following the Supreme Court's decision in *Brown v. Board of
Education*, 347 U.S. 483 (1954), declaring public schools segregated on the
basis of race to be unconstitutional, there was widespread resistance in
southern states. For example, the state of Arkansas amended its
constitution to require the legislature to oppose "in every Constitutional
manner the unconstitutional desegregation" decision in *Brown*. States
maintained, as they had before the Civil War, that they could
independently interpret the Constitution. A suit was brought in Little
Rock, Arkansas, by nine school children (John Aaron was listed first
alphabetically) against the school district (William Cooper was the
president of the school district) to integrate the public schools. On the basis
of *Brown*, the district court ordered the schools integrated, but the
governor, Orville Faubus, and the state legislature argued that they were
not bound by *Brown*, because they had not been parties to that suit, which
involved school districts in other states. The governor called out the
National Guard to prevent integration of the Little Rock Central High
School by the nine black students. The district court ordered the governor
to cease his interference, and he did, but it took troops from the 82d
Airborne Division dispatched to Little Rock by President Eisenhower to
maintain sufficient order to enable the students to enter the school.
Because of the riots and public disorder, the school district asked for a delay
of two and one half years in its requirement to integrate the schools. While
the district court granted that delay, it was reversed by the Eighth Circuit,
and the Supreme Court affirmed the circuit court's decision. In rendering
its decision, the Court did something it had never done before and has
never done since—all nine justices announced the opinion.* They clearly
meant to send a message to the resisting states that there was no hidden
reluctance on the Court to enforcing integration; that all the justices were
fully committed to this path.

In affirming the Eighth Circuit, the Court agreed that there was no
legal reason to delay integration and that concerted official resistance was
no basis for not enforcing the Constitution. However, the Court went
further.

---

* There are many unanimous decisions by the Supreme Court. Indeed, *Marbury* was such a
decision, but the opinion for the Court in *Marbury* was rendered by Chief Justice Marshall, with
which all members agreed. In *Cooper v. Aaron*, it was not an opinion by one justice with which all
the others agreed, it was *the* opinion of *all* the justices jointly.

COOPER V. AARON
United States Supreme Court, 1958.
358 U.S. 1, 78 S.Ct. 1401.

Opinion of the Court by THE CHIEF JUSTICE, MR. JUSTICE BLACK, MR. JUSTICE FRANKFURTER, MR. JUSTICE DOUGLAS, MR. JUSTICE BURTON, MR. JUSTICE CLARK, MR. JUSTICE HARLAN, MR. JUSTICE BRENNAN, and MR. JUSTICE WHITTAKER.

As this case reaches us it raises questions of the highest importance to the maintenance of our federal system of government. It necessarily involves a claim by the Governor and Legislature of a State that there is no duty on state officials to obey federal court orders resting on this Court's considered interpretation of the United States Constitution. Specifically it involves actions by the Governor and Legislature of Arkansas upon the premise that they are not bound by our holding in *Brown v. Board of Education.* That holding was that the Fourteenth Amendment forbids States to use their governmental powers to bar children on racial grounds from attending schools where there is state participation through any arrangement, management, funds or property. We are urged to uphold a suspension of the Little Rock School Board's plan to do away with segregated public schools in Little Rock until state laws and efforts to upset and nullify our holding in *Brown v. Board of Education* have been further challenged and tested in the courts. We reject these contentions.

[The Court then explained why it would not delay the integration plan.]

What has been said, in the light of the facts developed, is enough to dispose of the case. However, we should answer the premise of the actions of the Governor and Legislature that they are not bound by our holding in the *Brown* case. It is necessary only to recall some basic constitutional propositions which are settled doctrine.

Article VI of the Constitution makes the Constitution the "supreme Law of the Land." In 1803, Chief Justice Marshall, speaking for a unanimous Court, referring to the Constitution as "the fundamental and paramount law of the nation," declared in the notable case of *Marbury v. Madison* that "It is emphatically the province and duty of the judicial department to say what the law is." This decision declared the basic principle that the federal judiciary is supreme in the exposition of the law of the Constitution, and that principle has ever since been respected by this Court and the Country as a permanent and indispensable feature of our constitutional system. It follows that the interpretation of the Fourteenth Amendment enunciated by this Court in the *Brown* case is the supreme law of the land, and Art. VI of the Constitution makes it of binding effect on the States "any Thing in the Constitution or Laws of any State to the Contrary notwithstanding." Every state legislator and executive and judicial officer is solemnly committed by oath taken pursuant to Art. VI, ¶ 3 "to support this Constitution. . . ."

No state legislator or executive or judicial officer can war against the Constitution without violating his undertaking to support it. Chief Justice Marshall spoke for a unanimous Court in saying that: "If the legislatures of the several states may, at will, annul the judgments of the courts of the United States, and destroy the rights acquired under those judgments, the constitution itself becomes a solemn mockery * * *." *United States v. Peters,* 5 Cranch 115, 136, 3 L.Ed. 53. A Governor who asserts a power to nullify a federal court order is similarly restrained. . . .

The basic decision in *Brown* was unanimously reached by this Court only after the case had been briefed and twice argued and the issues had been given the most serious consideration. Since the first *Brown* opinion three new Justices have come to the Court. They are at one with the Justices still on the Court who participated in that basic decision as to its correctness, and that decision is now unanimously reaffirmed. The principles announced in that decision and the obedience of the States to them, according to the command of the Constitution, are indispensable for the protection of the freedoms guaranteed by our fundamental charter for all of us. . . .

COMMENTS AND QUESTIONS

1.   The actual decision in *Cooper* that the integration plan should not be delayed because of official resistance, the part of the opinion that has been edited out, is undoubtedly correct. Moreover, the Court's statement that persons must comply with final court orders is clearly the law.* However, the Court's statement that the Court's interpretation of the Constitution itself becomes the Constitution, which all state and federal officers have sworn to uphold, has engendered substantial debate. *Compare* Larry Alexander and Frederick Schauer, *On Extrajudicial Constitutional Interpretation,* 110 Harv. L. Rev. 1359 (1997), and Daniel A. Farber, *The Supreme Court and the Rule of Law:* Cooper v. Aaron *Revisited,* 1982 U. Ill. L. Rev. 387 (defending the statement) *with* Mark V. Tushnet, *The Hardest Question in Constitutional Law,* 81 Minn. L. Rev. 1, 25–28 (1996) and Edwin Meese III, *The Law of the Constitution,* 61 Tul. L. Rev. 979, 983–86 (1987)(challenging the statement). Would a congressman violate his oath of office if he introduced a bill making it a crime to burn the United States flag in public, inasmuch as the Supreme Court has twice declared flag-burning to be constitutionally protected expression? Would the President violate his oath of office if he vetoed a bill

---

*   In *United States v. Nixon,* 418 U.S. 683 (1974), the Supreme Court affirmed a lower court order requiring President Nixon to turn over tapes made of conversations in the White House Oval Office over his objection that they were constitutionally protected from disclosure. Inasmuch as those tapes revealed the so-called "smoking gun" of his participation in the cover-up of criminal activity, which sealed his fate as President, if ever there were a case where a President might refuse to comply with a court order, this would seem to be it. Nevertheless, he did comply.

because he believed it would be unconstitutional, even though the Supreme Court had upheld an identical law?

2.   Whatever the academic debates, for most practical purposes what the Supreme Court says the Constitution means is the last word. If a decision is sufficiently objectionable, the amendment process has been used to overturn it. However, again for most practical purposes, this is not a realistic option. Accordingly, courts hold tremendous power, and as Lord Acton said, "power tends to corrupt, and absolute power corrupts absolutely." Under a Constitution that uses checks and balances to keep any one branch from excessive power, the question becomes, what is the check on this judicial power?

C.   CHECKS ON JUDICIAL POWER

1.   LEGISLATIVE CHECKS

Already, prior to *Marbury,* we saw one legislative attempt at checking the judiciary. There Congress canceled the Supreme Court's then-scheduled August term because it feared the Court might declare the repeal of the Judiciary Act of 1801 unconstitutional, inasmuch as the Act terminated the tenure of the judges appointed under the Act. Can you see why this type of check might not be very effective on a long-term basis?

The following case involved a more targeted form of trying to deny Supreme Court review.

William McCardle

EX PARTE MCCARDLE

United States Supreme Court, 1869.
74 U.S. (7 Wall.) 506, 19 L.Ed. 264.

[In 1867, William McCardle, a former Colonel in the Confederate army and a current newspaper publisher, was arrested by the federal military authorities for publishing inflammatory articles opposing Reconstruction.* He was held in military custody awaiting trial by a military commission for four alleged offenses under the Military Reconstruction Act: disturbing the peace, inciting to insurrection and disorder, libel, and impeding reconstruction. McCardle, claiming that the Act was

---

*   Reconstruction is the term used to describe the period after the Civil War when Congress placed the former Confederate states under federal military occupation in order to protect the newly freed slaves and to attempt to enforce their newly acquired rights under the Civil War Amendments and the Civil Rights Acts. The state and local governments operated under military supervision.

unconstitutional, filed a petition for habeas corpus in federal circuit court pursuant to a new habeas statute that broadened the grounds for federal habeas relief. The court denied the petition, and McCardle appealed to the Supreme Court. The Supreme Court heard oral argument in early March, 1868, but members of Congress were concerned that the Court might declare the Military Reconstruction Act, the foundation for all reconstruction, unconstitutional, so they attached to an otherwise uncontroversial bill a rider* that withdrew Supreme Court jurisdiction over any appeal under the new habeas statute. The bill with its rider passed Congress, was vetoed by President Johnson (five days before his impeachment hearings began), and then repassed over his veto.]

The CHIEF JUSTICE [SALMON P. CHASE] delivered the opinion of the court.

The first question necessarily is that of jurisdiction; for, if the act of March, 1868 [the bill that contained the rider], takes away the jurisdiction defined by the act of February, 1867 [the new habeas statute that broadened the scope of habeas], it is useless, if not improper, to enter into any discussion of other questions.

It is quite true, as was argued by the counsel for the petitioner, that the appellate jurisdiction of this court is not derived from acts of Congress. It is, strictly speaking, conferred by the Constitution. But it is conferred "with such exceptions and under such regulations as Congress shall make."

It is unnecessary to consider whether, if Congress had made no exceptions and no regulations, this court might not have exercised general appellate jurisdiction under rules prescribed by itself. For among the earliest acts of the first Congress, at its first session, was the act of September 24th, 1789, to establish the judicial courts of the United States. That act provided for the organization of this court, and prescribed regulations for the exercise of its jurisdiction.

The source of that jurisdiction, and the limitations of it by the Constitution and by statute, have been on several occasions subjects of consideration here. In the case of *Durousseau v. The United States*, 10 U.S. 307 (1810), particularly, the whole matter was carefully examined, and the court held, that while "the appellate powers of this court are not given by the judicial act, but are given by the Constitution," they are, nevertheless, "limited and regulated by that act, and by such other acts as have been passed on the subject." The court said, further, that the judicial act was an exercise of the power given by the Constitution to Congress "of making exceptions to the appellate jurisdiction of the Supreme Court." "They have described affirmatively," said the court, "its jurisdiction, and this

---

* A "rider" is a provision attached to a legislative bill to which it has no substantial relationship, usually for the purposes of hiding it from scrutiny, thereby increasing its chances of passage.

affirmative description has been understood to imply a negation of the exercise of such appellate power as is not comprehended within it."

The principle that the affirmation of appellate jurisdiction implies the negation of all such jurisdiction not affirmed having been thus established, it was an almost necessary consequence that acts of Congress, providing for the exercise of jurisdiction, should come to be spoken of as acts granting jurisdiction, and not as acts making exceptions to the constitutional grant of it.

The exception to appellate jurisdiction in the case before us, however, is not an inference from the affirmation of other appellate jurisdiction. It is made in terms. The provision of the act of 1867, affirming the appellate jurisdiction of this court in cases of habeas corpus is expressly repealed. It is hardly possible to imagine a plainer instance of positive exception.

We are not at liberty to inquire into the motives of the legislature. We can only examine into its power under the Constitution; and the power to make exceptions to the appellate jurisdiction of this court is given by express words.

What, then, is the effect of the repealing act upon the case before us? We cannot doubt as to this. Without jurisdiction the court cannot proceed at all in any cause. Jurisdiction is power to declare the law, and when it ceases to exist, the only function remaining to the court is that of announcing the fact and dismissing the cause. And this is not less clear upon authority than upon principle. . . .

[T]he general rule, supported by the best elementary writers, is, that "when an act of the legislature is repealed, it must be considered, except as to transactions past and closed, as if it never existed." And the effect of repealing acts upon suits under acts repealed, has been determined by the adjudications of this court . . . [in which] it was held that no judgment could be rendered in a suit after the repeal of the act under which it was brought and prosecuted.

It is quite clear, therefore, that this court cannot proceed to pronounce judgment in this case, for it has no longer jurisdiction of the appeal; and judicial duty is not less fitly performed by declining ungranted jurisdiction than in exercising firmly that which the Constitution and the laws confer.

Counsel seem to have supposed, if effect be given to the repealing act in question, that the whole appellate power of the court, in cases of habeas corpus, is denied. But this is an error. The act of 1868 does not except from that jurisdiction any cases but appeals from Circuit Courts under the act of 1867. It does not affect the jurisdiction which was previously exercised.

COMMENTS AND QUESTIONS

1.   Again, who wins and who loses this case?

2.   In light of this ruling, would it be constitutional for Congress to pass a law creating an "exception" to the Supreme Court's appellate jurisdiction over any case dealing with the constitutionality of a law restricting ownership of handguns? How would such a law be different from or the same as *McCardle*? Would the difference compel a different conclusion from that in *McCardle*?

3.   What if Congress passed a law stating that the Supreme Court would have no appellate jurisdiction over any case brought by a person of color? Would such a law be constitutional? How would it be different from *McCardle*?

4.   *McCardle* upheld the power of Congress to restrict the appellate jurisdiction of the Supreme Court, relying upon the language in Article III that says the Court's appellate jurisdiction is subject to "such exceptions . . . as the Congress shall make." Article III grants to Congress the power to create lower federal courts. Does that mean that Congress can decide what jurisdiction those lower courts can exercise? As a general matter the answer must be "yes," because as noted earlier, Congress has never given the lower federal courts jurisdiction over all the cases within the judicial power of the United States as described in Article III. Their jurisdiction has always been restricted. The question is whether there is any limit to what restriction Congress can place on lower courts' jurisdiction. What if Congress limited jurisdiction to cases in which the plaintiff is a male? How about a law providing that no federal court shall have jurisdiction to hear any case challenging the constitutionality of a law restricting the ownership of handguns, would such a law be constitutional? If it were, might there be other reasons Congress might not want to pass it, even if Congress did not like federal courts ruling on this subject?

5.   Questions as to the meaning of *McCardle* are not just academic. In 2006 Congress passed a law that prohibited any court from exercising jurisdiction over an application for habeas corpus filed by an "alien detained by the United States who has been determined by the United States to have been properly detained as an enemy combatant or is awaiting such determination." And this act explicitly provided that it was applicable to habeas petitions that had already been filed. In *Boumediene v. Bush*, 553 U.S. 723 (2008), the Supreme Court found this law unconstitutional. Specifically, the Court held that the law violated the Suspension Clause of the Constitution, which prohibits the suspension of the writ of habeas corpus "unless when in cases of rebellion or invasion the public safety may require it." How did *Boumediene* differ from *McCardle*? Re-read the last paragraph of *McCardle*.

6.   The Court in *McCardle* notes the "general rule" that until a case is finished—that is, there is a final, unappealable judgment—changes in the law are given effect even in that on-going case. Thus, in *McCardle*, the fact that the case was still on-going did not stop Congress from eliminating the Court's jurisdiction over it. At the same time, the Court distinguished earlier cases, which it described as "the exercise of judicial power by the legislature, or of

legislative interference with courts in the exercising of continuing jurisdiction." These, it suggested, would not be permissible.

7.   *United States v. Klein*, 80 U.S. 128 (1871), was another post-Civil War case in which Congress did not like what it perceived to be the direction of the courts. As a result, it created a statute to try to foreclose the courts from reaching a decision the Congress would not like. There had been a law during the Civil War authorizing the confiscation of all property of persons who participated in the rebellion. However, as an inducement to people to abandon support of the Confederacy, there was another law to the effect that, if the President pardoned someone, subject to the condition that the person would swear thereafter to uphold the Constitution and support the Union, the proceeds from the property that had been confiscated would be returned upon a claim filed in the Court of Claims. The Radical Republicans after the war wished to punish those who had actually taken up arms against the United States, so they enacted a law requiring persons who wished to obtain the return of confiscated property to prove affirmatively that they had not supported the Confederacy during the war. The Supreme Court, however, in *United States v. Padelford*, 76 U.S. 531 (1869), held that a Presidential pardon in effect eliminated any disability related to participation in the rebellion, so that the person could obtain their property without having to make the affirmative proof. Klein was the executor of the estate of someone whose property had been seized, but who had taken the requisite oath and received a presidential pardon, and Klein filed suit in the Court of Claims for the proceeds from that property. The Court of Claims ruled in his favor, and the government appealed to the Supreme Court. Congress, however, upset with the decision in *Padelford*, enacted a proviso to an appropriation law saying that acceptance of such a pardon "shall be taken and deemed in such suit in the said Court of Claims, and on appeal therefrom, conclusive evidence that such person did take part in, and give aid and comfort to, the late rebellion, and did not maintain true allegiance or consistently adhere to the United States; and on proof of such pardon and acceptance . . ., the jurisdiction of the court in the case shall cease, and the court shall forthwith dismiss the suit of such claimant." This, the Court said went too far. Congress had not just decided the jurisdiction of the Court of Claims, it had instead told the court how to rule in a particular case.

8.   Another case in which the Court said Congress went too far was *Plaut v. Spendthrift Farm, Inc.* 514 U.S. 211 (1995). Earlier, the Supreme Court had interpreted the Securities Exchange Act of 1934 as requiring a suit alleging fraud in the sale of securities to be brought within one year of the discovery of the alleged fraud and within three years of the date of the alleged fraud. As a result, a number of securities fraud cases were dismissed as barred by the statute of limitations.* Congress, upset with these decisions, amended the Securities Exchange Act to provide specifically that the statute of limitations

---

*   A "statute of limitations" is a law that specifies the period within which a person must bring a lawsuit to avoid being time-barred, as well as a law that specifies the period within which the government must prosecute a person for a crime.

under the Act would be the limitations period applicable under state law (which normally would be longer than what the Supreme Court had interpreted the Act to require). That did not create any problem. Congress can change the limitations periods for suits under its statutes, but the new law went further. It also said that anyone who had had their case dismissed because of the prior statute of limitations (but who would not have had their case dismissed if the new law had then been in existence) could have their case reinstated by filing a motion with the court that had dismissed their case. This the Supreme Court said unconstitutionally intruded on the judicial function. Once a case has been finally decided by the courts, Congress cannot change the law applicable to that case.

9.   In *Robertson v. Seattle Audubon Society*, 503 U.S. 429 (1992), the Court upheld a novel congressional act. Upset with lawsuits brought by environmentalists alleging violations of various environmental laws, thereby delaying timber sales from certain federal lands, Congress enacted a law that contained the following provision:

> "[T]he Congress hereby determines and directs that management of areas according to subsections (b)(3) and (b)(5) of this section on the thirteen national forests in Oregon and Washington and Bureau of Land Management lands in western Oregon known to contain northern spotted owls is adequate consideration for the purpose of meeting the statutory requirements that are the basis for the consolidated cases captioned Seattle Audubon Society et al., v. F. Dale Robertson, Civil No. 89–160 and Washington Contract Loggers Assoc. et al., v. F. Dale Robertson, Civil No. 89–99 (order granting preliminary injunction). . . ."

On the basis of this language, the lower courts dismissed the lawsuits that had been brought alleging that the government had not given adequate consideration to the environment as required by certain environmental statutes. The environmental groups appealed. On its face, the provision looked like Congress was telling courts how to decide specific cases, something that *Klein* had said Congress was not allowed to do. The Supreme Court, however, cited to the canon of statutory construction that if there are two possible interpretations of a statute, one of which is unconstitutional, the constitutional interpretation should be adopted even if it is not the most natural interpretation of the language of the statute. This canon is based on the assumption that Congress would not have intended to enact an unconstitutional statute. Here, the Court said—unanimously—that Congress had not directed a decision in pending cases; it had merely changed the relevant environmental laws as they applied to the particular forest lands in question. Because the litigation had not gone to a final judgment, courts should apply this new law to the cases involved. Although not artfully worded, the provision should be interpreted merely as an amendment to existing law, changing the statutory requirements applicable to the particular timber sales.

10.   One can synthesize *Klein* and *Robertson* by understanding that in *Robertson* Congress was merely changing a statutory provision that it had

itself enacted, whereas in *Klein* Congress was trying to undo the effect of the Court's interpretation of the Constitution—specifically the effect of a Presidential pardon. Congress can prospectively change a law it enacts, even to avoid judicial interpretations of the prior law, but it cannot change the Constitution or the courts' interpretation of the Constitution. This issue arose again in *Bank Markazi v. Peterson*, 578 U.S. 212 (2016). Here, during the pendency of private litigation for damages against Iran for injuries caused by state-sponsored terrorism, Congress by law identified by reference to that particular case certain financial assets that could be used to satisfy any judgment. The defendants argued that this violated *Klein*, but the Court responded that this was a case like *Robertson* where Congress simply required a court to apply a new legal standard.

PROBLEM

Imagine that Congress passes a law, the No Abortions Now Act (NANA), prohibiting all abortions and stating that no court shall have jurisdiction to determine the constitutionality of NANA. Now imagine that a doctor does provide a woman an abortion, and both are prosecuted for violating NANA. The doctor and woman raise as a defense that NANA is unconstitutional, so their prosecutions should be dismissed. Does the court have jurisdiction to rule on their defense?

---

2. SELF-IMPOSED CHECKS

As may be seen, Congress actually has a fair amount of power to "check" the judicial power of the United States, although you may perceive some practical problems involved in using this checking power. At the same time, however, throughout our history the Supreme Court has been sensitive to the role of courts in American government. In a sense, it has imposed checks on itself (and lower courts) through its interpretation of the Constitution. It begins even before *Marbury*.

a. Advisory Opinions

In 1793, on behalf of President Washington, Secretary of State Thomas Jefferson wrote a letter to the Supreme Court justices asking for their opinion concerning certain legal matters relating to the United States' neutrality in the then ongoing war between France and Great Britain.

Gentlemen:

The war which has taken place among the powers of Europe produces frequent transactions within our ports and limits, on which questions arise of considerable difficulty, and of greater importance to the peace of the United States. Their questions depend for their solution on the construction of our treaties, on the laws of nature and nations, and on the laws of the land, and are often presented under circumstances which do not give a cognisance of them to the tribunals of the country. Yet their decision is so little analogous to the ordinary functions of the executive, as to occasion much embarrassment and difficulty to them. The President therefore would be much relieved if he found himself free to refer questions of this description to the opinions of the judges of the Supreme Court of the United States, whose knowledge of the subject would secure us against errors dangerous to the peace of the United States, and their authority insure the respect of all parties. He has therefore asked the attendance of such of the judges as could be collected in time for the occasion, to know, in the first place, their opinion, whether the public may, with propriety, be availed of their advice on these questions? And if they may, to present, for their advice, the abstract questions which have already occurred, or may soon occur, from which they will themselves strike out such as any circumstances might, in their opinion, forbid them to pronounce on.

Attached to the letter was a list of 29 questions. Ultimately, the Court responded:

We have considered the previous question stated in a letter written by your direction to us by the Secretary of State on the 18th of last month, [regarding] the lines of separation drawn by the Constitution between the three departments of the government. These being in certain respects checks upon each other, and our being judges of a court of the last resort, are considerations which afford strong arguments against the propriety of our extra-judicially deciding the questions alluded to, especially as the power given by the Constitution to the President, of calling on the heads of departments for opinions, seems to have been purposely as well as expressly united to the executive departments. We exceedingly regret every event that may cause embarrassment to your administration, but we derive consolation from the reflection that your judgment will discern what is right, and that your usual prudence, decision, and firmness will surmount every obstacle to the preservation of the rights, peace, and dignity of the United States.

In other words, Washington as President wished to know what the Supreme Court thought the law was, so that he could follow their advice. The Court, however, refused his invitation. Notice the basis for their refusal. The Court refers to the Constitution's separation of powers and checks of one branch on another. Then it characterizes what it is being asked to do as extra-judicial and therefore presumably inappropriate.

Rather, the Court says, the Constitution's explicit authority for the President to ask heads of departments for opinions suggests that it is those officers, rather than the Court, that the Constitution expects to render advice to the President.

The refusal of the Court to provide "advisory opinions," first expressed in this letter, has been followed ever since. *See, e.g., Massachusetts v. EPA*, 549 U.S. 497, 516 (2007). But why was the Court so reluctant to render an advisory opinion? What harm would it have caused? Canada's Supreme Court provides them; the constitution of the state of Massachusetts requires its Supreme Judicial Court to answer questions posed to it by the governor or either branch of the legislature.

Perhaps the answer lies in what transpired the year before. In 1792 a case was brought before the Supreme Court seeking it to order lower federal circuit courts to administer a law providing for pensions to disabled soldiers of the Revolutionary War. *See Hayburn's Case*, 2 U.S. 408 (1892). Three circuit courts had refused to comply with that law because they believed it unconstitutionally required them to perform non-judicial functions. The law required the courts to determine whether a person qualified for a pension. The courts' decisions were subject to review and reversal by the Secretary of War, and, if not reversed by the Secretary of War, to review and possible revision by Congress. Each of the circuits expressed a similar analysis: that each branch of government is separate and distinct with only the powers granted to it by the Constitution; that the judicial branch is only authorized to exercise judicial power; that to perform acts not in their nature judicial would be beyond its delegated judicial power; and that acts subject to revision by either the executive or the legislative branches would be acts not in their nature judicial. While the Supreme Court did not decide the issue, because Congress changed the law before the Court could render its decision, this case made the Court aware of lurking issues regarding the use of the judiciary for non-traditional, non-judicial functions and perhaps heightened its sensitivity to a request for an advisory opinion.

b. Standing

Imagine two law students who, having read the Constitution, discover that a Senator from South Carolina is a Colonel in the U.S. Air Force Reserves. They recall that Article I, Section 6, Clause 2, which is known as the Incompatibility Clause, states that "no person holding any office under the United States, shall be a Member of either House during his continuance in office." One student believes the Senator is in violation of the Constitution; the other does not. They argue but cannot convince one another. May they sue each other in federal court? After all, is this not a dispute arising under the Constitution? The answer, of course, is that they cannot sue one another to resolve this dispute, but why not? Could one of them sue the Secretary of Defense or the Secretary of the Army to have the person's commission as a Colonel taken away? In *Schlesinger v. Reservists Committee to Stop the War*, 418 U.S. 208 (1974), the Supreme Court dismissed a case challenging the constitutionality of members of Congress being reserve officers in the military, saying that the persons bringing the suit, whether as taxpayers or citizens, lacked a sufficient particularized adverse interest for them to bring the case. This necessary particularized adverse interest is called **standing**. In other words, the case was dismissed without any ruling on the constitutional question the plaintiff tried to raise. What it takes to establish standing, and even what its basis in the law is, has varied over the years. The case of *Flast v. Cohen*, 392 U.S. 83 (1968), reflected an activist stance by the Court, as it allowed a person to challenge a federal government expenditure on Establishment Clause grounds merely because the person was a taxpayer. The Court, in an opinion written by Chief Justice Earl Warren, said:

> The fundamental aspect of standing is that it focuses on the party seeking to get his complaint before a federal court and not on the issues he wishes to have adjudicated. The "gist of the question of standing" is whether the party seeking relief has "alleged such a personal stake in the outcome of the controversy as to assure that concrete adverseness which sharpens the presentation of issues upon which the court so largely depends for illumination of difficult constitutional questions." In other words, when standing is placed in issue in a case, the question is whether the person whose standing is challenged is a proper party to request an adjudication of a particular issue and not whether the issue itself is justiciable. . . . A proper party is demanded so that federal courts will not be asked to decide "ill defined controversies over constitutional issues," or a case which is of "a hypothetical or abstract character.". . .

> [T]he question whether a particular person is a proper party to maintain the action does not, by its own force, raise separation of powers problems related to improper judicial interference in areas committed to other branches of the Federal Government. Such problems arise, if at all, only from the substantive issues the individual seeks to have adjudicated. Thus, in terms of Article III limitations on federal court jurisdiction, the question of standing is related only to whether the dispute sought to be adjudicated will be presented in an adversary context and in a form historically viewed as capable of judicial resolution. . . . Therefore, we find no absolute bar in Article III to suits by federal taxpayers challenging allegedly unconstitutional federal taxing and spending programs. There remains, however, the problem of determining the circumstances under which a federal taxpayer will be deemed to have the personal stake and interest that impart the necessary concrete adverseness to such litigation so that

standing can be conferred on the taxpayer qua taxpayer consistent with the constitutional limitations of Article III.

392 U.S. at 99–100.

That was the last time the Supreme Court allowed a federal taxpayer to have standing to challenge a federal spending program,* and subsequent cases, if they have not overruled *Flast*, have limited it strictly to its facts. *See Valley Forge Christian College v. Americans United for Separation of Church and State, Inc.*, 454 U.S. 464 (1982)(finding no standing for taxpayers to challenge on Establishment Clause grounds the federal donation of land to a religious institution); *Hein v. Freedom From Religion Foundation, Inc.*, 551 U.S. 587 (2007)(finding no standing for taxpayers to bring an Establishment Clause challenge against federal agency's use of federal money to fund conferences to promote President's "faith-based initiatives"); *Arizona Christian School Tuition Org. v. Winn*, 563 U.S. 125 (2011)(finding no standing for taxpayers to bring Establishment Clause challenge against Arizona tax credit for persons who donated to a "student tuition organization" that funded religious schools). Moreover, later cases seem to have a different conception of the Article III nature of standing from that described in the *Flast* opinion, which focused not on separation of powers concerns but on assuring sufficient adverseness between the parties to ensure the case is well presented to the court. The following case is probably the current leading case on standing.

LUJAN V. DEFENDERS OF WILDLIFE
United States Supreme Court, 1992.
504 U.S. 555, 112 S.Ct. 2130.

JUSTICE SCALIA delivered the opinion of the Court with respect to Parts I, II, III-A, and IV, and an opinion with respect to Part III-B, in which THE CHIEF JUSTICE, JUSTICE WHITE, and JUSTICE THOMAS join.

This case involves a challenge to a rule promulgated by the Secretary of the Interior [Manuel Lujan] interpreting § 7 of the Endangered Species Act of 1973 (ESA) in such fashion as to render it applicable only to actions within the United States or on the high seas.

The preliminary issue, and the only one we reach, is whether respondents here, plaintiffs below, have standing to seek judicial review of the rule.

I

The ESA seeks to protect species of animals against threats to their continuing existence caused by man. . . . Section 7(a)(2) of the Act then

---

* It would, of course, be different if the taxpayer were challenging the lawfulness or constitutionality of a tax imposed on the taxpayer. A person clearly would have standing to challenge a tax the person was required to pay.

provides, in pertinent part: "Each Federal agency shall, in consultation with and with the assistance of the Secretary [of the Interior], insure that any action authorized, funded, or carried out by such agency . . . is not likely to jeopardize the continued existence of any endangered species or threatened species. . . ."

In 1978, the Fish and Wildlife Service (FWS) and the National Marine Fisheries Service (NMFS), on behalf of the Secretary of the Interior and the Secretary of Commerce respectively, promulgated a joint regulation stating that the obligations imposed by § 7(a)(2) extend to actions taken in foreign nations. The next year, however, the Interior Department began to reexamine its position. A revised joint regulation, reinterpreting § 7(a)(2) to require consultation only for actions taken in the United States or on the high seas, was proposed in 1983 and promulgated in 1986.

Shortly thereafter, respondents, organizations dedicated to wildlife conservation and other environmental causes, filed this action against the Secretary of the Interior, seeking a declaratory judgment that the new regulation is in error as to the geographic scope of § 7(a)(2) and an injunction requiring the Secretary to promulgate a new regulation restoring the initial interpretation. The District Court granted the Secretary's motion to dismiss for lack of standing. The Court of Appeals for the Eighth Circuit reversed by a divided vote. . . . We granted certiorari.

Antonin Scalia

Ronald Reagan appointed Antonin Scalia to the Supreme Court in 1986. A proponent of originalism, Justice Scalia often consulted old dictionaries to determine the then meaning of words in the Constitution or statutes. He also was "conservative" in the sense that he believed judges should decide cases only when necessary. Justice Scalia wrote well-crafted opinions replete with colorful phrases and occasionally used harsh language directed toward his fellow Justices. His wit, intelligence, and influence made him personally popular but a controversial member of the Court, gaining him both fans and opponents. Justice Scalia was one of the most recognized and influential members of the Rehnquist and Roberts Courts due to his strong personality, combative charm, and poignant written opinions, as well as being the most out-spoken member of the Court outside of the Court.

II

While the Constitution of the United States divides all power conferred upon the Federal Government into "legislative Powers," Art. I, § 1, "[t]he executive Power," Art. II, § 1, and "[t]he judicial Power," Art. III, § 1, it does not attempt to define those terms. To be sure, it limits the jurisdiction of federal courts to "Cases" and "Controversies," but an executive inquiry can bear the name "case" (the Hoffa case) and a legislative dispute can bear the name "controversy" (the Smoot-Hawley controversy). Obviously, then, the Constitution's central mechanism of separation of powers depends largely upon common understanding of what activities are appropriate to legislatures, to executives, and to courts. In The Federalist No. 48, Madison expressed the view that "[i]t is not infrequently a question of real nicety in legislative bodies whether the operation of a particular measure will, or will not, extend beyond the legislative sphere," whereas "the executive power [is] restrained within a narrower compass and . . . more simple in its nature," and "the judiciary [is] described by landmarks still less uncertain." One of those landmarks, setting apart the "Cases" and "Controversies" that are of the justiciable sort referred to in Article III—"serv[ing] to identify those disputes which are appropriately resolved through the judicial process,"—is the doctrine of standing. Though some of its elements express merely prudential considerations that are part of judicial self-government, the core component of standing is an essential and unchanging part of the case-or-controversy requirement of Article III.

Over the years, our cases have established that the irreducible constitutional minimum of standing contains three elements. First, the plaintiff must have suffered an "injury in fact"—an invasion of a legally protected interest which is (a) concrete and particularized[1] and (b) "actual or imminent, not 'conjectural' or 'hypothetical.' " Second, there must be a causal connection between the injury and the conduct complained of—the injury has to be "fairly . . . trace[able] to the challenged action of the defendant, and not . . . th[e] result [of] the independent action of some third party not before the court." Third, it must be "likely," as opposed to merely "speculative," that the injury will be "redressed by a favorable decision."

The party invoking federal jurisdiction bears the burden of establishing these elements. Since they are not mere pleading requirements but rather an indispensable part of the plaintiff's case, each element must be supported in the same way as any other matter on which the plaintiff bears the burden of proof, *i.e.*, with the manner and degree of evidence required at the successive stages of the litigation. At the pleading stage, general factual allegations of injury resulting from the defendant's conduct may suffice, for on a motion to dismiss we "presum[e] that general allegations embrace those specific facts that are necessary to support the claim." In response to a summary judgment motion, however, the plaintiff can no longer rest on such "mere allegations," but must "set forth" by affidavit or other evidence "specific facts," which for purposes of the summary judgment motion will be taken to be true. And at the final stage, those facts (if controverted) must be "supported adequately by the evidence adduced at trial."

When the suit is one challenging the legality of government action or inaction, the nature and extent of facts that must be averred (at the summary judgment stage) or proved (at the trial stage) in order to establish

---

[1] By particularized, we mean that the injury must affect the plaintiff in a personal and individual way.

standing depends considerably upon whether the plaintiff is himself an object of the action (or forgone action) at issue. If he is, there is ordinarily little question that the action or inaction has caused him injury, and that a judgment preventing or requiring the action will redress it. When, however, as in this case, a plaintiff's asserted injury arises from the government's allegedly unlawful regulation (or lack of regulation) of someone else, much more is needed. In that circumstance, causation and redressability ordinarily hinge on the response of the regulated (or regulable) third party to the government action or inaction—and perhaps on the response of others as well. The existence of one or more of the essential elements of standing "depends on the unfettered choices made by independent actors not before the courts and whose exercise of broad and legitimate discretion the courts cannot presume either to control or to predict," and it becomes the burden of the plaintiff to adduce facts showing that those choices have been or will be made in such manner as to produce causation and permit redressability of injury. Thus, when the plaintiff is not himself the object of the government action or inaction he challenges, standing is not precluded, but it is ordinarily "substantially more difficult" to establish.

III

We think the Court of Appeals failed to apply the foregoing principles in denying the Secretary's motion for summary judgment. Respondents had not made the requisite demonstration of (at least) injury and redressability.

A

Respondents' claim to injury is that the lack of consultation with respect to certain funded activities abroad "increas[es] the rate of extinction of endangered and threatened species." Of course, the desire to use or observe an animal species, even for purely esthetic purposes, is undeniably a cognizable interest for purpose of standing. *See, e.g., Sierra Club v. Morton,* 405 U.S. 727, at 734 (1972). "But the 'injury in fact' test requires more than an injury to a cognizable interest. It requires that the party seeking review be himself among the injured." To survive the Secretary's summary judgment motion, respondents had to submit affidavits or other evidence showing, through specific facts, not only that listed species were in fact being threatened by funded activities abroad, but also that one or more of respondents' members would thereby be "directly" affected apart from their " 'special interest' in th[e] subject."

With respect to this aspect of the case, the Court of Appeals focused on the affidavits of two Defenders' members—Joyce Kelly and Amy Skilbred. Ms. Kelly stated that she traveled to Egypt in 1986 and "observed the traditional habitat of the endangered Nile crocodile there and intend[s] to do so again, and hope[s] to observe the crocodile directly," and that she "will suffer harm in fact as the result of [the] American . . . role . . . in overseeing the rehabilitation of the Aswan High Dam on the Nile . . . and [in] develop [ing] . . . Egypt's . . . Master Water Plan." Ms. Skilbred averred that she traveled to Sri Lanka in 1981 and "observed th[e] habitat" of "endangered species such as the Asian elephant and the leopard" at what is now the site of the Mahaweli project funded by the Agency for International Development (AID), although she "was unable to see any of the endangered species"; "this development project," she continued, "will seriously reduce endangered, threatened, and endemic species habitat including areas that I visited . . . [, which] may severely shorten the future of these species"; that threat, she concluded, harmed her because she "intend[s] to return to Sri Lanka in the future and hope[s] to be more fortunate in spotting at least the endangered elephant and leopard." When Ms. Skilbred was asked at a subsequent deposition if and when she had any plans to return to Sri Lanka, she reiterated that "I intend to go back to Sri Lanka," but confessed that she had no current plans: "I don't know [when]. There is a civil war going on right now. I don't know. Not next year, I will say. In the future."

We shall assume for the sake of argument that these affidavits contain facts showing that certain agency-funded projects threaten listed species— though that is questionable. They plainly contain no facts, however, showing how damage to the species will produce "imminent" injury to Mses. Kelly and Skilbred. That the women "had visited" the areas of the projects before the projects commenced proves nothing. As we have said in a related context, " 'Past exposure to illegal conduct does not in itself show a present case or controversy regarding injunctive relief . . . if unaccompanied by any continuing, present adverse effects.' " And the affiants' profession of an "inten[t]" to return to the places they had visited before—where they will presumably, this time, be deprived of the opportunity to observe animals of the endangered species—is simply not enough. Such "some day" intentions—without any description of concrete plans, or indeed even any specification of when the some day will be—do not support a finding of the "actual or imminent" injury that our cases require.[2]

---

[2] The dissent acknowledges the settled requirement that the injury complained of be, if not actual, then at least imminent, but it contends that respondents could get past summary judgment because "a reasonable finder of fact could conclude . . . that . . . Kelly or Skilbred will soon return to the project sites." This analysis suffers either from a factual or from a legal defect, depending on what the "soon" is supposed to mean. If "soon" refers to the standard mandated by our precedents—that the injury be "imminent"—we are at a loss to see how, as a factual matter, the standard can be met by respondents' mere profession of an intent, some day, to return. But if, as we suspect, "soon" means nothing more than "in this lifetime," then the dissent has undertaken quite a departure from our precedents. Although "imminence" is concededly a somewhat elastic concept, it cannot be stretched beyond its purpose, which is to ensure that the alleged injury is not too speculative for Article III purposes-that the injury is " 'certainly impending,' " It has been stretched beyond the breaking point when, as here, the plaintiff alleges only an injury at some indefinite future time, and the acts necessary to make the injury happen are at least partly within the plaintiff's own control. In such circumstances we have insisted that the injury proceed with a high degree of immediacy, so as to reduce the possibility of deciding a case in which no injury would have occurred at all. . . .

Besides relying upon the Kelly and Skilbred affidavits, respondents propose a series of novel standing theories. The first, inelegantly styled "ecosystem nexus," proposes that any person who uses any part of a "contiguous ecosystem" adversely affected by a funded activity has standing even if the activity is located a great distance away. This approach, as the Court of Appeals correctly observed, is inconsistent with our opinion in *National Wildlife Federation*, which held that a plaintiff claiming injury from environmental damage must use the area affected by the challenged activity and not an area roughly "in the vicinity" of it. . . .

Respondents' other theories are called, alas, the "animal nexus" approach, whereby anyone who has an interest in studying or seeing the endangered animals anywhere on the globe has standing; and the "vocational nexus" approach, under which anyone with a professional interest in such animals can sue. Under these theories, anyone who goes to see Asian elephants in the Bronx Zoo, and anyone who is a keeper of Asian elephants in the Bronx Zoo, has standing to sue because the Director of the Agency for International Development (AID) did not consult with the Secretary regarding the AID-funded project in Sri Lanka. This is beyond all reason. Standing is not "an ingenious academic exercise in the conceivable," but as we have said requires, at the summary judgment stage, a factual showing of perceptible harm. It is clear that the person who observes or works with a particular animal threatened by a federal decision is facing perceptible harm, since the very subject of his interest will no longer exist. It is even plausible—though it goes to the outermost limit of plausibility—to think that a person who observes or works with animals of a particular species in the very area of the world where that species is threatened by a federal decision is facing such harm, since some animals that might have been the subject of his interest will no longer exist. It goes beyond the limit, however, and into pure speculation and fantasy, to say that anyone who observes or works with an endangered species, anywhere in the world, is appreciably harmed by a single project affecting some portion of that species with which he has no more specific connection.

B

Besides failing to show injury, respondents failed to demonstrate redressability. Instead of attacking the separate decisions to fund particular projects allegedly causing them harm, respondents chose to challenge a more generalized level of Government action (rules regarding consultation), the invalidation of which would affect all overseas projects. This programmatic approach has obvious practical advantages, but also obvious difficulties insofar as proof of causation or redressability is concerned. . . .

The most obvious problem in the present case is redressability. Since the agencies funding the projects were not parties to the case, the District Court could accord relief only against the Secretary: He could be ordered to revise his regulation to require consultation for foreign projects. But this would not remedy respondents' alleged injury unless the funding agencies were bound by the Secretary's regulation, which is very much an open question. . . . When the Secretary promulgated the regulation at issue here, he thought it was binding on the agencies. The Solicitor General, however, has repudiated that position here, and the agencies themselves apparently deny the Secretary's authority. (During the period when the Secretary took the view that § 7(a)(2) did apply abroad, AID and FWS engaged in a running controversy over whether consultation was required with respect to the Mahaweli project, AID insisting that consultation applied only to domestic actions.)

[T]he short of the matter is that redress of the only injury in fact respondents complain of requires action (termination of funding until consultation) by the individual funding agencies; and any relief the District Court could have provided in this suit against the Secretary was not likely to produce that action.

A further impediment to redressability is the fact that the agencies generally supply only a fraction of the funding for a foreign project. AID, for example, has provided less than 10% of the funding for the Mahaweli project. Respondents have produced nothing to indicate that the projects they have named will either be suspended, or do less harm to listed species, if that fraction is eliminated. [I]t is entirely conjectural whether the nonagency activity that affects respondents will be altered or affected by the agency activity they seek to achieve. There is no standing.

IV

The Court of Appeals found that respondents had standing for an additional reason: because they had suffered a "procedural injury." The so-called "citizen-suit" provision of the ESA provides, in pertinent part, that "any person may commence a civil suit on his own behalf (A) to enjoin any person, including the United States and any other governmental instrumentality or agency . . . who is alleged to be in violation of any provision of this chapter." The court held that, because § 7(a)(2) requires interagency consultation, the citizen-suit provision creates a "procedural righ[t]" to consultation in all "persons"—so that anyone can file suit in federal court to challenge the Secretary's (or presumably any other official's) failure to follow the assertedly correct consultative procedure, notwithstanding his or her inability to allege any discrete injury flowing from that failure. To understand the remarkable nature of this holding one must be clear about what it does not rest upon: This is not a case where plaintiffs are seeking to enforce a procedural requirement the disregard of which could impair a separate concrete interest of theirs (e.g., the procedural requirement for a hearing prior to denial of their license application, or the procedural requirement for an environmental impact statement before a federal facility is constructed next door to them).[7] Nor is it simply a case where concrete injury has been suffered by many persons, as in mass fraud or mass tort situations. Nor, finally, is it the unusual case in which Congress has created a concrete private interest in the outcome of a suit against a private party for the government's benefit, by providing a cash bounty for the victorious plaintiff. Rather, the court held that the injury-in-fact requirement had been satisfied by congressional conferral upon all persons of an abstract, self-contained, noninstrumental "right" to have the Executive observe the procedures required by law. We reject this view.[8]

We have consistently held that a plaintiff raising only a generally available grievance about government—claiming only harm to his and every citizen's interest in proper application of the Constitution and laws, and seeking relief that no more directly and tangibly benefits him than it does the public at large—does not state an Article III case or controversy. For example, in *Fairchild v. Hughes*, 258 U.S. 126, 129–130 (1922), we dismissed a suit challenging the propriety of the process by which the Nineteenth Amendment was ratified. Justice Brandeis wrote for the Court: "[This is] not a case within the meaning of . . . Article III. . . . Plaintiff has [asserted] only the right, possessed by every citizen, to require that the Government be administered according to law and that the public moneys be not wasted. Obviously this general right does not entitle a private citizen to institute in the federal courts a suit. . . ."

In *Massachusetts v. Mellon*, 262 U.S. 447 (1923), we dismissed for lack of Article III standing a taxpayer suit challenging the propriety of certain federal expenditures. We said: "The party who invokes the power [of

---

[7] There is this much truth to the assertion that "procedural rights" are special: The person who has been accorded a procedural right to protect his concrete interests can assert that right without meeting all the normal standards for redressability and immediacy. Thus, under our case law, one living adjacent to the site for proposed construction of a federally licensed dam has standing to challenge the licensing agency's failure to prepare an environmental impact statement, even though he cannot establish with any certainty that the statement will cause the license to be withheld or altered, and even though the dam will not be completed for many years. (That is why we do not rely, in the present case, upon the Government's argument that, even if the other agencies were obliged to consult with the Secretary, they might not have followed his advice.) What respondents' "procedural rights" argument seeks, however, is quite different from this: standing for persons who have no concrete interests affected-persons who live (and propose to live) at the other end of the country from the dam.

[8] The dissent's discussion of this aspect of the case distorts our opinion. We do not hold that an individual cannot enforce procedural rights; he assuredly can, so long as the procedures in question are designed to protect some threatened concrete interest of his that is the ultimate basis of his standing. The dissent, however, asserts that there exist "classes of procedural duties . . . so enmeshed with the prevention of a substantive, concrete harm that an individual plaintiff may be able to demonstrate a sufficient likelihood of injury just through the breach of that procedural duty." If we understand this correctly, it means that the Government's violation of a certain (undescribed) class of procedural duty satisfies the concrete-injury requirement by itself, without any showing that the procedural violation endangers a concrete interest of the plaintiff (apart from his interest in having the procedure observed). We cannot agree. The dissent is unable to cite a single case in which we actually found standing solely on the basis of a "procedural right" unconnected to the plaintiff's own concrete harm. . . .

judicial review] must be able to show not only that the statute is invalid but that he has sustained or is immediately in danger of sustaining some direct injury as the result of its enforcement, and not merely that he suffers in some indefinite way in common with people generally.... Here the parties plaintiff have no such case.... [T]heir complaint ... is merely that officials of the executive department of the government are executing and will execute an act of Congress asserted to be unconstitutional; and this we are asked to prevent. To do so would be not to decide a judicial controversy, but to assume a position of authority over the governmental acts of another and co-equal department, an authority which plainly we do not possess."
. . .

More recent cases are to the same effect. In *United States v. Richardson*, 418 U.S. 166 (1974), we dismissed for lack of standing a taxpayer suit challenging the Government's failure to disclose the expenditures of the Central Intelligence Agency, in alleged violation of the constitutional requirement, Art. I, § 9, cl. 7, that "a regular Statement and Account of the Receipts and Expenditures of all public Money shall be published from time to time." We held that such a suit rested upon an impermissible "generalized grievance," and was inconsistent with "the framework of Article III" because "the impact on [plaintiff] is plainly undifferentiated and 'common to all members of the public.'" And in *Schlesinger v. Reservists Comm. to Stop the War*, we dismissed for the same reasons a citizen-taxpayer suit contending that it was a violation of the Incompatibility Clause, Art. I, § 6, cl. 2, for Members of Congress to hold commissions in the military Reserves. We said that the challenged action, "standing alone, would adversely affect only the generalized interest of all citizens in constitutional governance...." And only two Terms ago, we rejected the notion that Article III permits a citizen suit to prevent a condemned criminal's execution on the basis of "'the public interest protections of the Eighth Amendment'"; once again, "[t]his allegation raise[d] only the 'generalized interest of all citizens in constitutional governance' ... and [was] an inadequate basis on which to grant ... standing."

To be sure, our generalized-grievance cases have typically involved Government violation of procedures assertedly ordained by the Constitution rather than the Congress. But there is absolutely no basis for making the Article III inquiry turn on the source of the asserted right. Whether the courts were to act on their own, or at the invitation of Congress, in ignoring the concrete injury requirement described in our cases, they would be discarding a principle fundamental to the separate and distinct constitutional role of the Third Branch—one of the essential elements that identifies those "Cases" and "Controversies" that are the business of the courts rather than of the political branches. "The province of the court," as Chief Justice Marshall said in *Marbury v. Madison*, "is, solely, to decide on the rights of individuals." Vindicating the public interest (including the public interest in Government observance of the

Constitution and laws) is the function of Congress and the Chief Executive. The question presented here is whether the public interest in proper administration of the laws (specifically, in agencies' observance of a particular, statutorily prescribed procedure) can be converted into an individual right by a statute that denominates it as such, and that permits all citizens . . . to sue. If the concrete injury requirement has the separation-of-powers significance we have always said, the answer must be obvious: To permit Congress to convert the undifferentiated public interest in executive officers' compliance with the law into an "individual right" vindicable in the courts is to permit Congress to transfer from the President to the courts the Chief Executive's most important constitutional duty, to "take Care that the Laws be faithfully executed," Art. II, § 3. It would enable the courts, with the permission of Congress, "to assume a position of authority over the governmental acts of another and co-equal department," and to become " 'virtually continuing monitors of the wisdom and soundness of Executive action.' " We have always rejected that vision of our role. . . .

Nothing in this contradicts the principle that "[t]he . . . injury required by Art. III may exist solely by virtue of 'statutes creating legal rights, the invasion of which creates standing.' " . . . As we said in *Sierra Club*, "[Statutory] broadening [of] the categories of injury that may be alleged in support of standing is a different matter from abandoning the requirement that the party seeking review must himself have suffered an injury." . . .

We hold that respondents lack standing to bring this action and that the Court of Appeals erred in denying the summary judgment motion filed by the United States. The opinion of the Court of Appeals is hereby reversed, and the cause is remanded for proceedings consistent with this opinion.

JUSTICE KENNEDY, with whom JUSTICE SOUTER joins, concurring in part and concurring in the judgment.

Although I agree with the essential parts of the Court's analysis, I write separately to make several observations.

I agree with the Court's conclusion in Part III-A that, on the record before us, respondents have failed to demonstrate that they themselves are "among the injured." . . .

While it may seem trivial to require that Mses. Kelly and Skilbred acquire airline tickets to the project sites or announce a date certain upon which they will return, this is not a case where it is reasonable to assume that the affiants will be using the sites on a regular basis nor do the affiants claim to have visited the sites since the projects commenced. With respect to the Court's discussion of respondents' "ecosystem nexus," "animal nexus," and "vocational nexus" theories, I agree that on this record respondents' showing is insufficient to establish standing on any of these bases. I am not willing to foreclose the possibility, however, that in different circumstances a nexus theory similar to those proffered here might support a claim to standing.

In light of the conclusion that respondents have not demonstrated a concrete injury here sufficient to support standing under our precedents, I would not reach the issue of redressability that is discussed by the plurality in Part III-B.

I also join Part IV of the Court's opinion with the following observations. As Government programs and policies become more complex and farreaching, we must be sensitive to the articulation of new rights of action that do not have clear analogs in our common-law tradition. Modern litigation has progressed far from the paradigm of Marbury suing Madison to get his commission. . . . In my view, Congress has the power to define injuries and articulate chains of causation that will give rise to a case or controversy where none existed before, and I do not read the Court's opinion to suggest a contrary view. In exercising this power, however, Congress must at the very least identify the injury it seeks to vindicate and relate the injury to the class of persons entitled to bring suit. The citizen-suit provision of the Endangered Species Act does not meet these minimal requirements, because while the statute purports to confer a right on "any person . . . to enjoin . . . the United States and any other governmental instrumentality or agency . . . who is alleged to be in violation of any provision of this chapter," it does not of its own force establish that there is an injury in "any person" by virtue of any "violation." . . .

With these observations, I concur in Parts I, II, III-A, and IV of the Court's opinion and in the judgment of the Court.

JUSTICE STEVENS, concurring in the judgment.

Because I am not persuaded that Congress intended the consultation requirement in § 7(a)(2) of the Endangered Species Act of 1973 (ESA) to apply to activities in foreign countries, I concur in the judgment of reversal. I do not, however, agree with the Court's conclusion that respondents lack standing because the threatened injury to their interest in protecting the environment and studying endangered species is not "imminent." Nor do I agree with the plurality's additional conclusion that respondents' injury is not "redressable" in this litigation.

In my opinion a person who has visited the critical habitat of an endangered species, has a professional interest in preserving the species and its habitat, and intends to revisit them in the future has standing to challenge agency action that threatens their destruction. Congress has found that a wide variety of endangered species of fish, wildlife, and plants are of "aesthetic, ecological, educational, historical, recreational, and scientific value to the Nation and its people." Given that finding, we have no license to demean the importance of the interest that particular individuals may have in observing any species or its habitat, whether those individuals are motivated by esthetic enjoyment, an interest in professional research, or an economic interest in preservation of the species. Indeed, this Court has often held that injuries to such interests are sufficient to confer standing and the Court reiterates that holding today.

The Court nevertheless concludes that respondents have not suffered "injury in fact" because they have not shown that the harm to the endangered species will produce "imminent" injury to them. I disagree. An injury to an individual's interest in studying or enjoying a species and its natural habitat occurs when someone (whether it be the Government or a private party) takes action that harms that species and habitat. In my judgment, therefore, the "imminence" of such an injury should be measured by the timing and likelihood of the threatened environmental harm, rather than—as the Court seems to suggest—by the time that might elapse between the present and the time when the individuals would visit the area if no such injury should occur.

To understand why this approach is correct and consistent with our precedent, it is necessary to consider the purpose of the standing doctrine. Concerned about "the proper—and properly limited—role of the courts in a democratic society," we have long held that "Art. III judicial power exists only to redress or otherwise to protect against injury to the complaining party." The plaintiff must have a "personal stake in the outcome" sufficient to "assure that concrete adverseness which sharpens the presentation of issues upon which the court so largely depends for illumination of difficult . . . questions." For that reason, "[a]bstract injury is not enough. It must be alleged that the plaintiff 'has sustained or is immediately in danger of sustaining some direct injury' as the result of the challenged statute or official conduct. . . . The injury or threat of injury must be both 'real and immediate,' not 'conjectural,' or 'hypothetical.' "

Consequently, we have denied standing to plaintiffs whose likelihood of suffering any concrete adverse effect from the challenged action was speculative. In this case, however, the likelihood that respondents will be injured by the destruction of the endangered species is not speculative. If respondents are genuinely interested in the preservation of the endangered species and intend to study or observe these animals in the future, their injury will occur as soon as the animals are destroyed. Thus the only potential source of "speculation" in this case is whether respondents' intent to study or observe the animals is genuine.[2] In my view, Joyce Kelly and

---

[2]   As we recognized in *Sierra Club v. Morton*, the impact of changes in the esthetics or ecology of a particular area does "not fall indiscriminately upon every citizen. The alleged injury will be felt directly only by those who use [the area,] and for whom the aesthetic and recreational values of the area will be lessened. . . ." Thus, respondents would not be injured by the challenged projects if they had not visited the sites or studied the threatened species and habitat. But, as discussed above, respondents did visit the sites; moreover, they have expressed an intent to do so again. This intent to revisit the area is significant evidence tending to confirm the genuine character of respondents' interest, but I am not at all sure that an intent to revisit would be indispensable in

Amy Skilbred have introduced sufficient evidence to negate petitioner's contention that their claims of injury are "speculative" or "conjectural." . . .

The plurality also concludes that respondents' injuries are not redressable in this litigation for two reasons. First, respondents have sought only a declaratory judgment that the Secretary of the Interior's regulation interpreting § 7(a)(2) to require consultation only for agency actions in the United States or on the high seas is invalid and an injunction requiring him to promulgate a new regulation requiring consultation for agency actions abroad as well. But, the plurality opines, even if respondents succeed and a new regulation is promulgated, there is no guarantee that federal agencies that are not parties to this case will actually consult with the Secretary. Furthermore, the plurality continues, respondents have not demonstrated that federal agencies can influence the behavior of the foreign governments where the affected projects are located. Thus, even if the agencies consult with the Secretary and terminate funding for foreign projects, the foreign governments might nonetheless pursue the projects and jeopardize the endangered species. Neither of these reasons is persuasive.

We must presume that if this Court holds that § 7(a)(2) requires consultation, all affected agencies would abide by that interpretation and engage in the requisite consultations. Certainly the Executive Branch cannot be heard to argue that an authoritative construction of the governing statute by this Court may simply be ignored by any agency head. Moreover, if Congress has required consultation between agencies, we must presume that such consultation will have a serious purpose that is likely to produce tangible results. As Justice BLACKMUN explains, it is not mere speculation to think that foreign governments, when faced with the threatened withdrawal of United States assistance, will modify their projects to mitigate the harm to endangered species. . . .

JUSTICE BLACKMUN, with whom JUSTICE O'CONNOR joins, dissenting.

[I] question the Court's breadth of language in rejecting standing for "procedural" injuries. I fear the Court seeks to impose fresh limitations on the constitutional authority of Congress to allow citizen suits in the federal courts for injuries deemed "procedural" in nature. I dissent. . . .

The Court expresses concern that allowing judicial enforcement of "agencies' observance of a particular, statutorily prescribed procedure" would "transfer from the President to the courts the Chief Executive's most important constitutional duty, to 'take Care that the Laws be faithfully executed,' Art. II, § 3." In fact, the principal effect of foreclosing judicial

---

every case. The interest that confers standing in a case of this kind is comparable, though by no means equivalent, to the interest in a relationship among family members that can be immediately harmed by the death of an absent member, regardless of when, if ever, a family reunion is planned to occur. Thus, if the facts of this case had shown repeated and regular visits by the respondents, proof of an intent to revisit might well be superfluous.

enforcement of such procedures is to transfer power into the hands of the Executive at the expense—not of the courts—but of Congress, from which that power originates and emanates. . . .

In conclusion, I cannot join the Court on what amounts to a slash-and-burn expedition through the law of environmental standing. In my view, "[t]he very essence of civil liberty certainly consists in the right of every individual to claim the protection of the laws, whenever he receives an injury." *Marbury v. Madison.*

I dissent.

COMMENTS AND QUESTIONS

1.   Note that this case is not a "constitutional case" in the sense that the plaintiff did not raise any constitutional claims nor did the defendant defend on the merits based on the Constitution. The Constitution is only involved in that its limitation of the "judicial power of the United States" to "cases or controversies" means that plaintiffs must have standing to bring any lawsuit in a federal court. In this opinion the Court identifies the three requirements for standing: Injury, Causation, and Redressability. Try to identify the different bases upon which the plaintiffs tried to establish injury and the basis upon which the Court rejected those bases.

2.   "Redress," it is worth noting, can be of two different types: after-the-fact redress in the form of damages for the injury and before-the-fact avoidance of the injury about to occur. It is the latter that is usually involved in standing cases, as it is here.

3.   Note that Justice Scalia's opinion regarding redressability does not command agreement from a majority of the Court. Justices Kennedy and Souter agree with the rest of his opinion for the Court, but not with respect to redressability, and Justices Stevens, Blackmun, and O'Connor disagree with all of Scalia's opinion. So, what does the Court decide regarding redressability?

4.   The Endangered Species Act states that "any person" may sue to enforce its provisions, but the Court in effect says that is unconstitutional, because only a person with standing can bring an action in federal court. Who can sue to enforce the ESA now?

5.   Does Justice Scalia's description of the purpose of the standing requirement seem consistent with the description in *Flast* or with Justice Stevens's description?

6.   Note that the plaintiff in the case is the organization Defenders of the Wildlife, but it is the failure of two of its members to establish standing that results in the case being lost. Groups like Defenders can establish standing in their own right if the group itself is injured by an allegedly unlawful action that can be redressed by a court. For example, a law denying a tax exemption to all non-profit organizations that try to protect the environment would directly injure the organization itself. However, in *Defenders* that is not the case. Instead, Defenders tries to establish standing based upon the doctrine of

"representational standing." In order to establish "representational standing," an organization needs to show three things: first, that one or more of its members would themselves have standing (hence the concern in *Defenders* with whether the two members can establish standing); second, that the purpose of the organization relates to the subject matter of the lawsuit (here, Defenders, an organization with the specific purpose of protecting endangered species, easily qualified); and third, that the member of the group with standing does not need to be a named party. This third requirement is a little confusing, but what it means in effect is that the action is either for an injunction or for a declaratory judgment, not for damages to one or more of the members.

7.   *Defenders* acknowledged that esthetic or recreational injury can satisfy the injury requirement for standing, so long as that injury is particularized and imminent. Thus, had Mses. Kelly and Skilbred regularly traveled to Egypt and Sir Lanka to see or study the endangered species, they would have had standing. Were it otherwise a broad range of environmental law suits could not be brought. Recently, Justice Neil Gorsuch, joined by Justice Clarence Thomas, questioned this acknowledgment. In *American Legion v. American Humanist Ass'n*, 139 S.Ct. 2067 (2019), the plaintiff argued that the presence of a large cross on government property violated the Establishment Clause of the First Amendment. The alleged injury was having to observe that cross at a busy intersection the plaintiff's members were forced to use. The Court held that the cross did not violate the Establishment Clause. Justice Gorsuch concurred in the judgment reversing the court below, but not on the basis of the Establishment Clause. In his view the plaintiff did not have standing, because "[o]ffended observer standing cannot be squared with this Court's longstanding teachings about the limits of Article III." He equated this type of injury to the generalized grievance that does not satisfy standing.

8.   The Court has made clear in the past that when the action is seeking an injunction or a declaratory judgment, then so long as one plaintiff has standing, other plaintiffs may proceed in the case as well without considering their separate standing. In other words, in *Defenders*, if a zoologist from the San Diego Zoo, who had regularly visited Egypt and Sri Lanka to view the endangered crocodile and elephant and had plans to return shortly, had also been a plaintiff, she would have had standing. Then, Defenders of Wildlife could have continued in the case even though it could not establish standing. The reasoning behind this is that it would be a waste of a court's resources to consider the standing of all of the plaintiffs when at least one plaintiff has standing, and the judgment of the case will equally affect them all. However, to the extent that different plaintiffs in the same case seek *different* relief, such as one seeking a particular injunction and another seeking a different injunction, then each plaintiff would need to establish standing in his own right.

9.   A recurring issue in standing law is how to treat the *risk* of injury. For example, imagine that the Environmental Protection Agency amended a current air standard to allow a greater amount of pollution than previously

allowed, and plaintiffs could show that this additional pollution would increase their risk of contracting lung cancer, would they have standing to challenge the amendment? The Supreme Court has decided three cases that bear upon this issue. The first was *Summers v. Earth Island Institute*, 555 U.S. 488 (2009). There, environmental organizations challenged a Forest Service regulation exempting certain small-scale timber salvage sales from having to undergo prior public notice and comment or be subject to administrative appeals, notwithstanding a statute that required such notice and comment and an appeals process for all timber sales. In order to establish standing, the environmental groups produced a member who hiked in an area that was to be subject to such a timber sale. The government consented to providing the requisite notice and comment and appeals process for that particular timber sale and then moved to dismiss the case challenging the regulation, arguing that plaintiffs no longer had standing because they had not produced a member who would use any other particular area that would be subject to such a timber sale. The Supreme Court agreed by a 5–4 vote.

The plaintiffs claimed that they suffered injury in not being able to comment on or administratively appeal other salvage timber sales that would occur, but the Court reiterated its statement in *Defenders of Wildlife* that a procedural injury alone, the inability to comment on or administratively appeal a timber sale, did not satisfy the constitutional requirement for injury.

The dissent by Justice Breyer made a different argument. He suggested that because the plaintiff environmental organizations had hundreds of thousands of members and the government conceded that there would be thousands of this type of timber sales, the likelihood that some member would use one of the areas involved was almost certain. Thus, an injury-in-fact by a member was virtually certain. This, he suggested, was sufficient injury to establish standing. Justice Scalia, writing for the majority, characterized this as a "hitherto unheard-of test for organizational standing" and rejected it. First, he said that prior cases required an organization to identify the particular members who would be injured and, second, allowing a statistical probability of an injury would substitute the requirement of an imminent harm with a requirement of a realistic threat of harm in the reasonably near future.

The second case follows.

MONSANTO CO. v. GEERTSON SEED FARMS

United States Supreme Court, 2010.
561 U.S. 139, 130 S.Ct. 2743.

JUSTICE ALITO delivered the opinion of the Court.

This case arises out of a decision by the Animal and Plant Health Inspection Service (APHIS) to deregulate a variety of genetically engineered alfalfa. The District Court held that APHIS violated the National Environmental Policy Act of 1969 (NEPA) by issuing its deregulation decision without first completing a detailed assessment of the environmental consequences of its proposed course of action. To remedy

Samuel A. Alito

Appointed by President George W. Bush to the Supreme Court in 2006, Justice Alito became the second Italian-American and only military veteran on the then current Court. Prior to the Supreme Court, Justice Alito had served on the Third Circuit for sixteen years, where he developed a reputation as a solid judge with conservative leanings, particularly in criminal cases, which was not surprising given his membership in the Federalist Society, his previous service in the Reagan administration's Justice Department, and his stint as a criminal prosecutor in the New Jersey U.S. Attorney's Office. His confirmation was actively opposed by liberals and the final vote was 58–42, largely along party lines. On the Supreme Court, he has been a reliable "conservative" vote. The leaking of his opinion for the Court overruling *Roe v. Wade* caused a scandal.

that violation, the District Court vacated the agency's decision completely deregulating the alfalfa variety in question; ordered APHIS not to act on the deregulation petition in whole or in part until it had completed a detailed environmental review; and enjoined almost all future planting of the genetically engineered alfalfa pending the completion of that review. The Court of Appeals affirmed the District Court's entry of permanent injunctive relief. . . .

We next consider petitioners' contention that respondents lack standing to seek injunctive relief. Petitioners argue that respondents have failed to show that any of the named respondents is likely to suffer a constitutionally cognizable injury absent injunctive relief. We disagree.

Respondents include conventional alfalfa farmers. Emphasizing "the undisputed concentration of alfalfa seed farms," the District Court found that those farmers had "established a 'reasonable probability'" that their organic and conventional alfalfa crops will be infected with the engineered gene" if Roundup Ready Alfalfa (RRA) is completely deregulated.[3] A substantial risk of gene flow injures respondents in several ways. For example, respondents represent that, in order to continue marketing their product to consumers who wish to buy non-genetically-engineered alfalfa, respondents would have to conduct testing to find out whether and to what extent their crops have been contaminated. See (Declaration of Phillip

---

[3]   At least one of the respondents in this case specifically alleges that he owns an alfalfa farm in a prominent seed-growing region and faces a significant risk of contamination from RRA ("Since alfalfa is pollinated by honey, bumble and leafcutter bees, the genetic contamination of the Roundup Ready seed will rapidly spread through the seed growing regions. Bees have a range of at least two to ten miles, and the alfalfa seed farms are much more concentrated"). Other declarations in the record provide further support for the District Court's conclusion that the deregulation of RRA poses a significant risk of contamination to respondents' crops. See (Declaration of Jim Munsch)(alleging risk of "significant contamination . . . due to the compact geographic area of the prime alfalfa seed producing areas and the fact that pollen is distributed by bees that have large natural range of activity"); (Declaration of Marc Asumendi)("Roundup alfalfa seed fields are currently being planted in all the major alfalfa seed production areas with little regard to contamination to non-GMO seed production fields").

Geertson in Support of Plaintiffs' Motion for Summary Judgment) (hereinafter Geertson Declaration) ("Due to the high potential for contamination, I will need to test my crops for the presence of genetically engineered alfalfa seed. This testing will be a new cost to my seed business and we will have to raise our seed prices to cover these costs, making our prices less competitive"); (Declaration of Patrick Trask in Support of Plaintiff's Motion for Summary Judgment)("To ensure that my seeds are pure, I will need to test my crops and obtain certification that my seeds are free of genetically engineered alfalfa"); see also ("There is zero tolerance for contaminated seed in the organic market"). Respondents also allege that the risk of gene flow will cause them to take certain measures to minimize the likelihood of potential contamination and to ensure an adequate supply of non-genetically-engineered alfalfa. See, *e.g.*, Geertson Declaration 3 (noting the "increased cost of alfalfa breeding due to potential for genetic contamination"); *id.*, at 6 ("Due to the threat of contamination, I have begun contracting with growers outside of the United States to ensure that I can supply genetically pure, conventional alfalfa seed. Finding new growers has already resulted in increased administrative costs at my seed business").

Such harms, which respondents will suffer even if their crops are not actually infected with the Roundup ready gene, are sufficiently concrete to satisfy the injury-in-fact prong of the constitutional standing analysis. Those harms are readily attributable to APHIS's deregulation decision, which, as the District Court found, gives rise to a significant risk of gene flow to non-genetically-engineered varieties of alfalfa. Finally, a judicial order prohibiting the growth and sale of all or some genetically engineered alfalfa would remedy respondents' injuries by eliminating or minimizing the risk of gene flow to conventional and organic alfalfa crops. We therefore conclude that respondents have constitutional standing to seek injunctive relief from the complete deregulation order at issue here. . . .

COMMENTS AND QUESTIONS

1.   The third case was *Clapper v. Amnesty International USA*, 568 U.S. 398 (2013). In *Clapper* the plaintiffs challenged the constitutionality of a provision of the Foreign Intelligence Surveillance Act (FISA) that authorizes the National Security Agency to target for interception the communications of non-United States persons overseas. The plaintiffs were American journalists and attorneys whose work required them to engage in sensitive international communications with individuals likely to be targeted, such as alleged terrorists and their families and friends. The question was whether the plaintiffs had standing to bring the suit. The plaintiffs seemed to take *Monsanto* as their play book, introducing evidence of the likelihood that their communications would be intercepted and of the expense and additional measures they had to take to avoid the risk of being intercepted. A lower court had found that there was "an objectively reasonable likelihood that their

communications will be acquired . . . at some point in the future," but the Supreme Court by a 5–4 vote, with Justice Alito writing for himself and the four other "conservative" justices, found this insufficient. Rather, the Court found that it was entirely speculative whether the plaintiffs would ever be subject to interception pursuant to the challenged provision of FISA. In order to establish standing, the Court said, the plaintiffs must establish that their interception pursuant to the FISA provision was "certainly impending." Moreover, the Court said that the fact that the plaintiffs suffered costs and burdens resulting from the fear of being intercepted was not sufficient, because the risk of harm they sought to avoid was not certainly impending. The dissent would have found the risk of interception sufficient, noting the Court's (and Justice Alito's!) opinion in *Monsanto* had found standing on the basis of a finding that there was a "reasonable probability" of injury or a "substantial risk" of harm and the fact that the organic alfalfa farmers had incurred costs to mitigate or avoid that risk.

2.   How to reconcile these three cases? First, Justice Breyer's dissent in *Summers*, concluding that standing is satisfied if an organization could show a high degree of probability that some one of its members would be injured in the future, would indeed have established a novel approach. And Justice Scalia was correct in saying that prior cases had always required that the organization seeking standing on the basis of representational standing had to establish that specific, named members of the organization would suffer injury, a requirement which Justice Breyer's approach would have dispensed with. However, Justice Scalia's further statement that a realistic threat of harm in the reasonably near future could not satisfy standing was not consistent with past lower court cases at least and is in tension with the unanimous Court's decision in *Monsanto*. Two statements by the Court in *Clapper* may explain why it distinguished the probability of injury there compared to the probability of injury in *Monsanto*. First, it said, "[o]ur standing inquiry has been especially rigorous when reaching the merits of the dispute would force us to decide whether an action taken by one of the other two branches of the Federal Government was unconstitutional." In *Monsanto*, the claim was that the government agency had not complied with a statute, not that its actions were unconstitutional. In *Clapper*, the claim was that Congress had enacted an unconstitutional law. Second, the Court said, "we have often found a lack of standing in cases in which the Judiciary has been requested to review actions of the political branches in the fields of intelligence gathering and foreign affairs."

3.   None of these cases seem to view the risk itself as an injury. Why not? Are you not injured as much when someone puts your life or health at risk as when you have to suffer the aesthetic injury of having to walk in a clear cut forest rather than in a magnificent old growth forest?

4.   The issue of risk is not the only recurring issue in standing. Congressmen have from time-to-time thought that they should have standing to challenge the constitutionality of laws which they thought violated the Constitution with respect to the procedures or prerogatives of Congress. In

Raines v. Byrd, 521 U.S. 811 (1997), the Court denied standing to congressmen challenging the Line Item Veto Act (which will be considered later in this book). The Act allowed the President to cancel specific line item appropriations after they became law, and the congressmen argued that this authority diluted their votes for the appropriations, because the appropriations could be canceled thereafter. This was not a sufficient injury for them to have standing. If Congress passed a law prohibiting certain members from voting on certain types of bills, that would be different.

5. Yet another recurring issue is that raised by Justice Kennedy's concurrence in *Defenders of Wildlife*. That is, to what extent can Congress create new rights, the violation of which would constitute injury for standing purposes. The following case addressed that issue.

SPOKEO, INC. V. ROBINS
United States Supreme Court, 2016.
578 U.S. 330, 136 S.Ct. 1540.

JUSTICE ALITO delivered the opinion of the Court.

This case presents the question whether respondent Robins has standing to maintain an action in federal court against petitioner Spokeo under the Fair Credit Reporting Act of 1970 (FCRA or Act).

Spokeo operates a "people search engine." If an individual visits Spokeo's Web site and inputs a person's name, a phone number, or an e-mail address, Spokeo conducts a computerized search in a wide variety of databases and provides information about the subject of the search. Spokeo performed such a search for information about Robins, and some of the information it gathered and then disseminated was incorrect. . . .

The FCRA seeks to ensure "fair and accurate credit reporting." To achieve this end, the Act regulates the creation and the use of "consumer report[s]" by "consumer reporting agenc[ies]" for certain specified purposes, including credit transactions, insurance, licensing, consumer-initiated business transactions, and employment. . . .

The FCRA imposes a host of requirements concerning the creation and use of consumer reports. . . .

The Act also provides that "[a]ny person who willfully fails to comply with any requirement [of the Act] with respect to any [individual] is liable to that [individual]" for, among other things, either "actual damages" or statutory damages of $100 to $1,000 per violation, costs of the action and attorney's fees, and possibly punitive damages.

Spokeo is alleged to qualify as a "consumer reporting agency" under the FCRA. . . .

At some point in time, someone (Robins' complaint does not specify who) made a Spokeo search request for information about Robins, and

Spokeo trawled its sources and generated a profile. By some means not detailed in Robins' complaint, he became aware of the contents of that profile and discovered that it contained inaccurate information. His profile, he asserts, states that he is married, has children, is in his 50's, has a job, is relatively affluent, and holds a graduate degree. According to Robins' complaint, all of this information is incorrect.

Robins filed a class-action complaint in the United States District Court for the Central District of California, claiming, among other things, that Spokeo willfully failed to comply with the FCRA requirements enumerated above.

The District Court ... dismissed the complaint with prejudice. The court found that Robins had not "properly pled" an injury in fact, as required by Article III.

The Court of Appeals for the Ninth Circuit reversed. Relying on Circuit precedent, the court began by stating that "the violation of a statutory right is usually a sufficient injury in fact to confer standing." The court recognized that "the Constitution limits the power of Congress to confer standing." But the court held that those limits were honored in this case because Robins alleged that "Spokeo violated *his* statutory rights, not just the statutory rights of other people," and because his "personal interests in the handling of his credit information are individualized rather than collective." The court thus concluded that Robins' "alleged violations of [his] statutory rights [were] sufficient to satisfy the injury-in-fact requirement of Article III." . . .

Standing to sue is a doctrine rooted in the traditional understanding of a case or controversy. The doctrine developed in our case law to ensure that federal courts do not exceed their authority as it has been traditionally understood. The doctrine limits the category of litigants empowered to maintain a lawsuit in federal court to seek redress for a legal wrong.

Our cases have established that the "irreducible constitutional minimum" of standing consists of three elements. The plaintiff must have (1) suffered an injury in fact, (2) that is fairly traceable to the challenged conduct of the defendant, and (3) that is likely to be redressed by a favorable judicial decision. . . .

This case primarily concerns injury in fact, the "[f]irst and foremost" of standing's three elements. Injury in fact is a constitutional requirement, and "[i]t is settled that Congress cannot erase Article III's standing requirements by statutorily granting the right to sue to a plaintiff who would not otherwise have standing."

To establish injury in fact, a plaintiff must show that he or she suffered "an invasion of a legally protected interest" that is "concrete and particularized" and "actual or imminent, not conjectural or hypothetical."
. . .

For an injury to be "particularized," it "must affect the plaintiff in a personal and individual way." Particularization is necessary to establish injury in fact, but it is not sufficient. An injury in fact must also be "concrete." Under the Ninth Circuit's analysis, however, that independent requirement was elided. As previously noted, the Ninth Circuit concluded that Robins' complaint alleges "concrete, *de facto*" injuries for essentially two reasons. First, the court noted that Robins "alleges that Spokeo violated *his* statutory rights, not just the statutory rights of other people." Second, the court wrote that "Robins's personal interests in the handling of his credit information are *individualized rather than collective*." Both of these observations concern particularization, not concreteness. We have made it clear time and time again that an injury in fact must be both concrete *and* particularized.

A "concrete" injury must be "*de facto*"; that is, it must actually exist. When we have used the adjective "concrete," we have meant to convey the usual meaning of the term—"real," and not "abstract." Concreteness, therefore, is quite different from particularization.

"Concrete" is not, however, necessarily synonymous with "tangible." Although tangible injuries are perhaps easier to recognize, we have confirmed in many of our previous cases that intangible injuries can nevertheless be concrete.

In determining whether an intangible harm constitutes injury in fact, both history and the judgment of Congress play important roles. Because the doctrine of standing derives from the case-or-controversy requirement, and because that requirement in turn is grounded in historical practice, it is instructive to consider whether an alleged intangible harm has a close relationship to a harm that has traditionally been regarded as providing a basis for a lawsuit in English or American courts. In addition, because Congress is well positioned to identify intangible harms that meet minimum Article III requirements, its judgment is also instructive and important. Thus, we said in *Lujan* that Congress may "elevat[e] to the status of legally cognizable injuries concrete, *de facto* injuries that were previously inadequate in law." Similarly, Justice Kennedy's concurrence in that case explained that "Congress has the power to define injuries and articulate chains of causation that will give rise to a case or controversy where none existed before."

Congress' role in identifying and elevating intangible harms does not mean that a plaintiff automatically satisfies the injury-in-fact requirement whenever a statute grants a person a statutory right and purports to authorize that person to sue to vindicate that right. Article III standing requires a concrete injury even in the context of a statutory violation. For that reason, Robins could not, for example, allege a bare procedural violation, divorced from any concrete harm, and satisfy the injury-in-fact requirement of Article III.

This does not mean, however, that the risk of real harm cannot satisfy the requirement of concreteness. For example, the law has long permitted recovery by certain tort victims even if their harms may be difficult to prove or measure [e.g., slander per se]. Just as the common law permitted suit in such instances, the violation of a procedural right granted by statute can be sufficient in some circumstances to constitute injury in fact. In other words, a plaintiff in such a case need not allege any *additional* harm beyond the one Congress has identified.

In the context of this particular case, these general principles tell us two things: On the one hand, Congress plainly sought to curb the dissemination of false information by adopting procedures designed to decrease that risk. On the other hand, Robins cannot satisfy the demands of Article III by alleging a bare procedural violation. A violation of one of the FCRA's procedural requirements may result in no harm. For example, even if a consumer reporting agency fails to provide the required notice to a user of the agency's consumer information, that information regardless may be entirely accurate. In addition, not all inaccuracies cause harm or present any material risk of harm. An example that comes readily to mind is an incorrect zip code. It is difficult to imagine how the dissemination of an incorrect zip code, without more, could work any concrete harm.

Because the Ninth Circuit failed to fully appreciate the distinction between concreteness and particularization, its standing analysis was incomplete. It did not address the question framed by our discussion, namely, whether the particular procedural violations alleged in this case entail a degree of risk sufficient to meet the concreteness requirement. We take no position as to whether the Ninth Circuit's ultimate conclusion— that Robins adequately alleged an injury in fact—was correct.

JUSTICE THOMAS, concurring.

[I] join the Court's opinion. I write separately to explain how, in my view, the injury-in-fact requirement applies to different types of rights. . . .

To understand the limits that standing imposes on "the judicial Power," . . . we must "refer directly to the traditional, fundamental limitations upon the powers of common-law courts." These limitations preserve separation of powers by preventing the judiciary's entanglement in disputes that are primarily political in nature. This concern is generally absent when a private plaintiff seeks to enforce only his personal rights against another private party.

Common-law courts imposed different limitations on a plaintiff's right to bring suit depending on the type of right the plaintiff sought to vindicate. Historically, common-law courts possessed broad power to adjudicate suits involving the alleged violation of private rights, even when plaintiffs alleged only the violation of those rights and nothing more. "Private rights" are rights "belonging to individuals, considered as individuals." "Private rights" have traditionally included rights of personal security (including security of reputation), property rights, and contract rights. In a suit for the violation of a private right, courts historically presumed that the plaintiff suffered a *de facto* injury merely from having his personal, legal rights invaded. Thus, when one man placed his foot on another's property, the property owner needed to show nothing more to establish a traditional case or controversy. Many traditional remedies for private-rights causes of action—such as for trespass, infringement of intellectual property, and unjust enrichment—are not contingent on a plaintiff's allegation of damages beyond the violation of his private legal right.

Common-law courts, however, have required a further showing of injury for violations of "public rights"—rights that involve duties owed "to the whole community, considered as a community, in its social aggregate capacity." Such rights include "free navigation of waterways, passage on public highways, and general compliance with regulatory law." Generally, only the government had the authority to vindicate a harm borne by the public at large, such as the violation of the criminal laws. Even in limited cases where private plaintiffs could bring a claim for the violation of public rights, they had to allege that the violation caused them "some extraordinary damage, beyond the rest of the [community]." 3 Blackstone *220 (discussing nuisance). . . . The existence of special, individualized damage had the effect of creating a private action for compensatory relief to an otherwise public-rights claim. . . .

These differences between legal claims brought by private plaintiffs for the violation of public and private rights underlie modern standing doctrine and explain the Court's description of the injury-in-fact requirement. . . . The injury-in-fact requirement often stymies a private plaintiff's attempt to vindicate the infringement of *public* rights. The Court has said time and again that, when a plaintiff seeks to vindicate a public right, the plaintiff must allege that he has suffered a "concrete" injury particular to himself. This requirement applies with special force when a plaintiff files suit to require an executive agency to "follow the law"; at that point, the citizen must prove that he "has sustained or is immediately in danger of sustaining a direct injury as a result of that [challenged] action and it is not sufficient that he has merely a general interest common to all members of the public." . . .

But the concrete-harm requirement does not apply as rigorously when a private plaintiff seeks to vindicate his own private rights. Our contemporary decisions have not required a plaintiff to assert an actual injury beyond the violation of his personal legal rights to satisfy the "injury-in-fact" requirement. . . .

When Congress creates new private causes of action to vindicate private or public rights, these Article III principles circumscribe federal courts' power to adjudicate a suit alleging the violation of those new legal rights. Congress can create new private rights and authorize private plaintiffs to sue based simply on the violation of those private rights. A plaintiff seeking to vindicate a statutorily created private right need not allege actual harm beyond the invasion of that private right. A plaintiff seeking to vindicate a public right embodied in a federal statute, however, must demonstrate that the violation of that public right has caused him a concrete, individual harm distinct from the general population. Thus, Congress cannot authorize private plaintiffs to enforce *public* rights in their own names, absent some showing that the plaintiff has suffered a concrete harm particular to him.

Given these principles, I agree with the Court's decision to vacate and remand. The Fair Credit Reporting Act creates a series of regulatory duties. Robins has no standing to sue Spokeo, in his own name, for violations of the duties that Spokeo owes to the public collectively, absent some showing that he has suffered concrete and particular harm. These consumer protection requirements include, for example, the requirement to "post a toll-free telephone number on [Spokeo's] website through which consumers can request free annual file disclosures."

But a remand is required because one claim in Robins' complaint rests on a statutory provision that could arguably establish a private cause of action to vindicate the violation of a privately held right. Section 1681e(b) requires Spokeo to "follow reasonable procedures to assure maximum possible accuracy of the information *concerning the individual about whom the report relates*." If Congress has created a private duty owed personally to Robins to protect *his* information, then the violation of the legal duty suffices for Article III injury in fact. If that provision, however, vests any and all consumers with the power to police the "reasonable procedures" of Spokeo, without more, then Robins has no standing to sue for its violation absent an allegation that he has suffered individualized harm. On remand, the Court of Appeals can consider the nature of this claim.

JUSTICE GINSBURG, with whom JUSTICE SOTOMAYOR joins, dissenting.

[I] agree with much of the Court's opinion. . . .

I part ways with the Court, however, on the necessity of a remand to determine whether Robins' particularized injury was "concrete." Judged by what we have said about "concreteness," Robins' allegations carry him across the threshold. . . .

Inspection of the Court's decisions suggests that the particularity requirement bars complaints raising generalized grievances, seeking relief that no more benefits the plaintiff than it does the public at large. Robins' claim does not present a question of that character. He seeks redress, not for harm to the citizenry, but for Spokeo's spread of misinformation specifically about him.

Concreteness as a discrete requirement for standing, the Court's decisions indicate, refers to the reality of an injury, harm that is real, not abstract, but not necessarily tangible.

Robins would not qualify, the Court observes, if he alleged a "bare" procedural violation, one that results in no harm, for example, "an incorrect zip code." Far from an incorrect zip code, Robins complains of misinformation about his education, family situation, and economic status, inaccurate representations that could affect his fortune in the job market. See Brief for Center for Democracy & Technology et al. as *Amici Curiae* 13 (Spokeo's inaccuracies bore on Robins' "ability to find employment by creating the erroneous impression that he was overqualified for the work he was seeking, that he might be unwilling to relocate for a job due to family commitments, or that his salary demands would exceed what prospective employers were prepared to offer him."); Brief for Restitution and Remedies Scholars et al. as *Amici Curiae* 35 ("An applicant can lose [a] job for being over-qualified; a suitor can lose a woman if she reads that he is married."). The FCRA's procedural requirements aimed to prevent such harm. I therefore see no utility in returning this case to the Ninth Circuit to underscore what Robins' complaint already conveys concretely: Spokeo's misinformation "cause[s] actual harm to [his] employment prospects."

COMMENTS AND QUESTIONS

1.   Justice Alito, writing for the Court, tries to explain what is necessary for an injury to be concrete. He admits that an intangible harm can constitute a concrete injury, but is it clear what is an "intangible harm," much less what kind of intangible harm can be a concrete injury? In addition to looking at history, he suggests the judgment of Congress reflected in the creation of a statutory right to sue is "instructive and important." However, he quickly reminds us that Congress cannot, simply by creating a statutory right and a right to sue for its infringement, create concrete injury. But, wait, "that does not mean . . . that the risk of real harm cannot satisfy the requirement of concreteness." And, "the violation of a procedural right granted by a statute can be sufficient in some circumstances [what circumstances?] to constitute injury in fact." So, "a plaintiff in such a case [what case?] need not allege any *additional* harm beyond the one Congress has identified." What is the judge to do to whom this case is remanded? Did Robins suffer concrete injury or not? On remand, the Ninth Circuit held that Robins had suffered concrete injury "because it is clear to us that Robins's allegations relate facts that are substantially more likely to harm his concrete interests than the Supreme Court's example of an incorrect zip code." *Robins v. Spokeo, Inc.*, 867 F.3d 1108, 1117 (9th Cir. 2017).

2.   Justice Thomas concurs but writes separately to present a different way of looking at the case. Instead of the Court's unclear expression of when intangible harms may be concrete injuries, he uses a private rights/public rights distinction to demonstrate when concrete injury is required to be shown

over and above the violation of a statutory right. This may be helpful, but is it always clear what is a private right and what is a public right? In the Fair Credit Reporting Act, for example, does the "procedural" requirement that a consumer reporting agency such as Spokeo "follow reasonable procedures to assure maximum possible accuracy of the information concerning the individual about whom the report relates" create a public right or a private right? Does Justice Thomas answer that question?

3.   Justice Ginsburg, joined by Justice Sotomayor, dissents, but apparently only over the need for a remand, because to her it is clear that Robins has suffered a concrete injury. Do you agree?

4.   In *Transunion LLC v. Ramirez*, 141 S.Ct. 2190 (2021), the Court again addressed a claim under the Fair Credit Reporting Act. In this case, a credit reporting agency provided a service to subscribing companies to identify terrorists, drug traffickers, and other serious criminals. It, however, did a particularly shoddy job by taking names from the Office of Foreign Assets Control and simply identifying anyone with the same first and last name as a terrorist, drug trafficker, or serious criminal. A class of over eight thousand persons sued for damages under the Act. As in *Spokeo*, the issue was whether the persons had been injured. Transunion had transmitted the false information to third parties with respect to over a thousand members of the class, but the false information with respect to the remaining members of the class had not been sent to anyone. The Court held that the false information was clearly defamatory and therefore created an injury when published to third parties. However, as yet there was no injury as to the class members about whom no information had been published. The Court acknowledged that a future risk of harm (that the information might be published in the future) can support standing, if the risk is sufficiently imminent and substantial, in a suit for injunctive relief. Here, however, the suit was for damages, *i.e.*, for past injury, so the future risk could not support standing in this case for those persons whose information had not been published to anyone.

5.   In *Uzuegbunam v. Preczewksi*, 141 S.Ct. 792 (2021), a public college student was prohibited from proselytizing his religion in the designated free speech zone. He sued, seeking nominal damages and injunctive relief. The college quickly revoked the policy that kept him from speaking, mooting the request for injunctive relief. The issue was whether a request for nominal damages was sufficient to establish standing. It was clear that the student had suffered a concrete injury that was directly traceable to the unlawful conduct of the college; the question was whether nominal damages would redress that injury. Interestingly, Justice Thomas's opinion for the Court, holding that it would, drew only one dissent—the Chief Justice. Justice Thomas's conclusion that "nominal damages satisfies the redressability element of standing where a plaintiff's claim is based on a completed violation of a legal right" was based on his analysis of the historical practice at common law; the Chief Justice read the history differently, believing that allowing for judicial decisions based on a claim of nominal damages was the equivalent of giving an advisory opinion.

6. In 2021, the Supreme Court in two cases avoided a harder constitutional decision by denying the plaintiff standing. In *California v. Texas*, 141 S.Ct. 2104 (2021), the Court ducked a challenge to the Affordable Care Act by finding that neither individuals nor states had an injury that was traceable to the individual mandate, because Congress had repealed its sole enforcement mechanism. In *Trump v. New York*, 141 S.Ct. 530 (2020), a suit for injunctive relief was brought against President Trump's memorandum directing exclusion of noncitizens who were not lawful immigrants from the apportionment base for congressional apportionment following the 2020 decennial census. The Court, however, in a *per curiam* opinion found that any potential injury to a state's apportionment was highly conjectural and speculative, not concrete and particularized.

PROBLEM

Under the National Traffic and Motor Vehicle Safety Act the National Highway Traffic Safety Administration (NHTSA) is supposed to adopt safety regulations to protect road safety for both those in automobiles and those outside. As a result of some highly publicized accidents involving parents backing over their own children in their driveways, NHTSA undertakes a rulemaking to protect persons behind automobiles when automobiles travel in reverse. Rather than adopt a rule requiring rear vision cameras, which would be quite expensive, but also quite effective, NHTSA adopts the cheaper, but less effective, alternative of an audible signal activated by the vehicle going in reverse. Public Citizen, a non-profit public interest group dedicated to improving automobile safety with hundreds of thousands of members, sues to challenge the lawfulness of the rule adopted, arguing that the Act requires NHTSA to adopt the more effective standard. What will Public Citizen have to show in order to have standing to bring the suit?

---

c. Political Questions

In *Marbury*, Chief Justice Marshall writes that, while executive acts may be reviewed if they are subject to law, "by the constitution of the United States, the President is invested with certain important political powers, in the exercise of which he is to use his own discretion, and is accountable only to his country in his political character, and to his own conscience." Thus, from the beginning, so to speak, the Court has recognized that certain matters are committed to the political arena, not the judicial arena, and the political arena is not limited to the Presidency. The difficulty is to determine which matters go where.

The case that is always referred to as best describing the taxonomy of political questions is *Baker v. Carr*, 369 U.S. 186 (1962). In this case, Baker was a voter living in an urban area of Tennessee, and Carr was the

Secretary of State of Tennessee, one of whose responsibilities was administering elections in Tennessee. Baker complained that the 99 representatives in the state House of Representatives and the 33 Senators were apportioned to districts in the state based upon a 1901 law. He argued that, as a result of changes in the population in the intervening 60 years, he and persons like him in urban areas were systematically discriminated against in terms of their representation in violation of the Equal Protection Clause of the Fourteenth Amendment. The initial question, however, was whether this was a case able to be heard by federal courts. In other words, was it "justiciable"? The Court first determined that Baker had standing to bring the case. Then, the Court addressed the defendant's argument that the apportionment of representatives was a political question left to state legislatures and was not a justiciable issue for judicial resolution.

The Court discussed how to address this issue as follows:

> We have said that "In determining whether a question falls within (the political question) category, the appropriateness under our system of government of attributing finality to the action of the political departments and also the lack of satisfactory criteria for a judicial determination are dominant considerations." The nonjusticiability of a political question is primarily a function of the separation of powers. Much confusion results from the capacity of the "political question" label to obscure the need for case-by-case inquiry. Deciding whether a matter has in any measure been committed by the Constitution to another branch of government, or whether the action of that branch exceeds whatever authority has been committed, is itself a delicate exercise in constitutional interpretation, and is a responsibility of this Court as ultimate interpreter of the Constitution. . . .

> It is apparent that several formulations which vary slightly according to the settings in which the questions arise may describe a political question, although each has one or more elements which identify it as essentially a function of the separation of powers. Prominent on the surface of any case held to involve a political question is found a textually demonstrable constitutional commitment of the issue to a coordinate political department; or a lack of judicially discoverable and manageable standards for resolving it; or the impossibility of deciding without an initial policy determination of a kind clearly for nonjudicial discretion; or the impossibility of a court's undertaking independent resolution without expressing lack of the respect due coordinate branches of government; or an unusual need for unquestioning adherence to a political decision already made; or the potentiality of embarrassment from multifarious pronouncements by various departments on one question. . . .

The Court concluded that the issue in *Baker* did not share any of the common characteristics with prior political question cases.

This decision occurs in the midst of an "activist" period in the Court's history. Justice Brennan, the author of the opinion, was a noted liberal and activist judge. Justice Frankfurter, who dissented, was a political liberal, appointed by President Franklin Roosevelt, but a judicial conservative— meaning that he conceived of the courts as a last shield, not as an active sword, in protecting individuals. Here, he believed the Court would be engaging in an essentially political function in second-guessing the apportionment decisions of states, notwithstanding that a rural voter had more than 10 times the representation in the Tennessee legislature as an urban voter. *Baker v. Carr* remanded the case to the district court to decide the merits, the Supreme Court having found only that the case was justiciable. While Baker prevailed on the merits, Tennessee did not appeal that decision, so that the Supreme Court finally decided the one person/one vote requirement (meaning that states had to apportion their state representatives and federal representatives in proportion to the population as derived from the decennial census) in a different, but factually similar case from Alabama, *Reynolds v. Sims*, 377 U.S. 533 (1964). The effects of that case were felt nationwide, because the misapportionment in Tennessee and Alabama was reproduced in almost every state. As a result, every ten years as a result of the decennial census, both federal and legislative districts get adjusted to generally satisfy the one person/one vote requirement.

The factors *Baker v. Carr* instructs us to consider leave a lot to judgment, but there is at least one provision of the Constitution that *Baker v. Carr* recognized as traditionally non-justiciable as raising a political question. That is the Guaranty Clause, Art. IV, Sec. 4, which provides that "The United States shall guarantee to every state a republican form of government. . . ." In 1841–42 there were two groups each proclaiming themselves to be the rightful government of Rhode Island, and a lawsuit in essence asked the federal courts to declare which was the rightful government. The Supreme Court in *Luther v. Borden*, 7 How. 1 (1849), held that there was no federal law relevant to decide that issue and specifically that issues under the Guaranty Clause were non-justiciable, because the clause committed the decision as to whether a state had a republican form of government to the political branches. By its terms, of course, the Guaranty Clause does not commit the decision to any particular branch, placing the responsibility on "the United States." Thus, the Court was inferring such a commitment.

Knowing the doctrine still leaves a lot to judgment in individual cases. The following two cases provide a sample of its application involving claims that there has been a constitutional commitment of the issue to a branch of government other than the judiciary. The third case is a very recent example of its application involving a claim that there was a lack of judicially discoverable and manageable standards for resolving the issue.

POWELL V. MCCORMACK

United States Supreme Court, 1969.
395 U.S. 486, 89 S.Ct. 1944.

Adam Clayton Powell

[Adam Clayton Powell was an African-American congressman elected from the district in New York City that included Harlem. Prior to being elected to Congress, Powell had been a charismatic pastor of a local church and a prominent civil rights leader, who went on to be the first black person elected to the New York City Council. Later, in 1944, Powell was elected to the U.S. House of Representatives—the first black congressman from New York. In 1961, on the basis of seniority, he became the Chair of the House Education and Labor Committee. There he championed a number of progressive bills that became law. However, by the mid-60s, his dedication to the cause, if not his popularity in his district, seemed to flag. He spent increasing amounts of time at his private villa on Bimini in the Bahamas, living a luxurious life style with various female friends, apparently sustained by funds taken from his committee's budget, even while his wife was on the committee payroll but not performing any functions. Moreover, because he was perpetually absent, his committee no longer met. Between those members who disliked him for the progressive things he had done and those who were upset with his present abandonment of his duties and misuse of committee funds, in 1967 the 90th Congress voted to exclude him from his seat despite his reelection. He sued the Speaker of the House, John McCormack to reclaim his seat.]

John McCormack

MR. CHIEF JUSTICE WARREN delivered the opinion of the Court.

In November 1966, petitioner Adam Clayton Powell, Jr., was duly elected from the 18th Congressional District of New York to serve in the United States House of Representatives for the 90th Congress. However, pursuant to a House resolution, he was not permitted to take his seat. Powell (and some of the voters of his district) then filed suit in Federal District Court, claiming that the House could exclude him only if it found he failed to meet the standing requirements of age, citizenship, and residence contained in Art. I, § 2, of the Constitution—requirements the

House specifically found Powell met—and thus had excluded him unconstitutionally. . . .

VI.

JUSTICIABILITY.

[W]e turn to the question whether the case is justiciable. [W]e must determine whether the structure of the Federal Government renders the issue presented a "political question"—that is, a question which is not justiciable in federal court because of the separation of powers provided by the Constitution.

B.   Political Question Doctrine.

1.   Textually Demonstrable Constitutional Commitment.

Respondents maintain that even if this case is otherwise justiciable, it presents only a political question. It is well established that the federal courts will not adjudicate political questions. In *Baker v. Carr* we noted that political questions are not justiciable primarily because of the separation of powers within the Federal Government. After reviewing our decisions in this area, we concluded that on the surface of any case held to involve a political question was at least one of the following formulations:

> a textually demonstrable constitutional commitment of the issue to a co-ordinate political department; or a lack of judicially discoverable and manageable standards for resolving it; or the impossibility of deciding without an initial policy determination of a kind clearly for nonjudicial discretion; or the impossibility of a court's undertaking independent resolution without expressing lack of the respect due co-ordinate branches of government; or an

Earl Warren

President Eisenhower appointed Earl Warren, the former Republican governor of California, to be Chief Justice in 1953. It was widely believed that Eisenhower was rewarding Warren for his support during the 1952 presidential campaign. Although Warren had been the Attorney General of California at the beginning of World War II, where he was a strong supporter of the Japanese internment, and an active Republican politician his whole life, as Chief Justice he moved the Court in a distinctly liberal and activist direction. This led Eisenhower allegedly to have remarked that appointing Warren was "the biggest damned fool mistake I ever made." Appointed to the Court, after the case of *Brown v. Bd. of Education* had been first argued but before it was decided, replacing the conservative Chief Justice Fred Vinson who had died suddenly, Warren managed to have the Court unanimously support the opinion he wrote declaring segregated schools unconstitutional.

unusual need for unquestioning adherence to a political decision already made; or the potentiality of embarrassment from multifarious pronouncements by various departments on one question.

Respondents' first contention is that this case presents a political question because under Art. I, § 5, there has been a "textually demonstrable constitutional commitment" to the House of the "adjudicatory power" to determine Powell's qualifications. Thus it is argued that the House, and the House alone, has power to determine who is qualified to be a member.

In order to determine whether there has been a textual commitment to a coordinate department of the Government, we must interpret the Constitution. In other words, we must first determine what power the Constitution confers upon the House through Art. I, § 5, before we can determine to what extent, if any, the exercise of that power is subject to judicial review. Respondents maintain that the House has broad power under § 5, and, they argue, the House may determine which are the qualifications necessary for membership. On the other hand, petitioners allege that the Constitution provides that an elected representative may be denied his seat only if the House finds he does not meet one of the standing qualifications expressly prescribed by the Constitution.

If examination of § 5 disclosed that the Constitution gives the House judicially unreviewable power to set qualifications for membership and to judge whether prospective members meet those qualifications, further review of the House determination might well be barred by the political question doctrine. On the other hand, if the Constitution gives the House power to judge only whether elected members possess the three standing qualifications set forth in the Constitution, further consideration would be necessary to determine whether any of the other formulations of the political question doctrine are "inextricable from the case at bar."[41]

In other words, whether there is a "textually demonstrable constitutional commitment of the issue to a coordinate political department" of government and what is the scope of such commitment are questions we must resolve for the first time in this case. For, as we pointed out in *Baker v. Carr*, "(d)eciding whether a matter has in any measure been committed by the Constitution to another branch of government, or whether the action of that branch exceeds whatever authority has been committed, is itself a delicate exercise in constitutional interpretation, and is a responsibility of this Court as ultimate interpreter of the Constitution."

---

[41] In addition to the three qualifications set forth in Art. I, § 2, Art. I, § 3, cl. 7, authorizes the disqualification of any person convicted in an impeachment proceeding from "any Office of honor, Trust or Profit under the United States"; Art. I, § 6, cl. 2, provides that "no Person holding any Office under the United States, shall be a Member of either House during his Continuance in Office"; and § 3 of the 14th Amendment disqualifies any person "who, having previously taken an oath * * * to support the Constitution of the United States, shall have engaged in insurrection or rebellion against the same, or given aid or comfort to the enemies thereof." It has been argued that each of these provisions, as well as the Guarantee Clause of Article IV and the oath requirement of Art. VI, cl. 3, is no less a "qualification" within the meaning of Art. I, § 5, than those set forth in Art. I, § 2. We need not reach this question, however, since both sides agree that Powell was not ineligible under any of these provisions.

In order to determine the scope of any "textual commitment" under Art. I, § 5, we necessarily must determine the meaning of the phrase to "be the Judge of the Qualifications of its own Members." Petitioners argue that the records of the debates during the Constitutional Convention; available commentary from the post-Convention, pre-ratification period; and early congressional applications of Art. I, § 5, support their construction of the section. Respondents insist, however, that a careful examination of the pre-Convention practices of the English Parliament and American colonial assemblies demonstrates that by 1787, a legislature's power to judge the qualifications of its members was generally understood to encompass exclusion or expulsion on the ground that an individual's character or past conduct rendered him unfit to serve. When the Constitution and the debates over its adoption are thus viewed in historical perspective, argue respondents, it becomes clear that the "qualifications" expressly set forth in the Constitution were not meant to limit the long-recognized legislative power to exclude or expel at will, but merely to establish "standing incapacities," which could be altered only by a constitutional amendment. Our examination of the relevant historical materials leads us to the conclusion that petitioners are correct and that the Constitution leaves the House without authority to exclude any person, duly elected by his constituents, who meets all the requirements for membership expressly prescribed in the Constitution.

[The Court considered the practice in England before independence and found that, while earlier parliament had excluded members who otherwise met the qualifications for office, there had been a strong reaction against that so that by the time of independence such exclusion was discredited. The Court then considered the ratification debates and found that they solidly, if not explicitly, supported the notion that exclusion could only be based on failure to meet the specified qualifications in the Constitution.]

c.   *Post-Ratification.*

[Respondents] suggest that far more relevant is Congress's own understanding of its power to judge qualifications as manifested in post-ratification exclusion cases. Unquestionably, both the House and the Senate have excluded members-elect for reasons other than their failure to meet the Constitution's standing qualifications. For almost the first 100 years of its existence, however, Congress strictly limited its power to judge the qualifications of its members to those enumerated in the Constitution. . . .

Had these congressional exclusion precedents been more consistent, their precedential value still would be quite limited. That an unconstitutional action has been taken before surely does not render that same action any less unconstitutional at a later date. Particularly in view of the Congress's own doubts in those few cases where it did exclude members-elect, we are not inclined to give its precedents controlling weight. The relevancy of prior exclusion cases is limited largely to the insight they afford in correctly ascertaining the draftsmen's intent. Obviously, therefore, the precedential value of these cases tends to increase in proportion to their proximity to the Convention in 1787. And, what evidence we have of Congress's early understanding confirms our conclusion that the House is without power to exclude any member-elect who meets the Constitution's requirements for membership. . . .

For these reasons, we have concluded that Art. I, § 5, is at most a "textually demonstrable commitment" to Congress to judge only the qualifications expressly set forth in the Constitution. Therefore, the "textual commitment" formulation of the political question doctrine does not bar federal courts from adjudicating petitioners' claims. . . .

MR. JUSTICE DOUGLAS [issued a concurring opinion].

MR. JUSTICE STEWART, dissent[ed on the grounds that the case was moot, because the session of Congress from which Powell was excluded had expired; he had been reelected and had been seated in the current Congress.]

NIXON V. UNITED STATES
United States Supreme Court, 1993.
506 U.S. 224, 113 S.Ct. 732.

CHIEF JUSTICE REHNQUIST delivered the opinion of the Court.

Petitioner Walter L. Nixon, Jr., asks this Court to decide whether Senate Rule XI, which allows a committee of Senators to hear evidence against an individual who has been impeached and to report that evidence to the full Senate, violates the Impeachment Trial Clause, Art. I, § 3, cl. 6.That Clause provides that the "Senate shall have the sole Power to try all Impeachments." But before we reach the merits of such a claim, we must decide whether it is "justiciable," that is, whether it is a claim that may be resolved by the courts. We conclude that it is not.

Nixon, a former Chief Judge of the United States District Court for the Southern District of Mississippi, was convicted by a jury of two counts of making false statements before a federal grand jury and sentenced to prison. . . . Because Nixon refused to resign from his office as a United States District Judge, he continued to collect his judicial salary while serving out his prison sentence.

On May 10, 1989, the House of Representatives adopted three articles of impeachment for high crimes and misdemeanors. The first two articles charged Nixon with giving false testimony before the grand jury and the third article charged him with bringing disrepute on the Federal Judiciary.

After the House presented the articles to the Senate, the Senate voted to invoke its own Impeachment Rule XI, under which the presiding officer appoints a committee of Senators to "receive evidence and take testimony." The Senate committee held four days of hearings, during which 10 witnesses, including Nixon, testified. Pursuant to Rule XI, the committee presented the full Senate with a complete transcript of the proceeding and a Report stating the uncontested facts and summarizing the evidence on the contested facts. Nixon and the House impeachment managers submitted extensive final briefs to the full Senate and delivered arguments from the Senate floor during the three hours set aside for oral argument in front of that body. Nixon himself gave a personal appeal, and several Senators posed questions directly to both parties. The Senate voted by more than the constitutionally required two-thirds majority to convict Nixon on the first two articles. . . .

Nixon thereafter commenced the present suit, arguing that Senate Rule XI violates the constitutional grant of authority to the Senate to "try" all impeachments because it prohibits the whole Senate from taking part in the evidentiary hearings. . . . The District Court held that his claim was nonjusticiable, and the Court of Appeals for the District of Columbia Circuit agreed. We granted certiorari.

William Rehnquist

Richard Nixon appointed Rehnquist as Associate Justice in 1971. In 1986, Chief Justice Burger resigned, and President Ronald Reagan appointed Rehnquist Chief Justice. Preferring to interpret the Constitution narrowly, Rehnquist penned several opinions that endorsed conservative ideals. In particular, he protected state interests relative to federal interests, authoring opinions finding federal statutes beyond Congress's power and upholding state sovereign immunity. Rehnquist also reflected conservative values by denying the existence of constitutional rights, like the right to privacy, that did not have a clear textual basis in the Constitution.

A controversy is nonjusticiable—*i.e.,* involves a political question— where there is "a textually demonstrable constitutional commitment of the issue to a coordinate political department; or a lack of judicially discoverable and manageable standards for resolving it. . . ." *Baker v. Carr.* But the courts must, in the first instance, interpret the text in question and determine whether and to what extent the issue is textually committed. *See ibid.*; *Powell v. McCormack.* As the discussion that follows makes clear, the concept of a textual commitment to a coordinate political department is not completely separate from the concept of a lack of judicially discoverable and manageable standards for resolving it; the lack of judicially manageable standards may strengthen the conclusion that there is a textually demonstrable commitment to a coordinate branch.

In this case, we must examine Art. I, § 3, cl. 6, to determine the scope of authority conferred upon the Senate by the Framers regarding impeachment. It provides:

"The Senate shall have the sole Power to try all Impeachments. When sitting for that Purpose, they shall be on Oath or Affirmation. When the President of the United States is tried, the Chief Justice shall preside: And no Person shall be convicted without the Concurrence of two thirds of the Members present."

[P]etitioner argues that the word "try" in the first sentence imposes by implication an additional requirement on the Senate in that the proceedings must be in the nature of a judicial trial. From there petitioner goes on to argue that this limitation precludes the Senate from delegating to a select committee the task of hearing the testimony of witnesses, as was done pursuant to Senate Rule XI. "[T]ry" means more than simply "vote on" or "review" or "judge." In 1787 and today, trying a case means hearing the evidence, not scanning a cold record. Brief for Petitioner 25. Petitioner concludes from this that courts may review whether or not the Senate "tried" him before convicting him.

There are several difficulties with this position which lead us ultimately to reject it. The word "try," both in 1787 and later, has considerably broader meanings than those to which petitioner would limit it. Older dictionaries define try as "[t]o examine" or "[t]o examine as a judge." *See* 2 S. Johnson, A Dictionary of the English Language (1785). In more modern usage the term has various meanings. For example, try can mean "to examine or investigate judicially," "to conduct the trial of," or "to put to the test by experiment, investigation, or trial." Webster's Third New International Dictionary 2457 (1971). Petitioner submits that "try," as contained in T. Sheridan, Dictionary of the English Language (1796), means "to examine as a judge; to bring before a judicial tribunal." Based on the variety of definitions, however, we cannot say that the Framers used the word "try" as an implied limitation on the method by which the Senate might proceed in trying impeachments. . . .

The conclusion that the use of the word "try" in the first sentence of the Impeachment Trial Clause lacks sufficient precision to afford any judicially manageable standard of review of the Senate's actions is fortified by the existence of the three very specific requirements that the Constitution does impose on the Senate when trying impeachments: The Members must be under oath, a two-thirds vote is required to convict, and the Chief Justice presides when the President is tried. These limitations are quite precise, and their nature suggests that the Framers did not intend to impose additional limitations on the form of the Senate proceedings by the use of the word "try" in the first sentence.

Petitioner devotes only two pages in his brief to negating the significance of the word "sole" in the first sentence of Clause 6. [T]hat sentence provides that "[t]he Senate shall have the sole Power to try all Impeachments." We think that the word "sole" is of considerable significance. Indeed, the word "sole" appears only one other time in the Constitution—with respect to the House of Representatives' "*sole* Power of Impeachment." Art. I, § 2, cl. 5 (emphasis added). The commonsense meaning of the word "sole" is that the Senate alone shall have authority to determine whether an individual should be acquitted or convicted. The dictionary definition bears this out. "Sole" is defined as "having no companion," "solitary," "being the only one," and "functioning . . . independently and without assistance or interference." Webster's Third New International Dictionary 2168 (1971). If the courts may review the actions of the Senate in order to determine whether that body "tried" an impeached official, it is difficult to see how the Senate would be "functioning . . . independently and without assistance or interference." . . .

Petitioner finally argues that even if significance be attributed to the word "sole" in the first sentence of the Clause, the authority granted is to the Senate, and this means that "the Senate—not the courts, not a lay jury, not a Senate Committee—shall try impeachments." It would be possible to read the first sentence of the Clause this way, but it is not a natural reading. Petitioner's interpretation would bring into judicial purview not merely the sort of claim made by petitioner, but other similar claims based on the conclusion that the word "Senate" has imposed by implication limitations on procedures which the Senate might adopt. Such limitations would be inconsistent with the construction of the Clause as a whole, which, as we have noted, sets out three express limitations in separate sentences.

The history and contemporary understanding of the impeachment provisions support our reading of the constitutional language. The parties do not offer evidence of a single word in the history of the Constitutional Convention or in contemporary commentary that even alludes to the possibility of judicial review in the context of the impeachment powers. This silence is quite meaningful in light of the several explicit references to the availability of judicial review as a check on the Legislature's power with respect to bills of attainder, *ex post facto* laws, and statutes. *See* The Federalist No. 78 ("Limitations . . . can be preserved in practice no other way than through the medium of the courts of justice").

The Framers labored over the question of where the impeachment power should lie. Significantly, in at least two considered scenarios the power was placed with the Federal Judiciary. Indeed, James Madison and the Committee of Detail proposed that the Supreme Court should have the power to determine impeachments. Despite these proposals, the Convention ultimately decided that the Senate would have "the sole Power to try all Impeachments." Art. I, § 3, cl. 6. According to Alexander Hamilton, the Senate was the "most fit depositary of this important trust" because its Members are representatives of the people. The Supreme Court was not the proper body because the Framers "doubted whether the members of that tribunal would, at all times, be endowed with so eminent a portion of fortitude as would be called for in the execution of so difficult a task" or whether the Court "would possess the degree of credit and authority" to carry out its judgment if it conflicted with the accusation brought by the Legislature—the people's representative. In addition, the Framers believed the Court was too small in number: "The awful discretion, which a court of impeachments must necessarily have, to doom to honor or to infamy the most confidential and the most distinguished characters of the community, forbids the commitment of the trust to a small number of persons."

[Moreover], judicial review would be inconsistent with the Framers' insistence that our system be one of checks and balances. In our constitutional system, impeachment was designed to be the *only* check on the Judicial Branch by the Legislature. . . .

Judicial involvement in impeachment proceedings, even if only for purposes of judicial review, is counterintuitive because it would eviscerate the "important constitutional check" placed on the Judiciary by the Framers. Nixon's argument would place final reviewing authority with respect to impeachments in the hands of the same body that the impeachment process is meant to regulate. . . .

In addition to the textual commitment argument, we are persuaded that the lack of finality and the difficulty of fashioning relief counsel against justiciability. We agree with the Court of Appeals that opening the door of judicial review to the procedures used by the Senate in trying impeachments would "expose the political life of the country to months, or perhaps years, of chaos." This lack of finality would manifest itself most dramatically if the President were impeached. The legitimacy of any successor, and hence his effectiveness, would be impaired severely, not merely while the judicial process was running its course, but during any retrial that a differently constituted Senate might conduct if its first judgment of conviction were invalidated. Equally uncertain is the question of what relief a court may give other than simply setting aside the judgment of conviction. Could it order the reinstatement of a convicted federal judge, or order Congress to create an additional judgeship if the seat had been filled in the interim?

Petitioner finally contends that a holding of nonjusticiability cannot be reconciled with our opinion in *Powell v. McCormack*. The relevant issue in *Powell* was whether courts could review the House of Representatives' conclusion that Powell was "unqualified" to sit as a Member because he had been accused of misappropriating public funds and abusing the process of the New York courts. We stated that the question of justiciability turned on whether the Constitution committed authority to the House to judge its

Members' qualifications, and if so, the extent of that commitment. Article I, § 5, provides that "Each House shall be the Judge of the Elections, Returns and Qualifications of its own Members." In turn, Art. I, § 2, specifies three requirements for membership in the House: The candidate must be at least 25 years of age, a citizen of the United States for no less than seven years, and an inhabitant of the State he is chosen to represent. We held that, in light of the three requirements specified in the Constitution, the word "qualifications"—of which the House was to be the Judge—was of a precise, limited nature.

Our conclusion in *Powell* was based on the fixed meaning of "[q]ualifications" set forth in Art. I, § 2. The claim by the House that its power to "be the Judge of the Elections, Returns and Qualifications of its own Members" was a textual commitment of unreviewable authority was defeated by the existence of this separate provision specifying the only qualifications which might be imposed for House membership. The decision as to whether a Member satisfied these qualifications *was* placed with the House, but the decision as to what these qualifications consisted of was not. . . .

JUSTICE STEVENS [wrote a concurring opinion that is omitted.]

JUSTICE WHITE, with whom JUSTICE BLACKMUN joins, concurring in the judgment.

Petitioner contends that the method by which the Senate convicted him on two articles of impeachment violates Art. I, § 3, cl. 6, of the Constitution, which mandates that the Senate "try" impeachments. The Court is of the view that the Constitution forbids us even to consider his contention. I find no such prohibition and would therefore reach the merits of the claim. I concur in the judgment because the Senate fulfilled its constitutional obligation to "try" petitioner.

It should be said at the outset that, as a practical matter, it will likely make little difference whether the Court's or my view controls this case. This is so because the Senate has very wide discretion in specifying impeachment trial procedures and because it is extremely unlikely that the Senate would abuse its discretion and insist on a procedure that could not be deemed a trial by reasonable judges. Even taking a wholly practical approach, I would prefer not to announce an unreviewable discretion in the Senate to ignore completely the constitutional direction to "try" impeachment cases. When asked at oral argument whether that direction would be satisfied if, after a House vote to impeach, the Senate, without any procedure whatsoever, unanimously found the accused guilty of being "a bad guy," counsel for the United States answered that the Government's theory "leads me to answer that question yes." Especially in light of this advice from the Solicitor General, I would not issue an invitation to the Senate to find an excuse, in the name of other pressing business, to be dismissive of its critical role in the impeachment process.

Practicalities aside, however, since the meaning of a constitutional provision is at issue, my disagreement with the Court should be stated.

The majority states that the question raised in this case meets two of the criteria for political questions set out in *Baker v. Carr.* It concludes first that there is "a textually demonstrable constitutional commitment of the issue to a coordinate political department." It also finds that the question cannot be resolved for "a lack of judicially discoverable and manageable standards."

Of course the issue in the political question doctrine is *not* whether the constitutional text commits exclusive responsibility for a particular governmental function to one of the political branches. There are numerous instances of this sort of textual commitment, *e.g.,* Art. I, § 8, and it is not thought that disputes implicating these provisions are nonjusticiable. Rather, the issue is whether the Constitution has given one of the political branches final responsibility for interpreting the scope and nature of such a power.

Although *Baker* directs the Court to search for "a textually demonstrable constitutional commitment" of such responsibility, there are few, if any, explicit and unequivocal instances in the Constitution of this sort of textual commitment. . . . The courts therefore are usually left to infer the presence of a political question from the text and structure of the Constitution. In drawing the inference that the Constitution has committed final interpretive authority to one of the political branches, courts are sometimes aided by textual evidence that the Judiciary was not meant to exercise judicial review—a coordinate inquiry expressed in *Baker*'s "lack of judicially discoverable and manageable standards" criterion. See, *e.g., Coleman v. Miller,* where the Court refused to determine the life span of a proposed constitutional amendment given Art. V's placement of the amendment process with Congress and the lack of any judicial standard for resolving the question.

The majority finds a clear textual commitment in the Constitution's use of the word "sole" in the phrase "[t]he Senate shall have the sole Power to try all Impeachments." It attributes "considerable significance" to the fact that this term appears in only one other passage in the Constitution. The Framers' sparing use of "sole" is thought to indicate that its employment in the Impeachment Trial Clause demonstrates a concern to give the Senate exclusive interpretive authority over the Clause.

In disagreeing with the Court, I note that the Solicitor General stated at oral argument that "[w]e don't rest our submission on sole power to try." The Government was well advised in this respect. The significance of the Constitution's use of the term "sole" lies not in the infrequency with which the term appears, but in the fact that it appears exactly twice, in parallel provisions concerning impeachment. That the word "sole" is found only in the House and Senate Impeachment Clauses demonstrates that its purpose is to emphasize the distinct role of each in the impeachment process. As the majority notes, the Framers, following English practice, were very much concerned to separate the prosecutorial from the adjudicative aspects of impeachment. Giving each House "sole" power with respect to its role in impeachments effected this division of labor. While the majority is thus right to interpret the term "sole" to indicate that the Senate ought to "functio[n] independently and without assistance or interference," it wrongly identifies the Judiciary, rather than the House, as the source of potential interference with which the Framers were concerned when they employed the term "sole."

Even if the Impeachment Trial Clause is read without regard to its Companion clause, the Court's willingness to abandon its obligation to review the constitutionality of legislative acts merely on the strength of the word "sole" is perplexing. Consider, by comparison, the treatment of Art. I, § 1, which grants "All legislative powers" to the House and Senate. As used in that context "all" is nearly synonymous with "sole"—both connote entire and exclusive authority. Yet the Court has never thought it would unduly interfere with the operation of the Legislative Branch to entertain difficult and important questions as to the extent of the legislative power. Quite the opposite, we have stated that the proper interpretation of the Clause falls within the province of the Judiciary. . . .

The majority also claims support in the history and early interpretations of the Impeachment Clauses. . . . In light of these materials there can be little doubt that the Framers came to the view at the Convention that the trial of officials' public misdeeds should be conducted by representatives of the people; that the fledgling Judiciary lacked the wherewithal to adjudicate political intrigues; that the Judiciary ought not to try both impeachments and subsequent criminal cases emanating from them; and that the impeachment power must reside in the Legislative Branch to provide a check on the largely unaccountable Judiciary.

The majority's review of the historical record thus explains why the power to try impeachments properly resides with the Senate. It does not explain, however, the sweeping statement that the Judiciary was "not chosen to have any role in impeachments." Not a single word in the historical materials cited by the majority addresses judicial review of the Impeachment Trial Clause. And a glance at the arguments surrounding the Impeachment Clauses negates the majority's attempt to infer nonjusticiability from the Framers' arguments in support of the Senate's power to try impeachments. . . .

The majority also contends that the term "try" does not present a judicially manageable standard. It notes that in 1787, as today, the word "try" may refer to an inquiry in the nature of a judicial proceeding, or, more generally, to experimentation or investigation. In light of the term's multiple senses, the Court finds itself unable to conclude that the Framers used the word "try" as "an implied limitation on the method by which the Senate might proceed in trying impeachments." . . .

It is apparently on this basis that the majority distinguishes *Powell v. McCormack*. . . . The majority finds this case different from *Powell* only on the grounds that, whereas the qualifications of Art. I, § 2, are readily susceptible to judicial interpretation, the term "try" does not provide an "identifiable textual limit on the authority which is committed to the Senate."

This argument comes in two variants. The first, which asserts that one simply cannot ascertain the sense of "try" which the Framers employed and hence cannot undertake judicial review, is clearly untenable. To begin with, one would intuitively expect that, in defining the power of a political body to conduct an inquiry into official wrongdoing, the Framers used "try" in its legal sense. That intuition is borne out by reflection on the alternatives. The third Clause of Art. I, § 3, cannot seriously be read to mean that the Senate shall "attempt" or "experiment with" impeachments. It is equally implausible to say that the Senate is charged with "investigating" impeachments given that this description would substantially overlap with the House of Representatives' "sole" power to draw up articles of impeachment. That these alternatives are not realistic possibilities is finally evidenced by the use of "tried" in the third sentence of the Impeachment Trial Clause ("[w]hen the President of the United States is tried . . ."), and by Art. III, § 2, cl. 3 ("[t]he Trial of all Crimes, except in Cases of Impeachment . . .").

The other variant of the majority position focuses not on which sense of "try" is employed in the Impeachment Trial Clause, but on whether the legal sense of that term creates a judicially manageable standard. The majority concludes that the term provides no "identifiable textual limit." Yet, as the Government itself conceded at oral argument, the term "try" is hardly so elusive as the majority would have it. Were the Senate, for example, to adopt the practice of automatically entering a judgment of conviction whenever articles of impeachment were delivered from the House, it is quite clear that the Senate will have failed to "try" impeachments. Indeed in this respect, "try" presents no greater, and perhaps fewer, interpretive difficulties than some other constitutional standards that have been found amenable to familiar techniques of judicial construction, including, for example, "Commerce . . . among the several States," Art. I, § 8, cl. 3, and "due process of law," Amdt. 5.[3]

---

[3] The majority's in terrorem argument against justiciability—that judicial review of impeachments might cause national disruption and that the courts would be unable to fashion effective relief—merits only brief attention. In the typical instance, court review of impeachments would no more render the political system dysfunctional than has this litigation. Moreover, the same capacity for disruption was noted and rejected as a basis for not hearing *Powell*. The relief granted for unconstitutional impeachment trials would presumably be similar to the relief granted to other unfairly tried public employee-litigants. Finally, as applied to the special case of the

The majority's conclusion that "try" is incapable of meaningful judicial construction is not without irony. One might think that if any class of concepts would fall within the definitional abilities of the Judiciary, it would be that class having to do with procedural justice. Examination of the remaining question—whether proceedings in accordance with Senate Rule XI are compatible with the Impeachment Trial Clause—confirms this intuition. [Justice White then analysed the procedures used under Senate Rule XI and found them compatible with the term "try." Consequently, the petitioner would lose on the merits.]

JUSTICE SOUTER, concurring in the judgment.

I agree with the Court that this case presents a nonjusticiable political question. Because my analysis differs somewhat from the Court's, however, I concur in its judgment by this separate opinion.

As we cautioned in *Baker v. Carr*, "the 'political question' label" tends "to obscure the need for case-by-case inquiry." The need for such close examination is nevertheless clear from our precedents, which demonstrate that the functional nature of the political question doctrine requires analysis of "the precise facts and posture of the particular case," and precludes "resolution by any semantic cataloguing." . . .

Whatever considerations feature most prominently in a particular case, the political question doctrine is "essentially a function of the separation of powers," existing to restrain courts "from inappropriate interference in the business of the other branches of Government," and deriving in large part from prudential concerns about the respect we owe the political departments. Not all interference is inappropriate or disrespectful, however, and application of the doctrine ultimately turns, as Learned Hand put it, on "how importunately the occasion demands an answer."

This occasion does not demand an answer. . . . It seems fair to conclude that the Clause contemplates that the Senate may determine, within broad boundaries, such subsidiary issues as the procedures for receipt and consideration of evidence necessary to satisfy its duty to "try" impeachments. . . .

One can, nevertheless, envision different and unusual circumstances that might justify a more searching review of impeachment proceedings. If the Senate were to act in a manner seriously threatening the integrity of its results, convicting, say, upon a coin toss, or upon a summary determination that an officer of the United States was simply " 'a bad guy,' " judicial interference might well be appropriate. In such

---

President, the majority's argument merely points out that, were the Senate to convict the President without any kind of a trial, a constitutional crisis might well result. It hardly follows that the Court ought to refrain from upholding the Constitution in all impeachment cases. Nor does it follow that, in cases of Presidential impeachment, the Justices ought to abandon their constitutional responsibilities because the Senate has precipitated a crisis.

circumstances, the Senate's action might be so far beyond the scope of its constitutional authority, and the consequent impact on the Republic so great, as to merit a judicial response despite the prudential concerns that would ordinarily counsel silence. . . .

COMMENTS AND QUESTIONS

1.   Are these two cases compatible? Why is the question whether the judge was "tried" by the Senate a political question, but whether Powell met the "qualifications" to be a congressman was not?

2.   What is the significance of the word "sole" in the Impeachment Clause? Is not the House the "sole" judge of the qualifications of its members?

3.   In what way does Justice White disagree with Chief Justice Rehnquist? Note that Justice White concurs in the "judgment" of the Court, not in its opinion. This means that he agrees with the outcome of the case— Walter Nixon loses—but Justice White does not agree with the Court's rationale. He has his own. What is it?

4.   What point is Justice Souter making? He also concurs in the judgment but not in the opinion. How does he disagree with the Chief Justice?

5.   Which opinions are "activist" and which are "conservative"?

6.   Both *Powell* and *Nixon* turn on an assessment whether the Constitution has placed the decision in question in a place other than the judiciary. This is the essence of what a "political question" is. Often, however, unlike both *Powell* and *Nixon*, there is no constitutional language suggesting the commitment of the question in another branch. In those cases, the commitment to another branch must be inferred from the circumstances, rather than from any textual commitment. Even in *Nixon* we see Chief Justice Rehnquist bolster his textual argument by reference to other factors that suggest courts should not be involved. One of these other factors is when there is no legal standard to apply. If there is no legal standard to apply, that would suggest the decision is inappropriate for courts, because courts apply legal standards. However, to say there is no legal standard, such as whether there is a time limit for proposed amendments to be ratified, *see Coleman v. Miller*, 307 U.S. 433 (1939)(finding the issue a political question because the Constitution provided no legal standard to apply), is different from saying the legal standard is unclear. Which do you think was the case in *Nixon*?

7.   Nevertheless, there are a number of cases we will come across where the Constitution is totally silent on an issue, but the Court demonstrates no reluctance to decide the case. For example, the Constitution says absolutely nothing about the removal of officers within the executive branch, other than by impeachment, and no one ever imagined that that was the sole manner of removing such officers; it is just the sole means by which *Congress* can remove such officers. The Court, however, has decided a number of cases dealing with how executive officers may be removed.

8. It is well to state explicitly that a "political question" that keeps a court from reaching the merits does not mean it is a question involving politics. There are many questions involving politics that are justiciable—*Bush v. Gore*, 531 U.S. 98 (2000), for example, that effectively decided the 2000 Presidential election.

9. Another political question case involved President Jimmy Carter's termination of a mutual defense treaty with Taiwan. Several senators sued, alleging that treaties could only be terminated in the same manner in which they were made—by the President with the concurrence of two-thirds of the Senate. Because this termination had not been submitted to the Senate for concurrence, they argued it was invalid. The Court held that the case was not justiciable, but there was no majority opinion. A plurality joined Justice Rehnquist's opinion that the case involved a "political question." The opinion relied principally upon the fact that this involved foreign relations and the President's authority. The opinion noted that this was really a dispute between co-equal branches of government, each of which had ample resources to press its points. In other words, those branches could settle the issue politically. Moreover, the Constitution says nothing about the termination of treaties, only their creation. Justice Powell, who concurred in the judgment, found no basis for a "political question," because there was no textual basis for a commitment of the question to another branch of government; instead, he found the decision not "ripe" for decision. Justice Brennan likewise did not believe the case raised a "political question," and he would have decided the case on the merits, albeit upholding the President's power to terminate treaties without Senate approval. *See Goldwater v. Carter*, 444 U.S. 996 (1979).

RUCHO V. COMMON CAUSE

United States Supreme Court, 2019.
139 S.Ct. 2484.

CHIEF JUSTICE ROBERTS delivered the opinion of the Court.

Voters and other plaintiffs in North Carolina and Maryland challenged their States' congressional districting maps as unconstitutional partisan gerrymanders. The North Carolina plaintiffs complained that the State's districting plan discriminated against Democrats; the Maryland plaintiffs complained that their State's plan discriminated against Republicans. The plaintiffs alleged that the gerrymandering violated the First Amendment, the Equal Protection Clause of the Fourteenth Amendment, the Elections Clause, and Article I, § 2, of the Constitution. The District Courts in both cases ruled in favor of the plaintiffs, and the defendants appealed directly to this Court.

These cases require us to consider once again whether claims of excessive partisanship in districting are "justiciable"—that is, properly suited for resolution by the federal courts. This Court has not previously struck down a districting plan as an unconstitutional partisan gerrymander, and has struggled without success over the past several

John Roberts

President George W. Bush appointed John Roberts Chief Justice in 2005. Previously Justice Roberts had been a judge on the D.C. Circuit Court of Appeals, to which he had been appointed in 2003. As a young attorney, Justice Roberts clerked for Justice William Rehnquist and then worked in the Reagan administration both in the White House and the Justice Department. He then joined a large Washington, D.C. private law firm for three years, where he focused on appellate litigation. This prepared him for a four-year stint in the Solicitor General's office, where he argued 39 cases before the Supreme Court. He then returned to private practice until his appointment to the D.C. Circuit. In his confirmation hearings, Roberts indicated a desire to bring the Court together, to avoid major split decisions. In that he has not been successful. Nevertheless, he is leading a Court that is moving in a conservative direction.

decades to discern judicially manageable standards for deciding such claims. The districting plans at issue here are highly partisan, by any measure. The question is whether the courts below appropriately exercised judicial power when they found them unconstitutional as well.

The first case involves a challenge to the congressional redistricting plan enacted by the Republican-controlled North Carolina General Assembly in 2016. The Republican legislators leading the redistricting effort instructed their mapmaker to use political data to draw a map that would produce a congressional delegation of ten Republicans and three Democrats. . . . One Democratic state senator objected that entrenching the 10–3 advantage for Republicans was not "fair, reasonable, [or] balanced" because, as recently as 2012, "Democratic congressional candidates had received more votes on a statewide basis than Republican candidates." The General Assembly was not swayed by that objection and approved the 2016 Plan by a party-line vote.

In November 2016, North Carolina conducted congressional elections using the 2016 Plan, and Republican candidates won 10 of the 13 congressional districts. . . .

The second case before us is *Lamone v. Benisek*. In 2011, the Maryland Legislature—dominated by Democrats—undertook to redraw the lines of that State's eight congressional districts. The Governor at the time, Democrat Martin O'Malley, led the process. He appointed a redistricting committee to help redraw the map, and asked Congressman Steny Hoyer, who has described himself as a "serial gerrymanderer," to advise the committee. The Governor later testified that his aim was to "use the redistricting process to change the overall composition of Maryland's congressional delegation to 7 Democrats and 1 Republican by flipping" one district. . . . The map was adopted by a party-line vote. It was used in the 2012 election and succeeded in flipping the Sixth District. A Democrat has held the seat ever since. . . .

Article III of the Constitution limits federal courts to deciding "Cases" and "Controversies." We have understood that limitation to mean that federal courts can address only questions "historically viewed as capable of resolution through the judicial process." In these cases we are asked to decide an important question of constitutional law. "But before we do so, we must find that the question is presented in a 'case' or 'controversy' that is, in James Madison's words, 'of a Judiciary Nature.' "

Chief Justice Marshall famously wrote that it is "the province and duty of the judicial department to say what the law is." Sometimes, however, "the law is that the judicial department has no business entertaining the claim of unlawfulness—because the question is entrusted to one of the political branches or involves no judicially enforceable rights." In such a case the claim is said to present a "political question" and to be nonjusticiable—outside the courts' competence and therefore beyond the courts' jurisdiction. Among the political question cases the Court has identified are those that lack "judicially discoverable and manageable standards for resolving [them]." . . .

The question here is whether there is an "appropriate role for the Federal Judiciary" in remedying the problem of partisan gerrymandering—whether such claims are claims of *legal* right, resolvable according to *legal* principles, or political questions that must find their resolution elsewhere.

Partisan gerrymandering is nothing new. Nor is frustration with it. The practice was known in the Colonies prior to Independence, and the Framers were familiar with it at the time of the drafting and ratification of the Constitution. During the very first congressional elections, George Washington and his Federalist allies accused Patrick Henry of trying to gerrymander Virginia's districts against their candidates—in particular James Madison, who ultimately prevailed over fellow future President James Monroe.

In 1812, Governor of Massachusetts and future Vice President Elbridge Gerry notoriously approved congressional districts that the legislature had drawn to aid the Democratic-Republican Party. The moniker "gerrymander" was born when an outraged Federalist newspaper observed that one of the misshapen districts resembled a salamander. "By 1840, the gerrymander was a recognized force in party politics and was generally attempted in all legislation enacted for the formation of election districts. It was generally conceded that each party would attempt to gain power which was not proportionate to its numerical strength."

The Framers addressed the election of Representatives to Congress in the Elections Clause. Art. I, § 4, cl. 1. That provision assigns to state legislatures the power to prescribe the "Times, Places and Manner of holding Elections" for Members of Congress, while giving Congress the power to "make or alter" any such regulations. . . .

Congress has regularly exercised its Elections Clause power, including to address partisan gerrymandering. The Apportionment Act of 1842, which required single-member districts for the first time, specified that those districts be "composed of contiguous territory," in "an attempt to forbid the practice of the gerrymander." Later statutes added requirements of compactness and equality of population. (Only the single member district requirement remains in place today.) . . .

Appellants suggest that, through the Elections Clause, the Framers set aside electoral issues such as the one before us as questions that only Congress can resolve. We do not agree. In two areas—one-person, one-vote and racial gerrymandering—our cases have held that there is a role for the courts with respect to at least some issues that could arise from a State's drawing of congressional districts.

But the history is not irrelevant. The Framers were aware of electoral districting problems and considered what to do about them. They settled on a characteristic approach, assigning the issue to the state legislatures, expressly checked and balanced by the Federal Congress. . . . At no point was there a suggestion that the federal courts had a role to play. Nor was there any indication that the Framers had ever heard of courts doing such a thing.

Courts have nevertheless been called upon to resolve a variety of questions surrounding districting. Early on, doubts were raised about the competence of the federal courts to resolve those questions.

In the leading case of *Baker v. Carr*, voters in Tennessee complained that the State's districting plan for state representatives "debase[d]" their votes, because the plan was predicated on a 60-year-old census that no longer reflected the distribution of population in the State. The District Court dismissed the action on the ground that the claim was not justiciable, relying on this Court's precedents . . . . This Court reversed. It identified various considerations relevant to determining whether a claim is a nonjusticiable political question, including whether there is "a lack of judicially discoverable and manageable standards for resolving it." The Court concluded that the claim of population inequality among districts did not fall into that category, because such a claim could be decided under basic equal protection principles. . . .

Another line of challenges to districting plans has focused on race. Laws that explicitly discriminate on the basis of race, as well as those that are race neutral on their face but are unexplainable on grounds other than race, are of course presumptively invalid. . . .

Partisan gerrymandering claims have proved far more difficult to adjudicate. The basic reason is that, while it is illegal for a jurisdiction to depart from the one-person, one-vote rule, or to engage in racial discrimination in districting, "a jurisdiction may engage in constitutional political gerrymandering." *Hunt v. Cromartie*, 526 U.S. 541 (1999)(citing *Bush v. Vera*, 517 U.S. 952 (1996)); *Shaw v. Hunt*, 517 U.S. 899 (1996); *Miller v. Johnson*, 515 U.S. 900 (1995); *Shaw v. Reno*, 509 U.S. 630 (1993). See also *Gaffney v. Cummings*, 412 U.S. 735 (1973)(recognizing that "[p]olitics and political considerations are inseparable from districting and apportionment").

To hold that legislators cannot take partisan interests into account when drawing district lines would essentially countermand the Framers' decision to entrust districting to political entities. The "central problem" is not determining whether a jurisdiction has engaged in partisan gerrymandering. It is "determining when political gerrymandering has gone too far."

We first considered a partisan gerrymandering claim in *Gaffney v. Cummings* in 1973. There we rejected an equal protection challenge to Connecticut's redistricting plan, which "aimed at a rough scheme of proportional representation of the two major political parties" by "wiggl[ing] and joggl[ing] boundary lines" to create the appropriate number of safe seats for each party. In upholding the State's plan, we reasoned that districting "inevitably has and is intended to have substantial political consequences."

Thirteen years later, in *Davis v. Bandemer*, we addressed a claim that Indiana Republicans had cracked and packed* Democrats in violation of the Equal Protection Clause. A majority of the Court agreed that the case was justiciable, but the Court splintered over the proper standard to apply.... Three Justices, meanwhile, would have held that the Equal Protection Clause simply "does not supply judicially manageable standards for resolving purely political gerrymandering claims." ... In any event, the Court held that the plaintiffs had failed to show that the plan violated the Constitution.

Eighteen years later, in *Vieth*, the plaintiffs complained that Pennsylvania's legislature "ignored all traditional redistricting criteria, including the preservation of local government boundaries," in order to benefit Republican congressional candidates. Justice Scalia wrote for a four-Justice plurality. He would have held that the plaintiffs' claims were nonjusticiable because there was no "judicially discernible and manageable standard" for deciding them. Justice Kennedy, concurring in the judgment, noted "the lack of comprehensive and neutral principles for drawing electoral boundaries [and] the absence of rules to limit and confine judicial

---

* The two principal tactics used in gerrymandering are "cracking" and "packing." Cracking is spreading like-minded voters apart across multiple districts to dilute their voting power in each. This denies them representation in multiple districts. Packing is concentrating like-minded voters together in one district to reduce their voting power in other districts. This gives them representation in a single district while denying them representation across districts. [author's note]

intervention." He nonetheless left open the possibility that "in another case a standard might emerge." . . .

In [*League of United Latin American Citizens v. Perry*], the plaintiffs challenged a mid-decade redistricting map approved by the Texas Legislature. Once again a majority of the Court could not find a justiciable standard for resolving the plaintiffs' partisan gerrymandering claims. . . .

In considering whether partisan gerrymandering claims are justiciable, we are mindful of Justice Kennedy's counsel in *Vieth*: Any standard for resolving such claims must be grounded in a "limited and precise rationale" and be "clear, manageable, and politically neutral." . . . An expansive standard requiring "the correction of all election district lines drawn for partisan reasons would commit federal and state courts to unprecedented intervention in the American political process."

As noted, the question is one of degree: How to "provid[e] a standard for deciding how much partisan dominance is too much." And it is vital in such circumstances that the Court act only in accord with especially clear standards: "With uncertain limits, intervening courts—even when proceeding with best intentions—would risk assuming political, not legal, responsibility for a process that often produces ill will and distrust." If federal courts are to "inject [themselves] into the most heated partisan issues" by adjudicating partisan gerrymandering claims, they must be armed with a standard that can reliably differentiate unconstitutional from "constitutional political gerrymandering."

Partisan gerrymandering claims rest on an instinct that groups with a certain level of political support should enjoy a commensurate level of political power and influence. Explicitly or implicitly, a districting map is alleged to be unconstitutional because it makes it too difficult for one party to translate statewide support into seats in the legislature. But such a claim is based on a "norm that does not exist" in our electoral system— "statewide elections for representatives along party lines."

Partisan gerrymandering claims invariably sound in a desire for proportional representation. As Justice O'Connor put it, such claims are based on "a conviction that the greater the departure from proportionality, the more suspect an apportionment plan becomes." "Our cases, however, clearly foreclose any claim that the Constitution requires proportional representation or that legislatures in reapportioning must draw district lines to come as near as possible to allocating seats to the contending parties in proportion to what their anticipated statewide vote will be."

The Founders certainly did not think proportional representation was required. For more than 50 years after ratification of the Constitution, many States elected their congressional representatives through at-large or "general ticket" elections. Such States typically sent single-party delegations to Congress. That meant that a party could garner nearly half of the vote statewide and wind up without any seats in the congressional delegation. . . .

Unable to claim that the Constitution requires proportional representation outright, plaintiffs inevitably ask the courts to make their own political judgment about how much representation particular political parties *deserve*—based on the votes of their supporters—and to rearrange the challenged districts to achieve that end. But federal courts are not equipped to apportion political power as a matter of fairness, nor is there any basis for concluding that they were authorized to do so. As Justice Scalia put it for the plurality in *Vieth*: " 'Fairness' does not seem to us a judicially manageable standard. . . . Some criterion more solid and more demonstrably met than that seems to us necessary to enable the state legislatures to discern the limits of their districting discretion, to meaningfully constrain the discretion of the courts, and to win public acceptance for the courts' intrusion into a process that is the very foundation of democratic decisionmaking."

The initial difficulty in settling on a "clear, manageable and politically neutral" test for fairness is that it is not even clear what fairness looks like in this context. There is a large measure of "unfairness" in any winner-take-all system. Fairness may mean a greater number of competitive districts. Such a claim seeks to undo packing and cracking so that supporters of the disadvantaged party have a better shot at electing their preferred candidates. But making as many districts as possible more competitive could be a recipe for disaster for the disadvantaged party. As Justice White has pointed out, "[i]f all or most of the districts are competitive . . . even a narrow statewide preference for either party would produce an overwhelming majority for the winning party in the state legislature."

On the other hand, perhaps the ultimate objective of a "fairer" share of seats in the congressional delegation is most readily achieved by yielding to the gravitational pull of proportionality and engaging in cracking and packing, to ensure each party its "appropriate" share of "safe" seats. Such an approach, however, comes at the expense of competitive districts and of individuals in districts allocated to the opposing party.

Or perhaps fairness should be measured by adherence to "traditional" districting criteria, such as maintaining political subdivisions, keeping communities of interest together, and protecting incumbents. But protecting incumbents, for example, enshrines a particular partisan distribution. And the "natural political geography" of a State—such as the fact that urban electoral districts are often dominated by one political party—can itself lead to inherently packed districts. . . .

Deciding among just these different visions of fairness (you can imagine many others) poses basic questions that are political, not legal. There are no legal standards discernible in the Constitution for making such judgments, let alone limited and precise standards that are clear, manageable, and politically neutral. Any judicial decision on what is "fair" in this context would be an "unmoored determination" of the sort characteristic of a political question beyond the competence of the federal courts.

And it is only after determining how to define fairness that you can even begin to answer the determinative question: "How much is too much?" At what point does permissible partisanship become unconstitutional?

[For example,] if a court . . . focused on the respective number of seats in the legislature, it would have to decide the ideal number of seats for each party and determine at what point deviation from that balance went too far. If a 5–3 allocation corresponds most closely to statewide vote totals, is a 6–2 allocation permissible, given that legislatures have the authority to engage in a certain degree of partisan gerrymandering? Which seats should be packed and which cracked? Or if the goal is as many competitive districts as possible, how close does the split need to be for the district to be considered competitive? Presumably not all districts could qualify, so how to choose? Even assuming the court knew which version of fairness to be looking for, there are no discernible and manageable standards for deciding whether there has been a violation. The questions are "unguided and ill-suited to the development of judicial standards." and "results from one gerrymandering case to the next would likely be disparate and inconsistent." . . .

Excessive partisanship in districting leads to results that reasonably seem unjust. But the fact that such gerrymandering is "incompatible with democratic principles," *Arizona State Legislature*, 135 S.Ct., at 2586, does not mean that the solution lies with the federal judiciary. We conclude that partisan gerrymandering claims present political questions beyond the reach of the federal courts. Federal judges have no license to reallocate political power between the two major political parties, with no plausible grant of authority in the Constitution, and no legal standards to limit and direct their decisions. "[J]udicial action must be governed by *standard*, by *rule*," and must be "principled, rational, and based upon reasoned distinctions" found in the Constitution or laws. Judicial review of partisan gerrymandering does not meet those basic requirements. . . .

Our conclusion does not condone excessive partisan gerrymandering. Nor does our conclusion condemn complaints about districting to echo into a void. The States, for example, are actively addressing the issue on a number of fronts. In 2015, the Supreme Court of Florida struck down that State's congressional districting plan as a violation of the Fair Districts Amendment to the Florida Constitution. The dissent wonders why we can't do the same. The answer is that there is no "Fair Districts Amendment" to the Federal Constitution. Provisions in state statutes and state constitutions can provide standards and guidance for state courts to apply.

Indeed, numerous other States are restricting partisan considerations in districting through legislation. One way they are doing so is by placing power to draw electoral districts in the hands of independent commissions. For example, in November 2018, voters in Colorado and Michigan approved constitutional amendments creating multimember commissions that will be responsible in whole or in part for creating and approving district maps for congressional and state legislative districts. Missouri is trying a different tack. Voters there overwhelmingly approved the creation of a new position—state demographer—to draw state legislative district lines. . . .

As noted, the Framers gave Congress the power to do something about partisan gerrymandering in the Elections Clause. The first bill introduced in the 116th Congress would require States to create 15-member independent commissions to draw congressional districts and would establish certain redistricting criteria, including protection for communities of interest, and ban partisan gerrymandering.

Dozens of other bills have been introduced to limit reliance on political considerations in redistricting. In 2010, H. R. 6250 would have required States to follow standards of compactness, contiguity, and respect for political subdivisions in redistricting. It also would have prohibited the establishment of congressional districts "with the major purpose of diluting the voting strength of any person, or group, including any political party," except when necessary to comply with the Voting Rights Act of 1965.

Another example is the Fairness and Independence in Redistricting Act, which was introduced in 2005 and has been reintroduced in every Congress since. That bill would require every State to establish an independent commission to adopt redistricting plans. The bill also set forth criteria for the independent commissions to use, such as compactness, contiguity, and population equality. It would prohibit consideration of voting history, political party affiliation, or incumbent Representative's residence. H. R. 2642,

We express no view on any of these pending proposals. We simply note that the avenue for reform established by the Framers, and used by Congress in the past, remains open.

JUSTICE KAGAN, with whom JUSTICE GINSBURG, JUSTICE BREYER, and JUSTICE SOTOMAYOR join, dissenting.

For the first time ever, this Court refuses to remedy a constitutional violation because it thinks the task beyond judicial capabilities.

And not just any constitutional violation. The partisan gerrymanders in these cases deprived citizens of the most fundamental of their constitutional rights: the rights to participate equally in the political process, to join with others to advance political beliefs, and to choose their political representatives. In so doing, the partisan gerrymanders here debased and dishonored our democracy, turning upside-down the core

American idea that all governmental power derives from the people. These gerrymanders enabled politicians to entrench themselves in office as against voters' preferences. They promoted partisanship above respect for the popular will. They encouraged a politics of polarization and dysfunction. If left unchecked, gerrymanders like the ones here may irreparably damage our system of government.

And checking them is *not* beyond the courts. The majority's abdication comes just when courts across the country, including those below, have coalesced around manageable judicial standards to resolve partisan gerrymandering claims. Those standards satisfy the majority's own benchmarks. They do not require—indeed, they do not permit—courts to rely on their own ideas of electoral fairness, whether proportional representation or any other. And they limit courts to correcting only egregious gerrymanders, so judges do not become omnipresent players in the political process. But yes, the standards used here do allow—as well they should—judicial intervention in the worst-of-the-worst cases of democratic subversion, causing blatant constitutional harms. In other words, they allow courts to undo partisan gerrymanders of the kind we face today from North Carolina and Maryland. In giving such gerrymanders a pass from judicial review, the majority goes tragically wrong. . . .

If there is a single idea that made our Nation (and that our Nation commended to the world), it is this one: The people are sovereign. The "power," James Madison wrote, "is in the people over the Government, and not in the Government over the people."

Free and fair and periodic elections are the key to that vision. The people get to choose their representatives. And then they get to decide, at regular intervals, whether to keep them. . . .

And partisan gerrymandering can make it meaningless. At its most extreme—as in North Carolina and Maryland—the practice amounts to "rigging elections." By drawing districts to maximize the power of some voters and minimize the power of others, a party in office at the right time can entrench itself there for a decade or more, no matter what the voters would prefer. Just ask the people of North Carolina and Maryland. The "core principle of republican government," this Court has recognized, is "that the voters should choose their representatives, not the other way around." Partisan gerrymandering turns it the other way around. By that mechanism, politicians can cherry-pick voters to ensure their reelection. And the power becomes, as Madison put it, "in the Government over the people."

The majority disputes none of this. I think it important to underscore that fact: The majority disputes none of what I have said (or will say) about how gerrymanders undermine democracy. Indeed, the majority concedes (really, how could it not?) that gerrymandering is "incompatible with democratic principles." And therefore what? That recognition would seem to demand a response. The majority offers two ideas that might qualify as such. One is that the political process can deal with the problem—a proposition so dubious on its face that I feel secure in delaying my answer for some time. The other is that political gerrymanders have always been with us. . . . The majority's idea . . . seems to be that if we have lived with partisan gerrymanders so long, we will survive.

That complacency has no cause. Yes, partisan gerrymandering goes back to the Republic's earliest days. (As does vociferous opposition to it.) But big data and modern technology—of just the kind that the mapmakers in North Carolina and Maryland used—make today's gerrymandering altogether different from the crude linedrawing of the past. Old-time efforts, based on little more than guesses, sometimes led to so-called dummymanders—gerrymanders that went spectacularly wrong. Not likely in today's world. Mapmakers now have access to more granular data about party preference and voting behavior than ever before. . . . Just as important, advancements in computing technology have enabled mapmakers to put that information to use with unprecedented efficiency and precision. While bygone mapmakers may have drafted three or four alternative districting plans, today's mapmakers can generate thousands of possibilities at the touch of a key—and then choose the one giving their party maximum advantage (usually while still meeting traditional districting requirements). The effect is to make gerrymanders far more effective and durable than before, insulating politicians against all but the most titanic shifts in the political tides. These are not your grandfather's—let alone the Framers'—gerrymanders. . . .

Partisan gerrymandering of the kind before us not only subverts democracy (as if that weren't bad enough). It violates individuals' constitutional rights as well. That statement is not the lonesome cry of a dissenting Justice. This Court has recognized extreme partisan gerrymandering as such a violation for many years.

Partisan gerrymandering operates through vote dilution—the devaluation of one citizen's vote as compared to others. A mapmaker draws district lines to "pack" and "crack" voters likely to support the disfavored party. He packs supermajorities of those voters into a relatively few districts, in numbers far greater than needed for their preferred candidates to prevail. Then he cracks the rest across many more districts, spreading them so thin that their candidates will not be able to win. Whether the person is packed or cracked, his vote carries less weight—has less consequence—than it would under a neutrally drawn (non-partisan) map. In short, the mapmaker has made some votes count for less, because they are likely to go for the other party.

That practice implicates the Fourteenth Amendment's Equal Protection Clause. The Fourteenth Amendment, we long ago recognized, "guarantees the opportunity for equal participation by all voters in the election" of legislators. And that opportunity "can be denied by a debasement or dilution of the weight of a citizen's vote just as effectively as by wholly prohibiting the free exercise of the franchise." Based on that principle, this Court in its one-person-one-vote decisions prohibited creating districts with significantly different populations. A State could not, we explained, thus "dilut[e] the weight of votes because of place of residence." The constitutional injury in a partisan gerrymandering case is much the same, except that the dilution is based on party affiliation. . . .

So the only way to understand the majority's opinion is as follows: In the face of grievous harm to democratic governance and flagrant infringements on individuals' rights—in the face of escalating partisan manipulation whose compatibility with this Nation's values and law no one defends—the majority declines to provide any remedy. For the first time in this Nation's history, the majority declares that it can do nothing about an acknowledged constitutional violation because it has searched high and low and cannot find a workable legal standard to apply.

The majority gives two reasons for thinking that the adjudication of partisan gerrymandering claims is beyond judicial capabilities. First and foremost, the majority says, it cannot find a neutral baseline—one not based on contestable notions of political fairness—from which to measure injury. . . . And second, the majority argues that even after establishing a baseline, a court would have no way to answer "the determinative question: 'How much is too much?'" No "discernible and manageable" standard is available, the majority claims—and so courts could willy-nilly become embroiled in fixing every districting plan. . . .

But in throwing up its hands, the majority misses something under its nose: What it says can't be done *has* been done. Over the past several years, federal courts across the country—including, but not exclusively, in the decisions below—have largely converged on a standard for adjudicating partisan gerrymandering claims (striking down both Democratic and Republican districting plans in the process). And that standard does what the majority says is impossible. The standard does not use any judge-made conception of electoral fairness—either proportional representation or any other; instead, it takes as its baseline a State's *own* criteria of fairness, apart from partisan gain. And by requiring plaintiffs to make difficult showings relating to both purpose and effects, the standard invalidates the most extreme, but only the most extreme, partisan gerrymanders. . . .

Start with the standard the lower courts used. . . . Both courts focused on the harm of vote dilution. . . . And both courts (like others around the country) used basically the same three-part test to decide whether the plaintiffs had made out a vote dilution claim. As many legal standards do, that test has three parts: (1) intent; (2) effects; and (3) causation. First, the plaintiffs challenging a districting plan must prove that state officials' "predominant purpose" in drawing a district's lines was to "entrench [their party] in power" by diluting the votes of citizens favoring its rival. Second, the plaintiffs must establish that the lines drawn in fact have the intended effect by "substantially" diluting their votes. And third, if the plaintiffs make those showings, the State must come up with a legitimate, non-partisan justification to save its map. If you are a lawyer, you know that this test looks utterly ordinary. It is the sort of thing courts work with every day.

Turn now to the test's application. First, did the North Carolina and Maryland districters have the predominant purpose of entrenching their own party in power? Here, the two District Courts catalogued the overwhelming direct evidence that they did. . . . The majority's response to the District Courts' purpose analysis is discomfiting. The majority does not contest the lower courts' findings; how could it? Instead, the majority says that state officials' intent to entrench their party in power is perfectly "permissible," even when it is the predominant factor in drawing district lines. But that is wrong. True enough, that the intent to inject "political considerations" into districting may not raise any constitutional concerns. . . . And true enough that even the naked purpose to gain partisan advantage may not rise to the level of constitutional notice when it is not the driving force in mapmaking or when the intended gain is slight. But when political actors have a specific and predominant intent to entrench themselves in power by manipulating district lines, that goes too far. . . . Just consider the purposes here. It cannot be permissible and thus irrelevant, as the majority claims, that state officials have as their purpose the kind of grotesquely gerrymandered map that, according to all this Court has ever said, violates the Constitution.

On to the second step of the analysis, where the plaintiffs must prove that the districting plan substantially dilutes their votes. The majority fails to discuss most of the evidence the District Courts relied on to find that the plaintiffs had done so. . . .

Consider the sort of evidence used in North Carolina. . . . There, the plaintiffs demonstrated the districting plan's effects mostly by relying on what might be called the "extreme outlier approach." (Here's a spoiler: the State's plan was one.) The approach—which also has recently been used in Michigan and Ohio litigation—begins by using advanced computing technology to randomly generate a large collection of districting plans that incorporate the State's physical and political geography and meet its declared districting criteria, *except for* partisan gain. For each of those maps, the method then uses actual precinct-level votes from past elections to determine a partisan outcome (*i.e.*, the number of Democratic and Republican seats that map produces). Suppose we now have 1,000 maps, each with a partisan outcome attached to it. We can line up those maps on a continuum—the most favorable to Republicans on one end, the most favorable to Democrats on the other. We can then find the median outcome—that is, the outcome smack dab in the center—in a world with no partisan manipulation. And we can see where the State's actual plan falls on the spectrum—at or near the median or way out on one of the tails? The further out on the tail, the more extreme the partisan distortion and the more significant the vote dilution.

Using that approach, the North Carolina plaintiffs offered a boatload of alternative districting plans—all showing that the State's map was an out-out-out-outlier. One expert produced 3,000 maps, adhering in the way described above to the districting criteria that the North Carolina redistricting committee had used, other than partisan advantage. . . . The results were, shall we say, striking. Every single one of the 3,000 maps would have produced at least one more Democratic House Member than the State's actual map, and 77% would have elected three or four more. A second expert obtained essentially the same results with maps conforming to more generic districting criteria (*e.g.*, compactness and contiguity of districts). Over 99% of that expert's 24,518 simulations would have led to the election of at least one more Democrat, and over 70% would have led to two or three more. Based on those and other findings, the District Court determined that the North Carolina plan substantially dilutes the plaintiffs' votes. . . .

The majority claims all these findings are mere "prognostications" about the future, in which no one "can have any confidence." But the courts below did not gaze into crystal balls, as the majority tries to suggest. Their findings about these gerrymanders' effects on voters—both in the past and predictably in the future—were evidence-based, data-based, statistics-based. Knowledge-based, one might say. . . . They looked at the evidence—at the facts about how these districts operated—and they could reach only one conclusion. By substantially diluting the votes of citizens favoring their rivals, the politicians of one party had succeeded in entrenching themselves in office. They had beat democracy. . . .

Contrary to the majority's suggestion, the District Courts did not have to—and in fact did not—choose among competing visions of electoral fairness. That is because they did not try to compare the State's actual map to an "ideally fair" one (whether based on proportional representation or some other criterion). Instead, they looked at the difference between what the State did and what the State would have done if politicians hadn't been intent on partisan gain. . . . The effects evidence in these cases accepted as a given the State's physical geography (*e.g.*, where does the Chesapeake run?) and political geography (*e.g.*, where do the Democrats live on top of each other?). So the courts did not, in the majority's words, try to "counteract 'natural' gerrymandering caused, for example, by the urban concentration of one party." . . .

The majority's "how much is too much" critique fares no better than its neutrality argument. How about the following for a first-cut answer:

This much is too much. By any measure, a map that produces a greater partisan skew than any of 3,000 randomly generated maps (all with the State's political geography and districting criteria built in) reflects "too much" partisanship. Think about what I just said: The absolute worst of 3,001 possible maps. The *only one* that could produce a 10–3 partisan split even as Republicans got a bare majority of the statewide vote. And again: How much is too much? This much is too much. . . . If the majority had done nothing else, it could have set the line here. How much is too much? At the least, any gerrymanders as bad as these.

And if the majority thought that approach too case-specific, it could have used the lower courts' general standard—focusing on "predominant" purpose and "substantial" effects—without fear of indeterminacy. I do not take even the majority to claim that courts are incapable of investigating whether legislators mainly intended to seek partisan advantage. That is for good reason. Although purpose inquiries carry certain hazards (which courts must attend to), they are a common form of analysis in constitutional cases. Those inquiries would be no harder here than in other contexts.

Nor is there any reason to doubt, as the majority does, the competence of courts to determine whether a district map "substantially" dilutes the votes of a rival party's supporters from the everything-but-partisanship baseline described above. . . . As this Court recently noted, "the law is full of instances" where a judge's decision rests on "estimating rightly . . . some matter of degree"—including the "substantial[ity]" of risk or harm. . . .

Illicit purpose was simple to show here only because politicians and mapmakers thought their actions could not be attacked in court. They therefore felt free to openly proclaim their intent to entrench their party in office. But if the Court today had declared that behavior justiciable, such smoking guns would all but disappear. . . . So plaintiffs would have to prove the intent to entrench through circumstantial evidence—essentially showing that no other explanation (no geographic feature or non-partisan districting objective) could explain the districting plan's vote dilutive effects. And that would be impossible unless those effects were even more than substantial—unless mapmakers had packed and cracked with abandon in unprecedented ways. As again, they did here. That the two courts below found constitutional violations does not mean their tests were unrigorous; it means that the conduct they confronted was constitutionally appalling—by even the strictest measure, inordinately partisan.

The majority, in the end, fails to understand both the plaintiffs' claims and the decisions below. Everything in today's opinion assumes that these cases grew out of a "desire for proportional representation" or, more generally phrased, a "fair share of political power." *Ante,* at 2499, 2502. And everything in it assumes that the courts below had to (and did) decide what that fair share would be. But that is not so. The plaintiffs objected to one specific practice—the extreme manipulation of district lines for partisan gain. Elimination of that practice could have led to proportional representation. Or it could have led to nothing close. What was left after the practice's removal could have been fair, or could have been unfair, by any number of measures. That was not the crux of this suit. The plaintiffs asked only that the courts bar politicians from entrenching themselves in power by diluting the votes of their rivals' supporters. And the courts, using neutral and manageable—and eminently legal—standards, provided that (and only that) relief. This Court should have cheered, not overturned, that restoration of the people's power to vote. . . .

The majority [concludes] its opinion with a paean to congressional bills limiting partisan gerrymanders. "Dozens of [those] bills have been introduced," the majority says. One was "introduced in 2005 and has been reintroduced in every Congress since." And might be reintroduced until the end of time. Because what all these *bills* have in common is that they are not *laws*. The politicians who benefit from partisan gerrymandering are unlikely to change partisan gerrymandering. And because those politicians maintain themselves in office through partisan gerrymandering, the chances for legislative reform are slight.

No worries, the majority says; it has another idea. The majority notes that voters themselves have recently approved ballot initiatives to put power over districting in the hands of independent commissions or other non-partisan actors. . . . Fewer than half the States offer voters an opportunity to put initiatives to direct vote; in all the rest (including North Carolina and Maryland), voters are dependent on legislators to make electoral changes (which for all the reasons already given, they are unlikely to do). . . .

The majority's most perplexing "solution" is to look to state courts. . . . But what do those courts know that this Court does not? If they can develop and apply neutral and manageable standards to identify unconstitutional gerrymanders, why couldn't we?[6]

We could have, and we should have. . . .

Of all times to abandon the Court's duty to declare the law, this was not the one. The practices challenged in these cases imperil our system of government. Part of the Court's role in that system is to defend its foundations. None is more important than free and fair elections. With respect but deep sadness, I dissent.

---

[6] Contrary to the majority's suggestion, state courts do not typically have more specific "standards and guidance" to apply than federal courts have. The Pennsylvania Supreme Court based its gerrymandering decision on a constitutional clause providing only that "elections shall be free and equal" and no one shall "interfere to prevent the free exercise of the right of suffrage."

PROBLEM

A congressional election in an Ohio district is extremely close. According to the tally by the Ohio electoral districts, certified by the Ohio Secretary of State, the Republican candidate won by 21 votes out of over 100,000 cast. The closeness of the election required an automatic recount under Ohio law, and the recount resulted in the Democratic candidate winning by 7 votes. Because of allegations of irregularities in the recount, another state recount was held, resulting this time in the Republican winning by 37 votes. By a straight party line vote, the U.S. House of Representatives decided to institute a proceeding to determine the winner of the election. After reviewing the various records of the count and recount, the House again by a straight party line vote voted to seat the Democratic candidate. If the Republican candidate sues in federal court to overturn that decision, how should the federal court rule on a motion to dismiss on the grounds that the suit raises only a "political question"?

PROBLEM

The United States participates in a United Nations Peacekeeping Operation. Pursuant to an authorization by Congress, the President orders a battalion of the 101st Airborne Division to report to Darfur, to don United Nations blue helmets and UN insignia, and to be subject to the local command of the UN commander, who is a French military officer. A soldier in the battalion seeks a declaratory judgment in federal court that the order is unconstitutional because war has not been declared and because having to report to a French officer violates the constitutional statement that the President is the Commander in Chief. How should a court rule on a motion to dismiss on the grounds that the suit raises a "political question"?

---

d. Mootness

Mootness is still another basis upon which the Court has refused to consider cases. Mootness refers to the situation where, although there may have been a valid case or controversy when the suit was brought, subsequent events have eliminated the complained of effects, or, stated differently, have rendered the case moot. In *Powell v. McCormack*, Justice Stewart dissented, because he believed the case was moot. By the time the case was before the Supreme Court, the session of Congress from which Adam Clayton Powell, Jr., was excluded had expired. Powell had been re-elected to the next Congress, and he had been seated (*i.e.*, not excluded).

As a result, his exclusion was totally in the past. Justice Stewart thought that this was no longer a live controversy requiring a judicial decision. The Court, however, noted that Congress had withheld his salary for the two years of the session of Congress from which he was excluded, so that his claim to that salary certainly made this a live controversy.

A recurring issue with regard to mootness is whether a case is mooted if, in an action for an injunction or declaratory judgment, the defendant simply stops engaging in the challenged conduct. Is there still a live controversy? For example, imagine that the President directs the National Security Agency to monitor all the international communications of persons in the United States of the Muslim faith. Members of that faith bring suit against the NSA, alleging that such monitoring would be unconstitutional and seeking an injunction ordering NSA to stop. After the suit is brought, but before the court has any opportunity to rule on it, the President withdraws the order, and the NSA stops monitoring. Should the case be dismissed as moot? Assume for a moment that it is. Then, the President revives his order, and NSA starts monitoring again; and again the Muslims bring suit; and again the President then tells NSA to stop. You can see the problem. As a result, the Court has established the rule that the voluntary cessation of the allegedly unlawful conduct will not necessarily moot a case. The burden is on the defendant to show by a preponderance of the evidence that the allegedly unlawful activity will not recur. Unless the defendant can satisfy that burden, which is not easy to do, the case will not be moot, and the court will go on to decide it. Note, however, that this is an "activist" approach, because it is asserting that, even though there is in fact no live controversy at the moment, courts can still decide the matter.

Another circumstance where the Court has allowed cases to go forward in the absence of an actual, continuing live controversy is where the facts giving rise to the plaintiff's case have passed, but they are likely to recur. For example, in *Roe v. Wade*, 410 U.S. 113 (1973), the case was brought by a pregnant woman challenging the law criminalizing abortion. By the time the case was before the Supreme Court, however, she was no longer pregnant. The defendants argued that the case was moot, but the Court held that there was an exception to mootness when a case was "capable of repetition yet evading review." In other words, any challenge to a law premised on the plaintiff being pregnant would never be able to reach the Supreme Court while the person was still pregnant, and thus the issue would always evade review, if mootness was applied strictly. Again, note that this is "activist" in the sense that the Court is deciding in favor of hearing the case, rather than not hearing the case, in order that the issue can be decided by a court.

e. Other Grounds for Avoiding Decision

The above rules for avoiding review are from the Court's perspective all commanded by the Constitution's requirement that the judicial power of the United States is limited to "case and controversies." Thus, Congress by statute cannot change those rules. As in *Defenders of Wildlife*, Congress cannot grant standing to persons who are not injured or about to be injured. There are, however, a number of "prudential" grounds for avoiding review. They are called "prudential" because the Court has invented them in the exercise of its "good judgment," not because the Constitution, as interpreted, commands them.

An example is "prudential standing." In addition to the constitutional requirements of injury, causation, and redressability, the Court has created some prudential requirements, one of which is that a person cannot raise the rights of another. For example, imagine a law that made it illegal for non-U.S. citizens to participate in professional sporting events in the United States. Rory McIlroy, the Northern Ireland citizen who won the U.S. Open in golf in 2011, would certainly have standing to challenge the law. But what about his caddy? Presumably, the caddy would suffer injury as well, because if his player could not compete in U.S. tournaments, it would decrease the caddy's income; the injury would be caused by the law, and a favorable court resolution would overturn the law, allowing the player to compete. Thus, even the caddy would have constitutional standing, but the caddy would lack prudential standing, because he would be asserting a claimed constitutional right of the foreign golfer to play, not a right of his own.

There are a host of exceptions to this general rule of prudential standing, and in 2011 the Court clarified the outcome of a recurring issue. A woman was convicted of a crime, and she claimed that the federal statute under which she was convicted was unconstitutional as a violation of the Tenth Amendment. Recall that the Tenth Amendment states that the powers not delegated to the United States are reserved to the States. The government initially argued that the woman did not have prudential standing to claim a violation of the Tenth Amendment; only a state could make such a claim, because that Amendment protects states' rights, not individuals' rights. The courts of appeals had split on this issue. The Supreme Court unanimously decided that she could bring the claim. *Bond v. United States*, 564 U.S. 211 (2011). Justice Kennedy wrote for the Court that the limits imposed on Congress by concepts of federalism, whether stemming from limitations on the grant of its power or restrictions on the exercise of its powers, were not to protect the interests of states alone but also, and most importantly, to protect the liberty of all people. Consequently, the woman was *not* invoking another's rights; she was invoking her own individual right not to be subjected to a law that was beyond Congress's power.

The Court is often not explicit as to whether its justiciability decisions are constitutionally or prudentially based. Indeed, occasionally a determination that a case is a "political question" seems more based upon a prudential judgment than a constitutional judgment. That is, the Court seems to say that it believes it would be better not to have the Court decide the issue, rather than say it is interpreting the Constitution to forbid the Court from deciding the issue. "Ripeness" is another example. In *Goldwater v. Carter*, Justice Powell's opinion concurring in the judgment, rejected the political question determination of the plurality and instead found that the case was not "ripe" for decision.

> Prudential considerations persuade me that a dispute between Congress and the President is not ready for judicial review unless and until each branch has taken action asserting its constitutional authority. Differences between the President and the Congress are commonplace under our system. The differences should, and almost invariably do, turn on political rather than legal considerations. The Judicial Branch should not decide issues affecting the allocation of power between the President and Congress until the political branches reach a constitutional impasse. Otherwise, we would encourage small groups or even individual Members of Congress to seek judicial resolution of issues before the normal political process has the opportunity to resolve the conflict.

444 U.S. at 996. This explanation seems to turn on the timing of the bringing of the case. If the political branches cannot work it out, and they have reached an impasse, then Justice Powell believes the case would be justiciable, but until that time the case would not be "ripe."

The main difference between a constitutionally based justiciability requirement and a prudentially based justiciability requirement is that Congress can overrule or create exceptions to the latter, while it cannot with respect to the former. Many of these prudential bases for avoiding review are covered either in courses on administrative law or on federal courts.

3. THE ELEVENTH AMENDMENT

Above we have addressed legislative checks on the judicial power and checks on judicial power the Court has found embedded in Article III's "case" and "controversy" language, as well as in general prudential considerations. The Eleventh Amendment provides yet another check on a particular application of judicial power.

During the Revolutionary War, Robert Farquhar, a citizen of South Carolina, supplied some goods to the state of Georgia on credit. In 1792, when Georgia did not pay, Alexander Chisholm, as executor of Farquhar's estate, sued Georgia in the Supreme Court for the money due, invoking the

Supreme Court's original jurisdiction. At first Georgia did not appear in court to answer the suit, so the case was put over until the next term. At the next term, lawyers for Georgia filed a formal protest against the Supreme Court exercising jurisdiction over the state of Georgia upon a suit filed by a citizen of another state. Their argument was that Georgia, as a sovereign state, was immune from private suit under the long-standing British tradition that one cannot sue the sovereign.

Four justices of the Supreme Court, however, read the Constitution literally.* Article III specifically provides that the judicial power of the United States extends "to controversies . . . between a state and citizens of another state," and that the Supreme Court has original jurisdiction over such cases. The Judiciary Act of 1789 also contained an explicit provision providing for the Supreme Court to exercise original jurisdiction over controversies between a state and citizens of another state. Consequently, the four justices read these provisions to override any state sovereign immunity that might exist in the absence of the Constitution. One justice, Justice Iredell, agreed with Georgia. Consequently, the Court issued an order that unless Georgia appeared at the term of court the following year, a default judgment would be entered against Georgia. *See Chisholm v. Georgia*, 2 U.S. 419 (1793). Georgia did not appear the next year, and a default judgment was entered against it.

The Court's decision issued in 1793 raised such a firestorm of protest in the states that Congress proposed an amendment to overrule the decision in early 1794, which was ratified by the requisite number of states in less than a year. The amendment, the Eleventh Amendment, provides:

> The Judicial power of the United States shall not be construed to extend to any suit in law or equity, commenced or prosecuted against one of the United States by Citizens of another State, or by Citizens or Subjects of any Foreign State.

This amendment thus eliminated some of the judicial power granted to the Court in Article III.

But, what about a suit against a state by a citizen of that state in a case "arising under th[e] Constitution [or] laws of the United States"? Article III says that the judicial power of the United States extends to "all cases" "arising under th[e] Constitution [or] laws of the United States," with no exception where the defendant is a state, and the Eleventh Amendment says nothing about a suit against a state brought by one of its own citizens.

---

*   As a case decided before John Marshall became Chief Justice, the practice was for each Justice to write his own opinion without regard to the others, with the opinions printed one after another in the opposite order of seniority.

HANS V. LOUISIANA
United States Supreme Court, 1890.
134 U.S. 1, 10 S.Ct. 504.

BRADLEY, J.

This is an action brought in the circuit court of the United States, in December, 1884, against the state of Louisiana, by Hans, a citizen of that state, to recover the amount [due him under certain bonds of the state issued in 1874. In 1879, Louisiana amended its constitution to provide that the state would not pay the monies due on these bonds. Hans argued that this state constitutional amendment was in violation of Article I, Section 10, Clause 1, the Contracts Clause, because it impaired the obligation of a lawful contract. The state of Louisiana filed an exception in circuit court, arguing that the plaintiff could not sue the state without its permission and that the constitution and laws do not give the courts jurisdiction of a suit against the state. The circuit court agreed with Louisiana and dismissed the case. Hans, however, appealed to the Supreme Court.] [T]he question is presented whether a state can be sued in a circuit court of the United States by one of its own citizens upon a suggestion that the case is one that arises under the constitution or laws of the United States.

The ground taken is that under the constitution, as well as under the act of congress passed to carry it into effect, a case is within the jurisdiction of the federal courts, without regard to the character of the parties, if it arises under the constitution or laws of the United States, or, which is the same thing, if it necessarily involves a question under said constitution or laws. The language relied on is that clause of the third article of the constitution, which declares that "the judicial power of the United States shall extend to all cases in law and equity arising under this constitution, the laws of the United States, and treaties made, or which shall be made, under their authority;" and the corresponding clause of the act conferring jurisdiction upon the circuit court. It is said that these jurisdictional clauses make no exception arising from the character of the parties, and therefore that a state can claim no exemption from suit, if the case is really one arising under the constitution, laws, or treaties of the United States. . . .

That a state cannot be sued by a citizen of another state, or of a foreign state, on the mere ground that the case is one arising under the constitution or laws of the United States, is clearly established by the decisions of this court in several recent cases. Those were cases arising under the constitution of the United States, upon laws complained of as impairing the obligation of contracts, one of which was the constitutional amendment of Louisiana, complained of in the present case. Relief was sought against state officers who professed to act in obedience to those laws. This court held that the suits were virtually against the states themselves, and were consequently violative of the eleventh amendment of the constitution, and could not be maintained. It was not denied that they presented cases arising under the constitution; but, notwithstanding that, they were held to be prohibited by the amendment referred to.

In the present case the plaintiff in error* contends that he, being a citizen of Louisiana, is not embarrassed by the obstacle of the eleventh amendment, inasmuch as that amendment only prohibits suits against a state which are brought by the citizens of another state, or by citizens or subjects of a foreign state. It is true the amendment does so read, and, if there were no other reason or ground for abating his suit, it might be maintainable; and then we should have this anomalous result, that, in cases arising under the constitution or laws of the United States, a state may be sued in the federal courts by its own citizens, though it cannot be sued for a like cause of action by the citizens of other states, or of a foreign state; and may be thus sued in the federal courts, although not allowing itself to be sued in its own courts. If this is the necessary consequence of the language of the constitution and the law, the result is no less startling and unexpected than was the original decision of this court, that, under the language of the constitution and of the judiciary act of 1789, a state was liable to be sued by a citizen of another state or of a foreign country. That decision was made in the case of *Chisholm v. Georgia* and created such a shock of surprise throughout the country that, at the first meeting of congress thereafter, the eleventh amendment to the constitution was almost unanimously proposed, and was in due course adopted by the legislatures of the states. This amendment, expressing the will of the ultimate sovereignty of the whole country, superior to all legislatures and all courts, actually reversed the decision of the supreme court. It did not in terms prohibit suits by individuals against the states, but declared that the constitution should not be construed to import any power to authorize the bringing of such suits. The language of the amendment is that "the judicial power of the United States shall not be construed to extend to any suit, in law or equity, commenced or prosecuted against one of the United States by citizens of another state, or by citizens or subjects of any foreign state." The supreme court had construed the judicial power as extending to such a suit, and its decision was thus overruled. The court itself so understood the effect of the amendment.

This view of the force and meaning of the amendment is important. It shows that, on this question of the suability of the states by individuals, the highest authority of this country** was in accord rather with the minority than with the majority of the court in the decision of the case of *Chisholm v. Georgia*; and this fact lends additional interest to the able

---

* The term "plaintiff in error" means the person who is appealing the lower court case, or stated otherwise, the plaintiff in the appellate court. Here it refers to Hans. [author's note]

** "[T]he highest authority of this country" to whom the Court is referring is the people of the United States who amended the Constitution to overrule *Chisholm*. [author's note]

opinion of Mr. Justice IREDELL* on that occasion. The other justices were more swayed by a close observance of the letter of the constitution,** without regard to former experience and usage; and because the letter said that the judicial power shall extend to controversies "between a state and citizens of another state;" and "between a state and foreign states, citizens or subjects," they felt constrained to see in this language a power to enable the individual citizens of one state, or of a foreign state, to sue another state of the Union in the federal courts. Justice IREDELL, on the contrary, contended that it was not the intention to create new and unheard of remedies, by subjecting sovereign states to actions at the suit of individuals, (which he conclusively showed was never done before,) but only, by proper legislation, to invest the federal courts with jurisdiction to hear and determine controversies and cases, between the parties designated, that were properly susceptible of litigation in courts. Looking back from our present stand-point at the decision in *Chisholm v. Georgia*, we do not greatly wonder at the effect which it had upon the country. Any such power as that of authorizing the federal judiciary to entertain suits by individuals against the states had been expressly disclaimed, and even resented, by the great defenders of the constitution while it was on its trial before the American people. As some of their utterances are directly pertinent to the question now under consideration, we deem it proper to quote them.

The eighty-first number of the Federalist, written by Hamilton, has the following profound remarks:

> [I]t is inherent in the nature of sovereignty not to be amenable to the suit of an individual without its consent. This is the general sense and the general practice of mankind; and the exemption, as one of the attributes of sovereignty, is now enjoyed by the government of every state in the Union. Unless, therefore, there is a surrender of this immunity in the plan of the convention, it will remain with the states, and the danger intimated must be merely ideal. [T]here is no color to pretend that the state governments would, by the adoption of that plan, be divested of the privilege of paying their own debts in their own way, free from every constraint but that which flows from the obligations of good faith. The contracts between a nation and individuals are only binding on the conscience of the sovereign, and have no pretension to a compulsive force. They confer no right of action independent of the sovereign will. . . .

---

* Justice Iredell was the one justice who agreed with Georgia in *Chisholm v. Georgia*. [author's note]

** The term, the "letter of the Constitution," shortened to just "the letter" subsequently in the opinion, means the literal words of the Constitution, as in the term "letter of the law." [author's note]

The obnoxious clause to which Hamilton's argument was directed, and which was the ground of the objections which he so forcibly met, was that which declared that "the judicial power shall extend to all * * * controversies between a state and citizens of another state, * * * and between a state and foreign states, citizens, or subjects." It was argued by the opponents of the constitution that this clause would authorize jurisdiction to be given to the federal courts to entertain suits against a state brought by the citizens of another state or of a foreign state. Adhering to the mere letter, it might be so, and so, in fact, the supreme court held in *Chisholm v. Georgia*; but looking at the subject as Hamilton did, and as Mr. Justice IREDELL did, in the light of history and experience and the established order of things, the views of the latter were clearly right, as the people of the United States in their sovereign capacity subsequently decided. . . .

It seems to us that these views of those great advocates and defenders of the constitution were most sensible and just, and they apply equally to the present case as to that then under discussion. The letter is appealed to now, as it was then, as a ground for sustaining a suit brought by an individual against a state. The reason against it is as strong in this case as it was in that. It is an attempt to strain the constitution and the law to a construction never imagined or dreamed of. Can we suppose that, when the eleventh amendment was adopted, it was understood to be left open for citizens of a state to sue their own state in the federal courts, while the idea of suits by citizens of other states, or of foreign states, was indignantly repelled? Suppose that congress, when proposing the eleventh amendment, had appended to it a proviso that nothing therein contained should prevent a state from being sued by its own citizens in cases arising under the constitution or laws of the United States, can we imagine that it would have been adopted by the states? The supposition that it would is almost an absurdity on its face.

The truth is that the cognizance of suits and actions unknown to the law, and forbidden by the law, was not contemplated by the constitution when establishing the judicial power of the United States. Some things, undoubtedly, were made justi[c]iable which were not known as such at the common law; such, for example, as controversies between states as to boundary lines, and other questions admitting of judicial solution. . . . The establishment of this new branch of jurisdiction seemed to be necessary from the extinguishment of diplomatic relations between the states. . . .

The suability of a state, without its consent, was a thing unknown to the law. This has been so often laid down and acknowledged by courts and jurists that it is hardly necessary to be formally asserted. It was fully shown by an exhaustive examination of the old law by Mr. Justice IREDELL in his opinion in *Chisholm v. Georgia*; and it has been conceded in every case since, where the question has, in any way, been presented. . . .

HARLAN, J.

I concur with the court in holding that a suit directly against a state by one of its own citizens is not one to which the judicial power of the United States extends, unless the state itself consents to be sued. Upon this ground alone I assent to the judgment. But I cannot give my assent to many things said in the opinion. The comments made upon the decision in *Chisholm v. Georgia* do not meet my approval. They are not necessary to the determination of the present case. Besides, I am of opinion that the decision in that case was based upon a sound interpretation of the constitution as that instrument then was.

COMMENTS AND QUESTIONS

1.   Although it does not use the term, the Court in *Hans* describes the rule of "sovereign immunity." The sovereign is immune from suit absent its consent. Moreover, as implied in *Hans*, and as was even recognized in *Chisholm*, the federal government also has sovereign immunity. A person cannot sue the federal government without its consent. After *Hans*, what is the rule—that a person may not sue either a state or the federal government for violating the person's constitutional rights? If so, what sort of protection is there for a person's constitutional and statutory rights?

2.   As an initial matter, a person might raise his constitutional or statutory rights as a defense when the government proceeds against him. For example, in a criminal trial the defendant might assert the unconstitutionality of the law under which he is being prosecuted. Or, a person in custody could file a petition for habeas corpus alleging he is being held unlawfully.

3.   Moreover, there are a number of exceptions to the general rule that a person may not sue the government. First, the state and federal governments can consent to suit. Given the strength of opposition to being sued that one sees reflected in the adoption of the Eleventh Amendment, one might wonder when, if ever, a state would consent to suit. In fact, states and the federal government have by law waived their sovereign immunity in numerous circumstances. For example, the federal government and all the states allow persons to sue them for various torts committed by agents of the government. In addition, they generally allow suits based on contracts with the government. They all allow suits based upon claims that government has unconstitutionally taken property without just compensation. In order for the state or federal government to consent to suit, however, the consent must be "unequivocally expressed"; consent cannot be inferred. Nevertheless, a state may be deemed to have waived its sovereign immunity as to particular actions (*i.e.*, consented to suit) by accepting federal funds when those funds have an express condition that by their acceptance a state waives its sovereign immunity for those types of actions. Still, any ambiguity as to what has been waived is interpreted in favor of the states retaining their immunity from suit.

4.   Second, in *Ex parte Young*, 209 U.S. 123 (1908), the Supreme Court allowed a suit against a state officer that alleged he was acting

unconstitutionally. This was not a suit against the state, the Court reasoned, but against the officer in his personal capacity, because if he were violating the constitution, he could not be acting officially. This is called a "legal fiction," because if he were not acting officially, he could not violate the Constitution, inasmuch as the Constitution (generally) only restricts governments, not individuals. For example, if a suit alleged a state officer was depriving a person of equal protection of the laws, the officer would have to be acting in his capacity as an officer of the state to violate the Equal Protection Clause, because it prohibits only "states" from denying equal protection. Nevertheless, the doctrine of *Ex parte Young* enables persons to sue state officers to enjoin them from violating the Constitution or laws of the United States. The same theory holds true for federal officers, but it is generally not necessary, because the federal Administrative Procedure Act waives sovereign immunity for suits against federal agency actions alleging they have violated federal laws or the Constitution.

5.　　Third, as will be addressed in more detail later in this book, if Congress acts pursuant to its legislative authority under the Fourteenth Amendment, it may override state sovereign immunity and provide a federal judicial forum for enforcement of rights under the Fourteenth Amendment or laws passed pursuant thereto. *See Fitzpatrick v. Bitzer*, 427 U.S. 445 (1976). The Court flirted with the idea that Congress could override a state's sovereign immunity and create judicially enforceable federal rights pursuant to Congress's authorities under Article I, *see Pennsylvania v. Union Gas Co.*, 491 U.S. 1 (1989), but in *Seminole Tribe of Florida v. Florida*, 517 U.S. 44 (1996), the Court by a 5–4 vote held that Congress had no such power, relying on *Hans*.

6.　　Fourth, the Court has recognized an exception where states gave up their immunity from congressionally authorized suits pursuant to the "plan of the Constitution," as part of "the structure of the original Constitution itself." This has been characterized as "structural waiver" of immunity. This includes suits by the United States against a state or one state against another state. More recently, the Court has said that the Constitution's Bankruptcy Clause constituted a waiver by states of immunity to private suits pursuant to federal bankruptcy laws. *Central Va. Comm. College v. Katz*, 546 U.S. 356 (2006). In addition, the clauses authorizing Congress to raise and support an Army and Navy constitute a waiver by states of immunity from at least some laws passed by Congress under those clauses. *Torres* v. *Texas Dept. of Public Safety*, 142 S.Ct. 2455 (2022). Both of these later cases were controversial and decided by 5–4 votes.

7.　　Local governments, such as cities and counties, although subdivisions of the state, do not enjoy sovereign immunity in federal courts. On the other hand, state "agencies" do have sovereign immunity in federal courts. A state university, for example, is a state "agency."

8.　　In *Hans*, consider the interpretive methodology the Court uses. Is it textual? Originalist? Does it try to determine original intent? Is it an activist decision or is it judicially conservative? Is the Court enforcing the Constitution or its view of what the law should be?

9.   The Eleventh Amendment is a constitutional check on the judicial power of the United States, but unlike most of the other types of checks we have considered, which were checks and balances within and among the three branches of the federal government, the Eleventh Amendment reflects federalism concerns. It is a check on the federal judiciary vis à vis the states, as opposed to a check on judicial power vis à vis the legislative and executive branches.

CHAPTER 3

THE LEGISLATIVE POWER

■ ■ ■

In the last chapter, on the judicial power of the United States, we learned that the judicial power is the power to decide cases. Moreover, when necessary to decide those cases, the judicial power includes the power to review laws passed by Congress and acts performed by the executive branch, as well as laws and executive acts of states, in order to determine their lawfulness under the Constitution and laws of the United States. In this chapter we will explore the legislative power of the United States—both its extent and its limitations.

The power of Congress to make laws is largely contained in Article I, Section 8. We will begin with the canonical case of *McCulloch v. Maryland* dealing with the Necessary and Proper Clause, and then we will explore in some depth the case law regarding the Commerce Clause, which has received more judicial attention than any of the other powers of Congress to make laws. We will then consider the Taxing and Spending Clause and the power to implement treaties. After a consideration of certain limitations on the exercise of the powers of Congress under the Tenth Amendment, the chapter concludes with a section on the powers of Congress under the Fourteenth Amendment.

Much of what we read regarding the checks on the judicial power involved checks in favor of one of the political branches of the federal government—the legislative and executive branches. This reflects the horizontal separation of powers, but the genius (or flaw depending upon your perspective) of the Constitution is that it separates powers not only horizontally, but also vertically—between the federal government and state governments. In this chapter regarding the legislative powers, the focus is on this vertical separation, or what is also called "federalism."

A. THE NECESSARY AND PROPER CLAUSE

The following case involves a challenge to the constitutionality of the Bank of the United States, a bank chartered in 1816 pursuant to an act of Congress. The state of Maryland required any bank not chartered by the state to pay an annual tax of $15,000. The Bank of the United States was the only bank not chartered by the state, and it did not pay the required tax. James McCulloch was the "cashier" of the Baltimore branch of the Bank; today we would call him the branch manager or president. Maryland fined him $100 for circulating a bank note from a bank that was neither a

Maryland chartered bank nor a bank that had paid the required tax. He refused to pay, and Maryland brought an action in state court to collect the fine. Of course, from the beginning this case was not about the $100 or even the $15,000; it was about the power of Congress to charter this bank.

McCulloch defended on the grounds that the state law imposing the fee on the Bank of the United States was unconstitutional, and Maryland argued that because chartering a bank was beyond the enumerated powers of Congress, its law was not unconstitutional, and even if the bank was constitutional, Maryland could still enact this tax. The trial court found against McCulloch, and he appealed to the Maryland Court of Appeals, the highest state court, which affirmed the lower court, finding the Bank unconstitutional. McCulloch then appealed to the United States Supreme Court.

Alexander Hamilton

This Bank of the United States is often called the Second Bank of the United States, although it might as well be called the third bank of the United States. In 1781, during the Revolutionary War and under the Articles of Confederation, Finance Minister Robert Morris proposed to the Continental Congress that it charter a Bank of North America pursuant to a plan devised by the then 23-year-old Alexander Hamilton. Questions were raised as to the authority of the Continental Congress to charter the bank, but James Wilson, a member of the Congress, argued in support of it, and the bank was chartered and handled the financing of the rest of the Revolutionary War.

In the Constitutional Convention, there was consideration given to authorizing Congress to charter canal corporations—canals being probably the most important means of transportation across land—there already having been agreement to authorize Congress to make post roads.* Some delegates suggested expanding the authority to any corporations, but the first motion to authorize canal corporations was defeated, so the broader authorization was never again raised. Robert Morris and James Wilson, as well as Hamilton, were among the framers in Philadelphia.

Nevertheless, in 1791, as part of his financial plan, Secretary of the Treasury Alexander Hamilton proposed that Congress charter a Bank of the United States to serve as a central bank for the country. Congress debated the creation of a Bank of the United States. Madison argued

---

*   A "post road" was a road used for the purposes of transporting mail, although obviously it could be used for other purposes as well.

strongly against it, saying that the
Constitution did not authorize it, but Congress
passed the measure and sent it to the
President for signature. Washington then
asked both Hamilton and Thomas Jefferson,
the Secretary of State, for their views on the
constitutionality of the Bank. Jefferson
opposed the Bank on the grounds that the
Constitution did not specifically give Congress
such a power, and that under a limited
government, Congress had no powers other
than those explicitly given to it. Hamilton

Thomas Jefferson

responded by arguing that Congress had all powers except those
specifically denied to it in the Constitution, and that moreover, the
"necessary and proper" clause of Article I required a broad reading of the
specified powers. President Washington backed Hamilton, and the bank
was given a twenty-year charter. The charter expired in 1811, and
Madison, now President, and his party of Democratic-Republicans, did not
renew it.

Financial difficulties arising out of the War of 1812, however, led
members of his own party to propose a second Bank of the United States,
and while Madison vetoed a bill to create one in 1815, later the same year
even he became convinced of its desirability and asked Congress to create
one, which it did in 1816. The bank quickly established branches
throughout the Union. If there was agreement at the federal level for a
Bank of the United States, however, there was not necessarily agreement
at the state level, and a number of states adopted anti-Bank legislation, of
which the Maryland $15,000 annual fee was an example.

Today, it may not be clear why first the Democratic-Republicans and
later the states would oppose a Bank of the United States. What was the
big deal? First, one has to appreciate the political and cultural divide
between the merchants and the farmers. Merchants tended to be
Federalists, nationalists, and supportive of financial institutions that
would support a strong economy. Farmers tended to be Democratic-
Republicans, states-rightists, and suspicious of financial institutions
generally and centralized financial institutions especially. States whose
economies were predominantly merchant oriented, such as Massachusetts,
New York, and Pennsylvania, for example, were in the nationalist camp.
States whose economies were predominately farmer oriented tended in the
other direction. In addition, state chartered banks saw the Bank of the
United States as a competitor generally and a monopolist with respect to
federal funds. That is, the federal government would utilize only the Bank
of the United States, at the expense of the state banks, and the state banks
looked to their state for protection. Finally, as a matter of principle, states
regarded the chartering of a federal corporation, potentially immune from

its laws, as a serious imposition on their sovereignty. This latter point is not just an historical issue; in 2007 states objected to national banks' immunity from state banking laws designed to protect consumers, but the Supreme Court upheld the immunity of the national banks from state regulation. *See Watters v. Wachovia Bank*, 550 U.S. 1 (2007).

What does it mean for a bank to be chartered by the United States, as opposed to by a state? In both cases, the bank is a private, for-profit institution whose investors hope to make a profit. In the former case, the legal existence of the bank depends upon federal law, while in the latter case the legal existence of the bank depends upon state law. That is, for the bank, as an entity, to be able to make contracts, sue, make loans, etc., it must be recognized as a legal entity. In order to have rights and responsibilities under the law, one must be a legal entity. Natural persons are by nature legal entities, but organizations, in order to be a legal entity, must be recognized as such by the government.* The government that charters a corporation, whether bank or otherwise, also establishes the rules under which it must operate. Private persons owned 80% of the stock in the Bank of the United States at issue in the following case. The federal government owned the remainder.

Oral argument in the case extended over nine days. At the time, lawyers did not submit written briefs, so the lawyers' oral presentations were the Court's sole exposure to the arguments for the parties. Representing McCulloch were both the Attorney General of the United States and Daniel Webster, the most famous lawyer of his day. Representing Maryland was Luther Martin, the long-time Attorney General of Maryland and a member of the Constitutional Convention, who had earlier participated in the successful defense of former Vice President Aaron Burr on charges of treason.

McCULLOCH V. MARYLAND

United States Supreme Court, 1819.
4 Wheat. (17 U.S.) 316, 4 L.Ed. 579.

MARSHALL, CH. J., delivered the opinion of the court.

In the case now to be determined, the defendant, a sovereign state, denies the obligation of a law enacted by the legislature of the Union, and the plaintiff, on his part, contests the validity of an act which has been passed by the legislature of that state. . . .

---

* Today, virtually all corporations are created under state law, rather than federal law. Even the biggest, multi-national corporations, like Amazon, Apple, General Motors, and Exxon, are creatures of state, rather than federal, law. They are, of course, regulated by federal law in various ways, but their existence derives from state law. For reasons you will learn when you take a course in Business Associations or Corporations, most big American corporations are creatures of Delaware law. For years, Ralph Nader lobbied to have corporations that do business nationally or internationally be incorporated (or in other words chartered) by the federal government, rather than by state governments. His lobbying on this issue was singularly unsuccessful.

The first question made in the cause is—has congress power to incorporate a bank? It has been truly said, that this can scarcely be considered as an open question, entirely unprejudiced by the former proceedings of the nation respecting it. The principle now contested was introduced at a very early period of our history, has been recognized by many successive legislatures, and has been acted upon by the judicial department, in cases of peculiar delicacy, as a law of undoubted obligation.

It will not be denied, that a bold and daring usurpation might be resisted, after an acquiescence still longer and more complete than this. But it is conceived that a doubtful question, one on which human reason may pause, and the human judgment be suspended, in the decision of which the great principles of liberty are not concerned, but the respective powers of those who are equally the representatives of the people are to be adjusted, if not put at rest by the practice of the government, ought to receive a considerable impression from that practice. An exposition of the constitution, deliberately established by legislative acts, on the faith of which an immense property has been advanced, ought not to be lightly disregarded.

The power now contested was exercised by the first congress elected under the present constitution. The bill for incorporating the Bank of the United States did not steal upon an unsuspecting legislature, and pass unobserved. Its principle was completely understood, and was opposed with equal zeal and ability. After being resisted, first, in the fair and open field of debate, and afterwards, in the executive cabinet, with as much persevering talent as any measure has ever experienced, and being supported by arguments which convinced minds as pure and as intelligent as this country can boast, it became a law. The original act was permitted to expire; but a short experience of the embarrassments to which the refusal to revive it exposed the government, convinced those who were most prejudiced against the measure of its necessity, and induced the passage of the present law. It would require no ordinary share of intrepidity, to assert that a measure adopted under these circumstances, was a bold and plain usurpation, to which the constitution gave no countenance. These observations belong to the cause; but they are not made under the impression, that, were the question entirely new, the law would be found irreconcilable with the constitution. . . .

This government is acknowledged by all, to be one of enumerated powers. . . . But the question respecting the extent of the powers actually granted, is perpetually arising, and will probably continue to arise, so long as our system shall exist. In discussing these questions, the conflicting powers of the general and state governments must be brought into view, and the supremacy of their respective laws, when they are in opposition, must be settled. . . .

Among the enumerated powers, we do not find that of establishing a bank or creating a corporation. But there is no phrase in the instrument which, like the articles of confederation, excludes incidental or implied powers; and which requires that everything granted shall be expressly and minutely described. Even the 10th amendment, which was framed for the purpose of quieting the excessive jealousies which had been excited, omits the word "expressly," and declares only, that the powers "not delegated to the United States, nor prohibited to the states, are reserved to the states or to the people;" thus leaving the question, whether the particular power which may become the subject of contest, has been delegated to the one government, or prohibited to the other, to depend on a fair construction of the whole instrument. The men who drew and adopted this amendment had experienced the embarrassments resulting from the insertion of this word ["expressly"] in the articles of confederation, and probably omitted it, to avoid those embarrassments. A constitution, to contain an accurate detail of all the subdivisions of which its great powers will admit, and of all the means by which they may be carried into execution, would partake of the prolixity of a legal code, and could scarcely be embraced by the human mind. It would, probably, never be understood by the public. Its nature, therefore, requires, that only its great outlines should be marked, its important objects designated, and the minor ingredients which compose those objects, be deduced from the nature of the objects themselves. That this idea was entertained by the framers of the American constitution, is not only to be inferred from the nature of the instrument, but from the language. Why else were some of the limitations, found in the 9th section of the 1st article, introduced? It is also, in some degree, warranted, by their having omitted to use any restrictive term which might prevent its receiving a fair and just interpretation. In considering this question, then, we must never forget that it is a constitution we are expounding.

Although, among the enumerated powers of government, we do not find the word "bank" or "incorporation," we find the great powers, to lay and collect taxes; to borrow money; to regulate commerce; to declare and conduct a war; and to raise and support armies and navies. The sword and the purse, all the external relations, and no inconsiderable portion of the industry of the nation, are intrusted to its government. It can never be pretended, that these vast powers draw after them others of inferior importance, merely because they are inferior. Such an idea can never be advanced. But it may with great reason be contended, that a government, intrusted with such ample powers, on the due execution of which the happiness and prosperity of the nation so vitally depends, must also be intrusted with ample means for their execution. The power being given, it is the interest of the nation to facilitate its execution. It can never be their interest, and cannot be presumed to have been their intention, to clog and embarrass its execution, by withholding the most appropriate means. Throughout this vast republic, from the St. Croix to the Gulf of Mexico, from the Atlantic to the Pacific, revenue is to be collected and expended, armies are to be marched and supported. The exigencies of the nation may require, that the treasure raised in the north should be transported to the south, that raised in the east, conveyed to the west, or that this order should be reversed. Is that construction of the constitution to be preferred, which would render these operations difficult, hazardous and expensive? Can we adopt that construction (unless the words imperiously require it), which would impute to the framers of that instrument, when granting these powers for the public good, the intention of impeding their exercise, by withholding a choice of means? If, indeed, such be the mandate of the constitution, we have only to obey; but that instrument does not profess to enumerate the means by which the powers it confers may be executed; nor does it prohibit the creation of a corporation, if the existence of such a being be essential, to the beneficial exercise of those powers. It is, then, the subject of fair inquiry, how far such means may be employed.

It is not denied, that the powers given to the government imply the ordinary means of execution. That, for example, of raising revenue, and applying it to national purposes, is admitted to imply the power of conveying money from place to place, as the exigencies of the nation may require, and of employing the usual means of conveyance. But it is denied, that the government has its choice of means; or, that it may employ the most convenient means, if, to employ them, it be necessary to erect a corporation. On what foundation does this argument rest? On this alone: the power of creating a corporation, is one appertaining to sovereignty, and is not expressly conferred on congress. This is true. But all legislative powers appertain to sovereignty. The original power of giving the law on any subject whatever, is a sovereign power; and if the government of the Union is restrained from creating a corporation, as a means for performing its functions, on the single reason that the creation of a corporation is an act of sovereignty; if the sufficiency of this reason be acknowledged, there would be some difficulty in sustaining the authority of congress to pass other laws for the accomplishment of the same objects. The government which has a right to do an act, and has imposed on it, the duty of performing that act, must, according to the dictates of reason, be allowed to select the means; and those who contend that it may not select any appropriate means, that one particular mode of effecting the object is excepted, take upon themselves the burden of establishing that exception.

The creation of a corporation, it is said, appertains to sovereignty. This is admitted. But to what portion of sovereignty does it appertain? Does it belong to one more than to another? In America, the powers of sovereignty are divided between the government of the Union, and those of the states. They are each sovereign, with respect to the objects committed to it, and neither sovereign, with respect to the objects committed to the other. . . . The power of creating a corporation, though appertaining to sovereignty, is not, like the power of making war, or levying taxes, or of regulating commerce, a great substantive and independent power, which cannot be implied as incidental to other powers, or used as a means of executing them. It is never the end for which other powers are exercised, but a means by which other objects are accomplished. . . . The power of creating a corporation is never used for its own sake, but for the purpose of effecting something else. No sufficient reason is, therefore, perceived, why it may not pass as incidental to those powers which are expressly given, if it be a direct mode of executing them.

But the constitution of the United States has not left the right of congress to employ the necessary means, for the execution of the powers conferred on the government, to general reasoning. To its enumeration of powers is added, that of making "all laws which shall be necessary and proper, for carrying into execution the foregoing powers, and all other powers vested by this constitution, in the government of the United States, or in any department thereof." The counsel for the state of Maryland have urged various arguments, to prove that this clause, though, in terms, a grant of power, is not so, in effect; but is really restrictive of the general right, which might otherwise be implied, of selecting means for executing the enumerated powers. . . .

[T]he argument on which most reliance is placed, is drawn from that peculiar language of this clause. Congress is not empowered by it to make all laws, which may have relation to the powers conferred on the government, but such only as may be "necessary and proper" for carrying them into execution. The word "necessary" is considered as controlling the whole sentence, and as limiting the right to pass laws for the execution of the granted powers, to such as are indispensable, and without which the power would be nugatory. That it excludes the choice of means, and leaves to congress, in each case, that only which is most direct and simple.

Is it true, that this is the sense in which the word "necessary" is always used? Does it always import an absolute physical necessity, so strong, that one thing to which another may be termed necessary, cannot exist without that other? We think it does not. If reference be had to its use, in the common affairs of the world, or in approved authors, we find that it frequently imports no more than that one thing is convenient, or useful, or essential to another. To employ the means necessary to an end, is generally understood as employing any means calculated to produce the end, and not as being confined to those single means, without which the end would be entirely unattainable. Such is the character of human language, that no word conveys to the mind, in all situations, one single definite idea; and nothing is more common than to use words in a figurative sense. . . . The word "necessary" is of this description. It has not a fixed character, peculiar to itself. It admits of all degrees of comparison; and is often connected with other words, which increase or diminish the impression the mind receives of the urgency it imports. A thing may be necessary, very necessary, absolutely or indispensably necessary. To no mind would the same idea be conveyed by these several phrases. The comment on the word is well illustrated by the . . . 10th section of the 1st article of the constitution. It is, we think, impossible to compare the sentence which prohibits a state from laying "imposts, or duties on imports or exports, except what may be absolutely necessary for executing its inspection laws," with that which authorizes congress "to make all laws which shall be necessary and proper for carrying into execution" the powers of the general government, without feeling a conviction, that the convention understood itself to change materially the meaning of the word "necessary," by prefixing the word "absolutely." This word, then, like others, is used in various senses; and, in its construction, the subject, the context, the intention of the person using them, are all to be taken into view.

Let this be done in the case under consideration. The subject is the execution of those great powers on which the welfare of a nation essentially depends. It must have been the intention of those who gave these powers, to insure, so far as human prudence could insure, their beneficial execution. This could not be done, by confiding the choice of means to such narrow limits as not to leave it in the power of congress to adopt any which might be appropriate, and which were conducive to the end. This provision is made in a constitution, intended to endure for ages to come, and consequently, to be adapted to the various crises of human affairs. To have prescribed the means by which government should, in all future time, execute its powers, would have been to change, entirely, the character of the instrument, and give it the properties of a legal code. It would have been an unwise attempt to provide, by immutable rules, for exigencies which, if foreseen at all, must have been seen dimly, and which can be best provided for as they occur. To have declared, that the best means shall not be used, but those alone, without which the power given would be nugatory, would have been to deprive the legislature of the capacity to avail itself of experience, to exercise its reason, and to accommodate its legislation to circumstances. . . .

Take, for example, the power "to establish post-offices and post-roads." This power is executed, by the single act of making the establishment. But, from this has been inferred the power and duty of carrying the mail along the post-road, from one post-office to another. And from this implied power, has again been inferred the right to punish those who steal letters from the post-office, or rob the mail. It may be said, with some plausibility, that the right to carry the mail, and to punish those who rob it, is not indispensably necessary to the establishment of a post-office and post-road. . . .

If the word "necessary" means "needful," "requisite," "essential," "conducive to," in order to let in the power of punishment for the infraction of law; why is it not equally comprehensive, when required to authorize the use of means which facilitate the execution of the powers of government, without the infliction of punishment? . . .

But the argument which most conclusively demonstrates the error of the construction contended for by the counsel for the state of Maryland [that the clause is a limitation on Congress's powers] is founded on the intention of the convention, as manifested in the whole clause. . . .

1st. The clause is placed among the powers of congress, not among the limitations on those powers. 2d. Its terms purport to enlarge, not to diminish the powers vested in the government. It purports to be an additional power, not a restriction on those already granted. No reason has been, or can be assigned, for thus concealing an intention to narrow the discretion of the national legislature, under words which purport to enlarge it. . . .

The result of the most careful and attentive consideration bestowed upon this clause is, that if it does not enlarge, it cannot be construed to restrain the powers of congress, or to impair the right of the legislature to exercise its best judgment in the selection of measures to carry into execution the constitutional powers of the government. If no other motive for its insertion can be suggested, a sufficient one is found in the desire to remove all doubts respecting the right to legislate on that vast mass of incidental powers which must be involved in the constitution, if that instrument be not a splendid bauble.

We admit, as all must admit, that the powers of the government are limited, and that its limits are not to be transcended. But we think the sound construction of the constitution must allow to the national legislature that discretion, with respect to the means by which the powers it confers are to be carried into execution, which will enable that body to perform the high duties assigned to it, in the manner most beneficial to the people. Let the end be legitimate, let it be within the scope of the constitution, and all means which are appropriate, which are plainly adapted to that end, which are not prohibited, but consist with the letter and spirit of the constitution, are constitutional.

That a corporation must be considered as a means not less usual, not of higher dignity, not more requiring a particular specification than other means, has been sufficiently proved. If we look to the origin of corporations, to the manner in which they have been framed in that government from which we have derived most of our legal principles and ideas, or to the uses to which they have been applied, we find no reason to suppose, that a constitution, omitting, and wisely omitting, to enumerate all the means for carrying into execution the great powers vested in government, ought to have specified this. Had it been intended to grant this power, as one which should be distinct and independent, to be exercised in any case whatever, it would have found a place among the enumerated powers of the government. But being considered merely as a means, to be employed only for the purpose of carrying into execution the given powers, there could be no motive for particularly mentioning it. . . .

If a corporation may be employed, indiscriminately with other means, to carry into execution the powers of the government, no particular reason can be assigned for excluding the use of a bank, if required for its fiscal operations. To use one must be within the discretion of congress, if it be an appropriate mode of executing the powers of government. That it is a convenient, a useful, and essential instrument in the prosecution of its fiscal operations, is not now a subject of controversy. All those who have been concerned in the administration of our finances, have concurred in representing its importance and necessity; and so strongly have they been felt, that statesmen of the first class, whose previous opinions against it had been confirmed by every circumstance which can fix the human judgment, have yielded those opinions to the exigencies of the nation. . . .

But were its necessity less apparent, none can deny its being an appropriate measure; and if it is, the decree of its necessity, as has been very justly observed, is to be discussed in another place. Should congress, in the execution of its powers, adopt measures which are prohibited by the constitution; or should congress, under the pretext of executing its powers, pass laws for the accomplishment of objects not intrusted to the government; it would become the painful duty of this tribunal, should a case requiring such a decision come before it, to say, that such an act was not the law of the land. But where the law is not prohibited, and is really calculated to effect any of the objects intrusted to the government, to undertake here to inquire into the decree of its necessity, would be to pass the line which circumscribes the judicial department, and to tread on legislative ground. This court disclaims all pretensions to such a power.

After this declaration, it can scarcely be necessary to say, that the existence of state banks can have no possible influence on the question. No trace is to be found in the constitution, of an intention to create a dependence of the government of the Union on those of the states, for the execution of the great powers assigned to it. Its means are adequate to its ends; and on those means alone was it expected to rely for the accomplishment of its ends. To impose on it the necessity of resorting to means which it cannot control, which another government may furnish or withhold, would render its course precarious, the result of its measures uncertain, and create a dependence on other governments, which might disappoint its most important designs, and is incompatible with the language of the constitution. But were it otherwise, the choice of means implies a right to choose a national bank in preference to state banks, and congress alone can make the election.

After the most deliberate consideration, it is the unanimous and decided opinion of this court, that the act to incorporate the Bank of the

United States is a law made in pursuance of the constitution, and is a part of the supreme law of the land. . . .

It being the opinion of the court, that the act incorporating the bank is constitutional; and that the power of establishing a branch in the state of Maryland might be properly exercised by the bank itself, we proceed to inquire—2. Whether the state of Maryland may, without violating the constitution, tax that branch?

[T]hat the power to tax involves the power to destroy; that the power to destroy may defeat and render useless the power to create; that there is a plain repugnance in conferring on one government a power to control the constitutional measures of another, which other, with respect to those very measures, is declared to be supreme over that which exerts the control, are propositions not to be denied. . . . This was not intended by the American people. They did not design to make their government dependent on the states.

COMMENTS AND QUESTIONS

1.   In many ways Marshall's opinion for the Court is a response to the original objections by Madison and Jefferson, and in that response established an expansive rather than restricted view of the Constitution's grants of authority to Congress.

2.   Recognize how the interests and arguments align. That is, Maryland argues for a narrow interpretation of the federal constitutional powers in order to preserve its own powers and prerogatives. The federal government argues for a broad interpretation to advance its own powers and prerogatives. Thus, this case is all about federalism.

3.   How does Marshall justify that "necessary" does not really mean "necessary"?

4.   How is it that a Bank of the United States facilitates the carrying into execution any of the specified powers of the United States?

5.   Marshall's statement that "we must never forget that it is a constitution we are expounding" has often been cited. What did he mean? How would this concept apply to Article III's description of the Supreme Court's original jurisdiction, or to the First Amendment?

6.   Clearly, Marshall's formulation of congressional power is expansive. What limitations on when the "necessary and proper" clause would authorize congressional action does he find in the Constitution?

7.   It is really not relevant to anything, but for constitutional trivia you may be interested to learn that McCulloch was later convicted for embezzling money from the Bank.

8.   In recent years, the Necessary and Proper Clause has played an important role in several cases. For example, *Gonzales v. Raich*, 545 U.S. 1 (2005), asked whether Congress had the power to prohibit the cultivation and

use of home-grown marijuana for medicinal purposes as authorized by state law. Justice Scalia's concurrence in the judgment upholding the law relied on the Necessary and Proper Clause. In his view, "[w]here necessary to make a regulation of interstate commerce effective, Congress may regulate even those intrastate activities that do not themselves substantially affect interstate commerce." In order to eliminate any interstate market in marijuana, it was necessary to eliminate not only any intrastate market but also activities likely to induce an intrastate market, such as simple possession of marijuana. In *United States v. Comstock*, 560 U.S. 126 (2010), a federal law provided for the civil commitment of persons in federal prisons who had served their criminal sentences but who were determined to have engaged in sexually violent conduct or child abuse and to be mentally ill and as a result of that illness would be sexually dangerous to others. The question was what constitutional authority justified that law. With only Justices Scalia and Thomas dissenting, the Court held that the Necessary and Proper Clause was that authority. The Court viewed the civil commitment of these prisoners who would otherwise be released to be justified on the same basis that escaped prisoners could be captured and returned to prison. In the case challenging the Affordable Care Act (otherwise known as Obamacare), *National Fed. of Ind. Business v. Sebelius*, 567 U.S. 519 (2012), the government tried to justify the individual mandate (the requirement that all persons have medical insurance) in part under the Necessary and Proper Clause, saying that it was a necessary means by which to regulate commerce in health care when persons could not be denied insurance coverage for pre-existing conditions. Otherwise, persons would simply wait until they were sick to obtain health insurance, driving insurance premiums sky high. A majority of the Court rejected the argument. We will see why later. Finally, in *United States v. Kebodeaux*, 570 U.S. 387 (2013), the Court relied on the Necessary and Proper Clause to uphold a registration requirement for persons convicted of federal sex offenses, because having to register would create a further disincentive to commit the underlying offense.

B. THE COMMERCE CLAUSE

As indicated earlier, the bulk of this chapter involves a close examination of the Court's jurisprudence under the Commerce Clause. It is presented in a chronological fashion from the earliest to the latest Court cases. Think of it as a journey through time. Like a journey, it reflects twists and turns, not a straight line. There are "good" cases and "bad" cases as viewed through our eyes today. The last cases in this section reflect "current law," but this is a journey that is not finished, and to perceive where we may be going, it is well to see where we have been.

1. THE FOUNDATIONS

Recall that the absence of the power to regulate commerce under the Articles of Confederation was one of the primary motivations for the Philadelphia Convention, and that under the Articles states engaged in trade wars. The mere ratification of the Constitution did not end those

A replica of Fulton's original steamboat

problems. The case that follows, the first Commerce Clause case, reflects the situation. The state of New York granted a monopoly to Robert Fulton (who invented the steamboat according to American history) and Robert Livingston, his financial backer, to operate steamboats within the state. They in turn had assigned this right to Aaron Ogden, presumably for a handsome sum. Granting monopoly rights to an entrepreneur to encourage investment in an enterprise is something that was frequently done at the time and still is done in certain situations. Thus, no one could operate a steamboat in New York without a license from Ogden. Operation without such a license could lead to forfeiture of the boat.

At the same time, Connecticut, interested in supporting its own steamboat fleet, prohibited anyone possessing a license from Fulton and Livingston from operating a steamboat in its waters. New Jersey had a law creating treble damages for any New Jersey citizen against any person who restrained the New Jersey citizen from operating a steamboat in New York.

Thomas Gibbons, who had a federal license to engage in "the coasting trade," began operating a steamboat between New York City and New Jersey. Ogden sought an injunction from the New York state courts prohibiting Gibbons from operating his steamboats in New York state. The New York courts granted the injunction, and Gibbons appealed to the United States Supreme Court.

GIBBONS V. OGDEN

United States Supreme Court, 1824.
9 Wheat. (22 U.S.) 1, 6 L.Ed. 23.

MR. CHIEF JUSTICE MARSHALL delivered the opinion of the Court, and, after stating the case, proceeded as follows:

The appellant contends that this decree is erroneous, because the laws which purport to give the exclusive privilege it sustains, are repugnant to the constitution and laws of the United States. . . .

The words are, "Congress shall have power to regulate commerce with foreign nations, and among the several States, and with the Indian tribes."

The subject to be regulated is commerce; and our constitution being, as was aptly said at the bar, one of enumeration, and not of definition, to ascertain the extent of the power, it becomes necessary to settle the meaning of the word. The counsel for the appellee would limit it to traffic, to buying and selling, or the interchange of commodities, and do not admit that it comprehends navigation. . . .

If commerce does not include navigation, the government of the Union has no direct power over that subject, and can make no law prescribing what shall constitute American vessels, or requiring that they shall be navigated by American seamen. Yet this power has been exercised from the commencement of the government, has been exercised with the consent of all, and has been understood by all to be a commercial regulation. All America understands, and has uniformly understood, the word "commerce," to comprehend navigation. It was so understood, and must have been so understood, when the constitution was framed. The power over commerce, including navigation, was one of the primary objects for which the people of America adopted their government, and must have been contemplated in forming it. The convention must have used the word in that sense, because all have understood it in that sense; and the attempt to restrict it comes too late. . . .

The word used in the constitution, then, comprehends, and has been always understood to comprehend, navigation within its meaning; and a power to regulate navigation, is as expressly granted, as if that term had been added to the word "commerce."

To what commerce does this power extend? The constitution informs us, to commerce "with foreign nations, and among the several States, and with the Indian tribes."

It has, we believe, been universally admitted, that these words comprehend every species of commercial intercourse between the United States and foreign nations. No sort of trade can be carried on between this country and any other, to which this power does not extend. It has been truly said, that commerce, as the word is used in the constitution, is a unit, every part of which is indicated by the term.

If this be the admitted meaning of the word, in its application to foreign nations, it must carry the same meaning throughout the sentence, and remain a unit, unless there be some plain intelligible cause which alters it.

The subject to which the power is next applied, is to commerce "among the several States." The word "among" means intermingled with. A thing which is among others, is intermingled with them. Commerce among the States, cannot stop at the external boundary line of each State, but may be introduced into the interior.

It is not intended to say that these words comprehend that commerce, which is completely internal, which is carried on between man and man in a State, or between different parts of the same State, and which does not extend to or affect other States. Such a power would be inconvenient, and is certainly unnecessary.

Comprehensive as the word "among" is, it may very properly be restricted to that commerce which concerns more States than one. The phrase is not one which would probably have been selected to indicate the completely interior traffic of a State, because it is not an apt phrase for that purpose; and the enumeration of the particular classes of commerce, to which the power was to be extended, would not have been made, had the intention been to extend the power to every description. The enumeration presupposes something not enumerated; and that something, if we regard the language or the subject of the sentence, must be the exclusively internal commerce of a State. The genius and character of the whole government seem to be, that its action is to be applied to all the external concerns of the nation, and to those internal concerns which affect the States generally; but not to those which are completely within a particular State, which do not affect other States, and with which it is not necessary to interfere, for the purpose of executing some of the general powers of the government. The completely internal commerce of a State, then, may be considered as reserved for the State itself.

But, in regulating commerce with foreign nations, the power of Congress does not stop at the jurisdictional lines of the several States. It would be a very useless power, if it could not pass those lines. The commerce of the United States with foreign nations, is that of the whole United States. Every district has a right to participate in it. The deep streams which penetrate our country in every direction, pass through the interior of almost every State in the Union, and furnish the means of exercising this right. If Congress has the power to regulate it, that power must be exercised whenever the subject exists. If it exists within the States, if a foreign voyage may commence or terminate at a port within a State, then the power of Congress may be exercised within a State.

This principle is, if possible, still more clear, when applied to commerce "among the several States." They either join each other, in which case they are separated by a mathematical line, or they are remote from each other, in which case other States lie between them. . . . Commerce among the States must, of necessity, be commerce with the States. . . . The power of Congress, then, whatever it may be, must be exercised within the territorial jurisdiction of the several States. . . .

We are now arrived at the inquiry—What is this power?

It is the power to regulate; that is, to prescribe the rule by which commerce is to be governed. This power, like all others vested in Congress, is complete in itself, may be exercised to its utmost extent, and acknowledges no limitations, other than are prescribed in the constitution. . . . If, as has always been understood, the sovereignty of Congress, though limited to specified objects, is plenary as to those objects, the power over commerce with foreign nations, and among the several States, is vested in Congress as absolutely as it would be in a single government, having in its constitution the same restrictions on the exercise of the power as are found in the constitution of the United States. The wisdom and the discretion of Congress, their identity with the people, and the influence which their constituents possess at elections, are, in this, as in many other instances, as that, for example, of declaring war, the sole restraints on which they have relied, to secure them from its abuse. They are the restraints on which the people must often rely solely, in all representative governments.

The power of Congress, then, comprehends navigation, within the limits of every State in the Union; so far as that navigation may be, in any manner, connected with "commerce with foreign nations, or among the several States, or with the Indian tribes." It may, of consequence, pass the jurisdictional line of New York, and act upon the very waters to which the prohibition now under consideration applies.

But it has been urged with great earnestness, that, although the power of Congress to regulate commerce with foreign nations, and among the several States, be co-extensive with the subject itself, and have no other limits than are prescribed in the constitution, yet the States may severally exercise the same power, within their respective jurisdictions. . . .

In discussing the question, whether this power is still in the States, in the case under consideration, we may dismiss from it the inquiry, whether it is surrendered by the mere grant to Congress, or is retained until Congress shall exercise the power. We may dismiss that inquiry, because it has been exercised, and the regulations which Congress deemed it proper to make, are now in full operation. . . .

[T]he State of New York cannot prevent an enrolled and licensed vessel, proceeding from Elizabethtown, in New Jersey, to New York, from enjoying, in her course, and on her entrance into port, all the privileges conferred by the act of Congress. . . . To the Court it seems very clear, that the whole act on the subject of the coasting trade, according to those principles which govern the construction of statutes, implies, unequivocally, an authority to licensed vessels to carry on the coasting trade. . . .

COMMENTS AND QUESTIONS

1.   While Chief Justice Marshall's language may sometimes be difficult to decipher, the case seems hardly a difficult one. If Congress could not regulate the interstate transportation of passengers by steamboat, the Commerce Clause would have accomplished little. It does not take a nationalist like Marshall to see the necessity of this outcome. Nevertheless, the effect of the case is to seriously diminish the sovereignty of New York state. It no longer can further its domestic industries by establishing monopolies with respect to

industries engaged in interstate commerce, at least if Congress does not agree. Imagine that today Congress enacted a law authorizing persons to import toys from China. Would a state be able to ban toys dangerous to children if they came from China?

2.   In a portion of *Gibbons v. Ogden* that has been edited out here, Marshall discusses what had been a major point of argument before the Court: that the New York law was unconstitutional even if Gibbons had not had a license to engage in the coastal trade. Indeed, one justice concurred with the Court on the basis of that argument. We will address that issue later in this book, when we deal with something called the "dormant Commerce Clause."

THE DANIEL BALL*
United States Supreme Court, 1870.
77 U.S. 557, 19 L.Ed. 999.

The steamboat Sultana explodes,
killing 1700 passengers

[This is another steamboat case. Steamboats were, of course, an important invention, providing the first mechanical means of propulsion, significantly reducing the time required to transport people and goods by ship. Steamboats work by using steam under pressure to drive pistons, which then drive the propeller or paddle wheel. Steam under pressure, however, can be very dangerous, and in the early days boiler explosions occurred all too often, and the effects were disastrous, rapidly sinking the boats and killing large numbers of passengers and crew. As a result, beginning in 1833, the federal government passed laws regulating boilers used on steamboats engaged in commerce on navigable waters of the United States and requiring their regular inspection. Failure to comply with this law would subject the owners to substantial penalties.

In March, 1868, the Daniel Ball, a one hundred and twenty-three ton steamboat, was engaged in the transportation of merchandise and passengers on the Grand River, in the State of Michigan, between the cities of Grand Rapids and Grand Haven, without having been inspected or licensed under the laws of the United States. The United States filed suit to impose a penalty. The answer of the owners, who appeared in the case, admitted the employment of the steamer as alleged, but set up as a defense that the Grand River was not a navigable water of the United States, and that the steamer was engaged solely in domestic trade and commerce, and

---

*   Note that this case is not entitled *someone v. someone*. It is what is known as an *in rem* action, in which the plaintiff, here the United States, proceeds directly against an object alleged to be in violation of the law, here the good ship Daniel Ball.

was not engaged in trade or commerce between two or more States, or in any trade by reason of which she was subject to the navigation laws of the United States, or was required to be inspected and licensed. It was conceded that the Daniel Ball only operated between the two cities in Michigan and never left the state. It was also conceded that some of the goods that she loaded at Grand Rapids and carried to Grand Haven were destined and marked for places in other states than Michigan, and that some of the goods which she loaded at Grand Haven came from other states and were destined for places within Michigan. Finally, it was also conceded that the Grand River connected to other waters (in particular Lake Michigan), which enabled vessels to travel interstate. The district court dismissed the suit on the basis that the federal law, as applied to the Daniel Ball, was beyond the powers of Congress under the Commerce Clause. The circuit court reversed, and appeal was taken to the Supreme Court.]

MR. JUSTICE FIELD, after stating the case, delivered the opinion of the court, as follows:

Two questions are presented in this case for our determination.

First: Whether the steamer was at the time . . . engaged in transporting merchandise and passengers on a navigable water of the United States within the meaning of the acts of Congress; and,

Second: Whether those acts are applicable to a steamer engaged as a common carrier between places in the same State, when a portion of the merchandise transported by her is destined to places in other States, or comes from places without the State, she not running in connection with or in continuation of any line of steamers or other vessels, or any railway line leading to or from another State.

Upon the first of these questions we entertain no doubt. . . . [A test must] be applied to determine the navigability of our rivers, and that is found in their navigable capacity. Those rivers must be regarded as public navigable rivers in law which are navigable in fact. And they are navigable in fact when they are used, or are susceptible of being used, in their ordinary condition, as highways for commerce, over which trade and travel are or may be conducted in the customary modes of trade and travel on water. And they constitute navigable waters of the United States within the meaning of the acts of Congress, in contradistinction from the navigable waters of the States, when they form in their ordinary condition by themselves, or by uniting with other waters, a continued highway over which commerce is or may be carried on with other States or foreign countries in the customary modes in which such commerce is conducted by water.

If we apply this test to Grand River, the conclusion follows that it must be regarded as a navigable water of the United States. From the conceded facts in the case the stream is capable of bearing a steamer of one hundred and twenty-three tons burden, laden with merchandise and passengers, as far as Grand Rapids, a distance of forty miles from its mouth in Lake Michigan. And by its junction with the lake it forms a continued highway for commerce, both with other States and with foreign countries, and is thus brought under the direct control of Congress in the exercise of its commercial power.

That power authorizes all appropriate legislation for the protection or advancement of either interstate or foreign commerce, and for that purpose such legislation as will insure the convenient and safe navigation of all the navigable waters of the United States, whether that legislation consists in requiring the removal of obstructions to their use, in prescribing the form and size of the vessels employed upon them, or in subjecting the vessels to inspection and license, in order to insure their proper construction and equipment. . . .

But it is contended that the steamer Daniel Ball was only engaged in the internal commerce of the State of Michigan, and was not, therefore, required to be inspected or licensed, even if it be conceded that Grand River is a navigable water of the United States; and this brings us to the consideration of the second question presented.

There is undoubtedly an internal commerce which is subject to the control of the States. The power delegated to Congress is limited to commerce "among the several States," with foreign nations, and with the Indian tribes. This limitation necessarily excludes from Federal control all commerce not thus designated, and of course that commerce which is carried on entirely within the limits of a State, and does not extend to or affect other States.[7] In this case it is admitted that the steamer was engaged in shipping and transporting down Grand River, goods destined and marked for other States than Michigan, and in receiving and transporting up the river goods brought within the State from without its limits; but inasmuch as her agency in the transportation was entirely within the limits of the State, and she did not run in connection with, or in continuation of, any line of vessels or railway leading to other States, it is contended that she was engaged entirely in domestic commerce. But this conclusion does not follow. So far as she was employed in transporting goods destined for other States, or goods brought from without the limits of Michigan and destined to places within that State, she was engaged in commerce between the States, and however limited that commerce may have been, she was, so far as it went, subject to the legislation of Congress. She was employed as an instrument of that commerce; for whenever a commodity has begun to move as an article of trade from one State to another, commerce in that commodity between the States has commenced. The fact that several different and independent agencies are employed in transporting the commodity, some acting entirely in one State, and some

---

[7]   Gibbons v. Ogden, 9 Wheat. (22 U.S.) 1, 194 (1824).

acting through two or more States, does in no respect affect the character of the transaction. To the extent in which each agency acts in that transportation, it is subject to the regulation of Congress.

It is said that if the position here asserted be sustained, there is no such thing as the domestic trade of a State; that Congress may take the entire control of the commerce of the country, and extend its regulations to the railroads within a State on which grain or fruit is transported to a distant market.

We answer that the present case relates to transportation on the navigable waters of the United States, and we are not called upon to express an opinion upon the power of Congress over interstate commerce when carried on by land transportation. And we answer further, that we are unable to draw any clear and distinct line between the authority of Congress to regulate an agency employed in commerce between the States, when that agency extends through two or more States, and when it is confined in its action entirely within the limits of a single State. If its authority does not extend to an agency in such commerce, when that agency is confined within the limits of a State, its entire authority over interstate commerce may be defeated. Several agencies combining, each taking up the commodity transported at the boundary line at one end of a State, and leaving it at the boundary line at the other end, the Federal jurisdiction would be entirely ousted, and the constitutional provision would become a dead letter.

COMMENTS AND QUESTIONS

1.   The Court begins by posing two questions. When it concludes that the Grand River is a "navigable water of the United States," what is the consequence of that decision in terms of the powers of Congress over that water?

2.   With respect to the second question, how is it that regulating the Daniel Ball is regulating commerce among the states, when the Daniel Ball never leaves Michigan? Is it even necessary that the Daniel Ball was on "navigable waters of the United States"?

3.   Even if the Daniel Ball were traveling between states, how is regulating a boiler on the ship and requiring its inspection regulating "commerce among the states"? Would it be more accurate to say that regulating the boiler and requiring its inspection are necessary and proper to regulating commerce?

4.   The owners of the Daniel Ball argue that, if Congress can regulate things that occur totally within a state simply because they involve in some way goods traveling in interstate commerce, there would be no limit on Congress's power. What do you think? Could Congress set the standards for the safety equipment on your bicycle because you sometimes carry items that

came from out-of-state? And if it could, it could preclude the state from setting a different standard.

2. THE PROGRESSIVE ERA

The Progressive Era in American history spans roughly 1890–1920. Progressives supported women's suffrage, the temperance movement (banning alcohol), government regulation of business, legislation to restrict labor exploitation generally, but particularly of women and children, and increasing citizen participation in government through the enactment of initiative and referendum provisions in state constitutions. The judicial response to Progressive measures depended upon the orientation of the Court.

The Sherman Antitrust Act of 1890 was one piece of Progressive legislation arising from the emergence of great monopolies (or trusts) of industrial companies, such as John D. Rockefeller's Standard Oil Company that controlled virtually all oil refining in the United States. Under the Act, the creation of these monopolies was made unlawful. In 1892, Henry Havemeyer, who controlled the American Sugar Refining Company, which then owned 65% of all the sugar refining capacity in the United States, undertook to buy four of the five remaining independent sugar refineries, which would give it 98% control. The United States sued both the American Sugar Refining Company and the four independent refineries to set aside the sales under the authority of the Sherman Antitrust Act. One of those independent refineries was the E.C. Knight Co.

UNITED STATES V. E.C. KNIGHT CO.

United States Supreme Court, 1895.
156 U.S. 1, 15 S.Ct. 249.

MR. CHIEF JUSTICE FULLER . . . delivered the opinion of the court.

[T]he fundamental question is whether, conceding that the existence of a monopoly in manufacture is established by the evidence, that monopoly can be directly suppressed under the act of congress in the mode attempted by this bill.

It cannot be denied that the power of a state to protect the lives, health, and property of its citizens, and to preserve good order and the public morals, "the power to govern men and things within the limits of its dominion,"* is a power originally and always belonging to the states, not surrendered by them to the general government, nor directly restrained by the constitution of the United States, and essentially exclusive. The relief of the citizens of each state from the burden of monopoly and the evils

---

* This power is known as the "police power"—the power to place restraints on personal freedom and property rights for the protection of the safety, health, welfare, and morals of the community. It is an inherent power of the state that arises out of sovereignty. It does not refer to the officers of the law that we today call "the police." [author's note]

resulting from the restraint of trade among such citizens was left with the states to deal with. . . . On the other hand, the power of congress to regulate commerce among the several states is also exclusive. "Commerce undoubtedly is traffic," said Chief Justice Marshall, "but it is something more; it is intercourse. It describes the commercial intercourse between nations and parts of nations in all its branches, and is regulated by prescribing rules for carrying on that intercourse." That which belongs to commerce is within the jurisdiction of the United States, but that which does not belong to commerce is within the jurisdiction of the police power of the state.

The argument is that the power to control the manufacture of refined sugar is a monopoly over a necessary of life, to the enjoyment of which by a large part of the population of the United States interstate commerce is indispensable, and that, therefore, the general government, in the exercise of the power to regulate commerce, may repress such monopoly directly, and set aside the instruments which have created it. But this argument cannot be confined to necessaries of life merely, and must include all articles of general consumption. Doubtless the power to control the manufacture of a given thing involves, in a certain sense, the control of its disposition, but this is a secondary, and not the primary, sense; and, although the exercise of that power may result in bringing the operation of commerce into play, it does not control it, and affects it only incidentally and indirectly. Commerce succeeds to manufacture, and is not a part of it. The power to regulate commerce is the power to prescribe the rule by which commerce shall be governed, and is a power independent of the power to suppress monopoly. But it may operate in repression of monopoly whenever that comes within the rules by which commerce is governed, or whenever the transaction is itself a monopoly of commerce.

It is vital that the independence of the commercial power and of the police power, and the delimitation between them, however sometimes perplexing, should always be recognized and observed, for, while the one furnishes the strongest bond of union, the other is essential to the preservation of the autonomy of the states as required by our dual form of government; and acknowledged evils, however grave and urgent they may appear to be, had better be borne, than the risk be run, in the effort to suppress them, of more serious consequences by resort to expedients of even doubtful constitutionality.

It will be perceived how far-reaching the proposition is that the power of dealing with a monopoly directly may be exercised by the general government whenever interstate or international commerce may be ultimately affected. The regulation of commerce applies to the subjects of commerce, and not to matters of internal police. Contracts to buy, sell, or exchange goods to be transported among the several states, the transportation and its instrumentalities, and articles bought, sold, or exchanged for the purposes of such transit among the states, or put in the way of transit, may be regulated; but this is because they form part of interstate trade or commerce. The fact that an article is manufactured for export to another state does not of itself make it an article of interstate commerce, and the intent of the manufacturer does not determine the time when the article or product passes from the control of the state and belongs to commerce. . . . There must be a point of time when they cease to be governed exclusively by the domestic law, and begin to be governed and protected by the national law of commercial regulation; and that moment seems to us to be a legitimate one for this purpose in which they commence their final movement from the state of their origin to that of their destination.

"[N]o distinction is more popular to the common mind, or more clearly expressed in economic and political literature, than that between manufacture and commerce. Manufacture is transformation,—the fashioning of raw materials into a change of form for use. The functions of commerce are different. The buying and selling, and the transportation incidental thereto, constitute commerce; and the regulation of commerce in the constitutional sense embraces the regulation at least of such transportation. * * * If it be held that the term includes the regulation of all such manufactures as are intended to be the subject of commercial transactions in the future, it is impossible to deny that it would also include all productive industries that contemplate the same thing. The result would be that congress would be invested, to the exclusion of the states, with the power to regulate, not only manufactures, but also agriculture, horticulture, stock-raising, domestic fisheries, mining; in short, every branch of human industry. For is there one of them that does not contemplate, more or less clearly, an interstate or foreign market? Does not the wheat grower of the Northwest, and the cotton planter of the South, plant, cultivate, and harvest his crop with an eye on the prices at Liverpool, New York, and Chicago? The power being vested in congress and denied to the states, it would follow as an inevitable result that the duty would devolve on congress to regulate all of these delicate, multiform, and vital interests,—interests which in their nature are, and must be, local in all the details of their successful management. . . ."

Contracts, combinations, or conspiracies to control domestic enterprise in manufacture, agriculture, mining, production in all its forms, or to raise or lower prices or wages, might unquestionably tend to restrain external as well as domestic trade, but the restraint would be an indirect result, however inevitable. . . . Slight reflection will show that, if the national power extends to all contracts and combinations in manufacture, agriculture, mining, and other productive industries, whose ultimate result may affect external commerce, comparatively little of business operations and affairs would be left for state control. . . .

MR. JUSTICE HARLAN, dissenting.

In its consideration of the important constitutional question presented this court assumes on the record before us that the result of the transactions disclosed by the pleadings and proof was the creation of a monopoly in the manufacture of a necessary of life. If this combination, so far as its operations necessarily or directly affect interstate commerce, cannot be restrained or suppressed under some power granted to congress, it will be cause for regret that the patriotic statesmen who framed the constitution did not foresee the necessity of investing the national government with power to deal with gigantic monopolies holding in their grasp, and injuriously controlling in their own interest, the entire trade among the states in food products that are essential to the comfort of every household in the land.

John Marshall Harlan

President Rutherford B. Hayes appointed Harlan to the Supreme Court in 1877. From Kentucky, Harlan had been a slave owner and a defender of slavery prior to the Civil War, but he supported maintaining the Union and became an officer in the Union Army. After the war, he became a Republican and repudiated his earlier support of slavery. He is known as the "Great Dissenter" because of his dissents in *Plessy v. Ferguson*, which established the doctrine of "separate but equal" to support segregation, the *Civil Rights Cases*, which narrowly construed the Fourteenth Amendment, and *Lochner v. New York*, which limited the ability of government to regulate labor conditions.

The court holds it to be vital in our system of government to recognize and give effect to both the commercial power of the nation and the police powers of the states, to the end that the Union be strengthened, and the autonomy of the states preserved. In this view I entirely concur. Undoubtedly, the preservation of the just authority of the states is an object of deep concern to every lover of his country. . . . But it is equally true that the preservation of the just authority of the general government is essential as well to the safety of the states as to the attainment of the important ends for which that government was ordained by the people of the United States; and the destruction of that authority would be fatal to the peace and well-being of the American people. The constitution, which enumerates the powers committed to the nation for objects of interest to the people of all the states, should not, therefore, be subjected to an interpretation so rigid, technical, and narrow that those objects cannot be accomplished. . . .

COMMENTS AND QUESTIONS

1. Why was the United States unable to regulate the monopolization of the manufacture of sugar?

2.   Do you think *E.C. Knight* and *The Daniel Ball* are consistent in their approaches to the Commerce Clause?

3.   Note that in *The Daniel Ball* the Court rejects the argument that if the United States could regulate the Daniel Ball, it could regulate anything, but in *E.C. Knight* the Court accepts the argument that if Congress could regulate manufacture because it might end up in interstate commerce, it could regulate anything. Why is it concerned about whether Congress can regulate anything or everything? Is it a concern for regulation, or is it a concern about who can regulate? Recall that the inability of Congress to regulate manufacture does not prevent the ability of the states to regulate it.

CHAMPION V. AMES (LOTTERY CASE)
United States Supreme Court, 1903.
188 U.S. 321, 23 S.Ct. 321.

MR. JUSTICE HARLAN delivered the opinion of the court:

The general question arising upon this appeal involves the constitutionality of the 1st section of the act of Congress . . . entitled An Act for the Suppression of Lottery Traffic through National and Interstate Commerce and the Postal Service, Subject to the Jurisdiction and Laws of the United States. . . .

The 1st section of the act 1895 . . . is as follows:

§ 1. That any person who shall cause to be brought within the United States from abroad, for the purpose of disposing of the same, or deposited in or carried by the mails of the United States, or carried from one state to another in the United States, any paper, certificate, or instrument purporting to be or represent a ticket, chance, share, or interest in or dependent upon the event of a lottery, . . . or similar enterprise, offering prizes dependent upon lot or chance . . . shall be punishable [for] the first offense by imprisonment for not more than two years, or by a fine of not more than $1,000, or both, and in the second and after offenses by such imprisonment only.

[Charles Champion was arrested for conspiracy to commit this offense by shipping] from Dallas, in the state of Texas, to Fresno, in the state of California, certain papers, certificates, and instruments purporting to be and representing tickets, as [he] then and there well knew, chances, shares, and interests in and dependent upon the event of a lottery, offering prizes dependent upon lot and chance. . . . [He sued for a writ of habeas corpus, arguing that the law was beyond the power of Congress.]

The appellant insists that the carrying of lottery tickets from one state to another state by an express company engaged in carrying freight and packages from state to state, although such tickets may be contained in a box or package, does not constitute, and cannot by any act of Congress be legally made to constitute, commerce among the states within the meaning of the clause of the Constitution of the United States providing that Congress shall have power "to regulate commerce with foreign nations, and among the several states, and with the Indian tribes;" consequently, that Congress cannot make it an offense to cause such tickets to be carried from one state to another.

The government insists that express companies, when engaged, for hire, in the business of transportation from one state to another, are instrumentalities of commerce among the states; that the carrying of lottery tickets from one state to another is commerce which Congress may regulate; and that as a means of executing the power to regulate interstate commerce Congress may make it an offense against the United States to cause lottery tickets to be carried from one state to another. . . .

What is the import of the word "commerce" as used in the Constitution? It is not defined by that instrument. Undoubtedly, the carrying from one state to another by independent carriers of things or commodities that are ordinary subjects of traffic, and which have in themselves a recognized value in money, constitutes interstate commerce. But does not commerce among the several states include something more? Does not the carrying from one state to another, by independent carriers, of lottery tickets that entitle the holder to the payment of a certain amount of money therein specified, also constitute commerce among the states?

[The Court reviewed its past decisions interpreting the Commerce Clause, concluding that the transporting lottery tickets would be commerce within the meaning of the Clause.]

This reference to prior adjudications could be extended if it were necessary to do so. The cases cited, however, sufficiently indicate the grounds upon which this court has proceeded when determining the meaning and scope of the commerce clause. They show that commerce among the states embraces navigation, intercourse, communication, traffic, the transit of persons, and the transmission of messages by telegraph. They also show that the power to regulate commerce among the several states is vested in Congress as absolutely as it would be in a single government, having in its constitution the same restrictions on the exercise of the power as are found in the Constitution of the United States; that such power is plenary, complete in itself, and may be exerted by Congress to its utmost extent, subject only to such limitations as the Constitution imposes upon the exercise of the powers granted by it. . . .

We come, then, to inquire whether there is any solid foundation upon which to rest the contention that Congress may not regulate the carrying of lottery tickets from one state to another, at least by corporations or companies whose business it is, for hire, to carry tangible property from one state to another. . . .

But it is said that the statute in question does not regulate the carrying of lottery tickets from state to state, but by punishing those who cause them to be so carried Congress in effect prohibits such carrying; that . . . the authority given Congress was not to prohibit, but only to regulate. This view was earnestly pressed at the bar by learned counsel, and must be examined.

It is to be remarked that the Constitution does not define what is to be deemed a legitimate regulation of interstate commerce. In *Gibbons v. Ogden* it was said that the power to regulate such commerce is the power to prescribe the rule by which it is to be governed. But this general observation leaves it to be determined, when the question comes before the court, whether Congress, in prescribing a particular rule, has exceeded its power under the Constitution. . . .

We have said that the carrying from state to state of lottery tickets constitutes interstate commerce, and that the regulation of such commerce is within the power of Congress under the Constitution. Are we prepared to say that a provision which is, in effect, a prohibition of the carriage of such articles from state to state is not a fit or appropriate mode for the regulation of that particular kind of commerce? If lottery traffic, carried on through interstate commerce, is a matter of which Congress may take cognizance and over which its power may be exerted, can it be possible that it must tolerate the traffic, and simply regulate the manner in which it may be carried on? Or may not Congress, for the protection of the people of all the states, and under the power to regulate interstate commerce, devise such means, within the scope of the Constitution, and not prohibited by it, as will drive that traffic out of commerce among the states?

In determining whether regulation may not under some circumstances properly take the form or have the effect of prohibition, the nature of the interstate traffic which it was sought by the act of May 2d, 1895, to suppress cannot be overlooked. When enacting that statute Congress no doubt shared the views upon the subject of lotteries heretofore expressed by this court. [A]fter observing that the suppression of nuisances injurious to public health or morality is among the most important duties of government, this court said: "Experience has shown that the common forms of gambling are comparatively innocuous when placed in contrast with the widespread pestilence of lotteries. The former are confined to a few persons and places, but the latter infests the whole community; it enters every dwelling; it reaches every class; it preys upon the hard earnings of the poor; it plunders the ignorant and simple.". . . .

If a state, when considering legislation for the suppression of lotteries within its own limits, may properly take into view the evils that inhere in the raising of money, in that mode, why may not Congress, invested with the power to regulate commerce among the several states, provide that such commerce shall not be polluted by the carrying of lottery tickets from one state to another? In this connection it must not be forgotten that the power of Congress to regulate commerce among the states is plenary, is complete in itself, and is subject to no limitations except such as may be found in the Constitution. What provision in that instrument can be regarded as limiting the exercise of the power granted? What clause can be cited which, in any degree, countenances the suggestion that one may, of right, carry or cause to be carried from one state to another that which will harm the public morals? . . .

Besides, Congress, by that act, does not assume to interfere with traffic or commerce in lottery tickets carried on exclusively within the limits of any state, but has in view only commerce of that kind among the several states. It has not assumed to interfere with the completely internal affairs of any state, and has only legislated in respect of a matter which concerns the people of the United States. As a state may, for the purpose of guarding the morals of its own people, forbid all sales of lottery tickets within its limits, so Congress, for the purpose of guarding the people of the United States against the "widespread pestilence of lotteries" and to protect the commerce which concerns all the states, may prohibit the carrying of lottery tickets from one state to another. In legislating upon the subject of the traffic in lottery tickets, as carried on through interstate commerce, Congress only supplemented the action of those states—perhaps all of them—which, for the protection of the public morals, prohibit the drawing of lotteries, as well as the sale or circulation of lottery tickets, within their respective limits. It said, in effect, that it would not permit the declared policy of the states, which sought to protect their people against the mischiefs of the lottery business, to be overthrown or disregarded by the agency of interstate commerce. . . .

That regulation may sometimes appropriately assume the form of prohibition is also illustrated by the case of diseased cattle, transported from one state to another. Such cattle may have, notwithstanding their condition, a value in money for some purposes, and yet it cannot be doubted that Congress, under its power to regulate commerce, may either provide for their being inspected before transportation begins, or, in its discretion, may prohibit their being transported from one state to another. . . .

It is said, however, that if, in order to suppress lotteries carried on through interstate commerce, Congress may exclude lottery tickets from such commerce, that principle leads necessarily to the conclusion that Congress may arbitrarily exclude from commerce among the states any article, commodity, or thing, of whatever kind or nature, or however useful or valuable, which it may choose, no matter with what motive, to declare shall not be carried from one state to another. It will be time enough to consider the constitutionality of such legislation when we must do so. The present case does not require the court to declare the full extent of the power that Congress may exercise in the regulation of commerce among the states. We may, however, repeat, in this connection, what the court has heretofore said, that the power of Congress to regulate commerce among the states, although plenary, cannot be deemed arbitrary, since it is subject to such limitations or restrictions as are prescribed by the Constitution. . . . But, as often said, the possible abuse of a power is not an argument against its existence. There is probably no governmental power that may not be exerted to the injury of the public. If what is done by Congress is manifestly in excess of the powers granted to it, then upon the courts will rest the duty of adjudging that its action is neither legal nor binding upon the people. But if what Congress does is within the limits of its power, and is simply unwise or injurious, the remedy is that suggested by Chief Justice Marshall in *Gibbons v. Ogden*, when he said: "The wisdom and the discretion of Congress, their identity with the people, and the influence which their constituents possess at elections, are, in this, as in many other instances, as that, for example, of declaring war, the sole restraints on which they have relied, to secure them from its abuse. They are the restraints on which the people must often rely solely, in all representative governments." . . .

MR. CHIEF JUSTICE FULLER, with whom concur MR. JUSTICE BREWER, MR. JUSTICE SHIRAS, and MR. JUSTICE PECKHAM, dissenting:

[T]he naked question is whether the prohibition by Congress of the carriage of lottery tickets from one state to another by means other than the mails is within the powers vested in that body by the Constitution of the United States. That the purpose of Congress in this enactment was the suppression of lotteries cannot reasonably be denied. That purpose is avowed in the title of the act, and is its natural and reasonable effect, and by that its validity must be tested.

The power of the state to impose restraints and burdens on persons and property in conservation and promotion of the public health, good order, and prosperity is a power originally and always belonging to the states, not surrendered by them to the general government, nor directly restrained by the Constitution of the United States, and essentially exclusive, and the suppression of lotteries as a harmful business falls within this power, commonly called, of police.*

It is urged, however, that because Congress is empowered to regulate commerce between the several states, it, therefore, may suppress lotteries by prohibiting the carriage of lottery matter. Congress may, indeed, make all laws necessary and proper for carrying the powers granted to it into execution, and doubtless an act prohibiting the carriage of lottery matter would be necessary and proper to the execution of a power to suppress lotteries; but that power belongs to the states and not to Congress. To hold that Congress has general police power would be to hold that it may

---

* Recall that the "police power" is the power to place restraints on the personal freedom and property rights for the protection of the safety, health, welfare, and morals of the community. It does not refer to the officers of the law that we today call "the police." [author's note]

accomplish objects not intrusted to the general government, and to defeat the operation of the 10th Amendment, declaring that "the powers not delegated to the United States by the Constitution, nor prohibited by it to the states, are reserved to the states respectively, or to the people." . . .

But apart from the question of bona fides, this act cannot be brought within the power to regulate commerce among the several states, unless lottery tickets are articles of commerce, and, therefore, when carried across state lines, of interstate commerce; or unless the power to regulate interstate commerce includes the absolute and exclusive power to prohibit the transportation of anything or anybody from one state to another. . . . [The opinion then argues that lottery tickets are not articles of commerce.]

If a lottery ticket is not an article of commerce, how can it become so when placed in an envelope or box or other covering, and transported by an express company? To say that the mere carrying of an article which is not an article of commerce in and of itself nevertheless becomes such the moment it is to be transported from one state to another, is to transform a non-commercial article into a commercial one simply because it is transported. I cannot conceive that any such result can properly follow.

It would be to say that everything is an article of commerce the moment it is taken to be transported from place to place, and of interstate commerce if from state to state.

An invitation to dine, or to take a drive, or a note of introduction, all become articles of commerce under the ruling in this case, by being deposited with an express company for transportation. This in effect breaks down all the differences between that which is, and that which is not, an article of commerce, and the necessary consequence is to take from the states all jurisdiction over the subject so far as interstate communication is concerned. It is a long step in the direction of wiping out all traces of state lines, and the creation of a centralized government.

Does the grant to Congress of the power to regulate interstate commerce import the absolute power to prohibit it? . . .

It will not do to say—a suggestion which has heretofore been made in this case—that state laws have been found to be ineffective for the suppression of lotteries, and therefore Congress should interfere. The scope of the commerce clause of the Constitution cannot be enlarged because of present views of public interest. . . .

COMMENTS AND QUESTIONS

1.   This is a close case, 5–4, but why is it a close case? What is it that leads four justices to say that the law is beyond the power of Congress under the Commerce Clause?

2.   Prior to the Constitution, the "police power" resided in the states, not the United States. The dissent maintains that the Constitution did not alter

the placement of the police power and that only the states have the police power—nothing in Article I, Section 8 grants Congress any police power. What do you think?

3.   What do you think of the majority's argument that Congress needed to pass this law in order to protect those states that wished to ban lotteries, because absent this law it would be difficult to suppress lotteries in states? What do you think of the dissent's response?

4.   Is the dissent correct that if Congress can regulate the carriage of lottery tickets across state lines, it can regulate the carriage of anything across state lines, and if that is so, the notion of a federal government of limited powers would be destroyed?

5.   Two years later the Court decided another case that broadened the scope of the Commerce Clause. In *Swift & Co. v. United States*, 196 U.S. 375 (1905), the Court upheld the constitutionality of an application of the Sherman Antitrust Act against meat dealers. Recall that in *E.C. Knight Co.*, ten years before, the Court had found the application of the Sherman Antitrust Act against sugar manufacturers was beyond Congress's power. The Court in an opinion by Justice Oliver Wendell Holmes distinguished *E.C. Knight* as involving something occurring wholly within a state—manufacture—but here the combination was between sellers of meat. While sales of meat might occur only within a state,

> [w]hen cattle are sent for sale from a place in one state, with the expectation that they will end their transit, after purchase, in another, and when in effect they do so, with only the interruption necessary to find a purchaser at the stock yards, and when this is a typical, constantly recurring course, the current thus existing is a current of commerce among the states, and the purchase of the cattle is a part and incident of such commerce.

196 U.S. at 398–99. This "current of commerce" became a "stream of commerce" in a later case, *Stafford v. Wallace*, 258 U.S. 495 (1922). There the Court said:

> The application of the commerce clause of the Constitution in the *Swift Case* was the result of the natural development of interstate commerce under modern conditions. It was the inevitable recognition of the great central fact that such streams of commerce from one part of the country to another, which are ever flowing, are in their very essence the commerce among the states and with foreign nations, which historically it was one of the chief purposes of the Constitution to bring under national protection and control. This court declined to defeat this purpose in respect of such a stream and take it out of complete national regulation by a nice and technical inquiry into the noninterstate character of some of its necessary incidents and facilities, when considered alone and without reference to their association with the movement of which they were an essential but subordinate part.

258 U.S. at 518–19. Thus, if something occurred in the "stream of commerce," it was subject to national regulation under the Commerce Clause even if the actual matter regulated only occurred within a state. Does this remind you at all of *Gibbons v. Ogden? The Daniel Ball?*

HAMMER V. DAGENHART (CHILD LABOR CASE)
United States Supreme Court, 1918.
247 U.S. 251, 38 S.Ct. 529.

MR. JUSTICE DAY delivered the opinion of the Court.

A bill was filed in the United States District Court for the Western District of North Carolina by a father in his own behalf and as next friend of his two minor sons, one under the age of fourteen years and the other between the ages of fourteen and sixteen years, employees in a cotton mill at Charlotte, North Carolina, to enjoin the enforcement of the act of Congress intended to prevent interstate commerce in the products of child labor.

The District Court held the act unconstitutional and entered a decree enjoining its enforcement. This appeal brings the case here. . . .

The controlling question for decision is: Is it within the authority of Congress in regulating commerce among the states to prohibit the transportation in interstate commerce of manufactured goods, the product of a factory in which, within thirty days prior to their removal therefrom, children under the age of fourteen have been employed or permitted to work, or children between the ages of fourteen and sixteen years have been employed or permitted to work more than eight hours in any day, or more than six days in any week, or after the hour of 7 o'clock p. m., or before the hour of 6 o'clock a. m.?

Children working in a cotton mill

The power essential to the passage of this act, the government contends, is found in the commerce clause of the Constitution which authorizes Congress to regulate commerce with foreign nations and among the states.

In *Gibbons v. Ogden*, Chief Justice Marshall, speaking for this court, and defining the extent and nature of the commerce power, said, "It is the power to regulate; that is, to prescribe the rule by which commerce is to be governed." In other words, the power is one to control the means by which commerce is carried on, which is directly the contrary of the assumed right to forbid commerce from moving and thus destroying it as to particular commodities. But it is insisted that adjudged cases in this court establish the doctrine that the power to regulate given to Congress incidentally includes the authority to prohibit the movement of ordinary commodities and therefore that the subject is not open for discussion. The cases demonstrate the contrary. They rest upon the character of the particular subjects dealt with and the fact that the scope of governmental authority, state or national, possessed over them is such that the authority to prohibit is as to them but the exertion of the power to regulate.

The first of these cases is *Champion v. Ames*, the so-called *Lottery Case*, in which it was held that Congress might pass a law having the effect to keep the channels of commerce free from use in the transportation of tickets used in the promotion of lottery schemes. In *Hipolite Egg Co. v. United States*, 220 U. S. 45 (1911), this court sustained the power of Congress to pass the Pure Food and Drug Act, which prohibited the introduction into the states by means of interstate commerce of impure foods and drugs. In *Hoke v. United States*, 227 U. S. 308 (1913), this court sustained the constitutionality of the so-called "White Slave Traffic Act," whereby the transportation of a woman in interstate commerce for the purpose of prostitution was forbidden. . . . In *Caminetti v. United States*, 242 U. S. 470 (1917), we held that Congress might prohibit the transportation of women in interstate commerce for the purposes of debauchery and kindred purposes. In *Clark Distilling Co. v. Western Maryland Railway Co.*, 242 U. S. 311 (1917), the power of Congress over the transportation of intoxicating liquors was sustained. . . . And concluding the discussion which sustained the authority of the Government to prohibit the transportation of liquor in interstate commerce, the court said: "* * * The exceptional nature of the subject here regulated is the basis upon which the exceptional power exerted must rest and affords no ground for any fear that such power may be constitutionally extended to things which it may not, consistently with the guaranties of the Constitution embrace."

In each of these instances the use of interstate transportation was necessary to the accomplishment of harmful results. In other words, although the power over interstate transportation was to regulate, that could only be accomplished by prohibiting the use of the facilities of interstate commerce to effect the evil intended.

This element is wanting in the present case. The thing intended to be accomplished by this statute is the denial of the facilities of interstate commerce to those manufacturers in the states who employ children within the prohibited ages. The act in its effect does not regulate transportation among the states, but aims to standardize the ages at which children may be employed in mining and manufacturing within the states. The goods shipped are of themselves harmless. The act permits them to be freely shipped after thirty days from the time of their removal from the factory. When offered for shipment, and before transportation begins, the labor of their production is over, and the mere fact that they were intended for interstate commerce transportation does not make their production subject to federal control under the commerce power.

Commerce "consists of intercourse and traffic * * * and includes the transportation of persons and property, as well as the purchase, sale and exchange of commodities." The making of goods and the mining of coal are not commerce, nor does the fact that these things are to be afterwards shipped, or used in interstate commerce, make their production a part thereof.

Over interstate transportation, or its incidents, the regulatory power of Congress is ample, but the production of articles, intended for interstate commerce, is a matter of local regulation.... If it were otherwise, all manufacture intended for interstate shipment would be brought under federal control to the practical exclusion of the authority of the states, a result certainly not contemplated by the framers of the Constitution when they vested in Congress the authority to regulate commerce among the States.

It is further contended that the authority of Congress may be exerted to control interstate commerce in the shipment of childmade goods because of the effect of the circulation of such goods in other states where the evil of this class of labor has been recognized by local legislation, and the right to thus employ child labor has been more rigorously restrained than in the state of production. In other words, that the unfair competition, thus engendered, may be controlled by closing the channels of interstate commerce to manufacturers in those states where the local laws do not meet what Congress deems to be the more just standard of other states.

There is no power vested in Congress to require the states to exercise their police power so as to prevent possible unfair competition. Many causes may co-operate to give one state, by reason of local laws or conditions, an economic advantage over others. The commerce clause was not intended to give to Congress a general authority to equalize such conditions. In some of the states laws have been passed fixing minimum wages for women, in others the local law regulates the hours of labor of women in various employments. Business done in such states may be at an economic disadvantage when compared with states which have no such regulations; surely, this fact does not give Congress the power to deny transportation in interstate commerce to those who carry on business where the hours of labor and the rate of compensation for women have not been fixed by a standard in use in other states and approved by Congress.

The grant of power of Congress over the subject of interstate commerce was to enable it to regulate such commerce, and not to give it authority to control the states in their exercise of the police power over local trade and manufacture.

The grant of authority over a purely federal matter was not intended to destroy the local power always existing and carefully reserved to the states in the Tenth Amendment to the Constitution. . . .

That there should be limitations upon the right to employ children in mines and factories in the interest of their own and the public welfare, all will admit. That such employment is generally deemed to require regulation is shown by the fact that the brief of counsel states that every state in the Union has a law upon the subject, limiting the right to thus employ children. In North Carolina, the state wherein is located the factory in which the employment was had in the present case, no child under twelve years of age is permitted to work.

It may be desirable that such laws be uniform, but our federal government is one of enumerated powers; "this principle," declared Chief Justice Marshall in *McCulloch v. Maryland*, "is universally admitted."

A statute must be judged by its natural and reasonable effect. The control by Congress over interstate commerce cannot authorize the exercise of authority not entrusted to it by the Constitution. The maintenance of the authority of the states over matters purely local is as essential to the preservation of our institutions as is the conservation of the supremacy of the federal power in all matters entrusted to the nation by the federal Constitution.

In interpreting the Constitution it must never be forgotten that the nation is made up of states to which are entrusted the powers of local government. And to them and to the people the powers not expressly delegated to the national government are reserved. The power of the states to regulate their purely internal affairs by such laws as seem wise to the local authority is inherent and has never been surrendered to the general government. To sustain this statute would not be in our judgment a recognition of the lawful exertion of congressional authority over interstate commerce, but would sanction an invasion by the federal power of the control of a matter purely local in its character, and over which no authority has been delegated to Congress in conferring the power to regulate commerce among the states. . . .

In our view the necessary effect of this act is, by means of a prohibition against the movement in interstate commerce of ordinary commercial commodities to regulate the hours of labor of children in factories and mines within the states, a purely state authority. Thus the act in a two-fold sense is repugnant to the Constitution. It not only transcends the authority delegated to Congress over commerce but also exerts a power as to a purely local matter to which the federal authority does not extend. The far reaching result of upholding the act cannot be more plainly indicated than by pointing out that if Congress can thus regulate matters entrusted to local authority by prohibition of the movement of commodities in interstate commerce, all freedom of commerce will be at an end, and the power of the states over local matters may be eliminated, and thus our system of government be practically destroyed.

For these reasons we hold that this law exceeds the constitutional authority of Congress.

MR. JUSTICE HOLMES, dissenting.

The single question in this case is whether Congress has power to prohibit the shipment in interstate or foreign commerce of any product of a cotton mill situated in the United States, in which within thirty days before the removal of the product children under fourteen have been employed, or children between fourteen and sixteen have been employed more than eight hours in a day, or more than six days in any week, or between seven in the evening and six in the morning. The objection urged against the power is that the States have exclusive control over their methods of production and that Congress cannot meddle with them, and taking the proposition in the sense of direct intermeddling I agree to it and suppose that no one denies it. But if an act is within the powers specifically conferred upon Congress, it seems to me that it is not made any less constitutional because of the indirect effects that it may have, however obvious it may be that it will have those effects, and that we are not at liberty upon such grounds to hold it void.

The first step in my argument is to make plain what no one is likely to dispute—that the statute in question is within the power expressly given to Congress if considered only as to its immediate effects and that if invalid it is so only upon some collateral ground. The statute confines itself to prohibiting the carriage of certain goods in interstate or foreign commerce. Congress is given power to

Oliver Wendell Holmes, Jr.
Theodore Roosevelt appointed Holmes to the Court in 1902 when he was 61 years old and where he served until 1932, when he was 91. An uncommonly strong writer, Holmes is notable both for a number of his dissents and his decisions for the Court. He expressed a view of judicial restraint in construing the legislative powers of Congress and the states during the Progressive era, while believing in an active judiciary to protect rights enumerated in the Bill of Rights. His dissents in particular have virtually all been vindicated by later decisions of the Court. Later, during the New Deal, however, he joined the majority in finding various New Deal laws unconstitutional.

regulate such commerce in unqualified terms. It would not be argued today that the power to regulate does not include the power to prohibit. Regulation means the prohibition of something, and when interstate commerce is the matter to be regulated I cannot doubt that the regulation may prohibit any part of such commerce that Congress sees fit to forbid. At all events it is established by the *Lottery Case* and others that have followed it that a law is not beyond the regulative power of Congress merely because it prohibits certain transportation out and out. So I repeat that this statute in its immediate operation is clearly within the Congress's constitutional power.

The question then is narrowed to whether the exercise of its otherwise constitutional power by Congress can be pronounced unconstitutional because of its possible reaction upon the conduct of the States in a matter upon which I have admitted that they are free from direct control. I should have thought that that matter had been disposed of so fully as to leave no room for doubt. . . .

The notion that prohibition is any less prohibition when applied to things now thought evil I do not understand. But if there is any matter upon which civilized countries have agreed—far more unanimously than they have with regard to intoxicants and some other matters over which this country is now emotionally aroused—it is the evil of premature and excessive child labor. I should have thought that if we were to introduce our own moral conceptions where is my opinion they do not belong, this was preeminently a case for upholding the exercise of all its powers by the United States.

But I had thought that the propriety of the exercise of a power admitted to exist in some cases was for the consideration of Congress alone and that this Court always had disavowed the right to intrude its judgment upon questions of policy or morals. It is not for this Court to pronounce when prohibition is necessary to regulation if it ever may be necessary—to say that it is permissible as against strong drink but not as against the product of ruined lives.

The Act does not meddle with anything belonging to the States. They may regulate their internal affairs and their domestic commerce as they like. But when they seek to send their products across the State line they are no longer within their rights. If there were no Constitution and no Congress their power to cross the line would depend upon their neighbors. Under the Constitution such commerce belongs not to the States but to Congress to regulate. It may carry out its views of public policy whatever indirect effect they may have upon the activities of the States. Instead of being encountered by a prohibitive tariff at her boundaries the State encounters the public policy of the United States which it is for Congress to express. The public policy of the United States is shaped with a view to the benefit of the nation as a whole. If, as has been the case within the memory of men still living, a State should take a different view of the propriety of sustaining a lottery from that which generally prevails, I cannot believe that the fact would require a different decision from that reached in *Champion v. Ames*. Yet in that case it would be said with quite as much force as in this that Congress was attempting to intermeddle with the State's domestic affairs. The national welfare as understood by Congress may require a different attitude within its sphere from that of some self-seeking State. It seems to me entirely constitutional for Congress to enforce its understanding by all the means at its command.

MR. JUSTICE MCKENNA, MR. JUSTICE BRANDEIS, and MR. JUSTICE CLARKE concur in this opinion.

COMMENTS AND QUESTIONS

1.   Between the *Lottery Case* and the *Child Labor Case*, six justices had been replaced. Nevertheless, the closeness of the case remained, but this time with the majority finding the law beyond Congress's powers. Is this case consistent with the *Lottery Case*? How does the majority in the *Child Labor Case* distinguish the *Lottery Case*?

2.   Do you agree with the majority that if Congress could regulate the shipment across state lines of goods from factories employing child labor, it could regulate anything, destroying the notion of limited federal powers?

3.   What limit on Congress's power does Holmes envision?

4.   Do you think Congress's power to "regulate" includes the power to "prohibit"?

5.   Should Congress be able in effect to override a state's considered judgment with respect to the working conditions in a state? Should Congress be able to override some states' views in order to eliminate their competitive advantage over other states that have chosen a different view on the appropriate working conditions?

3. THE NEW DEAL

The Progressive era stalled in the tumultuous period of the Twenties, with its celebration of the modern and the exuberance of an expansive post-war economy after World War I. A succession of Republican presidents and congresses took a hands-off approach to business and social issues while engaged in a concerted repression of socialists and communists at both national and state levels. The Great Depression, initiated by the stock market crash in 1929, resulted in a political upheaval. In 1932 Franklin Roosevelt was elected President with the promise of a New Deal, and he was supported by Democratic majorities in the House and Senate. The Court, however, reflected the past, with seven of the nine justices appointed by a Republican president, and it demonstrated its hostility to New Deal legislation by its consistent rulings against the constitutionality

of the various acts designed to ameliorate or overcome the Great
Depression. The Court's conservative approach to the Commerce Clause
reflected in the *Child Labor Case* continued into the New Deal. In 1935 the
Court invalidated two New Deal laws on Commerce Clause grounds. In
Railroad Retirement Bd. v. Alton R. Co., 295 U.S. 330 (1935) the Court
found the Railroad Retirement Act, which established a mandatory
retirement and pension program for railroads, beyond Congress's
Commerce Clause authority. In *A.L.A. Schechter Poultry Corp. v. United
States*, 295 U.S. 495 (1935), the Court found the National Industrial
Recovery Act unconstitutional, in part as beyond Congress's Commerce
Clause authority. The next year it held the Bituminous Coal Conservation
Act, which regulated the price at which coal could be sold and set minimum
wages and maximum hours for coal workers, beyond the Commerce Clause
as well. *See Carter v. Carter Coal Co.*, 298 U.S. 238 (1936). Nevertheless,
most of the cases were decided by slender 5–4 majorities.

The obstacles the Court placed in the way of legislative and executive
attempts to deal with the depression resulted in President Roosevelt's so-
called Court-packing plan. In 1937, following an overwhelming Democratic
victory in the 1936 election, Roosevelt proposed that Congress enact a law
to add a new seat to the Supreme Court for every member of the Court who
was over 70½ years old, which at that time was six members. Billed as a
measure to relieve the burden on elderly justices, it was transparently a
means by which Roosevelt would be able to add six new justices. Despite
the substantial Democratic majority in both houses, the plan was not
generally supported. There was a widespread feeling that, notwithstanding
the errors of the Court in the view of Congress, playing politics with the
Court to overturn its decisions was inappropriate. Moreover, within two
months of the introduction of the proposed law, the narrow majority
against the New Deal legislation seemed to crumble in a case in which one
justice switched sides. This led to the expression—the switch in time that
saved the nine*—reflecting a belief that one justice may have switched in
order to make the proposed law unnecessary. Subsequent historical inquiry
suggests this belief was incorrect.

Shortly thereafter, the Court upheld by a 5–4 vote the constitutionality
of the National Labor Relations Act, the basic federal law permitting
unions to exist. *See NLRB v. Jones & Laughlin Steel Corp.*, 301 U.S. 1
(1937). This case involved an order by the National Labor Relations Board
to the steel company, prohibiting it from discriminating against employees
because of union activity. The company argued that the law was beyond
Congress's Commerce Clause authority, because it regulated labor
relations wholly within one state. The Court, however, noted that the
company was a vertically integrated firm, owning iron ore mines in

---

* This is a play on the adage, "a stitch in time saves nine," meaning preventive maintenance
can eliminate the need for major repairs later.

Minnesota, steamships that carried the ore on the Great Lakes, coal mines in Pennsylvania, two railroads, steel mills in Pennsylvania, and fabricating plants in New York and Louisiana. The Court found that a labor disruption in one place would affect the entire chain of commerce from mining to ultimate sale of finished steel products. Building on the "stream of commerce" theory from earlier cases, the Court said that Congress could regulate labor relations at one plant in one state, because of its effect on the entire stream of commerce.

While Congress did not adopt Roosevelt's Court-packing plan, it did adopt a generous retirement plan—full pay for judges who retired over the age of 70—with the result that one of the "four horsemen,"* the conservative core of the Court, retired, allowing Roosevelt to appoint Justice Hugo Black, a New Deal Democratic Senator, in 1937. This assured a "liberal" majority on the Court, and the cases reflected the new orientation.

UNITED STATES V. DARBY
United States Supreme Court, 1941.
312 U.S. 100, 61 S.Ct. 451.

MR. JUSTICE STONE delivered the opinion of the Court.

The two principal questions raised by the record in this case are, first, whether Congress has constitutional power to prohibit the shipment in interstate commerce of lumber manufactured by employees whose wages are less than a prescribed minimum or whose weekly hours of labor at that wage are greater than a prescribed maximum, and, second, whether it has power to prohibit the employment of workmen in the production of goods "for interstate commerce" at other than prescribed wages and hours. . . . [Darby, a Georgia lumber manufacturer, was indicted for violating the Fair Labor Standards Act, which imposed these requirements in § 15(a)(1) & (2). The district court quashed the indictment on the grounds that the Act was unconstitutional, and the case came directly to the Supreme Court pursuant to a statute at the time that authorized the direct appeal to the Court when the district court judgment "is based upon the invalidity, or construction of the statute upon which the indictment is founded."]

The Fair Labor Standards Act set up a comprehensive legislative scheme for preventing the shipment in interstate commerce of certain products and commodities produced in the United States under labor conditions as respects wages and hours which fail to conform to standards set up by the Act. Its purpose [as reflected in its findings and declaration of policy[1]] is to exclude from interstate commerce goods produced for the

---

* This is a reference to the four horsemen of the apocalypse described in the Book of Revelations.

[1] The Congress hereby finds that the existence, in industries engaged in commerce or in the production of goods for commerce, of labor conditions detrimental to the maintenance of the

Harlan Fiske Stone

President Calvin Coolidge appointed Stone to the Supreme Court in 1925. Stone had been a partner in a law firm, a professor, and then dean of Columbia Law School. When the Attorney General was forced to resign in a scandal, Coolidge needed a person above reproach for the position, and he reached out to Stone. As a reward, when a vacancy on the Court arose, Coolidge appointed Stone. Although appointed by a Republican, Stone was one of the "Three Musketeers" (opposed to the "Four Horsemen") who dissented from the Court's invalidation of most of the New Deal legislation. Consequently, when the Chief Justice retired, Franklin Roosevelt appointed Stone Chief Justice.

commerce and to prevent their production for interstate commerce, under conditions detrimental to the maintenance of the minimum standards of living necessary for health and general well-being; and to prevent the use of interstate commerce as the means of competition in the distribution of goods so produced, and as the means of spreading and perpetuating such substandard labor conditions among the workers of the several states. . . .

The district court quashed the indictment in its entirety upon the broad grounds that the Act, which it interpreted as a regulation of manufacture within the states, is unconstitutional. It declared that manufacture is not interstate commerce and that the regulation by the Fair Labor Standards Act of wages and hours of employment of those engaged in the manufacture of goods which it is intended at the time of production "may or will be" after production "sold in interstate commerce in part or in whole" is not within the congressional power to regulate interstate commerce.

The effect of the court's decision and judgment are thus to deny the power of Congress to prohibit shipment in interstate commerce of lumber produced for interstate commerce under the proscribed substandard labor conditions of wages and hours [and] its power to penalize the employer for his failure to conform to the wage and hour provisions in the case of employees engaged in the production of lumber which he intends thereafter to ship in interstate commerce in part or in whole according to the normal course of his business. . . .

---

minimum standard of living necessary for health, efficiency, and general well-being of workers (1) causes commerce and the channels and instrumentalities of commerce to be used to spread and perpetuate such labor conditions among the workers of the several States; (2) burdens commerce and the free flow of goods in commerce; (3) constitutes an unfair method of competition in commerce; (4) leads to labor disputes burdening and obstructing commerce and the free flow of goods in commerce; and (5) interferes with the orderly and fair marketing of goods in commerce.

The prohibition of shipment of the proscribed goods in interstate commerce.
[§ 15(a)(1)]

[W]hile manufacture is not of itself interstate commerce, the shipment of manufactured goods interstate is such commerce and the prohibition of such shipment by Congress is indubitably a regulation of the commerce. The power to regulate commerce is the power "to prescribe the rule by which commerce is to be governed." *Gibbons v. Ogden.* It extends not only to those regulations which aid, foster and protect the commerce, but embraces those which prohibit it. *Lottery Case (Champion v. Ames).* . . .

But it is said that the present prohibition falls within the scope of none of these categories; that while the prohibition is nominally a regulation of the commerce its motive or purpose is regulation of wages and hours of persons engaged in manufacture, the control of which has been reserved to the states and upon which Georgia and some of the states of destination have placed no restriction; that the effect of the present statute is not to exclude the prescribed articles from interstate commerce in aid of state regulation . . . but instead, under the guise of a regulation of interstate commerce, it undertakes to regulate wages and hours within the state contrary to the policy of the state which has elected to leave them unregulated.

The power of Congress over interstate commerce "is complete in itself, may be exercised to its utmost extent, and acknowledges no limitations, other than are prescribed by the constitution." *Gibbons v. Ogden.* . . . Congress, following its own conception of public policy concerning the restrictions which may appropriately be imposed on interstate commerce, is free to exclude from the commerce articles whose use in the states for which they are destined it may conceive to be injurious to the public health, morals or welfare, even though the state has not sought to regulate their use.

Such regulation is not a forbidden invasion of state power merely because either its motive or its consequence is to restrict the use of articles of commerce within the states of destination and is not prohibited unless by other Constitutional provisions. It is no objection to the assertion of the power to regulate interstate commerce that its exercise is attended by the same incidents which attend the exercise of the police power of the states.

The motive and purpose of the present regulation are plainly to make effective the Congressional conception of public policy that interstate commerce should not be made the instrument of competition in the distribution of goods produced under substandard labor conditions, which competition is injurious to the commerce and to the states from and to which the commerce flows. The motive and purpose of a regulation of interstate commerce are matters for the legislative judgment upon the exercise of which the Constitution places no restriction and over which the courts are given no control. . . . Whatever their motive and purpose, regulations of commerce which do not infringe some constitutional prohibition are within the plenary power conferred on Congress by the Commerce Clause. Subject only to that limitation, presently to be considered, we conclude that the prohibition of the shipment interstate of goods produced under the forbidden substandard labor conditions is within the constitutional authority of Congress.

In the more than a century which has elapsed since the decision of *Gibbons v. Ogden*, these principles of constitutional interpretation have been so long and repeatedly recognized by this Court as applicable to the Commerce Clause, that there would be little occasion for repeating them now were it not for the decision of this Court twenty-two years ago in *Hammer v. Dagenhart*. In that case it was held by a bare majority of the Court over the powerful and now classic dissent of Mr. Justice Holmes setting forth the fundamental issues involved, that Congress was without power to exclude the products of child labor from interstate commerce. The reasoning and conclusion of the Court's opinion there cannot be reconciled with the conclusion which we have reached, that the power of Congress under the Commerce Clause is plenary to exclude any article from interstate commerce subject only to the specific prohibitions of the Constitution.

Hammer v. Dagenhart has not been followed. The distinction on which the decision was rested that Congressional power to prohibit interstate commerce is limited to articles which in themselves have some harmful or deleterious property—a distinction which was novel when made and unsupported by any provision of the Constitution—has long since been abandoned. The thesis of the opinion that the motive of the prohibition or its effect to control in some measure the use or production within the states of the article thus excluded from the commerce can operate to deprive the regulation of its constitutional authority has long since ceased to have force. And finally we have declared "The authority of the Federal Government over interstate commerce does not differ in extent or character from that retained by the states over intrastate commerce." *United States v. Rock Royal Co-Operative, Inc.*, 307 U.S. 533 (1939).

The conclusion is inescapable that *Hammer v. Dagenhart*, was a departure from the principles which have prevailed in the interpretation of the commerce clause both before and since the decision and that such vitality, as a precedent, as it then had has long since been exhausted. It should be and now is overruled.

Validity of the wage and hour requirements—[§ 15(a)(2)]

[T]he validity of the prohibition turns on the question whether the employment, under other than the prescribed labor standards, of employees engaged in the production of goods for interstate commerce is so related to the commerce and so affects it as to be within the reach of the power of Congress to regulate it. . . .

[T]he power of Congress over interstate commerce is not confined to the regulation of commerce among the states. It extends to those activities intrastate which so affect interstate commerce or the exercise of the power of Congress over it as to make regulation of them appropriate means to the attainment of a legitimate end, the exercise of the granted power of Congress to regulate interstate commerce. *See McCulloch v. Maryland.*

[I]n the absence of Congressional legislation on the subject state laws which are not regulations of the commerce itself or its instrumentalities are not forbidden even though they affect interstate commerce.

But it does not follow that Congress may not by appropriate legislation regulate intrastate activities where they have a substantial effect on interstate commerce. A recent example is the National Labor Relations Act for the regulation of employer and employee relations in industries in which strikes, induced by unfair labor practices named in the Act, tend to disturb or obstruct interstate commerce. *See National Labor Relations Board v. Jones & Laughlin Steel Corp.* But long before the adoption of the National Labor Relations Act, this Court had many times held that the power of Congress to regulate interstate commerce extends to the regulation through legislative action of activities intrastate which have a substantial effect on the commerce or the exercise of the Congressional power over it.

[C]ongress, having by the present Act adopted the policy of excluding from interstate commerce all goods produced for the commerce which do not conform to the specified labor standards, it may choose the means reasonably adapted to the attainment of the permitted end, even though they involve control of intrastate activities. Such legislation has often been sustained with respect to powers, other than the commerce power granted to the national government, when the means chosen, although not themselves within the granted power, were nevertheless deemed appropriate aids to the accomplishment of some purpose within an admitted power of the national government.

[W]e think also that § 15(a)(2), now under consideration, is sustainable independently of § 15(a)(1), which prohibits shipment or transportation of the proscribed goods. As we have said the evils aimed at by the Act are the spread of substandard labor conditions through the use of the facilities of interstate commerce for competition by the goods so produced with those produced under the prescribed or better labor conditions; and the consequent dislocation of the commerce itself caused by the impairment or destruction of local businesses by competition made effective through interstate commerce. The Act is thus directed at the suppression of a method or kind of competition in interstate commerce which it has in effect condemned as "unfair." . . .

The means adopted by § 15(a)(2) for the protection of interstate commerce by the suppression of the production of the condemned goods for interstate commerce is so related to the commerce and so affects it as to be within the reach of the commerce power. . . .

COMMENTS AND QUESTIONS

1.   This is our first "modern" Commerce Clause case, modern in the sense that its doctrine is still good law. Note, by the way, that it is unanimous. In essence, it has three separate parts: the power of Congress to regulate commerce that crosses state lines, the power of Congress under the Necessary and Proper Clause to take measures to implement that power, and the power of Congress to regulate intrastate matters that have a substantial effect on interstate commerce. Can you see where the Court addresses these three separate issues?

2.   Note that the opinion restates the conclusion of *E.C. Knight* that "manufacture is not of itself interstate commerce." That so, how is it that the Court upholds the regulation of hours and wages by manufacturing employees?

3.   What are the last two paragraphs of the opinion saying?

4.   If the federal government can regulate anything that crosses a state line, anything that substantially affects something that crosses a state line, or anything that happens in one state that would substantially affect competition in goods or services between states, what is beyond Congress's power to regulate?

WICKARD V. FILBURN
United States Supreme Court, 1942.
317 U.S. 111, 63 S.Ct. 82.

MR. JUSTICE JACKSON delivered the opinion of the Court.

The appellee [Roscoe Filburn] filed his complaint against the Secretary of Agriculture of the United States [Claude Wickard]. . . . He sought to enjoin enforcement against himself of the marketing penalty imposed by . . . the Agricultural Adjustment Act of 1938 upon that part of his 1941 wheat crop which was available for marketing in excess of the marketing quota established for his farm. He also sought a declaratory judgment that the wheat marketing quota provisions of the Act as amended and applicable to him were unconstitutional because not sustainable under the Commerce Clause. . . .

The appellee for many years past has owned and operated a small farm in Montgomery County, Ohio, maintaining a herd of dairy cattle, selling milk, raising poultry, and selling poultry and eggs. It has been his practice to raise a small acreage of winter wheat, sown in the Fall and harvested in the following July; to sell a portion of the crop; to feed part to poultry and livestock on the farm, some of which is sold; to use some in making flour for home consumption; and to keep the rest for the following seeding. The intended disposition of the crop here involved has not been expressly stated.

In July of 1940, pursuant to the Agricultural Adjustment Act of 1938 . . ., there were established for the appellee's 1941 crop a wheat acreage allotment of 11.1 acres and a normal yield of 20.1 bushels of wheat an acre. . . . He sowed, however, 23 acres, and harvested from his 11.9 acres of excess acreage 239 bushels, which under the terms of the Act as amended on May 26, 1941, constituted farm marketing excess, subject to a penalty of 49 cents a bushel, or $117.11 in all. . . . The general scheme of the Agricultural Adjustment Act of 1938 as related to wheat is to control the volume moving in interstate and foreign commerce in order to avoid surpluses and shortages and the consequent abnormally low or high wheat prices and obstructions to commerce.* Within prescribed limits and by prescribed standards the Secretary of Agriculture is directed to ascertain and proclaim each year a national acreage allotment for the next crop of wheat, which is then apportioned to the states and their counties, and is eventually broken up into allotments for individual farms. . . .

It is urged that under the Commerce Clause of the Constitution, Article I, § 8, clause 3, Congress does not possess the power it has in this instance sought to exercise. The question would merit little consideration

Robert Jackson

President Franklin Roosevelt appointed Jackson to the Supreme Court in 1941. Previously he served as Roosevelt's Attorney General, where he earned the President's trust through a number of legal opinions supporting the President's actions in supporting Great Britain and preparing for our seemingly inevitable entry into World War II. As a Justice, Jackson was known for his writing style, as well as his opinions in several famous cases. In 1945 he took a leave from the Court to be the Chief Prosecutor at the Nuremburg War Crimes trial. Thereafter he returned to the Court until his death in 1954.

since our decision in *United States v. Darby*, sustaining the federal power to regulate production of goods for commerce except for the fact that this Act extends federal regulation to production not intended in any part for commerce but wholly for consumption on the farm. The Act includes a

---

* As you may recall, one of the features of the Great Depression was a surplus of goods relative to the demand for them. The demand was low because people did not have enough money to buy very much. Just as inflation results when there is more money relative to the supply of goods and services, thereby bidding up the price of those goods and services, deflation results when there are not enough bidders to maintain the previous prices. The Agricultural Adjustment Act was intended to restrict the supply of commodity crops, so that the price would naturally rise.[This type of regulatory system to maintain prices at a certain level, rather than at the level the "free market" would set, continues to exist today with respect to certain commodities, for example, milk and hazelnuts. [author's note]

Roscoe Filburn

definition of "market" and its derivatives so that as related to wheat in addition to its conventional meaning it also means to dispose of "by feeding (in any form) to poultry or livestock which, or the products of which, are sold, bartered, or exchanged, or to be so disposed of." Hence, marketing quotas not only embrace all that may be sold without penalty but also what may be consumed on the premises. . . . The sum of this is that the Federal Government fixes a quota including all that the farmer may harvest for sale or for his own farm needs, and declares that wheat produced on excess acreage may neither be disposed of nor used except upon payment of the penalty or except it is stored as required by the Act or delivered to the Secretary of Agriculture.

Appellee says that this is a regulation of production and consumption of wheat. Such activities are, he urges, beyond the reach of Congressional power under the Commerce Clause, since they are local in character, and their effects upon interstate commerce are at most "indirect." In answer the Government argues that the statute regulates neither production nor consumption, but only marketing; and, in the alternative, that if the Act does go beyond the regulation of marketing it is sustainable as a "necessary and proper" implementation of the power of Congress over interstate commerce.

The Government's concern lest the Act be held to be a regulation of production or consumption rather than of marketing is attributable to a few dicta and decisions of this Court which might be understood to lay it down that activities such as "production," "manufacturing," and "mining" are strictly "local" and, except in special circumstances which are not present here, cannot be regulated under the commerce power because their effects upon interstate commerce are, as matter of law, only "indirect." Even today, when this power has been held to have great latitude, there is no decision of this Court that such activities may be regulated where no part of the product is intended for interstate commerce or intermingled with the subjects thereof. We believe that a review of the course of decision under the Commerce Clause will make plain, however, that questions of the power of Congress are not to be decided by reference to any formula which would give controlling force to nomenclature such as "production" and "indirect" and foreclose consideration of the actual effects of the activity in question upon interstate commerce.

At the beginning Chief Justice Marshall described the Federal commerce power with a breadth never yet exceeded. *Gibbons v. Ogden.* He made emphatic the embracing and penetrating nature of this power by warning that effective restraints on its exercise must proceed from political rather than from judicial processes.

For nearly a century [thereafter], however, decisions of this Court under the Commerce Clause dealt rarely with questions of what Congress might do in the exercise of its granted power under the Clause. . . .

It was not until 1887 with the enactment of the Interstate Commerce Act that the interstate commerce power began to exert positive influence in American law and life. This first important federal resort to the commerce power was followed in 1890 by the Sherman Anti-Trust Act and, thereafter, mainly after 1903, by many others. These statutes ushered in new phases of adjudication, which required the Court to approach the interpretation of the Commerce Clause in the light of an actual exercise by Congress of its power thereunder.

When it first dealt with this new legislation, the Court . . . allowed but little scope to the power of Congress. *United States v. E. C. Knight Co.* . . .

Even while important opinions in this line of restrictive authority were being written, however, other cases called forth broader interpretations of the Commerce Clause destined to supersede the earlier ones, and to bring about a return to the principles first enunciated by Chief Justice Marshall in *Gibbons v. Ogden*.

Not long after the decision of *United States v. E. C. Knight Co.*, Mr. Justice Holmes, in sustaining the exercise of national power over intrastate activity, stated for the Court that "commerce among the states is not a technical legal conception, but a practical one, drawn from the course of business." *Swift & Co. v. United States*. . . .

The Court's recognition of the relevance of the economic effects in the application of the Commerce Clause exemplified by this statement has made the mechanical application of legal formulas no longer feasible. Once an economic measure of the reach of the power granted to Congress in the Commerce Clause is accepted, questions of federal power cannot be decided simply by finding the activity in question to be "production" nor can consideration of its economic effects be foreclosed by calling them "indirect." . . .

Whether the subject of the regulation in question was "production," "consumption," or "marketing" is, therefore, not material for purposes of deciding the question of federal power before us. That an activity is of local character may help in a doubtful case to determine whether Congress intended to reach it. . . . But even if appellee's activity be local and though it may not be regarded as commerce, it may still, whatever its nature, be reached by Congress if it exerts a substantial economic effect on interstate commerce and this irrespective of whether such effect is what might at some earlier time have been defined as "direct" or "indirect."

The parties have stipulated a summary of the economics of the wheat industry. Commerce among the states in wheat is large and important. Although wheat is raised in every state but one, production in most states is not equal to consumption. Sixteen states on average have had a surplus of wheat above their own requirements for feed, seed, and food. Thirty-two states and the District of Columbia, where production has been below consumption, have looked to these surplus-producing states for their supply as well as for wheat for export and carryover.

The wheat industry has been a problem industry for some years. Largely as a result of increased foreign production and import restrictions, annual exports of wheat and flour from the United States during the ten-year period ending in 1940 averaged less than 10 per cent of total production, while during the 1920's they averaged more than 25 per cent. The decline in the export trade has left a large surplus in production. . . .

The effect of consumption of homegrown wheat on interstate commerce is due to the fact that it constitutes the most variable factor in the disappearance of the wheat crop. Consumption on the farm where grown appears to vary in an amount greater than 20 per cent of average production. The total amount of wheat consumed as food varies but relatively little, and use as seed is relatively constant.

The maintenance by government regulation of a price for wheat undoubtedly can be accomplished as effectively by sustaining or increasing the demand as by limiting the supply. The effect of the statute before us is to restrict the amount which may be produced for market and the extent as well to which one may forestall resort to the market by producing to meet his own needs. That appellee's own contribution to the demand for wheat may be trivial by itself is not enough to remove him from the scope of federal regulation where, as here, his contribution, taken together with that of many others similarly situated, is far from trivial.

It is well established by decisions of this Court that the power to regulate commerce includes the power to regulate the prices at which commodities in that commerce are dealt in and practices affecting such prices. One of the primary purposes of the Act in question was to increase the market price of wheat and to that end to limit the volume thereof that could affect the market. It can hardly be denied that a factor of such volume and variability as home-consumed wheat would have a substantial influence on price and market conditions. This may arise because being in marketable condition such wheat overhangs the market and if induced by rising prices tends to flow into the market and check price increases. But if we assume that it is never marketed, it supplies a need of the man who grew it which would otherwise be reflected by purchases in the open market. Home-grown wheat in this sense competes with wheat in commerce. The stimulation of commerce is a use of the regulatory function quite as definitely as prohibitions or restrictions thereon. This record leaves us in no doubt that Congress may properly have considered that wheat consumed on the farm where grown if wholly outside the scheme of regulation would have a substantial effect in defeating and obstructing its purpose to stimulate trade therein at increased prices.

It is said, however, that this Act, forcing some farmers into the market to buy what they could provide for themselves, is an unfair promotion of the markets and prices of specializing wheat growers. It is of the essence of regulation that it lays a restraining hand on the self interest of the regulated and that advantages from the regulation commonly fall to others. The conflicts of economic interest between the regulated and those who advantage by it are wisely left under our system to resolution by the Congress under its more flexible and responsible legislative process. Such conflicts rarely lend themselves to judicial determination. And with the wisdom, workability, or fairness, of the plan of regulation we have nothing to do. . . .

COMMENTS AND QUESTIONS

1. *Wickard* makes two notable expansions of Congress's Commerce Clause power. First, even though the actual case does not involve commerce (no buying or selling, merely consumption on the farm of wheat grown on the farm), it affects commerce because otherwise the farmer would have to engage in commerce (by buying wheat to feed to his animals). Second, the aggregation doctrine says that, even though a small amount may be involved in an individual case, if it is aggregated with all the cases like it, there would be a substantial effect on interstate commerce and that is sufficient. Thus, while Filburn did not himself engage in any relevant commerce at all, and his measly 239 bushels of wheat would have no effect on interstate commerce, if all farmers were able to do what he did, in aggregate they would have had a substantial effect on interstate commerce. Or stated another way, if Congress could *not* regulate the small amount, then all the small amounts together could escape regulation even though together they would have a substantial effect on interstate commerce.

2. In light of this justification, is there anything left that the federal government cannot regulate? And if so, so what?

3. Does *Wickard* really change the law from what Justice Field suggested it was in the *Daniel Ball*? From what Marshall suggested it was in *Gibbons*? Or, has the economy itself changed from one that was basically local with some interstate characteristics to one that is almost totally interstate and international with almost no totally local characteristics?

4. THE MODERN AND POST-MODERN PERIOD

Darby and *Wickard* seemed to settle the Commerce Clause question for a number of years. The Supreme Court only granted certiorari in a few cases in which lower courts had found something beyond the Commerce

Clause, and the Supreme Court reversed. For example, in *United States v. Sullivan*, 332 U.S. 689 (1948), a druggist in Columbus, Georgia, had purchased a bottle of pills from a wholesaler in Atlanta, which had bought a large number of such bottles from a company in Chicago that manufactured the pills. While the bottle was properly labeled, the druggist took twelve pills out of the bottle, put them in a pill box that was not properly labeled, and sold them to a customer. He was prosecuted for violation of the Food, Drug and Cosmetic Act's provision that prohibits "misbranding" of drugs "held for sale after shipment in interstate commerce." The court of appeals reversed his conviction, refusing to apply the law literally, because in its view to do so would raise grave doubts about its constitutionality under the Commerce Clause. The Supreme Court reversed the court of appeals, finding no constitutional problem with application of the law to the facts involved.

Heart of Atlanta Motel

The civil rights era of the 1960s, however, raised some new questions. The Civil Rights Act of 1964 prohibited discrimination on the basis of race in any "place of public accommodation." A "place of public accommodation" was defined to include, among other things, motels and restaurants if their "operations affect commerce." The statute provided that any motel that offered lodging to transient guests, other than an owner-occupied structure with less than five rooms, was *per se* an operation affecting commerce. It also provided that any restaurant that either served interstate travelers or served food that had moved in interstate commerce was also an operation affecting commerce. In *Heart of Atlanta Motel, Inc. v. United States*, 379 U.S. 241 (1964), the Court considered whether the law was constitutional as applied to the Heart of Atlanta Motel, a motel that had 216 rooms and 75% of whose customers were from out-of-state, but which refused to rent rooms to African-Americans. The Court noted that Congress had found that racial discrimination in the hotel industry had obstructed interstate commerce by making it difficult for African-American travelers to find accommodations and thereby created a disincentive for them to travel. The fact that the motive for the law might be moral, rather than economic, was held to be irrelevant.

A companion case, *Katzenbach v. McClung*, 379 U.S. 294 (1964), involved Ollie's Barbecue, a family-owned restaurant in Birmingham, Alabama. There was no evidence that interstate travelers used the restaurant, but 46% of the meat sold (worth $69,000) came from out-of-state. African-American customers could not be seated in the restaurant,

although they could purchase
food for takeout from a takeout
window dedicated to African-
American customers. Again,
Congress had found that
discrimination against African-
Americans in restaurants
resulted in lower per capita
expenditures, corrected for
income differentials. Thus, but
for the discrimination, there
would be more spent in

Ollie's Bar-B-Q

restaurants obtaining food from interstate commerce, thereby increasing
the amount traveling in interstate commerce. Even though Ollie's effect on
interstate commerce would not be significant, the Court cited to *Wickard*
as a basis to reach Ollie's actions. Moreover, the Court held it was not
necessary to determine whether Ollie's discrimination affected the amount
of out-of-state food it bought. Because Congress's determination was
reasonable that racial discrimination in restaurants would generally affect
the amount of out-of-state food bought, that was sufficient. So long as the
defined class was within the power of Congress, and Ollie's was within the
defined class, there was no basis for courts to excise individual instances.
See also Perez v. United States, 402 U.S. 146 (1971)(federal law
criminalizing loan sharking was within the Commerce Clause power).

     In addition, the environmental movement raised new questions. In
Hodel v. Virginia Surface Mining and Reclamation Assn., 452 U.S. 264
(1981), and *Hodel v. Indiana*, 452 U.S. 314 (1981), the Court considered the
constitutionality of the Surface Mining Control and Reclamation Act. That
act required companies engaged in surface mining of coal to meet certain
standards in the mining and to reclaim the land when done. Congress made
findings that surface mining had various negative environmental effects.
The Court cited three separate reasons for upholding the law under the
Commerce Clause. First, Congress can regulate local conditions that have
an adverse effect on interstate commerce, suggesting that the
environmental effects would have such an effect on interstate commerce.
Second, citing *Darby*, the Court said Congress can regulate local activities
in order to protect fair competition between the states, suggesting that
allowing some states to avoid surface mining controls would be unfair
competition with those states that would regulate surface mining. Third,
the Court said it agreed with the lower courts that had held the Commerce
Clause authority was broad enough to regulate "activities causing air or
water pollution, or other environmental hazards that may have effects in
more than one State."

     At this point, many observers believed that the Supreme Court had
given up trying to police any restrictions on Congress's Commerce Clause

authority, leaving that to the political processes. Then the Court decided the following case.

UNITED STATES V. LOPEZ

United States Supreme Court, 1995.
514 U.S. 549, 115 S.Ct. 1624.

CHIEF JUSTICE REHNQUIST delivered the opinion of the Court.

In the Gun-Free School Zones Act of 1990, Congress made it a federal offense for any individual knowingly to possess a firearm at a place that the individual knows, or has reasonable cause to believe, is a school zone. 18 U.S.C. § 922(q). . . .

On March 10, 1992, respondent, who was then a 12th-grade student, arrived at Edison High School in San Antonio, Texas, carrying a concealed .38-caliber handgun and five bullets. Acting upon an anonymous tip, school authorities confronted respondent, who admitted that he was carrying the weapon. [Lopez stated that "Gilbert" had given him the gun so that he (Lopez) could deliver it after school to "Jason," who planned to use it in a "gang war." Lopez was to receive $40 for his services.] He was arrested and charged under Texas law with firearm possession on school premises. The next day, the state charges were dismissed after federal agents charged respondent by complaint with violating the Gun-Free School Zones Act of 1990.[1]

[He was convicted, and o]n appeal respondent challenged his conviction based on his claim that § 922(q) exceeded Congress's power to legislate under the Commerce Clause. The Court of Appeals for the Fifth Circuit agreed and reversed respondent's conviction. . . . Because of the importance of the issue, we granted certiorari, and we now affirm. . . .

The Constitution delegates to Congress the power [t]o regulate Commerce with foreign Nations, and among the several States, and with the Indian Tribes. The Court, through Chief Justice Marshall, first defined the nature of Congress's commerce power in *Gibbons v. Ogden*. . . . The *Gibbons* Court, however, acknowledged that limitations on the commerce power are inherent in the very language of the Commerce Clause. . . .

Jones & Laughlin Steel, *Darby*, and *Wickard* ushered in an era of Commerce Clause jurisprudence that greatly expanded the previously defined authority of Congress under that Clause. In part, this was a recognition of the great changes that had occurred in the way business was carried on in this country. Enterprises that had once been local or at most regional in nature had become national in scope. But the doctrinal change

---

[1]   The term school zone is defined as in, or on the grounds of, a public, parochial or private school or within a distance of 1,000 feet from the grounds of a public, parochial or private school.

also reflected a view that earlier Commerce Clause cases artificially had constrained the authority of Congress to regulate interstate commerce.

But even these modern-era precedents which have expanded congressional power under the Commerce Clause confirm that this power is subject to outer limits. . . . In *Jones & Laughlin Steel*, the Court warned that the scope of the interstate commerce power must be considered in the light of our dual system of government and may not be extended so as to embrace effects upon interstate commerce so indirect and remote that to embrace them, in view of our complex society, would effectually obliterate the distinction between what is national and what is local and create a completely centralized government. Since that time, the Court has heeded that warning and undertaken to decide whether a rational basis existed for concluding that a regulated activity sufficiently affected interstate commerce. See, *e.g.*, *Hodel v. Virginia Surface Mining & Reclamation Assn., Inc.*; *Perez v. United States*; *Katzenbach v. McClung*; *Heart of Atlanta Motel, Inc. v. United States.* . . .

Consistent with this structure, we have identified three broad categories of activity that Congress may regulate under its commerce power. First, Congress may regulate the use of the channels of interstate commerce. Second, Congress is empowered to regulate and protect the instrumentalities of interstate commerce, or persons or things in interstate commerce, even though the threat may come only from intrastate activities. Finally, Congress's commerce authority includes the power to regulate those activities having a substantial relation to interstate commerce, *i.e.*, those activities that substantially affect interstate commerce.

Within this final category, admittedly, our case law has not been clear whether an activity must affect or substantially affect interstate commerce in order to be within Congress's power to regulate it under the Commerce Clause. We conclude, consistent with the great weight of our case law, that the proper test requires an analysis of whether the regulated activity substantially affects interstate commerce.

We now turn to consider the power of Congress, in the light of this framework, to enact § 922(q). The first two categories of authority may be quickly disposed of: § 922(q) is not a regulation of the use of the channels of interstate commerce, nor is it an attempt to prohibit the interstate transportation of a commodity through the channels of commerce; nor can § 922(q) be justified as a regulation by which Congress has sought to protect an instrumentality of interstate commerce or a thing in interstate commerce. Thus, if § 922(q) is to be sustained, it must be under the third category as a regulation of an activity that substantially affects interstate commerce.

First, we have upheld a wide variety of congressional Acts regulating intrastate economic activity where we have concluded that the activity substantially affected interstate commerce. Examples include the regulation of intrastate coal mining; *Hodel*, intrastate extortionate credit transactions, *Perez*, restaurants utilizing substantial interstate supplies, *McClung*, inns and hotels catering to interstate guests, *Heart of Atlanta Motel*, and production and consumption of homegrown wheat, *Wickard v. Filburn*. These examples are by no means exhaustive, but the pattern is clear. Where economic activity substantially affects interstate commerce, legislation regulating that activity will be sustained.

Even *Wickard*, which is perhaps the most far reaching example of Commerce Clause authority over intrastate activity, involved economic activity in a way that the possession of a gun in a school zone does not. . . .

Section 922(q) is a criminal statute that by its terms has nothing to do with commerce or any sort of economic enterprise, however broadly one might define those terms.[3] Section 922(q) is not an essential part of a larger regulation of economic activity, in which the regulatory scheme could be undercut unless the intrastate activity were regulated. It cannot, therefore, be sustained under our cases upholding regulations of activities that arise out of or are connected with a commercial transaction, which viewed in the aggregate, substantially affects interstate commerce.

Second, § 922(q) contains no jurisdictional element which would ensure, through case-by-case inquiry, that the firearm possession in question affects interstate commerce. . . . [Section] 922(q) has no express jurisdictional element which might limit its reach to a discrete set of firearm possessions that additionally have an explicit connection with or effect on interstate commerce. . . .

The Government's essential contention, in fine, is that we may determine here that § 922(q) is valid because possession of a firearm in a local school zone does indeed substantially affect interstate commerce. The Government argues that possession of a firearm in a school zone may result in violent crime and that violent crime can be expected to affect the functioning of the national economy in two ways. First, the costs of violent crime are substantial, and, through the mechanism of insurance, those costs are spread throughout the population. Second, violent crime reduces the willingness of individuals to travel to areas within the country that are perceived to be unsafe. The Government also argues that the presence of guns in schools poses a substantial threat to the educational process by

---

[3]   Under our federal system, the "States possess primary authority for defining and enforcing the criminal law." When Congress criminalizes conduct already denounced as criminal by the States, it effects a change in the sensitive relation between federal and state criminal jurisdiction. The Government acknowledges that § 922(q) displace[s] state policy choices in . . . that its prohibitions apply even in States that have chosen not to outlaw the conduct in question. *See also* Statement of President George Bush on Signing the Crime Control Act of 1990, 26 Weekly Comp. of Pres. Doc. 1944, 1945 (Nov. 29, 1990)("Most egregiously, section [922(q)] inappropriately overrides legitimate State firearms laws with a new and unnecessary Federal law. The policies reflected in these provisions could legitimately be adopted by the States, but they should not be imposed upon the States by the Congress").

threatening the learning environment. A handicapped educational process, in turn, will result in a less productive citizenry. That, in turn, would have an adverse effect on the Nation's economic well-being. As a result, the Government argues that Congress could rationally have concluded that § 922(q) substantially affects interstate commerce.

We pause to consider the implications of the Government's arguments. The Government admits, under its costs of crime reasoning, that Congress could regulate not only all violent crime, but all activities that might lead to violent crime, regardless of how tenuously they relate to interstate commerce. Similarly, under the Government's national productivity reasoning, Congress could regulate any activity that it found was related to the economic productivity of individual citizens: family law (including marriage, divorce, and child custody), for example. Under the theories that the Government presents in support of § 922(q), it is difficult to perceive any limitation on federal power, even in areas such as criminal law enforcement or education where States historically have been sovereign. Thus, if we were to accept the Government's arguments, we are hard pressed to posit any activity by an individual that Congress is without power to regulate.

Justice BREYER focuses, for the most part, on the threat that firearm possession in and near schools poses to the educational process and the potential economic consequences flowing from that threat. Specifically, the dissent reasons that (1) gun-related violence is a serious problem; (2) that problem, in turn, has an adverse effect on classroom learning; and (3) that adverse effect on classroom learning, in turn, represents a substantial threat to trade and commerce. This analysis would be equally applicable, if not more so, to subjects such as family law and direct regulation of education.

For instance, if Congress can, pursuant to its Commerce Clause power, regulate activities that adversely affect the learning environment, then, a fortiori, it also can regulate the educational process directly. Congress could determine that a school's curriculum has a significant effect on the extent of classroom learning. As a result, Congress could mandate a federal curriculum for local elementary and secondary schools because what is taught in local schools has a significant effect on classroom learning, and that, in turn, has a substantial effect on interstate commerce. . . .

To uphold the Government's contentions here, we would have to pile inference upon inference in a manner that would bid fair to convert congressional authority under the Commerce Clause to a general police power of the sort retained by the States. Admittedly, some of our prior cases have taken long steps down that road, giving great deference to congressional action. The broad language in these opinions has suggested the possibility of additional expansion, but we decline here to proceed any further. To do so would require us to conclude that the Constitution's enumeration of powers does not presuppose something not enumerated, and that there never will be a distinction between what is truly national and what is truly local. This we are unwilling to do.

For the foregoing reasons the judgment of the Court of Appeals is Affirmed.

JUSTICE KENNEDY, with whom JUSTICE O'CONNOR joins, concurring.

The history of the judicial struggle to interpret the Commerce Clause during the transition from the economic system the Founders knew to the single, national market still emergent in our own era counsels great restraint before the Court determines that the Clause is insufficient to support an exercise of the national power. That history gives me some pause about today's decision, but I join the Court's opinion with these observations on what I conceive to be its necessary though limited holding. . . .

The history of our Commerce Clause decisions contains at least two lessons of relevance to this case. The first . . . is the imprecision of content-based boundaries used without more to define the limits of the Commerce Clause. The second, related to the first but of even greater consequence, is that the Court as an institution and the legal system as a whole have an immense stake in the stability of our Commerce Clause jurisprudence as it has evolved to this point. *Stare decisis* operates with great force in counseling us not to call in question the essential principles now in place respecting the congressional power to regulate transactions of a commercial nature. That fundamental restraint on our power forecloses us from reverting to an understanding of commerce that would serve only an 18th-century economy, dependent then upon production and trading practices that had changed but little over the preceding centuries; it also mandates against returning to the time when congressional authority to regulate undoubted commercial activities was limited by a judicial determination that those matters had an insufficient connection to an interstate system. Congress can regulate in the commercial sphere on the assumption that we have a single market and a unified purpose to build a stable national economy. . . .

Of the various structural elements in the Constitution, separation of powers, checks and balances, judicial review, and federalism, only concerning the last does there seem to be much uncertainty respecting the existence, and the content, of standards that allow the Judiciary to play a significant role in maintaining the design contemplated by the Framers. . . .

There is irony in this, because of the four structural elements in the Constitution just mentioned, federalism was the unique contribution of the Framers to political science and political theory. Though on the surface the idea may seem counterintuitive, it was the insight of the Framers that freedom was enhanced by the creation of two governments, not one. In the compound republic of America, the power surrendered by the people is first divided between two distinct governments, and then the portion allotted to each subdivided among distinct and separate departments. Hence a double security arises to the rights of the people. The different governments will control each other, at the same time that each will be controlled by itself. The Federalist No. 51 (J. Madison).

[W]ere the Federal Government to take over the regulation of entire areas of traditional state concern, areas having nothing to do with the regulation of commercial activities, the boundaries between the spheres of federal and state authority would blur and political responsibility would become illusory. . . .

As THE CHIEF JUSTICE explains, unlike the earlier cases to come before the Court here neither the actors nor their conduct has a commercial character, and neither the purposes nor the design of the statute has an evident commercial nexus. . . . If Congress attempts that extension, then at the least we must inquire whether the exercise of national power seeks to intrude upon an area of traditional state concern.

An interference of these dimensions occurs here, for it is well established that education is a traditional concern of the States. The proximity to schools, including of course schools owned and operated by the States or their subdivisions, is the very premise for making the conduct criminal. In these circumstances, we have a particular duty to ensure that the federal-state balance is not destroyed. . . .

JUSTICE THOMAS, concurring.

[A]lthough I join the majority, I write separately to observe that our case law has drifted far from the original understanding of the Commerce Clause.

We have said that Congress may regulate not only Commerce . . . among the several States, but also anything that has a substantial effect on such commerce. This test, if taken to its logical extreme, would give Congress a police power over all aspects of American life. . . .

In an appropriate case, I believe that we must further reconsider our substantial effects test with an eye toward constructing a standard that reflects the text and history of the Commerce Clause without totally rejecting our more recent Commerce Clause jurisprudence. . . .

JUSTICE STEVENS, dissenting. [omitted]

JUSTICE SOUTER, dissenting. [omitted]

JUSTICE BREYER, with whom JUSTICE STEVENS, JUSTICE SOUTER, and JUSTICE GINSBURG join, dissenting.

The issue in this case is whether the Commerce Clause authorizes Congress to enact a statute that makes it a crime to possess a gun in, or near, a school. In my view, the statute falls well within the scope of the commerce power as this Court has understood that power over the last half century.

In reaching this conclusion, I apply three basic principles of Commerce Clause interpretation. First, the power to regulate Commerce . . . among the several States encompasses the power to regulate local activities insofar as they significantly affect interstate commerce. *See, e.g., Gibbons v. Ogden; Wickard v. Filburn.* . . .

Second, in determining whether a local activity will likely have a significant effect upon interstate commerce, a court must consider, not the effect of an individual act (a single instance of gun possession), but rather the cumulative effect of all similar instances (*i.e.*, the effect of all guns possessed in or near schools). *See, e.g., Wickard.* . . .

Third, the Constitution requires us to judge the connection between a regulated activity and interstate commerce, not directly, but at one remove. Courts must give Congress a degree of leeway in determining the existence of a significant factual connection between the regulated activity and interstate commerce—both because the Constitution delegates the commerce power directly to Congress and because the determination requires an empirical judgment of a kind that a legislature is more likely than a court to make with accuracy. The traditional words rational basis capture this leeway. Thus, the specific question before us, as the Court recognizes, is not whether the regulated activity sufficiently affected interstate commerce, but, rather, whether Congress could have had a rational basis for so concluding. . . .

Applying these principles to the case at hand, we must ask whether Congress could have had a rational basis for finding a significant (or substantial) connection between gun-related school violence and interstate commerce. As long as one views the commerce connection, not as a technical legal conception, but as a practical one, *Swift & Co. v. United States* (Holmes, J.), the answer to this question must be yes. Numerous reports and studies—generated both inside and outside government— make clear that Congress could reasonably have found the empirical connection that its law, implicitly or explicitly, asserts.

For one thing, reports, hearings, and other readily available literature make clear that the problem of guns in and around schools is widespread and extremely serious. . . . And, they report that this widespread violence in schools throughout the Nation significantly interferes with the quality of education in those schools. Based on reports such as these, Congress obviously could have thought that guns and learning are mutually exclusive. Congress could therefore have found a substantial educational problem—teachers unable to teach, students unable to learn—and concluded that guns near schools contribute substantially to the size and scope of that problem.

Having found that guns in schools significantly undermine the quality of education in our Nation's classrooms, Congress could also have found, given the effect of education upon interstate and foreign commerce, that gun-related violence in and around schools is a commercial, as well as a human, problem. Education, although far more than a matter of economics, has long been inextricably intertwined with the Nation's economy. . . . Scholars estimate that nearly a quarter of America's economic growth in the early years of this century is traceable directly to increased schooling; that investment in human capital (through spending on education) exceeded investment in physical capital by a ratio of almost two to one; and that the economic returns to this investment in education exceeded the returns to conventional capital investment.

In recent years the link between secondary education and business has strengthened, becoming both more direct and more important. Scholars on the subject report that technological changes and innovations in management techniques have altered the nature of the workplace so that more jobs now demand greater educational skills. . . .

[T]he economic links I have just sketched seem fairly obvious. Why then is it not equally obvious, in light of those links, that a widespread, serious, and substantial physical threat to teaching and learning also substantially threatens the commerce to which that teaching and learning is inextricably tied? . . .

To hold this statute constitutional is not to obliterate the distinction between what is national and what is local; nor is it to hold that the Commerce Clause permits the Federal Government to regulate any activity that it found was related to the economic productivity of individual citizens, to regulate marriage, divorce, and child custody, or to regulate any and all aspects of education. First, this statute is aimed at curbing a particularly acute threat to the educational process—the possession (and use) of life-threatening firearms in, or near, the classroom. . . . Second, the immediacy of the connection between education and the national economic well-being is documented by scholars and accepted by society at large in a way and to a degree that may not hold true for other social institutions. It must surely be the rare case, then, that a statute strikes at conduct that (when considered in the abstract) seems so removed from commerce, but which (practically speaking) has so significant an impact upon commerce. . . .

COMMENTS AND QUESTIONS

1.   *Lopez* was a shock to the legal community. It was the first case in over a half-century to find a limit to Congress's power under the Commerce Clause. That it was not a flash in the pan was shown by the Court's decision five years later in *United States v. Morrison*, 529 U.S. 598 (2000). In that case the statute in question was the civil damages portion of the Violence Against Women Act (VAWA), which despite the title, provided for damages against any

person who "commits a crime of violence motivated by gender." Christy Brzonkala alleged that she had been raped by two college football players, and she sued them in federal court under VAWA. In passing VAWA, informed by the Court's decision in *Lopez*, Congress made extensive findings that gender-motivated violence affects interstate commerce "by deterring potential victims from traveling interstate, from engaging in employment in interstate business, and from transacting with business, and in places involved in interstate commerce; . . . by diminishing national productivity, increasing medical and other costs, and decreasing the supply or and the demand for interstate products." Nevertheless, the Court, by the same 5–4 split, found the damages provision unconstitutional under the rationale of *Lopez*. If these listed impacts on interstate commerce were sufficient to authorize federal regulation, the Court said, Congress would be able to regulate any criminal activity. Gender-motivated violence, the Court found, was not any part of economic or commercial activity.

2.   *Lopez* was decided before the Columbine, Newtown, Sandy Hook, and other school and mass shooting incidents. Do you think the lack of federal regulation had any causal relationship to those incidents? If some of those incidents had predated *Lopez*, do you think the Court (or at least one member of the majority) might have reached a different conclusion as to the constitutionality of the law?

3.   Justice Thomas in both *Lopez* and *Morrison* called for abolition of the "substantial effects" test, arguing that the Constitution only authorizes regulation *of* commerce, not regulation of things that affect commerce. This is typical of Justice Thomas to suggest radical revisions of existing doctrine on the basis of his perceived understanding of the original meaning of the Constitution. In this regard, he went further than Justice Scalia, who despite his originalist rhetoric seemed more willing to accept long-standing precedent. Now it is Justice Gorsuch who joins Justice Thomas, and vice-versa, penning dissents and concurrences arguing for radical new interpretations.

4.   What is the point of Justice Kennedy's concurrence? Recall Justice Kennedy's concurrence in *Lujan v. Defenders of Wildlife*.

5.   A year after *Lopez*, Congress amended § 922(q) to read: "It shall be unlawful for any individual knowingly to possess a firearm that has moved in or that otherwise affects interstate or foreign commerce at a place that the individual knows, or has reasonable cause to believe, is a school zone." The amendment has been upheld by every circuit court of appeals to have considered it, and the Court has not granted certiorari in any of those cases. Similarly, the criminal provision of VAWA provides: "A person who travels across a State line or enters or leaves Indian country with the intent to injure, harass, or intimidate that person's spouse or intimate partner, and who, in the course of or as a result of such travel, intentionally commits a crime of violence and thereby causes bodily injury to such spouse or intimate partner, shall be punished. . . ." The Court in *Morrison* noted without criticism that this law had been upheld by all the circuits that had considered it.

6.   Assuming that Alfonso Lopez's gun was not manufactured in Texas, and the amended law had been in place at the time of his arrest, would his prosecution under this law be constitutional? If so, what is the point of the Court's parade of horribles as to what would happen if Congress could prohibit such behavior?

7.   How would a law prohibiting persons from having guns within 500 feet of a federal building be different from the law in *Lopez*? Would it be constitutional? How about a law prohibiting guns within commercial establishments? How about a law prohibiting the possession of marijuana anywhere?

8.   This last question was raised in *Gonzales v. Raich*, 545 U.S. 1 (2005), in the context of persons personally growing and possessing marijuana for medicinal purposes as authorized by state law. The Court by a vote of 6–3 upheld the federal statute banning the possession of marijuana anywhere. Here, unlike in *Lopez*, Congress was regulating commercial activities, specifically the interstate marijuana market, by trying to eliminate that market entirely, and just as in *Wickard* the home production and consumption of the product could, aggregated with all other home production and consumption, affect the price and market conditions of marijuana in the marketplace. Moreover, Congress could rationally conclude that homegrown marijuana could be diverted into the interstate market.

9.   Subsequent to *Lopez*, there have been a number of challenges to the authority of Congress to enact the Endangered Species Act (ESA) to protect species for which there is no commercial market and which have no known value for any purpose. Among them, one involved the Arroyo Southwestern Toad which lives only in southern California; one involved the Delhi Sands Flower-Loving Fly, which lives only in two counties in California; and one involved four spiders and two beetles that only live underground in two counties in Texas. While each of the courts upheld the ESA, the nine judges involved authored seven different opinions. One judge thought the ESA unconstitutional as beyond Congress's power under the Commerce Clause in light of *Lopez*. Among the judges who upheld the ESA there were a number of theories. One was that the ESA was within Congress's authority because, even if the species itself had no effect on interstate commerce, the activity that was prohibited (in order to protect the endangered species) was closely related to interstate commerce—*e.g.*, building an on-ramp to an interstate highway or building a new subdivision. Another justification was that the destruction of biodiversity generally would have a substantial effect on interstate commerce, so it is necessary for Congress to be able to protect each aspect of biodiversity, or else all of biodiversity could be destroyed one species at a time. Still another justification was that it is necessary for Congress to be able to protect endangered species in order to protect against unfair competition between states that might occur if some states protected such species and others did not. The Supreme Court denied certiorari in all three cases. What do you think?

10.   In 2012, the Court was faced with a challenge to the constitutionality of two parts of the Affordable Care Act. One part involved the so-called

individual mandate that generally requires persons to purchase health insurance if they are not otherwise covered by health insurance, Medicare, or Medicaid. The government's principal defense was that the mandate was authorized by the Commerce Clause as means of regulating the interstate market in health insurance. The other part challenged was the Act's expansion of Medicaid. That aspect of the case will be covered in the next section of this chapter.

NATIONAL FEDERATION OF INDEPENDENT BUSINESS V. SEBELIUS, SECRETARY OF HEALTH AND HUMAN SERVICES
United States Supreme Court, 2012.
567 U.S. 519, 132 S.Ct. 2566.

CHIEF JUSTICE ROBERTS announced the judgment of the Court and delivered the opinion of the Court with respect to Parts I, II, and III-C, an opinion with respect to Part IV, in which JUSTICE BREYER and JUSTICE KAGAN join, and an opinion with respect to Parts III-A, III-B, and III-D.

Today we resolve constitutional challenges to two provisions of the Patient Protection and Affordable Care Act of 2010: the individual mandate, which requires individuals to purchase a health insurance policy providing a minimum level of coverage; and the Medicaid expansion, which gives funds to the States on the condition that they provide specified health care to all citizens whose income falls below a certain threshold. . . .

[T]his case concerns two powers that the Constitution does grant the Federal Government, but which must be read carefully to avoid creating a general federal authority akin to the police power. The Constitution authorizes Congress to "regulate Commerce with foreign Nations, and among the several States, and with the Indian Tribes." Our precedents read that to mean that Congress may regulate "the channels of interstate commerce," "persons or things in interstate commerce," and "those activities that substantially affect interstate commerce.". . .

Congress may also "lay and collect Taxes, Duties, Imposts and Excises, to pay the Debts and provide for the common Defence and general Welfare of the United States." Put simply, Congress may tax and spend. [The portion of this opinion relating to the Taxing and Spending Clause is contained in the section of this book under the Taxing and Spending Clause. See Section D of this chapter.]

The reach of the Federal Government's enumerated powers is broader still because the Constitution authorizes Congress to "make all Laws which shall be necessary and proper for carrying into Execution the foregoing Powers." Art. I, § 8, cl. 18. We have long read this provision to give Congress great latitude in exercising its powers: "Let the end be legitimate, let it be within the scope of the constitution, and all means which are appropriate, which are plainly adapted to that end, which are not prohibited, but consist

with the letter and spirit of the constitution, are constitutional."
McCulloch, 4 Wheat., at 421. . . .

I

In 2010, Congress enacted the Patient Protection and Affordable Care
Act. The Act aims to increase the number of Americans covered by health
insurance and decrease the cost of health care. The Act's 10 titles stretch
over 900 pages and contain hundreds of provisions. . . .

The individual mandate requires most Americans to maintain
"minimum essential" health insurance coverage. . . . Beginning in 2014,
those who do not comply with the mandate must make a "[s]hared
responsibility payment" to the Federal Government. That payment, which
the Act describes as a "penalty," is calculated as a percentage of household
income, subject to a floor based on a specified dollar amount and a ceiling
based on the average annual premium the individual would have to pay for
qualifying private health insurance. . . . The Act provides that the penalty
will be paid to the Internal Revenue Service with an individual's taxes, and
"shall be assessed and collected in the same manner" as tax penalties, such
as the penalty for claiming too large an income tax refund. The Act,
however, bars the IRS from using several of its normal enforcement tools,
such as criminal prosecutions and levies. And some individuals who are
subject to the mandate are nonetheless exempt from the penalty—for
example, those with income below a certain threshold and members of
Indian tribes.

On the day the President signed the Act into law, Florida and 12 other
States filed a complaint in the Federal District Court for the Northern
District of Florida. Those plaintiffs . . . were subsequently joined by 13
more States, several individuals, and the National Federation of
Independent Business. The plaintiffs alleged, among other things, that the
individual mandate provisions of the Act exceeded Congress's powers
under Article I of the Constitution. . . .

III

A

The Government's first argument is that the individual mandate is a
valid exercise of Congress's power under the Commerce Clause and the
Necessary and Proper Clause. According to the Government, the health
care market is characterized by a significant cost-shifting problem.
Everyone will eventually need health care at a time and to an extent they
cannot predict, but if they do not have insurance, they often will not be able
to pay for it. Because state and federal laws nonetheless require hospitals
to provide a certain degree of care to individuals without regard to their
ability to pay, hospitals end up receiving compensation for only a portion
of the services they provide. To recoup the losses, hospitals pass on the cost
to insurers through higher rates, and insurers, in turn, pass on the cost to

policy holders in the form of higher premiums. Congress estimated that the cost of uncompensated care raises family health insurance premiums, on average, by over $1,000 per year.

In the Affordable Care Act, Congress addressed the problem of those who cannot obtain insurance coverage because of preexisting conditions or other health issues. It did so through the Act's "guaranteed-issue" and "community-rating" provisions. These provisions together prohibit insurance companies from denying coverage to those with such conditions or charging unhealthy individuals higher premiums than healthy individuals.

The guaranteed-issue and community-rating reforms do not, however, address the issue of healthy individuals who choose not to purchase insurance to cover potential health care needs. In fact, the reforms sharply exacerbate that problem, by providing an incentive for individuals to delay purchasing health insurance until they become sick, relying on the promise of guaranteed and affordable coverage. The reforms also threaten to impose massive new costs on insurers, who are required to accept unhealthy individuals but prohibited from charging them rates necessary to pay for their coverage. This will lead insurers to significantly increase premiums on everyone.

The individual mandate was Congress's solution to these problems. By requiring that individuals purchase health insurance, the mandate prevents cost-shifting by those who would otherwise go without it. In addition, the mandate forces into the insurance risk pool more healthy individuals, whose premiums on average will be higher than their health care expenses. This allows insurers to subsidize the costs of covering the unhealthy individuals the reforms require them to accept. The Government claims that Congress has power under the Commerce and Necessary and Proper Clauses to enact this solution.

The Government contends that the individual mandate is within Congress's power because the failure to purchase insurance "has a substantial and deleterious effect on interstate commerce" by creating the cost-shifting problem. The path of our Commerce Clause decisions has not always run smooth, but it is now well established that Congress has broad authority under the Clause. . . .

Given its expansive scope, it is no surprise that Congress has employed the commerce power in a wide variety of ways to address the pressing needs of the time. But Congress has never attempted to rely on that power to compel individuals not engaged in commerce to purchase an unwanted product.[3] Legislative novelty is not necessarily fatal; there is a first time

---

[3]   The examples of other congressional mandates cited by JUSTICE GINSBURG are not to the contrary. Each of those mandates—to report for jury duty, to register for the draft, to purchase firearms in anticipation of militia service, to exchange gold currency for paper currency, and to file a tax return—are based on constitutional provisions other than the Commerce Clause.

for everything. But sometimes "the most telling indication of [a] severe constitutional problem . . . is the lack of historical precedent" for Congress's action. . . .

The Constitution grants Congress the power to "*regulate* Commerce." Art. I, § 8, cl. 3 (emphasis added). The power to *regulate* commerce presupposes the existence of commercial activity to be regulated. . . . The language of the Constitution reflects the natural understanding that the power to regulate assumes there is already something to be regulated.

Our precedent also reflects this understanding. As expansive as our cases construing the scope of the commerce power have been, they all have one thing in common: They uniformly describe the power as reaching "activity." It is nearly impossible to avoid the word when quoting them. See, *e.g.*, *Lopez* ("Where economic activity substantially affects interstate commerce, legislation regulating that activity will be sustained"); *Wickard* ("[E]ven if appellee's activity be local and though it may not be regarded as commerce, it may still, whatever its nature, be reached by Congress if it exerts a substantial economic effect on interstate commerce"); *NLRB v. Jones & Laughlin Steel Corp* ("Although activities may be intrastate in character when separately considered, if they have such a close and substantial relation to interstate commerce that their control is essential or appropriate to protect that commerce from burdens and obstructions, Congress cannot be denied the power to exercise that control").

The individual mandate, however, does not regulate existing commercial activity. It instead compels individuals to *become* active in commerce by purchasing a product, on the ground that their failure to do so affects interstate commerce. Construing the Commerce Clause to permit Congress to regulate individuals precisely *because* they are doing nothing would open a new and potentially vast domain to congressional authority. . . . Allowing Congress to justify federal regulation by pointing to the effect of inaction on commerce would bring countless decisions an individual could *potentially* make within the scope of federal regulation, and—under the Government's theory—empower Congress to make those decisions for him.

Applying the Government's logic to the familiar case of *Wickard* v. *Filburn* shows how far that logic would carry us from the notion of a government of limited powers. . . .

Wickard has long been regarded as "perhaps the most far reaching example of Commerce Clause authority over intrastate activity," but the Government's theory in this case would go much further. Under *Wickard* it is within Congress's power to regulate the market for wheat by supporting its price. But price can be supported by increasing demand as well as by decreasing supply. The aggregated decisions of some consumers not to purchase wheat have a substantial effect on the price of wheat, just as decisions not to purchase health insurance have on the price of insurance. Congress can therefore command that those not buying wheat do so, just as it argues here that it may command that those not buying health insurance do so. The farmer in *Wickard* was at least actively engaged in the production of wheat, and the Government could regulate that activity because of its effect on commerce. The Government's theory here would effectively override that limitation, by establishing that individuals may be regulated under the Commerce Clause whenever enough of them are not doing something the Government would have them do.

Indeed, the Government's logic would justify a mandatory purchase to solve almost any problem. To consider a different example in the health care market, many Americans do not eat a balanced diet. The failure of that group to have a healthy diet increases health care costs, to a greater extent than the failure of the uninsured to purchase insurance. Those increased costs are borne in part by other Americans who must pay more, just as the uninsured shift costs to the insured. Congress addressed the insurance problem by ordering everyone to buy insurance. Under the Government's theory, Congress could address the diet problem by ordering everyone to buy vegetables.

People, for reasons of their own, often fail to do things that would be good for them or good for society. Those failures—joined with the similar failures of others—can readily have a substantial effect on interstate commerce. Under the Government's logic, that authorizes Congress to use its commerce power to compel citizens to act as the Government would have them act.

That is not the country the Framers of our Constitution envisioned. . . . While Congress's authority under the Commerce Clause has of course expanded with the growth of the national economy, our cases have "always recognized that the power to regulate commerce, though broad indeed, has limits." . . . Congress already enjoys vast power to regulate much of what we do. Accepting the Government's theory would give Congress the same license to regulate what we do not do, fundamentally changing the relation between the citizen and the Federal Government.

To an economist, perhaps, there is no difference between activity and inactivity; both have measurable economic effects on commerce. But the distinction between doing something and doing nothing would not have been lost on the Framers, who were "practical statesmen," not metaphysical philosophers. . . . The Framers gave Congress the power to *regulate* commerce, not to *compel* it, and for over 200 years both our decisions and Congress's actions have reflected this understanding. There is no reason to depart from that understanding now. . . .

The Government argues that the individual mandate can be sustained as a sort of exception to this rule, because health insurance is a unique product. . . .

The Government says that health insurance and health care financing are "inherently integrated." But that does not mean the compelled purchase of the first is properly regarded as a regulation of the second. No matter how "inherently integrated" health insurance and health care consumption may be, they are not the same thing: They involve different transactions, entered into at different times, with different providers. And for most of those targeted by the mandate, significant health care needs will be years, or even decades, away. The proximity and degree of connection between the mandate and the subsequent commercial activity is too lacking to justify an exception of the sort urged by the Government. The individual mandate forces individuals into commerce precisely because they elected to refrain from commercial activity. Such a law cannot be sustained under a clause authorizing Congress to "regulate Commerce."

The Government next contends that Congress has the power under the Necessary and Proper Clause to enact the individual mandate because the mandate is an "integral part of a comprehensive scheme of economic regulation"—the guaranteed-issue and community-rating insurance reforms. Under this argument, it is not necessary to consider the effect that an individual's inactivity may have on interstate commerce; it is enough that Congress regulate commercial activity in a way that requires regulation of inactivity to be effective. The power to "make all Laws which shall be necessary and proper for carrying into Execution" the powers enumerated in the Constitution vests Congress with authority to enact provisions "incidental to the [enumerated] power, and conducive to its beneficial exercise," *McCulloch*.

As our jurisprudence under the Necessary and Proper Clause has developed, we have been very deferential to Congress's determination that a regulation is "necessary." We have thus upheld laws that are " 'convenient, or useful' or 'conducive' to the authority's 'beneficial exercise.' " But we have also carried out our responsibility to declare unconstitutional those laws that undermine the structure of government established by the Constitution. Such laws, which are not "consist[ent] with the letter and spirit of the constitution," *McCulloch*, are not "*proper* [means] for carrying into Execution" Congress's enumerated powers. . . .

Applying these principles, the individual mandate cannot be sustained under the Necessary and Proper Clause as an essential component of the insurance reforms. Each of our prior cases upholding laws under that Clause involved exercises of authority derivative of, and in service to, a granted power. For example, we have upheld provisions permitting continued confinement of those *already in federal custody* when they could not be safely released, *Comstock*; criminalizing bribes involving organizations *receiving federal funds*; and tolling state statutes of limitations while cases are *pending in federal court*. The individual mandate, by contrast, vests Congress with the extraordinary ability to create the necessary predicate to the exercise of an enumerated power.

This is in no way an authority that is "narrow in scope," *Comstock*, or "incidental" to the exercise of the commerce power, *McCulloch*. Rather, such a conception of the Necessary and Proper Clause would work a substantial expansion of federal authority. No longer would Congress be limited to regulating under the Commerce Clause those who by some preexisting activity bring themselves within the sphere of federal regulation. Instead, Congress could reach beyond the natural limit of its authority and draw within its regulatory scope those who otherwise would be outside of it. Even if the individual mandate is "necessary" to the Act's insurance reforms, such an expansion of federal power is not a "proper" means for making those reforms effective.

The Government relies primarily on our decision in *Gonzales* v. *Raich*. In *Raich*, we considered "comprehensive legislation to regulate the interstate market" in marijuana. Certain individuals sought an exemption from that regulation on the ground that they engaged in only intrastate possession and consumption. We denied any exemption, on the ground that marijuana is a fungible commodity, so that any marijuana could be readily diverted into the interstate market. Congress's attempt to regulate the interstate market for marijuana would therefore have been substantially undercut if it could not also regulate intrastate possession and consumption. Accordingly, we recognized that "Congress was acting well within its authority" under the Necessary and Proper Clause even though its "regulation ensnare[d] some purely intrastate activity." *Raich* thus did not involve the exercise of any "great substantive and independent power" of the sort at issue here. Instead, it concerned only the constitutionality of "individual *applications* of a concededly valid statutory scheme." . . .

[The portions of Chief Justice Roberts's opinion on the constitutionality of the individual mandate under the Taxing and Spending Clause and the constitutionality of the expansion of Medicaid is contained in the book's Section on the Taxing and Spending Clause.]

JUSTICE GINSBURG, with whom JUSTICE SOTOMAYOR joins, and with whom JUSTICE BREYER and JUSTICE KAGAN join as to Parts I, II, III, and IV, concurring in part, concurring in the judgment in part, and dissenting in part. [The portions of this opinion relating to the Taxing and Spending Clause are contained in this book's section on the Taxing and Spending Clause. See Section D of this chapter.]

[I] would hold . . . that the Commerce Clause authorizes Congress to enact the minimum coverage provision. . . .

I

The provision of health care is today a concern of national dimension, just as the provision of old-age and survivors' benefits was in the 1930s. In the Social Security Act, Congress installed a federal system to provide monthly benefits to retired wage earners and, eventually, to their survivors. Beyond question, Congress could have adopted a similar scheme for health care. Congress chose, instead, to preserve a central role for private insurers and state governments. According to THE CHIEF JUSTICE, the Commerce Clause does not permit that preservation. This rigid reading of the Clause makes scant sense and is stunningly retrogressive. Since 1937, our precedent has recognized Congress's large authority to set the Nation's course in the economic and social welfare realm. THE CHIEF JUSTICE's crabbed reading of the Commerce Clause harks back to the era in which the Court routinely thwarted Congress's efforts to regulate the national economy in the interest of those who labor to sustain it. It is a reading that should not have staying power.

In enacting the Patient Protection and Affordable Care Act (ACA), Congress comprehensively reformed the national market for health-care products and services. By any measure, that market is immense. Collectively, Americans spent $2.5 trillion on health care in 2009, accounting for 17.6% of our Nation's economy. Within the next decade, it is anticipated, spending on health care will nearly double. The health-care market's size is not its only distinctive feature. Unlike the market for almost any other product or service, the market for medical care is one in which all individuals inevitably participate. Virtually every person residing in the United States, sooner or later, will visit a doctor or other health-care professional. Most people will do so repeatedly.

When individuals make those visits, they face another reality of the current market for medical care: its high cost. . . .

Although every U. S. domiciliary will incur significant medical expenses during his or her lifetime, the time when care will be needed is often unpredictable. An accident, a heart attack, or a cancer diagnosis commonly occurs without warning. Inescapably, we are all at peril of needing medical care without a moment's notice.

To manage the risks associated with medical care—its high cost, its unpredictability, and its inevitability—most people in the United States obtain health insurance. Many (approximately 170 million in 2009) are insured by private insurance companies. Others, including those over 65 and certain poor and disabled persons, rely on government-funded insurance programs, notably Medicare and Medicaid. Combined, private health insurers and State and Federal Governments finance almost 85% of the medical care administered to U. S. residents.

Not all U. S. residents, however, have health insurance. In 2009, approximately 50 million people were uninsured, either by choice or, more likely, because they could not afford private insurance and did not qualify for government aid. As a group, uninsured individuals annually consume more than $100 billion in health-care services, nearly 5% of the Nation's total. Over 60% of those without insurance visit a doctor's office or emergency room in a given year.

The large number of individuals without health insurance, Congress found, heavily burdens the national health-care market. As just noted, the cost of emergency care or treatment for a serious illness generally exceeds what an individual can afford to pay on her own. Unlike markets for most products, however, the inability to pay for care does not mean that an uninsured individual will receive no care. Federal and state law, as well as professional obligations and embedded social norms, require hospitals and physicians to provide care when it is most needed, regardless of the patient's ability to pay. As a consequence, medical-care providers deliver significant amounts of care to the uninsured for which the providers receive no payment. In 2008, for example, hospitals, physicians, and other health-care professionals received no compensation for $43 billion worth of the $116 billion in care they administered to those without insurance.

Health-care providers do not absorb these bad debts. Instead, they raise their prices, passing along the cost of uncompensated care to those who do pay reliably: the government and private insurance companies. In response, private insurers increase their premiums, shifting the cost of the elevated bills from providers onto those who carry insurance. The net result: Those with health insurance subsidize the medical care of those without it. As economists would describe what happens, the uninsured "free ride" on those who pay for health insurance. . . .

Aware that a national solution was required, Congress could have taken over the health-insurance market by establishing a tax-and-spend federal program like Social Security. Such a program, commonly referred to as a single-payer system (where the sole payer is the Federal Government), would have left little, if any, room for private enterprise or the States. Instead of going this route, Congress enacted the ACA, a solution that retains a robust role for private insurers and state governments. To make its chosen approach work, however, Congress had to use some new tools, including a requirement that most individuals obtain private health insurance coverage. As explained below, by employing these tools, Congress was able to achieve a practical, altogether reasonable, solution. . . .

Before the ACA's enactment, private insurance companies took an applicant's medical history into account when setting insurance rates or deciding whether to insure an individual. Because individuals with preexisting medical conditions cost insurance companies significantly more than those without such conditions, insurers routinely refused to insure these individuals, charged them substantially higher premiums, or offered only limited coverage that did not include the preexisting illness.

To ensure that individuals with medical histories have access to affordable insurance, Congress devised a three-part solution. First,

Congress imposed a "guaranteed issue" requirement, which bars insurers from denying coverage to any person on account of that person's medical condition or history. Second, Congress required insurers to use "community rating" to price their insurance policies. Community rating, in effect, bars insurance companies from charging higher premiums to those with preexisting conditions.

But these two provisions, Congress comprehended, could not work effectively unless individuals were given a powerful incentive to obtain insurance.

In the 1990s, several States—including New York, New Jersey, Washington, Kentucky, Maine, New Hampshire, and Vermont—enacted guaranteed-issue and community-rating laws without requiring universal acquisition of insurance coverage. The results were disastrous. "All seven states suffered from skyrocketing insurance premium costs, reductions in individuals with coverage, and reductions in insurance products and providers."

Congress comprehended that guaranteed-issue and community-rating laws alone will not work. When insurance companies are required to insure the sick at affordable prices, individuals can wait until they become ill to buy insurance. Pretty soon, those in need of immediate medical care—*i.e.,* those who cost insurers the most—become the insurance companies' main customers. This "adverse selection" problem leaves insurers with two choices: They can either raise premiums dramatically to cover their ever-increasing costs or they can exit the market. In the seven States that tried guaranteed-issue and community-rating requirements without a minimum coverage provision, that is precisely what insurance companies did.

Massachusetts, Congress was told, cracked the adverse selection problem. By requiring most residents to obtain insurance, the Commonwealth ensured that insurers would not be left with only the sick as customers. As a result, federal lawmakers observed, Massachusetts succeeded where other States had failed. *See* Brief for Commonwealth of Massachusetts as *Amicus Curiae* in No. 11–398, p. 3 (noting that the Commonwealth's reforms reduced the number of uninsured residents to less than 2%, the lowest rate in the Nation, and cut the amount of uncompensated care by a third). In coupling the minimum coverage provision with guaranteed-issue and community-rating prescriptions, Congress followed Massachusetts's lead. . . .

In sum, Congress passed the minimum coverage provision as a key component of the ACA to address an economic and social problem that has plagued the Nation for decades: the large number of U. S. residents who are unable or unwilling to obtain health insurance. Whatever one thinks of the policy decision Congress made, it was Congress's prerogative to make it. Reviewed with appropriate deference, the minimum coverage provision, allied to the guaranteed-issue and community-rating prescriptions, should survive measurement under the Commerce and Necessary and Proper Clauses.

II

The Commerce Clause, it is widely acknowledged, "was the Framers' response to the central problem that gave rise to the Constitution itself." Under the Articles of Confederation, the Constitution's precursor, the regulation of commerce was left to the States. This scheme proved unworkable, because the individual States, understandably focused on their own economic interests, often failed to take actions critical to the success of the Nation as a whole. . . . The Framers' solution was the Commerce Clause, which, as they perceived it, granted Congress the authority to enact economic legislation "in all Cases for the general Interests of the Union, and also in those Cases to which the States are separately incompetent." 2 Records of the Federal Convention of 1787 (M. Farrand rev. 1966).

The Framers understood that the "general Interests of the Union" would change over time, in ways they could not anticipate. Accordingly, they recognized that the Constitution was of necessity a "great outlin[e]," not a detailed blueprint, see *McCulloch* v. *Maryland*. . . .

Consistent with the Framers' intent, we have repeatedly emphasized that Congress's authority under the Commerce Clause is dependent upon "practical" considerations, including "actual experience." *Jones & Laughlin Steel Corp.*; see *Wickard* v. *Filburn*; *United States* v. *Lopez* (KENNEDY, J., concurring)(emphasizing "the Court's definitive commitment to the practical conception of the commerce power"). . . . Until today, this Court's pragmatic approach to judging whether Congress validly exercised its commerce power was guided by two familiar principles. First, Congress has the power to regulate economic activities "that substantially affect interstate commerce." This capacious power extends even to local activities that, viewed in the aggregate, have a substantial impact on interstate commerce.

Second, we owe a large measure of respect to Congress when it frames and enacts economic and social legislation. *See Raich*. When appraising such legislation, we ask only (1) whether Congress had a "rational basis" for concluding that the regulated activity substantially affects interstate commerce, and (2) whether there is a "reasonable connection between the regulatory means selected and the asserted ends." *Id*. In answering these questions, we presume the statute under review is constitutional and may strike it down only on a "plain showing" that Congress acted irrationally. . . .

Not only do those without insurance consume a large amount of health care each year; critically, as earlier explained, their inability to pay for a significant portion of that consumption drives up market prices, foists costs on other consumers, and reduces market efficiency and stability. Given these far-reaching effects on interstate commerce, the decision to forgo insurance is hardly inconsequential or equivalent to "doing nothing"; it is, instead, an economic decision Congress has the authority to address under the Commerce Clause. . . .

Congress . . . acted reasonably in requiring uninsured individuals, whether sick or healthy, either to obtain insurance or to pay the specified penalty. As earlier observed, because every person is at risk of needing care at any moment, all those who lack insurance, regardless of their current health status, adversely affect the price of health care and health insurance. . . .

Rather than evaluating the constitutionality of the minimum coverage provision in the manner established by our precedents, THE CHIEF JUSTICE relies on a newly minted constitutional doctrine. The commerce power does not, THE CHIEF JUSTICE announces, permit Congress to "compe[l] individuals to become active in commerce by purchasing a product."

THE CHIEF JUSTICE's novel constraint on Congress's commerce power gains no force from our precedent and for that reason alone warrants disapprobation. But even assuming, for the moment, that Congress lacks authority under the Commerce Clause to "compel individuals not engaged in commerce to purchase an unwanted product," such a limitation would be inapplicable here. Everyone will, at some point, consume health-care products and services. Thus, if THE CHIEF JUSTICE is correct that an insurance-purchase requirement can be applied only to those who "actively" consume health care, the minimum coverage provision fits the bill. . . .

[C]ontrary to THE CHIEF JUSTICE's contention, our precedent does indeed support "[t]he proposition that Congress may dictate the conduct of an individual today because of prophesied future activity." In *Wickard*, the Court upheld a penalty the Federal Government imposed on a farmer who grew more wheat than he was permitted to grow under the Agricultural Adjustment Act of 1938 (AAA). He could not be penalized, the farmer argued, as he was growing the wheat for home consumption, not for sale on the open market. The Court rejected this argument. Wheat intended for home consumption, the Court noted, "overhangs the market, and if induced by rising prices, tends to flow into the market and check price increases [intended by the AAA]."

Similar reasoning supported the Court's judgment in *Raich*, which upheld Congress's authority to regulate marijuana grown for personal use. Homegrown marijuana substantially affects the interstate market for marijuana, we observed, for "the high demand in the interstate market will [likely] draw such marijuana into that market."

Our decisions thus acknowledge Congress's authority, under the Commerce Clause, to direct the conduct of an individual today (the farmer in *Wickard*, stopped from growing excess wheat; the plaintiff in *Raich*, ordered to cease cultivating marijuana) because of a prophesied future transaction (the eventual sale of that wheat or marijuana in the interstate market). Congress's actions are even more rational in this case, where the future activity (the consumption of medical care) is certain to occur, the sole uncertainty being the time the activity will take place. . . .

Nor is it accurate to say that the minimum coverage provision "compel[s] individuals . . . to purchase an unwanted product," or "suite of products." If unwanted today, medical service secured by insurance may be desperately needed tomorrow. Virtually everyone, I reiterate, consumes health care at some point in his or her life. Health insurance is a means of paying for this care, nothing more. In requiring individuals to obtain insurance, Congress is therefore not mandating the purchase of a discrete, unwanted product. Rather, Congress is merely defining the terms on which individuals pay for an interstate good they consume: Persons subject to the mandate must now pay for medical care in advance (instead of at the point of service) and through insurance (instead of out of pocket). Establishing payment terms for goods in or affecting interstate commerce is quintessential economic regulation well within Congress's domain. . . .

In any event, THE CHIEF JUSTICE's limitation of the commerce power to the regulation of those actively engaged in commerce finds no home in the text of the Constitution or our decisions. Article I, § 8, of the Constitution grants Congress the power "[t]o regulate Commerce . . . among the several States." Nothing in this language implies that Congress's commerce power is limited to regulating those actively engaged in commercial transactions. . . .

Underlying THE CHIEF JUSTICE's view that the Commerce Clause must be confined to the regulation of active participants in a commercial market is a fear that the commerce power would otherwise know no limits. The joint dissenters express a similar apprehension. This concern is unfounded.

First, THE CHIEF JUSTICE could certainly uphold the individual mandate without giving Congress *carte blanche* to enact any and all purchase mandates. As several times noted, the unique attributes of the health-care market render everyone active in that market and give rise to a significant free-riding problem that does not occur in other markets.

Nor would the commerce power be unbridled, absent THE CHIEF JUSTICE's "activity" limitation. Congress would remain unable to regulate noneconomic conduct that has only an attenuated effect on interstate commerce and is traditionally left to state law. *See Lopez*; *Morrison*. . . .

An individual's decision to self-insure, I have explained, is an economic act with the requisite connection to interstate commerce. Other choices individuals make are unlikely to fit the same or similar description. As an example of the type of regulation he fears, THE CHIEF JUSTICE cites a Government mandate to purchase green vegetables. One could call this concern "the broccoli horrible." Congress, THE CHIEF JUSTICE posits, might adopt such a mandate, reasoning that an individual's failure to eat a healthy diet, like the failure to purchase health insurance, imposes costs on others.

Consider the chain of inferences the Court would have to accept to conclude that a vegetable-purchase mandate was likely to have a substantial effect on the health-care costs borne by lithe Americans. The Court would have to believe that individuals forced to buy vegetables would then eat them (instead of throwing or giving them away), would prepare the vegetables in a healthy way (steamed or raw, not deep-fried), would cut back on unhealthy foods, and would not allow other factors (such as lack of exercise or little sleep) to trump the improved diet.[9] Such "pil[ing of] inference upon inference" is just what the Court refused to do in *Lopez* and *Morrison*. . . .

When contemplated in its extreme, almost any power looks dangerous. The commerce power, hypothetically, would enable Congress to prohibit the purchase and home production of all meat, fish, and dairy goods, effectively compelling Americans to eat only vegetables. Cf. *Raich*; *Wickard*. Yet no one would offer the "hypothetical and unreal possibilit[y]" of a vegetarian state as a credible reason to deny Congress the authority ever to ban the possession and sale of goods. . . .

To bolster his argument that the minimum coverage provision is not valid Commerce Clause legislation, THE CHIEF JUSTICE emphasizes the provision's novelty. While an insurance-purchase mandate may be novel, THE CHIEF JUSTICE's argument certainly is not. See, *e.g.,* Brief for Petitioner in *Perez* v. *United States* ("unprecedented exercise of power"); Supplemental Brief for Appellees in *Katzenbach* v. *McClung* ("novel assertion of federal power"); Brief for Appellee in *Wickard* v. *Filburn* ("complete departure"). For decades, the Court has declined to override legislation because of its novelty, and for good reason. As our national economy grows and changes, we have recognized, Congress must adapt to the changing "economic and financial realities." Hindering Congress's

---

[9]   The failure to purchase vegetables in THE CHIEF JUSTICE's hypothetical, then, is not what leads to higher health-care costs for others; rather, it is the failure of individuals to maintain a healthy diet, and the resulting obesity, that creates the cost-shifting problem. Requiring individuals to purchase vegetables is thus several steps removed from solving the problem. The failure to obtain health insurance, by contrast, is the immediate cause of the cost-shifting Congress sought to address through the ACA. Requiring individuals to obtain insurance attacks the source of the problem directly, in a single step.

ability to do so is shortsighted; if history is any guide, today's constriction of the Commerce Clause will not endure.

III

For the reasons explained above, the minimum coverage provision is valid Commerce Clause legislation. When viewed as a component of the entire ACA, the provision's constitutionality becomes even plainer. The Necessary and Proper Clause "empowers Congress to enact laws in effectuation of its [commerce] powe[r] that are not within its authority to enact in isolation." *Raich* (SCALIA, J., concurring in judgment). . . .

Recall that one of Congress's goals in enacting the Affordable Care Act was to eliminate the insurance industry's practice of charging higher prices or denying coverage to individuals with preexisting medical conditions. The commerce power allows Congress to ban this practice, a point no one disputes.

Congress knew, however, that simply barring insurance companies from relying on an applicant's medical history would not work in practice. . . . When complemented by an insurance mandate, on the other hand, guaranteed issue and community rating would work as intended, increasing access to insurance and reducing uncompensated care. The minimum coverage provision is thus an "essential par[t] of a larger regulation of economic activity"; without the provision, "the regulatory scheme [w]ould be undercut." *Raich.* Put differently, the minimum coverage provision, together with the guaranteed-issue and community-rating requirements, is " 'reasonably adapted' to the attainment of a legitimate end under the commerce power": the elimination of pricing and sales practices that take an applicant's medical history into account. . . .

JUSTICE SCALIA, JUSTICE KENNEDY, JUSTICE THOMAS, and JUSTICE ALITO, dissenting.

[T]his case is in one respect difficult: it presents two questions of first impression. The first of those is whether failure to engage in economic activity (the purchase of health insurance) is subject to regulation under the Commerce Clause. Failure to act does result in an effect on commerce, and hence might be said to come under this Court's "affecting commerce" criterion of Commerce Clause jurisprudence. But in none of its decisions has this Court extended the Clause that far. The second question is whether the congressional power to tax and spend, permits the conditioning of a State's continued receipt of all funds under a massive state-administered federal welfare program upon its acceptance of an expansion to that program. [The portions of this opinion relating to the Taxing and Spending Clause are contained in the section of this book under the Taxing and Spending Clause. See Section D of this chapter.] Those questions are difficult.

The case is easy and straightforward, however, in another respect. What is absolutely clear, affirmed by the text of the 1789 Constitution, by the Tenth Amendment ratified in 1791, and by innumerable cases of ours in the 220 years since, is that there are structural limits upon federal power—upon what it can prescribe with respect to private conduct, and upon what it can impose upon the sovereign States. Whatever may be the conceptual limits upon the Commerce Clause and upon the power to tax and spend, they cannot be such as will enable the Federal Government to regulate all private conduct. . . .

That clear principle carries the day here. The striking case of *Wickard* v. *Filburn*, which held that the economic activity of growing wheat, even for one's own consumption, affected commerce sufficiently that it could be regulated, always has been regarded as the *ne plus ultra* of expansive Commerce Clause jurisprudence. To go beyond that, and to say the *failure* to grow wheat (which is *not* an economic activity, or any activity at all) nonetheless affects commerce and therefore can be federally regulated, is to make mere breathing in and out the basis for federal prescription and to extend federal power to virtually all human activity. . . .

[T]he Individual Mandate in the Act commands that every "applicable individual shall for each month beginning after 2013 ensure that the individual, and any dependent of the individual who is an applicable individual, is covered under minimum essential coverage." If this provision "regulates" anything, it is the *failure* to maintain minimum essential coverage. . . . But that failure—that abstention from commerce—is not "Commerce." To be sure, *purchasing* insurance *is* "Commerce"; but one does not regulate commerce that does not exist by compelling its existence.

In *Gibbons* v. *Ogden* Chief Justice Marshall wrote that the power to regulate commerce is the power "to prescribe the rule by which commerce is to be governed." That understanding is consistent with the original meaning of "regulate" at the time of the Constitution's ratification, when "to regulate" meant "[t]o adjust by rule, method or established mode," 2 N. Webster, An American Dictionary of the English Language (1828); "[t]o adjust by rule or method," 2 S. Johnson, A Dictionary of the English Language (7th ed. 1785); "[t]o adjust, to direct according to rule," 2 J. Ash, New and Complete Dictionary of the English Language (1775); "to put in order, set to rights, govern or keep in order," T. Dyche & W. Pardon, A New General English Dictionary (16th ed. 1777). It can mean to direct the manner of something but not to direct that something come into being. . . .

We do not doubt that the buying and selling of health insurance contracts is commerce generally subject to federal regulation. But when Congress provides that (nearly) all citizens must buy an insurance contract, it goes beyond "adjust[ing] by rule or method," or "direct[ing] according to rule"; it directs the creation of commerce.

In response, the Government offers two theories as to why the Individual Mandate is nevertheless constitutional. Neither theory suffices to sustain its validity.

First, the Government submits that § 5000A is "integral to the Affordable Care Act's insurance reforms" and "necessary to make effective the Act's core reforms." Congress included a "finding" to similar effect in the Act itself. . . .

The Government presents the Individual Mandate as a unique feature of a complicated regulatory scheme governing many parties with countervailing incentives that must be carefully balanced. Congress has imposed an extensive set of regulations on the health insurance industry, and compliance with those regulations will likely cost the industry a great deal. If the industry does not respond by increasing premiums, it is not likely to survive. And if the industry does increase premiums, then there is a serious risk that its products—insurance plans—will become economically undesirable for many and prohibitively expensive for the rest.

This is not a dilemma unique to regulation of the health-insurance industry. Government regulation typically imposes costs on the regulated industry. . . Congress might protect the imperiled industry by prohibiting low-cost competition, or by according it preferential tax treatment, or even by granting it a direct subsidy.

Here, however, Congress has impressed into service third parties, healthy individuals who could be but are not customers of the relevant industry, to offset the undesirable consequences of the regulation. Congress's desire to force these individuals to purchase insurance is motivated by the fact that they are further removed from the market than unhealthy individuals with pre-existing conditions, because they are less likely to need extensive care in the near future. If Congress can reach out and command even those furthest removed from an interstate market to participate in the market, then the Commerce Clause becomes a font of unlimited power . . . .

The case upon which the Government principally relies to sustain the Individual Mandate under the Necessary and Proper Clause is *Gonzales* v. *Raich.* . . . *Raich* is no precedent for what Congress has done here. That case's prohibition of growing (cf. *Wickard*), and of possession (cf. innumerable federal statutes) did not represent the expansion of the federal power to direct into a broad new field. The mandating of economic activity does, and since it is a field so limitless that it converts the Commerce Clause into a general authority to direct the economy, that mandating is not "consist[ent] with the letter and spirit of the constitution." *McCulloch* v. *Maryland.* . . .

The Government was invited, at oral argument, to suggest what federal controls over private conduct (other than those explicitly prohibited by the Bill of Rights or other constitutional controls) could *not* be justified as necessary and proper for the carrying out of a general regulatory scheme. It was unable to name any. As we said at the outset, whereas the precise scope of the Commerce Clause and the Necessary and Proper Clause is uncertain, the proposition that the Federal Government cannot do everything is a fundamental precept. *See Lopez* ("[I]f we were to accept the Government's arguments, we are hard pressed to posit any activity by an individual that Congress is without power to regulate"). . . .

JUSTICE THOMAS, dissenting.

I dissent for the reasons stated in our joint opinion, but I write separately to say a word about the Commerce Clause. . . . I adhere to my view that "the very notion of a 'substantial effects' test under the Commerce Clause is inconsistent with the original understanding of Congress's powers and with this Court's early Commerce Clause cases." . . .

COMMENTS AND QUESTIONS

1.   This case was the blockbuster of the 2011 October Session of the Supreme Court. Its outcome, or at least the way the outcome was reached, was predicted by virtually no one. Spoiler alert! The Chief Justice in the portion of his opinion discussed in Section D of this chapter, relating to Congress's powers under the Taxing and Spending Clause, finds that the "penalty" that cannot be imposed under the Commerce Clause for failing to comply with the individual mandate can be imposed as a tax under the Taxing Clause. Joined by the four "liberals" on this point, he saves the individual mandate, much to the consternation of the "conservatives."

2.   As you can see from the excerpts of the case here (all the opinions run 193 pages), a majority of the Court found that the individual mandate was not authorized under the Commerce Clause. However, there is no majority opinion on that issue. Indeed, the Chief Justice's opinion is joined by no one. Why do you suppose the four joint dissenters (Justice Scalia, *et al.*), who also conclude that the mandate cannot be justified under the Commerce Clause, do not join the Chief Justice's opinion? What is the precedential status of *NFIB* with respect to the Commerce Clause?

3.   In *Lopez* and *Morrison* the Court found that the laws did not relate to commercial or economic matters, even if guns in schools or gender-motivated violence might indirectly have economic effects. Those indirect effects were simply too attenuated from the matter regulated to be justified by the Commerce Clause. In *NFIB*, however, the law involved regulation of the national health care insurance system, clearly commercial and economic matters. Why then did a majority of the Court find the law not authorized by the Commerce Clause?

4.   What do you think about the fact that all the previous cases that upheld a Commerce Clause power involved regulation of "activities," not inactivity? If economists agree that there is no economic difference between

activity and inactivity, why should the law erect a difference when the government is regulating economic matters? Are economists "metaphysical philosophers? Isn't it "practical" to recognize the economic consequences of persons not purchasing health insurance?

5.   The Chief Justice states that the Commerce Clause authorizes regulating activity, not compelling activity. When Congress passes a law requiring auto manufacturers to install airbags and seatbelts, is it regulating activity or compelling activity? How about when Congress passes a law requiring persons who emit air pollutants to install devices to remove the pollutants from their emissions?

6.   Why is it that no one questions (and no one challenged) the employer mandate in the Affordable Care Act? That portion of the Act requires employers of a certain size to provide health insurance for their employees. Why isn't this also a requirement for activity not authorized by the Commerce Clause?

7.   Do you think this case is likely to have much fall out with respect to other regulatory laws now or in the future, or is it a decision limited to an "individual mandate to purchase a good or service"?

PROBLEMS

1.   Congress passes a law creating a federal crime to transport any drug in interstate commerce for the purposes of facilitating suicide. Is this law constitutional?

2.   Congress passes a law creating a federal crime for anyone to possess a loaded firearm within the firearm's range of any runway of any airport. Is this law within Congress's Commerce Clause authority?

3.   Congress makes findings that arson of owner-occupied residential housing affects commerce by raising the price of fire insurance for residential housing, by raising the price of housing generally by decreasing the supply, by destroying the collateral for mortgages, by interfering with the delivery of electricity and gas or oil used by the residence, and by increasing the cost of fire protection. These findings are then included in a federal law creating a crime for anyone who commits arson of an owner-occupied residence. Max travels from California to Arizona to firebomb the home of a businessman who had not paid the gambling debts he incurred in Nevada. Max is caught and prosecuted under the federal law. He defends on the basis that the law is unconstitutional. How should the court rule?

C. THE TENTH AMENDMENT

So far in this chapter, we have been exploring the extent of Congress's powers under the Commerce Clause and the Necessary and Proper Clause. If a law is beyond Congress's powers, as in *Lopez*, that law is unconstitutional. Of course, something may be within Congress's positive authority, such as regulating the channels of commerce, but unconstitutional because of an express limitation of the Constitution. For example, Congress could not deny the use of the interstate highways to anyone who criticized the President of the United States. That would clearly violate the First Amendment's Free Speech Clause. A question we have already seen adverted to is whether the Tenth Amendment is a limitation on Congress's authority in the same manner as, for example, the First Amendment.

The text of the Tenth Amendment is relatively clear as constitutional provisions go:

> The powers not delegated to the United States by the Constitution, nor prohibited by it to the States, are reserved to the states respectively, or to the people.

Thus, if the power *is* delegated to the United States, the Tenth Amendment simply does not apply. Of course, if the power is *not* delegated to the United States, then its exercise is unconstitutional separate from the Tenth Amendment; it is beyond Congress's authority, as the Court found in *Lopez*. This textual construction led the Court in a number of cases to refer to the amendment as a truism. *See, e.g., United States v. Darby*, 312 U.S. 100, 124 (1941). This construction, however, was interrupted by *National League of Cities v. Usery*, 426 U.S. 833 (1976). That case challenged the application of a federal minimum wage, maximum hours law to almost all state employees. It was conceded that the wages and hours paid to state employees had a substantial effect on interstate commerce, but the Court, in a 5–4 decision written by then Justice Rehnquist, held that the Tenth Amendment in effect prohibited the application of the law to these state employees, overruling a case decided eight years before, *Maryland v. Wirtz*, 392 U.S. 183 (1968), that had upheld federal minimum wages and maximum hours laws applied to certain state workers. Nine years later, however, the Court changed its mind again.

GARCIA v. SAN ANTONIO METROPOLITAN TRANSIT AUTHORITY

United States Supreme Court, 1985.
469 U.S. 528, 105 S.Ct. 1005.

JUSTICE BLACKMUN delivered the opinion of the Court.

We revisit in these cases an issue raised in *National League of Cities v. Usery*. In that litigation, this Court, by a sharply divided vote, ruled that the Commerce Clause does not empower Congress to enforce the minimum-wage and overtime provisions of the Fair Labor Standards Act (FLSA) against the States in areas of traditional governmental functions. Although *National League of Cities* supplied some examples of traditional governmental functions, it did not offer a general explanation of how a traditional function is to be distinguished from a nontraditional one. Since then, federal and state courts have struggled with the task, thus imposed, of identifying a traditional function for purposes of state immunity under the Commerce Clause.

In the present cases, a Federal District Court concluded that municipal ownership and operation of a mass-transit system is a traditional governmental function and thus, under *National League of Cities*, is exempt from the obligations imposed by the FLSA. Faced with the identical question, three Federal Courts of Appeals and one state appellate court have reached the opposite conclusion.

Our examination of this function standard applied in these and other cases over the last eight years now persuades us that the attempt to draw the boundaries of state regulatory immunity in terms of traditional governmental function is not only unworkable but is also inconsistent with established principles of federalism and, indeed, with those very federalism principles on which *National League of Cities* purported to rest. That case, accordingly, is overruled.

[The San Antonio Metropolitan Transit Authority (SAMTA) sued the Secretary of Labor, seeking a declaratory judgment that FLSA was unconstitutional in light of *National League of Cities*. At the same time, a SAMTA worker, Joe Garcia, sued SAMTA seeking overtime pay as mandated by FLSA. The latter case was stayed, but Garcia was allowed to intervene in the other case. The district court found for SAMTA, and the Secretary and Garcia appealed directly to the Supreme Court.]

Appellees have not argued that SAMTA is immune from regulation under the FLSA on the ground that it is a local transit system engaged in intrastate commercial activity. In a practical sense, SAMTA's operations might well be characterized as local. Nonetheless, it long has been settled that Congress's authority under the Commerce Clause extends to intrastate economic activities that affect interstate commerce. Were SAMTA a privately owned and operated enterprise, it could not credibly argue that Congress exceeded the bounds of its Commerce Clause powers in prescribing minimum wages and overtime rates for SAMTA's employees. Any constitutional exemption from the requirements of the FLSA therefore must rest on SAMTA's status as a governmental entity rather than on the local nature of its operations.

The prerequisites for governmental immunity under *National League of Cities* [have been] summarized by this Court. . . . Under that summary, four conditions must be satisfied before a state activity may be deemed immune from a particular federal regulation under the Commerce Clause. First, it is said that the federal statute at issue must regulate the States as States. Second, the statute must address matters that are indisputably attribute[s] of state sovereignty. Third, state compliance with the federal obligation must directly impair [the States'] ability to structure integral operations in areas of traditional governmental functions. Finally, the relation of state and federal interests must not be such that the nature of the federal interest . . . justifies state submission.

The controversy in the present cases has focused on the third . . . requirement—that the challenged federal statute trench on traditional governmental functions. The District Court voiced a common concern: Despite the abundance of adjectives, identifying which particular state functions are immune remains difficult. Just how troublesome the task has been is revealed by the results reached in other federal cases. Thus, courts have held that regulating ambulance services; licensing automobile drivers; operating a municipal airport; performing solid waste disposal; and operating a highway authority are functions protected under *National League of Cities*. At the same time, courts have held that issuance of industrial development bonds; regulation of intrastate natural gas sales; regulation of traffic on public roads; regulation of air transportation; operation of a telephone system; leasing and sale of natural gas; operation of a mental health facility; and provision of in-house domestic services for the aged and handicapped are not entitled to immunity. We find it difficult, if not impossible, to identify an organizing principle that places each of the cases in the first group on one side of a line and each of the cases in the second group on the other side. . . .

The most obvious defect of a historical approach to state immunity is that it prevents a court from accommodating changes in the historical functions of States, changes that have resulted in a number of once-private functions like education being assumed by the States and their subdivisions.[9] At the same time, the only apparent virtue of a rigorous historical standard, namely, its promise of a reasonably objective measure for state immunity, is illusory. . . .

A nonhistorical standard for selecting immune governmental functions is likely to be just as unworkable as is a historical standard. The goal of identifying uniquely governmental functions, for example, has been rejected by the Court in the field of governmental tort liability in part

---

[9]   Indeed, the traditional nature of a particular governmental function can be a matter of historical nearsightedness; today's self-evidently traditional function is often yesterday's suspect innovation. Thus, *National League of Cities* offered the provision of public parks and recreation as an example of a traditional governmental function. A scant 80 years earlier, however, the Court pointed out that city commons originally had been provided not for recreation but for grazing domestic animals in common, and that [i]n the memory of men now living, a proposition to take private property [by eminent domain] for a public park . . . would have been regarded as a novel exercise of legislative power.

because the notion of a uniquely governmental function is unmanageable. . . .

We believe, however, that there is a more fundamental problem at work here. . . . The problem is that neither the governmental/proprietary distinction nor any other that purports to separate out important governmental functions can be faithful to the role of federalism in a democratic society. The essence of our federal system is that within the realm of authority left open to them under the Constitution, the States must be equally free to engage in any activity that their citizens choose for the common weal, no matter how unorthodox or unnecessary anyone else— including the judiciary—deems state involvement to be. Any rule of state immunity that looks to the traditional, integral, or necessary nature of governmental functions inevitably invites an unelected federal judiciary to make decisions about which state policies it favors and which ones it dislikes. . . .

We therefore now reject, as unsound in principle and unworkable in practice, a rule of state immunity from federal regulation that turns on a judicial appraisal of whether a particular governmental function is integral or traditional. Any such rule leads to inconsistent results at the same time that it disserves principles of democratic self-governance, and it breeds inconsistency precisely because it is divorced from those principles. If there are to be limits on the Federal Government's power to interfere with state functions—as undoubtedly there are—we must look elsewhere to find them. We accordingly return to the underlying issue that confronted this Court in *National League of Cities*—the manner in which the Constitution insulates States from the reach of Congress's power under the Commerce Clause.

The central theme of *National League of Cities* was that the States occupy a special position in our constitutional system and that the scope of Congress's authority under the Commerce Clause must reflect that position. Of course, the Commerce Clause by its specific language does not provide any special limitation on Congress's actions with respect to the States. . . . *National League of Cities* reflected the general conviction that the Constitution precludes the National Government [from] devour[ing] the essentials of state sovereignty. . . .

The States unquestionably do retai[n] a significant measure of sovereign authority. They do so, however, only to the extent that the Constitution has not divested them of their original powers and transferred those powers to the Federal Government. . . .

When we look for the States' residuary and inviolable sovereignty, in the shape of the constitutional scheme rather than in predetermined notions of sovereign power, a different measure of state sovereignty emerges. Apart from the limitation on federal authority inherent in the delegated nature of Congress's Article I powers, the principal means chosen by the Framers to ensure the role of the States in the federal system lies in the structure of the Federal Government itself. It is no novelty to observe that the composition of the Federal Government was designed in large part to protect the States from overreaching by Congress. The Framers thus gave the States a role in the selection both of the Executive and the Legislative Branches of the Federal Government. The States were vested with indirect influence over the House of Representatives and the Presidency by their control of electoral qualifications and their role in Presidential elections. They were given more direct influence in the Senate, where each State received equal representation and each Senator was to be selected by the legislature of his State. . . .

The extent to which the structure of the Federal Government itself was relied on to insulate the interests of the States is evident in the views of the Framers. . . . In short, the Framers chose to rely on a federal system in which special restraints on federal power over the States inhered principally in the workings of the National Government itself, rather than in discrete limitations on the objects of federal authority. State sovereign interests, then, are more properly protected by procedural safeguards inherent in the structure of the federal system than by judicially created limitations on federal power.

The effectiveness of the federal political process in preserving the States' interests is apparent even today in the course of federal legislation. On the one hand, the States have been able to direct a substantial proportion of federal revenues into their own treasuries in the form of general and program-specific grants in aid. . . . Moreover, at the same time that the States have exercised their influence to obtain federal support, they have been able to exempt themselves from a wide variety of obligations imposed by Congress under the Commerce Clause. . . . The fact that some federal statutes such as the FLSA extend general obligations to the States cannot obscure the extent to which the political position of the States in the federal system has served to minimize the burdens that the States bear under the Commerce Clause.

[A]gainst this background, we are convinced that the fundamental limitation that the constitutional scheme imposes on the Commerce Clause to protect the States as States is one of process rather than one of result. Any substantive restraint on the exercise of Commerce Clause powers must find its justification in the procedural nature of this basic limitation, and it must be tailored to compensate for possible failings in the national political process rather than to dictate a sacred province of state autonomy.

Insofar as the present cases are concerned, then, we need go no further than to state that we perceive nothing in the overtime and minimum-wage requirements of the FLSA, as applied to SAMTA, that is destructive of state sovereignty or violative of any constitutional provision. SAMTA faces nothing more than the same minimum-wage and overtime obligations that hundreds of thousands of other employers, public as well as private, have to meet.

This analysis makes clear that Congress's action in affording SAMTA employees the protections of the wage and hour provisions of the FLSA contravened no affirmative limit on Congress's power under the Commerce Clause. The judgment of the District Court therefore must be reversed.

Of course, we continue to recognize that the States occupy a special and specific position in our constitutional system and that the scope of Congress's authority under the Commerce Clause must reflect that position. But the principal and basic limit on the federal commerce power is that inherent in all congressional action—the built-in restraints that our system provides through state participation in federal governmental action. The political process ensures that laws that unduly burden the States will not be promulgated. In the factual setting of these cases the internal safeguards of the political process have performed as intended.

These cases do not require us to identify or define what affirmative limits the constitutional structure might impose on federal action affecting the States under the Commerce Clause. . . .

JUSTICE POWELL, with whom THE CHIEF JUSTICE, JUSTICE REHNQUIST, and JUSTICE O'CONNOR join, dissenting.

The Court today, in its 5–4 decision, overrules *National League of Cities v. Usery*, a case in which we held that Congress lacked authority to impose the requirements of the Fair Labor Standards Act on state and local governments. Because I believe this decision substantially alters the federal system embodied in the Constitution, I dissent.

There are, of course, numerous examples over the history of this Court in which prior decisions have been reconsidered and overruled. There have been few cases, however, in which the principle of stare decisis and the rationale of recent decisions were ignored as abruptly as we now witness.[1]
. . .

Whatever effect the Court's decision may have in weakening the application of stare decisis, it is likely to be less important than what the Court has done to the Constitution itself. A unique feature of the United States is the federal system of government guaranteed by the Constitution and implicit in the very name of our country. Despite some genuflecting in the Court's opinion to the concept of federalism, today's decision effectively reduces the Tenth Amendment to meaningless rhetoric when Congress acts pursuant to the Commerce Clause. . . .

---

[1]   *National League of Cities*, following some changes in the composition of the Court, had overruled *Maryland v. Wirtz*. Unlike *National League of Cities*, the rationale of *Wirtz* had not been repeatedly accepted by our subsequent decisions.

To leave no doubt about its intention, the Court renounces its decision in *National League of Cities* because it inevitably invites an unelected federal judiciary to make decisions about which state policies it favors and which ones it dislikes. In other words, the extent to which the States may exercise their authority, when Congress purports to act under the Commerce Clause, henceforth is to be determined from time to time by political decisions made by members of the Federal Government, decisions the Court says will not be subject to judicial review. I note that it does not seem to have occurred to the Court that it—an unelected majority of five Justices—today rejects almost 200 years of the understanding of the constitutional status of federalism. In doing so, there is only a single passing reference to the Tenth Amendment. Nor is so much as a dictum of any court cited in support of the view that the role of the States in the federal system may depend upon the grace of elected federal officials, rather than on the Constitution as interpreted by this Court. . . .

[M]ore troubling than the logical infirmities in the Court's reasoning is the result of its holding, *i.e.*, that federal political officials, invoking the Commerce Clause, are the sole judges of the limits of their own power. This result is inconsistent with the fundamental principles of our constitutional system. At least since *Marbury v. Madison*, it has been the settled province of the federal judiciary to say what the law is with respect to the constitutionality of Acts of Congress. . . .

In our federal system, the States have a major role that cannot be pre-empted by the National Government. As contemporaneous writings and the debates at the ratifying conventions make clear, the States' ratification of the Constitution was predicated on this understanding of federalism. Indeed, the Tenth Amendment was adopted specifically to ensure that the important role promised the States by the proponents of the Constitution was realized.

Much of the initial opposition to the Constitution was rooted in the fear that the National Government would be too powerful and eventually would eliminate the States as viable political entities. This concern was voiced repeatedly until proponents of the Constitution made assurances that a Bill of Rights, including a provision explicitly reserving powers in the States, would be among the first business of the new Congress. . . .

This history, which the Court simply ignores, documents the integral role of the Tenth Amendment in our constitutional theory. It exposes as well, I believe, the fundamental character of the Court's error today. Far from being unsound in principle, judicial enforcement of the Tenth Amendment is essential to maintaining the federal system so carefully designed by the Framers and adopted in the Constitution. . . .

The Framers believed that the separate sphere of sovereignty reserved to the States would ensure that the States would serve as an effective counterpoise to the power of the Federal Government. The States would serve this essential role because they would attract and retain the loyalty of their citizens. The roots of such loyalty, the Founders thought, were found in the objects peculiar to state government. . . .

Thus, the harm to the States that results from federal overreaching under the Commerce Clause is not simply a matter of dollars and cents. . . . Rather, by usurping functions traditionally performed by the States, federal overreaching under the Commerce Clause undermines the constitutionally mandated balance of power between the States and the Federal Government, a balance designed to protect our fundamental liberties. . . .

[T]he Court today propounds a view of federalism that pays only lipservice to the role of the States. Although it says that the States unquestionably do retai[n] a significant measure of sovereign authority, it fails to recognize the broad, yet specific areas of sovereignty that the Framers intended the States to retain. Indeed, the Court barely acknowledges that the Tenth Amendment exists. . . .

As I view the Court's decision today as rejecting the basic precepts of our federal system and limiting the constitutional role of judicial review, I dissent.

JUSTICE REHNQUIST, dissenting.

I join both Justice POWELL'S and Justice O'CONNOR's thoughtful dissents. . . . But . . . I do not think it incumbent on those of us in dissent to spell out further the fine points of a principle that will, I am confident, in time again command the support of a majority of this Court.

JUSTICE O'CONNOR, with whom JUSTICE POWELL and JUSTICE REHNQUIST join, dissenting.

The Court today surveys the battle scene of federalism and sounds a retreat. Like Justice POWELL, I would prefer to hold the field and, at the very least, render a little aid to the wounded. I join Justice POWELL'S opinion. I also write separately to note my fundamental disagreement with the majority's views of federalism and the duty of this Court. . . .

In my view, federalism cannot be reduced to the weak essence distilled by the majority today. . . .

Due to the emergence of an integrated and industrialized national economy, this Court has been required to examine and review a breathtaking expansion of the powers of Congress. In doing so the Court correctly perceived that the Framers of our Constitution intended Congress to have sufficient power to address national problems. . . . Just as surely as the Framers envisioned a National Government capable of solving national problems, they also envisioned a republic whose vitality was assured by the diffusion of power not only among the branches of the Federal Government, but also between the Federal Government and the States. . . .

The operative language of [our] cases varies, but the underlying principle is consistent: state autonomy is a relevant factor in assessing the means by which Congress exercises its powers.

This principle requires the Court to enforce affirmative limits on federal regulation of the States to complement the judicially crafted expansion of the interstate commerce power. *National League of Cities v. Usery* represented an attempt to define such limits. The Court today rejects *National League of Cities* and washes its hands of all efforts to protect the States. In the process, the Court opines that unwarranted federal encroachments on state authority are and will remain horrible possibilities that never happen in the real world. There is ample reason to believe to the contrary. . . .

The problems of federalism in an integrated national economy are capable of more responsible resolution than holding that the States as States retain no status apart from that which Congress chooses to let them retain. The proper resolution, I suggest, lies in weighing state autonomy as a factor in the balance when interpreting the means by which Congress can exercise its authority on the States as States. It is insufficient, in assessing the validity of congressional regulation of a State pursuant to the commerce power, to ask only whether the same regulation would be valid if enforced against a private party. That reasoning, embodied in the majority opinion, is inconsistent with the spirit of our Constitution. It remains relevant that a State is being regulated. . . . I share Justice REHNQUIST's belief that this Court will in time again assume its constitutional responsibility.

I respectfully dissent.

COMMENTS AND QUESTIONS

1.   The dissent complains that *SAMTA* overrules *National League of Cities* a mere nine years after it was decided. However, the dissent does not mention the irony that *National League of Cities* overruled *Maryland v. Wirtz*, only eight years after it was decided; that *National League of Cities* was decided by a split Court 5–4; and that *National League of Cities* had rejected over a century of jurisprudence that the Tenth Amendment did not have substantive effect.

2.   The only change in the membership of the Court between *National League of Cities* and *SAMTA* was the replacement of Justice Stewart with Justice O'Connor, an even stronger advocate of states rights. Instead, Justice Blackmun, who had concurred in *National League of Cities*, saying that he was "not untroubled by certain possible implications of the Court's opinion," switched sides and wrote the new majority opinion. The other members of the Court making up the majority had dissented in *National League of Cities* on the basis that the Tenth Amendment simply was not a restriction on Congress's Commerce Clause authority. Is this what Justice Blackmun's

opinion for the Court says, or does he adopt a different theory to uphold the law?

3.　　The Court's opinion faithfully describes the *National League of Cities'* test for whether a law would transgress the Tenth Amendment. The Court focuses on the difficulty of determining whether a particular activity is a traditional state function, but another of the criteria is whether the federal statute regulates "states as states." Does the FLSA regulate states as states? Does it not just regulate employers whoever they are, making no exceptions for states? Should this make a difference? Consider that in light of the next case.

4.　　The Court concludes that the role of states in our federal system can be adequately protected through the political process. How does the political process protect the role of states? How would you feel about a decision that left protection of First Amendment rights to the political process? Is that a fair analogy?

5.　　The dissenters in *SAMTA* confidently predict that in time *SAMTA* will be overruled and *National League of Cities* reinstated. Is that what the next case does?

NEW YORK V. UNITED STATES

United States Supreme Court, 1992.
505 U.S. 144, 112 S.Ct. 2408.

JUSTICE O'CONNOR delivered the opinion of the Court.

These cases implicate one of our Nation's newest problems of public policy and perhaps our oldest question of constitutional law. The public policy issue involves the disposal of radioactive waste: In these cases, we address the constitutionality of three provisions of the Low-Level Radioactive Waste Policy Amendments Act of 1985. The constitutional question is as old as the Constitution: It consists of discerning the proper division of authority between the Federal Government and the States. We conclude that while Congress has substantial power under the Constitution to encourage the States to provide for the disposal of the radioactive waste generated within their borders, the Constitution does not confer upon Congress the ability simply to compel the States to do so. We therefore find that only two of the Act's three provisions at issue are consistent with the Constitution's allocation of power to the Federal Government.

We live in a world full of low level radioactive waste. Radioactive material is present in luminous watch dials, smoke alarms, measurement devices, medical fluids, research materials, and the protective gear and construction materials used by workers at nuclear power plants. . . . Millions of cubic feet of low level radioactive waste must be disposed of each year.

[S]ince 1979 only three disposal sites—those in Nevada, Washington, and South Carolina—have been in operation. Waste generated in the rest of the country must be shipped to one of these three sites for disposal. . . . The Governors of Washington and Nevada announced plans to shut their sites permanently.

Faced with the possibility that the Nation would be left with no disposal sites for low level radioactive waste, Congress responded by enacting the Low-Level Radioactive Waste Policy Act. . . . The . . . Act was . . . based largely on a proposal submitted by the National Governors' Association. In broad outline, the Act embodies a compromise among the sited and unsited States. . . .

The mechanics of this compromise are intricate. [It requires each state to be responsible for providing for the disposal of low-level radioactive waste generated within the State, either by itself or in cooperation with other States through adoption of an interstate compact.]

The Act provides three types of incentives to encourage the States to comply with their statutory obligation to provide for the disposal of waste generated within their borders.

1. *Monetary incentives.* [The Secretary of Energy makes payments to each state that complies with the Act.]

2. *Access incentives.* The second type of incentive involves the denial of access to disposal sites. States that fail to meet the [requirements] may be denied access to disposal facilities thereafter [by those states that have disposal facilities.]

Sandra Day O'Connor
President Reagan appointed O'Connor to the Supreme Court in 1981, the first woman to serve on the Court. She was known for her support of women's rights and states' rights. After dissenting from several decisions upholding *Roe v. Wade,* she provided a necessary fifth vote in the crucial final case of *Planned Parenthood v. Casey* to continue a woman's right to an abortion. Her jurisprudence was characterized by an attempt to decide only the particular case before her rather than to make broad, sweeping rules on the basis of the particular case. She retired from the Court in 2006 and was replaced by Samuel Alito.

3. *The take title provision.* The third type of incentive is the most severe. The Act provides [that if a State in which low-level radioactive waste is generated is unable to provide for the disposal of all such waste generated within such State or compact region by January 1, 1996, each State in which such waste is generated, upon the request of the generator or owner of the waste, shall take title to the waste, be obligated to take possession of the waste, and shall be liable for all damages directly or indirectly incurred by such generator or owner as a consequence of the failure of the State to take possession of the waste.]

These three incentives are the focus of petitioners' constitutional challenge.

[P]etitioners—the State of New York and . . . two counties—filed this suit against the United States in 1990. They sought a declaratory judgment that the Act is inconsistent with the Tenth . . . Amendment[ ] to the Constitution . . . and with the Guarantee Clause of Article IV of the Constitution. . . .

At least as far back as [1816], the Court has resolved questions of great importance and delicacy in determining whether particular sovereign powers have been granted by the Constitution to the Federal Government or have been retained by the States. These questions can be viewed in either of two ways. In some cases the Court has inquired whether an Act of Congress is authorized by one of the powers delegated to Congress in Article I of the Constitution. *See, e.g., Perez v. United States; McCulloch v. Maryland.* In other cases the Court has sought to determine whether an Act of Congress invades the province of state sovereignty reserved by the Tenth Amendment. *See, e.g., Garcia v. San Antonio Metropolitan Transit Authority.* In a case like these, involving the division of authority between federal and state governments, the two inquiries are mirror images of each other. If a power is delegated to Congress in the Constitution, the Tenth Amendment expressly disclaims any reservation of that power to the States; if a power is an attribute of state sovereignty reserved by the Tenth Amendment, it is necessarily a power the Constitution has not conferred on Congress. It is in this sense that the Tenth Amendment states but a truism that all is retained which has not been surrendered. *United States v. Darby* . . . .

Congress exercises its conferred powers subject to the limitations contained in the Constitution. Thus, for example, under the Commerce Clause Congress may regulate publishers engaged in interstate commerce, but Congress is constrained in the exercise of that power by the First Amendment. The Tenth Amendment likewise restrains the power of Congress, but this limit is not derived from the text of the Tenth Amendment itself, which, as we have discussed, is essentially a tautology. Instead, the Tenth Amendment confirms that the power of the Federal Government is subject to limits that may, in a given instance, reserve power to the States. The Tenth Amendment thus directs us to determine, as in this case, whether an incident of state sovereignty is protected by a limitation on an Article I power. . . .

Petitioners do not contend that Congress lacks the power to regulate the disposal of low level radioactive waste. . . . Petitioners likewise do not dispute that under the Supremacy Clause Congress could, if it wished, pre-empt state radioactive waste regulation. Petitioners contend only that the Tenth Amendment limits the power of Congress to regulate in the way it has chosen. Rather than addressing the problem of waste disposal by directly regulating the generators and disposers of waste, petitioners argue, Congress has impermissibly directed the States to regulate in this field.

Most of our recent cases interpreting the Tenth Amendment have concerned the authority of Congress to subject state governments to generally applicable laws. The Court's jurisprudence in this area has traveled an unsteady path. *See Maryland v. Wirtz*; *National League of Cities v. Usery*; *Garcia v. San Antonio Metropolitan Transit Authority*. This litigation presents no occasion to apply or revisit the holdings of any of these cases, as this is not a case in which Congress has subjected a State to the same legislation applicable to private parties.

This litigation instead concerns the circumstances under which Congress may use the States as implements of regulation; that is, whether Congress may direct or otherwise motivate the States to regulate in a particular field or a particular way. Our cases have established a few principles that guide our resolution of the issue.

As an initial matter, Congress may not simply commandee[r] the legislative processes of the States by directly compelling them to enact and enforce a federal regulatory program. . . . While Congress has substantial powers to govern the Nation directly, including in areas of intimate concern to the States, the Constitution has never been understood to confer upon Congress the ability to require the States to govern according to Congress's instructions. . . . Indeed, the question whether the Constitution should permit Congress to employ state governments as regulatory agencies was a topic of lively debate among the Framers. Under the Articles of Confederation, Congress lacked the authority in most respects to govern the people directly. . . .

The [Constitutional] Convention generated a great number of proposals for the structure of the new Government, but two quickly took center stage. Under the Virginia Plan, . . . Congress would exercise legislative authority directly upon individuals, without employing the States as intermediaries. Under the New Jersey Plan, . . . Congress would continue to require the approval of the States before legislating, as it had under the Articles of Confederation. . . . In the end, the Convention opted for a Constitution in which Congress would exercise its legislative authority directly over individuals rather than over States; for a variety of reasons, it rejected the New Jersey Plan in favor of the Virginia Plan. . . . In providing for a stronger central government, therefore, the Framers explicitly chose a Constitution that confers upon Congress the power to regulate individuals, not States. The allocation of power contained in the Commerce Clause, for example, authorizes Congress to regulate interstate commerce directly; it does not authorize Congress to regulate state governments' regulation of interstate commerce.

This is not to say that Congress lacks the ability to encourage a State to regulate in a particular way, or that Congress may not hold out incentives to the States as a method of influencing a State's policy choices. Our cases have identified a variety of methods, short of outright coercion, by which Congress may urge a State to adopt a legislative program consistent with federal interests. Two of these methods are of particular relevance here.

First, under Congress's spending power, Congress may attach conditions on the receipt of federal funds. *South Dakota v. Dole*. . . . Where the recipient of federal funds is a State, . . . the conditions attached to the funds by Congress may influence a State's legislative choices. . . .

Second, where Congress has the authority to regulate private activity under the Commerce Clause, we have recognized Congress's power to offer States the choice of regulating that activity according to federal standards or having state law pre-empted by federal regulation. This arrangement, which has been termed a program of cooperative federalism, is replicated in numerous federal statutory schemes. These include the Clean Water Act; the Occupational Safety and Health Act of 1970; the Resource Conservation and Recovery Act of 1976; and the Alaska National Interest Lands Conservation Act.

By either of these methods, as by any other permissible method of encouraging a State to conform to federal policy choices, the residents of the State retain the ultimate decision as to whether or not the State will comply. If a State's citizens view federal policy as sufficiently contrary to local interests, they may elect to decline a federal grant. If state residents would prefer their government to devote its attention and resources to problems other than those deemed important by Congress, they may choose to have the Federal Government rather than the State bear the expense of a federally mandated regulatory program, and they may continue to supplement that program to the extent state law is not pre-empted. Where Congress encourages state regulation rather than compelling it, state governments remain responsive to the local electorate's preferences; state officials remain accountable to the people.

By contrast, where the Federal Government compels States to regulate, the accountability of both state and federal officials is diminished. If the citizens of New York, for example, do not consider that making provision for the disposal of radioactive waste is in their best interest, they may elect state officials who share their view. That view can always be pre-empted under the Supremacy Clause if it is contrary to the national view, but in such a case it is the Federal Government that makes the decision in full view of the public, and it will be federal officials that suffer the consequences if the decision turns out to be detrimental or unpopular. But where the Federal Government directs the States to regulate, it may be state officials who will bear the brunt of public disapproval, while the federal officials who devised the regulatory program may remain insulated from the electoral ramifications of their decision. Accountability is thus diminished when, due to federal coercion, elected state officials cannot regulate in accordance with the views of the local electorate in matters not pre-empted by federal regulation.

With these principles in mind, we turn to the three challenged provisions of the [Act].

The first set of incentives [essentially provides funds to states as they achieve a series of milestones toward disposing of the waste.] [This] is a conditional exercise of Congress's authority under the Spending Clause: Congress has placed conditions—the achievement of the milestones—on the receipt of federal funds. Petitioners do not contend that Congress has exceeded its [Spending Clause] authority in any of the . . . respects our cases have identified. . . . The Act's first set of incentives, in which Congress has conditioned grants to the States upon the States' attainment of a series of milestones, is thus well within the authority of Congress under the Commerce and Spending Clauses. Because the first set of incentives is supported by affirmative constitutional grants of power to Congress, it is not inconsistent with the Tenth Amendment.

In the second set of incentives, Congress has authorized States and regional compacts with disposal sites . . . to deny access altogether to radioactive waste generated in States that do not meet federal deadlines. . . . [In other words,] States may either regulate the disposal of radioactive waste according to federal standards by attaining local or regional self-sufficiency, or their residents who produce radioactive waste will be subject to federal regulation authorizing sited States and regions to deny access to their disposal sites. The affected States are not compelled by Congress to regulate, because any burden caused by a State's refusal to regulate will fall on those who generate waste and find no outlet for its disposal, rather than on the State as a sovereign. . . . The Act's second set of incentives thus represents a conditional exercise of Congress's commerce power, along the lines of those we have held to be within Congress's authority. As a result, the second set of incentives does not intrude on the sovereignty reserved to the States by the Tenth Amendment.

The take title provision is of a different character. This third so-called incentive offers States, as an alternative to regulating pursuant to Congress's direction, the option of taking title to and possession of the low level radioactive waste generated within their borders and becoming liable for all damages waste generators suffer as a result of the States' failure to do so promptly. In this provision, Congress has crossed the line distinguishing encouragement from coercion.

[T]he take title provision offers state governments a choice of either accepting ownership of waste or regulating according to the instructions of Congress. . . . Because an instruction to state governments to take title to waste, standing alone, would be beyond the authority of Congress, and because a direct order to regulate, standing alone, would also be beyond the authority of Congress, it follows that Congress lacks the power to offer the States a choice between the two. Unlike the first two sets of incentives, the take title incentive does not represent the conditional exercise of any congressional power enumerated in the Constitution. In this provision, Congress has not held out the threat of exercising its spending power or its commerce power; it has instead held out the threat, should the States not regulate according to one federal instruction, of simply forcing the States to submit to another federal instruction. A choice between two unconstitutionally coercive regulatory techniques is no choice at all. Either way, the Act commandeers the legislative processes of the States by directly compelling them to enact and enforce a federal regulatory program, an outcome that has never been understood to lie within the authority conferred upon Congress by the Constitution. . .

[S]tates are not mere political subdivisions of the United States. State governments are neither regional offices nor administrative agencies of the Federal Government. The positions occupied by state officials appear nowhere on the Federal Government's most detailed organizational chart. The Constitution instead leaves to the several States a residuary and inviolable sovereignty, reserved explicitly to the States by the Tenth Amendment.

Whatever the outer limits of that sovereignty may be, one thing is clear: The Federal Government may not compel the States to enact or administer a federal regulatory program. The Constitution permits both the Federal Government and the States to enact legislation regarding the disposal of low level radioactive waste. The Constitution enables the Federal Government to pre-empt state regulation contrary to federal interests, and it permits the Federal Government to hold out incentives to the States as a means of encouraging them to adopt suggested regulatory schemes. It does not, however, authorize Congress simply to direct the States to provide for the disposal of the radioactive waste generated within their borders. While there may be many constitutional methods of achieving regional self-sufficiency in radioactive waste disposal, the method Congress has chosen is not one of them.

JUSTICE WHITE, with whom JUSTICE BLACKMUN and JUSTICE STEVENS join, concurring in part and dissenting in part.

[T]he Court strikes down and severs [the] third component of the 1985 Act, the take title provision, which requires a noncomplying State to take title to or to assume liability for its low-level radioactive waste if it fails to provide for the disposal of such waste by January 1, 1996. The Court deems this last provision unconstitutional under principles of federalism. Because I believe the Court has mischaracterized the essential inquiry, misanalyzed the inquiry it has chosen to undertake, and undervalued the effect the seriousness of this public policy problem should have on the constitutionality of the take title provision, I can only join Parts III-A and

III-B, and I respectfully dissent from the rest of its opinion and the judgment reversing in part the judgment of the Court of Appeals. . . .

To justify its holding that the take title provision contravenes the Constitution, the Court posits that [i]n this provision, Congress has crossed the line distinguishing encouragement from coercion. . . .

Curiously absent from the Court's analysis is any effort to place the take title provision within the overall context of the legislation. . . . Congress could have pre-empted the field by directly regulating the disposal of this waste pursuant to its powers under the Commerce and Spending Clauses, but instead it unanimously assented to the States' request for congressional ratification of agreements to which they had acceded. As the floor statements of Members of Congress reveal, the States wished to take the lead in achieving a solution to this problem and agreed among themselves to the various incentives and penalties implemented by Congress to ensure adherence to the various deadlines and goals. The chief executives of the States proposed this approach, and I am unmoved by the Court's vehemence in taking away Congress's authority to sanction a recalcitrant unsited State now that New York has reaped the benefits of the sited States' concessions. . . .

The Court's distinction between a federal statute's regulation of States and private parties for general purposes, as opposed to a regulation solely on the activities of States, is unsupported by our recent Tenth Amendment cases. In no case has the Court rested its holding on such a distinction. . . . Certainly one would be hard-pressed to read the spirited exchanges between the Court and dissenting Justices in *National League of Cities* and in *Garcia v. San Antonio Metropolitan Transit Authority* as having been based on the distinction now drawn by the Court. An incursion on state sovereignty hardly seems more constitutionally acceptable if the federal statute that commands specific action also applies to private parties. The alleged diminution in state authority over its own affairs is not any less because the federal mandate restricts the activities of private parties. . . .

The ultimate irony of the decision today is that in its formalistically rigid obeisance to federalism, the Court gives Congress fewer incentives to defer to the wishes of state officials in achieving local solutions to local problems. This legislation was a classic example of Congress acting as arbiter among the States in their attempts to accept responsibility for managing a problem of grave import. The States urged the National Legislature not to impose from Washington a solution to the country's low-level radioactive waste management problems. Instead, they sought a reasonable level of local and regional autonomy consistent with Art. I, § 10, cl. 3, of the Constitution. . . .

JUSTICE STEVENS, concurring in part and dissenting in part.

Under the Articles of Confederation, the Federal Government had the power to issue commands to the States. *See* Arts. VIII, IX. Because that indirect exercise of federal power proved ineffective, the Framers of the Constitution empowered the Federal Government to exercise legislative authority directly over individuals within the States, even though that direct authority constituted a greater intrusion on state sovereignty. Nothing in that history suggests that the Federal Government may not also impose its will upon the several States as it did under the Articles. The Constitution enhanced, rather than diminished, the power of the Federal Government.

The notion that Congress does not have the power to issue a simple command to state governments to implement legislation enacted by Congress is incorrect and unsound. There is no such limitation in the Constitution. The Tenth Amendment surely does not impose any limit on Congress's exercise of the powers delegated to it by Article I. Nor does the structure of the constitutional order or the values of federalism mandate such a formal rule. To the contrary, the Federal Government directs state governments in many realms. The Government regulates state-operated railroads, state school systems, state prisons, state elections, and a host of other state functions. Similarly, there can be no doubt that, in time of war, Congress could either draft soldiers itself or command the States to supply their quotas of troops. I see no reason why Congress may not also command the States to enforce federal water and air quality standards or federal standards for the disposition of low-level radioactive wastes.

COMMENTS AND QUESTIONS

1. What is the status of *Garcia v. SAMTA* after *New York v. United States*?

2. How is *New York v. United States* a Tenth Amendment case?

3. The Court says that the Constitution rejected the plan of the Articles of Confederation, in which the laws of the United States directed the states to take action, in favor of laws of the United States that would act directly on people. Justice Stevens argues that the Constitution added the power for Congress to make laws that would act directly on people without taking away the power to direct states to take action. What do you think? Does it make any difference that the Articles provided that "[e]ach state retains its sovereignty, freedom, and independence, and every power, jurisdiction, and right, which is not by this Confederation expressly delegated to the United States . . .," and the Tenth Amendment only provides that "[t]he powers not delegated to the United States by the Constitution . . . are reserved to the states respectively, or the people"?

4. There is an irony, noted by the dissent, that the law is held unconstitutional as improperly interfering with states' rights even though it was suggested to Congress by the National Governors Association. Moreover,

persons normally can waive their rights under the Bill of Rights. For example, you can waive your right to a trial; you can consent to a search without a warrant. Why can states not waive their rights under the Tenth Amendment?

5.   What is the difference between the first two parts of the Act and the third part that makes only the latter unconstitutional?

6.   Five years later, the Court applied the anti-commandeering principle of *New York v. United States* to a provision of the Brady Handgun Violence Prevention Act, which required state and local law enforcement officers to conduct background checks on prospective handgun purchasers pending the development of a national instant background check. *Printz v. United States*, 521 U.S. 898 (1997). While *New York v. United States* had involved the "commandeering" of state legislatures, *Printz* involved "commandeering" of state officers. While this made a difference to Justice Souter, who had joined the Court's opinion in *New York v. United States*, but dissented in *Printz*, the other members of the Court essentially saw them as indistinguishable.

7.   Three years after *Printz*, South Carolina challenged the Driver's Privacy Protection Act (DPPA), which restricted the ability of any person to sell or disclose to private parties the personal information contained on drivers' licenses without the consent of the driver involved. States routinely sold this information to businesses that then used it for marketing purposes. The state argued that this law was like *Printz* and *New York* in that it directed what the state could and could not do, essentially requiring it to carry out the federal law. The Court disagreed. In a unanimous opinion for the Court, Chief Justice Rehnquist distinguished those two cases. In those cases states were required to regulate citizens on behalf of the federal government, but here the states themselves were subject to the regulation. Moreover, this information was clearly an article in commerce and therefore clearly something subject to federal regulation. The statute did not single out states as the only entity subject to the law; indeed, the law applied to anyone who sold this information. *See Reno v. Condon*, 528 U.S. 141 (2000). It is not surprising, perhaps, that Chief Justice Rehnquist did not cite *Garcia v. SAMTA* in support of his position. Nevertheless, does not this case suggest the continued vitality of that case?

8.   *Murphy v. NCAA*, 138 S.Ct. 1461 (2018), raised an interesting twist to the anti-commandeering doctrine. Gambling on most sports events was for a long time illegal in every state (except Nevada). However, in 1992 as restrictions on various forms of gambling were being eliminated, Congress enacted the Professional and Amateur Sports Protection Act (PASPA) which made it unlawful for any state to "authorize by law" gambling on competitive sports events (with a grandfather exception to Nevada). New Jersey, seeking to make its casinos more attractive, repealed its law prohibiting sports betting with respect to casinos. This was challenged as violative of PASPA. The Court held that PASPA "unequivocally dictates what a state legislature may and may not do." "A more direct affront to state sovereignty is not easy to imagine." While *New York* and *Printz* involved laws commanding affirmative actions, as opposed to a law containing a prohibition, "[t]he basic principle—that Congress

cannot issue direct orders to state legislatures—applies in either event." The Court did not question the authority of Congress itself to ban sports gambling.

9.   As will be seen below, the doctrine of *New York* and *Printz* was important in the arguments over the Medicaid expansion in the Affordable Care Act.

PROBLEM

Congress finds that overfishing of various types of fish in navigable waters poses a threat to their continued use for recreation and commerce. Accordingly, it passes a law requiring states to adopt state laws regulating the catching of those fish, which laws must meet federal standards as set by the United States Fish and Wildlife Service (USFWS). If a state does not pass such a law, then the USFWS will regulate the catching of those fish in that state to the exclusion of the state. Is the law constitutional?

D. THE TAXING AND SPENDING CLAUSE

The so-called Taxing and Spending Clause is Article I, Section 8, Clause 1: "The Congress shall have the power to lay and collect taxes, duties, imposts, and excises, to pay the debts and provide for the common defense and general welfare of the United States. . . ." Compared to the Commerce Clause, the Taxing and Spending Clause has not engendered as many disputes. An early dispute was whether Congress could only tax and spend for the purposes enumerated in the subsequent clauses of Section 8, or whether it could tax and spend for anything that paid the Nation's debts, involved defense, or furthered the general welfare. Obviously, if it was only the former, many of the same issues we have seen with regard to the Commerce Clause would come into play, whereas if it was the latter, there would seem to be little if any substantive limit on what Congress could tax or spend for—what is not for the general welfare? Hamilton was emphatic that the latter was the right interpretation, while Madison espoused the former. The Court did not definitively decide this issue until 1936 in *United States v. Butler*, 297 U.S. 1 (1936), holding that Hamilton's position was correct.

Nevertheless, despite that determination, the Court in *Butler* found the Agricultural Adjustment Act of 1933 unconstitutional as a violation of the Taxing and Spending Clause. In reaching this conclusion, it relied on an earlier case, *Bailey v. Drexel Furniture Co.* (*Child Labor Tax Case*), 259 U.S. 20 (1922). Recall that the Court had found federal regulation of child labor beyond Congress's authority under the Commerce Clause in *Hammer v. Dagenhart*, 247 U.S. 251 (1918). Congress responded by enacting a tax of 10% on the net profits of any company employing children under the age of fourteen. In *Bailey*, the Court correctly discerned that the purpose of the tax was not to raise revenue but to force employers to stop employing children under fourteen, something the Court had denied it the power to do under the Commerce Clause. The Court viewed this as an attempt to avoid its decision in *Hammer* and struck the tax down. Similarly, in *Butler*, the Court interpreted the tax as not intended to raise revenue to be spent for the general welfare but to regulate the volume of production of agricultural commodities.* As such, the Court found it beyond Congress's power because Congress had no power, the Court believed, to regulate agricultural production. Today, of course, we recognize that Congress does have the power to regulate child labor and agricultural production to the extent that they substantially affect interstate commerce, so this element of *Butler* and *Bailey* is no longer good law. What is worth remembering, however, is that, denied the authority to act under one of its Article I, Section 8 powers, Congress responded by trying to use one of its other authorities, and the question became whether it could achieve that regulatory end through another means. This type of issue continues to arise.

It arose in the *National Fed. of Ind. Business v. Sebelius* case involving the Affordable Care Act. Recall that five members of the Court held that Congress could not enact the individual mandate under the Commerce Clause. The government argued in the alternative that the penalty one must pay if one did not buy health insurance under the mandate was actually a tax for constitutional purposes and therefore was authorized under the Taxing and Spending Clause. The four justices who did believe the mandate was authorized by the Commerce Clause also believed that the penalty was authorized by the Taxing and Spending Clause. Chief Justice Roberts, who had concluded that the mandate was not authorized by the Commerce Clause, allowed that the penalty was a tax authorized by the Taxing and Spending Clause, providing the fifth vote to uphold the individual mandate/penalty.

In reaching this conclusion, he noted that, although denominated a penalty, the characteristics of the payment were consistent with being a tax—its amount was assessed depending upon amount of income and marital status, the payment was to the Treasury as part of one's income tax payment, and the "penalty" was expected to raise significant amounts of money for the general budget. The fact that the "penalty" had regulatory effects—inducing people to purchase insurance rather than pay the "penalty"—and that those regulatory effects were intentional did not distinguish it from many other taxes, such as the federal excise tax on cigarettes. The Chief Justice noted that it was perhaps strange that Congress could not require persons to purchase insurance under the

---

* Recall *Wickard v. Filburn*, in which the Court upheld an amended version of this act years later.

Commerce Clause but that it could require people to pay a tax for not purchasing insurance. Nevertheless, he found ample precedent for such a tax scheme; after all, tax policy is used to encourage people to buy homes, why not to buy health insurance? Moreover, unlike a mandate imposed under the Commerce Clause, which could be enforced by civil and criminal sanctions (although the mandate in the Affordable Car Act was not), the encouragement to people to purchase insurance still left the choice to individuals whether to purchase the insurance or pay a tax. In short, as long as something qualifies as a tax, Congress is not subject to the same limits on its powers that it is when it regulates under the Commerce Clause.

One is left to wonder, however, why, if enforcing the individual mandate under the Commerce Clause would have such grave consequences for the expansion of federal power as the Chief Justice envisioned, allowing the federal government to achieve the same end through the taxing power would not have the same consequences.

In *National Fed. of Ind. Business v. Sebelius* the Court recognized and allowed that Congress could use its taxing power for regulatory purposes. But Congress can also use its spending power to "regulate." And again there are questions about the extent of its powers.

SOUTH DAKOTA V. DOLE
United States Supreme Court, 1987.
483 U.S. 203, 107 S.Ct. 2793.

CHIEF JUSTICE REHNQUIST delivered the opinion of the Court.

Petitioner South Dakota permits persons 19 years of age or older to purchase beer containing up to 3.2% alcohol. In 1984 Congress enacted 23 U.S.C. § 158 (1982 ed., Supp. III), which directs the Secretary of Transportation to withhold a percentage of federal highway funds otherwise allocable from States in which the purchase or public possession . . . of any alcoholic beverage by a person who is less than twenty-one years of age is lawful. The State sued in United States District Court seeking a declaratory judgment that § 158 violates the constitutional limitations on congressional exercise of the spending power. . . . The District Court rejected the State's claims, and the Court of Appeals for the Eighth Circuit affirmed. . . .

The Constitution empowers Congress to lay and collect Taxes, Duties, Imposts, and Excises, to pay the Debts and provide for the common Defence and general Welfare of the United States. Incident to this power, Congress may attach conditions on the receipt of federal funds, and has repeatedly employed the power to further broad policy objectives by conditioning receipt of federal moneys upon compliance by the recipient with federal statutory and administrative directives. The breadth of this power was made clear in *United States v. Butler*, where the Court, resolving a longstanding debate over the scope of the Spending Clause, determined that the power of Congress to authorize expenditure of public moneys for public purposes is not limited by the direct grants of legislative power found in the Constitution. Thus, objectives not thought to be within Article I's enumerated legislative fields may nevertheless be attained through the use of the spending power and the conditional grant of federal funds.

The spending power is of course not unlimited, but is instead subject to several general restrictions articulated in our cases. The first of these limitations is derived from the language of the Constitution itself: the exercise of the spending power must be in pursuit of the general welfare. In considering whether a particular expenditure is intended to serve general public purposes, courts should defer substantially to the judgment of Congress.[2] Second, we have required that if Congress desires to condition the States' receipt of federal funds, it must do so unambiguously . . ., enabl[ing] the States to exercise their choice knowingly, cognizant of the consequences of their participation. Third, our cases have suggested (without significant elaboration) that conditions on federal grants might be illegitimate if they are unrelated to the federal interest in particular national projects or programs. Finally, we have noted that other constitutional provisions may provide an independent bar to the conditional grant of federal funds.

South Dakota does not seriously claim that § 158 is inconsistent with any of the first three restrictions mentioned above. We can readily conclude that the provision is designed to serve the general welfare, especially in light of the fact that the concept of welfare or the opposite is shaped by Congress. . . . Congress found that the differing drinking ages in the States created particular incentives for young persons to combine their desire to drink with their ability to drive, and that this interstate problem required a national solution. The means it chose to address this dangerous situation were reasonably calculated to advance the general welfare. The conditions upon which States receive the funds, moreover, could not be more clearly stated by Congress. And the State itself, rather than challenging the germaneness of the condition to federal purposes, admits that it has never contended that the congressional action was . . . unrelated to a national concern. . . . Indeed, the condition imposed by Congress is directly related to one of the main purposes for which highway funds are expended—safe interstate travel.[3] This goal of the interstate highway system had been

---

[2]   The level of deference to the congressional decision is such that the Court has more recently questioned whether general welfare is a judicially enforceable restriction at all.

[3]   Our cases have not required that we define the outer bounds of the germaneness or relatedness limitation on the imposition of conditions under the spending power. Amici urge that we take this occasion to establish that a condition on federal funds is legitimate only if it relates directly to the purpose of the expenditure to which it is attached. Because petitioner has not sought such a restriction, and because we find any such limitation on conditional federal grants satisfied

frustrated by varying drinking ages among the States. . . . By enacting § 158, Congress conditioned the receipt of federal funds in a way reasonably calculated to address this particular impediment to a purpose for which the funds are expended.

The remaining question about the validity of § 158 . . . is whether the Twenty-first Amendment constitutes an independent constitutional bar to the conditional grant of federal funds. Petitioner, relying on its view that the Twenty-first Amendment prohibits direct regulation of drinking ages by Congress, asserts that Congress may not use the spending power to regulate that which it is prohibited from regulating directly under the Twenty-first Amendment. But our cases . . . establish that the independent constitutional bar limitation on the spending power is not, as petitioner suggests, a prohibition on the indirect achievement of objectives which Congress is not empowered to achieve directly. Instead, we think that the language in our earlier opinions stands for the unexceptionable proposition that the power may not be used to induce the States to engage in activities that would themselves be unconstitutional. Thus, for example, a grant of federal funds conditioned on invidiously discriminatory state action or the infliction of cruel and unusual punishment would be an illegitimate exercise of the Congress's broad spending power. But no such claim can be or is made here. Were South Dakota to succumb to the blandishments offered by Congress and raise its drinking age to 21, the State's action in so doing would not violate the constitutional rights of anyone.

Our decisions have recognized that in some circumstances the financial inducement offered by Congress might be so coercive as to pass the point at which pressure turns into compulsion. Here, however, Congress has directed only that a State desiring to establish a minimum drinking age lower than 21 lose a relatively small percentage of certain federal highway funds. Petitioner contends that the coercive nature of this program is evident from the degree of success it has achieved. We cannot conclude, however, that a conditional grant of federal money of this sort is unconstitutional simply by reason of its success in achieving the congressional objective.

When we consider, for a moment, that all South Dakota would lose if she adheres to her chosen course as to a suitable minimum drinking age is 5% of the funds otherwise obtainable under specified highway grant programs, the argument as to coercion is shown to be more rhetoric than fact. . . .

Here Congress has offered relatively mild encouragement to the States to enact higher minimum drinking ages than they would otherwise choose. But the enactment of such laws remains the prerogative of the States not merely in theory but in fact. Even if Congress might lack the power to

---

in this case in any event, we do not address whether conditions less directly related to the particular purpose of the expenditure might be outside the bounds of the spending power.

impose a national minimum drinking age directly, we conclude that encouragement to state action found in § 158 is a valid use of the spending power. Accordingly, the judgment of the Court of Appeals is

Affirmed.

JUSTICE BRENNAN, dissenting. [omitted]

JUSTICE O'CONNOR, dissenting.

[M]y disagreement with the Court is relatively narrow on the spending power issue: it is a disagreement about the application of a principle rather than a disagreement on the principle itself. I agree with the Court that Congress may attach conditions on the receipt of federal funds to further the federal interest in particular national projects or programs. I also subscribe to the established proposition that the reach of the spending power is not limited by the direct grants of legislative power found in the Constitution. Finally, I agree that there are four separate types of limitations on the spending power: the expenditure must be for the general welfare, the conditions imposed must be unambiguous, they must be reasonably related to the purpose of the expenditure, and the legislation may not violate any independent constitutional prohibition. Insofar as two of those limitations are concerned, the Court is clearly correct that § 158 is wholly unobjectionable. Establishment of a national minimum drinking age certainly fits within the broad concept of the general welfare and the statute is entirely unambiguous. I am also willing to assume, arguendo, that the Twenty-first Amendment does not constitute an independent constitutional bar to a spending condition.

But the Court's application of the requirement that the condition imposed be reasonably related to the purpose for which the funds are expended is cursory and unconvincing. . . . In my view, establishment of a minimum drinking age of 21 is not sufficiently related to interstate highway construction to justify so conditioning funds appropriated for that purpose. . . .

[T]he Court asserts the reasonableness of the relationship between the supposed purpose of the expenditure—safe interstate travel—and the drinking age condition. The Court reasons that Congress wishes that the roads it builds may be used safely, that drunken drivers threaten highway safety, and that young people are more likely to drive while under the influence of alcohol under existing law than would be the case if there were a uniform national drinking age of 21. It hardly needs saying, however, that if the purpose of § 158 is to deter drunken driving, it is far too over and under-inclusive. It is over-inclusive because it stops teenagers from drinking even when they are not about to drive on interstate highways. It is under-inclusive because teenagers pose only a small part of the drunken driving problem in this Nation. *See, e.g.,* 130 Cong.Rec. 18648

(1984)(remarks of Sen. Humphrey)(Eighty-four percent of all highway fatalities involving alcohol occur among those whose ages exceed 21).

When Congress appropriates money to build a highway, it is entitled to insist that the highway be a safe one. But it is not entitled to insist as a condition of the use of highway funds that the State impose or change regulations in other areas of the State's social and economic life because of an attenuated or tangential relationship to highway use or safety. Indeed, if the rule were otherwise, the Congress could effectively regulate almost any area of a State's social, political, or economic life on the theory that use of the interstate transportation system is somehow enhanced. . . .

There is a clear place at which the Court can draw the line between permissible and impermissible conditions on federal grants. It is the line identified in the Brief for the National Conference of State Legislatures et al. as Amici Curiae:

> Congress has the power to spend for the general welfare, it has the power to legislate only for delegated purposes. . . . The appropriate inquiry, then, is whether the spending requirement or prohibition is a condition on a grant or whether it is regulation. The difference turns on whether the requirement specifies in some way how the money should be spent, so that Congress's intent in making the grant will be effectuated. Congress has no power under the Spending Clause to impose requirements on a grant that go beyond specifying how the money should be spent. A requirement that is not such a specification is not a condition, but a regulation, which is valid only if it falls within one of Congress's delegated regulatory powers.

This approach harks back to *United States v. Butler*, the last case in which this Court struck down an Act of Congress as beyond the authority granted by the Spending Clause. There the Court wrote that [t]here is an obvious difference between a statute stating the conditions upon which moneys shall be expended and one effective only upon assumption of a contractual obligation to submit to a regulation which otherwise could not be enforced. The *Butler* Court saw the Agricultural Adjustment Act for what it was— an exercise of regulatory, not spending, power. The error in *Butler* was not the Court's conclusion that the Act was essentially regulatory, but rather its crabbed view of the extent of Congress's regulatory power under the Commerce Clause. The Agricultural Adjustment Act was regulatory but it was regulation that today would likely be considered within Congress's commerce power.

While *Butler*'s authority is questionable insofar as it assumes that Congress has no regulatory power over farm production, its discussion of the spending power and its description of both the power's breadth and its limitations remain sound. The Court's decision in *Butler* also properly recognizes the gravity of the task of appropriately limiting the spending power. If the spending power is to be limited only by Congress's notion of the general welfare, the reality, given the vast financial resources of the Federal Government, is that the Spending Clause gives power to the Congress to tear down the barriers, to invade the states' jurisdiction, and to become a parliament of the whole people, subject to no restrictions save such as are self-imposed. This, of course, as *Butler* held, was not the Framers' plan and it is not the meaning of the Spending Clause. . . .

COMMENTS AND QUESTIONS

1.   The disagreement between Justice O'Connor and the Court is the degree to which the condition on the expenditure must relate to the expenditure itself. The Court looks to the general purpose of the expenditure and asks whether there is some relationship between that purpose and the condition. Justice O'Connor would require a much narrower relationship; the condition would have to be directly on how the money was to be spent. Here, for example, a condition could specify the width and composition of the roads to be funded.

2.   Left unanswered in *Dole* was when financial inducement would be "so coercive as to pass the point at which pressure turns into compulsion." Lower courts struggled with this issue in subsequent cases but never found a particular threat of reduction of funds to be so coercive. The issue arose before the Supreme Court in the challenge to the Affordable Care Act's Medicaid expansion provision.

NATIONAL FEDERATION OF INDEPENDENT BUSINESS V. SEBELIUS, SECRETARY OF HEALTH AND HUMAN SERVICES
United States Supreme Court, 2012.
567 U.S. 519, 132 S.Ct. 2566.

CHIEF JUSTICE ROBERTS announced the judgment of the Court and delivered the opinion of the Court with respect to Parts I, II, and III-C, an opinion with respect to Part IV, in which JUSTICE BREYER and JUSTICE KAGAN join, and an opinion with respect to Parts III-A, III-B, and III-D.

Today we resolve constitutional challenges to two provisions of the Patient Protection and Affordable Care Act of 2010: the individual mandate, which requires individuals to purchase a health insurance policy providing a minimum level of coverage; and the Medicaid expansion, which gives funds to the States on the condition that they provide specified health care to all citizens whose income falls below a certain threshold. . . .

[T]his case concerns two powers that the Constitution does grant the Federal Government, but which must be read carefully to avoid creating a general federal authority akin to the police power. [The portion of this opinion relating to the Commerce Clause is contained in the section of this book concerning the Commerce Clause. See Section B of this chapter.]

Congress may also "lay and collect Taxes, Duties, Imposts and Excises, to pay the Debts and provide for the common Defence and general Welfare of the United States." Put simply, Congress may tax and spend. This grant gives the Federal Government considerable influence even in areas where it cannot directly regulate. The Federal Government may enact a tax on an activity that it cannot authorize, forbid, or otherwise control. And in exercising its spending power, Congress may offer funds to the States, and may condition those offers on compliance with specified conditions. These offers may well induce the States to adopt policies that the Federal Government itself could not impose. *See, e.g., South Dakota v. Dole.* . . .

The second provision of the Affordable Care Act directly challenged here is the Medicaid expansion. Enacted in 1965, Medicaid offers federal funding to States to assist pregnant women, children, needy families, the blind, the elderly, and the disabled in obtaining medical care. In order to receive that funding, States must comply with federal criteria governing matters such as who receives care and what services are provided at what cost. By 1982 every State had chosen to participate in Medicaid. Federal funds received through the Medicaid program have become a substantial part of state budgets, now constituting over 10 percent of most States' total revenue.

The Affordable Care Act expands the scope of the Medicaid program and increases the number of individuals the States must cover. For example, the Act requires state programs to provide Medicaid coverage to adults with incomes up to 133 percent of the federal poverty level, whereas many States now cover adults with children only if their income is considerably lower, and do not cover childless adults at all. The Act increases federal funding to cover the States' costs in expanding Medicaid coverage, although States will bear a portion of the costs on their own. If a State does not comply with the Act's new coverage requirements, it may lose not only the federal funding for those requirements, but all of its federal Medicaid funds.

Along with their challenge to the individual mandate, the state plaintiffs in the Eleventh Circuit argued that the Medicaid expansion exceeds Congress's constitutional powers. . . .

IV

The States also contend that the Medicaid expansion exceeds Congress's authority under the Spending Clause. They claim that Congress is coercing the States to adopt the changes it wants by threatening to withhold all of a State's Medicaid grants, unless the State accepts the new expanded funding and complies with the conditions that come with it. This, they argue, violates the basic principle that the "Federal Government may not compel the States to enact or administer a federal regulatory program." *New York v. United States.* There is no doubt that the Act dramatically increases state obligations under Medicaid. The current Medicaid program requires States to cover only certain discrete categories of needy individuals—pregnant women, children, needy families, the blind, the elderly, and the disabled. There is no mandatory coverage for most childless adults, and the States typically do not offer any such coverage. . . .

The Spending Clause grants Congress the power "to pay the Debts and provide for the . . . general Welfare of the United States." U. S. Const., Art. I, § 8, cl. 1. We have long recognized that Congress may use this power to grant federal funds to the States, and may condition such a grant upon the States' "taking certain actions that Congress could not require them to take." Such measures "encourage a State to regulate in a particular way, [and] influenc[e] a State's policy choices." The conditions imposed by Congress ensure that the funds are used by the States to "provide for the . . . general Welfare" in the manner Congress intended.

At the same time, our cases have recognized limits on Congress's power under the Spending Clause to secure state compliance with federal objectives. "We have repeatedly characterized . . . Spending Clause legislation as 'much in the nature of a *contract*.'" The legitimacy of Congress's exercise of the spending power "thus rests on whether the State voluntarily and knowingly accepts the terms of the 'contract.'" Respecting this limitation is critical to ensuring that Spending Clause legislation does not undermine the status of the States as independent sovereigns in our federal system. . . . For this reason, "the Constitution has never been understood to confer upon Congress the ability to require the States to govern according to Congress's instructions." *New York*. Otherwise the two-government system established by the Framers would give way to a system that vests power in one central government, and individual liberty would suffer.

That insight has led this Court to strike down federal legislation that commandeers a State's legislative or administrative apparatus for federal purposes. See, *e.g., Printz*; *New York*. It has also led us to scrutinize Spending Clause legislation to ensure that Congress is not using financial inducements to exert a "power akin to undue influence." Congress may use its spending power to create incentives for States to act in accordance with federal policies. But when "pressure turns into compulsion," the legislation runs contrary to our system of federalism. "[T]he Constitution simply does not give Congress the authority to require the States to regulate." *New York*. That is true whether Congress directly commands a State to regulate or indirectly coerces a State to adopt a federal regulatory system as its own. . . .

[C]ongress may attach appropriate conditions to federal taxing and spending programs to preserve its control over the use of federal funds. In the typical case we look to the States to defend their prerogatives by adopting "the simple expedient of not yielding" to federal blandishments when they do not want to embrace the federal policies as their own. The

States are separate and independent sovereigns. Sometimes they have to act like it.

The States, however, argue that the Medicaid expansion is far from the typical case. They object that Congress has "crossed the line distinguishing encouragement from coercion" in the way it has structured the funding. Instead of simply refusing to grant the new funds to States that will not accept the new conditions, Congress has also threatened to withhold those States' existing Medicaid funds. The States claim that this threat serves no purpose other than to force unwilling States to sign up for the dramatic expansion in health care coverage effected by the Act.

Given the nature of the threat and the programs at issue here, we must agree. We have upheld Congress's authority to condition the receipt of funds on the States' complying with restrictions on the use of those funds, because that is the means by which Congress ensures that the funds are spent according to its view of the "general Welfare." Conditions that do not here govern the use of the funds, however, cannot be justified on that basis. When, for example, such conditions take the form of threats to terminate other significant independent grants, the conditions are properly viewed as a means of pressuring the States to accept policy changes.

In *South Dakota v. Dole*, we considered a challenge to a federal law that threatened to withhold five percent of a State's federal highway funds if the State did not raise its drinking age to 21. . . .

We . . . asked whether "the financial inducement offered by Congress" was "so coercive as to pass the point at which 'pressure turns into compulsion.'" By "financial inducement" the Court meant the threat of losing five percent of highway funds; no new money was offered to the States to raise their drinking ages. We found that the inducement was not impermissibly coercive, because Congress was offering only "relatively mild encouragement to the States." We observed that "all South Dakota would lose if she adheres to her chosen course as to a suitable minimum drinking age is 5%" of her highway funds. In fact, the federal funds at stake constituted less than half of one percent of South Dakota's budget at the time. In consequence, "we conclude[d] that [the] encouragement to state action [was] a valid use of the spending power." Whether to accept the drinking age change "remain[ed] the prerogative of the States not merely in theory but in fact."

In this case, the financial "inducement" Congress has chosen is much more than "relatively mild encouragement"—it is a gun to the head. Section 1396c of the Medicaid Act provides that if a State's Medicaid plan does not comply with the Act's requirements, the Secretary of Health and Human Services may declare that "further payments will not be made to the State." A State that opts out of the Affordable Care Act's expansion in health care coverage thus stands to lose not merely "a relatively small percentage" of its existing Medicaid funding, but *all* of it. Medicaid spending accounts for over 20 percent of the average State's total budget, with federal funds covering 50 to 83 percent of those costs. . . . The threatened loss of over 10 percent of a State's overall budget . . . is economic dragooning that leaves the States with no real option but to acquiesce in the Medicaid expansion.

JUSTICE GINSBURG claims that *Dole* is distinguishable because here "Congress has not threatened to withhold funds earmarked for any other program." But that begs the question: The States contend that the expansion is in reality a new program and that Congress is forcing them to accept it by threatening the funds for the existing Medicaid program. We cannot agree that existing Medicaid and the expansion dictated by the Affordable Care Act are all one program simply because "Congress styled" them as such. If the expansion is not properly viewed as a modification of the existing Medicaid program, Congress's decision to so title it is irrelevant.

Here, the Government claims that the Medicaid expansion is properly viewed merely as a modification of the existing program because the States agreed that Congress could change the terms of Medicaid when they signed on in the first place. . . .

The Medicaid expansion, however, accomplishes a shift in kind, not merely degree. The original program was designed to cover medical services for four particular categories of the needy: the disabled, the blind, the elderly, and needy families with dependent children. Previous amendments to Medicaid eligibility merely altered and expanded the boundaries of these categories. Under the Affordable Care Act, Medicaid is transformed into a program to meet the health care needs of the entire nonelderly population with income below 133 percent of the poverty level. It is no longer a program to care for the neediest among us, but rather an element of a comprehensive national plan to provide universal health insurance coverage.[14] . . .

The Court [previously has not attempted] to "fix the outermost line" where persuasion gives way to coercion. The Court found it "[e]nough for present purposes that wherever the line may be, this statute is within it." We have no need to fix a line either. It is enough for today that wherever that line may be, this statute is surely beyond it. Congress may not simply "conscript state [agencies] into the national bureaucratic army," and that is what it is attempting to do with the Medicaid expansion.

Nothing in our opinion precludes Congress from offering funds under the Affordable Care Act to expand the availability of health care, and

---

[14] JUSTICE GINSBURG suggests that the States can have no objection to the Medicaid expansion, because "Congress could have repealed Medicaid [and,] [t]hereafter, . . . could have enacted Medicaid II, a new program combining the pre-2010 coverage with the expanded coverage required by the ACA." But it would certainly not be that easy. Practical constraints would plainly inhibit, if not preclude, the Federal Government from repealing the existing program and putting every feature of Medicaid on the table for political reconsideration. Such a massive undertaking would hardly be "ritualistic." . . .

requiring that States accepting such funds comply with the conditions on their use. What Congress is not free to do is to penalize States that choose not to participate in that new program by taking away their existing Medicaid funding. . . . In light of the Court's holding, the Secretary cannot apply § 1396c to withdraw existing Medicaid funds for failure to comply with the requirements set out in the expansion. That fully remedies the constitutional violation we have identified. . . .

JUSTICE GINSBURG, with whom JUSTICE SOTOMAYOR joins, and with whom JUSTICE BREYER and JUSTICE KAGAN join as to Parts I, II, III, and IV, concurring in part, concurring in the judgment in part, and dissenting in part.

[I] would . . . hold that the Spending Clause permits the Medicaid expansion exactly as Congress enacted it.

* * *

V

Through Medicaid, Congress has offered the States an opportunity to furnish health care to the poor with the aid of federal financing. To receive federal Medicaid funds, States must provide health benefits to specified categories of needy persons, including pregnant women, children, parents, and adults with disabilities. Guaranteed eligibility varies by category: for some it is tied to the federal poverty level (incomes up to 100% or 133%); for others it depends on criteria such as eligibility for designated state or federal assistance programs. The ACA enlarges the population of needy people States must cover to include adults under age 65 with incomes up to 133% of the federal poverty level. The spending power conferred by the Constitution, the Court has never doubted, permits Congress to define the contours of programs financed with federal funds. And to expand coverage, Congress could have recalled the existing legislation, and replaced it with a new law making Medicaid as embracive of the poor as Congress chose. The question posed by the 2010 Medicaid expansion, then, is essentially this: To cover a notably larger population, must Congress take the repeal/reenact route, or may it achieve the same result by amending existing law? The answer should be that Congress may expand by amendment the classes of needy persons entitled to Medicaid benefits. A ritualistic requirement that Congress repeal and reenact spending legislation in order to enlarge the population served by a federally funded program would advance no constitutional principle and would scarcely serve the interests of federalism. To the contrary, such a requirement would rigidify Congress's efforts to empower States by partnering with them in the implementation of federal programs. . . .

THE CHIEF JUSTICE acknowledges that Congress may "condition the receipt of [federal] funds on the States' complying with restrictions on the use of those funds," but nevertheless concludes that the 2010 expansion is unduly coercive. His conclusion rests on three premises, each of them essential to his theory. First, the Medicaid expansion is, in THE CHIEF JUSTICE's view, a new grant program, not an addition to the Medicaid program existing before the ACA's enactment. Congress, THE CHIEF JUSTICE maintains, has threatened States with the loss of funds from an old program in an effort to get them to adopt a new one. Second, the expansion was unforeseeable by the States when they first signed on to Medicaid. Third, the threatened loss of funding is so large that the States have no real choice but to participate in the Medicaid expansion. THE CHIEF JUSTICE therefore—*for the first time ever*—finds an exercise of Congress's spending power unconstitutionally coercive.

Medicaid, as amended by the ACA, however, is not two spending programs; it is a single program with a constant aim—to enable poor persons to receive basic health care when they need it. Given past expansions, plus express statutory warning that Congress may change the requirements participating States must meet, there can be no tenable claim that the ACA fails for lack of notice. Moreover, States have no entitlement to receive any Medicaid funds; they enjoy only the opportunity to accept funds on Congress's terms. Future Congresses are not bound by their predecessors' dispositions; they have authority to spend federal revenue as they see fit. The Federal Government, therefore, is not, as THE CHIEF JUSTICE charges, threatening States with the loss of "existing" funds from one spending program in order to induce them to opt into another program. Congress is simply requiring States to do what States have long been required to do to receive Medicaid funding: comply with the conditions Congress prescribes for participation.

A majority of the Court, however, buys the argument that prospective withholding of funds formerly available exceeds Congress's spending power. Given that holding, I entirely agree with THE CHIEF JUSTICE as to the appropriate remedy. It is to bar the withholding found impermissible. . . . Because THE CHIEF JUSTICE finds the withholding—not the granting—of federal funds incompatible with the Spending Clause, Congress's extension of Medicaid remains available to any State that affirms its willingness to participate. . . .

JUSTICE SCALIA, JUSTICE KENNEDY, JUSTICE THOMAS, and JUSTICE ALITO, dissenting. [The portion of this opinion dealing with the Commerce Clause is contained in this book's section on the Commerce Clause. See Section B in this chapter.]

[T]his case is in one respect difficult: it presents two questions of first impression. . . . The second question is whether the congressional power to tax and spend, permits the conditioning of a State's continued receipt of all funds under a massive state-administered federal welfare program upon its acceptance of an expansion to that program. Several of our opinions have suggested that the power to tax and spend cannot be used to coerce state administration of a federal program, but we have never found a law enacted under the spending power to be coercive. . . .

As for the constitutional power to tax and spend for the general welfare: The Court has long since expanded that beyond (what Madison thought it meant) taxing and spending for those aspects of the general welfare that were within the Federal Government's enumerated powers. . . . The principal practical obstacle that prevents Congress from using the tax-and-spend power to assume all the general-welfare responsibilities traditionally exercised by the States is the sheer impossibility of managing a Federal Government large enough to administer such a system. That obstacle can be overcome by granting funds to the States, allowing them to administer the program. That is fair and constitutional enough when the States freely agree to have their powers employed and their employees enlisted in the federal scheme. But it is a blatant violation of the constitutional structure when the States have no choice. . . .

[W]hen Congress makes grants to the States, it customarily attaches conditions, and this Court has long held that the Constitution generally permits Congress to do this.

This practice of attaching conditions to federal funds greatly increases federal power. "[O]bjectives not thought to be within Article I's enumerated legislative fields, may nevertheless be attained through the use of the spending power and the conditional grant of federal funds." *Dole.*

This formidable power, if not checked in any way, would present a grave threat to the system of federalism created by our Constitution. If Congress's "Spending Clause power to pursue objectives outside of Article I's enumerated legislative fields" is "limited only by Congress's notion of the general welfare, the reality, given the vast financial resources of the Federal Government, is that the Spending Clause gives 'power to the Congress to tear down the barriers, to invade the states' jurisdiction, and to become a parliament of the whole people, subject to no restrictions save such as are self-imposed,'" *Dole* (O'Connor, J., dissenting). . . .

Recognizing this potential for abuse, our cases have long held that the power to attach conditions to grants to the States has limits. . . .

If a federal spending program coerces participation the States have not "exercise[d] their choice"—let alone made an "informed choice." Coercing States to accept conditions risks the destruction of the "unique role of the States in our system." . . . Where all Congress has done is to "encourag[e] state regulation rather than compe[l] it, state governments remain responsive to the local electorate's preferences; state officials remain accountable to the people. . . .

Whether federal spending legislation crosses the line from enticement to coercion is often difficult to determine, and courts should not conclude that legislation is unconstitutional on this ground unless the coercive nature of an offer is unmistakably clear. In this case, however, there can be no doubt. In structuring the ACA, Congress unambiguously signaled its belief that every State would have no real choice but to go along with the Medicaid Expansion. If the anticoercion rule does not apply in this case, then there is no such rule. . . .

[I]n crafting the ACA, Congress clearly expressed its informed view that no State could possibly refuse the offer that the ACA extends. The stated goal of the ACA is near-universal health care coverage. To achieve this goal, the ACA mandates that every person obtain a minimum level of coverage. . . . [F]or low-income individuals who are simply not able to obtain insurance, Congress expanded Medicaid, transforming it from a program covering only members of a limited list of vulnerable groups into a program that provides at least the requisite minimum level of coverage for the poor. This design was intended to provide at least a specified minimum level of coverage for all Americans, but the achievement of that goal obviously depends on participation by every single State. If any State—not to mention all of the 26 States that brought this suit—chose to decline the federal offer, there would be a gaping hole in the ACA's coverage. . . .

These features of the ACA convey an unmistakable message: Congress never dreamed that any State would refuse to go along with the expansion of Medicaid. Congress well understood that refusal was not a practical option. . . .

In sum, it is perfectly clear from the goal and structure of the ACA that the offer of the Medicaid Expansion was one that Congress understood no State could refuse. The Medicaid Expansion therefore exceeds Congress's spending power and cannot be implemented. . . .

COMMENTS AND QUESTIONS

1. If Congress repealed the current Medicaid program and replaced it with the expanded Medicaid program, would that pass muster with the Chief Justice? With the joint dissenters?

2. The Chief Justice finds that conditioning a state's continuation of the existing Medicaid program on the state's acceptance of the expansion of the program to be unconstitutional. Therefore, he severs the unconstitutional condition from the law, meaning that the Medicaid expansion is constitutional, but states that do not want to accept it do not lose their existing Medicaid funding. Two of the Court's four "liberals," at the time, Justices Breyer and Kagan, agree with the Chief Justice. The other two "liberals," Justices Ginsburg and Sotomayor, however, believe the Medicaid expansion and its condition are both constitutional. The joint dissenters agree with the Chief Justice that the Medicaid expansion in the law is unconstitutional because of the condition, but their remedy is to declare the entire expansion of Medicaid

unconstitutional. What's the status of the Medicaid expansion, given these three different positions.

3.   Are you surprised that two of the "liberals" on the Court joined the Chief Justice on this issue?

4.   Twenty-six states challenged the constitutionality of the Medicaid expansion. How many do you think refused to sign onto the expansion when they were allowed to without losing their existing Medicaid funding? As of February 4, 2023, thirty-nine states have agreed to the Medicaid expansion, including seventeen of those who sued to declare it unconstitutional. I guess they changed their minds, or their citizens convinced them to do so. *See* https://www.kff.org/medicaid/issue-brief/status-of-state-medicaid-expansion-decisions-interactive-map/.

PROBLEM

Congress passes a law to amend the law providing federal funding to states for K–12 education that requires states as a condition of receiving that funding to pass laws banning the possession of firearms within 500 feet of a school benefitting from that funding. Is this law constitutional?

E. IMPLEMENTING TREATIES

The Necessary and Proper Clause states that Congress may make all laws necessary and proper, not only "for carrying into execution the foregoing powers" [the powers in the earlier enumerated powers provisions], but also "for carrying into execution . . . all other powers vested by this Constitution in the Government of the United States. . . ." Another power vested by the Constitution in the federal government is the power to make treaties with foreign nations. Article II, Section 2, Clause 2 states that the President "shall have the power, by and with the advice and consent of the Senate, to make treaties, provided two thirds of the Senators present concur." The following case is an example of the use of the Necessary and Proper Clause to carry into execution the power to make treaties.

MISSOURI V. HOLLAND
United States Supreme Court, 1920.
252 U.S. 416, 40 S.Ct. 382.

MR. JUSTICE HOLMES delivered the opinion of the Court.

This is a bill in equity brought by the State of Missouri to prevent a game warden of the United States from attempting to enforce the Migratory Bird Treaty Act of July 3, 1918, and the regulations made by the Secretary of Agriculture in pursuance of the same. The ground of the bill is that the statute is an unconstitutional interference with the rights reserved to the States by the Tenth Amendment, and that the acts of the defendant done and threatened under that authority invade the sovereign right of the State and contravene its will manifested in statutes. The State also alleges a pecuniary interest, as owner of the wild birds within its borders and otherwise, admitted by the Government to be sufficient, but it is enough that the bill is a reasonable and proper means to assert the alleged quasi sovereign rights of a State. A motion to dismiss was sustained by the District Court on the ground that the Act of Congress is constitutional. The State appeals.

On December 8, 1916, a treaty between the United States and Great Britain* was proclaimed by the President. It recited that many species of birds in their annual migrations traversed many parts of the United States and of Canada, that they were of great value as a source of food and in destroying insects injurious to vegetation, but were in danger of extermination through lack of adequate protection. It therefore provided for specified closed seasons and protection in other forms, and agreed that the two powers would take or propose to their lawmaking bodies the necessary measures for carrying the treaty out. The above mentioned act of July 3, 1918, entitled an act to give effect to the convention, prohibited the killing, capturing or selling any of the migratory birds included in the terms of the treaty except as permitted by regulations compatible with those terms, to be made by the Secretary of Agriculture. Regulations were proclaimed on July 31, and October 25, 1918. It is unnecessary to go into any details, because, as we have said, the question raised is the general one whether the treaty and statute are void as an interference with the rights reserved to the States.

To answer this question it is not enough to refer to the Tenth Amendment, reserving the powers not delegated to the United States, because by Article 2, Section 2, the power to make treaties is delegated expressly, and by Article 6 treaties made under the authority of the United States, along with the Constitution and laws of the United States made in pursuance thereof, are declared the supreme law of the land. If the treaty is valid there can be no dispute about the validity of the statute under Article 1, Section 8, as a necessary and proper means to execute the powers of the Government. The language of the Constitution as to the supremacy of treaties being general, the question before us is narrowed to an inquiry into the ground upon which the present supposed exception is placed.

It is said that a treaty cannot be valid if it infringes the Constitution, that there are limits, therefore, to the treaty-making power, and that one such limit is that what an act of Congress could not do unaided, in derogation of the powers reserved to the States, a treaty cannot do. An

---

* At this time, Great Britain still exercised the foreign affairs powers for Canada, so the treaty, although relating to Canada, was contracted with Great Britain. [author's note]

earlier act of Congress that attempted by itself and not in pursuance of a treaty to regulate the killing of migratory birds within the States had been held bad in the District Court.** Those decisions were supported by arguments that migratory birds were owned by the States in their sovereign capacity for the benefit of their people, and that . . . this control was one that Congress had no power to displace. The same argument is supposed to apply now with equal force.

Whether the [district court cases] were decided rightly or not they cannot be accepted as a test of the treaty power. Acts of Congress are the supreme law of the land only when made in pursuance of the Constitution, while treaties are declared to be so when made under the authority of the United States. It is open to question whether the authority of the United States means more than the formal acts prescribed to make the convention. We do not mean to imply that there are no qualifications to the treaty-making power; but they must be ascertained in a different way. It is obvious that there may be matters of the sharpest exigency for the national well being that an act of Congress could not deal with but that a treaty followed by such an act could, and it is not lightly to be assumed that, in matters requiring national action, "a power which must belong to and somewhere reside in every civilized government" is not to be found. Wh[ile this] was said . . . with regard to the powers of the States[, it] applies with equal force to the powers of the nation in cases where the States individually are incompetent to act. We are not yet discussing the particular case before us but only are considering the validity of the test proposed. With regard to that we may add that when we are dealing with words that also are a constituent act, like the Constitution of the United States, we must realize that they have called into life a being the development of which could not have been foreseen completely by the most gifted of its begetters. It was enough for them to realize or to hope that they had created an organism; it has taken a century and has cost their successors much sweat and blood to prove that they created a nation. The case before us must be considered in the light of our whole experience and not merely in light of what was said a hundred years ago. The treaty in question does not contravene any prohibitory words to be found in the Constitution. The only question is whether it is forbidden by some invisible radiation from the general terms of the Tenth Amendment. We must consider what this country has become in deciding what that amendment has reserved.

The State as we have intimated founds its claim of exclusive authority upon an assertion of title to migratory birds, an assertion that is embodied in statute. No doubt it is true that as between a State and its inhabitants the State may regulate the killing and sale of such birds, but it does not

---

** Actually, two separate district court decisions, one in Arkansas and one in Kansas, had held that the earlier act was unconstitutional as not authorized by any provision of the Constitution. [author's note]

follow that its authority is exclusive of paramount powers. To put the claim of the State upon title is to lean upon a slender reed. Wild birds are not in the possession of anyone; and possession is the beginning of ownership. The whole foundation of the State's rights is the presence within their jurisdiction of birds that yesterday had not arrived, tomorrow may be in another State and in a week a thousand miles away. If we are to be accurate we cannot put the case of the State upon higher ground than that the treaty deals with creatures that for the moment are within the state borders, that it must be carried out by officers of the United States within the same territory, and that but for the treaty the State would be free to regulate this subject itself.

As most of the laws of the United States are carried out within the States and as many of them deal with matters which in the silence of such laws the State might regulate, such general grounds are not enough to support Missouri's claim. . . .

Here a national interest of very nearly the first magnitude is involved. It can be protected only by national action in concert with that of another power. The subject matter is only transitorily within the State and has no permanent habitat therein. But for the treaty and the statute there soon might be no birds for any powers to deal with. We see nothing in the Constitution that compels the Government to sit by while a food supply is cut off and the protectors of our forests and our crops are destroyed. It is not sufficient to rely upon the States. The reliance is vain, and were it otherwise, the question is whether the United States is forbidden to act. We are of opinion that the treaty and statute must be upheld.

MR. JUSTICE VAN DEVANTER and MR. JUSTICE PITNEY dissent.

COMMENTS AND QUESTIONS

1. Here we see again a situation in which a law passed by Congress, the 1913 Act, was deemed unconstitutional, and thereafter the federal government (here the President and the Senate by treaty, followed by Congress in passing the law) attempt to achieve the same end by a different means—using the Necessary and Proper Clause to implement the treaty. The Court upholds this action.

2. Note that the Treaty Clause does not contain any limitation regarding the subject matter of a treaty. Justice Holmes adverts to this when he asks whether anything is required to make a treaty valid other than its "formal acts," meaning the President has made it with the advice and consent of two thirds of the Senate. This would be unlike laws passed by Congress under Article I, Section 8, where not only the "formal acts" (passage by both houses and the signature of the President) are required, but the law must be within one of the powers listed in the Constitution. If Congress can under the Necessary and Proper Clause implement any treaty adopted by the United States, is there any limitation what Congress can regulate?

This issue arose in *Bond v. United States*, 572 U.S. 844 (2014). Carol Bond's best friend had an affair with Carol's husband, who made her friend pregnant. Upon learning this, Ms. Bond undertook to punish her former friend by putting chemical poisons on the person's mailbox, car door handles, and house doorknob on numerous occasions. Ms. Bond was photographed by postal inspectors who had been alerted to tampering with the mailbox and was subsequently prosecuted under a federal statute making it a crime to "use . . . chemical weapons," part of the Chemical Weapons Convention Implementation Act of 1998, passed to implement the nation's responsibilities under the 1993 Chemical Weapons Convention (a convention is another name for a treaty). Convicted and sentenced to six years in prison, despite the fact that her intended victim suffered no more than a slight chemical burn on her hand, Ms. Bond raised the question whether the law was constitutional as applied to her. The Court unanimously overturned her conviction, although three justices concurred in the judgment, not the opinion of the Court.

The Chief Justice wrote the majority opinion, concluding that it was not necessary to reach the constitutional question because interpreting the statute in a manner consistent with the principles of federalism inherent in our constitutional structure indicated that Congress did not intend to reach such local activity. Although the explicit text of the statute seemed to encompass Ms. Bond's actions, the Court said that, in light of the basic principles of federalism, the "improbably broad reach" of the statute, the "deeply serious consequences of adopting such a boundless reading," and "the lack of any apparent need to do so in light of the context from which the statute arose" rendered the statute ambiguous. Consequently, the Court said it could insist on a clear indication that Congress meant to reach purely local crimes, before interpreting the statute's expansive language in a way that intrudes on the police power of the States.

Justices Scalia, Thomas, and Alito all concurred in the judgment, but they all believed that the statute by its terms applied to Ms. Bond's actions so that the constitutional question could not be avoided. Justice Scalia found the statute unconstitutional because in his view *Missouri v. Holland* was simply wrong; the Necessary and Proper Clause does not authorize Congress to legislate to implement treaties. Instead, any power to implement treaties must come from the specified powers granted to Congress in Article I, Section 8. Justice Thomas agreed with Justice Scalia but would go further. In his view the treaty power itself is limited; it can be used to arrange intercourse with other nations but not to regulate purely domestic affairs. Justice Alito agreed with Justice Thomas that the treaty power is so limited, but he noted that the control of true chemical weapons is a matter of great international concern, and therefore the heart of the Convention clearly represented a valid exercise of the treaty power. However, to the extent that the Convention might be read to obligate the United States to enact domestic legislation criminalizing conduct of the sort at issue in this case, which typically is the sort of conduct regulated by the States, the Convention exceeded the treaty power. Thus, the provision criminalizing Ms. Bond's activities was not necessary and proper to carry into execution the treaty power.

Each of these opinions raises novel arguments. The Court's reading of a textually explicit provision as ambiguous because it would trench upon the states' historic criminal law enforcement powers raises significant questions (as noted by Justice Scalia in his concurrence). For example, the Boston Marathon bomber engaged in what appears to have been a local crime, but he was prosecuted for a federal offense of using a weapon of mass destruction. No one has questioned the constitutionality or applicability of the law to this offense. Of course, instead of mild burns to a hand, three persons were killed and 180 wounded by the Boston Marathon bomb, but is the severity of the actual injury the key to the applicability of a federal criminal provision to what would otherwise be a local crime? What if Ms. Bond had instead poisoned a city's water system, killing hundreds, would the statute still not have applied to her? Justice Scalia's argument that the only authority to implement treaties is to be found in the specified powers granted to Congress in Article I, Section 8, has its own problems. While the modern Commerce Clause powers of Congress are vast and might authorize implementation of many treaty provisions, we have found those powers are not without limit. For example, imagine that the United States entered a treaty with a nation where U.S. citizens are especially at risk of being assaulted or kidnaped, agreeing to provide special criminal law protections for citizens of that nation in the United States in exchange for special criminal law protections of our citizens in that nation. Protecting our citizens abroad is clearly an appropriate exercise of our treaty power, but protection of persons in the United States generally from assault and kidnaping is a paradigmatic exercise of the police powers of the states. Finally, Justice Thomas's argument that the treaty power itself is limited raises a host of problems, especially because nothing in the text of the Constitution provides a guide to what that limit is. Rather it would be judges who would ultimately decide, exercising their sense of what is properly a matter of international concern, not the President and the Senate, who probably have a better idea of what is a matter of international concern.

3. Imagine that the United States enters into a multilateral United Nations convention pledging to protect women from violence. Can Congress then constitutionally adopt the damage provisions in the Violence Against Women Act that the Court found unconstitutional in *United States v. Morrison*?

4. Of course, a treaty may not violate a constitutional right, any more than a statute may, so a law violating the First Amendment, for example, could not be justified on the basis that it was necessary to implement a treaty to which the United States was a party. *See, e.g., Reid v. Covert*, 354 U.S. 1 (1957)(treaty with Japan that the U.S. would try by military commission civilian dependents accompanying the military in Japan unconstitutionally deprived them of their right to a trial by jury).

5. Consider Justice Holmes's discussion in *Missouri v. Holland* of the proper way of interpreting a "constituent act" like the Constitution: "The case before us must be considered in the light of our whole experience and not merely in light of what was said a hundred years ago." And in considering the

Tenth Amendment: "We must consider what this country has become in deciding what that amendment has reserved." This is not Originalism.

F. THE CIVIL WAR AMENDMENTS

Up to this point, we have been dealing with the legislative powers contained in the original Constitution. Each of the Civil War Amendments (the Thirteenth, Fourteenth, and Fifteenth Amendments), however, also contains a provision stating that Congress shall have the power to enforce the provisions of the amendment. The Thirteenth Amendment, adopted in 1865, prohibits slavery, and in 1866 Congress enacted the Civil Rights Act of 1866 to implement that amendment. That act, however, went well beyond merely prohibiting slavery. Intending to overturn the "black codes"* by which southern states were attempting to maintain the newly freed slaves in a subjugated state, Congress provided that all persons "of every race and color" born in the United States were citizens of the United States and entitled to a list of specified rights, including the same right to contract and to own property "as is enjoyed by white citizens." The act made violations of those rights federal crimes. Because of serious questions raised as to the constitutionality of that Act under the Thirteenth Amendment, supporters of the Act introduced the Fourteenth Amendment, which was adopted in 1868. The Fifteenth Amendment was adopted in 1870, and Congress passed the 1870 Civil Rights Act to protect against state denials of voting rights. Congress passed new Civil Rights Acts in 1871 and 1875. The 1871 Act, known as the Ku Klux Klan Act, created a private cause of action against persons who, under color of state law, deprive a person of rights established by the Constitution or federal law. This provision, codified today as 42 U.S.C. § 1983, continues to be a frequent basis for suits alleging a violation of federal or constitutional rights by state officers. The 1875 Act prohibited discrimination on the basis of race in public accommodations, such as common carriers (*e.g.*, railroads), inns, and theaters. The constitutionality of this Act was challenged in the so-called *Civil Rights Cases*, 109 U.S. 3 (1883).

While today such a law would be authorized under the Commerce Clause, *see Heart of Atlanta Motel, Inc. v. United States*, 379 U.S. 241 (1964), in 1883 the Commerce Clause was not construed so broadly. The government maintained that the law was authorized by both the Thirteenth and Fourteenth Amendments. The Court, however, over the

---

* The so-called "Black Codes" were enacted by every southern state after the Thirteenth Amendment. Although they differed in detail, in essence they required all freedmen to be employed upon pain of being arrested as a vagrant, for which there was a large fine that would be paid off by leasing the "vagrant" at a public cry out (think: auction) and using all the wages so earned to pay the fine. Employment contracts provided that the freedman could not quit, and if he did, he could be arrested and returned to his employer. The employment contracts typically provided that the freedman would work from sun-up to sun-down six days a week. Freedmen employees were termed "servants" and their employers "masters." Freed children were to be apprenticed. Freedmen could not possess firearms, knives, or alcoholic beverages.

dissent of Justice Harlan, held the law unconstitutional under both amendments. First, the Court said that, while the Thirteenth Amendment authorized Congress to address the "badges and incidents of slavery," mere racial discrimination was not such a badge or incident of slavery because people had discriminated against black freemen who had never been slaves. [What do you think of that rationale?] Second, the Court held that the Fourteenth Amendment did not authorize Congress to prohibit activity by private persons. The Fourteenth Amendment by its terms prohibits states from doing various things, but it does not operate on private persons, so Congress's enforcement powers were likewise limited to acting upon states.

The first holding in the *Civil Rights Cases* was effectively overruled in 1968 by *Jones v. Alfred H. Mayer Co.*, 392 U.S. 409 (1968). That case involved a federal statute that stated that all citizens had the same right "as is enjoyed by white citizens" to purchase, sell, or lease real and personal property. The Court held that Congress could rationally determine that private discrimination on the basis of race with respect to property was a badge or incident of slavery. Thus, the Thirteenth Amendment has become a basis for legislation banning racial discrimination by private persons as well as by governments.

The second holding in the *Civil Rights Cases*, however, continues to be the law. Congress cannot act with regard to private persons under the authority of the Fourteenth Amendment; it may only act with regard to state (and local) government. *See United States v. Morrison*, 529 U.S. 598 (2000).

Given the current ability of Congress to act against discrimination of various sorts pursuant to its Commerce Clause power, one might wonder why one would still care about the Thirteenth and Fourteenth Amendment powers. First, there are some situations of discrimination that lie beyond Congress's powers under the Commerce Clause. The first case below is a case in point. The more frequent reason to care is the Eleventh Amendment and the Court's interpretation of it in *Hans v. Louisiana*, 134 U.S. 1 (1890), and subsequent cases. That is, while Congress can usually regulate state activity pursuant to the Commerce Clause, *see Garcia v. SAMTA*, 469 U.S. 528 (1985), private persons cannot sue states for damages even when states violate those federal laws. However, as mentioned in the section of the book on the Eleventh Amendment, when Congress legislates pursuant to the Fourteenth Amendment, as opposed to the Commerce Clause, Congress *can* authorize private suits for damages against states. Thus, in cases where private persons sue a state or state agency for damages alleging it has violated a federal law, it may be necessary to determine whether the federal law was enacted under the authority of the Fourteenth Amendment.

During the 1960s, the Court deferred to congressional determinations as to whether the evil Congress was addressing fell within the authority of Congress to enforce the provisions of the Fourteenth Amendment. *See, e.g., Katzenbach v. Morgan*, 384 U.S. 641 (1966)(deferring to Congress's determination in the Voting Rights Act that an English-language literacy test for voting in New York elections constituted invidious discrimination). By 1990, however, the Court took a different turn.

CITY OF BOERNE V. FLORES
United States Supreme Court, 1997.
521 U.S. 507, 117 S.Ct. 2157.

JUSTICE KENNEDY delivered the opinion of the Court.

A decision by local zoning authorities to deny a church a building permit was challenged under the Religious Freedom Restoration Act of 1993 (RFRA or Act). The case calls into question the authority of Congress to enact RFRA. We conclude the statute exceeds Congress's power.

St. Peter Catholic Church

Situated on a hill in the city of Boerne, Texas, . . . is St. Peter Catholic Church. Built in 1923, the church's structure replicates the mission style of the region's earlier history. The church seats about 230 worshippers, a number too small for its growing parish. . . . In order to meet the needs of the congregation the Archbishop of San Antonio gave permission to the parish to plan alterations to enlarge the building.

A few months later, the Boerne City Council passed an ordinance authorizing the city's Historic Landmark Commission to prepare a preservation plan with proposed historic landmarks and districts. Under the ordinance, the commission must preapprove construction affecting historic landmarks or buildings in a historic district.

Soon afterwards, the Archbishop applied for a building permit so construction to enlarge the church could proceed. City authorities, relying on the ordinance and the designation of a historic district (which, they argued, included the church), denied the application. The Archbishop brought this suit challenging the permit denial. . . .

The complaint contained various claims, but to this point the litigation has centered on RFRA and the question of its constitutionality. The Archbishop relied upon RFRA as one basis for relief from the refusal to issue the permit. The District Court concluded that by enacting RFRA Congress exceeded the scope of its enforcement power under § 5 of the Fourteenth Amendment. The court certified its order for interlocutory appeal and the Fifth Circuit reversed, finding RFRA to be constitutional. We granted certiorari and now reverse.

Congress enacted RFRA in direct response to the Court's decision in *Employment Div. v. Smith*. There we considered a Free Exercise Clause claim brought by members of the Native American Church who were denied unemployment benefits when they lost their jobs because they had used peyote. Their practice was to ingest peyote for sacramental purposes, and they challenged an Oregon statute of general applicability which made use of the drug criminal. In evaluating the claim, we declined to apply the balancing test set forth in *Sherbert v. Verner,* 374 U.S. 398 (1963), under which we would have asked whether Oregon's prohibition substantially burdened a religious practice and, if it did, whether the burden was justified by a compelling government interest. . . . By contrast, where a general prohibition, such as Oregon's, is at issue, "the sounder approach, and the approach in accord with the vast majority of our precedents, is to hold the test inapplicable to [free exercise] challenges." *Smith* held that neutral, generally applicable laws may be applied to religious practices even when not supported by a compelling governmental interest. . . .

These points of constitutional interpretation were debated by Members of Congress in hearings and floor debates. Many criticized the Court's reasoning, and this disagreement resulted in the passage of RFRA. . . .

The Act's stated purposes are: "(1) to restore the compelling interest test as set forth in *Sherbert v. Verner* and to guarantee its application in all cases where free exercise of religion is substantially burdened"; and "(2) to provide a claim or defense to persons whose religious exercise is substantially burdened by government."

RFRA prohibits "[g]overnment" from "substantially burden[ing]" a person's exercise of religion even if the burden results from a rule of general applicability unless the government can demonstrate the burden "(1) is in furtherance of a compelling governmental interest; and (2) is the least restrictive means of furthering that compelling governmental interest." The Act's mandate applies to any "branch, department, agency, instrumentality, and official (or other person acting under color of law) of the United States," as well as to any "State, or . . . subdivision of a State." . . .

[C]ongress relied on its Fourteenth Amendment enforcement power in enacting the most far-reaching and substantial of RFRA's provisions, those which impose its requirements on the States. . . .

The parties disagree over whether RFRA is a proper exercise of Congress's § 5 power "to enforce" by "appropriate legislation" the constitutional guarantee that no State shall deprive any person of "life, liberty, or property, without due process of law" nor deny any person "equal protection of the laws."

In defense of the Act, respondent the Archbishop contends, with support from the United States, that RFRA is permissible enforcement legislation. Congress, it is said, is only protecting by legislation one of the liberties guaranteed by the Fourteenth Amendment's Due Process Clause, the free exercise of religion, beyond what is necessary under *Smith*. It is said the congressional decision to dispense with proof of deliberate or overt discrimination and instead concentrate on a law's effects accords with the settled understanding that § 5 includes the power to enact legislation designed to prevent, as well as remedy, constitutional violations. It is further contended that Congress's § 5 power is not limited to remedial or preventive legislation. . . .

[I]n assessing the breadth of § 5's enforcement power, we begin with its text. Congress has been given the power "to enforce" the "provisions of this article." We agree with respondent, of course, that Congress can enact legislation under § 5 enforcing the constitutional right to the free exercise of religion. The "provisions of this article," to which § 5 refers, include the Due Process Clause of the Fourteenth Amendment. Congress's power to enforce the Free Exercise Clause follows from our holding . . . that the "fundamental concept of liberty embodied in [the Fourteenth Amendment's Due Process Clause] embraces the liberties guaranteed by the First Amendment."

Congress's power under § 5, however, extends only to "enforc[ing]" the provisions of the Fourteenth Amendment. The Court has described this power as "remedial." The design of the Amendment and the text of § 5 are inconsistent with the suggestion that Congress has the power to decree the substance of the Fourteenth Amendment's restrictions on the States. Legislation which alters the meaning of the Free Exercise Clause cannot be said to be enforcing the Clause. Congress does not enforce a constitutional right by changing what the right is. It has been given the power "to enforce," not the power to determine what constitutes a constitutional violation. Were it not so, what Congress would be enforcing would no longer be, in any meaningful sense, the "provisions of [the Fourteenth Amendment]."

While the line between measures that remedy or prevent unconstitutional actions and measures that make a substantive change in the governing law is not easy to discern, and Congress must have wide latitude in determining where it lies, the distinction exists and must be observed. There must be a congruence and proportionality between the injury to be prevented or remedied and the means adopted to that end.

Lacking such a connection, legislation may become substantive in operation and effect. History and our case law support drawing the distinction, one apparent from the text of the Amendment. . . .

There is language in our opinion in *Katzenbach v. Morgan,* which could be interpreted as acknowledging a power in Congress to enact legislation that expands the rights contained in § 1 of the Fourteenth Amendment. This is not a necessary interpretation, however, or even the best one. . . . The Court provided two related rationales for its conclusion that § 4(e) could "be viewed as a measure to secure for the Puerto Rican community residing in New York nondiscriminatory treatment by government." . . . Both rationales for upholding § 4(e) rested on unconstitutional discrimination by New York and Congress's reasonable attempt to combat it. . . .

If Congress could define its own powers by altering the Fourteenth Amendment's meaning, no longer would the Constitution be "superior paramount law, unchangeable by ordinary means." It would be "on a level with ordinary legislative acts, and, like other acts, . . . alterable when the legislature shall please to alter it." . . . Shifting legislative majorities could change the Constitution and effectively circumvent the difficult and detailed amendment process contained in Article V.

We now turn to consider whether RFRA can be considered enforcement legislation under § 5 of the Fourteenth Amendment.

Respondent contends that RFRA is a proper exercise of Congress's remedial or preventive power. The Act, it is said, is a reasonable means of protecting the free exercise of religion as defined by *Smith*. It prevents and remedies laws which are enacted with the unconstitutional object of targeting religious beliefs and practices. To avoid the difficulty of proving such violations, it is said, Congress can simply invalidate any law which imposes a substantial burden on a religious practice unless it is justified by a compelling interest and is the least restrictive means of accomplishing that interest. . . .

While preventive rules are sometimes appropriate remedial measures, there must be a congruence between the means used and the ends to be achieved. The appropriateness of remedial measures must be considered in light of the evil presented. Strong measures appropriate to address one harm may be an unwarranted response to another, lesser one.

A comparison between RFRA and the Voting Rights Act is instructive. In contrast to the record which confronted Congress and the Judiciary in the voting rights cases, RFRA's legislative record lacks examples of modern instances of generally applicable laws passed because of religious bigotry. The history of persecution in this country detailed in the hearings mentions no episodes occurring in the past 40 years. . . . Rather, the emphasis of the hearings [on RFRA] was on laws of general applicability which place incidental burdens on religion. . . . This lack of support in the legislative record, however, is not RFRA's most serious shortcoming. Judicial deference, in most cases, is based not on the state of the legislative record Congress compiles but "on due regard for the decision of the body constitutionally appointed to decide." As a general matter, it is for Congress to determine the method by which it will reach a decision.

Regardless of the state of the legislative record, RFRA cannot be considered remedial, preventive legislation, if those terms are to have any meaning. RFRA is so out of proportion to a supposed remedial or preventive object that it cannot be understood as responsive to, or designed to prevent, unconstitutional behavior. It appears, instead, to attempt a substantive change in constitutional protections. Preventive measures prohibiting certain types of laws may be appropriate when there is reason to believe that many of the laws affected by the congressional enactment have a significant likelihood of being unconstitutional. Remedial legislation under § 5 "should be adapted to the mischief and wrong which the [Fourteenth] [A]mendment was intended to provide against."

RFRA is not so confined. Sweeping coverage ensures its intrusion at every level of government, displacing laws and prohibiting official actions of almost every description and regardless of subject matter. . . . RFRA applies to all federal and state law, statutory or otherwise, whether adopted before or after its enactment. RFRA has no termination date or termination mechanism. Any law is subject to challenge at any time by any individual who alleges a substantial burden on his or her free exercise of religion.

The reach and scope of RFRA distinguish it from other measures passed under Congress's enforcement power, even in the area of voting rights. In *South Carolina v. Katzenbach,* the challenged provisions were confined to those regions of the country where voting discrimination had been most flagrant and affected a discrete class of state laws, *i.e.,* state voting laws. . . . The provisions restricting and banning literacy tests, upheld in *Katzenbach v. Morgan* and *Oregon v. Mitchell,* attacked a particular type of voting qualification, one with a long history as a "notorious means to deny and abridge voting rights on racial grounds." . . . This is not to say, of course, that § 5 legislation requires termination dates, geographic restrictions, or egregious predicates. Where, however, a congressional enactment pervasively prohibits constitutional state action in an effort to remedy or to prevent unconstitutional state action, limitations of this kind tend to ensure Congress's means are proportionate to ends legitimate under § 5.

The stringent test RFRA demands of state laws reflects a lack of proportionality or congruence between the means adopted and the legitimate end to be achieved. If an objector can show a substantial burden on his free exercise, the State must demonstrate a compelling governmental interest and show that the law is the least restrictive means of furthering its interest. Claims that a law substantially burdens someone's exercise of religion will often be difficult to contest.... Laws valid under *Smith* would fall under RFRA without regard to whether they had the object of stifling or punishing free exercise. We make these observations not to reargue the position of the majority in *Smith* but to illustrate the substantive alteration of its holding attempted by RFRA....

The substantial costs RFRA exacts, both in practical terms of imposing a heavy litigation burden on the States and in terms of curtailing their traditional general regulatory power, far exceed any pattern or practice of unconstitutional conduct under the Free Exercise Clause as interpreted in *Smith*. Simply put, RFRA is not designed to identify and counteract state laws likely to be unconstitutional because of their treatment of religion. In most cases, the state laws to which RFRA applies are not ones which will have been motivated by religious bigotry. If a state law disproportionately burdened a particular class of religious observers, this circumstance might be evidence of an impermissible legislative motive. RFRA's substantial-burden test, however, is not even a discriminatory effects or disparate-impact test. It is a reality of the modern regulatory state that numerous state laws, such as the zoning regulations at issue here, impose a substantial burden on a large class of individuals. When the exercise of religion has been burdened in an incidental way by a law of general application, it does not follow that the persons affected have been burdened any more than other citizens, let alone burdened because of their religious beliefs....

Our national experience teaches that the Constitution is preserved best when each part of the Government respects both the Constitution and the proper actions and determinations of the other branches. When the Court has interpreted the Constitution, it has acted within the province of the Judicial Branch, which embraces the duty to say what the law is. When the political branches of the Government act against the background of a judicial interpretation of the Constitution already issued, it must be understood that in later cases and controversies the Court will treat its precedents with the respect due them under settled principles, including *stare decisis,* and contrary expectations must be disappointed. RFRA was designed to control cases and controversies, such as the one before us; but as the provisions of the federal statute here invoked are beyond congressional authority, it is this Court's precedent, not RFRA, which must control....

JUSTICE STEVENS, concurring. [omitted]

JUSTICE SCALIA, with whom JUSTICE STEVENS joins, concurring in part. [omitted]

JUSTICE O'CONNOR, with whom JUSTICE BREYER joins except as to the first paragraph of Part I, dissenting.

I dissent from the Court's disposition of this case. I agree with the Court that the issue before us is whether the Religious Freedom Restoration Act of 1993 (RFRA) is a proper exercise of Congress's power to enforce § 5 of the Fourteenth Amendment. But as a yardstick for measuring the constitutionality of RFRA, the Court uses its holding in *Employment Div., Dept. of Human Resources of Oregon v. Smith,* the decision that prompted Congress to enact RFRA as a means of more rigorously enforcing the Free Exercise Clause. I remain of the view that *Smith* was wrongly decided, and I would use this case to reexamine the Court's holding there. . . .

I

I agree with much of the reasoning set forth in . . . the Court's opinion. Indeed, if I agreed with the Court's standard in *Smith,* I would join the opinion. As the Court's careful and thorough historical analysis shows, Congress lacks the "power to decree the *substance* of the Fourteenth Amendment's restrictions on the States." Rather, its power under § 5 of the Fourteenth Amendment extends only to *enforcing* the Amendment's provisions. In short, Congress lacks the ability independently to define or expand the scope of constitutional rights by statute. Accordingly, whether Congress has exceeded its § 5 powers turns on whether there is a "congruence and proportionality between the injury to be prevented or remedied and the means adopted to that end." This recognition does not, of course, in any way diminish Congress's obligation to draw its own conclusions regarding the Constitution's meaning. Congress, no less than this Court, is called upon to consider the requirements of the Constitution and to act in accordance with its dictates. But when it enacts legislation in furtherance of its delegated powers, Congress must make its judgments consistent with this Court's exposition of the Constitution and with the limits placed on its legislative authority by provisions such as the Fourteenth Amendment. . . .

JUSTICE SOUTER, dissenting.

To decide whether the Fourteenth Amendment gives Congress sufficient power to enact the Religious Freedom Restoration Act of 1993, the Court measures the legislation against the free-exercise standard of *Employment Div., Dept. of Human Resources of Oregon v. Smith.* . . . I have serious doubts about the precedential value of the *Smith* rule and its entitlement to adherence. . . .

JUSTICE BREYER, dissenting. [omitted]

COMMENTS AND QUESTIONS

1. *Boerne* (pronounced "bernie") makes several things clear. First, it makes clear that Congress can indeed enforce Free Exercise rights with respect to the states pursuant to Section 5 of the Fourteenth Amendment, but it also

makes clear that it is the Court, not Congress, that gets to define what those rights are. The suggestion in *Katzenbach* that Congress might be able to define the contours of constitutional rights subject to its enforcement powers is rejected. Second, *Boerne* makes clear that Congress in enforcing constitutional rights is not limited merely to prohibiting or punishing violations of those rights; it can engage in preventative and remedial measures. Third, the Court is clear that, if Congress engages in preventative or remedial measures under its Section 5 enforcement powers, those measures must be congruent and proportional to actual violations that have existed or are about to exist.

2.   What specifically was wrong with RFRA? Was it that Congress had defined the right, not the Court? Was it that Congress had no preventative or remedial measure in mind? Was it that any preventative or remedial measure was not congruent and proportional?

BOARD OF TRUSTEES OF THE UNIVERSITY OF ALABAMA V. GARRETT

United States Supreme Court, 2001.
531 U.S. 356, 121 S.Ct. 955.

CHIEF JUSTICE REHNQUIST delivered the opinion of the Court.

We decide here whether employees of the State of Alabama may recover money damages by reason of the State's failure to comply with the provisions of Title I of the Americans with Disabilities Act of 1990 (ADA or Act). We hold that such suits are barred by the Eleventh Amendment.

The ADA prohibits certain employers, including the States, from "discriminat[ing] against a qualified individual with a disability because of the disability of such individual in regard to job application procedures, the hiring, advancement, or discharge of employees, employee compensation, job training, and other terms, conditions, and privileges of employment." . . .

Respondent Patricia Garrett, a registered nurse, was employed as the Director of Nursing, OB/Gyn/Neonatal Services, for the University of Alabama in Birmingham Hospital. In 1994, Garrett was diagnosed with breast cancer and subsequently underwent a lumpectomy, radiation treatment, and chemotherapy. Garrett's treatments required her to take substantial leave from work. Upon returning to work in July 1995, Garrett's supervisor informed Garrett that she would have to give up her Director position. Garrett then applied for and received a transfer to another, lower paying position as a nurse manager. . . .

Garrett . . . filed [a lawsuit] in the District Court, both seeking money damages under the ADA. Petitioners moved for summary judgment, claiming that the ADA exceeds Congress's authority to abrogate the State's Eleventh Amendment immunity. [T]he District Court agreed with petitioner['s] position and granted [her motion] for summary judgment. . . .

The Court of Appeals reversed. . . . We granted certiorari to resolve a split among the Courts of Appeals on the question whether an individual may sue a State for money damages in federal court under the ADA. . . .

Although by its terms the Amendment applies only to suits against a State by citizens of another State, our cases have extended the Amendment's applicability to suits by citizens against their own States. The ultimate guarantee of the Eleventh Amendment is that nonconsenting States may not be sued by private individuals in federal court.

We have recognized, however, that Congress may abrogate the States' Eleventh Amendment immunity when it both unequivocally intends to do so and "act[s] pursuant to a valid grant of constitutional authority." The first of these requirements is not in dispute here. The question, then, is whether Congress acted within its constitutional authority by subjecting the States to suits in federal court for money damages under the ADA.

Congress may not, of course, base its abrogation of the States' Eleventh Amendment immunity upon the powers enumerated in Article I. In *Fitzpatrick v. Bitzer,* 427 U.S. 445 (1976), however, we held that "the Eleventh Amendment, and the principle of state sovereignty which it embodies, are necessarily limited by the enforcement provisions of § 5 of the Fourteenth Amendment." As a result, we concluded, Congress may subject nonconsenting States to suit in federal court when it does so pursuant to a valid exercise of its § 5 power. . . . Accordingly, the ADA can apply to the States only to the extent that the statute is appropriate § 5 legislation. . . .

Section 5 of the Fourteenth Amendment grants Congress the power to enforce the substantive guarantees contained in Section 1 of [the Fourteenth Amendment] by enacting "appropriate legislation." *See City of Boerne v. Flores.* Congress is not limited to mere legislative repetition of this Court's constitutional jurisprudence. "Rather, Congress's power 'to enforce' the Amendment includes the authority both to remedy and to deter violation of rights guaranteed thereunder by prohibiting a somewhat broader swath of conduct, including that which is not itself forbidden by the Amendment's text."

City of Boerne also confirmed, however, the long-settled principle that it is the responsibility of this Court, not Congress, to define the substance of constitutional guarantees. Accordingly, § 5 legislation reaching beyond the scope of § 1's actual guarantees must exhibit "congruence and proportionality between the injury to be prevented or remedied and the means adopted to that end."

The first step in applying these now familiar principles is to identify with some precision the scope of the constitutional right at issue. Here, that inquiry requires us to examine the limitations § 1 of the Fourteenth Amendment places upon States' treatment of the disabled. . . .

[The Court assessed how it had in the past analyzed Equal Protection claims regarding the disabled and concluded that it only required a "rational-basis review." This contrasts with "strict scrutiny" applicable to racial discrimination and "quasi-suspect scrutiny" applicable to sex discrimination.]

Under rational-basis review, where a group possesses "distinguishing characteristics relevant to interests the State has the authority to implement," a State's decision to act on the basis of those differences does not give rise to a constitutional violation. "Such a classification cannot run afoul of the Equal Protection Clause if there is a rational relationship between the disparity of treatment and some legitimate governmental purpose." Moreover, the State need not articulate its reasoning at the moment a particular decision is made. Rather, the burden is upon the challenging party to negative " 'any reasonably conceivable state of facts that could provide a rational basis for the classification.' " . . .

Thus, the result of [our past cases] is that States are not required by the Fourteenth Amendment to make special accommodations for the disabled, so long as their actions toward such individuals are rational. They could quite hardheadedly—and perhaps hardheartedly—hold to job-qualification requirements which do not make allowance for the disabled. If special accommodations for the disabled are to be required, they have to come from positive law and not through the Equal Protection Clause.

Once we have determined the metes and bounds of the constitutional right in question, we examine whether Congress identified a history and pattern of unconstitutional employment discrimination by the States against the disabled. Just as § 1 of the Fourteenth Amendment applies only to actions committed "under color of state law," Congress's § 5 authority is appropriately exercised only in response to state transgressions. The legislative record of the ADA, however, simply fails to show that Congress did in fact identify a pattern of irrational state discrimination in employment against the disabled.

Respondents contend that the inquiry as to unconstitutional discrimination should extend not only to States themselves, but to units of local governments, such as cities and counties. All of these, they say, are "state actors" for purposes of the Fourteenth Amendment. This is quite true, but the Eleventh Amendment does not extend its immunity to units of local government. These entities are subject to private claims for damages under the ADA without Congress's ever having to rely on § 5 of the Fourteenth Amendment to render them so. It would make no sense to consider constitutional violations on their part, as well as by the States themselves, when only the States are the beneficiaries of the Eleventh Amendment. . . .

Respondents in their brief cite half a dozen examples from the record that did involve States. . . . Several of these incidents undoubtedly evidence an unwillingness on the part of state officials to make the sort of accommodations for the disabled required by the ADA. Whether they were irrational under our decision[s] is more debatable, particularly when the incident is described out of context. But even if it were to be determined that each incident upon fuller examination showed unconstitutional action on the part of the State, these incidents taken together fall far short of even suggesting the pattern of unconstitutional discrimination on which § 5 legislation must be based. . . .

Even were it possible to squeeze out of these examples a pattern of unconstitutional discrimination by the States, the rights and remedies created by the ADA against the States would raise the same sort of concerns as to congruence and proportionality as were found in *City of Boerne*. For example, whereas it would be entirely rational (and therefore constitutional) for a state employer to conserve scarce financial resources by hiring employees who are able to use existing facilities, the ADA requires employers to "mak[e] existing facilities used by employees readily accessible to and usable by individuals with disabilities." The ADA does except employers from the "reasonable accommodatio[n]" requirement where the employer "can demonstrate that the accommodation would impose an undue hardship on the operation of the business of such covered entity." However, even with this exception, the accommodation duty far exceeds what is constitutionally required in that it makes unlawful a range of alternative responses that would be reasonable but would fall short of imposing an "undue burden" upon the employer. The Act also makes it the employer's duty to prove that it would suffer such a burden, instead of requiring (as the Constitution does) that the complaining party negate reasonable bases for the employer's decision. . . .

The ADA's constitutional shortcomings are apparent when the Act is compared to Congress's efforts in the Voting Rights Act of 1965 to respond to a serious pattern of constitutional violations. In *South Carolina v. Katzenbach,* we considered whether the Voting Rights Act was "appropriate" legislation to enforce the Fifteenth Amendment's protection against racial discrimination in voting. Concluding that it was a valid exercise of Congress's enforcement power under § 2 of the Fifteenth Amendment, we noted that "[b]efore enacting the measure, Congress explored with great care the problem of racial discrimination in voting." In that Act, Congress documented a marked pattern of unconstitutional action by the States. State officials, Congress found, routinely applied voting tests in order to exclude African-American citizens from registering to vote. Congress also determined that litigation had proved ineffective and that there persisted an otherwise inexplicable 50-percentage-point gap in the registration of white and African-American voters in some States. Congress's response was to promulgate in the Voting Rights Act a detailed but limited remedial scheme designed to guarantee meaningful enforcement of the Fifteenth Amendment in those areas of the Nation where abundant evidence of States' systematic denial of those rights was identified.

The contrast between this kind of evidence, and the evidence that Congress considered in the present case, is stark. Congressional enactment of the ADA represents its judgment that there should be a "comprehensive national mandate for the elimination of discrimination against individuals with disabilities." Congress is the final authority as to desirable public policy, but in order to authorize private individuals to recover money damages against the States, there must be a pattern of discrimination by the States which violates the Fourteenth Amendment, and the remedy imposed by Congress must be congruent and proportional to the targeted violation. Those requirements are not met here, and to uphold the Act's application to the States would allow Congress to rewrite the Fourteenth Amendment law laid down by this Court.[9] . . .

JUSTICE KENNEDY, with whom JUSTICE O'CONNOR joins, concurring.

[F]or the reasons explained by the Court, an equal protection violation has not been shown with respect to the several States in this case. . . .

It must be noted, moreover, that what is in question is not whether the Congress, acting pursuant to a power granted to it by the Constitution, can compel the States to act. What is involved is only the question whether the States can be subjected to liability in suits brought not by the Federal Government . . ., but by private persons seeking to collect moneys from the state treasury without the consent of the State. The predicate for money damages against an unconsenting State in suits brought by private persons must be a federal statute enacted upon the documentation of patterns of constitutional violations committed by the State in its official capacity. That predicate, for reasons discussed here and in the decision of the Court, has not been established. With these observations, I join the Court's opinion.

JUSTICE BREYER, with whom JUSTICE STEVENS, JUSTICE SOUTER, and JUSTICE GINSBURG join, dissenting.

Reviewing the congressional record as if it were an administrative agency record, the Court holds the statutory provision before us unconstitutional. The Court concludes that Congress assembled insufficient evidence of unconstitutional discrimination, that Congress improperly attempted to "rewrite" the law we established in [our past

---

[9] Our holding here that Congress did not validly abrogate the States' sovereign immunity from suit by private individuals for money damages under Title I does not mean that persons with disabilities have no federal recourse against discrimination. Title I of the ADA still prescribes standards applicable to the States. Those standards can be enforced by the United States in actions for money damages, as well as by private individuals in actions for injunctive relief under *Ex parte Young*. In addition, state laws protecting the rights of persons with disabilities in employment and other aspects of life provide independent avenues of redress.

cases], and that the law is not sufficiently tailored to address unconstitutional discrimination.

Section 5, however, grants Congress the "power to enforce, by appropriate legislation," the Fourteenth Amendment's equal protection guarantee. As the Court recognizes, state discrimination in employment against persons with disabilities might " 'run afoul of the Equal Protection Clause' " where there is no " 'rational relationship between the disparity of treatment and some legitimate governmental purpose.' " In my view, Congress reasonably could have concluded that the remedy before us constitutes an "appropriate" way to enforce this basic equal protection requirement. And that is all the Constitution requires.

COMMENTS AND QUESTIONS

1.   *Garrett* is a more common type of case raising Congress's Section 5 powers than is *Boerne*. That is, in *Garrett*, everyone agrees that Congress can enact the Americans with Disabilities Act (ADA) under its Commerce Clause powers, and that under those powers Congress can bind the states like other employers. Recall *Garcia v. SAMTA*. The problem is the Eleventh Amendment. As we discovered in Chapter 2, the Eleventh Amendment as interpreted by the Supreme Court generally precludes private damage actions against states (including state agencies). The notes at the end of the Eleventh Amendment section listed the exceptions to this general rule. One of those exceptions is when Congress authorizes the suit pursuant to its enforcement powers under the Fourteenth Amendment. In *Garrett*, because the suit is one for damages against a state agency, the Court must determine whether the ADA is authorized not only by the Commerce Clause but also by Section 5 of the Fourteenth Amendment.

2.   *Garrett* gives us some feel for how to apply the "congruent and proportional" test, especially where Congress is purportedly enforcing the Equal Protection Clause. First, one must determine what constitutional violations may exist. In *Garrett*, the Court concludes that discriminating against the handicapped is not generally a constitutional violation under the tests the Court uses for determining whether discrimination is unconstitutional.* Next, one must determine whether the identified constitutional violations are widespread or rare. In *Garrett*, because discrimination against the handicapped generally is not unconstitutional, although in some circumstances the discrimination may be so irrational as to be unconstitutional, unconstitutional discrimination against the handicapped is relatively rare. Finally, one must assess whether the protections provided

---

* While the ins and outs of the Equal Protection Clause are treated later in the "rights" portion of this book, it is sufficient to know here that some types of discrimination are subject to stricter judicial scrutiny than other types. As you might imagine, racial discrimination is subject to strict judicial scrutiny, whereas many other forms of discrimination (such as disability, age, obesity, drug addiction, poverty) are subject to a very lax form of scrutiny—rational basis review— because discrimination on these bases is usually rational, even if not nice. And discrimination on these bases is often illegal, even if not unconstitutional, because Congress, states, or localities have adopted laws banning such discrimination.

by the law are "congruent and proportional" to the extent of the constitutional violations. The greater the extent of the violations, the greater the appropriate remedial or preventative power may be. In *Garrett* the law is broad (generally banning discrimination against the handicapped in employment) while the constitutional violations are rare, hence the remedies provided are not congruent and proportional to the violations.

3.   Prior to *Garrett*, the Court decided *Kimel v. Florida Board of Regents*, 528 U.S. 62 (2000), involving a private damages action by employees of Florida State University under the Age Discrimination in Employment Act (ADEA), which prohibits employers from discriminating against employees because of age. There too the Court by a 5–4 vote held that the law was not authorized under Section 5 of the Fourteenth Amendment and therefore could not provide a basis for a private damages action. The Court noted that its past cases had upheld discrimination based upon age in cases alleging a violation of the Equal Protection Clause, so a broad prohibition against such discrimination was not congruent or proportional to any unconstitutional conduct shown to exist.

NEVADA DEPARTMENT OF HUMAN RESOURCES V. HIBBS

United States Supreme Court, 2003.
538 U.S. 721, 123 S.Ct. 1972.

CHIEF JUSTICE REHNQUIST delivered the opinion of the Court.

The Family and Medical Leave Act of 1993 (FMLA or Act) entitles eligible employees to take up to 12 work weeks of unpaid leave annually for any of several reasons, including the onset of a "serious health condition" in an employee's spouse, child, or parent. The Act creates a private right of action to seek both equitable relief and money damages "against any employer (including a public agency) in any Federal or State court of competent jurisdiction," should that employer "interfere with, restrain, or deny the exercise of" FMLA rights. We hold that employees of the State of Nevada may recover money damages in the event of the State's failure to comply with the family-care provision of the Act.

Petitioners include the Nevada Department of Human Resources (Department). . . . Respondent William Hibbs (hereinafter respondent) worked for the Department's Welfare Division. In April and May 1997, he sought leave under the FMLA to care for his ailing wife, who was recovering from a car accident and neck surgery. . . . [He was granted some leave, but he refused to return to work when told to and was then fired.]

Respondent sued petitioners in the United States District Court seeking damages and injunctive and declaratory relief for violations of [FMLA]. The District Court awarded petitioners summary judgment on the grounds that the FMLA claim was barred by the Eleventh Amendment and that respondent's Fourteenth Amendment rights had not been violated. Respondent appealed, and the United States intervened . . . to defend the validity of the FMLA's application to the States. The Ninth Circuit reversed.

We granted certiorari to resolve a split among the Courts of Appeals on the question whether an individual may sue a State for money damages in federal court for violation of [FMLA].

For over a century now, we have made clear that the Constitution does not provide for federal jurisdiction over suits against nonconsenting States. Congress may, however, abrogate such immunity in federal court if it makes its intention to abrogate unmistakably clear in the language of the statute and acts pursuant to a valid exercise of its power under § 5 of the Fourteenth Amendment. The clarity of Congress's intent here is not fairly debatable. . . . This case turns, then, on whether Congress acted within its constitutional authority when it sought to abrogate the States' immunity for purposes of the FMLA's family-leave provision.

In enacting the FMLA, Congress relied on two of the powers vested in it by the Constitution: its Article I commerce power and its power under § 5 of the Fourteenth Amendment to enforce that Amendment's guarantees. Congress may not abrogate the States' sovereign immunity pursuant to its Article I power over commerce. Congress may, however, abrogate States' sovereign immunity through a valid exercise of its § 5 power, for "the Eleventh Amendment, and the principle of state sovereignty which it embodies, are necessarily limited by the enforcement provisions of § 5 of the Fourteenth Amendment."

Two provisions of the Fourteenth Amendment are relevant here: Section 5 grants Congress the power "to enforce" the substantive guarantees of § 1—among them, equal protection of the laws—by enacting "appropriate legislation." Congress may, in the exercise of its § 5 power, do more than simply proscribe conduct that we have held unconstitutional. " 'Congress's power "to enforce" the Amendment includes the authority both to remedy and to deter violation of rights guaranteed thereunder by prohibiting a somewhat broader swath of conduct, including that which is not itself forbidden by the Amendment's text." In other words, Congress may enact so-called prophylactic legislation that proscribes facially constitutional conduct, in order to prevent and deter unconstitutional conduct.

City of Boerne also confirmed, however, that it falls to this Court, not Congress, to define the substance of constitutional guarantees. . . . Section 5 legislation reaching beyond the scope of § 1's actual guarantees must be an appropriate remedy for identified constitutional violations, not "an attempt to substantively redefine the States' legal obligations." We distinguish appropriate prophylactic legislation from "substantive redefinition of the Fourteenth Amendment right at issue," by applying the test set forth in City of Boerne: Valid § 5 legislation must exhibit "congruence and proportionality between the injury to be prevented or remedied and the means adopted to that end."

The FMLA aims to protect the right to be free from gender-based discrimination in the workplace. We have held that statutory classifications that distinguish between males and females are subject to heightened scrutiny. For a gender-based classification to withstand such scrutiny, it must "serv[e] important governmental objectives," and "the discriminatory means employed [must be] substantially related to the achievement of those objectives." . . . We now inquire whether Congress had evidence of a pattern of constitutional violations on the part of the States in this area.

The history of the many state laws limiting women's employment opportunities is chronicled in—and, until relatively recently, was sanctioned by—this Court's own opinions. For example, . . . the Court upheld state laws prohibiting women from practicing law and tending bar, respectively. State laws frequently subjected women to distinctive restrictions, terms, conditions, and benefits for those jobs they could take. [F]or example, this Court approved a state law limiting the hours that women could work for wages, and observed that 19 States had such laws at the time. Such laws were based on the related beliefs that (1) a woman is, and should remain, "the center of home and family life," and (2) "a proper discharge of [a woman's] maternal functions—having in view not merely her own health, but the well-being of the race—justif[ies] legislation to protect her from the greed as well as the passion of man." Until our decision in *Reed v. Reed*, 404 U.S. 71 (1971), "it remained the prevailing doctrine that government, both federal and state, could withhold from women opportunities accorded men so long as any 'basis in reason' "—such as the above beliefs—"could be conceived for the discrimination."

Congress responded to this history of discrimination by abrogating States' sovereign immunity in Title VII of the Civil Rights Act of 1964 and we sustained this abrogation in *Fitzpatrick*. But state gender discrimination did not cease. . . . According to evidence that was before Congress when it enacted the FMLA, States continue to rely on invalid gender stereotypes in the employment context, specifically in the administration of leave benefits. Reliance on such stereotypes cannot justify the States' gender discrimination in this area. The long and extensive history of sex discrimination prompted us to hold that measures that differentiate on the basis of gender warrant heightened scrutiny; here, as in *Fitzpatrick,* the persistence of such unconstitutional discrimination by the States justifies Congress's passage of prophylactic § 5 legislation.

As the FMLA's legislative record reflects, a 1990 Bureau of Labor Statistics (BLS) survey stated that 37 percent of surveyed private-sector employees were covered by maternity leave policies, while only 18 percent were covered by paternity leave policies. . . . Thus, stereotype-based beliefs about the allocation of family duties remained firmly rooted, and employers' reliance on them in establishing discriminatory leave policies remained widespread.[3]

Congress also heard testimony that "[p]arental leave for fathers . . . is rare. Even . . . [w]here child-care leave policies do exist, men, *both in the public and private sectors,* receive notoriously discriminatory treatment in their requests for such leave." . . . This and other differential leave policies were not attributable to any differential physical needs of men and women, but rather to the pervasive sex-role stereotype that caring for family members is women's work. . . .

In sum, the States' record of unconstitutional participation in, and fostering of, gender-based discrimination in the administration of leave benefits is weighty enough to justify the enactment of prophylactic § 5 legislation.

We reached the opposite conclusion in *Garrett* and *Kimel.* In those cases, the § 5 legislation under review responded to a purported tendency of state officials to make age- or disability-based distinctions. Under our equal protection case law, discrimination on the basis of such characteristics is not judged under a heightened review standard, and passes muster if there is "a rational basis for doing so at a class-based level, even if it 'is probably not true' that those reasons are valid in the majority of cases." Thus, in order to impugn the constitutionality of state discrimination against the disabled or the elderly, Congress must identify, not just the existence of age- or disability-based state decisions, but a "widespread pattern" of irrational reliance on such criteria. We found no such showing with respect to the ADEA and Title I of the Americans with Disabilities Act of 1990 (ADA).

Here, however, Congress directed its attention to state gender discrimination, which triggers a heightened level of scrutiny. Because the standard for demonstrating the constitutionality of a gender-based classification is more difficult to meet than our rational-basis test—it must "serv[e] important governmental objectives" and be "substantially related to the achievement of those objectives,"—it was easier for Congress to show a pattern of state constitutional violations. Congress was similarly successful in *South Carolina v. Katzenbach,* where we upheld the Voting Rights Act of 1965: Because racial classifications are presumptively invalid, most of the States' acts of race discrimination violated the Fourteenth Amendment.

The impact of the discrimination targeted by the FMLA is significant. Congress determined:

---

[3] While this and other material described leave policies in the private sector, a 50-state survey also before Congress demonstrated that "[t]he proportion and construction of leave policies available to public sector employees differs little from those offered private sector employees." . . .

"Historically, denial or curtailment of women's employment opportunities has been traceable directly to the pervasive presumption that women are mothers first, and workers second. This prevailing ideology about women's roles has in turn justified discrimination against women when they are mothers or mothers-to-be."

Stereotypes about women's domestic roles are reinforced by parallel stereotypes presuming a lack of domestic responsibilities for men. Because employers continued to regard the family as the woman's domain, they often denied men similar accommodations or discouraged them from taking leave. These mutually reinforcing stereotypes created a self-fulfilling cycle of discrimination that forced women to continue to assume the role of primary family caregiver, and fostered employers' stereotypical views about women's commitment to work and their value as employees. Those perceptions, in turn, Congress reasoned, lead to subtle discrimination that may be difficult to detect on a case-by-case basis.

We believe that Congress's chosen remedy, the family-care leave provision of the FMLA, is "congruent and proportional to the targeted violation." Congress had already tried unsuccessfully to address this problem through Title VII and the amendment of Title VII by the Pregnancy Discrimination Act. Here, as in *Katzenbach*, Congress again confronted a "difficult and intractable proble[m], where previous legislative attempts had failed. Such problems may justify added prophylactic measures in response.

By creating an across-the-board, routine employment benefit for all eligible employees, Congress sought to ensure that family-care leave would no longer be stigmatized as an inordinate drain on the workplace caused by female employees, and that employers could not evade leave obligations simply by hiring men. By setting a minimum standard of family leave for *all* eligible employees, irrespective of gender, the FMLA attacks the formerly state-sanctioned stereotype that only women are responsible for family caregiving, thereby reducing employers' incentives to engage in discrimination by basing hiring and promotion decisions on stereotypes. . . .

Unlike the statutes at issue in *City of Boerne, Kimel*, and *Garrett*, which applied broadly to every aspect of state employers' operations, the FMLA is narrowly targeted at the faultline between work and family—precisely where sex-based overgeneralization has been and remains strongest—and affects only one aspect of the employment relationship.

We also find significant the many other limitations that Congress placed on the scope of this measure. The FMLA requires only unpaid leave and applies only to employees who have worked for the employer for at least one year and provided 1,250 hours of service within the last 12 months. Employees in high-ranking or sensitive positions are simply ineligible for FMLA leave; of particular importance to the States, the FMLA expressly excludes from coverage state elected officials, their staffs, and appointed policymakers. Employees must give advance notice of foreseeable leave, and employers may require certification by a health care provider of the need for leave. In choosing 12 weeks as the appropriate leave floor, Congress chose "a middle ground, a period long enough to serve 'the needs of families' but not so long that it would upset 'the legitimate interests of employers.'" Moreover, the cause of action under the FMLA is a restricted one: The damages recoverable are strictly defined and measured by actual monetary losses, and the accrual period for backpay is limited by the Act's 2-year statute of limitations (extended to three years only for willful violations).

For the above reasons, we conclude that § 2612(a)(1)(C) is congruent and proportional to its remedial object, and can "be understood as responsive to, or designed to prevent, unconstitutional behavior."

JUSTICE SOUTER, with whom JUSTICE GINSBURG and JUSTICE BREYER join, concurring.

Even on this Court's view of the scope of congressional power under § 5 of the Fourteenth Amendment, the Family and Medical Leave Act of 1993 is undoubtedly valid legislation, and application of the Act to the States is constitutional; the same conclusions follow *a fortiori* from my own understanding of § 5. I join the Court's opinion here without conceding [my former] dissenting positions. . . .

JUSTICE STEVENS, concurring in the judgment.

Because I have never been convinced that an Act of Congress can amend the Constitution and because I am uncertain whether the congressional enactment before us was truly "'needed to secure the guarantees of the Fourteenth Amendment,'" I write separately to explain why I join the Court's judgment. [Justice Stevens goes on to explain why he believes Congress under the Commerce Clause can override states' Eleventh Amendment sovereign immunity in a case brought by a citizen of the state.]

JUSTICE SCALIA, dissenting.

I join Justice KENNEDY's dissent, and add one further observation: The constitutional violation that is a prerequisite to "prophylactic" congressional action to "enforce" the Fourteenth Amendment is a violation *by the State against which the enforcement action is taken.* There is no guilt by association, enabling the sovereignty of one State to be abridged under § 5 of the Fourteenth Amendment because of violations by another State, or by most other States, or even by 49 other States. . . .

JUSTICE KENNEDY, with whom JUSTICE SCALIA and JUSTICE THOMAS join, dissenting.

[T]he Court is unable to show that States have engaged in a pattern of unlawful conduct which warrants the remedy of opening state treasuries to private suits. The inability to adduce evidence of alleged discrimination, coupled with the inescapable fact that the federal scheme is not a remedy but a benefit program, demonstrates the lack of the requisite link between any problem Congress has identified and the program it mandated.

In examining whether Congress was addressing a demonstrated "pattern of unconstitutional employment discrimination by the States," the Court gives superficial treatment to the requirement that we "identify with some precision the scope of the constitutional right at issue." The Court suggests the issue is "the right to be free from gender-based discrimination in the workplace," and then it embarks on a survey of our precedents speaking to "[t]he history of the many state laws limiting women's employment opportunities." All would agree that women historically have been subjected to conditions in which their employment opportunities are more limited than those available to men. As the Court acknowledges, however, Congress responded to this problem by abrogating States' sovereign immunity in Title VII of the Civil Rights Act of 1964 The provision now before us has a different aim than Title VII. It seeks to ensure that eligible employees, irrespective of gender, can take a minimum amount of leave time to care for an ill relative.

The relevant question, as the Court seems to acknowledge, is whether, notwithstanding the passage of Title VII and similar state legislation, the States continued to engage in widespread discrimination on the basis of gender in the provision of family leave benefits. If such a pattern were shown, the Eleventh Amendment would not bar Congress from devising a congruent and proportional remedy. The evidence to substantiate this charge must be far more specific, however, than a simple recitation of a general history of employment discrimination against women. When the federal statute seeks to abrogate state sovereign immunity, the Court should be more careful to insist on adherence to the analytic requirements set forth in its own precedents. Persisting overall effects of gender-based discrimination at the workplace must not be ignored; but simply noting the problem is not a substitute for evidence which identifies some real discrimination the family leave rules are designed to prevent. . . .

Respondents fail to make the requisite showing.

As the Court seems to recognize, the evidence considered by Congress concerned discriminatory practices of the private sector, not those of state employers. . . . The Court seeks to connect the evidence of private discrimination to an alleged pattern of unconstitutional behavior by States through inferences drawn from two sources [both of which related to parenting leave, not family medical leave, in 1986. . . .]

Even if this isolated testimony could support an inference that private sector's gender-based discrimination in the provision of parenting leave was parallel to the behavior by state actors in 1986, the evidence would not be probative of the States' conduct some seven years later with respect to a statutory provision conferring a different benefit. . . .

The Court's reliance on evidence suggesting States provided men and women with the parenting leave of different length suffers from the same flaw. This evidence concerns the Act's grant of parenting leave and is too attenuated to justify the family leave provision. . . . The charge that a State has engaged in a pattern of unconstitutional discrimination against its citizens is a most serious one. It must be supported by more than conjecture.

The Court maintains the evidence pertaining to the parenting leave is relevant because both parenting and family leave provisions respond to "the same gender stereotype: that women's family duties trump those of the workplace." This sets the contours of the inquiry at too high a level of abstraction. The question is not whether the family leave provision is a congruent and proportional response to general gender-based stereotypes in employment which "ha[ve] historically produced discrimination in the hiring and promotion of women," the question is whether it is a proper remedy to an alleged pattern of unconstitutional discrimination by States in the grant of family leave. The evidence of gender-based stereotypes is too remote to support the required showing. . . .

Considered in its entirety, the evidence fails to document a pattern of unconstitutional conduct sufficient to justify the abrogation of States' sovereign immunity. The few incidents identified by the Court "fall far short of even suggesting the pattern of unconstitutional discrimination on which § 5 legislation must be based." . . .

Our concern with gender discrimination, which is subjected to heightened scrutiny, as opposed to age- or disability-based distinctions, which are reviewed under rational standard does not alter this conclusion. The application of heightened scrutiny is designed to ensure gender-based classifications are not based on the entrenched and pervasive stereotypes which inhibit women's progress in the workplace. This consideration does not divest respondents of their burden to show that "Congress identified a history and pattern of unconstitutional employment discrimination by the States." The Court seems to reaffirm this requirement. In my submission, however, the Court does not follow it. Given the insufficiency of the evidence that States discriminated in the provision of family leave, the unfortunate fact that stereotypes about women continue to be a serious and pervasive social problem would not alone support the charge that a State has engaged in a practice designed to deny its citizens the equal protection of the laws.

The paucity of evidence to support the case the Court tries to make demonstrates that Congress was not responding with a congruent and proportional remedy to a perceived course of unconstitutional conduct.

Instead, it enacted a substantive entitlement program of its own. If Congress had been concerned about different treatment of men and women with respect to family leave, a congruent remedy would have sought to ensure the benefits of any leave program enacted by a State are available to men and women on an equal basis. Instead, the Act imposes, across the board, a requirement that States grant a minimum of 12 weeks of leave per year. . . .

It bears emphasis that, even were the Court to bar unconsented federal suits by private individuals for money damages from a State, individuals whose rights under the Act were violated would not be without recourse. The Act is likely a valid exercise of Congress's power under the Commerce Clause, and so the standards it prescribes will be binding upon the States. The United States may enforce these standards in actions for money damages; and private individuals may bring actions against state officials for injunctive relief under *Ex parte Young*. What is at issue is only whether the States can be subjected, without consent, to suits brought by private persons seeking to collect moneys from the state treasury. Their immunity cannot be abrogated without documentation of a pattern of unconstitutional acts by the States, and only then by a congruent and proportional remedy. There has been a complete failure by respondents to carry their burden to establish each of these necessary propositions. I would hold that the Act is not a valid abrogation of state sovereign immunity and dissent with respect from the Court's conclusion to the contrary.

COMMENTS AND QUESTIONS

1.   *Hibbs* is another case involving a private damages suit against a state agency, and again the issue is whether the federal statute authorizing the suit can be an exercise of Congress's Section 5 enforcement authority under the Fourteenth Amendment, which would override the state's Eleventh Amendment sovereign immunity. *Hibbs*, however, comes out differently from *Garrett*. Chief Justice Rehnquist and Justice O'Connor have switched sides. What are the factors that lead them to find that the FMLA is within Congress's Section 5 powers? Does the dissent disagree on the test to be applied?

2.   What are the equal protection violations the majority says states have engaged in, justifying the FMLA's preventative and remedial measures? And, then, why are FMLA's preventative and remedial measures "congruent and proportional" to those violations?

3.   What is the relevance of the fact that discrimination based on sex is subject to a higher level of scrutiny than age and disability?

4.   In 2012, the Court was faced with another FMLA case raising a Section 5 question. In *Coleman v. Court of Appeals of Maryland*, 566 U.S. 30 (2012), Coleman sought the same mandated twelve-week unpaid leave that the Court in *Hibbs* had said Congress could require under Section 5 of the

Fourteenth Amendment, but in his case he needed the leave due to his own serious health condition, not the need to care for a family member. While the FMLA expressly provides that an employee's own serious health condition qualifies for such leave, Coleman's employer, the Maryland Court of Appeals, refused, and Coleman sued for damages under the Act. The Court by a 5–4 vote held that Congress could not under Section 5 of the Fourteenth Amendment require the state to grant the leave for the employee's own serious health condition. There was, however, no majority opinion. Justice Kennedy, writing for the plurality, said that *Hibbs* had found the leave provision justified under Section 5 because it was based upon extensive congressional findings of unconstitutional sex-based discrimination by states in family-leave policies. Consequently, requiring states to provide all employees equally the opportunity to take family-care leave was congruent and proportional to the underlying constitutional violations. The provision in the Act allowing employees to take leave because of their own health conditions, however, had nothing to do with the unconstitutional sex-based discrimination. Thus, requiring leave for such employees was not congruent and proportional to any pattern of unconstitutional state practices. Justice Scalia concurred only in the judgment, stating his view that Congress's powers under Section 5 are limited to regulating conduct that itself violates the Fourteenth Amendment unless, for reasons of *stare decisis*, the conduct involves racial discrimination. The four "liberal" justices would have found the leave policy authorized by Section 5. It is well to recall, however, that, while Coleman's employer, the Maryland Court of Appeals, could not be required to pay damages under the FMLA for failure to provide sick leave, it could be ordered to provide such leave in the future under the FMLA pursuant to Congress's powers under the Commerce Clause and the exception to sovereign immunity for injunction suits against state officers.

5.   *Tennessee v. Lane*, 541 U.S. 509 (2004), is still another private damages suit against a state, this time under Title II of the ADA. Title II of the ADA, unlike the employment portion—Title I—involved in *Garrett*, provides that: "no qualified individual with a disability shall, by reason of such disability, be excluded from participation or denied the benefits of the services, programs or activities of a public entity." Lane was a paraplegic who was a defendant in a state criminal case, whose case was to be heard on the second floor of a courthouse that had no elevator. At his first appearance, Lane crawled up two flights of stairs in order to reach his courtroom. At his second appearance, he refused to crawl or be carried by officers and was arrested for failing to appear. He sued for damages under Title II of the ADA. The Court in a 5–4 vote held that Congress could enact Title II of the ADA under the authority of Section 5 of the Fourteenth Amendment to the extent that it prohibited discrimination against disabled persons in access to essential government functions, such as access to the courts. The Court did not rely on evidence of equal protection violations, but rather looked to evidence of state violations of due process, which of course are also prohibited by the Fourteenth Amendment. The Court noted its past cases finding a due process right of access to courts and the fact that state laws that limited access to courts were

subject to heightened judicial scrutiny. This made *Lane* like *Hibbs* in that Congress was acting in an area that the Court had found laws presumptively unconstitutional, rather than presumptively constitutional. The dissent argued that the evidence of state constitutional violations was inadequate to justify this wide-ranging remedy, and in particular that the wide ranging prohibition in Title II involved many situations other than courthouses and other state functions to which persons have a due process right of access. For example, Title II would apply to state-owned theaters and hockey stadiums, to which there is no due process right of access. The Court, however, said that the fact that there might be instances under which Title II's prohibitions might not be authorized under Section 5 did not mean that there could not be other instances in which it would be so authorized—such as the instance in *Lane*.

PROBLEM

Congress finds that discrimination in employment against overweight persons results in those persons not being fully productive members of society and are more likely to end up on public assistance. Accordingly, it passes the Body Appearance Non-Discrimination Act (BANDA) prohibiting employers in an industry affecting commerce, including government industries, from discriminating in employment against overweight persons, and it provides a private cause of action for injunctive and monetary relief against anyone who violates BANDA. A state university Provost asks its General Counsel whether the university could constitutionally be sued by a private person for injunctive or monetary relief pursuant to BANDA.

G. PREEMPTION

When a state or local law is rendered invalid under the Supremacy Clause (Article VI, Clause 2) because it conflicts with a federal law, we say that the federal law preempts the state law, or that the state law is preempted, rather than saying that the state law is unconstitutional. We have run into preemption before. In *Gibbons v. Ogden*, for example, the New York law granting the monopoly to Ogden conflicted with the federal law granting Gibbons a license to engage in the coastal trade, and as a result the New York law was rendered invalid to the extent of that conflict, and Gibbons could carry passengers between New Jersey and New York.

Whether state law is preempted by federal law depends on the particulars of the federal law. The federal law may explicitly preempt state law. This is called express preemption. For example, imagine that Congress passes a law under its Commerce Clause powers stating that no person may practice law in the United States unless they have graduated from an American Bar Association accredited law school. The law further provides that no state may impose any other requirement on the ability to practice law in the state. This federal law expressly preempts any state law providing different or additional requirements, so that existing state requirements that a person must, in addition to graduating from an ABA accredited law school, pass the state bar exam in order to practice law in the state would be preempted by the federal law.

Often, however, the language of the federal statute may not be entirely clear, so there may be a question to what extent it preempts state law. For example, a recurring issue today is whether a federal statute expressly preempting any state "requirement or prohibition" preempts state common law tort law or only preempts state statutory or regulatory requirements or prohibitions. *See Cipollone v. Liggett Group, Inc.,* 505 U.S. 504 (1992)(federal prohibition of other state requirements held to include state tort law). Thus, often a court must interpret an unclear federal statutory preemption provision to determine what Congress intended.

Frequently, if not usually, there is no express preemption language, and a court must interpret the federal statute to determine whether Congress intended to preempt state law. This is called "implied preemption." For example, imagine that Congress had passed the same law establishing graduation from an ABA-accredited law school as the federal requirement for the practice of law in the United States, but that it left off the provision that no state could impose any other requirement on the ability to practice law in the state. The question then might arise whether there was a conflict between the federal law and existing state laws. Congress might have intended the federal requirement to be a floor, not a ceiling, on the requirements to practice law, so that an additional state requirement that a person must also pass a state bar exam would not conflict with the federal law. On the other hand, Congress might have intended that the federal requirement be the only requirement for a person to practice law in the United States, in which case any additional requirement imposed by a state, such as a requirement to pass a state bar exam, would conflict with the intent of the federal law. In this case, the additional state requirement would be preempted by the federal law.

There are actually three forms of implied preemption: field preemption, direct conflict preemption, and obstacle preemption. Field preemption refers to the situation where the federal government so fully regulates the field that any state regulation, whether or not it actually conflicts with the federal regulation, is seen as incompatible with exclusive federal regulation. For example, in *United States v. Locke,* 529 U.S. 89 (2000), the Court found that the federal Ports and Waterways Safety Act, governing the design, construction, alteration, repair, maintenance, operation, equipping, personnel qualification, and manning of oil tankers occupied the entire field, so that Congress left no room for state regulation of these matters. Direct conflict preemption occurs when a person cannot comply with both the state and the federal laws at the same time, such as in *Gibbons v. Ogden*. Obstacle preemption is when the state law does not actually conflict with a federal law, but it "stands as an obstacle to the accomplishment and execution of the full purposes and objectives of Congress." This is perhaps the hardest of the preemption categories to apply.

In recent years the Court has decided a plethora of preemption cases, many of them involving alleged preemption of state tort laws by federal regulatory statutes, which supposedly set a uniform health or safety standard which would be undermined if each state's tort law could impose liability notwithstanding the person's compliance with the federal regulation. The outcome in the cases has varied greatly, making general statements about how to apply preemption doctrine, especially obstacle preemption, difficult. It has led Justice Thomas to call for elimination of obstacle preemption altogether.

Many of the cases are close, with 5–4 decisions, but the line-ups do not always break down on "liberal" or "conservative" lines. Conservatives generally like to protect state prerogatives, but they also are hostile to tort law. Liberals, on the other hand, usually like federal regulation, but they tend to be partial to tort law. Thus, both groups are conflicted in their normal predilections.

The issue in these cases, however, are statutory in nature—what does the federal statute say and what did Congress intend—not constitutional, so in-depth consideration here is not possible.

CHAPTER 4

OTHER FEDERALISM LIMITATIONS IN THE CONSTITUTION

■ ■ ■

In the previous chapter, the recurring issue was one of federalism—the respective roles of the Federal and state governments. The issue was always whether Congress could enact the laws in question (and what the effect of those laws would be) under our constitutional structure. In the face of uncertain constitutional text, the Court attempted to define the appropriate roles of the state and federal governments. This chapter addresses two aspects of the Constitution that restrict state powers in favor of national concerns: the so-called Dormant Commerce Clause and the Privileges and Immunities Clause of Article IV.

A. THE DORMANT COMMERCE CLAUSE

1. THE ORIGINS

We return to the Commerce Clause. Previously we considered the extent of Congress's authority to enact legislation under the Commerce Clause. Recall the first Commerce Clause case, *Gibbons v. Ogden*. There the Court concluded that the New York state law granting a monopoly to Ogden conflicted with the federal law granting a license to Gibbons to engage in the coastal trade, and because the federal law was constitutional under the Commerce Clause, the federal law governed. In a portion of the opinion that was edited out of the version we read earlier, Chief Justice Marshall discussed the possibility that even in the absence of the federal law the New York state law might be invalid under the Commerce Clause itself. And Justice Johnson, who concurred in the judgment, wrote an opinion finding New York's law unconstitutional on precisely that ground. The idea that the Commerce Clause by itself, without any action by Congress, can preclude some state action is what is known today as the "Dormant Commerce Clause" or sometimes as the "Negative Commerce Clause."

GIBBONS V. OGDEN

United States Supreme Court, 1824.
9 Wheat. (22 U.S.) 1, 6 L.Ed. 23.

MR. CHIEF JUSTICE MARSHALL delivered the opinion of the Court:

[After its analysis the Court went on. I]t has been urged with great earnestness, that, although the power of Congress to regulate commerce with foreign nations, and among the several States, be co-extensive with the subject itself, and have no other limits than are prescribed in the constitution, yet the States may severally exercise the same power, within their respective jurisdictions. In support of this argument, it is said, that they possessed it as an inseparable attribute of sovereignty, before the formation of the constitution, and still retain it, except so far as they have surrendered it by that instrument; that this principle results from the nature of the government, and is secured by the tenth amendment; that an affirmative grant of power is not exclusive, unless in its own nature it be such that the continued exercise of it by the former possessor is inconsistent with the grant, and that this is not of that description.

The appellant, conceding these postulates, except the last, contends, that full power to regulate a particular subject, implies the whole power, and leaves no residuum; that a grant of the whole is incompatible with the existence of a right in another to any part of it. . . .

The grant of the power to lay and collect taxes is, like the power to regulate commerce, made in general terms, and has never been understood to interfere with the exercise of the same power by the State; and hence has been drawn an argument which has been applied to the question under consideration. But the two grants are not, it is conceived, similar in their terms or their nature. Although many of the powers formerly exercised by the States, are transferred to the government of the Union, yet the State governments remain, and constitute a most important part of our system. The power of taxation is indispensable to their existence, and is a power which, in its own nature, is capable of residing in, and being exercised by, different authorities at the same time. We are accustomed to see it placed, for different purposes, in different hands. . . . When, then, each government exercises the power of taxation, neither is exercising the power of the other. But, when a State proceeds to regulate commerce with foreign nations, or among the several States, it is exercising the very power that is granted to Congress, and is doing the very thing which Congress is authorized to do. There is no analogy, then, between the power of taxation and the power of regulating commerce. . . .

It has been contended by the counsel for the appellant, that, as the word "to regulate'" implies in its nature, full power over the thing to be regulated, it excludes, necessarily, the action of all others that would perform the same operation on the same thing. That regulation is designed for the entire result, applying to those parts which remain as they were, as well as to those which are altered. It produces a uniform whole, which is as much disturbed and deranged by changing what the regulating power designs to leave untouched, as that on which it has operated.

There is great force in this argument, and the Court is not satisfied that it has been refuted. . . . [The Court concluded, however, that it need not decide that question because here the New York law conflicted with the federal law that authorized Gibbons to engage in the coastal trade and therefore was unconstitutional under the Supremacy Clause.]

MR. JUSTICE JOHNSON.

The judgment entered by the Court in this cause, has my entire approbation; but having adopted my conclusions on views of the subject materially different from those of my brethren, I feel it incumbent on me to exhibit those views. I have, also, another inducement: in questions of great importance and great delicacy, I feel my duty to the public best discharged, by an effort to maintain my opinions in my own way. . . .

The words of the constitution are, "Congress shall have power to regulate commerce with foreign nations, and among the several States, and with the Indian tribes." . . .

The "power to regulate commerce," here meant to be granted, was that power to regulate commerce which previously existed in the States. But what was that power? The States were, unquestionably, supreme; and each possessed that power over commerce, which is acknowledged to reside in every sovereign State. . . . The power of a sovereign state over commerce . . . amounts to nothing more than a power to limit and restrain it at pleasure. And since the power to prescribe the limits to its freedom, necessarily implies the power to determine what shall remain unrestrained, it follows, that the power must be exclusive; it can reside but in one potentate; and hence, the grant of this power carries with it the whole subject, leaving nothing for the State to act upon.

And such has been the practical construction of the act. Were every law on the subject of commerce repealed tomorrow, all commerce would be lawful; and, in practice, merchants never inquire what is permitted, but what is forbidden commerce. Of all the endless variety of branches of foreign commerce, now carried on to every quarter of the world, I know of no one that is permitted by act of Congress, any otherwise than by not being forbidden. No statute of the United States, that I know of, was ever passed to permit a commerce, unless in consequence of its having been prohibited by some previous statute. . . .

The grant to Livingston and Fulton, interferes with the freedom of intercourse and on this principle its constitutionality is contested. . . .

Commerce, in its simplest signification, means an exchange of goods; but in the advancement of society, labour, transportation, intelligence, care, and various mediums of exchange, become commodities, and enter into commerce; the subject, the vehicle, the agent, and their various operations, become the objects of commercial regulation. Ship building, the carrying trade, and propagation of seamen, are such vital agents of commercial prosperity, that the nation which could not legislate over these subjects, would not possess power to regulate commerce. . . .

It is impossible, with the views which I entertain of the principle on which the commercial privileges of the people of the United States, among themselves, rests, to concur in the view which this Court takes of the effect of the coasting license in this cause. I do not regard it as the foundation of the right set up in behalf of the appellant. If there was any one object riding over every other in the adoption of the constitution, it was to keep the commercial intercourse among the States free from all invidious and partial restraints. And I cannot overcome the conviction, that if the licensing act was repealed tomorrow, the rights of the appellant to a reversal of the decision complained of, would be as strong as it is under this license. . . .

COMMENTS AND QUESTIONS

1.   Recall that Chief Justice Marshall instituted the tradition of there being one opinion for the Court, rather than separate opinions by each justice. Justice Johnson's opening paragraph suggests he was not fully supportive of that change.

2.   Chief Justice Marshall's discussion and Justice Johnson's opinion would read the positive grant of authority to Congress to regulate commerce among the states as a prohibition on the ability of states to regulate commerce among the states. Unlike the taxing power, which Chief Justice Marshall suggested could be exercised by both sovereigns, he believed that the power of regulation could only be held by one sovereign. If the matter were one subject to federal regulation, it could not be regulated by the states. Clearly, that theory was not the basis for *Gibbons*, which ultimately relied on the fact that Congress had exercised its authority and the federal law conflicted with New York's law. Nevertheless, the notion persisted that, if something was within Congress's power under the Commerce Clause, then it was no longer subject to state power. This perhaps explains some of the reluctance of the Court to extend the federal commerce power at various points in history—not just concern about the federal government having the power, but the implication that perhaps the mere possession of the power would disable the states from regulating in that field *even when the federal government did not exercise its power*.

3.   While the original notion suggested by Marshall and Johnson—that federal authority under the Commerce Clause would preempt the entire field—never commanded a Court majority, the Court did overturn some state actions solely on the grounds that it interfered with interstate commerce in a particular way, even in the absence of any federal legislation. For example, in

Pennsylvania v. Wheeling & Belmont Bridge Co., 54 U.S. 518 (1851), the state of Virginia authorized the construction of a bridge over the Ohio River at a height that would not allow steamships to go under it. Pennsylvania brought a suit alleging that the bridge obstructed navigation and therefore was a violation of the negative implications of the Commerce Clause. While the Court's decision finding the bridge unlawful is particularly opaque, many have read it to be based upon the Dormant Commerce Clause.

4.   Attempts to discern the dividing line between what states could regulate and what was forbidden by the Dormant Commerce Clause were not very successful. Early on there were attempts to distinguish between exercises of the state police power (which would be authorized) and exercises of commercial regulation (which would be precluded), *see, e.g., Mayor of the City of New York v. Miln*, 36 U.S. 102 (1837); between state regulation of things local (which would be authorized) and things national (which would be precluded), *see, e.g., Cooley v. Board of Wardens*, 53 U.S. 299 (1851); and between state regulation that only indirectly affected interstate commerce (which would be authorized) and state regulation that directly regulated interstate commerce (which would be precluded), *see, e.g., Di Santo v. Pennsylvania*, 273 U.S. 34 (1927). Some would say that this lack of success in providing a bright line continues today.

2.   THE MODERN APPROACH

The modern (since the 1930s) Dormant Commerce Clause Doctrine comes in two flavors—discriminatory state laws and non-discriminatory state laws. Each has its own particular test for whether the law is unconstitutional under the Dormant Commerce Clause. We begin with the easier of the two strands.

a.   Discriminatory State Laws

PHILADELPHIA V. NEW JERSEY
United States Supreme Court, 1978.
437 U.S. 617, 98 S.Ct. 2531.

MR. JUSTICE STEWART delivered the opinion of the Court.

A New Jersey law prohibits the importation of most "solid or liquid waste which originated or was collected outside the territorial limits of the State. . . ." In this case we are required to decide whether this statutory prohibition violates the Commerce Clause of the United States Constitution.

Immediately affected by th[is law] were the operators of private landfills in New Jersey, and several cities in other States that had agreements with these operators for waste disposal. They brought suit against New Jersey and its Department of Environmental Protection in state court, attacking the statute and regulations on a number of state and federal grounds. In an oral opinion granting the plaintiffs' motion for summary judgment, the trial court declared the law unconstitutional because it discriminated against interstate commerce. The New Jersey Supreme Court ... found that [the law] advanced vital health and environmental objectives with no economic discrimination against, and with little burden upon, interstate commerce, and that the law was therefore permissible under the Commerce Clause of the Constitution.

The plaintiffs then appealed to this Court. . . . The dispositive question . . . is whether the law is constitutionally permissible in light of the Commerce Clause of the Constitution. . . .

Although the Constitution gives Congress the power to regulate commerce among the States, many subjects of potential federal regulation under that power inevitably escape congressional attention "because of their local character and their number and diversity." In the absence of federal legislation, these subjects are open to control by the States so long as they act within the restraints imposed by the Commerce Clause itself. The bounds of these restraints appear nowhere in the words of the Commerce Clause, but have emerged gradually in the decisions of this Court giving effect to its basic purpose. . . .

The opinions of the Court through the years have reflected an alertness to the evils of "economic isolation" and protectionism, while at the same time recognizing that incidental burdens on interstate commerce may be unavoidable when a State legislates to safeguard the health and safety of its people. Thus, where simple economic protectionism is effected by state legislation, a virtually *per se* rule of invalidity has been erected. The clearest example of such legislation is a law that overtly blocks the flow of interstate commerce at a State's borders. But where other legislative objectives are credibly advanced and there is no patent discrimination against interstate trade, the Court has adopted a much more flexible approach, the general contours of which were outlined in *Pike v. Bruce Church, Inc.*, 397 U.S. 137, 142:

> "Where the statute regulates evenhandedly to effectuate a legitimate local public interest, and its effects on interstate commerce are only incidental, it will be upheld unless the burden imposed on such commerce is clearly excessive in relation to the putative local benefits. . . . If a legitimate local purpose is found, then the question becomes one of degree. And the extent of the burden that will be tolerated will of course depend on the nature of the local interest involved, and on whether it could be promoted as well with a lesser impact on interstate activities."

The crucial inquiry, therefore, must be directed to determining whether [the New Jersey law] is basically a protectionist measure, or whether it can fairly be viewed as a law directed to legitimate local concerns, with effects upon interstate commerce that are only incidental.

The purpose of [the law] is set out in the statute itself as follows:

"The Legislature finds and determines that . . . the volume of solid and liquid waste continues to rapidly increase, that the treatment and disposal of these wastes continues to pose an even greater threat to the quality of the environment of New Jersey, that the available and appropriate land fill sites within the State are being diminished, that the environment continues to be threatened by the treatment and disposal of waste which originated or was collected outside the State, and that the public health, safety and welfare require that the treatment and disposal within this State of all wastes generated outside of the State be prohibited."

The New Jersey Supreme Court accepted this statement of the state legislature's purpose. The state court additionally found that New Jersey's existing landfill sites will be exhausted within a few years; that to go on using these sites or to develop new ones will take a heavy environmental toll, both from pollution and from loss of scarce open lands; that new techniques to divert waste from landfills to other methods of disposal and resource recovery processes are under development, but that these changes will require time; and finally, that "the extension of the lifespan of existing landfills, resulting from the exclusion of out-of-state waste, may be of crucial importance in preventing further virgin wetlands or other undeveloped lands from being devoted to landfill purposes." Based on these findings, the court concluded that [the law] was designed to protect, not the State's economy, but its environment, and that its substantial benefits outweigh its "slight" burden on interstate commerce.

The appellants strenuously contend that [the law], "while outwardly cloaked 'in the currently fashionable garb of environmental protection,' . . . is actually no more than a legislative effort to suppress competition and stabilize the cost of solid waste disposal for New Jersey residents. . . ." They cite passages of legislative history suggesting that the problem addressed by [the law] is primarily financial: Stemming the flow of out-of-state waste into certain landfill sites will extend their lives, thus delaying the day when New Jersey cities must transport their waste to more distant and expensive sites.

The appellees, on the other hand, deny that [the law] was motivated by financial concerns or economic protectionism. In the words of their brief, "[n]o New Jersey commercial interests stand to gain advantage over competitors from outside the state as a result of the ban on dumping out-of-state waste." Noting that New Jersey landfill operators are among the plaintiffs, the appellee's brief argues that "[t]he complaint is not that New Jersey has forged an economic preference for its own commercial interests, but rather that it has denied a small group of its entrepreneurs an economic opportunity to traffic in waste in order to protect the health, safety and welfare of the citizenry at large."

This dispute about ultimate legislative purpose need not be resolved, because its resolution would not be relevant to the constitutional issue to be decided in this case. Contrary to the evident assumption of the state court and the parties, the evil of protectionism can reside in legislative means as well as legislative ends. Thus, it does not matter whether the ultimate aim of [the law] is to reduce the waste disposal costs of New Jersey residents or to save remaining open lands from pollution, for we assume New Jersey has every right to protect its residents' pocketbooks as well as their environment. And it may be assumed as well that New Jersey may pursue those ends by slowing the flow of *all* waste into the State's remaining landfills, even though interstate commerce may incidentally be affected. But whatever New Jersey's ultimate purpose, it may not be accomplished by discriminating against articles of commerce coming from outside the State unless there is some reason, apart from their origin, to treat them differently. Both on its face and in its plain effect, [the law] violates this principle of nondiscrimination.

The Court has consistently found parochial legislation of this kind to be constitutionally invalid, whether the ultimate aim of the legislation was to assure a steady supply of milk by erecting barriers to allegedly ruinous outside competition, or to create jobs by keeping industry within the State, or to preserve the State's financial resources from depletion by fencing out indigent immigrants. In each of these cases, a presumably legitimate goal was sought to be achieved by the illegitimate means of isolating the State from the national economy.

Also relevant here are the Court's decisions holding that a State may not accord its own inhabitants a preferred right of access over consumers in other States to natural resources located within its borders. These cases stand for the basic principle that a "State is without power to prevent privately owned articles of trade from being shipped and sold in interstate commerce on the ground that they are required to satisfy local demands or because they are needed by the people of the State."[6] The New Jersey law at issue in this case falls squarely within the area that the Commerce Clause puts off limits to state regulation. On its face, it imposes on out-of-state commercial interests the full burden of conserving the State's remaining landfill space. It is true that in our previous cases the scarce natural resource was itself the article of commerce, whereas here the scarce resource and the article of commerce are distinct. But that difference is without consequence. In both instances, the State has overtly moved to slow or freeze the flow of commerce for protectionist reasons. It does not matter that the State has shut the article of commerce inside the State in one case and outside the State in the other. What is crucial is the attempt

---

[6] We express no opinion about New Jersey's power, consistent with the Commerce Clause, to restrict to state residents access to state-owned resources, or New Jersey's power to spend state funds solely on behalf of state residents and businesses.

by one State to isolate itself from a problem common to many by erecting a barrier against the movement of interstate trade.

The appellees argue that not all laws which facially discriminate against out-of-state commerce are forbidden protectionist regulations. In particular, they point to quarantine laws, which this Court has repeatedly upheld even though they appear to single out interstate commerce for special treatment. In the appellees' view, [the New Jersey law] is analogous to such health-protective measures, since it reduces the exposure of New Jersey residents to the allegedly harmful effects of landfill sites.

It is true that certain quarantine laws have not been considered forbidden protectionist measures, even though they were directed against out-of-state commerce. But those quarantine laws banned the importation of articles such as diseased livestock that required destruction as soon as possible because their very movement risked contagion and other evils. Those laws thus did not discriminate against interstate commerce as such, but simply prevented traffic in noxious articles, whatever their origin.

The New Jersey statute is not such a quarantine law. There has been no claim here that the very movement of waste into or through New Jersey endangers health, or that waste must be disposed of as soon and as close to its point of generation as possible. The harms caused by waste are said to arise after its disposal in landfill sites, and at that point, as New Jersey concedes, there is no basis to distinguish out-of-state waste from domestic waste. If one is inherently harmful, so is the other. Yet New Jersey has banned the former while leaving its landfill sites open to the latter. The New Jersey law blocks the importation of waste in an obvious effort to saddle those outside the State with the entire burden of slowing the flow of refuse into New Jersey's remaining landfill sites. That legislative effort is clearly impermissible under the Commerce Clause of the Constitution.

Today, cities in Pennsylvania and New York find it expedient or necessary to send their waste into New Jersey for disposal, and New Jersey claims the right to close its borders to such traffic. Tomorrow, cities in New Jersey may find it expedient or necessary to send their waste into Pennsylvania or New York for disposal, and those States might then claim the right to close their borders. The Commerce Clause will protect New Jersey in the future, just as it protects her neighbors now, from efforts by one State to isolate itself in the stream of interstate commerce from a problem shared by all.

MR. JUSTICE REHNQUIST, with whom THE CHIEF JUSTICE joins, dissenting.

A growing problem in our Nation is the sanitary treatment and disposal of solid waste. . . . In [the New Jersey law], the State of New Jersey legislatively recognized the unfortunate fact that landfills also present extremely serious health and safety problems. First, in New Jersey, "virtually all sanitary landfills can be expected to produce leachate, a noxious and highly polluted liquid which is seldom visible and frequently pollutes . . . ground and surface waters." The natural decomposition process which occurs in landfills also produces large quantities of methane and thereby presents a significant explosion hazard. Landfills can also generate "health hazards caused by rodents, fires and scavenger birds" and, "needless to say, do not help New Jersey's aesthetic appearance nor New Jersey's noise or water or air pollution problems."

The health and safety hazards associated with landfills present appellees with a currently unsolvable dilemma. Other, hopefully safer, methods of disposing of solid wastes are still in the development stage and cannot presently be used. But appellees obviously cannot completely stop the tide of solid waste that its citizens will produce in the interim. For the moment, therefore, appellees must continue to use sanitary landfills to dispose of New Jersey's own solid waste despite the critical environmental problems thereby created.

The question presented in this case is whether New Jersey must also continue to receive and dispose of solid waste from neighboring States, even though these will inexorably increase the health problems discussed above. The Court answers this question in the affirmative. New Jersey must either prohibit *all* landfill operations, leaving itself to cast about for a presently nonexistent solution to the serious problem of disposing of the waste generated within its own borders, or it must accept waste from every portion of the United States, thereby multiplying the health and safety problems which would result if it dealt only with such wastes generated within the State. Because past precedents establish that the Commerce Clause does not present appellees with such a Hobson's choice, I dissent. . . .

The Supreme Court of New Jersey expressly found that [the law] was passed "to preserve the health of New Jersey residents by keeping their exposure to solid waste and landfill areas to a minimum." The Court points to absolutely no evidence that would contradict this finding by the New Jersey Supreme Court. Because I find no basis for distinguishing the laws under challenge here from our past cases upholding state laws that prohibit the importation of items that could endanger the population of the State, I dissent.

COMMENTS AND QUESTIONS

1. *Philadelphia* is a good example of a case involving facial discrimination against interstate commerce. That is, the law itself on its face discriminates against commerce from out-of-state. The state argues that trash is not commerce, because it has no value, but that is clearly wrong when there is an active trade in its treatment and disposal and when there is active commerce in its transportation. *Philadelphia* is also a good case for demonstrating how the evil of this discrimination is "protectionism."

Protectionism is when a state (or locality) enacts a law to benefit or protect a state or local business or economic interest at the expense of out-of-state businesses or interests. The Court asserts that the Dormant Commerce Clause maintains a national common market, so that goods and services can flow freely within the United States, benefitting all through free trade.

2.   Free trade across international boundaries is today a debated political issue, but economically it is difficult to fault the logic and history of free trade as a powerful tool for growing economies—whether it was the common market that the Constitution originally established among the thirteen states or the common market that was established in western Europe after World War II.

DEAN MILK CO. V. MADISON
United States Supreme Court, 1951.
340 U.S. 349, 71 S.Ct. 295.

MR. JUSTICE CLARK delivered the opinion of the Court.

This appeal challenges the constitutional validity . . . of an ordinance of the City of Madison, Wisconsin, regulating the sale of milk and milk products within the municipality's jurisdiction. [The ordinance] makes it unlawful to sell any milk as pasteurized unless it has been processed and bottled at an approved pasteurization plant within a radius of five miles from the central square of Madison. . . .

Appellant is an Illinois corporation engaged in distributing milk and milk products in Illinois and Wisconsin. It contended below, as it does here, that . . . the five-mile limit on pasteurization plants . . . violate[s] the Commerce Clause. . . . The Supreme Court of Wisconsin upheld the five-mile limit on pasteurization. . . .

The City of Madison is the county seat of Dane County. Within the county are some 5,600 dairy farms with total raw milk production in excess of 600,000,000 pounds annually and more than ten times the requirements of Madison. Aside from the milk supplied to Madison, fluid milk produced in the county moves in large quantities to Chicago and more distant consuming areas, and the remainder is used in making cheese, butter and other products. At the time of trial the Madison milkshed was not of "Grade A" quality by the standards recommended by the United States Public Health Service, and no milk labeled "Grade A" was distributed in Madison.

The area defined by the ordinance with respect to milk sources encompasses practically all of Dane County and includes some 500 farms which supply milk for Madison. Within the five-mile area for pasteurization are plants of five processors, only three of which are engaged in the general wholesale and retail trade in Madison. Inspection of these farms and plants is scheduled once every thirty days and is performed by two municipal inspectors, one of whom is full-time. The courts below found that the ordinance in question promotes convenient, economical and efficient plant inspection.

Appellant purchases and gathers milk from approximately 950 farms in northern Illinois and southern Wisconsin, none being within twenty-five miles of Madison. Its pasteurization plants are located at Chemung and Huntley, Illinois, about 65 and 85 miles respectively from Madison. Appellant was denied a license to sell its products within Madison solely because its pasteurization plants were more than five miles away.

It is conceded that the milk which appellant seeks to sell in Madison is supplied from farms and processed in plants licensed and inspected by public health authorities of Chicago, and is labeled "Grade A" under the Chicago ordinance which adopts the rating standards recommended by the United States Public Health Service. . . . Madison contends and we assume that in some particulars its ordinance is more rigorous than that of Chicago.

Upon these facts we find it necessary to determine only the issue raised under the Commerce Clause, for we agree with appellant that the ordinance imposes an undue burden on interstate commerce. . . .

[There can be no] objection to the avowed purpose of this enactment. We assume that difficulties in sanitary regulation of milk and milk products originating in remote areas may present a situation in which "upon a consideration of all the relevant facts and circumstances it appears that the matter is one which may appropriately be regulated in the interest of the safety, health and well-being of local communities * * *." . . .

But this regulation . . . in practical effect excludes from distribution in Madison wholesome milk produced and pasteurized in Illinois. . . . In thus erecting an economic barrier protecting a major local industry against competition from without the State, Madison plainly discriminates against interstate commerce.[4] This it cannot do, even in the exercise of its unquestioned power to protect the health and safety of its people, if reasonable nondiscriminatory alternatives, adequate to conserve legitimate local interests, are available. A different view, that the ordinance is valid simply because it professes to be a health measure, would mean that the Commerce Clause of itself imposes no limitations on state action other than those laid down by the Due Process Clause, save for the rare instance where a state artlessly discloses an avowed purpose to discriminate against interstate goods. Our issue then is whether the discrimination inherent in the Madison ordinance can be justified in view of the character of the local interests and the available methods of protecting them.

---

[4] It is immaterial that Wisconsin milk from outside the Madison area is subjected to the same proscription as that moving in interstate commerce.

It appears that reasonable and adequate alternatives are available. If the City of Madison prefers to rely upon its own officials for inspection of distant milk sources, such inspection is readily open to it without hardship for it could charge the actual and reasonable cost of such inspection to the importing producers and processors. Moreover, appellee Health Commissioner of Madison testified that as proponent of the local milk ordinance he had submitted the provisions here in controversy and an alternative proposal based on § 11 of the Model Milk Ordinance recommended by the United States Public Health Service. The model provision imposes no geographical limitation on location of milk sources and processing plants but excludes from the municipality milk not produced and pasteurized conformably to standards as high as those enforced by the receiving city. In implementing such an ordinance, the importing city obtains milk ratings based on uniform standards and established by health authorities in the jurisdiction where production and processing occur. The receiving city may determine the extent of enforcement of sanitary standards in the exporting area by verifying the accuracy of safety ratings of specific plants or of the milkshed in the distant jurisdiction through the United States Public Health Service, which routinely and on request spot checks the local ratings. The Commissioner testified that Madison consumers "would be safeguarded adequately" under either proposal and that he had expressed no preference. The milk sanitarian of the Wisconsin State Board of Health testified that the State Health Department recommends the adoption of a provision based on the Model Ordinance. Both officials agreed that a local health officer would be justified in relying upon the evaluation by the Public Health Service of enforcement conditions in remote producing areas.

To permit Madison to adopt a regulation not essential for the protection of local health interests and placing a discriminatory burden on interstate commerce would invite a multiplication of preferential trade areas destructive of the very purpose of the Commerce Clause. . . .

For these reasons we conclude that the judgment below sustaining the five-mile provision as to pasteurization must be reversed. . . .

MR. JUSTICE BLACK, with whom MR. JUSTICE DOUGLAS and MR. JUSTICE MINTON concur, dissenting.

Today's holding invalidates § 7.21 of the Madison, Wisconsin, ordinance on the following reasoning: (1) the section excludes wholesome milk coming from Illinois; (2) this imposes a discriminatory burden on interstate commerce; (3) such a burden cannot be imposed where, as here, there are reasonable, nondiscriminatory and adequate alternatives available. I disagree with the Court's premises, reasoning, and judgment.

(1) This ordinance does not exclude wholesome milk coming from Illinois or anywhere else. It does require that all milk sold in Madison must be pasteurized within five miles of the center of the city. But there was no

finding in the state courts, nor evidence to justify a finding there or here, that appellant, Dean Milk Company, is unable to have its milk pasteurized within the defined geographical area. As a practical matter, so far as the record shows, Dean can easily comply with the ordinance whenever it wants to. Therefore, Dean's personal preference to pasteurize in Illinois, not the ordinance, keeps Dean's milk out of Madison.

(2) Characterization of § 7.21 as a "discriminatory burden" on interstate commerce is merely a statement of the Court's result, which I think incorrect. The section does prohibit the sale of milk in Madison by interstate and intrastate producers who prefer to pasteurize over five miles distant from the city. But both state courts below found that § 7.21 represents a good-faith attempt to safeguard public health by making adequate sanitation inspection possible. While we are not bound by these findings, I do not understand the Court to overturn them. Therefore, the fact that § 7.21, like all health regulations, imposes some burden on trade, does not mean that it "discriminates" against interstate commerce.

(3) This health regulation should not be invalidated merely because the Court believes that alternative milk-inspection methods might insure the cleanliness and healthfulness of Dean's Illinois milk. . . . Since the days of Chief Justice Marshall, federal courts have left states and municipalities free to pass bona fide health regulations subject only "to the paramount authority of Congress if it decides to assume control * * *." This established judicial policy of refusing to invalidate genuine local health laws under the Commerce Clause has been approvingly noted even in our recent opinions measuring state regulation by stringent standards. No case is cited, and I have found none, in which a bona fide health law was struck down on the ground that some other method of safeguarding health would be as good as, or better than, the one the Court was called on to review. In my view, to use this ground now elevates the right to traffic in commerce for profit above the power of the people to guard the purity of their daily diet of milk. . . .

C & A CARBONE, INC. V. CLARKSTOWN

United States Supreme Court, 1994.
511 U.S. 383, 114 S.Ct. 1677.

JUSTICE KENNEDY delivered the opinion of the Court.

As solid waste output continues apace and landfill capacity becomes more costly and scarce, state and local governments are expending significant resources to develop trash control systems that are efficient, lawful, and protective of the environment. The difficulty of their task is evident from the number of recent cases that we have heard involving waste transfer and treatment. The case decided today, while perhaps a small new chapter in that course of decisions, rests nevertheless upon well-settled principles of our Commerce Clause jurisprudence.

We consider a so-called flow control ordinance, which requires all solid waste to be processed at a designated transfer station before leaving the municipality. The avowed purpose of the ordinance is to retain the processing fees charged at the transfer station to amortize the cost of the facility. Because it attains this goal by depriving competitors, including out-of-state firms, of access to a local market, we hold that the flow control ordinance violates the Commerce Clause.

[I]n August 1989, Clarkstown entered into a consent decree with the New York State Department of Environmental Conservation. The town agreed to close its landfill located on Route 303 in West Nyack and build a new solid waste transfer station on the same site. The station would receive bulk solid waste and separate recyclable from nonrecyclable items. Recyclable waste would be baled for shipment to a recycling facility; nonrecyclable waste, to a suitable landfill or incinerator.

The cost of building the transfer station was estimated at $1.4 million. A local private contractor agreed to construct the facility and operate it for five years, after which the town would buy it for $1. During those five years, the town guaranteed a minimum waste flow of 120,000 tons per year, for which the contractor could charge the hauler a so-called tipping fee of $81 per ton. If the station received less than 120,000 tons in a year, the town promised to make up the tipping fee deficit. The object of this arrangement was to amortize the cost of the transfer station: The town would finance its new facility with the income generated by the tipping fees.

The problem, of course, was how to meet the yearly guarantee. This difficulty was compounded by the fact that the tipping fee of $81 per ton exceeded the disposal cost of unsorted solid waste on the private market. The solution the town adopted was the flow control ordinance here in question. The ordinance requires all

Anthony Kennedy

Anthony Kennedy was appointed to the Supreme Court by President Reagan in 1988 after the failed nominations of Robert Bork and Douglas Ginsburg. Prior to his appointment to the Court, Justice Kennedy had been a judge on the Ninth Circuit since 1975. Kennedy became the swing vote on the Court, sometimes siding with the liberals, such as in the case of *Planned Parenthood v. Casey,* in which his vote was crucial to upholding a right to abortion, *Lawrence v. Texas,* in which he wrote the Court's opinion finding state sodomy laws unconstitutional, and *Obergefell v. Hodges,* which found a constitutional right to same sex marriage. More often, however he sided with the conservatives, such as in *Gonzales v. Carhart,* in which he wrote the opinion upholding the federal ban on partial-birth abortions. In the 2006 Term, Justice Kennedy was the fifth vote in each of the 24 cases decided by a 5–4 vote. In his last year on the Court, he was the fifth vote in 16 of the 19 cases decided by a 5–4 vote. In 14 of the 16, he sided with the conservatives.

nonhazardous solid waste within the town to be deposited at the Route 303 transfer station. . . .

The petitioners in this case are C & A Carbone, Inc., a company engaged in the processing of solid waste. . . . Carbone operates a recycling center in Clarkstown, where it receives bulk solid waste, sorts and bales it, and then ships it to other processing facilities—much as occurs at the town's new transfer station. While the flow control ordinance permits recyclers like Carbone to continue receiving solid waste, it requires them to bring the nonrecyclable residue from that waste to the Route 303 station. It thus forbids Carbone to ship the nonrecyclable waste itself, and it requires Carbone to pay a tipping fee on trash that Carbone has already sorted. . . .

[Carbone was found to be violating the ordinance, so Clarkstown sued in state court seeking an injunction requiring Carbone to comply with the ordinance.] [T]he New York court granted summary judgment to [Clarkstown]. The court declared the flow control ordinance constitutional and enjoined Carbone to comply with it. . . .

The Appellate Division affirmed. The court found that the ordinance did not discriminate against interstate commerce because it "applies evenhandedly to all solid waste processed within the Town, regardless of point of origin." The New York Court of Appeals denied Carbone's motion for leave to appeal. We granted certiorari and now reverse.

At the outset we confirm that the flow control ordinance does regulate interstate commerce, despite the town's position to the contrary. The town says that its ordinance reaches only waste within its jurisdiction and is in practical effect a quarantine: It prevents garbage from entering the stream of interstate commerce until it is made safe. This reasoning is premised, however, on an outdated and mistaken concept of what constitutes interstate commerce.

While the immediate effect of the ordinance is to direct local transport of solid waste to a designated site within the local jurisdiction, its economic effects are interstate in reach. The Carbone facility in Clarkstown receives and processes waste from places other than Clarkstown, including from out of State. By requiring Carbone to send the nonrecyclable portion of this waste to the Route 303 transfer station at an additional cost, the flow control ordinance drives up the cost for out-of-state interests to dispose of their solid waste. Furthermore, even as to waste originating in Clarkstown, the ordinance prevents everyone except the favored local operator from performing the initial processing step. The ordinance thus deprives out-of-state businesses of access to a local market. These economic effects are more than enough to bring the Clarkstown ordinance within the purview of the Commerce Clause. It is well settled that actions are within the domain of the Commerce Clause if they burden interstate commerce or impede its free flow.

The real question is whether the flow control ordinance is valid despite its undoubted effect on interstate commerce. For this inquiry, our case law yields two lines of analysis: first, whether the ordinance discriminates against interstate commerce, *Philadelphia v. New Jersey*; and second, whether the ordinance imposes a burden on interstate commerce that is "clearly excessive in relation to the putative local benefits," *Pike v. Bruce Church, Inc.*, 397 U.S. 137 (1970). As we find that the ordinance discriminates against interstate commerce, we need not resort to the *Pike* test.

The central rationale for the rule against discrimination is to prohibit state or municipal laws whose object is local economic protectionism, laws that would excite those jealousies and retaliatory measures the Constitution was designed to prevent. We have interpreted the Commerce Clause to invalidate local laws that impose commercial barriers or discriminate against an article of commerce by reason of its origin or destination out of State. *See, e.g., Philadelphia, supra* (striking down New Jersey statute that prohibited the import of solid waste); *Hughes v. Oklahoma*, 441 U.S. 322 (1979)(striking down Oklahoma law that prohibited the export of natural minnows).

Clarkstown protests that its ordinance does not discriminate because it does not differentiate solid waste on the basis of its geographic origin. All solid waste, regardless of origin, must be processed at the designated transfer station before it leaves the town. Unlike the statute in *Philadelphia,* says the town, the ordinance erects no barrier to the import or export of any solid waste but requires only that the waste be channeled through the designated facility.

Our initial discussion of the effects of the ordinance on interstate commerce goes far toward refuting the town's contention that there is no discrimination in its regulatory scheme. The town's own arguments go the rest of the way. As the town itself points out, what makes garbage a profitable business is not its own worth but the fact that its possessor must pay to get rid of it. In other words, the article of commerce is not so much the solid waste itself, but rather the service of processing and disposing of it.

With respect to this stream of commerce, the flow control ordinance discriminates, for it allows only the favored operator to process waste that is within the limits of the town. The ordinance is no less discriminatory because in-state or in-town processors are also covered by the prohibition. In *Dean Milk Co. v. Madison,* we struck down a city ordinance that required all milk sold in the city to be pasteurized within five miles of the city lines. We found it "immaterial that Wisconsin milk from outside the Madison area is subjected to the same proscription as that moving in interstate commerce."

In this light, the flow control ordinance is just one more instance of local processing requirements that we long have held invalid. *See Minnesota v. Barber,* 136 U.S. 313 (1890)(striking down a Minnesota statute that required any meat sold within the State, whether originating within or without the State, to be examined by an inspector within the State); *Foster-Fountain Packing Co. v. Haydel,* 278 U.S. 1 (1928)(striking down a Louisiana statute that forbade shrimp to be exported unless the heads and hulls had first been removed within the State); *Johnson v. Haydel,* 278 U.S. 16 (1928)(striking down analogous Louisiana statute for oysters); *Toomer v. Witsell,* 334 U.S. 385 (1948)(striking down South Carolina statute that required shrimp fishermen to unload, pack, and stamp their catch before shipping it to another State); *Pike v. Bruce Church, Inc., supra* (striking down Arizona statute that required all Arizona-grown cantaloupes to be packaged within the State prior to export); *South-Central Timber Development, Inc. v. Wunnicke,* 467 U.S. 82 (1984)(striking down an Alaska regulation that required all Alaska timber to be processed within the State prior to export). The essential vice in laws of this sort is that they bar the import of the processing service. Out-of-state meat inspectors, or shrimp hullers, or milk pasteurizers, are deprived of access to local demand for their services. Put another way, the offending local laws hoard a local resource—be it meat, shrimp, or milk—for the benefit of local businesses that treat it.

The flow control ordinance has the same design and effect. It hoards solid waste, and the demand to get rid of it, for the benefit of the preferred processing facility. The only conceivable distinction from the cases cited above is that the flow control ordinance favors a single local proprietor. But this difference just makes the protectionist effect of the ordinance more acute. . . .

Discrimination against interstate commerce in favor of local business or investment is *per se* invalid, save in a narrow class of cases in which the municipality can demonstrate, under rigorous scrutiny, that it has no other means to advance a legitimate local interest. *Maine v. Taylor,* 477 U.S. 131 (1986)(upholding Maine's ban on the import of baitfish because Maine had no other way to prevent the spread of parasites and the adulteration of its native fish species). A number of *amici* contend that the flow control ordinance fits into this narrow class. They suggest that as landfill space diminishes and environmental cleanup costs escalate, measures like flow control become necessary to ensure the safe handling and proper treatment of solid waste.

The teaching of our cases is that these arguments must be rejected absent the clearest showing that the unobstructed flow of interstate commerce itself is unable to solve the local problem. The Commerce Clause presumes a national market free from local legislation that discriminates in favor of local interests. Here Clarkstown has any number of nondiscriminatory alternatives for addressing the health and environmental problems alleged to justify the ordinance in question. The most obvious would be uniform safety regulations enacted without the object to discriminate. These regulations would ensure that competitors like Carbone do not underprice the market by cutting corners on environmental safety.

Nor may Clarkstown justify the flow control ordinance as a way to steer solid waste away from out-of-town disposal sites that it might deem harmful to the environment. To do so would extend the town's police power beyond its jurisdictional bounds. States and localities may not attach restrictions to exports or imports in order to control commerce in other States.

The flow control ordinance does serve a central purpose that a nonprotectionist regulation would not: It ensures that the town-sponsored facility will be profitable, so that the local contractor can build it and Clarkstown can buy it back at nominal cost in five years. In other words, as the most candid of *amici* and even Clarkstown admit, the flow control ordinance is a financing measure. By itself, of course, revenue generation is not a local interest that can justify discrimination against interstate commerce. Otherwise States could impose discriminatory taxes against solid waste originating outside the State. *See Chemical Waste Management, Inc. v. Hunt,* 504 U.S. 334 (1992)(striking down Alabama statute that imposed additional fee on all hazardous waste generated outside the State and disposed of within the State); *Oregon Waste Systems, Inc. v. Department of Environmental Quality of Ore.,* 511 U.S. 93 (1994)(striking down Oregon statute that imposed additional fee on solid waste generated outside the State and disposed of within the State).

Clarkstown maintains that special financing is necessary to ensure the long-term survival of the designated facility. If so, the town may subsidize the facility through general taxes or municipal bonds. But having elected to use the open market to earn revenues for its project, the town may not employ discriminatory regulation to give that project an advantage over rival businesses from out of State. . . .

State and local governments may not use their regulatory power to favor local enterprise by prohibiting patronage of out-of-state competitors or their facilities. We reverse the judgment and remand the case for proceedings not inconsistent with this decision.

JUSTICE O'CONNOR, concurring in the judgment. [omitted]

JUSTICE SOUTER, with whom THE CHIEF JUSTICE and JUSTICE BLACKMUN join, dissenting.

The majority may invoke "well-settled principles of our Commerce Clause jurisprudence," but it does so to strike down an ordinance unlike anything this Court has ever invalidated. Previous cases have held that the "negative" or "dormant" aspect of the Commerce Clause renders state or local legislation unconstitutional when it discriminates against out-of-state or out-of-town businesses such as those that pasteurize milk, hull shrimp, or mill lumber, and the majority relies on these cases because of what they have in common with this one: out-of-state processors are excluded from the local market (here, from the market for trash processing services). What the majority ignores, however, are the differences between our local processing cases and this one: the exclusion worked by Clarkstown's Local Law 9 bestows no benefit on a class of local private actors, but instead directly aids the government in satisfying a traditional governmental responsibility. The law does not differentiate between all local and all out-of-town providers of a service, but instead between the one entity responsible for ensuring that the job gets done and all other enterprises, regardless of their location. The ordinance thus falls outside that class of tariff or protectionist measures that the Commerce Clause has traditionally been thought to bar States from enacting against each other, and when the majority subsumes the ordinance within the class of laws this Court has struck down as facially discriminatory, the majority is in fact greatly extending the Clause's dormant reach.

There are, however, good and sufficient reasons against expanding the Commerce Clause's inherent capacity to trump exercises of state authority such as the ordinance at issue here. There is no indication in the record that any out-of-state trash processor has been harmed, or that the interstate movement or disposition of trash will be affected one whit. To the degree Local Law 9 affects the market for trash processing services, it does so only by subjecting Clarkstown residents and businesses to burdens far different from the burdens of local favoritism that dormant Commerce Clause jurisprudence seeks to root out. The town has found a way to finance a public improvement, not by transferring its cost to out-of-state economic interests, but by spreading it among the local generators of trash, an equitable result with tendencies that should not disturb the Commerce Clause and should not be disturbed by us.

HUNT V. WASHINGTON STATE APPLE ADVERTISING COMM'N

United States Supreme Court, 1977.
432 U.S. 333, 97 S.Ct. 2434.

MR. CHIEF JUSTICE BURGER delivered the opinion of the Court.

In 1973, North Carolina enacted a statute which required, inter alia, all closed containers of apples sold, offered for sale, or shipped into the State to bear "no grade other than the applicable U.S. grade or standard." In an action brought by the Washington State Apple Advertising Commission, a three-judge Federal District Court invalidated the statute insofar as it prohibited the display of Washington State apple grades on the ground that it unconstitutionally discriminated against interstate commerce.

The specific question[ ] presented on appeal [is] whether the challenged North Carolina statute constitutes an unconstitutional burden on interstate commerce.

Washington State is the Nation's largest producer of apples, its crops accounting for approximately 30% of all apples grown domestically and nearly half of all apples shipped in closed containers in interstate commerce. As might be expected, the production and sale of apples on this scale is a multimillion dollar enterprise which plays a significant role in Washington's economy. Because of the importance of the apple industry to the State, its legislature has undertaken to protect and enhance the reputation of Washington apples by establishing a stringent, mandatory inspection program, administered by the State's Department of Agriculture, which requires all apples shipped in interstate commerce to be tested under strict quality standards and graded accordingly. In all cases, the Washington State grades, which have gained substantial acceptance in the trade, are the equivalent of, or superior to, the comparable grades and standards adopted by the United States Department of Agriculture (USDA). Compliance with the Washington inspection scheme costs the State's growers approximately $1 million each year.

In addition to the inspection program, the state legislature has sought to enhance the market for Washington apples through the creation of a state agency, the Washington State Apple Advertising Commission, charged with the statutory duty of promoting and protecting the State's apple industry. . . .

Warren Burger

President Nixon appointed Burger Chief Justice in 1969, fulfilling a promise to appoint persons to the Court who were "strict constructionists." Previously, Burger had served on the United States Court of Appeals for the District of Columbia Circuit for thirteen years, where he enjoyed a solid if undistinguished reputation. While President Nixon undoubtedly wished him to undo the effects of the so-called liberal Warren Court, the Court under Chief Justice Burger in essence solidified the Warren Court jurisprudence, generally not extending it but also not overruling it. Indeed, in *Roe v. Wade,* Burger voted with the majority, finding a woman's constitutional right to obtain an abortion. Moreover, although he was appointed by President Nixon, it was Chief Justice Burger who wrote the unanimous opinion in *Nixon v. United States,* holding that Nixon was required to disclose the tapes recorded in the Oval Office to the grand jury investigating the Watergate conspiracy, which opinion inexorably led to Nixon's resignation.

In 1972, the North Carolina Board of Agriculture adopted an administrative regulation, unique in the 50 States, which in effect required all closed containers of apples shipped into or sold in the State to display either the applicable USDA grade or none at all. State grades were expressly prohibited. In addition to its obvious consequence prohibiting the display of Washington State apple grades on containers of apples shipped into North Carolina, the regulation presented the Washington apple industry with a marketing problem of potentially nationwide significance. Washington apple growers annually ship in commerce approximately 40 million closed containers of apples, nearly 500,000 of which eventually find their way into North Carolina, stamped with the applicable Washington State variety and grade. It is the industry's practice to purchase these containers preprinted with the various apple varieties and grades, prior to harvest. After these containers are filled with apples of the appropriate type and grade, a substantial portion of them are placed in cold-storage warehouses where the grade labels identify the product and facilitate its handling. These apples are then shipped as needed throughout the year; after February 1 of each year, they constitute approximately two-thirds of all apples sold in fresh markets in this country. Since the ultimate destination of these apples is unknown at the time they are placed in storage, compliance with North Carolina's unique regulation would have required Washington growers to obliterate the printed labels on containers shipped to North Carolina, thus giving their product a damaged appearance. Alternatively, they could have changed their marketing practices to accommodate the needs of the North Carolina market, i. e., repack apples to be shipped to North Carolina in containers bearing only the USDA grade, and/or store the estimated portion of the harvest destined for that market in such special containers. As a last resort, they could discontinue the use of the preprinted containers entirely. None of these costly and less efficient options was very attractive to the industry. Moreover, in the event a number of other States followed North Carolina's lead, the resultant inability to display the Washington grades could force the Washington growers to abandon the State's expensive inspection and grading system which their customers had come to know and rely on over the 60-odd years of its existence. . . .

Unsuccessful in its attempts to secure administrative relief, the Commission instituted this action challenging the constitutionality of the statute in the United States District Court for the Eastern District of North Carolina. . . . A three-judge Federal District Court was convened. . . .

After a hearing, the District Court granted the requested relief. . . . This appeal followed. . . .

We turn finally to the appellants' claim that the District Court erred in holding that the North Carolina statute violated the Commerce Clause insofar as it prohibited the display of Washington State grades on closed containers of apples shipped into the State. Appellants do not really contest the District Court's determination that the challenged statute burdened the Washington apple industry by increasing its costs of doing business in the North Carolina market and causing it to lose accounts there. Rather, they maintain that any such burdens on the interstate sale of Washington apples were far outweighed by the local benefits flowing from what they contend was a valid exercise of North Carolina's inherent police powers designed to protect its citizenry from fraud and deception in the marketing of apples.

Prior to the statute's enactment, appellants point out, apples from 13 different States were shipped into North Carolina for sale. Seven of those States, including the State of Washington, had their own grading systems which, while differing in their standards, used similar descriptive labels (e. g., fancy, extra fancy, etc.). This multiplicity of inconsistent state grades, as the District Court itself found, posed dangers of deception and confusion not only in the North Carolina market, but in the Nation as a whole. The North Carolina statute, appellants claim, was enacted to eliminate this source of deception and confusion by replacing the numerous state grades with a single uniform standard. Moreover, it is contended that North Carolina sought to accomplish this goal of uniformity in an evenhanded manner as evidenced by the fact that its statute applies to all apples sold in closed containers in the State without regard to their point of origin. Nonetheless, appellants argue that the District Court gave "scant attention" to the obvious benefits flowing from the challenged legislation and to the long line of decisions from this Court holding that the States possess "broad powers" to protect local purchasers from fraud and deception in the marketing of foodstuffs.

As the appellants properly point out, not every exercise of state authority imposing some burden on the free flow of commerce is invalid. Although the Commerce Clause acts as a limitation upon state power even without congressional implementation, our opinions have long recognized that, "in the absence of conflicting legislation by Congress, there is a residuum of power in the state to make laws governing matters of local concern which nevertheless in some measure affect interstate commerce or even, to some extent, regulate it."

Moreover, as appellants correctly note, that "residuum" is particularly strong when the State acts to protect its citizenry in matters pertaining to the sale of foodstuffs. By the same token, however, a finding that state legislation furthers matters of legitimate local concern, even in the health and consumer protection areas, does not end the inquiry. . . . Rather, when such state legislation comes into conflict with the Commerce Clause's overriding requirement of a national "common market," we are confronted with the task of effecting an accommodation of the competing national and local interests. *Pike v. Bruce Church, Inc.* We turn to that task.

As the District Court correctly found, the challenged statute has the practical effect of not only burdening interstate sales of Washington apples, but also discriminating against them. This discrimination takes various forms. The first, and most obvious, is the statute's consequence of raising the costs of doing business in the North Carolina market for Washington apple growers and dealers, while leaving those of their North Carolina counterparts unaffected. As previously noted, this disparate effect results from the fact that North Carolina apple producers, unlike their Washington competitors, were not forced to alter their marketing practices in order to comply with the statute. They were still free to market their wares under the USDA grade or none at all as they had done prior to the statute's enactment. Obviously, the increased costs imposed by the statute would tend to shield the local apple industry from the competition of Washington apple growers and dealers who are already at a competitive disadvantage because of their great distance from the North Carolina market.

Second, the statute has the effect of stripping away from the Washington apple industry the competitive and economic advantages it has earned for itself through its expensive inspection and grading system. The record demonstrates that the Washington apple-grading system has gained nationwide acceptance in the apple trade. Indeed, it contains numerous affidavits from apple brokers and dealers located both inside and outside of North Carolina who state their preference, and that of their customers, for apples graded under the Washington, as opposed to the USDA, system because of the former's greater consistency, its emphasis on color, and its supporting mandatory inspections. Once again, the statute had no similar impact on the North Carolina apple industry and thus operated to its benefit.

Third, by prohibiting Washington growers and dealers from marketing apples under their State's grades, the statute has a leveling effect which insidiously operates to the advantage of local apple producers. As noted earlier, the Washington State grades are equal or superior to the USDA grades in all corresponding categories. Hence, with free market forces at work, Washington sellers would normally enjoy a distinct market advantage vis-a-vis local producers in those categories where the Washington grade is superior. However, because of the statute's operation, Washington apples which would otherwise qualify for and be sold under the superior Washington grades will now have to be marketed under their inferior USDA counterparts. Such "downgrading" offers the North Carolina apple industry the very sort of protection against competing out-of-state products that the Commerce Clause was designed to prohibit. At worst, it will have the effect of an embargo against those Washington apples in the superior grades as Washington dealers withhold them from the North Carolina market. At best, it will deprive Washington sellers of the market premium that such apples would otherwise command.

Despite the statute's facial neutrality, the Commission suggests that its discriminatory impact on interstate commerce was not an unintended byproduct and there are some indications in the record to that effect. The most glaring is the response of the North Carolina Agriculture Commissioner to the Commission's request for an exemption following the statue's passage in which he indicated that before he could support such an exemption, he would "want to have the sentiment from our apple producers since they were mainly responsible for this legislation being passed. . . ." Moreover, we find it somewhat suspect that North Carolina singled out only closed containers of apples, the very means by which apples are transported in commerce, to effectuate the statute's ostensible consumer protection purpose when apples are not generally sold at retail in their shipping containers. However, we need not ascribe an economic protection motive to the North Carolina Legislature to resolve this case; we conclude that the challenged statute cannot stand insofar as it prohibits the display of Washington State grades even if enacted for the declared purpose of protecting consumers from deception and fraud in the marketplace.

When discrimination against commerce of the type we have found is demonstrated, the burden falls on the State to justify it both in terms of the local benefits flowing from the statute and the unavailability of nondiscriminatory alternatives adequate to preserve the local interests at stake. North Carolina has failed to sustain that burden on both scores.

The several States unquestionably possess a substantial interest in protecting their citizens from confusion and deception in the marketing of foodstuffs, but the challenged statute does remarkably little to further that laudable goal at least with respect to Washington apples and grades. The statute, as already noted, permits the marketing of closed containers of apples under no grades at all. Such a result can hardly be thought to eliminate the problems of deception and confusion created by the multiplicity of differing state grades; indeed, it magnifies them by depriving purchasers of all information concerning the quality of the contents of closed apple containers. Moreover, although the statute is ostensibly a consumer protection measure, it directs its primary efforts, not at the consuming public at large, but at apple wholesalers and brokers who are the principal purchasers of closed containers of apples. And those individuals are presumably the most knowledgeable individuals in this area. Since the statute does nothing at all to purify the flow of information at the retail level, it does little to protect consumers against the problems it was designed to eliminate. Finally, we note that any potential for confusion and deception created by the Washington grades was not of the type that led to the statute's enactment. Since Washington grades are in all cases equal or superior to their USDA counterparts, they could only "deceive" or "confuse" a consumer to his benefit, hardly a harmful result.

In addition, it appears that nondiscriminatory alternatives to the outright ban of Washington State grades are readily available. For example, North Carolina could effectuate its goal by permitting out-of-state growers to utilize state grades only if they also marked their shipments with the applicable USDA label. In that case, the USDA grade would serve as a benchmark against which the consumer could evaluate the quality of the various state grades. If this alternative was for some reason inadequate to eradicate problems caused by state grades inferior to those adopted by the USDA, North Carolina might consider banning those state grades which, unlike Washington's could not be demonstrated to be equal or superior to the corresponding USDA categories. Concededly, even in this latter instance, some potential for "confusion" might persist. However, it is the type of "confusion" that the national interest in the free flow of goods between the States demands be tolerated.

MR. JUSTICE REHNQUIST took no part in the consideration or decision of the case.

COMMENTS AND QUESTIONS

1.   In *Philadelphia v. New Jersey*, *Dean Milk Co. v. Madison*, and *C & A Carbone, Inc. v. Clarkstown*, the state or local law had an explicit geographical restriction involved—out-of-state waste could not be brought into New Jersey, milk pasteurized outside a 5-mile limit of Madison could not be sold in Madison, and no waste generated in Clarkstown could be sent out of Clarkstown and no waste could be sent into Clarkstown, unless processed in the particular Clarkstown facility. Thus, there was a clear discrimination against the movement interstate of the commerce in question. We call this facial discrimination, because the discrimination can be found in the text of the law itself. *Hunt* is different. Here the law itself does not treat apples differently with respect to where they come from or where they go. Nevertheless, the Court finds that the law is discriminatory. We call this discriminatory in fact or in effect; that is, the discrimination or discriminatory effect depends on the particular facts. What facts does the Court identify as making this law discriminatory?

2.   The Court in *Hunt* does not conclude that the purpose of the law is protectionism, although that is its effect, but the Court does make mention of something that might support a protectionist purpose behind the law. Why does the Court do that? Do you think it affected the Court's decision?

3.   The only reason the North Carolina law is found unconstitutional is that it interferes with Washington apple growers obtaining the benefit of a Washington state law. That is, it is only because Washington state had already established its unique and special apple grading system that the North Carolina ban on out-of-state grades on apple crates interfered with interstate commerce. In the absence of the Washington law, the North Carolina law would be constitutional. Is it fair that Washington's law to benefit its apple growers can trump North Carolina's law that benefits its apple growers?

WEST LYNN CREAMERY, INC. V. HEALY

United States Supreme Court, 1994.
512 U.S. 186, 114 S.Ct. 2205.

JUSTICE STEVENS delivered the opinion of the Court.

A Massachusetts pricing order imposes an assessment on all fluid milk sold by dealers to Massachusetts retailers. About two-thirds of that milk is produced out of State. The entire assessment, however, is distributed to Massachusetts dairy farmers. The question presented is whether the pricing order unconstitutionally discriminates against interstate commerce. We hold that it does.

Petitioner West Lynn Creamery, Inc., is a milk dealer licensed to do business in Massachusetts. It purchases raw milk, which it processes, packages, and sells to wholesalers, retailers, and other milk dealers. About 97% of the raw milk it purchases is produced by out-of-state farmers. . . .

[I]n the 1980s and early 1990s, Massachusetts dairy farmers began to lose market share to lower cost producers in neighboring States. In response, the Governor of Massachusetts appointed a Special Commission to study the dairy industry. The commission found that many producers had sold their dairy farms during the past decade and that if prices paid to farmers for their milk were not significantly increased, a majority of the remaining farmers in Massachusetts would be "forced out of business within the year." . . . [Consequently, Healy, the Commissioner of the Massachusetts Department of Food and Agriculture,] issued the pricing order that is challenged in this proceeding.

John Paul Stevens

President Gerald Ford appointed Stevens to the Court in 1975, from which he retired in 2010 as the then oldest and longest serving member of the Court. After law school and clerking for Justice Wiley Rutledge, he undertook a 20-plus year career in a private law firm in Chicago, specializing in antitrust law. His work as General Counsel for a special commission to investigate corruption brought him some prominence and probably led to President Richard Nixon appointing him to the Seventh Circuit. There he had a reputation as a moderate conservative, which he maintained in his first years on the Supreme Court. Thereafter, however, he gravitated to the liberal wing of the Court and with the retirement of Justice William Brennan was considered the most liberal member of the Court.

The order requires every "dealer"[4] in Massachusetts to make a monthly "premium payment" into the "Massachusetts Dairy Equalization

---

[4] A "dealer" is defined as "any person who is engaged within the Commonwealth in the business of receiving, purchasing, pasteurizing, bottling, processing, distributing, or otherwise handling milk, purchases or receives milk for sale as the consignee or agent of a producer, and shall include a producer-dealer, dealer-retailer, and sub-dealer."

Fund." . . . Each month the fund is distributed to Massachusetts producers.[7] Each Massachusetts producer receives a share of the total fund equal to his proportionate contribution to the State's total production of raw milk.

[Petitioner West Lynn refused to make the premium payments, and respondent commenced license revocation proceedings. Petitioner] then filed an action in state court seeking an injunction against enforcement of the order on the ground that it violated the Commerce Clause of the Federal Constitution. The state court denied relief and . . . the Supreme Judicial Court of Massachusetts . . . affirmed, because it concluded that "the pricing order does not discriminate on its face, is evenhanded in its application, and only incidentally burdens interstate commerce." . . . We granted certiorari and now reverse.

[T]he Commerce Clause . . . limits the power of the Commonwealth of Massachusetts to adopt regulations that discriminate against interstate commerce. "This 'negative' aspect of the Commerce Clause prohibits economic protectionism—that is, regulatory measures designed to benefit in-state economic interests by burdening out-of-state competitors. . . . Thus, state statutes that clearly discriminate against interstate commerce are routinely struck down . . . unless the discrimination is demonstrably justified by a valid factor unrelated to economic protectionism.

The paradigmatic example of a law discriminating against interstate commerce is the protective tariff or customs duty, which taxes goods imported from other States, but does not tax similar products produced in State. A tariff is an attractive measure because it simultaneously raises revenue and benefits local producers by burdening their out-of-state competitors. Nevertheless, it violates the principle of the unitary national market by handicapping out-of-state competitors, thus artificially encouraging in-state production even when the same goods could be produced at lower cost in other States. . . .

Under these cases, Massachusetts's pricing order is clearly unconstitutional. Its avowed purpose and its undisputed effect are to enable higher cost Massachusetts dairy farmers to compete with lower cost dairy farmers in other States. The "premium payments" are effectively a tax which makes milk produced out of State more expensive. Although the tax also applies to milk produced in Massachusetts, its effect on Massachusetts producers is entirely (indeed more than) offset by the subsidy provided exclusively to Massachusetts dairy farmers. Like an ordinary tariff, the tax is thus effectively imposed only on out-of-state products. The pricing order thus allows Massachusetts dairy farmers who produce at higher cost to sell at or below the price charged by lower cost out-of-state producers. . . . The Massachusetts pricing order thus will

---

[7]   A "producer" is defined as "any person producing milk from dairy cattle."

almost certainly "cause local goods to constitute a larger share, and goods with an out-of-state source to constitute a smaller share, of the total sales in the market." In fact, this effect was the motive behind the promulgation of the pricing order. This effect renders the program unconstitutional, because it, like a tariff, "neutraliz[es] advantages belonging to the place of origin."

In some ways, the Massachusetts pricing order is most similar to the law at issue in *Bacchus Imports, Ltd. v. Dias,* 468 U.S. 263 (1984). Both involve a broad-based tax on a single kind of good and special provisions for in-state producers. *Bacchus* involved a 20% excise tax on all liquor sales, coupled with an exemption for fruit wine manufactured in Hawaii and for okolehao, a brandy distilled from the root of a shrub indigenous to Hawaii. The Court held that Hawaii's law was unconstitutional because it "had both the purpose and effect of discriminating in favor of local products." By granting a tax exemption for local products, Hawaii in effect created a protective tariff. Goods produced out of State were taxed, but those produced in State were subject to no net tax. It is obvious that the result in *Bacchus* would have been the same if instead of exempting certain Hawaiian liquors from tax, Hawaii had rebated the amount of tax collected from the sale of those liquors. . . .

Respondent's principal argument is that . . . the payments to Massachusetts dairy farmers from the Dairy Equalization Fund are valid, because subsidies are constitutional exercises of state power, and that the order premium which provides money for the fund is valid, because it is a nondiscriminatory tax. Therefore the pricing order is constitutional, because it is merely the combination of two independently lawful regulations. In effect, respondent argues, if the State may impose a valid tax on dealers, it is free to use the proceeds of the tax as it chooses; and if it may independently subsidize its farmers, it is free to finance the subsidy by means of any legitimate tax.

Even granting respondent's assertion that both components of the pricing order would be constitutional standing alone,[15] the pricing order nevertheless must fall. A pure subsidy funded out of general revenue ordinarily imposes no burden on interstate commerce, but merely assists local business. The pricing order in this case, however, is funded principally from taxes on the sale of milk produced in other States. By so funding the subsidy, respondent not only assists local farmers, but burdens interstate commerce. The pricing order thus violates the cardinal principle that a State may not "benefit in-state economic interests by burdening out-of-state competitors."

---

[15] We have never squarely confronted the constitutionality of subsidies, and we need not do so now. We have, however, noted that "[d]irect subsidization of domestic industry does not ordinarily run afoul" of the negative Commerce Clause.

[N]ondiscriminatory measures, like the evenhanded tax at issue here, are generally upheld, in spite of any adverse effects on interstate commerce, in part because "[t]he existence of major in-state interests adversely affected . . . is a powerful safeguard against legislative abuse." However, when a nondiscriminatory tax is coupled with a subsidy to one of the groups hurt by the tax, a State's political processes can no longer be relied upon to prevent legislative abuse, because one of the in-state interests which would otherwise lobby against the tax has been mollified by the subsidy. So, in this case, one would ordinarily have expected at least three groups to lobby against the order premium, which, as a tax, raises the price (and hence lowers demand) for milk: dairy farmers, milk dealers, and consumers. But because the tax was coupled with a subsidy, one of the most powerful of these groups, Massachusetts dairy farmers, instead of exerting their influence against the tax, were in fact its primary supporters.

Respondent's argument would require us to analyze separately two parts of an integrated regulation, but we cannot divorce the premium payments from the use to which the payments are put. It is the entire program—not just the contributions to the fund or the distributions from that fund—that simultaneously burdens interstate commerce and discriminates in favor of local producers. The choice of constitutional means—nondiscriminatory tax and local subsidy—cannot guarantee the constitutionality of the program as a whole. . . . Similarly, the law held unconstitutional in *Bacchus Imports, Ltd. v. Dias,* 468 U.S. 263, 104 S.Ct. 3049, 82 L.Ed.2d 200 (1984), involved the exercise of Hawaii's undisputed power to tax and to grant tax exemptions.

Our Commerce Clause jurisprudence is not so rigid as to be controlled by the form by which a State erects barriers to commerce. Rather our cases have eschewed formalism for a sensitive, case-by-case analysis of purposes and effects. As the Court declared over 50 years ago: "The commerce clause forbids discrimination, whether forthright or ingenious. In each case it is our duty to determine whether the statute under attack, whatever its name may be, will in its practical operation work discrimination against interstate commerce." . . .

"Our system, fostered by the Commerce Clause, is that every farmer and every craftsman shall be encouraged to produce by the certainty that he will have free access to every market in the Nation, that no home embargoes will withhold his exports, and no foreign state will by customs duties or regulations exclude them. Likewise, every consumer may look to the free competition from every producing area in the Nation to protect him from exploitation by any. Such was the vision of the Founders; such has been the doctrine of this Court which has given it reality."

The judgment of the Supreme Judicial Court of Massachusetts is reversed.

JUSTICE SCALIA, with whom JUSTICE THOMAS joins, concurring in the judgment. [omitted]

CHIEF JUSTICE REHNQUIST, with whom JUSTICE BLACKMUN joins, dissenting.

The Court is less than just in its description of the reasons which lay behind the Massachusetts law which it strikes down. The law undoubtedly sought to aid struggling Massachusetts dairy farmers, beset by steady or declining prices and escalating costs. . . . The value of agricultural land located near metropolitan areas is driven up by the demand for housing and similar urban uses; distressed farmers eventually sell out to developers. Not merely farm produce is lost, as is the milk production in this case, but, as the Massachusetts Special Commission whose report was the basis for the order in question here found:

> "Without the continued existence of dairy farmers, the Commonwealth will lose its supply of locally produced fresh milk, together with the open lands that are used as wildlife refuges, for recreation, hunting, fishing, tourism, and education."

Massachusetts has dealt with this problem by providing a subsidy to aid its beleaguered dairy farmers. In case after case, we have approved the validity under the Commerce Clause of such enactments. . . . But today the Court relegates these well-established principles to a footnote and, at the same time, gratuitously casts doubt on the validity of state subsidies, observing that "[w]e have never squarely confronted" their constitutionality. . . .

The Court concludes that the combined effect of the milk order "simultaneously burdens interstate commerce and discriminates in favor of local producers." In support of this conclusion, the Court cites . . . *Bacchus Imports, Ltd. v. Dias, supra,* as [an example] in which constitutional means were held to have unconstitutional effects on interstate commerce. But . . . *Bacchus* [is] a far cry from this case. . . .

In *Bacchus,* the State of Hawaii combined its undisputed power to tax and grant exemptions in a manner that the Court found violative of the Commerce Clause. There, the State exempted a local wine from the burdens of an excise tax levied on all other liquor sales. Despite the Court's strained attempt to compare the scheme in *Bacchus* to the milk order in this case, it is clear that the milk order does not produce the same effect on interstate commerce as the tax exemption in *Bacchus.* . . . No decided case supports the Court's conclusion that the negative Commerce Clause prohibits the State from using money that it has lawfully obtained through a neutral tax on milk dealers and distributing it as a subsidy to dairy farmers. . . .

Comments and Questions

1. As in *Hunt*, the Massachusetts pricing order does not distinguish between in-state and out-of-state milk or milk dealers; they all must pay the same assessment. Again, however, the Court finds that Massachusetts is discriminating against interstate commerce in milk. Do you agree with the majority or the dissent as whether the Massachusetts's milk system is like Hawaii's tax exemption for Hawaiian-made alcoholic beverages?

2. The Twenty-first Amendment, which repealed Prohibition, includes the following language: "The transportation or importation into any State, Territory, or Possession of the United States for delivery or use therein of intoxicating liquors, in violation of the laws thereof, is hereby prohibited." Over the years, some have interpreted this language to constitutionalize state laws regulating alcoholic beverage commercial activities, even to exempt such state laws from inconsistent federal laws and constitutional limitations. The Supreme Court, however, has made clear that this is not the case. In *Bacchus*, discussed in *West Lynn Creamery*, the Court explained that the Amendment did not necessarily insulate a state's discriminatory conduct from the Dormant Commerce Clause. More recently, in *Tennessee Wine and Spirits Ass'n v. Thomas*, 139 S.Ct. 2449 (2019), the Court declared that this language in the Amendment simply had the effect of returning the law regarding alcoholic beverage commercial activities to what it had been before Prohibition. Because Tennessee's requirement that licenses for retail liquor stores could only be granted to persons who had been resident in the state for more than two years was blatantly discriminatory against interstate commerce, it violated the Dormant Commerce Clause under traditional standards, and the Amendment was no defense.

b. Nondiscriminatory State Laws

Above we have considered discriminatory state laws, and while it is sometimes difficult to discern whether a law is or is not discriminatory, once it is determined to be discriminatory against interstate commerce, then it is usually not difficult to determine the validity of the law, given the high hurdle it must overcome—there is no less discriminatory means to achieve a legitimate government interest. If a law is not discriminatory, as we have already seen described in cases above, the "test" announced in *Pike v. Bruce Church* is used:

> "Where the statute regulates even-handedly to effectuate a legitimate local public interest, and its effects on interstate commerce are only incidental, it will be upheld unless the burden imposed on such commerce is clearly excessive in relation to the putative local benefits."

MINNESOTA V. CLOVER LEAF CREAMERY CO.

United States Supreme Court, 1981.
449 U.S. 456, 101 S.Ct. 715.

JUSTICE BRENNAN delivered the opinion of the Court:

In 1977, the Minnesota Legislature enacted a statute banning the retail sale of milk in plastic nonreturnable, nonrefillable containers, but permitting such sale in other nonreturnable, nonrefillable containers, such as paperboard milk cartons. Respondents[1] contend that the statute violates the Equal Protection and Commerce Clauses of the Constitution.

The purpose of the Minnesota statute is set out as § 1:

"The legislature finds that the use of nonreturnable, nonrefillable containers for the packaging of milk and other milk products presents a solid waste management problem for the state, promotes energy waste, and depletes natural resources. The legislature therefore, in furtherance of the policies stated in Minnesota Statutes, determines that the use of nonreturnable, nonrefillable containers for packaging milk and other milk products should be discouraged and that the use of returnable and reusable packaging for these products is preferred and should be encouraged."

Section 2 of the Act forbids the retail sale of milk and fluid milk products, other than sour cream, cottage cheese, and yogurt, in nonreturnable, nonrefillable rigid or semi-rigid containers composed at least 50% of plastic.[3]

The Act was introduced with the support of the state Pollution Control Agency, Department of Natural Resources, Department of Agriculture, Consumer Services Division, and Energy Agency, and debated vigorously in both houses of the state legislature. Proponents of the legislation argued that it would promote resource conservation, ease solid waste disposal problems, and conserve energy. Relying on the results of studies and other information, they stressed the need to stop introduction of the plastic nonreturnable container before it became entrenched in the market. Opponents of the Act, also presenting empirical evidence, argued that the Act would not promote the goals asserted by the proponents, but would merely increase costs of retail milk products and prolong the use of ecologically undesirable paperboard milk cartons.

---

[1]   Respondents, plaintiffs below, are a Minnesota dairy that owns equipment for producing plastic nonreturnable milk jugs, a Minnesota dairy that leases such equipment, a non-Minnesota company that manufactures such equipment, a Minnesota company that produces plastic nonreturnable milk jugs, a non-Minnesota dairy that sells milk products in Minnesota in plastic nonreturnable milk jugs, a Minnesota milk retailer, a non-Minnesota manufacturer of polyethylene resin that sells such resin in many States, including Minnesota, and a plastics industry trade association.

[3]   Minnesota is apparently the first State so to regulate milk containers.

After the Act was passed, respondents filed suit in Minnesota District Court, seeking to enjoin its enforcement. The court conducted extensive evidentiary hearings into the Act's probable consequences, and found the evidence "in sharp conflict." Nevertheless, finding itself "as factfinder . . . obliged to weigh and evaluate this evidence," the court resolved the evidentiary conflicts in favor of respondents, and concluded that the Act "will not succeed in effecting the Legislature's published policy goals. . . ." The court further found that, contrary to the statement of purpose in § 1, the "actual basis" for the Act "was to promote the economic interests of certain segments of the local dairy and pulpwood industries at the expense of the economic interests of other segments of the dairy industry and the plastics industry." The court therefore declared the Act "null, void, and unenforceable" and enjoined its enforcement. . . . The State appealed to the Supreme Court of Minnesota, which affirmed the District Court. . . . Unlike the District Court, the State Supreme Court found that the purpose of the Act was "to promote the state interests of encouraging the reuse and recycling of materials and reducing the amount and type of material entering the solid waste stream," and acknowledged the legitimacy of this purpose. Nevertheless, relying on the District Court's findings of fact, the full record, and an independent review of documentary sources, the State Supreme Court held that "the evidence conclusively demonstrates that the discrimination against plastic nonrefillables is not rationally related to the Act's objectives." We granted certiorari and now reverse. . . .

The District Court also held that the Minnesota statute is unconstitutional under the Commerce Clause because it imposes an unreasonable burden on interstate commerce. We cannot agree.

When legislating in areas of legitimate local concern, such as environmental protection and resource conservation, States are nonetheless limited by the Commerce Clause. If a state law purporting to promote environmental purposes is in reality "simple economic protectionism," we have applied a "virtually *per se* rule of invalidity." *Philadelphia v. New Jersey.* Even if a statute regulates "evenhandedly," and imposes only "incidental" burdens on interstate commerce, the courts must nevertheless strike it down if "the burden imposed on such commerce is clearly excessive in relation to the putative local benefits." *Pike v. Bruce Church, Inc.,* 397 U.S. 137 (1970). Moreover, "the extent of the burden that will be tolerated will of course depend on the nature of the local interest involved, and on whether it could be promoted as well with a lesser impact on interstate activities."

Minnesota's statute does not effect "simple protectionism," but "regulates evenhandedly" by prohibiting all milk retailers from selling their products in plastic, nonreturnable milk containers, without regard to whether the milk, the containers, or the sellers are from outside the State.

This statute is therefore unlike statutes discriminating against interstate commerce, which we have consistently struck down. . . .

Since the statute does not discriminate between interstate and intrastate commerce, the controlling question is whether the incidental burden imposed on interstate commerce by the Minnesota Act is "clearly excessive in relation to the putative local benefits." We conclude that it is not.

The burden imposed on interstate commerce by the statute is relatively minor. Milk products may continue to move freely across the Minnesota border, and since most dairies package their products in more than one type of container, the inconvenience of having to conform to different packaging requirements in Minnesota and the surrounding States should be slight. Within Minnesota, business will presumably shift from manufacturers of plastic nonreturnable containers to producers of paperboard cartons, refillable bottles, and plastic pouches, but there is no reason to suspect that the gainers will be Minnesota firms, or the losers out-of-state firms. Indeed, two of the three dairies, the sole milk retailer, and the sole milk container producer challenging the statute in this litigation are Minnesota firms.

Pulpwood producers are the only Minnesota industry likely to benefit significantly from the Act at the expense of out-of-state firms. Respondents point out that plastic resin, the raw material used for making plastic nonreturnable milk jugs, is produced entirely by non-Minnesota firms, while pulpwood, used for making paperboard, is a major Minnesota product. Nevertheless, it is clear that respondents exaggerate the degree of burden on out-of-state interests, both because plastics will continue to be used in the production of plastic pouches, plastic returnable bottles, and paperboard itself, and because out-of-state pulpwood producers will presumably absorb some of the business generated by the Act.

Even granting that the out-of-state plastics industry is burdened relatively more heavily than the Minnesota pulpwood industry, we find that this burden is not "clearly excessive" in light of the substantial state interest in promoting conservation of energy and other natural resources and easing solid waste disposal problems. . . . We find these local benefits ample to support Minnesota's decision under the Commerce Clause. Moreover, we find that no approach with "a lesser impact on interstate activities," is available. Respondents have suggested several alternative statutory schemes, but these alternatives are either more burdensome on commerce than the Act (as, for example, banning all nonreturnables) or less likely to be effective (as, for example, providing incentives for recycling). . . .

The judgment of the Minnesota Supreme Court is *Reversed*.

JUSTICE REHNQUIST took no part in the consideration or decision of this case.

JUSTICE POWELL, concurring in part and dissenting in part. [omitted]

JUSTICE STEVENS, dissenting. [omitted]

COMMENTS AND QUESTIONS

1. Applying the *Pike v. Bruce Church* test is not an exact science. As with many balancing tests, different people can end up with different predictions of how a court may rule. The one thing that is for sure is that this test places the burden on those challenging a law to show that the burden not only outweighs, but clearly outweighs, the legitimate benefits. If, however, the law were considered discriminatory, the burden would be on the person trying to uphold the law to show that there was indeed a legitimate local interest and that it could not be achieved in any less discriminatory way. This shift of burden in itself may be decisive.

2. What do you think is most important to the Court's decision here—the benefit to the environment or the lack of adverse effect on interstate commerce?

c. The Special Case of Transportation

BIBB v. NAVAJO FREIGHT LINES, INC.

United States Supreme Court, 1959.
359 U.S. 520, 79 S.Ct. 962.

MR. JUSTICE DOUGLAS delivered the opinion of the Court.

We are asked in this case to hold that an Illinois statute requiring the use of a certain type of [contoured] rear fender mudguard on trucks and trailers operated on the highways of that State conflicts with the Commerce Clause of the Constitution. . . .[3]

Appellees, interstate motor carriers holding certificates from the Interstate Commerce Commission, challenged the constitutionality of the Illinois Act. A specially constituted three-judge District Court* concluded that it unduly and unreasonably burdened and obstructed interstate commerce, because it made the conventional or straight mudflap, which is legal in at least 45 States, illegal in Illinois, and because the statute, taken together with a Rule of the Arkansas Commerce Commission requiring straight mudflaps, rendered the use of the same motor vehicle equipment

---

[3] No contention is here made that the statute discriminates against interstate commerce, and it is clear that its provisions apply alike to vehicles in intrastate as well as in interstate commerce.

* At the time of this case, cases challenging the constitutionality of state laws in federal courts were held before a three-judge district court composed of two district court judges and one circuit court judge. Decisions from these courts then could be appealed directly to the Supreme Court as of right (as opposed to by petition for certiorari). [author's note]

in both States impossible. The statute was declared to be violative of the Commerce Clause and appellants were enjoined from enforcing it. An appeal was taken and we noted probable jurisdiction.

The power of the State to regulate the use of its highways is broad and pervasive. We have recognized the peculiarly local nature of this subject of safety, and have upheld state statutes applicable alike to interstate and intrastate commerce, despite the fact that they may have an impact on interstate commerce. The regulation of highways "is akin to quarantine measures, same laws, and like local regulations of rivers, harbors, piers, and docks, with respect to which the state has exceptional scope for the exercise of its regulatory power, and which, Congress not acting, have been sustained even though they materially interfere with interstate commerce."

These safety measures carry a strong presumption of validity when challenged in court. If there are alternative ways of solving a problem, we do not sit to determine which of them is best suited to achieve a valid state objective. Policy decisions are for the state legislature, absent federal entry into the field. Unless we can conclude on the whole record that "the total effect of the law as a safety measure in reducing accidents and casualties is so slight or problematical as not to outweigh the national interest in keeping interstate commerce free from interferences which seriously impede it" we must uphold the statute.

The District Court found that "since it is impossible for a carrier operating in interstate commerce to determine which of its equipment will be used in a particular area, or on a particular day, or days, carriers operating into or through Illinois * * * will be required to equip all their trailers in accordance with the requirements of the Illinois Splash Guard statute." With two possible exceptions the mudflaps required in those States which have mudguard regulations would not meet the standards required by the Illinois statute. The cost of installing the contour mudguards is $30 or more per vehicle. The District Court found that the initial cost of installing those mudguards on all the trucks owned by the appellees ranged from $4,500 to $45,840. There was also evidence in the record to indicate that the cost of maintenance and replacement of these guards is substantial.

Illinois introduced evidence seeking to establish that contour mudguards had a decided safety factor in that they prevented the throwing of debris into the faces of drivers of passing cars and into the windshields of a following vehicle. But the District Court in its opinion stated that it was "conclusively shown that the contour mud flap possesses no advantages over the conventional or straight mud flap previously required in Illinois and presently required in most of the states," and that "there is rather convincing testimony that use of the contour flap creates hazards previously unknown to those using the highways." These hazards were found to be occasioned by the fact that this new type of mudguard tended to cause an accumulation of heat in the brake drum, thus decreasing the effectiveness of brakes, and by the fact that they were susceptible of being hit and bumped when the trucks were backed up and of falling off on the highway.

These findings on cost and on safety are not the end of our problem. . . . State control of the width and weight of motor trucks and trailers sustained in *South Carolina State Highway Dept. v. Barnwell Bros.*, 303 U.S. 177 (1938), involved nice questions of judgment concerning the need of those regulations so far as the issue of safety was concerned. That case also presented the problem whether interstate motor carriers, who were required to replace all equipment or keep out of the State, suffered an unconstitutional restraint on interstate commerce. The matter of safety was said to be one essentially for the legislative judgment; and the burden of redesigning or replacing equipment was said to be a proper price to exact from interstate and intrastate motor carriers alike. . . . Cost taken into consideration with other factors might be relevant in some cases to the issue of burden on commerce. But it has assumed no such proportions here. If we had here only a question whether the cost of adjusting an interstate operation to these new local safety regulations prescribed by Illinois unduly burdened interstate commerce, we would have to sustain the law under the authority of [prior] cases. The same result would obtain if we had to resolve the much discussed issues of safety presented in this case.

This case presents a different issue. The equipment in the [prior] cases could pass muster in any State, so far as the records in those cases reveal. We were not faced there with the question whether one State could prescribe standards for interstate carriers that would conflict with the standards of another State, making it necessary, say, for an interstate carrier to shift its cargo to differently designed vehicles once another state line was reached. We had a related problem in *Southern Pacific Co. v. State of Arizona*, 325 U.S. 761 (1945), where the Court invalidated a statute of Arizona prescribing a maximum length of 70 cars for freight trains moving through that State. Those cases indicate the dimensions of our present problem.

An order of the Arkansas Commerce Commission, already mentioned, requires that trailers operating in that State be equipped with straight or conventional mudflaps. Vehicles equipped to meet the standards of the Illinois statute would not comply with Arkansas standards, and vice versa. Thus if a trailer is to be operated in both States, mudguards would have to be interchanged, causing a significant delay in an operation where prompt movement may be of the essence. It was found that from two to four hours of labor are required to install or remove a contour mudguard. Moreover, the contour guard is attached to the trailer by welding and if the trailer is conveying a cargo of explosives (*e.g.*, for the United States Government) it would be exceedingly dangerous to attempt to weld on a contour mudguard without unloading the trailer.

It was also found that the Illinois statute seriously interferes with the "interline" operations of motor carriers—that is to say, with the interchanging of trailers between an originating carrier and another carrier when the latter serves an area not served by the former. These "interline" operations provide a speedy through-service for the shipper. Interlining contemplates the physical transfer of the entire trailer; there is no unloading and reloading of the cargo. The interlining process is particularly vital in connection with shipment of perishables, which would spoil if unloaded before reaching their destination, or with the movement of explosives carried under seal. Of course, if the originating carrier never operated in Illinois, it would not be expected to equip its trailers with contour mudguards. Yet if an interchanged trailer of that carrier were hauled to or through Illinois, the statute would require that it contain contour guards. Since carriers which operate in and through Illinois cannot compel the originating carriers to equip their trailers with contour guards, they may be forced to cease interlining with those who do not meet the Illinois requirements. Over 60 percent of the business of 5 of the 6 plaintiffs is interline traffic. For the other it constitutes 30 percent. All of the plaintiffs operate extensively in interstate commerce, and the annual mileage in Illinois of none of them exceeds 7 percent of total mileage.

This is [a] summary [of] the rather massive showing of burden on interstate commerce which appellees made at the hearing.

Appellants did not attempt to rebut the appellees' showing that the statute in question severely burdens interstate commerce. Appellants' showing was aimed at establishing that contour mudguards prevented the throwing of debris into the faces of drivers of passing cars and into the windshields of a following vehicle. They concluded that, because the Illinois statute is a reasonable exercise of the police power, a federal court is precluded from weighing the relative merits of the contour mudguard against any other kind of mudguard and must sustain the validity of the statute notwithstanding the extent of the burden it imposes on interstate commerce. They rely in the main on *South Carolina State Highway Dept. v. Barnwell Bros.* There is language in that opinion which, read in isolation from such later decisions as *Southern Pacific Co. v. State of Arizona*, would suggest that no showing of burden on interstate commerce is sufficient to invalidate local safety regulations in absence of some element of discrimination against interstate commerce.

The various exercises by the States of their police power stand, however, on an equal footing. All are entitled to the same presumption of validity ... when measured against the Commerce Clause.... Like any local law that conflicts with federal regulatory measures state regulations that run afoul of the policy of free trade reflected in the Commerce Clause must also bow.

This is one of those cases—few in number—where local safety measures that are nondiscriminatory place an unconstitutional burden on interstate commerce. This conclusion is especially underlined by the deleterious effect which the Illinois law will have on the "interline" operation of interstate motor carriers. The conflict between the Arkansas regulation and the Illinois regulation also suggests that this regulation of mudguards is not one of those matters "admitting of diversity of treatment, according to the special requirements of local conditions." . . . A State which insists on a design out of line with the requirements of almost all the other States may sometimes place a great burden of delay and inconvenience on those interstate motor carriers entering or crossing its territory. Such a new safety device—out of line with the requirements of the other States— may be so compelling that the innovating State need not be the one to give way. But the present showing—balanced against the clear burden on commerce—is far too inconclusive to make this mudguard meet that test.

We deal not with absolutes but with questions of degree. The state legislatures plainly have great leeway in providing safety regulations for all vehicles—interstate as well as local. Our decisions so hold. Yet the heavy burden which the Illinois mudguard law places on the interstate movement of trucks and trailers seems to us to pass the permissible limits even for safety regulations.

MR. JUSTICE HARLAN, whom MR. JUSTICE STEWART joins, concurring. [omitted]

COMMENTS AND QUESTIONS

1.   This section is entitled "the special case of transportation" because transportation cases raise special problems with respect to nondiscriminatory laws. *Bibb* is a good example. There is no suggestion by anyone that Illinois adopts its mudflap rule for any reason other than a good faith belief that it protects motorists from spray and objects thrown from tires on the trailers of large trucks. For whatever reason, its safety engineers believe that contoured mudflaps are preferable to straight mudflaps. If no other state had any mudflap rule, it is clear that Illinois's law would be constitutional, despite the unequivocal findings by the district court that the contoured flaps were less safe, rather than more safe, than straight flaps. However, other states do have mudflap rules. At the time Illinois adopts its rule, apparently 45 states have mudflap rules that allow straight mudflaps, with the result that virtually all large trucks have straight mudflaps. However, all but two apparently would also allow the contoured mudflaps. Arkansas in particular requires the straight mudflaps. What is a trucker to do? He currently has straight mudflaps, but if he wants to take his trailer to Illinois he will have to replace them. That will be relatively expensive. Moreover, the poor trucker will have to change mudflaps every time he goes between Arkansas and Illinois, and,

even more important to the Court, it will make "interlining" very difficult, because it will be impossible to know which trailers will go where. This leads to an unacceptable burden on interstate commerce. Courts have reached similar conclusions with respect to state-mandated train lengths that differ from one state to another and with respect to different state restrictions regarding double- and triple-trailer trucks.

2.　Note that Illinois's law is only unconstitutional because Arkansas has a directly contradictory law. Why is it that Illinois's law is unconstitutional rather than Arkansas's. Could Congress pass a law now requiring contoured mudflaps on all the nation's highways?

3.　Obviously, what's special about transportation cases is that trucks, trains, ships, and airplanes are forever crossing state lines, and different state standards applicable to these modes of transportation could wreak havoc with an efficient national transportation system. What is not so obvious is why it is that we think courts are supposed to sort out what are the appropriate standards when states disagree, rather than Congress or some federal agency. Isn't that what the Commerce Clause was all about—empowering Congress to regulate commerce among the states? Why do you think the Court has taken up this responsibility?

PROBLEM

State A has had unfortunate experiences with hazardous waste disposal sites leaking into underground aquifers, even from EPA regulated sites. Consequently, it passes a law banning the disposal on land of any hazardous waste. An out-of-state chemical company that has historically disposed of its hazardous waste at a regulated site in State A sues, alleging the law violates the Dormant Commerce Clause. How should the court rule?

---

d.　The Special Case of Taxation

Just as states may violate the Dormant Commerce Clause through discriminatory regulation, they may also violate it through discriminatory taxation, such as taxing goods coming from out-of-state while not taxing the same goods from in-state. This would be discriminatory. In several cases the Court has used what it calls the "internal consistency test" to determine if a state's tax law discriminates in violation of the Dormant Commerce Clause. As described in *Comptroller of the Treasury of Maryland v. Wynne*, 575 U.S. 542 (2015), the test asks if every state adopted such a tax would such a tax discriminate against out-of-state commerce. For example, if a state has a sales tax on goods sold within the state and imposes an identical use tax on goods bought in another state but brought into the state, but also credits against the use tax any sales tax paid in the other state, then there is no discrimination. *See Henneford v. Silas Mason Co.*, 300 U.S. 577 (1937). If every state imposed such a tax, there would be no greater tax imposed on goods coming from out-of-state than imposed on goods sold within the state. In *Wynne*, Maryland imposed a county income tax on income of residents earned both in Maryland and out-of-state and on income earned in Maryland by non-residents. If every state imposed the same tax, then a resident of Maryland who earned out-of-state income would pay more tax on the same total income than a resident of Maryland who earned all her income in Maryland, because the first resident would be taxed both by Maryland and the state in which his income was earned, whereas the second resident would only be taxed by Maryland. This, the Court said, violated the "internal consistency test."

Similarly, just as states may sometimes violate the Dormant Commerce Clause even when the regulation is not discriminatory, they also can possibly violate it through non-discriminatory taxation. Here, the Court uses a test from *Complete Auto Transit, Inc. v. Brady*, 430 U.S. 272 (1977). Like the *Pike v. Bruce Church Test*, this test does not always lead to predictable results. The Court's most recent use of the test reflects this.

SOUTH DAKOTA V. WAYFAIR, INC.
United States Supreme Court, 2018.
138 S.Ct. 2080.

JUSTICE KENNEDY delivered the opinion of the Court.

When a consumer purchases goods or services, the consumer's State often imposes a sales tax. This case requires the Court to determine when an out-of-state seller can be required to collect and remit that tax. All concede that taxing the sales in question here is lawful. The question is whether the out-of-state seller can be held responsible for its payment, and this turns on a proper interpretation of the Commerce Clause.

In two earlier cases the Court held that an out-of-state seller's liability to collect and remit the tax to the consumer's State depended on whether the seller had a physical presence in that State, but that mere shipment of goods into the consumer's State, following an order from a catalog, did not satisfy the physical presence requirement. *National Bellas Hess, Inc. v. Department of Revenue of Ill.,* 386 U.S. 753 (1967); *Quill Corp. v. North Dakota,* 504 U.S. 298 (1992). The Court granted certiorari here to reconsider the scope and validity of the physical presence rule mandated by those cases.

Like most States, South Dakota has a sales tax. It taxes the retail sales of goods and services in the State. Sellers are generally required to collect and remit this tax to the Department of Revenue. If for some reason the sales tax is not remitted by the seller, then in-state consumers are separately responsible for paying a use tax at the same rate. Many States employ this kind of complementary sales and use tax regime.

Under this Court's decisions in *Bellas Hess* and *Quill,* South Dakota may not require a business to collect its sales tax if the business lacks a physical presence in the State. Without that physical presence, South Dakota instead must rely on its residents to pay the use tax owed on their purchases from out-of-state sellers. "[T]he impracticability of [this] collection from the multitude of individual purchasers is obvious." And consumer compliance rates are notoriously low. It is estimated that *Bellas Hess* and *Quill* cause the States to lose between $8 and $33 billion every year. . . .

In 2016, South Dakota confronted the serious inequity *Quill* imposes by enacting S. 106—"An Act to provide for the collection of sales taxes from certain remote sellers, to establish certain Legislative findings, and to declare an emergency." . . . To that end, the Act requires out-of-state sellers to collect and remit sales tax "as if the seller had a physical presence in the state." The Act applies only to sellers that, on an annual basis, deliver more than $100,000 of goods or services into the State or engage in 200 or more separate transactions for the delivery of goods or services into the State. The Act also forecloses the retroactive application of this requirement and provides means for the Act to be appropriately stayed until the constitutionality of the law has been clearly established.

Respondents Wayfair, Inc., Overstock.com, Inc., and Newegg, Inc., are merchants with no employees or real estate in South Dakota. . . . Each of these three companies ships its goods directly to purchasers throughout the United States, including South Dakota. Each easily meets the minimum sales or transactions requirement of the Act, but none collects South Dakota sales tax. . . .

The Constitution grants Congress the power "[t]o regulate Commerce . . . among the several States." Although the Commerce Clause is written as an affirmative grant of authority to Congress, this Court has long held that in some instances it imposes limitations on the States absent congressional action. Of course, when Congress exercises its power to regulate commerce by enacting legislation, the legislation controls. But this Court has observed that "in general Congress has left it to the courts to formulate the rules" to preserve "the free flow of interstate commerce." . . .

The[ ] principles [underlying the Court's precedents in the regulatory field] also animate the Court's Commerce Clause precedents addressing the validity of state taxes. The Court explained the now-accepted framework for state taxation in *Complete Auto Transit, Inc. v. Brady.* The Court held that a State "may tax exclusively interstate commerce so long as the tax does not create any effect forbidden by the Commerce Clause." . . . The Court will sustain a tax so long as it (1) applies to an activity with a substantial nexus with the taxing State, (2) is fairly apportioned, (3) does not discriminate against interstate commerce, and (4) is fairly related to the services the State provides.

Before *Complete Auto,* the Court had addressed a challenge to an Illinois tax that required out-of-state retailers to collect and remit taxes on sales made to consumers who purchased goods for use within Illinois. *Bellas Hess.* The Court held that a mail-order company "whose only connection with customers in the State is by common carrier or the United States mail" lacked the requisite minimum contacts with the State required by both the Due Process Clause and the Commerce Clause. Unless the retailer maintained a physical presence such as "retail outlets, solicitors, or property within a State," the State lacked the power to require that retailer to collect a local use tax. The dissent disagreed: "There should be no doubt that this large-scale, systematic, continuous solicitation and exploitation of the Illinois consumer market is a sufficient 'nexus' to require Bellas Hess to collect from Illinois customers and to remit the use tax." (opinion of Fortas, J., joined by Black and Douglas, JJ.).

In 1992, the Court reexamined the physical presence rule in *Quill.* That case presented a challenge to North Dakota's "attempt to require an out-of-state mail-order house that has neither outlets nor sales representatives in the State to collect and pay a use tax on goods purchased for use within the State." Despite the fact that *Bellas Hess* linked due process and the Commerce Clause together, the Court in *Quill* overruled the due process holding, but not the Commerce Clause holding; and it thus reaffirmed the physical presence rule.

The Court in *Quill* recognized that intervening precedents, specifically *Complete Auto,* "might not dictate the same result were the issue to arise for the first time today." But, nevertheless, the *Quill* majority concluded that the physical presence rule was necessary to prevent undue burdens on interstate commerce. It grounded the physical presence rule in *Complete Auto*'s requirement that a tax have a " 'substantial nexus' " with the activity being taxed.

Three Justices based their decision to uphold the physical presence rule on *stare decisis* alone. (SCALIA, J., joined by KENNEDY and THOMAS, JJ., concurring in part and concurring in judgment). Dissenting in relevant part, Justice White argued that "there is no relationship between the physical-presence/nexus rule the Court retains and Commerce Clause considerations that allegedly justify it."

The physical presence rule has "been the target of criticism over many years from many quarters." *Quill,* it has been said, was "premised on assumptions that are unfounded" and "riddled with internal inconsistencies." *Quill* created an inefficient "online sales tax loophole" that gives out-of-state businesses an advantage. And "while nexus rules are clearly necessary," the Court "should focus on rules that are appropriate to the twenty-first century, not the nineteenth." Each year, the physical presence rule becomes further removed from economic reality and results in significant revenue losses to the States. These critiques underscore that the physical presence rule, both as first formulated and as applied today, is an incorrect interpretation of the Commerce Clause.

Quill is flawed on its own terms. First, the physical presence rule is not a necessary interpretation of the requirement that a state tax must be "applied to an activity with a substantial nexus with the taxing State." Second, *Quill* creates rather than resolves market distortions. And third, *Quill* imposes the sort of arbitrary, formalistic distinction that the Court's modern Commerce Clause precedents disavow.

All agree that South Dakota has the authority to tax these transactions. S.B. 106 applies to sales of "tangible personal property, products transferred electronically, or services *for delivery into South Dakota.*" § 1 (emphasis added). "It has long been settled" that the sale of goods or services "has a sufficient nexus to the State in which the sale is consummated to be treated as a local transaction taxable by that State."

The central dispute is whether South Dakota may require remote sellers to collect and remit the tax without some additional connection to the State. The Court has previously stated that "[t]he imposition on the seller of the duty to insure collection of the tax from the purchaser does not violate the [C]ommerce [C]lause." It is a " 'familiar and sanctioned device.' " There just must be "a substantial nexus with the taxing State."

This nexus requirement is "closely related" to the due process requirement that there be "some definite link, some minimum connection, between a state and the person, property or transaction it seeks to tax," It is settled law that a business need not have a physical presence in a State to satisfy the demands of due process. Although physical presence " 'frequently will enhance' " a business' connection with a State, " 'it is an inescapable fact of modern commercial life that a substantial amount of business is transacted . . . [with no] need for physical presence within a State in which business is conducted.' " *Quill* itself recognized that "[t]he requirements of due process are met irrespective of a corporation's lack of physical presence in the taxing State."

When considering whether a State may levy a tax, Due Process and Commerce Clause standards may not be identical or coterminous, but there are significant parallels. The reasons given in *Quill* for rejecting the physical presence rule for due process purposes apply as well to the question whether physical presence is a requisite for an out-of-state seller's liability to remit sales taxes. Physical presence is not necessary to create a substantial nexus. . . .

Quill puts both local businesses and many interstate businesses with physical presence at a competitive disadvantage relative to remote sellers. Remote sellers can avoid the regulatory burdens of tax collection and can offer *de facto* lower prices caused by the widespread failure of consumers to pay the tax on their own. This "guarantees a competitive benefit to certain firms simply because of the organizational form they choose" while the rest of the Court's jurisprudence "is all about preventing discrimination between firms." In effect, *Quill* has come to serve as a judicially created tax shelter for businesses that decide to limit their physical presence and still sell their goods and services to a State's consumers—something that has become easier and more prevalent as technology has advanced.

Worse still, the rule produces an incentive to avoid physical presence in multiple States. Distortions caused by the desire of businesses to avoid tax collection mean that the market may currently lack storefronts, distribution points, and employment centers that otherwise would be efficient or desirable. The Commerce Clause must not prefer interstate commerce only to the point where a merchant physically crosses state borders. Rejecting the physical presence rule is necessary to ensure that artificial competitive advantages are not created by this Court's precedents. This Court should not prevent States from collecting lawful taxes through a physical presence rule that can be satisfied only if there is an employee or a building in the State. . . .

The *Quill* Court itself acknowledged that the physical presence rule is "artificial at its edges." That was an understatement when *Quill* was decided; and when the day-to-day functions of marketing and distribution in the modern economy are considered, it is all the more evident that the physical presence rule is artificial in its entirety.

Modern e-commerce does not align analytically with a test that relies on the sort of physical presence defined in *Quill.* . . . The "dramatic technological and social changes" of our "increasingly interconnected economy" mean that buyers are "closer to most major retailers" than ever before—"regardless of how close or far the nearest storefront." Between targeted advertising and instant access to most consumers via any internet-enabled device, "a business may be present in a State in a meaningful way without" that presence "being physical in the traditional sense of the term." A virtual showroom can show far more inventory, in far more detail, and with greater opportunities for consumer and seller interaction than might be possible for local stores. Yet the continuous and pervasive virtual presence of retailers today is, under *Quill,* simply irrelevant. This Court should not maintain a rule that ignores these substantial virtual connections to the State. . . .

"Although we approach the reconsideration of our decisions with the utmost caution, *stare decisis* is not an inexorable command." Here, *stare decisis* can no longer support the Court's prohibition of a valid exercise of the States' sovereign power.

If it becomes apparent that the Court's Commerce Clause decisions prohibit the States from exercising their lawful sovereign powers in our federal system, the Court should be vigilant in correcting the error. While it can be conceded that Congress has the authority to change the physical presence rule, Congress cannot change the constitutional default rule. It is inconsistent with the Court's proper role to ask Congress to address a false constitutional premise of this Court's own creation. Courts have acted as the front line of review in this limited sphere; and hence it is important that their principles be accurate and logical, whether or not Congress can or will act in response. It is currently the Court, and not Congress, that is limiting the lawful prerogatives of the States.

Further, the real world implementation of Commerce Clause doctrines now makes it manifest that the physical presence rule as defined by *Quill* must give way to the "far-reaching systemic and structural changes in the economy" and "many other societal dimensions" caused by the Cyber Age. Though *Quill* was wrong on its own terms when it was decided in 1992, since then the Internet revolution has made its earlier error all the more egregious and harmful.

The *Quill* Court did not have before it the present realities of the interstate marketplace. . . . When it decided *Quill,* the Court could not have envisioned a world in which the world's largest retailer would be a remote seller. The Internet's prevalence and power have changed the dynamics of the national economy. . . .

Reliance interests are a legitimate consideration when the Court weighs adherence to an earlier but flawed precedent. But even on its own terms, the physical presence rule as defined by *Quill* is no longer a clear or easily applicable standard, so arguments for reliance based on its clarity are misplaced. And, importantly, *stare decisis* accommodates only "legitimate reliance interest[s]." Here, the tax distortion created by *Quill* exists in large part because consumers regularly fail to comply with lawful use taxes. Some remote retailers go so far as to advertise sales as tax free. A business "is in no position to found a constitutional right on the practical opportunities for tax avoidance." . . .

For these reasons, the Court concludes that the physical presence rule of *Quill* is unsound and incorrect. The Court's decisions in *Quill Corp. v. North Dakota* and *National Bellas Hess, Inc. v. Department of Revenue of Ill.* should be, and now are, overruled.

In the absence of *Quill* and *Bellas Hess,* the first prong of the *Complete Auto* test simply asks whether the tax applies to an activity with a substantial nexus with the taxing State. "[S]uch a nexus is established when the taxpayer [or collector] 'avails itself of the substantial privilege of carrying on business' in that jurisdiction."

Here, the nexus is clearly sufficient based on both the economic and virtual contacts respondents have with the State. The Act applies only to sellers that deliver more than $100,000 of goods or services into South Dakota or engage in 200 or more separate transactions for the delivery of goods and services into the State on an annual basis. This quantity of business could not have occurred unless the seller availed itself of the substantial privilege of carrying on business in South Dakota. And respondents are large, national companies that undoubtedly maintain an extensive virtual presence. Thus, the substantial nexus requirement of *Complete Auto* is satisfied in this case.

The question remains whether some other principle in the Court's Commerce Clause doctrine might invalidate the Act. Because the *Quill* physical presence rule was an obvious barrier to the Act's validity, these issues have not yet been litigated or briefed, and so the Court need not resolve them here. That said, South Dakota's tax system includes several features that appear designed to prevent discrimination against or undue burdens upon interstate commerce. First, the Act applies a safe harbor to those who transact only limited business in South Dakota. Second, the Act ensures that no obligation to remit the sales tax may be applied retroactively. Third, South Dakota is one of more than 20 States that have adopted the Streamlined Sales and Use Tax Agreement. This system standardizes taxes to reduce administrative and compliance costs: It requires a single, state level tax administration, uniform definitions of products and services, simplified tax rate structures, and other uniform rules. It also provides sellers access to sales tax administration software paid for by the State. Sellers who choose to use such software are immune from audit liability. Any remaining claims regarding the application of the Commerce Clause in the absence of *Quill* and *Bellas Hess* may be addressed in the first instance on remand.

JUSTICE THOMAS, concurring. [Opinion omitted. Justice Thomas wrote to restate his view that the Court's "entire negative Commerce Clause jurisprudence" "can no longer be rationally justified." In other words, no more dormant commerce clause.]

JUSTICE GORSUCH, concurring. [Opinion omitted. Justice Gorsuch wrote to make clear that by concurring in this opinion he does not mean to indicate that he agrees with the Court's dormant commerce clause jurisprudence generally. While not going so far as Justice Thomas, he indicated that he is open to reconsidering the Court's entire dormant commerce clause jurisprudence.]

CHIEF JUSTICE ROBERTS, with whom JUSTICE BREYER, JUSTICE SOTOMAYOR, and JUSTICE KAGAN join, dissenting. [Opinion omitted. The thrust of the dissent is that as bad as *Bellas Hess* and *Quill* might be, it is more appropriate for Congress to address the issue than for the Court to overrule those cases. He noted that the Court "does not overturn its precedents lightly." Departing from the doctrine of *stare decisis* is an "exceptional action" demanding "special justification," and the bar is even higher in fields in which Congress "exercises primary authority" and can, if it wishes, override the Court's decisions with contrary legislation.]

COMMENTS AND QUESTIONS

1.   The outcome in this case was widely anticipated given the negative effects of the physical presence rule, yet the decision was still 5–4, because of the doctrine of *stare decisis*, which is stronger in statutory cases than in constitutional cases, because of the ability of Congress to "correct" the Court's decisions based on statutory law. Why didn't Congress correct the "problem" caused by *Bellas Hess* and *Quill* years ago?

2.   As one of the most recent Dormant Commerce Clause cases from the Supreme Court, *Wayfair* gives hints as to the future of Dormant Commerce Clause jurisprudence. Justice Kennedy writing for the majority makes much of the increasingly pragmatic nature of that jurisprudence and he calls out the fact that the Dormant Commerce Clause involves the Court interfering with the sovereignty of states. Justice Thomas clearly and Justice Gorsuch apparently seem willing to jettison the Dormant Commerce Clause entirely on the basis that there is no textual support for it in the Constitution. If they prevailed, it would certainly shorten the Constitutional Law casebooks.

3.   THE MARKET PARTICIPANT DOCTRINE

In all of the above Dormant Commerce Clause cases, the state or locality acted as a market regulator. Does it make any difference if the state or locality's restriction on interstate commerce occurs as a market participant?

REEVES, INC. V. STAKE
United States Supreme Court, 1980.
447 U.S. 429, 100 S.Ct. 2271.

MR. JUSTICE BLACKMUN delivered the opinion of the Court.

The issue in this case is whether, consistent with the Commerce Clause, the State of South Dakota, in a time of shortage, may confine the sale of the cement it produces solely to its residents.

In 1919, South Dakota undertook plans to build a cement plant. The project, a product of the State's then prevailing Progressive political movement, was initiated in response to recent regional

Dacotah Cement plant in Rapid City, S.D.

cement shortages that "interfered with and delayed both public and private enterprises," and that were "threatening the people of this state." In 1920, the South Dakota Cement Commission anticipated "[t]hat there would be a ready market for the entire output of the plant within the state." The plant, however, . . . soon produced more cement than South Dakotans could use. Over the years, buyers in no less than nine nearby States purchased cement from the State's plant. Between 1970 and 1977, some 40% of the plant's output went outside the State.

The plant's list of out-of-state cement buyers included petitioner Reeves, Inc. . . . For 20 years the relationship between Reeves and the South Dakota cement plant was amicable, uninterrupted, and mutually profitable.

As the 1978 construction season approached, difficulties at the plant slowed production. Meanwhile, a booming construction industry spurred demand for cement both regionally and nationally. The plant found itself unable to meet all orders. Faced with the same type of "serious cement shortage" that inspired the plant's construction, the Commission "reaffirmed its policy of supplying all South Dakota customers first and to honor all contract commitments, with the remaining volume allocated on a first come, first served basis."

Reeves, which had no pre-existing long-term supply contract, was hit hard and quickly by this development. . . . On July 19, Reeves brought this suit against the Commission, challenging the plant's policy of preferring South Dakota buyers, and seeking injunctive relief. [T]he District Court found no substantial issue of material fact and permanently enjoined the Commission's practice. The court reasoned that South Dakota's "hoarding" was inimical to the national free market envisioned by the Commerce Clause.

The United States Court of Appeals for the Eighth Circuit reversed. . . . We granted Reeves's petition for certiorari to consider once again. the impact of the Commerce Clause on state proprietary activity.

[In *Hughes v. Alexandria Scrap Corp.*, 426 U.S. 794 (1976) we considered] a Maryland program designed to remove abandoned automobiles from the State's roadways and junkyards. To encourage recycling, a "bounty" was offered for every Maryland-titled junk car converted into scrap. . . . [T]he . . . law imposed more exacting documentation requirements on out-of-state than in-state processors. . . . Indeed, "[t]he practical effect was substantially the same as if Maryland had withdrawn altogether the availability of bounties on hulks delivered by . . . suppliers to . . . non-Maryland processors."

Invoking the Commerce Clause, a three-judge District Court struck down the legislation. . . .

This Court reversed. . . . In the Court's view . . . *Alexandria Scrap* did not involve "the kind of action with which the Commerce Clause is concerned." Unlike prior cases voiding state laws inhibiting interstate trade, "Maryland has not sought to prohibit the flow of hulks, or to regulate the conditions under which it may occur. Instead, it has entered into the market itself to bid up their price," "as a purchaser, in effect, of a potential article of interstate commerce," and has restricted "its trade to its own citizens or businesses within the State."

Having characterized Maryland as a market participant, rather than as a market regulator, the Court found no reason to "believe the Commerce Clause was intended to require independent justification for [the State's] action." The Court couched its holding in unmistakably broad terms. "Nothing in the purposes animating the Commerce Clause prohibits a State, in the absence of congressional action, from participating in the market and exercising the right to favor its own citizens over others."

The basic distinction drawn in *Alexandria Scrap* between States as market participants and States as market regulators makes good sense and sound law. As that case explains, the Commerce Clause responds principally to state taxes and regulatory measures impeding free private trade in the national marketplace. There is no indication of a constitutional plan to limit the ability of the States themselves to operate freely in the free market. The precedents comport with this distinction.

Restraint in this area is also counseled by considerations of state sovereignty, the role of each State " 'as guardian and trustee for its people,' " and "the long recognized right of trader or manufacturer, engaged in an entirely private business, freely to exercise his own independent discretion as to parties with whom he will deal."[12] Moreover, state proprietary activities may be, and often are, burdened with the same restrictions imposed on private market participants. Evenhandedness suggests that, when acting as proprietors, States should similarly share existing freedoms from federal constraints, including the inherent limits of the Commerce Clause. Finally, as this case illustrates, the competing considerations in cases involving state proprietary action often will be subtle, complex, politically charged, and difficult to assess under traditional Commerce Clause analysis. Given these factors, *Alexandria Scrap* wisely recognizes that, as a rule, the adjustment of interests in this context is a task better suited for Congress than this Court.

---

[12] When a State buys or sells, it has the attributes of both a political entity and a private business. Nonetheless, the dissent would dismiss altogether the "private business" element of such activity and focus solely on the State's political character. The Court, however, heretofore has recognized that "[l]ike private individuals and businesses, the Government enjoys the unrestricted power to produce its own supplies, to determine those with whom it will deal, and to fix the terms and conditions upon which it will make needed purchases." While acknowledging that there may be limits on this sweepingly phrased principle, we cannot ignore the similarities of private businesses and public entities when they function in the marketplace.

South Dakota, as a seller of cement, unquestionably fits the "market participant" label more comfortably than a State acting to subsidize local scrap processors. Thus, the general rule of *Alexandria Scrap* plainly applies here. Petitioner argues, however, that the exemption for marketplace participation necessarily admits of exceptions. While conceding that possibility, we perceive in this case no sufficient reason to depart from the general rule. . . .

Undaunted by these considerations, petitioner advances [other] arguments for reversal:

> "If a state in this union, were allowed to hoard its commodities or resources for the use of their own residents only, a drastic situation might evolve. For example, Pennsylvania or Wyoming might keep their coal, the northwest its timber, and the mining states their minerals. The result being that embargo may be retaliated by embargo and commerce would be halted at state lines."

This argument, although rooted in the core purpose of the Commerce Clause, does not fit the present facts. Cement is not a natural resource, like coal, timber, wild game, or minerals. It is the end product of a complex process whereby a costly physical plant and human labor act on raw materials. South Dakota has not sought to limit access to the State's limestone or other materials used to make cement. Nor has it restricted the ability of private firms or sister States to set up plants within its borders. Moreover, petitioner has not suggested that South Dakota possesses unique access to the materials needed to produce cement. Whatever limits might exist on a State's ability to invoke the *Alexandria Scrap* exemption to hoard resources which by happenstance are found there, those limits do not apply here. . . .

MR. JUSTICE POWELL, with whom MR. JUSTICE BRENNAN, MR. JUSTICE WHITE, and MR. JUSTICE STEVENS join, dissenting.

The South Dakota Cement Commission has ordered that in times of shortage the state cement plant must turn away out-of-state customers until all orders from South Dakotans are filled. This policy represents precisely the kind of economic protectionism that the Commerce Clause was intended to prevent.[1] The Court, however, finds no violation of the Commerce Clause, solely because the State produces the cement. I agree with the Court that the State of South Dakota may provide cement for its public needs without violating the Commerce Clause. But I cannot agree

---

[1]   By "protectionism," I refer to state policies designed to protect private economic interests within the State from the forces of the interstate market. I would exclude from this term policies relating to traditional governmental functions, such as education, and subsidy programs like the one at issue in *Hughes v. Alexandria Scrap Corp.*

that South Dakota may withhold its cement from interstate commerce in order to benefit private citizens and businesses within the State. . . .

This case presents a novel constitutional question. The Commerce Clause would bar legislation imposing on private parties the type of restraint on commerce adopted by South Dakota. Conversely, a private business constitutionally could adopt a marketing policy that excluded customers who come from another State. This case falls between those polar situations. The State, through its Commission, engages in a commercial enterprise and restricts its own interstate distribution. The question is whether the Commission's policy should be treated like state regulation of private parties or like the marketing policy of a private business.

The application of the Commerce Clause to this case should turn on the nature of the governmental activity involved. If a public enterprise undertakes an "integral operatio[n] in areas of traditional governmental functions," *National League of Cities v. Usery*, the Commerce Clause is not directly relevant. If, however, the State enters the private market and operates a commercial enterprise for the advantage of its private citizens, it may not evade the constitutional policy against economic Balkanization.

This distinction derives from the power of governments to supply their own needs and from the purpose of the Commerce Clause itself, which is designed to protect "the natural functioning of the interstate market." In procuring goods and services for the operation of government, a State may act without regard to the private marketplace and remove itself from the reach of the Commerce Clause. But when a State itself becomes a participant in the private market for other purposes, the Constitution forbids actions that would impede the flow of interstate commerce. . . .

The Court holds that South Dakota, like a private business, should not be governed by the Commerce Clause when it enters the private market. But precisely because South Dakota is a State, it cannot be presumed to behave like an enterprise " 'engaged in an entirely private business.' " A State frequently will respond to market conditions on the basis of political rather than economic concerns. To use the Court's terms, a State may attempt to act as a "market regulator" rather than a "market participant." In that situation, it is a pretense to equate the State with a private economic actor. State action burdening interstate trade is no less state action because it is accomplished by a public agency authorized to participate in the private market. . . .

Unlike the market subsidies at issue in *Alexandria Scrap*, the marketing policy of the South Dakota Cement Commission has cut off interstate trade. The State can raise such a bar when it enters the market to supply its own needs. In order to ensure an adequate supply of cement for public uses, the State can withhold from interstate commerce the cement needed for public projects.

The State, however, has no parallel justification for favoring private, in-state customers over out-of-state customers. In response to political concerns that likely would be inconsequential to a private cement producer, South Dakota has shut off its cement sales to customers beyond its borders. That discrimination constitutes a direct barrier to trade "of the type forbidden by the Commerce Clause, and involved in previous cases. . . ." The effect on interstate trade is the same as if the state legislature had imposed the policy on private cement producers. The Commerce Clause prohibits this severe restraint on commerce. . . .

COMMENTS AND QUESTIONS

1.   Both the majority and the dissent recognize that this case falls between the two endpoints of clear law—the Commerce Clause forbids states to enact protectionist regulatory laws, but the Commerce Clause imposes no limits on whom private companies can choose to deal with. The question in *Reeves* is which of these two endpoints is closer to the facts in that case. The dissent believes it is the former, while the majority believes it is the latter. Which do you think is closer?

2.   The majority relies heavily on *Alexandria Scrap*, but the dissent distinguishes that case on the basis that there the state was using state funds to subsidize the scrapping of old automobiles, while here the state, at least by this time, is running the cement plant out of the plant's operating funds. Do you think that is relevant? The dissent also distinguishes producing cement for the state's own needs as opposed to being a market participant, citing *National League of Cities*. Do you recall that case under the Tenth Amendment portion of this chapter? It was overruled in *Garcia v. SAMTA*.

3.   The petitioner tries to characterize the facts in *Reeves* as the state hoarding a natural resource, and the majority distinguishes a cement plant from a state's natural resources, such as coal, timber, wild game, or minerals. Do you think restricting the output of the state's cement plant is like hoarding the natural resources in the state? Consider the following case.

SOUTH-CENTRAL TIMBER DEVELOPMENT, INC. V. WUNNICKE

United States Supreme Court, 1984.
467 U.S. 82, 104 S.Ct. 2237.

JUSTICE WHITE announced the judgment of the Court and delivered the opinion of the Court with respect to Parts I and II, and an opinion with respect to Parts III and IV, in which JUSTICE BRENNAN, JUSTICE BLACKMUN, and JUSTICE STEVENS joined.

* * *

I

In September 1980, the Alaska Department of Natural Resources published a notice that it would sell approximately 49 million board-feet of timber in the area of Icy Cape, Alaska, on October 23, 1980. The notice of sale, the prospectus, and the proposed contract for the sale all provided, pursuant to [Alaska law] that "[p]rimary manufacture within the State of Alaska will be required as a special provision of the contract." Under the primary-manufacture requirement, the successful bidder must partially process the timber prior to shipping it outside of the State. The requirement is imposed by contract and does not limit the export of unprocessed timber not owned by the State. . . . When it imposes the requirement, the State charges a significantly lower price for the timber than it otherwise would.

Petitioner, South-Central Timber Development, Inc., is an Alaska corporation engaged in the business of purchasing standing timber, logging the timber, and shipping the logs into foreign commerce, almost exclusively to Japan. . . . [I]t brought an action in Federal District Court seeking an injunction, arguing that the requirement violated the negative implications of the Commerce Clause. The District Court agreed and issued an injunction. The Court of Appeals for the Ninth Circuit reversed, finding it unnecessary to reach the question whether, standing alone, the requirement would violate the Commerce Clause, because it found implicit congressional authorization in the federal policy of imposing a primary-manufacture requirement on timber taken from federal land in Alaska.

II

[The Court concluded that the fact that Congress imposed a primary-manufacture requirement on timber from federal land in Alaska did not implicitly authorize Alaska to impose a similar requirement with respect to state lands.]

III

We now turn to the issues left unresolved by the Court of Appeals. The first of these issues is whether Alaska's restrictions on export of unprocessed timber from state-owned lands are exempt from Commerce Clause scrutiny under the "market-participant doctrine."

Our cases make clear that if a State is acting as a market participant, rather than as a market regulator, the dormant Commerce Clause places no limitation on its activities. The precise contours of the market-participant doctrine have yet to be established, however, the doctrine having been applied in only three cases of this Court to date.

The first of the cases, *Hughes v. Alexandria Scrap Corp.*, involved a Maryland program designed to reduce the number of junked automobiles in the State. A "bounty" was established on Maryland-licensed junk cars, and the State imposed more stringent documentation requirements on out-of-state scrap processors than on in-state ones. The Court rejected a Commerce Clause attack on the program, although it noted that under traditional Commerce Clause analysis the program might well be invalid because it had the effect of reducing the flow of goods in interstate commerce. . . .

In *Reeves, Inc. v. Stake*, the Court upheld a South Dakota policy of restricting the sale of cement from a state-owned plant to state residents, declaring that "[t]he basic distinction drawn in Alexandria Scrap between States as market participants and States as market regulators makes good sense and sound law." The Court relied upon " 'the long recognized right of trader or manufacturer, engaged in an entirely private business, freely to exercise his own independent discretion as to parties with whom he will deal.' " In essence, the Court recognized the principle that the Commerce Clause places no limitations on a State's refusal to deal with particular parties when it is participating in the interstate market in goods.

The most recent of this Court's cases developing the market-participant doctrine is *White v. Massachusetts Council of Construction Employers, Inc.*, 460 U.S. 204 (1983), in which the Court sustained against a Commerce Clause challenge an executive order of the Mayor of Boston that required all construction projects funded in whole or in part by city funds or city-administered funds to be performed by a work force of at least 50% city residents. The Court rejected the argument that the city was not entitled to the protection of the doctrine because the order had the effect of regulating employment contracts between public contractors and their employees. Recognizing that "there are some limits on a state or local government's ability to impose restrictions that reach beyond the immediate parties with which the government transacts business," the Court found it unnecessary to define those limits because "[e]veryone affected by the order [was], in a substantial if informal sense, 'working for the city.' " The fact that the employees were "working for the city" was "crucial" to the market-participant analysis in *White*.

The State of Alaska contends that its primary-manufacture requirement fits squarely within the market-participant doctrine, arguing that "Alaska's entry into the market may be viewed as precisely the same type of subsidy to local interests that the Court found unobjectionable in *Alexandria Scrap*." However, when Maryland became involved in the scrap market it was as a purchaser of scrap; Alaska, on the other hand, participates in the timber market, but imposes conditions downstream in the timber-processing market. Alaska is not merely subsidizing local timber processing in an amount "roughly equal to the difference between the price the timber would fetch in the absence of such a requirement and the amount the state actually receives." If the State directly subsidized the timber-processing industry by such an amount, the purchaser would retain the option of taking advantage of the subsidy by processing timber in the State or forgoing the benefits of the subsidy and exporting unprocessed timber. Under the Alaska requirement, however, the choice is made for him: if he buys timber from the State he is not free to take the timber out of state prior to processing.

The State also would have us find *Reeves* controlling. It states that "*Reeves* made it clear that the Commerce Clause imposes no limitation on Alaska's power to choose the terms on which it will sell its timber." Such an unrestrained reading of *Reeves* is unwarranted. Although the Court in *Reeves* did strongly endorse the right of a State to deal with whomever it chooses when it participates in the market, it did not—and did not purport to—sanction the imposition of any terms that the State might desire. For example, the Court expressly noted in *Reeves* that Commerce Clause scrutiny may well be more rigorous when a restraint on foreign commerce is alleged; that a natural resource "like coal, timber, wild game, or minerals," was not involved, but instead the cement was "the end product of a complex process whereby a costly physical plant and human labor act on raw materials,"; and that South Dakota did not bar resale of South Dakota cement to out-of-state purchasers. In this case, all three of the elements that were not present in *Reeves*—foreign commerce, a natural resource, and restrictions on resale—are present.

Finally, Alaska argues that since the Court in *White* upheld a requirement that reached beyond "the boundary of formal privity of contract," then, a fortiori, the primary-manufacture requirement is permissible, because the State is not regulating contracts for resale of timber or regulating the buying and selling of timber, but is instead "a seller of timber, pure and simple." Yet it is clear that the State is more than merely a seller of timber. In the commercial context, the seller usually has no say over, and no interest in, how the product is to be used after sale; in this case, however, payment for the timber does not end the obligations of the purchaser, for, despite the fact that the purchaser has taken delivery of the timber and has paid for it, he cannot do with it as he pleases. Instead, he is obligated to deal with a stranger to the contract after completion of the sale.

That privity of contract is not always the outer boundary of permissible state activity does not necessarily mean that the Commerce Clause has no application within the boundary of formal privity. The market-participant doctrine permits a State to influence "a discrete, identifiable class of economic activity in which [it] is a major participant." *White*. Contrary to the State's contention, the doctrine is not carte blanche to impose any conditions that the State has the economic power to dictate, and does not validate any requirement merely because the State imposes it upon someone with whom it is in contractual privity.

The limit of the market-participant doctrine must be that it allows a State to impose burdens on commerce within the market in which it is a participant, but allows it to go no further. The State may not impose conditions, whether by statute, regulation, or contract, that have a substantial regulatory effect outside of that particular market. Unless the "market" is relatively narrowly defined, the doctrine has the potential of swallowing up the rule that States may not impose substantial burdens on interstate commerce even if they act with the permissible state purpose of fostering local industry. . . .

There are sound reasons for distinguishing between a State's preferring its own residents in the initial disposition of goods when it is a market participant and a State's attachment of restrictions on dispositions subsequent to the goods coming to rest in private hands. First, simply as a matter of intuition a state market participant has a greater interest as a "private trader" in the immediate transaction than it has in what its purchaser does with the goods after the State no longer has an interest in them. . . .

Second, downstream restrictions have a greater regulatory effect than do limitations on the immediate transaction. Instead of merely choosing its own trading partners, the State is attempting to govern the private, separate economic relationships of its trading partners; that is, it restricts the post-purchase activity of the purchaser, rather than merely the purchasing activity. In contrast to the situation in *White*, this restriction on private economic activity takes place after the completion of the parties' direct commercial obligations, rather than during the course of an ongoing commercial relationship in which the city retained a continuing proprietary interest in the subject of the contract. In sum, the State may not avail itself of the market-participant doctrine to immunize its downstream regulation of the timber-processing market in which it is not a participant. . . .

IV

[Justice White then concluded that the primary-manufacture requirement substantially burdened foreign commerce and thus was prohibited by the Dormant Commerce Clause.]

JUSTICE MARSHALL took no part in the decision of this case.

JUSTICE BRENNAN, concurring. [omitted]

JUSTICE POWELL, with whom THE CHIEF JUSTICE joins, concurring in part and concurring in the judgment.

I join Parts I and II of Justice WHITE's opinion. I would remand the case to the Court of Appeals to allow that court to consider whether Alaska was acting as a "market participant" and whether Alaska's primary-manufacture requirement substantially burdened interstate commerce under the holding of *Pike v. Bruce Church, Inc.*

JUSTICE REHNQUIST, with whom JUSTICE O'CONNOR joins, dissenting.

In my view, the line of distinction drawn in the plurality opinion between the State as market participant and the State as market regulator is both artificial and unconvincing. The plurality draws this line "simply as a matter of intuition," but then seeks to bolster its intuition through a series of remarks more appropriate to antitrust law than to the Commerce Clause.[1] For example, the plurality complains that the State is using its "leverage" in the timber market to distort consumer choice in the timber-processing market, a classic example of a tying arrangement. And the plurality cites the common-law doctrine of restraints on alienation and the antitrust limits on vertical restraints in dismissing the State's claim that it could accomplish exactly the same result in other ways.

Perhaps the State's actions do raise antitrust problems. But what the plurality overlooks is that the antitrust laws apply to a State only when it is acting as a market participant. When the State acts as a market regulator, it is immune from antitrust scrutiny. Of course, the line of distinction in cases under the Commerce Clause need not necessarily parallel the line drawn in antitrust law. But the plurality can hardly justify placing Alaska in the market-regulator category, in this Commerce Clause case, by relying on antitrust cases that are relevant only if the State is a market participant.

The contractual term at issue here no more transforms Alaska's sale of timber into "regulation" of the processing industry than the resident-hiring preference imposed by the city of Boston in *White* constituted regulation of the construction industry. Alaska is merely paying the buyer of the timber indirectly, by means of a reduced price, to hire Alaska residents to process the timber. Under existing precedent, the State could accomplish that same result in any number of ways. For example, the State could choose to sell its timber only to those companies that maintain active primary-processing plants in Alaska. *Reeves.* Or the State could directly subsidize the primary-processing industry within the State. *Hughes v. Alexandria Scrap Corp.* The State could even pay to have the logs processed and then enter the market only to sell processed logs. It seems to me unduly formalistic to conclude that the one path chosen by the State as best suited to promote its concerns is the path forbidden it by the Commerce Clause.

---

[1]   The plurality does offer one other reason for its demarcation of the boundary between these two concepts. "[D]ownstream restrictions have a greater regulatory effect than do limitations on the immediate transaction. Instead of merely choosing its own trading partners, the State is attempting to govern the private, separate economic relationships of its trading partners; that is, it restricts the post-purchase activity of the purchaser, rather than merely the purchasing activity." But, of course, this is not a "reason" at all, but merely a restatement of the conclusion. The line between participation and regulation is what we are trying to determine. To invoke that very distinction in support of the line drawn is merely to fall back again on intuition.

COMMENTS AND QUESTIONS

1.   Count the votes in this case. Is there an opinion for the Court on the Market Participant Doctrine?

2.   Note that *Reeves* was a 5–4 decision, with Justice Blackmun writing the majority opinion, but in *Wunnicke* Justice Blackmun joins the *Reeves*'s dissenters. Recall that it was Justice Blackmun who defected from the 5–4 majority of *National League of Cities v. Usery* to write the opinion in *Garcia v. SAMTA* overruling *National League of Cities*. Is this another signal of the judicial conversion of Justice Blackmun from a "conservative" to a "liberal" justice?

3.   *Wunnicke* involves a state's natural resources. Is that what results in a different outcome from *Reeves*? When *Reeves* referred to a state's natural resources, it was probably referring to natural resources that simply happened to be found within the state, not to resources actually owned by the state. Here the timber was actually owned by the state.

4.   Justice Rehnquist's dissent points out that private sellers can, and sometimes do, impose "downstream conditions" on customers, although under certain circumstances such tying arrangements may run afoul of the antitrust laws. Why does the plurality not treat Alaska like such a private seller?

5.   Do you find it strange that the federal government by statute would restrict sales of federal timber in Alaska to persons who would process it in Alaska, and yet the Court finds no federal approval of Alaska making an identical restriction for state-owned timber?

6.   Justice Rehnquist's last paragraph identifies certain ways Alaska could reach the same result without running afoul of the Dormant Commerce Clause. Why then should the Dormant Commerce Clause prohibit this particular way? In our past cases, have we ever seen the Court strike down a law whose result could have been achieved through a different means?

7.   In *McBurney v. Young*, 569 U.S. 221 (2013), the Court utilized the market participant exception to uphold a state's refusal to extend its public records law to out-of-staters.

UNITED HAULERS ASS'N V. ONEIDA-HERKIMER SOLID WASTE MANAGEMENT AUTHORITY

United States Supreme Court, 2007.
550 U.S. 330, 127 S.Ct. 1786.

CHIEF JUSTICE ROBERTS delivered the opinion of the Court, except as to Part II-D.

"Flow control" ordinances require trash haulers to deliver solid waste to a particular waste processing facility. In *C & A Carbone, Inc. v. Clarkstown*, this Court struck down under the Commerce Clause a flow control ordinance that forced haulers to deliver waste to a particular *private* processing facility. In this case, we face flow control ordinances quite similar to the one invalidated in *Carbone*. The only salient difference is that the laws at issue here require haulers to bring waste to facilities owned and operated by a state-created public benefit corporation. We find this difference constitutionally significant. Disposing of trash has been a traditional government activity for years, and laws that favor the government in such areas—but treat every private business, whether in-state or out-of-state, exactly the same—do not discriminate against interstate commerce for purposes of the Commerce Clause. Applying the Commerce Clause test reserved for regulations that do not discriminate against interstate commerce, we uphold these ordinances because any incidental burden they may have on interstate commerce does not outweigh the benefits they confer on the citizens of Oneida and Herkimer Counties.

I

[R]esponding to [a number of local] problems involving the disposal of solid waste, the Counties requested and New York's Legislature and Governor created the Oneida-Herkimer Solid Waste Management Authority (Authority), a public benefit corporation. . . .

In 1989, the Authority and the Counties entered into a Solid Waste Management Agreement, under which the Authority agreed to manage all solid waste within the Counties. Private haulers would remain free to pick up citizens' trash from the curb, but the Authority would take over the job of processing the trash, sorting it, and sending it off for disposal. To fulfill its part of the bargain, the Authority agreed to purchase and develop facilities for the processing and disposal of solid waste and recyclables generated in the Counties.

The Authority collected "tipping fees"[1] to cover its operating and maintenance costs for these facilities. The tipping fees significantly exceeded those charged for waste removal on the open market, but they allowed the Authority to do more than the average private waste disposer. In addition to landfill transportation and solid waste disposal, the fees enabled the Authority to provide recycling of 33 kinds of materials, as well as composting, household hazardous waste disposal, and a number of other services. . . .

As described, the agreement had a flaw: Citizens might opt to have their waste hauled to facilities with lower tipping fees. To avoid being stuck with the bill for facilities that citizens voted for but then chose not to use, the Counties enacted "flow control" ordinances requiring that all solid waste generated within the Counties be delivered to the Authority's processing sites. Private haulers must obtain a permit from the Authority

---

[1]   Tipping fees are disposal charges levied against collectors who drop off waste at a processing facility. They are called "tipping" fees because garbage trucks literally tip their back end to dump out the carried waste. . . .

to collect waste in the Counties. Penalties for noncompliance with the ordinances include permit revocation, fines, and imprisonment.

Petitioners are United Haulers Association, Inc., a trade association made up of solid waste management companies, and six haulers that operated in Oneida and Herkimer Counties when this action was filed. In 1995, they sued the Counties and the Authority . . ., alleging that the flow control laws violate the Commerce Clause by discriminating against interstate commerce. They submitted evidence that without the flow control laws and the associated $86-per-ton tipping fees, they could dispose of solid waste at out-of-state facilities for between $37 and $55 per ton, including transportation.

The District Court read our decision in *Carbone* as categorically rejecting nearly all flow control laws. The court ruled in the haulers' favor, enjoining enforcement of the Counties' laws. The Second Circuit reversed. . . . Because the Sixth Circuit had recently issued a conflicting decision holding that a flow control ordinance favoring a public entity *does* facially discriminate against interstate commerce, we granted certiorari.

II

A

[T]o determine whether a law violates this so-called "dormant" aspect of the Commerce Clause, we first ask whether it discriminates on its face against interstate commerce. In this context, " 'discrimination' simply means differential treatment of in-state and out-of-state economic interests that benefits the former and burdens the latter." Discriminatory laws motivated by "simple economic protectionism" are subject to a "virtually *per se* rule of invalidity," which can only be overcome by a showing that the State has no other means to advance a legitimate local purpose.

B

[T]he haulers argue vigorously that the Counties' ordinances discriminate against interstate commerce under *Carbone*. . . . [There the] Court struck down the ordinance, holding that it discriminated against interstate commerce by "hoard[ing] solid waste, and the demand to get rid of it, for the benefit of the preferred processing facility." . . .

The *Carbone* majority viewed Clarkstown's flow control ordinance as "just one more instance of local processing requirements that we long have held invalid." It then cited six local processing cases, every one of which involved discrimination in favor of *private* enterprise. The Court's own description of the cases acknowledges that the "offending local laws hoard a local resource—be it meat, shrimp, or milk—for the benefit of *local businesses* that treat it." If the Court were extending this line of local processing cases to cover discrimination in favor of local government, one would expect it to have said so. . . .

C

The flow control ordinances in this case benefit a clearly public facility, while treating all private companies exactly the same. Because the question is now squarely presented on the facts of the case before us, we decide that such flow control ordinances do not discriminate against interstate commerce for purposes of the dormant Commerce Clause.

Compelling reasons justify treating these laws differently from laws favoring particular private businesses over their competitors. [S]tates and municipalities are not private businesses—far from it. Unlike private enterprise, government is vested with the responsibility of protecting the health, safety, and welfare of its citizens. These important responsibilities set state and local government apart from a typical private business.

Given these differences, it does not make sense to regard laws favoring local government and laws favoring private industry with equal skepticism. As our local processing cases demonstrate, when a law favors in-state business over out-of-state competition, rigorous scrutiny is appropriate because the law is often the product of "simple economic protectionism." Laws favoring local government, by contrast, may be directed toward any number of legitimate goals unrelated to protectionism. Here the flow control ordinances enable the Counties to pursue particular policies with respect to the handling and treatment of waste generated in the Counties, while allocating the costs of those policies on citizens and businesses according to the volume of waste they generate.

The contrary approach of treating public and private entities the same under the dormant Commerce Clause would lead to unprecedented and unbounded interference by the courts with state and local government. The dormant Commerce Clause is not a roving license for federal courts to decide what activities are appropriate for state and local government to undertake, and what activities must be the province of private market competition. In this case, the citizens of Oneida and Herkimer Counties have chosen the government to provide waste management services, with a limited role for the private sector in arranging for transport of waste from the curb to the public facilities. The citizens could have left the entire matter for the private sector, in which case any regulation they undertook could not discriminate against interstate commerce. But it was also open to them to vest responsibility for the matter with their government, and to adopt flow control ordinances to support the government effort. It is not the office of the Commerce Clause to control the decision of the voters on whether government or the private sector should provide waste management services.

We should be particularly hesitant to interfere with the Counties' efforts under the guise of the Commerce Clause because "[w]aste disposal is both typically and traditionally a local government function." . . .

Finally, it bears mentioning that the most palpable harm imposed by the ordinances—more expensive trash removal—is likely to fall upon the very people who voted for the laws. Our dormant Commerce Clause cases often find discrimination when a State shifts the costs of regulation to other States, because when "the burden of state regulation falls on interests outside the state, it is unlikely to be alleviated by the operation of those political restraints normally exerted when interests within the state are affected." . . .

We hold that the Counties' flow control ordinances, which treat in-state private business interests exactly the same as out-of-state ones, do not "discriminate against interstate commerce" for purposes of the dormant Commerce Clause.[7]

D

The Counties' flow control ordinances are properly analyzed under the test set forth in *Pike v. Bruce Church, Inc.* . . . Under the *Pike* test, we will uphold a nondiscriminatory statute like this one "unless the burden imposed on [interstate] commerce is clearly excessive in relation to the putative local benefits."

After years of discovery, both the Magistrate Judge and the District Court could not detect *any* disparate impact on out-of-state as opposed to in-state businesses. . . . We find it unnecessary to decide whether the ordinances impose any incidental burden on interstate commerce because any arguable burden does not exceed the public benefits of the ordinances.

The ordinances give the Counties a convenient and effective way to finance their integrated package of waste-disposal services. While "revenue generation is not a local interest that can justify *discrimination* against interstate commerce," we think it is a cognizable benefit for purposes of the *Pike* test.

At the same time, the ordinances are more than financing tools. They increase recycling . . ., conferring significant health and environmental benefits upon the citizens of the Counties. For these reasons, any arguable burden the ordinances impose on interstate commerce does not exceed their public benefits. . . .

JUSTICE SCALIA, concurring in part.

I join Part I and Parts II-A through II-C of the Court's opinion. I write separately to reaffirm my view that "the so-called 'negative' Commerce

---

[7] The Counties and their amicus were asked at oral argument if affirmance would lead to the "Oneida-Herkimer Hamburger Stand," accompanied by a "flow control" law requiring citizens to purchase their burgers only from the state-owned producer. We doubt it. . . . Recognizing that local government may facilitate a customary and traditional government function such as waste disposal, without running afoul of the Commerce Clause, is hardly a prescription for state control of the economy. In any event, Congress retains authority under the Commerce Clause as written to regulate interstate commerce, whether engaged in by private or public entities. . . .

Clause is an unjustified judicial invention, not to be expanded beyond its existing domain."

I am unable to join Part II-D of the principal opinion, in which the plurality performs so-called "*Pike* balancing." Generally speaking, the balancing of various values is left to Congress—which is precisely what the Commerce Clause (the *real* Commerce Clause) envisions.

JUSTICE THOMAS, concurring in the judgment.

I concur in the judgment. Although I joined *C & A Carbone, Inc. v. Clarkstown,* I no longer believe it was correctly decided. The negative Commerce Clause has no basis in the Constitution and has proved unworkable in practice. As the debate between the majority and dissent shows, application of the negative Commerce Clause turns solely on policy considerations, not on the Constitution. Because this Court has no policy role in regulating interstate commerce, I would discard the Court's negative Commerce Clause jurisprudence. . . .

Because I believe that the power to regulate interstate commerce is a power given to Congress and not the Court, I concur in the judgment of the Court.

JUSTICE ALITO, with whom JUSTICE STEVENS and JUSTICE KENNEDY join, dissenting.

In *C & A Carbone, Inc. v. Clarkstown,* we held that "a so-called flow control ordinance, which require[d] all solid waste to be processed at a designated transfer station before leaving the municipality," discriminated against interstate commerce and was invalid under the Commerce Clause because it "depriv[ed] competitors, including out-of-state firms, of access to a local market." Because the provisions challenged in this case are essentially identical to the ordinance invalidated in *Carbone,* I respectfully dissent. . . .

This case cannot be meaningfully distinguished from *Carbone.* As the Court itself acknowledges, "[t]he only salient difference" between the cases is that the ordinance invalidated in *Carbone* discriminated in favor of a privately owned facility, whereas the laws at issue here discriminate in favor of "facilities owned and operated by a state-created public benefit corporation." The Court relies on the distinction between public and private ownership to uphold the flow-control laws, even though a straightforward application of *Carbone* would lead to the opposite result. The public-private distinction drawn by the Court is both illusory and without precedent.

The fact that the flow control laws at issue discriminate in favor of a government-owned enterprise does not meaningfully distinguish this case from *Carbone.* The preferred facility in *Carbone* was, to be sure, nominally owned by a private contractor who had built the facility on the town's behalf, but it would be misleading to describe the facility as private. In exchange for the contractor's promise to build the facility for the town free of charge and then to sell it to the town five years later for $1, the town guaranteed that, during the first five years of the facility's existence, the contractor would receive "a minimum waste flow of 120,000 tons per year" and that the contractor could charge an above-market tipping fee. If the facility "received less than 120,000 tons in a year, the town [would] make up the tipping fee deficit." To prevent residents, businesses, and trash haulers from taking their waste elsewhere in pursuit of lower tipping fees (leaving the town responsible for covering any shortfall in the contractor's guaranteed revenue stream), the town enacted an ordinance "requir[ing] all nonhazardous solid waste within the town to be deposited at" the preferred facility.

This Court observed that "[t]he object of this arrangement was to amortize the cost of the transfer station: The town would finance *its new facility* with the income generated by the tipping fees." "In other words," the Court explained, "the flow control ordinance [wa]s a financing measure," for what everyone—including the Court—regarded as *the town's* new transfer station.

The only real difference between the facility at issue in *Carbone* and its counterpart in this case is that title to the former had not yet formally passed to the municipality. The Court exalts form over substance in adopting a test that turns on this technical distinction, particularly since, barring any obstacle presented by state law, the transaction in *Carbone* could have been restructured to provide for the passage of title at the beginning, rather than the end, of the 5-year period.

In any event, we have never treated discriminatory legislation with greater deference simply because the entity favored by that legislation was a government-owned enterprise.... The Court has long subjected discriminatory legislation to strict scrutiny, and has never, until today, recognized an exception for discrimination in favor of a state-owned entity....

Nor has this Court ever suggested that discriminatory legislation favoring a state-owned enterprise is entitled to favorable treatment. To be sure, state-owned entities are accorded special status under the market-participant doctrine. But that doctrine is not applicable here.

Under the market-participant doctrine, a State is permitted to exercise " 'independent discretion as to parties with whom [it] will deal.' " The doctrine thus allows States to engage in certain otherwise-discriminatory practices (*e.g.,* selling exclusively to, or buying exclusively from, the State's own residents), so long as the State is "acting as a market participant, *rather than as a market regulator*," *South-Central Timber Development, Inc. v. Wunnicke.*

Respondents are doing exactly what the market-participant doctrine says they cannot: While acting as market participants by operating a fee-for-service business enterprise in an area in which there is an established interstate market, respondents are also regulating that market in a discriminatory manner and claiming that their special governmental status somehow insulates them from a dormant Commerce Clause challenge.

Respondents insist that the market-participant doctrine has no application here because they are not asserting a defense under the market-participant doctrine, but that argument misses the point. Regardless of whether respondents can assert a defense under the market-participant doctrine, this Court's cases make clear that States cannot discriminate against interstate commerce unless they are acting solely as market participants. Today, however, the Court suggests, contrary to its prior holdings, that States can discriminate in favor of in-state interests while acting both as a market participant *and* as a market regulator.

Despite precedent condemning discrimination in favor of government-owned enterprises, the Court attempts to develop a logical justification for the rule it creates today. That justification rests on three principal assertions. First, the Court insists that it simply "does not make sense to regard laws favoring local government and laws favoring private industry with equal skepticism," because the latter are "often the product of 'simple economic protectionism,'" while the former "may be directed toward any number of legitimate goals unrelated to protectionism." Second, the Court reasons that deference to legislation discriminating in favor of a municipal landfill is especially appropriate considering that " '[w]aste disposal is both typically and traditionally a local government function.' " Third, the Court suggests that respondents' flow-control laws are not discriminatory because they "treat in-state private business interests exactly the same as out-of-state ones." I find each of these arguments unpersuasive. . . .

COMMENTS AND QUESTIONS

1.   *United Haulers* is not a Market Participant Doctrine case. The majority never refers to it. Instead, it is the dissent that raises the doctrine. Why does the dissent raise that issue?

2.   Do you understand why the counties could not use the Market Participant Doctrine to defend their action despite the fact that they indeed were a market participant in supplying waste management services?

3.   Justices Breyer, Ginsburg, and Souter, who are generally considered "liberals," were the justices who fully joined the opinion of Chief Justice Roberts, who is generally considered "conservative." Justice Stevens is definitely considered "liberal," but he joins the dissent authored by Justice Alito, who is generally considered "conservative." Does this suggest a problem with these labels?

4. The majority holds that a facially discriminatory law favoring a "public" entity is exempt from the test applicable to discriminatory laws under the Dormant Commerce Clause. Four of these justices, however, hold that the *Pike v. Bruce Church* test for non-discriminatory laws still applies. What is it about the "publicness" of the entity receiving the benefit of the discrimination that leads the Chief Justice (and three others) to exempt it from one Dormant Commerce Clause test but to leave it subject to another one? Note that this portion of the opinion does not command a majority of the Court. What is its status as precedent?

5. Consider the dissent's discussion of *Wunnicke*. Does the dissent recognize that the language it quotes from *Wunnicke* was not subscribed to by a majority of the Court?

6. Justice Thomas would make a lot of law students happy by simply eliminating the Dormant Commerce Clause altogether, because, as he says, there is no textual basis for it in the Constitution. He is right on that score, is he not? If so, why is it that no other justice seemed inclined to go along with him, at least until Justice Gorsuch joined the Court? Do they think there is a textual basis for it, or is there another reason?

7. Subsequent to *United Haulers*, the Court was faced with a challenge to the widespread and century-old practice of states exempting from their state income tax the interest paid on their own state bonds but not the interest paid on other states' bonds. *See Department of Revenue of Kentucky v. Davis*, 553 U.S. 328 (2008). Kentucky's tax law explicitly distinguished between the income from interest on its own bonds and the interest from other states' bonds and provided a benefit to its bonds not provided to other states. Consequently, the claim was that the law discriminated on its face against out-of-state bonds in violation of the Dormant Commerce Clause. The Court, however, relied upon its decision in *United Haulers* to explain that when a state discriminates in favor of a government function, as opposed to in favor of in-state private interests, the concerns of economic protectionism do not arise. The Court noted that the state law did not favor bonds issued by in-state private entities. Only Justices Kennedy and Alito dissented, although Justice Thomas concurred in the result simply because he believes there is no constitutional basis for the Dormant Commerce Clause, and Justice Scalia restated his position that he would enforce the Dormant Commerce Clause only when stare decisis demands it.

PROBLEM

State A, which has a harsh view of what should be done with undocumented aliens, is upset with State B, which allows cities within the state to be "sanctuary cities," cities which follow certain procedures to shelter illegal immigrants. As a result, State A enacts a law directing that state procurement officers shall not purchase any goods or services from State B. A business in State B

> sues to invalidate State A's law, alleging it is in violation of the Dormant Commerce Clause.

B. THE PRIVILEGES AND IMMUNITIES CLAUSE

There are actually two Privileges and Immunities Clauses in the Constitution. One is Article IV, Section 2, Clause 1: The citizens of each state shall be entitled to all privileges and immunities of citizens in the several states. The other is the second sentence of Section 1 of the Fourteenth Amendment: No state shall make or enforce any law which shall abridge the privileges or immunities of citizens of the United States. Although both these provisions refer to "privileges" and "immunities," the terms in each provision have been interpreted to mean entirely different things. Later, when addressing rights under the Fourteenth Amendment, we will consider these terms' meaning there. Here we deal with the former clause, because of its similarity to the Dormant Commerce Clause in terms of judicial oversight of a national common market.

The Privileges and Immunities Clause of Article IV has its origin in an almost identical provision in the Articles of Confederation, and there as here it means that a state cannot deny to the citizens of another state the privileges and immunities enjoyed by its own citizens. Or, stated another way, one state cannot discriminate against the citizens of another state with respect to the privileges and immunities enjoyed by its own citizens. This prohibited discrimination against out-of-staters is one of the factors that makes this clause similar to the Dormant Commerce Clause. Another similarity is that a local ordinance discriminating against all persons from outside that locality (and therefore necessarily someone from outside the state) can violate the Privileges and Immunities Clause. *See, e.g., United Building & Construction Trades Council v. Mayor and Council of Camden*, 465 U.S. 208 (1984)(local ordinance required city contractors to have at least 40% of their employees be residents of the city).

The two major issues that arise under the Privileges and Immunities Clause are: 1) what are privileges and immunities, and 2) what constitutes prohibited discrimination with respect to those privileges and immunities, as opposed to legitimate differentiation.

The Supreme Court often refers to a formulation of privileges and immunities made by Justice Bushrod Washington, sitting as a circuit judge in *Corfield v. Coryell*, 6 F. Cas. 546, 551 (C.C.E.D. Pa. 1823):

> We feel no hesitation in confining these expressions to those privileges and immunities which are, in their nature, fundamental; which belong, of right, to the citizens of all free governments; and which have, at all times, been enjoyed by the citizens of the several states which compose this Union, from the time of their becoming free, independent, and sovereign. What

these fundamental principles are, it would perhaps be more tedious than difficult to enumerate. They may, however, be all comprehended under the following general heads: Protection by the government; the enjoyment of life and liberty, with the right to acquire and possess property of every kind, and to pursue and obtain happiness and safety; subject nevertheless to such restraints as the government may justly prescribe for the general good of the whole. The right of a citizen of one state to pass through, or to reside in any other state, for purposes of trade, agriculture, professional pursuits, or otherwise; to claim the benefit of the writ of habeas corpus; to institute and maintain actions of any kind in the courts of the state; to take, hold and dispose of property, either real or personal; and an exemption from higher taxes or impositions than are paid by the other citizens of the state; may be mentioned as some of the particular privileges and immunities of citizens, which are clearly embraced by the general description of privileges deemed to be fundamental. . . .

The Court has from time-to-time pointed to one or another of Justice Washington's examples to rule that something was a protected privilege or immunity, but the most common example referred to is "[t]he right of a citizen of one state to pass through, or to reside in any other state, for purposes of trade, agriculture, professional pursuits, or otherwise." Sometimes this is referred to as the right to engage in or pursue a "common calling." *See, e.g., Hicklin v. Orbeck*, 437 U.S. 518 (1978)(Alaskan law giving preference to residents in hiring for work on oil or gas pipelines in the state discriminated against the right to engage in a common calling); *Toomer v. Witsell*, 334 U.S. 385 (1948)(South Carolina's restriction of commercial shrimp fishing to residents of the state discriminated against the right to engage in a common calling). *Compare McBurney v. Young*, 569 U.S. 221 (2013)(Privileges and Immunities Clause does not cover a broad right of access to state public information for out-of-staters on equal terms with citizens of the state); *Baldwin v. Fish & Game Comm'n of Montana*, 436 U.S. 371 (1978)("[w]hatever rights or activities may be 'fundamental' under the Privileges and Immunities Clause, . . . [recreational] elk hunting by nonresidents in Montana is not one of them").

The following case addresses both what is a privilege and immunity and what circumstances might justify a state treating out-of-state citizens differently from its own citizens with respect to their "privileges and immunities."

SUPREME COURT OF NEW HAMPSHIRE V. PIPER

United States Supreme Court, 1985.
470 U.S. 274, 105 S.Ct. 1272.

JUSTICE POWELL delivered the opinion of the Court.

The Rules of the Supreme Court of New Hampshire limit bar admission to state residents. We here consider whether this restriction violates the Privileges and Immunities Clause of the United States Constitution, Art. IV, § 2.

Kathryn Piper lives in Lower Waterford, Vermont, about 400 yards from the New Hampshire border. In 1979, she applied to take the February 1980 New Hampshire bar examination.... She was allowed to take, and passed, the examination. Piper was informed by the Board that she would have to establish a home address in New Hampshire prior to being sworn in.

On May 7, 1980, Piper requested from the Clerk of the New Hampshire Supreme Court a dispensation from the residency requirement.... On May 13, 1980, the Clerk informed Piper that her request had been denied....

On March 22, 1982, Piper filed this action in the United States District Court for the District of New

Kathryn Piper and children

Hampshire. She named as defendants the State Supreme Court, its five Justices, and its Clerk. She alleged that Rule 42 of the New Hampshire Supreme Court, that excludes nonresidents from the bar, violates the Privileges and Immunities Clause of Art. IV, § 2, of the United States Constitution.

On May 17, 1982, the District Court granted Piper's motion for summary judgment.... An evenly divided Court of Appeals for the First Circuit, sitting en banc, affirmed the judgment in favor of Piper....

The Supreme Court of New Hampshire filed a timely notice of appeal, and we noted probable jurisdiction. We now affirm the judgment of the court below.

Article IV, § 2, of the Constitution provides that the "Citizens of each State shall be entitled to all Privileges and Immunities of Citizens in the several States."[6] This Clause was intended to "fuse into one Nation a collection of independent, sovereign States." Recognizing this purpose, we have held that it is "[o]nly with respect to those 'privileges' and 'immunities' bearing on the vitality of the Nation as a single entity" that a State must accord residents and nonresidents equal treatment. *Baldwin v. Montana Fish & Game Comm'n.* In *Baldwin,* for example, we concluded that a State may charge a nonresident more than it charges a resident for the same elk-hunting license. Because elk hunting is "recreation" rather than a "means of a livelihood," we found that the right to a hunting license was not "fundamental" to the promotion of interstate harmony.

Derived . . . from the fourth of the Articles of Confederation, the Privileges and Immunities Clause was intended to create a national economic union. It is therefore not surprising that this Court repeatedly has found that "one of the privileges which the Clause guarantees to citizens of State A is that of doing business in State B on terms of substantial equality with the citizens of that State." In *Ward v. Maryland,* 12 Wall. 418 (1871), the Court invalidated a statute under which nonresidents were required to pay $300 per year for a license to trade in goods not manufactured in Maryland, while resident traders paid a fee varying from $12 to $150. Similarly, in *Toomer v. Witsell,* the Court held that nonresident fishermen could not be required to pay a license fee of $2,500 for each shrimp boat owned when residents were charged only $25 per boat. Finally, in *Hicklin v. Orbeck,* we found violative of the Privileges and Immunities Clause a statute containing a resident hiring preference for all employment related to the development of the State's oil and gas resources.[9]

There is nothing in *Ward, Toomer,* or *Hicklin* suggesting that the practice of law should not be viewed as a "privilege" under Art. IV, § 2. Like the occupations considered in our earlier cases, the practice of law is important to the national economy. . . .

Appellant asserts that the Privileges and Immunities Clause should be held inapplicable to the practice of law because a lawyer's activities are "bound up with the exercise of judicial power and the administration of justice." Its contention is based on the premise that the lawyer is an "officer of the court," who "exercises state power on a daily basis." Appellant concludes that if the State cannot exclude nonresidents from the bar, its ability to function as a sovereign political body will be threatened.

---

[6] Under this Clause, the terms "citizen" and "resident" are used interchangeably. Under the Fourteenth Amendment, of course, "[a]ll persons born or naturalized in the United States . . . are citizens . . . of the State wherein they reside."

[9] In *United Building & Construction Trades Council v. Mayor & Council of Camden,* 465 U.S. 208 (1984), we stated that "the pursuit of a common calling is one of the most fundamental of those privileges protected by the Clause." We noted that "[m]any, if not most, of our cases expounding the Privileges and Immunities Clause have dealt with this basic and essential activity."

Lawyers do enjoy a "broad monopoly . . . to do things other citizens may not lawfully do." We do not believe, however, that the practice of law involves an "exercise of state power" justifying New Hampshire's residency requirement. [We have] held that the State could not exclude an alien from the bar on the ground that a lawyer is an " 'officer of the Court who' . . . is entrusted with the 'exercise of actual governmental power.' " [H]e " 'makes his own decisions, follows his own best judgment, collects his own fees and runs his own business.' " Moreover, we held that the state powers entrusted to lawyers do not "involve matters of state policy or acts of such unique responsibility as to entrust them only to citizens."

Because . . . a lawyer is not an "officer" of the State in any political sense, there is no reason for New Hampshire to exclude from its bar nonresidents. We therefore conclude that the right to practice law is protected by the Privileges and Immunities Clause.

The conclusion that Rule 42 deprives nonresidents of a protected privilege does not end our inquiry. The Court has stated that "[l]ike many other constitutional provisions, the privileges and immunities clause is not an absolute." The Clause does not preclude discrimination against nonresidents where (i) there is a substantial reason for the difference in treatment; and (ii) the discrimination practiced against nonresidents bears a substantial relationship to the State's objective. In deciding whether the discrimination bears a close or substantial relationship to the State's objective, the Court has considered the availability of less restrictive means.

The Supreme Court of New Hampshire offers several justifications for its refusal to admit nonresidents to the bar. It asserts that nonresident members would be less likely (i) to become, and remain, familiar with local rules and procedures; (ii) to behave ethically; (iii) to be available for court proceedings; and (iv) to do *pro bono* and other volunteer work in the State. We find that none of these reasons meets the test of "substantiality," and that the means chosen do not bear the necessary relationship to the State's objectives.[18]

There is no evidence to support appellant's claim that nonresidents might be less likely to keep abreast of local rules and procedures. Nor may we assume that a nonresident lawyer—any more than a resident—would disserve his clients by failing to familiarize himself with the rules. As a practical matter, we think that unless a lawyer has, or anticipates, a

---

[18] A former president of the American Bar Association has suggested another possible reason for the rule: "Many of the states that have erected fences against out-of-state lawyers have done so primarily to protect their own lawyers from professional competition." This reason is not "substantial." The Privileges and Immunities Clause was designed primarily to prevent such economic protectionism.

considerable practice in the New Hampshire courts, he would be unlikely to take the bar examination and pay the annual dues of $125.[19]

We also find the appellant's second justification to be without merit, for there is no reason to believe that a nonresident lawyer will conduct his practice in a dishonest manner. . . .

There is more merit to the appellant's assertion that a nonresident member of the bar at times would be unavailable for court proceedings. In the course of litigation, pretrial hearings on various matters often are held on short notice. At times a court will need to confer immediately with counsel. Even the most conscientious lawyer residing in a distant State may find himself unable to appear in court for an unscheduled hearing or proceeding. Nevertheless, we do not believe that this type of problem justifies the exclusion of nonresidents from the state bar. One may assume that a high percentage of nonresident lawyers willing to take the state bar examination and pay the annual dues will reside in places reasonably convenient to New Hampshire. Furthermore, in those cases where the nonresident counsel will be unavailable on short notice, the State can protect its interests through less restrictive means. The trial court, by rule or as an exercise of discretion, may require any lawyer who resides at a great distance to retain a local attorney who will be available for unscheduled meetings and hearings.

The final reason advanced by appellant is that nonresident members of the state bar would be disinclined to do their share of *pro bono* and volunteer work. Perhaps this is true to a limited extent, particularly where the member resides in a distant location. . . . [However], a nonresident bar member, like the resident member, could be required to represent indigents and perhaps to participate in formal legal-aid work.

In summary, appellant neither advances a "substantial reason" for its discrimination against nonresident applicants to the bar, nor demonstrates that the discrimination practiced bears a close relationship to its proffered objectives.

JUSTICE WHITE, concurring in the result. [omitted]

JUSTICE REHNQUIST, dissenting.

Today the Court holds that New Hampshire cannot decide that a New Hampshire lawyer should live in New Hampshire. This may not be surprising to those who view law as just another form of business frequently practiced across state lines by interchangeable actors; the

---

[19] Because it is markedly overinclusive, the residency requirement does not bear a substantial relationship to the State's objective. A less restrictive alternative would be to require mandatory attendance at periodic seminars on state practice. . . . New Hampshire's "simple residency" requirement is underinclusive as well, because it permits lawyers who move away from the State to retain their membership in the bar. There is no reason to believe that a former resident would maintain a more active practice in the New Hampshire courts than would a nonresident lawyer who had never lived in the State.

Privileges and Immunities Clause of Art. IV, § 2, has long been held to apply to States' attempts to discriminate against nonresidents who seek to ply their trade interstate. The decision will be surprising to many, however, because it so clearly disregards the fact that the practice of law is—almost by definition—fundamentally different from those other occupations that are practiced across state lines without significant deviation from State to State. The fact that each State is free, in a large number of areas, to establish *independently* of the other States its own laws for the governance of its citizens, is a fundamental precept of our Constitution that, I submit, is of equal stature with the need for the States to form a cohesive union. What is at issue here is New Hampshire's right to decide that those people who in many ways will intimately deal with New Hampshire's self-governance should reside within that State. . . .

It is but a small step from these facts to the recognition that a State has a very strong interest in seeing that its legislators and its judges come from among the constituency of state residents, so that they better understand the local interests to which they will have to respond. The Court does not contest this point; it recognizes that a State may require its lawmakers to be residents without running afoul of the Privileges and Immunities Clause of Art. IV, § 2.

Unlike the Court, I would take the next step, and recognize that the State also has a very "substantial" interest in seeing that its lawyers also are members of that constituency. I begin with two important principles that the Court seems to have forgotten: first, that in reviewing state statutes under this Clause "States should have considerable leeway in analyzing local evils and prescribing appropriate cures," and second, that regulation of the practice of law generally has been "left exclusively to the States. . . ." My belief that the practice of law differs from other trades and businesses for Art. IV, § 2, purposes is not based on some notion that law is for some reason a superior profession. The reason that the practice of law should be treated differently is that law is one occupation that does not readily translate across state lines.[1] Certain aspects of legal practice are distinctly and intentionally *nonnational;* in this regard one might view this country's legal system as the antithesis of the norms embodied in the Art. IV Privileges and Immunities Clause. Put simply, the State has a substantial interest in creating its own set of laws responsive to its own local interests, and it is reasonable for a State to decide that those people who have been trained to analyze law and policy are better equipped to write those state laws and adjudicate cases arising under them. . . .

---

[1] I do not mean to suggest that the practice of law, unlike other occupations, is not a "fundamental" interest subject to the two-step analysis outlined by the Court. It makes little difference to me which prong of the Court's analysis is implicated, although the thrust of my position is that there are significant state interests justifying this type of interstate discrimination. . . .

It is no answer to these arguments that many lawyers simply will not perform these functions, or that out-of-state lawyers can perform them equally well, or that the State can devise less restrictive alternatives for accomplishing these goals. Conclusory second-guessing of difficult legislative decisions, such as the Court resorts to today, is not an attractive way for federal courts to engage in judicial review. Thus, whatever the reality of how much New Hampshire can expect to gain from having the members of its bar reside within that State, the point is that New Hampshire is entitled to believe and hope that its lawyers will provide the various unique services mentioned above, just as it is entitled to believe that the residency requirement is the appropriate way to that end. . . .

In addition, I find the Court's "less restrictive means" analysis both ill-advised and potentially unmanageable. Initially I would note . . . that such an analysis, when carried too far, will ultimately lead to striking down almost any statute on the ground that the Court could think of another "less restrictive" way to write it. This approach to judicial review, far more than the usual application of a standard of review, tends to place courts in the position of second-guessing legislators on legislative matters. Surely this is not a consequence to be desired. . . .

COMMENTS AND QUESTIONS

1. The Court finds that to be a lawyer is to follow a common calling. Justice Rehnquist appears to disagree. Do you think he is right to compare lawyers to judges and legislators?

2. What does the Court mean that a lawyer may be an "officer of the court" but "not an 'officer' of the State in any political sense"?

3. After deciding that lawyers are a common calling, the Court first asks whether "(i) there is a substantial reason for the difference in treatment." Obviously, a substantial reason must also be a legitimate reason. Thus, the state cannot rely on impermissible reasons, such as protecting state jobs for state residents; this would be protectionism, as impermissible under the Privileges and Immunities Clause as under the Dormant Commerce Clause. In *Piper* the state argues that it has four legitimate purposes. The Court dismisses all as not substantial reasons.

4. Although the Court finds that New Hampshire did not advance a "substantial reason" for its discrimination, it also addresses whether "(ii) the discrimination practiced against nonresidents bears a substantial relationship to the State's objective. In deciding whether the discrimination bears a close or substantial relationship to the State's objective, the Court has considered the availability of less restrictive means." In other words, if there is a less discriminatory means available to achieve the substantial, legitimate purpose, the State must use it. Here, it suggests that there is not a substantial relationship between the discrimination and the legitimate purpose. The Court finds that there are less discriminatory ways to achieve the purposes of

assuring non-resident lawyers' availability at court proceedings and willingness to engage in pro bono activity.

5.   Justice Rehnquist takes issue with the "less restrictive means" test used by the Court to determine if the discrimination has a substantial relationship to the state's legitimate objective. He indicates it is unmanageable and will have terrible effects, but this is and was the test used for discriminatory laws under the Dormant Commerce Clause. Should it be any different for discrimination under the Privileges and Immunities Clause? Perhaps he objects because in an earlier case he had identified the appropriate inquiry to be whether it can be shown that the nonresidents "constitute a peculiar source of the evil at which the statute is aimed." *See United Building & Construction Trades Council v. Mayor and Council of Camden*, 465 U.S. 208, 222 (1984). How would one apply that test to the facts in *Piper* and would it result in any different outcome?

6.   In *McBurney v. Young*, 569 U.S. 221 (2013), the Court made clear that a law did not run afoul of the Privileges and Immunities Clause if it did not directly or intentionally interfere with a person's ability to exercise a fundamental right protected by the clause but only incidentally and marginally burdened that exercise.

7.   As you can see there are a number of similarities between Dormant Commerce Clause doctrine and Privileges and Immunities Clause doctrine. As a result, cases are often filed asserting a violation of both the Dormant Commerce Clause and the Privileges and Immunities Clause. There are, however, a few notable differences between the two doctrines:

- Corporations and other non-natural persons are not protected by the Privileges and Immunities Clause, because it only protects "citizens," and only natural persons can be citizens.

- There is no market participant exception to the Privileges and Immunities Clause prohibition on discriminatory state and local laws, *see United Building & Construction Trades Council v. Mayor and Council of Camden, supra.*

- While Congress can reverse a decision made by the Court under the Dormant Commerce Clause to authorize something the Court found unconstitutional or to prohibit something the Court found constitutional, Congress cannot reverse a decision by the Court under the Privileges and Immunities Clause.

PROBLEM

State B (from the previous problem) in retaliation to State A's procurement law contemplates a law prohibiting the employment by State B in any position of any citizen of State A. State B's Legislative Counsel is asked whether this law would be constitutional.

CHAPTER 5

EXECUTIVE V. LEGISLATIVE POWER— THE SEPARATION OF POWERS

■ ■ ■

In Chapter 3 we surveyed the legislative powers vested in Congress by the Constitution. There we saw that the tension was between federal lawmaking and state lawmaking and the proper roles and responsibilities of the state and federal governments—or what is called federalism or sometimes the vertical separation of powers. In this chapter we survey the executive powers and privileges vested in the President by Article II of the Constitution. Here we will see that the tension is between executive powers and congressional powers and the proper roles and responsibilities of President and the Congress—or what is called the separation of powers (or horizontal separation of powers) and checks and balances. In addition, we will find that there are limitations on the ability of the President and Congress, even when acting together, to alter the roles and responsibilities the Court believes mandated by the Constitution.

As The Federalist papers recognized, "The accumulation of all powers legislative, executive and judiciary in the same hands, whether of one, a few or many, and whether hereditary, self-appointed, or elective, may justly be pronounced the very definition of tyranny." It is Civics 101 that to avoid tyranny the United States government is divided into three branches—the judicial, the legislative, and the executive. This division is called the separation of powers. At the same time, the branches are not hermetically sealed from one another. To the contrary, the Constitution mandates necessary interactions between them, what we call "checks and balances." For example, Congress is the legislative branch but the President is empowered to veto bills passed by Congress. The President is authorized to make treaties and appoint officers of the United States, but the former is subject to Senate ratification and the latter to Senate confirmation. The President appoints judges, but Congress can remove them through impeachment. The President is the Commander-in-Chief, but Congress raises and supports armies and provides the rules for the regulation of armed forces. These interactions provide a wealth of opportunities for clashes between the branches. During periods when the presidency and Congress are controlled by different political parties, the conflicts between them are sometimes partisan, rather than institutional, but even when the presidency and Congress are both controlled by the same party, with shared political orientations, there are often conflicts between the branches arising out of institutional concerns.

A. BACKGROUND

This chapter will begin with two canonical cases involving the power of the President.

UNITED STATES V. CURTISS-WRIGHT EXPORT CORP.

United States Supreme Court, 1936.
299 U.S. 304, 57 S.Ct. 216.

Chaco combatants with machine gun

[This case needs some introduction. A longstanding border dispute between Paraguay and Bolivia over an area known as the Chaco broke out into war in 1932. The League of Nations imposed an international arms embargo to keep foreign weapons out of the war, and Congress passed a law authorizing the President by resolution to forbid the sale of weapons to persons involved in that dispute and provided criminal penalties for anyone violating such a Presidential resolution. This occurred during the period in which the Court was striking down various New Deal laws passed by Congress to deal with the Great Depression. Indeed, in the year prior to this case, in two cases the Court had found that laws authorizing the President to take certain actions were unconstitutional delegations of legislative power. *See Panama Refining Co. v. Ryan*, 293 U.S. 388 (1935); *A.L.A. Schechter Poultry Corporation v. United States*, 295 U.S. 495 (1935). The theory was that the Constitution vests the legislative authority in Congress, and Congress cannot delegate that authority to the President in a manner that gives him largely unfettered discretion. For example, imagine a law that said: the President may make all the laws for the next four years. Of course, the laws invalidated by the Court were not nearly so stark, and the law involved in *Panama Refining*, authorizing the President to ban from interstate commerce any oil produced in a state in violation of that state's law and creating criminal penalties for anyone violating that ban, looked much like the law in this case. Thus, Curtiss-Wright had some reason to believe that it might win on the argument that the law here was an unconstitutional delegation of legislative authority.]

MR. JUSTICE SUTHERLAND delivered the opinion of the Court.

On January 27, 1936, an indictment was returned in the court below, the first count of which charges that appellees . . . conspired to sell in the United States certain arms of war, namely, fifteen machine guns, to Bolivia, a country then engaged in armed conflict in the Chaco, in violation of the Joint Resolution of Congress approved May 28, 1934, and the provisions of a proclamation issued on the same day by the President of the United States pursuant to authority conferred by . . . the resolution. . . .

Appellees severally demurred to the first count of the indictment. . . . [One point] urged in support of the demurrers [was] that the Joint Resolution effects an invalid delegation of legislative power to the executive. . . .

Whether, if the Joint Resolution had related solely to internal affairs, it would be open to the challenge that it constituted an unlawful delegation of legislative power to the Executive, we find it unnecessary to determine. The whole aim of the resolution is to affect a situation entirely external to the United States, and falling within the category of foreign affairs. The determination which we are called to make, therefore, is whether the Joint Resolution, as applied to that situation, is vulnerable to attack under the rule that forbids a delegation of the lawmaking power. In other words, assuming (but not deciding) that the challenged delegation, if it were confined to internal affairs, would be invalid, may it nevertheless be sustained on the ground that its exclusive aim is to afford a remedy for a hurtful condition within foreign territory?

It will contribute to the elucidation of the question if we first consider the differences between the powers of the federal government in respect of foreign or external affairs and those in respect of domestic or internal affairs. . . .

The two classes of powers are different, both in respect of their origin and their nature. The broad statement that the federal government can exercise no powers except those specifically enumerated in the Constitution, and such implied powers as are necessary and proper to carry into effect the enumerated powers, is categorically true only in respect of our internal affairs. In that field, the primary purpose of the Constitution was to carve from the general mass of legislative powers then possessed by the states such portions as it was thought desirable to vest in the federal government, leaving those not included in the enumeration still in the states. That this doctrine applies only to powers which the states had is self-evident. And since the states severally never possessed international powers, such powers could not have been carved from the mass of state powers but obviously were transmitted to the United States from some other source. During the Colonial period, those powers were possessed exclusively by and were entirely under the control of the Crown. By the Declaration of Independence, "the Representatives of the United States of

America" declared the United (not the several) Colonies to be free and independent states, and as such to have "full Power to levy War, conclude Peace, contract Alliances, establish Commerce and to do all other Acts and Things which Independent States may of right do."

As a result of the separation from Great Britain by the colonies, acting as a unit, the powers of external sovereignty passed from the Crown not to the colonies severally, but to the colonies in their collective and corporate capacity as the United States of America. Even before the Declaration, the colonies were a unit in foreign affairs, acting through a common agency— namely, the Continental Congress, composed of delegates from the thirteen colonies. That agency exercised the powers of war and peace, raised an army, created a navy, and finally adopted the Declaration of Independence. Rulers come and go; governments end and forms of government change; but sovereignty survives. A political society cannot endure without a supreme will somewhere. Sovereignty is never held in suspense. When, therefore, the external sovereignty of Great Britain in respect of the colonies ceased, it immediately passed to the Union. That fact was given practical application almost at once. The treaty of peace, made on September 3, 1783, was concluded between his Brittanic Majesty and the "United States of America."

The Union existed before the Constitution, which was ordained and established among other things to form "a more perfect Union." Prior to that event, it is clear that the Union, declared by the Articles of Confederation to be "perpetual," was the sole possessor of external sovereignty, and in the Union it remained without change save in so far as the Constitution in express terms qualified its exercise. The Framers' Convention was called and exerted its powers upon the irrefutable postulate that though the states were several their people in respect of foreign affairs were one. . . .

It results that the investment of the federal government with the powers of external sovereignty did not depend upon the affirmative grants of the Constitution. The powers to declare and wage war, to conclude peace, to make treaties, to maintain diplomatic relations with other sovereignties, if they had never been mentioned in the Constitution, would have vested in the federal government as necessary concomitants of nationality. . . .

Not only, as we have shown, is the federal power over external affairs in origin and essential character different from that over internal affairs, but participation in the exercise of the power is significantly limited. In this vast external realm, with its important, complicated, delicate and manifold problems, the President alone has the power to speak or listen as a representative of the nation. He makes treaties with the advice and consent of the Senate; but he alone negotiates. Into the field of negotiation the Senate cannot intrude; and Congress itself is powerless to invade it. As Marshall said in his great argument of March 7, 1800, in the House of

Representatives, "The President is the sole organ of the nation in its external relations, and its sole representative with foreign nations." The Senate Committee on Foreign Relations at a very early day in our history (February 15, 1816), reported to the Senate, among other things, as follows:

> "The President is the constitutional representative of the United States with regard to foreign nations. He manages our concerns with foreign nations and must necessarily be most competent to determine when, how, and upon what subjects negotiation may be urged with the greatest prospect of success. For his conduct he is responsible to the Constitution. The committee considers this responsibility the surest pledge for the faithful discharge of his duty. They think the interference of the Senate in the direction of foreign negotiations calculated to diminish that responsibility and thereby to impair the best security for the national safety. The nature of transactions with foreign nations, moreover, requires caution and unity of design, and their success frequently depends on secrecy and dispatch."

It is important to bear in mind that we are here dealing not alone with an authority vested in the President by an exertion of legislative power, but with such an authority plus the very delicate, plenary and exclusive power of the President as the sole organ of the federal government in the field of international relations—a power which does not require as a basis for its exercise an act of Congress, but which, of course, like every other governmental power, must be exercised in subordination to the applicable provisions of the Constitution. It is quite apparent that if, in the maintenance of our international relations, embarrassment—perhaps serious embarrassment—is to be avoided and success for our aims achieved, congressional legislation which is to be made effective through negotiation and inquiry within the international field must often accord to the President a degree of discretion and freedom from statutory restriction which would not be admissible were domestic affairs alone involved. Moreover, he, not Congress, has the better opportunity of knowing the conditions which prevail in foreign countries, and especially is this true in time of war. He has his confidential sources of information. He has his agents in the form of diplomatic, consular and other officials. Secrecy in respect of information gathered by them may be highly necessary, and the premature disclosure of it productive of harmful results. Indeed, so clearly is this true that the first President refused to accede to a request to lay before the House of Representatives the instructions, correspondence and documents relating to the negotiation of the Jay Treaty—a refusal the wisdom of which was recognized by the House itself and has never since been doubted. In his reply to the request, President Washington said:

> "The nature of foreign negotiations requires caution, and their success must often depend on secrecy; and even when brought to

a conclusion a full disclosure of all the measures, demands, or eventual concessions which may have been proposed or contemplated would be extremely impolitic; for this might have a pernicious influence on future negotiations, or produce immediate inconveniences, perhaps danger and mischief, in relation to other powers. The necessity of such caution and secrecy was one cogent reason for vesting the power of making treaties in the President, with the advice and consent of the Senate, the principle on which that body was formed confining it to a small number of members. To admit, then, a right in the House of Representatives to demand and to have as a matter of course all the papers respecting a negotiation with a foreign power would be to establish a dangerous precedent."

[W]hen the President is to be authorized by legislation to act in respect of a matter intended to affect a situation in foreign territory, the legislator properly bears in mind the important consideration that the form of the President's action—or, indeed, whether he shall act at all—may well depend, among other things, upon the nature of the confidential information which he has or may thereafter receive, or upon the effect which his action may have upon our foreign relations. This consideration, in connection with what we have already said on the subject discloses the unwisdom of requiring Congress in this field of governmental power to lay down narrowly definite standards by which the President is to be governed. . . .

In the light of the foregoing observations, it is evident that this court should not be in haste to apply a general rule which will have the effect of condemning legislation like that under review as constituting an unlawful delegation of legislative power. The principles which justify such legislation find overwhelming support in the unbroken legislative practice which has prevailed almost from the inception of the national government to the present day.

MR. JUSTICE MCREYNOLDS does not agree. He is of the opinion that the court below reached the right conclusion and its judgment ought to be affirmed.

MR. JUSTICE STONE took no part in the consideration or decision of this case.

COMMENTS AND QUESTIONS

1.   Analytically, the outcome of this case is unremarkable—when Congress delegates power to the President, it can provide him more discretion regarding foreign affairs than would be the case in domestic affairs. Moreover, subsequent case law concerning even domestic delegations of legislative authority to the President has made clear that so long as there is an intelligible standard to govern the President's actions, the delegation is not excessive. For

example, the Clean Air Act's delegation of legislative authority to reduce air pollution "requisite to protect the public health" is easily an adequate standard. *See Whitman v. American Trucking Ass'ns*, 531 U.S. 457 (2001). In fact, no federal law has been found unconstitutional under the Delegation Doctrine since 1935. In 2019, however, the Court almost did. The Sex Offender Registration and Notification Act (SORNA) established a uniform national system for registering sex offenders convicted after SORNA's enactment. In addition, for persons convicted *before* SORNA's enactment, it authorized the Attorney General to "specify the applicability" of SORNA's registration requirements and "to prescribe rules for [their] registration." The Attorney General did, and a person consequently required to register challenged this authorization to the Attorney General as an unconstitutional delegation of legislative authority. In *Gundy v. United States*, 139 S.Ct. 2116 (2019), the Court by a 5–3 vote upheld the delegation, finding that the statute contained an intelligible principle to guide and cabin the Attorney General's discretion. However, Justice Alito only concurred in the judgment. He agreed that the statute contained a discernable standard as articulated in past decisions but said that "[i]f a majority of this Court were willing to reconsider the approach we have taken for the past 84 years, I would support that effort." Justice Gorsuch, joined by the Chief Justice and Justice Thomas, dissented. They would throw out the intelligible principle test. Justice Kavanaugh, who had not yet been appointed to the Court when the case was argued, recused himself. Thus, in the next case to raise seriously the Delegation Doctrine, the continued vitality of the intelligible principle test may depend upon Justice Kavanaugh's opinion. Because the SORNA provision could be viewed as particularly egregious in its lack of any clear and express principle, even a very general one, it was a good vehicle for testing the limits of the intelligible principle test. Such a vehicle may not arise again soon. That said, even the potential for overruling such an established principle is shocking.

2. However, *Curtiss-Wright* is not remembered for its discussion of the Delegation Doctrine. Instead, it is most often cited for the proposition that the President is "the sole organ of the nation in its external relations." This characterization, first made by John Marshall when he was a member of Congress, is often mischaracterized as saying the President is solely or primarily responsible for our nation's foreign affairs. *See, e.g.*, the Wikipedia entry for *United States v. Curtiss-Wright Export Corp.* Marshall and the Court in *Curtiss-Wright* meant that the President is the actor through whom the nation's foreign affairs are conducted, not that the President is solely responsible for them. Recall the various provisions of Article I, Section 8, that authorize Congress to make laws regarding foreign and military affairs, not to mention the Senate's role in ratifying treaties.

3. *Curtiss-Wright* is also known for its historical analysis of the transfer of sovereignty from Great Britain directly to the United States as a nation, and not to the states separately and then from them to the United States through the Articles or the Constitution. While this history has been quite conclusively proven wrong, *see* Charles Lofgren, *United States v. Curtiss-Wright Export Corporation: A Historical Reassessment*, 83 Yale L.J. 1, 32 (1973), the theory

that the United States possesses all the powers that any nation has under international law by reason of being a nation-state, even though some of these powers may not be mentioned in the Constitution, is largely unquestioned. To say that, however, is not necessarily to say that these unenumerated powers are possessed by the President, as opposed to possessed by the President and Congress together. Look back at the Court's opinion. Do you think it unequivocally states that these powers rest in the President?

YOUNGSTOWN SHEET & TUBE CO. V. SAWYER (THE STEEL SEIZURE CASE)

United States Supreme Court, 1952.
343 U.S. 579, 72 S.Ct. 863.

[Since 1910 Japan had ruled Korea. In the closing days of World War II, the Soviet Union declared war on Japan and upon Japan's surrender occupied the northern half of Korea, while the United States occupied its southern half. In 1948 two separate governments were established, both claiming to be the rightful government of all Korea, and over the next two years Soviet and U.S. forces left Korea. On June 25, 1950, North Korean troops carried out a surprise attack against the south. In five days, three quarters of the South Korean forces had been killed, wounded, captured, or dispersed. The United Nations Security Council, seizing an opportunity when the Soviet representative left in protest, voted to authorize defense of South Korea. Nevertheless, by September, the North Korean forces had occupied all of South Korea except the Pusan peninsula in the southeast corner of Korea. At that point, American forces reinforced from Japan counterattacked in the Pusan, and General Douglas MacArthur led an invasion at Inchon, 100 miles behind the North Korean lines. The result was to push back North Korean forces back across the pre-war border, capturing Pyongyang, the capital of North Korea, and reaching in some places to the border of China in October. This caused the Chinese government to enter the war, hurling 200,000 troops across the border in a surprise attack. Overwhelmed, the United States and U.N. forces retreated back into South Korea, suffering terrible losses, and Seoul, the capital of South Korea, fell once again to the enemy. By December, 1950, the allied forces had recovered and began pushing the Chinese back to approximately the pre-war border of North and South Korea. By July, 1951, the war had become something of a stalemate, with each side making attacks costly to both sides, even as they were negotiating a possible armistice.

Back in the United States, a dispute arose between the steel companies and their employees over terms and conditions that should be included in new collective bargaining agreements. Long-continued conferences failed to resolve the dispute, and on April 4, 1952, the union gave notice of a nation-wide strike called to begin at 12:01 a.m. April 9. The indispensability of steel as a component of substantially all weapons and other war materials led President Harry Truman to believe that the proposed work stoppage would immediately jeopardize our national defense

President Harry Truman

and the war effort in Korea. Consequently, he decided that governmental seizure of the steel mills was necessary in order to assure the continued availability of steel. Reciting these considerations for his action, the President, a few hours before the strike was to begin, issued Executive Order 10340. The order directed the Secretary of Commerce to take possession of most of the steel mills and keep them running. The next morning the President sent a message to Congress reporting his action.

Obeying the Secretary's orders under protest, the companies brought proceedings against him in the District Court. The District Court on April 30 issued a preliminary injunction restraining the Secretary from continuing the seizure and possession of the plant. On the same day the Court of Appeals stayed the District Court's injunction. The Supreme Court, deeming it best that the issues raised be promptly decided, granted certiorari on May 3 and set the cause for argument on May 12. On June 2, the Court issued its decision.]

MR. JUSTICE BLACK delivered the opinion of the Court.

We are asked to decide whether [President Truman] was acting within his constitutional power when he issued an order directing the Secretary of Commerce to take possession of and operate most of the Nation's steel mills. The mill owners argue that the President's order amounts to lawmaking, a legislative function which the Constitution has expressly confided to the Congress and not to the President. The Government's position is that the order was made on findings of the President that his action was necessary to avert a national catastrophe which would inevitably result from a stoppage of steel production, and that in meeting this grave emergency the President was acting within the aggregate of his constitutional powers as the Nation's Chief Executive and the Commander in Chief of the Armed Forces of the United States. . . . The President's power, if any, to issue the order must stem either from an act of Congress or from the Constitution itself. There is no statute that expressly

Hugo Black

Hugo Black, a Democratic Senator from Alabama, was President Franklin Roosevelt's first appointment to the Court. He shared the President's belief that the Court was overstepping its bounds in declaring the New Deal legislation unconstitutional. He is an example of a liberal politician and conservative jurist. He believed that the Fourteenth Amendment incorporated all of the Bill of Rights but denied there were any unenumerated rights protected by the Due Process Clause. He tended toward literalism, notably the First Amendment's statement that Congress could make "no law" abridging the freedom of speech or the press. Despite his background, including one-time membership in the Ku Klux Klan, he was a dependable vote in favor of civil rights.

authorizes the President to take possession of property as he did here. Nor is there any act of Congress to which our attention has been directed from which such a power can fairly be implied. Indeed, we do not understand the Government to rely on statutory authorization for this seizure. There are two statutes which do authorize the President to take both personal and real property under certain conditions. However, the Government admits that these conditions were not met and that the President's order was not rooted in either of the statutes. The Government refers to the seizure provisions of one of these statutes (§ 201(b) of the Defense Production Act) as much too cumbersome, involved, and time-consuming for the crisis which was at hand.

Moreover, the use of the seizure technique to solve labor disputes in order to prevent work stoppages was not only unauthorized by any congressional enactment; prior to this controversy, Congress had refused to adopt that method of settling labor disputes. When the Taft-Hartley Act was under consideration in 1947, Congress rejected an amendment which would have authorized such governmental seizures in cases of emergency. . . . Instead, the plan sought to bring about settlements by use of the customary devices of mediation, conciliation, investigation by boards of inquiry, and public reports. In some instances temporary injunctions were authorized to provide cooling-off periods. All this failing, unions were left free to strike. . . .

It is clear that if the President had authority to issue the order he did, it must be found in some provisions of the Constitution. And it is not claimed that express constitutional language grants this power to the President. The contention is that presidential power should be implied from the aggregate of his powers under the Constitution. Particular reliance is placed on provisions in Article II which say that the executive Power shall be vested in a President * * *; that he shall take Care that the Laws be faithfully executed; and that he shall be Commander in Chief of the Army and Navy of the United States.

The order cannot properly be sustained as an exercise of the President's military power as Commander in Chief of the Armed Forces. The Government attempts to do so by citing a number of cases upholding broad powers in military commanders engaged in day-to-day fighting in a theater of war. Such cases need not concern us here. Even though theater of war be an expanding concept, we cannot with faithfulness to our constitutional system hold that the Commander in Chief of the Armed Forces has the ultimate power as such to take possession of private property in order to keep labor disputes from stopping production. This is a job for the Nation's lawmakers, not for its military authorities.

Nor can the seizure order be sustained because of the several constitutional provisions that grant executive power to the President. In the framework of our Constitution, the President's power to see that the laws are faithfully executed refutes the idea that he is to be a lawmaker. The Constitution limits his functions in the lawmaking process to the recommending of laws he thinks wise and the vetoing of laws he thinks bad. And the Constitution is neither silent nor equivocal about who shall make laws which the President is to execute. . . .

[T]he power of Congress to adopt such public policies as those proclaimed by the order is beyond question. It can authorize the taking of private property for public use. It can make laws regulating the relationships between employers and employees, prescribing rules designed to settle labor disputes, and fixing wages and working conditions in certain fields of our economy. The Constitution did not subject this law-making power of Congress to presidential or military supervision or control. . . .

The Founders of this Nation entrusted the law making power to the Congress alone in both good and bad times. It would do no good to recall the historical events, the fears of power and the hopes for freedom that lay behind their choice. Such a review would but confirm our holding that this seizure order cannot stand.

MR. JUSTICE JACKSON, concurring in the judgment and opinion of the Court.

[T]he actual art of governing under our Constitution does not and cannot conform to judicial definitions of the power of any of its branches based on isolated clauses or even single Articles torn from context. While the Constitution diffuses power the better to secure liberty, it also contemplates that practice will integrate the dispersed powers into a workable government. It enjoins upon its branches separateness but interdependence, autonomy but reciprocity. Presidential powers are not fixed but fluctuate, depending upon their disjunction or conjunction with those of Congress. We may well begin by a somewhat over-simplified grouping of practical situations in which a President may doubt, or others may challenge, his powers, and by distinguishing roughly the legal consequences of this factor of relativity.

1.   When the President acts pursuant to an express or implied authorization of Congress, his authority is at its maximum, for it includes all that he possesses in his own right plus all that Congress can delegate.[2] In these circumstances, and in these only, may he be said (for what it may be worth), to personify the federal sovereignty. If his act is held unconstitutional under these circumstances, it usually means that the Federal Government as an undivided whole lacks power. A seizure executed by the President pursuant to an Act of Congress would be supported by the strongest of presumptions and the widest latitude of judicial interpretation, and the burden of persuasion would rest heavily upon any who might attack it.

2.   When the President acts in absence of either a congressional grant or denial of authority, he can only rely upon his own independent powers, but there is a zone of twilight in which he and Congress may have concurrent authority, or in which its distribution is uncertain. Therefore, congressional inertia, indifference or quiescence may sometimes, at least as a practical matter, enable, if not invite, measures on independent presidential responsibility. In this area, any actual test of power is likely to depend on the imperatives of events and contemporary imponderables rather than on abstract theories of law.[3]

3.   When the President takes measures incompatible with the expressed or implied will of Congress, his power is at its lowest ebb, for then he can rely only upon his own constitutional powers minus any constitutional powers of Congress over the matter. Courts can sustain exclusive Presidential control in such a case only by disabling the Congress from acting upon the subject. Presidential claim to a power at once so conclusive and preclusive must be scrutinized with caution, for what is at stake is the equilibrium established by our constitutional system.

Into which of these classifications does this executive seizure of the steel industry fit? It is eliminated from the first by admission, for it is conceded that no congressional authorization exists for this seizure. Can it then be defended under flexible tests available to the second category? It

---

    [2]   It is in this class of cases that we find the broadest recent statements of presidential power, including those relied on here. *United States v. Curtiss-Wright Export Corp.* involved, not the question of the President's power to act without congressional authority, but the question of his right to act under and in accord with an Act of Congress. . . . That case does not solve the present controversy. It recognized internal and external affairs as being in separate categories, and held that the strict limitation upon congressional delegations of power to the President over internal affairs does not apply with respect to delegations of power in external affairs. It was intimated that the President might act in external affairs without congressional authority, but not that he might act contrary to an Act of Congress. . . .

    [3]   Since the Constitution implies that the writ of habeas corpus may be suspended in certain circumstances but does not say by whom, President Lincoln asserted and maintained it as an executive function in the face of judicial challenge and doubt. Congress eventually ratified his action.

seems clearly eliminated from that class because Congress has not left seizure of private property an open field but has covered it by three statutory policies inconsistent with this seizure. In cases where the purpose is to supply needs of the Government itself, two courses are provided: one, seizure of a plant which fails to comply with obligatory orders placed by the Government, another, condemnation of facilities, including temporary use under the power of eminent domain. The third is applicable where it is the general economy of the country that is to be protected rather than exclusive governmental interests. None of these were invoked. In choosing a different and inconsistent way of his own, the President cannot claim that it is necessitated or invited by failure of Congress to legislate upon the occasions, grounds and methods for seizure of industrial properties.

This leaves the current seizure to be justified only by the severe tests under the third grouping, where it can be supported only by any remainder of executive power after subtraction of such powers as Congress may have over the subject. In short, we can sustain the President only by holding that seizure of such strike-bound industries is within his domain and beyond control by Congress. Thus, this Court's first review of such seizures occurs under circumstances which leave Presidential power most vulnerable to attack and in the least favorable of possible constitutional postures.

I did not suppose, and I am not persuaded, that history leaves it open to question, at least in the courts, that the executive branch, like the Federal Government as a whole, possesses only delegated powers. The purpose of the Constitution was not only to grant power, but to keep it from getting out of hand. However, because the President does not enjoy unmentioned powers does not mean that the mentioned ones should be narrowed by a niggardly construction. Some clauses could be made almost unworkable, as well as immutable, by refusal to indulge some latitude of interpretation for changing times. I have heretofore, and do now, give to the enumerated powers the scope and elasticity afforded by what seem to be reasonable practical implications instead of the rigidity dictated by a doctrinaire textualism.

The Solicitor General seeks the power of seizure in three clauses of the Executive Article, the first reading, The executive Power shall be vested in a President of the United States of America. Lest I be thought to exaggerate, I quote the interpretation which his brief puts upon it: "In our view, this clause constitutes a grant of all the executive powers of which the Government is capable." If that be true, it is difficult to see why the forefathers bothered to add several specific items, including some trifling ones.

The example of such unlimited executive power that must have most impressed the forefathers was the prerogative exercised by George III, and the description of its evils in the Declaration of Independence leads me to doubt that they were creating their new Executive in his image. . . . I cannot accept the view that this clause is a grant in bulk of all conceivable executive power but regard it as an allocation to the presidential office of the generic powers thereafter stated.

The clause on which the Government next relies is that "The President shall be Commander in Chief of the Army and Navy of the United States * * *." These cryptic words have given rise to some of the most persistent controversies in our constitutional history. Of course, they imply something more than an empty title. But just what authority goes with the name has plagued Presidential advisers who would not waive or narrow it by nonassertion yet cannot say where it begins or ends. It undoubtedly puts the Nation's armed forces under Presidential command. Hence, this loose appellation is sometimes advanced as support for any Presidential action, internal or external, involving use of force, the idea being that it vests power to do anything, anywhere, that can be done with an army or navy. . . .

I cannot foresee all that it might entail if the Court should indorse this argument. Nothing in our Constitution is plainer than that declaration of a war is entrusted only to Congress. Of course, a state of war may in fact exist without a formal declaration. But no doctrine that the Court could promulgate would seem to me more sinister and alarming than that a President whose conduct of foreign affairs is so largely uncontrolled, and often even is unknown, can vastly enlarge his mastery over the internal affairs of the country by his own commitment of the Nation's armed forces to some foreign venture. . . .

Assuming that we are in a war *de facto*, whether it is or is not a war *de jure*, does that empower the Commander-in-Chief to seize industries he thinks necessary to supply our army? The Constitution expressly places in Congress power "to raise and support Armies" and "to provide and maintain a Navy." This certainly lays upon Congress primary responsibility for supplying the armed forces. Congress alone controls the raising of revenues and their appropriation and may determine in what manner and by what means they shall be spent for military and naval procurement. . . .

There are indications that the Constitution did not contemplate that the title Commander-in-Chief of the Army and Navy will constitute him also Commander-in-Chief of the country, its industries and its inhabitants. He has no monopoly of "war powers," whatever they are. While Congress cannot deprive the President of the command of the army and navy, only Congress can provide him an army or navy to command. It is also empowered to make rules for the Government and Regulation of land and naval forces, by which it may to some unknown extent impinge upon even command functions. . . .

We should not use this occasion to circumscribe, much less to contract, the lawful role of the President as Commander-in-Chief. I should indulge the widest latitude of interpretation to sustain his exclusive function to command the instruments of national force, at least when turned against the outside world for the security of our society. But, when it is turned inward, not because of rebellion but because of a lawful economic struggle between industry and labor, it should have no such indulgence. His command power is not such an absolute as might be implied from that office in a militaristic system but is subject to limitations consistent with a constitutional Republic whose law and policy-making branch is a representative Congress. The purpose of lodging dual titles in one man was to insure that the civilian would control the military, not to enable the military to subordinate the presidential office. No penance would ever expiate the sin against free government of holding that a President can escape control of executive powers by law through assuming his military role. What the power of command may include I do not try to envision, but I think it is not a military prerogative, without support of law, to seize persons or property because they are important or even essential for the military and naval establishment.

The third clause in which the Solicitor General finds seizure powers is that "he shall take Care that the Laws be faithfully executed * * *." That authority must be matched against words of the Fifth Amendment that "No person shall be * * * deprived of life, liberty, or property, without due process of law * * *." One gives a governmental authority that reaches so far as there is law, the other gives a private right that authority shall go no farther. These signify about all there is of the principle that ours is a government of laws, not of men, and that we submit ourselves to rulers only if under rules.

The Solicitor General lastly grounds support of the seizure upon nebulous, inherent powers never expressly granted but said to have accrued to the office from the customs and claims of preceding administrations. The plea is for a resulting power to deal with a crisis or an emergency according to the necessities of the case, the unarticulated assumption being that necessity knows no law.

Loose and irresponsible use of adjectives colors all non-legal and much legal discussion of presidential powers. "Inherent" powers, "implied" powers, "incidental" powers, "plenary" powers, "war" powers and "emergency" powers are used, often interchangeably and without fixed or ascertainable meanings. . . .

The appeal, however, that we declare the existence of inherent powers *ex necessitate* to meet an emergency asks us to do what many think would be wise, although it is something the forefathers omitted. They knew what emergencies were, knew the pressures they engender for authoritative action, knew, too, how they afford a ready pretext for usurpation. We may also suspect that they suspected that emergency powers would tend to kindle emergencies. Aside from suspension of the privilege of the writ of habeas corpus in time of rebellion or invasion, when the public safety may require it, they made no express provision for exercise of extraordinary authority because of a crisis. I do not think we rightfully may so amend their work, and, if we could, I am not convinced it would be wise to do so. . . .

In the practical working of our Government we already have evolved a technique within the framework of the Constitution by which normal executive powers may be considerably expanded to meet an emergency. Congress may and has granted extraordinary authorities which lie dormant in normal times but may be called into play by the Executive in war or upon proclamation of a national emergency. . . . Under this procedure we retain Government by law—special, temporary law, perhaps, but law nonetheless. The public may know the extent and limitations of the powers that can be asserted, and persons affected may be informed from the statute of their rights and duties.

In view of the ease, expedition and safety with which Congress can grant and has granted large emergency powers, certainly ample to embrace this crisis, I am quite unimpressed with the argument that we should affirm possession of them without statute. . . .

But I have no illusion that any decision by this Court can keep power in the hands of Congress if it is not wise and timely in meeting its problems. A crisis that challenges the President equally, or perhaps primarily, challenges Congress. . . . We may say that power to legislate for emergencies belongs in the hands of Congress, but only Congress itself can prevent power from slipping through its fingers. . . .

With all its defects, delays and inconveniences, men have discovered no technique for long preserving free government except that the Executive be under the law, and that the law be made by parliamentary deliberations. Such institutions may be destined to pass away. But it is the duty of the Court to be last, not first, to give them up.

MR. JUSTICE BURTON, concurring in both the opinion and judgment of the Court. [omitted]

MR. JUSTICE CLARK, concurring in the judgment of the Court.

One of this Court's first pronouncements upon the powers of the President under the Constitution was made by Chief Justice John Marshall some one hundred and fifty years ago. In *Little v. Barreme*, [2 Cranch 170 (1804)] he used this characteristically clear language in discussing the power of the President to instruct the seizure of the "Flying-Fish," a vessel bound from a French port: "It is by no means clear that the President of the United States whose high duty it is to take care that the laws be faithfully executed, and who is commander in chief of the armies and navies of the United States, might not, without any special authority for that purpose, in the then existing state of things, have empowered the officers commanding the armed vessels of the United States, to seize and send into port for adjudication, American vessels which were forfeited by being engaged in this illicit commerce. But when it is observed that (an act of Congress) gives a special authority to seize on the high seas, and limits that authority to the seizure of vessels bound or sailing to a French port, the legislature seem to have prescribed that the manner in which this law shall be carried into execution, was to exclude a seizure of any vessel not bound to a French port." Accordingly, a unanimous Court held that the President's instructions had been issued without authority and that they could not legalize an act which without those instructions would have been a plain trespass. I know of no subsequent holding of this Court to the contrary.

The limits of presidential power are obscure. However, Article II, no less than Article I, is part of a constitution intended to endure for ages to come, and, consequently, to be adapted to the various crises of human affairs. Some of our Presidents, such as Lincoln, felt that measures otherwise unconstitutional might become lawful by becoming indispensable to the preservation of the Constitution through the preservation of the nation. Others, such as Theodore Roosevelt, thought the President to be capable, as a "steward" of the people, of exerting all power save that which is specifically prohibited by the Constitution or the Congress. In my view—taught me not only by the decision of Chief Justice Marshall in *Little v. Barreme*, but also by a score of other pronouncements of distinguished members of this bench—the Constitution does grant to the President extensive authority in times of grave and imperative national emergency. In fact, to my thinking, such a grant may well be necessary to the very existence of the Constitution itself. As Lincoln aptly said, (is) it possible to lose the nation and yet preserve the Constitution? In describing this authority I care not whether one calls it "residual," "inherent," "moral," "implied," "aggregate," "emergency," or otherwise. I am of the conviction that those who have had the gratifying experience of being the President's lawyer have used one or more of these adjectives only with the utmost of sincerity and the highest of purpose.

I conclude that where Congress has laid down specific procedures to deal with the type of crisis confronting the President, he must follow those procedures in meeting the crisis; but that in the absence of such action by Congress, the President's independent power to act depends upon the gravity of the situation confronting the nation. I cannot sustain the seizure in question because here, as in *Little v. Barreme*, Congress had prescribed methods to be followed by the President in meeting the emergency at hand. . . .

MR. JUSTICE DOUGLAS, concurring.

[T]he President can act more quickly than the Congress. The President with the armed services at his disposal can move with force as well as with speed. All executive power—from the reign of ancient kings to the rule of modern dictators—has the outward appearance of efficiency.

Legislative power, by contrast, is slower to exercise. There must be delay while the ponderous machinery of committees, hearings, and debates is put into motion. That takes time; and while the Congress slowly moves into action, the emergency may take its toll. . . . Legislative action may indeed often be cumbersome, time-consuming, and apparently inefficient. . . .

We therefore cannot decide this case by determining which branch of government can deal most expeditiously with the present crisis. The answer must depend on the allocation of powers under the Constitution. . . .

The legislative nature of the action taken by the President seems to me to be clear. When the United States takes over an industrial plant to settle a labor controversy, it is condemning property. . . .

The power of the Federal Government to condemn property is well established. . . . The command of the Fifth Amendment is that no private property be taken for public use, without just compensation."

[T]he President might seize and the Congress by subsequent action might ratify the seizure.[1] But until and unless Congress acted, no condemnation would be lawful. The branch of government that has the power to pay compensation for a seizure is the only one able to authorize a seizure or make lawful one that the President had effected.

MR. JUSTICE FRANKFURTER, concurring.

[T]he Founders of this Nation were not imbued with the modern cynicism that the only thing that history teaches is that it teaches nothing. They acted on the conviction that the experience of man sheds a good deal of light on his nature. It sheds a good deal of light not merely on the need for effective power, if a society is to be at once cohesive and civilized, but also on the need for limitations on the power of governors over the governed.

[T]he content of the three authorities of government is not to be derived from an abstract analysis. The areas are partly interacting, not wholly disjointed. The Constitution is a framework for government. Therefore the way the framework has consistently operated fairly establishes that it has operated according to its true nature. Deeply embedded traditional ways of conducting government cannot supplant the

---

[1] What a President may do as a matter of expediency or extremity may never reach a definitive constitutional decision. For example, President Lincoln suspended the writ of habeas corpus, claiming the constitutional right to do so. Congress ratified his action.

Constitution or legislation, but they give meaning to the words of a text or supply them. It is an inadmissibly narrow conception of American constitutional law to confine it to the words of the Constitution and to disregard the gloss which life has written upon them. In short, a systematic, unbroken, executive practice, long pursued to the knowledge of the Congress and never before questioned, engaged in by Presidents who have also sworn to uphold the Constitution, making as it were such exercise of power part of the structure of our government, may be treated as a gloss on "executive Power" vested in the President. . . .

[Justice Frankfurter then considered executive practice from the beginning of the Republic.] Down to the World War II period, then, the record is barren of instances comparable to the one before us. Of twelve seizures by President Roosevelt prior to the enactment of the War Labor Disputes Act in June, 1943, three were sanctioned by existing law, and six others were effected after Congress, on December 8, 1941, had declared the existence of a state of war. In this case, reliance on the powers that flow from declared war has been commendably disclaimed by the Solicitor General. Thus the list of executive assertions of the power of seizure in circumstances comparable to the present reduces to three in the six-month period from June to December of 1941. We need not split hairs in comparing those actions to the one before us, though much might be said by way of differentiation. Without passing on their validity, as we are not called upon to do, it suffices to say that these three isolated instances do not add up, either in number, scope, duration or contemporaneous legal justification, to the kind of executive construction of the Constitution [often exercised over a long period of time with full acquiescence of Congress].

MR. CHIEF JUSTICE VINSON, with whom MR. JUSTICE REED and MR. JUSTICE MINTON join, dissenting.

The President of the United States directed the Secretary of Commerce to take temporary possession of the Nation's steel mills during the existing emergency because a work stoppage would immediately jeopardize and imperil our national defense and the defense of those joined with us in resisting aggression, and would add to the continuing danger of our soldiers, sailors and airmen engaged in combat in the field. . . .

Some members of the Court are of the view that the President is without power to act in time of crisis in the absence of express statutory authorization. Other members of the Court affirm on the basis of their reading of certain statutes. Because we cannot agree that affirmance is proper on any ground, and because of the transcending importance of the questions presented not only in this critical litigation but also to the powers the President and of future Presidents to act in time of crisis, we are compelled to register this dissent.

In passing upon the question of Presidential powers in this case, we must first consider the context in which those powers were exercised.

Those who suggest that this is a case involving extraordinary powers should be mindful that these are extraordinary times. A world not yet recovered from the devastation of World War II has been forced to face the threat of another and more terrifying global conflict.

[I]n 1950, when the United Nations called upon member nations "to render every assistance" to repel aggression in Korea, the United States furnished its vigorous support. For almost two full years, our armed forces have been fighting in Korea, suffering casualties of over 108,000 men. Hostilities have not abated. The determination of the United Nations to continue its action in Korea to meet the aggression has been reaffirmed. Congressional support of the action in Korea has been manifested by provisions for increased military manpower and equipment and for economic stabilization, as hereinafter described. . . .

Our treaties represent not merely legal obligations but show congressional recognition that mutual security for the free world is the best security against the threat of aggression on a global scale. The need for mutual security is shown by the very size of the armed forces outside the free world. Defendant's brief informs us that the Soviet Union maintains the largest air force in the world and maintains ground forces much larger than those presently available to the United States and the countries joined with us in mutual security arrangements. Constant international tensions are cited to demonstrate how precarious is the peace. . . .

Congress also directed the President to build up our own defenses. Congress, recognizing "the grim fact * * * that the United States is now engaged in a struggle for survival" and that "it is imperative that we now take those necessary steps to make our strength equal to the peril of the hour," granted authority to draft men into the armed forces. As a result, we now have over 3,500,000 men in our armed forces. . . .

Secretary of Defense Lovett swore that a work stoppage in the steel industry will result immediately in serious curtailment of production of essential weapons and munitions of all kinds. . . .The Secretary of Defense stated that: We are holding the line (in Korea) with ammunition and not with the lives of our troops. . . .

[T]he central fact of this case [is] that the Nation's entire basic steel production would have shut down completely if there had been no Government seizure. Even ignoring for the moment whatever confidential information the President may possess as the Nation's organ for foreign affairs, the uncontroverted affidavits in this record amply support the finding that a work stoppage would immediately jeopardize and imperil our national defense. . . .

Accordingly, if the President has any power under the Constitution to meet a critical situation in the absence of express statutory authorization, there is no basis whatever for criticizing the exercise of such power in this case. . . .

A review of executive action demonstrates that our Presidents have on many occasions exhibited the leadership contemplated by the Framers when they made the President Commander in Chief, and imposed upon him the trust to take Care that the Laws be faithfully executed. With or without explicit statutory authorization, Presidents have at such times dealt with national emergencies by acting promptly and resolutely to enforce legislative programs, at least to save those programs until Congress could act. Congress and the courts have responded to such executive initiative with consistent approval.

Our first President displayed at once the leadership contemplated by the Framers. When the national revenue laws were openly flouted in some sections of Pennsylvania, President Washington, without waiting for a call from the state government, summoned the militia and took decisive steps to secure the faithful execution of the laws. When international disputes engendered by the French revolution threatened to involve this country in war, and while congressional policy remained uncertain, Washington issued his Proclamation of Neutrality. Hamilton, whose defense of the Proclamation has endured the test of time, invoked the argument that the Executive has the duty to do that which will preserve peace until Congress acts and, in addition, pointed to the need for keeping the Nation informed of the requirements of existing laws and treaties as part of the faithful execution of the laws. . . .

Without declaration of war, President Lincoln took energetic action with the outbreak of the War Between the States. He summoned troops and paid them out of the Treasury without appropriation therefor. He proclaimed a naval blockade of the Confederacy and seized ships violating that blockade. Congress, far from denying the validity of these acts, gave them express approval. The most striking action of President Lincoln was the Emancipation Proclamation, issued in aid of the successful prosecution of the War Between the States, but wholly without statutory authority.

[The dissent then details a large number of circumstances in which a President took action in response to one crisis or another, which action was not previously authorized by Congress.]

This is but a cursory summary of executive leadership. But it amply demonstrates that Presidents have taken prompt action to enforce the laws and protect the country whether or not Congress happened to provide in advance for the particular method of execution. At the minimum, the executive actions reviewed herein sustain the action of the President in this case. . . .

History bears out the genius of the Founding Fathers, who created a Government subject to law but not left subject to inertia when vigor and initiative are required. . . .

Much of the argument in this case has been directed at straw men. We do not now have before us the case of a President acting solely on the basis of his own notions of the public welfare. Nor is there any question of unlimited executive power in this case. The President himself closed the door to any such claim when he sent his Message to Congress stating his purpose to abide by any action of Congress, whether approving or disapproving his seizure action. Here, the President immediately made sure that Congress was fully informed of the temporary action he had taken only to preserve the legislative programs from destruction until Congress could act. . . .

There is no statute prohibiting seizure as a method of enforcing legislative programs. . . .

Whatever the extent of Presidential power on more tranquil occasions, and whatever the right of the President to execute legislative programs as he sees fit without reporting the mode of execution to Congress, the single Presidential purpose disclosed on this record is to faithfully execute the laws by acting in an emergency to maintain the status quo, thereby preventing collapse of the legislative programs until Congress could act. . . . Consequently, there is no evidence whatever of any Presidential purpose to defy Congress or act in any way inconsistent with the legislative will. . . .

The broad executive power granted by Article II to an officer on duty 365 days a year cannot, it is said, be invoked to avert disaster. Instead, the President must confine himself to sending a message to Congress recommending action. Under this messenger-boy concept of the Office, the President cannot even act to preserve legislative programs from destruction so that Congress will have something left to act upon. There is no judicial finding that the executive action was unwarranted because there was in fact no basis for the President's finding of the existence of an emergency for, under this view, the gravity of the emergency and the immediacy of the threatened disaster are considered irrelevant as a matter of law. . . .

COMMENTS AND QUESTIONS

1. Consider the timeline of this case. The President issues his proclamation on April 8, 1952. Within a half hour attorneys from leading New York law firms filed an action in federal district court in the District of Columbia seeking a temporary restraining order. That request was denied, and the case was heard on an expedited basis, with the district court rendering an opinion on April 30 enjoining the seizure of the steel mills. The government immediately sought a stay of the order, which was denied by the district court

but granted by the *en banc* United States Court of Appeals for the District of Columbia Circuit on the same day. Rather than have the case go through the normal process of an appeal to a court of appeals, the Supreme Court granted certiorari three days later, with briefs due in one week and oral argument two days later. The government in its week filed a 175 page brief, with much of it devoted to listing all the examples of Presidential actions taken without statutory authorization in the history of the nation. The Court allowed five hours for oral argument, and on June 2, three weeks later, rendered its decision in six separate opinions. And all of this was done without Westlaw, Lexis, the internet, or word processing.

2.   After the decision, President Truman immediately ordered the Secretary of Commerce to return the steel mills to their owners, and shortly thereafter the strike began. While it went on for 50 days, there was no apparent effect on the "war" effort, as there had been a significant stockpile of steel created during the period of the federal takeover.

3.   One might wonder why the steelworkers who were set to go on strike would come back to work just because the government seized the mills. The answer is simple; the first act of the Secretary of Commerce after seizing the mills was to grant the workers the wage demands they had sought before going on strike. Indeed, the owners' first argument in court was not to overturn the seizure but to overturn the requirement to pay the higher wages. That is, the owners' real objection was not to the seizure, but to the requirement to pay the increased wages.

4.   One might also wonder why President Truman did not use one of the three statutory mechanisms alluded to in the Court's opinion. The two statutory systems for seizing factories would have taken more time and had not been created to deal with labor/management problems. The Taft-Hartley Act, which specifically dealt with labor/management problems and which would have allowed the President to delay the strike, had been passed over President Truman's veto, so he did not wish to utilize it. Moreover, because it would have maintained the status quo as to wages, it would have disadvantaged the workers, and Truman believed that in the labor/management dispute labor was in the right.

5.   While Justice Black's opinion is for the Court, it is not the opinion that has become the canonical opinion. That place is reserved for Justice Jackson's concurrence. While Justice Black's opinion is what scholars would call "formalistic," because it draws bright lines based on the Constitution's text, Justice Jackson's opinion is what scholars would call "functional," because it tries to accommodate the realities of governing in modern times with the Constitution's ambiguous provisions. Justice Black's approach provides clear answers—the President's action is unlawful because no statute authorizes it and there is no constitutional text authorizing it. End of case. The "functional" approach, however, is less determinative; it requires balancing. Justice Jackson's three groupings, which have become a standard approach to assessing the constitutionality of Presidential actions, provide guidance but no firm answer. For example, even after he determines that the seizure of the

steel mills is in the third category—contrary to Congress' commands—that still does not by itself determine that the action is unconstitutional.

6.   Justice Douglas's opinion appears to allow for the possibility that Congress can ratify after-the-fact a Presidential action that would have been unconstitutional without it, and in that sense approving of a President taking action without authority but in the expectation (or hope) that Congress will ratify it later—as indeed President Truman obviously hoped here.

7.   Justice Frankfurter's opinion stresses the relevance of historical practice in assessing the constitutionality of Presidential action where the Constitution is unclear. Here, he finds no historical practice justifying the seizure. The dissent, by contrast, reads the history just the opposite—as a clear justification for the seizure. Inasmuch as they are both using the same history, does this suggest the indeterminacy of history as a guide to constitutional decisionmaking? Of course, that is not to say that other guides are not indeterminate as well.

8.   Justice Clark's opinion reflects an approach much like Justice Jackson's, but a bit more categorical. He is willing to accept a broad executive power in the absence of congressional action, but when Congress has spoken, the President must comply. It is interesting that our old friend John Marshall even had something to say about this, and that it remains on point today.

9.   Justices Jackson, Clark, Frankfurter, and Burton all characterize the statutes in issue as reflecting a congressional decision that the President could not seize the mills as he did. The dissent, however, correctly notes that neither these laws nor any other law state that the President may not do what he did. They all provide other means to accomplish the same end but do not in terms forbid other means. Who do you think is right?

PROBLEM

Prior to the American-led invasion of Afghanistan in response to the attack on the World Trade Center and the Pentagon on September 11, 2001, Congress authorized the use of "all necessary and appropriate force" against the "nations, organizations, or persons" associated with the September 11, 2001, attacks. After fighting the Taliban and Al Qaeda in Afghanistan for a number of years, the United States withdrew from Afghanistan. Nevertheless, the President continued to authorize the use of drones to hunt down and kill senior Al Qaeda officers involved in Al Qaeda activities in other nations. In light of *Curtiss-Wright* and the *Steel Seizure Case,* is this extension of military force by the President constitutional?

B. WARS AND EMERGENCIES

The text of the Constitution would not seem to give much power or responsibility to the President with respect to wars and national emergencies. The President is the Commander-in-Chief of the army and navy and of the militia, when called into national service, a not inconsiderable power, but nonetheless a relatively subordinate role when compared to Congress's power and authority to declare war; to grant letters of marque and reprisal; to make rules for captures on land and water; to raise and support armies; to provide and maintain a navy; to make rules for the government and regulation of the land and naval forces; to provide for calling forth the militia to execute the laws, suppress insurrections, and repel invasions; and to provide for the organizing, arming, disciplining, and governing the militia when called into national service. In other words, it would appear that the President is to be the top General, but always subject to congressional control.

The Federalist papers likewise do not provide much support for expansive Presidential authority in wars or emergencies. Reflecting their purpose to convince people to ratify the Constitution, the Federalist papers had to tread a narrow line. On the one hand, they needed to portray the powers of the President as less than those of the king of Great Britain and not dissimilar to those of some state governors. This would reassure people that the President would not be too strong. *See* The Federalist, No. 69. On the other hand, The Federalist papers needed to justify why the executive power was to be lodged in one person's hands, rather than a Council, which had been an alternative recommendation. Here, the Federalist papers stress the importance of energy and vigor in the executive, and they argue that "unity" is a necessity for such energy and vigor. *See* The Federalist, No. 70. Another necessity for energy and vigor, the Federalist papers state, is the provision of adequate powers. In Numbers 73–77, Hamilton identifies the various powers provided the President. The discussion of the powers of Commander-in-Chief is amazingly short.

> The propriety of this provision is so evident in itself, and it is, at the same time, so consonant to the precedents of the State constitutions in general, that little need be said to explain or enforce it. Even those of them which have, in other respects, coupled the chief magistrate with a council, have for the most part concentrated the military authority in him alone. Of all the cares or concerns of government, the direction of war most peculiarly demands those qualities which distinguish the exercise of power by a single hand. The direction of war implies the direction of the common strength; and the power of directing and employing the common strength, forms a usual and essential part in the definition of the executive authority.

The Federalist, No. 74. He explains that the President's authority as Commander-in-Chief is:

> nominally the same with that of the king of Great Britain, but in substance much inferior to it. It would amount to nothing more than the supreme command and direction of the military and naval forces, as first General and admiral of the Confederacy; while that of the British king extends to the declaring of war and to the raising and regulating of fleets and armies, all which, by the Constitution under consideration, would appertain to the legislature.

The Federalist, No. 69. Nowhere do the Federalist papers suggest any authority in the President beyond the listed powers. Instead, Hamilton finishes his discussion of the powers of the President by explaining the safeguards against a misuse or abuse of those powers: the limited term of office, possible impeachment, and possible subsequent criminal prosecution. Then Hamilton concludes:

> But these precautions, great as they are, are not the only ones which the plan of the convention has provided in favor of the public security. In the only instances in which the abuse of the executive authority was materially to be feared, the Chief Magistrate of the United States would, by that plan, be subjected to the control of a branch of the legislative body. What more could be desired by an enlightened and reasonable people?

The Federalist, No. 77.

Perhaps, however, Hamilton had his fingers crossed, because, after all, he was trying to reassure potential ratifiers that the President was not to be feared. Later, defending President Washington's declaration of neutrality in the war between France and Great Britain against claims that the President had no authority to make such a determination, Hamilton wrote that such a declaration clearly is not for the legislative branch, because it "is not the organ of intercourse between the United States and foreign nations." Equally clearly, it was not an appropriate exercise of judicial functions. Thus, because this power did not belong to the legislative or the judicial branches, it "of course, must belong to the executive." That is, all residual powers of the government not expressly granted to the legislative and judicial branches must reside in the executive. Moreover, Hamilton wrote,

> It deserves to be remarked, that as the participation of the senate in the making of treaties, and the power of the legislature to declare war, are exceptions out of the general "executive power" vested in the President, they are to be construed strictly, and ought to be extended no further than is essential to their execution.

The "general 'executive power' " Hamilton refers to here was the executive power that historically resided in the king of Great Britain, who alone could declare war and make treaties. Here Hamilton tells us what he really thinks.

Hamilton's view was not unopposed at the time. Madison, then a member of Congress, wrote in opposition, reflecting the views of the Democratic-Republicans of a more limited executive authority than envisaged by the Federalists.

Whoever one believes has the better argument in theory or from the constitutional text, historical practice has definitely reflected the notion of a strong executive, especially in wars, emergencies, and foreign affairs. From Washington's declaration of neutrality, Jefferson's action against the Barbary pirates, Lincoln's actions during the Civil War, Wilson's actions preceding and during the First World War, and Roosevelt's actions preceding and during the Second World War, presidents did not shy from using their military and diplomatic powers to protect the nation and its interests—as understood by those presidents. Although the United States has only declared war on five occasions, the President has dispatched American armed forces abroad on more than 200 occasions. For various reasons, almost all of these actions escaped judicial review.

THE PRIZE CASES

United States Supreme Court, 1862.
67 U.S. 635, 17 L.Ed. 459.

[On April 12, 1861, Confederate batteries in Charleston, South Carolina, opened fire on Fort Sumter, a federal fort located in the harbor, when it refused to surrender. This was the first outbreak of hostilities between the Union and the Confederacy. One week later, President Lincoln announced a naval blockade of the Confederate States, and subsequently some commercial ships from South America destined for Confederate ports, having no knowledge of the state of hostilities or the blockade, were seized by the U.S. Navy. The practice at the time was to sell captured ships and any goods thereon as "prizes" at auction, with a portion of the funds being used to reward the crew of the capturing ship. The owners of these ships challenged the lawfulness of their seizure on the grounds that the blockade was unlawful, because there was as a matter of law no "war" then existing that would authorize a blockade.]

MR. JUSTICE GRIER.

[H]ad the President a right to institute a blockade of ports in possession of persons in armed rebellion against the Government, on the principles of international law, as known and acknowledged among civilized States? . . . Let us enquire whether, at the time this blockade was instituted, a state of war existed which would justify a resort to these means of subduing the hostile force. . . .

Insurrection against a government may or may not culminate in an organized rebellion, but a civil war always begins by insurrection against the lawful authority of the Government. A civil war is never solemnly declared; it becomes such by its accidents—the number, power, and organization of the persons who originate and carry it on. When the party in rebellion occupy and hold in a hostile manner a certain portion of territory; have declared their independence; have cast off their allegiance; have organized armies; have commenced hostilities against their former sovereign, the world acknowledges them as belligerents, and the contest a *war*. *They* claim to be in arms to establish their liberty and independence, in order to become a sovereign State, while the sovereign party treats them as insurgents and rebels who owe allegiance, and who should be punished with death for their treason. . . .

"A civil war," says Vattel,* "breaks the bands of society and government, or at least suspends their force and effect; it produces in the nation two independent parties, who consider each other as enemies, and acknowledge no common judge. Those two parties, therefore, must necessarily be considered as constituting, at least for a time, two separate bodies, two distinct societies. Having no common superior to judge between them, they stand in precisely the same predicament as two nations who engage in a contest and have recourse to arms. This being the case, it is very evident that the common laws of war—those maxims of humanity, moderation, and honor—ought to be observed by both parties in every civil war. . . ." As a civil war is never publicly proclaimed, *eo nomine*,** against insurgents, its actual existence is a fact in our domestic history which the Court is bound to notice and to know.

The true test of its existence, as found in the writings of the sages of the common law, may be thus summarily stated: "When the regular course of justice is interrupted by revolt, rebellion, or insurrection, so that the Courts of Justice cannot be kept open, *civil war exists* and hostilities may be prosecuted on the same footing as if those opposing the Government were foreign enemies invading the land."

By the Constitution, Congress alone has the power to declare a national or foreign war. It cannot declare war against a State, or any number of States, by virtue of any clause in the Constitution. The Constitution confers on the President the whole Executive power. He is bound to take care that the laws be faithfully executed. He is Commander-in-chief of the Army and Navy of the United States, and of the militia of the several States when called into the actual service of the United States.

---

    *   Emer de Vattel was a famous 18th-century expert on international law whose work, Law of Nations, was well known to the Founding Fathers. [author's note]

   ** Latin for "in the name of." [author's note]

He has no power to initiate or declare a war either against a foreign nation or a domestic State. But by the Acts of Congress of February 28th, 1795, and 3d of March, 1807, he is authorized to call out the militia and use the military and naval forces of the United States in case of invasion by foreign nations, and to suppress insurrection against the government of a State or of the United States.

If a war be made by invasion of a foreign nation, the President is not only authorized but bound to resist force by force. He does not initiate the war, but is bound to accept the challenge without waiting for any special legislative authority. And whether the hostile party be a foreign invader, or States organized in rebellion, it is none the less a war, although the declaration of it be "*unilateral.*" . . . It is not the less a war on *that account*, for war may exist without a declaration on either side. It is so laid down by the best writers on the law of nations. A declaration of war by one country only, is not a mere challenge to be accepted or refused at pleasure by the other. . . .

This greatest of civil wars was not gradually developed by popular commotion, tumultuous assemblies, or local unorganized insurrections. However long may have been its previous conception, it nevertheless sprung forth suddenly from the parent brain, a Minerva in the full panoply of *war*.* The President was bound to meet it in the shape it presented itself, without waiting for Congress to baptize it with a name; and no name given to it by him or them could change the fact. . . .

Whether the President in fulfilling his duties, as Commander-in-chief, in suppressing an insurrection, has met with such armed hostile resistance, and a civil war of such alarming proportions as will compel him to accord to them the character of belligerents, is a question to be decided *by him*, and this Court must be governed by the decisions and acts of the political department of the Government to which this power was entrusted. "He must determine what degree of force the crisis demands." The proclamation of blockade is itself official and conclusive evidence to the Court that a state of war existed which demanded and authorized a recourse to such a measure, under the circumstances peculiar to the case. . . .

If it were necessary to the technical existence of a war, that it should have a legislative sanction, we find it in almost every act passed at the extraordinary session of the Legislature of 1861, which was wholly employed in enacting laws to enable the Government to prosecute the war with vigor and efficiency. And finally, in 1861, we find Congress "*ex majore cautela*"** and in anticipation of such astute objections, passing an act

---

* A reference to the Roman goddess of wisdom and war (Athena in Greek mythology) who was supposed to have been born by springing full grown from the head of Jupiter, the king of the gods. [author's note]

** Latin for "in an abundance of caution." [author's note]

"approving, legalizing, and making valid all the acts, proclamations, and orders of the President, &c., as if they had been *issued and done under the previous express authority* and direction of the Congress of the United States." . . .

On this first question therefore we are of the opinion that the President had a right, *jure belli*,* to institute a blockade of ports in possession of the States in rebellion, which neutrals are bound to regard. . . .

MR. JUSTICE NELSON, dissenting.

[A]nother objection taken to the seizure of this vessel and cargo is, that there was no existing war between the United States and the States in insurrection within the meaning of the law of nations, which drew after it the consequences of a public or civil war. A contest by force between independent sovereign States is called a public war; and, when duly commenced by proclamation or otherwise, it entitles both of the belligerent parties to all the rights of war against each other, and as respects neutral nations. Chancellor Kent observes, "Though a solemn declaration, or previous notice to the enemy, be now laid aside, it is essential that some formal public act, proceeding directly from the competent source, should announce to the people at home their new relations and duties growing out of a state of war, and which should equally apprize neutral nations of the fact, to enable them to conform their conduct to the rights belonging to the new state of things." . . . He further observes, "as war cannot lawfully be commenced on the part of the United States without an act of Congress, such act is, of course, a formal notice to all the world, and equivalent to the most solemn declaration." . . .

In the case of a rebellion or resistance of a portion of the people of a country against the established government, there is no doubt, if in its progress and enlargement the government thus sought to be overthrown sees fit, it may by the competent power recognize or declare the existence of a state of civil war, which will draw after it all the consequences and rights of war between the contending parties as in the case of a public war. . . . But before this insurrection against the established Government can be dealt with on the footing of a civil war, within the meaning of the law of nations and the Constitution of the United States, and which will draw after it belligerent rights, it must be recognized or declared by the war-making power of the Government. No power short of this can change the legal status of the Government or the relations of its citizens from that of peace to a state of war, or bring into existence all those duties and obligations of neutral third parties growing out of a state of war. The war power of the Government must be exercised before this changed condition of the Government and people and of neutral third parties can be admitted. There is no difference in this respect between a civil or a public war. . . .

---

* Latin for "the law of war." [author's note]

An idea seemed to be entertained that all that was necessary to constitute a war was organized hostility in the district of country in a state of rebellion—that conflicts on land and on sea—the taking of towns and capture of fleets—in fine, the magnitude and dimensions of the resistance against the Government—constituted war with all the belligerent rights belonging to civil war. . . . It was said that war was to be ascertained by looking at the armies and navies or public force of the contending parties, and the battles lost and won—that in the language of one of the learned counsel, "Whenever the situation of opposing hostilities has assumed the proportions and pursued the methods of war, then peace is driven out, the ordinary authority and administration of law are suspended, and war in fact and by necessity is the *status* of the nation until peace is restored and the laws resumed their dominion."

Now, in one sense, no doubt this is war, and may be a war of the most extensive and threatening dimensions and effects, but it is a statement simply of its existence in a material sense, and has no relevancy or weight when the question is what constitutes war in a legal sense, in the sense of the law of nations, and of the Constitution of the United States? For it must be a war in this sense to attach to it all the consequences that belong to belligerent rights. Instead, therefore, of inquiring after armies and navies, and victories lost and won, or organized rebellion against the general Government, the inquiry should be into the law of nations and into the municipal fundamental laws of the Government. For we find there that to constitute a civil war in the sense in which we are speaking, before it can exist, in contemplation of law, it must be recognized or declared by the sovereign power of the State, and which sovereign power by our Constitution is lodged in the Congress of the United States—civil war, therefore, under our system of government, can exist only by an act of Congress, which requires the assent of two of the great departments of the Government, the Executive and Legislative.

We have thus far been speaking of the war power under the Constitution of the United States, and as known and recognized by the law of nations. But we are asked, what would become of the peace and integrity of the Union in case of an insurrection at home or invasion from abroad if this power could not be exercised by the President in the recess of Congress, and until that body could be assembled?

The framers of the Constitution fully comprehended this question, and provided for the contingency. . . . The Constitution declares that Congress shall have power "to provide for calling forth the militia to execute the laws of the Union, suppress insurrections, and repel invasions." . . . Congress passed laws on this subject in 1792 and 1795.

The last Act provided that whenever the United States shall be invaded or be in imminent danger of invasion from a foreign nation, it shall be lawful for the President to call forth such number of the militia most convenient to the place of danger, and in case of insurrection in any State against the Government thereof, it shall be lawful for the President, on the application of the Legislature of such State, if in session, or if not, of the Executive of the State, to call forth such number of militia of any other State or States as he may judge sufficient to suppress such insurrection. [A]nd by the Act 3 March, 1807, it is provided that in case of insurrection or obstruction of the laws, either in the United States or of any State of Territory, where it is lawful for the President to call forth the militia for the purpose of suppressing such insurrection, and causing the laws to be executed, it shall be lawful to employ for the same purpose such part of the land and naval forces of the United States as shall be judged necessary.

It will be seen, therefore, that ample provision has been made under the Constitution and laws against any sudden and unexpected disturbance of the public peace from insurrection at home or invasion from abroad. The whole military and naval power of the country is put under the control of the President to meet the emergency. . . .

Congress assembled on the call for an extra session the 4th of July, 1861, and among the first acts passed was one in which the President was authorized by proclamation to interdict all trade and intercourse between all the inhabitants of States in insurrection and the rest of the United States, subjecting vessel and cargo to capture and condemnation as prize, and also to direct the capture of any ship or vessel belonging in whole or in part to any inhabitant of a State whose inhabitants are declared by the proclamation to be in a state of insurrection, found at sea or in any part of the rest of the United States. Act of Congress of 13th of July, 1861, secs. 5, 6. . . .

This Act of Congress, we think, recognized a state of civil war between the Government and the Confederate States, and made it territorial. . . . We agree, therefore, that the Act 13th July, 1861, recognized a state of civil war between the Government and the people of the State described in that proclamation. . . .

Upon the whole, after the most careful consideration of this case which the pressure of other duties has admitted, I am compelled to the conclusion that no civil war existed between this Government and the States in insurrection till recognized by the Act of Congress 13th of July, 1861; . . . and, consequently, that the President had no power to set on foot a blockade under the law of nations, and that the capture of the vessel and cargo in this case, and in all cases before us in which the capture occurred before the 13th of July, 1861, for breach of blockade . . . are illegal and void, and that the decrees of condemnation should be reversed and the vessel and cargo restored.

MR. CHIEF JUSTICE TANEY, MR. JUSTICE CATRON and MR. JUSTICE CLIFFORD, concurred in the dissenting opinion of MR. JUSTICE NELSON.

COMMENTS AND QUESTIONS

1.   Everyone on the Court agrees that a civil war can be a "war" within the meaning of international law and the Constitution, just as they all agree that hostilities between nations can be a war within the meaning of international law and the Constitution. The disagreement between the majority and the dissent is what it takes to transform a state of hostilities, whether between nations or within a nation, into a "war" for legal purposes. What does the majority say? What does the dissent say?

2.   If the President can characterize any given state of hostilities as a "war" for legal purposes, what does the Constitution mean that Congress has the power to declare war?

3.   Do you agree with the dissent that the only way hostilities can be a "war" for legal purposes is for Congress to so declare it? What difference does it make today whether something is a "war" for legal purposes as opposed to for practical purposes? After all, we don't take "prizes" anymore.

4.   The dissent seems to think it is important that the President pursuant to the several militia acts can call out the militia as well as utilize all the armed forces on his own say so. If these did not exist, would it make a difference to the dissent's analysis?

5.   Both the majority and dissent agree that the Act of 13 July, 1861, had the effect of declaring war, although it did not say so in so many words. What does it take to characterize a legislative act as a declaration of war? Is it enough that it authorizes action that would be illegal (domestically or internationally) but for a state of war?

6.   In 1973, in response to the Vietnam War and over President Nixon's veto, Congress passed the War Powers Resolution. Among other things the Resolution requires the President to submit a report to Congress within 48 hours "in any case in which United States Armed Forces are introduced into hostilities or into situations where imminent involvement in hostilities is clearly indicated by the circumstances." Moreover, unless Congress declares war or specifically authorizes the involvement within 60 days, the President is required to terminate any such use of United States Armed Forces. Virtually every President since Nixon has indicated that he believes the Resolution is unconstitutional, but Presidents have usually complied with the reporting requirement (while denying that the report is required) and have usually received authorization in one form or another for continued involvement in hostilities. An issue arose with respect to the United States' participation in NATO activities in aid of Libyan rebels. President Obama did not make the required report, claiming that US troops were not involved in hostilities; our only involvement was support of other nations' activities and the use of drones, which did not subject US forces to hostile action. This conclusion has been roundly criticized and was not unanimous within the administration itself; apparently both the Justice Department and Defense Department thought the action fell within the terms of the Resolution, whereas the White House Counsel and the State Department thought it did not. Similarly, President

Trump did not make a report to Congress regarding the raid to capture or kill the ISIS leader, Abu Bakr al-Baghdadi, although his explanation for not reporting was different. What do you think? Do you think this issue could or would ever be resolved by a court?

EX PARTE QUIRIN

United States Supreme Court, 1942.
317 U.S. 1, 63 S.Ct. 2.

[On the night of June 13, 1942, a German submarine deposited on Amagansett Beach on Long Island, New York, four persons equipped with explosives, fuses, and incendiary and timing devices. Four nights later a

The German Saboteurs

German submarine deposited four more persons similarly equipped on Ponte Vedra Beach, near Jacksonville, Florida. All proceeded in civilian clothes with orders to destroy war industries and war facilities in the United States. Two of the persons who landed in New York turned themselves into the Federal Bureau of Investigation, and as a result the remainder were taken into custody shortly thereafter in New York or Chicago by FBI agents. All of these persons had been born in Germany, lived for some period in the United States, but had returned to Germany between 1933 and 1941. All but one were German citizens. One claimed to be an American citizen. All had received training at a sabotage school near Berlin, Germany, where they were instructed in the use of explosives and in methods of secret writing.

Pursuant to an order of President Roosevelt, they were charged before a military commission for spying in violation of the laws of war. They sought habeas corpus review in a federal district court, which denied review. They sought immediate review of that decision in the Supreme Court, which the Court granted. It heard argument on July 29 and 30, while their trial before the Military Commission was still underway, but denied the writ on July 31 with a brief *per curiam* opinion, stating that a full opinion would come later. They were all convicted and sentenced to death, but President Roosevelt commuted the sentences for the two who had turned themselves in, requiring instead a life sentence for one and 30 years for the other. On August 8, the remaining six were executed. On October 29, the Supreme Court filed its full opinion, which follows.]

MR. CHIEF JUSTICE STONE delivered the opinion of the Court.

[T]he question for decision is whether the detention of petitioners by respondent for trial by Military Commission, appointed by Order of the President of July 2, 1942, on charges preferred against them purporting to set out their violations of the law of war and of the Articles of War, is in conformity to the laws and Constitution of the United States. . . .

The President, as President and Commander in Chief of the Army and Navy, by Order of July 2, 1942, appointed a Military Commission and directed it to try petitioners for offenses against the law of war and the Articles of War, and prescribed regulations for the procedure on the trial and for review of the record of the trial and of any judgment or sentence of the Commission. On the same day, by Proclamation, the President declared that "all persons who are subjects, citizens or residents of any nation at war with the United States or who give obedience to or act under the direction of any such nation, and who during time of war enter or attempt to enter the United States * * * through coastal or boundary defenses, and are charged with committing or attempting or preparing to commit sabotage, espionage, hostile or warlike acts, or violations of the law of war, shall be subject to the law of war and to the jurisdiction of military tribunals."

The Proclamation also stated in terms that all such persons were denied access to the courts. . . .

Petitioners' main contention is that the President is without any statutory or constitutional authority to order the petitioners to be tried by military tribunal for offenses with which they are charged; that in consequence they are entitled to be tried in the civil courts with the safeguards, including trial by jury, which the Fifth and Sixth Amendments guarantee to all persons charged in such courts with criminal offenses. In any case it is urged that the President's Order, in prescribing the procedure of the Commission and the method for review of its findings and sentence, and the proceedings of the Commission under the Order, conflict with Articles of War adopted by Congress—particularly Articles 38, 43, 46, 50 1/2 and 70—and are illegal and void.

The Government challenges each of these propositions. But regardless of their merits, it also insists that petitioners must be denied access to the courts, both because they are enemy aliens or have entered our territory as enemy belligerents, and because the President's Proclamation undertakes in terms to deny such access to the class of persons defined by the Proclamation, which aptly describes the character and conduct of petitioners. It is urged that if they are enemy aliens or if the Proclamation has force no court may afford the petitioners a hearing. But there is certainly nothing in the Proclamation to preclude access to the courts for determining its applicability to the particular case. And neither the Proclamation nor the fact that they are enemy aliens forecloses consideration by the courts of petitioners' contentions that the Constitution and laws of the United States constitutionally enacted forbid their trial by military commission. . . .

We are not here concerned with any question of the guilt or innocence of petitioners. Constitutional safeguards for the protection of all who are charged with offenses are not to be disregarded in order to inflict merited punishment on some who are guilty. But the detention and trial of petitioners—ordered by the President in the declared exercise of his powers as Commander in Chief of the Army in time of war and of grave public danger—are not to be set aside by the courts without the clear conviction that they are in conflict with the Constitution or laws of Congress constitutionally enacted.

Congress and the President, like the courts, possess no power not derived from the Constitution. But one of the objects of the Constitution, as declared by its preamble, is to "provide for the common defence." As a means to that end the Constitution gives to Congress [a number of powers.]

The Constitution confers on the President the "executive Power," and imposes on him the duty to "take Care that the Laws be faithfully executed." It makes him the Commander in Chief of the Army and Navy, and empowers him to appoint and commission officers of the United States.

The Constitution thus invests the President as Commander in Chief with the power to wage war which Congress has declared, and to carry into effect all laws passed by Congress for the conduct of war and for the government and regulation of the Armed Forces, and all laws defining and punishing offences against the law of nations, including those which pertain to the conduct of war.

By the Articles of War, Congress has provided rules for the government of the Army. [T]he Articles . . . recognize the "military commission" appointed by military command as an appropriate tribunal for the trial and punishment of offenses against the law of war not ordinarily tried by court martial. Articles 38 and 46 authorize the President, with certain limitations, to prescribe the procedure for military commissions. Articles 81 and 82 authorize trial, either by court martial or military commission, of those charged with relieving, harboring or corresponding with the enemy and those charged with spying. . . .

Similarly the Espionage Act of 1917, which authorizes trial in the district courts of certain offenses that tend to interfere with the prosecution of war, provides that nothing contained in the act "shall be deemed to limit the jurisdiction of the general courts-martial, military commissions, or naval courts-martial."

[B]y the Articles of War, . . . Congress has explicitly provided, so far as it may constitutionally do so, that military tribunals shall have jurisdiction to try offenders or offenses against the law of war in appropriate cases.

Congress, in addition to making rules for the government of our Armed Forces, has thus exercised its authority to define and punish offenses against the law of nations by sanctioning, within constitutional limitations, the jurisdiction of military commissions to try persons for offenses which, according to the rules and precepts of the law of nations, and more particularly the law of war, are cognizable by such tribunals. And the President, as Commander in Chief, by his Proclamation in time of war has invoked that law. By his Order creating the present Commission he has undertaken to exercise the authority conferred upon him by Congress, and also such authority as the Constitution itself gives the Commander in Chief, to direct the performance of those functions which may constitutionally be performed by the military arm of the nation in time of war.

[I]t is unnecessary for present purposes to determine to what extent the President as Commander in Chief has constitutional power to create military commissions without the support of Congressional legislation. For here Congress has authorized trial of offenses against the law of war before such commissions. We are concerned only with the question whether it is within the constitutional power of the national government to place petitioners upon trial before a military commission for the offenses with which they are charged. We must therefore first inquire whether any of the acts charged is an offense against the law of war cognizable before a military tribunal, and if so whether the Constitution prohibits the trial. We may assume that there are acts . . . which would not be triable by military tribunal here, . . . because they are of that class of offenses constitutionally triable only by a jury. It was upon such grounds that the Court denied the right to proceed by military tribunal in *Ex parte Milligan*. But as we shall show, these petitioners were charged with an offense against the law of war which the Constitution does not require to be tried by jury. . . .

By universal agreement and practice the law of war draws a distinction between the armed forces and the peaceful populations of belligerent nations and also between those who are lawful and unlawful combatants. Lawful combatants are subject to capture and detention as prisoners of war by opposing military forces. Unlawful combatants are likewise subject to capture and detention, but in addition they are subject to trial and punishment by military tribunals for acts which render their belligerency unlawful. The spy who secretly and without uniform passes the military lines of a belligerent in time of war, seeking to gather military information and communicate it to the enemy, or an enemy combatant who without uniform comes secretly through the lines for the purpose of waging war by destruction of life or property, are familiar examples of belligerents who are generally deemed not to be entitled to the status of prisoners of war, but to be offenders against the law of war subject to trial and punishment by military tribunals. . . .

Our Government, by thus defining lawful belligerents entitled to be treated as prisoners of war, has recognized that there is a class of unlawful belligerents not entitled to that privilege, including those who though combatants do not wear "fixed and distinctive emblems." And by Article 15 of the Articles of War Congress has made provision for their trial and punishment by military commission, according to "the law of war." . . .

Citizenship in the United States of an enemy belligerent does not relieve him from the consequences of a belligerency which is unlawful because in violation of the law of war. Citizens who associate themselves with the military arm of the enemy government, and with its aid, guidance and direction enter this country bent on hostile acts are enemy belligerents within the meaning of the Hague Convention and the law of war. . . .

But petitioners insist that even if the offenses with which they are charged are offenses against the law of war, their trial is subject to the requirement of the Fifth Amendment that no person shall be held to answer for a capital or otherwise infamous crime unless on a presentment or indictment of a grand jury, and that such trials by Article III, § 2, and the Sixth Amendment must be by jury in a civil court. . . .

Presentment by a grand jury and trial by a jury of the vicinage where the crime was committed were at the time of the adoption of the Constitution familiar parts of the machinery for criminal trials in the civil courts. But they were procedures unknown to military tribunals, which are not courts in the sense of the Judiciary Article. . . . In the light of this long-continued and consistent interpretation we must conclude that § 2 of Article III and the Fifth and Sixth Amendments cannot be taken to have extended the right to demand a jury to trials by military commission, or to have required that offenses against the law of war not triable by jury at common law be tried only in the civil courts.

Since the Amendments, like § 2 of Article III, do not preclude all trials of offenses against the law of war by military commission without a jury when the offenders are aliens not members of our Armed Forces, it is plain that they present no greater obstacle to the trial in like manner of citizen enemies who have violated the law of war applicable to enemies. . . .

Petitioners, and especially petitioner Haupt, stress the pronouncement of this Court in the *Milligan* case, that the law of war "can never be applied to citizens in states which have upheld the authority of the government, and where the courts are open and their process unobstructed." Elsewhere in its opinion, the Court was at pains to point out that Milligan, a citizen twenty years resident in Indiana, who had never been a resident of any of the states in rebellion, was not an enemy belligerent either entitled to the status of a prisoner of war or subject to the penalties imposed upon unlawful belligerents. We construe the Court's statement as to the inapplicability of the law of war to Milligan's case as having particular reference to the facts before it. From them the Court concluded that Milligan, not being a part of or associated with the armed forces of the enemy, was a non-belligerent, not subject to the law of war save as—in circumstances found not there to be present and not involved here—martial law might be constitutionally established.

The Court's opinion is inapplicable to the case presented by the present record. We have no occasion now to define with meticulous care the ultimate boundaries of the jurisdiction of military tribunals to try persons according to the law of war. It is enough that petitioners here, upon the conceded facts, were plainly within those boundaries, and were held in good faith for trial by military commission, charged with being enemies who, with the purpose of destroying war materials and utilities, entered or after entry remained in our territory without uniform—an offense against the law of war. We hold only that those particular acts constitute an offense against the law of war which the Constitution authorizes to be tried by military commission. . . .

There remains the contention that the President's Order of July 2, 1942, so far as it lays down the procedure to be followed on the trial before the Commission and on the review of its findings and sentence, and the procedure in fact followed by the Commission, are in conflict with Articles of War 38, 43, 46, 50 1/2 and 70. . . .

Petitioners do not argue and we do not consider the question whether the President is compelled by the Articles of War to afford unlawful enemy belligerents a trial before subjecting them to disciplinary measures. Their contention is that, if Congress has authorized their trial by military commission upon the charges preferred—violations of the law of war and the 81st and 82nd Articles of War—it has by the Articles of War prescribed the procedure by which the trial is to be conducted; and that since the President has ordered their trial for such offenses by military commission, they are entitled to claim the protection of the procedure which Congress has commanded shall be controlling.

We need not inquire whether Congress may restrict the power of the Commander in Chief to deal with enemy belligerents. For the Court is unanimous in its conclusion that the Articles in question could not at any stage of the proceedings afford any basis for issuing the writ. But a majority of the full Court are not agreed on the appropriate grounds for decision. Some members of the Court are of opinion that Congress did not intend the Articles of War to govern a Presidential military commission convened for the determination of questions relating to admitted enemy invaders and that the context of the Articles makes clear that they should not be construed to apply in that class of cases. Others are of the view that—even though this trial is subject to whatever provisions of the Articles of War Congress has in terms made applicable to "commissions"—the particular Articles in question, rightly construed, do not foreclose the procedure prescribed by the President or that shown to have been employed by the

Commission in a trial of offenses against the law of war and the 81st and 82nd Articles of War, by a military commission appointed by the President.

Accordingly, we conclude that Charge I, on which petitioners were detained for trial by the Military Commission, alleged an offense which the President is authorized to order tried by military commission; that his Order convening the Commission was a lawful order and that the Commission was lawfully constituted; that the petitioners were held in lawful custody and did not show cause for their discharge. It follows that the orders of the District Court should be affirmed, and that leave to file petitions for habeas corpus in this Court should be denied.

MR. JUSTICE MURPHY took no part in the consideration or decision of these cases.

COMMENTS AND QUESTIONS

1. Here there is no question that there is a declared war. Rather the question is what power the President has to detain, try, and execute a sentence with regard to persons alleged to be unlawful enemy combatants acting in violation of the laws of war. The alternative, sought by the petitioners, was that they be tried by civilian courts for violations of the criminal law. They cite the Civil War case of *Ex parte Milligan*, 71 U.S. 2 (1866), in which the Court set Milligan free from military custody and held that he could not be tried by military commission. The Court in *Quirin* finds the facts in *Milligan* distinguishable, but the language in *Milligan* is unconditional: "[the laws of war] can never be applied to citizens in states which have upheld the authority of the government [*i.e.*, not Confederate states], and where the courts are open and their process unobstructed." Haupt, the saboteur who claimed American citizenship, argued this language applied to him, because he was found in a state upholding the authority of the government and where the courts were open and unobstructed. And there were (and are) federal laws criminalizing sabotage and conspiracy to commit sabotage, not to mention treason. Do you think the *Quirin* Court's factual distinction is sufficient?

2. How important is it in *Quirin* that Congress had authorized the use of military commissions in such cases? What is the disagreement on the Court regarding the claim that the commission did not follow the procedures required by the Articles of War?

3. *Quirin* has become very topical because of the "War on Terror," the federal military detention of a large number of alleged unlawful combatants at the Guantanamo naval base in Cuba, and the desire by the government to try at least some of them by military commission. How would *Quirin*'s analysis of who can be subjected to military commissions apply to Jose Padilla, the citizen arrested by the FBI in Chicago for allegedly being involved in a plot to detonate a "dirty bomb," who was then turned over to the military and held in military custody as an alleged unlawful enemy combatant? Could he be tried by military commission? The government at first took the position that he could, but when the case looked like it would go to the Supreme Court, the government released

him from military custody, took him into civilian custody, and charged him with several federal criminal violations. In August 2007 he was convicted on all charges by a federal jury.

HAMDI V. RUMSFELD

United States Supreme Court, 2004.
542 U.S. 507, 124 S.Ct. 2633.

JUSTICE O'CONNOR announced the judgment of the Court and delivered an opinion, in which THE CHIEF JUSTICE, JUSTICE KENNEDY, and JUSTICE BREYER join.

At this difficult time in our Nation's history, we are called upon to consider the legality of the Government's detention of a United States citizen on United States soil as an "enemy combatant" and to address the process that is constitutionally owed to one who seeks to challenge his classification as such. . . . We hold that although Congress authorized the detention of combatants in the narrow circumstances alleged here, due process demands that a citizen held in the United States as an enemy combatant be given a meaningful opportunity to contest the factual basis for that detention before a neutral decisionmaker.

On September 11, 2001, the al Qaeda terrorist network used hijacked commercial airliners to attack prominent targets in the United States. . . . One week later, . . . Congress passed a resolution authorizing the President to "use all necessary and appropriate force against those nations, organizations, or persons he determines planned, authorized, committed, or aided the terrorist attacks" or "harbored such organizations or persons, in order to prevent any future acts of international terrorism against the United States by such nations, organizations or persons." Authorization for Use of Military Force (AUMF). Soon thereafter, the President ordered United States Armed Forces to Afghanistan, with a mission to subdue al Qaeda and quell the Taliban regime that was known to support it.

This case arises out of the detention of a man whom the Government alleges took up arms with the Taliban during this conflict. His name is Yaser Esam Hamdi. Born in Louisiana in 1980, Hamdi moved with his family to Saudi Arabia as a child. By 2001, the parties agree, he resided in Afghanistan. At some point that year, he was seized by members of the Northern Alliance, a coalition of military groups opposed to the Taliban government, and eventually was turned over to the United States military. . . . The Government contends that Hamdi is an "enemy combatant," and that this status justifies holding him in the United States indefinitely—without formal charges or proceedings—unless and until it makes the determination that access to counsel or further process is warranted.

The threshold question before us is whether the Executive has the authority to detain citizens who qualify as "enemy combatants." There is some debate as to the proper scope of this term, and the Government has never provided any court with the full criteria that it uses in classifying individuals as such. It has made clear, however, that, for purposes of this case, the "enemy combatant" that it is seeking to detain is an individual who, it alleges, was " 'part of or supporting forces hostile to the United States or coalition partners' " in Afghanistan and who " 'engaged in an armed conflict against the United States' " there. We therefore answer only the narrow question before us: whether the detention of citizens falling within that definition is authorized.

The Government maintains that no explicit congressional authorization is required, because the Executive possesses plenary authority to detain pursuant to Article II of the Constitution. We do not reach the question whether Article II provides such authority, however, because we agree with the Government's alternative position, that Congress has in fact authorized Hamdi's detention, through the AUMF.

[F]or the reasons that follow, we conclude that the AUMF is explicit congressional authorization for the detention of individuals in the narrow category we describe (assuming, without deciding, that such authorization is required). . . .

The AUMF authorizes the President to use "all necessary and appropriate force" against "nations, organizations, or persons" associated with the September 11, 2001, terrorist attacks. There can be no doubt that individuals who fought against the United States in Afghanistan as part of the Taliban, an organization known to have supported the al Qaeda terrorist network responsible for those attacks, are individuals Congress sought to target in passing the AUMF. We conclude that detention of individuals falling into the limited category we are considering, for the duration of the particular conflict in which they were captured, is so fundamental and accepted an incident to war as to be an exercise of the "necessary and appropriate force" Congress has authorized the President to use.

The capture and detention of lawful combatants and the capture, detention, and trial of unlawful combatants, by "universal agreement and practice," are "important incident[s] of war." *Ex parte Quirin.* The purpose of detention is to prevent captured individuals from returning to the field of battle and taking up arms once again.

There is no bar to this Nation's holding one of its own citizens as an enemy combatant. In *Quirin,* one of the detainees, Haupt, alleged that he was a naturalized United States citizen. We held that "[c]itizens who associate themselves with the military arm of the enemy government, and with its aid, guidance and direction enter this country bent on hostile acts, are enemy belligerents within the meaning of . . . the law of war." . . .

In light of these principles, it is of no moment that the AUMF does not use specific language of detention. Because detention to prevent a combatant's return to the battlefield is a fundamental incident of waging war, in permitting the use of "necessary and appropriate force," Congress has clearly and unmistakably authorized detention in the narrow circumstances considered here.

Hamdi objects, nevertheless, that Congress has not authorized the *indefinite* detention to which he is now subject. . . . We take Hamdi's objection to be not to the lack of certainty regarding the date on which the conflict will end, but to the substantial prospect of perpetual detention. We recognize that the national security underpinnings of the "war on terror," although crucially important, are broad and malleable. As the Government concedes, "given its unconventional nature, the current conflict is unlikely to end with a formal cease-fire agreement." The prospect Hamdi raises is therefore not farfetched. If the Government does not consider this unconventional war won for two generations, and if it maintains during that time that Hamdi might, if released, rejoin forces fighting against the United States, then the position it has taken throughout the litigation of this case suggests that Hamdi's detention could last for the rest of his life. . . .

Hamdi contends that the AUMF does not authorize indefinite or perpetual detention. Certainly, we agree that indefinite detention for the purpose of interrogation is not authorized. Further, we understand Congress' grant of authority for the use of "necessary and appropriate force" to include the authority to detain for the duration of the relevant conflict, and our understanding is based on longstanding law-of-war principles. If the practical circumstances of a given conflict are entirely unlike those of the conflicts that informed the development of the law of war, that understanding may unravel. But that is not the situation we face as of this date. Active combat operations against Taliban fighters apparently are ongoing in Afghanistan. The United States may detain, for the duration of these hostilities, individuals legitimately determined to be Taliban combatants who "engaged in an armed conflict against the United States." If the record establishes that United States troops are still involved in active combat in Afghanistan, those detentions are part of the exercise of "necessary and appropriate force," and therefore are authorized by the AUMF. . . .

Even in cases in which the detention of enemy combatants is legally authorized, there remains the question of what process is constitutionally due to a citizen who disputes his enemy-combatant status. . . . Though they reach radically different conclusions on the process that ought to attend the present proceeding, the parties begin on common ground. All agree that, absent suspension, the writ of habeas corpus remains available to every individual detained within the United States. . . .

The [Government argues] that further factual exploration is unwarranted and inappropriate in light of the extraordinary constitutional interests at stake. Under the Government's most extreme rendition of this argument, "[r]espect for separation of powers and the limited institutional capabilities of courts in matters of military decision-making in connection with an ongoing conflict" ought to eliminate entirely any individual process, restricting the courts to investigating only whether legal authorization exists for the broader detention scheme. At most, the Government argues, courts should review its determination that a citizen is an enemy combatant under a very deferential "some evidence" standard. Under this review, a court would assume the accuracy of the Government's articulated basis for Hamdi's detention. . . .

In response, Hamdi emphasizes that this Court consistently has recognized that an individual challenging his detention may not be held at the will of the Executive without recourse to some proceeding before a neutral tribunal to determine whether the Executive's asserted justifications for that detention have basis in fact and warrant in law. . . .

Both of these positions highlight legitimate concerns. And both emphasize the tension that often exists between the autonomy that the Government asserts is necessary in order to pursue effectively a particular goal and the process that a citizen contends he is due before he is deprived of a constitutional right. . . .

We . . . hold that a citizen-detainee seeking to challenge his classification as an enemy combatant must receive notice of the factual basis for his classification, and a fair opportunity to rebut the Government's factual assertions before a neutral decisionmaker. . . .

At the same time, the exigencies of the circumstances may demand that, aside from these core elements, enemy-combatant proceedings may be tailored to alleviate their uncommon potential to burden the Executive at a time of ongoing military conflict. Hearsay, for example, may need to be accepted as the most reliable available evidence from the Government in such a proceeding. Likewise, the Constitution would not be offended by a presumption in favor of the Government's evidence, so long as that presumption remained a rebuttable one and fair opportunity for rebuttal were provided. Thus, once the Government puts forth credible evidence that the habeas petitioner meets the enemy-combatant criteria, the onus could shift to the petitioner to rebut that evidence with more persuasive evidence that he falls outside the criteria. A burden-shifting scheme of this sort would meet the goal of ensuring that the errant tourist, embedded journalist, or local aid worker has a chance to prove military error while giving due regard to the Executive once it has put forth meaningful support for its conclusion that the detainee is in fact an enemy combatant. . . .

In so holding, we necessarily reject the Government's assertion that separation of powers principles mandate a heavily circumscribed role for the courts in such circumstances. . . . We have long since made clear that a state of war is not a blank check for the President when it comes to the rights of the Nation's citizens. *Youngstown Sheet & Tube.* Whatever power the United States Constitution envisions for the Executive in its exchanges with other nations or with enemy organizations in times of conflict, it most assuredly envisions a role for all three branches when individual liberties are at stake. . . .

The judgment of the [court of appeals] is vacated, and the case is remanded for further proceedings.

JUSTICE SOUTER, with whom JUSTICE GINSBURG joins, concurring in part, dissenting in part, and concurring in the judgment.

According to Yaser Hamdi's petition for writ of habeas corpus, brought on his behalf by his father, the Government of the United States is detaining him, an American citizen on American soil, with the explanation that he was seized on the field of battle in Afghanistan, having been on the enemy side. It is undisputed that the Government has not charged him with espionage, treason, or any other crime under domestic law. It is likewise undisputed that for one year and nine months, on the basis of an Executive designation of Hamdi as an "enemy combatant," the Government denied him the right to send or receive any communication beyond the prison where he was held and, in particular, denied him access to counsel to represent him. The Government asserts a right to hold Hamdi under these conditions indefinitely, that is, until the Government determines that the United States is no longer threatened by the terrorism exemplified in the attacks of September 11, 2001. . . .

The Government [argues] that Hamdi's incommunicado imprisonment as an enemy combatant seized on the field of battle falls within the President's power as Commander in Chief under the laws and usages of war, and is in any event authorized by two statutes. Accordingly, the Government contends that Hamdi has no basis for any challenge by petition for habeas except to his own status as an enemy combatant; and even that challenge may go no further than to enquire whether "some evidence" supports Hamdi's designation; if there is "some evidence," Hamdi should remain locked up at the discretion of the Executive. At the argument of this case, in fact, the Government went further and suggested that as long as a prisoner could challenge his enemy combatant designation when responding to interrogation during incommunicado detention he was accorded sufficient process to support his designation as an enemy combatant. ("[H]e has an opportunity to explain it in his own words" "[d]uring interrogation"). Since on either view judicial enquiry so limited would be virtually worthless as a way to contest detention, the Government's concession of jurisdiction to hear Hamdi's habeas claim is more theoretical than practical, leaving the assertion of Executive authority close to unconditional.

The plurality rejects any such limit on the exercise of habeas jurisdiction and so far I agree with its opinion. The plurality does, however, accept the Government's position that if Hamdi's designation as an enemy combatant is correct, his detention (at least as to some period) is authorized by an Act of Congress . . ., that is, by the Authorization for Use of Military Force. Here, I disagree and respectfully dissent. The Government has failed to demonstrate that the Force Resolution authorizes the detention complained of here even on the facts the Government claims. . . .

[T]here is the Government's claim, accepted by the plurality, that the terms of the Force Resolution are adequate to authorize detention of an enemy combatant under the circumstances described. . . . Since the Force Resolution was adopted one week after the attacks of September 11, 2001, it naturally speaks with some generality, but its focus is clear, and that is on the use of military power. It is fairly read to authorize the use of armies and weapons, whether against other armies or individual terrorists. But, . . . it never so much as uses the word detention, and there is no reason to think Congress might have perceived any need to augment Executive power to deal with dangerous citizens within the United States, given the well-stocked statutory arsenal of defined criminal offenses covering the gamut of actions that a citizen sympathetic to terrorists might commit. . . .

Subject to these qualifications, I join with the plurality in a judgment of the Court vacating the Fourth Circuit's judgment and remanding the case.

JUSTICE SCALIA, with whom JUSTICE STEVENS joins, dissenting.

Petitioner Yaser Hamdi, a presumed American citizen, has been imprisoned without charge or hearing in the Norfolk and Charleston Naval Brigs for more than two years, on the allegation that he is an enemy combatant who bore arms against his country for the Taliban. His father claims to the contrary, that he is an inexperienced aid worker caught in the wrong place at the wrong time. This case brings into conflict the competing demands of national security and our citizens' constitutional right to personal liberty. Although I share the plurality's evident unease as it seeks to reconcile the two, I do not agree with its resolution.

Where the Government accuses a citizen of waging war against it, our constitutional tradition has been to prosecute him in federal court for treason or some other crime. Where the exigencies of war prevent that, the Constitution's Suspension Clause, Art. I, § 9, cl. 2, allows Congress to relax the usual protections temporarily. Absent suspension, however, the Executive's assertion of military exigency has not been thought sufficient to permit detention without charge. . . . Accordingly, I would reverse the judgment below.

The very core of liberty secured by our Anglo-Saxon system of separated powers has been freedom from indefinite imprisonment at the will of the Executive. . . .

To be sure, certain types of permissible *non* criminal detention—that is, those not dependent upon the contention that the citizen had committed a criminal act—did not require the protections of criminal procedure. However, these fell into a limited number of well-recognized exceptions—civil commitment of the mentally ill, for example, and temporary detention in quarantine of the infectious. It is unthinkable that the Executive could render otherwise criminal grounds for detention noncriminal merely by disclaiming an intent to prosecute, or by asserting that it was incapacitating dangerous offenders rather than punishing wrongdoing. . . .

The allegations here, of course, are no ordinary accusations of criminal activity. Yaser Esam Hamdi has been imprisoned because the Government believes he participated in the waging of war against the United States. The relevant question, then, is whether there is a different, special procedure for imprisonment of a citizen accused of wrongdoing *by aiding the enemy in wartime.*

Justice O'CONNOR, writing for a plurality of this Court, asserts that captured enemy combatants (other than those suspected of war crimes) have traditionally been detained until the cessation of hostilities and then released. That is probably an accurate description of wartime practice with respect to enemy *aliens.* The tradition with respect to American citizens, however, has been quite different. Citizens aiding the enemy have been treated as traitors subject to the criminal process. . . .

There are times when military exigency renders resort to the traditional criminal process impracticable. . . . Where the Executive has not pursued the usual course of charge, committal, and conviction, it has historically secured the Legislature's explicit approval of a suspension. . . . Our Federal Constitution contains a provision explicitly permitting suspension, but limiting the situations in which it may be invoked. . . .

The Suspension Clause was by design a safety valve, the Constitution's only "express provision for exercise of extraordinary authority because of a crisis," *Youngstown Sheet & Tube Co. v. Sawyer* (Jackson, concurring).

The Government argues that our more recent jurisprudence ratifies its indefinite imprisonment of a citizen within the territorial jurisdiction of federal courts. It places primary reliance upon *Ex parte Quirin,* a World War II case upholding the trial by military commission of eight German saboteurs, one of whom, Herbert Haupt, was a U.S. citizen. The case was not this Court's finest hour. . . .

But . . . *Quirin* would still not justify denial of the writ here. In *Quirin* it was uncontested that the petitioners were members of enemy forces. . . .

The specific holding of the Court was only that, "upon the *conceded* facts," the petitioners were "plainly within [the] boundaries" of military jurisdiction. But where those jurisdictional facts are *not* conceded where the petitioner insists that he is *not* a belligerent—*Quirin* left the pre-existing law in place: Absent suspension of the writ, a citizen held where the courts are open is entitled either to criminal trial or to a judicial decree requiring his release. . . .

Several limitations give my views in this matter a relatively narrow compass. They apply only to citizens, accused of being enemy combatants, who are detained within the territorial jurisdiction of a federal court. This is not likely to be a numerous group; currently we know of only two, Hamdi and Jose Padilla. Where the citizen is captured outside and held outside the United States, the constitutional requirements may be different. Moreover, even within the United States, the accused citizen-enemy combatant may lawfully be detained once prosecution is in progress or in contemplation. . . . If civil rights are to be curtailed during wartime, it must be done openly and democratically, as the Constitution requires, rather than by silent erosion through an opinion of this Court. . . .

JUSTICE THOMAS, dissenting.

The Executive Branch, acting pursuant to the powers vested in the President by the Constitution and with explicit congressional approval, has determined that Yaser Hamdi is an enemy combatant and should be detained. This detention falls squarely within the Federal Government's war powers, and we lack the expertise and capacity to second-guess that decision. As such, petitioners' habeas challenge should fail, and there is no reason to remand the case. The plurality reaches a contrary conclusion by failing adequately to consider basic principles of the constitutional structure as it relates to national security and foreign affairs. . . .

The Founders intended that the President have primary responsibility—along with the necessary power—to protect the national security and to conduct the Nation's foreign relations. They did so principally because the structural advantages of a unitary Executive are essential in these domains. . . .

These structural advantages are most important in the national-security and foreign-affairs contexts. . . .

This Court has long recognized these features and has accordingly held that the President has *constitutional* authority to protect the national security and that this authority carries with it broad discretion.

> "If a war be made by invasion of a foreign nation, the President is not only authorized but bound to resist force by force. He does not initiate the war, but is bound to accept the challenge without waiting for any special legislative authority. . . . Whether the President in fulfilling his duties, as Commander in-chief, in

suppressing an insurrection, has met with such armed hostile resistance . . . is a question to be decided *by him.*" *Prize Cases.*

[W]ith respect to foreign affairs as well, the Court has recognized the President's independent authority and need to be free from interference. See, *e.g., United States v. Curtiss-Wright Export Corp.*

Congress, to be sure, has a substantial and essential role in both foreign affairs and national security. But it is crucial to recognize that *judicial* interference in these domains destroys the purpose of vesting primary responsibility in a unitary Executive. . . . First, with respect to certain decisions relating to national security and foreign affairs, the courts simply lack the relevant information and expertise to second-guess determinations made by the President based on information properly withheld. Second, even if the courts could compel the Executive to produce the necessary information, such decisions are simply not amenable to judicial determination because "[t]hey are delicate, complex, and involve large elements of prophecy." Third, the Court . . . has correctly recognized the primacy of the political branches in the foreign-affairs and national-security contexts. . . .

I acknowledge that the question whether Hamdi's executive detention is lawful is a question properly resolved by the Judicial Branch, though the question comes to the Court with the strongest presumptions in favor of the Government. The plurality agrees that Hamdi's detention is lawful if he is an

Clarence Thomas

President George H.W. Bush appointed Justice Thomas to the Court in 1991 to replace the retiring Thurgood Marshall, the first African-American justice of the Supreme Court. The nomination was highly controversial, first because of Justice Thomas's lack of clear qualifications and his known strong conservative leanings and later because of allegations of sexual harassment against him. Ultimately, he was confirmed by a vote of 52–48, at the time the narrowest margin in over a century. On the Court Justice Thomas is known for his extreme originalist views, giving little credit to *stare decisis* when he believes the Court has deviated from the original meaning of the Constitution. Justice Thomas was also known as a justice who normally did not ask questions during oral argument, until the Court held oral argument by Zoom during the pandemic.

enemy combatant. But the question whether Hamdi is actually an enemy combatant is "of a kind for which the Judiciary has neither aptitude, facilities nor responsibility and which has long been held to belong in the domain of political power not subject to judicial intrusion or inquiry." That is, although it is appropriate for the Court to determine the judicial question whether the President has the asserted authority, we lack the information and expertise to question whether Hamdi is actually an enemy combatant, a question the resolution of which is committed to other branches. . . .

COMMENTS AND QUESTIONS

1. Hamdi was eventually released on condition that he give up his American citizenship and leave the United States to return to Saudi Arabia.

2. As you can see, there is no majority opinion, but eight of the nine justices reject the government's arguments that the Court should simply defer to the President's determinations as to the need to keep an American citizen in custody indefinitely simply because he was captured in a country in which the United States was engaged in hostilities. The plurality reads the AUMF as authorization to detain captured combatants for the duration of the hostilities. Does the plurality read the AUMF as the equivalent of a declaration of war? Does Justice Souter or Justice Scalia or Justice Thomas? Were you surprised to see Justice Scalia write the most "liberal" opinion?

3. Based upon the plurality's opinion, the government created "Combat Status Review Tribunals" (CSRTs) to hold hearings to determine whether detainees were really enemy combatants. These are not military commissions, because they do not assess whether the detainee committed any violation of the laws of war and do not impose any punishment; they merely determine whether the detainee is properly kept in custody until the "war" in Afghanistan is over.

4. The government did, however, also create military commissions to try alleged war criminals. Ahmed Hamdan, a Yemeni national and not a United States citizen, was captured during fighting in Afghanistan, brought to Guantanamo, and ultimately charged with "conspiracy to commit war crimes." Hamdan petitioned for habeas corpus, which was granted by the district court but then reversed by the Court of Appeals for the D.C. Circuit. Justice Stevens in an opinion for the Court on most issues held that the military commissions that had been established were not in accordance with statutory authorization and therefore were unauthorized, citing the *Steel Seizure* case. *Hamdan v. Rumsfeld*, 548 U.S. 557 (2006). Congress responded by enacting the Military Commissions Act of 2006, which among other things prohibited the exclusion of the defendant from the proceedings (which the presidentially created commissions could do) but also limited judicial review of the outcomes of the proceedings. This Act was challenged by another person designated to be tried by commission, and the D.C. Circuit by a 2–1 vote found the act constitutional. The Supreme Court, after first denying certiorari, in a most unusual move vacated the denial of certiorari, granted certiorari, and after hearing the case held that the Act unconstitutionally suspended habeas corpus with respect to those detainees. *See Boumediene v. Bush*, 553 U.S. 723 (2008).

5. If you were writing the Constitution today, how would you address these issues?

C. TREATIES, INTERNATIONAL LAW, AND FOREIGN AFFAIRS

The Constitution states that treaties, along with the Constitution and laws of the United States, are "the supreme law of the land." We have already seen how the Constitution and federal laws are supreme over state law, but what about treaties? And what about international law?

MEDELLÍN V. TEXAS

United States Supreme Court, 2008.
552 U.S. 491, 128 S.Ct. 1346.

[In 1969, the United States ratified the Vienna Convention on Consular Relations as well as its Optional Protocol Concerning the Compulsory Settlement of Disputes to the Vienna Convention. Among other things the Convention requires a nation detaining a person from another nation to inform that person of the right to request assistance from the consul of his nation and to notify the detainee's consul without delay. The Optional Protocol provides that the International Court of Justice (ICJ) has compulsory jurisdiction over disputes under the Vienna Convention between parties to the Convention. Moreover, the United Nations Charter requires each member to comply with any decision of the ICJ to which the member is a party.]

[José Ernesto Medellín was a Mexican national who was convicted by a Texas court of the rape and murder of two girls, one 14 years old and one 16 years old, and was sentenced to death. However, he was never informed of his right to request assistance from the Mexican consul, nor was the Mexican consul ever notified of Medellín's detention. His conviction and sentence were affirmed on appeal. Only in a motion for post-conviction relief in state court did he raise the violation of the Convention, asking that his conviction and sentencing be reviewed and reconsidered, but the state courts held that his claim was procedurally defaulted because he had failed to raise it at trial or on direct review. He brought a federal habeas corpus action making the same claim, which was denied by the district court on the same basis as the state courts.]

[While Medellín's federal habeas case was being appealed, the ICJ rendered a decision in a case, the *Avena* case, brought by Mexico against the United States on behalf of 51 named Mexican nationals, including Medellín, none of whom were informed of their ability to request assistance of their consul. There the ICJ held that the United States had violated the Convention and required the United States to review and reconsider the convictions and sentences of the affected Mexican nationals. The ICJ specifically held that such review was required without regard to state procedural default rules. The Fifth Circuit still denied habeas, relying on an earlier Supreme Court decision that Vienna Convention claims can be procedurally defaulted.]

[At this point President George W. Bush sent a memorandum to the Attorney General of the United States saying:

> I have determined, pursuant to the authority vested in me as President by the Constitution and the laws of the United States of America, that the United States will discharge its international obligations under the decision of the International Court of Justice in [*Avena*], by having State courts give effect to the decision in accordance with general principles of comity in cases filed by the 51 Mexican nationals addressed in that decision.

Medellín, relying on the President's memorandum again sought post conviction relief in state court. The Texas Court of Criminal Appeal dismissed the petition, stating that neither the ICJ decision nor the President's memorandum was "binding federal law" that could displace state procedural default law.]

[Medellín sought and the Supreme Court granted certiorari.]

CHIEF JUSTICE ROBERTS delivered the opinion of the Court.

[W]e granted certiorari to decide two questions. *First,* is the ICJ's judgment in *Avena* directly enforceable as domestic law in a state court in the United States? *Second,* does the President's Memorandum independently require the States to provide review and reconsideration of the claims of the 51 Mexican nationals named in *Avena* without regard to state procedural default rules? We conclude that neither *Avena* nor the President's Memorandum constitutes directly enforceable federal law that pre-empts state limitations on the filing of successive habeas petitions. We therefore affirm the decision below. . . .

Medellín first contends that the ICJ's judgment in *Avena* constitutes a "binding" obligation on the state and federal courts of the United States. He argues that "by virtue of the Supremacy Clause, the treaties requiring compliance with the *Avena* judgment are *already* the 'Law of the Land' by which all state and federal courts in this country are 'bound.' " Accordingly, Medellín argues, *Avena* is a binding federal rule of decision that pre-empts contrary state limitations. . . .

No one disputes that the *Avena* decision—a decision that flows from the treaties through which the United States submitted to ICJ jurisdiction with respect to Vienna Convention disputes—constitutes an *international* law obligation on the part of the United States. But not all international law obligations automatically constitute binding federal law enforceable in United States courts. The question we confront here is whether the *Avena* judgment has automatic *domestic* legal effect such that the judgment of its own force applies in state and federal courts.

This Court has long recognized the distinction between treaties that automatically have effect as domestic law, and those that—while they constitute international law commitments—do not by themselves function as binding federal law. The distinction was well explained by Chief Justice Marshall's opinion in *Foster v. Neilson*, 2 Pet. 253, 315, 7 L.Ed. 415 (1829) . . . which held that a treaty is "equivalent to an act of the legislature," and hence self-executing, when it "operates of itself without the aid of any legislative provision." When, in contrast, "[treaty] stipulations are not self-executing they can only be enforced pursuant to legislation to carry them into effect." In sum, while treaties "may comprise international commitments . . . they are not domestic law unless Congress has either enacted implementing statutes or the treaty itself conveys an intention that it be 'self-executing' and is ratified on these terms."[2]

A treaty is, of course, "primarily a compact between independent nations." It ordinarily "depends for the enforcement of its provisions on the interest and the honor of the governments which are parties to it." *See also* The Federalist No. 33, p. 207 (J. Cooke ed. 1961)(A. Hamilton)(comparing laws that individuals are "bound to observe" as "the supreme law of the land" with "a mere treaty, dependent on the good faith of the parties"). "If these [interests] fail, its infraction becomes the subject of international negotiations and reclamations. . . . It is obvious that with all this the judicial courts have nothing to do and can give no redress." Only "[i]f the treaty contains stipulations which are self-executing, that is, require no legislation to make them operative, [will] they have the force and effect of a legislative enactment."[3]

Medellín and his *amici* nonetheless contend that the Optional Protocol, United Nations Charter, and ICJ Statute supply the "relevant obligation" to give the *Avena* judgment binding effect in the domestic courts of the United States.[4] Because none of these treaty sources creates binding federal law in the absence of implementing legislation, and because it is

---

[2]   The label "self-executing" has on occasion been used to convey different meanings. What we mean by "self-executing" is that the treaty has automatic domestic effect as federal law upon ratification. Conversely, a "non-self-executing" treaty does not by itself give rise to domestically enforceable federal law. Whether such a treaty has domestic effect depends upon implementing legislation passed by Congress.

[3]   Even when treaties are self-executing in the sense that they create federal law, the background presumption is that "[i]nternational agreements, even those directly benefiting private persons, generally do not create private rights or provide for a private cause of action in domestic courts." Accordingly, a number of the Courts of Appeals have presumed that treaties do not create privately enforceable rights in the absence of express language to the contrary.

[4]   The question is whether the *Avena* judgment has binding effect in domestic courts under the Optional Protocol, ICJ Statute, and U.N. Charter. Consequently, it is unnecessary to resolve whether the Vienna Convention is itself "self-executing" or whether it grants Medellín individually enforceable rights. [W]e thus assume, without deciding, that Article 36 grants foreign nationals "an individually enforceable right to request that their consular officers be notified of their detention, and an accompanying right to be informed by authorities of the availability of consular notification."

uncontested that no such legislation exists, we conclude that the *Avena* judgment is not automatically binding domestic law.

The interpretation of a treaty, like the interpretation of a statute, begins with its text. Because a treaty ratified by the United States is "an agreement among sovereign powers," we have also considered as "aids to its interpretation" the negotiation and drafting history of the treaty as well as "the postratification understanding" of signatory nations.

As a signatory to the Optional Protocol, the United States agreed to submit disputes arising out of the Vienna Convention to the ICJ. . . . Of course, submitting to jurisdiction and agreeing to be bound are two different things. A party could, for example, agree to compulsory nonbinding arbitration. Such an agreement would require the party to appear before the arbitral tribunal without obligating the party to treat the tribunal's decision as binding.

The most natural reading of the Optional Protocol is as a bare grant of jurisdiction. . . . The Protocol says nothing about the effect of an ICJ decision and does not itself commit signatories to comply with an ICJ judgment. The Protocol is similarly silent as to any enforcement mechanism.

The obligation on the part of signatory nations to comply with ICJ judgments derives not from the Optional Protocol, but rather from Article 94 of the United Nations Charter—the provision that specifically addresses the effect of ICJ decisions. Article 94(1) provides that "[e]ach Member of the United Nations *undertakes to comply* with the decision of the [ICJ] in any case to which it is a party." The Executive Branch contends that the phrase "undertakes to comply" is not "an acknowledgement that an ICJ decision will have immediate legal effect in the courts of U.N. members," but rather "a *commitment* on the part of U.N. Members to take *future* action through their political branches to comply with an ICJ decision."

We agree with this construction of Article 94. The Article is not a directive to domestic courts. It does not provide that the United States "shall" or "must" comply with an ICJ decision, nor indicate that the Senate that ratified the U.N. Charter intended to vest ICJ decisions with immediate legal effect in domestic courts. [T]he U.N. Charter reads like "a compact between independent nations" that "depends for the enforcement of its provisions on the interest and the honor of the governments which are parties to it."[5]

---

[5] We do not read "undertakes" to mean that " '[t]he United States . . . shall be at liberty to make respecting th[e] matter, such laws as they think proper.' " Whether or not the United States "undertakes" to comply with a treaty says nothing about what laws it may enact. The United States is always "at liberty to make . . . such laws as [it] think[s] proper." Indeed, a later-in-time federal statute supersedes inconsistent treaty provisions. Rather, the "undertakes to comply" language confirms that further action to give effect to an ICJ judgment was contemplated, contrary to the dissent's position that such judgments constitute directly enforceable federal law, without more.

The remainder of Article 94 confirms that the U.N. Charter does not contemplate the automatic enforceability of ICJ decisions in domestic courts. Article 94(2)—the enforcement provision—provides the sole remedy for noncompliance: referral to the United Nations Security Council by an aggrieved state.

The U.N. Charter's provision of an express diplomatic—that is, nonjudicial—remedy is itself evidence that ICJ judgments were not meant to be enforceable in domestic courts. . . .

This was the understanding of the Executive Branch when the President agreed to the U.N. Charter and the declaration accepting general compulsory ICJ jurisdiction.

If ICJ judgments were instead regarded as automatically enforceable domestic law, they would be immediately and directly binding on state and federal courts pursuant to the Supremacy Clause. Mexico or the ICJ would have no need to proceed to the Security Council to enforce the judgment in this case. . . .

In sum, Medellín's view that ICJ decisions are automatically enforceable as domestic law is fatally undermined by the enforcement structure established by Article 94. His construction would eliminate the option of noncompliance contemplated by Article 94(2), undermining the ability of the political branches to determine whether and how to comply with an ICJ judgment. Those sensitive foreign policy decisions would instead be transferred to state and federal courts charged with applying an ICJ judgment directly as domestic law. And those courts would not be empowered to decide whether to comply with the judgment—again, always regarded as an option by the political branches—any more than courts may consider whether to comply with any other species of domestic law. This result would be particularly anomalous in light of the principle that "[t]he conduct of the foreign relations of our Government is committed by the Constitution to the Executive and Legislative—'the political'—Departments." . . .

It is, moreover, well settled that the United States' interpretation of a treaty "is entitled to great weight." The Executive Branch has unfailingly adhered to its view that the relevant treaties do not create domestically enforceable federal law.[9]

---

[9] In interpreting our treaty obligations, we also consider the views of the ICJ itself, "giv[ing] respectful consideration to the interpretation of an international treaty rendered by an international court with jurisdiction to interpret [the treaty]." It is not clear whether that principle would apply when the question is the binding force of ICJ judgments themselves, rather than the substantive scope of a treaty the ICJ must interpret in resolving disputes. In any event, nothing suggests that the ICJ views its judgments as automatically enforceable in the domestic courts of signatory nations. The *Avena* judgment itself directs the United States to provide review and reconsideration of the affected convictions and sentences "by means of its own choosing." This language, as well as the ICJ's mere suggestion that the "judicial process" is best suited to provide

The pertinent international agreements, therefore, do not provide for implementation of ICJ judgments through direct enforcement in domestic courts, and "where a treaty does not provide a particular remedy, either expressly or implicitly, it is not for the federal courts to impose one on the States through lawmaking of their own." . . .

Our conclusion that *Avena* does not by itself constitute binding federal law is confirmed by the "postratification understanding" of signatory nations. There are currently 47 nations that are parties to the Optional Protocol and 171 nations that are parties to the Vienna Convention. Yet neither Medellín nor his *amici* have identified a single nation that treats ICJ judgments as binding in domestic courts. [T]he lack of any basis for supposing that any other country would treat ICJ judgments as directly enforceable as a matter of their domestic law strongly suggests that the treaty should not be so viewed in our courts. . . .

Our prior decisions identified by the dissent as holding a number of treaties to be self-executing stand only for the unremarkable proposition that some international agreements are self-executing and others are not. It is well settled that the "[i]nterpretation of [a treaty] . . . must, of course, begin with the language of the Treaty itself." As a result, we have held treaties to be self-executing when the textual provisions indicate that the President and Senate intended for the agreement to have domestic effect. . . .

We do not suggest that treaties can never afford binding domestic effect to international tribunal judgments—only that the U.N. Charter, the Optional Protocol, and the ICJ Statute do not do so. And whether the treaties underlying a judgment are self-executing so that the judgment is directly enforceable as domestic law in our courts is, of course, a matter for this Court to decide.

Our holding does not call into question the ordinary enforcement of foreign judgments or international arbitral agreements. Indeed, we agree with Medellín that, as a general matter, "an agreement to abide by the result" of an international adjudication—or what he really means, an agreement to give the result of such adjudication domestic legal effect—can be a treaty obligation like any other, so long as the agreement is consistent with the Constitution. The point is that the particular treaty obligations on which Medellín relies do not of their own force create domestic law. . . .

In sum, while the ICJ's judgment in *Avena* creates an international law obligation on the part of the United States, it does not of its own force constitute binding federal law that pre-empts state restrictions on the filing of successive habeas petitions. [A] contrary conclusion would be extraordinary, given that basic rights guaranteed by our own Constitution

---

such review, confirm that domestic enforceability in court is not part and parcel of an ICJ judgment.

do not have the effect of displacing state procedural rules. Nothing in the text, background, negotiating and drafting history, or practice among signatory nations suggests that the President or Senate intended the improbable result of giving the judgments of an international tribunal a higher status than that enjoyed by "many of our most fundamental constitutional protections."

Medellín next argues that the ICJ's judgment in *Avena* is binding on state courts by virtue of the President's February 28, 2005 Memorandum. The United States contends that while the *Avena* judgment does not of its own force require domestic courts to set aside ordinary rules of procedural default, that judgment became the law of the land with precisely that effect pursuant to the President's Memorandum and his power "to establish binding rules of decision that preempt contrary state law." Accordingly, we must decide whether the President's declaration alters our conclusion that the *Avena* judgment is not a rule of domestic law binding in state and federal courts.

The United States maintains that the President's constitutional role "uniquely qualifies" him to resolve the sensitive foreign policy decisions that bear on compliance with an ICJ decision and "to do so expeditiously." We do not question these propositions. In this case, the President seeks to vindicate United States interests in ensuring the reciprocal observance of the Vienna Convention, protecting relations with foreign governments, and demonstrating commitment to the role of international law. These interests are plainly compelling.

Such considerations, however, do not allow us to set aside first principles. The President's authority to act, as with the exercise of any governmental power, "must stem either from an act of Congress or from the Constitution itself."

Justice Jackson's familiar tripartite scheme provides the accepted framework for evaluating executive action in this area. . . .

The United States marshals two principal arguments in favor of the President's authority "to establish binding rules of decision that preempt contrary state law." The Solicitor General first argues that the relevant treaties give the President the authority to implement the *Avena* judgment and that Congress has acquiesced in the exercise of such authority. The United States also relies upon an "independent" international dispute-resolution power wholly apart from the asserted authority based on the pertinent treaties. Medellín adds the additional argument that the President's Memorandum is a valid exercise of his power to take care that the laws be faithfully executed.

The United States maintains that the President's Memorandum is authorized by the Optional Protocol and the U.N. Charter. That is, because the relevant treaties "create an obligation to comply with *Avena*," they "*implicitly* give the President authority to implement that treaty-based obligation." As a result, the President's Memorandum is well grounded in the first category of the *Youngstown* framework.

We disagree. The President has an array of political and diplomatic means available to enforce international obligations, but unilaterally converting a non-self-executing treaty into a self-executing one is not among them. The responsibility for transforming an international obligation arising from a non-self-executing treaty into domestic law falls to Congress. As this Court has explained, when treaty stipulations are "not self-executing they can only be enforced pursuant to legislation to carry them into effect." Moreover, "[u]ntil such act shall be passed, the Court is not at liberty to disregard the existing laws on the subject."

The requirement that Congress, rather than the President, implement a non-self-executing treaty derives from the text of the Constitution, which divides the treaty-making power between the President and the Senate. The Constitution vests the President with the authority to "make" a treaty. If the Executive determines that a treaty should have domestic effect of its own force, that determination may be implemented "in mak[ing]" the treaty, by ensuring that it contains language plainly providing for domestic enforceability. If the treaty is to be self-executing in this respect, the Senate must consent to the treaty by the requisite two-thirds vote, consistent with all other constitutional restraints.

Once a treaty is ratified without provisions clearly according it domestic effect, however, whether the treaty will ever have such effect is governed by the fundamental constitutional principle that " '[t]he power to make the necessary laws is in Congress; the power to execute in the President.' " As already noted, the terms of a non-self-executing treaty can become domestic law only in the same way as any other law—through passage of legislation by both Houses of Congress, combined with either the President's signature or a congressional override of a Presidential veto. Indeed, "the President's power to see that the laws are faithfully executed refutes the idea that he is to be a lawmaker."

A non-self-executing treaty, by definition, is one that was ratified with the understanding that it is not to have domestic effect of its own force. That understanding precludes the assertion that Congress has implicitly authorized the President-acting on his own-to achieve precisely the same result. We therefore conclude, given the absence of congressional legislation, that the non-self-executing treaties at issue here did not "express[ly] or implied[ly]" vest the President with the unilateral authority to make them self-executing. Accordingly, the President's Memorandum does not fall within the first category of the *Youngstown* framework.

Indeed, the preceding discussion should make clear that the non-self-executing character of the relevant treaties not only refutes the notion that the ratifying parties vested the President with the authority to unilaterally make treaty obligations binding on domestic courts, but also implicitly prohibits him from doing so. When the President asserts the power to "enforce" a non-self-executing treaty by unilaterally creating domestic law, he acts in conflict with the implicit understanding of the ratifying Senate. His assertion of authority, insofar as it is based on the pertinent non-self-executing treaties, is therefore within Justice Jackson's third category, not the first or even the second. . . .

None of this is to say, however, that the combination of a non-self-executing treaty and the lack of implementing legislation precludes the President from acting to comply with an international treaty obligation. It is only to say that the Executive cannot unilaterally execute a non-self-executing treaty by giving it domestic effect. That is, the non-self-executing character of a treaty constrains the President's ability to comply with treaty commitments by unilaterally making the treaty binding on domestic courts. The President may comply with the treaty's obligations by some other means, so long as they are consistent with the Constitution. But he may not rely upon a non-self-executing treaty to "establish binding rules of decision that preempt contrary state law."

We thus turn to the United States' claim that—independent of the United States' treaty obligations—the Memorandum is a valid exercise of the President's foreign affairs authority to resolve claims disputes with foreign nations. The United States relies on a series of cases in which this Court has upheld the authority of the President to settle foreign claims pursuant to an executive agreement. In these cases this Court has explained that, if pervasive enough, a history of congressional acquiescence can be treated as a "gloss on 'Executive Power' vested in the President by § 1 of Art. II."

This argument is of a different nature than the one rejected above. Rather than relying on the United States' treaty obligations, the President relies on an independent source of authority in ordering Texas to put aside its procedural bar to successive habeas petitions. Nevertheless, we find that our claims-settlement cases do not support the authority that the President asserts in this case.

The claims-settlement cases involve a narrow set of circumstances: the making of executive agreements to settle civil claims between American citizens and foreign governments or foreign nationals. They are based on the view that "a systematic, unbroken, executive practice, long pursued to the knowledge of the Congress and never before questioned," can "raise a presumption that the [action] had been [taken] in pursuance of its consent." . . .

Even still, the limitations on this source of executive power are clearly set forth and the Court has been careful to note that "[p]ast practice does not, by itself, create power."

The President's Memorandum is not supported by a "particularly longstanding practice" of congressional acquiescence, but rather is what the United States itself has described as "unprecedented action," Indeed, the Government has not identified a single instance in which the President has attempted (or Congress has acquiesced in) a Presidential directive issued to state courts, much less one that reaches deep into the heart of the State's police powers and compels state courts to reopen final criminal judgments and set aside neutrally applicable state laws. The Executive's narrow and strictly limited authority to settle international claims disputes pursuant to an executive agreement cannot stretch so far as to support the current Presidential Memorandum. . . .

The judgment of the Texas Court of Criminal Appeals is affirmed.

JUSTICE STEVENS, concurring in the judgment. [omitted]

JUSTICE BREYER, with whom JUSTICE SOUTER and JUSTICE GINSBURG join, dissenting.

[T]he critical question here is whether the Supremacy Clause requires Texas to follow, *i.e.,* to enforce, this ICJ judgment. The Court says "no." And it reaches its negative answer by interpreting the labyrinth of treaty provisions as creating a legal obligation that binds the United States internationally, but which, for Supremacy Clause purposes, is not automatically enforceable as domestic law. In the majority's view, the Optional Protocol simply sends the dispute to the ICJ; the ICJ statute says that the ICJ will subsequently reach a judgment; and the U.N. Charter contains no more than a promise to " 'undertak[e] to comply' " with that judgment. Such a promise, the majority says, does not as a domestic law matter (in Chief Justice Marshall's words) "operat[e] of itself without the aid of any legislative provision." Rather, here (and presumably in any other ICJ judgment rendered pursuant to any of the approximately 70 U.S. treaties in force that contain similar provisions for submitting treaty-based disputes to the ICJ for decisions that bind the parties) Congress must enact specific legislation before ICJ judgments entered pursuant to our consent to compulsory ICJ jurisdiction can become domestic law.

In my view, the President has correctly determined that Congress need not enact additional legislation. The majority places too much weight upon treaty language that says little about the matter. The words "undertak[e] to comply," for example, do not tell us whether an ICJ judgment rendered pursuant to the parties' consent to compulsory ICJ jurisdiction does, or does not, automatically become part of our domestic law. To answer that question we must look instead to our own domestic law, in particular, to the many treaty-related cases interpreting the Supremacy Clause. Those cases, including some written by Justices well aware of the Founders' original intent, lead to the conclusion that the ICJ judgment before us is enforceable as a matter of domestic law without further legislation. [Justice Breyer then relates from his perspective Supreme Court cases starting in

1796, coming to the conclusion that they] make clear that self-executing treaty provisions are not uncommon or peculiar creatures of our domestic law; that they cover a wide range of subjects; that the Supremacy Clause itself answers the self-execution question by applying many, but not all, treaty provisions directly to the States; and that the Clause answers the self-execution question differently than does the law in many other nations. . . .

The case law provides no simple magic answer to the question whether a particular treaty provision is self-executing. But the case law does make clear that, insofar as today's majority looks for language about "self-execution" in the treaty itself and insofar as it erects "clear statement" presumptions designed to help find an answer, it is misguided. . . .

The case law also suggests practical, context-specific criteria that this Court has previously used to help determine whether, for Supremacy Clause purposes, a treaty provision is self-executing. The provision's text matters very much. . . . Drafting history is also relevant. But, again, that is not because it will explicitly address the relevant question. Instead text and history, along with subject matter and related characteristics will help our courts determine whether, as Chief Justice Marshall put it, the treaty provision "addresses itself to the political . . . department[s]" for further action or to "the judicial department" for direct enforcement.

In making this determination, this Court has found the provision's subject matter of particular importance. Does the treaty provision declare peace? Does it promise not to engage in hostilities? If so, it addresses itself to the political branches. Alternatively, does it concern the adjudication of traditional private legal rights such as rights to own property, to conduct a business, or to obtain civil tort recovery? If so, it may well address itself to the Judiciary. Enforcing such rights and setting their boundaries is the bread-and-butter work of the courts.

One might also ask whether the treaty provision confers specific, detailed individual legal rights. Does it set forth definite standards that judges can readily enforce? Other things being equal, where rights are specific and readily enforceable, the treaty provision more likely "addresses" the judiciary. . . .

Such questions, drawn from case law stretching back 200 years, do not create a simple test, let alone a magic formula. But they do help to constitute a practical, context-specific judicial approach, seeking to separate run-of-the-mill judicial matters from other matters, sometimes more politically charged, sometimes more clearly the responsibility of other branches, sometimes lacking those attributes that would permit courts to act on their own without more ado. And such an approach is all that we need to find an answer to the legal question now before us.

Applying the approach just described, I would find the relevant treaty provisions self-executing as applied to the ICJ judgment before us (giving that judgment domestic legal effect) for the following reasons, taken together.

First, the language of the relevant treaties strongly supports direct judicial enforceability, at least of judgments of the kind at issue here. . . .

The upshot is that treaty language says that an ICJ decision is legally binding, but it leaves the implementation of that binding legal obligation to the domestic law of each signatory nation. In this Nation, the Supremacy Clause, as long and consistently interpreted, indicates that ICJ decisions rendered pursuant to provisions for binding adjudication must be domestically legally binding and enforceable in domestic courts *at least sometimes.* And for purposes of this argument, that conclusion is all that I need. The remainder of the discussion will explain why, if ICJ judgments *sometimes* bind domestic courts, then they have that effect here. . . .

Because the majority concludes that the Nation's international legal obligation to enforce the ICJ's decision is not automatically a domestic legal obligation, it must then determine whether the President has the constitutional authority to enforce it. And the majority finds that he does not.

In my view, that second conclusion has broader implications than the majority suggests. The President here seeks to implement treaty provisions in which the United States agrees that the ICJ judgment is binding with respect to the *Avena* parties. Consequently, his actions draw upon his constitutional authority in the area of foreign affairs. In this case, his exercise of that power falls within that middle range of Presidential authority where Congress has neither specifically authorized nor specifically forbidden the Presidential action in question. *See Youngstown Sheet & Tube Co. v. Sawyer* (Jackson, J., concurring). At the same time, if the President were to have the authority he asserts here, it would require setting aside a state procedural law.

It is difficult to believe that in the exercise of his Article II powers pursuant to a ratified treaty, the President can *never* take action that would result in setting aside state law. . . . Does the Constitution require the President in each and every such instance to obtain a special statute authorizing his action? On the other hand, the Constitution must impose significant restrictions upon the President's ability, by invoking Article II treaty-implementation authority, to circumvent ordinary legislative processes and to pre-empt state law as he does so.

Previously this Court has said little about this question. It has held that the President has a fair amount of authority to make and to implement executive agreements, at least in respect to international claims settlement, and that this authority can require contrary state law to be set aside. . . . But it has reserved judgment as to "the scope of the President's power to preempt state law pursuant to authority delegated by . . . a ratified treaty"—a fact that helps to explain the majority's inability to find support in precedent for its own conclusions.

Given the Court's comparative lack of expertise in foreign affairs; given the importance of the Nation's foreign relations; given the difficulty of finding the proper constitutional balance among state and federal, executive and legislative, powers in such matters; and given the likely future importance of this Court's efforts to do so, I would very much hesitate before concluding that the Constitution implicitly sets forth broad prohibitions (or permissions) in this area.

I would thus be content to leave the matter in the constitutional shade from which it has emerged. Given my view of this case, I need not answer the question. And I shall not try to do so. That silence, however, cannot be taken as agreement with the majority's Part III conclusion.

COMMENTS AND QUESTIONS

1.   *Medellín* is a major case that addresses two important questions: 1) when does a treaty which obligates the nation under international law constitute binding domestic law enforceable in state and federal courts, and 2) what power does the President have on his own to create binding domestic law as a result of international obligations. These are important issues with ramifications well beyond the fate of Mr. Medellín and the other 50 Mexican citizens in Texas prisons.

2.   According to both the majority and the dissent, had the ICJ decision been self-executing, then the President's memorandum would have been unnecessary; the decision of the ICJ would have been binding on the Texas courts. For the ICJ decision to be self-executing, the treaties relating to the ICJ—the Optional Protocol, the United Nations Charter, and the so-called ICJ Statute—would have to be self-executing. The Court finds they are not self-executing. Note that the Court assumes, without deciding, that the Vienna Convention's requirements are self-executing and provide a private right of action. *See* footnote 4. That is, the Court assumes that Medellín had a right enforceable in state court (if he had raised it at the proper time) to be notified of his ability to request assistance of his consul.

3.   Do you think the Senate, when it ratified the treaties applicable to the ICJ, intended to allow a decision of the ICJ to bind state and federal courts here? Why does the majority say it did not, and why does the dissent say it did? What tests do the majority and dissent use to determine if the treaties are self-executing?

4.   If the treaties here are not self-executing, then the question is what is the authority for the President to order the Texas courts to give effect to the ICJ decision? Everyone agrees that Congress could pass a law implementing the ICJ decision or making such decisions in the future binding domestic law,

but what can the President do on his own? What does the majority say? What does the dissent say? With whom do you agree?

5.   The ICJ in the *Avena* case specifically held that state procedural default rules could not bar a person from raising a claim of a Vienna Convention violation in a post-conviction relief petition. Edited from Chief Justice Roberts's lengthy opinion in *Medellín* is the acknowledgment that the U.S. Supreme Court had previously decided in a different case that a state's procedural default rules could preclude raising violations of the Vienna Convention on post-conviction review petitions. *See Sanchez-Llamas v. Oregon*, 548 U.S. 331 (2006). In other words, the ICJ interpreted the interplay between the Convention's requirements and state procedural rules relating to criminal trials differently than the United States Supreme Court's interpretation of the very same matter. Moreover, were the ICJ's decision to be given effect, it would in effect be overruling the U.S. Supreme Court's decision on the issue. Do you think that may have affected how the justices viewed the ICJ decision? Would it surprise you to learn that Justices Breyer, Souter, and Ginsburg all dissented from the Court's decision in *Sanchez-Llamas*? That is, the justices who believed that state procedural default rules did *not* necessarily preclude raising a Vienna Convention violation on postconviction review also believed that the ICJ's decision to require such post-conviction review despite state procedural default rules should be given effect.

6.   Four months after the Supreme Court's decision, Texas executed Medellín by lethal injection.

ZIVOTOFSKY V. KERRY
United States Supreme Court, 2015.
576 U.S. 1, 135 S.Ct. 2076.

[A U.S. passport contains an identification of the person's place of birth, which in the case of persons born abroad normally states the nation in which the person was born. However, the State Department for some time identified the place of birth of persons born in Jerusalem as "Jerusalem" rather than Israel. This was done for diplomatic reasons because of a dispute between Israel and Jordan as to sovereignty over Jerusalem. Congress, however, for political reasons, provided by law that persons born in Jerusalem could at their request have their place of birth listed as Israel. Menachem Zivotofsky, whose parents were both American citizens, was born in Jerusalem. He asked to have his passport reflect his place of birth as "Israel," rather than "Jerusalem," but the State Department refused. When he sued, the lower courts held the case was non-justiciable as a political question, but the Supreme Court reversed, holding that the issue was simply a question of the constitutionality of the statute and therefore justiciable and remanding for consideration of the merits. The lower court held the statute unconstitutional.]

JUSTICE KENNEDY delivered the opinion of the Court.

[T]he Court addresses two questions to resolve the interbranch dispute now before it. First, it must determine whether the President has the exclusive power to grant formal recognition to a foreign sovereign. Second, if he has that power, the Court must determine whether Congress can command the President and his Secretary of State to issue a formal statement that contradicts the earlier recognition. The statement in question here is a congressional mandate that allows a United States citizen born in Jerusalem to direct the President and Secretary of State, when issuing his passport, to state that his place of birth is "Israel."

Jerusalem's political standing has long been, and remains, one of the most sensitive issues in American foreign policy, and indeed it is one of the most delicate issues in current international affairs. In 1948, President Truman formally recognized Israel in a signed statement of "recognition." That statement did not recognize Israeli sovereignty over Jerusalem. Over the last 60 years, various actors have sought to assert full or partial sovereignty over the city, including Israel, Jordan, and the Palestinians. Yet, in contrast to a consistent policy of formal recognition of Israel, neither President Truman nor any later United States President has issued an official statement or declaration acknowledging any country's sovereignty over Jerusalem. Instead, the Executive Branch has maintained that " 'the status of Jerusalem . . . should be decided not unilaterally but in consultation with all concerned.' " . . .

[U]nderstanding that passports will be construed as reflections of American policy, the State Department's Foreign Affairs Manual (FAM) instructs its employees, in general, to record the place of birth on a passport as the "country [having] present sovereignty over the actual area of birth." . . . Because the United States does not recognize any country as having sovereignty over Jerusalem, the FAM instructs employees to record the place of birth for citizens born there as "Jerusalem."

In 2002, Congress passed the Act at issue here. . . . Section 214 of the Act is titled "United States Policy with Respect to Jerusalem as the Capital of Israel." The subsection that lies at the heart of this case, § 214(d), addresses passports. That subsection seeks to override the FAM by allowing citizens born in Jerusalem to list their place of birth as "Israel." . . .

In considering claims of Presidential power this Court refers to Justice Jackson's familiar tripartite framework from *Youngstown Sheet & Tube Co. v. Sawyer*, 343 U.S. 579 (1952)(concurring opinion). . . .

In this case the Secretary contends that § 214(d) infringes on the President's exclusive recognition power by "requiring the President to contradict his recognition position regarding Jerusalem in official communications with foreign sovereigns." In so doing the Secretary acknowledges the President's power is "at its lowest ebb." Because the

President's refusal to implement § 214(d) falls into Justice Jackson's third category, his claim must be "scrutinized with caution," and he may rely solely on powers the Constitution grants to him alone.

Recognition is a "formal acknowledgement" that a particular "entity possesses the qualifications for statehood" or "that a particular regime is the effective government of a state." It may also involve the determination of a state's territorial bounds. Recognition is often effected by an express "written or oral declaration." It may also be implied—for example, by concluding a bilateral treaty or by sending or receiving diplomatic agents.

Legal consequences follow formal recognition. Recognized sovereigns may sue in United States courts and may benefit from sovereign immunity when they are sued. The actions of a recognized sovereign committed within its own territory also receive deference in domestic courts under the act of state doctrine. Recognition at international law, furthermore, is a precondition of regular diplomatic relations. Recognition is thus "useful, even necessary," to the existence of a state.

Despite the importance of the recognition power in foreign relations, the Constitution does not use the term "recognition," either in Article II or elsewhere. The Secretary asserts that the President exercises the recognition power based on the Reception Clause, which directs that the President "shall receive Ambassadors and other public Ministers." Art. II, § 3. As Zivotofsky notes, the Reception Clause received little attention at the Constitutional Convention. . . .

At the time of the founding, however, prominent international scholars suggested that receiving an ambassador was tantamount to recognizing the sovereignty of the sending state. It is a logical and proper inference, then, that a Clause directing the President alone to receive ambassadors would be understood to acknowledge his power to recognize other nations.

This in fact occurred early in the Nation's history when President Washington recognized the French Revolutionary Government by receiving its ambassador. . . . As a result, the Reception Clause provides support, although not the sole authority, for the President's power to recognize other nations.

The inference that the President exercises the recognition power is further supported by his additional Article II powers. It is for the President, "by and with the Advice and Consent of the Senate," to "make Treaties, provided two thirds of the Senators present concur." Art. II, § 2, cl. 2. In addition, "he shall nominate, and by and with the Advice and Consent of the Senate, shall appoint Ambassadors" as well as "other public Ministers and Consuls."

As a matter of constitutional structure, these additional powers give the President control over recognition decisions. At international law, recognition may be effected by different means, but each means is dependent upon Presidential power. In addition to receiving an ambassador, recognition may occur on "the conclusion of a bilateral treaty," or the "formal initiation of diplomatic relations," including the dispatch of an ambassador. The President has the sole power to negotiate treaties, see *United States v. Curtiss-Wright Export Corp.*, 299 U.S. 304 (1936), and the Senate may not conclude or ratify a treaty without Presidential action. The President, too, nominates the Nation's ambassadors and dispatches other diplomatic agents. Congress may not send an ambassador without his involvement. Beyond that, the President himself has the power to open diplomatic channels simply by engaging in direct diplomacy with foreign heads of state and their ministers. The Constitution thus assigns the President means to effect recognition on his own initiative. Congress, by contrast, has no constitutional power that would enable it to initiate diplomatic relations with a foreign nation. Because these specific Clauses confer the recognition power on the President, the Court need not consider whether or to what extent the Vesting Clause, which provides that the "executive Power" shall be vested in the President, provides further support for the President's action here. Art. II, § 1, cl. 1.

The text and structure of the Constitution grant the President the power to recognize foreign nations and governments. The question then becomes whether that power is exclusive. The various ways in which the President may unilaterally effect recognition—and the lack of any similar power vested in Congress—suggest that it is. So, too, do functional considerations. Put simply, the Nation must have a single policy regarding which governments are legitimate in the eyes of the United States and which are not. Foreign countries need to know, before entering into diplomatic relations or commerce with the United States, whether their ambassadors will be received; whether their officials will be immune from suit in federal court; and whether they may initiate lawsuits here to vindicate their rights. These assurances cannot be equivocal.

[B]etween the two political branches, only the Executive has the characteristic of unity at all times. And with unity comes the ability to exercise, to a greater degree, "[d]ecision, activity, secrecy, and dispatch." The President is capable, in ways Congress is not, of engaging in the delicate and often secret diplomatic contacts that may lead to a decision on recognition. . . .

[T]he President since the founding has exercised this unilateral power to recognize new states—and the Court has endorsed the practice. . . .

It remains true, of course, that many decisions affecting foreign relations—including decisions that may determine the course of our relations with recognized countries—require congressional action. Congress may "regulate Commerce with foreign Nations," "establish an uniform Rule of Naturalization," "define and punish Piracies and Felonies committed on the high Seas, and Offences against the Law of Nations," "declare War," "grant Letters of Marque and Reprisal," and "make Rules for the Government and Regulation of the land and naval Forces." U.S. Const., Art. I, § 8. In addition, the President cannot make a treaty or appoint an ambassador without the approval of the Senate. Art. II, § 2, cl. 2. The President, furthermore, could not build an American Embassy abroad without congressional appropriation of the necessary funds. Art. I, § 8, cl. 1. Under basic separation-of-powers principles, it is for the Congress to enact the laws, including "all Laws which shall be necessary and proper for carrying into Execution" the powers of the Federal Government. § 8, cl. 18.

In foreign affairs, as in the domestic realm, the Constitution "enjoins upon its branches separateness but interdependence, autonomy but reciprocity." *Youngstown*, (Jackson, J., concurring). Although the President alone effects the formal act of recognition, Congress' powers, and its central role in making laws, give it substantial authority regarding many of the policy determinations that precede and follow the act of recognition itself. If Congress disagrees with the President's recognition policy, there may be consequences. Formal recognition may seem a hollow act if it is not accompanied by the dispatch of an ambassador, the easing of trade restrictions, and the conclusion of treaties. And those decisions require action by the Senate or the whole Congress.

In practice, then, the President's recognition determination is just one part of a political process that may require Congress to make laws. The President's exclusive recognition power encompasses the authority to acknowledge, in a formal sense, the legitimacy of other states and governments, including their territorial bounds. Albeit limited, the exclusive recognition power is essential to the conduct of Presidential duties. The formal act of recognition is an executive power that Congress may not qualify. If the President is to be effective in negotiations over a formal recognition determination, it must be evident to his counterparts abroad that he speaks for the Nation on that precise question. . . .

No single precedent resolves the question whether the President has exclusive recognition authority and, if so, how far that power extends. In part that is because, until today, the political branches have resolved their disputes over questions of recognition. [The Court then reviews the relevant cases and concludes] In the end, however, a fair reading of the cases shows that the President's role in the recognition process is both central and exclusive. . . .

[J]udicial precedent and historical practice teach that it is for the President alone to make the specific decision of what foreign power he will recognize as legitimate, both for the Nation as a whole and for the purpose of making his own position clear within the context of recognition in discussions and negotiations with foreign nations. Recognition is an act with immediate and powerful significance for international relations, so the President's position must be clear. Congress cannot require him to contradict his own statement regarding a determination of formal recognition. . . .

Having examined the Constitution's text and this Court's precedent, it is appropriate to turn to accepted understandings and practice. In separation-of-powers cases this Court has often "put significant weight upon historical practice." Here, history is not all on one side, but on balance it provides strong support for the conclusion that the recognition power is the President's alone. . . .

As the power to recognize foreign states resides in the President alone, the question becomes whether § 214(d) infringes on the Executive's consistent decision to withhold recognition with respect to Jerusalem. . . .

Section 214(d) requires . . . the President, through the Secretary, to identify citizens born in Jerusalem who so request as being born in Israel. But according to the President, those citizens were not born in Israel. As a matter of United States policy, neither Israel nor any other country is acknowledged as having sovereignty over Jerusalem. In this way, § 214(d) "directly contradicts" the "carefully calibrated and longstanding Executive branch policy of neutrality toward Jerusalem."

If the power over recognition is to mean anything, it must mean that the President not only makes the initial, formal recognition determination but also that he may maintain that determination in his and his agent's statements. This conclusion is a matter of both common sense and necessity. If Congress could command the President to state a recognition position inconsistent with his own, Congress could override the President's recognition determination. . . .

As Justice Jackson wrote in *Youngstown*, when a Presidential power is "exclusive," it "disabl[es] the Congress from acting upon the subject." Here, the subject is quite narrow: The Executive's exclusive power extends no further than his formal recognition determination. But as to that determination, Congress may not enact a law that directly contradicts it. This is not to say Congress may not express its disagreement with the President in myriad ways. For example, it may enact an embargo, decline to confirm an ambassador, or even declare war. But none of these acts would alter the President's recognition decision.

If Congress may not pass a law, speaking in its own voice, that effects formal recognition, then it follows that it may not force the President himself to contradict his earlier statement. That congressional command would not only prevent the Nation from speaking with one voice but also prevent the Executive itself from doing so in conducting foreign relations.

Although the statement required by § 214(d) would not itself constitute a formal act of recognition, it is a mandate that the Executive contradict his prior recognition determination in an official document issued by the Secretary of State. As a result, it is unconstitutional. . . .

JUSTICE BREYER, concurring.

I continue to believe that this case presents a political question inappropriate for judicial resolution. But because precedent precludes resolving this case on political question grounds, I join the Court's opinion.

JUSTICE THOMAS, concurring in the judgment in part and dissenting in part. [omitted]

CHIEF JUSTICE ROBERTS, with whom JUSTICE ALITO joins, dissenting.

Today's decision is a first: Never before has this Court accepted a President's direct defiance of an Act of Congress in the field of foreign affairs. We have instead stressed that the President's power reaches "its lowest ebb" when he contravenes the express will of Congress, "for what is at stake is the equilibrium established by our constitutional system." *Youngstown Sheet & Tube Co. v. Sawyer* (1952). . . .

The first principles in this area are firmly established. The Constitution allocates some foreign policy powers to the Executive, grants some to the Legislature, and enjoins the President to "take Care that the Laws be faithfully executed." The Executive may disregard "the expressed or implied will of Congress" only if the Constitution grants him a power "at once so conclusive and preclusive" as to "disable[e] the Congress from acting upon the subject." *Youngstown.*

Assertions of exclusive and preclusive power leave the Executive "in the least favorable of possible constitutional postures," and such claims have been "scrutinized with caution" throughout the Court's history. For our first 225 years, no President prevailed when contradicting a statute in the field of foreign affairs. . . .

In this case, the President claims the exclusive and preclusive power to recognize foreign sovereigns. . . . I have grave doubts about that position. The majority places great weight on the Reception Clause. . . . But that provision, framed as an obligation rather than an authorization, appears alongside the duties imposed on the President by Article II, Section 3, not the powers granted to him by Article II, Section 2. Indeed, the People ratified the Constitution with Alexander Hamilton's assurance that the executive reception of ambassadors "is more a matter of dignity than of authority" and "will be without consequence in the administration of the government." In short, at the time of the founding, "there was no reason to view the reception clause as a source of discretionary authority for the president.". . . .

As for history, the majority admits that it too points in both directions. Some Presidents have claimed an exclusive recognition power, but others have expressed uncertainty about whether such preclusive authority exists. Those in the skeptical camp include Andrew Jackson and Abraham Lincoln, leaders not generally known for their cramped conceptions of Presidential power. Congress has also asserted its authority over recognition determinations at numerous points in history. The majority therefore falls short of demonstrating that "Congress has accepted" the President's exclusive recognition power. In any event, we have held that congressional acquiescence is only "pertinent" when the President acts in the absence of express congressional authorization, not when he asserts power to disregard a statute, as the Executive does here. . . .

JUSTICE SCALIA, with whom THE CHIEF JUSTICE and JUSTICE ALITO join, dissenting.

Before this country declared independence, the law of England entrusted the King with the exclusive care of his kingdom's foreign affairs. . . . The People of the United States had other ideas when they organized our Government. They considered a sound structure of balanced powers essential to the preservation of just government and international relations formed no exception to that principle. . . .

The Constitution contemplates that the political branches will make policy about the territorial claims of foreign nations the same way they make policy about other international matters. The President will exercise his powers on the basis of his views, Congress its powers on the basis of its views. That is just what has happened here. . . .

Congress's power to "establish an uniform Rule of Naturalization" enables it to grant American citizenship to someone born abroad. The naturalization power also enables Congress to furnish the people it makes citizens with papers verifying their citizenship. . . . Even on the most miserly understanding of Congress's incidental authority, Congress may make grants of citizenship "effectual" by providing for the issuance of certificates authenticating them.

One would think that if Congress may grant Zivotofsky a passport and a birth report, it may also require these papers to record his birthplace as "Israel." The birthplace specification promotes the document's citizenship authenticating function by identifying the bearer, distinguishing people with similar names but different birthplaces from each other. . . . To be sure, recording Zivotofksy's birthplace as "Jerusalem" rather than "Israel" would fulfill these objectives, but when faced with alternative ways to carry its power into execution, Congress has the "discretion" to choose the one it deems "most beneficial to the people.". . .

The Court frames this case as a debate about recognition. . . .

The Court holds that the Constitution makes the President alone responsible for recognition and that [this statute] invades this exclusive power. I agree that the Constitution empowers the President to extend recognition on behalf of the United States, but I find it a much harder question whether it makes that power exclusive.... To take a stark example, Congress legislated in 1934 to grant independence to the Philippines, which were then an American colony. In the course of doing so, Congress directed the President to "recognize the independence of the Philippine Islands as a separate and self-governing nation." ... Constitutional? And if Congress may control recognition when exercising its power "to dispose of . . . the Territory or other Property belonging to the United States," why not when exercising other enumerated powers? Neither text nor history nor precedent yields a clear answer to these questions. . . .

[This statute] does not require the Secretary to make a formal declaration about Israel's sovereignty over Jerusalem. And nobody suggests that international custom infers acceptance of sovereignty from the birthplace designation on a passport or birth report, as it does from bilateral treaties or exchanges of ambassadors. . . . [M]aking a notation in a passport or birth report does not encumber the Republic with any international obligations. It leaves the Nation free (so far as international law is concerned) to change its mind in the future. That would be true even if the statute required all passports to list "Israel" for which the citizen (or his guardian) requests "Israel." ... It is utterly impossible for this deference to private requests to constitute an act that unequivocally manifests an intention to grant recognition.

[A]lthough normal protocol requires specifying the bearer's country of birth in is passport, the State Department will, if the bearer protests, specify the city instead—so that an Irish nationalist may have his birthplace recorded as "Belfast" rather than "United Kingdom." And although normal protocol requires specifying the country with present sovereignty over the bearer's place of birth, a special exception allows a bearer born before 1948 in what was then Palestine to have his birthplace listed as "Palestine." [This statute] requires the State Department to make a further accommodation. . . . Granting a request to specify "Israel" rather than "Jerusalem" does not recognize Israel's sovereignty over Jerusalem, just as granting a request to specify "Belfast" rather than "United Kingdom" does not derecognize the United Kingdom's sovereignty over Northern Ireland.

[E]ven if the Constitution gives the President sole power to extend recognition, it does not give him sole power to make all decisions relating to foreign disputes over sovereignty. To the contrary, a fair reading of Article I allows Congress to decide for itself how its laws should handle these controversies. . . .

History does not even support an exclusive Presidential power to make what the Court calls "formal statements" about the "legitimacy of a state or government and its territorial bounds." For a long time, the Houses of

Congress have made formal statements announcing their own positions on these issues, again without provoking constitutional objections. . . .

The Court's error could be made more apparent by applying its reasoning to the President's power "to make Treaties." There is no question that Congress may, if it wishes, pass laws that openly flout treaties made by the President. Would anyone have dreamt that the President may refuse to carry out such laws . . . so that the Executive may "speak with one voice" about the country's international obligations? To ask is to answer. Today's holding puts the implied power to recognize territorial claims . . . on a higher footing than the express power to make treaties. . . .

In the end, the Court's decision does not rest on text or history or precedent. It instead comes down to "functional considerations"—principally the Court's perception that the Nation "must speak with one voice" about the status of Jerusalem. The vices of this mode of analysis go beyond mere lack of footing in the Constitution. Functionalism of the sort the Court practices today will systematically favor the unitary President over the plural Congress in disputes involving foreign affairs. It is possible that this approach will make for more effective foreign policy, perhaps as effective as that of a monarchy. It is certain that, in the long run, it will erode the structure of separated powers that the People established for the protection of their liberty. . . .

COMMENTS AND QUESTIONS

1.   There is nothing novel in the conclusion that the Reception Clause authorizes the President to recognize what the United States considers the legitimate government of a foreign nation, but the dissenters are less sure whether that clause makes the President's power exclusive. The Court suggests that our government must speak with one voice, but even it acknowledges that the Senate might effectively blunt that voice by refusing to confirm an ambassador to that nation on the grounds that the Senate does not believe it to be the legitimate government of that nation.

2.   Whether Menachem Zivotosky's passport states his place of birth as Israel or Jerusalem seems less than compelling either to him or the United States government. After all, to Menachem the desire to have Israel listed is simply a desire to have his view that Jerusalem is part of Israel recognized by the United States government. On the other hand, if the passport listed Israel, no one simply seeing his passport would know that this was a statement about who had sovereignty over Jerusalem. For all anyone would know by looking at his passport, Menachem could have been born in Tel Aviv, not Jerusalem. Nevertheless, this case, as the Chief Justice notes, is historic for being the first time the Court approved the President's flouting of a law passed by Congress in the field of foreign affairs. Are there other foreign affairs areas now where the President may ignore laws passed by Congress?

3.   The Chief Justice in dissent points out that the Reception Clause is contained in Article II, Section 3, which he characterizes as listing the President's *duties*, not his *powers*, as compared to Article II, Section 2, which literally refers to the President's powers. This is not a distinction that is often made. Do you think it is a valid distinction? Even if the President has the *duty* to receive ambassadors from foreign nations, he must still have the *power* to receive them. And while the President has the *power* to appoint officers of the United States under Section 2, does he not also have the *duty* to appoint them?

4.   President Donald Trump, by moving the United States embassy from Tel Aviv to Jerusalem, apparently has decided that Jerusalem is in Israel. Imagine that Congress passed a law providing that a person born in Jerusalem, rather than having their place of birth listed as Israel, may, like those persons born in Belfast, choose to have their place of birth listed as the city of their birth. Would it be constitutional for the President to ignore that law and insist that the passport list Israel?

D. THE UNITARY EXECUTIVE

The "unitary executive" should not be confused with the "imperial presidency." However, these terms often are. The latter term is a derogatory term used to characterize the claim that "the executive power" extends to everything that is not expressly legislative or judicial—that is, it is a derogatory term for a broad reading of "executive power." Presidents from Andrew Jackson to Theodore Roosevelt to Franklin Roosevelt to George W. Bush to Donald Trump have made claims for such executive power. Often, although not always, the claimed power is in the foreign affairs or national security realm. Thus, such a characterization might be made if the President claimed a constitutional authority to commit American troops abroad without the approval of Congress and even contrary to congressional enactments. The cases we have been considering might be said to address this concept.

The term "unitary executive" refers instead to the idea that the "executive power" (whatever it is) resides in the President alone and cannot be divested from him. For example, those who believe in a strong form of the "unitary executive" would say that Congress cannot by law place the responsibility for executing a particular law in the head of an agency as opposed to the President. This has been an area of active legal scholarship in recent years. *Compare, e.g.,* Peter Strauss, *Overseer, or "The Decider"? The President in Administrative Law*, 75 Geo. Wash. L.Rev. 696 (2007)(critiquing the unitary executive) *with* Christopher Yoo, Steven Calabresi, and Anthony Colangelo, *The Unitary Executive in the Modern Era, 1945–2004*, 90 Iowa L. Rev. 601 (2005)(defending the unitary executive). In terms of case law, the issue has most often come up in the context of legislative restrictions on appointments to positions in the government and on the removal of persons from such positions.

1. APPOINTMENTS

The Appointments Clause, Article II, Section 2, Clause 2, provides that the President, with the advice and consent of the Senate, "shall appoint . . . officers of the United States . . ., but the Congress may by law vest the appointment of such inferior officers, as they think proper, in the President alone, in the courts of law, or in the heads of departments." It is, however, not uncommon for statutes creating agencies and specifying the officers to administer them to place some limits on whom the President may appoint. For example, the Solicitor General, who assists the Attorney General and by regulation is responsible for the position of the United States in litigation in courts, must be "learned in the law." 28 U.S.C. § 505. The Secretary of Defense must be a civilian. 10 U.S.C. § 113. The Administrator of the Federal Emergency Management Agency (as a result of the Katrina disaster) is now required to have "a demonstrated ability in and knowledge of emergency management and homeland security and not less than 5 years of executive leadership and management experience in the public or private sector." 6 U.S.C. § 313(c)(2). While none of these restrictions have been subject to any judicial challenge, in a case involving statutory restrictions on the President's use of advisory committees, Justice Kennedy (joined by Chief Justice Rehnquist and Justice O'Connor) opined that any statutory limitation on the President's power to nominate and, with Senate confirmation, to appoint officers of the United States would be unconstitutional. Moreover, Presidents since Ronald Reagan have regularly stated that such restrictions unconstitutionally limit the President's authority (subject to the Senate's confirmation) to appoint officers of the United States. As a practical matter, the issue is academic. The President is unlikely to nominate someone who does not meet the statutory criteria, even if he deems them unconstitutional, because of the likelihood of Senate rejection of the nominee.

a. Distinguishing Between Principal and Inferior Officers

The Appointments Clause also provides that "Congress may by law vest the appointment of such inferior officers, as they think proper, in the President alone, in the courts of law, or in the heads of departments." Of course, if Congress does not so provide, inferior officers would be appointed in the same manner as principal officers—by the President with the advice and consent of the Senate. Because the methods of appointment may differ between inferior and principal officers, it is important to be able to distinguish between them. In *Morrison v. Olson*, 487 U.S. 654 (1988), the Court addressed this issue. Under provisions of the Ethics in Government Act of 1978, upon a report by the Attorney General that there were sufficient grounds to investigate possible violations of federal criminal laws by federal officials, a Special Division of the United States Court of Appeals for the District of Columbia Circuit was required to appoint an independent counsel to investigate those possible violations. Thus, if the independent counsel was a principal officer, her appointment was unconstitutional, because it would be made by a court of law, rather than by the President with the advice and consent of the Senate.

The Court said that the line between principal and inferior officers is unclear, but that the independent counsel was "clearly" an inferior officer in light of four factors. First, the statute provided that the counsel was subject to removal by the Attorney General, someone superior to the counsel but below the President; thus, she was inferior to a principal officer. Second, the statute authorized her only to perform certain limited duties—the investigation and possible prosecution of certain specified offenses. This distinguished her from United States Attorneys, for example, who have the authority, among other things, to investigate and prosecute any federal crimes by any person. Third, the statute limited her jurisdiction to what was granted to her by the Special Division, which like the second factor distinguished her from other federal prosecutors. Finally, the statute limited her tenure to accomplishing the particular task she was assigned. Thus, in a real sense, her appointment was a temporary one.

There remained a question whether "interbranch appointments" were constitutional. The claim was that a court of law could only appoint inferior officers in the judicial branch, because it was inappropriate for courts of law to appoint executive officers, and the independent counsel concededly was an executive officer. The Court rejected this argument as well. It noted that the Appointments Clause contained no such limitation and indeed by its terms seemed to leave the issue to the discretion of Congress ("as [Congress] think[s] proper"). The Court did leave open the possibility of some constitutional limitation if "there was some 'incongruity' between the functions normally performed by the courts" and the functions of the officer they were to appoint. But, the Court said, "This is not a case in which judges are given power to appoint an officer in an area in which they have no special knowledge or expertise, as in, for example, a statute authorizing the courts to appoint officials in the Department of Agriculture or the Federal Energy Regulatory Commission."

Subsequent to *Morrison v. Olson*, the Court decided *Edmond v. United States*, 520 U.S. 651 (1997), in which the question was whether the Secretary of Transportation could appoint judges of the Coast Guard Court of Criminal Appeals. If they were principal officers, they would have to have been appointed by the President with the advice and consent of the Senate. The Court, in an opinion by Justice Scalia, who dissented in *Morrison*, held the appointment was of an inferior officer, but in reaching that conclusion, he did not utilize the *Morrison* test. Instead, the Court said:

> Generally speaking, the term "inferior officer" connotes a relationship with some higher ranking officer or officers below the President: Whether one is an "inferior" officer depends on whether

he has a superior. It is not enough that other officers may be identified who formally maintain a higher rank, or possess responsibilities of a greater magnitude. . . . Rather, in the context of a Clause designed to preserve political accountability relative to important Government assignments, we think it evident that "inferior officers" are officers whose work is directed and supervised at some level by others who were appointed by Presidential nomination with the advice and consent of the Senate.

Because these judges were subject to the supervision of the Judge Advocate General, who could remove them without cause, and because the Court of Appeals for the Armed Forces exercised appellate jurisdiction over their judgments, these judges were inferior officers.

Later, in *Free Enterprise Fund v. Public Company Accounting Oversight Board*, 561 U.S. 477 (2010), the Court followed *Edmonds* without mentioning *Morrison* in finding that members of the Public Company Accounting Oversight Board were inferior officers because they were in effect supervised by the members of the Security and Exchange Commission and, as interpreted by the Court, were able to be removed without cause by the Commission.

Whether these later cases reflect a tacit rejection of *Morrison* or, as suggested in *Edmond*, simply an alternative test, either of which might be used, is unknown. One distinguishing factor between the officers in *Edmond* and *Free Enterprise Fund* and the officer in *Morrison* is that in *Morrison* the officer could only be removed for cause, which would restrict the supervisory power of the superior officer, while in the other two cases the officer could be removed at will by the superior officer. This might suggest that the *Morrison* factors come into play only when the superior officer's supervisory authority is in some way restricted.

The Court's most recent case follows.

UNITED STATES v. ARTHREX, INC.

United States Supreme Court, 2021.
141 S.Ct. 1970.

CHIEF JUSTICE ROBERTS delivered the opinion of the Court with respect to Parts I and II.

The validity of a patent previously issued by the Patent and Trademark Office can be challenged before the Patent Trial and Appeal Board, an executive tribunal within the PTO. The Board, composed largely of Administrative Patent Judges appointed by the Secretary of Commerce, has the final word within the Executive Branch on the validity of a challenged patent. Billions of dollars can turn on a Board decision.

Under the Constitution, "[t]he executive Power" is vested in the President, who has the responsibility to "take Care that the Laws be faithfully executed." Art. II, § 1, cl. 1; § 3. The Appointments Clause provides that he may be assisted in carrying out that responsibility by officers nominated by him and confirmed by the Senate, as well as by other officers not appointed in that manner but whose work, we have held, must be directed and supervised by an officer who has been. § 2, cl. 2. The question presented is whether the authority of the Board to issue decisions on behalf of the Executive Branch is consistent with these constitutional provisions.

I

[T]his suit centers on the Patent Trial and Appeal Board (PTAB), an executive adjudicatory body within the PTO. . . . The PTAB sits in panels of at least three members drawn from the Director, the Deputy Director, the Commissioner for Patents, the Commissioner for Trademarks, and more than 200 Administrative Patent Judges (APJs). The Secretary of Commerce appoints the members of the PTAB (except for the Director), including the APJs at issue in this dispute. . . .

Through a variety of procedures, the PTAB can . . . take a second look at patents previously issued by the PTO. One such procedure is inter partes review. Established in 2011, inter partes review is an adversarial process by which members of the PTAB reconsider whether existing patents satisfy the novelty and nonobviousness requirements for inventions. . . . Congress has committed the decision to institute inter partes review to the Director's unreviewable discretion. By regulation, the Director has delegated this authority to the PTAB itself.

The Director designates at least three members of the PTAB (typically three APJs) to conduct an inter partes proceeding. The PTAB then assumes control of the process, which resembles civil litigation in many respects. The PTAB must issue a final written decision on all of the challenged patent claims within 12 to 18 months of institution. A party who disagrees with a decision may request rehearing by the PTAB.

The PTAB is the last stop for review within the Executive Branch. A party dissatisfied with the final decision may seek judicial review in the Court of Appeals for the Federal Circuit. At this stage, the Director can intervene before the court to defend or disavow the Board's decision. The Federal Circuit reviews the PTAB's application of patentability standards *de novo* and its underlying factual determinations for substantial evidence. Upon expiration of the time to appeal or termination of any appeal, "the Director shall issue and publish a certificate canceling any claim of the patent finally determined to be unpatentable, confirming any claim of the patent determined to be patentable, and incorporating in the patent by operation of the certificate any new or amended claim determined to be patentable."

[I]n 2015, [Arthrex] secured a patent on a surgical device for reattaching soft tissue to bone without tying a knot. Arthrex soon claimed that Smith & Nephew, Inc. and ArthroCare Corp. (collectively, Smith & Nephew) had infringed the . . . patent, and the dispute eventually made its way to inter partes review in the PTO. Three APJs formed the PTAB panel that conducted the proceeding and ultimately concluded that a prior patent application "anticipated" the invention claimed by the . . . patent, so that Arthrex's patent was invalid.

On appeal to the Federal Circuit, Arthrex raised for the first time an argument premised on the Appointments Clause of the Constitution. That Clause specifies how the President may appoint officers who assist him in carrying out his responsibilities. *Principal* officers must be appointed by the President with the advice and consent of the Senate, while *inferior* officers may be appointed by the President alone, the head of an executive department, or a court. Art. II, § 2, cl. 2. Arthrex argued that the APJs were principal officers and therefore that their appointment by the Secretary of Commerce was unconstitutional. The Government intervened to defend the appointment procedure.

The Federal Circuit agreed with Arthrex that APJs were principal officers. Neither the Secretary nor Director had the authority to review their decisions or to remove them at will. The Federal Circuit held that these restrictions meant that APJs were themselves principal officers, not inferior officers under the direction of the Secretary or Director.

To fix this constitutional violation, the Federal Circuit invalidated the tenure protections for APJs. Making APJs removable at will by the Secretary, the panel held, prospectively "renders them inferior rather than principal officers." The Federal Circuit vacated the PTAB's decision and remanded for a fresh hearing before a new panel of APJs, who would no longer enjoy protection against removal. . . .

II

Only the President, with the advice and consent of the Senate, can appoint noninferior officers, called "principal" officers as shorthand in our cases. The "default manner of appointment" for inferior officers is also nomination by the President and confirmation by the Senate. But the Framers foresaw that "when offices became numerous, and sudden removals necessary, this mode might be inconvenient." Reflecting this concern for "administrative convenience," the Appointments Clause permits Congress to dispense with joint appointment, but only for inferior officers. Congress may vest the appointment of such officers "in the President alone, in the Courts of Law, or in the Heads of Departments."

Congress provided that APJs would be appointed as inferior officers, by the Secretary of Commerce as head of a department. The question presented is whether the nature of their responsibilities is consistent with their method of appointment. . . .

The starting point for each party's analysis is our opinion in *Edmond v. United States*, 520 U.S. 651 (1997). There we explained that "[w]hether one is an 'inferior' officer depends on whether he has a superior" other than the President. An inferior officer must be "directed and supervised at some level by others who were appointed by Presidential nomination with the advice and consent of the Senate."

In *Edmond*, we applied this test to adjudicative officials within the Executive Branch—specifically, Coast Guard Court of Criminal Appeals judges appointed by the Secretary of Transportation. We held that the judges were inferior officers because they were effectively supervised by a combination of Presidentially nominated and Senate confirmed officers in the Executive Branch: first, the Judge Advocate General, who "exercise[d] administrative oversight over the Court of Criminal Appeals" by prescribing rules of procedure and formulating policies for court-martial cases, and could also "remove a Court of Criminal Appeals judge from his judicial assignment without cause"; and second, the Court of Appeals for the Armed Forces, an executive tribunal that could review the judges' decisions under a *de novo* standard for legal issues and a deferential standard for factual issues. "What is significant," we concluded, "is that the judges of the Court of Criminal Appeals have no power to render a final decision on behalf of the United States unless permitted to do so by other Executive officers."

Congress structured the PTAB differently, providing only half of the "divided" supervision to which judges of the Court of Criminal Appeals were subject. Like the Judge Advocate General, the PTO Director possesses powers of "administrative oversight." The Director fixes the rate of pay for APJs, controls the decision whether to institute inter partes review, and selects the APJs to reconsider the validity of the patent. The Director also promulgates regulations governing inter partes review, issues prospective guidance on patentability issues, and designates past PTAB decisions as "precedential" for future panels. He is the boss, except when it comes to the one thing that makes the APJs officers exercising "significant authority" in the first place—their power to issue decisions on patentability. In contrast to the scheme approved by *Edmond*, no principal officer at any level within the Executive Branch "direct[s] and supervise[s]" the work of APJs in that regard.

Edmond goes a long way toward resolving this dispute. What was "significant" to the outcome there—review by a superior executive officer— is absent here: APJs have the "power to render a final decision on behalf of the United States" without any such review by their nominal superior or any other principal officer in the Executive Branch.

This "diffusion of power carries with it a diffusion of accountability." The restrictions on review relieve the Director of responsibility for the final decisions rendered by APJs purportedly under his charge. . . .

The Government contends that the Director may respond after the fact by removing an APJ "from his judicial assignment without cause" and refusing to designate that APJ on *future* PTAB panels. Even assuming that is true, reassigning an APJ to a different task going forward gives the Director no means of countermanding the final decision already on the books. Nor are APJs "meaningfully controlled" by the threat of removal from federal service entirely, because the Secretary can fire them after a decision only "for such cause as will promote the efficiency of the service." In all the ways that matter to the parties who appear before the PTAB, the buck stops with the APJs, not with the Secretary or Director. . . .

Given the insulation of PTAB decisions from any executive review, the President can neither oversee the PTAB himself nor "attribute the Board's failings to those whom he *can* oversee." APJs accordingly exercise power that conflicts with the design of the Appointments Clause "to preserve political accountability." . . .

The Government and Smith & Nephew point to a handful of contemporary officers who are appointed by heads of departments but who nevertheless purportedly exercise final decisionmaking authority. Several examples, however, involve inferior officers whose decisions a superior executive officer can review or implement a system for reviewing. For instance, the special trial judges in *Freytag v. Commissioner*, 501 U.S. 868 (1991), may enter a decision on behalf of the Tax Court—whose members are nominated by the President and confirmed by the Senate—but only "subject to such conditions and review as the court may provide." And while the Board of Veterans' Appeals does make the final decision within the Department of Veterans Affairs, its decisions are reviewed by the Court of Appeals for Veterans Claims, an Executive Branch entity. Other examples are potentially distinguishable, such as the Benefits Review Board members who appear to serve at the pleasure of the appointing department head.

Perhaps the Civilian and Postal Boards of Contract Appeals are most similar to the PTAB. The Administrator of General Services and the Postmaster General appoint the members of the respective Boards, whose decisions are appealable to the Federal Circuit. Congress established both entities in 2006 and gave them jurisdiction over disputes involving public contractors. Whatever distinct issues that scheme might present, the Boards of Contract Appeals—both young entrants to the regulatory landscape—provide the PTAB no "foothold in history or tradition" across the Executive Branch. . . .

We hold that the unreviewable authority wielded by APJs during inter partes review is incompatible with their appointment by the Secretary to an inferior office. The principal dissent repeatedly charges that we never say whether APJs are principal officers who were not appointed in the manner required by the Appointments Clause, or instead inferior officers exceeding the permissible scope of their duties under that Clause. But both formulations describe the same constitutional violation: Only an officer properly appointed to a principal office may issue a final decision binding the Executive Branch in the proceeding before us. . . .

III

We turn now to the appropriate way to resolve this dispute given this violation of the Appointments Clause. In general, "when confronting a constitutional flaw in a statute, we try to limit the solution to the problem" by disregarding the "problematic portions while leaving the remainder intact." This approach derives from the Judiciary's "negative power to disregard an unconstitutional enactment" in resolving a legal dispute. In a case that presents a conflict between the Constitution and a statute, we give "full effect" to the Constitution and to whatever portions of the statute are "not repugnant" to the Constitution, effectively severing the unconstitutional portion of the statute. This principle explains our "normal rule that partial, rather than facial, invalidation is the required course."

Arthrex asks us to hold the entire regime of inter partes review unconstitutional. In its view, any more tailored declaration of unconstitutionality would necessitate a policy decision best left to Congress in the first instance. Because the good cannot be separated from the bad, Arthrex continues, the appropriate remedy is to order outright dismissal of the proceeding below. The partial dissent, similarly forswearing the need to do anything beyond "identifying the constitutional violation," would grant full relief to Arthrex. . . .

In our view, the structure of the PTO and the governing constitutional principles chart a clear course: Decisions by APJs must be subject to review by the Director. Congress vested the Director with the "powers and duties" of the PTO, tasked him with supervising APJs, and placed the PTAB "in" the PTO. . . . While shielding the ultimate decisions of the 200-plus APJs from review, Congress also provided the Director means of control over the institution and conduct of inter partes review. In every respect save the insulation of their decisions from review within the Executive Branch, APJs appear to be inferior officers—an understanding consistent with their appointment in a manner permissible for inferior but not principal officers.

We conclude that a tailored approach is the appropriate one: Section 6(c) cannot constitutionally be enforced to the extent that its requirements prevent the Director from reviewing final decisions rendered by APJs. Because Congress has vested the Director with the "power and duties" of the PTO, the Director has the authority to provide for a means of reviewing PTAB decisions. The Director accordingly may review final PTAB decisions and, upon review, may issue decisions himself on behalf of the Board. . . .

This does not result in an incomplete or unworkable statutory scheme. To the contrary, review by the Director would follow the almost-universal model of adjudication in the Executive Branch and aligns the PTAB with the *other* adjudicative body in the PTO, the Trademark Trial and Appeal Board.

The Government defends the different approach adopted by the Federal Circuit. The Court of Appeals held unenforceable APJs' protection against removal except "for such cause as will promote the efficiency of the service." If the for-cause provision were unenforceable, the Secretary could remove APJs at will. The Government contends that APJs would then be inferior officers under *Free Enterprise Fund*. But regardless whether the Government is correct that at-will removal by the Secretary would cure the constitutional problem, review by the Director better reflects the structure of supervision within the PTO and the nature of APJs' duties, for the reasons we have explained.

JUSTICE GORSUCH, concurring in part and dissenting in part.

[I] join Parts I and II of the Court's opinion. Respectfully, however, I am unable to join the Court's severability discussion in Part III. . . . [Justice Gorsuch critiques the Court's severability doctrine and says that the proper remedy here is simply to set aside the PTAB's decision in this case.]

JUSTICE BREYER, with whom JUSTICE SOTOMAYOR and JUSTICE KAGAN join, concurring in the judgment in part and dissenting in part. [omitted]

JUSTICE THOMAS, with whom JUSTICE BREYER, JUSTICE SOTOMAYOR, and JUSTICE KAGAN join as to Parts I and II, dissenting.

For the very first time, this Court holds that Congress violated the Constitution by vesting the appointment of a federal officer in the head of a department. Just who are these "principal" officers that Congress unsuccessfully sought to smuggle into the Executive Branch without Senate confirmation? About 250 administrative patent judges who sit at the bottom of an organizational chart, nestled under at least two levels of authority. Neither our precedent nor the original understanding of the Appointments Clause requires Senate confirmation of officers inferior to not one, but *two* officers below the President.

I

The Executive Branch is large, and the hierarchical path from President to administrative patent judge is long. At the top sits the President, in whom the executive power is vested. U.S. Const., Art. II, § 1. Below him is the Secretary of Commerce, who oversees the Department of Commerce and its work force of about 46,000. Within that Department is the United States Patent and Trademark Office led by a Director. In the Patent and Trademark Office is the Patent Trial and Appeal Board. Serving on this Board are administrative patent judges. . . .

That both the Federal Circuit and this Court would take so much care to ensure that administrative patent judges, appointed as inferior officers, would remain inferior officers at the end of the day suggests that perhaps they were inferior officers to begin with. Instead of rewriting the Director's statutory powers, I would simply leave intact the patent scheme Congress has created.

II

[T]he Court has been careful not to create a rigid test to divide principal officers—those who must be Senate confirmed—from inferior ones. Instead, the Court's opinions have traditionally used a case-by-case analysis. And those analyses invariably result in this Court deferring to Congress' choice of which constitutional appointment process works best. No party (nor the majority) has identified any instance in which this Court has found unconstitutional an appointment that aligns with one of the two processes outlined in the Constitution.

Our most exhaustive treatment of the inferior-officer question is found in *Edmond*. . . . Recognizing that no "definitive test" existed for distinguishing between inferior and principal officers, the Court set out two general guidelines. First, there is a formal, definitional requirement. The officer must be lower in rank to "a superior." But according to the Court in *Edmond*, formal inferiority is "not enough." So the Court imposed a functional requirement: The inferior officer's work must be "directed and supervised at some level by others who were appointed by Presidential nomination with advice and consent of the Senate." Because neither side asks us to overrule our precedent, I would apply this two-part guide.

There can be no dispute that administrative patent judges are, in fact, inferior: They are lower in rank to at least two different officers. . . .

As a comparison to the facts in *Edmond* illustrates, the Director and Secretary are also functionally superior because they supervise and direct the work administrative patent judges perform. . . .

The Director here possesses even greater functional power over the Board than that possessed by the Judge Advocate General [in *Edmond*]. . . .

Also like the Judge Advocate General in *Edmond*, the Director prescribes uniform procedural rules and formulates policies and procedures for Board proceedings. He may issue binding policy directives that govern the Board. And he may release "instructions that include exemplary applications of patent laws to fact patterns, which the Board can refer to when presented with factually similar cases." His oversight is not just administrative; it is substantive as well.

The Director has yet another "powerful tool for control." He may designate which of the 250-plus administrative patent judges hear certain cases and may remove administrative patent judges from their specific assignments without cause. So, if any administrative patent judges depart from the Director's direction, he has ample power to rein them in to avoid erroneous decisions. And, if an administrative patent judge consistently fails to follow instructions, the Secretary has the authority to fire him.

To be sure, the Director's power over administrative patent judges is not complete. He cannot singlehandedly reverse decisions. Still, he has two powerful checks on Board decisions not found in *Edmond*. . . .

The Court today appears largely to agree with all of this. "In every respect" save one, the plurality says, "[administrative patent judges] appear to be inferior officers." All that matters is whether the Director has the statutory authority to individually reverse Board decisions. . . .

[I]nterpreting the Appointments Clause to bar any nonprincipal officer from taking "final" action poses serious line-drawing problems. The majority assures that not every decision by an inferior officer must be reviewable by a superior officer. But this sparks more questions than it answers. Can a line prosecutor offer a plea deal without sign off from a principal officer? If faced with a life-threatening scenario, can an FBI agent use deadly force to subdue a suspect? Or if an inferior officer temporarily fills a vacant office tasked with making final decisions, do those decisions violate the Appointments Clause? . . .

III

[Justice Thomas argues that even if it is unconstitutional to prohibit the Director's ability to review the PTAB's decisions, the Court's remedy does not follow. This is so, because if the prohibition is unconstitutional, it has always been unconstitutional, so the Director has always had the power to review the PTAB's decisions, so there is no need to remand for him to decide anew whether to review the decision in this case.]

COMMENTS AND QUESTIONS

1.   Note the strange alignment. The Chief Justice's opinion is the opinion of the Court as to the existence of a constitutional violation because it is joined by Justices Alito, Gorsuch, Kavanaugh, and Barrett, but it is the opinion of the Court for the remedy because it is joined by Justices Alito, Kavanaugh, Barrett, Breyer, Kagan, and Sotomayor. Because Justice Gorsuch does not agree with the Chief Justice's opinion as to remedy, that opinion would not muster a majority of the Court without the "liberals" joining that part of the Chief Justice's opinion. Also, isn't it interesting that Justice Thomas joins the "liberals" in finding no constitutional violation. One would search a long time to find another opinion in which Thomas alone joins the liberals.

2.   *Edmond* says that inferior officers must be "directed and supervised at some level by others" who are principal officers. Does *Arthrex* now say that such direction and supervision must include the ability to review what the inferior officer does in each case? Or only if the person cannot be removed at

will? The Constitution says that the President is responsible to take care that the laws be faithfully executed. Art. II, cl. 1, § 3. Does *Arthrex* suggest that the President must be able to review what each principal officer does in each case, at least where the principal officer can only be removed for cause?

3.   In addition to normal appointments, the Constitution provides for what are called "recess appointments." Article II, Section 2, Clause 3, states that "The President shall have Power to fill up all vacancies that may happen during the Recess of the Senate, by granting commissions which shall expire at the end of their next session." One would think that the Founding Fathers put this into the Constitution because they did not want appointments to offices that would require Senate confirmation to be held up because the Senate was in recess. Recall that at the time of the founding, Congress was not in session for much of the year, and transportation took a lot longer than today.

Today, however, much is changed. Congress is in session for most of the year, and precisely to avoid the President making a recess appointment when the Senate does take a recess for a short period of time, the Senate has used the tactic of holding pro forma sessions, where one Senator is present, calls the Senate to order and then adjourns it for three days. President Obama, frustrated by the Senate's failure to take a vote on numerous nominees for principal officer positions, made several recess appointments during one of the three-day adjournments.

In *NLRB v. Noel Canning*, 573 U.S. 513 (2014), by a 5–4 vote the Supreme Court held the appointments invalid. The initial question was whether the term, "the recess of the Senate," referred only to an end of session recess and not to intra-session recesses. The second question was whether the Constitution's words, "vacancies that may happen during the recess," referred only to those vacancies that arose during the recess, not to vacancies that happened to exist during the recess. Justice Breyer, writing for the Court, found that the language in question was ambiguous:

> In light of these ambiguities, the Court looked at the historical practice, finding that ever since intra-session recesses became common in the mid-19th century Presidents had made recess appointments during those recesses, and ever since President Madison Presidents have made recess appointments where the vacancy occurred prior to the recess. Moreover, this was done with the general understanding of the Senate that such appointments were constitutional. Consequently, the Court concluded that recess appointments could be made during intra-session recesses as well as inter-session recesses with respect to vacancies that existed during those recesses, not just those that arose during the recesses. The question then became whether the appointments in question made by President Obama during a 3-day adjournment between two *pro forma* sessions was made during a "recess" at all. The Court said no. Three days was simply too short a period to be deemed a recess, and only when the Senate itself says it is in recess can it be a recess. The Court suggested that presumptively a recess would have to be at least

10 days long in order to trigger the President's recess appointment power. The four "conservative" dissenters, led by Justice Scalia, took issue with both the conclusion that the language of the clause was ambiguous and that the Court should defer to the two branches' historical practice (which was argued not to be as consistent as the Court suggested). Nevertheless, given the Senate's current practices, it would seem that Presidents will no longer be able to make recess appointments.

4.   In *Arthrex*, the Court said the case should be remanded to the "Acting Director [of the Patent and Trademark Office] for him to decide whether to rehear the petition." The Commissioner of Patents was the Acting Director, because there was a vacancy in the positions of both the Director and Deputy Director, and the Commissioner of Patents is not a position appointed by the President with the advice and consent of the Senate. On remand, the Acting Director decided not to rehear the petition, and Arthrex appealed to the Federal Circuit, arguing that, because the Acting Director, the Commissioner of Patents, was only an inferior officer, Arthrex did not receive what the Supreme Court required—a decision reviewable by a principal officer. The Federal Circuit acknowledged that in light of *Arthrex* "ordinarily" an inferior officer cannot issue a final, unreviewable decision binding on the Executive Branch. However, it cited to *United States v. Eaton*, 169 U.S. 331 (1898), which had in fact been cited by the Court in *Arthrex*, for the rule that an inferior officer "charged with the performance of the duty of [a] superior for a limited time, and under special and temporary conditions" need not be Presidentially appointed and Senate confirmed. Here, the offices of both the Director and Deputy Director were vacant, and a new Director had not yet been confirmed, so the situation was akin to that in *Eaton*. Moreover, a standing directive from a former Director provided that if there were vacancies in the offices of both the Director and Deputy Director, then the functions of the Director should be performed by the Commissioner of Patents. *Arthrex, Inc. v. Smith & Nephew, Inc.*, 35 F.4th 1328 (Fed. Cir. 2022).

5.   Another workaround when a principal officer vacancy occurs is the Federal Vacancy Reform Act (FVRA). It states that the first assistant to the principal officer may fill the vacancy for a specified period or the President may appoint certain types of persons, identified in the Act, for a specified period of time to carry out the functions of the office. There is some question when the FVRA is applicable, but the Federal Circuit in *Arthrex* said it only applies to functions and duties which are non delegable; that is, which by statute may only be performed by the principal officer.

b.   Distinguishing Between Inferior Officers and Employees

Just as the line between principal and inferior officers is not clear, the line between inferior officers and mere employees is not clear. The Constitution does not address the appointment, or more accurately the hiring, of employees. In *Buckley v. Valeo*, 424 U.S. 1 (1976), the Court said that "employees are lesser functionaries subordinate to officers of the

United States." Employees are not authorized to make policy; they merely carry it out. On the other hand, a person "exercising significant authority pursuant to the laws of the United States is an 'Officer of the United States.'" Nevertheless, some inferior officers may be fairly indistinguishable from an employee. For example, the clerk of a district court was deemed an inferior officer. *See Ex parte Hennen*, 38 U.S. (13 Pet.) 230 (1839).

In *Freytag v. Commissioner*, 501 U.S. 868 (1991), the Court found that Special Trial Judges (STJs) of the United States Tax Court* were inferior officers, not mere employees. In reaching that conclusion, the Court said that they held a "continuing office established by law"; they served on an ongoing, not temporary, basis; and their duties, salary, and means of appointment are specified in statute. In addressing *Buckley*'s "significant authority test," the Court said that the STJs had significant duties and discretion, whether or not they could render final decisions for the tax court. Specifically, they could "take testimony, conduct trials, rule on the admissibility of evidence, and have the power to enforce compliance with discovery orders." This was sufficient to make them officers rather than employees. The government had argued that so long as a person could not make a binding decision on behalf of an agency, the person should be an employee; only persons with the power to make final, binding decisions for the agency should be officers. The Court responded to this argument by noting that in minor matters STJs were authorized to make final decisions for the agency. Thus, even under that test STJs would be officers.

More recently, in *Lucia v. SEC*, 138 S.Ct. 2044 (2018), a similar issue arose. Are the roughly 1500 Administrative Law Judges (ALJs) employed by various agencies also officers or only employees? Like the STJs, ALJs take testimony, conduct adjudications, rule on the admissibility of evidence, and have the power to enforce compliance with discovery orders. Moreover, they hold a continuing office established by law; they serve on an ongoing, not temporary, basis; and their duties, salary, and means of appointment are specified in statute. However, their decisions are always subject to review by the agency, so unlike the STJs they cannot make final decisions for the agency (although the agency can adopt their decisions as its own). This led some courts to hold that ALJs were not officers. The Supreme Court disagreed, saying that *Freytag* governed this case; ALJs were indistinguishable from STJs, other than their inability sometimes to make final decisions for the agency, and in *Freytag* the ability to make final decisions for the agency was an alternative basis, not a necessary requirement, for someone to qualify as an officer.

---

* It should be noted that despite the title the U.S. Tax Court is not an Article III court made up of judges who hold their offices "during good behavior." Instead, it is what is known as a legislative court, but which is considered part of the executive branch. *See Free Enterprise Fund v. Public Company Accounting Oversight Board*, 561 U.S. 477, 511 (2010).

2. REMOVAL

While Article II has a specific clause governing appointments that is fairly clear as constitutional provisions go, the Constitution nowhere says anything about who may remove officers, other than that Congress may remove them through impeachment. The history is clear, however, that impeachment was intended to be an extraordinary power to be exercised in rare circumstances demanding a check by the legislative branch over the executive or judicial branches; it was not to be the means by which to manage executive or judicial personnel.

The Constitution states that federal judges hold their offices "during good behavior," but again it says nothing about who should determine when a judge fails to behave well. Historically, there has never been an attempt to remove a judge except through impeachment, but from time-to-time there have been suggestions to institutionalize a system within the judicial branch by which it would be able to remove judges upon a determination that they no longer are acting in "good behavior." These suggestions, however, have not had traction.

Again, historically, appointment to federal office was often patronage bestowed on political supporters. One would be hard pressed to say that some appointments today are not made on that basis. Because they were based on patronage, the assumption was that the person who hired you could fire you and replace you with a new supporter, and the assumption was that a new administration would replace virtually all the principal officers and many, if not most, of the inferior officers. It is standard practice today for principal officers in executive agencies to offer their resignations to the new incoming President.

There are and have been exceptions to this standard practice, however. For example, when Andrew Johnson became President after Lincoln's assassination, the Congress controlled by radical Republicans wished to limit his power, because, as a southern Democrat (part of Lincoln's plan to suggest national unity), he would go easy on the defeated Confederacy. One way to do that was by passing the Tenure in Office Act, which prohibited the removal of any principal officer without the consent of the Senate. The theory was that, if such an officer could only be appointed with the consent of the Senate, that officer should only be able to be removed with the consent of the Senate. Johnson, however, did not abide by the law and fired the Secretary of War, who was in league with the radical Republicans against Johnson. This violation of the Tenure in Office Act became the principal basis for bringing impeachment charges against Johnson, but it, like the other articles of impeachment, failed by one vote to obtain the necessary two-thirds majority in the Senate, and Johnson remained in office.

The Tenure in Office Act remained in effect until it was repealed in 1887, but an 1876 law provided that Postmasters "shall be appointed and may be removed by the President with the advice and consent of the Senate," and in 1920 President Woodrow Wilson fired the Postmaster of Portland, Oregon, without seeking the advice and consent of the Senate. The Postmaster sued for his salary.

MYERS V. UNITED STATES

United States Supreme Court, 1926.
272 U.S. 52, 47 S.Ct. 21.

MR. CHIEF JUSTICE TAFT delivered the opinion of the Court.

This case presents the question whether under the Constitution the President has the exclusive power of removing executive officers of the United States whom he has appointed by and with the advice and consent of the Senate. . . .

The Senate did not consent to the President's removal of Myers during his term. If this statute in its requirement [that he can be removed by the President only] with the consent of the Senate is valid, the appellant, Myers's administratrix,* is entitled to recover his unpaid salary for his full term. . . . The government maintains that the requirement is invalid, for the reason that under article 2 of the Constitution the President's power of removal of executive officers appointed by him with the advice and consent of the Senate is full and complete without consent of the Senate. If this view is sound, the removal of Myers by the President without the Senate's consent was legal. . . .

There is no express provision respecting removals in the Constitution, except as section 4 of article 2 provides for removal from office by impeachment. The subject was not discussed in the Constitutional Convention. Under the Articles of Confederation, Congress was given the power of appointing certain executive officers of the Confederation, and during the Revolution and while the articles were given effect, Congress exercised the power of removal. . . .

In the House of Representatives of the First Congress. . . . Mr. Madison moved in the committee of the whole that there should be established three executive departments, . . . at the head of each of which there should be a Secretary, to be appointed by the President by and with the advice and consent of the Senate, and to be removable by the President. [The Court then provides an extensive history of the debates over the

---

* An administratrix is a female administrator. The term is no longer in use; both males and females are now called administrators. An administrator in this context is a person appointed by a court to handle the affairs of a person who has died without a will. Here, Myers, the Postmaster, had died without a will, and his wife was the administrator of his affairs, including continuing this lawsuit. [author's note]

provision that the heads of these departments would be removable by the President.]

It is very clear from this history that the exact question which the House voted upon was whether it should recognize and declare the power of the President under the Constitution to remove the Secretary of Foreign Affairs without the advice and consent of the Senate. That was what the vote was taken for. Some effort has been made to question whether the decision carries the result claimed for it, but there is not the slightest doubt, after an examination of the record, that the vote was, and was intended to be, a legislative declaration that the power to remove officers appointed by the President and the Senate vested in the President alone, and until the Johnson impeachment trial in 1868 its meaning was not doubted, even by those who questioned its soundness. . . .

The vesting of the executive power in the President was essentially a grant of the power to execute the laws. But the President alone and unaided could not execute the laws. He must execute them by the assistance of subordinates. . . . As he is charged specifically to take care that they be faithfully executed, the reasonable implication, even in the absence of express words, was that as part of his executive power he should select those who were to act for him under his direction in the execution of the laws. The further

William Howard Taft

Taft was a protégé of President Theodore Roosevelt, serving in several positions in his administration. Roosevelt anointed him as his successor, but after Taft's election as President, Taft took his own course, alienating Roosevelt, who then ran as a third party candidate against him in the next election, assuring Taft's defeat by Democrat Woodrow Wilson. Taft retreated to Yale Law School as a professor, but the next Republican President, Warren G. Harding, appointed him to the Supreme Court as Chief Justice in 1921. Although he authored over 200 opinions before his retirement in 1930, Taft's legacy is not in his jurisprudence but in the Supreme Court building which he lobbied to have built.

implication must be, in the absence of any express limitation respecting removals, that as his selection of administrative officers is essential to the execution of the laws by him, so must be his power of removing those for whom he cannot continue to be responsible. . . .

Second. The view of Mr. Madison and his associates was that not only did the grant of executive power to the President in the first section of article 2 carry with it the power of removal, but the express recognition of the power of appointment in the second section enforced this view on the well-approved principle of constitutional and statutory construction that the power of removal of executive officers was incident to the power of appointment. . . . The reason for the principle is that those in charge of and responsible for administering functions of government, who select their executive subordinates, need in meeting their responsibility to have the power to remove those whom they appoint. . . .

Fourth. Mr. Madison and his associates pointed out with great force the unreasonable character of the view that the convention intended, without express provision, to give to Congress or the Senate, in case of political or other differences, the means of thwarting the executive in the exercise of his great powers and in the bearing of his great responsibility by fastening upon him, as subordinate executive officers, men who by their inefficient service under him, by their lack of loyalty to the service, or by their different views of policy might make his taking care that the laws be faithfully executed most difficult or impossible.

Made responsible under the Constitution for the effective enforcement of the law, the President needs as an indispensable aid to meet it the disciplinary influence upon those who act under him of a reserve power of removal. But it is contended that executive officers appointed by the President with the consent of the Senate are bound by the statutory law, and are not his servants to do his will, and that his obligation to care for the faithful execution of the laws does not authorize him to treat them as such. The degree of guidance in the discharge of their duties that the President may exercise over executive officers varies with the character of their service as prescribed in the law under which they act. The highest and most important duties which his subordinates perform are those in which they act for him. In such cases they are exercising not their own but his discretion. This field is a very large one. It is sometimes described as political. Each head of a department is and must be the President's alter ego in the matters of that department where the President is required by law to exercise authority. . . .

In . . . cases [in which the President acts under his constitutional powers], the discretion to be exercised is that of the President in determining the national public interest and in directing the action to be taken by his executive subordinates to protect it. In this field his cabinet officers must do his will. He must place in each member of his official family, and his chief executive subordinates, implicit faith. The moment that he loses confidence in the intelligence, ability, judgment, or loyalty of any one of them, he must have the power to remove him without delay. To require him to file charges and submit them to the consideration of the Senate might make impossible that unity and coordination in executive administration essential to effective action. . . .

But this is not to say that there are not strong reasons why the President should have a like power to remove his appointees charged with other duties than those above described. The ordinary duties of officers prescribed by statute come under the general administrative control of the President by virtue of the general grant to him of the executive power, and he may properly supervise and guide their construction of the statutes under which they act in order to secure that unitary and uniform execution of the laws which article 2 of the Constitution evidently contemplated in vesting general executive power in the President alone. Laws are often passed with specific provision for adoption of regulations by a department or bureau head to make the law workable and effective. The ability and judgment manifested by the official thus empowered, as well as his energy and stimulation of his subordinates, are subjects which the President must consider and supervise in his administrative control. Finding such officers to be negligent and inefficient, the President should have the power to remove them. Of course there may be duties so peculiarly and specifically committed to the discretion of a particular officer as to raise a question whether the President may overrule or revise the officer's interpretation of his statutory duty in a particular instance. Then there may be duties of a quasi judicial character imposed on executive officers and members of executive tribunals whose decisions after hearing affect interests of individuals, the discharge of which the President cannot in a particular case properly influence or control. But even in such a case he may consider the decision after its rendition as a reason for removing the officer, on the ground that the discretion regularly entrusted to that officer by statute has not been on the whole intelligently or wisely exercised. Otherwise he does not discharge his own constitutional duty of seeing that the laws be faithfully executed.

We have devoted much space to this discussion and decision of the question of the presidential power of removal in the First Congress, not because a congressional conclusion on a constitutional issue is conclusive, but first because of our agreement with the reasons upon which it was avowedly based, second because this was the decision of the First Congress on a question of primary importance in the organization of the government made within two years after the Constitutional Convention and within a much shorter time after its ratification, and third because that Congress numbered among its leaders those who had been members of the convention, it must necessarily constitute a precedent upon which many future laws supplying the machinery of the new government would be based and, if erroneous, would be likely to evoke dissent and departure in future Congresses. . . .

The power to remove inferior executive officers, like that to remove superior executive officers, is an incident of the power to appoint them, and is in its nature an executive power. The authority of Congress given by the excepting clause to vest the appointment of such inferior officers in the heads of departments carries with it authority incidentally to invest the heads of departments with power to remove. It has been the practice of Congress to do so and this court has recognized that power. . . .

For the reasons given, we must therefore hold that the provision of the law of 1876 by which the unrestricted power of removal of first-class postmasters is denied to the President is in violation of the Constitution and invalid. . . .

The separate opinion of MR. JUSTICE MCREYNOLDS.

May the President oust at will all postmasters appointed with the Senate's consent for definite terms under an act which inhibits removal without consent of that body? . . . I think there is no such power. Certainly it is not given by any plain words of the Constitution; and the argument advanced to establish it seems to me forced and unsubstantial. . . .

Again and again Congress has enacted statutes prescribing restrictions on removals, and by approving them many Presidents have affirmed its power therein. The following are some of the officers who have been or may be appointed with consent of the Senate under such restricting statutes: Members of the Interstate Commerce Commission, Board of General Appraisers, Federal Reserve Board, Federal Trade Commission, Tariff Commission, Shipping Board, Federal Farm Loan Board, Railroad Labor Board; officers of the Army and Navy; Comptroller General; Postmaster General and his assistants; Postmasters of the first, second, and third classes; judge of the United States Court for China; judges of the Court of Claims, established in 1855, the judges to serve "during good behavior"; judges of territorial (statutory) courts; judges of the Supreme Court and Court of Appeals for the District of Columbia (statutory courts), appointed to serve "during good behavior." . . . Every one of these officers, we are now told in effect, holds his place subject to the President's pleasure or caprice. . . . Nothing short of language clear beyond serious disputation should be held to clothe the President with authority wholly beyond congressional control arbitrarily to dismiss every officer whom he appoints except a few judges. There are no such words in the Constitution, and the asserted inference conflicts with the heretofore accepted theory that this government is one of carefully enumerated powers under an intelligible charter. . . .

MR. JUSTICE BRANDEIS, dissenting.

[P]ostmasters are inferior officers. Congress might have vested their appointment in the head of the department. . . . May the President, having acted under the statute in so far as it creates the office and authorizes the appointment, ignore, while the Senate is in session, the provision which prescribes the condition under which a removal may take place?

It is this narrow question, and this only, which we are required to decide. We need not consider what power the President, being Commander-in-Chief, has over officers in the Army and the Navy. We need not determine whether the President, acting alone, may remove high political officers. . . .

Over removal from inferior civil offices, Congress has, from the foundation of our government, exercised continuously some measure of control by legislation. The instances of such laws are many. . . .

The practice of Congress to control the exercise of the executive power of removal from inferior offices is evidenced by many statutes which restrict it in many ways besides the removal clause here in question. Each of these restrictive statutes became law with the approval of the President. Every President who has held office since 1861, except President Garfield, approved one or more of such statutes. Some of these statutes, prescribing a fixed term, provide that removal shall be made only for one of several specified causes. Some provide a fixed term, subject generally to removal for cause. Some provide for removal only after hearing. Some provide a fixed term, subject to removal for reasons to be communicated by the President to the Senate. Some impose the restriction in still other ways. . . .

The assertion that the mere grant by the Constitution of executive power confers upon the President as a prerogative the unrestricted power of appointment and of removal from executive offices, except so far as otherwise expressly provided by the Constitution, is clearly inconsistent also with those statutes which restrict the exercise by the President of the power of nomination. There is not a word in the Constitution which

Louis Brandeis

After graduating from Harvard Law School, Brandeis became a successful lawyer representing business clients. He also authored one of the most significant law review articles: The Right of Privacy. His practice evolved more into representing progressive causes—workers' rights and attacking monopolies—and his briefs departed from the customary legal argument by providing data and factual information, so-called Brandeis briefs. President Woodrow Wilson, nominated him for the Supreme Court, but the nomination was highly controversial, partly for the unstated reason that he was Jewish and partly because he was considered a radical by the establishment. Ultimately, he was confirmed by an almost party line vote. On the Court, Brandeis was one of the more liberal justices, but he was hardly a radical.

in terms authorizes Congress to limit the President's freedom of choice in making nominations for executive offices. . . . But a multitude of laws have been enacted which limit the President's power to make nominations, and which through the restrictions imposed, may prevent the selection of the person deemed by him best fitted. Such restriction upon the power to nominate has been exercised by Congress continuously since the foundation of the government. Every President has approved one or more of such acts. Every President has consistently observed them. This is true of those offices to which he makes appointments without the advice and consent of the Senate as well as of those for which its consent is required. . . .

The separation of the powers of government did not make each branch completely autonomous. It left each in some measure, dependent upon the others, as it left to each power to exercise, in some respects, functions in their nature executive, legislative and judicial. Obviously the President cannot secure full execution of the laws, if Congress denies to him adequate means of doing so. Full execution may be defeated because Congress declines to create offices indispensable for that purpose; or because Congress, having created the office, declines to make the indispensable appropriation; or because Congress, having both created the office and made the appropriation, prevents, by restrictions which it imposes, the appointment of officials who in quality and character are indispensable to the efficient execution of the law. If, in any such way, adequate means are denied to the President, the fault will lie with Congress. The President performs his full constitutional duty, if, with the means and instruments provided by Congress and within the limitations prescribed by it, he uses his best endeavors to secure the faithful execution of the laws enacted.

MR. JUSTICE HOLMES, dissenting.

[T]he arguments drawn from the executive power of the President, and from his duty to appoint officers of the United States (when Congress does not vest the appointment elsewhere), to take care that the laws be faithfully executed, and to commission all officers of the United States, seem to me spiders' webs inadequate to control the dominant facts.

We have to deal with an office that owes its existence to Congress and that Congress may abolish tomorrow. Its duration and the pay attached to it while it lasts depend on Congress alone. Congress alone confers on the President the power to appoint to it and at any time may transfer the power to other hands. With such power over its own creation, I have no more trouble in believing that Congress has power to prescribe a term of life for it free from any interference than I have in accepting the undoubted power of Congress to decree its end. I have equally little trouble in accepting its power to prolong the tenure of an incumbent until Congress or the Senate shall have assented to his removal. The duty of the President to see that the laws be executed is a duty that does not go beyond the laws or require him to achieve more than Congress sees fit to leave within his power.

COMMENTS AND QUESTIONS

1.   The opinion for the Court is written by Chief Justice Taft, who had been President of the United States from 1909–13. Thus, it is perhaps not surprising that he comes out on the side of presidential power rather than congressional power.

2.   It is well to keep in mind that the law in question in *Myers* did not impose just any restriction on the power of the President to remove postmasters; it required the approval of the Senate. That is, it did not just restrict the President's absolute power to remove, as, for example, a limitation

that he could remove someone only for good cause; it subjected his decisions to the approval of a portion of a different branch of government. In the First Congress, this too was the issue; could Congress subject the President's removal power to the supervision of a portion of Congress? While aspects of the Court's opinion do recognize the nature of the specific limitation in the case before it, much of the rhetoric is not so restricted, and it is that rhetoric that Presidents and the Supreme Court subsequently have drawn upon.

3. Justice McReynolds's dissent likewise makes little of the nature of the particular restriction on the President's removal authority in *Myers*. Rather he treats it like any other restriction, of which he notes there had been many in many statutes.

4. What is the focus of Justice Brandeis's dissent? How does the majority opinion respond to Brandeis's argument?

5. What about Justice Holmes's dissent? Under his interpretation of the Constitution could Congress prohibit the President from either directing or removing any officer of the United States? If so, how could the President take care that the laws are faithfully executed? Could Congress place the entire removal power in the Senate under Holmes's theory? If so, what would be the purpose of the Impeachment Clause of the Constitution?

6. *Myers* is important not just for its interpretation of the President's removal authority, and the basis for it, but also for its imposition of limitations on Congress's powers as a result of structural implications implied by the Constitution. Implications from the structure of the Constitution can extend much more broadly than questions regarding removal.

HUMPHREY'S EXECUTOR V. UNITED STATES

United States Supreme Court, 1935.
295 U.S. 602, 55 S.Ct. 869.

MR. JUSTICE SUTHERLAND delivered the opinion of the Court.

[William E. Humphrey the decedent, was a former Republican politician appointed to the Federal Trade Commission first by Republican President Calvin Coolidge in 1926 and reappointed by Republican President Herbert Hoover in 1931. In July 1933, President Roosevelt asked for his resignation, on the ground "that the aims and purposes of the Administration with respect to the work of the Commission can be carried out most effectively with personnel of my own selection." Later, the President wrote the commissioner saying: "You will, I know, realize that I do not feel that your mind and my mind go along together on either the

William E. Humphrey

policies or the administering of the Federal Trade Commission, and, frankly, I think it is best for the people of this country that I should have a full confidence." The commissioner declined to resign; and the President removed him.]

Plaintiff brought suit in the Court of Claims against the United States to recover a sum of money alleged to be due the deceased for salary as a Federal Trade Commissioner from October 8, 1933, when the President undertook to remove him from office, to the time of his death on February 14, 1934. . . .

The Federal Trade Commission Act creates a commission of five members to be appointed by the President by and with the advice and consent of the Senate, and section 1 provides: ". . . Any commissioner may be removed by the President for inefficiency, neglect of duty, or malfeasance in office. * * *". . .

The commission is to be nonpartisan; and it must, from the very nature of its duties, act with entire impartiality. It is charged with the enforcement of no policy except the policy of the law. Its duties are neither political nor executive, but predominantly quasi judicial and quasi legislative. Like the Interstate Commerce Commission, its members are called upon to exercise the trained judgment of a body of experts "appointed by law and informed by experience."

The legislative reports in both houses of Congress clearly reflect the view that a fixed term was necessary to the effective and fair administration of the law. . . . The [Senate] report declares that one advantage which the commission possessed over the Bureau of Corporations (an executive subdivision in the Department of Commerce which was abolished by the act) lay in the fact of its independence, and that it was essential that the commission should not be open to the suspicion of partisan direction. . . .

The debates in both houses demonstrate that the prevailing view was that the Commission was not to be "subject to anybody in the government but * * * only to the people of the United States"; free from "political domination or control" or the "probability or possibility of such a thing"; to be "separate and apart from any existing department of the government— not subject to the orders of the President.". . .

To support its contention that the removal provision of section 1, as we have just construed it, is an unconstitutional interference with the executive power of the President, the government's chief reliance is *Myers v. United States*. That case has been so recently decided, and the prevailing and dissenting opinions so fully review the general subject of the power of executive removal, that further discussion would add little of value to the wealth of material there collected. These opinions examine at length the historical, legislative, and judicial data bearing upon the question, beginning with what is called "the decision of 1789" in the first Congress and coming down almost to the day when the opinions were delivered. They occupy 243 pages of the volume in which they are printed. Nevertheless, the narrow point actually decided was only that the President had power to remove a postmaster of the first class, without the advice and consent of the Senate as required by act of Congress. In the course of the opinion of the court, expressions occur which tend to sustain the government's contention, but these are beyond the point involved and, therefore, do not come within the rule of *stare decisis*. In so far as they are out of harmony with the views here set forth, these expressions are disapproved.

The office of a postmaster is so essentially unlike the office now involved that the decision in the *Myers Case* cannot be accepted as controlling our decision here. A postmaster is an executive officer restricted to the performance of executive functions. He is charged with no duty at all related to either the legislative or judicial power. The actual decision in the *Myers Case* finds support in the theory that such an officer is merely one of the units in the executive department and, hence, inherently subject to the exclusive and illimitable power of removal by the Chief Executive, whose subordinate and aid he is. Putting aside dicta, which may be followed if sufficiently persuasive but which are not controlling, the necessary reach of the decision goes far enough to include all purely executive officers. It goes no farther; much less does it include an officer who occupies no place in the executive department and who exercises no part of the executive power vested by the Constitution in the President.

The Federal Trade Commission is an administrative body created by Congress to carry into effect legislative policies embodied in the statute in accordance with the legislative standard therein prescribed, and to perform other specified duties as a legislative or as a judicial aid. Such a body cannot in any proper sense be characterized as an arm or an eye of the executive. Its duties are performed without executive leave and, in the contemplation of the statute, must be free from executive control. In administering the provisions of the statute in respect of "unfair methods of competition," that is to say, in filling in and administering the details embodied by that general standard, the commission acts in part quasi legislatively and in part quasi judicially. . . . To the extent that it exercises any executive function, as distinguished from executive power in the constitutional sense, it does so in the discharge and effectuation of its quasi legislative or quasi judicial powers, or as an agency of the legislative or judicial departments of the government. . . .

[T]he authority of Congress, in creating quasi legislative or quasi judicial agencies, to require them to act in discharge of their duties independently of executive control cannot well be doubted; and that authority includes, as an appropriate incident, power to fix the period during which they shall continue, and to forbid their removal except for cause in the meantime. For it is quite evident that one who holds his office only during the pleasure of another cannot be depended upon to maintain an attitude of independence against the latter's will.

The fundamental necessity of maintaining each of the three general departments of government entirely free from the control or coercive influence, direct or indirect, of either of the others, has often been stressed and is hardly open to serious question. So much is implied in the very fact of the separation of the powers of these departments by the Constitution; and in the rule which recognizes their essential coequality. The sound application of a principle that makes one master in his own house precludes him from imposing his control in the house of another who is master there. . . .

The power of removal here claimed for the President falls within this principle, since its coercive influence threatens the independence of a commission, which is not only wholly disconnected from the executive department, but which, as already fully appears, was created by Congress as a means of carrying into operation legislative and judicial powers, and as an agency of the legislative and judicial departments. . . .

The result of what we now have said is this: Whether the power of the President to remove an officer shall prevail over the authority of Congress to condition the power by fixing a definite term and precluding a removal except for cause will depend upon the character of the office; the *Myers* decision, affirming the power of the President alone to make the removal, is confined to purely executive officers; and as to officers of the kind here under consideration, we hold that no removal can be made during the prescribed term for which the officer is appointed, except for one or more of the causes named in the applicable statute. . . .

MR. JUSTICE MCREYNOLDS [concurs in the judgment]. [omitted]

COMMENTS AND QUESTIONS

1.   On the question of the constitutionality of the limitation on the President's ability to remove commissioners, what's happened? The Court's opinion in *Myers* declaring a broad immunity of the President from limitations on his power of removal has changed to a unanimous decision that creating a "for cause" removal requirement for certain principal officers of the United States is fully within the power of Congress. First, the composition of the Court has changed. McReynolds, Brandeis, and Holmes, all of whom dissented in *Myers*, are all still on the Court, but Taft, the presidentially oriented Chief Justice, has been replaced. Second, the year is 1935, the year in which the Court found two statutes unconstitutional delegations of legislative authority to the President, and in which it was imposing judicial barriers to the New Deal. In other words, the Court was strongly hostile to President Roosevelt and his policies. Strengthening the independence of certain agencies was a way of thwarting Roosevelt's attempt to take control of the government to achieve his

policies. Third, *Humphreys* is a different case from *Myers*, whether *Myers* is viewed as involving a purely executive officer (the point of distinction relied upon by the *Humphreys* Court), only an inferior officer, or a removal subject to approval by a portion of Congress as opposed to simply a limitation on the President's unfettered discretion.

2.   The Court suggests that the Federal Trade Commission is not part of the executive branch because it is "an administrative body created by Congress to carry into effect legislative policies embodied in the statute in accordance with the legislative standard therein prescribed." But why would that be so? First, all administrative agencies are created by Congress; the Constitution neither creates nor identifies any department or agency. Second, wouldn't this description equally fit the Department of Interior, the Department of Commerce, the Department of Labor, and the Department of Agriculture—to mention some of the other departments then in existence? Indeed, other than perhaps the Department of State, the Department of Defense, and the Department of Justice, are not all departments and agencies of the United States created by Congress exclusively to carry into effect legislative policies embodied in statute? And certainly the Departments of State, Defense, and Justice at least in part are created to carry out legislative policies. Does this mean that it is a matter of congressional policy, discretion, or whim whether a department or agency is "within the executive branch" or instead must be able to act "without executive leave and . . . free from executive control"? To ask that question is to answer it.

3.   The Court says that if the Federal Trade Commission performs any executive function, it does it in the discharge of its "quasi-legislative" and "quasi-judicial" functions. What does the Court mean by "quasi-legislative" and "quasi-judicial" functions? If you take Administrative Law, you will learn that when agencies adopt rules or regulations, they engage in quasi-legislative functions, and when they perform adjudication, they engage in quasi-judicial functions. But virtually all departments and agencies perform these functions. Again, could Congress make them all independent of the President? What would this mean with respect to the President's constitutional duty to take care that the laws are faithfully executed?

MORRISON V. OLSON

United States Supreme Court, 1988.
487 U.S. 654, 108 S.Ct. 2597.

CHIEF JUSTICE REHNQUIST delivered the opinion of the Court.

[In 1982, during the Reagan administration, two Subcommittees of the House of Representatives issued subpoenas directing the Environmental Protection Agency (EPA) to produce certain documents. Acting on the advice of the Justice Department, the President ordered the Administrator of EPA to invoke executive privilege to withhold certain of the documents on the ground that they contained "enforcement sensitive information." Later, however, the administration agreed to give the House

Subcommittees limited access to the documents. The following year, the House Judiciary Committee began an investigation into the Justice Department's role in the controversy over the EPA documents. During this investigation, Assistant Attorney General Theodore Olson testified before a House Subcommittee. Later, the majority members of the Judiciary Committee published a lengthy report on the Committee's investigation. The report not only criticized various officials in the Department of Justice for their role in the EPA executive privilege dispute, but it also suggested that Olson had given false and misleading testimony to the Subcommittee. The Chairman of the Judiciary Committee forwarded a copy of the report to the Attorney General with a request that he seek the appointment of an independent counsel to investigate the allegations pursuant to the independent counsel provisions of the Ethics in Government Act of 1978. As a result, the Special Division of the United States Court of Appeals for the District of Columbia Circuit appointed Alexia Morrison independent counsel. She in turn subpoenaed various documents from Olson. He moved to quash the subpoenas on the ground that the independent counsel provisions of the Act were unconstitutional. Recall from the discussion of this case in the previous section on Appointments that one of the claims was that the independent counsel was a principal officer and therefore had to be appointed by the President with the advice and consent of the Senate. The Court rejected that claim, finding the independent counsel an inferior officer. In addition, Olson argued that because the statute provided that the independent counsel could only be removed by the Attorney General "for good cause," the statute was unconstitutional under *Myers v. United States*.]

We now turn to consider whether the Act is invalid under the constitutional principle of separation of powers. Two related issues must be addressed: The first is whether the provision of the Act restricting the Attorney General's power to remove the independent counsel to only those instances in which he can show "good cause," taken by itself, impermissibly interferes with the President's exercise of his constitutionally appointed functions. The second is whether, taken as a whole, the Act violates the separation of powers by reducing the President's ability to control the prosecutorial powers wielded by the independent counsel.

Two Terms ago we had occasion to consider whether it was consistent with the separation of powers for Congress to pass a statute that authorized a Government official who is removable only by Congress to participate in what we found to be "executive powers." *Bowsher v. Synar,* 478 U.S. 714 (1986). We held in *Bowsher* that "Congress cannot reserve for itself the power of removal of an officer charged with the execution of the laws except by impeachment." A primary antecedent for this ruling was our 1926 decision in *Myers v. United States. . . .* There too, Congress's attempt to involve itself in the removal of an executive official was found to be sufficient grounds to render the statute invalid. As we observed in

Bowsher, the essence of the decision in *Myers* was the judgment that the Constitution prevents Congress from "draw[ing] to itself . . . the power to remove or the right to participate in the exercise of that power." . . .

Unlike both *Bowsher* and *Myers,* this case does not involve an attempt by Congress itself to gain a role in the removal of executive officials other than its established powers of impeachment and conviction. The Act instead puts the removal power squarely in the hands of the Executive Branch; an independent counsel may be removed from office, "only by the personal action of the Attorney General, and only for good cause." . . . In our view, the removal provisions of the Act make this case more analogous to *Humphrey's Executor v. United States* . . . than to *Myers* or *Bowsher.*

In *Humphrey's Executor,* [w]e stated that whether Congress can "condition the [President's power of removal] by fixing a definite term and precluding a removal except for cause, will depend upon the character of the office.". . .

Appellees contend that *Humphrey's Executor* [is] distinguishable from this case because [it] did not involve officials who performed a "core executive function." They argue that our decision in *Humphrey's Executor* rests on a distinction between "purely executive" officials and officials who exercise "quasi-legislative" and "quasi-judicial" powers. In their view, when a "purely executive" official is involved, the governing precedent is *Myers,* not *Humphrey's Executor.* And, under *Myers,* the President must have absolute discretion to discharge "purely" executive officials at will.

We undoubtedly did rely on the terms "quasi-legislative" and "quasi-judicial" to distinguish the officials involved in *Humphrey's Executor* . . . from those in *Myers,* but our present considered view is that the determination of whether the Constitution allows Congress to impose a "good cause"-type restriction on the President's power to remove an official cannot be made to turn on whether or not that official is classified as "purely executive." The analysis contained in our removal cases is designed not to define rigid categories of those officials who may or may not be removed at will by the President,[28] but to ensure that Congress does not

---

[28] The difficulty of defining such categories of "executive" or "quasi-legislative" officials is illustrated by a comparison of our decisions in cases such as *Humphrey's Executor, Buckley v. Valeo,* and *Bowsher.* In *Buckley,* we indicated that the functions of the Federal Election Commission are "administrative," and "more legislative and judicial in nature," and are "of kinds usually performed by independent regulatory agencies or by some department in the Executive Branch under the direction of an Act of Congress." In *Bowsher,* we found that the functions of the Comptroller General were "executive" in nature, in that he was required to exercise judgment concerning facts that affect the application of the Act, and he must "interpret the provisions of the Act to determine precisely what budgetary calculations are required." Compare this with the description of the FTC's powers in *Humphrey's Executor,* which we stated "occupie[d] no place in the executive department": "The [FTC] is an administrative body created by Congress to carry into effect legislative policies embodied in the statute in accordance with the legislative standard therein prescribed, and to perform other specified duties as a legislative or as a judicial aid." As Justice WHITE noted in his dissent in *Bowsher,* it is hard to dispute that the powers of the FTC at the time of *Humphrey's Executor* would at the present time be considered "executive," at least to some degree.

interfere with the President's exercise of the "executive power" and his constitutionally appointed duty to "take care that the laws be faithfully executed" under Article II. *Myers* was undoubtedly correct in its holding, and in its broader suggestion that there are some "purely executive" officials who must be removable by the President at will if he is to be able to accomplish his constitutional role. . . .

At the other end of the spectrum from *Myers,* the characterization of the agencies in *Humphrey's Executor* . . . as "quasi-legislative" or "quasi-judicial" in large part reflected our judgment that it was not essential to the President's proper execution of his Article II powers that these agencies be headed up by individuals who were removable at will. We do not mean to suggest that an analysis of the functions served by the officials at issue is irrelevant. But the real question is whether the removal restrictions are of such a nature that they impede the President's ability to perform his constitutional duty, and the functions of the officials in question must be analyzed in that light.

Considering for the moment the "good cause" removal provision in isolation from the other parts of the Act at issue in this case, we cannot say that the imposition of a "good cause" standard for removal by itself unduly trammels on executive authority. There is no real dispute that the functions performed by the independent counsel are "executive" in the sense that they are law enforcement functions that typically have been undertaken by officials within the Executive Branch. As we noted above, however, the independent counsel is an inferior officer under the Appointments Clause, with limited jurisdiction and tenure and lacking policymaking or significant administrative authority. Although the counsel exercises no small amount of discretion and judgment in deciding how to carry out his or her duties under the Act, we simply do not see how the President's need to control the exercise of that discretion is so central to the functioning of the Executive Branch as to require as a matter of constitutional law that the counsel be terminable at will by the President.

Nor do we think that the "good cause" removal provision at issue here impermissibly burdens the President's power to control or supervise the independent counsel, as an executive official, in the execution of his or her duties under the Act. This is not a case in which the power to remove an executive official has been completely stripped from the President, thus providing no means for the President to ensure the "faithful execution" of the laws. Rather, because the independent counsel may be terminated for "good cause," the Executive, through the Attorney General, retains ample authority to assure that the counsel is competently performing his or her statutory responsibilities in a manner that comports with the provisions of the Act. Although we need not decide in this case exactly what is encompassed within the term "good cause" under the Act, the legislative history of the removal provision also makes clear that the Attorney General may remove an independent counsel for "misconduct." . . . We do not think that this limitation as it presently stands sufficiently deprives the President of control over the independent counsel to interfere impermissibly with his constitutional obligation to ensure the faithful execution of the laws.

The final question to be addressed is whether the Act, taken as a whole, violates the principle of separation of powers by unduly interfering with the role of the Executive Branch. Time and again we have reaffirmed the importance in our constitutional scheme of the separation of governmental powers into the three coordinate branches. . . .

We observe first that this case does not involve an attempt by Congress to increase its own powers at the expense of the Executive Branch. Unlike some of our previous cases, most recently *Bowsher v. Synar,* this case simply does not pose a "dange[r] of congressional usurpation of Executive Branch functions." . . .

Finally, we do not think that the Act "impermissibly undermine[s]" the powers of the Executive Branch or "disrupts the proper balance" between the coordinate branches [by] prevent[ing] the Executive Branch from accomplishing its constitutionally assigned functions. It is undeniable that the Act reduces the amount of control or supervision that the Attorney General and, through him, the President exercises over the investigation and prosecution of a certain class of alleged criminal activity. . . . Nonetheless, the Act does give the Attorney General several means of supervising or controlling the prosecutorial powers that may be wielded by an independent counsel. Most importantly, the Attorney General retains the power to remove the counsel for "good cause," a power that we have already concluded provides the Executive with substantial ability to ensure that the laws are "faithfully executed" by an independent counsel. No independent counsel may be appointed without a specific request by the Attorney General, and the Attorney General's decision not to request appointment if he finds "no reasonable grounds to believe that further investigation is warranted" is committed to his unreviewable discretion. The Act thus gives the Executive a degree of control over the power to initiate an investigation by the independent counsel. In addition, the jurisdiction of the independent counsel is defined with reference to the facts submitted by the Attorney General, and once a counsel is appointed, the Act requires that the counsel abide by Justice Department policy unless it is not "possible" to do so. Notwithstanding the fact that the counsel is to some degree "independent" and free from executive supervision to a greater extent than other federal prosecutors, in our view these features of the Act give the Executive Branch sufficient control over the independent counsel to ensure that the President is able to perform his constitutionally assigned duties. . . .

JUSTICE KENNEDY took no part in the consideration or decision of this case.

Justice Scalia, dissenting. . . .

[T]his suit is about ... [p]ower. The allocation of power among Congress, the President, and the courts in such fashion as to preserve the equilibrium the Constitution sought to establish—so that "a gradual concentration of the several powers in the same department can effectively be resisted. Frequently an issue of this sort will come before the Court clad, so to speak, in sheep's clothing: the potential of the asserted principle to effect important change in the equilibrium of power is not immediately evident, and must be discerned by a careful and perceptive analysis. But this wolf comes as a wolf. . . .

The Court concedes that "[t]here is no real dispute that the functions performed by the independent counsel are 'executive.' " . . . Governmental investigation and prosecution of crimes is a quintessentially executive function. . . .

The Court has, nonetheless, replaced the clear constitutional prescription that the executive power belongs to the President with a "balancing test." What are the standards to determine how the balance is to be struck, that is, how much removal of Presidential power is too much? . . . Once we depart from the text of the Constitution, just where short of that do we stop? The most amazing feature of the Court's opinion is that it does not even purport to give an answer. It simply announces, with no analysis, that the ability to control the decision whether to investigate and prosecute the President's closest advisers, and indeed the President himself, is not "so central to the functioning of the Executive Branch" as to be constitutionally required to be within the President's control. Apparently that is so because we say it is so. Having abandoned as the basis for our decision-making the text of Article II that "the executive Power" must be vested in the President, the Court does not even attempt to craft a substitute criterion—a "justiciable standard," however remote from the Constitution—that today governs, and in the future will govern, the decision of such questions. Evidently, the governing standard is to be what might be called the unfettered wisdom of a majority of this Court, revealed to an obedient people on a case-by-case basis. This is not only not the government of laws that the Constitution established; it is not a government of laws at all. . . .

Comments and Questions

1. After three years and $2 million, the independent counsel closed its investigation with no charges brought.

2. The Court says that the outcomes in both *Myers* and *Humphreys* were correct, but it rejects the analyses of both.

3. The Court discusses the case of *Bowsher v. Synar*, decided two years before. There Congress had passed a statute designed to change the federal

budgeting process in order to try to rein in the consistent deficits. An integral part of the statute was the ability of the Comptroller General to make a report assessing the proposed income and expenditures of the government, and if the expenditures exceeded the income by specified amounts, the Comptroller General would direct the President to cut expenditures to bring the difference within the specified figures. Such power, the Court held, could only be performed by an officer of the executive branch of government, and the question was whether the Comptroller General could be such an officer in light of the manner in which he could be removed—by an act of Congress finding any of the following: permanent disability, inefficiency, neglect of duty, malfeasance, or a felony or conduct involving moral turpitude. The Court held that by assigning the removal power to Congress, Congress made the Comptroller General subservient to it, allowing Congress to play a role in the execution of the laws. This, the Court held, Congress could not do. Consequently, the role assigned to the Comptroller General was unconstitutional. Recall that *Myers* to a large extent was about the role the Senate would play in the removal of the postmaster.

4.   In *Bowsher* the Court discussed the grounds upon which the Comptroller General could be removed. "The statute permits removal for 'inefficiency,' 'neglect of duty,' or 'malfeasance.' These terms are very broad and, as interpreted by Congress, could sustain removal of a Comptroller General for any number of actual or perceived transgressions of the legislative will." 478 U.S. at 729. Recall, however, the grounds upon which a commissioner of the Federal Trade Commission may be removed by the President: inefficiency, neglect of duty, or malfeasance in office. If these terms are so broad that the President could interpret them to sustain removal of a commissioner for any number of transgressions of his will, how "independent" are the so-called independent regulatory agencies? Is this a reason why such limitations might not interfere with the President's responsibility to take care that the laws are faithfully executed?

5.   Note that in footnote 28 the Court acknowledges that today the so-called independent regulatory agencies, like the Federal Trade Commission, are considered "executive" agencies, "at least to some degree."

6.   A more recent removal case is *Free Enterprise Fund v. Public Company Accounting Oversight Board*, 561 U.S. 477 (2010). There members of the Board, deemed inferior officers, could only be removed for cause by the Securities and Exchange Commission (SEC), which also appointed them. However, the members of the SEC, who are principal officers, themselves could only be removed for cause, as understood by the Court. By a 5–4 vote, the Court found this "dual for-cause" removal limitation unconstitutional. Chief Justice Roberts wrote for the Court:

Since 1789, the Constitution has been understood to empower the President to keep these officers accountable—by removing them from office, if necessary. *See* generally *Myers v. United States*, 272 U.S. 52 (1926). This Court has determined, however, that this authority is not without limit. In *Humphrey's Executor v. United*

States, 295 U.S. 602 (1935), we held that Congress can, under certain circumstances, create independent agencies run by principal officers appointed by the President, whom the President may not remove at will but only for good cause. Likewise, in *United States* v. *Perkins*, 116 U.S. 483 (1886), and *Morrison* v. *Olson*, 487 U.S. 654 (1988), the Court sustained similar restrictions on the power of principal executive officers—themselves responsible to the President—to remove their own inferiors. The parties do not ask us to reexamine any of these precedents, and we do not do so.

We are asked, however, to consider a new situation not yet encountered by the Court. The question is whether these separate layers of protection may be combined. May the President be restricted in his ability to remove a principal officer, who is in turn restricted in his ability to remove an inferior officer, even though that inferior officer determines the policy and enforces the laws of the United States?

We hold that such multilevel protection from removal is contrary to Article II's vesting of the executive power in the President. The President cannot "take Care that the Laws be faithfully executed" if he cannot oversee the faithfulness of the officers who execute them. Here the President cannot remove an officer who enjoys more than one level of good-cause protection, even if the President determines that the officer is neglecting his duties or discharging them improperly. That judgment is instead committed to another officer, who may or may not agree with the President's determination, and whom the President cannot remove simply because that officer disagrees with him. This contravenes the President's "constitutional obligation to ensure the faithful execution of the laws."

Is this just an application of the *Morrison* test, asking whether a removal limitation unduly burdens the President in the exercise of his authority to take care that the laws are faithfully executed, or is this something new?

7.   *Lucia v. SEC*, discussed earlier under Appointments, finding that ALJs are inferior officers, not employees, raises the question whether their insulation from removal except for cause is unconstitutional under *Free Enterprise Fund*. ALJs can only be removed for cause by the Merit Systems Protection Board, whose members also can only be removed for cause. This creates the dual for-cause removal problem identified in *Free Enterprise Fund*. Even worse, the Merit Systems Protection Board only can remove an ALJ after the agency that employs the ALJ files a complaint alleging the for-cause basis for removal, and many agencies employing ALJs are themselves made up of members who can only be removed for cause—a triple for-cause removal situation. This issue is at the time of this writing working its way through the lower courts and likely will reach the Supreme Court. There is, however, an easy way to distinguish *Free Enterprise Fund* from the ALJ situation. In *Free Enterprise Fund* the Court noted that the PCAOB had wide-ranging powers, the power to enforce requirements, make rules governing the industry, and

adjudicate cases alleging violations. ALJs, on the other hand, only have the power of adjudication, and the Supreme Court in an old case, *Wiener v. United States*, 357 U.S. 349 (1958), read a for-cause removal limitation into a law that did not provide it where the agency performed solely adjudicative functions. The idea is that the President has less legitimate basis for direct supervision of persons acting as adjudicators than he does of persons making policy or engaging in enforcement decisions.

The Court's most recent removal case follows:

SEILA LAW LLC v. CONSUMER FINANCIAL PROTECTION BUREAU

United States Supreme Court, 2020.
140 S.Ct. 2183.

CHIEF JUSTICE ROBERTS delivered the opinion of the Court with respect to Parts I, II, and III.

In the wake of the 2008 financial crisis, Congress established the Consumer Financial Protection Bureau (CFPB), an independent regulatory agency tasked with ensuring that consumer debt products are safe and transparent. In organizing the CFPB, Congress deviated from the structure of nearly every other independent administrative agency in our history. Instead of placing the agency under the leadership of a board with multiple members, Congress provided that the CFPB would be led by a single Director, who serves for a longer term than the President and cannot be removed by the President except for inefficiency, neglect, or malfeasance. The CFPB Director has no boss, peers, or voters to report to. Yet the Director wields vast rulemaking, enforcement, and adjudicatory authority over a significant portion of the U. S. economy. The question before us is whether this arrangement violates the Constitution's separation of powers.

Under our Constitution, the "executive Power"—all of it—is "vested in a President," who must "take Care that the Laws be faithfully executed." Art. II, § 1, cl. 1; *id.*, § 3. Because no single person could fulfill that responsibility alone, the Framers expected that the President would rely on subordinate officers for assistance. Ten years ago, in *Free Enterprise Fund* v. *Public Company Accounting Oversight Bd.* (2010), we reiterated that, "as a general matter," the Constitution gives the President "the authority to remove those who assist him in carrying out his duties." "Without such power, the President could not be held fully accountable for discharging his own responsibilities; the buck would stop somewhere else."

The President's power to remove—and thus supervise—those who wield executive power on his behalf follows from the text of Article II, was settled by the First Congress, and was confirmed in the landmark decision *Myers* v. *United States* (1926). Our precedents have recognized only two exceptions to the President's unrestricted removal power. In *Humphrey's Executor* v. *United States* (1935), we held that Congress could create expert agencies led by a *group* of principal officers removable by the President only for good cause. And in *United States* v. *Perkins* (1886), and *Morrison* v. *Olson* (1988), we held that Congress could provide tenure protections to certain *inferior* officers with narrowly defined duties.

We are now asked to extend these precedents to a new configuration: an independent agency that wields significant executive power and is run by a single individual who cannot be removed by the President unless certain statutory criteria are met. We decline to take that step. While we need not and do not revisit our prior decisions allowing certain limitations on the President's removal power, there are compelling reasons not to extend those precedents to the novel context of an independent agency led by a single Director. Such an agency lacks a foundation in historical practice and clashes with constitutional structure by concentrating power in a unilateral actor insulated from Presidential control. . . .

I

In 2010, Congress . . . created the Consumer Financial Protection Bureau (CFPB) as an independent financial regulator within the Federal Reserve System. Congress tasked the CFPB with "implement[ing]" and "enforc[ing]" a large body of financial consumer protection laws to "ensur[e] that all consumers have access to markets for consumer financial products and services and that markets for consumer financial products and services are fair, transparent, and competitive." . . .

Congress also vested the CFPB with potent enforcement powers. The agency has the authority to conduct investigations, issue subpoenas and civil investigative demands, initiate administrative adjudications, and prosecute civil actions in federal court. . . .

The CFPB's rulemaking and enforcement powers are coupled with extensive adjudicatory authority. The agency may conduct administrative proceedings to "ensure or enforce compliance with" the statutes and regulations it administers. . . .

Congress elected to place the CFPB under the leadership of a single Director. The CFPB Director is appointed by the President with the advice and consent of the Senate. The Director serves for a term of five years, during which the President may remove the Director from office only for "inefficiency, neglect of duty, or malfeasance in office."

Unlike most other agencies, the CFPB does not rely on the annual appropriations process for funding. Instead, the CFPB receives funding directly from the Federal Reserve, which is itself funded outside the appropriations process through bank assessments. . . .

Seila Law LLC is a California-based law firm that provides debt-related legal services to clients. In 2017, the CFPB issued a civil investigative demand to Seila Law to determine whether the firm had "engag[ed] in unlawful acts or practices in the advertising, marketing, or sale of debt relief services." . . .

Seila Law asked the CFPB to set aside the demand, objecting that the agency's leadership by a single Director removable only for cause violated the separation of powers. [The CFPB refused. When the CFPB sued to enforce the demand, Seila Law renewed its constitutional objection, which was refused by the District Court and by the Court of Appeals. The Supreme Court granted certiorari.]

III

We hold that the CFPB's leadership by a single individual removable only for inefficiency, neglect, or malfeasance violates the separation of powers.

Article II provides that "[t]he executive Power shall be vested in a President," who must "take Care that the Laws be faithfully executed." Art. II, § 1, cl. 1; *id.*, § 3. The entire "executive Power" belongs to the President alone. But because it would be "impossib[le]" for "one man" to "perform all the great business of the State," the Constitution assumes that lesser executive officers will "assist the supreme Magistrate in discharging the duties of his trust." Writings of George Washington (1939).

These lesser officers must remain accountable to the President, whose authority they wield. As Madison explained, "[I]f any power whatsoever is in its nature Executive, it is the power of appointing, overseeing, and controlling those who execute the laws." That power, in turn, generally includes the ability to remove executive officials, for it is "only the authority that can remove" such officials that they "must fear and, in the performance of [their] functions, obey." *Bowsher v Synar*, 478 U.S. 714 (1986).

The President's removal power has long been confirmed by history and precedent. The First Congress's recognition of the President's removal power in 1789 "provides contemporaneous and weighty evidence of the Constitution's meaning," *Bowsher*, and has long been the "settled and well understood construction of the Constitution," *Ex parte Hennen* (1839).

The Court recognized the President's prerogative to remove executive officials in *Myers* v. *United States*. Just as the President's "selection of administrative officers is essential to the execution of the laws by him, so must be his power of removing those for whom he cannot continue to be responsible." "[T]o hold otherwise," the Court reasoned, "would make it impossible for the President . . . to take care that the laws be faithfully executed."

We recently reiterated the President's general removal power in *Free Enterprise Fund.* . . .

Free Enterprise Fund left in place two exceptions to the President's unrestricted removal power. First, in *Humphrey's Executor*, decided less than a decade after *Myers*, the Court upheld a statute that protected the Commissioners of the FTC from removal except for "inefficiency, neglect of duty, or malfeasance in office." In reaching that conclusion, the Court stressed that Congress's ability to impose such removal restrictions "will depend upon the character of the office."

Because the Court limited its holding "to officers of the kind here under consideration," the contours of the *Humphrey's Executor* exception depend upon the characteristics of the agency before the Court. Rightly or wrongly, the Court viewed the FTC (as it existed in 1935) as exercising "no part of the executive power." Instead, it was "an administrative body" that performed "specified duties as a legislative or as a judicial aid." It acted "as a legislative agency" in "making investigations and reports" to Congress and "as an agency of the judiciary" in making recommendations to courts as a master in chancery. "To the extent that [the FTC] exercise[d] any executive *function*[,] as distinguished from executive *power* in the constitutional sense," it did so only in the discharge of its "quasi-legislative or quasi-judicial powers." *Ibid.* (emphasis added).[2]

The Court identified several organizational features that helped explain its characterization of the FTC as non-executive. Composed of five members—no more than three from the same political party—the Board was designed to be "non-partisan" and to "act with entire impartiality." The FTC's duties were "neither political nor executive," but instead called for "the trained judgment of a body of experts" "informed by experience." And the Commissioners' staggered, seven-year terms enabled the agency to accumulate technical expertise and avoid a "complete change" in leadership "at any one time."

In short, *Humphrey's Executor* permitted Congress to give for-cause removal protections to a multimember body of experts, balanced along partisan lines, that performed legislative and judicial functions and was said not to exercise any executive power. . . .

While recognizing an exception for multimember bodies with "quasi-judicial" or "quasi-legislative" functions, *Humphrey's Executor* reaffirmed the core holding of *Myers* that the President has "unrestrictable power . . . to remove purely executive officers." The Court acknowledged that between purely executive officers on the one hand, and officers that closely

---

[2]   The Court's conclusion that the FTC did not exercise executive power has not withstood the test of time. As we observed in *Morrison v. Olson* (1988), "[I]t is hard to dispute that the powers of the FTC at the time of *Humphrey's Executor* would at the present time be considered 'executive,' at least to some degree."

resembled the FTC Commissioners on the other, there existed "a field of doubt" that the Court left "for future consideration."

We have recognized a second exception for *inferior* officers in two cases, *United States* v. *Perkins* and *Morrison* v. *Olson*. . . . Backing away from the reliance in *Humphrey's Executor* on the concepts of "quasi-legislative" and "quasi-judicial" power, [in *Morrison*] we viewed the ultimate question as whether a removal restriction is of "such a nature that [it] impede[s] the President's ability to perform his constitutional duty." Although the independent counsel was a single person and performed "law enforcement functions that typically have been undertaken by officials within the Executive Branch," we concluded that the removal protections did not unduly interfere with the functioning of the Executive Branch because "the independent counsel [was] an inferior officer under the Appointments Clause, with limited jurisdiction and tenure and lacking policymaking or significant administrative authority."

These two exceptions—one for multimember expert agencies that do not wield substantial executive power, and one for inferior officers with limited duties and no policymaking or administrative authority— "represent what up to now have been the outermost constitutional limits of permissible congressional restrictions on the President's removal power." *PHH Corp.* v. *CFPB*, 881 F.3d 75, 196 (D.C. Cir. 2018)(Kavanaugh, J., dissenting).

Neither *Humphrey's Executor* nor *Morrison* resolves whether the CFPB Director's insulation from removal is constitutional. Start with *Humphrey's Executor*. Unlike the New Deal-era FTC upheld there, the CFPB is led by a single Director who cannot be described as a "body of experts" and cannot be considered "non-partisan" in the same sense as a group of officials drawn from both sides of the aisle. Moreover, while the staggered terms of the FTC Commissioners prevented complete turnovers in agency leadership and guaranteed that there would always be some Commissioners who had accrued significant expertise, the CFPB's single-Director structure and five-year term guarantee abrupt shifts in agency leadership and with it the loss of accumulated expertise.

In addition, the CFPB Director is hardly a mere legislative or judicial aid. Instead of making reports and recommendations to Congress, as the 1935 FTC did, the Director possesses the authority to promulgate binding rules fleshing out 19 federal statutes, including a broad prohibition on unfair and deceptive practices in a major segment of the U. S. economy. And instead of submitting recommended dispositions to an Article III court, the Director may unilaterally issue final decisions awarding legal and equitable relief in administrative adjudications. Finally, the Director's enforcement authority includes the power to seek daunting monetary penalties against private parties on behalf of the United States in federal court—a quintessentially executive power not considered in *Humphrey's Executor*.[4]

The logic of *Morrison* also does not apply. Everyone agrees the CFPB Director is not an inferior officer, and her duties are far from limited. . . .

In light of these differences, the constitutionality of the CFPB Director's insulation from removal cannot be settled by *Humphrey's Executor* or *Morrison* alone.

The question instead is whether to extend those precedents to the "new situation" before us, namely an independent agency led by a single Director and vested with significant executive power. *Free Enterprise Fund*. We decline to do so. Such an agency has no basis in history and no place in our constitutional structure.

"Perhaps the most telling indication of [a] severe constitutional problem" with an executive entity "is [a] lack of historical precedent" to support it. An agency with a structure like that of the CFPB is almost wholly unprecedented.

After years of litigating the agency's constitutionality, the Courts of Appeals, parties, and *amici* have identified "only a handful of isolated" incidents in which Congress has provided good-cause tenure to principal officers who wield power alone rather than as members of a board or commission. "[T]hese few scattered examples"—four to be exact—shed little light.

First, the CFPB's defenders point to the Comptroller of the Currency, who enjoyed removal protection for *one year* during the Civil War. That example has rightly been dismissed as an aberration. It was "adopted without discussion" during the heat of the Civil War and abandoned before it could be "tested by executive or judicial inquiry."

Second, the supporters of the CFPB point to the Office of the Special Counsel (OSC), which has been headed by a single officer since 1978. But this first enduring single-leader office, created nearly 200 years after the Constitution was ratified, drew a contemporaneous constitutional objection from the Office of Legal Counsel under President Carter and a subsequent veto on constitutional grounds by President Reagan. . . . In any event, the OSC exercises only limited jurisdiction to enforce certain rules governing Federal Government employers and employees. It does not bind private parties at all or wield regulatory authority comparable to the CFPB.

---

[4] The dissent would have us ignore the reasoning of *Humphrey's Executor* and instead apply the decision only as part of a reimagined *Humphrey's*-through-*Morrison* framework. But we take the decision on its own terms, not through gloss added by a later Court in dicta. The dissent also criticizes us for suggesting that the 1935 FTC may have had lesser responsibilities than the present FTC. Perhaps the FTC possessed broader rulemaking, enforcement, and adjudicatory powers than the *Humphrey's* Court appreciated. Perhaps not. Either way, what matters is the set of powers the Court considered as the basis for its decision, not any latent powers that the agency may have had not alluded to by the Court.

Third, the CFPB's defenders note that the Social Security Administration (SSA) has been run by a single Administrator since 1994. . . . [T]he SSA lacks the authority to bring enforcement actions against private parties. Its role is largely limited to adjudicating claims for Social Security benefits.

The only remaining example is the Federal Housing Finance Agency (FHFA), created in 2008 to assume responsibility for Fannie Mae and Freddie Mac. That agency is essentially a companion of the CFPB, established in response to the same financial crisis. It regulates primarily Government-sponsored enterprises, not purely private actors. And its single-Director structure is a source of ongoing controversy. Indeed, it was recently held unconstitutional by the Fifth Circuit, sitting en banc. See *Collins* v. *Mnuchin* (2019).

With the exception of the one-year blip for the Comptroller of the Currency, these isolated examples are modern and contested. And they do not involve regulatory or enforcement authority remotely comparable to that exercised by the CFPB. The CFPB's single-Director structure is an innovation with no foothold in history or tradition.

In addition to being a historical anomaly, the CFPB's single-Director configuration is incompatible with our constitutional structure. Aside from the sole exception of the Presidency, that structure scrupulously avoids concentrating power in the hands of any single individual.

"The Framers recognized that, in the long term, structural protections against abuse of power were critical to preserving liberty." *Bowsher.* Their solution to governmental power and its perils was simple: divide it. . . . At the highest level, they "split the atom of sovereignty" itself into one Federal Government and the States. They then divided the "powers of the new Federal Government into three defined categories, Legislative, Executive, and Judicial."

They did not stop there. Most prominently, the Framers bifurcated the federal legislative power into two Chambers: the House of Representatives and the Senate, each composed of multiple Members and Senators. The Executive Branch is a stark departure from all this division. The Framers viewed the legislative power as a special threat to individual liberty, so they divided that power to ensure that "differences of opinion" and the "jarrings of parties" would "promote deliberation and circumspection" and "check excesses in the majority." By contrast, the Framers thought it necessary to secure the authority of the Executive so that he could carry out his unique responsibilities. . . .

To justify and check *that* authority—unique in our constitutional structure—the Framers made the President the most democratic and politically accountable official in Government. Only the President (along with the Vice President) is elected by the entire Nation. And the President's political accountability is enhanced by the solitary nature of the Executive Branch, which provides "a single object for the jealousy and watchfulness of the people." The President "cannot delegate ultimate responsibility or the active obligation to supervise that goes with it," because Article II "makes a single President responsible for the actions of the Executive Branch." The resulting constitutional strategy is straightforward: divide power everywhere except for the Presidency, and render the President directly accountable to the people through regular elections. In that scheme, individual executive officials will still wield significant authority, but that authority remains subject to the ongoing supervision and control of the elected President. Through the President's oversight, "the chain of dependence [is] preserved," so that "the lowest officers, the middle grade, and the highest" all "depend, as they ought, on the President, and the President on the community." 1 Annals of Cong. (J. Madison).

The CFPB's single-Director structure contravenes this carefully calibrated system by vesting significant governmental power in the hands of a single individual accountable to no one. The Director is neither elected by the people nor meaningfully controlled (through the threat of removal) by someone who is. The Director does not even depend on Congress for annual appropriations.... Yet the Director may *unilaterally*, without meaningful supervision, issue final regulations, oversee adjudications, set enforcement priorities, initiate prosecutions, and determine what penalties to impose on private parties. With no colleagues to persuade, and no boss or electorate looking over her shoulder, the Director may dictate and enforce policy for a vital segment of the economy affecting millions of Americans.

The CFPB Director's insulation from removal by an accountable President is enough to render the agency's structure unconstitutional. But several other features of the CFPB combine to make the Director's removal protection even more problematic. In addition to lacking the most direct method of presidential control—removal at will—the agency's unique structure also forecloses certain indirect methods of Presidential control.

Because the CFPB is headed by a single Director with a five-year term, some Presidents may not have any opportunity to shape its leadership and thereby influence its activities.... That means an unlucky President might get elected on a consumer-protection platform and enter office only to find herself saddled with a holdover Director from a competing political party who is dead set *against* that agenda....

The CFPB's receipt of funds outside the appropriations process further aggravates the agency's threat to Presidential control....

[T]ext, first principles, the First Congress's decision in 1789, *Myers*, and *Free Enterprise Fund* all establish that the President's removal power is the rule, not the exception. While we do not revisit *Humphrey's Executor* or any other precedent today, we decline to elevate it into a freestanding invitation for Congress to impose additional restrictions on the President's removal authority.[11]

[A]micus contends that if we identify a constitutional problem with the CFPB's structure, we should avoid it by broadly construing the statutory grounds for removing the CFPB Director from office. The Dodd-Frank Act provides that the Director may be removed for "inefficiency, neglect of duty, or malfeasance in office. In amicus' view, that language could be interpreted to reserve substantial discretion to the President.

We are not persuaded. For one, *Humphrey's Executor* implicitly rejected an interpretation that would leave the President free to remove an officer based on disagreements about agency policy. In addition, while both amicus and the House of Representatives invite us to adopt whatever construction would cure the constitutional problem, they have not advanced any workable standard derived from the statutory language. . . . We decline to embrace such an uncertain and elastic approach to the text. . . .

IV

Having concluded that the CFPB's leadership by a single independent Director violates the separation of powers, we now turn to the appropriate remedy. . . .

"Generally speaking, when confronting a constitutional flaw in a statute, we try to limit the solution to the problem, severing any problematic portions while leaving the remainder intact." . . .

The only constitutional defect we have identified in the CFPB's structure is the Director's insulation from removal. If the Director were removable at will by the President, the constitutional violation would disappear. . . .

So too here. The provisions of the Dodd-Frank Act bearing on the CFPB's structure and duties remain fully operative without the offending tenure restriction. Those provisions are capable of functioning

---

[11] [T]he dissent would endorse whatever "the times demand, so long as the President retains the ability to carry out his constitutional functions." But that amorphous test provides no real limiting principle. The "clearest" (and only) "example" the dissent can muster for what may be prohibited is a for-cause removal restriction placed on the President's "close military or diplomatic advisers." But that carveout makes no logical or constitutional sense. In the dissent's view, for-cause removal restrictions are permissible because they guarantee the President "meaningful control" over his subordinates. If that is the theory, then what is the harm in giving the President the same "meaningful control" over his close advisers? The dissent claims to see a constitutional distinction between the President's "own constitutional duties in foreign relations and war" and his duty to execute laws passed by Congress. But the same Article that establishes the President's foreign relations and war duties expressly entrusts him to take care that the laws be faithfully executed. And, from the perspective of the governed, it is far from clear that the President's core and traditional powers present greater cause for concern than peripheral and modern ones. If anything, "[t]he growth of the Executive Branch, which now wields vast power and touches almost every aspect of daily life, heightens the concern that it may slip from the Executive's control, and thus from that of the people."

independently, and there is nothing in the text or history of the Dodd-Frank Act that demonstrates Congress would have preferred *no* CFPB to a CFPB supervised by the President. Quite the opposite . . .

JUSTICE THOMAS, with whom JUSTICE GORSUCH joins, concurring in part and dissenting in part. [Opinion omitted. Justice Thomas concurred in the opinion that the removal protection provision was unconstitutional, but he would go further and overrule *Humphrey's Executor*. In addition, he would not reach the severability question, because the case could be decided simply by dismissing the CFPB's enforcement action against Seila Law. Moreover, he questioned the Court's historical treatment of severability.]

Elena Kagan

President Obama appointed Justice Kagan to the Supreme Court in 2010. She is the only current justice not to have previously served as an appellate judge before being appointed to the Supreme Court. Immediately prior to her appointment she had been the Solicitor General of the United States, the first woman ever to hold that position. Prior to that she had been Dean and Professor of Law at Harvard Law School. She also had worked in the Clinton White House, where she developed a belief in strong Presidential powers. On the Court she has been a consistent liberal on most issues, although more likely to compromise than her other female colleagues.

JUSTICE KAGAN, joined by JUSTICES GINSBURG, BREYER, and SOTOMAYOR, concurred in the judgment on severability and dissented from the decision on the Constitutionality of the removal protection provision.

Throughout the Nation's history, this Court has left most decisions about how to structure the Executive Branch to Congress and the President, acting through legislation they both agree to. In particular, the Court has commonly allowed those two branches to create zones of administrative independence by limiting the President's power to remove agency heads. The Federal Reserve Board. The Federal Trade Commission (FTC). The National Labor Relations Board. Statute after statute establishing such entities instructs the President that he may not discharge their directors except for cause—most often phrased as inefficiency, neglect of duty, or malfeasance in office. Those statutes, whose language the Court has repeatedly approved, provide the model for the removal restriction before us today. If precedent were any guide, that provision would have survived its encounter with this Court—and so would the intended independence of the Consumer Financial Protection Bureau (CFPB).

Our Constitution and history demand that result. The text of the Constitution allows these common for-cause removal limits. Nothing in it speaks of removal. And it grants Congress authority to organize all the institutions of American governance, provided only that those arrangements allow the

President to perform his own constitutionally assigned duties. Still more, the Framers' choice to give the political branches wide discretion over administrative offices has played out through American history in ways that have settled the constitutional meaning. From the first, Congress debated and enacted measures to create spheres of administration—especially of financial affairs—detached from direct presidential control. As the years passed, and governance became ever more complicated, Congress continued to adopt and adapt such measures—confident it had latitude to do so under a Constitution meant to "endure for ages to come." Not every innovation in governance—not every experiment in administrative independence—has proved successful. And debates about the prudence of limiting the President's control over regulatory agencies, including through his removal power, have never abated. But the Constitution—both as originally drafted and as practiced—mostly leaves disagreements about administrative structure to Congress and the President, who have the knowledge and experience needed to address them. Within broad bounds, it keeps the courts—who do not—out of the picture.

The Court today fails to respect its proper role. It recognizes that this Court has approved limits on the President's removal power over heads of agencies much like the CFPB. The majority's explanation is that the heads of those agencies fall within an "exception"—one for multimember bodies and another for inferior officers—to a "general rule" of unrestricted presidential removal power. And the majority says the CFPB Director does not. That account, though, is wrong in every respect. The majority's general rule does not exist. Its exceptions, likewise, are made up for the occasion—gerrymandered so the CFPB falls outside them. And the distinction doing most of the majority's work—between multimember bodies and single directors—does not respond to the constitutional values at stake. If a removal provision violates the separation of powers, it is because the measure so deprives the President of control over an official as to impede his own constitutional functions. But with or without a for-cause removal provision, the President has at least as much control over an individual as over a commission—and possibly more. That means the constitutional concern is, if anything, ameliorated when the agency has a single head. . . .

What does the Constitution say about the separation of powers—and particularly about the President's removal authority? (Spoiler alert: about the latter, nothing at all.)

[B]lackstone, whose work influenced the Framers on this subject as on others, observed that "every branch" of government "supports and is supported, regulates and is regulated, by the rest." Or as Justice Story reiterated a half-century later: "[W]hen we speak of a separation of the three great departments of government," it is "not meant to affirm, that they must be kept wholly and entirely separate." Instead, the branches have—as they must for the whole arrangement to work—"common link[s] of connexion [and] dependence."

One way the Constitution reflects that vision is by giving Congress broad authority to establish and organize the Executive Branch. Article II presumes the existence of "Officer[s]" in "executive Departments." § 2, cl. 1. But it does not, as you might think from reading the majority opinion, give the President authority to decide what kinds of officers—in what departments, with what responsibilities—the Executive Branch requires. Instead, Article I's Necessary and Proper Clause puts those decisions in the legislature's hands. Similarly, the Appointments Clause reflects Congress's central role in structuring the Executive Branch. Yes, the President can appoint principal officers, but only as the legislature "shall . . . establish[ ] by Law" (and of course subject to the Senate's advice and consent). Art. II, § 2, cl. 2. And Congress has plenary power to decide not only what inferior officers will exist but also who (the President or a head of department) will appoint them. So as Madison told the first Congress, the legislature gets to "create[ ] the office, define[ ] the powers, [and] limit[ ] its duration." The President, as to the construction of his own branch of government, can only try to work his will through the legislative process.[3]

The majority relies for its contrary vision on Article II's Vesting Clause, but the provision can't carry all that weight. Or as Chief Justice Rehnquist wrote of a similar claim in *Morrison* v. *Olson* (1988), "extrapolat[ing]" an unrestricted removal power from such "general constitutional language"—which says only that "[t]he executive Power shall be vested in a President"—is "more than the text will bear." . . . For now, note two points about practice before the Constitution's drafting. First, in that era, Parliament often restricted the King's power to remove royal officers—and the President, needless to say, wasn't supposed to be a king. Second, many States at the time allowed limits on gubernatorial removal power even though their constitutions had similar vesting clauses. Historical understandings thus belie the majority's "general rule."

Nor can the Take Care Clause come to the majority's rescue. That Clause cannot properly serve as a "placeholder for broad judicial judgments" about presidential control. . . . [T]he text of the Take Care Clause requires only enough authority to make sure "the laws [are] faithfully executed"—meaning with fidelity to the law itself, not to every presidential policy preference. As this Court has held, a President can ensure " 'faithful execution' of the laws"—thereby satisfying his "take care"

---

[3] Article II's Opinions Clause also demonstrates the possibility of limits on the President's control over the Executive Branch. Under that Clause, the President "may require the Opinion, in writing, of the principal Officer in each of the executive Departments, upon any Subject relating to the Duties of their respective Offices." § 2, cl. 1. For those in the majority's camp, that Clause presents a puzzle: If the President must always have the direct supervisory control they posit, including by threat of removal, why would he ever need a constitutional warrant to demand agency heads' opinions? The Clause becomes at least redundant—though really, inexplicable—under the majority's idea of executive power.

obligation—with a removal provision like the one here. A for-cause standard gives him "ample authority to assure that [an official] is competently performing [his] statutory responsibilities in a manner that comports with the [relevant legislation's] provisions."

Finally, recall the Constitution's telltale silence: Nowhere does the text say anything about the President's power to remove subordinate officials at will. The majority professes unconcern. After all, it says, "neither is there a 'separation of powers clause' or a 'federalism clause.'" But those concepts are carved into the Constitution's text—the former in its first three articles separating powers, the latter in its enumeration of federal powers and its reservation of all else to the States. . . .

History no better serves the majority's cause. . . .

Begin with evidence from the Constitution's ratification. And note that this moment is indeed the beginning: Delegates to the Constitutional Convention never discussed whether or to what extent the President would have power to remove executive officials. As a result, the Framers advocating ratification had no single view of the matter. In Federalist No. 77, Hamilton presumed that under the new Constitution "[t]he consent of [the Senate] would be necessary to displace as well as to appoint" officers of the United States. By contrast, Madison thought the Constitution allowed Congress to decide how any executive official could be removed. . . . Neither view, of course, at all supports the majority's story.[4]

The second chapter is the Decision of 1789, when Congress addressed the removal power while considering the bill creating the Department of Foreign Affairs. Speaking through Chief Justice Taft—a judicial presidentialist if ever there was one—this Court in *Myers* v. *United States* (1926), read that debate as expressing Congress's judgment that the Constitution gave the President illimitable power to remove executive officials. The majority rests its own historical claim on that analysis (though somehow also finding room for its two exceptions). But Taft's historical research has held up even worse than *Myers'* holding (which was mostly reversed). As Dean Manning has concluded after reviewing decades' worth of scholarship on the issue, "the implications of the debate, properly understood, [are] highly ambiguous and prone to overreading."

The best view is that the First Congress was "deeply divided" on the President's removal power, and "never squarely addressed" the central issue here. The congressional debates revealed three main positions. Some shared Hamilton's Federalist No. 77 view: The Constitution required Senate consent for removal. At the opposite extreme, others claimed that the Constitution gave absolute removal power to the President. And a third faction maintained that the Constitution placed Congress in the driver's

---

⁴ The majority dismisses Federalist Nos. 77 and 39 as "reflect[ing] initial impressions later abandoned." . . . In any event, such changing minds and inconstant opinions don't usually prove the existence of constitutional rules.

seat: The legislature could regulate, if it so chose, the President's authority to remove. In the end, Congress passed a bill saying nothing about removal, leaving the President free to fire the Secretary of Foreign Affairs at will. But the only one of the three views definitively rejected was Hamilton's theory of necessary Senate consent. As even strong proponents of executive power have shown, Congress never "endorse[d] the view that [it] lacked authority to modify" the President's removal authority when it wished to. The summer of 1789 thus ended without resolution of the critical question: Was the removal power "beyond the reach of congressional regulation?" Contrary to the majority's view, then, the founding era closed without any agreement that Congress lacked the power to curb the President's removal authority. . . .

And then, nearly a century and a half ago, the floodgates opened. In 1887, the growing power of the railroads over the American economy led Congress to create the Interstate Commerce Commission. Under that legislation, the President could remove the five Commissioners only "for inefficiency, neglect of duty, or malfeasance in office"—the same standard Congress applied to the CFPB Director. More—many more—for-cause removal provisions followed. In 1913, Congress gave the Governors of the Federal Reserve Board for-cause protection to ensure the agency would resist political pressure and promote economic stability. The next year, Congress provided similar protection to the FTC in the interest of ensuring "a continuous policy" "free from the effect" of "changing [White House] incumbency." The Federal Deposit Insurance Corporation (FDIC), the Securities and Exchange Commission (SEC), the Commodity Futures Trading Commission. By one count, across all subject matter areas, 48 agencies have heads (and below them hundreds more inferior officials) removable only for cause. So year by year by year, the broad sweep of history has spoken to the constitutional question before us: Independent agencies are everywhere. . . .

[W]hat the majority does not say is that within a decade the Court abandoned that view (much as later scholars rejected Taft's one-sided history). In *Humphrey's Executor* v. *United States*, the Court unceremoniously—and unanimously—confined *Myers* to its facts. "[T]he narrow point actually decided" there, *Humphrey's* stated, was that the President could "remove a postmaster of the first class, without the advice and consent of the Senate." Nothing else in Chief Justice Taft's prolix opinion "c[a]me within the rule of stare decisis." (Indeed, the Court went on, everything in *Myers* "out of harmony" with *Humphrey's* was expressly "disapproved." . . .

And *Humphrey's* found constitutional a statute identical to the one here, providing that the President could remove FTC Commissioners for "inefficiency, neglect of duty, or malfeasance in office." . . .

Another three decades on, *Morrison* both extended *Humphrey's* domain and clarified the standard for addressing removal issues. The *Morrison* Court, over a one-Justice dissent, upheld for-cause protections afforded to an independent counsel with power to investigate and prosecute crimes committed by high-ranking officials. . . . The key question in all the cases, *Morrison* saw, was whether such a restriction would "impede the President's ability to perform his constitutional duty." Only if it did so would it fall outside Congress's power. . . .

So caselaw joins text and history in establishing the general permissibility of for-cause provisions giving some independence to agencies. For almost a century, this Court has made clear that Congress has broad discretion to enact for-cause protections in pursuit of good governance. . . .

The analysis is as simple as simple can be. The CFPB Director exercises the same powers, and receives the same removal protections, as the heads of other, constitutionally permissible independent agencies. How could it be that this opinion is a dissent?

The majority focuses on one (it says sufficient) reason: The CFPB Director is singular, not plural.[11] And a solo CFPB Director does not fit within either of the majority's supposed exceptions. Further, the majority argues, "[a]n agency with a [unitary] structure like that of the CFPB" is "novel"—or, if not quite that, "almost wholly unprecedented." Finally, the CFPB's organizational form violates the "constitutional structure" because it vests power in a "single individual" who is "insulated from Presidential control." . . .

First, as I'm afraid you've heard before, the majority's "exceptions" (like its general rule) are made up. . . .

Similarly, *Humphrey's* and later precedents give no support to the majority's view that the number of people at the apex of an agency matters to the constitutional issue. Those opinions mention the "groupness" of the agency head only in their background sections. The majority picks out that until-now-irrelevant fact to distinguish the CFPB, and constructs around it an until-now-unheard-of exception. So if the majority really wants to see something "novel," it need only look to its opinion.

---

[11] The majority briefly mentions, but understandably does not rely on, two other features of Congress's scheme. First, the majority notes that the CFPB receives its funding outside the normal appropriations process. But so too do other financial regulators, including the Federal Reserve Board and the FDIC. And budgetary independence comes mostly at the expense of Congress's control over the agency, not the President's. (Because that is so, it actually works to the President's advantage.) Second, the majority complains that the Director's five-year term may prevent a President from "shap[ing the agency's] leadership" through appointments. But again that is true, to one degree or another, of quite a few longstanding independent agencies, including the Federal Reserve, the FTC, the Merit Systems Protection Board, and the Postal Service Board of Governors.)

By contrast, the CFPB's single-director structure has a fair bit of precedent behind it. The Comptroller of the Currency. The Office of the Special Counsel (OSC). The Social Security Administration (SSA). The Federal Housing Finance Agency (FHFA). Maybe four prior agencies is in the eye of the beholder, but it's hardly nothing. . . .

Still more important, novelty is not the test of constitutionality when it comes to structuring agencies. See *Mistretta* v. *United States* (1989)("[M]ere anomaly or innovation" does not violate the separation of powers). Congress regulates in that sphere under the Necessary and Proper Clause, not (as the majority seems to think) a Rinse and Repeat Clause. The Framers understood that new times would often require new measures, and exigencies often demand innovation. See *McCulloch*. . . .

But if the demand is for generalization, then the majority's distinction cuts the opposite way: More powerful control mechanisms are needed (if anything) for commissions. Holding everything else equal, those are the agencies more likely to "slip from the Executive's control." Just consider your everyday experience: It's easier to get one person to do what you want than a gaggle. So too, you know exactly whom to blame when an individual—but not when a group—does a job badly. The same is true in bureaucracies. A multimember structure reduces accountability to the President because it's harder for him to oversee, to influence—or to remove, if necessary—a group of five or more commissioners than a single director. Indeed, that is *why* Congress so often resorts to hydra-headed agencies. . . .

Because it has no answer on that score, the majority slides to a different question: Assuming presidential control of any independent agency is vanishingly slim, is a single-head or a multi-head agency more capable of exercising power, and so of endangering liberty? The majority says a single head is the greater threat because he may wield power "*unilaterally*" and "[w]ith no colleagues to persuade." So the CFPB falls victim to what the majority sees as a constitutional anti-power-concentration principle (with an exception for the President).

If you've never heard of a statute being struck down on that ground, you're not alone. . . .

COMMENTS AND QUESTIONS

1.   Justice Thomas, joined by Justice Gorsuch, in an opinion omitted here for length, makes the case for overruling *Humphrey's Executor*. Does the majority opinion provide a map for how that might be done in a subsequent case? Or would overruling more than a century of law with countless examples of multi-member agencies with removal protection for members be a bridge too far for some of those in the majority?

2.   Isn't Justice Kagan right that it is harder for the President to control a multi-member agency than to control an agency with a single head, where

both have protections against removal at will? If so, how is the CFPB unconstitutional but the FTC not?

3.   The majority places significant weight on the original understanding as reflected in the so-called decision of 1789, but as the dissent points out, historians looking at that decision have almost all concluded that there was no decision that the President had a constitutional right to remove executive officers at will. Chief Justice Taft's contrary conclusion, which even at the time was contradicted by the dissent written by Justice Brandeis, nevertheless, is held to be truth by the majority. Is incorrect history protected by *stare decisis*?

4.   In *Humphrey's*, the Court rejected the reasoning of *Myers*, but did not overrule it. In *Morrison*, the Court rejected the reasoning of *Humphrey's*, but did not overrule it. In *Seila Law*, the Court rejects the reasoning of *Morrison*, but does not overrule it. What does this bode for the reasoning of *Seila Law*?

5.   As the Court notes, the CFPB was not the only agency to be headed by a single individual with for cause removal protection. In *Collins v. Yellen*, 141 S.Ct. 1761 (2021), the Court reached the same conclusion with respect to the Federal Housing Finance Agency. Subsequently, the Office of Legal Counsel opined that the President may remove the Administrator of the Social Security Administration at will despite the statutory removal protection, based on *Seila Law* and *Collins*. President Biden then removed the Administrator.

PROBLEM

Imagine that Congress has decided that in its view the Environmental Protection Agency has become too politicized and that it needs some degree of independence from the President. Currently, the Administrator serves at the pleasure of the President. Two different options are being considered. The first would provide that the Administrator of EPA could only be removed for failure to faithfully execute the laws. The second would replace EPA with a new Environmental Protection Commission, made up of five commissioners appointed by the President with the advice and consent of the Senate for a term of five years, with staggered terms, so that every year one commissioner's term would end. In addition, the commissioners could only be removed for inefficiency, neglect of duty, or malfeasance in office. Would either or both of these be constitutional?

E. ATTEMPTS TO ADDRESS STRUCTURAL ISSUES

The next two cases involve attempts by Congress and the President to address structural difficulties encountered in modern government.

IMMIGRATION AND NATURALIZATION SERVICE V. CHADHA

United States Supreme Court, 1983.
462 U.S. 919, 103 S.Ct. 2764.

[Historically, if an illegal alien was found, he was subject to deportation, no matter how long he had managed to stay in the United States and no matter what ties he had established, such as a wife and family and steady job. One way of avoiding the harshness of deportation in such cases was by way of a "private bill." A private bill is a bill introduced into Congress for the relief of a particular individual (or company), as opposed to being for the good of the general public. If the alien's lawyer or congressman could convince enough members of the House and Senate, they could pass a law and submit it to the President for signature, in order to adjust the alien's status from deportable to immigrant. In order to replace this very cumbersome and inadequate process, which relied more on influence and contacts than justice, Congress eventually passed the Immigration and Nationality Act in 1952.]

[Under Section 244 of that Act, an alien who was ordered deported could apply to the Attorney General for a "suspension" of deportation on the grounds that he had been physically present in the United States for a continuous period of not less than seven years, that he was of good moral character, and that he or his immediate family would suffer "extreme hardship" if he was deported. If the Attorney General in his discretion granted the "suspension," the Act required the Attorney General to report the "suspension" with a detailed statement of facts and reasons to both houses of Congress. If before the end of the next session of Congress either house of Congress voted a resolution of disapproval, the "suspension" would be terminated, and the alien would have to be deported. If, however, neither house voted such a resolution before the end of the next session of Congress, then the Attorney General would cancel the deportation proceedings, and the alien was allowed to remain in the United States.]

[Jagdish Rai Chadha was an East Indian from Kenya admitted into the United States on a student visa in 1966. His visa expired in 1972, and the following year the Immigration and Naturalization Service, the agency then responsible for immigration matters, ordered him to show cause why he should not be deported. At the immigration hearing the following year, Chadha conceded his deportability, but the hearing was stayed to enable him to file an application for a suspension of deportation. In June 1974, an immigration judge, operating under a delegation of authority from the Attorney General, granted Chadha a suspension of deportation. The suspension was reported to Congress, and in December 1975 the House of Representatives without debate or recorded vote, on the basis of the recommendation of the House Committee on the Judiciary, passed a resolution of disapproval.]

[Chadha, unlike numerous other aliens in identical circumstances, challenged the constitutionality of this process. The Board of Immigration Appeals held it had no authority to rule on the constitutionality of the law. Chadha then appealed to the Ninth Circuit. Before the Ninth Circuit, the Immigration and Naturalization Service agreed with Chadha that the one-house veto provision of § 244(c)(2) of the Act was unconstitutional. The House and Senate sought to intervene in the case, and the court granted them intervention but, nonetheless, held the one-house veto provision unconstitutional in an opinion by then-Judge Anthony Kennedy. The House and Senate petitioned the Supreme Court for certiorari, which was granted.]

CHIEF JUSTICE BURGER delivered the opinion of the Court.

[W]e turn now to the question whether action of one House of Congress under § 244(c)(2) violates strictures of the Constitution. . . .

[T]he fact that a given law or procedure is efficient, convenient, and useful in facilitating functions of government, standing alone, will not save it if it is contrary to the Constitution. Convenience and efficiency are not the primary objectives—or the hallmarks—of democratic government and our inquiry is sharpened rather than blunted by the fact that Congressional veto provisions are appearing with increasing frequency in statutes which delegate authority to executive and independent agencies:

> "Since 1932, when the first veto provision was enacted into law, 295 congressional veto-type procedures have been inserted in 196 different statutes as follows: from 1932 to 1939, five statutes were affected; from 1940–49, nineteen statutes; between 1950–59, thirty-four statutes; and from 1960–69, forty-nine. From the year 1970 through 1975, at least one hundred sixty-three such provisions were included in eighty-nine laws."

[E]xplicit and unambiguous provisions of the Constitution prescribe and define the respective functions of the Congress and of the Executive in the legislative process. . . . These provisions of Art. I are integral parts of the constitutional design for the separation of powers. . . .

The decision to provide the President with a limited and qualified power to nullify proposed legislation by veto was based on the profound conviction of the Framers that the powers conferred on Congress were the powers to be most carefully circumscribed. It is beyond doubt that lawmaking was a power to be shared by both Houses and the President. . . .

The President's role in the lawmaking process also reflects the Framers' careful efforts to check whatever propensity a particular Congress might have to enact oppressive, improvident, or ill-considered measures. . . . The Court also has observed that the Presentment Clauses serve the important purpose of assuring that a "national" perspective is grafted on the legislative process: "The President is a representative of the people just as the members of the Senate and of the House are, and it may be, at some times, on some subjects, that the President elected by all the people is rather more representative of them all than are the members of either body of the Legislature whose constituencies are local and not countrywide. . . ." *Myers v. United States.*

The bicameral requirement of Art. I, §§ 1, 7 was of scarcely less concern to the Framers than was the Presidential veto and indeed the two concepts are interdependent. By providing that no law could take effect without the concurrence of the prescribed majority of the Members of both Houses, the Framers reemphasized their belief, already remarked upon in connection with the Presentment Clauses, that legislation should not be enacted unless it has been carefully and fully considered by the Nation's elected officials. . . .

We see therefore that the Framers were acutely conscious that the bicameral requirement and the Presentment Clauses would serve essential constitutional functions. The President's participation in the legislative process was to protect the Executive Branch from Congress and to protect the whole people from improvident laws. The division of the Congress into two distinctive bodies assures that the legislative power would be exercised only after opportunity for full study and debate in separate settings. The President's unilateral veto power, in turn, was limited by the power of two thirds of both Houses of Congress to overrule a veto thereby precluding final arbitrary action of one person. It emerges clearly that the prescription for legislative action in Art. I, §§ 1, 7 represents the Framers' decision that the legislative power of the Federal government be exercised in accord with a single, finely wrought and exhaustively considered, procedure.

The Constitution sought to divide the delegated powers of the new federal government into three defined categories, legislative, executive and judicial, to assure, as nearly as possible, that each Branch of government would confine itself to its assigned responsibility. The hydraulic pressure inherent within each of the separate Branches to exceed the outer limits of its power, even to accomplish desirable objectives, must be resisted.

Although not "hermetically" sealed from one another, the powers delegated to the three Branches are functionally identifiable. When any Branch acts, it is presumptively exercising the power the Constitution has delegated to it. When the Executive acts, it presumptively acts in an executive or administrative capacity as defined in Art. II. And when, as here, one House of Congress purports to act, it is presumptively acting within its assigned sphere.

Beginning with this presumption, we must nevertheless establish that the challenged action under § 244(c)(2) is of the kind to which the procedural requirements of Art. I, § 7 apply. Not every action taken by either House is subject to the bicameralism and presentment requirements of Art. I. Whether actions taken by either House are, in law and fact, an exercise of legislative power depends not on their form but upon "whether they contain matter which is properly to be regarded as legislative in its character and effect."

Examination of the action taken here by one House pursuant to § 244(c)(2) reveals that it was essentially legislative in purpose and effect. [T]he House took action that had the purpose and effect of altering the legal rights, duties and relations of persons, including the Attorney General, Executive Branch officials and Chadha, all outside the legislative branch.... The one-House veto operated in this case to overrule the Attorney General and mandate Chadha's deportation; absent the House action, Chadha would remain in the United States. Congress has *acted* and its action has altered Chadha's status.

The legislative character of the one-House veto in this case is confirmed by the character of the Congressional action it supplants. Neither the House of Representatives nor the Senate contends that, absent the veto provision in § 244(c)(2), either of them, or both of them acting together, could effectively require the Attorney General to deport an alien once the Attorney General, in the exercise of legislatively delegated authority, had determined the alien should remain in the United States. Without the challenged provision in § 244(c)(2), this could have been achieved, if at all, only by legislation requiring deportation....

The nature of the decision implemented by the one-House veto in this case further manifests its legislative character. After long experience with the clumsy, time consuming private bill procedure, Congress made a deliberate choice to delegate to the Executive Branch, and specifically to the Attorney General, the authority to allow deportable aliens to remain in this country in certain specified circumstances. It is not disputed that this choice to delegate authority is precisely the kind of decision that can be implemented only in accordance with the procedures set out in Art. I. Disagreement with the Attorney General's decision on Chadha's deportation—that is, Congress's decision to deport Chadha—no less than Congress's original choice to delegate to the Attorney General the authority to make that decision, involves determinations of policy that Congress can implement in only one way; bicameral passage followed by presentment to the President. Congress must abide by its delegation of authority until that delegation is legislatively altered or revoked.

Finally, we see that when the Framers intended to authorize either House of Congress to act alone and outside of its prescribed bicameral legislative role, they narrowly and precisely defined the procedure for such action. There are but four provisions in the Constitution, explicit and unambiguous, by which one House may act alone with the unreviewable force of law, not subject to the President's veto:

(a) The House of Representatives alone was given the power to initiate impeachments. Art. I, § 2, cl. 6;

(b) The Senate alone was given the power to conduct trials following impeachment on charges initiated by the House and to convict following trial. Art. I, § 3, cl. 5;

(c) The Senate alone was given final unreviewable power to approve or to disapprove presidential appointments. Art. II, § 2, cl. 2;

(d) The Senate alone was given unreviewable power to ratify treaties negotiated by the President. Art. II, § 2, cl. 2.

Clearly, when the Draftsmen sought to confer special powers on one House, independent of the other House, or of the President, they did so in explicit, unambiguous terms. These carefully defined exceptions from presentment and bicameralism underscore the difference between the legislative functions of Congress and other unilateral but important and binding one-House acts provided for in the Constitution. These exceptions are narrow, explicit, and separately justified; none of them authorize the action challenged here. On the contrary, they provide further support for the conclusion that Congressional authority is not to be implied and for the conclusion that the veto provided for in § 244(c)(2) is not authorized by the constitutional design of the powers of the Legislative Branch.

Since it is clear that the action by the House under § 244(c)(2) was not within any of the express constitutional exceptions authorizing one House to act alone, and equally clear that it was an exercise of legislative power, that action was subject to the standards prescribed in Article I. . . .

JUSTICE POWELL, concurring in the judgment.

The Court's decision, based on the Presentment Clauses, Art. I, § 7, cls. 2 and 3, apparently will invalidate every use of the legislative veto. The breadth of this holding gives one pause. Congress has included the veto in literally hundreds of statutes, dating back to the 1930s. Congress clearly views this procedure as essential to controlling the delegation of power to administrative agencies. One reasonably may disagree with Congress's assessment of the veto's utility, but the respect due its judgment as a coordinate branch of Government cautions that our holding should be no more extensive than necessary to decide this case. In my view, the case may be decided on a narrower ground. When Congress finds that a particular person does not satisfy the statutory criteria for permanent residence in this country it has assumed a judicial function in violation of the principle of separation of powers. Accordingly, I concur only in the judgment.

JUSTICE WHITE, dissenting.

Today the Court not only invalidates § 244(c)(2) of the Immigration and Nationality Act, but also sounds the death knell for nearly 200 other statutory provisions in which Congress has reserved a "legislative veto."

For this reason, the Court's decision is of surpassing importance. And it is for this reason that the Court would have been well-advised to decide the case, if possible, on the narrower grounds of separation of powers, leaving for full consideration the constitutionality of other congressional review statutes operating on such varied matters as war powers and agency rulemaking, some of which concern the independent regulatory agencies.

The prominence of the legislative veto mechanism in our contemporary political system and its importance to Congress can hardly be overstated. It has become a central means by which Congress secures the accountability of executive and independent agencies. Without the legislative veto, Congress is faced with a Hobson's choice: either to refrain from delegating the necessary authority, leaving itself with a hopeless task of writing laws with the requisite specificity to cover endless special circumstances across the entire policy landscape, or in the alternative, to abdicate its law-making function to the executive branch and independent agencies. To choose the former leaves major national problems unresolved; to opt for the latter risks unaccountable policymaking by those not elected to fill that role. Accordingly, over the past five decades, the legislative veto has been placed in nearly 200 statutes. The device is known in every field of governmental concern: reorganization, budgets, foreign affairs, war powers, and regulation of trade, safety, energy, the environment and the economy. . . .

[T]he legislative veto is more than "efficient, convenient, and useful." It is an important if not indispensable political invention that allows the President and Congress to resolve major constitutional and policy differences, assures the accountability of independent regulatory agencies, and preserves Congress's control over lawmaking. Perhaps there are other means of accommodation and accountability, but the increasing reliance of Congress upon the legislative veto suggests that the alternatives to which Congress must now turn are not entirely satisfactory.[10] . . .

If the legislative veto were as plainly unconstitutional as the Court strives to suggest, its broad ruling today would be more comprehensible. But, the constitutionality of the legislative veto is anything but clearcut. The issue divides scholars, courts, attorneys general, and the two other branches of the National Government. If the veto devices so flagrantly disregarded the requirements of Article I as the Court today suggests, I find it incomprehensible that Congress, whose members are bound by oath to uphold the Constitution, would have placed these mechanisms in nearly 200 separate laws over a period of 50 years.

---

[10]   While Congress could write certain statutes with greater specificity, it is unlikely that this is a realistic or even desirable substitute for the legislative veto. . . . Oversight hearings and congressional investigations have their purpose, but unless Congress is to be rendered a think tank or debating society, they are no substitute for the exercise of actual authority. . . . Finally, the passage of corrective legislation after agency regulations take effect or Executive Branch officials have acted entail the drawbacks endemic to a retroactive response.

The reality of the situation is that the constitutional question posed today is one of immense difficulty over which the executive and legislative branches—as well as scholars and judges—have understandably disagreed. That disagreement stems from the silence of the Constitution on the precise question: The Constitution does not directly authorize or prohibit the legislative veto. Thus, our task should be to determine whether the legislative veto is consistent with the purposes of Art. I and the principles of Separation of Powers which are reflected in that Article and throughout the Constitution. . . . Only within the last half century has the complexity and size of the Federal Government's responsibilities grown so greatly that the Congress must rely on the legislative veto as the most effective if not the only means to insure their role as the nation's lawmakers. But the wisdom of the Framers was to anticipate that the nation would grow and new problems of governance would require different solutions. Accordingly, our Federal Government was intentionally chartered with the flexibility to respond to contemporary needs without losing sight of fundamental democratic principles. . . .

This is the perspective from which we should approach the novel constitutional questions presented by the legislative veto. In my view, neither Article I of the Constitution nor the doctrine of separation of powers is violated by this mechanism by which our elected representatives preserve their voice in the governance of the nation. . . .

[T]he power to exercise a legislative veto is not the power to write new law without bicameral approval or presidential consideration. The veto must be authorized by statute and may only negative what an Executive department or independent agency has proposed. On its face, the legislative veto no more allows one House of Congress to make law than does the presidential veto confer such power upon the President. . . .

If Congress may delegate lawmaking power to independent and executive agencies, it is most difficult to understand Article I as forbidding Congress from also reserving a check on legislative power for itself. Absent the veto, the agencies receiving delegations of legislative or quasi-legislative power may issue regulations having the force of law without bicameral approval and without the President's signature. It is thus not apparent why the reservation of a veto over the exercise of that legislative power must be subject to a more exacting test. In both cases, it is enough that the initial statutory authorizations comply with the Article I requirements. . . .

JUSTICE REHNQUIST, with whom JUSTICE WHITE joins, dissenting.

[B]ecause I believe that Congress did not intend the one-House veto provision of § 244(c)(2) to be severable, I dissent. . . .

COMMENTS AND QUESTIONS

1.   Unlike many constitutional law cases, *Chadha* establishes a clear rule of law—one-house vetoes and two-house vetoes of executive action are unconstitutional, the former because it lacks both bicameralism and presentment and the latter because it lacks presentment. Some laws have provided for a single congressional committee to be able to veto executive action, but of course those provisions would likewise be unconstitutional for the same reason.

2.   What happens to § 244(c)(2) of the Act after *Chadha*? Justice Rehnquist argued that the one-house veto provision was not "severable" from the other portions of the provision allowing for suspension of deportation by the Attorney General. In his view, shared by Justice White, Congress would not have granted the Attorney General the authority to suspend deportation without retaining the ability to veto that decision. Thus, if the one-house veto provision was unconstitutional, so was the entire section, meaning that Chadha would have to be deported, because the Attorney General's suspension of deportation itself would be part of the provision declared unconstitutional. For this reason, Justice Rehnquist said, Chadha did not have standing to bring this action, because his injury would not be redressed by a favorable court decision—he would still have to be deported. The Court, however, found that the one-house veto provision was severable. The general presumption is that Congress would intend its acts to remain in effect even if one provision was found unconstitutional, and the Act here contained a severability provision stating explicitly that if any provision of the Act was found unconstitutional, the remainder of the Act should stay in effect. As a result, those portions of the statute that provide for the Attorney General to suspend deportation and to report it to Congress remain in effect. At the end of the next session of Congress, the temporary suspension of deportation is ended but the alien's deportation proceedings are also terminated, so he or she may remain in the United States.

3.   *Chadha* is often cited as an example of formalistic, as opposed to functional, constitutional analysis. Recall Justice Black's decision for the majority in the *Steel Seizure Case*, another formalistic opinion. There as here the Court states that what is being done is "legislative action." In the *Steel Seizure Case* that made the seizure unconstitutional, because the President is not a lawmaker. In *Chadha* the fact that the action is legislative action makes the one-house veto unconstitutional, because lawmaking must go through both houses and be presented to the President. In both cases the characterization of the action as legislative action dictates the outcome, but what makes the one-house veto "legislative action"? Is it that it is action by a branch of the legislature? Or is it that the action has legal effect? Or is it both together? Why does Justice Powell think it is judicial action rather than legislative action?

4.   Justice White's opinion in *Chadha*, on the other hand, is a functional opinion. That is, rather than dealing with the issue on a formalistic basis of deciding what box the action falls within, he discusses how the provision acts in the real world—as a balance to broad delegations to the executive, thereby

serving the checks and balances of the separation of powers. No one agrees with him, however.

5.   Imagine that after *Chadha* both houses of Congress pass a bill containing a one-house veto provision and submit it to the President. Imagine further that but for that provision, the President supports the policies in the bill. Must the President veto the bill, because he believes the one-house veto provision is unconstitutional, or may he sign the bill with the caveat that he will not recognize the validity of any one-house veto that might be made pursuant to the law? Congress has in fact passed such bills subsequent to *Chadha*, and Presidents have signed them while announcing that they will not give effect to the one-house veto provisions.

6.   Statements made by Presidents when signing bills into law are known as signing statements. Generally, they enable the President to make politically suitable remarks, and they have never had any particular legal effect. Often these statements express an intention either to interpret the law to avoid what the President views as its unconstitutionality or to ignore those portions of the law he views as unconstitutional. Virtually every President since James Monroe has made signing statements of such effect. Do you see anything wrong with a President making such a signing statement if he believes the law he signs has a constitutional problem? Would it be better if he just kept it a secret what his views were? Do you think he is required by the Constitution to veto any bill that he believes contains an unconstitutional provision? Is it constitutional for a President to enforce a law he believes is unconstitutional?

PROBLEMS

1.   In 1996, Congress enacted the Congressional Review Act. That Act requires the executive to send to Congress each regulation adopted by a federal agency before it becomes effective. "Major" regulations, generally those with more than $100 million effect on the economy, may not go into effect until at least 60 days after they have been reported to Congress. During that period the Act provides an expedited procedure by which Congress may enact a joint resolution of disapproval of the regulation. The joint resolution is sent to the President for his signature or veto (as are all joint resolutions).* Is this constitutional?

2.   Imagine that Congress amends the Act involved in *Chadha* to provide that the Attorney General, instead of reporting the temporary suspension to Congress, must report the suspension

---

*   A "joint resolution" is the equivalent of a "bill," in that it is voted on by both houses and sent to the President for his approval or veto, and the result is the same—they become law. The only distinction is a parliamentary one. Bills may be amended on the floor of either house, but resolutions cannot be amended on the floor of either house; they must be voted on as they are introduced. Joint resolutions are distinct from "concurrent resolutions," which are voted on by both houses but not sent to the President. Therefore, they do not become law.

to the Secretary of State, and if the Secretary of State does nothing for 18 months, then the suspension is permanent, but if the Secretary of State vetoes the suspension, then the alien must be deported. Would this be constitutional?

CLINTON V. NEW YORK

United States Supreme Court, 1998.
524 U.S. 417, 118 S.Ct. 2091.

[The Presentment Clause refers to "every bill" passed by the House and Senate being presented to the President before it becomes a law. It then states that the President shall sign "it" if he approves, but if not, he shall return "it" with his objections. Then Congress may reconsider "it," and if two thirds approve, "it" becomes law. This language has been interpreted by every President since George Washington as requiring the President to accept or veto the entire bill presented to him. He is not allowed to veto a particular article, section, or provision. This makes possible a particular legislative strategy for Congress, allowing it to include in a bill, which for

President Bill Clinton

various reasons a President feels the need to approve, a provision that otherwise the President would veto, a provision that may have nothing to do with the rest of the bill and that is included solely for the purpose of attaching it to a veto-proof bill. This strategy can be used particularly in the appropriations area. Congress may include various appropriations that the President thinks are inappropriate or unnecessary in an appropriation bill that is otherwise absolutely necessary—*e.g.*, salaries for military forces.]

[Recognizing the problems created by this arrangement, especially in the context of federal deficits in part created by unnecessary expenditures, Congress passed with the President's support the Line Item Veto Act in 1996, effective on January 1, 1997. That Act authorized the President to "cancel" three types of provisions within laws that he signs into effect: "(1) any dollar amount of discretionary budget authority; (2) any item of new direct spending; or (3) any limited tax benefit." In August, President Bill Clinton "cancelled" an "item of new direct spending"—approximately $2.6 billion for the City of New York—contained in the Balanced Budget Act of 1997 that he signed into effect. As a result, New York sued, arguing that the Line Item Veto Act was unconstitutional.]

JUSTICE STEVENS delivered the opinion of the Court.

The Act requires the President to adhere to precise procedures whenever he exercises his cancellation authority. In identifying items for cancellation he must consider the legislative history, the purposes, and other relevant information about the items. He must determine, with respect to each cancellation, that it will "(i) reduce the Federal budget deficit; (ii) not impair any essential Government functions; and (iii) not harm the national interest." Moreover, he must transmit a special message to Congress notifying it of each cancellation within five calendar days (excluding Sundays) after the enactment of the canceled provision. It is undisputed that the President meticulously followed these procedures in these cases.

A cancellation takes effect upon receipt by Congress of the special message from the President. If, however, a "disapproval bill" pertaining to a special message is enacted into law, the cancellations set forth in that message become "null and void." The Act sets forth a detailed expedited procedure for the consideration of a "disapproval bill," but no such bill was passed for either of the cancellations involved in these cases. A majority vote of both Houses is sufficient to enact a disapproval bill. The Act does not grant the President the authority to cancel a disapproval bill, but he does, of course, retain his constitutional authority to veto such a bill.

The effect of a cancellation is plainly stated . . . in the Act. With respect to . . . an item of new direct spending . . ., the cancellation prevents the item "from having legal force or effect." Thus, under the plain text of the statute, . . . the action[ ] of the President that [is] challenged in these cases prevented one section of the Balanced Budget Act of 1997 . . . "from having legal force or effect." . . .

In both legal and practical effect, the President has amended [an Act] of Congress by repealing a portion of [it]. "[R]epeal of statutes, no less than enactment, must conform with Art. I." *INS v. Chadha*. There is no provision in the Constitution that authorizes the President to enact, to amend, or to repeal statutes. . . .

There are important differences between the President's "return" of a bill pursuant to Article I, § 7, and the exercise of the President's cancellation authority pursuant to the Line Item Veto Act. The constitutional return takes place *before* the bill becomes law; the statutory cancellation occurs *after* the bill becomes law. The constitutional return is of the entire bill; the statutory cancellation is of only a part. Although the Constitution expressly authorizes the President to play a role in the process of enacting statutes, it is silent on the subject of unilateral Presidential action that either repeals or amends parts of duly enacted statutes.

There are powerful reasons for construing constitutional silence on this profoundly important issue as equivalent to an express prohibition. The procedures governing the enactment of statutes set forth in the text of Article I were the product of the great debates and compromises that produced the Constitution itself. Familiar historical materials provide abundant support for the conclusion that the power to enact statutes may only "be exercised in accord with a single, finely wrought and exhaustively considered, procedure.". . . What has emerged in these cases from the President's exercise of his statutory cancellation powers, however, are truncated versions of two bills that passed both Houses of Congress. They are not the product of the "finely wrought" procedure that the Framers designed.

The Government advances two related arguments to support its position that despite the unambiguous provisions of the Act, cancellations do not amend or repeal properly enacted statutes in violation of the Presentment Clause. First, relying primarily on *Field v. Clark,* 143 U.S. 649 (1892), the Government contends that the cancellations were merely exercises of discretionary authority granted to the President by the Balanced Budget Act and the Taxpayer Relief Act read in light of the previously enacted Line Item Veto Act. Second, the Government submits that the substance of the authority to cancel tax and spending items "is, in practical effect, no more and no less than the power to 'decline to spend' specified sums of money, or to 'decline to implement' specified tax measures." Neither argument is persuasive.

In *Field v. Clark,* the Court upheld the constitutionality of the Tariff Act of 1890. That statute contained a "free list" of almost 300 specific articles that were exempted from import duties "unless otherwise specially provided for in this act." Section 3 was a special provision that directed the President to suspend that exemption for sugar, molasses, coffee, tea, and hides "whenever, and so often" as he should be satisfied that any country producing and exporting those products imposed duties on the agricultural products of the United States that he deemed to be "reciprocally unequal and unreasonable. . . ." The section then specified the duties to be imposed on those products during any such suspension. The Court provided this explanation for its conclusion that § 3 had not delegated legislative power to the President:

> "Nothing involving the expediency or the just operation of such legislation was left to the determination of the President. . . . [W]hen he ascertained the fact that duties and exactions, reciprocally unequal and unreasonable, were imposed upon the agricultural or other products of the United States by a country producing and exporting sugar, molasses, coffee, tea or hides, it became his duty to issue a proclamation declaring the suspension, as to that country, which Congress had determined should occur. He had no discretion in the premises except in respect to the duration of the suspension so ordered. But that related only to the enforcement of the policy established by Congress. As the suspension was absolutely required when the President

ascertained the existence of a particular fact, it cannot be said that in ascertaining that fact and in issuing his proclamation, in obedience to the legislative will, he exercised the function of making laws. . . . It was a part of the law itself as it left the hands of Congress that the provisions, full and complete in themselves, permitting the free introduction of sugars, molasses, coffee, tea and hides, from particular countries, should be suspended, in a given contingency, and that in case of such suspensions certain duties should be imposed."

This passage identifies three critical differences between the power to suspend the exemption from import duties and the power to cancel portions of a duly enacted statute. First, the exercise of the suspension power was contingent upon a condition that did not exist when the Tariff Act was passed: the imposition of "reciprocally unequal and unreasonable" import duties by other countries. In contrast, the exercise of the cancellation power within five days after the enactment of the Balanced Budget and Tax Reform Acts necessarily was based on the same conditions that Congress evaluated when it passed those statutes. Second, under the Tariff Act, when the President determined that the contingency had arisen, he had a duty to suspend; in contrast, while it is true that the President was required by the Act to make three determinations before he canceled a provision, those determinations did not qualify his discretion to cancel or not to cancel. Finally, whenever the President suspended an exemption under the Tariff Act, he was executing the policy that Congress had embodied in the statute. In contrast, whenever the President cancels an item of new direct spending or a limited tax benefit he is rejecting the policy judgment made by Congress and relying on his own policy judgment. Thus, the conclusion in *Field v. Clark* that the suspensions mandated by the Tariff Act were not exercises of legislative power does not undermine our opinion that cancellations pursuant to the Line Item Veto Act are the functional equivalent of partial repeals of Acts of Congress that fail to satisfy Article I, § 7. . . .

[W]hen enacting the statutes discussed in *Field,* Congress itself made the decision to suspend or repeal the particular provisions at issue upon the occurrence of particular events subsequent to enactment, and it left only the determination of whether such events occurred up to the President. The Line Item Veto Act authorizes the President himself to effect the repeal of laws, for his own policy reasons, without observing the procedures set out in Article I, § 7. The fact that Congress intended such a result is of no moment. Although Congress presumably anticipated that the President might cancel some of the items in the Balanced Budget Act and in the Taxpayer Relief Act, Congress cannot alter the procedures set out in Article I, § 7, without amending the Constitution.

Neither are we persuaded by the Government's contention that the President's authority to cancel new direct spending . . . is no greater than his traditional authority to decline to spend appropriated funds. The Government has reviewed in some detail the series of statutes in which Congress has given the Executive broad discretion over the expenditure of appropriated funds. For example, the First Congress appropriated "sum[s] not exceeding" specified amounts to be spent on various Government operations. In those statutes, as in later years, the President was given wide discretion with respect to both the amounts to be spent and how the money would be allocated among different functions. It is argued that the Line Item Veto Act merely confers comparable discretionary authority over the expenditure of appropriated funds. The critical difference between this statute and all of its predecessors, however, is that unlike any of them, this Act gives the President the unilateral power to change the text of duly enacted statutes. None of the Act's predecessors could even arguably have been construed to authorize such a change.

Although they are implicit in what we have already written, the profound importance of these cases makes it appropriate to emphasize three points.

First, we express no opinion about the wisdom of the procedures authorized by the Line Item Veto Act. . . .

Second, although appellees challenge the validity of the Act on alternative grounds, the only issue we address concerns the "finely wrought" procedure commanded by the Constitution. We have been favored with extensive debate about the scope of Congress's power to delegate lawmaking authority, or its functional equivalent, to the President[,] but [it] does not really bear on the narrow issue that is dispositive of these cases.

Third, our decision rests on the narrow ground that the procedures authorized by the Line Item Veto Act are not authorized by the Constitution. . . . If the Line Item Veto Act were valid, it would authorize the President to create a different law—one whose text was not voted on by either House of Congress or presented to the President for signature. Something that might be known as "Public Law 105–33 as modified by the President" may or may not be desirable, but it is surely not a document that may "become a law" pursuant to the procedures designed by the Framers of Article I, § 7, of the Constitution. . . .

JUSTICE KENNEDY, concurring.

[I] write to respond to my colleague Justice BREYER, who observes that the statute does not threaten the liberties of individual citizens, a point on which I disagree. The argument is related to his earlier suggestion that our role is lessened here because the two political branches are adjusting their own powers between themselves. To say the political branches have a somewhat free hand to reallocate their own authority would seem to require acceptance of two premises: first, that the public good demands it, and second, that liberty is not at risk. The former premise is inadmissible. The Constitution's structure requires a stability which transcends the convenience of the moment. The latter premise, too, is flawed. Liberty is always at stake when one or more of the branches seek to transgress the separation of powers.

Separation of powers was designed to implement a fundamental insight: Concentration of power in the hands of a single branch is a threat to liberty. . . .

In recent years, perhaps, we have come to think of liberty as defined by that word in the Fifth and Fourteenth Amendments and as illuminated by the other provisions of the Bill of Rights. The conception of liberty embraced by the Framers was not so confined. They used the principles of separation of powers and federalism to secure liberty in the fundamental political sense of the term, quite in addition to the idea of freedom from intrusive governmental acts. . . .

JUSTICE SCALIA, with whom JUSTICE O'CONNOR joins, and with whom JUSTICE BREYER joins as to Part III, concurring in part and dissenting in part.

III

[T]he Presentment Clause requires, in relevant part, that "[e]very Bill which shall have passed the House of Representatives and the Senate, shall, before it become a Law, be presented to the President of the United States; If he approve he shall sign it, but if not he shall return it." There is no question that enactment of the Balanced Budget Act complied with these requirements: the House and Senate passed the bill, and the President signed it into law. It was only *after* the requirements of the Presentment Clause had been satisfied that the President exercised his authority under the Line Item Veto Act to cancel the spending item. Thus, the Court's problem with the Act is not that it authorizes the President to veto parts of a bill and sign others into law, but rather that it authorizes him to "cancel"—prevent from "having legal force or effect"—certain parts of duly enacted statutes.

Article I, § 7, of the Constitution obviously prevents the President from canceling a law that Congress has not authorized him to cancel. Such action cannot possibly be considered part of his execution of the law, and if it is legislative action, as the Court observes, " 'repeal of statutes, no less than enactment, must conform with Art. I.' " But that is not this case. It was certainly arguable, as an original matter, that Art. I, § 7, also prevents the President from canceling a law which itself *authorizes* the President to cancel it. But as the Court acknowledges, that argument has long since been made and rejected. . . . The Tariff Act of 1890 authorized the

President to "suspend, by proclamation to that effect" certain of its provisions if he determined that other countries were imposing "reciprocally unequal and unreasonable" duties. This Court upheld the constitutionality of that Act in *Field v. Clark*, reciting the history since 1798 of statutes conferring upon the President the power to "discontinue the prohibitions and restraints hereby enacted and declared," "suspend the operation of the aforesaid act," and "declare the provisions of this act to be inoperative."

As much as the Court goes on about Art. I, § 7, therefore, that provision does not demand the result the Court reaches. It no more categorically prohibits the Executive *reduction* of congressional dispositions in the course of implementing statutes that authorize such reduction, than it categorically prohibits the Executive *augmentation* of congressional dispositions in the course of implementing statutes that authorize such augmentation—generally known as substantive rulemaking. There are, to be sure, limits upon the former just as there are limits upon the latter— and I am prepared to acknowledge that the limits upon the former may be much more severe. Those limits are established, however, not by some categorical prohibition of Art. I, § 7, which our cases conclusively disprove, but by what has come to be known as the doctrine of unconstitutional delegation of legislative authority: When authorized Executive reduction or augmentation is allowed to go too far, it usurps the nondelegable function of Congress and violates the separation of powers.

It is this doctrine, and not the Presentment Clause, that was discussed in the *Field* opinion, and it is this doctrine, and not the Presentment Clause, that is the issue presented by the statute before us here. . . .

I turn, then, to the crux of the matter: whether Congress's authorizing the President to cancel an item of spending gives him a power that our history and traditions show must reside exclusively in the Legislative Branch. I may note, to begin with, that the Line Item Veto Act is not the first statute to authorize the President to "cancel" spending items. In *Bowsher v. Synar,* we addressed the constitutionality of the Balanced Budget and Emergency Deficit Control Act of 1985, which required the President, if the federal budget deficit exceeded a certain amount, to issue a "sequestration" order mandating spending reductions specified by the Comptroller General. The effect of sequestration was that "amounts sequestered . . . shall be *permanently cancelled.*" We held that the Act was unconstitutional, not because it impermissibly gave the Executive legislative power, but because it gave the Comptroller General, an officer of the Legislative Branch over whom Congress retained removal power, "the ultimate authority to determine the budget cuts to be made," "functions . . . plainly entailing execution of the law in constitutional terms." The President's discretion under the Line Item Veto Act is certainly broader than the Comptroller General's discretion was under the 1985 Act, but it is no broader than the discretion traditionally granted the President in his execution of spending laws.

Insofar as the degree of political, "lawmaking" power conferred upon the Executive is concerned, there is not a dime's worth of difference between Congress's authorizing the President to *cancel* a spending item, and Congress's authorizing money to be spent on a particular item at the President's discretion. And the latter has been done since the founding of the Nation. . . .

Certain Presidents have claimed Executive authority to withhold appropriated funds even *absent* an express conferral of discretion to do so. . . . President Nixon, the Mahatma Gandhi of all impounders, asserted at a press conference in 1973 that his "constitutional right" to impound appropriated funds was "absolutely clear." Our decision two years later in *Train v. City of New York,* 420 U.S. 35 (1975), proved him wrong, but it implicitly confirmed that Congress may confer discretion upon the Executive to withhold appropriated funds, even funds appropriated for a specific purpose. . . . This Court held, as a matter of statutory interpretation, that the statute *did not grant* the Executive discretion to withhold the funds, but required allotment of the full amount authorized.

The short of the matter is this: Had the Line Item Veto Act authorized the President to "decline to spend" any item of spending contained in the Balanced Budget Act of 1997, there is not the slightest doubt that authorization would have been constitutional. What the Line Item Veto Act does instead—authorizing the President to "cancel" an item of spending— is technically different. But the technical difference does *not* relate to the technicalities of the Presentment Clause, which have been fully complied with; and the doctrine of unconstitutional delegation, which *is* at issue here, is preeminently *not* a doctrine of technicalities. The title of the Line Item Veto Act, which was perhaps designed to simplify for public comprehension, or perhaps merely to comply with the terms of a campaign pledge, has succeeded in faking out the Supreme Court. The President's action it authorizes in fact is not a line-item veto and thus does not offend Art. I, § 7; and insofar as the substance of that action is concerned, it is no different from what Congress has permitted the President to do since the formation of the Union.

JUSTICE BREYER, with whom JUSTICE O'CONNOR and JUSTICE SCALIA join as to Part III, dissenting.

I

[I]n my view the Line Item Veto Act (Act) does not violate any specific textual constitutional command, nor does it violate any implicit separation-of-powers principle. Consequently, I believe that the Act is constitutional.

II

I approach the constitutional question before us with three general considerations in mind. *First,* the Act represents a legislative effort to provide the President with the power to give effect to some, but not to all, of the expenditure and revenue-diminishing provisions contained in a single massive appropriations bill. And this objective is constitutionally proper. . . .

Second, the case in part requires us to focus upon the Constitution's generally phrased structural provisions, provisions that delegate all "legislative" power to Congress and vest all "executive" power in the President. . . .

Third, we need not here referee a dispute among the other two branches. . . .

The background circumstances also mean that we are to interpret nonliteral separation-of-powers principles in light of the need for "workable government." *Youngstown Sheet and Tube Co.* If we apply those principles in light of that objective, as this Court has applied them in the past, the Act is constitutional.

III

The Court believes that the Act violates the literal text of the Constitution. A simple syllogism captures its basic reasoning:

Major Premise: The Constitution sets forth an exclusive method for enacting, repealing, or amending laws.

Minor Premise: The Act authorizes the President to "repea[l] or amen[d]" laws in a different way, namely by announcing a cancellation of a portion of a previously enacted law.

Conclusion: The Act is inconsistent with the Constitution.

I find this syllogism unconvincing, however, because its Minor Premise is faulty. When the President "canceled" the . . . appropriation measure[ ] now before us, he did not *repeal* any law nor did he *amend* any law. He simply *followed* the law, leaving the statutes, as they are literally written, intact.

To understand why one cannot say, *literally speaking,* that the President has repealed or amended any law, imagine how the provisions of law before us might have been, but were not, written. Imagine that the canceled New York health care tax provision at issue here had instead said the following:

"Section One. Taxes . . . that were collected by the State of New York from a health care provider before June 1, 1997, and for which a waiver of the provisions [requiring payment] have been sought . . . are deemed to be permissible health care related taxes

. . . provided however that the President may prevent the just-mentioned provision from having legal force or effect if he determines x, y, and z. (Assume x, y and z to be the same determinations required by the Line Item Veto Act).

Whatever a person might say, or think, about the constitutionality of this imaginary law, there is one thing the English language would prevent one from saying. One could not say that a President who "prevent[s]" the deeming language from "having legal force or effect" has either *repealed* or *amended* this particular hypothetical statute. Rather, the President has *followed* that law to the letter. He has exercised the power it explicitly delegates to him. He has executed the law, not repealed it.

It could make no significant difference to this linguistic point were the italicized proviso to appear, not as part of what I have called Section One, but, instead, at the bottom of the statute page, say, referenced by an asterisk, with a statement that it applies to every spending provision in the Act next to which a similar asterisk appears. And that being so, it could make no difference if that proviso appeared, instead, in a different, earlier enacted law, along with legal language that makes it applicable to every future spending provision picked out according to a specified formula.

But, of course, this last mentioned possibility is this very case. . . . In sum, I recognize that the Act before us is novel. In a sense, it skirts a constitutional edge. But that edge has to do with means, not ends. The means chosen do not amount literally to the enactment, repeal, or amendment of a law. Nor, for that matter, do they amount literally to the "line item veto" that the Act's title announces. Those means do not violate any basic separation-of-powers principle. They do not improperly shift the constitutionally foreseen balance of power from Congress to the President. Nor, since they comply with separation-of-powers principles, do they threaten the liberties of individual citizens. They represent an experiment that may, or may not, help representative government work better. The Constitution, in my view, authorizes Congress and the President to try novel methods in this way. Consequently, with respect, I dissent.

COMMENTS AND QUESTIONS

1.   Is the majority not correct that the Line Item Veto Act allows the President to do precisely what he could not do under the Presentment Clause, at least with respect to the three specific types of laws that the Act covers? That is, is there any distinction between the effect of an actual line-item veto, which is not provided for in the Presentment Clause, and what the President can do under the Line Item Veto Act with respect to specific appropriations within one appropriations law?

2.   Even if this is so, is there a reason for finding a law unconstitutional just because it allows something that the Constitution did not provide for? That is, did the allowance in the Constitution for the President to veto a bill at all

(albeit only the whole bill) constitute a prohibition on Congress allowing him to veto a part of a bill? There would seem to be a difference between limitations on what the Constitution allows the President to do absent congressional action and what the Constitution might allow Congress to permit in specified circumstances. Does the latter really threaten the constitutional arrangement?

3. If the Constitution really does prohibit that which it did not allow with respect to line-item vetoes, how is it that everyone agrees that Congress can write an appropriation bill that leaves to the President's discretion whether particular appropriations in that bill will be spent? What is it about *Field v. Clark* that would distinguish it from the line-item veto in the *Clinton* case? What would *Field v. Clark* say about a law that authorized the President not to spend certain line items within that very same law?

4. Is the problem in the Line Item Veto Act that one Congress, the one that passed the Line Item Veto Act, is authorizing the President to reduce the spending contained in a subsequent law passed by a possibly different Congress? Can one Congress pass a law binding a subsequent Congress? If not, presumably Congress also cannot delegate a power to the President that would bind a subsequent Congress. Is that what the Line Item Veto Act does?

5. Would this explain why this is not simply a delegation issue, as argued by Justice Scalia?

6. In the two cases of *Chadha* and *Clinton*, we see that attempts by Congress, even with presidential support, to structure relations between the executive and legislative branches in ways not explicitly authorized by constitutional text are struck down by the Court. In the discussion of Removals, there was also mention of *Bowsher v. Synar*, in which Congress also attempted a structural solution to chronic deficits, providing the Comptroller General authority over total spending, which solution also was found unconstitutional.

Nevertheless, not all such structural solutions are struck down. For example, in order to address complaints of radically inconsistent sentencing by federal judges, Congress enacted the Sentencing Reform Act of 1984, which created the United States Sentencing Commission and tasked it with developing rules to guide sentencing discretion in federal courts. The Commission was composed of seven members appointed by the President with the advice and consent of the Senate, at least three of whom had to be federal judges "selected after considering a list of six judges recommended to the President by the Judicial Conference of the United States." The commission was described as "an independent commission in the judicial branch." This structure was challenged as unconstitutional under the separation of powers, in that it delegated legislative authority to the judicial branch. In *Mistretta v. United States*, 488 U.S. 361 (1989), the Court upheld the structure, although acknowledging that the Commission was a "peculiar institution." The Court recognized that normally it was inappropriate for the judicial branch to perform administrative duties of a nonjudicial nature, but placement of the Commission in the judicial branch for the purpose of adopting rules governing sentencing—a paradigmatic judicial function—was not inconsistent with the duties and responsibilities of the judicial branch. Moreover, utilizing judges on the Commission for such work did not impermissibly involve judges in nonjudicial activities in ways that would undermine their independence. Justice Scalia, as in *Morrison*, was the lone dissenter. Reflecting his belief in a unitary executive, he did not believe it was constitutional to assign this function to the judicial branch.

7.   *Clinton* is an example of a law that would fit in Justice Jackson's first category in the *Steel Seizure case*—Presidential actions authorized by statute—the category in which the President's authority is at its greatest. Nevertheless, the Court finds the action unconstitutional.

PROBLEM

Congress passes a statute appropriating $2 billion for the operations of the Environmental Protection Agency, and that statute contains a provision that states: "The President may at any time after this bill becomes law withhold from spending any funds appropriated herein which he determines are not necessary for the EPA fully to execute its responsibilities." Is this provision constitutional?

F. PRIVILEGES AND IMMUNITIES OF THE CONGRESS AND PRESIDENT

When we considered federalism issues, we identified the two Privileges and Immunities Clauses in the Constitution: Article IV, Section 2, Clause 1 and the Fourteenth Amendment, Section 1. Both those clauses deal with the privileges and immunities of ordinary persons or, as we might say, individual rights. Here the "privileges" and "immunities" are special privileges and immunities arising out of the office of President or membership in the House of Representatives or the Senate. They have no relationship to "privileges and immunities" enjoyed by ordinary persons.

1. CONGRESSIONAL PRIVILEGES AND IMMUNITIES

Article I, Section 6, Clause 1 of the Constitution, provides that Senators and Representatives:

shall in all cases, except treason, felony and breach of the peace, be privileged from arrest during their attendance at the session of their respective houses, and in going to and returning from the same; and for any speech or debate in either house, they shall not be questioned in any other place.

The Supreme Court has interpreted this privilege from arrest to apply only to arrests in civil cases, which were common in 1789 but no longer exist, because the phrase "treason, felony and breach of the peace" was read to mean all criminal laws. *See Williamson v. United States*, 207 U.S. 425 (1908). In other words, this privilege is meaningless today. Is that disturbing? It means that the executive branch can criminally prosecute members of the legislative branch, and the only protection is the same protection afforded any member of the public. Is that consistent with the separation of powers? Moreover, it means that a local prosecutor, a local district attorney, for example, might be able to incapacitate a member of the House or a Senator, depriving the state or a district of representation.

However, the prohibition against questioning Senators and Representatives "for any speech or debate in either house," known as the "Speech and Debate Clause," is alive and well.

GRAVEL V. UNITED STATES

United States Supreme Court, 1972.
408 U.S. 606, 92 S.Ct. 2614.

[On June 13, 1971, during the height of the antiwar sentiment against the war in Vietnam, the New York Times began publishing excerpts from a leaked, highly classified history of the war prepared by the Defense Department, known today as the Pentagon Papers. The excerpts indicated that President Lyndon Johnson had systematically misled the public in order to drum up support for large-scale United States military intervention in Vietnam. The Nixon administration sought and obtained a preliminary injunction against the Times to stop the publication on June 15, the only time

Senator Mike Gravel

in the nation's history when the federal government sought to restrain the publication of information in a newspaper. The court of appeals affirmed that decision on June 23, and the Supreme Court granted certiorari on June 25, heard argument on June 26, and rendered its decision on June 30, overturning the injunction. *See New York Times Co. v. United States*, 403 U.S. 713 (1971).

On the eve of the Supreme Court decision, with its outcome still unknown, Senator Mike Gravel of Alaska called a meeting of the Subcommittee on Buildings and Grounds of the Senate Public Works Committee, of which he was chair, and proceeded to read from the Pentagon Papers, which had also been leaked to him after the injunction against the Times' publication.]

Opinion of the Court by MR. JUSTICE WHITE, announced by MR. JUSTICE BLACKMUN.

These cases arise out of the investigation by a federal grand jury into possible criminal conduct with respect to the release and publication of a classified Defense Department study entitled History of the United States Decision-Making Process on Viet Nam Policy. This document, popularly known as the Pentagon Papers, bore a Defense security classification of Top Secret-Sensitive. . . .

Among the witnesses subpoenaed were Leonard S. Rodberg, an assistant to Senator Mike Gravel of Alaska and a resident fellow at the Institute of Policy Studies. . . . Senator Gravel, as intervenor,[1] filed motions to quash the subpoenas. . . . He asserted that requiring these witnesses to appear and testify would violate his privilege under the Speech or Debate Clause of the United States Constitution, Art. I, § 6, cl. 1.

It appeared that on the night of June 29, 1971, Senator Gravel, as Chairman of the Subcommittee on Buildings and Grounds of the Senate Public Works Committee, convened a meeting of the subcommittee and there read extensively from a copy of the Pentagon Papers. He then placed the entire 47 volumes of the study in the public record. Rodberg had been added to the Senator's staff earlier in the day and assisted Gravel in preparing for and conducting the hearing. Some weeks later there were press reports that Gravel had arranged for the papers to be published by Beacon Press. . . .

The District Court [held that the Speech and Debate Clause protected whatever the Senator did in the committee meeting as well anything done by his assistant that would have been protected if done by the Senator. However, the trial court held the private publication of the documents was not privileged by the Speech or Debate Clause.]

The Court of Appeals affirmed the [trial court's rulings under the Speech and Debate Clause.]. . . .

The United States petitioned for certiorari challenging the ruling that aides and other persons may not be questioned with respect to legislative acts. . . . Senator Gravel also petitioned for certiorari seeking reversal of the Court of Appeals insofar as it held private publication unprotected by the Speech or Debate Clause. . . . We granted both petitions.

Because the claim is that a Member's aide shares the Member's constitutional privilege, we consider first whether and to what extent Senator Gravel himself is exempt from process or inquiry by a grand jury investigating the commission of a crime. Our frame of reference is Art. I, § 6, cl. 1, of the Constitution. . . .

---

[1] The District Court permitted Senator Gravel to intervene in the proceeding on Dr. Rodberg's motion to quash the subpoena ordering his appearance before the grand jury and accepted motions from Gravel to quash the subpoena and to specify the exact nature of the questions to be asked Rodberg.

Senator Gravel ... points out that the last portion of § 6 affords Members of Congress [a] vital privilege—they may not be questioned in any other place for any speech or debate in either House. [H]is insistence is that the Speech or Debate Clause at the very least protects him from criminal or civil liability and from questioning elsewhere than in the Senate, with respect to the events occurring at the subcommittee hearing at which the Pentagon Papers were introduced into the public record. To us this claim is incontrovertible. The Speech or Debate Clause was designed to assure a co-equal branch of the government wide freedom of speech, debate, and deliberation without intimidation or threats from the Executive Branch. It thus protects Members against prosecutions that directly impinge upon or threaten the legislative process. We have no doubt that Senator Gravel may not be made to answer—either in terms of questions or in terms of defending himself from prosecution—for the events that occurred at the subcommittee meeting. Our decision is made easier by the fact that the United States appears to have abandoned whatever position it took to the contrary in the lower courts.

Even so, the United States strongly urges that because the Speech or Debate Clause confers a privilege only upon "Senators and Representatives," Rodberg himself has no valid claim to constitutional immunity from grand jury inquiry. In our view, both courts below correctly rejected this position. We agree with the Court of Appeals that for the purpose of construing the privilege a Member and his aide are to be "treated as one," [T]he "Speech or Debate Clause prohibits inquiry into things done by Dr. Rodberg as the Senator's agent or assistant which would have been legislative acts, and therefore privileged, if performed by the Senator personally." [I]t is literally impossible, in view of the complexities of the modern legislative process, with Congress almost constantly in session and matters of legislative concern constantly proliferating, for Members of Congress to perform their legislative tasks without the help of aides and assistants; that the day-to-day work of such aides is so critical to the Members' performance that they must be treated as the latter's alter egos; and that if they are not so recognized, the central role of the Speech or Debate Clause—to prevent intimidation of legislators by the Executive and accountability before a possibly hostile judiciary—will inevitably be diminished and frustrated. . . .

It is true that the Clause itself mentions only "Senators and Representatives," but prior cases have plainly not taken a literalistic approach in applying the privilege. The Clause also speaks only of "Speech or Debate," but the Court's consistent approach has been that to confine the protection of the Speech or Debate Clause to words spoken in debate would be an unacceptably narrow view. Committee reports, resolutions, and the act of voting are equally covered; "(i)n short, . . . things generally done in a session of the House by one of its members in relation to the business before it." Rather than giving the clause a cramped construction, the Court has sought to implement its fundamental purpose of freeing the legislator from executive and judicial oversight that realistically threatens to control his conduct as a legislator. We have little doubt that we are neither exceeding our judicial powers nor mistakenly construing the Constitution by holding that the Speech or Debate Clause applies not only to a Member but also to his aides insofar as the conduct of the latter would be a protected legislative act if performed by the Member himself. . . .

The United States fears the abuses that history reveals have occurred when legislators are invested with the power to relieve others from the operation of otherwise valid civil and criminal laws. But these abuses, it seems to us, are for the most part obviated if the privilege applicable to the aide is viewed, as it must be, as the privilege of the Senator, and invocable only by the Senator or by the aide on the Senator's behalf, and if in all events the privilege available to the aide is confined to those services that would be immune legislative conduct if performed by the Senator himself. This view places beyond the Speech or Debate Clause a variety of services characteristically performed by aides for Members of Congress, even though within the scope of their employment. It likewise provides no protection for criminal conduct threatening the security of the person or property of others, whether performed at the direction of the Senator in preparation for or in execution of a legislative act or done without his knowledge or direction. Neither does it immunize Senator or aide from testifying at trials or grand jury proceedings involving third-party crimes where the questions do not require testimony about or impugn a legislative act. Thus our refusal to distinguish between Senator and aide in applying the Speech or Debate Clause does not mean that Rodberg is for all purposes exempt from grand jury questioning.

We are convinced also that the Court of Appeals correctly determined that Senator Gravel's alleged arrangement with Beacon Press to publish the Pentagon Papers was not protected speech or debate within the meaning of Art. I, § 6, cl. 1, of the Constitution.

Historically, the English legislative privilege was not viewed as protecting republication of an otherwise immune libel on the floor of the House. . . .

Prior cases have read the Speech or Debate Clause "broadly to effectuate its purposes," and have included within its reach anything "generally done in a session of the House by one of its members in relation to the business before it." Thus, voting by Members and committee reports are protected; and we recognize today—as the Court has recognized before—that a Member's conduct at legislative committee hearings, although subject to judicial review in various circumstances, as is legislation itself, may not be made the basis for a civil or criminal judgment against a Member because that conduct is within the "sphere of legitimate legislative activity."

But the Clause has not been extended beyond the legislative sphere. That Senators generally perform certain acts in their official capacity as Senators does not necessarily make all such acts legislative in nature. Members of Congress are constantly in touch with the Executive Branch of the Government and with administrative agencies—they may cajole, and exhort with respect to the administration of a federal statute—but such conduct, though generally done, is not protected legislative activity. . . .

Here, private publication by Senator Gravel through the cooperation of Beacon Press was in no way essential to the deliberations of the Senate; nor does questioning as to private publication threaten the integrity or independence of the Senate by impermissibly exposing its deliberations to executive influence. The Senator had conducted his hearings; the record and any report that was forthcoming were available both to his committee and the Senate. Insofar as we are advised, neither Congress nor the full committee ordered or authorized the publication. We cannot but conclude that the Senator's arrangements with Beacon Press were not part and parcel of the legislative process.[16]

There are additional considerations. Article I, § 6, cl. 1, as we have emphasized, does not purport to confer a general exemption upon Members of Congress from liability or process in criminal cases. Quite the contrary is true. While the Speech or Debate Clause recognizes speech, voting, and other legislative acts as exempt from liability that might otherwise attach, it does not privilege either Senator or aide to violate an otherwise valid criminal law in preparing for or implementing legislative acts. If republication of these classified papers would be a crime under an Act of Congress, it would not be entitled to immunity under the Speech or Debate Clause. It also appears that the grand jury was pursuing this very subject in the normal course of a valid investigation. The Speech or Debate Clause does not in our view extend immunity to Rodberg, as a Senator's aide, from testifying before the grand jury about the arrangement between Senator Gravel and Beacon Press or about his own participation, if any, in the alleged transaction, so long as legislative acts of the Senator are not impugned.

MR. JUSTICE DOUGLAS, dissenting. [omitted]

MR. JUSTICE BRENNAN, with whom MR. JUSTICE DOUGLAS, and MR. JUSTICE MARSHALL, join, dissenting.

The facts of this litigation, which are detailed by the Court, and the objections to overclassification of documents by the Executive. . . need not be repeated here. My concern is with the narrow scope accorded the Speech or Debate Clause by today's decision. I fully agree with the Court that a

---

[16] The sole constitutional claim asserted here is based on the Speech or Debate Clause. We need not address issues that may arise when Congress or either House, as distinguished from a single Member, orders the publication and/or public distribution of committee hearings, reports, or other materials. . . .

Congressman's immunity under the Clause must also be extended to his aides if it is to be at all effective. . . . The scope of that immunity, however, is as important as the persons to whom it extends. In my view, today's decision so restricts the privilege of speech or debate as to endanger the continued performance of legislative tasks that are vital to the workings of our democratic system.

In holding that Senator Gravel's alleged arrangement with Beacon Press to publish the Pentagon Papers is not shielded from extra-senatorial inquiry by the Speech or Debate Clause, the Court adopts what for me is a far too narrow view of the legislative function. The Court seems to assume that words spoken in debate or written in congressional reports are protected by the Clause, so that if Senator Gravel had recited part of the Pentagon Papers on the Senate floor or copied them into a Senate report, those acts could not be questioned "in any other Place." Yet because he sought a wider audience, to publicize information deemed relevant to matters pending before his own committee, the Senator suddenly loses his immunity and is exposed to grand jury investigation and possible prosecution for the republication. The explanation for this anomalous result is the Court's belief that "Speech or Debate" encompasses only acts necessary to the internal deliberations of Congress concerning proposed legislation. . . .

Thus, the Court excludes from the sphere of protected legislative activity a function that I had supposed lay at the heart of our democratic system. I speak, of course, of the legislator's duty to inform the public about matters affecting the administration of government. That this "informing function" falls into the class of things "generally done in a session of the House by one of its members in relation to the business before it," [has been] explicitly acknowledged by the Court. . . .

We need look no further than Congress itself to find evidence supporting the Court's observation. . . . Congress has provided financial support for communications between its Members and the public, including the franking privilege for letters, telephone and telegraph allowances, stationery allotments, and favorable prices on reprints from the Congressional Record. Congressional hearings, moreover, are not confined to gathering information for internal distribution, but are often widely publicized, sometimes televised, as a means of alerting the electorate to matters of public import and concern. . . .

Though I fully share these and related views on the educational values served by the informing function, there is yet another, and perhaps more fundamental, interest at stake. It requires no citation of authority to state that public concern over current issues—the war, race relations, governmental invasions of privacy—has transformed itself in recent years into what many believe is a crisis of confidence, in our system of government and its capacity to meet the needs and reflect the wants of the

American people. Communication between Congress and the electorate tends to alleviate that doubt by exposing and clarifying the workings of the political system, the policies underlying new laws and the role of the Executive in their administration. To the extent that the informing function succeeds in fostering public faith in the responsiveness of Government, it is not only an "ordinary" task of the legislator but one that is essential to the continued vitality of our democratic institutions.

Unlike the Court, therefore, I think that the activities of Congressmen in communicating with the public are legislative acts protected by the Speech or Debate Clause. I agree with the Court that not every task performed by a legislator is privileged; intervention before Executive departments is one that is not. But the informing function carries a far more persuasive claim to the protections of the Clause. . . . To say in the face of these facts that the informing function is not privileged merely because it is not necessary to the internal deliberations of Congress is to give the Speech or Debate Clause an artificial and narrow reading unsupported by reason. . . .

MR. JUSTICE STEWART, dissenting in part. [opinion omitted]

COMMENTS AND QUESTIONS

1.   This case gives a good sense of the judicial approach to the Speech or Debate Clause—a functional, rather than formalist view, even though there is clear text that could be used for strict line drawing. The difficulty with a functional approach is also apparent in this case, because it does not provide a clear answer where to draw the line. The majority draws the line at what happens in the context of the committee hearing, an official, congressional function, whereas three of the justices would extend protection to the private publication of information by the congressman, inasmuch as informing the public is in their view an important and recognized function of Congress, Senators, and Representatives.

2.   Ultimately, Beacon Press did publish the Pentagon Papers without legal incident. The administration determined that Daniel Ellsberg, a former Defense Department employee, had leaked the papers and prosecuted him for various criminal acts. The trial court, however, dismissed the charges because of prosecutorial misconduct—the illegal burglarizing of Ellsberg's psychiatrist's office (by the same people who later burglarized the Watergate on behalf of the Nixon reelection committee).

3.   Not all congressional acts of making information public seem as public spirited as Senator Gravel's. For example, in 1970, a special select subcommittee of the House Committee on the District of Columbia published a report critical of the District's school system. The report included some 45 pages of supporting documents, including: absentee lists identifying by name "frequent class cutters," actual test papers with student names that bore failing grades, and letters, memoranda, and other documents relating to disciplinary problems of specifically named students. The parents of the named

children sued seeking an injunction against further publication of this and other information about the students and seeking damages. The defendants to the suit included the members of the House committee; the Clerk, Staff Director, and Counsel of the Committee; a consultant and an investigator for the Committee; and the Superintendent of Documents and the Public Printer. The Court in *Doe v. McMillan*, 412 U.S. 306 (1973), held that all the congressional actors, including the consultant and investigator, were immune from suit, but that the Superintendent of Documents and Public Printer were subject to suit for the publication of the report "beyond the reasonable bounds of the legislative task." To a great extent, this seems quite consistent with *Gravel*. However, while *Gravel* found no protection for the private publishers of the Pentagon Papers, in *McMillan* the government printers found no protection under the Speech and Debate Clause even for the official publication to the public at large of the committee report, although the congressional actors and publication for legislative purposes were still protected.

4.   In *Hutchinson v. Proxmire*, 443 U.S. 111 (1979), a Senator found he had no Speech and Debate Clause protection when he personally published derogatory information about a person in press releases and constituent newsletters.

5.   A recurring issue under the Speech and Debate Clause is to what extent the government may use evidence of a Senator's or Representative's official actions in a criminal prosecution of the Senator or Representative for bribery or similar crime. For example, in *United States v. Johnson*, 383 U.S. 169 (1966), a congressman was convicted for taking money for the purpose of making a speech on the floor of the House defending certain indicted savings and loan companies, so that the companies could use the speech to reassure customers. The Court held that the use of his speech against him in the prosecution violated the Speech and Debate Clause. In *United States v. Helstoski*, 442 U.S. 477 (1979), a congressman was prosecuted for accepting bribes to introduce private bills to allow illegal aliens to remain in the United States. The Court held that the government could not introduce into evidence either the bills he introduced or any reference to them after the fact. The Court distinguished between promises to perform a legislative act (not protected) and references to a past legislative act (protected). Thus, the government may enter into evidence a tape recorded promise to introduce a bill in consideration for a bribe, but it may not introduce into evidence the fact—available in public records for all to see—that the congressman did indeed introduce the bill.

6.   Remember that even if members of Congress are protected by the Speech and Debate Clause from being questioned "in any other place," their respective houses are fully able to question and sanction members, including expulsion from the House or Senate, for speech and acts performed in their legislative capacities.

2.   EXECUTIVE PRIVILEGES AND IMMUNITIES

Unlike members of Congress, nothing in the Constitution mentions or even hints at any privilege or immunity arising out of the office of the

President. That, however, like the absence of any mention of the President's removal powers, has not stopped the Court from inferring privileges and immunities from the Constitution's text and structure.

UNITED STATES V. NIXON

United States Supreme Court, 1974.
418 U.S. 683, 94 S.Ct. 3090.

[On June 17, 1972, during the presidential campaign between incumbent President Richard Nixon and the Democratic Party nominee, George McGovern, there was a burglary at the headquarters of the National Committee of the Democratic Party, located in the Watergate apartment building in Washington, D.C. The burglars, who were attempting to install listening devices in the office to replace malfunctioning devices they had earlier installed, were caught on the scene as a result of their own incompetence. The five men were former contract personnel for the Central Intelligence Agency but were presently associated with the Committee to ReElect the President (CREEP, as it was known at the time). They implicated two others, E. Howard Hunt, Jr. and Gordon Liddy, both of whom were directly employed by CREEP. All seven were convicted of conspiracy, burglary, and violation of federal wiretapping laws. One of the seven, who felt betrayed because he was not "taken care of," wrote a letter to the sentencing judge stating that the conspiracy went much further.

This led to the appointment of a Special Prosecutor, Archibald Cox, a professor at Harvard Law School and former Solicitor General. His aggressive investigation of White House involvement in a conspiracy to obstruct justice by covering up White House involvement led to indictments of John N. Mitchell, the former Attorney General and director of CREEP; H. R. Haldeman, the White House Chief of Staff; John D. Ehrlichman, the Advisor to the President for Domestic Affairs; Charles W. Colson, Special Counsel to the President; Robert C. Mardian, Assistant Attorney General for the Internal Security Division; Kenneth W.

Archibald Cox

Parkinson, Counsel to CREEP; and Gordon Strachan, an aide to H.R. Haldeman. The grand jury named President Nixon an unindicted co-conspirator.

Revelations in congressional testimony that President Nixon had bugged the Oval Office to record the conversations there led Cox to subpoena President Nixon for copies of the tapes of those conversations in order to obtain further evidence against the indicted individuals. Nixon refused and instead ordered Attorney General Elliot Richardson to fire Cox. Richardson resigned rather than carry out the order, as did Deputy Attorney General William Ruckelshaus. This event, because it happened on a Saturday night, is known as the "Saturday Night Massacre." The next in line of succession at the Justice Department was Solicitor General Robert Bork, who carried out the order, firing Cox. The political firestorm that followed led to the appointment of a new Special Prosecutor, Leon Jaworski, a Texas lawyer who had supported Nixon in the previous election. Nevertheless, Jaworski continued the subpoena for the tapes. The President's personal counsel filed a motion to quash the subpoena on the grounds that the information sought was constitutionally privileged that the President was bound to maintain confidential. At the same time the House Judiciary Committee began hearings into the possible impeachment of the President. The district court denied the President's motion to quash and ordered the President to produce the tapes in court. The President appealed to the court of appeals, but the United States (*i.e.*, the Special Prosecutor) petitioned for certiorari directly to the Supreme Court, and the President cross-petitioned. The Court granted the petition.]

Leon Jaworski

MR. CHIEF JUSTICE BURGER delivered the opinion of the Court.

[W]e turn to the claim that the subpoena should be quashed because it demands "confidential conversations between a President and his close advisors that it would be inconsistent with the public interest to produce." The first contention is a broad claim that the separation of powers doctrine precludes judicial review of a President's claim of privilege. The second contention is that if he does not prevail on the claim of absolute privilege, the court should hold as a matter of constitutional law that the privilege prevails over the subpoena duces tecum.

In the performance of assigned constitutional duties each branch of the Government must initially interpret the Constitution, and the interpretation of its powers by any branch is due great respect from the others. The President's counsel, as we have noted, reads the Constitution as providing an absolute privilege of confidentiality for all Presidential communications. Many decisions of this Court, however, have unequivocally reaffirmed the holding of *Marbury v. Madison*, that "(i)t is emphatically the province and duty of the judicial department to say what the law is." . . .

In support of his claim of absolute privilege, the President's counsel urges two grounds, one of which is common to all governments and one of which is peculiar to our system of separation of powers. The first ground is the valid need for protection of communications between high Government officials and those who advise and assist them in the performance of their manifold duties; the importance of this confidentiality is too plain to require further discussion. Human experience teaches that those who expect public dissemination of their remarks may well temper candor with a concern for appearances and for their own interests to the detriment of the decisionmaking process.[15] Whatever the nature of the privilege of confidentiality of Presidential communications in the exercise of Art. II powers, the privilege can be said to derive from the supremacy of each branch within its own assigned area of constitutional duties. Certain powers and privileges flow from the nature of enumerated powers; the protection of the confidentiality of Presidential communications has similar constitutional underpinnings.

The second ground asserted by the President's counsel in support of the claim of absolute privilege rests on the doctrine of separation of powers. Here it is argued that the independence of the Executive Branch within its own sphere insulates a President from a judicial subpoena in an ongoing criminal prosecution, and thereby protects confidential Presidential communications.

However, neither the doctrine of separation of powers, nor the need for confidentiality of high-level communications, without more, can sustain an absolute, unqualified Presidential privilege of immunity from judicial process under all circumstances. The President's need for complete candor and objectivity from advisers calls for great deference from the courts. However, when the privilege depends solely on the broad, undifferentiated claim of public interest in the confidentiality of such conversations, a confrontation with other values arises. Absent a claim of need to protect military, diplomatic, or sensitive national security secrets, we find it difficult to accept the argument that even the very important interest in confidentiality of Presidential communications is significantly diminished by production of such material for in camera inspection with all the protection that a district court will be obliged to provide.

The impediment that an absolute, unqualified privilege would place in the way of the primary constitutional duty of the Judicial Branch to do

---

[15] There is nothing novel about governmental confidentiality. The meetings of the Constitutional Convention in 1787 were conducted in complete privacy. Moreover, all records of those meetings were sealed for more than 30 years after the Convention. Most of the Framers acknowledge that without secrecy no constitution of the kind that was developed could have been written.

justice in criminal prosecutions would plainly conflict with the function of the courts under Art. III. . . .

To read the Art. II powers of the President as providing an absolute privilege as against a subpoena essential to enforcement of criminal statutes on no more than a generalized claim of the public interest in confidentiality of nonmilitary and nondiplomatic discussions would upset the constitutional balance of "a workable government" and gravely impair the role of the courts under Art. III.

Since we conclude that the legitimate needs of the judicial process may outweigh Presidential privilege, it is necessary to resolve those competing interests in a manner that preserves the essential functions of each branch. . . .

The expectation of a President to the confidentiality of his conversations and correspondence, like the claim of confidentiality of judicial deliberations, for example, has all the values to which we accord deference for the privacy of all citizens and, added to those values, is the necessity for protection of the public interest in candid, objective, and even blunt or harsh opinions in Presidential decisionmaking. A President and those who assist him must be free to explore alternatives in the process of shaping policies and making decisions and to do so in a way many would be unwilling to express except privately. These are the considerations justifying a presumptive privilege for Presidential communications. The privilege is fundamental to the operation of Government and inextricably rooted in the separation of powers under the Constitution. . . .

But this presumptive privilege must be considered in light of our historic commitment to the rule of law. This is nowhere more profoundly manifest than in our view that "the twofold aim (of criminal justice) is that guilt shall not escape or innocence suffer." We have elected to employ an adversary system of criminal justice in which the parties contest all issues before a court of law. The need to develop all relevant facts in the adversary system is both fundamental and comprehensive. The ends of criminal justice would be defeated if judgments were to be founded on a partial or speculative presentation of the facts. The very integrity of the judicial system and public confidence in the system depend on full disclosure of all the facts, within the framework of the rules of evidence. To ensure that justice is done, it is imperative to the function of courts that compulsory process be available for the production of evidence needed either by the prosecution or by the defense.

Only recently the Court restated the ancient proposition of law, albeit in the context of a grand jury inquiry rather than a trial, "that 'the public . . . has a right to every man's evidence,' except for those persons protected by a constitutional, common-law, or statutory privilege."

The privileges referred to by the Court are designed to protect weighty and legitimate competing interests. . . . Whatever their origins, these exceptions to the demand for every man's evidence are not lightly created nor expansively construed, for they are in derogation of the search for truth.

In this case the President challenges a subpoena served on him as a third party requiring the production of materials for use in a criminal prosecution; he does so on the claim that he has a privilege against disclosure of confidential communications. He does not place his claim of privilege on the ground they are military or diplomatic secrets. As to these areas of Art. II duties the courts have traditionally shown the utmost deference to Presidential responsibilities. . . .

No case of the Court, however, has extended this high degree of deference to a President's generalized interest in confidentiality. Nowhere in the Constitution . . . is there any explicit reference to a privilege of confidentiality, yet to the extent this interest relates to the effective discharge of a President's powers, it is constitutionally based.

The right to the production of all evidence at a criminal trial similarly has constitutional dimensions. The Sixth Amendment explicitly confers upon every defendant in a criminal trial the right "to be confronted with the witnesses against him" and "to have compulsory process for obtaining witnesses in his favor." Moreover, the Fifth Amendment also guarantees that no person shall be deprived of liberty without due process of law. It is the manifest duty of the courts to vindicate those guarantees, and to accomplish that it is essential that all relevant and admissible evidence be produced.

In this case we must weigh the importance of the general privilege of confidentiality of Presidential communications in performance of the President's responsibilities against the inroads of such a privilege on the fair administration of criminal justice.[19] The interest in preserving confidentiality is weighty indeed and entitled to great respect. However, we cannot conclude that advisers will be moved to temper the candor of their remarks by the infrequent occasions of disclosure because of the possibility that such conversations will be called for in the context of a criminal prosecution.

On the other hand, the allowance of the privilege to withhold evidence that is demonstrably relevant in a criminal trial would cut deeply into the guarantee of due process of law and gravely impair the basic function of

---

[19] We are not here concerned with the balance between the President's generalized interest in confidentiality and the need for relevant evidence in civil litigation, nor with that between the confidentiality interest and congressional demands for information, nor with the President's interest in preserving state secrets. We address only the conflict between the President's assertion of a generalized privilege of confidentiality and the constitutional need for relevant evidence in criminal trials.

the courts. A President's acknowledged need for confidentiality in the communications of his office is general in nature, whereas the constitutional need for production of relevant evidence in a criminal proceeding is specific and central to the fair adjudication of a particular criminal case in the administration of justice. . . .

We conclude that when the ground for asserting privilege as to subpoenaed materials sought for use in a criminal trial is based only on the generalized interest in confidentiality, it cannot prevail over the fundamental demands of due process of law in the fair administration of criminal justice. The generalized assertion of privilege must yield to the demonstrated, specific need for evidence in a pending criminal trial.

[I]f a President concludes that compliance with a subpoena would be injurious to the public interest he may properly, as was done here, invoke a claim of privilege on the return of the subpoena. Upon receiving a claim of privilege from the Chief Executive, it became the further duty of the District Court to treat the subpoenaed material as presumptively privileged and to require the Special Prosecutor to demonstrate that the Presidential material was "essential to the justice of the (pending criminal) case." Here the District Court treated the material as presumptively privileged, proceeded to find that the Special Prosecutor had made a sufficient showing to rebut the presumption, and ordered an in camera examination of the subpoenaed material. On the basis of our examination of the record we are unable to conclude that the District Court erred in ordering the inspection. Accordingly we affirm the order of the District Court that subpoenaed materials be transmitted to that court. We now turn to the important question of the District Court's responsibilities in conducting the in camera examination of Presidential materials or communications delivered under the compulsion of the subpoena duces tecum.

[S]tatements that meet the test of admissibility and relevance must be isolated; all other material must be excised. . . . It is elementary that in camera inspection of evidence is always a procedure calling for scrupulous protection against any release or publication of material not found by the court, at that stage, probably admissible in evidence and relevant to the issues of the trial for which it is sought. . . .

MR. JUSTICE REHNQUIST took no part in the consideration or decision of these cases.

COMMENTS AND QUESTIONS

1. Prior to the Court's opinion there was some question whether President Nixon would comply with an adverse decision, especially if it was a split decision. Apparently the Court felt some need to have a unanimous opinion, and it was rendered in some haste given the unfolding political events. The President did comply with the Court's decision, and information on the

tapes confirming Nixon's complicity in the cover up, as well as an unexplained 18 minute gap where the tapes had been mysteriously erased, made impeachment a certainty and a conviction in the Senate a near certainty. As a result, President Nixon resigned two and a half weeks after the Court's decision.

2.   On what basis does the Court find a constitutionally based executive privilege? How is the privilege for confidential advice different from an executive privilege based on national security secrets?

3.   Inasmuch as the President loses the case, what does it mean that the Court found an executive privilege? What good is it?

4.   What does the Court mean by the "constitutional duty of the Judicial Branch to do justice in criminal prosecutions"? Reliable, probative evidence is inadmissible in criminal prosecutions for a variety of reasons. Would a prosecutor have a right to obtain common-law privileged information, such as attorney-client, doctor-patient, priest-penitent, or husband-wife communications? If these common law privileges are "absolute," why is the President's constitutionally based privilege only a "qualified" privilege?

5.   Would the Court's analysis be any different if it were a local prosecutor investigating a local crime?

6.   A case should always be viewed in light of its historical circumstances, and *Nixon* is a good example of how a case might be driven more by those circumstances than by legal logic. Hopefully, a similar circumstance will not arise again. However, executive privilege issues arise with some frequency with respect to congressional demands for information. Recall that the event that triggered the appointment of the independent counsel in *Morrison v. Olson*: an invocation of executive privilege with regard to subpoenas from House subcommittees by the Administrator of the Environmental Protection Agency on the legal advice of the Olson, the Assistant Attorney General for the Office of Legal Counsel in the Justice Department.

7.   In George W. Bush's administration, the House Judiciary Committee subpoenaed certain testimony and information from executive branch officials regarding the highly publicized firing of several U.S. Attorneys, allegedly for political reasons. The President invoked executive privilege, instructing those subject to the subpoenas to ignore them. As a result, in 2008 the House voted contempt against the persons to whom the subpoenas were directed and forwarded the contempt citations to the U.S. Attorney for the District of Columbia for prosecution under the contempt of Congress criminal provisions, 2 U.S.C. §§ 192, 194. The Attorney General then directed the U.S. Attorney not to prosecute, stating "that the contempt of Congress statute was not intended to apply and could not constitutionally be applied to an Executive Branch official who asserts the President's claim of executive privilege." Consequently, the House filed a civil suit against the persons to whom the subpoenas were directed, seeking a judicial resolution of the validity of the claim of executive privilege. Before any decision was rendered, the House withdrew its complaint

in light of substantial (but not complete) compliance by the executive. Historically, courts have been very reluctant to decide these disputes between the executive and legislative branches, finding various excuses to avoid decision. As a result no court has yet ruled on the power of the President to invoke executive privilege with regard to a congressional investigation. Is this a "political question"?

8.   President Barack Obama invoked executive privilege with respect to many thousands of pages of Justice Department documents subpoenaed by the Republican-controlled House Committee on Oversight and Government Reform regarding the so-called Operation Fast and Furious, in which the government allowed illegally purchased firearms to be exported to Mexican drug cartels. In response, the House voted contempt against Attorney General Eric Holder.

9.   Two separate cases in 2020 involved subpoenas for President Trump's tax records. In *Trump v. Vance*, 140 S.Ct. 2412, the New York County District Attorney on behalf of a grand jury investigating business transactions possibly involving violations of state law served a subpoena on the President's personal accounting firm. In *Trump v. Mazars USA*, 140 S.Ct. 2019, three committees of the House of Representatives issued subpoenas for financial records related to the President both to the President's accounting firm as well as to banks with which the President had done business. The justification for the subpoenas was to determine whether new legislation was necessary. Chief Justice Roberts wrote for the Court in both cases. In *Vance*, the Court began by describing the uninterrupted history since 1807 of Presidents complying with subpoenas in *federal* criminal cases. The question was whether there should be a different rule or standard for subpoenas in state criminal cases. The Court said that the President was neither absolutely immune nor entitled to a heightened standard, but that under Article II the President may raise the claim that a subpoena would impede his constitutional duties. The case was remanded to the district court, where the President could raise such a claim, although the suggestion was that in this case—a subpoena for personal documents in the control of someone else—the claim would fail. In *Trump v. Mazars*, the Court said that this was a case of first impression. A subpoena by a congressional committee in support of broad legislative objectives was different from a subpoena in connection with a particular judicial proceeding. The Court noted that historically demands from Congress for information from the President "have been hashed out in the 'hurly-burly, the give-and-take of the political process between the legislative and the executive'." The Court has long recognized a constitutionally-based authority for Congress to obtain information, including by subpoena, in order to inform its legislative powers. Nevertheless, a congressional subpoena "is valid only if it is 'related to, and in furtherance of, a legitimate task of the Congress.'" Moreover, if the subpoena were for presidential documents that were arguably privileged as executive privileged or as state secrets, a heightened standard would apply. Here, however, the documents sought were not privileged. Nevertheless, the Court concluded that in light of separation of powers concerns courts must "perform a careful analysis" that takes accounts of the interests of both branches of

government. First, "courts must carefully assess whether the asserted legislative purpose warrants the significant step of involving the President and his papers" Second, courts should insist that the subpoena is "no broader than reasonably necessary to support Congress's legislative objective." Third, courts should "be attentive to the nature of the evidence offered by Congress to establish that a subpoena advances a valid legislative purpose." Fourth, courts should be "careful to assess the burdens imposed on the President" by the subpoena. Again, the case was remanded for the lower courts to engage in this careful analysis.

10.   As this is edition is being written, there are ongoing judicial cases in which former President Trump is attempting to claim executive privilege as a way of retaining and not disclosing documents from his administration. The Supreme Court has never addressed whether a former President can invoke executive privilege over the objection of the sitting President. What do you think?

NIXON V. FITZGERALD
United States Supreme Court, 1982.
457 U.S. 731, 102 S.Ct. 2690.

[In 1970, A. Ernest Fitzgerald lost his job as a management analyst with the Department of the Air Force pursuant to an alleged reduction in force. Because he had recently exposed embarrassing cost-overruns on a major Air Force contract, including testifying before a Senate committee on the subject, there was general speculation that he had instead been terminated in retaliation for causing the administration embarrassment. He sought review of his termination by the Civil Service Commission. After hearing over 4,000 pages of testimony, the Chief Examiner for the Civil Service Commission issued his decision in 1973, finding that Fitzgerald's dismissal had offended applicable civil service regulations. Following the Commission's order, respondent ultimately was reassigned to his former position, but Fitzgerald also filed a suit for damages in the United States District Court, alleging a continuing conspiracy to deprive him of his job, to deny him reemployment, and to besmirch his reputation. This suit was dismissed because of a 3-year statute of limitations, but on appeal the court held that the statute had not run as to one of the several original defendants. After remand and extensive discovery, Fitzgerald filed a second amended complaint in 1978. In this complaint he included as a defendant former President Nixon, who sought dismissal on the grounds that he was absolutely immune from suit for actions taken in his official capacity as President. The trial court rejected the immunity claim, and its decision was affirmed by the court of appeals.]

JUSTICE POWELL delivered the opinion of the Court.

[A]s this Court has not ruled on the scope of immunity available to a President of the United States, we granted certiorari to decide this important issue. . . .

This Court consistently has recognized that government officials are entitled to some form of immunity from suits for civil damages. . . .

In *Scheuer v. Rhodes*, 416 U.S. 232 (1974), the Court considered the immunity available to state executive officials in a § 1983 suit alleging the violation of constitutional rights. In that case we rejected the officials' claim to absolute immunity . . ., finding instead that state executive officials possessed a good faith immunity from § 1983 suits alleging constitutional violations.* Balancing the purposes of § 1983 against the imperatives of public policy, the Court held that in varying scope, a qualified immunity is available to officers of the executive branch of government, the variation being dependent upon the scope of discretion and responsibilities of the office and all the circumstances as they reasonably appeared at the time of the action on which liability is sought to be based.

As construed by subsequent cases, *Scheuer* established a two-tiered division of immunity defenses in § 1983 suits. To most executive officers *Scheuer* accorded qualified immunity. For them the scope of the defense varied in proportion to the nature of their official functions and the range of decisions that conceivably might be taken in good faith. This functional approach also defined a second tier, however, at which the especially sensitive duties of certain officials—notably judges and prosecutors— required the continued recognition of absolute immunity.

This approach was reviewed in detail in *Butz v. Economou*, 438 U.S. 478 (1978), when we considered for the first time the kind of immunity possessed by *federal* executive officials who are sued for constitutional violations. In *Butz* the Court rejected an argument, based on decisions involving federal officials charged with common-law torts, that all high federal officials have a right to absolute immunity from constitutional damages actions. Concluding that a blanket recognition of absolute immunity would be anomalous in light of the qualified immunity standard applied to state executive officials, we held that federal officials generally have the same qualified immunity possessed by state officials in cases under § 1983. In so doing we reaffirmed our holdings that some officials, notably judges and prosecutors, because of the special nature of their responsibilities, require a full exemption from liability. . . .

This case now presents the claim that the President of the United States is shielded by absolute immunity from civil damages liability. . . .

---

*   42 U.S.C. § 1983 provides a private right of action for injunctive relief or damages against any person acting under color of law to deprive a person of their rights under the Constitution or any federal law. [author's note]

Here a former President asserts his immunity from civil damages claims of two kinds. He stands named as a defendant in a direct action under the Constitution and in two statutory actions under federal laws of general applicability. In neither case has Congress taken express legislative action to subject the President to civil liability for his official acts.[27]

Applying the principles of our cases to claims of this kind, we hold that petitioner, as a former President of the United States, is entitled to absolute immunity from damages liability predicated on his official acts. We consider this immunity a functionally mandated incident of the President's unique office, rooted in the constitutional tradition of the separation of powers and supported by our history. . . .

The President occupies a unique position in the constitutional scheme. [T]he President [is] the chief constitutional officer of the Executive Branch, entrusted with supervisory and policy responsibilities of utmost discretion and sensitivity. These include the enforcement of federal law . . .; the conduct of foreign affairs . . .; and management of the Executive Branch. . . .

In arguing that the President is entitled only to qualified immunity, the respondent relies on cases in which we have recognized immunity of this scope for governors and cabinet officers. We find these cases to be inapposite. The President's unique status under the Constitution distinguishes him from other executive officials.[31]

Because of the singular importance of the President's duties, diversion of his energies by concern with private lawsuits would raise unique risks to the effective functioning of government. As is the case with prosecutors and judges—for whom absolute immunity now is established—a President must concern himself with matters likely to arouse the most intense feelings. Yet, as our decisions have recognized, it is in precisely such cases that there exists the greatest public interest in providing an official the maximum ability to deal fearlessly and impartially with the duties of his office. This concern is compelling where the officeholder must make the most sensitive and far-reaching decisions entrusted to any official under our constitutional system.[32] Nor can the sheer prominence of the President's office be ignored. In view of the visibility of his office and the effect of his actions on countless people, the President would be an easily

---

[27] In the present case we therefore are presented only with implied causes of action, and we need not address directly the immunity question as it would arise if Congress expressly had created a damages action against the President of the United States. . . .

[31] Noting that the Speech and Debate Clause provides a textual basis for congressional immunity, respondent argues that the Framers must be assumed to have rejected any similar grant of executive immunity. This argument is unpersuasive. First, a specific textual basis has not been considered a prerequisite to the recognition of immunity. No provision expressly confers judicial immunity. Yet the immunity of judges is well settled. . . .

[32] Among the most persuasive reasons supporting official immunity is the prospect that damages liability may render an official unduly cautious in the discharge of his official duties. . . .

identifiable target for suits for civil damages. Cognizance of this personal vulnerability frequently could distract a President from his public duties, to the detriment of not only the President and his office but also the Nation that the Presidency was designed to serve. . . .

In defining the scope of an official's absolute privilege, this Court has recognized that the sphere of protected action must be related closely to the immunity's justifying purposes. Frequently our decisions have held that an official's absolute immunity should extend only to acts in performance of particular functions of his office. But the Court also has refused to draw functional lines finer than history and reason would support. In view of the special nature of the President's constitutional office and functions, we think it appropriate to recognize absolute Presidential immunity from damages liability for acts within the outer perimeter of his official responsibility. . . .

A rule of absolute immunity for the President will not leave the Nation without sufficient protection against misconduct on the part of the Chief Executive. There remains the constitutional remedy of impeachment. In addition, there are formal and informal checks on Presidential action that do not apply with equal force to other executive officials. The President is subjected to constant scrutiny by the press. Vigilant oversight by Congress also may serve to deter Presidential abuses of office, as well as to make credible the threat of impeachment. Other incentives to avoid misconduct may include a desire to earn reelection, the need to maintain prestige as an element of Presidential influence, and a President's traditional concern for his historical stature.

The existence of alternative remedies and deterrents establishes that absolute immunity will not place the President above the law. For the President, as for judges and prosecutors, absolute immunity merely precludes a particular private remedy for alleged misconduct in order to advance compelling public ends.

CHIEF JUSTICE BURGER, concurring. [opinion omitted]

JUSTICE WHITE, with whom JUSTICE BRENNAN, JUSTICE MARSHALL, and JUSTICE BLACKMUN join, dissenting.

The four dissenting Members of the Court in *Butz v. Economou* argued that all federal officials are entitled to absolute immunity from suit for any action they take in connection with their official duties. That immunity would extend even to actions taken with express knowledge that the conduct was clearly contrary to the controlling statute or clearly violative of the Constitution. Fortunately, the majority of the Court rejected that approach: We held that although public officials perform certain functions that entitle them to absolute immunity, the immunity attaches to particular functions—not to particular offices. Officials performing functions for which immunity is not absolute enjoy qualified immunity;

they are liable in damages only if their conduct violated well-established law and if they should have realized that their conduct was illegal.

The Court now applies the dissenting view in *Butz* to the Office of the President: A President, acting within the outer boundaries of what Presidents normally do, may, without liability, deliberately cause serious injury to any number of citizens even though he knows his conduct violates a statute or tramples on the constitutional rights of those who are injured. Even if the President in this case ordered Fitzgerald fired by means of a trumped-up reduction in force, knowing that such a discharge was contrary to the civil service laws, he would be absolutely immune from suit. By the same token, if a President, without following the statutory procedures which he knows apply to himself as well as to other federal officials, orders his subordinates to wiretap or break into a home for the purpose of installing a listening device, and the officers comply with his request, the President would be absolutely immune from suit. He would be immune regardless of the damage he inflicts, regardless of how violative of the statute and of the Constitution he knew his conduct to be, and regardless of his purpose.[1]

The Court intimates that its decision is grounded in the Constitution. If that is the case, Congress cannot provide a remedy against Presidential misconduct and the criminal laws of the United States are wholly inapplicable to the President. I find this approach completely unacceptable. I do not agree that if the Office of President is to operate effectively, the holder of that Office must be permitted, without fear of liability and regardless of the function he is performing, deliberately to inflict injury on others by conduct that he knows violates the law. . . .

Attaching absolute immunity to the Office of the President, rather than to particular activities that the President might perform, places the President above the law. It is a reversion to the old notion that the King can do no wrong. Until now, this concept had survived in this country only in the form of sovereign immunity. . . . Now, however, the Court clothes the Office of the President with sovereign immunity, placing it beyond the law. . . .

The functional approach to the separation-of-powers doctrine and the Court's more recent immunity decisions converge on the following principle: The scope of immunity is determined by function, not office. The wholesale claim that the President is entitled to absolute immunity in all of his actions stands on no firmer ground than did the claim that all Presidential communications are entitled to an absolute privilege, which was rejected in favor of a functional analysis, by a unanimous Court in *United States v. Nixon*. Therefore, whatever may be true of the necessity of

---

[1] This, of course, is not simply a hypothetical example. *See Halperin v. Kissinger*, 606 F.2d 1192 (1979), *aff'd by an equally divided Court*, 452 U.S. 713 (1981).

such a broad immunity in certain areas of executive responsibility,[30] the only question that must be answered here is whether the dismissal of employees falls within a constitutionally assigned executive function, the performance of which would be substantially impaired by the possibility of a private action for damages. I believe it does not.

JUSTICE BLACKMUN, with whom JUSTICE BRENNAN and JUSTICE MARSHALL join, dissenting. [opinion omitted]

COMMENTS AND QUESTIONS

1.   The dispute in this case is whether the President should enjoy absolute immunity for his official acts, as found by the five member majority, or only qualified immunity, as argued by the four person dissent. Absolute immunity means what it sounds like; any suit filed against the President for an "official act," broadly construed, will be subject to a motion to dismiss. Judges and prosecutors, as the Court notes, enjoy absolute immunity for their official acts. Qualified immunity, which is what most executive officials in state and federal government enjoy, means that they enjoy immunity if their conduct "does not violate clearly established statutory or constitutional rights of which a reasonable person would have known." *Harlow v. Fitzgerald*, 457 U.S. 800, 818 (1982). The *Harlow* case was a companion case to *Nixon v. Fitzgerald*. Harlow was an adviser to the President and was sued by Fitzgerald as being involved in the conspiracy to fire him in violation of the Civil Service Laws as well as the Constitution.

2.   In setting this standard for qualified immunity, the Court balanced the need to vindicate the violation of a person's individual rights against the need to avoid requiring government officials to go to trial on insubstantial claims. Accordingly, the Court altered the prior standard for establishing qualified immunity, which included a subjective, "good faith" element, which almost necessarily called for a trial on that issue, with what it said was a wholly objective standard—the reasonable person standard. The problem with even this "objective" standard for qualified immunity is that it often cannot be determined what the official actually did—a necessary precondition to deciding if he violated a clearly established right—before there has been substantial discovery or even a trial. For example, in the *Harlow* case, Harlow denied that he had any role whatsoever in Fitzgerald's firing, but that is a factual question, not a legal question. Fitzgerald alleged that Harlow had been involved in firing him in retaliation for providing Congress with truthful information simply because that information was embarrassing to the administration, and that firing a protected civil servant for such a reason was clearly unlawful. Such an allegation would survive the motion to dismiss, because in a motion to dismiss the alleged facts are presumed to be true. Consequently, there would have to be discovery to determine whether there was any basis to the allegations. Indeed, in the *Harlow* case, discovery went on for eight years, at which point

---

[30]   I will not speculate on the Presidential functions which may require absolute immunity, but a clear example would be instances in which the President participates in prosecutorial decisions.

the trial court found that there were disputed facts that would need to go to trial. In short, the qualified immunity standard is not very successful at "permit[ting] the defeat of insubstantial claims without resort to trial," one of the goals that the Court sought to achieve.

3. What is it about the Presidency that leads the Court to grant the President absolute immunity, unlike other executive officers? Should it be a relevant consideration that Nixon was no longer President when he was sued?

4. What kind of immunity do you think the Vice President should enjoy? Vice President Cheney was sued by Valerie Plame, a Central Intelligence Agency employee allegedly outed by the administration to discredit a report undermining the administration's claim that Iraq was developing nuclear weapons. The case was dismissed on other grounds.

CLINTON V. JONES

United States Supreme Court, 1997.
520 U.S. 681, 117 S.Ct. 1636.

JUSTICE STEVENS delivered the opinion of the Court.

This case raises a constitutional and a prudential question concerning the Office of the President of the United States. Respondent, a private citizen, seeks to recover damages from the current occupant of that office based on actions allegedly taken before his term began. The President submits that in all but the most exceptional cases the Constitution requires federal courts to defer such litigation until his term ends and that, in any event, respect for the office warrants such a stay. Despite the force of the arguments supporting the President's submissions, we conclude that they must be rejected.

Petitioner, William Jefferson Clinton, was elected to the Presidency in 1992, and re-elected in 1996. His term of office expires on January 20, 2001. In 1991 he was the Governor of the State of Arkansas. Respondent, Paula Corbin Jones, is a resident of California. In 1991 she lived in Arkansas, and was an employee of the Arkansas Industrial Development Commission.

On May 6, 1994, she commenced this action in the United States District Court for the Eastern District of Arkansas by filing a complaint naming petitioner and Danny Ferguson, a former Arkansas State Police officer, as defendants. The complaint alleges two federal claims, and two state-law claims over which the federal court has jurisdiction because of the diverse citizenship of the parties. As the case comes to us, we are required to assume the truth of the detailed—but as yet untested—factual allegations in the complaint.

Those allegations principally describe events that are said to have occurred on the afternoon of May 8, 1991, during an official conference held at the Excelsior Hotel in Little Rock, Arkansas. The Governor delivered a speech at the conference; respondent—working as a state employee—

staffed the registration desk. She alleges that Ferguson persuaded her to leave her desk and to visit the Governor in a business suite at the hotel, where he made abhorrent sexual advances that she vehemently rejected. She further claims that her superiors at work subsequently dealt with her in a hostile and rude manner, and changed her duties to punish her for rejecting those advances. Finally, she alleges that after petitioner was elected President, Ferguson defamed her by making a statement to a reporter that implied she had accepted petitioner's alleged overtures, and that various persons authorized to speak for the President publicly branded her a liar by denying that the incident had occurred.

Respondent seeks actual damages of $75,000 and punitive damages of $100,000. . . . [I]t is perfectly clear that the alleged misconduct of petitioner was unrelated to any of his official duties as President of the United States and, indeed, occurred before he was elected to that office.

In response to the complaint, petitioner . . . filed a motion to dismiss . . . without prejudice and to toll any statutes of limitation [that may be applicable] until he is no longer President, at which time the plaintiff may refile the instant suit. . . .

The District Judge denied the motion to dismiss on immunity grounds and ruled that discovery in the case could go forward, but ordered any trial stayed until the end of petitioner's Presidency. . . .

Both parties appealed. A divided panel of the Court of Appeals affirmed the denial of the motion to dismiss, but because it regarded the order postponing the trial until the President leaves office as the functional equivalent of a grant of temporary immunity, it reversed that order. . . .

The President, represented by private counsel, filed a petition for certiorari. The Acting Solicitor General, representing the United States, supported the petition, arguing that the decision of the Court of Appeals was fundamentally mistaken and created serious risks for the institution of the Presidency. . . .

[It is] appropriate to identify two important constitutional issues not encompassed within the questions presented by the petition for certiorari that we need not address today.

First, because the claim of immunity is asserted in a federal court and relies heavily on the doctrine of separation of powers that restrains each of the three branches of the Federal Government from encroaching on the domain of the other two, it is not necessary to consider or decide whether a comparable claim might succeed in a state tribunal. If this case were being heard in a state forum, instead of advancing a separation-of-powers argument, petitioner would presumably rely on federalism and comity concerns, as well as the interest in protecting federal officials from possible local prejudice that underlies the authority to remove certain cases brought against federal officers from a state to a federal court. Whether those concerns would present a more compelling case for immunity is a question that is not before us.

Second, our decision rejecting the immunity claim and allowing the case to proceed does not require us to confront the question whether a court may compel the attendance of the President at any specific time or place. We assume that the testimony of the President, both for discovery and for use at trial, may be taken at the White House at a time that will accommodate his busy schedule, and that, if a trial is held, there would be no necessity for the President to attend in person, though he could elect to do so.[14]

Petitioner's principal submission—that in all but the most exceptional cases, the Constitution affords the President temporary immunity from civil damages litigation arising out of events that occurred before he took office—cannot be sustained on the basis of precedent.

Only three sitting Presidents have been defendants in civil litigation involving their actions prior to taking office. Complaints against Theodore Roosevelt and Harry Truman had been dismissed before they took office; the dismissals were affirmed after their respective inaugurations. Two companion cases arising out of an automobile accident were filed against John F. Kennedy in 1960 during the Presidential campaign. After taking office, he unsuccessfully argued that his status as Commander in Chief gave him a right to a stay under the Soldiers' and Sailors' Civil Relief Act of 1940. The motion for a stay was denied by the District Court, and the matter was settled out of court. Thus, none of those cases sheds any light on the constitutional issue before us.

The principal rationale for affording certain public servants immunity from suits for money damages arising out of their official acts is inapplicable to unofficial conduct. In cases involving prosecutors, legislators, and judges we have repeatedly explained that the immunity serves the public interest in enabling such officials to perform their designated functions effectively without fear that a particular decision may give rise to personal liability.

That rationale provided the principal basis for our holding that a former President of the United States was entitled to absolute immunity from damages liability predicated on his official acts, *Nixon v. Fitzgerald.* Our central concern was to avoid rendering the President unduly cautious in the discharge of his official duties.[19]

---

[14] Although Presidents have responded to written interrogatories, given depositions, and provided videotaped trial testimony, no sitting President has ever testified, or been ordered to testify, in open court.

[19] Petitioner draws our attention to dicta in *Fitzgerald*, which he suggests are helpful to his cause. We noted there that [b]ecause of the singular importance of the President's duties, diversion of his energies by concern with private lawsuits would raise unique risks to the effective functioning of government, and suggested further that [c]ognizance of . . . personal vulnerability frequently could distract a President from his public duties. Petitioner argues that in this aspect

This reasoning provides no support for an immunity for *unofficial* conduct. As we explained in *Fitzgerald,* the sphere of protected action must be related closely to the immunity's justifying purposes. Because of the President's broad responsibilities, we recognized in that case an immunity from damages claims arising out of official acts extending to the outer perimeter of his authority. But we have never suggested that the President, or any other official, has an immunity that extends beyond the scope of any action taken in an official capacity. . . .

Petitioner's effort to construct an immunity from suit for unofficial acts grounded purely in the identity of his office is unsupported by precedent.

We are also unpersuaded by the evidence from the historical record to which petitioner has called our attention. . . . Respondent, in turn, has called our attention to conflicting historical evidence. . . .

In the end, as applied to the particular question before us, we reach the same conclusion about these historical materials that Justice Jackson described when confronted with an issue concerning the dimensions of the President's power. . . . They largely cancel each other.

Petitioner's strongest argument supporting his immunity claim is based on the text and structure of the Constitution. He does not contend that the occupant of the Office of the President is above the law, in the sense that his conduct is entirely immune from judicial scrutiny. The President argues merely for a postponement of the judicial proceedings that will determine whether he violated any law. His argument is grounded in the character of the office that was created by Article II of the Constitution, and relies on separation-of-powers principles that have structured our constitutional arrangement since the founding.

As a starting premise, petitioner contends that he occupies a unique office with powers and responsibilities so vast and important that the public interest demands that he devote his undivided time and attention to his public duties. He submits that—given the nature of the office—the doctrine of separation of powers places limits on the authority of the Federal Judiciary to interfere with the Executive Branch that would be transgressed by allowing this action to proceed.

We have no dispute with the initial premise of the argument. . . .

It does not follow, however, that separation-of-powers principles would be violated by allowing this action to proceed. . . . The litigation of questions that relate entirely to the unofficial conduct of the individual who happens

the Court's concern was parallel to the issue he suggests is of great importance in this case, the possibility that a sitting President might be distracted by the need to participate in litigation during the pendency of his office. In context, however, it is clear that our dominant concern was with the diversion of the President's attention during the decisionmaking process caused by needless worry as to the possibility of damages actions stemming from any particular official decision. Moreover, *Fitzgerald* did not present the issue raised in this case because that decision involved claims against a former President.

to be the President poses no perceptible risk of misallocation of either judicial power or executive power.

Rather than arguing that the decision of the case will produce either an aggrandizement of judicial power or a narrowing of executive power, petitioner contends that—as a byproduct of an otherwise traditional exercise of judicial power—burdens will be placed on the President that will hamper the performance of his official duties. We have recognized that [e]ven when a branch does not arrogate power to itself . . . the separation-of-powers doctrine requires that a branch not impair another in the performance of its constitutional duties. As a factual matter, petitioner contends that this particular case—as well as the potential additional litigation that an affirmance of the Court of Appeals judgment might spawn—may impose an unacceptable burden on the President's time and energy, and thereby impair the effective performance of his office.

Petitioner's predictive judgment finds little support in either history or the relatively narrow compass of the issues raised in this particular case. As we have already noted, in the more than 200-year history of the Republic, only three sitting Presidents have been subjected to suits for their private actions. If the past is any indicator, it seems unlikely that a deluge of such litigation will ever engulf the Presidency. As for the case at hand, if properly managed by the District Court, it appears to us highly unlikely to occupy any substantial amount of petitioner's time.

Of greater significance, petitioner errs by presuming that interactions between the Judicial Branch and the Executive, even quite burdensome interactions, necessarily rise to the level of constitutionally forbidden impairment of the Executive's ability to perform its constitutionally mandated functions. The fact that a federal court's exercise of its traditional Article III jurisdiction may significantly burden the time and attention of the Chief Executive is not sufficient to establish a violation of the Constitution. Two long-settled propositions, first announced by Chief Justice Marshall, support that conclusion.

First, we have long held that when the President takes official action, the Court has the authority to determine whether he has acted within the law. . . .

Second, it is also settled that the President is subject to judicial process in appropriate circumstances. Although Thomas Jefferson apparently thought otherwise, Chief Justice Marshall, when presiding in the treason trial of Aaron Burr, ruled that a subpoena *duces tecum* could be directed to the President. We unequivocally and emphatically endorsed Marshall's position when we held that President Nixon was obligated to comply with a subpoena commanding him to produce certain tape recordings of his conversations with his aides.

Sitting Presidents have responded to court orders to provide testimony and other information with sufficient frequency that such interactions between the Judicial and Executive Branches can scarcely be thought a novelty. President Ford complied with an order to give a deposition in a criminal trial, and President Clinton has twice given videotaped testimony in criminal proceedings. Moreover, sitting Presidents have also voluntarily complied with judicial requests for testimony. President Grant gave a lengthy deposition in a criminal case under such circumstances, and President Carter similarly gave videotaped testimony for use at a criminal trial.

In sum, [i]t is settled law that the separation-of-powers doctrine does not bar every exercise of jurisdiction over the President of the United States. If the Judiciary may severely burden the Executive Branch by reviewing the legality of the President's official conduct, and if it may direct appropriate process to the President himself, it must follow that the federal courts have power to determine the legality of his unofficial conduct. The burden on the President's time and energy that is a mere byproduct of such review surely cannot be considered as onerous as the direct burden imposed by judicial review and the occasional invalidation of his official actions.[40] We therefore hold that the doctrine of separation of powers does not require federal courts to stay all private actions against the President until he leaves office.

[W]e turn to the question whether the District Court's decision to stay the trial until after petitioner leaves office was an abuse of discretion. . . .

Strictly speaking the stay was not the functional equivalent of the constitutional immunity that petitioner claimed, because the District Court ordered discovery to proceed. Moreover, a stay of either the trial or discovery might be justified by considerations that do not require the recognition of any constitutional immunity. The District Court has broad discretion to stay proceedings as an incident to its power to control its own docket. As we have explained, [e]specially in cases of extraordinary public moment, [a plaintiff] may be required to submit to delay not immoderate in extent and not oppressive in its consequences if the public welfare or convenience will thereby be promoted. Although we have rejected the argument that the potential burdens on the President violate separation-of-powers principles, those burdens are appropriate matters for the District Court to evaluate in its management of the case. The high respect that is owed to the office of the Chief Executive, though not justifying a rule of

---

[40] [W]e recognize that a President, like any other official or private citizen, may become distracted or preoccupied by pending litigation. Presidents and other officials face a variety of demands on their time, however, some private, some political, and some as a result of official duty. While such distractions may be vexing to those subjected to them, they do not ordinarily implicate constitutional separation-of-powers concerns.

categorical immunity, is a matter that should inform the conduct of the entire proceeding, including the timing and scope of discovery.

Nevertheless, we are persuaded that it was an abuse of discretion for the District Court to defer the trial until after the President leaves office. Such a lengthy and categorical stay takes no account whatever of the respondent's interest in bringing the case to trial. . . .

The decision to postpone the trial was, furthermore, premature. . . . We think the District Court may have given undue weight to the concern that a trial might generate unrelated civil actions that could conceivably hamper the President in conducting the duties of his office. If and when that should occur, the court's discretion would permit it to manage those actions in such fashion (including deferral of trial) that interference with the President's duties would not occur. But no such impingement upon the President's conduct of his office was shown here. . . .

JUSTICE BREYER, concurring in the judgment.

I agree with the majority that the Constitution does not automatically grant the President an immunity from civil lawsuits based upon his private conduct. Nor does the doctrine of separation of powers . . . require federal courts to stay virtually all private actions against the President until he leaves office. To obtain a postponement the President must bea[r] the burden of establishing its need.

In my view, however, once the President sets forth and explains a conflict between judicial proceeding and public duties, the matter changes. At that point, the Constitution permits a judge to schedule a trial in an ordinary civil damages action (where postponement normally is possible without overwhelming damage to a plaintiff) only within the constraints of a constitutional principle—a principle that forbids a federal judge in such a case to interfere with the President's discharge of his public duties. I have no doubt that the Constitution contains such a principle applicable to civil suits, based upon Article II's vesting of the entire executive Power in a single individual, implemented through the Constitution's structural separation of powers, and revealed both by history and case precedent. . . .

COMMENTS AND QUESTIONS

1.   Subsequent to the Court's decision, the plaintiff's attorneys sought to depose the President regarding all past extramarital affairs for the purpose of showing a pattern of behavior. The judge, over the objection of Clinton's lawyers, required President Clinton to answer these questions. As part of that deposition, Clinton denied having "sexual relations" with Monica Lewinsky, a White House intern. Later the judge decided that evidence regarding past affairs was not admissible and ultimately ruled against Jones on all claims. While the case was on appeal, Clinton settled with Jones for $850,000.

2.   His denial of sexual relations with Monica Lewinsky in the *Jones* deposition led Independent Counsel Ken Starr to include possible perjury in the *Jones* case to his ongoing investigation of the President regarding certain real estate transactions the Clintons had made while he was Governor of Arkansas. As part of this new investigation, the President was required to testify before a grand jury regarding his relationship with Monica Lewinsky, and there he testified that he did not have sexual intercourse with her and that he believed his responses in the *Jones* case were truthful, because he understood the questions there to have related to sexual intercourse. As to whether there was oral intercourse, the President refused to answer, admitting only to an inappropriate intimate relationship. While Starr did not bring any criminal charges against the President, he referred the matter to the House of Representatives for use in possible impeachment proceedings. Alleged perjury in the *Jones* suit and before the grand jury constituted two of the four counts considered by the House. On party lines, the House voted to impeach the President for the alleged grand jury perjury as well as for obstruction of justice in impeding the grand jury investigation. The Senate acquitted him on both counts, with 10 Republicans joining all the Democrats for acquittal on the perjury charge and five Republicans joining all the Democrats for acquittal on the obstruction of justice charge. The judge in the *Jones* case, however, held Clinton in civil contempt for lying in the deposition, fined him $90,000, and referred the matter to the Arkansas Supreme Court, for possible disciplinary action. Later, as part of a deal with Starr's successor to avoid criminal prosecution after leaving office, Clinton admitted to giving false testimony in the *Jones* case and agreed to a five-year suspension of his bar membership. Subsequently, he resigned his membership to avoid permanent disbarment.

3.   Given the fallout from the *Jones* deposition, what do you think of the Supreme Court's statement that "if properly managed by the District Court, it appears to us highly unlikely [that the case will] occupy any substantial amount of petitioner's time"? Does this suggest the case was *not* properly managed by the trial judge? Given the stakes involved, do you think it appropriate to leave the fate of the Presidency to the judgment of one of almost 700 federal district court judges? Or is what happened simply Bill Clinton's fault for lying in the deposition? How many people in public life would want to be asked under oath about all their extramarital affairs?

4.   One might ask why the Independent Counsel did not bring any criminal charges. The final report of the Independent Counsel explained:

> In the Independent Counsel's judgment, there was sufficient evidence to prosecute President Clinton for violating federal criminal laws within this Office's jurisdiction. Nonetheless, in light of: (1) President Clinton's admission of providing false testimony that was knowingly misleading, evasive, and prejudicial to the administration of justice before the United States District Court for the Eastern District of Arkansas; (2) his acknowledgement that his conduct violated the Rules of Professional Conduct of the Arkansas Supreme Court; (3) the five-year suspension of his license to practice law and $25,000 fine

imposed on him by the Circuit Court of Pulaski County, Arkansas; (4) the civil contempt penalty of more than $90,000 imposed on President Clinton by the federal court for violating its orders; (5) the payment of more than $850,000 in settlement to Paula Jones; (6) the express finding by the federal court that President Clinton had engaged in contemptuous conduct; and (7) the substantial public condemnation of President Clinton arising from his impeachment, the Independent Counsel concluded, consistent with the Principles of Federal Prosecution, that further proceedings against President Clinton for his conduct should not be initiated.

5.   There is substantial dispute concerning whether a sitting President may be prosecuted criminally. This undoubtedly affected the Independent Counsel in the Clinton case as well as the Special Prosecutor in the Nixon case. Recall that the grand jury named Nixon as an *unindicted* co-conspirator in the obstruction of justice charges. It was even an issue with respect to Nixon's Vice President, Spiro Agnew, who, in light of evidence that he had accepted bribes when he was governor of Maryland and continuing while he was Vice President, was induced to resign the Vice Presidency in return for a plea agreement to income tax evasion and money laundering charges that imposed only a $10,000 fine and three years probation. Most recently, it was a major issue with respect to the Special Counsel's investigation of President Trump, in which Robert Mueller, the Special Counsel, said that as a Justice Department employee he was bound to follow the legal opinions of the Office of Legal Counsel in the Department, two of which had concluded that the President cannot be indicted while in office.

PROBLEM

Imagine that the new President of the United States is a former businessman, who was notorious for being a rough competitor in the business world. After the President's inauguration, a former business competitor, who had lost out to the President in a competition for building a hotel/casino, files suit against the President for damages, alleging that the President had engaged in unlawful actions to obtain the building rights. The President moves to have the suit dismissed or delayed. The lower courts on the basis of *Jones v. Clinton* deny the President's motions. The President seeks certiorari from the Supreme Court. How do you think it should rule?

CHAPTER 6

THE SECOND AMENDMENT AND INCORPORATION OF THE BILL OF RIGHTS

■ ■ ■

In the previous chapters, we addressed the powers granted to the federal government and the powers withdrawn from the states under the Constitution, as well as the separation of powers and checks and balances between the legislative, executive, and judicial branches of the federal government. This and the following chapters address the "rights" protected by the Constitution. We start with the Second Amendment, not because of its relative importance, but because it is a matter of current concern; it provides a good introduction to competing methods of interpretation of the Bill of Rights; and it explains the "incorporation" of the Bill of Rights to the states.

DISTRICT OF COLUMBIA V. HELLER
United States Supreme Court, 2008.
554 U.S. 570, 128 S.Ct. 2783.

JUSTICE SCALIA delivered the opinion of the Court.

We consider whether a District of Columbia prohibition on the possession of usable handguns in the home violates the Second Amendment to the Constitution. . . .

The Second Amendment provides: "A well regulated Militia, being necessary to the security of a free State, the right of the people to keep and bear Arms, shall not be infringed." In interpreting this text, we are guided by the principle that "[t]he Constitution was written to be understood by the voters; its words and phrases were used in their normal and ordinary as distinguished from technical meaning." . . .

The two sides in this case have set out very different interpretations of the Amendment. Petitioners and today's dissenting Justices believe that it protects only the right to possess and carry a firearm in connection with militia service. Respondent argues that it protects an individual right to possess a firearm unconnected with service in a militia, and to use that arm for traditionally lawful purposes, such as self-defense within the home.

The Second Amendment is naturally divided into two parts: its prefatory clause and its operative clause. The former does not limit the latter grammatically, but rather announces a purpose. The Amendment could be rephrased, "Because a well regulated Militia is necessary to the security of a free State, the right of the people to keep and bear Arms shall not be infringed." . . .

Logic demands that there be a link between the stated purpose and the command. . . . That requirement of logical connection may cause a prefatory clause to resolve an ambiguity in the operative clause. . . . But apart from that clarifying function, a prefatory clause does not limit or expand the scope of the operative clause. . . . Therefore, while we will begin our textual analysis with the operative clause, we will return to the prefatory clause to ensure that our reading of the operative clause is consistent with the announced purpose. . . .

The first salient feature of the operative clause is that it codifies a "right of the people." The unamended Constitution and the Bill of Rights use the phrase "right of the people" two other times, in the First Amendment's Assembly-and-Petition Clause and in the Fourth Amendment's Search-and-Seizure Clause. The Ninth Amendment uses very similar terminology ("The enumeration in the Constitution, of certain rights, shall not be construed to deny or disparage others retained by the people"). All three of these instances unambiguously refer to individual rights, not "collective" rights, or rights that may be exercised only through participation in some corporate body. . . . Nowhere else in the Constitution does a "right" attributed to "the people" refer to anything other than an individual right. . . .

We start therefore with a strong presumption that the Second Amendment right is exercised individually and belongs to all Americans.

We move now from the holder of the right—"the people"—to the substance of the right: "to keep and bear Arms."

Before addressing the verbs "keep" and "bear," we interpret their object: "Arms." The 18th-century meaning is no different from the meaning today. The 1773 edition of Samuel Johnson's dictionary defined "arms" as "weapons of offence, or armour of defence." Timothy Cunningham's important 1771 legal dictionary defined "arms" as "any thing that a man wears for his defence, or takes into his hands, or useth in wrath to cast at or strike another."

The term was applied, then as now, to weapons that were not specifically designed for military use and were not employed in a military capacity. For instance, Cunningham's legal dictionary gave as an example of usage: "Servants and labourers shall use bows and arrows on *Sundays,* & c. and not bear other arms." Although one founding-era thesaurus limited "arms" (as opposed to "weapons") to "instruments of offence *generally* made use of in war," even that source stated that all firearms constituted "arms."

Some have made the argument, bordering on the frivolous, that only those arms in existence in the 18th century are protected by the Second Amendment. We do not interpret constitutional rights that way. Just as the First Amendment protects modern forms of communications, and the Fourth Amendment applies to modern forms of search, the Second Amendment extends, prima facie, to all instruments that constitute bearable arms, even those that were not in existence at the time of the founding.

We turn to the phrases "keep arms" and "bear arms." Johnson defined "keep" as, most relevantly, "[t]o retain; not to lose," and "[t]o have in custody." Webster defined it as "[t]o hold; to retain in one's power or possession." No party has apprised us of an idiomatic meaning of "keep Arms." Thus, the most natural reading of "keep Arms" in the Second Amendment is to "have weapons."

The phrase "keep arms" was not prevalent in the written documents of the founding period that we have found, but there are a few examples, all of which favor viewing the right to "keep Arms" as an individual right unconnected with militia service. William Blackstone, for example, wrote that Catholics convicted of not attending service in the Church of England suffered certain penalties, one of which was that they were not permitted to "keep arms in their houses.". . .

At the time of the founding, as now, to "bear" meant to "carry." When used with "arms," however, the term has a meaning that refers to carrying for a particular purpose—confrontation. . . . Although the phrase implies that the carrying of the weapon is for the purpose of "offensive or defensive action," it in no way connotes participation in a structured military organization.

From our review of founding-era sources, we conclude that this natural meaning was also the meaning that "bear arms" had in the 18th century. In numerous instances, "bear arms" was unambiguously used to refer to the carrying of weapons outside of an organized militia. The most prominent examples are those most relevant to the Second Amendment: Nine state constitutional provisions written in the 18th century or the first two decades of the 19th, which enshrined a right of citizens to "bear arms in defense of themselves and the state" or "bear arms in defense of himself and the state." It is clear from those formulations that "bear arms" did not refer only to carrying a weapon in an organized military unit. . . . These provisions demonstrate—again, in the most analogous linguistic context— that "bear arms" was not limited to the carrying of arms in a militia. . . .

Petitioners justify their limitation of "bear arms" to the military context by pointing out the unremarkable fact that it was often used in that context. . . . Other legal sources frequently used "bear arms" in nonmilitary contexts. . . . And if one looks beyond legal sources, "bear arms" was frequently used in nonmilitary contexts. . . .

Putting all of these textual elements together, we find that they guarantee the individual right to possess and carry weapons in case of confrontation. This meaning is strongly confirmed by the historical background of the Second Amendment. We look to this because it has always been widely understood that the Second Amendment, like the First and Fourth Amendments, codified a *pre-existing* right. The very text of the Second Amendment implicitly recognizes the pre-existence of the right and declares only that it "shall not be infringed.". . .

Between the Restoration and the Glorious Revolution, the Stuart Kings Charles II and James II succeeded in using select militias loyal to them to suppress political dissidents, in part by disarming their opponents. . . . These experiences caused Englishmen to be extremely wary of concentrated military forces run by the state and to be jealous of their arms. They accordingly obtained an assurance from William and Mary, in the Declaration of Right (which was codified as the English Bill of Rights), that Protestants would never be disarmed: "That the subjects which are Protestants may have arms for their defense suitable to their conditions and as allowed by law." This right has long been understood to be the predecessor to our Second Amendment. . . .

And, of course, what the Stuarts had tried to do to their political enemies, George III had tried to do to the colonists. In the tumultuous decades of the 1760s and 1770s, the Crown began to disarm the inhabitants of the most rebellious areas. That provoked polemical reactions by Americans invoking their rights as Englishmen to keep arms. . . .

There seems to us no doubt, on the basis of both text and history, that the Second Amendment conferred an individual right to keep and bear arms. Of course the right was not unlimited, just as the First Amendment's right of free speech was not. Thus, we do not read the Second Amendment to protect the right of citizens to carry arms for *any sort* of confrontation, just as we do not read the First Amendment to protect the right of citizens to speak for *any purpose*. Before turning to limitations upon the individual right, however, we must determine whether the prefatory clause of the Second Amendment comports with our interpretation of the operative clause.

The prefatory clause reads: "A well regulated Militia, being necessary to the security of a free State . . . ."

In *United States v. Miller,* 307 U.S. 174 (1939), we explained that "the Militia comprised all males physically capable of acting in concert for the common defense." That definition comports with founding-era sources. . . .

Finally, the adjective "well-regulated" implies nothing more than the imposition of proper discipline and training. . . .

We reach the question, then: Does the preface fit with an operative clause that creates an individual right to keep and bear arms? It fits perfectly, once one knows the history that the founding generation knew and that we have described above. That history showed that the way tyrants had eliminated a militia consisting of all the able-bodied men was not by banning the militia but simply by taking away the people's arms, enabling a select militia or standing army to suppress political opponents. This is what had occurred in England that prompted codification of the right to have arms in the English Bill of Rights.

The debate with respect to the right to keep and bear arms, as with other guarantees in the Bill of Rights, was not over whether it was desirable (all agreed that it was) but over whether it needed to be codified in the Constitution. During the 1788 ratification debates, the fear that the federal government would disarm the people in order to impose rule through a standing army or select militia was pervasive in Antifederalist rhetoric. . . . It was understood across the political spectrum that the right helped to secure the ideal of a citizen militia, which might be necessary to oppose an oppressive military force if the constitutional order broke down.

It is therefore entirely sensible that the Second Amendment's prefatory clause announces the purpose for which the right was codified: to prevent elimination of the militia. The prefatory clause does not suggest that preserving the militia was the only reason Americans valued the ancient right; most undoubtedly thought it even more important for self-defense and hunting. But the threat that the new Federal Government would destroy the citizens' militia by taking away their arms was the reason that right—unlike some other English rights—was codified in a written Constitution. . . .

Our interpretation is confirmed by analogous arms-bearing rights in state constitutions that preceded and immediately followed adoption of the Second Amendment. Four States adopted analogues to the Federal Second Amendment in the period between independence and the ratification of the Bill of Rights. Two of them—Pennsylvania and Vermont—clearly adopted individual rights unconnected to militia service. Pennsylvania's Declaration of Rights of 1776 said: "That the people have a right to bear arms *for the defence of themselves,* and the state. . . ." In 1777, Vermont adopted the identical provision, except for inconsequential differences in punctuation and capitalization. . . .

We therefore believe that the most likely reading of all four of these pre-Second Amendment state constitutional provisions is that they secured an individual right to bear arms for defensive purposes. . . .

We now address how the Second Amendment was interpreted from immediately after its ratification through the end of the 19th century. . . .

Three important founding-era legal scholars interpreted the Second Amendment in published writings. All three understood it to protect an individual right unconnected with militia service. . . .

The 19th-century cases that interpreted the Second Amendment universally support an individual right unconnected to militia service. . . .

It was plainly the understanding in the post-Civil War Congress that the Second Amendment protected an individual right to use arms for self-defense.

Every late-19th-century legal scholar that we have read interpreted the Second Amendment to secure an individual right unconnected with militia service. . . .

One example . . . will convey the general flavor.

"[The purpose of the Second Amendment is] to secure a well-armed militia . . . . But a militia would be useless unless the citizens were enabled to exercise themselves in the use of warlike weapons. To preserve this privilege, and to secure to the people the ability to oppose themselves in military force against the usurpations of government, as well as against enemies from without, that government is forbidden by any law or proceeding to invade or destroy the right to keep and bear arms . . . .

We now ask whether any of our precedents forecloses the conclusions we have reached about the meaning of the Second Amendment. . . .

Justice STEVENS places overwhelming reliance upon this Court's decision in *United States v. Miller,* 307 U.S. 174 (1939). . . . And what is, according to Justice STEVENS, the holding of *Miller* . . .? That the Second Amendment "protects the right to keep and bear arms for certain military purposes, but that it does not curtail the legislature's power to regulate the nonmilitary use and ownership of weapons."

Nothing so clearly demonstrates the weakness of Justice STEVENS's case. *Miller* did not hold that and cannot possibly be read to have held that. The judgment in the case upheld against a Second Amendment challenge two men's federal indictment for transporting an unregistered short-barreled shotgun in interstate commerce, in violation of the National Firearms Act. It is entirely clear that the Court's basis for saying that the Second Amendment did not apply was *not* that the defendants were "bear[ing] arms" not "for . . . military purposes" but for "nonmilitary use." Rather, it was that the *type of weapon at issue* was not eligible for Second Amendment protection: "In the absence of any evidence tending to show that the possession or use of a [short-barreled shotgun] at this time has some reasonable relationship to the preservation or efficiency of a well regulated militia, we cannot say that the Second Amendment guarantees the right to keep and bear *such an instrument.*" "Certainly," the Court continued, "it is not within judicial notice that this weapon is any part of the ordinary military equipment or that its use could contribute to the common defense." Beyond that, the opinion provided no explanation of the content of the right.

This holding is not only consistent with, but positively suggests, that the Second Amendment confers an individual right to keep and bear arms (though only arms that "have some reasonable relationship to the preservation or efficiency of a well regulated militia"). Had the Court believed that the Second Amendment protects only those serving in the militia, it would have been odd to examine the character of the weapon rather than simply note that the two crooks were not militiamen. . . . *Miller* stands only for the proposition that the Second Amendment right, whatever its nature, extends only to certain types of weapons. . . .

We may as well consider at this point (for we will have to consider eventually) *what* types of weapons *Miller* permits. Read in isolation, *Miller*'s phrase "part of ordinary military equipment" could mean that only those weapons useful in warfare are protected. That would be a startling reading of the opinion, since it would mean that the National Firearms Act's restrictions on machineguns (not challenged in *Miller*) might be unconstitutional, machineguns being useful in warfare in 1939. We think that *Miller*'s "ordinary military equipment" language must be read in tandem with what comes after: "[O]rdinarily when called for [militia] service [able-bodied] men were expected to appear bearing arms supplied by themselves and of the kind in common use at the time." The traditional militia was formed from a pool of men bringing arms "in common use at the time" for lawful purposes like self-defense. . . . Indeed, that is precisely the way in which the Second Amendment's operative clause furthers the purpose announced in its preface. We therefore read *Miller* to say only that the Second Amendment does not protect those weapons not typically possessed by law-abiding citizens for lawful purposes, such as short-barreled shotguns. That accords with the historical understanding of the scope of the right. . . .

We conclude that nothing in our precedents forecloses our adoption of the original understanding of the Second Amendment. . . .

Like most rights, the right secured by the Second Amendment is not unlimited. From Blackstone through the 19th-century cases, commentators and courts routinely explained that the right was not a right to keep and carry any weapon whatsoever in any manner whatsoever and for whatever purpose. For example, the majority of the 19th-century courts to consider the question held that prohibitions on carrying concealed weapons were lawful under the Second Amendment or state analogues. [N]othing in our opinion should be taken to cast doubt on longstanding prohibitions on the possession of firearms by felons and the mentally ill, or laws forbidding the carrying of firearms in sensitive places such as schools and government buildings, or laws imposing conditions and qualifications on the commercial sale of arms.

We also recognize another important limitation on the right to keep and carry arms. *Miller* said, as we have explained, that the sorts of weapons protected were those "in common use at the time." We think that limitation is fairly supported by the historical tradition of prohibiting the carrying of "dangerous and unusual weapons."

It may be objected that if weapons that are most useful in military service—M-16 rifles and the like—may be banned, then the Second Amendment right is completely detached from the prefatory clause. But as we have said, the conception of the militia at the time of the Second Amendment's ratification was the body of all citizens capable of military service, who would bring the sorts of lawful weapons that they possessed at home to militia duty. It may well be true today that a militia, to be as effective as militias in the 18th century, would require sophisticated arms that are highly unusual in society at large. Indeed, it may be true that no amount of small arms could be useful against modern-day bombers and tanks. But the fact that modern developments have limited the degree of fit between the prefatory clause and the protected right cannot change our interpretation of the right.

We turn finally to the law at issue here. As we have said, the law totally bans handgun possession in the home. It also requires that any lawful firearm in the home be disassembled or bound by a trigger lock at all times, rendering it inoperable.

As the quotations earlier in this opinion demonstrate, the inherent right of self-defense has been central to the Second Amendment right. The handgun ban amounts to a prohibition of an entire class of "arms" that is overwhelmingly chosen by American society for that lawful purpose. The prohibition extends, moreover, to the home, where the need for defense of self, family, and property is most acute. Under any of the standards of scrutiny that we have applied to enumerated constitutional rights, banning from the home "the most preferred firearm in the nation to 'keep' and use for protection of one's home and family" would fail constitutional muster. . . .

We must . . . address the District's requirement (as applied to respondent's handgun) that firearms in the home be rendered and kept inoperable at all times. This makes it impossible for citizens to use them for the core lawful purpose of self-defense and is hence unconstitutional. . . .

Justice BREYER [makes] a broad jurisprudential point: He criticizes us for declining to establish a level of scrutiny for evaluating Second Amendment restrictions. He proposes . . . a judge-empowering "interest-balancing inquiry" that "asks whether the statute burdens a protected interest in a way or to an extent that is out of proportion to the statute's salutary effects upon other important governmental interests.". . .

We know of no other enumerated constitutional right whose core protection has been subjected to a freestanding "interest-balancing" approach. The very enumeration of the right takes out of the hands of government—even the Third Branch of Government—the power to decide on a case-by-case basis whether the right is *really worth* insisting upon. . . .

JUSTICE STEVENS, with whom JUSTICE SOUTER, JUSTICE GINSBURG, and JUSTICE BREYER join, dissenting.

The question presented by this case is not whether the Second Amendment protects a "collective right" or an "individual right." Surely it protects a right that can be enforced by individuals. But a conclusion that the Second Amendment protects an individual right does not tell us anything about the scope of that right.

Guns are used to hunt, for self-defense, to commit crimes, for sporting activities, and to perform military duties. The Second Amendment plainly does not protect the right to use a gun to rob a bank; it is equally clear that it *does* encompass the right to use weapons for certain military purposes. Whether it also protects the right to possess and use guns for nonmilitary purposes like hunting and personal self-defense is the question presented by this case. The text of the Amendment, its history, and our decision in *United States v. Miller* provide a clear answer to that question.

The Second Amendment was adopted to protect the right of the people of each of the several States to maintain a well-regulated militia. . . . Neither the text of the Amendment nor the arguments advanced by its proponents evidenced the slightest interest in limiting any legislature's authority to regulate private civilian uses of firearms. Specifically, there is no indication that the Framers of the Amendment intended to enshrine the common-law right of self-defense in the Constitution.

In 1934, Congress enacted the National Firearms Act, the first major federal firearms law. Sustaining an indictment under the Act, this Court held that, "[i]n the absence of any evidence tending to show that possession or use of a 'shotgun having a barrel of less than eighteen inches in length' at this time has some reasonable relationship to the preservation or efficiency of a well regulated militia, we cannot say that the Second Amendment guarantees the right to keep and bear such an instrument." *Miller*. The view of the Amendment we took in *Miller*—that it protects the right to keep and bear arms for certain military purposes, but that it does not curtail the Legislature's power to regulate the nonmilitary use and ownership of weapons—is both the most natural reading of the Amendment's text and the interpretation most faithful to the history of its adoption.

Since our decision in *Miller,* hundreds of judges have relied on the view of the Amendment we endorsed there;[2] we ourselves affirmed it in 1980. . . .

---

[2]   Until the Fifth Circuit's decision in *United States v. Emerson*, 270 F.3d 203 (2001), every Court of Appeals to consider the question had understood *Miller* to hold that the Second Amendment does not protect the right to possess and use guns for purely private, civilian purposes.

Even if the textual and historical arguments on both sides of the issue were evenly balanced, respect for the well-settled views of all of our predecessors on this Court, and for the rule of law itself would prevent most jurists from endorsing such a dramatic upheaval in the law. . . .

The text of the Second Amendment is brief. It provides: "A well regulated Militia, being necessary to the security of a free State, the right of the people to keep and bear Arms, shall not be infringed."

Three portions of that text merit special focus: the introductory language defining the Amendment's purpose, the class of persons encompassed within its reach, and the unitary nature of the right that it protects.

"A well regulated Militia, being necessary to the security of a free State"

The preamble to the Second Amendment makes three important points. It identifies the preservation of the militia as the Amendment's purpose; it explains that the militia is necessary to the security of a free State; and it recognizes that the militia must be "well regulated." . . . While the need for state militias has not been a matter of significant public interest for almost two centuries, that fact should not obscure the contemporary concerns that animated the Framers. . . .

The preamble thus both sets forth the object of the Amendment and informs the meaning of the remainder of its text. Such text should not be treated as mere surplusage, for "[i]t cannot be presumed that any clause in the constitution is intended to be without effect." *Marbury*. . . .

"The right of the people"

The centerpiece of the Court's textual argument is its insistence that the words "the people" as used in the Second Amendment must have the same meaning, and protect the same class of individuals, as when they are used in the First and Fourth Amendments. . . . But the Court *itself* reads the Second Amendment to protect a "subset" significantly narrower than the class of persons protected by the First and Fourth Amendments; when it finally drills down on the substantive meaning of the Second Amendment, the Court limits the protected class to "law-abiding, responsible citizens." But the class of persons protected by the First and Fourth Amendments is *not* so limited; for even felons (and presumably irresponsible citizens as well) may invoke the protections of those constitutional provisions. The Court offers no way to harmonize its conflicting pronouncements. . . .

"To keep and bear Arms"

Although the Court's discussion of these words treats them as two "phrases"—as if they read "to keep" and "to bear"—they describe a unitary

---

[citing eleven cases] And a number of courts have remained firm in their prior positions, even after considering *Emerson*. [citing seven cases]

right: to possess arms if needed for military purposes and to use them in conjunction with military activities. . .

The term "bear arms" is a familiar idiom; when used unadorned by any additional words, its meaning is "to serve as a soldier, do military service, fight." 1 Oxford English Dictionary 634 (2d ed.1989). . . . Had the Framers wished to expand the meaning of the phrase "bear arms" to encompass civilian possession and use, they could have done so by the addition of phrases such as "for the defense of themselves," as was done in the Pennsylvania and Vermont Declarations of Rights. The *unmodified* use of "bear arms," by contrast, refers most naturally to a military purpose, as evidenced by its use in literally dozens of contemporary texts.[9] . . .

"[K]eep and bear arms" thus perfectly describes the responsibilities of a framing-era militia member. . . .

When each word in the text is given full effect, the Amendment is most naturally read to secure to the people a right to use and possess arms in conjunction with service in a well-regulated militia. . . . Until today, it has been understood that legislatures may regulate the civilian use and misuse of firearms so long as they do not interfere with the preservation of a well-regulated militia. The Court's announcement of a new constitutional right to own and use firearms for private purposes upsets that settled understanding, but leaves for future cases the formidable task of defining the scope of permissible regulations. . . . I fear that the District's policy choice may well be just the first of an unknown number of dominoes to be knocked off the table. . . .

JUSTICE BREYER, with whom JUSTICE STEVENS, JUSTICE SOUTER, and JUSTICE GINSBURG join, dissenting.

We must decide whether a District of Columbia law that prohibits the possession of handguns in the home violates the Second Amendment. The Court, relying upon its view that the Second Amendment seeks to protect a right of personal self-defense, holds that this law violates that Amendment. In my view, it does not.

The majority's conclusion is wrong for two independent reasons. The first reason is that set forth by Justice STEVENS—namely, that the Second Amendment protects militia-related, not self-defense-related, interests. These two interests are sometimes intertwined. To assure 18th-century

---

[9] Amici professors of Linguistics and English reviewed uses of the term "bear arms" in a compilation of books, pamphlets, and other sources disseminated in the period between the Declaration of Independence and the adoption of the Second Amendment. Amici determined that of 115 texts that employed the term, all but five usages were in a clearly military context, and in four of the remaining five instances, further qualifying language conveyed a different meaning.

The Court allows that the phrase "bear Arms" did have as an idiomatic meaning, " 'to serve as a soldier, do military service, fight,' " but asserts that it "unequivocally bore that idiomatic meaning only when followed by the preposition 'against,' which was in turn followed by the target of the hostilities." But contemporary sources make clear that the phrase "bear arms" was often used to convey a military meaning without those additional words.

citizens that they could keep arms for militia purposes would necessarily have allowed them to keep arms that they could have used for self-defense as well. But self-defense alone, detached from any militia-related objective, is not the Amendment's concern.

The second independent reason is that the protection the Amendment provides is not absolute. The Amendment permits government to regulate the interests that it serves. Thus, irrespective of what those interests are— whether they do or do not include an independent interest in self-defense— the majority's view cannot be correct unless it can show that the District's regulation is unreasonable or inappropriate in Second Amendment terms. This the majority cannot do.

[I]n this opinion I shall focus upon the second reason. I shall show that the District's law is consistent with the Second Amendment even if that Amendment is interpreted as protecting a wholly separate interest in individual self-defense. That is so because the District's regulation, which focuses upon the presence of handguns in high-crime urban areas, represents a permissible legislative response to a serious, indeed life-threatening, problem.

Thus I here assume that one objective of those who wrote the Second Amendment was to help assure citizens that they would have arms available for purposes of self-defense. Even so, a legislature could reasonably conclude that the law will advance goals of great public importance, namely, saving lives, preventing injury, and reducing crime. The law is tailored to the urban crime problem in that it is local in scope and thus affects only a geographic area both limited in size and entirely urban; the law concerns handguns, which are specially linked to urban gun deaths and injuries, and which are the overwhelmingly favorite weapon of armed criminals; and at the same time, the law imposes a burden upon gun owners that seems proportionately no greater than restrictions in existence at the time the Second Amendment was adopted. In these circumstances, the District's law falls within the zone that the Second Amendment leaves open to regulation by legislatures. . . .

[C]olonial history itself offers important examples of the kinds of gun regulation that citizens would then have thought compatible with the "right to keep and bear arms," whether embodied in Federal or State Constitutions, or the background common law. And those examples include substantial regulation of firearms in urban areas, including regulations that imposed obstacles to the use of firearms for the protection of the home.

Boston, Philadelphia, and New York City, the three largest cities in America during that period, all restricted the firing of guns within city limits to at least some degree.

Furthermore, several towns and cities (including Philadelphia, New York, and Boston) regulated, for fire-safety reasons the storage of gunpowder, a necessary component of an operational firearm. Boston's law in particular impacted the use of firearms in the home very much as the District's law does today. Boston's gunpowder law imposed a £10 fine upon "any Person" who "shall take into any Dwelling-House, Stable, Barn, Out-house, Ware-house, Store, Shop, or other Building, within the Town of Boston, any . . . Fire-Arm, loaded with, or having Gun-Powder.". . .

And Massachusetts residents must have believed this kind of law compatible with the provision in the Massachusetts Constitution that granted "the people . . . a right to keep and to bear arms for the common defence"—a provision that the majority says was interpreted as "secur[ing] an individual right to bear arms for defensive purposes." . . .

[A]lmost every gun-control regulation will seek to advance (as the one here does) a "primary concern of every government—a concern for the safety and indeed the lives of its citizens." The Court has deemed that interest, as well as "the Government's general interest in preventing crime," to be "compelling," and the Court has in a wide variety of constitutional contexts found such public-safety concerns sufficiently forceful to justify restrictions on individual liberties, [including First Amendment free speech rights, First Amendment religious rights, Fourth Amendment protection of the home, Fifth Amendment rights, and Eighth Amendment bail rights]. Thus, any attempt *in theory* to apply strict scrutiny to gun regulations will *in practice* turn into an interest-balancing inquiry, with the interests protected by the Second Amendment on one side and the governmental public-safety concerns on the other, the only question being whether the regulation at issue impermissibly burdens the former in the course of advancing the latter. . . .

In applying this kind of standard the Court normally defers to a legislature's empirical judgment in matters where a legislature is likely to have greater expertise and greater institutional factfinding capacity. Nonetheless, a court, not a legislature, must make the ultimate constitutional conclusion, exercising its "independent judicial judgment" in light of the whole record to determine whether a law exceeds constitutional boundaries. . . .

No one doubts the constitutional importance of the statute's basic objective, saving lives. But there is considerable debate about whether the District's statute helps to achieve that objective. . . .

[Justice BREYER then recounts the statistics and arguments provided by supporters of the law as to the link between easy access to handguns and violent crime, especially in urban areas, as well as the statistics and arguments provided by opponents of the law that a statutory ban on handguns in the District of Columbia will not reduce violent crime or gun deaths.]

These empirically based arguments [by those opposed to the law] may have proved strong enough to convince many legislatures, as a matter of legislative policy, not to adopt total handgun bans. But the question here is whether they are strong enough to destroy judicial confidence in the reasonableness of a legislature that rejects them. And that they are not. . . .

COMMENTS AND QUESTIONS

1.   Justice Scalia's opinion for the Court is a perfect example of his method of interpreting the Constitution—"originalism," or "original public meaning." It does not focus on the intent of those who wrote the Second Amendment but upon how those who would read it—those people for whom the right was enacted—would interpret it. Thus, he relies upon dictionaries from that time as well as other writings of the time. Moreover, the meaning at the time does not change over time. The "arms" protected may change in light of what today would be arms "in common use" by ordinary persons, so that semi-automatic pistols (and rifles), not just muskets and single shot pistols, would qualify for protection, but the absence of state militias today would not change the nature of the right to keep and bear arms.

2.   Justices Scalia and Stevens engage in a historical duel, most of which has been edited from their combined 110 pages of opinions. The former finds clear historical evidence that the Second Amendment protects a right to keep and bear arms for domestic self-protection. The latter finds equally clear evidence that the Second Amendment only protects a right to keep and bear arms in the service of an organized militia. Is it a coincidence that the "conservatives," who generally dislike government regulation, happen to read the history to prohibit this regulation, and the "liberals," who are more forgiving of government regulation, happen to read the history in a way that would uphold this regulation? Or does this again demonstrate that history does not provide clear answers and no more constrains judges' discretion than does an explicit balancing approach, such as favored by Justice Breyer?

3.   Justice Breyer states that even if there is a Second Amendment right to keep and bear guns for self-defense, it is not an absolute right, as the majority concedes. The question then is: how to determine the limits of the right. The majority indicates some historical exceptions (such as limits on possession by felons and the mentally ill, limits on carrying arms in certain sensitive places, and conditions on their commercial sale), but Justice Breyer uses an interest balancing methodology, weighing the needs for self-defense against the needs of society to protect against misuse of handguns. Which method do you prefer? Is a historical exception test less "judge empowering"?

4.   Why are M-4 carbines (the automatic rifle that is the standard equipment for the U.S. Army) not a weapon a law-abiding, responsible citizen can keep and bear? Wouldn't it be a very popular weapon, if it were legal to own one? Not to mention machine guns and fragmentation grenades.

5.   Prior to the passage of the 14th Amendment, it was clear that none of the protections of the Bill of Rights applied to the states. As far as the United

States Constitution was involved, states could restrict speech, make unwarranted and unreasonable searches, take private property without paying just compensation, convict persons of crimes in a secret trial where the defendant could be forced to testify against himself, and impose cruel and unusual punishments. Beginning in the late 19th Century, the Supreme Court bit-by-bit began to "incorporate" many of the rights in the Bill of Rights against the states as well. Prior to *Heller*, however, the Court had never incorporated the Second Amendment against the states. Consequently, immediately after *Heller* a case was brought against a Chicago city ordinance that was virtually identical to the ordinance in *Heller*.

MCDONALD V. CITY OF CHICAGO
United States Supreme Court, 2010.
561 U.S. 742, 130 S.Ct. 3020.

JUSTICE ALITO announced the judgment of the Court and delivered the opinion of the Court with respect to Parts I, II-A, II-B, II-D, III-A, and III-B, in which THE CHIEF JUSTICE, JUSTICE SCALIA, JUSTICE KENNEDY, and JUSTICE THOMAS join, and an opinion with respect to Parts II-C, IV, and V, in which THE CHIEF JUSTICE, JUSTICE SCALIA, and JUSTICE KENNEDY join.

Two years ago, in *District of Columbia v. Heller*, we held that the Second Amendment protects the right to keep and bear arms for the purpose of self-defense, and we struck down a District of Columbia law that banned the possession of handguns in the home. The city of Chicago (City) and the village of Oak Park, a Chicago suburb, have laws that are similar to the District of Columbia's, but Chicago and Oak Park argue that their laws are constitutional because the Second Amendment has no application to the States. We have previously held that most of the provisions of the Bill of Rights apply with full force to both the Federal Government and the States. Applying the standard that is well established in our case law, we hold that the Second Amendment right is fully applicable to the States.

I

Otis McDonald, Adam Orlov, Colleen Lawson, and David Lawson (Chicago petitioners) are Chicago residents who would like to keep handguns in their homes for self-defense but are prohibited from doing so by Chicago's firearms laws. . . .

Chicago enacted its handgun ban to protect its residents "from the loss of property and injury or death from firearms.". . .

II

A

Petitioners argue that the Chicago and Oak Park laws violate the right to keep and bear arms for two reasons. Petitioners' primary submission is that this right is among the "privileges or immunities of citizens of the United States" and that the narrow interpretation of the Privileges or

Immunities Clause adopted in the *Slaughter-House Cases,* 83 U.S. 36 (1873), should now be rejected. As a secondary argument, petitioners contend that the Fourteenth Amendment's Due Process Clause "incorporates" the Second Amendment right. . . .

Chicago and Oak Park (municipal respondents) maintain that a right set out in the Bill of Rights applies to the States only if that right is an indispensable attribute of *any* " 'civilized' " legal system. If it is possible to imagine a civilized country that does not recognize the right, the municipal respondents tell us, then that right is not protected by due process. And since there are civilized countries that ban or strictly regulate the private possession of handguns, the municipal respondents maintain that due process does not preclude such measures. . . .

B

The Bill of Rights, including the Second Amendment, originally applied only to the Federal Government. In *Barron ex rel. Tiernan v. Mayor of Baltimore,* 7 Pet. 243, 8 L.Ed. 672 (1833), the Court, in an opinion by Chief Justice Marshall, explained that this question was "of great importance" but "not of much difficulty." In less than four pages, the Court firmly rejected the proposition that the first eight Amendments operate as limitations on the States, holding that they apply only to the Federal Government.

The constitutional Amendments adopted in the aftermath of the Civil War fundamentally altered our country's federal system. The provision at issue in this case, § 1 of the Fourteenth Amendment, provides, among other things, that a State may not abridge "the privileges or immunities of citizens of the United States" or deprive "any person of life, liberty, or property, without due process of law.". . .

D

In the late 19th century, the Court began to consider whether the Due Process Clause prohibits the States from infringing rights set out in the Bill of Rights. Five features of the approach taken during the ensuing era should be noted.

First, the Court viewed the due process question as entirely separate from the question whether a right was a privilege or immunity of national citizenship.

Second, the Court explained that the only rights protected against state infringement by the Due Process Clause were those rights "of such a nature that they are included in the conception of due process of law." While it was "possible that some of the personal rights safeguarded by the first eight Amendments against National action [might] also be safeguarded against state action," the Court stated, this was "not because those rights are enumerated in the first eight Amendments."

The Court used different formulations in describing the boundaries of due process. For example, in [one case] the Court referred to "immutable principles of justice which inhere in the very idea of free government which no member of the Union may disregard." In [another], the Court spoke of rights that are "so rooted in the traditions and conscience of our people as to be ranked as fundamental." And in [a third] the Court famously said that due process protects those rights that are "the very essence of a scheme of ordered liberty" and essential to "a fair and enlightened system of justice."

Third, in some cases decided during this era the Court "can be seen as having asked, when inquiring into whether some particular procedural safeguard was required of a State, if a civilized system could be imagined that would not accord the particular protection." Thus, in holding that due process prohibits a State from taking private property without just compensation, the Court described the right as "a principle of natural equity, recognized by all temperate and civilized governments, from a deep and universal sense of its justice." . . .

Fourth, the Court during this era was not hesitant to hold that a right set out in the Bill of Rights failed to meet the test for inclusion within the protection of the Due Process Clause. The Court found that some such rights qualified. But others did not.

Finally, even when a right set out in the Bill of Rights was held to fall within the conception of due process, the protection or remedies afforded against state infringement sometimes differed from the protection or remedies provided against abridgment by the Federal Government. . . .

An alternative theory regarding the relationship between the Bill of Rights and § 1 of the Fourteenth Amendment was championed by Justice Black. This theory held that § 1 of the Fourteenth Amendment totally incorporated all of the provisions of the Bill of Rights. As Justice Black noted, the chief congressional proponents of the Fourteenth Amendment espoused the view that the Amendment made the Bill of Rights applicable to the States and, in so doing, overruled this Court's decision in *Barron*. Nonetheless, the Court never has embraced Justice Black's "total incorporation" theory.

While Justice Black's theory was never adopted, the Court eventually moved in that direction by initiating what has been called a process of "selective incorporation," *i.e.*, the Court began to hold that the Due Process Clause fully incorporates particular rights contained in the first eight Amendments.

The decisions during this time abandoned three of the previously noted characteristics of the earlier period. The Court made it clear that the governing standard is not whether *any* "civilized system [can] be imagined that would not accord the particular protection." Instead, the Court inquired whether a particular Bill of Rights guarantee is fundamental to *our* scheme of ordered liberty and system of justice.

The Court also shed any reluctance to hold that rights guaranteed by the Bill of Rights met the requirements for protection under the Due Process Clause. The Court eventually incorporated almost all of the provisions of the Bill of Rights. Only a handful of the Bill of Rights protections remain unincorporated.[13]

Finally, the Court abandoned "the notion that the Fourteenth Amendment applies to the States only a watered-down, subjective version of the individual guarantees of the Bill of Rights.". . . Instead, the Court decisively held that incorporated Bill of Rights protections "are all to be enforced against the States under the Fourteenth Amendment according to the same standards that protect those personal rights against federal encroachment."[14]

Employing this approach, the Court overruled earlier decisions in which it had held that particular Bill of Rights guarantees or remedies did not apply to the States.

III

With this framework in mind, we now turn directly to the question whether the Second Amendment right to keep and bear arms is incorporated in the concept of due process. In answering that question, as just explained, we must decide whether the right to keep and bear arms is fundamental to *our* scheme of ordered liberty, or as we have said in a related context, whether this right is "deeply rooted in this Nation's history and tradition."

A

Our decision in *Heller* points unmistakably to the answer. Self-defense is a basic right, recognized by many legal systems from ancient times to the present day, and in *Heller,* we held that individual self-defense is "the *central component*" of the Second Amendment right. Explaining that "the need for defense of self, family, and property is most acute" in the home, we found that this right applies to handguns because they are "the most preferred firearm in the nation to 'keep' and use for protection of one's home

---

[13] In addition to the right to keep and bear arms (and the Sixth Amendment right to a unanimous jury verdict), the only rights not fully incorporated are (1) the Third Amendment's protection against quartering of soldiers; (2) the Fifth Amendment's grand jury indictment requirement; (3) the Seventh Amendment right to a jury trial in civil cases; and (4) the Eighth Amendment's prohibition on excessive fines. We never have decided whether the Third Amendment or the Eighth Amendment's prohibition of excessive fines applies to the States through the Due Process Clause. Our governing decisions regarding the Grand Jury Clause of the Fifth Amendment and the Seventh Amendment's civil jury requirement long predate the era of selective incorporation.

[14] There is one exception to this general rule. The Court has held that although the Sixth Amendment right to trial by jury requires a unanimous jury verdict in federal criminal trials, it does not require a unanimous jury verdict in state criminal trials. . . .

and family." Thus, we concluded, citizens must be permitted "to use [handguns] for the core lawful purpose of self-defense."

Heller makes it clear that this right is "deeply rooted in this Nation's history and tradition." [The opinion reiterates the history from the founding to the Civil War recounted in *Heller* regarding the right to keep and bear arms.]

B

[The opinion then restates the history regarding the adoption of the Fourteenth Amendment and the right to keep and bear arms.]

In sum, it is clear that the Framers and ratifiers of the Fourteenth Amendment counted the right to keep and bear arms among those fundamental rights necessary to our system of ordered liberty. . . .

IV

Municipal respondents' remaining arguments are at war with our central holding in *Heller*: that the Second Amendment protects a personal right to keep and bear arms for lawful purposes, most notably for self-defense within the home. Municipal respondents, in effect, ask us to treat the right recognized in *Heller* as a second-class right, subject to an entirely different body of rules than the other Bill of Rights guarantees that we have held to be incorporated into the Due Process Clause.

Municipal respondents' main argument is nothing less than a plea to disregard 50 years of incorporation precedent and return (presumably for this case only) to a bygone era. . . .

Municipal respondents maintain that the Second Amendment differs from all of the other provisions of the Bill of Rights because it concerns the right to possess a deadly implement and thus has implications for public safety. And they note that there is intense disagreement on the question whether the private possession of guns in the home increases or decreases gun deaths and injuries.

The right to keep and bear arms, however, is not the only constitutional right that has controversial public safety implications. All of the constitutional provisions that impose restrictions on law enforcement and on the prosecution of crimes fall into the same category. . . . Municipal respondents cite no case in which we have refrained from holding that a provision of the Bill of Rights is binding on the States on the ground that the right at issue has disputed public safety implications.

We likewise reject municipal respondents' argument that we should depart from our established incorporation methodology on the ground that making the Second Amendment binding on the States and their subdivisions is inconsistent with principles of federalism and will stifle experimentation. . . .

There is nothing new in the argument that, in order to respect federalism and allow useful state experimentation, a federal constitutional right should not be fully binding on the States. This argument was made repeatedly and eloquently by Members of this Court who rejected the concept of incorporation and urged retention of the two-track approach to incorporation. . . .

Time and again, however, those pleas failed. Unless we turn back the clock or adopt a special incorporation test applicable only to the Second Amendment, municipal respondents' argument must be rejected. Under our precedents, if a Bill of Rights guarantee is fundamental from an American perspective, then, unless *stare decisis* counsels otherwise, that guarantee is fully binding on the States and thus *limits* (but by no means eliminates) their ability to devise solutions to social problems that suit local needs and values. As noted by the 38 States that have appeared in this case as *amici* supporting petitioners, "[s]tate and local experimentation with reasonable firearms regulations will continue under the Second Amendment." . . .

We made it clear in *Heller* that our holding did not cast doubt on such longstanding regulatory measures as "prohibitions on the possession of firearms by felons and the mentally ill," "laws forbidding the carrying of firearms in sensitive places such as schools and government buildings, or laws imposing conditions and qualifications on the commercial sale of arms." We repeat those assurances here. Despite municipal respondents' doomsday proclamations, incorporation does not imperil every law regulating firearms. . . .

V

[J]ustice BREYER's dissent makes several points to which we briefly respond. . . .

Justice BREYER's conclusion that the Fourteenth Amendment does not incorporate the right to keep and bear arms appears to rest primarily on four factors: First, "there is no popular consensus" that the right is fundamental; second, the right does not protect minorities or persons neglected by those holding political power; third, incorporation of the Second Amendment right would "amount to a significant incursion on a traditional and important area of state concern, altering the constitutional relationship between the States and the Federal Government" and preventing local variations; and fourth, determining the scope of the Second Amendment right in cases involving state and local laws will force judges to answer difficult empirical questions regarding matters that are outside their area of expertise. Even if we believed that these factors were relevant to the incorporation inquiry, none of these factors undermines the case for incorporation of the right to keep and bear arms for self-defense.

First, we have never held that a provision of the Bill of Rights applies to the States only if there is a "popular consensus" that the right is fundamental, and we see no basis for such a rule. But in this case, as it turns out, there is evidence of such a consensus. An *amicus* brief submitted by 58 Members of the Senate and 251 Members of the House of Representatives urges us to hold that the right to keep and bear arms is fundamental. Another brief submitted by 38 States takes the same position.

Second, petitioners and many others who live in high-crime areas dispute the proposition that the Second Amendment right does not protect minorities and those lacking political clout.... *Amici* supporting incorporation of the right to keep and bear arms contend that the right is especially important for women and members of other groups that may be especially vulnerable to violent crime. . . .

Third, Justice BREYER is correct that incorporation of the Second Amendment right will to some extent limit the legislative freedom of the States, but this is always true when a Bill of Rights provision is incorporated. . . . This conclusion is no more remarkable with respect to the Second Amendment than it is with respect to all the other limitations on state power found in the Constitution.

Finally, Justice BREYER is incorrect that incorporation will require judges to assess the costs and benefits of firearms restrictions and thus to make difficult empirical judgments in an area in which they lack expertise. As we have noted, while his opinion in *Heller* recommended an interest-balancing test, the Court specifically rejected that suggestion. . . .

JUSTICE SCALIA, concurring. [Justice Scalia's concurrence is omitted. It is a rebuttal of Justice Stevens's dissent, which also has been omitted.]

JUSTICE THOMAS, concurring in part and concurring in the judgment.

[Justice Thomas accepted the petitioner's invitation to reconsider the longstanding precedent regarding the Privileges and Immunities Clause of the Fourteenth Amendment and would have held that it, rather than the Due Process Clause, protected the Second Amendment right as well as the other rights in the Bill of Rights.]

JUSTICE STEVENS, dissenting. [omitted]

JUSTICE BREYER, with whom JUSTICE GINSBURG and JUSTICE SOTOMAYOR join, dissenting.

[I]n my view, taking *Heller* as a given, the Fourteenth Amendment does not incorporate the Second Amendment right to keep and bear arms for purposes of private self-defense. . . .

The majority here, like that in *Heller,* relies almost exclusively upon history to make the necessary showing. But to do so for incorporation purposes is both wrong and dangerous. . . .

[T]his Court, in considering an incorporation question, has never stated that the historical status of a right is the only relevant consideration. Rather, the Court has either explicitly or implicitly made clear in its opinions that the right in question has remained fundamental over time. . . .

I thus think it proper, above all where history provides no clear answer, to look to other factors in considering whether a right is sufficiently "fundamental" to remove it from the political process in every State. I would include among those factors the nature of the right; any contemporary disagreement about whether the right is fundamental; the extent to which incorporation will further other, perhaps more basic, constitutional aims; and the extent to which incorporation will advance or hinder the Constitution's structural aims, including its division of powers among different governmental institutions (and the people as well) . . .

How do these considerations apply here? For one thing, I would apply them only to the private self-defense right directly at issue.

[A]s *Heller* concedes, the private self-defense right that the Court would incorporate has nothing to do with "the *reason*" the Framers "codified" the right to keep and bear arms "in a written Constitution." . . .

Further, there is no popular consensus that the private self-defense right described in *Heller* is fundamental. . . .

Moreover, there is no reason here to believe that incorporation of the private self-defense right will further any other or broader constitutional objective. We are aware of no argument that gun-control regulations target or are passed with the purpose of targeting "discrete and insular minorities." Nor will incorporation help to assure equal respect for individuals. Unlike the First Amendment's rights of free speech, free press, assembly, and petition, the private self-defense right does not comprise a necessary part of the democratic process that the Constitution seeks to establish. Unlike the First Amendment's religious protections, the Fourth Amendment's protection against unreasonable searches and seizures, the Fifth and Sixth Amendments' insistence upon fair criminal procedure, and the Eighth Amendment's protection against cruel and unusual punishments, the private self-defense right does not significantly seek to protect individuals who might otherwise suffer unfair or inhumane treatment at the hands of a majority. Unlike the protections offered by many of these same Amendments, it does not involve matters as to which judges possess a comparative expertise, by virtue of their close familiarity with the justice system and its operation. And, unlike the Fifth Amendment's insistence on just compensation, it does not involve a matter where a majority might unfairly seize for itself property belonging to a minority.

Finally, incorporation of the right *will* work a significant disruption in the constitutional allocation of decisionmaking authority, thereby interfering with the Constitution's ability to further its objectives.

First, on any reasonable accounting, the incorporation of the right recognized in *Heller* would amount to a significant incursion on a traditional and important area of state concern, altering the constitutional relationship between the States and the Federal Government. . . .

Second, determining the constitutionality of a particular state gun law requires finding answers to complex empirically based questions of a kind that legislatures are better able than courts to make. And it may require this kind of analysis in virtually every case. . . .

Consider . . . that countless gun regulations of many shapes and sizes are in place in every State and in many local communities. Does the right to possess weapons for self-defense extend outside the home? To the car? To work? What sort of guns are necessary for self-defense? Handguns? Rifles? Semiautomatic weapons? When is a gun semi-automatic? Where are different kinds of weapons likely needed? Does time-of-day matter? Does the presence of a child in the house matter? Does the presence of a convicted felon in the house matter? Do police need special rules permitting patdowns designed to find guns? When do registration requirements become severe to the point that they amount to an unconstitutional ban? Who can possess guns and of what kind? Aliens? Prior drug offenders? Prior alcohol abusers? How would the right interact with a state or local government's ability to take special measures during, say, national security emergencies? . . .

Third, the ability of States to reflect local preferences and conditions—both key virtues of federalism—here has particular importance. The incidence of gun ownership varies substantially as between crowded cities and uncongested rural communities, as well as among the different geographic regions of the country. Thus, approximately 60% of adults who live in the relatively sparsely populated Western States of Alaska, Montana, and Wyoming report that their household keeps a gun, while fewer than 15% of adults in the densely populated Eastern States of Rhode Island, New Jersey, and Massachusetts say the same.

The nature of gun violence also varies as between rural communities and cities. Urban centers face significantly greater levels of firearm crime and homicide, while rural communities have proportionately greater problems with nonhomicide gun deaths, such as suicides and accidents. And idiosyncratic local factors can lead to two cities finding themselves in dramatically different circumstances: For example, in 2008, the murder rate was 40 times higher in New Orleans than it was in Lincoln, Nebraska.

It is thus unsurprising that States and local communities have historically differed about the need for gun regulation as well as about its proper level. Nor is it surprising that "primarily, and historically," the law has treated the exercise of police powers, including gun control, as "matter[s] of local concern.". . .

COMMENTS AND QUESTIONS

1.   The dissents clearly have not changed their minds about the correctness of *Heller*, and if they believe *Heller* is not correct, then they certainly do not believe that the right to have a handgun in your home for self defense is a fundamental right incorporated against the states. But some of the argumentation, and especially that which has not been edited out, seems an attempt to deny incorporation, even if *Heller* were correct. Assuming *Heller* is correct, who do you think has the better argument regarding incorporation?

2.   On what basis did the Court here and in *Heller* conclude that guns could be kept from felons and the mentally ill as well as from sensitive places? Is Justice Breyer correct that these conclusions reflect the very balancing he advocates and the Court rejects?

3.   *McDonald* provides a good history and the current test for determining whether a right protected under the Bill of Rights against the federal government is likewise protected against state governments under the Due Process Clause of the Fourteenth Amendment. In addition, it discusses the alternate theory for incorporation based upon the Privileges and Immunities Clause of the Fourteenth Amendment, which has never been accepted, although Justice Thomas in *McDonald* and Justice Gorsuch today would adopt that theory in place of the Due Process theory. Since *McDonald*, the Court addressed whether the prohibition on excessive fines contained in the Eighth Amendment, still an outstanding question at the time of *McDonald*, should be incorporated. In *Timbs v. Indiana*, 139 S.Ct. 682 (2019), the Court unanimously held that it is. Moreover, in 2020 the Court overruled its earlier case that allowed nonunanimous jury verdicts in state criminal cases, despite the requirement for unanimity in federal criminal cases under the Sixth Amendment. *Ramos v. Louisiana*, 140 S.Ct. 1390 (2020). This leaves unincorporated only the Third Amendment, the right to a grand jury indictment in the Fifth Amendment, and the Seventh Amendment's right to a jury trial in common law cases where the amount in controversy exceeds twenty dollars.

4.   Just as the original Bill of Rights only applied to the Federal government, once one of those rights becomes protected against the states under the Due Process Clause of the Fourteenth Amendment, the question sometimes arises whether the complained of action is "state action." Obviously, if the action is a law passed by the state legislature or an act by a state agency or officer it is state action. The same is true for municipalities (cities, towns, counties, etc.) in a state. Sometimes, however, it is claimed that private actors have taken on the role of a state government and hence should be subject to the prohibitions of the incorporated rights in the Bill of Rights. The test for the "state-action doctrine" is whether the private entity exercises "powers traditionally exclusively reserved to the State." That is, the government must

have traditionally *and* exclusively performed the function. At least since the 1970's the Court has stressed that "very few" functions meet the test. In a recent case, *Manhattan Community Access Corp. v. Halleck*, 139 S.Ct. 1921 (2019), the Court, in the course of holding that a private corporation operating a public access television channel was not a state actor, listed a number of functions that do not qualify as making the private entity a state actor: running sports associations and leagues (*e.g.*, NCAA), administering insurance payments, operating nursing homes, providing special education, representing indigent criminal defendants, resolving private disputes, and supplying electricity. In addition, actions by a private entity as a result of a government requirement or pursuant to government funding does not make the private entity a state actor.

NEW YORK STATE RIFLE & PISTOL ASS'N V. BRUEN

United States Supreme Court, 2022.
142 S.Ct. 2111.

JUSTICE THOMAS delivered the opinion of the Court.

In *District of Columbia* v. *Heller* (2008), and *McDonald* v. *Chicago* (2010), we recognized that the Second and Fourteenth Amendments protect the right of an ordinary, law-abiding citizen to possess a handgun in the home for self-defense. In this case, petitioners and respondents agree that ordinary, law-abiding citizens have a similar right to carry handguns publicly for their self-defense. We too agree, and now hold, consistent with *Heller* and *McDonald*, that the Second and Fourteenth Amendments protect an individual's right to carry a handgun for self-defense outside the home.

The parties nevertheless dispute whether New York's licensing regime respects the constitutional right to carry handguns publicly for self-defense. . . .

New York State has regulated the public carry of handguns at least since the early 20th century. . . .

Today's licensing scheme largely tracks that of the early 1900s. It is a crime in New York to possess "any firearm" without a license, whether inside or outside the home, punishable by up to four years in prison or a $5,000 fine for a felony offense, and one year in prison or a $1,000 fine for a misdemeanor. Meanwhile, possessing a loaded firearm outside one's home or place of business without a license is a felony punishable by up to 15 years in prison.

A license applicant who wants to possess a firearm *at home* (or in his place of business) must convince a "licensing officer"—usually a judge or law enforcement officer—that, among other things, he is of good moral character, has no history of crime or mental illness, and that "no good cause exists for the denial of the license." If he wants to carry a firearm *outside* his home or place of business for self-defense, the applicant must obtain an unrestricted license to "have and carry" a concealed "pistol or revolver." To secure that license, the applicant must prove that "proper cause exists" to issue it. If an applicant cannot make that showing, he can receive only a "restricted" license for public carry, which allows him to carry a firearm for a limited purpose, such as hunting, target shooting, or employment.

No New York statute defines "proper cause." But New York courts have held that an applicant shows proper cause only if he can "demonstrate a special need for self-protection distinguishable from that of the general community." This "special need" standard is demanding. For example, living or working in an area " 'noted for criminal activity' " does not suffice. Rather, New York courts generally require evidence "of particular threats, attacks or other extraordinary danger to personal safety."

New York is not alone in requiring a permit to carry a handgun in public. But the vast majority of States—43 by our count—are "shall issue" jurisdictions, where authorities must issue concealed-carry licenses whenever applicants satisfy certain threshold requirements, without granting licensing officials discretion to deny licenses based on a perceived lack of need or suitability. Meanwhile, only six States and the District of Columbia have "may issue" licensing laws, under which authorities have discretion to deny concealed-carry licenses even when the applicant satisfies the statutory criteria, usually because the applicant has not demonstrated cause or suitability for the relevant license. Aside from New York, then, only California, the District of Columbia, Hawaii, Maryland, Massachusetts, and New Jersey have analogues to the "proper cause" standard.

As set forth in the pleadings below, petitioners Brandon Koch and Robert Nash are law-abiding, adult citizens of Rensselaer County, New York. . . . Petitioner New York State Rifle & Pistol Association, Inc., is a public-interest group organized to defend the Second Amendment rights of New Yorkers. Both Koch and Nash are members.

In 2014, Nash applied for an unrestricted license to carry a handgun in public. Nash did not claim any unique danger to his personal safety; he simply wanted to carry a handgun for self-defense. In early 2015, the State denied Nash's application for an unrestricted license. . . .

Between 2008 and 2017, Koch was in the same position as Nash: He faced no special dangers, wanted a handgun for general self-defense, and had only a restricted license permitting him to carry a handgun outside the home for hunting and target shooting. . . .

In *Heller* and *McDonald*, we held that the Second and Fourteenth Amendments protect an individual right to keep and bear arms for self-defense. In doing so, we held unconstitutional two laws that prohibited the possession and use of handguns in the home. . . .

Heller and *McDonald* do not support applying means-end scrutiny in the Second Amendment context. Instead, the government must affirmatively prove that its firearms regulation is part of the historical tradition that delimits the outer bounds of the right to keep and bear arms.

Heller's methodology centered on constitutional text and history. Whether it came to defining the character of the right (individual or militia dependent), suggesting the outer limits of the right, or assessing the constitutionality of a particular regulation, *Heller* relied on text and history. It did not invoke any means-end test such as strict or intermediate scrutiny.

Moreover, *Heller* and *McDonald* expressly rejected the application of any "judge-empowering 'interest balancing inquiry' that 'asks whether the statute burdens a protected interest in a way or to an extent that is out of proportion to the statute's salutary effects upon other important governmental interests.' " We declined to engage in means-end scrutiny because "[t]he very enumeration of the right takes out of the hands of government—even the Third Branch of Government—the power to decide on a case-by-case basis whether the right is *really worth* insisting upon." We then concluded: "A constitutional guarantee subject to future judges' assessments of its usefulness is no constitutional guarantee at all."

[W]e reiterate that the standard for applying the Second Amendment is as follows: When the Second Amendment's plain text covers an individual's conduct, the Constitution presumptively protects that conduct. The government must then justify its regulation by demonstrating that it is consistent with the Nation's historical tradition of firearm regulation. Only then may a court conclude that the individual's conduct falls outside the Second Amendment's "unqualified command."

This Second Amendment standard accords with how we protect other constitutional rights. Take, for instance, the freedom of speech in the First Amendment, to which *Heller* repeatedly compared the right to keep and bear arms. In that context, "[w]hen the Government restricts speech, the Government bears the burden of proving the constitutionality of its actions.". . . . And to carry that burden, the government must generally point to *historical* evidence about the reach of the First Amendment's protections.

And beyond the freedom of speech, our focus on history also comports with how we assess many other constitutional claims. If a litigant asserts the right in court to "be confronted with the witnesses against him," U. S. Const., Amdt. 6, we require courts to consult history to determine the scope of that right. Similarly, when a litigant claims a violation of his rights under the Establishment Clause, Members of this Court "loo[k] to history for guidance." We adopt a similar approach here.

To be sure, "[h]istorical analysis can be difficult; it sometimes requires resolving threshold questions, and making nuanced judgments about which evidence to consult and how to interpret it." But reliance on history to inform the meaning of constitutional text—especially text meant to codify a *pre-existing* right—is, in our view, more legitimate, and more administrable, than asking judges to "make difficult empirical judgments" about "the costs and benefits of firearms restrictions," especially given their "lack [of] expertise" in the field.[6]

The test that we set forth in *Heller* and apply today requires courts to assess whether modern firearms regulations are consistent with the Second Amendment's text and historical understanding. In some cases, that inquiry will be fairly straightforward. For instance, when a challenged regulation addresses a general societal problem that has persisted since the 18th century, the lack of a distinctly similar historical regulation addressing that problem is relevant evidence that the challenged regulation is inconsistent with the Second Amendment. Likewise, if earlier generations addressed the societal problem, but did so through materially different means, that also could be evidence that a modern regulation is unconstitutional. And if some jurisdictions actually attempted to enact analogous regulations during this timeframe, but those proposals were rejected on constitutional grounds, that rejection surely would provide some probative evidence of unconstitutionality.

New York's proper-cause requirement concerns the same alleged societal problem addressed in *Heller*: "handgun violence," primarily in "urban area[s]." Following the course charted by *Heller*, we will consider whether "historical precedent" from before, during, and even after the founding evinces a comparable tradition of regulation. And, as we explain below, we find no such tradition in the historical materials that respondents and their *amici* have brought to bear on that question. . . .

Much like we use history to determine which modern "arms" are protected by the Second Amendment, so too does history guide our consideration of modern regulations that were unimaginable at the founding. When confronting such present-day firearm regulations, this historical inquiry that courts must conduct will often involve reasoning by analogy. Like all analogical reasoning, determining whether a historical regulation is a proper analogue for a distinctly modern firearm regulation

---

[6]   The dissent claims that Heller's text-and-history test will prove unworkable compared to means-end scrutiny in part because judges are relatively ill equipped to "resolv[e] difficult historical questions" or engage in "searching historical surveys." We are unpersuaded. The job of judges is not to resolve historical questions in the abstract; it is to resolve legal questions presented in particular cases or controversies. That "legal inquiry is a refined subset" of a broader "historical inquiry," and it relies on "various evidentiary principles and default rules" to resolve uncertainties. For example, "[i]n our adversarial system of adjudication, we follow the principle of party presentation." Courts are thus entitled to decide a case based on the historical record compiled by the parties.

requires a determination of whether the two regulations are "relevantly similar."

As we stated in *Heller* and repeated in *McDonald*, "individual self-defense is 'the *central component*' of the Second Amendment right." Therefore, whether modern and historical regulations impose a comparable burden on the right of armed self-defense and whether that burden is comparably justified are " '*central*' " considerations when engaging in an analogical inquiry.

Consider, for example, *Heller*'s discussion of "longstanding" "laws forbidding the carrying of firearms in sensitive places such as schools and government buildings." Although the historical record yields relatively few 18th- and 19th-century "sensitive places" where weapons were altogether prohibited—*e.g.,* legislative assemblies, polling places, and courthouses— we are also aware of no disputes regarding the lawfulness of such prohibitions. We therefore can assume it settled that these locations were "sensitive places" where arms carrying could be prohibited consistent with the Second Amendment. And courts can use analogies to those historical regulations of "sensitive places" to determine that modern regulations prohibiting the carry of firearms in *new* and analogous sensitive places are constitutionally permissible.

Although we have no occasion to comprehensively define "sensitive places" in this case, we do think respondents err in their attempt to characterize New York's proper-cause requirement as a "sensitive-place" law. [E]xpanding the category of "sensitive places" simply to all places of public congregation that are not isolated from law enforcement defines the category of "sensitive places" far too broadly. Respondents' argument would in effect exempt cities from the Second Amendment and would eviscerate the general right to publicly carry arms for self-defense that we discuss in detail below. Put simply, there is no historical basis for New York to effectively declare the island of Manhattan a "sensitive place" simply because it is crowded and protected generally by the New York City Police Department.

Having made the constitutional standard endorsed in *Heller* more explicit, we now apply that standard to New York's proper-cause requirement.

It is undisputed that petitioners Koch and Nash—two ordinary, law-abiding, adult citizens—are part of "the people" whom the Second Amendment protects. Nor does any party dispute that handguns are weapons "in common use" today for self-defense. We therefore turn to whether the plain text of the Second Amendment protects Koch's and Nash's proposed course of conduct—carrying handguns publicly for self-defense.

We have little difficulty concluding that it does. Respondents do not dispute this. Nor could they. Nothing in the Second Amendment's text draws a home/public distinction with respect to the right to keep and bear arms. . . .

This definition of "bear" naturally encompasses public carry. Most gun owners do not wear a holstered pistol at their hip in their bedroom or while sitting at the dinner table. Although individuals often "keep" firearms in their home, at the ready for self-defense, most do not "bear" (*i.e.*, carry) them in the home beyond moments of actual confrontation. To confine the right to "bear" arms to the home would nullify half of the Second Amendment's operative protections.

Moreover, confining the right to "bear" arms to the home would make little sense given that self-defense is "the *central component* of the [Second Amendment] right itself." *Heller*. After all, the Second Amendment guarantees an "individual right to possess and carry weapons in case of confrontation," and confrontation can surely take place outside the home.

Although we remarked in *Heller* that the need for armed self-defense is perhaps "most acute" in the home, we did not suggest that the need was insignificant elsewhere. Many Americans hazard greater danger outside the home than in it. See *Moore* v. *Madigan* (CA7 2012) [(Posner, J.)] ("[A] Chicagoan is a good deal more likely to be attacked on a sidewalk in a rough neighborhood than in his apartment on the 35th floor of the Park Tower"). The text of the Second Amendment reflects that reality.

The Second Amendment's plain text thus presumptively guarantees petitioners Koch and Nash a right to "bear" arms in public for self-defense.

Conceding that the Second Amendment guarantees a general right to public carry, respondents instead claim that the Amendment "permits a State to condition handgun carrying in areas 'frequented by the general public' on a showing of a non-speculative need for armed self-defense in those areas." To support that claim, the burden falls on respondents to show that New York's proper-cause requirement is consistent with this Nation's historical tradition of firearm regulation. Only if respondents carry that burden can they show that the pre-existing right codified in the Second Amendment, and made applicable to the States through the Fourteenth, does not protect petitioners' proposed course of conduct.

Throughout modern Anglo-American history, the right to keep and bear arms in public has traditionally been subject to well-defined restrictions governing the intent for which one could carry arms, the manner of carry, or the exceptional circumstances under which one could not carry arms. But apart from a handful of late-19th-century jurisdictions, the historical record compiled by respondents does not demonstrate a tradition of broadly prohibiting the public carry of commonly used firearms for self-defense. Nor is there any such historical tradition limiting public carry only to those law-abiding citizens who demonstrate a special need for self-defense.[9] We conclude that respondents have failed to meet their burden to identify an American tradition justifying New York's proper-cause requirement. Under *Heller*'s text-and-history standard, the proper-cause requirement is therefore unconstitutional.

[Justice Thomas analyzes in some depth the various laws the respondents and the Dissent cite as evidence of a historical pattern of denying lawful citizens from generally carrying arms in public, but finds that the laws are not relevantly similar or are sufficiently unusual so that they cannot establish a history of such regulation.]

To summarize: The historical evidence from antebellum America does demonstrate that *the manner* of public carry was subject to reasonable regulation. Under the common law, individuals could not carry deadly weapons in a manner likely to terrorize others. Similarly, although surety statutes did not directly restrict public carry, they did provide financial incentives for responsible arms carrying. Finally, States could lawfully eliminate one kind of public carry—concealed carry—so long as they left open the option to carry openly.

None of these historical limitations on the right to bear arms approach New York's proper-cause requirement because none operated to prevent law-abiding citizens with ordinary self-defense needs from carrying arms in public for that purpose.

[Justice Thomas continues his analysis of laws adopted after the Civil War and reaches the same conclusion as he had with respect to the ante bellum laws.]

At the end of this long journey through the Anglo-American history of public carry, we conclude that respondents have not met their burden to identify an American tradition justifying the State's proper-cause requirement.

New York's proper-cause requirement violates the Fourteenth Amendment in that it prevents law-abiding citizens with ordinary self-

---

[9] To be clear, nothing in our analysis should be interpreted to suggest the unconstitutionality of the 43 States' "shall issue" licensing regimes, under which "a general desire for self-defense is sufficient to obtain a [permit]." Because these licensing regimes do not require applicants to show an atypical need for armed self-defense, they do not necessarily prevent "law-abiding, responsible citizens" from exercising their Second Amendment right to public carry. Rather, it appears that these shall-issue regimes, which often require applicants to undergo a background check or pass a firearms safety course, are designed to ensure only that those bearing arms in the jurisdiction are, in fact, "law-abiding, responsible citizens." And they likewise appear to contain only "narrow, objective, and definite standards" guiding licensing officials, *Shuttlesworth* v. *Birmingham* (1969), rather than requiring the "appraisal of facts, the exercise of judgment, and the formation of an opinion," *Cantwell* v. *Connecticut* (1940)—features that typify proper-cause standards like New York's. That said, because any permitting scheme can be put toward abusive ends, we do not rule out constitutional challenges to shall-issue regimes where, for example, lengthy wait times in processing license applications or exorbitant fees deny ordinary citizens their right to public carry.

defense needs from exercising their right to keep and bear arms. We therefore reverse the judgment of the Court of Appeals and remand the case for further proceedings consistent with this opinion.

JUSTICE ALITO, concurring.

I join the opinion of the Court in full but add the following comments in response to the dissent. [He asked what relevance the Dissent's parade of horribles in its introductory section had with respect to what the Court actually held. He also took issue with the Dissent's idea that the validity of a gun regulation should be assessed through a means/end relationship. Such an approach places no firm limits on the ability of judges to sustain any law restricting the possession or use of a gun.]

JUSTICE KAVANAUGH, with whom THE CHIEF JUSTICE joins, concurring.

I join the Court's opinion, and I write separately to underscore two important points about the limits of the Court's decision.

First, the Court's decision does not prohibit States from imposing licensing requirements for carrying a handgun for self-defense. In particular, the Court's decision does not affect the existing licensing regimes—known as "shall-issue" regimes—that are employed in 43 States.

[T]hose shall-issue regimes may require a license applicant to undergo fingerprinting, a background check, a mental health records check, and training in firearms handling and in laws regarding the use of force, among other possible requirements. . . .

Going forward, therefore, the 43 States that employ objective shall-issue licensing regimes for carrying handguns for self-defense may continue to do so. Likewise, the 6 States including New York potentially affected by today's decision may continue to require licenses for carrying handguns for self-defense so long as those States employ objective licensing requirements like those used by the 43 shall-issue States.

Second, as *Heller* and *McDonald* established and the Court today again explains, the Second Amendment "is neither a regulatory straightjacket nor a regulatory blank check." Properly interpreted, the Second Amendment allows a "variety" of gun regulations. . . .

JUSTICE BARRETT, concurring.

I join the Court's opinion in full. I write separately to highlight two methodological points that the Court does not resolve. First, the Court does not conclusively determine the manner and circumstances in which post-ratification practice may bear on the original meaning of the Constitution. The historical inquiry presented in this case does not require us to answer such questions, which might make a difference in another case.

Second and relatedly, the Court avoids another "ongoing scholarly debate on whether courts should primarily rely on the prevailing understanding of an individual right when the Fourteenth Amendment was ratified in 1868" or when the Bill of Rights was ratified in 1791. Here, the lack of support for New York's law in either period makes it unnecessary to choose between them.

JUSTICE BREYER, with whom JUSTICE SOTOMAYOR and JUSTICE KAGAN join, dissenting.

In 2020, 45,222 Americans were killed by firearms. Since the start of this year (2022), there have been 277 reported mass shootings—an average of more than one per day. Gun violence has now surpassed motor vehicle crashes as the leading cause of death among children and adolescents.

In my view, when courts interpret the Second Amendment, it is constitutionally proper, indeed often necessary, for them to consider the serious dangers and consequences of gun violence that lead States to regulate firearms. . . .

In 2017, there were an estimated 393.3 million civilian-held firearms in the United States, or about 120 fire-arms per 100 people. That is more guns per capita than in any other country in the world. Unsurprisingly, the United States also suffers a disproportionately high rate of firearm-related deaths and injuries. In 2015, approximately 36,000 people were killed by firearms nationwide. Of those deaths, 22,018 (or about 61%) were suicides, 13,463 (37%) were homicides, and 489 (1%) were unintentional injuries. Worse yet, gun violence appears to be on the rise. By 2020, the number of firearm-related deaths had risen to 45,222, or by about 25% since 2015. That means that, in 2020, an average of about 124 people died from gun violence every day. As I mentioned above, gun violence has now become the leading cause of death in children and adolescents, surpassing car crashes, which had previously been the leading cause of death in that age group for over 60 years. And the consequences of gun violence are borne disproportionately by communities of color, and Black communities in particular. The dangers posed by firearms can take many forms. Since the start of this year alone (2022), there have already been 277 reported mass shootings—an average of more than one per day. And mass shootings are just one part of the problem. Easy access to firearms can also make many other aspects of American life more dangerous. Consider, for example, the effect of guns on road rage. Some of those deaths might have been avoided if there had not been a loaded gun in the car.

The same could be said of protests: A study of 30,000 protests between January 2020 and June 2021 found that armed protests were nearly six times more likely to become violent or destructive than unarmed protests. . . . Or domestic disputes: Another study found that a woman is five times more likely to be killed by an abusive partner if that partner has access to a gun. . . . Or suicides: A study found that men who own handguns are three times as likely to commit suicide than men who do not and women who own handguns are seven times as likely to commit suicide than women who do not.

Consider, too, interactions with police officers. The presence of a gun in the hands of a civilian poses a risk to both officers and civilians. *Amici* prosecutors and police chiefs tell us that most officers who are killed in the line of duty are killed by firearms; they explain that officers in States with high rates of gun ownership are three times as likely to be killed in the line of duty as officers in States with low rates of gun ownership.

These are just some examples of the dangers that firearms pose. There is, of course, another side to the story. I am not simply saying that "guns are bad." Some Americans use guns for legitimate purposes, such as sport (*e.g.,* hunting or target shooting), certain types of employment (*e.g.,* as a private security guard), or self-defense. Balancing these lawful uses against the dangers of firearms is primarily the responsibility of elected bodies, such as legislatures. It requires consideration of facts, statistics, expert opinions, predictive judgments, relevant values, and a host of other circumstances, which together make decisions about how, when, and where to regulate guns more appropriately legislative work. That consideration counsels modesty and restraint on the part of judges when they interpret and apply the Second Amendment. . . .

Justice Alito asks why I have begun my opinion by reviewing some of the dangers and challenges posed by gun violence and what relevance that has to today's case. All of the above considerations illustrate that the question of firearm regulation presents a complex problem—one that should be solved by legislatures rather than courts.

[Justice Breyer goes on to criticize the majority's reliance on history alone as a basis for decision, its reading of the history, and its failure to weigh the dangers to society against the individual right to keep and bear arms in assessing the constitutionality of particular regulations.]

COMMENTS AND QUESTIONS

1.   *Bruen* is just the first of a number of cases likely to go to the Supreme Court as states and lower courts try to assess the contours of the right to keep and bear arms. In one notable federal district court case trying to apply *Bruen*'s historical test faithfully, the court found there was no historical antecedent for banning guns at summer camps. Indeed, a ban on guns on buses was unconstitutional, because history actually showed that in the past the right to have a gun was especially protected when traveling—after all there were bandits attacking the stage coaches. *See Antonyuk v. Hochul*, 2022 WL 16744700 (N.D. N.Y. 2022).

PROBLEM

What may New York do now?

1)   Retain the current concealed handgun permit requirement but allow an open carry license after undergoing a background check and passing a firearms safety course?

2)   Make it a felony for any person to bring a firearm into a private dwelling or business without the express permission of the owner?

3)   Ban the sale or possession of an assault rifle (defined as a semi-automatic rifle with the appearance of a military rifle)?

4)   Ban the possession of a firearm in Times Square and in the New York City subways and buses?

CHAPTER 7

SUBSTANTIVE DUE PROCESS

■ ■ ■

A. INTRODUCTION

In Chapter 1 we read two due process clauses, one in the Fifth Amendment and the other in the Fourteenth Amendment. Both prohibit the deprivation of a person's life, liberty, or property without due process of law. The Fifth Amendment applies to the federal government, and the Fourteenth Amendment applies to the states.

In a course on administrative law, you will learn about procedural due process, or the procedures that governments must provide before they deprive a person of liberty or property, such as prior notice and a hearing before a neutral decisionmaker. Here we study what is called substantive due process, or the substantive limits on what laws government may make. In the chapter on legislative powers we explored the extent of the powers granted to Congress, but even if something is within one of those powers, other provisions of the Constitution may limit what Congress can do. We just saw an example of that in *District of Columbia v. Heller*. We have also seen substantive limits on what laws states can make, limits imposed by the Dormant Commerce Clause and the Privileges and Immunities Clause of Article IV. Moreover, Sections 9 and 10 of Article I impose substantive limits on what laws Congress and the states, respectively, may pass.

The structural elements of the Constitution that create a government of separated powers with checks and balances operating under an umbrella of federalism also serve to protect liberty and property, as Justice Anthony Kennedy in particular was wont to point out. However, when we think of constitutional *rights*, we usually think of the Bill of Rights and the Fourteenth Amendment. The rights of free speech, freedom of religion; the right to bear arms; the right not to have troops quartered in your home, and the right to be free of unreasonable searches and seizures, for example, are all *enumerated rights*, because they are specifically addressed in the Constitution. Recall, however, that the Ninth Amendment suggested that there were rights beyond those listed in the Constitution. We might call these *unenumerated rights*.

Whether courts could enforce such unenumerated rights, however, was unclear. In a very early case, *Calder v. Bull*, 3 Dall. (3 U.S. 386 (1798), when each justice wrote an opinion in every case, one justice stated that courts could enforce unenumerated rights, while one justice denied courts had such power. In 1810, the Court in an opinion by Chief Justice Marshall held that the law there was invalid "either by general principles which are common to our free institutions, or by the particular provisions of the constitution of the United States." *Fletcher v. Peck*, 10 U.S. 87, 139 (1810). States all had their own bills of rights, including due process clauses, and state courts showed greater willingness to find and enforce rights outside those explicitly provided for, relying on due process; its textual antecedent, the Magna Carta's guarantee of the "law of the land"; or general principles of law. *See Washington v. Glucksberg*, 521 U.S. 702, 756–57 (1997)(Souter, J., concurring in the judgment). It was not until the notorious case of *Dred Scott v. Sandford*, 60 U.S. 393 (1857) that the Supreme Court found a statute unconstitutional based on an unenumerated right enforced through the Due Process Clause.

The Fourteenth Amendment created three new constitutional limitations on states. They could not "abridge the privileges or immunities of citizens of the United States"; they could not "deprive any person of life, liberty, or property without due process of law"; and they could not "deny to any person within its jurisdiction the equal protection of the laws." One of the first cases to reach the Supreme Court involving these provisions follows.

SLAUGHTER-HOUSE CASES

United States Supreme Court, 1873.
83 U.S. 36, 21 L.Ed. 394.

[A Louisiana law granted a monopoly to operate slaughterhouses in New Orleans to the Crescent City Slaughter House. Other butchers, now deprived of the ability to ply their trade in New Orleans, sued, alleging that the law violated each of these provisions in the Fourteenth Amendment. Recall that one of the privileges and immunities recognized under Article IV of the Constitution was the right to engage in a common calling or profession. Here the butchers argued they were being denied that right.]

The Crescent City Slaughter House in 1874

MR. JUSTICE MILLER delivered the opinion of the Court.

[The Court relates the history leading up to the adoption of the Thirteenth, Fourteenth, and Fifteenth Amendments.] We repeat, then, in the light of this recapitulation of events, almost too recent to be called history, but which are familiar to us all; and on the most casual examination of the language of these amendments, no one can fail to be impressed with the one pervading purpose found in them all, lying at the foundation of each, and without which none of them would have been even suggested; we mean the freedom of the slave race, the security and firm establishment of that freedom, and the protection of the newly-made freeman and citizen from the oppressions of those who had formerly exercised unlimited dominion over him. It is true that only the fifteenth amendment, in terms, mentions the negro by speaking of his color and his slavery. But it is just as true that each of the other articles was addressed to the grievances of that race, and designed to remedy them as the fifteenth.

We do not say that no one else but the negro can share in this protection. Both the language and spirit of these articles are to have their fair and just weight in any question of construction. . . . And so if other rights are assailed by the States which properly and necessarily fall within the protection of these articles, that protection will apply, though the party interested may not be of African descent. But what we do say, and what we wish to be understood is, that in any fair and just construction of any section or phrase of these amendments, it is necessary to look to the purpose which we have said was the pervading spirit of them all, the evil which they were designed to remedy, and the process of continued addition to the Constitution, until that purpose was supposed to be accomplished, as far as constitutional law can accomplish it.

[The Court then describes the first sentence of the Fourteenth Amendment—providing that all persons born in the United States are "citizens of the United States and of the State wherein they reside"—as distinguishing between citizens of a state and citizens of the United States.] We think this distinction and its explicit recognition in this amendment of great weight in this argument, because the next [sentence] of this same section, which is the one mainly relied on by the plaintiffs in error, speaks only of privileges and immunities of citizens of the United States, and does not speak of those of citizens of the several States. The argument, however, in favor of the plaintiffs rests wholly on the assumption that the citizenship is the same, and the privileges and immunities guaranteed by the clause are the same.

The language is, "No State shall make or enforce any law which shall abridge the privileges or immunities of citizens of the United States." It is a little remarkable, if this clause was intended as a protection to the citizen of a State against the legislative power of his own State, that the word citizen of the State should be left out when it is so carefully used, and used in contradistinction to citizens of the United States, in the very sentence which precedes it. It is too clear for argument that the change in phraseology was adopted understandingly and with a purpose.

Of the privileges and immunities of the citizen of the United States, and of the privileges and immunities of the citizen of the State, and what they respectively are, we will presently consider; but we wish to state here that it is only the former which are placed by this clause under the protection of the Federal Constitution, and that the latter, whatever they may be, are not intended to have any additional protection by this [sentence] of the amendment.

If, then, there is a difference between the privileges and immunities belonging to a citizen of the United States as such, and those belonging to the citizen of the State as such the latter must rest for their security and protection where they have heretofore rested; for they are not embraced by this paragraph of the amendment.

[The Court notes that Article IV of the Constitution speaks of the privileges and immunities of citizens of a state. It is these privileges and immunities that belong as of right to a citizen of a state. The Court then cites to what the Court in previous cases described as those privileges and immunities.] [T]he entire domain of the privileges and immunities of citizens of the States, as above defined, lay within the constitutional and legislative power of the States, and without that of the Federal government. Was it the purpose of the fourteenth amendment, by the simple declaration that no State should make or enforce any law which shall abridge the privileges and immunities of citizens of the United States, to transfer the security and protection of all the civil rights which we have mentioned, from the States to the Federal government? And where it is declared that Congress shall have the power to enforce that article, was it intended to bring within the power of Congress the entire domain of civil rights heretofore belonging exclusively to the States? . . .

We are convinced that no such results were intended by the Congress which proposed these amendments, nor by the legislatures of the States which ratified them.

Having shown that the privileges and immunities relied on in the argument are those which belong to citizens of the States as such, and that they are left to the State governments for security and protection, and not by this article placed under the special care of the Federal government, we may hold ourselves excused from defining the privileges and immunities of citizens of the United States which no State can abridge, until some case involving those privileges may make it necessary to do so.

But lest it should be said that no such privileges and immunities are to be found if those we have been considering are excluded, we venture to suggest some which own their existence to the Federal government, its National character, its Constitution, or its laws.

One of these is . . . the right of the citizen of this great country, protected by implied guarantees of its Constitution, "to come to the seat of government to assert any claim he may have upon that government, to transact any business he may have with it, to seek its protection, to share its offices, to engage in administering its functions. He has the right of free access to its seaports, through which all operations of foreign commerce are conducted, to the subtreasuries, land offices, and courts of justice in the several States." . . .

Another privilege of a citizen of the United States is to demand the care and protection of the Federal government over his life, liberty, and property when on the high seas or within the jurisdiction of a foreign government. The right to peaceably assemble and petition for redress of grievances, the privilege of the writ of habeas corpus, are rights of the citizen guaranteed by the Federal Constitution. The right to use the navigable waters of the United States, however they may penetrate the territory of the several States, all rights secured to our citizens by treaties with foreign nations, are dependent upon citizenship of the United States, and not citizenship of a State. . . .

But it is useless to pursue this branch of the inquiry, since we are of opinion that the rights claimed by these plaintiffs in error, if they have any existence, are not privileges and immunities of citizens of the United States within the meaning of the clause of the fourteenth amendment under consideration.

The argument has not been much pressed in these cases that the defendant's charter deprives the plaintiffs of their property without due process of law, or that it denies to them the equal protection of the law. The first of these paragraphs has been in the Constitution since the adoption of the fifth amendment, as a restraint upon the Federal power. It is also to be found in some form of expression in the constitutions of nearly all the States, as a restraint upon the power of the States. This law then, has practically been the same as it now is during the existence of the government, except so far as the present amendment may place the restraining power over the States in this matter in the hands of the Federal government.

We are not without judicial interpretation, therefore, both State and National, of the meaning of this clause. And it is sufficient to say that under no construction of that provision that we have ever seen, or any that we deem admissible, can the restraint imposed by the State of Louisiana upon the exercise of their trade by the butchers of New Orleans be held to be a deprivation of property within the meaning of that provision.

Nor shall any State deny to any person within its jurisdiction the equal protection of the laws.

In the light of the history of these amendments, and the pervading purpose of them, which we have already discussed, it is not difficult to give a meaning to this clause. The existence of laws in the States where the newly emancipated negroes resided, which discriminated with gross injustice and hardship against them as a class, was the evil to be remedied by this clause, and by it such laws are forbidden.

[W]e doubt very much whether any action of a State not directed by way of discrimination against the negroes as a class, or on account of their race, will ever be held to come within the purview of this provision. It is so clearly a provision for that race and that emergency, that a strong case would be necessary for its application to any other. . . . We find no such case in the one before us. . . .

MR. JUSTICE FIELD, dissenting (joined by the CHIEF JUSTICE, MR. JUSTICE SWAYNE, and MR. JUSTICE BRADLEY):

[T]he question presented is, therefore, one of the gravest importance, not merely to the parties here, but to the whole country. It is nothing less than the question whether the recent amendments to the Federal Constitution protect the citizens of the United States against the deprivation of their common rights by State legislation. In my judgment the fourteenth amendment does afford such protection, and was so intended by the Congress which framed and the States which adopted it.

The amendment was adopted to obviate objections which had been raised and pressed with great force to the validity of the Civil Rights Act, and to place the common rights of American citizens under the protection of the National government. . . .

[T]he amendment does not attempt to confer any new privileges or immunities upon citizens, or to enumerate or define those already existing. It assumes that there are such privileges and immunities which belong of right to citizens as such, and ordains that they shall not be abridged by State legislation. If this inhibition has no reference to privileges and immunities of this character, but only refers, as held by the majority of the court in their opinion, to such privileges and immunities as were before its adoption specially designated in the Constitution or necessarily implied as belonging to citizens of the United States, it was a vain and idle enactment, which accomplished nothing, and most unnecessarily excited Congress and the people on its passage. With privileges and immunities thus designated or implied no State could ever have interfered by its laws, and no new constitutional provision was required to inhibit such interference. The supremacy of the Constitution and the laws of the United States always controlled any State legislation of that character. But if the amendment refers to the natural and inalienable rights which belong to all citizens, the inhibition has a profound significance and consequence.

What, then, are the privileges and immunities which are secured against abridgment by State legislation?

In the first section of the Civil Rights Act Congress has given its interpretation to these terms, or at least has stated some of the rights which, in its judgment, these terms include; it has there declared that they include the right "to make and enforce contracts, to sue, be parties and give evidence, to inherit, purchase, lease, sell, hold, and convey real and personal property, and to full and equal benefit of all laws and proceedings for the security of person and property."

The terms, privileges and immunities, are not new in the amendment; they were in the Constitution before the amendment was adopted. They are found in the second section of the fourth article, which declares that "the citizens of each State shall be entitled to all privileges and immunities of citizens in the several States," and they have been the subject of frequent consideration in judicial decisions. In *Corfield v. Coryell*, Mr. Justice Washington said he had "no hesitation in confining these expressions to those privileges and immunities which were, in their nature, fundamental; which belong of right to citizens of all free governments, and which have at all times been enjoyed by the citizens of the several States which compose the Union, from the time of their becoming free, independent, and sovereign;" and, in considering what those fundamental privileges were, he said that perhaps it would be more tedious than difficult to enumerate them, but that they might be "all comprehended under the following general heads: protection by the government; the enjoyment of life and liberty, with the right to acquire and possess property of every kind, and to pursue and obtain happiness and safety, subject, nevertheless, to such restraints as the government may justly prescribe for the general good of the whole." This appears to me to be a sound construction of the clause in question. The privileges and immunities designated are those which of right belong to the citizens of all free governments. Clearly among these must be placed the right to pursue a lawful employment in a lawful manner, without other restraint than such as equally affects all persons.

MR. JUSTICE BRADLEY, also dissenting:

I concur in the opinion which has just been read by Mr. Justice Field; but desire to add a few observations for the purpose of more fully illustrating my views on the important question decided in these cases. . . .

The [fourteenth] amendment also prohibits any State from depriving any person (citizen or otherwise) of life, liberty, or property, without due process of law.

In my view, a law which prohibits a large class of citizens from adopting a lawful employment, or from following a lawful employment previously adopted, does deprive them of liberty as well as property, without due process of law. Their right of choice is a portion of their liberty; their occupation is their property. Such a law also deprives those citizens of the equal protection of the laws, contrary to the last clause of the section. . . .

It is futile to argue that none but persons of the African race are intended to be benefited by this amendment. They may have been the primary cause of the amendment, but its language is general, embracing all citizens, and I think it was purposely so expressed.

The mischief to be remedied was not merely slavery and its incidents and consequences; but that spirit of insubordination and disloyalty to the National government which had troubled the country for so many years in some of the States, and that intolerance of free speech and free discussion which often rendered life and property insecure, and led to much unequal legislation. The amendment was an attempt to give voice to the strong National yearning for that time and that condition of things, in which American citizenship should be a sure guaranty of safety, and in which every citizen of the United States might stand erect on every portion of its soil, in the full enjoyment of every right and privilege belonging to a freeman, without fear of violence or molestation.

MR. JUSTICE SWAYNE dissenting. [omitted]

COMMENTS AND QUESTIONS

1.   A mere four years after the adoption of the Fourteenth Amendment, the Court cannot agree whether or not the amendment radically altered the federal-state relationship by placing protection of basic, fundamental rights in the federal government rather than state governments.

2.   Historians and law professors have opined on the subject ever since. One thread suggests that the Privileges and Immunities Clause of the Fourteenth Amendment was intended to extend the restrictions of the Bill of Rights to the states, and there is legislative history to support this conclusion. The other thread is that, while some legislators may have had this intent, others did not, and the absence of clear support for such an intent in the ratification debates in the states would be inconsistent with a dramatic limitation on state powers.

3.   Whatever the truth may be, today the *Slaughter-House Cases* is still good law with respect to its interpretation of the Privileges and Immunities Clause. As a result, that Clause has had virtually no impact on the law, with one exception. In 1999 the Court found a California law unconstitutional under the Fourteenth Amendment's Privileges and Immunities Clause. *Saenz v. Roe*, 526 U.S. 489 (1999). The law limited for one year the maximum welfare benefits available to newly arrived residents of the state to that amount that they would have received in their original state. The purpose was to eliminate an incentive to move to California merely to obtain greater welfare benefits. The Court said that even the *Slaughter-House Cases* had said that one of the benefits of United States citizenship was the right to become a citizen of another state "with the same rights as other citizens of that state." Some thought that *Saenz* might indicate a new willingness by the Court to breathe life into the Fourteenth Amendment's Privileges and Immunities clause, but it was not to be. *See McDonald v. City of Chicago*, 561 U.S. 742 (2010)(rejecting

by an 8–1 vote a claim that the Privileges and Immunities Clause extended the Second Amendment's right to bear arms to the states, but holding, 5–4, that instead the Due Process Clause did). Nevertheless, Justices Thomas and Gorsuch have indicated their willingness to overrule the *Slaughter-House Cases* on this point.

4. While the *Slaughter-House Cases* remains good law with respect to the Privileges and Immunities Clause, it is not good law with respect to the Due Process and Equal Protection clauses. As the following case demonstrates, by the turn of the Twentieth Century the Court had found that the Due Process Clause of the Fourteenth Amendment did indeed place substantive obstacles in the path of state legislation. Moreover, this concept of the Due Process Clause protecting persons from state actions that interfered with important liberty interests led the Court to its "incorporation" of provisions of the Bill of Rights. The case arises at the beginning of an era in which some states were beginning to adopt laws championed by the Progressive movement to protect workers.

LOCHNER V. NEW YORK

United States Supreme Court, 1905.
198 U.S. 45, 25 S.Ct. 539.

JUSTICE PECKHAM delivered the opinion of the Court.

[A New York law prohibited employment in a bakery for more than 10 hours a day or 60 hours a week. Lochner, who owned a bakery, violated the statute by requiring his workers to work longer than the law allowed. The state prosecuted him, and he defended on the grounds that the statute was unconstitutional.]

The statute necessarily interferes with the right of contract between the employer and employees. . . . The general right to make a contract in relation to his business is part of the liberty of the individual protected by the 14th Amendment of the Federal Constitution. Under that provision no state can deprive any person of life, liberty, or property without due process of law. The right to purchase or to sell labor is part of the liberty protected by this amendment, unless there are circumstances which exclude the right. There are, however, certain powers, existing in the sovereignty of each state in the Union, somewhat vaguely termed police powers. . . . Those powers, broadly stated . . . relate to the safety, health, morals, and general welfare of the public. Both property and liberty are held on such reasonable conditions as may be imposed by the governing power of the state in the exercise of those powers, and with such conditions the 14th Amendment was not designed to interfere.

The state, therefore, has power to prevent the individual from making certain kinds of contracts, and in regard to them the Federal Constitution offers no protection. If the contract be one which the state, in the legitimate exercise of its police power, has the right to prohibit, it is not prevented from prohibiting it by the 14th Amendment. . . .

This court has recognized the existence and upheld the exercise of the police powers of the states in many cases which might fairly be considered as border ones, and it has, in the course of its determination of questions regarding the asserted invalidity of such statutes, on the ground of their violation of the rights secured by the Federal Constitution, been guided by rules of a very liberal nature, the application of which has resulted, in numerous instances, in upholding the validity of state statutes thus assailed. [The Court discussed a case in which it upheld a limit on the hours worked by miners in underground mines and persons working in smelters. There the Court concluded:] "This law applies only to the classes subjected by their employment to the peculiar conditions and effects attending underground mining and work in smelters . . . . Therefore it is not necessary to discuss or decide whether the legislature can fix the hours of labor in other employments." . . .

It must, of course, be conceded that there is a limit to the valid exercise of the police power by the state. There is no dispute concerning this general proposition. Otherwise the 14th Amendment would have no efficacy and the legislatures of the states would have unbounded power, and it would be enough to say that any piece of legislation was enacted to conserve the morals, the health, or the safety of the people; such legislation would be valid, no matter how absolutely without foundation the claim might be. . . . In every case that comes before this court, therefore, where legislation of this character is concerned, and where the protection of the Federal Constitution is sought, the question necessarily arises: Is this a fair, reasonable, and appropriate exercise of the police power of the state, or is it an unreasonable, unnecessary, and arbitrary interference with the right of the individual to his personal liberty, or to enter into those contracts in relation to labor which may seem to him appropriate or necessary for the support of himself and his family? . . .

This is not a question of substituting the judgment of the court for that of the legislature. If the act be within the power of the state it is valid, although the judgment of the court might be totally opposed to the enactment of such a law. . . .

The question whether this act is valid as a labor law, pure and simple, may be dismissed in a few words. There is no reasonable ground for interfering with the liberty of person or the right of free contract, by determining the hours of labor, in the occupation of a baker. There is no contention that bakers as a class are not equal in intelligence and capacity to men in other trades or manual occupations, or that they are not able to assert their rights and care for themselves without the protecting arm of the state, interfering with their independence of judgment and of action. They are in no sense wards of the state. Viewed in the light of a purely labor law, with no reference whatever to the question of health, we think that a law like the one before us involves neither the safety, the morals, nor the welfare, of the public, and that the interest of the public is not in the slightest degree affected by such an act. The law must be upheld, if at all, as a law pertaining to the health of the individual engaged in the occupation of a baker. . . .

It is a question of which of two powers or rights shall prevail, the power of the state to legislate or the right of the individual to liberty of person and freedom of contract. The mere assertion that the subject relates, though but in a remote degree, to the public health does not necessarily render the enactment valid. The act must have a more direct relation, as a means to an end, and the end itself must be appropriate and legitimate, before an act can be held to be valid which interferes with the general right of an individual to be free in his person and in his power to contract in relation to his own labor. . . .

We think the limit of the police power has been reached and passed in this case. There is, in our judgment, no reasonable foundation for holding this to be necessary or appropriate as a health law to safeguard the public health, or the health of the individuals who are following the trade of a baker. If this statute be valid, and if, therefore, a proper case is made out in which to deny the right of an individual . . . to make contracts for . . . labor . . . under the protection of the provisions of the Federal Constitution, there would seem to be no length to which legislation of this nature might not go. . . .

We think that there can be no fair doubt that the trade of a baker, in and of itself, is not an unhealthy one to that degree which would authorize the legislature to interfere with the right to labor, and with the right of free contract on the part of the individual, either as employer or employee. In looking through statistics regarding all trades and occupations, it may be true that the trade of a baker does not appear to be as healthy as some other trades, and is also vastly more healthy than still others. To the common understanding the trade of a baker has never been regarded as an unhealthy one. . . . Some occupations are more healthy than others, but we think there are none which might not come under the power of the legislature to supervise and control the hours of working therein, if the mere fact that the occupation is not absolutely and perfectly healthy is to confer that right upon the legislative department of the government. . . .

It is also urged, pursuing the same line of argument, that it is to the interest of the state that its population should be strong and robust, and therefore any legislation which may be said to tend to make people healthy must be valid as health laws, enacted under the police power. If this be a valid argument and a justification for this kind of legislation, it follows that the protection of the Federal Constitution from undue interference with liberty of person and freedom of contract is visionary, wherever the law is sought to be justified as a valid exercise of the police power. Scarcely any law but might find shelter under such assumptions. . . .

When assertions such as we have adverted to become necessary in order to give, if possible, a plausible foundation for the contention that the law is a "health law," it gives rise to at least a suspicion that there was some other motive dominating the legislature than the purpose to subserve the public health or welfare.

This interference on the part of the legislatures of the several states with the ordinary trades and occupations of the people seems to be on the increase. . . .

It is impossible for us to shut our eyes to the fact that many of the laws of this character, while passed under what is claimed to be the police power for the purpose of protecting the public health or welfare, are, in reality, passed from other motives. . . .

It is manifest to us that the limitation of the hours of labor as provided for in this section of the statute has no such direct relation to, and no such substantial effect upon, the health of the employee, as to justify us in regarding the section as really a health law. It seems to us that the real object and purpose were simply to regulate the hours of labor between the master and his employees . . . in a private business, not dangerous in any degree to morals, or in any real and substantial degree to the health of the employees. Under such circumstances the freedom of master and employee to contract with each other in relation to their employment, and in defining the same, cannot be prohibited or interfered with, without violating the Federal Constitution.

JUSTICE HOLMES dissenting:

This case is decided upon an economic theory which a large part of the country does not entertain. If it were a question whether I agreed with that theory, I should desire to study it further and long before making up my mind. But I do not conceive that to be my duty, because I strongly believe that my agreement or disagreement has nothing to do with the right of a majority to embody their opinions in law. It is settled by various decisions of this court that state constitutions and state laws may regulate life in many ways which we as legislators might think as injudicious, or if you like as tyrannical, as this, and which, equally with this, interfere with the liberty to contract. Sunday laws and usury laws are ancient examples. A more modern one is the prohibition of lotteries. The liberty of the citizen to do as he likes so long as he does not interfere with the liberty of others to do the same, which has been a shibboleth for some well-known writers, is interfered with by school laws, by the Post Office, by every state or municipal institution which takes his money for purposes thought desirable, whether he likes it or not. The 14th Amendment does not enact Mr. Herbert Spencer's Social Statics. . . .

I think that the word 'liberty,' in the 14th Amendment, is perverted when it is held to prevent the natural outcome of a dominant opinion, unless it can be said that a rational and fair man necessarily would admit that the statute proposed would infringe fundamental principles as they have been understood by the traditions of our people and our law. It does not need research to show that no such sweeping condemnation can be passed upon the statute before us. A reasonable man might think it a proper measure on the score of health. Men whom I certainly could not pronounce unreasonable would uphold it as a first installment of a general regulation of the hours of work. . . .

JUSTICE HARLAN (with whom JUSTICE WHITE and JUSTICE DAY concur) dissenting:

Granting . . . that there is a liberty of contract which cannot be violated even under the sanction of direct legislative enactment, but assuming, as according to settled law we may assume, that such liberty of contract is subject to such regulations as the state may reasonably prescribe for the common good and the well-being of society, what are the conditions under which the judiciary may declare such regulations to be in excess of legislative authority and void? Upon this point there is no room for dispute; for the rule is universal that a legislative enactment, Federal or state, is never to be disregarded or held invalid unless it be, beyond question, plainly and palpably in excess of legislative power. . . . If there be doubt as to the validity of the statute, that doubt must therefore be resolved in favor of its validity, and the courts must keep their hands off, leaving the legislature to meet the responsibility for unwise legislation. If the end which the legislature seeks to accomplish be one to which its power extends, and if the means employed to that end, although not the wisest or best, are yet not plainly and palpably unauthorized by law, then the court cannot interfere. . . .

It is plain that this statute was enacted in order to protect the physical well-being of those who work in bakery and confectionery establishments. It may be that the statute had its origin, in part, in the belief that employers and employees in such establishments were not upon an equal footing, and that the necessities of the latter often compelled them to submit to such exactions as unduly taxed their strength. Be this as it may, the statute must be taken as expressing the belief of the people of New York that, as a general rule, and in the case of the average man, labor in excess of sixty hours during a week in such establishments may endanger the health of those who thus labor. Whether or not this be wise legislation it is not the province of the court to inquire. Under our systems of government the courts are not concerned with the wisdom or policy of legislation. So that, in determining the question of power to interfere with liberty of contract, the court may inquire whether the means devised by the state are germane to an end which may be lawfully accomplished and have a real or substantial relation to the protection of health, as involved in the daily work of the persons, male and female, engaged in bakery and confectionery establishments. But when this inquiry is entered upon I find it impossible, in view of common experience, to say that there is here no real or substantial relation between the means employed by the state and the end sought to be accomplished by its legislation. . . . Therefore I submit that this court will transcend its functions if it assumes to annul the statute of New York. . . .

We judicially know that the question of the number of hours during which a workman should continuously labor has been, for a long period, and is yet, a subject of serious consideration among civilized peoples, and by those having special knowledge of the laws of health. Suppose the statute prohibited labor in bakery and confectionery establishments in excess of eighteen hours each day. No one, I take it, could dispute the power of the state to enact such a statute. But the statute before us does not embrace extreme or exceptional cases. It may be said to occupy a middle ground in respect of the hours of labor. What is the true ground for the state to take between legitimate protection, by legislation, of the public health and liberty of contract is not a question easily solved, nor one in respect of which there is or can be absolute certainty.

I do not stop to consider whether any particular view of this economic question presents the sounder theory. What the precise facts are it may be difficult to say. It is enough for the determination of this case, and it is enough for this court to know, that the question is one about which there is room for debate and for an honest difference of opinion.

COMMENTS AND QUESTIONS

1.   New York defends its law as being directed at the physical health and safety of the bakery workers. There is some support in the legislative record that flour dust harms the health of bakery workers. Why is this not enough for the majority? Why is it enough for the dissents?

2.   Note that the majority first determines that if the law is a "labor law" unrelated to the health or safety of the bakers, it cannot be justified under the police powers of the state. It is simply not a legitimate state interest. What does the majority mean by a "labor law"? What do the dissents say about a "labor law" per se?

3.   *Lochner* and its doctrine were responsible over the next thirty-some years for invalidating a host of state laws regulating the hours and wages of employees in various industries, forbidding discrimination against unions, and regulating the prices of products. What "Progressives" and labor unions were able to win in state legislatures were often overturned in the courts. Recall the Court's initial reaction to federal New Deal legislation on these issues. It is no surprise that during this period the courts were viewed as deeply conservative and antagonistic to liberal legislation.

4. The doctrine of substantive due process protecting "fundamental liberties" from arbitrary state action was not limited to the economic arena. Two cases relying on *Lochner* recognized different fundamental liberties. In *Meyer v. Nebraska*, 262 U.S. 390 (1923), the Court held unconstitutional Nebraska's law that banned the teaching of German in private schools or by private tutors (and it was not taught in the public schools). The Court recognized as important liberties, the freedom to "acquire useful knowledge, to marry, establish a home and bring up children, [and] to worship God according to the dictates of [one's] own conscience." Similarly, in *Pierce v. Society of Sisters*, 268 U.S. 510 (1925), the Court invalidated an Oregon law that required all children to attend public school through the eighth grade. The purpose was to close down parochial schools operated by the Catholic church. This law was found to "unreasonably interfere[ ] with the liberty of parents . . . to direct the upbringing and education of [their] children." Moreover, as indicated earlier, the notion that the Due Process Clause protected important liberty interests was the origin of the incorporation of most of the Bill of Rights against the states. While *Lochner* has not stood the test of time, *Meyer* and *Pierce* continue to be cited positively, and, of course, the incorporation doctrine is alive and well.

5. The case that signaled the end of *Lochner* was *Nebbia v. New York*, 291 U.S. 502 (1934). In that case, New York had established a minimum retail price for milk. Nebbia was prosecuted for selling two quarts of milk for a total of thirteen cents when the required minimum price was nine cents per quart. The purpose of the law was to assist dairy farmers during the Depression by artificially raising the price at which their milk was sold. Although there was some question as to how raising consumers' prices at retail would necessarily aid dairy farmers who sold at wholesale, the Court held that:

> So far as the requirement of due process is concerned, a state is free to adopt whatever economic policy may reasonably be deemed to promote public welfare, and to enforce that policy by legislation adapted to its purpose. The courts are without authority either to declare such policy, or, when it is declared by the legislature, to override it. If the laws passed are seen to have a reasonable relation to a proper legislative purpose, and are neither arbitrary nor discriminatory, the requirements of due process are satisfied. . . . [I]t is equally clear that if the legislative policy be to curb unrestrained and harmful competition by measures which are not arbitrary or discriminatory it does not lie with the courts to determine that the rule is unwise. With the wisdom of the policy adopted, with the adequacy or practicability of the law enacted to forward it, the courts are both incompetent and unauthorized to deal.
>
> The Constitution does not secure to any one liberty to conduct his business in such fashion as to inflict injury upon the public at large, or upon any substantial group of the people. Price control, like any other form of regulation, is unconstitutional only if arbitrary, discriminatory, or demonstrably irrelevant to the policy the

> Legislature is free to adopt, and hence an unnecessary and unwarranted interference with individual liberty.

Four justices dissented, saying:

> [P]lainly, I think, this Court must have regard to the wisdom of the enactment. At least, we must inquire concerning its purpose and decide whether the means proposed have reasonable relation to something within legislative power—whether the end is legitimate, and the means appropriate. . . . Here, we find direct interference with guaranteed rights defended upon the ground that the purpose was to promote the public welfare by increasing milk prices at the farm. Unless we can affirm that the end proposed is proper and the means adopted have reasonable relation to it, this action is unjustifiable.
>
> The court below has not definitely affirmed this necessary relation. . . . Not only does the statute interfere arbitrarily with the rights of the little grocer to conduct his business according to standards long accepted. . .; but it takes away the liberty of 12,000,000 consumers to buy a necessity of life in an open market. It imposes direct and arbitrary burdens upon those already seriously impoverished with the alleged immediate design of affording special benefits to others. . . . *The Legislature cannot lawfully destroy guaranteed rights of one man with the prime purpose of enriching another, even if for the moment, this may seem advantageous to the public*. . . . Grave concern for embarrassed farmers is everywhere; but this should neither obscure the rights of others nor obstruct judicial appraisement of measures proposed for relief. (emphasis added by author)

Both the majority and dissent say that due process requires a "reasonable relation" between a proper purpose and the means used, so where is the disagreement? Is it the italicized language?

    6.   In *United States v. Carolene Products Co.*, 304 U.S. 144 (1938), the Court upheld the constitutionality of a federal statute that prohibited interstate shipment of "filled milk," where vegetable oil is added to skimmed milk to increase its fat content. Properly labeled it can be used for a number of pure milk uses but is cheaper than pure milk. Probably the law was simply an attempt to assist the dairy industry by eliminating a lower cost alternative to pure milk. Nevertheless, the Court said that economic regulation such as this was entitled to a presumption of constitutionality and would be upheld if supported by any rational basis. Moreover, anyone challenging the rational basis had the burden of proving the lack of facts supporting the legislation. The Court then dropped probably the most famous footnote in Supreme Court history. Footnote four stated:

> There may be narrower scope for operation of the presumption of constitutionality when legislation appears on its face to be within a specific prohibition of the Constitution, such as those of the first ten Amendments, which are deemed equally specific when held to be

embraced within the Fourteenth. It is unnecessary to consider now whether legislation which restricts those political processes which can ordinarily be expected to bring about repeal of undesirable legislation, is to be subjected to more exacting judicial scrutiny under the general prohibitions of the Fourteenth Amendment than are most other types of legislation. . . . Nor need we enquire whether similar considerations enter into the review of statutes directed at particular religious or national or racial minorities [or] whether prejudice against discrete and insular minorities may be a special condition, which tends seriously to curtail the operation of those political processes ordinarily to be relied upon to protect minorities, and which may call for a correspondingly more searching judicial inquiry.

B. MODERN SUBSTANTIVE DUE PROCESS

1. ECONOMIC REGULATION

WILLIAMSON V. LEE OPTICAL OF OKLAHOMA

United States Supreme Court, 1955.
348 U.S. 483, 75 S.Ct. 461.

JUSTICE DOUGLAS delivered the opinion of the Court:

[An Oklahoma law made it unlawful for opticians to fit or duplicate lenses without a prescription from an ophthalmologist or optometrist.] In practical effect, it means that no optician can fit old glasses into new frames or supply a lens, whether it be a new lens or one to duplicate a lost or broken lens, without a prescription. The District Court conceded that it was in the competence of the police power of a State to regulate the examination of the eyes. But it rebelled at the notion that a State could require a prescription from an optometrist or ophthalmologist "to take old lenses and place them in new frames and then fit the completed spectacles to the face of the eyeglass wearer." It held that such a requirement was not "reasonably and rationally related to the health and welfare of the people." The court found that through mechanical devices and ordinary skills the optician could take a broken lens or a fragment thereof, measure its power, and reduce it to prescriptive terms. . . . It was, accordingly, the opinion of the court that this provision of the law violated the Due Process Clause by arbitrarily interfering with the optician's right to do business.

The Oklahoma law may exact a needless, wasteful requirement in many cases. But it is for the legislature, not the courts, to balance the advantages and disadvantages of the new requirement. It appears that in many cases the optician can easily supply the new frames or new lenses without reference to the old written prescription. It also appears that many written prescriptions contain no directive data in regard to fitting spectacles to the face. But in some cases the directions contained in the prescription are essential, if the glasses are to be fitted so as to correct the particular defects of vision or alleviate the eye condition. The legislature might have concluded that the frequency of occasions when a prescription is necessary was sufficient to justify this regulation of the fitting of eyeglasses. Likewise, when it is necessary to duplicate a lens, a written prescription may or may not be necessary. But the legislature might have concluded that one was needed often enough to require one in every case. Or the legislature may have concluded that eye examinations were so critical, not only for correction of vision but also for detection of latent ailments or diseases, that every change in frames and every duplication of a lens should be accompanied by a prescription from a medical expert. To be sure, the present law does not require a new examination of the eyes every time the frames are changed or the lenses duplicated. For if the old prescription is on file with the optician, he can go ahead and make the new fitting or duplicate the lenses. But the law need not be in every respect logically consistent with its aims to be constitutional. It is enough that there is an evil at hand for correction, and that it might be thought that the particular legislative measure was a rational way to correct it.

The day is gone when this Court uses the Due Process Clause of the Fourteenth Amendment to strike down state laws, regulatory of business and industrial conditions, because they may be unwise, improvident, or out of harmony with a particular school of thought.

COMMENTS AND QUESTIONS

1.   What do you think was the real reason for this law? The optometrist and ophthalmologist lobby? When, if ever, would a law regulating economic affairs violate due process?

2.   Is this near abdication of meaningful judicial review appropriate because the Court is in essence making up an unenumerated right?

3.   Article I, Section 10, Clause 1 of the Constitution contains the Contracts Clause, which prohibits states from "impairing the obligation of contracts." No similar restriction is placed on the federal government. One might imagine that as an enumerated right courts would be more likely to apply it strictly, as compared with their application of substantive due process. Not really. For example, in *Home Building & Loan Ass'n v. Blaisdell*, 290 U.S. 398 (1934), the Court upheld a state mortgage moratorium law that allowed a court to delay foreclosure for up to two years if it required the owner to pay all or a reasonable portion of the rental value of the property toward taxes, insurance, and the interest and principal of the mortgage. The Court noted that this was an emergency measure; that it did not extinguish the debt; that it was addressed to a legitimate end, the protection of a basic interest of society; and that the relief provided was "of a character appropriate to the emergency" and could be granted "only upon reasonable conditions." The four dissenters in *Nebbia* dissented here as well.

Subsequent cases established a two-part test. First, does the state law operate as a substantial impairment of a contractual relationship? Factors relevant to that consideration include "the extent to which the law undermines the contractual bargain, interferes with a party's reasonable expectations, and prevents the party from safeguarding or reinstating his rights." *Sveen v. Melin*, 138 S.Ct. 1815, 1822. Second, if it does impose a substantial impairment, a court must ask whether the law is drawn in an " 'appropriate' and 'reasonable' way to advance 'a significant and legitimate public purpose.' " *Id.* Nevertheless, the application of the test is faithful to the deferential approach in *Blaisdell*. For example, state and local mortgage and rental moratoriums enacted during the Covid pandemic were usually upheld. *See, e.g., Apartment Ass'n of Los Angeles County v. City of Los Angeles*, 10 F.4th 905 (9th Cir. 2021).

The one area in which the Court has been strict in applying the Contracts Clause is when the government changing the obligations of the contract is itself a party to the contract and benefits from its change. *See United States Trust Co. v. New Jersey*, 431 U.S. 1 (1977).

PROBLEM

Consider a state law intended to reduce lawyer malpractice by requiring that only persons who graduate in the top half of their law school class may take the state bar examination. Or, in order to assure that law students spend adequate time on their studies, a state law prohibiting them from working for pay during the school year. Would either of these laws violate the Due Process Clause?

---

2. RIGHT TO PRIVACY OR PERSONAL AUTONOMY

As indicated earlier, while the close look that *Lochner* epitomized for substantive due process protections against government regulation of economic matters is no longer good law, the 1960s saw a rebirth of substantive due process, although usually not under that name, to protect the newly discovered **right to privacy**, which sometimes is recharacterized as a right to personal autonomy. Recall that the police powers have traditionally included the power to regulate for the health, safety, welfare, and morals of the community. And historically states have regulated familial and sexual matters to protect the morals of the community as viewed by the majority. Today there is generally less interest in criminalizing what was considered immoral behavior, but many old laws remain on the books and new laws are passed as moral concerns evolve. For example, consider the justification for laws that require the humane treatment of animals.

The bellwether case for this new right follows.

GRISWOLD V. CONNECTICUT

United States Supreme Court, 1965.
381 U.S. 479, 85 S.Ct. 1678.

William Douglas

Douglas came from a poor background but managed to attend Columbia Law School, after which he taught there and at Yale. President Roosevelt first appointed him to the newly created Securities and Exchange Commission and in 1939, as a committed New Dealer, to the Supreme Court. Retiring in 1975, Douglas was the longest serving Justice in history. He also authored more Court opinions, more dissents, and more books than any other Justice. At Yale Douglas was identified with the Legal Realist movement, which critiqued the traditional claim that courts rendered neutral decisions on the basis of text, precedent, and legal analysis, arguing instead that decisions reflected the courts' political and social views. Douglas's own decisions clearly reflected his liberal political and social views, rather than text, precedent, and legal analysis. Douglas was an ardent supporter of civil rights, civil liberties, and environmentalism.

JUSTICE DOUGLAS delivered the opinion of the Court.

Appellant Griswold is Executive Director of the Planned Parenthood League of Connecticut. Appellant Buxton is a licensed physician . . . for the League at its Center in New Haven. . . .

They gave information, instruction, and medical advice to *married persons* as to the means of preventing conception. They examined the wife and prescribed the best contraceptive device or material for her use. . . . [As a result, they were arrested and charged with violating a Connecticut law criminalizing the assisting of persons to "use[ ] any drug, medicinal article or instrument for the purpose of preventing conception."]

[W]e are met with a wide range of questions that implicate the Due Process Clause of the Fourteenth Amendment. Overtones of some arguments suggest that *Lochner* should be our guide. But we decline that invitation. . . . We do not sit as a super-legislature to determine the wisdom, need, and propriety of laws that touch economic problems, business affairs, or social conditions. This law, however, operates directly on an intimate relation of husband and wife and their physician's role in one aspect of that relation.

The association of people is not mentioned in the Constitution nor in the Bill of Rights. The right to educate a child in a school of the parents' choice—whether public or private or parochial—is also not mentioned. Nor is the right to study any particular subject or any foreign language. Yet the First Amendment has been construed to include certain of those rights. [*See Pierce v. Society of Sisters*; *Meyer v. Nebraska*.]

The right of freedom of speech and press includes not only the right to utter or to print, but the right to distribute, the right to receive, the right to read and freedom of inquiry, freedom of thought, and freedom to teach— indeed the freedom of the entire university community. Without those peripheral rights the specific rights would be less secure. And so we reaffirm the principle of the *Pierce* and the *Meyer* cases.

In *NAACP v. State of Alabama*, 357 U.S. 449 (1958), we protected the "freedom to associate and privacy in one's associations," noting that freedom of association was a peripheral First Amendment right. Disclosure of membership lists of a constitutionally valid association, we held, was invalid "as entailing the likelihood of a substantial restraint upon the exercise by petitioner's members of their right to freedom of association." In other words, the First Amendment has a penumbra where privacy is protected from governmental intrusion. . . .

The right of "association," like the right of belief is more than the right to attend a meeting; it includes the right to express one's attitudes or philosophies by membership in a group or by affiliation with it or by other lawful means. Association in that context is a form of expression of opinion; and while it is not expressly included in the First Amendment its existence is necessary in making the express guarantees fully meaningful.

The foregoing cases suggest that specific guarantees in the Bill of Rights have penumbras, formed by emanations from those guarantees that help give them life and substance. Various guarantees create zones of privacy. The right of association contained in the penumbra of the First Amendment is one, as we have seen. The Third Amendment in its prohibition against the quartering of soldiers "in any house" in time of peace without the consent of the owner is another facet of that privacy. The Fourth Amendment explicitly affirms the "right of the people to be secure in their persons, houses, papers, and effects, against unreasonable searches and seizures." The Fifth Amendment in its Self-Incrimination Clause enables the citizen to create a zone of privacy which government may not force him to surrender to his detriment. The Ninth Amendment provides: "The enumeration in the Constitution, of certain rights, shall not be construed to deny or disparage others retained by the people." . . .

The present case, then, concerns a relationship lying within the zone of privacy created by several fundamental constitutional guarantees. And it concerns a law which, in forbidding the use of contraceptives rather than regulating their manufacture or sale, seeks to achieve its goals by means having a maximum destructive impact upon that relationship. Such a law cannot stand in light of the familiar principle, so often applied by this Court, that a "governmental purpose to control or prevent activities constitutionally subject to state regulation may not be achieved by means which sweep unnecessarily broadly and thereby invade the area of protected freedoms." *NAACP v. Alabama.* Would we allow the police to search the sacred precincts of marital bedrooms for telltale signs of the use of contraceptives? The very idea is repulsive to the notions of privacy surrounding the marriage relationship.

We deal with a right of privacy older than the Bill of Rights—older than our political parties, older than our school system. Marriage is a coming together for better or for worse, hopefully enduring, and intimate to the degree of being sacred.* It is an association that promotes a way of life, not causes; a harmony in living, not political faiths; a bilateral loyalty, not commercial or social projects. Yet it is an association for as noble a purpose as any involved in our prior decisions.

MR. JUSTICE GOLDBERG, whom THE CHIEF JUSTICE and MR. JUSTICE BRENNAN join, concurring.

I agree with the Court that Connecticut's birth-control law unconstitutionally intrudes upon the right of marital privacy, and I join in its opinion and judgment. Although I have not accepted the view that "due process" as used in the Fourteenth Amendment includes all of the first eight Amendments, I do agree that the concept of liberty protects those personal rights that are fundamental, and is not confined to the specific terms of the Bill of Rights. My conclusion that the concept of liberty is not so restricted and that it embraces the right of marital privacy though that right is not mentioned explicitly in the Constitution is supported both by numerous decisions of this Court, referred to in the Court's opinion, and by the language and history of the Ninth Amendment. In reaching the conclusion that the right of marital privacy is protected, as being within the protected penumbra of specific guarantees of the Bill of Rights, the Court refers to the Ninth Amendment. I add these words to emphasize the relevance of that Amendment to the Court's holding.

The Court stated many years ago that the Due Process Clause protects those liberties that are "so rooted in the traditions and conscience of our people as to be ranked as fundamental." In *Gitlow v. People of State of New York*, 268 U.S. 652, 666 (1925), the Court said:

> For present purposes we may and do assume that freedom of speech and of the press—which are protected by the First Amendment from abridgment by Congress—are among the fundamental personal rights and "liberties" protected by the due process clause of the Fourteenth Amendment from impairment by the States. . . .

This Court, in a series of decisions, has held that the Fourteenth Amendment absorbs and applies to the States those specifics of the first

---

    * It is probably not relevant, but Justice Douglas when he wrote this was on his third marriage, after two divorces, and within a few months at the age of 67 would be wooing a 22-year-old college student, who became his fourth wife three weeks after his third divorce the following year. [author's note]

eight amendments which express fundamental personal rights. The language and history of the Ninth Amendment reveal that the Framers of the Constitution believed that there are additional fundamental rights, protected from governmental infringement, which exist alongside those fundamental rights specifically mentioned in the first eight constitutional amendments. . . .

While this Court has had little occasion to interpret the Ninth Amendment, "(i)t cannot be presumed that any clause in the constitution is intended to be without effect." *Marbury v. Madison.* . . . The Ninth Amendment to the Constitution may be regarded by some as a recent discovery and may be forgotten by others, but since 1791 it has been a basic part of the Constitution which we are sworn to uphold. To hold that a right so basic and fundamental and so deeprooted in our society as the right of privacy in marriage may be infringed because that right is not guaranteed in so many words by the first eight amendments to the Constitution is to ignore the Ninth Amendment and to give it no effect whatsoever. Moreover, a judicial construction that this fundamental right is not protected by the Constitution because it is not mentioned in explicit terms by one of the first eight amendments or elsewhere in the Constitution would violate the Ninth Amendment, which specifically states that "(t)he enumeration in the Constitution, of certain rights shall not be construed to deny or disparage others retained by the people." . . .

In sum, the Ninth Amendment simply lends strong support to the view that the "liberty" protected by the Fifth And Fourteenth Amendments from infringement by the Federal Government or the States is not restricted to rights specifically mentioned in the first eight amendments.

In determining which rights are fundamental, judges are not left at large to decide cases in light of their personal and private notions. Rather, they must look to the "traditions and (collective) conscience of our people" to determine whether a principle is "so rooted (there) * * * as to be ranked as fundamental." The inquiry is whether a right involved "is of such a character that it cannot be denied without violating those 'fundamental principles of liberty and justice which lie at the base of all our civil and political institutions' * * *."

I agree fully with the Court that, applying these tests, the right of privacy is a fundamental personal right, emanating "from the totality of the constitutional scheme under which we live." . . .

The entire fabric of the Constitution and the purposes that clearly underlie its specific guarantees demonstrate that the rights to marital privacy and to marry and raise a family are of similar order and magnitude as the fundamental rights specifically protected. . . .

In a long series of cases this Court has held that where fundamental personal liberties are involved, they may not be abridged by the States simply on a showing that a regulatory statute has some rational relationship to the effectuation of a proper state purpose. "Where there is a significant encroachment upon personal liberty, the State may prevail only upon showing a subordinating interest which is compelling." The law must be shown "necessary, and not merely rationally related to, the accomplishment of a permissible state policy."

Although the Connecticut birth-control law obviously encroaches upon a fundamental personal liberty, the State does not show that the law serves any "subordinating (state) interest which is compelling" or that it is "necessary * * * to the accomplishment of a permissible state policy." The State, at most, argues that there is some rational relation between this statute and what is admittedly a legitimate subject of state concern—the discouraging of extra-marital relations. It says that preventing the use of birth-control devices by married persons helps prevent the indulgence by some in such extra-marital relations. The rationality of this justification is dubious, particularly in light of the admitted widespread availability to all persons in the State of Connecticut, unmarried as well as married, of birth-control devices for the prevention of disease, as distinguished from the prevention of conception. But, in any event, it is clear that the state interest in safeguarding marital fidelity can be served by a more discriminately tailored statute, which does not, like the present one, sweep unnecessarily broadly, reaching far beyond the evil sought to be dealt with and intruding upon the privacy of all married couples. . . . The State of Connecticut does have statutes, the constitutionality of which is beyond doubt, which prohibit adultery and fornication. These statutes demonstrate that means for achieving the same basic purpose of protecting marital fidelity are available to Connecticut without the need to "invade the area of protected freedoms."

Finally, it should be said of the Court's holding today that it in no way interferes with a State's proper regulation of sexual promiscuity or misconduct. As my Brother Harlan [has] so well stated . . .

Adultery, homosexuality and the like are sexual intimacies which the State forbids * * * but the intimacy of husband and wife is necessarily an essential and accepted feature of the institution of marriage, an institution which the State not only must allow, but which always and in every age it has fostered and protected. It is one thing when the State exerts its power either to forbid extra-marital sexuality * * * or to say who may marry, but it is quite another when, having acknowledged a marriage and the intimacies inherent in it, it undertakes to regulate by means of the criminal law the details of that intimacy. . . .

MR. JUSTICE HARLAN, concurring in the judgment.

I fully agree with the judgment of reversal, but find myself unable to join the Court's opinion. The reason is that it seems to me to evince an approach to this case very much like that taken by my Brothers BLACK and

STEWART in dissent, namely: the Due Process Clause of the Fourteenth Amendment does not touch this Connecticut statute unless the enactment is found to violate some right assured by the letter or penumbra of the Bill of Rights. . . .

In my view, the proper constitutional inquiry in this case is whether this Connecticut statute infringes the Due Process Clause of the Fourteenth Amendment because the enactment violates basic values "implicit in the concept of ordered liberty." I believe that it does. While the relevant inquiry may be aided by resort to one or more of the provisions of the Bill of Rights, it is not dependent on them or any of their radiations. The Due Process Clause of the Fourteenth Amendment stands, in my opinion, on its own bottom.

MR. JUSTICE WHITE, concurring in the judgment.

In my view this Connecticut law as applied to married couples deprives them of "liberty" without due process of law, as that concept is used in the Fourteenth Amendment. I therefore concur in the judgment of the Court reversing these convictions under Connecticut's aiding and abetting statute.

It would be unduly repetitious, and belaboring the obvious, to expound on the impact of this statute on the liberty guaranteed by the Fourteenth Amendment against arbitrary or capricious denials or on the nature of this liberty. Suffice it to say that this is not the first time this Court has had occasion to articulate that the liberty entitled to protection under the Fourteenth Amendment includes the right "to marry, establish a home and bring up children," and "the liberty * * * to direct the upbringing and education of children," and that these are among "the basic civil rights of man." These decisions affirm that there is a "realm of family life which the state cannot enter" without substantial justification. Surely the right invoked in this case, to be free of regulation of the intimacies of the marriage relationship, "come(s) to this Court with a momentum for respect lacking when appeal is made to liberties which derive merely from shifting economic arrangements."

The Connecticut anti-contraceptive statute deals rather substantially with this relationship. For it forbids all married persons the right to use birth-control devices, regardless of whether their use is dictated by considerations of family planning, health, or indeed even of life itself. . . .

An examination of the justification offered, however, cannot be avoided by saying that the Connecticut anti-use statute invades a protected area of privacy and association or that it demands the marriage relationship. The nature of the right invaded is pertinent, to be sure, for statutes regulating sensitive areas of liberty do, under the cases of this Court, require "strict scrutiny," and "must be viewed in the light of less drastic means for achieving the same basic purpose." But such statutes, if reasonably necessary for the effectuation of a legitimate and substantial state interest, and not arbitrary or capricious in application, are not invalid under the Due Process Clause. . . .

As I read the opinions of the Connecticut courts and the argument of Connecticut in this Court, the State claims but one justification for its anti-use statute. There is no serious contention that Connecticut thinks the use of artificial or external methods of contraception immoral or unwise in itself, or that the anti-use statute is founded upon any policy of promoting population expansion. Rather, the statute is said to serve the State's policy against all forms of promiscuous or illicit sexual relationships, be they premarital or extramarital, concededly a permissible and legitimate legislative goal.

Without taking issue with the premise that the fear of conception operates as a deterrent to such relationships in addition to the criminal proscriptions Connecticut has against such conduct, I wholly fail to see how the ban on the use of contraceptives by married couples in any way reinforces the State's ban on illicit sexual relationships. . . .

I find nothing in this record justifying the sweeping scope of this statute, with its telling effect on the freedoms of married persons, and therefore conclude that it deprives such persons of liberty without due process of law.

MR. JUSTICE BLACK, with whom MR. JUSTICE STEWART joins, dissenting.

In order that there may be no room at all to doubt why I vote as I do, I feel constrained to add that the law is every bit as offensive to me as it is my Brethren of the majority and my Brothers HARLAN, WHITE and GOLDBERG who, reciting reasons why it is offensive to them, hold it unconstitutional. There is no single one of the graphic and eloquent strictures and criticisms fired at the policy of this Connecticut law either by the Court's opinion or by those of my concurring Brethren to which I cannot subscribe—except their conclusion that the evil qualities they see in the law make it unconstitutional.

Had the doctor defendant here, or even the nondoctor defendant, been convicted for doing nothing more than expressing opinions to persons coming to the clinic that certain contraceptive devices, medicines or practices would do them good and would be desirable, or for telling people how devices could be used, I can think of no reasons at this time why their expressions of views would not be protected by the First and Fourteenth Amendments, which guarantee freedom of speech. But speech is one thing; conduct and physical activities are quite another. The [defendant] here [was an] active participant[ ] in an organization which gave physical examinations to women, advised them what kind of contraceptive devices or medicines would most likely be satisfactory for them, and then supplied the devices themselves, all for a graduated scale of fees, based on the family income. Thus these defendants admittedly engaged with others in a planned course of conduct to help people violate the Connecticut law. Merely because some speech was used in carrying on the conduct—just as in ordinary life some speech accompanies most kinds of conduct—we are not in my view justified in holding that the First Amendment forbids the State to punish their conduct. . . .

The Court talks about a constitutional "right of privacy" as though there is some constitutional provision or provisions forbidding any law ever to be passed which might abridge the "privacy" of individuals. But there is not. There are, of course, guarantees in certain specific constitutional provisions which are designed in part to protect privacy at certain times and places with respect to certain activities. . . .

For these reasons I get nowhere in this case by talk about a constitutional "right of privacy" as an emanation from one or more constitutional provisions. I like my privacy as well as the next one, but I am nevertheless compelled to admit that government has a right to invade it unless prohibited by some specific constitutional provision. For these reasons I cannot agree with the Court's judgment and the reasons it gives for holding this Connecticut law unconstitutional. . . .

The due process argument which my Brothers HARLAN and WHITE adopt here is based, as their opinions indicate, on the premise that this Court is vested with power to invalidate all state laws that it consider to be arbitrary, capricious, unreasonable, or oppressive, or this Court's belief that a particular state law under scrutiny has no "rational or justifying" purpose, or is offensive to a "sense of fairness and justice." If these formulas based on "natural justice," or others which mean the same thing,[4] are to prevail, they require judges to determine what is or is not constitutional on the basis of their own appraisal of what laws are unwise or unnecessary. The power to make such decisions is of course that of a legislative body. Surely it has to be admitted that no provision of the Constitution specifically gives such blanket power to courts to exercise such a supervisory veto over the wisdom and value of legislative policies and to hold unconstitutional those laws which they believe unwise or dangerous. [I] do not believe that we are granted power by the Due Process Clause or any other constitutional provision or provisions to measure

---

[4]   A collection of the catchwords and catch phrases invoked by judges who would strike down under the Fourteenth Amendment laws which offend their notions of natural justice would fill many pages. Thus it has been said that this Court can forbid state action which "shocks the conscience," sufficiently to "shock itself into the protective arms of the Constitution," It has been urged that States may not run counter to the "decencies of civilized conduct," or "some principle of justice so rooted in the traditions and conscience of our people as to be ranked as fundamental," or to "those canons of decency and fairness which express the notions of justice of English-speaking peoples," or to "the community's sense of fair play and decency." It has been said that we must decide whether a state law is "fair, reasonable and appropriate," or is rather "an unreasonable, unnecessary, and arbitrary interference with the right of the individual to his personal liberty, or to enter into * * * contracts," States, under this philosophy, cannot act in conflict with "deeply rooted feelings of the community," or with "fundamental notions of fairness and justice."

constitutionality by our belief that legislation is arbitrary, capricious or unreasonable, or accomplishes no justifiable purpose, or is offensive to our own notions of "civilized standards of conduct." . . .

Of the cases on which my Brothers WHITE and GOLDBERG rely so heavily, undoubtedly the reasoning of two of them supports their result here—as would that of a number of others which they do not bother to name, *e.g.*, *Lochner*. The two they do cite and quote from, *Meyer v. Nebraska* and *Pierce v. Society of Sisters* were both decided in opinions . . . which elaborated the same natural law due process philosophy found in *Lochner*. [T]the reasoning stated in *Meyer* and *Pierce* was the same natural law due process philosophy which many later opinions repudiated, and which I cannot accept. . . .

I repeat so as not to be misunderstood that this Court does have power, which it should exercise, to hold laws unconstitutional where they are forbidden by the Federal Constitution. My point is that there is no provision of the Constitution which either expressly or impliedly vests power in this Court to sit as a supervisory agency over acts of duly constituted legislative bodies and set aside their laws because of the Court's belief that the legislative policies adopted are unreasonable, unwise, arbitrary, capricious or irrational. The adoption of such a loose, flexible, uncontrolled standard for holding laws unconstitutional, if ever it is finally achieved, will amount to a great unconstitutional shift of power to the courts which I believe and am constrained to say will be bad for the courts and worse for the country. Subjecting federal and state laws to such an unrestrained and unrestrainable judicial control as to the wisdom of legislative enactments would, I fear, jeopardize the separation of governmental powers that the Framers set up and at the same time threaten to take away much of the power of States to govern themselves which the Constitution plainly intended them to have. . . .

I realize that many good and able men have eloquently spoken and written, sometimes in rhapsodical strains, about the duty of this Court to keep the Constitution in tune with the times. The idea is that the Constitution must be changed from time to time and that this Court is charged with a duty to make those changes. For myself, I must with all deference reject that philosophy. The Constitution makers knew the need for change and provided for it. Amendments suggested by the people's elected representatives can be submitted to the people or their selected agents for ratification. . . .

MR. JUSTICE STEWART, whom MR. JUSTICE BLACK joins, dissenting.

Since 1879 Connecticut has had on its books a law which forbids the use of contraceptives by anyone. I think this is an uncommonly silly law. As a practical matter, the law is obviously unenforceable, except in the oblique context of the present case. As a philosophical matter, I believe the use of contraceptives in the relationship of marriage should be left to personal and private choice, based upon each individual's moral, ethical, and religious beliefs. As a matter of social policy, I think professional counsel about methods of birth control should be available to all, so that each individual's choice can be meaningfully made. But we are not asked in this case to say whether we think this law is unwise, or even asinine. We are asked to hold that it violates the United States Constitution. And that I cannot do.

In the course of its opinion the Court refers to no less than six Amendments to the Constitution: the First, the Third, the Fourth, the Fifth, the Ninth, and the Fourteenth. But the Court does not say which of these Amendments, if any, it thinks is infringed by this Connecticut law.

We are told that the Due Process Clause of the Fourteenth Amendment is not, as such, the 'guide' in this case. With that much I agree. There is no claim that this law, duly enacted by the Connecticut Legislature, is unconstitutionally vague. There is no claim that the appellants were denied any of the elements of procedural due process at their trial, so as to make their convictions constitutionally invalid. And, as the Court says, the day has long passed since the Due Process Clause was regarded as a proper instrument for determining "the wisdom, need, and propriety" of state laws. . . .

As to the First, Third, Fourth, and Fifth Amendments, I can find nothing in any of them to invalidate this Connecticut law. . . .

The Court also quotes the Ninth Amendment, and my Brother GOLDBERG's concurring opinion relies heavily upon it. But to say that the Ninth Amendment has anything to do with this case is to turn somersaults with history. The Ninth Amendment, like its companion the Tenth, . . . was framed by James Madison and adopted by the States simply to make clear that the adoption of the Bill of Rights did not alter the plan that the Federal Government was to be a government of express and limited powers, and that all rights and powers not delegated to it were retained by the people and the individual States. Until today no member of this Court has ever suggested that the Ninth Amendment meant anything else, and the idea that a federal court could ever use the Ninth Amendment to annul a law passed by the elected representatives of the people of the State of Connecticut would have caused James Madison no little wonder. . . .

COMMENTS AND QUESTIONS

1.   The Court's opinion attempts to tie the right of married couples to use contraceptives to various enumerated rights. The opinions concurring in the opinion and in the judgment, reflecting the views of five justices, however, make a case for an unenumerated right of privacy arising out of the due process clause itself. The dissent straightforwardly states that there is no right of privacy in the text of the Constitution, so it does not exist as a constitutional right. Which approach do you find more persuasive?

2.   The dissent says that the Ninth Amendment's purpose was to assure that the Federal Government was to be a government of express and limited powers, and that all rights and powers not delegated to it were retained by the people and the individual States. Is that not what the Tenth Amendment says? Doesn't the Ninth Amendment address something different?

3.   What are the critical facts in *Griswold*? Is it that the law applies to married couples? Is it that the law applies to the use of contraceptives, as opposed to their sale? Is it about choices to procreate or about sexual intimacy?

4.   Subsequent cases broadened *Griswold* substantially. In *Eisenstadt v. Baird*, 405 U.S. 438 (1972), the Court found a Massachusetts statute unconstitutional that prohibited the distribution of contraceptives, with an exception for doctors or licensed pharmacists distributing to married persons. First, the Court characterized *Griswold* as prohibiting a ban on distribution to married persons, because if married persons cannot obtain contraceptives, they will not be able to use them. Next, the Court said, "If the right of privacy means anything, it is the right of the *individual*, married or single, to be free from unwarranted government intrusion into matters so fundamentally affecting a person as the decision whether to bear or beget a child." In *Carey v. Population Services International*, 431 U.S. 678 (1977), the Court invalidated a New York law that prohibited the sale of non-prescription contraceptives except by licensed pharmacists and prohibited absolutely the sale of such contraceptives to persons under 16 years old. The Court said, "in light of its progeny, the teaching of *Griswold* is that the Constitution protects individual decisions in matters of childbearing from unjustified intrusion by the State." Here the intrusion was unjustified because there was no health or safety concern with respect to the non-prescription contraceptives, and the Court rejected as invalid a purpose to deter sexual activity by increasing the hazards of the woman becoming pregnant.

ROE V. WADE

United States Supreme Court, 1973.
410 U.S. 113, 93 S.Ct. 705.

JUSTICE BLACKMUN delivered the opinion of the Court.

[A pregnant single woman (Roe) brought a class action challenging the constitutionality of the Texas criminal abortion laws, which proscribe procuring or attempting an abortion except on medical advice for the purpose of saving the mother's life.]

The Texas statutes under attack here are typical of those that have been in effect in many States for approximately a century. . . .

We forthwith acknowledge our awareness of the sensitive and emotional nature of the abortion controversy, of the vigorous opposing views, even among physicians, and of the deep and seemingly absolute convictions that the subject inspires. One's philosophy, one's experiences, one's exposure to the raw edges of human existence, one's religious training, one's attitudes toward life and family and their values, and the moral standards one establishes and seeks to observe, are all likely to influence and to color one's thinking and conclusions about abortion.

In addition, population growth, pollution, poverty, and racial overtones tend to complicate and not to simplify the problem.

Our task, of course, is to resolve the issue by constitutional measurement, free of emotion and of predilection. We seek earnestly to do this, and, because we do, we have inquired into, and in this opinion place some emphasis upon, medical and medical-legal history and what that history reveals about man's attitudes toward the abortion procedure over the centuries. . . .

The principal thrust of appellant's attack on the Texas statutes is that they improperly invade a right, said to be possessed by the pregnant woman, to choose to terminate her pregnancy. Appellant would discover this right in the concept of personal 'liberty' embodied in the Fourteenth Amendment's Due Process Clause; or in personal marital, familial, and sexual privacy said to be protected by the Bill of Rights or its penumbras, *see Griswold v. Connecticut*; *Eisenstadt v. Baird*. . . .

Harry Blackmun

Justice Blackmun, formerly a judge on the Eighth Circuit and a close friend of Chief Justice Warren Burger, was in 1970 President Nixon's second appointment to the Supreme Court. Billed as a "strict constructionist," he tended to follow the Chief Justice's lead in his first years on the Court, but his future as a member of the "liberal" wing of the Court was heralded by his opinion for the Court in *Roe v. Wade,* which became his defining achievement on the Court. It is rumored that he was lobbied by his wife and daughters before his decision in *Roe,* but his nine years as resident counsel for the Mayo Clinic also led him to consider himself something of an expert on medical matters.

Three reasons have been advanced to explain historically the enactment of criminal abortion laws in the 19th century and to justify their continued existence.

It has been argued occasionally that these laws were the product of a Victorian social concern to discourage illicit sexual conduct. Texas, however, does not advance this justification in the present case, and it appears that no court or commentator has taken the argument seriously. . . .

A second reason is concerned with abortion as a medical procedure. When most criminal abortion laws were first enacted, the procedure was a hazardous one for the woman. . . . Thus, it has been argued that a State's real concern in enacting a criminal abortion law was to protect the pregnant woman, that is, to restrain her from submitting to a procedure that placed her life in serious jeopardy. . . .

Modern medical techniques have altered this situation. Appellants and various amici refer to medical data indicating that abortion in early pregnancy, that is, prior to the end of the first trimester, although not without its risk, is now relatively safe. Mortality rates for women undergoing early abortions, where the procedure is legal, appear to be as low as or lower than the rates for normal childbirth. Consequently, any interest of the State in protecting the woman from an inherently hazardous procedure, except when it would be equally dangerous for her to forgo it, has largely disappeared. . . . [However,] the risk to the woman increases as her pregnancy continues. Thus, the State retains a definite interest in protecting the woman's own health and safety when an abortion is proposed at a late stage of pregnancy.

The third reason is the State's interest—some phrase it in terms of duty—in protecting prenatal life. Some of the argument for this justification rests on the theory that a new human life is present from the moment of conception. The State's interest and general obligation to protect life then extends, it is argued, to prenatal life. Only when the life of the pregnant mother herself is at stake, balanced against the life she carries within her, should the interest of the embryo or fetus not prevail. Logically, of course, a legitimate state interest in this area need not stand or fall on acceptance of the belief that life begins at conception or at some other point prior to live birth. In assessing the State's interest, recognition may be given to the less rigid claim that as long as at least potential life is involved, the State may assert interests beyond the protection of the pregnant woman alone. . . .

It is with these interests, and the weight to be attached to them, that this case is concerned.

The Constitution does not explicitly mention any right of privacy. In a line of decisions, however, . . . the Court has recognized that a right of personal privacy, or a guarantee of certain areas or zones of privacy, does exist under the Constitution. In varying contexts, the Court or individual Justices have, indeed, found at least the roots of that right in the First Amendment, in the Fourth and Fifth Amendments, in the penumbras of the Bill of Rights, in the Ninth Amendment, or in the concept of liberty guaranteed by the first section of the Fourteenth Amendment. These decisions make it clear that only personal rights that can be deemed "fundamental" or "implicit in the concept of ordered liberty," are included in this guarantee of personal privacy. They also make it clear that the right has some extension to activities relating to marriage, procreation, contraception, family relationships, and child rearing and education.

This right of privacy, whether it be founded in the Fourteenth Amendment's concept of personal liberty and restrictions upon state action, as we feel it is, or . . . in the Ninth Amendment's reservation of rights to the people, is broad enough to encompass a woman's decision whether or not to terminate her pregnancy. The detriment that the State would impose upon the pregnant woman by denying this choice altogether is apparent. Specific and direct harm medically diagnosable even in early pregnancy may be involved. Maternity, or additional offspring, may force upon the woman a distressful life and future. Psychological harm may be imminent. Mental and physical health may be taxed by child care. There is also the distress, for all concerned, associated with the unwanted child, and there is the problem of bringing a child into a family already unable, psychologically and otherwise, to care for it. In other cases, as in this one, the additional difficulties and continuing stigma of unwed motherhood may be involved. All these are factors the woman and her responsible physician necessarily will consider in consultation.

On the basis of elements such as these, appellant and some amici argue that the woman's right is absolute and that she is entitled to terminate her pregnancy at whatever time, in whatever way, and for whatever reason she alone chooses. With this we do not agree. Appellant's arguments that Texas either has no valid interest at all in regulating the abortion decision, or no interest strong enough to support any limitation upon the woman's sole determination, are unpersuasive. The Court's decisions recognizing a right of privacy also acknowledge that some state regulation in areas protected by that right is appropriate. As noted above, a State may properly assert important interests in safeguarding health, in maintaining medical standards, and in protecting potential life. At some point in pregnancy, these respective interests become sufficiently compelling to sustain regulation of the factors that govern the abortion decision. The privacy right involved, therefore, cannot be said to be absolute. . . .

We, therefore, conclude that the right of personal privacy includes the abortion decision, but that this right is not unqualified and must be considered against important state interests in regulation. . . .

Where certain "fundamental rights" are involved, the Court has held that regulation limiting these rights may be justified only by a "compelling state interest," and that legislative enactments must be narrowly drawn to express only the legitimate state interests at stake. . . .

The appellee and certain amici argue that the fetus is a "person" within the language and meaning of the Fourteenth Amendment. . . . If this suggestion of personhood is established, the appellant's case, of course, collapses, for the fetus's right to life would then be guaranteed specifically by the Amendment. [However,] the appellee conceded . . . that no case could be cited that holds that a fetus is a person within the meaning of the Fourteenth Amendment.

The Constitution does not define "person" in so many words. . . . But [where the term is used in the Constitution], the use of the word is such that it has application only postnatally. None indicates, with any assurance, that it has any possible prenatal application.

All this, together with our observation that throughout the major portion of the 19th century prevailing legal abortion practices were far freer than they are today, persuades us that the word "person," as used in the Fourteenth Amendment, does not include the unborn. . . .

This conclusion, however, does not of itself fully answer the contentions raised by Texas, and we pass on to other considerations.

The pregnant woman cannot be isolated in her privacy. She carries an embryo and, later, a fetus. The situation therefore is inherently different from marital intimacy, . . . or marriage, or procreation, or education, with which [our earlier cases} were . . . concerned. As we have intimated above, it is reasonable and appropriate for a State to decide that at some point in time another interest, that of health of the mother or that of potential human life, becomes significantly involved. The woman's privacy is no longer sole and any right of privacy she possesses must be measured accordingly.

Texas urges that, apart from the Fourteenth Amendment, life begins at conception and is present throughout pregnancy, and that, therefore, the State has a compelling interest in protecting that life from and after conception. We need not resolve the difficult question of when life begins. When those trained in the respective disciplines of medicine, philosophy, and theology are unable to arrive at any consensus, the judiciary, at this point in the development of man's knowledge, is not in a position to speculate as to the answer. . . .

In view of all this, we do not agree that, by adopting one theory of life, Texas may override the rights of the pregnant woman that are at stake. We repeat, however, that the State does have an important and legitimate interest in preserving and protecting the health of the pregnant woman . . . and that it has still another important and legitimate interest in protecting the potentiality of human life. These interests are separate and distinct. Each grows in substantiality as the woman approaches term and, at a point during pregnancy, each becomes "compelling."

With respect to the State's important and legitimate interest in the health of the mother, the "compelling" point, in the light of present medical knowledge, is at approximately the end of the first trimester. This is so because of the now-established medical fact . . . that until the end of the first trimester mortality in abortion may be less than mortality in normal childbirth. It follows that, from and after this point, a State may regulate the abortion procedure to the extent that the regulation reasonably relates to the preservation and protection of maternal health. . . .

This means, on the other hand, that, for the period of pregnancy prior to this "compelling" point, the attending physician, in consultation with his patient, is free to determine, without regulation by the State, that, in his medical judgment, the patient's pregnancy should be terminated. If that decision is reached, the judgment may be effectuated by an abortion free of interference by the State.

With respect to the State's important and legitimate interest in potential life, the "compelling" point is at viability. This is so because the fetus then presumably has the capability of meaningful life outside the mother's womb. State regulation protective of fetal life after viability thus has both logical and biological justifications. If the State is interested in protecting fetal life after viability, it may go so far as to proscribe abortion during that period, except when it is necessary to preserve the life or health of the mother.

Measured against these standards, Art. 1196 of the Texas Penal Code, in restricting legal abortions to those "procured or attempted by medical advice for the purpose of saving the life of the mother," sweeps too broadly. The statute makes no distinction between abortions performed early in pregnancy and those performed later, and it limits to a single reason, "saving" the mother's life, the legal justification for the procedure. The statute, therefore, cannot survive the constitutional attack made upon it here. . . .

MR. JUSTICE STEWART, concurring. [omitted]

MR. CHIEF JUSTICE BURGER, concurring.

I agree that, under the Fourteenth Amendment to the Constitution, the abortion statutes of Texas impermissibly limit the performance of abortions necessary to protect the health of pregnant women, using the term health in its broadest medical context. . . .

I do not read the Court's holdings today as having the sweeping consequences attributed to them by the dissenting Justices; the dissenting views discount the reality that the vast majority of physicians observe the standards of their profession, and act only on the basis of carefully deliberated medical judgments relating to life and health. Plainly, the Court today rejects any claim that the Constitution requires abortions on demand.

MR. JUSTICE DOUGLAS, concurring. [omitted]

MR. JUSTICE WHITE, with whom MR. JUSTICE REHNQUIST joins, dissenting.

At the heart of the controversy in these cases are those recurring pregnancies that pose no danger whatsoever to the life or health of the mother but are, nevertheless, unwanted for any one or more of a variety of reasons—convenience, family planning, economics, dislike of children, the embarrassment of illegitimacy, etc., The common claim before us is that for any one of such reasons, or for no reason at all, and without asserting or claiming any threat to life or health, any woman is entitled to an abortion at her request if she is able to find a medical advisor willing to undertake the procedure.

The Court for the most part sustains this position: During the period prior to the time the fetus becomes viable, the Constitution of the United States values the convenience, whim, or caprice of the pregnant woman more than the life or potential life of the fetus; the Constitution, therefore, guarantees the right to an abortion as against any state law or policy seeking to protect the fetus from an abortion not prompted by more compelling reasons of the mother.

With all due respect, I dissent. I find nothing in the language or history of the Constitution to support the Court's judgments. The Court simply fashions and announces a new constitutional right for pregnant women and, with scarcely any reason or authority for its action, invests that right with sufficient substance to override most existing state abortion statutes. The upshot is that the people and the legislatures of the 50 States are constitutionally disentitled to weigh the relative importance of the continued existence and development of the fetus, on the one hand, against a spectrum of possible impacts on the mother, on the other hand. . . .

The Court apparently values the convenience of the pregnant woman more than the continued existence and development of the life or potential life that she carries. Whether or not I might agree with that marshaling of values, I can in no event join the Court's judgment because I find no constitutional warrant for imposing such an order of priorities on the people and legislatures of the States. In a sensitive area such as this, involving as it does issues over which reasonable men may easily and heatedly differ, I cannot accept the Court's exercise of its clear power of choice by interposing a constitutional barrier to state efforts to protect human life and by investing women and doctors with the constitutionally protected right to exterminate it. This issue, for the most part, should be left with the people and to the political processes the people have devised to govern their affairs. . . .

MR. JUSTICE REHNQUIST, dissenting.

[I] have difficulty in concluding, as the Court does, that the right of "privacy" is involved in this case. Texas, by the statute here challenged, bars the performance of a medical abortion by a licensed physician on a plaintiff such as Roe. A transaction resulting in an operation such as this is not 'private' in the ordinary usage of that word. . . .

If the Court means by the term 'privacy' no more than that the claim of a person to be free from unwanted state regulation of consensual transactions may be a form of "liberty" protected by the Fourteenth Amendment, there is no doubt that similar claims have been upheld in our earlier decisions on the basis of that liberty. I agree with the statement of Mr. Justice STEWART in his concurring opinion that the "liberty," against deprivation of which without due process the Fourteenth Amendment protects, embraces more than the rights found in the Bill of Rights. But that liberty is not guaranteed absolutely against deprivation, only against deprivation without due process of law. The test traditionally applied in the area of social and economic legislation is whether or not a law such as that challenged has a rational relation to a valid state objective. *Williamson v. Lee Optical Inc.* . . . But the Court's sweeping invalidation of any restrictions on abortion during the first trimester is impossible to justify under that standard, and the conscious weighing of competing factors that the Court's opinion apparently substitutes for the established test is far more appropriate to a legislative judgment than to a judicial one. . . .

The fact that a majority of the States reflecting, after all the majority sentiment in those States, have had restrictions on abortions for at least a century is a strong indication, it seems to me, that the asserted right to an abortion is not "so rooted in the traditions and conscience of our people as to be ranked as fundamental." Even today, when society's views on abortion are changing, the very existence of the debate is evidence that the "right" to an abortion is not so universally accepted as the appellant would have us believe. . . .

COMMENTS AND QUESTIONS

1.   *Roe* for all the controversy that it created was not a close case in terms of votes: 7–2. Of President Nixon's three appointments to the Court, all supposedly "strict constructionists," only Justice Rehnquist dissented.

2.   *Doe v. Bolton*, 410 U.S. 179 (1973), was a companion case to *Roe*, involving Georgia's more modern abortion law based on a model abortion law drafted by the respected American Law Institute. That law allowed abortion if it was "based upon [a physician's] best clinical judgment [that] an abortion is necessary" because the pregnancy would endanger the woman's life or would seriously and permanently injure her health; or the fetus would very likely be born with a grave, permanent, and irremediable mental or physical defect; or the pregnancy resulted from forcible or statutory rape or incest. The Court interpreted this standard as allowing the physician to exercise his "medical judgment . . . in light of all factors—physical, emotional, psychological, familial, and the woman's age—relevant to the well-being of the patient." So interpreted, the Court did not strike down the law, although it did invalidate three procedural requirements: a requirement that the abortion be performed in an accredited hospital, that it be approved by a hospital staff abortion committee, and that in addition to the woman's physician, two other physicians would independently examine the woman and concur in the decision.

3.   Chief Justice Burger, concurring in both *Roe* and *Doe*, states that the Court rejected "abortion on demand." Justice White clearly reads the Court's opinion differently. Who do you think was right?

4.   The majority behind *Roe* did not extend to creating a right to government-funded abortions. *See Maher v. Roe*, 432 U.S. 464 (1977)(upholding Connecticut law disallowing use of Medicaid funds for elective or nontherapeutic abortions); *Harris v. McRae*, 448 U.S. 297 (1980)(upholding federal law denying Medicaid funds for abortions except to save the life of the mother or in cases of rape or incest, even if the government did fund live child births). The rationale was that *Roe* had created a right not to have the government interfere with a woman's decision to have an abortion; it did not forbid the government from favoring childbirth over abortion and providing funding consistent with that value judgment.

5.   Subsequent to *Roe*, many states passed laws designed either to thwart any woman's ability to obtain an abortion or to limit the circumstances in which an abortion might be obtained. In the early years, the Court applied its default test for laws restricting an enumerated right—"strict scrutiny"—to determine if the restrictions were necessary to achieve a compelling state interest. In *Connecticut v. Menillo*, 423 U.S. 9 (1975)(per curiam), the Court upheld a law requiring abortions to be performed by a licensed physician. In *Planned Parenthood of Central Missouri v. Danforth*, 428 U.S. 52 (1976), the Court upheld certain recordkeeping requirements and a requirement that the woman consent in writing, but it struck provisions requiring spousal consent and parental consent for persons under 18, requiring the abortion to be necessary to preserve the mother's life, and prohibiting saline amniocentesis as a method of second trimester abortions. In *Colautti v. Franklin*, 439 U.S. 379 (1979), the Court found unconstitutionally vague a Pennsylvania law requiring doctors, "if there is sufficient reason to believe that the fetus may be viable," to use best efforts to deliver the fetus alive. In *Akron v. Akron Center for Reproductive Health, Inc.*, 462 U.S. 416 (1983), the Court invalidated requirements that second trimester abortions be performed in a hospital; that the physician must orally inform the woman as to the development of her fetus, the date of possible viability, the physical and emotional complications that might result from an abortion, and the availability of agencies to assist in childbirth and adoption; and that the woman must wait 24 hours after signing a consent form before she could obtain the abortion. In *Thornburgh v. American College of Obstetricians and Gynecologists*, 476 U.S. 747 (1986), the Court held unconstitutional requirements that the woman be advised that medical assistance may be available for pre-natal care and the child's delivery and that the father is responsible for financial assistance in support of child; that the physician inform the woman of detrimental physical and psychological effects of an abortion and of all particular medical risks; that the facility keep various records concerning the patient, which would be available to the public; that, with respect to post-viability abortions, care be taken to try to preserve the life of the child, unless it would significantly increase the risk to the mother's life or health; and that, with respect to post-viability abortions, a second physician be present to be responsible for the child.

However, the clear majority in *Roe* evaporated with new appointments of Justices O'Connor, Scalia, and Kennedy to the Court by President Reagan. Now, depending how Justice O'Connor voted, the cases tended to be 5–4 upholding or overturning the state law. For example, in *Webster v. Reproductive Health Services*, 492 U.S. 490 (1989), the Court upheld a Missouri law requiring a doctor to determine if a fetus of twenty or more weeks is viable by using the degree of care normally exercised by a prudent physician." This conclusion, however, resulted from a plurality opinion by Chief Justice Rehnquist that said the trimester system of *Roe* should be thrown out; an opinion concurring in the judgment by Justice O'Connor, saying that the viability testing provision in the statute did not implicate the trimester system in *Roe*; and an opinion concurring in the judgment by Justice Scalia, saying he would overrule *Roe*. In *Hodgson v. Minnesota*, 497 U.S. 417 (1990), Justice O'Connor joined the four "liberals" to strike a requirement that both parents be notified 48 hours before a minor's abortion but joined the four "conservatives" to uphold the same requirement if it provided a judicial bypass by which the minor could go to court to show that she is "mature and capable of giving informed consent" or that an abortion without notice to both parents would be in her best interest.

6.   Republican President George H.W. Bush's appointments of David Souter and Clarence Thomas to replace Justices Brennan and Marshall, two "liberals," left only Justices Blackmun and Stevens from the *Roe* Court. Many believed *Roe*'s days were numbered. They were wrong, or at least its days were not as numbered as they thought. To the surprise of most observers, in a case challenging a Pennsylvania law placing various restrictions on obtaining an abortion, Justices O'Connor, Kennedy, and Souter authored a joint opinion, in which Justices Blackmun and Stevens concurred, upholding the essence of *Roe*. *Planned Parenthood of Southeastern Pennsylvania v. Casey*, 505 U.S. 833 (1992). The joint opinion suggested that the authors might not have found for Roe in the original case, but *Roe*'s status as precedent led them to reaffirm its central holding, albeit with some tweaking. In place of *Roe*'s trimester system, *Casey* established viability as the dividing point at which the state could ban abortion except as necessary to protect the life of the mother. In addition, rather than use a test of "strict scrutiny" for each attempted state regulation pre-viability, it established an "undue burden" test. That is, if a state regulation had "the purpose or effect of placing a substantial obstacle in the path of a woman seeking an abortion pre-viability," it would constitute an unconstitutional undue burden. *Casey* became the leading abortion case in the years that followed.

The four dissenters would have overruled *Roe*, finding its precedential weight insufficient.

Nevertheless, the joint opinion, applying the undue burden test, did in effect overrule some earlier cases that had applied the strict scrutiny test. Specifically, it upheld the portion of the state law requiring the woman to be provided various materials intended to dissuade her from obtaining an abortion and the portion that required a woman to wait 24 hours from receiving this information before she could receive the abortion. Justices Stevens and Blackmun did not concur in this part of the joint opinion, but because the four dissenters would have upheld the entire law, the parts of the law that the joint authors upheld received the votes of seven members of the Court.

We will return to the question of a right to abortion after consideration of some intervening cases in other areas of a right to privacy or personal autonomy between *Roe* and *Dobbs v. Jackson Women's Health Org.*, 142 S.Ct. 2228 (2022).

BOWERS V. HARDWICK
United States Supreme Court, 1986.
478 U.S. 186, 106 S.Ct. 2841.

JUSTICE WHITE delivered the opinion of the Court.

In August 1982, respondent Hardwick (hereafter respondent) was charged with violating the Georgia statute criminalizing sodomy[1] by committing that act with another adult male in the bedroom of respondent's home. . . .

This case does not require a judgment on whether laws against sodomy between consenting adults in general, or between homosexuals in particular, are wise or desirable. It raises no question about the right or propriety of state legislative decisions to repeal their laws that criminalize homosexual sodomy, or of state-court decisions invalidating those laws on state constitutional grounds. The issue presented is whether the Federal Constitution confers a fundamental right upon homosexuals to engage in sodomy and hence invalidates the laws of the many States that still make such conduct illegal and have done so for a very long time. The case also calls for some judgment about the limits of the Court's role in carrying out its constitutional mandate.

We first register our disagreement with the . . . respondent that the Court's prior cases have construed the Constitution to confer a right of privacy that extends to homosexual sodomy and for all intents and purposes have decided this case. The reach of this line of cases was sketched in *Carey v. Population Services International. Pierce v. Society of Sisters* and *Meyer v. Nebraska* were described as dealing with child rearing and education; *Prince v. Massachusetts,* 321 U.S. 158 (1944), with family relationships; *Skinner v. Oklahoma ex rel. Williamson,* 316 U.S. 535 (1942), with procreation; *Loving v. Virginia,* 388 U.S. 1 (1967), with marriage; *Griswold v. Connecticut* and *Eisenstadt v. Baird* with contraception; and *Roe v. Wade* with abortion. The latter three cases were interpreted as

---

[1] Georgia Code Ann. § 16–6–2 (1984) provides, in pertinent part, as follows:

"(a) A person commits the offense of sodomy when he performs or submits to any sexual act involving the sex organs of one person and the mouth or anus of another. . . .

"(b) A person convicted of the offense of sodomy shall be punished by imprisonment for not less than one nor more than 20 years. . . ."

construing the Due Process Clause of the Fourteenth Amendment to confer a fundamental individual right to decide whether or not to beget or bear a child.

Accepting the decisions in these cases and the above description of them, we think it evident that none of the rights announced in those cases bears any resemblance to the claimed constitutional right of homosexuals to engage in acts of sodomy that is asserted in this case. No connection between family, marriage, or procreation on the one hand and homosexual activity on the other has been demonstrated . . . by respondent. Moreover, any claim that these cases nevertheless stand for the proposition that any kind of private sexual conduct between consenting adults is constitutionally insulated from state proscription is unsupportable. Indeed, the Court's opinion in *Carey* twice asserted that the privacy right, which the *Griswold* line of cases found to be one of the protections provided by the Due Process Clause, did not reach so far.

Precedent aside, however, respondent would have us announce . . . a fundamental right to engage in homosexual sodomy. This we are quite unwilling to do. It is true that despite the language of the Due Process Clauses of the Fifth and Fourteenth Amendments, which appears to focus only on the processes by which life, liberty, or property is taken, the cases are legion in which those Clauses have been interpreted to have substantive content, subsuming rights that to a great extent are immune from federal or state regulation or proscription. . . .

Striving to assure itself and the public that announcing rights not readily identifiable in the Constitution's text involves much more than the imposition of the Justices' own choice of values on the States and the Federal Government, the Court has sought to identify the nature of the rights qualifying for heightened judicial protection. In [prior cases], it was said that this category includes those fundamental liberties that are "implicit in the concept of ordered liberty," such that "neither liberty nor justice would exist if [they] were sacrificed," [or] . . . those liberties that are "deeply rooted in this Nation's history and tradition."

It is obvious to us that neither of these formulations would extend a fundamental right to homosexuals to engage in acts of consensual sodomy. Proscriptions against that conduct have ancient roots. Sodomy was a criminal offense at common law and was forbidden by the laws of the original thirteen States when they ratified the Bill of Rights. In 1868, when the Fourteenth Amendment was ratified, all but 5 of the 37 States in the Union had criminal sodomy laws. In fact, until 1961, all 50 States outlawed sodomy, and today, 24 States and the District of Columbia continue to provide criminal penalties for sodomy performed in private and between consenting adults. Against this background, to claim that a right to engage in such conduct is "deeply rooted in this Nation's history and tradition" or "implicit in the concept of ordered liberty" is, at best, facetious.

Nor are we inclined to take a more expansive view of our authority to discover new fundamental rights imbedded in the Due Process Clause. The Court is most vulnerable and comes nearest to illegitimacy when it deals with judge-made constitutional law having little or no cognizable roots in the language or design of the Constitution. . . .

Even if the conduct at issue here is not a fundamental right, respondent asserts that there must be a rational basis for the law and that there is none in this case other than the presumed belief of a majority of the electorate in Georgia that homosexual sodomy is immoral and unacceptable. This is said to be an inadequate rationale to support the law. The law, however, is constantly based on notions of morality, and if all laws representing essentially moral choices are to be invalidated under the Due Process Clause, the courts will be very busy indeed. . . .

CHIEF JUSTICE BURGER, concurring. [opinion omitted]

JUSTICE POWELL, concurring. [opinion omitted]

JUSTICE BLACKMUN, with whom JUSTICE BRENNAN, JUSTICE MARSHALL, and JUSTICE STEVENS join, dissenting.

[T]he statute at issue denies individuals the right to decide for themselves whether to engage in particular forms of private, consensual sexual activity. The Court concludes that § 16–6–2 is valid essentially because "the laws of . . . many States . . . still make such conduct illegal and have done so for a very long time." But the fact that the moral judgments expressed by statutes like § 16–6–2 may be " 'natural and familiar . . . ought not to conclude our judgment upon the question whether statutes embodying them conflict with the Constitution of the United States.' " *Roe v. Wade*, quoting *Lochner v. New York* (Holmes, J., dissenting). . . . I believe we must analyze Hardwick's claim in the light of the values that underlie the constitutional right to privacy. If that right means anything, it means that, before Georgia can prosecute its citizens for making choices about the most intimate aspects of their lives, it must do more than assert that the choice they have made is an " 'abominable crime not fit to be named among Christians.' " *Herring v. State,* 119 Ga. 709 (1904).

[T]he Court's almost obsessive focus on homosexual activity is particularly hard to justify in light of the broad language Georgia has used. . . . The sex or status of the persons who engage in the act is irrelevant as a matter of state law. . . . I therefore see no basis for the Court's decision . . . to defend § 16–6–2 solely on the grounds that it prohibits homosexual activity. . . .

"Our cases long have recognized that the Constitution embodies a promise that a certain private sphere of individual liberty will be kept largely beyond the reach of government." In construing the right to privacy, the Court has proceeded along two somewhat distinct, albeit complementary, lines. First, it has recognized a privacy interest with reference to certain *decisions* that are properly for the individual to make. *E.g., Roe v. Wade*; *Pierce v. Society of Sisters*. Second, it has recognized a privacy interest with reference to certain *places* without regard for the particular activities in which the individuals who occupy them are engaged. The case before us implicates both the decisional and the spatial aspects of the right to privacy.

The Court concludes today that none of our prior cases dealing with various decisions that individuals are entitled to make free of governmental interference "bears any resemblance to the claimed constitutional right of homosexuals to engage in acts of sodomy that is asserted in this case." While it is true that these cases may be characterized by their connection to protection of the family, . . . we protect those rights not because they contribute, in some direct and material way, to the general public welfare, but because they form so central a part of an individual's life. . . .

Only the most willful blindness could obscure the fact that sexual intimacy is "a sensitive, key relationship of human existence, central to family life, community welfare, and the development of human personality." . . . The Court claims that its decision today merely refuses to recognize a fundamental right to engage in homosexual sodomy; what the Court really has refused to recognize is the fundamental interest all individuals have in controlling the nature of their intimate associations with others. . . .

The Court's failure to comprehend the magnitude of the liberty interests at stake in this case leads it to slight the question whether petitioner, on behalf of the State, has justified Georgia's infringement on these interests. I believe that neither of the two general justifications for § 16–6–2 that petitioner has advanced warrants dismissing respondent's challenge for failure to state a claim.

First, petitioner asserts that the acts made criminal by the statute may have serious adverse consequences for "the general public health and welfare," such as spreading communicable diseases or fostering other criminal activity. Inasmuch as this case was dismissed by the District Court on the pleadings, it is not surprising that the record before us is barren of any evidence to support petitioner's claim. . . .

The core of petitioner's defense of § 16–6–2, however, is that respondent and others who engage in the conduct prohibited by § 16–6–2 interfere with Georgia's exercise of the " 'right of the Nation and of the States to maintain a decent society.' " Essentially, petitioner argues, and the Court agrees, that the fact that the acts described in § 16–6–2 "for hundreds of years, if not thousands, have been uniformly condemned as immoral" is a sufficient reason to permit a State to ban them today. . . .

Nor can § 16–6–2 be justified as a "morally neutral" exercise of Georgia's power to "protect the public environment." Certainly, some private behavior can affect the fabric of society as a whole. . . . Petitioner and the Court fail to see the difference between laws that protect public sensibilities and those that enforce private morality. Statutes banning public sexual activity are entirely consistent with protecting the individual's liberty interest in decisions concerning sexual relations . . . . But the mere fact that intimate behavior may be punished when it takes place in public cannot dictate how States can regulate intimate behavior that occurs in intimate places.

JUSTICE STEVENS, with whom JUSTICE BRENNAN and JUSTICE MARSHALL join, dissenting.

[O]ur prior cases make two propositions abundantly clear. First, the fact that the governing majority in a State has traditionally viewed a particular practice as immoral is not a sufficient reason for upholding a law prohibiting the practice; neither history nor tradition could save a law prohibiting miscegenation from constitutional attack. Second, individual decisions by married persons, concerning the intimacies of their physical relationship, even when not intended to produce offspring, are a form of "liberty" protected by the Due Process Clause of the Fourteenth Amendment. *Griswold.* Moreover, this protection extends to intimate choices by unmarried as well as married persons. *Carey v. Population Services International*; *Eisenstadt v. Baird.*

In consideration of claims of this kind, the Court has emphasized the individual interest in privacy, but its decisions have actually been animated by an even more fundamental concern. As I wrote some years ago:

> These cases do not deal with the individual's interest in protection from unwarranted public attention, comment, or exploitation. They deal, rather, with the individual's right to make certain unusually important decisions that will affect his own, or his family's, destiny. The Court has referred to such decisions as implicating "basic values," as being "fundamental," and as being dignified by history and tradition. The character of the Court's language in these cases brings to mind the origins of the American heritage of freedom—the abiding interest in individual liberty that makes certain state intrusions on the citizen's right to decide how he will live his own life intolerable. Guided by history, our tradition of respect for the dignity of individual choice in matters of conscience and the restraints implicit in the federal system, federal judges have accepted the responsibility for recognition and protection of these rights in appropriate cases.

Society has every right to encourage its individual members to follow particular traditions in expressing affection for one another and in gratifying their personal desires. It, of course, may prohibit an individual from imposing his will on another to satisfy his own selfish interests. It also may prevent an individual from interfering with, or violating, a legally sanctioned and protected relationship, such as marriage. And it may explain the relative advantages and disadvantages of different forms of intimate expression. But when individual married couples are isolated from observation by others, the way in which they voluntarily choose to conduct their intimate relations is a matter for them-not the State-to decide. The essential "liberty" that animated the development of the law in cases like *Griswold, Eisenstadt,* and *Carey* surely embraces the right to engage in nonreproductive, sexual conduct that others may consider offensive or immoral.

Paradoxical as it may seem, our prior cases thus establish that a State may not prohibit sodomy within "the sacred precincts of marital bedrooms," *Griswold* or, indeed, between unmarried heterosexual adults. *Eisenstadt.* In all events, it is perfectly clear that the State of Georgia may not totally prohibit the conduct proscribed by § 16–6–2 of the Georgia Criminal Code. . . .

COMMENTS AND QUESTIONS

1.   Note that the Georgia statute criminalized heterosexual sodomy as well as homosexual sodomy. Do you see any basis for distinguishing *Bowers* in a challenge to the law brought by a male and female couple? What if they were married?

2.   A year after *Bowers*, the Court addressed whether a Washington law that banned physician assisted suicide for terminally ill patients violated a constitutional right for such patients to choose to die. In *Washington v. Glucksberg*, 521 U.S. 702 (1997), the Court unanimously held there was no such general right, but only a bare majority agreed with the following justification for that decision:

> We begin, as we do in all due process cases, by examining our Nation's history, legal traditions, and practices. In almost every State—indeed, in almost every western democracy—it is a crime to assist a suicide. The States' assisted-suicide bans are not innovations. Rather, they are longstanding expressions of the States' commitment to the protection and preservation of all human life. . . . Indeed, opposition to and condemnation of suicide—and, therefore, of assisting suicide—are consistent and enduring themes of our philosophical, legal, and cultural heritages. . . .

> The Due Process Clause guarantees more than fair process, and the "liberty" it protects includes more than the absence of physical restraint. The Clause also provides heightened protection against government interference with certain fundamental rights and liberty interests. . . .

But we "ha[ve] always been reluctant to expand the concept of substantive due process because guideposts for responsible decisionmaking in this unchartered area are scarce and open-ended." By extending constitutional protection to an asserted right or liberty interest, we, to a great extent, place the matter outside the arena of public debate and legislative action. We must therefore "exercise the utmost care whenever we are asked to break new ground in this field," lest the liberty protected by the Due Process Clause be subtly transformed into the policy preferences of the Members of this Court.

Our established method of substantive-due-process analysis has two primary features: First, we have regularly observed that the Due Process Clause specially protects those fundamental rights and liberties which are, objectively, "deeply rooted in this Nation's history and tradition" and "implicit in the concept of ordered liberty," such that "neither liberty nor justice would exist if they were sacrificed." Second, we have required in substantive-due-process cases a "careful description" of the asserted fundamental liberty interest. . . .

LAWRENCE V. TEXAS

United States Supreme Court, 2003.
539 U.S. 558, 123 S.Ct. 2472.

JUSTICE KENNEDY delivered the opinion of the Court.

[I]n Houston, Texas, officers of the Harris County Police Department were dispatched to a private residence in response to a reported weapons disturbance. They entered an apartment where one of the petitioners, John Geddes Lawrence, resided. . . . The officers observed Lawrence and another man . . . engaging in a sexual act. The two petitioners were arrested, . . . charged and convicted. . . .

The complaints described their crime as "deviate sexual intercourse, namely anal sex, with a member of the same sex (man)." The applicable state law . . . provides: "A person commits an offense if he engages in deviate sexual intercourse with another individual of the same sex." The statute defines "[d]eviate sexual intercourse" as follows:

"(A) any contact between any part of the genitals of one person and the mouth or anus of another person; or

"(B) the penetration of the genitals or the anus of another person with an object."

[Lawrence was convicted, and the Court of Appeals rejected his appeal claiming that the law was unconstitutional under both the Equal Protection and Due Process Clauses of the Fourteenth Amendment.] The majority opinion indicates that the Court of Appeals considered our decision in *Bowers v. Hardwick* to be controlling on the federal due process aspect of the case. *Bowers* then being authoritative, this was proper.

We granted certiorari to consider three questions:

1.   Whether petitioners' criminal convictions under the Texas 'Homosexual Conduct' law—which criminalizes sexual intimacy by same-sex couples, but not identical behavior by different-sex couples—violate the Fourteenth Amendment guarantee of equal protection of the laws.

2.   Whether petitioners' criminal convictions for adult consensual sexual intimacy in the home violate their vital interests in liberty and privacy protected by the Due Process Clause of the Fourteenth Amendment.

3.   Whether *Bowers v. Hardwick, supra,* should be overruled. . . .

We conclude the case should be resolved by determining whether the petitioners were free as adults to engage in the private conduct in the exercise of their liberty under the Due Process Clause of the Fourteenth Amendment to the Constitution. For this inquiry we deem it necessary to reconsider the Court's holding in *Bowers.* . . .

The facts in *Bowers* had some similarities to the instant case. . . . One difference between the two cases is that the Georgia statute prohibited the conduct whether or not the participants were of the same sex, while the Texas statute, as we have seen, applies only to participants of the same sex. . . .

The Court began its substantive discussion in *Bowers* as follows: "The issue presented is whether the Federal Constitution confers a fundamental right upon homosexuals to engage in sodomy and hence invalidates the laws of the many States that still make such conduct illegal and have done so for a very long time." That statement, we now conclude, discloses the Court's own failure to appreciate the extent of the liberty at stake. To say that the issue in *Bowers* was simply the right to engage in certain sexual conduct demeans the claim the individual put forward, just as it would demean a married couple were it to be said marriage is simply about the right to have sexual intercourse. The laws involved in *Bowers* and here are, to be sure, statutes that purport to do no more than prohibit a particular sexual act. Their penalties and purposes, though, have more far-reaching consequences, touching upon the most private human conduct, sexual behavior, and in the most private of places, the home. The statutes do seek to control a personal relationship that, whether or not entitled to formal recognition in the law, is within the liberty of persons to choose without being punished as criminals.

This, as a general rule, should counsel against attempts by the State, or a court, to define the meaning of the relationship or to set its boundaries absent injury to a person or abuse of an institution the law protects. It suffices for us to acknowledge that adults may choose to enter upon this relationship in the confines of their homes and their own private lives and still retain their dignity as free persons. When sexuality finds overt expression in intimate conduct with another person, the conduct can be but one element in a personal bond that is more enduring. The liberty protected by the Constitution allows homosexual persons the right to make this choice.

Having misapprehended the claim of liberty there presented to it, and thus stating the claim to be whether there is a fundamental right to engage in consensual sodomy, the *Bowers* Court said: "Proscriptions against that conduct have ancient roots." In academic writings, and in many of the scholarly *amicus* briefs filed to assist the Court in this case, there are fundamental criticisms of the historical premises relied upon by the majority and concurring opinions in *Bowers*. We need not enter this debate in the attempt to reach a definitive historical judgment . . ., but the following considerations counsel against adopting the definitive conclusions upon which *Bowers* placed such reliance.

At the outset it should be noted that there is no longstanding history in this country of laws directed at homosexual conduct as a distinct matter. . . . [E]arly American sodomy laws were not directed at homosexuals as such but instead sought to prohibit nonprocreative sexual activity more generally. This does not suggest approval of homosexual conduct. It does tend to show that this particular form of conduct was not thought of as a separate category from like conduct between heterosexual persons.

Laws prohibiting sodomy do not seem to have been enforced against consenting adults acting in private. A substantial number of sodomy prosecutions and convictions for which there are surviving records were for predatory acts against those who could not or did not consent, as in the case of a minor or the victim of an assault. . . . Instead of targeting relations between consenting adults in private, 19th-century sodomy prosecutions typically involved relations between men and minor girls or minor boys, relations between adults involving force, relations between adults implicating disparity in status, or relations between men and animals. . . .

The longstanding criminal prohibition of homosexual sodomy upon which the *Bowers* decision placed such reliance is as consistent with a general condemnation of nonprocreative sex as it is with an established tradition of prosecuting acts because of their homosexual character.

[A]merican laws targeting same-sex couples did not develop until the last third of the 20th century.

It was not until the 1970s that any State singled out same-sex relations for criminal prosecution, and only nine States have done so. Post-*Bowers* even some of these States did not adhere to the policy of suppressing homosexual conduct. Over the course of the last decades, States with same-sex prohibitions have moved toward abolishing them.

In summary, the historical grounds relied upon in *Bowers* are more complex than the majority opinion and the concurring opinion by Chief Justice Burger indicate. Their historical premises are not without doubt and, at the very least, are overstated.

It must be acknowledged, of course, that the Court in *Bowers* was making the broader point that for centuries there have been powerful voices to condemn homosexual conduct as immoral. The condemnation has been shaped by religious beliefs, conceptions of right and acceptable behavior, and respect for the traditional family. For many persons these are not trivial concerns but profound and deep convictions accepted as ethical and moral principles to which they aspire and which thus determine the course of their lives. These considerations do not answer the question before us, however. The issue is whether the majority may use the power of the State to enforce these views on the whole society through operation of the criminal law. "Our obligation is to define the liberty of all, not to mandate our own moral code." *Planned Parenthood of Southeastern Pa. v. Casey.*

[I]n all events we think that our laws and traditions in the past half century are of most relevance here. These references show an emerging awareness that liberty gives substantial protection to adult persons in deciding how to conduct their private lives in matters pertaining to sex. "[H]istory and tradition are the starting point but not in all cases the ending point of the substantive due process inquiry."

This emerging recognition should have been apparent when *Bowers* was decided. In 1955 the American Law Institute promulgated the Model Penal Code and made clear that it did not recommend or provide for "criminal penalties for consensual sexual relations conducted in private." It justified its decision on three grounds: (1) The prohibitions undermined respect for the law by penalizing conduct many people engaged in; (2) the statutes regulated private conduct not harmful to others; and (3) the laws were arbitrarily enforced and thus invited the danger of blackmail. In 1961 Illinois changed its laws to conform to the Model Penal Code. Other States soon followed.

In *Bowers* the Court referred to the fact that before 1961 all 50 States had outlawed sodomy, and that at the time of the Court's decision 24 States and the District of Columbia had sodomy laws. . . .

Of even more importance, almost five years before *Bowers* was decided the European Court of Human Rights considered a case with parallels to *Bowers* and to today's case. . . . The court held that the laws proscribing the conduct were invalid under the European Convention on Human Rights. Authoritative in all countries that are members of the Council of Europe (21 nations then, 45 nations now), the decision is at odds with the premise in *Bowers* that the claim put forward was insubstantial in our Western civilization.

In our own constitutional system the deficiencies in *Bowers* became even more apparent in the years following its announcement. The 25 States with laws prohibiting the relevant conduct referenced in the *Bowers* decision are reduced now to 13, of which 4 enforce their laws only against homosexual conduct. In those States where sodomy is still proscribed, whether for same-sex or heterosexual conduct, there is a pattern of nonenforcement with respect to consenting adults acting in private. The State of Texas admitted in 1994 that as of that date it had not prosecuted anyone under those circumstances.

Two principal cases decided after *Bowers* cast its holding into even more doubt. In *Planned Parenthood of Southeastern Pa. v. Casey,* the Court reaffirmed the substantive force of the liberty protected by the Due Process Clause. The *Casey* decision again confirmed that our laws and tradition afford constitutional protection to personal decisions relating to marriage, procreation, contraception, family relationships, child rearing, and education. In explaining the respect the Constitution demands for the autonomy of the person in making these choices, we stated as follows:

> These matters, involving the most intimate and personal choices a person may make in a lifetime, choices central to personal dignity and autonomy, are central to the liberty protected by the Fourteenth Amendment. At the heart of liberty is the right to define one's own concept of existence, of meaning, of the universe, and of the mystery of human life. Beliefs about these matters could not define the attributes of personhood were they formed under compulsion of the State.

Persons in a homosexual relationship may seek autonomy for these purposes, just as heterosexual persons do. The decision in *Bowers* would deny them this right.

The second post-*Bowers* case of principal relevance is *Romer v. Evans,* 517 U.S. 620 (1996). There the Court struck down class-based legislation directed at homosexuals as a violation of the Equal Protection Clause. *Romer* invalidated an amendment to Colorado's Constitution which named as a solitary class persons who were homosexuals, lesbians, or bisexual either by "orientation, conduct, practices or relationships," and deprived them of protection under state antidiscrimination laws. We concluded that the provision was "born of animosity toward the class of persons affected" and further that it had no rational relation to a legitimate governmental purpose.

As an alternative argument in this case, counsel for the petitioners and some *amici* contend that *Romer* provides the basis for declaring the Texas statute invalid under the Equal Protection Clause. That is a tenable argument, but we conclude the instant case requires us to address whether *Bowers* itself has continuing validity. Were we to hold the statute invalid under the Equal Protection Clause some might question whether a prohibition would be valid if drawn differently, say, to prohibit the conduct both between same-sex and different-sex participants.

[T]he central holding of *Bowers* has been brought in question by this case, and it should be addressed. Its continuance as precedent demeans the lives of homosexual persons.

[T]he foundations of *Bowers* have sustained serious erosion from our recent decisions in *Casey* and *Romer*. When our precedent has been thus weakened, criticism from other sources is of greater significance. In the United States criticism of *Bowers* has been substantial and continuing, disapproving of its reasoning in all respects, not just as to its historical assumptions. The courts of five different States[, including Georgia,] have declined to follow it in interpreting provisions in their own state constitutions parallel to the Due Process Clause of the Fourteenth Amendment.

To the extent *Bowers* relied on values we share with a wider civilization, it should be noted that the reasoning and holding in *Bowers* have been rejected elsewhere. . . . The right the petitioners seek in this case has been accepted as an integral part of human freedom in many other countries. There has been no showing that in this country the governmental interest in circumscribing personal choice is somehow more legitimate or urgent.

[T]he holding in Bowers . . . has not induced detrimental reliance comparable to some instances where recognized individual rights are involved. Indeed, there has been no individual or societal reliance on *Bowers* of the sort that could counsel against overturning its holding once there are compelling reasons to do so. *Bowers* itself causes uncertainty, for the precedents before and after its issuance contradict its central holding.

The rationale of *Bowers* does not withstand careful analysis. In his dissenting opinion in *Bowers* Justice STEVENS came to these conclusions:

> Our prior cases make two propositions abundantly clear. First, the fact that the governing majority in a State has traditionally viewed a particular practice as immoral is not a sufficient reason for upholding a law prohibiting the practice; neither history nor tradition could save a law prohibiting miscegenation from constitutional attack. Second, individual decisions by married persons, concerning the intimacies of their physical relationship, even when not intended to produce offspring, are a form of 'liberty' protected by the Due Process Clause of the Fourteenth Amendment. Moreover, this protection extends to intimate choices by unmarried as well as married persons.

Justice STEVENS's analysis, in our view, should have been controlling in *Bowers* and should control here.

Bowers was not correct when it was decided, and it is not correct today. It ought not to remain binding precedent. *Bowers v. Hardwick* should be and now is overruled.

The present case does not involve minors. It does not involve persons who might be injured or coerced or who are situated in relationships where consent might not easily be refused. It does not involve public conduct or prostitution. It does not involve whether the government must give formal recognition to any relationship that homosexual persons seek to enter. The case does involve two adults who, with full and mutual consent from each other, engaged in sexual practices common to a homosexual lifestyle. The petitioners are entitled to respect for their private lives. The State cannot demean their existence or control their destiny by making their private sexual conduct a crime. Their right to liberty under the Due Process Clause gives them the full right to engage in their conduct without intervention of the government. "It is a promise of the Constitution that there is a realm of personal liberty which the government may not enter." The Texas statute furthers no legitimate state interest which can justify its intrusion into the personal and private life of the individual.

Had those who drew and ratified the Due Process Clauses of the Fifth Amendment or the Fourteenth Amendment known the components of liberty in its manifold possibilities, they might have been more specific. They did not presume to have this insight. They knew times can blind us to certain truths and later generations can see that laws once thought necessary and proper in fact serve only to oppress. As the Constitution endures, persons in every generation can invoke its principles in their own search for greater freedom.

JUSTICE O'CONNOR, concurring in the judgment. [Her opinion, concluding that the Texas statute violated the Equal Protection Clause because it discriminated against homosexuals and thereby finding it unnecessary to reach the due process question, is omitted here.]

JUSTICE SCALIA, with whom THE CHIEF JUSTICE and JUSTICE THOMAS join, dissenting.

[M]ost of . . . today's opinion has no relevance to its actual holding— that the Texas statute "furthers no legitimate state interest which can justify" its application to petitioners under rational-basis review (overruling *Bowers* to the extent it sustained Georgia's antisodomy statute under the rational-basis test). Though there is discussion of "fundamental proposition[s]," and "fundamental decisions," nowhere does the Court's opinion declare that homosexual sodomy is a "fundamental right" under the Due Process Clause; nor does it subject the Texas law to the standard of review that would be appropriate (strict scrutiny) if homosexual sodomy *were* a "fundamental right." Thus, while overruling the *outcome* of *Bowers,* the Court leaves strangely untouched its central legal conclusion: "[R]espondent would have us announce . . . a fundamental right to engage in homosexual sodomy. This we are quite unwilling to do." Instead the Court simply describes petitioners' conduct as "an exercise of their liberty"—which it undoubtedly is—and proceeds to apply an unheard-of form of rational-basis review that will have far-reaching implications beyond this case. . . .

Texas Penal Code Ann. § 21.06(a)(2003) undoubtedly imposes constraints on liberty. So do laws prohibiting prostitution, recreational use of heroin, and, for that matter, working more than 60 hours per week in a bakery. But there is no right to "liberty" under the Due Process Clause, though today's opinion repeatedly makes that claim. The Fourteenth Amendment *expressly allows* States to deprive their citizens of "liberty," so long as "due process of law" is provided. . . .

Our opinions applying the doctrine known as "substantive due process" hold that the Due Process Clause prohibits States from infringing *fundamental* liberty interests, unless the infringement is narrowly tailored to serve a compelling state interest. We have held repeatedly, in cases the Court today does not overrule, that *only* fundamental rights qualify for this so-called "heightened scrutiny" protection—that is, rights which are " 'deeply rooted in this Nation's history and tradition,' " All other liberty interests may be abridged or abrogated pursuant to a validly enacted state law if that law is rationally related to a legitimate state interest. . . .

I turn now to the ground on which the Court squarely rests its holding: the contention that there is no rational basis for the law here under attack. This proposition is so out of accord with our jurisprudence—indeed, with the jurisprudence of *any* society we know—that it requires little discussion.

The Texas statute undeniably seeks to further the belief of its citizens that certain forms of sexual behavior are "immoral and unacceptable"—the same interest furthered by criminal laws against fornication, bigamy, adultery, adult incest, bestiality, and obscenity. *Bowers* held that this *was* a legitimate state interest. The Court today reaches the opposite conclusion. The Texas statute, it says, "furthers *no legitimate state interest* which can justify its intrusion into the personal and private life of the individual." The Court embraces instead Justice STEVENS's declaration in his *Bowers* dissent, that " 'the fact that the governing majority in a State has traditionally viewed a particular practice as immoral is not a sufficient reason for upholding a law prohibiting the practice.' " This effectively decrees the end of all morals legislation. If, as the Court asserts, the promotion of majoritarian sexual morality is not even a *legitimate* state interest, none of the above-mentioned laws can survive rational-basis review. . . .

Today's opinion is the product of a Court, which is the product of a law-profession culture, that has largely signed on to the so-called homosexual agenda, by which I mean the agenda promoted by some homosexual activists directed at eliminating the moral opprobrium that has traditionally attached to homosexual conduct. . . .

One of the most revealing statements in today's opinion is the Court's grim warning that the criminalization of homosexual conduct is "an invitation to subject homosexual persons to discrimination both in the public and in the private spheres." It is clear from this that the Court has taken sides in the culture war, departing from its role of assuring, as neutral observer, that the democratic rules of engagement are observed. Many Americans do not want persons who openly engage in homosexual conduct as partners in their business, as scoutmasters for their children, as teachers in their children's schools, or as boarders in their home. They view this as protecting themselves and their families from a lifestyle that they believe to be immoral and destructive. The Court views it as "discrimination" which it is the function of our judgments to deter. So imbued is the Court with the law profession's anti-anti-homosexual culture, that it is seemingly unaware that the attitudes of that culture are not obviously "mainstream"; that in most States what the Court calls "discrimination" against those who engage in homosexual acts is perfectly legal; that proposals to ban such "discrimination" under Title VII have repeatedly been rejected by Congress; that in some cases such "discrimination" is *mandated* by federal statute, *see* 10 U.S.C. § 654(b)(1)(mandating discharge from the Armed Forces of any service member who engages in or intends to engage in homosexual acts)*; and that in some cases such "discrimination" is a constitutional right, *see Boy Scouts of America v. Dale,* 530 U.S. 640 (2000).

Let me be clear that I have nothing against homosexuals, or any other group, promoting their agenda through normal democratic means. Social perceptions of sexual and other morality change over time, and every group has the right to persuade its fellow citizens that its view of such matters is the best. That homosexuals have achieved some success in that enterprise is attested to by the fact that Texas is one of the few remaining States that criminalize private, consensual homosexual acts. But persuading one's fellow citizens is one thing, and imposing one's views in absence of democratic majority will is something else. I would no more *require* a State to criminalize homosexual acts—or, for that matter, display *any* moral disapprobation of them—than I would *forbid* it to do so. What Texas has chosen to do is well within the range of traditional democratic action, and its hand should not be stayed through the invention of a brand-new "constitutional right" by a Court that is impatient of democratic change. It is indeed true that "later generations can see that laws once thought necessary and proper in fact serve only to oppress," and when that happens, later generations can repeal those laws. But it is the premise of our system

---

*   This law was repealed effective September 20, 2011. [author's note]

that those judgments are to be made by the people, and not imposed by a governing caste that knows best.

One of the benefits of leaving regulation of this matter to the people rather than to the courts is that the people, unlike judges, need not carry things to their logical conclusion. The people may feel that their disapprobation of homosexual conduct is strong enough to disallow homosexual marriage, but not strong enough to criminalize private homosexual acts—and may legislate accordingly. The Court today pretends that it possesses a similar freedom of action, so that we need not fear judicial imposition of homosexual marriage. . . . At the end of its opinion—after having laid waste the foundations of our rational-basis jurisprudence—the Court says that the present case "does not involve whether the government must give formal recognition to any relationship that homosexual persons seek to enter." Do not believe it. More illuminating than this bald, unreasoned disclaimer is the progression of thought displayed by an earlier passage in the Court's opinion, which notes the constitutional protections afforded to "personal decisions relating to *marriage,* procreation, contraception, family relationships, child rearing, and education," and then declares that "[p]ersons in a homosexual relationship may seek autonomy for these purposes, just as heterosexual persons do." Today's opinion dismantles the structure of constitutional law that has permitted a distinction to be made between heterosexual and homosexual unions, insofar as formal recognition in marriage is concerned. If moral disapprobation of homosexual conduct is "no legitimate state interest" for purposes of proscribing that conduct, and if, as the Court coos (casting aside all pretense of neutrality), "[w]hen sexuality finds overt expression in intimate conduct with another person, the conduct can be but one element in a personal bond that is more enduring," what justification could there possibly be for denying the benefits of marriage to homosexual couples exercising "[t]he liberty protected by the Constitution"? Surely not the encouragement of procreation, since the sterile and the elderly are allowed to marry. This case "does not involve" the issue of homosexual marriage only if one entertains the belief that principle and logic have nothing to do with the decisions of this Court. Many will hope that, as the Court comfortingly assures us, this is so. . . .

JUSTICE THOMAS, dissenting.

I join Justice SCALIA's dissenting opinion. I write separately to note that the law before the Court today "is . . . uncommonly silly." If I were a member of the Texas Legislature, I would vote to repeal it. Punishing someone for expressing his sexual preference through noncommercial consensual conduct with another adult does not appear to be a worthy way to expend valuable law enforcement resources.

Notwithstanding this, I recognize that as a Member of this Court I am not empowered to help petitioners and others similarly situated. My duty, rather, is to "decide cases 'agreeably to the Constitution and laws of the United States.' " And . . . I "can find [neither in the Bill of Rights nor any other part of the Constitution a] general right of privacy," or as the Court terms it today, the "liberty of the person both in its spatial and more transcendent dimensions."

COMMENTS AND QUESTIONS

1. Here we see Justice Kennedy joining the "liberals" as he did in *Planned Parenthood of Southeastern Pennsylvania v. Casey.* As in *Casey,* Justice Kennedy did not characterize the interest involved as a "fundamental right," with the concomitant "strict scrutiny" requirement for a narrowly tailored means to achieve a compelling state interest. Rather, Justice Kennedy merely refers to the person's liberty interest. In *Romer v. Evans,* involving Colorado's constitutional provision prohibiting state and local antidiscrimination laws aimed at protecting homosexuals, however, he wrote for the Court overturning the provision on equal protection grounds, rather than due process. There too, however, he avoided classifying the right involved as fundamental.

2. Does the avoidance of characterizing the interest as a "fundamental right" explain why Justice Kennedy does not address the lack of an historical tradition of a right to homosexual sodomy?

3. What about same-sex marriage? Justice Scalia says the analysis in *Lawrence* means states may not ban same-sex marriage? What do you think?

PROBLEM

After *Lawrence,* what may a state do? May it criminalize adult incest? Adultery? Group sex? Bestiality?

In *Loving v. Virginia,* 388 U.S. 1 (1967), the Supreme Court unanimously overturned Virginia's law (and in effect the law of fifteen other states) banning marriage between persons of different races. After concluding that the law denied the Lovings equal protection of the laws, the Court went on to say:

These statutes also deprive the Lovings of liberty without due process of law in violation of the Due Process Clause of the Fourteenth Amendment. The freedom to marry has long been recognized as one of the vital personal rights essential to the orderly pursuit of happiness by free men. Marriage is one of the "basic civil rights of man," fundamental to our very existence and survival. To deny this fundamental freedom on so unsupportable a basis as the racial classifications embodied in these statutes, classifications so directly subversive of the principle of equality at the heart of the Fourteenth Amendment, is surely to deprive all the State's citizens of liberty without due process of law.

Eleven years later, in *Zablocki v. Redhail*, 434 U.S. 374 (1978), the Court again referred to the fundamental right to marry in overturning a Wisconsin law that prohibited a person from receiving a marriage license if the person was delinquent in supporting a non-custodial child that the person was under obligation to support by any court order. While the Court's decision rested on the Equal Protection Clause, rather than the Due Process Clause, one justice concurred on substantive due process grounds, and what is a fundamental right for purposes of the Equal Protection Clause is also a fundamental right for purposes of the Due Process Clause, and vice versa.

In *Turner v. Safely*, 482 U.S. 78 (1987), a unanimous Court found facially unconstitutional a state law effectively prohibiting inmates from marrying. However, the opinion for the Court by Justice O'Connor, while citing *Loving* and *Zablocki*, did not utilize strict or heightened scrutiny. Rather it said that the law failed even a rational basis test, because a complete ban was not necessary to serve the security and rehabilitation purposes claimed by the state. The Court allowed that reasonable restrictions on inmates' marriages could be imposed to serve these interests without forbidding marriages altogether. The fact that the federal prison system generally allowed for inmates' marriages unless they posed a threat to the security or order of the prison proved as much. Four justices concurred in the opinion but noted that the Court's analysis of the rationality of the marriage ban was stricter than the traditional "any rational basis" review, because it required the state to provide actual justifications for the restriction imposed.

The cases dealing with marriage establish that the right to marry is fundamental, but they do not provide much guidance on what limits states may place on the exercise of that right or even on what test is appropriate for measuring those limits. In *Zablocki*, for example, Justice Stewart concurred in the judgment on due process grounds, but he also said that "Surely . . . a State may legitimately say that no one can marry his or her sibling, that no one can marry who is not at least 14 years old, that no one can marry without first passing an examination for venereal disease, or that no one can marry who has a living husband or wife. But, just as surely, in regulating the intimate human relationship of marriage, there is a limit beyond which a State may not constitutionally go." He did not, however, leave any clue as to how to draw the line, or why his list of examples was so surely within the state's powers. Of course, they were all conditions that had generally existed in the law for many years. Note that he does not even mention a requirement that the persons be of opposite sexes. Why do you suppose he left that out?

In 1996, as some States were beginning to consider the concept of same-sex marriage and before any State had acted to permit it, Congress enacted the Defense of Marriage Act (DOMA). Section 3 of DOMA amended the Dictionary Act in Title 1, § 7, of the United States Code, to provide a federal definition of "marriage" and "spouse" so that they would exclude same sex marriages. This amendment had the effect of barring same sex partners, lawfully married under a state's law, from any of the benefits under federal law applicable to married persons. In *United States v. Windsor*, 570 U.S. 744 (2013), the Court held this provision unconstitutional. Justice Kennedy writing for the majority, said the provision discriminated against same sex married couples. Moreover, this discrimination could not be justified, because "the principal purpose and the necessary effect of this law [was] to demean those persons who are in a lawful same-sex marriage." Although the principal thrust of the opinion involved equal protection principles, Justice Kennedy also relied on the Due Process Clause's protection of an individual's liberty. Chief Justice Roberts and Justices Scalia, Thomas, and Alito dissented.

OBERGEFELL V. HODGES

United States Supreme Court, 2015.
576 U.S. 644, 135 S.Ct. 2584.

JUSTICE KENNEDY delivered the opinion of the Court.

[T]hese cases come from Michigan, Kentucky, Ohio, and Tennessee, States that define marriage as a union between one man and one woman. The petitioners are 14 same-sex couples and two men whose same-sex partners are deceased. The respondents are state officials responsible for enforcing the laws in question. The petitioners claim the respondents violate the Fourteenth Amendment by denying them the right to marry or to have their marriages, lawfully performed in another State, given full recognition. . . .

From their beginning to their most recent page, the annals of human history reveal the transcendent importance of marriage. The lifelong union of a man and a woman always has promised nobility and dignity to all persons, without regard to their station in life. Marriage is sacred to those who live by their religions and offers unique fulfillment to those who find meaning in the secular realm. Its dynamic allows two people to find a life that could not be found alone, for a marriage becomes greater than just the two persons. Rising from the most basic human needs, marriage is essential to our most profound hopes and aspirations. . . .

There are untold references to the beauty of marriage in religious and philosophical texts spanning time, cultures, and faiths, as well as in art and literature in all their forms. It is fair and necessary to say these references were based on the understanding that marriage is a union between two persons of the opposite sex.

That history is the beginning of these cases. The respondents say it should be the end as well. To them, it would demean a timeless institution if the concept and lawful status of marriage were extended to two persons of the same sex. Marriage, in their view, is by its nature a gender-differentiated union of man and woman. This view long has been held—and continues to be held—in good faith by reasonable and sincere people here and throughout the world.

The petitioners acknowledge this history but contend that these cases cannot end there. Were their intent to demean the revered idea and reality of marriage, the petitioners' claims would be of a different order. But that is neither their purpose nor their submission. To the contrary, it is the enduring importance of marriage that underlies the petitioners' contentions. This, they say, is their whole point. Far from seeking to devalue marriage, the petitioners seek it for themselves because of their respect—and need—for its privileges and responsibilities. And their immutable nature dictates that same-sex marriage is their only real path to this profound commitment. . . .

The ancient origins of marriage confirm its centrality, but it has not stood in isolation from developments in law and society. The history of marriage is one of both continuity and change. That institution—even as confined to opposite-sex relations—has evolved over time.

For example, marriage was once viewed as an arrangement by the couple's parents based on political, religious, and financial concerns; but by the time of the Nation's founding it was understood to be a voluntary contract between a man and a woman. As the role and status of women changed, the institution further evolved. Under the centuries-old doctrine of coverture, a married man and woman were treated by the State as a single, male-dominated legal entity. As women gained legal, political, and property rights, and as society began to understand that women have their own equal dignity, the law of coverture was abandoned. These and other developments in the institution of marriage over the past centuries were not mere superficial changes. Rather, they worked deep transformations in its structure, affecting aspects of marriage long viewed by many as essential.

These new insights have strengthened, not weakened, the institution of marriage. Indeed, changed understandings of marriage are characteristic of a Nation where new dimensions of freedom become apparent to new generations, often through perspectives that begin in pleas or protests and then are considered in the political sphere and the judicial process.

This dynamic can be seen in the Nation's experiences with the rights of gays and lesbians. [The Court then describes both the historical discrimination and evolving legal and social acceptance of gays and lesbians.]

Against this background, the legal question of same-sex marriage arose. [The Court then described the history of litigation over same-sex marriage in state and federal courts.]

Under the Due Process Clause of the Fourteenth Amendment, no State shall "deprive any person of life, liberty, or property, without due process of law." The fundamental liberties protected by this Clause include most of the rights enumerated in the Bill of Rights. In addition these liberties extend to certain personal choices central to individual dignity and autonomy, including intimate choices that define personal identity and beliefs.

The identification and protection of fundamental rights is an enduring part of the judicial duty to interpret the Constitution. [I]t requires courts to exercise reasoned judgment in identifying interests of the person so fundamental that the State must accord them its respect. That process is guided by many of the same considerations relevant to analysis of other constitutional provisions that set forth broad principles rather than specific requirements. History and tradition guide and discipline this inquiry but do not set its outer boundaries. That method respects our history and learns from it without allowing the past alone to rule the present.

The nature of injustice is that we may not always see it in our own times. The generations that wrote and ratified the Bill of Rights and the Fourteenth Amendment did not presume to know the extent of freedom in all of its dimensions, and so they entrusted to future generations a charter protecting the right of all persons to enjoy liberty as we learn its meaning. When new insight reveals discord between the Constitution's central protections and a received legal stricture, a claim to liberty must be addressed.

Applying these established tenets, the Court has long held the right to marry is protected by the Constitution. In *Loving v. Virginia*, which invalidated bans on interracial unions, a unanimous Court held marriage is "one of the vital personal rights essential to the orderly pursuit of happiness by free men." The Court reaffirmed that holding in *Zablocki v. Redhail,* which held the right to marry was burdened by a law prohibiting fathers who were behind on child support from marrying. The Court again applied this principle in *Turner v. Safley,* which held the right to marry was abridged by regulations limiting the privilege of prison inmates to marry. . . .

It cannot be denied that this Court's cases describing the right to marry presumed a relationship involving opposite-sex partners. The Court, like many institutions, has made assumptions defined by the world and time of which it is a part. . . .

This analysis compels the conclusion that same-sex couples may exercise the right to marry. The four principles and traditions to be discussed demonstrate that the reasons marriage is fundamental under the Constitution apply with equal force to same-sex couples.

A first premise of the Court's relevant precedents is that the right to personal choice regarding marriage is inherent in the concept of individual autonomy. This abiding connection between marriage and liberty is why *Loving* invalidated interracial marriage bans under the Due Process Clause. Like choices concerning contraception, family relationships, procreation, and childrearing, all of which are protected by the Constitution, decisions concerning marriage are among the most intimate that an individual can make. . . .

The nature of marriage is that, through its enduring bond, two persons together can find other freedoms, such as expression, intimacy, and spirituality. This is true for all persons, whatever their sexual orientation. There is dignity in the bond between two men or two women who seek to marry and in their autonomy to make such profound choices.

A second principle in this Court's jurisprudence is that the right to marry is fundamental because it supports a two-person union unlike any other in its importance to the committed individuals. . . . Suggesting that marriage is a right "older than the Bill of Rights," *Griswold* described marriage this way: "Marriage is a coming together for better or for worse, hopefully enduring, and intimate to the degree of being sacred. It is an association that promotes a way of life, not causes; a harmony in living, not political faiths; a bilateral loyalty, not commercial or social projects. Yet it is an association for as noble a purpose as any involved in our prior decisions.". . . The right to marry thus dignifies couples who "wish to define themselves by their commitment to each other." *Windsor*. Marriage responds to the universal fear that a lonely person might call out only to find no one there. It offers the hope of companionship and understanding and assurance that while both still live there will be someone to care for the other.

As this Court held in *Lawrence,* same-sex couples have the same right as opposite-sex couples to enjoy intimate association. . . . But while *Lawrence* confirmed a dimension of freedom that allows individuals to engage in intimate association without criminal liability, it does not follow that freedom stops there. Outlaw to outcast may be a step forward, but it does not achieve the full promise of liberty.

A third basis for protecting the right to marry is that it safeguards children and families and thus draws meaning from related rights of childrearing, procreation, and education. The Court has recognized these connections by describing the varied rights as a unified whole: "[T]he right to 'marry, establish a home and bring up children' is a central part of the liberty protected by the Due Process Clause." Under the laws of the several States, some of marriage's protections for children and families are material. But marriage also confers more profound benefits. By giving recognition and legal structure to their parents' relationship, marriage allows children "to understand the integrity and closeness of their own family and its concord with other families in their community and in their daily lives." *Windsor*. Marriage also affords the permanency and stability important to children's best interests.

As all parties agree, many same-sex couples provide loving and nurturing homes to their children, whether biological or adopted. And hundreds of thousands of children are presently being raised by such couples. Most States have allowed gays and lesbians to adopt, either as individuals or as couples, and many adopted and foster children have same-sex parents. This provides powerful confirmation from the law itself that gays and lesbians can create loving, supportive families.

Excluding same-sex couples from marriage thus conflicts with a central premise of the right to marry. Without the recognition, stability, and predictability marriage offers, their children suffer the stigma of knowing their families are somehow lesser. They also suffer the significant material costs of being raised by unmarried parents, relegated through no fault of their own to a more difficult and uncertain family life. The marriage laws at issue here thus harm and humiliate the children of same-sex couples. . . .

Fourth and finally, this Court's cases and the Nation's traditions make clear that marriage is a keystone of our social order. Alexis de Tocqueville recognized this truth on his travels through the United States almost two centuries ago: "There is certainly no country in the world where the tie of marriage is so much respected as in America . . . [W]hen the American retires from the turmoil of public life to the bosom of his family, he finds in it the image of order and of peace. . . . [H]e afterwards carries [that image] with him into public affairs." In *Maynard v. Hill,* 125 U.S. 190 (1888), the Court echoed de Tocqueville, explaining that marriage is "the foundation of the family and of society, without which there would be neither civilization nor progress." . . . This idea has been reiterated even as the institution has evolved in substantial ways over time, superseding rules related to parental consent, gender, and race once thought by many to be essential. Marriage remains a building block of our national community.

For that reason, just as a couple vows to support each other, so does society pledge to support the couple, offering symbolic recognition and material benefits to protect and nourish the union. . . . These aspects of marital status include: taxation; inheritance and property rights; rules of intestate succession; spousal privilege in the law of evidence; hospital access; medical decisionmaking authority; adoption rights; the rights and benefits of survivors; birth and death certificates; professional ethics rules; campaign finance restrictions; workers' compensation benefits; health insurance; and child custody, support, and visitation rules. Valid marriage under state law is also a significant status for over a thousand provisions of federal law. . . .

There is no difference between same- and opposite-sex couples with respect to this principle. Yet by virtue of their exclusion from that institution, same-sex couples are denied the constellation of benefits that the States have linked to marriage. This harm results in more than just material burdens. Same-sex couples are consigned to an instability many opposite-sex couples would deem intolerable in their own lives. As the State itself makes marriage all the more precious by the significance it attaches to it, exclusion from that status has the effect of teaching that gays and lesbians are unequal in important respects. It demeans gays and lesbians for the State to lock them out of a central institution of the Nation's society. Same-sex couples, too, may aspire to the transcendent purposes of marriage and seek fulfillment in its highest meaning. . . .

Objecting that this does not reflect an appropriate framing of the issue, the respondents refer to *Washington v. Glucksberg* (1997), which called for a " 'careful description' " of fundamental rights. They assert the petitioners do not seek to exercise the right to marry but rather a new and nonexistent "right to same-sex marriage." *Glucksberg* did insist that liberty under the Due Process Clause must be defined in a most circumscribed manner, with central reference to specific historical practices. Yet while that approach may have been appropriate for the asserted right there involved (physician-assisted suicide), it is inconsistent with the approach this Court has used in discussing other fundamental rights, including marriage and intimacy. *Loving* did not ask about a "right to interracial marriage"; *Turner* did not ask about a "right of inmates to marry"; and *Zablocki* did not ask about a "right of fathers with unpaid child support duties to marry." Rather, each case inquired about the right to marry in its comprehensive sense, asking if there was a sufficient justification for excluding the relevant class from the right.

That principle applies here. If rights were defined by who exercised them in the past, then received practices could serve as their own continued justification and new groups could not invoke rights once denied. This Court has rejected that approach, both with respect to the right to marry and the rights of gays and lesbians.

[T]he right of same-sex couples to marry that is part of the liberty promised by the Fourteenth Amendment is derived, too, from that Amendment's guarantee of the equal protection of the laws. The Due Process Clause and the Equal Protection Clause are connected in a profound way, though they set forth independent principles. Rights implicit in liberty and rights secured by equal protection may rest on different precepts and are not always co-extensive, yet in some instances each may be instructive as to the meaning and reach of the other. In any particular case one Clause may be thought to capture the essence of the right in a more accurate and comprehensive way, even as the two Clauses may converge in the identification and definition of the right. This interrelation of the two principles furthers our understanding of what freedom is and must become.

The Court's cases touching upon the right to marry reflect this dynamic. In *Loving* the Court invalidated a prohibition on interracial marriage under both the Equal Protection Clause and the Due Process Clause. The Court first declared the prohibition invalid because of its unequal treatment of interracial couples. . . . With this link to equal protection the Court proceeded to hold the prohibition offended central precepts of liberty: "To deny this fundamental freedom on so unsupportable a basis as the racial classifications embodied in these statutes, classifications so directly subversive of the principle of equality at the heart of the Fourteenth Amendment, is surely to deprive all the State's citizens of liberty without due process of law.". . .

This dynamic also applies to same-sex marriage. It is now clear that the challenged laws burden the liberty of same-sex couples, and it must be further acknowledged that they abridge central precepts of equality. Here the marriage laws enforced by the respondents are in essence unequal: same-sex couples are denied all the benefits afforded to opposite-sex couples and are barred from exercising a fundamental right. Especially against a long history of disapproval of their relationships, this denial to same-sex couples of the right to marry works a grave and continuing harm. The imposition of this disability on gays and lesbians serves to disrespect and subordinate them. And the Equal Protection Clause, like the Due Process Clause, prohibits this unjustified infringement of the fundamental right to marry.

These considerations lead to the conclusion that the right to marry is a fundamental right inherent in the liberty of the person, and under the Due Process and Equal Protection Clauses of the Fourteenth Amendment couples of the same-sex may not be deprived of that right and that liberty. . . .

Finally, it must be emphasized that religions, and those who adhere to religious doctrines, may continue to advocate with utmost, sincere conviction that, by divine precepts, same-sex marriage should not be condoned. The First Amendment ensures that religious organizations and persons are given proper protection as they seek to teach the principles that are so fulfilling and so central to their lives and faiths, and to their own deep aspirations to continue the family structure they have long revered. The same is true of those who oppose same-sex marriage for other reasons. In turn, those who believe allowing same-sex marriage is proper or indeed essential, whether as a matter of religious conviction or secular belief, may engage those who disagree with their view in an open and searching debate. The Constitution, however, does not permit the State to bar same-sex couples from marriage on the same terms as accorded to couples of the opposite sex. . . .

CHIEF JUSTICE ROBERTS, with whom JUSTICE SCALIA and JUSTICE THOMAS join, dissenting.

Petitioners make strong arguments rooted in social policy and considerations of fairness. They contend that same-sex couples should be allowed to affirm their love and commitment through marriage, just like opposite-sex couples. That position has undeniable appeal; over the past six years, voters and legislators in eleven States and the District of Columbia have revised their laws to allow marriage between two people of the same sex.

But this Court is not a legislature. Whether same-sex marriage is a good idea should be of no concern to us. Under the Constitution, judges have power to say what the law is, not what it should be. . . .

Although the policy arguments for extending marriage to same-sex couples may be compelling, the legal arguments for requiring such an extension are not. The fundamental right to marry does not include a right to make a State change its definition of marriage. And a State's decision to maintain the meaning of marriage that has persisted in every culture throughout human history can hardly be called irrational. In short, our Constitution does not enact any one theory of marriage. The people of a State are free to expand marriage to include same-sex couples, or to retain the historic definition. . . .

The majority's decision is an act of will, not legal judgment. The right it announces has no basis in the Constitution or this Court's precedent. The majority expressly disclaims judicial "caution" and omits even a pretense of humility, openly relying on its desire to remake society according to its own "new insight" into the "nature of injustice." As a result, the Court invalidates the marriage laws of more than half the States and orders the transformation of a social institution that has formed the basis of human society for millennia, for the Kalahari Bushmen and the Han Chinese, the Carthaginians and the Aztecs. Just who do we think we are?

It can be tempting for judges to confuse our own preferences with the requirements of the law. But as this Court has been reminded throughout our history, the Constitution "is made for people of fundamentally differing views." *Lochner v. New York* (1905)(Holmes, J., dissenting). Accordingly, "courts are not concerned with the wisdom or policy of legislation." *Id.* (Harlan, J., dissenting). The majority today neglects that restrained conception of the judicial role. It seizes for itself a question the Constitution leaves to the people, at a time when the people are engaged in a vibrant debate on that question. And it answers that question based not on neutral principles of constitutional law, but on its own "understanding of what freedom is and must become." I have no choice but to dissent.

Understand well what this dissent is about: It is not about whether, in my judgment, the institution of marriage should be changed to include same-sex couples. It is instead about whether, in our democratic republic, that decision should rest with the people acting through their elected representatives, or with five lawyers who happen to hold commissions authorizing them to resolve legal disputes according to law. The Constitution leaves no doubt about the answer.

Petitioners and their *amici* base their arguments on the "right to marry" and the imperative of "marriage equality." There is no serious dispute that, under our precedents, the Constitution protects a right to marry and requires States to apply their marriage laws equally. The real question in these cases is what constitutes "marriage," or—more precisely—*who decides* what constitutes "marriage"?

The majority largely ignores these questions. . . .

This universal definition of marriage as the union of a man and a woman is no historical coincidence. . . . It arose in the nature of things to meet a vital need: ensuring that children are conceived by a mother and father committed to raising them in the stable conditions of a lifelong relationship.

The premises supporting this concept of marriage are so fundamental that they rarely require articulation. The human race must procreate to survive. Procreation occurs through sexual relations between a man and a woman. When sexual relations result in the conception of a child, that child's prospects are generally better if the mother and father stay together rather than going their separate ways. Therefore, for the good of children and society, sexual relations that can lead to procreation should occur only between a man and a woman committed to a lasting bond.

Society has recognized that bond as marriage. And by bestowing a respected status and material benefits on married couples, society encourages men and women to conduct sexual relations within marriage rather than without. . . .

As the majority notes, some aspects of marriage have changed over time. Arranged marriages have largely given way to pairings based on romantic love. States have replaced coverture, the doctrine by which a married man and woman became a single legal entity, with laws that respect each participant's separate status. Racial restrictions on marriage, which "arose as an incident to slavery" to promote "White Supremacy," were repealed by many States and ultimately struck down by this Court.

The majority observes that these developments "were not mere superficial changes" in marriage, but rather "worked deep transformations in its structure." They did not, however, work any transformation in the core structure of marriage as the union between a man and a woman. . . .

The majority purports to identify four "principles and traditions" in this Court's due process precedents that support a fundamental right for same-sex couples to marry. In reality, however, the majority's approach has no basis in principle or tradition, except for the unprincipled tradition of judicial policymaking that characterized discredited decisions such as *Lochner v. New York*. Stripped of its shiny rhetorical gloss, the majority's argument is that the Due Process Clause gives same-sex couples a fundamental right to marry because it will be good for them and for society. If I were a legislator, I would certainly consider that view as a matter of social policy. But as a judge, I find the majority's position indefensible as a matter of constitutional law. . . .

Rejecting *Lochner* does not require disavowing the doctrine of implied fundamental rights, and this Court has not done so. But to avoid repeating *Lochner*'s error of converting personal preferences into constitutional mandates, our modern substantive due process cases have stressed the need for "judicial self-restraint." Our precedents have required that implied fundamental rights be "objectively, deeply rooted in this Nation's history and tradition," and "implicit in the concept of ordered liberty, such that neither liberty nor justice would exist if they were sacrificed." . . .

When the majority turns to the law, it relies primarily on precedents discussing the fundamental "right to marry." These cases do not hold, of course, that anyone who wants to get married has a constitutional right to do so. They instead require a State to justify barriers to marriage as that institution has always been understood. In *Loving*, the Court held that racial restrictions on the right to marry lacked a compelling justification. In *Zablocki*, restrictions based on child support debts did not suffice. In *Turner*, restrictions based on status as a prisoner were deemed impermissible.

None of the laws at issue in those cases purported to change the core definition of marriage as the union of a man and a woman. . . . Removing racial barriers to marriage therefore did not change what a marriage was any more than integrating schools changed what a school was.

In short, the "right to marry" cases stand for the important but limited proposition that particular restrictions on access to marriage *as traditionally defined* violate due process. These precedents say nothing at all about a right to make a State change its definition of marriage, which is the right petitioners actually seek here. Neither petitioners nor the majority cites a single case or other legal source providing any basis for such a constitutional right. None exists, and that is enough to foreclose their claim. . . .

The majority opens its opinion by announcing petitioners' right to "define and express their identity." The majority later explains that "the right to personal choice regarding marriage is inherent in the concept of individual autonomy." This freewheeling notion of individual autonomy echoes nothing so much as "the general right of an individual to be *free in his person* and in his power to contract in relation to his own labor." *Lochner* (emphasis added).

To be fair, the majority does not suggest that its individual autonomy right is entirely unconstrained. The constraints it sets are precisely those that accord with its own "reasoned judgment," informed by its "new insight" into the "nature of injustice," which was invisible to all who came before but has become clear "as we learn [the] meaning" of liberty. The truth is that today's decision rests on nothing more than the majority's own conviction that same-sex couples should be allowed to marry because they want to, and that "it would disparage their choices and diminish their personhood to deny them this right." Whatever force that belief may have as a matter of moral philosophy, it has no more basis in the Constitution than did the naked policy preferences adopted in *Lochner*. . . .

One immediate question invited by the majority's position is whether States may retain the definition of marriage as a union of two people. Although the majority randomly inserts the adjective "two" in various places, it offers no reason at all why the two-person element of the core definition of marriage may be preserved while the man-woman element may not. Indeed, from the standpoint of history and tradition, a leap from opposite-sex marriage to same-sex marriage is much greater than one from a two-person union to plural unions, which have deep roots in some cultures around the world. If the majority is willing to take the big leap, it is hard to see how it can say no to the shorter one. . . .

In addition to their due process argument, petitioners contend that the Equal Protection Clause requires their States to license and recognize same-sex marriages. The majority does not seriously engage with this claim. Its discussion is, quite frankly, difficult to follow. The central point seems to be that there is a "synergy between" the Equal Protection Clause and the Due Process Clause, and that some precedents relying on one Clause have also relied on the other. Absent from this portion of the opinion, however, is anything resembling our usual framework for deciding equal protection cases. It is casebook doctrine that the "modern Supreme Court's treatment of equal protection claims has used a means-ends methodology in which judges ask whether the classification the government is using is sufficiently related to the goals it is pursuing." The majority's approach today is different. . . .

The majority goes on to assert in conclusory fashion that the Equal Protection Clause provides an alternative basis for its holding. Yet the majority fails to provide even a single sentence explaining how the Equal Protection Clause supplies independent weight for its position. . . . In any event, the marriage laws at issue here do not violate the Equal Protection Clause, because distinguishing between opposite-sex and same-sex couples is rationally related to the States' "legitimate state interest" in "preserving the traditional institution of marriage.". . .

JUSTICE SCALIA, with whom JUSTICE THOMAS joins, dissenting.

I join THE CHIEF JUSTICE's opinion in full. I write separately to call attention to this Court's threat to American democracy. . . .

Today's decree says that my Ruler, and the Ruler of 320 million Americans coast-to-coast, is a majority of the nine lawyers on the Supreme Court. The opinion in these cases is the furthest extension in fact—and the furthest extension one can even imagine—of the Court's claimed power to create "liberties" that the Constitution and its Amendments neglect to mention. This practice of constitutional revision by an unelected committee of nine, always accompanied (as it is today) by extravagant praise of liberty, robs the People of the most important liberty they asserted in the Declaration of Independence and won in the Revolution of 1776: the freedom to govern themselves. . . .

Since there is no doubt whatever that the People [who adopted the 14th Amendment] never decided to prohibit the limitation of marriage to opposite-sex couples, the public debate over same-sex marriage must be allowed to continue. But the Court ends this debate, in an opinion lacking even a thin veneer of law. Buried beneath the mummeries and straining-to-be-memorable passages of the opinion is a candid and startling assertion: No matter *what* it was the People ratified, the Fourteenth Amendment protects those rights that the Judiciary, in its "reasoned judgment," thinks the Fourteenth Amendment ought to protect. That is so because "[t]he generations that wrote and ratified the Bill of Rights and the Fourteenth Amendment did not presume to know the extent of freedom in all of its dimensions. . . ." One would think that sentence would continue: ". . . and therefore they provided for a means by which the People could amend the Constitution," or perhaps ". . . and therefore they left the creation of additional liberties, such as the freedom to marry someone of the same sex, to the People, through the never-ending process of legislation." But no. What logically follows, in the majority's judge-empowering estimation, is: "and so they entrusted to future generations a charter protecting the right of all persons to enjoy liberty as we learn its meaning." The "we," needless to say, is the nine of us. "History and tradition guide and discipline [our] inquiry but do not set its outer boundaries." Thus, rather than focusing on *the People's* understanding of "liberty"—at the time of ratification or even today—the majority focuses on four "principles and traditions" that, *in the majority's view,* prohibit States from defining marriage as an institution consisting of one man and one woman. . . .

Judges are selected precisely for their skill as lawyers; whether they reflect the policy views of a particular constituency is not (or should not be) relevant. Not surprisingly then, the Federal Judiciary is hardly a cross-section of America. Take, for example, this Court, which consists of only nine men and women, all of them successful lawyers who studied at Harvard or Yale Law School. Four of the nine are natives of New York City. Eight of them grew up in east- and west-coast States. Only one hails from the vast expanse in-between. Not a single Southwesterner or even, to tell the truth, a genuine Westerner (California does not count). Not a single evangelical Christian (a group that comprises about one quarter of Americans), or even a Protestant of any denomination. The strikingly unrepresentative character of the body voting on today's social upheaval would be irrelevant if they were functioning as *judges,* answering the legal question whether the American people had ever ratified a constitutional provision that was understood to proscribe the traditional definition of marriage. But of course the Justices in today's majority are not voting on that basis; *they say they are not.* And to allow the policy question of same-sex marriage to be considered and resolved by a select, patrician, highly unrepresentative panel of nine is to violate a principle even more fundamental than no taxation without representation: no social transformation without representation.

But what really astounds is the hubris reflected in today's judicial Putsch. The five Justices who compose today's majority are entirely comfortable concluding that every State violated the Constitution for all of the 135 years between the Fourteenth Amendment's ratification and Massachusetts' permitting of same-sex marriages in 2003. They have discovered in the Fourteenth Amendment a "fundamental right" overlooked by every person alive at the time of ratification, and almost everyone else in the time since. . . .

The opinion is couched in a style that is as pretentious as its content is egotistic. It is one thing for separate concurring or dissenting opinions to contain extravagances, even silly extravagances, of thought and expression; it is something else for the official opinion of the Court to do so.[22] Of course the opinion's showy profundities are often profoundly incoherent. "The nature of marriage is that, through its enduring bond, two persons together can find other freedoms, such as expression, intimacy, and spirituality." (Really? Who ever thought that intimacy and spirituality [whatever that means] were freedoms? And if intimacy is, one would think Freedom of Intimacy is abridged rather than expanded by marriage. Ask the nearest hippie. Expression, sure enough, *is* a freedom, but anyone in a long-lasting marriage will attest that that happy state constricts, rather than expands, what one can prudently say.) Rights, we are told, can "rise . . . from a better informed understanding of how constitutional

---

[22] If, even as the price to be paid for a fifth vote, I ever joined an opinion for the Court that began: "The Constitution promises liberty to all within its reach, a liberty that includes certain specific rights that allow persons, within a lawful realm, to define and express their identity," I would hide my head in a bag. The Supreme Court of the United States has descended from the disciplined legal reasoning of John Marshall and Joseph Story to the mystical aphorisms of the fortune cookie.

imperatives define a liberty that remains urgent in our own era." (Huh? How can a better informed understanding of how constitutional imperatives [whatever that means] define [whatever that means] an urgent liberty [never mind], give birth to a right?). . . . I could go on. The world does not expect logic and precision in poetry or inspirational pop-philosophy; it demands them in the law. The stuff contained in today's opinion has to diminish this Court's reputation for clear thinking and sober analysis. . . .

JUSTICE THOMAS, with whom JUSTICE SCALIA joins, dissenting.

The Court's decision today is at odds not only with the Constitution, but with the principles upon which our Nation was built. Since well before 1787, liberty has been understood as freedom from government action, not entitlement to government benefits. . . . Yet the majority invokes our Constitution in the name of a "liberty" that the Framers would not have recognized, to the detriment of the liberty they sought to protect. . . .

State decisions interpreting [due process clauses] between the founding and the ratification of the Fourteenth Amendment almost uniformly construed the word "liberty" to refer only to freedom from physical restraint. . . . [T]his Court's earliest Fourteenth Amendment decisions appear to interpret the Clause as using "liberty" to mean freedom from physical restraint. In *Munn v. Illinois* (1877), for example, the Court recognized the relationship between the two Due Process Clauses and Magna Carta and implicitly rejected the dissent's argument that " 'liberty' " encompassed "something more . . . than mere freedom from physical restraint or the bounds of a prison."

Even assuming that the "liberty" in those Clauses encompasses something more than freedom from physical restraint, it would not include the types of rights claimed by the majority. In the American legal tradition, liberty has long been understood as individual freedom from governmental action, not as a right to a particular governmental entitlement. . . .

Petitioners cannot claim, under the most plausible definition of "liberty," that they have been imprisoned or physically restrained by the States for participating in same-sex relationships. To the contrary, they have been able to cohabitate and raise their children in peace. They have been able to hold civil marriage ceremonies in States that recognize same-sex marriages and private religious ceremonies in all States. They have been able to travel freely around the country, making their homes where they please. Far from being incarcerated or physically restrained, petitioners have been left alone to order their lives as they see fit.

Nor, under the broader definition, can they claim that the States have restricted their ability to go about their daily lives as they would be able to absent governmental restrictions. Petitioners do not ask this Court to order the States to stop restricting their ability to enter same-sex relationships, to engage in intimate behavior, to make vows to their partners in public ceremonies, to engage in religious wedding ceremonies, to hold themselves out as married, or to raise children. The States have imposed no such restrictions. Nor have the States prevented petitioners from approximating a number of incidents of marriage through private legal means, such as wills, trusts, and powers of attorney.

Instead, the States have refused to grant them governmental entitlements. Petitioners claim that as a matter of "liberty," they are entitled to access privileges and benefits that exist solely because of the government. . . .

JUSTICE ALITO, with whom JUSTICE SCALIA and JUSTICE THOMAS join, dissenting.

[T]oday's decision usurps the constitutional right of the people to decide whether to keep or alter the traditional understanding of marriage. The decision will also have other important consequences.

It will be used to vilify Americans who are unwilling to assent to the new orthodoxy. In the course of its opinion, the majority compares traditional marriage laws to laws that denied equal treatment for African-Americans and women. The implications of this analogy will be exploited by those who are determined to stamp out every vestige of dissent.

Perhaps recognizing how its reasoning may be used, the majority attempts, toward the end of its opinion, to reassure those who oppose same-sex marriage that their rights of conscience will be protected. We will soon see whether this proves to be true. I assume that those who cling to old beliefs will be able to whisper their thoughts in the recesses of their homes, but if they repeat those views in public, they will risk being labeled as bigots and treated as such by governments, employers, and schools.

[B]y imposing its own views on the entire country, the majority facilitates the marginalization of the many Americans who have traditional ideas. Recalling the harsh treatment of gays and lesbians in the past, some may think that turnabout is fair play. But if that sentiment prevails, the Nation will experience bitter and lasting wounds. . . .

COMMENTS AND QUESTIONS

1.   *Obergefell* is a notable case not only for its outcome but also for its methodology. Most people, including the Solicitor General as amicus curiae and most of the lower courts that had addressed same-sex marriage, thought of the case in terms of equal protection, the subject of the following chapter in this book, not in terms of fundamental rights. Justice Kennedy, writing for the Court, does of course discuss the Equal Protection Clause, but the thrust of the opinion is on marriage as a fundamental right and a fundamental right arising out of the liberty protected by the Due Process Clause. Recall that in *Lawrence v. Texas* he also eschewed equal protection in favor of a finding based upon the

liberty protected by the Due Process Clause. And in *United States v. Windsor*, he also stressed liberty in addition to equal protection. Why do you suppose he does that?

2.   Justice Kennedy's opinion in *Obergefell* goes to some lengths to establish that marriage is a fundamental right, as opposed to simply a liberty interest. Nevertheless, the Court has traditionally held that even fundamental rights may be curtailed consistent with the Due Process Clause if necessary to achieve a compelling government interest. Does Justice Kennedy's opinion assess whether the states' limitation of marriage to persons of the opposite sex meets or fails this test?

3.   The Chief Justice in dissent argues that the very definition of marriage is a union of one man and one woman and that none of the Court's prior cases involved a challenge to the definition of marriage but only challenges to restrictions on persons being able to enter into marriage as so defined. This may be an accurate characterization of the Court's cases, but does it help to answer the question whether that very definition is itself unconstitutional?

4.   Because the people who adopted the 14th Amendment clearly never believed that it prohibited limiting marriage to one man and one woman, Justice Scalia argues that the issue should be left to the political process. However, as you will discover in the next chapter on equal protection, the people who adopted the 14th Amendment clearly never believed that it prohibited racially segregated schools or provided equal protection to women. Should these issues be left to the political process?

5.   Justice Scalia also derides Justice Kennedy's opinion for its lofty language. Indeed, Justice Kennedy does tend to wax eloquent in his rights-based decisions. Consider the joint opinion in *Casey* (*e.g.*, "At the heart of liberty is the right to define one's own concept of existence, of meaning, of the universe, and of the mystery of human life"), his opinion in *Carhart* ("Respect for human life finds an ultimate expression in the bond of love the mother has for her child"), and his opinion in *Lawrence* ("When sexuality finds overt expression in intimate conduct with another person, the conduct can be one element of a personal bond that is more enduring"). Do you think this makes his opinions more convincing, or less convincing?

6.   Justice Thomas argues that "liberty" in the Due Process Clause refers to freedom from physical constraint or, perhaps more broadly, freedom to do as you please without government restraint. If so, then denying someone legal marriage, that is, marriage recognized by the state for various benefits, simply would not interfere with anyone's liberty. He distinguishes *Loving* on the basis that the law there was a criminal statute providing for terms of imprisonment for violations and therefore clearly affected the Lovings' liberty. Could Virginia revive its anti-miscegenation statutes by simply not recognizing interracial marriage, as opposed to penalizing them? Justice Thomas might respond that they could as far the Due Process Clause of the 14th Amendment is involved, but that they would violate the Equal Protection Clause.

7.   Justice Alito is concerned that the effect of the Court's decision will be to brand persons with traditional views as bigots, just as those who favor separation of the races and historical views of women are viewed today. Do you think that it was the Court's decisions on desegregation or the equality of women that had that effect, or did the Court's decisions themselves reflect the evolving notions of society? In any case, has Justice Alito's prediction as to the marginalization of persons with traditional values come true? Perhaps it depends on where you live.

8.   Recall that two of the early substantive due process cases involved references to rights arising out of family relationships. In *Meyer v. Nebraska*, 262 U.S. 390 (1923), the Court said that the liberty protected by the due process clause included the right "to marry, establish a home and bring up children." And in *Pierce v. Society of Sisters*, 268 U.S. 510 (1925), the Court referred to the right of parents "to direct the upbringing and education of children under their control."

In a more modern case, *Troxel v. Granville*, 530 U.S. 57 (2000), the Court affirmed this right in finding unconstitutional a Washington state law that authorized grandparents' visitation rights over the objections of the sole surviving parent. There, the statute authorized a court to grant visitation rights to any person seeking them, if the court determined it was in the best interests of the child. The plurality opinion concluded that "so long as a parent adequately cares for his or her children (*i.e.,* is fit), there will normally be no reason for the State to inject itself into the private realm of the family to further question the ability of that parent to make the best decisions concerning the rearing of that parent's children." Two other justices were not willing to draw such a bright line rule. While agreeing that the statute here was too broad, they believed that determination of the best interests of the child by a court might overcome a fit parent's objections depending upon who was seeking the visitation rights and the reasons for the objections.

Michael H. v. Gerald D., 491 U.S. 110 (1989), involved a California statute that created a presumption that a child born to a married woman living with her husband is the child of the husband. The presumption could be rebutted only in certain rare circumstances. Michael H. had had an affair with Gerald D.'s wife, and she had a daughter, Victoria. Despite a blood test establishing that there was a 98.07% probability that Michael H. was the father of Victoria, this was insufficient to rebut the presumption that Victoria was Gerald D.'s daughter. Both Michael H. and Victoria challenged the California law as an unconstitutional violation of substantive due process, because it deprived them of having a familial relationship that would enable visitation rights. Four members of the Court, in an opinion by Justice Scalia, held that the presumption codified in the California law was of ancient lineage, so that there was no history and tradition of recognizing Michael H.'s or Victoria's interest in establishing their familial relationship. Consequently, there was no fundamental right that would trigger strict scrutiny under the Due Process Clause. In short, in determining who was a father entitled to the fundamental right with respect to his child, the law triumphed over biology. Justice Stevens concurred in the judgment because he found that California law established a means by which visitation rights could be granted to Michael H., but that the California courts had correctly decided that it was not in the best interests of Victoria to grant those visitation rights. Four justices dissented, believing that a biological parent could not be deprived of the fundamental right of a parent without some better justification than that the child was born to a woman married to another with whom she resided.

What constituted a "family" was the issue in *Moore v. City of East Cleveland*, 431 U.S. 494 (1977). A zoning ordinance limited the occupants of a house to members of a family, but it defined "family" in such a way that a grandmother, living with one of her sons, his son, and the son of her other son, did not qualify. She was subject to criminal prosecution for violating the ordinance. The Supreme Court held that the ordinance was unconstitutional, but again there was no majority opinion. Four members of the Court concluded that the ordinance violated substantive due process because it involved intrusive regulation of the family without any justifiable reason. Specifically rejected was the claim that the Constitution only protected the nuclear family of a couple and their children. Justice Stevens concurred in the judgment on the grounds that it was an arbitrary restriction on the owner's use of her property. That is, he relied on the owner's property rights under the Constitution, not on any consideration of the owner's family. Three justices did not believe the restriction unconstitutionally interfered with family values protected by the Constitution, and one justice would have dismissed the case on technical grounds.

As can be seen, while these cases have by narrow margins policed government actions interfering with families under the rubric of substantive due process, they have not produced any coherent doctrine as to when or how government may either define or regulate family matters.

PROBLEM

The Chief Justice suggests that the majority's analysis would seem to justify a fundamental right for polygamous marriages. What do you think? And what about incestuous marriages, *e.g.*, mother and son, brother and sister, or sister and sister, assuming both parties are mentally competent adults?

We now return to abortion. Recall the division on the Court in *Casey*, where two justices would have kept *Roe* intact, four justices wished to overrule *Roe*, and the three justice joint opinion reaffirmed "the essential holding of *Roe*," but changed *Roe*'s trimester system and overruled some post-*Roe* decisions. Nevertheless, the Court did not hear another abortion case until eight years later. By then Justices White and Blackmun had retired, replaced by Justices Breyer and Ginsburg, appointed by the President Clinton. Inasmuch as Justice White had dissented in *Roe* originally and would have overruled it later, his replacement by Justice Ginsburg, a known advocate for women's issues, and Justice Blackmun's replacement by Justice Breyer, an apparently "liberal" judge, seemed to provide additional support for *Roe/Casey*. That next case, *Stenberg v. Carhart*, 530 U.S. 914 (2000), involved so-called "partial birth abortions." In an opinion by Justice Breyer, the Court invalidated a Nebraska statute prohibiting such abortions except when necessary to save the life of the mother. The Court rested on two separate grounds: first, the statute did not have an exception for the "health of the mother," which the *Casey* plurality had said was a necessary prerequisite for banning abortions even after viability; and second, the statute, as worded, imposed "an undue burden" on a woman's ability to choose a commonly used abortion procedure, "thereby unduly burdening the right to choose abortion itself." The vote, however, was only 5–4; Justice Kennedy, one of the authors of the joint plurality in *Casey*, dissented, saying that the Court's decision repudiated a central premise of *Casey*, that the states "retain a critical and legitimate role in legislating on the subject of abortion. . . . The political processes of the State are not to be foreclosed from enacting laws to promote the life of the unborn and to ensure respect for all human life and its potential."

Seven years later the issue arose again, this time in a federal statute banning partial birth abortions, and this time the outcome was different. Chief Justice Rehnquist, who had dissented in *Stenberg*, was replaced by Chief Justice Roberts, and Justice Alito replaced Justice O'Connor, who had joined the liberals in *Stenberg*. In *Gonzales v. Carhart*, 550 U.S. 124 (2007), the Court upheld the federal ban on "intact" dilation and evacuation (D&E) abortions, one of the methods used for abortions in the second trimester. Justice Kennedy authored the opinion. First, after describing the gruesome details involved in intact D&E's, he found that the Act's purpose to promote respect for the dignity of human life by prohibiting "such a brutal and inhumane" procedure to be a legitimate government purpose. Next, he found that the ban did not impose a substantial burden on women's right to an abortion, because other methods of abortion were still available, thereby distinguishing the law from the state law in *Stenberg*, which banned all D&E abortions, not just the "intact" D&E's. Finally, he found that the absence of an exception for when such a procedure is necessary for the health of the mother was not fatal, because here there was "uncertainty over whether the barred procedure is ever necessary to preserve a woman's health, given the availability of other abortion procedures." Moreover, he went on, if in a particular case it was thought that an intact D&E really was necessary, then an as-applied challenge could be brought. The four dissenters took issue with the adequacy of the moral justification for the law to overrule the interests of the woman, and they pointed out that there was a medical consensus, as expressed by the American College of Obstetricians and Gynecologists, that intact D&E's were the safest form of abortion in certain types of cases.

Nine years passed before the Court decided its next abortion rights case. *Whole Woman's Health v. Hellerstedt*, 579 U.S. 582 (2016). By then, Justices Souter and Stevens had left the Court but were replaced by Justices Elena Kagan and Sonia Sotomayor. Texas passed a law that would have had the effect of reducing the number facilities that could provide abortions in the state. Applying the "undue burden" test from *Casey*, the four "liberals," again joined by Justice Kennedy, held that the burden imposed on women from obtaining an abortion outweighed whatever benefits the law purported to further and thereby was undue. Chief Justice Roberts and Justices Alito and Thomas dissented. Due to Justice Scalia's recent death, his seat was vacant. Justice Thomas reiterated that he believed *Roe* and *Casey* should be overruled, but he and the others also disputed that the majority had properly applied the undue burden test.

Not long after *Whole Woman's Health*, Justice Gorsuch was appointed to fill Justice Scalia's seat and Justice Kavanaugh was appointed to replace the retiring Justice Kennedy. Thus, given this new alignment, when Louisiana passed an almost identical law to that in *Whole Woman's Health*, it seemed likely that Court would overrule *Whole Woman's Health* and perhaps even *Roe*. It was not to be. In *June Medical Services v. Russo*, 140 S.Ct. 2103 (2020), the Chief Justice concurred with the four remaining "liberals" to strike down the law. He noted that he had dissented in *Whole Woman's Health*, but "[t]he legal doctrine of stare decisis requires us, absent special circumstances, to treat like cases alike. The Louisiana law imposes a burden on access to abortion just as severe as that imposed by the Texas law, for the same reasons. Therefore Louisiana's law cannot stand under our precedents."

Within two months Justice Ginsburg passed away, and the Trump Administration, with a Republican majority in the Senate, quickly nominated and confirmed Justice Barrett. Although Justices Gorsuch, Kavanaugh, and Barrett had all agreed that *Roe* was an important precedent in their confirmation hearings, important precedents, as we have seen in this chapter and will see in subsequent chapters, are not immune from being overruled by liberal as well as conservative courts. Several states, believing there was a majority for overruling *Roe/Casey*, passed laws clearly unconstitutional under those precedents. Only a miracle could save *Roe/Casey*. There was no miracle.

DOBBS V. JACKSON WOMEN'S HEALTH ORGANIZATION

United States Supreme Court, 2022.
142 S.Ct. 2228.

JUSTICE ALITO delivered the opinion of the Court.

Abortion presents a profound moral issue on which Americans hold sharply conflicting views. Some believe fervently that a human person comes into being at conception and that abortion ends an innocent life. Others feel just as strongly that any regulation of abortion invades a woman's right to control her own body and prevents women from achieving full equality. Still others in a third group think that abortion should be allowed under some but not all circumstances, and those within this group hold a variety of views about the particular restrictions that should be imposed.

For the first 185 years after the adoption of the Constitution, each State was permitted to address this issue in accordance with the views of its citizens. Then, in 1973, this Court decided *Roe* v. *Wade*. Even though the Constitution makes no mention of abortion, the Court held that it confers a broad right to obtain one. It did not claim that American law or the common law had ever recognized such a right, and its survey of history ranged from the constitutionally irrelevant (*e.g.*, its discussion of abortion in antiquity) to the plainly incorrect (*e.g.*, its assertion that abortion was probably never a crime under the common law). After cataloging a wealth of other information having no bearing on the meaning of the Constitution, the opinion concluded with a numbered set of rules much like those that might be found in a statute enacted by a legislature.

Under this scheme, each trimester of pregnancy was regulated differently, but the most critical line was drawn at roughly the end of the second trimester, which, at the time, corresponded to the point at which a fetus was thought to achieve "viability," *i.e.*, the ability to survive outside the womb. Although the Court acknowledged that States had a legitimate interest in protecting "potential life," it found that this interest could not justify any restriction on pre-viability abortions. The Court did not explain the basis for this line, and even abortion supporters have found it hard to defend *Roe*'s reasoning.

At the time of *Roe*, 30 States still prohibited abortion at all stages. In the years prior to that decision, about a third of the States had liberalized their laws, but *Roe* abruptly ended that political process. It imposed the same highly restrictive regime on the entire Nation, and it effectively struck down the abortion laws of every single State.

Eventually, in *Planned Parenthood of Southeastern Pa.* v. *Casey*, the Court revisited *Roe*, but the Members of the Court split three ways. Two Justices expressed no desire to change *Roe* in any way. Four others wanted to overrule the decision in its entirety. And the three remaining Justices, who jointly signed the controlling opinion, took a third position. Their opinion did not endorse *Roe*'s reasoning, and it even hinted that one or more of its authors might have "reservations" about whether the Constitution protects a right to abortion. But the opinion concluded that *stare decisis*, which calls for prior decisions to be followed in most instances, required adherence to what it called *Roe*'s "central holding"—that a State may not constitutionally protect fetal life before "viability"—even if that holding was wrong. Anything less, the opinion claimed, would undermine respect for this Court and the rule of law.

Paradoxically, the judgment in *Casey* did a fair amount of overruling. Several important abortion decisions were overruled *in toto*, and *Roe* itself was overruled in part. *Casey* threw out *Roe*'s trimester scheme and substituted a new rule of uncertain origin under which States were forbidden to adopt any regulation that imposed an "undue burden" on a woman's right to have an abortion. The decision provided no clear guidance about the difference between a "due" and an "undue" burden. But the three Justices who authored the controlling opinion "call[ed] the contending sides of a national controversy to end their national division" by treating the Court's decision as the final settlement of the question of the constitutional right to abortion.

As has become increasingly apparent in the intervening years, *Casey* did not achieve that goal. Americans continue to hold passionate and widely divergent views on abortion, and state legislatures have acted accordingly. Some have recently enacted laws allowing abortion, with few restrictions, at all stages of pregnancy. Others have tightly restricted abortion beginning well before viability. And in this case, 26 States have expressly asked this Court to overrule *Roe* and *Casey* and allow the States to regulate or prohibit pre-viability abortions.

Before us now is one such state law. The State of Mississippi asks us to uphold the constitutionality of a law that generally prohibits an abortion after the 15th week of pregnancy—several weeks before the point at which a fetus is now regarded as "viable" outside the womb.

We hold that *Roe* and *Casey* must be overruled. The Constitution makes no reference to abortion, and no such right is implicitly protected by any constitutional provision, including the one on which the defenders of *Roe* and *Casey* now chiefly rely—the Due Process Clause of the Fourteenth Amendment. That provision has been held to guarantee some rights that are not mentioned in the Constitution, but any such right must be "deeply rooted in this Nation's history and tradition" and "implicit in the concept of ordered liberty." *Washington* v. *Glucksberg,* 521 U. S. 702, 721 (1997).

The right to abortion does not fall within this category. Until the latter part of the 20th century, such a right was entirely unknown in American law. Indeed, when the Fourteenth Amendment was adopted, three quarters of the States made abortion a crime at all stages of pregnancy.

The abortion right is also critically different from any other right that this Court has held to fall within the Fourteenth Amendment's protection of "liberty." *Roe*'s defenders characterize the abortion right as similar to the rights recognized in past decisions involving matters such as intimate sexual relations, contraception, and marriage, but abortion is fundamentally different, as both *Roe* and *Casey* acknowledged, because it destroys what those decisions called "fetal life" and what the law now before us describes as an "unborn human being."

Stare decisis, the doctrine on which *Casey*'s controlling opinion was based, does not compel unending adherence to *Roe*'s abuse of judicial authority. *Roe* was egregiously wrong from the start. Its reasoning was exceptionally weak, and the decision has had damaging consequences. And far from bringing about a national settlement of the abortion issue, *Roe* and *Casey* have enflamed debate and deepened division.

It is time to heed the Constitution and return the issue of abortion to the people's elected representatives. "The permissibility of abortion, and the limitations, upon it, are to be resolved like most important questions in our democracy: by citizens trying to persuade one another and then voting." *Casey* (Scalia, J., concurring in judgment in part and dissenting in part). That is what the Constitution and the rule of law demand.

We begin by considering the critical question whether the Constitution, properly understood, confers a right to obtain an abortion.

We . . . address that question in three steps. First, we explain the standard that our cases have used in determining whether the Fourteenth Amendment's reference to "liberty" protects a particular right. Second, we examine whether the right at issue in this case is rooted in our Nation's history and tradition and whether it is an essential component of what we have described as "ordered liberty." Finally, we consider whether a right to obtain an abortion is part of a broader entrenched right that is supported by other precedents.

Constitutional analysis must begin with "the language of the instrument," which offers a "fixed standard" for ascertaining what our founding document means. The Constitution makes no express reference to a right to obtain an abortion, and therefore those who claim that it protects such a right must show that the right is somehow implicit in the constitutional text.

Roe, however, was remarkably loose in its treatment of the constitutional text. It held that the abortion right, which is not mentioned in the Constitution, is part of a right to privacy, which is also not mentioned. And that privacy right, *Roe* observed, had been found to spring from no fewer than five different constitutional provisions—the First, Fourth, Fifth, Ninth, and Fourteenth Amendments.

The Court's discussion left open at least three ways in which some combination of these provisions could protect the abortion right. One possibility was that the right was "founded . . . in the Ninth Amendment's reservation of rights to the people." Another was that the right was rooted in the First, Fourth, or Fifth Amendment, or in some combination of those provisions, and that this right had been "incorporated" into the Due Process Clause of the Fourteenth Amendment just as many other Bill of Rights provisions had by then been incorporated. And a third path was that the First, Fourth, and Fifth Amendments played no role and that the right was simply a component of the "liberty" protected by the Fourteenth Amendment's Due Process Clause. *Roe* expressed the "feel[ing]" that the Fourteenth Amendment was the provision that did the work, but its message seemed to be that the abortion right could be found *somewhere* in the Constitution and that specifying its exact location was not of paramount importance. The *Casey* Court did not defend this unfocused analysis and instead grounded its decision solely on the theory that the right to obtain an abortion is part of the "liberty" protected by the Fourteenth Amendment's Due Process Clause.

The underlying theory on which this argument rests—that the Fourteenth Amendment's Due Process Clause provides substantive, as well as procedural, protection for "liberty"—has long been controversial. But our decisions have held that the Due Process Clause protects two categories of substantive rights.

The first consists of rights guaranteed by the first eight Amendments. Those Amendments originally applied only to the Federal Government, but this Court has held that the Due Process Clause of the Fourteenth Amendment "incorporates" the great majority of those rights and thus makes them equally applicable to the States. The second category—which is the one in question here—comprises a select list of fundamental rights that are not mentioned anywhere in the Constitution.

In deciding whether a right falls into either of these categories, the Court has long asked whether the right is "deeply rooted in [our] history and tradition" and whether it is essential to our Nation's "scheme of ordered liberty." And in conducting this inquiry, we have engaged in a careful analysis of the history of the right at issue.

Historical inquiries of this nature are essential whenever we are asked to recognize a new component of the "liberty" protected by the Due Process Clause because the term "liberty" alone provides little guidance.In interpreting what is meant by the Fourteenth Amendment's reference to "liberty," we must guard against the natural human tendency to confuse what that Amendment protects with our own ardent views about the liberty that Americans should enjoy. That is why the Court has long been "reluctant" to recognize rights that are not mentioned in the Constitution.

On occasion, when the Court has ignored the "[a]ppropriate limits" imposed by " 'respect for the teachings of history,' " it has fallen into the freewheeling judicial policymaking that characterized discredited decisions such as *Lochner* v. *New York*. The Court must not fall prey to such an unprincipled approach. Instead, guided by the history and tradition that map the essential components of our Nation's concept of ordered liberty, we must ask what the *Fourteenth Amendment* means by the term "liberty." When we engage in that inquiry in the present case, the clear answer is that the Fourteenth Amendment does not protect the right to an abortion.

Until the latter part of the 20th century, there was no support in American law for a constitutional right to obtain an abortion. No state constitutional provision had recognized such a right. Until a few years before *Roe* was handed down, no federal or state court had recognized such a right. Nor had any scholarly treatise of which we are aware. And although law review articles are not reticent about advocating new rights, the earliest article proposing a constitutional right to abortion that has come to our attention was published only a few years before *Roe*.

Not only was there no support for such a constitutional right until shortly before *Roe*, but abortion had long been a *crime* in every single State. At common law, abortion was criminal in at least some stages of pregnancy and was regarded as unlawful and could have very serious consequences at all stages. American law followed the common law until a wave of statutory restrictions in the 1800s expanded criminal liability for abortions. By the time of the adoption of the Fourteenth Amendment, three-quarters of the States had made abortion a crime at any stage of pregnancy, and the remaining States would soon follow. . . .

This overwhelming consensus endured until the day *Roe* was decided. At that time, also by the *Roe* Court's own count, a substantial majority— 30 States—still prohibited abortion at all stages except to save the life of the mother. And though *Roe* discerned a "trend toward liberalization" in about "one-third of the States," those States still criminalized some abortions and regulated them more stringently than *Roe* would allow. In short, the "Court's opinion in *Roe* itself convincingly refutes the notion that the abortion liberty is deeply rooted in the history or tradition of our people."

The inescapable conclusion is that a right to abortion is not deeply rooted in the Nation's history and traditions. On the contrary, an unbroken tradition of prohibiting abortion on pain of criminal punishment persisted from the earliest days of the common law until 1973.

Instead of seriously pressing the argument that the abortion right itself has deep roots, supporters of *Roe* and *Casey* contend that the abortion right is an integral part of a broader entrenched right. *Roe* termed this a right to privacy, and *Casey* described it as the freedom to make "intimate and personal choices" that are "central to personal dignity and autonomy."

Casey elaborated: "At the heart of liberty is the right to define one's own concept of existence, of meaning, of the universe, and of the mystery of human life."

The Court did not claim that this broadly framed right is absolute, and no such claim would be plausible. While individuals are certainly free *to think* and *to say* what they wish about "existence," "meaning," the "universe," and "the mystery of human life," they are not always free *to act* in accordance with those thoughts. License to act on the basis of such beliefs may correspond to one of the many understandings of "liberty," but it is certainly not "ordered liberty."

Ordered liberty sets limits and defines the boundary between competing interests. *Roe* and *Casey* each struck a particular balance between the interests of a woman who wants an abortion and the interests of what they termed "potential life." But the people of the various States may evaluate those interests differently. Our Nation's historical understanding of ordered liberty does not prevent the people's elected representatives from deciding how abortion should be regulated.

Nor does the right to obtain an abortion have a sound basis in precedent. *Casey* relied on cases involving the right to marry a person of a different race, the right to marry while in prison, the right to obtain contraceptives, the right to reside with relatives, the right to make decisions about the education of one's children, the right not to be sterilized without consent, and the right in certain circumstances not to undergo involuntary surgery, forced administration of drugs, or other substantially similar procedures. Respondents and the Solicitor General also rely on post-*Casey* decisions like *Lawrence* v. *Texas* (right to engage in private, consensual sexual acts), and *Obergefell* v. *Hodges* (right to marry a person of the same sex).

These attempts to justify abortion through appeals to a broader right to autonomy and to define one's "concept of existence" prove too much. Those criteria, at a high level of generality, could license fundamental rights to illicit drug use, prostitution, and the like. None of these rights has any claim to being deeply rooted in history.

What sharply distinguishes the abortion right from the rights recognized in the cases on which *Roe* and *Casey* rely is something that both those decisions acknowledged: Abortion destroys what those decisions call "potential life" and what the law at issue in this case regards as the life of an "unborn human being." None of the other decisions cited by *Roe* and *Casey* involved the critical moral question posed by abortion. They are therefore inapposite. They do not support the right to obtain an abortion, and by the same token, our conclusion that the Constitution does not confer such a right does not undermine them in any way.

In drawing this critical distinction between the abortion right and other rights, it is not necessary to dispute *Casey*'s claim (which we accept for the sake of argument) that "the specific practices of States at the time of the adoption of the Fourteenth Amendment" do not "mar[k] the outer limits of the substantive sphere of liberty which the Fourteenth Amendment protects." Abortion is nothing new. It has been addressed by lawmakers for centuries, and the fundamental moral question that it poses is ageless.

Defenders of *Roe* and *Casey* do not claim that any new scientific learning calls for a different answer to the underlying moral question, but they do contend that changes in society require the recognition of a constitutional right to obtain an abortion. Without the availability of abortion, they maintain, people will be inhibited from exercising their freedom to choose the types of relationships they desire, and women will be unable to compete with men in the workplace and in other endeavors.

Americans who believe that abortion should be restricted press countervailing arguments about modern developments. They note that attitudes about the pregnancy of unmarried women have changed drastically; that federal and state laws ban discrimination on the basis of pregnancy; that leave for pregnancy and childbirth are now guaranteed by law in many cases; that the costs of medical care associated with pregnancy are covered by insurance or government assistance; that States have increasingly adopted "safe haven" laws, which generally allow women to drop off babies anonymously; and that a woman who puts her newborn up for adoption today has little reason to fear that the baby will not find a suitable home.

Both sides make important policy arguments, but supporters of *Roe* and *Casey* must show that this Court has the authority to weigh those arguments and decide how abortion may be regulated in the States. They have failed to make that showing, and we thus return the power to weigh those arguments to the people and their elected representatives.

We next consider whether the doctrine of *stare decisis* counsels continued acceptance of *Roe* and *Casey*. *Stare decisis* plays an important role in our case law, and we have explained that it serves many valuable ends.

We have long recognized, however, that *stare decisis* is "not an inexorable command," and it "is at its weakest when we interpret the Constitution," [W]hen one of our constitutional decisions goes astray, the country is usually stuck with the bad decision unless we correct our own mistake. An erroneous constitutional decision can be fixed by amending the Constitution, but our Constitution is notoriously hard to amend. Therefore, in appropriate circumstances we must be willing to reconsider and, if necessary, overrule constitutional decisions.

Some of our most important constitutional decisions have overruled prior precedents. We mention three. In *Brown* v. *Board of Education*, the Court repudiated the "separate but equal" doctrine, which had allowed States to maintain racially segregated schools and other facilities. In so doing, the Court overruled the infamous decision in *Plessy* v. *Ferguson*, along with six other Supreme Court precedents that had applied the separate-but-equal rule.

In *West Coast Hotel Co.* v. *Parrish*, 300 U. S. 379 (1937), the Court overruled *Adkins* v. *Children's Hospital of D. C.*, 261 U. S. 525 (1923), which had held that a law setting minimum wages for women violated the "liberty" protected by the Fifth Amendment's Due Process Clause.

Finally, in *West Virginia Bd. of Ed.* v. *Barnette*, 319 U. S. 624 (1943), after the lapse of only three years, the Court overruled *Minersville School Dist.* v. *Gobitis*, 310 U. S. 586 (1940), and held that public school students could not be compelled to salute the flag in violation of their sincere beliefs. *Barnette* stands out because nothing had changed during the intervening period other than the Court's belated recognition that its earlier decision had been seriously wrong.

On many other occasions, this Court has overruled important constitutional decisions. Without these decisions, American constitutional law as we know it would be unrecognizable, and this would be a different country.

In this case, five factors weigh strongly in favor of overruling *Roe* and *Casey*: the nature of their error, the quality of their reasoning, the "workability" of the rules they imposed on the country, their disruptive effect on other areas of the law, and the absence of concrete reliance.

The nature of the Court's error. An erroneous interpretation of the Constitution is always important, but some are more damaging than others. The infamous decision in *Plessy* v. *Ferguson*, was one such decision. *Roe* was also egregiously wrong and deeply damaging. For reasons already explained, *Roe*'s constitutional analysis was far outside the bounds of any reasonable interpretation of the various constitutional provisions to which it vaguely pointed.

The quality of the reasoning. Under our precedents, the quality of the reasoning in a prior case has an important bearing on whether it should be reconsidered.

Workability. Our precedents counsel that another important consideration in deciding whether a precedent should be overruled is whether the rule it imposes is workable—that is, whether it can be understood and applied in a consistent and predictable manner. *Casey*'s "undue burden" test has scored poorly on the workability scale.

The difficulty of applying *Casey*'s new rules surfaced in that very case. The controlling opinion found that Pennsylvania's 24-hour waiting period requirement and its informed-consent provision did not impose "undue burden[s]," but Justice Stevens, applying the same test, reached the opposite result. The ambiguity of the "undue burden" test also produced disagreement in later cases. *Casey* has generated a long list of Circuit conflicts. *Casey*'s "undue burden" test has proved to be unworkable.

Effect on other areas of law. Roe and *Casey* have led to the distortion of many important but unrelated legal doctrines, and that effect provides further support for overruling those decisions. The Court's abortion cases have diluted the strict standard for facial constitutional challenges. They have ignored the Court's third-party standing doctrine. They have disregarded standard *res judicata* principles. They have flouted the ordinary rules on the severability of unconstitutional provisions, as well as the rule that statutes should be read where possible to avoid unconstitutionality. And they have distorted First Amendment doctrines.

Reliance interests. We last consider whether overruling *Roe* and *Casey* will upend substantial reliance interests.

Traditional reliance interests arise "where advance planning of great precision is most obviously a necessity." In *Casey*, the controlling opinion conceded that those traditional reliance interests were not implicated because getting an abortion is generally "unplanned activity," and "reproductive planning could take virtually immediate account of any sudden restoration of state authority to ban abortions." For these reasons, we agree with the *Casey* plurality that conventional, concrete reliance interests are not present here.

[U]nable to find reliance in the conventional sense, the controlling opinion in *Casey* perceived a more intangible form of reliance. It wrote that "people [had] organized intimate relationships and made choices that define their views of themselves and their places in society . . . in reliance on the availability of abortion in the event that contraception should fail" and that "[t]he ability of women to participate equally in the economic and social life of the Nation has been facilitated by their ability to control their reproductive lives." But this Court is ill-equipped to assess "generalized assertions about the national psyche." *Casey*'s notion of reliance thus finds little support in our cases, which instead emphasize very concrete reliance interests, like those that develop in "cases involving property and contract rights."

Unable to show concrete reliance on *Roe* and *Casey* themselves, the Solicitor General suggests that overruling those decisions would "threaten the Court's precedents holding that the Due Process Clause protects other rights." That is not correct for reasons we have already discussed. And to ensure that our decision is not misunderstood or mischaracterized, we emphasize that our decision concerns the constitutional right to abortion and no other right. Nothing in this opinion should be understood to cast doubt on precedents that do not concern abortion.

We therefore hold that the Constitution does not confer a right to abortion. *Roe* and *Casey* must be overruled, and the authority to regulate abortion must be returned to the people and their elected representatives. . . .

We must now decide what standard will govern if state abortion regulations undergo constitutional challenge and whether the law before us satisfies the appropriate standard. Under our precedents, rational-basis review is the appropriate standard for such challenges. As we have explained, procuring an abortion is not a fundamental constitutional right because such a right has no basis in the Constitution's text or in our Nation's history. It follows that the States may regulate abortion for legitimate reasons, and when such regulations are challenged under the Constitution, courts cannot "substitute their social and economic beliefs for the judgment of legislative bodies." A law regulating abortion, like other health and welfare laws, is entitled to a "strong presumption of validity." It must be sustained if there is a rational basis on which the legislature could have thought that it would serve legitimate state interests. These legitimate interests include respect for and preservation of prenatal life at all stages of development, the protection of maternal health and safety, the elimination of particularly gruesome or barbaric medical procedures, the preservation of the integrity of the medical profession, the mitigation of fetal pain, and the prevention of discrimination on the basis of race, sex, or disability.

These legitimate interests justify Mississippi's Gestational Age Act.

JUSTICE THOMAS, concurring. [Justice Thomas reiterated his view that the Due Process Clause does not have a substantive component and does not protect so-called fundamental rights from abrogation by the legislature. Consequently, all of the Court's decision based substantive due process should be overruled. Moreover, the incorporation of most of the Bill of Rights by operation of the 14th Amendment's Due Process Clause is erroneous. The rights specified in the Bill of Rights are protected against state action by reason of the Privileges and Immunities Clause of the 14th Amendment. He leaves as an open question whether any unenumerated rights are also protected by the Privileges and Immunities Clause.]

JUSTICE KAVANAUGH, concurring.

Some *amicus* briefs argue that the Court today should not only overrule *Roe* and return to a position of judicial neutrality on abortion, but should go further and hold that the Constitution *outlaws* abortion throughout the United States. No Justice of this Court has ever advanced that position. I respect those who advocate for that position, just as I respect those who argue that this Court should hold that the Constitution

Brett Kavanaugh

In 2006 President George W. Bush appointed Kavanaugh to the U.S. Court of Appeals for the D.C. Circuit. Prior to that he had clerked for Justice Anthony Kennedy, become a partner in a D.C. law firm, and participated in the Independent Counsel's investigation of President Bill Clinton. On the D.C. Circuit Judge Kavanaugh quickly established himself as a conservative jurisprude, reflecting his long membership in the Federalist Society, and one who took novel legal positions. Nevertheless, of the fourteen of his opinions in cases that went to the Supreme Court, the Court adopted his position thirteen times. President Trump nominated Judge Kavanaugh to the Supreme Court, and his confirmation was highly contentious, largely relating to alleged sexual assaults committed while he was in high school or college. He was confirmed, with two exceptions, on a strictly party line vote in 2018.

legalizes pre-viability abortion throughout the United States. But both positions are wrong as a constitutional matter, in my view. The Constitution neither outlaws abortion nor legalizes abortion.

To be clear, then, the Court's decision today *does not outlaw* abortion throughout the United States. On the contrary, the Court's decision properly leaves the question of abortion for the people and their elected representatives in the democratic process. Through that democratic process, the people and their representatives may decide to allow or limit abortion. . . .

But the parties' arguments have raised other related questions, and I address some of them here.

First is the question of how this decision will affect other precedents involving issues such as contraception and marriage. I emphasize what the Court today states: Overruling *Roe* does *not* mean the overruling of those precedents, and does *not* threaten or cast doubt on those precedents.

Second, as I see it, some of the other abortion-related legal questions raised by today's decision are not especially difficult as a constitutional matter. For example, may a State bar a resident of that State from traveling to another State to obtain an abortion? In my view, the answer is no based on the constitutional right to interstate travel. May a State retroactively impose liability or punishment for an abortion that occurred before today's decision takes effect? In my view, the answer is no based on the Due Process Clause or the *Ex Post Facto* Clause.

CHIEF JUSTICE ROBERTS, concurring in the judgment.

We granted certiorari to decide one question: "Whether all pre-viability prohibitions on elective abortions are unconstitutional." In urging our review, Mississippi stated that its case was "an ideal vehicle" to "reconsider the bright-line viability rule," and that a judgment in its favor would "not require the Court to overturn" *Roe* v. *Wade* and *Planned*

Parenthood of Southeastern Pa. v. *Casey*. Today, the Court nonetheless rules for Mississippi by doing just that. I would take a more measured course. I agree with the Court that the viability line established by *Roe* and *Casey* should be discarded under a straightforward *stare decisis* analysis. That line never made any sense. Our abortion precedents describe the right at issue as a woman's right to choose to terminate her pregnancy. That right should therefore extend far enough to ensure a reasonable opportunity to choose, but need not extend any further—certainly not all the way to viability. I see no sound basis for questioning the adequacy of that opportunity. But that is all I would say, out of adherence to a simple yet fundamental principle of judicial restraint: If it is not necessary to decide more to dispose of a case, then it is necessary *not* to decide more.

JUSTICE BREYER, JUSTICE SOTOMAYOR, and JUSTICE KAGAN, dissenting.

For half a century, *Roe* v. *Wade* and *Planned Parenthood of Southeastern Pa.* v. *Casey* have protected the liberty and equality of women. *Roe* held, and *Casey* reaffirmed, that the Constitution safeguards a woman's right to decide for herself whether to bear a child. *Roe* held, and *Casey* reaffirmed, that in the first stages of pregnancy, the government could not make that choice for women. The government could not control a woman's body or the course of a woman's life: It could not determine what the woman's future would be. Respecting a woman as an autonomous being, and granting her full equality, meant giving her substantial choice over this most personal and most consequential of all life decisions.

Roe and *Casey* well understood the difficulty and divisiveness of the abortion issue. And the Court recognized that "the State has legitimate interests from the outset of the pregnancy in protecting" the "life of the fetus that may become a child." So the Court struck a balance, as it often does when values and goals compete. It held that the State could prohibit abortions after fetal viability, so long as the ban contained exceptions to safeguard a woman's life or health. It held that even before viability, the State could regulate the abortion procedure in multiple and meaningful ways. But until the viability line was crossed, the Court held, a State could not impose a "substantial obstacle" on a woman's "right to elect the procedure" as she (not the government) thought proper, in light of all the circumstances and complexities of her own life.

Today, the Court discards that balance. It says that from the very moment of fertilization, a woman has no rights to speak of. A State can force her to bring a pregnancy to term, even at the steepest personal and familial costs. An abortion restriction, the majority holds, is permissible whenever rational, the lowest level of scrutiny known to the law. And because, as the Court has often stated, protecting fetal life is rational, States will feel free to enact all manner of restrictions. The Mississippi law at issue here bars abortions after the 15th week of pregnancy. Under the majority's ruling, though, another State's law could do so after ten weeks, or five or three or one—or, again, from the moment of fertilization. States have already passed such laws, in anticipation of today's ruling. More will follow. Some States have enacted laws extending to all forms of abortion procedure, including taking medication in one's own home. They have passed laws without any exceptions for when the woman is the victim of rape or incest. Under those laws, a woman will have to bear her rapist's child or a young girl her father's—no matter if doing so will destroy her life. So too, after today's ruling, some States may compel women to carry to term a fetus with severe physical anomalies—for example, one afflicted with Tay-Sachs disease, sure to die within a few years of birth. States may even argue that a prohibition on abortion need make no provision for protecting a woman from risk of death or physical harm. Across a vast array of circumstances, a State will be able to impose its moral choice on a woman and coerce her to give birth to a child.

Enforcement of all these draconian restrictions will also be left largely to the States' devices. A State can of course impose criminal penalties on abortion providers, including lengthy prison sentences. But some States will not stop there. Perhaps, in the wake of today's decision, a state law will criminalize the woman's conduct too, incarcerating or fining her for daring to seek or obtain an abortion. And as Texas has recently shown, a State can turn neighbor against neighbor, enlisting fellow citizens in the effort to root out anyone who tries to get an abortion, or to assist another in doing so.

The majority tries to hide the geographically expansive effects of its holding. Today's decision, the majority says, permits "each State" to address abortion as it pleases. That is cold comfort, of course, for the poor woman who cannot get the money to fly to a distant State for a procedure. Above all others, women lacking financial resources will suffer from today's decision. In any event, interstate restrictions will also soon be in the offing. After this decision, some States may block women from traveling out of State to obtain abortions, or even from receiving abortion medications from out of State. Some may criminalize efforts, including the provision of information or funding, to help women gain access to other States' abortion services. Most threatening of all, no language in today's decision stops the Federal Government from prohibiting abortions nationwide, once again from the moment of conception and without exceptions for rape or incest. If that happens, "the views of [an individual State's] citizens" will not matter. The challenge for a woman will be to finance a trip not to "New York [or] California" but to Toronto.

Whatever the exact scope of the coming laws, one result of today's decision is certain: the curtailment of women's rights, and of their status as free and equal citizens. Yesterday, the Constitution guaranteed that a woman confronted with an unplanned pregnancy could (within reasonable limits) make her own decision about whether to bear a child, with all the life-transforming consequences that act involves. And in thus safeguarding each woman's reproductive freedom, the Constitution also protected "[t]he ability of women to participate equally in [this Nation's] economic and social life." But no longer. As of today, this Court holds, a State can always force a woman to give birth, prohibiting even the earliest abortions. A State can thus transform what, when freely undertaken, is a wonder into what, when forced, may be a nightmare. Some women, especially women of means, will find ways around the State's assertion of power. Others—those without money or childcare or the ability to take time off from work—will not be so fortunate. Maybe they will try an unsafe method of abortion, and come to physical harm, or even die. Maybe they will undergo pregnancy and have a child, but at significant personal or familial cost. At the least, they will incur the cost of losing control of their lives. The Constitution will, today's majority holds, provide no shield, despite its guarantees of liberty and equality for all.

And no one should be confident that this majority is done with its work. The right *Roe* and *Casey* recognized does not stand alone. To the contrary, the Court has linked it for decades to other settled freedoms involving bodily integrity, familial relationships, and procreation. Most obviously, the right to terminate a pregnancy arose straight out of the right to purchase and use contraception. In turn, those rights led, more recently, to rights of same-sex intimacy and marriage. They are all part of the same constitutional fabric, protecting autonomous decisionmaking over the most personal of life decisions. The majority (or to be more accurate, most of it) is eager to tell us today that nothing it does "cast[s] doubt on precedents that do not concern abortion." But how could that be? The lone rationale for what the majority does today is that the right to elect an abortion is not "deeply rooted in history": Not until *Roe*, the majority argues, did people think abortion fell within the Constitution's guarantee of liberty. The same could be said, though, of most of the rights the majority claims it is not tampering with. The majority could write just as long an opinion showing, for example, that until the mid-20th century, "there was no support in American law for a constitutional right to obtain [contraceptives]." So one of two things must be true. Either the majority does not really believe in its own reasoning. Or if it does, all rights that have no history stretching back to the mid-19th century are insecure. Either the mass of the majority's opinion is hypocrisy, or additional constitutional rights are under threat. It is one or the other.

One piece of evidence on that score seems especially salient: The majority's cavalier approach to overturning this Court's precedents. *Stare decisis* is the Latin phrase for a foundation stone of the rule of law: that things decided should stay decided unless there is a very good reason for change. It is a doctrine of judicial modesty and humility. Those qualities are not evident in today's opinion. The majority has no good reason for the upheaval in law and society it sets off. *Roe* and *Casey* have been the law of the land for decades, shaping women's expectations of their choices when an unplanned pregnancy occurs.

[The dissent goes on at great length to reargue the validity of *Roe* and *Casey* and to reargue the importance of *stare decisis* to upholding long-held rights.]

PROBLEM

In the State of Z, it is a crime for any man to engage in intercourse with any woman under the age of 16. For the purpose of enforcing this law, the State of Z requires that any woman under 16 years old who desires an abortion must name whoever may have fathered the fetus as a condition of obtaining an abortion, if she knows who the father was. The law allows for an exception where the life or health of the mother is in danger. Assess the constitutionality of this requirement.

COMMENTS AND QUESTIONS

1.   Justice Kavanaugh writes that overruling *Roe* does not cast doubt on *Griswold* or *Obergefell*. Note he does not mention sodomy and *Lawrence*. Justice Alito's opinion for the Court similarly states that "[n]othing in this opinion should be understood to cast doubt on precedents that do not concern abortion." But note that in his list of historic cases overruling precedents he does not include *Lawrence*.

2.   How could *Lawrence* survive if one uses the type of analysis used in *Dobbs*? At least with respect to *Obergefell*, there would be a strong reliance argument against overruling. However, if *Obergefell* could be upheld, how could you rationally allow the criminalization of sodomy?

CHAPTER 8

EQUAL PROTECTION

■ ■ ■

The Fourteenth Amendment declares: "nor shall any state . . . deny to any person within its jurisdiction the equal protection of the laws." This is the Equal Protection Clause. Today we often think of this as meaning that government should treat all people equally, but that cannot be. The income tax laws make all sorts of distinctions between people: married people versus singles, higher income people versus lower income people, people with home mortgage interest payments versus renters, etc. You cannot obtain a driver's license unless you are of a certain age and can pass various tests. You cannot be admitted to a state law school unless you have graduated from college. You cannot become a member of the bar unless you fulfill certain requirements. All of these laws and more distinguish between people. At the same time, today we all know without reading any cases that if a state law said that black people and women cannot attend the state university or law school, that law would be unconstitutional under the Equal Protection Clause. What is it in the language of the Equal Protection Clause that would tell us this?

A. ECONOMIC MATTERS

Recall the *Slaughter-House Cases*, 83 U.S. 36 (1873), where Louisiana had granted a monopoly to butcher animals to one company and other butchers challenged the law as a violation of the Fourteenth Amendment. One of the claims was that the law denied the butchers equal protection of the laws. The law certainly treated them differently than the one company that was granted the monopoly. The Court, however, wrote:

> In the light of the history of these amendments, and the pervading purpose of them, . . . it is not difficult to give a meaning to this clause. The existence of laws in the States where the newly emancipated negroes resided, which discriminated with gross injustice and hardship against them as a class, was the evil to be remedied by this clause, and by it such laws are forbidden. . . . We doubt very much whether any action of a State not directed by way of discrimination against the negroes as a class, or on account of their race, will ever be held to come within the purview of this provision. It is so clearly a provision for that race and that emergency, that a strong case would be necessary for its application to any other.

Despite the lack of any text to support such a restriction, the Court seemed to limit the Clause to discrimination against African-Americans, not even to racial discrimination generally.

That limitation, however, did not endure for long. Within almost twenty years the Court was overturning state regulations of business on the basis of the Equal Protection Clause, stating that a classification must be "based upon some reasonable ground—some difference which bears a just and proper relation to the attempted classification—and is not a mere arbitrary selection." *Gulf, C. & S. F. Ry. Co. v. Ellis*, 165 U.S. 150, 165–66 (1897). *See also F. S. Royster Guano Co. v. Virginia*, 253 U.S. 412 (1920)(overturning a state law imposing an income tax on income earned outside of the state by out-of-state corporations but not by in-state corporations). Like *Lochner* under the Due Process Clause, this serious policing of economic classifications under the Equal Protection Clause also evaporated.

By 1949 the Court was willing to defer to state and local authorities if they might have thought the classification had some possible relation to its purpose. The following recent case gives an example of that deference in action.

ARMOUR V. CITY OF INDIANAPOLIS, INDIANA
United States Supreme Court, 2012.
566 U.S. 673, 132 S.Ct. 2073.

JUSTICE BREYER delivered the opinion of the Court.

For many years, an Indiana statute, the "Barrett Law," authorized Indiana's cities to impose upon benefited lot owners the cost of sewer improvement projects. The Law also permitted those lot owners to pay either immediately in the form of a lump sum or over time in installments. In 2005, the city of Indianapolis (City) adopted a new assessment and payment method, . . . and it forgave any Barrett Law installments that lot owners had not yet paid.

A group of lot owners who had already paid their entire Barrett Law assessment in a lump sum believe that the City should have provided them with equivalent refunds. And we must decide whether the City's refusal to do so unconstitutionally discriminates against them in violation of the Equal Protection Clause. We hold that the City had a rational basis for distinguishing between those lot owners who had already paid their share of project costs and those who had not. And we conclude that there is no equal protection violation. . . .

As long as the City's distinction has a rational basis, that distinction does not violate the Equal Protection Clause. This Court has long held that "a classification neither involving fundamental rights nor proceeding along suspect lines . . . cannot run afoul of the Equal Protection Clause if there is a rational relationship between the disparity of treatment and some legitimate governmental purpose." We have made clear in analogous contexts that, where "ordinary commercial transactions" are at issue, rational basis review requires deference to reasonable underlying legislative judgments. *United States v. Carolene Products Co.,* 304 U.S. 144 (1938)(due process); *see also New Orleans v. Dukes,* 427 U.S. 297 (1976)(*per curiam*)(equal protection). And we have repeatedly pointed out that "[l]egislatures have especially broad latitude in creating classifications and distinctions in tax statutes."

Indianapolis's classification involves neither a "fundamental right" nor a "suspect" classification. Its subject matter is local, economic, social, and commercial. It is a tax classification.... Hence, this case falls directly within the scope of our precedents holding such a law constitutionally valid if "there is a plausible policy reason for the classification, the legislative facts on which the classification is apparently based rationally may have been considered to be true by the governmental decisionmaker, and the relationship of the classification to its goal is not so attenuated as to render the distinction arbitrary or irrational." And it falls within the scope of our precedents holding that there is such a plausible reason if "there is any reasonably conceivable state of facts that could provide a rational basis for the classification."

Stephen Breyer

President Bill Clinton appointed Breyer to the Supreme Court in 1994, after he had served for fourteen years on the United States Court of Appeals for the First Circuit. Prior to that Breyer had been a professor at Harvard Law School since 1967, although he took time off to serve as special counsel and then as chief counsel to the Senate Committee on the Judiciary. Breyer was generally considered to be part of the liberal wing of the Court, but his background in administrative law led him to place a high value on the views and actions of government agencies, often deferring to them because of their perceived expertise. His constitutional interpretations eschewed bright line rules in favor of multi-factor balancing tests. He retired in 2022.

[F]urther, because the classification is presumed constitutional, the "burden is on the one attacking the legislative arrangement to negative every conceivable basis which might support it."

In our view, Indianapolis's classification has a rational basis. Ordinarily, administrative considerations can justify a tax-related distinction. And the City's decision to stop collecting outstanding Barrett Law debts finds rational support in related administrative concerns.

The City had decided to switch to the [new] system. After that change, to continue Barrett Law unpaid-debt collection could have proved complex and expensive. It would have meant maintaining an administrative system that for years to come would have had to collect debts arising out of 20-plus different construction projects built over the course of a decade, involving monthly payments as low as $25 per household, with the possible need to maintain credibility by tracking down defaulting debtors and bringing legal action. . . .

Consistent with these facts, the Director of the City's Department of Public Works later explained that the City decided to forgive outstanding debt in part because "[t]he administrative costs to service and process remaining balances on Barrett Law accounts long past the transition to the STEP program would not benefit the taxpayers" and would defeat the purpose of the transition. The four other members of the City's Board of Public Works have said the same. . . .

Finally, the rationality of the distinction draws support from the fact that the line that the City drew—distinguishing past payments from future obligations—is a line well known to the law. Sometimes such a line takes the form of an amnesty program, involving, say, mortgage payments, taxes, or parking tickets. *E.g.,* 26 U.S.C. § 108(a)(1)(E)(2006 ed., Supp. IV)(federal income tax provision allowing homeowners to omit from gross income newly forgiven home mortgage debt); *United States v. Martin,* 523 F.3d 281, 284 (C.A.4 2008)(tax amnesty program whereby State newly forgave penalties and liabilities if taxpayer satisfied debt); *Horn v. Chicago,* 860 F.2d 700, 704, n. 9 (C.A.7 1988)(city parking ticket amnesty program whereby outstanding tickets could be newly settled for a fraction of amount specified). This kind of line is consistent with the distinction that the law often makes between actions previously taken and those yet to come. . . .

[T]he Indiana Supreme Court wrote that the City's classification was "rationally related" in part "to its legitimate interests *in reducing its administrative costs.*"(emphasis added). The record of the City's proceedings is consistent with that determination. In any event, a legislature need not "actually articulate at any time the purpose or rationale supporting its classification." Rather, the "burden is on the one attacking the legislative arrangement to negative every conceivable basis which might support it." Petitioners have not "negative[d]" the Indiana Supreme Court's first listed justification, namely the administrative concerns we have discussed.

Petitioners go on to propose various other forgiveness systems that would have included refunds for at least some of those who had already paid in full. They argue that those systems are superior to the system that the City chose. . . . But even if petitioners have found a superior system, the Constitution does not require the City to draw the perfect line nor even to draw a line superior to some other line it might have drawn. It requires only that the line actually drawn be a rational line. And for the reasons we have set forth . . ., we believe that the line the City drew here is rational.

Petitioners further argue that administrative considerations alone should not justify a tax distinction, lest a city arbitrarily allocate taxes among a few citizens while forgiving many similarly situated citizens on the ground that it is cheaper and easier to collect taxes from a few people than from many. Petitioners are right that administrative considerations could not justify such an unfair system. But that is not because administrative considerations can *never* justify tax differences (any more than they can *always* do so). The question is whether reducing those expenses, in the particular circumstances, provides a rational basis justifying the tax difference in question.

In this case, "in the light of the facts made known or generally assumed," it is reasonable to believe that to graft a refund system onto the City's forgiveness decision could have (for example) imposed an administrative burden of both collecting and paying out small sums (say, $25 per month) for years. As we have said, it is rational for the City to draw a line that avoids that burden. Petitioners, who are the ones "attacking the legislative arrangement," have the burden of showing that the circumstances are otherwise, *i.e.*, that the administrative burden is too insubstantial to justify the classification. That they have not done. . . .

[Petitioners point to one case where we held a tax classification unconstitutional under the Equal Protection Clause. That case is] *Allegheny Pittsburgh Coal Co. v. Commission of Webster Cty.*, 488 U.S. 336 (1989). The Court there took into account a state constitution and related laws that required equal valuation of equally valuable property. It considered the constitutionality of a county tax assessor's practice (over a period of many years) of determining property values as of the time of the property's last sale; that practice meant highly unequal valuations for two identical properties that were sold years or decades apart. The Court first found that the assessor's practice was not rationally related to the county's avowed purpose of assessing properties equally at true current value because of the intentional systemic discrepancies the practice created. The Court then noted that, in light of the state constitution and related laws requiring equal valuation, there could be no other rational basis for the practice. Therefore, the Court held, the assessor's discriminatory policy violated the Federal Constitution's insistence upon "equal protection of the law."

Petitioners argue that the City's refusal to add refunds to its forgiveness decision is similar, for it constitutes a refusal to apply "equally" an Indiana state law that says that the costs of a Barrett Law project shall be equally "apportioned." In other words, petitioners say that even if the City's decision might otherwise be related to a rational purpose, state law (as in *Allegheny*) makes this the rare case where the facts preclude any rational basis for the City's decision other than to comply with the state mandate of equality.

Allegheny, however, involved a clear state law requirement clearly and dramatically violated. Indeed, we have described *Allegheny* as "the rare case where the facts precluded" any alternative reading of state law and thus any alternative rational basis. Here, the City followed state law by apportioning the cost of its Barrett Law projects equally. State law says nothing about forgiveness, how to design a forgiveness program, or whether or when rational distinctions in doing so are permitted. To adopt petitioners' view would risk transforming ordinary violations of ordinary state tax law into violations of the Federal Constitution.

CHIEF JUSTICE ROBERTS, with whom JUSTICE SCALIA and JUSTICE ALITO join, dissenting.

Twenty-three years ago, we released a succinct and unanimous opinion striking down a property tax scheme in West Virginia on the ground that it clearly violated the Equal Protection Clause. In *Allegheny Pittsburgh,* we held that a county failed to comport with equal protection requirements when it assessed property taxes primarily on the basis of purchase price, with no appropriate adjustments over time. The result was that new property owners were assessed at "roughly 8 to 35 times" the rate of those who had owned their property longer. We found such a "gross disparit[y]" in tax levels could not be justified in a state system that demanded that "taxation . . . be equal and uniform." The case affirmed the common sense proposition that the Equal Protection Clause is violated by state action that deprives a citizen of even "rough equality in tax treatment," when state law itself specifically provides that all the affected taxpayers are in the same category for tax purposes.

In this case, . . . [s]ome of the property owners—petitioners here—paid the full $9,278 up front. Others elected the option of paying in installments. Shortly after hook-up, the City switched to a new financing system and decided to forgive the hook-up debts of those paying on an installment plan. The City refused, however, to refund any portion of the payments made by their identically situated neighbors who had already paid the full amount due. The result was that while petitioners each paid the City $9,278 for their hook-ups, more than half their neighbors paid less than $500 for the same improvement—some as little as $309.27. Another quarter paid less than $1,000. Petitioners thus paid between 10 and 30 times as much for their sewer hook-ups as their neighbors.

In seeking to justify this gross disparity, the City explained that it was presented with three choices: First, it could have continued to collect the installment plan payments of those who had not yet settled their debts under the old system. Second, it could have forgiven all those debts and given equivalent refunds to those who had made lump sum payments up front. Or third, it could have forgiven the future payments and not refunded payments that had already been made. The first two choices had the benefit of complying with state law, treating all of Indianapolis's citizens equally, and comporting with the Constitution. The City chose the third option.

And what did the City believe was sufficient to justify a system that would effectively charge petitioners *30 times more* than their neighbors for the *same* service—when state law promised equal treatment? Two things: the desire to avoid administrative hassle and the "fiscal[ ] challeng[e]" of giving back money it wanted to keep. I cannot agree that those reasons pass constitutional muster, even under rational basis review.

The City argues that either of the other options for transitioning away from the Barrett Law would have been "immensely difficult from an administrative standpoint." The Court accepts this rationale, observing that "[o]rdinarily, administrative considerations can justify a tax-related distinction." The cases the Court cites, however, stand only for the proposition that a legislature crafting a tax scheme may take administrative concerns into consideration when creating classes of taxable entities that may be taxed differently.

Here, however, Indiana's tax scheme explicitly provides that costs will "be primarily apportioned *equally* among all abutting lands or lots." The legislature has therefore decreed that all abutting landowners are within the same class. We have never before held that administrative burdens justify grossly disparate tax treatment of those the State has provided should be treated alike. Indeed, in *Allegheny Pittsburgh* the County argued that its unequal assessments were based on "[a]dministrative cost[ ]" concerns, to no avail. The reason we have rejected this argument is obvious: The Equal Protection Clause does not provide that no State shall "deny to any person within its jurisdiction the equal protection of the laws, unless it's too much of a bother." . . .

To the extent a ruling for petitioners would require issuing refunds . . ., I think the city workers are up to the task. The City has in fact already produced records showing exactly how much each lump-sum payer overpaid in *every* active Barrett Law Project—to the penny. What the city employees would need to do, therefore, is cut the checks and mail them out. . . .

The Court suggests that the City's administrative convenience argument is one with which the law is comfortable. The Court compares the City's decision to forgive the installment balances to the sort of parking ticket and mortgage payment amnesty programs that currently abound. This analogy is misplaced: Amnesty programs are designed to entice those who are unlikely ever to pay their debts to come forward and pay at least a portion of what they owe. It is not administrative convenience alone that justifies such schemes. In a sense, these schemes help remedy payment inequities by prompting those who would pay nothing to pay at least some of their fair share. The same cannot be said of the City's system.

The Court is willing to concede that "administrative considerations could not justify . . . an unfair system" in which "a city arbitrarily allocate[s] taxes among a few citizens while forgiving many others on the ground that it is cheaper and easier to collect taxes from a few people than from many." Cold comfort, that. If the quoted language does not accurately describe this case, I am not sure what it would reach. . . .

Equally unconvincing is the Court's attempt to distinguish *Allegheny Pittsburgh*. The Court claims that case was different because it involved "a clear state law requirement clearly and dramatically violated." Nothing less is at stake here. Indiana law requires that the costs of sewer projects be "apportioned equally among all abutting lands." The City has instead apportioned the costs of the Brisbane/Manning project such that petitioners paid between 10 and 30 times as much as their neighbors. Worse still, it has done so in order to avoid administrative hassle and save a bit of money. . . .

Our precedents do not ask for much from government in this area— only "rough equality in tax treatment." The Court reminds us that *Allegheny Pittsburgh* is a "rare case." It is and should be; we give great leeway to taxing authorities in this area, for good and sufficient reasons. But every generation or so a case comes along when this Court needs to say enough is enough, if the Equal Protection Clause is to retain any force in this context. *Allegheny Pittsburgh* was such a case; so is this one. Indiana law promised neighboring homeowners that they would be treated equally when it came to paying for sewer hook-ups. The City then ended up charging some homeowners *30 times* what it charged their neighbors for the same hook-ups. The equal protection violation is plain. I would accordingly reverse the decision of the Indiana Supreme Court, and respectfully dissent from the Court's decision to do otherwise.

COMMENTS AND QUESTIONS

1.   Note the established tests quoted by the Court for deciding equal protection cases involving commercial or tax matters. What does the dissent say about these tests?

2.   The dissent says the *Allegheny Pittsburgh* case is directly on point. The Court distinguishes it. What do you think?

3.   Why should a federal constitutional claim of denial of equal protection in taxation have to rely on a state constitutional or statutory provision requiring equal treatment in taxation? Why don't the taxpayers simply sue under state law?

4.   The city argues that there would be substantial administrative costs for it to require the taxpayers using the installment plan to continue to make their payments and that there would be significant out-of-pocket, unbudgeted expenditures if it were to pay the lump-sum taxpayers refunds, money that would have to come from some other city funded activity. The majority finds

these justifications reasonable. The dissent does not. The dissent emphasizes that some of the lump-sum payers here will pay *30 times* as much for the sewer hook-ups as those who were on the installment plan. What if it had been only twice as much? Would the city's justifications been sufficient for the dissent then?

B. RACE

1. SEGREGATION

The *Slaughter-House Cases* identified the purpose of the Fourteenth Amendment as protecting the newly freed slaves, but it was not until 1880, eight years later, and after a number of equal protection cases involving economic discrimination, that the first racial discrimination case found its way to the Court. *Strauder v. West Virginia*, 100 U.S. 303 (1880), involved a state law that did not allow blacks on juries. The Court overturned the conviction of a black man for murder. It explained:

> [The Fourteenth Amendment] was designed to assure to the colored race the enjoyment of all the civil rights that under the law are enjoyed by white persons, and to give to that race the protection of the general government, in that enjoyment, whenever it should be denied by the States. . . .
>
> It ordains that no State shall . . . deny to any person within its jurisdiction the equal protection of the laws. What is this but declaring that the law in the States shall be the same for the black as for the white; that all persons, whether colored or white, shall stand equal before the laws of the States, and, in regard to the colored race, for whose protection the amendment was primarily designed, that no discrimination shall be made against them by law because of their color? The words of the amendment, it is true, are prohibitory, but they contain a necessary implication of a positive immunity, or right, most valuable to the colored race— the right to exemption from unfriendly legislation against them distinctively as colored—exemption from legal discriminations, implying inferiority in civil society, lessening the security of their enjoyment of the rights which others enjoy, and discriminations which are steps towards reducing them to the condition of a subject race.
>
> That the West Virginia statute respecting juries . . . is such a discrimination ought not to be doubted. Nor would it be if the persons excluded by it were white men. If in those States where the colored people constitute a majority of the entire population a law should be enacted excluding all white men from jury service, thus denying to them the privilege of participating equally with the blacks in the administration of justice, we apprehend no one

would be heard to claim that it would not be a denial to white men of the equal protection of the laws. . . . The very fact that colored people are singled out and expressly denied by a statute all right to participate in the administration of the law, as jurors, because of their color, though they are citizens, and may be in other respects fully qualified, is practically a brand upon them, affixed by the law, an assertion of their inferiority, and a stimulant to that race prejudice which is an impediment to securing to individuals of the race that equal justice which the law aims to secure to all others. . . .

In view of these considerations, it is hard to see why the statute of West Virginia should not be regarded as discriminating against a colored man when he is put upon trial for an alleged criminal offence against the State. It is not easy to comprehend how it can be said that while every white man is entitled to a trial by a jury selected from persons of his own race or color, or, rather, selected without discrimination against his color, and a negro is not, the latter is equally protected by the law with the former. Is not protection of life and liberty against race or color prejudice, a right, a legal right, under the constitutional amendment? And how can it be maintained that compelling a colored man to submit to a trial for his life by a jury drawn from a panel from which the State has expressly excluded every man of his race, because of color alone, however well qualified in other respects, is not a denial to him of equal legal protection?

The Court, however, had a short memory, as is evidenced by the following infamous case.

PLESSY V. FERGUSON
United States Supreme Court, 1896.
163 U.S. 537, 16 S.Ct. 1138.

JUSTICE BROWN delivered the opinion of the Court.

This case turns upon the constitutionality of an act of the general assembly of the state of Louisiana, passed in 1890, providing for separate railway carriages for the white and colored races.

The first section of the statute enacts "that all railway companies carrying passengers in their coaches in this state, shall provide equal but separate accommodations for the white, and colored races, by providing two or more passenger coaches for each passenger train, or by dividing the passenger coaches by a partition so as to secure separate accommodations. No person or persons shall be permitted to occupy seats in coaches, other than the ones assigned to them, on account of the race they belong to."

[T]he constitutionality of this act is attacked upon the ground that it conflicts . . . [with] the fourteenth amendment, which prohibits certain restrictive legislation on the part of the states.

[B]y the fourteenth amendment, all persons born or naturalized in the United States, and subject to the jurisdiction thereof, are made citizens of the United States and of the state wherein they reside; and the states are forbidden from making or enforcing any law which shall abridge the privileges or immunities of citizens of the United States, or shall deprive any person of life, liberty, or property without due process of law, or deny to any person within their jurisdiction the equal protection of the laws.

[T]he object of the amendment was undoubtedly to enforce the absolute equality of the two races before the law, but, in the nature of things, it could not have been intended to abolish distinctions based upon color, or to enforce social, as distinguished from political, equality, or a commingling of the two races upon terms unsatisfactory to either. Laws permitting, and even requiring, their separation, in places where they are liable to be brought into contact, do not necessarily imply the inferiority of either race to the other, and have been generally, if not universally, recognized as within the competency of the state legislatures in the exercise of their police power. The most common instance of this is connected with the establishment of separate schools for white and colored children, which have been held to be a valid exercise of the legislative power even by courts of states where the political rights of the colored race have been longest and most earnestly enforced. . . .

Laws forbidding the intermarriage of the two races may be said in a technical sense to interfere with the freedom of contract, and yet have been universally recognized as within the police power of the state.

The distinction between laws interfering with the political equality of the negro and those requiring the separation of the two races in schools, theaters, and railway carriages has been frequently drawn by this court. Thus, in *Strauder v. West Virginia*, it was held that a law of West Virginia limiting to white male persons 21 years of age, and citizens of the state, the right to sit upon juries, was a discrimination which implied a legal inferiority in civil society, which lessened the security of the right of the colored race, and was a step towards reducing them to a condition of servility. . . .

[I]t is also suggested by the learned counsel for the plaintiff in error that the same argument that will justify the state legislature in requiring railways to provide separate accommodations for the two races will also authorize them to require separate cars to be provided for people whose hair is of a certain color, or who are aliens, or who belong to certain nationalities, or to enact laws requiring colored people to walk upon one side of the street, and white people upon the other, or requiring white men's houses to be painted white, and colored men's black, or their vehicles or business signs to be of different colors, upon the theory that one side of the street is as good as the other, or that a house or vehicle of one color is as good as one of another color. The reply to all this is that every exercise of the police power must be reasonable, and extend only to such laws as are enacted in good faith for the promotion of the public good, and not for the annoyance or oppression of a particular class. . . .

So far, then, as a conflict with the fourteenth amendment is concerned, the case reduces itself to the question whether the statute of Louisiana is a reasonable regulation, and with respect to this there must necessarily be a large discretion on the part of the legislature. In determining the question of reasonableness, it is at liberty to act with reference to the established usages, customs, and traditions of the people, and with a view to the promotion of their comfort, and the preservation of the public peace and good order. Gauged by this standard, we cannot say that a law which authorizes or even requires the separation of the two races in public conveyances is unreasonable, or more obnoxious to the fourteenth amendment than the acts of congress requiring separate schools for colored children in the District of Columbia, the constitutionality of which does not seem to have been questioned, or the corresponding acts of state legislatures.

We consider the underlying fallacy of the plaintiff's argument to consist in the assumption that the enforced separation of the two races stamps the colored race with a badge of inferiority. If this be so, it is not by reason of anything found in the act, but solely because the colored race chooses to put that construction upon it. The argument necessarily assumes that if, as has been more than once the case, and is not unlikely to be so again, the colored race should become the dominant power in the state legislature, and should enact a law in precisely similar terms, it would thereby relegate the white race to an inferior position. We imagine that the white race, at least, would not acquiesce in this assumption. The argument also assumes that social prejudices may be overcome by legislation, and that equal rights cannot be secured to the negro except by an enforced commingling of the two races. We cannot accept this proposition. If the two races are to meet upon terms of social equality, it must be the result of natural affinities, a mutual appreciation of each other's merits, and a voluntary consent of individuals. . . .

MR. JUSTICE BREWER did not hear the argument or participate in the decision of this case.

MR. JUSTICE HARLAN dissenting.

In respect of civil rights, common to all citizens, the constitution of the United States does not, I think, permit any public authority to know the race of those entitled to be protected in the enjoyment of such rights. Every true man has pride of race, and under appropriate circumstances, when the rights of others, his equals before the law, are not to be affected, it is his privilege to express such pride and to take such action based upon it as to him seems proper. But I deny that any legislative body or judicial tribunal may have regard to the race of citizens when the civil rights of those citizens are involved. Indeed, such legislation as that here in question is inconsistent not only with that equality of rights which pertains to citizenship, national and state, but with the personal liberty enjoyed by every one within the United States. . . .

It was said in argument that the statute of Louisiana does not discriminate against either race, but prescribes a rule applicable alike to white and colored citizens. But this argument does not meet the difficulty. Every one knows that the statute in question had its origin in the purpose, not so much to exclude white persons from railroad cars occupied by blacks, as to exclude colored people from coaches occupied by or assigned to white persons. . . . The thing to accomplish was, under the guise of giving equal accommodation for whites and blacks, to compel the latter to keep to themselves while traveling in railroad passenger coaches. No one would be so wanting in candor as to assert the contrary. The fundamental objection, therefore, to the statute, is that it interferes with the personal freedom of citizens. . . . If a white man and a black man choose to occupy the same public conveyance on a public highway, it is their right to do so; and no government, proceeding alone on grounds of race, can prevent it without infringing the personal liberty of each. . . .

The white race deems itself to be the dominant race in this country. And so it is, in prestige, in achievements, in education, in wealth, and in power. So, I doubt not, it will continue to be for all time, if it remains true to its great heritage, and holds fast to the principles of constitutional liberty. But in view of the constitution, in the eye of the law, there is in this country no superior, dominant, ruling class of citizens. There is no caste here. Our constitution is color-blind, and neither knows nor tolerates classes among citizens. In respect of civil rights, all citizens are equal before the law. The humblest is the peer of the most powerful. The law regards man as man, and takes no account of his surroundings or of his color when his civil rights as guaranteed by the supreme law of the land are involved. It is therefore to be regretted that this high tribunal, the final expositor of the fundamental law of the land, has reached the conclusion that it is competent for a state to regulate the enjoyment by citizens of their civil rights solely upon the basis of race.

In my opinion, the judgment this day rendered will, in time, prove to be quite as pernicious as the decision made by this tribunal in the *Dred Scott Case*.

It was adjudged in that case that the descendants of Africans who were imported into this country, and sold as slaves, were not included nor intended to be included under the word "citizens" in the constitution, and could not claim any of the rights and privileges which that instrument provided for and secured to citizens of the United States; that, at time of the adoption of the constitution, they were "considered as a subordinate and inferior class of beings, who had been subjugated by the dominant race, and, whether emancipated or not, yet remained subject to their authority, and had no rights or privileges but such as those who held the power and the government might choose to grant them." The recent amendments of the constitution, it was supposed, had eradicated these principles from our institutions. But it seems that we have yet, in some of the states, a dominant race—a superior class of citizens—which assumes to regulate the enjoyment of civil rights, common to all citizens, upon the basis of race. The present decision, it may well be apprehended, will not only stimulate aggressions, more or less brutal and irritating, upon the admitted rights of colored citizens, but will encourage the belief that it is possible, by means of state enactments, to defeat the beneficent purposes which the people of the United States had in view when they adopted the recent amendments of the constitution, by one of which the blacks of this country were made citizens of the United States and of the states in which they respectively reside, and whose privileges and immunities, as citizens, the states are forbidden to abridge. Sixty millions of whites are in no danger from the presence here of eight millions of blacks. The destinies of the two races, in this country, are indissolubly linked together, and the interests of both require that the common government of all shall not permit the seeds of race hate to be planted under the sanction of law. What can more certainly arouse race hate, what more certainly create and perpetuate a feeling of distrust between these races, than state enactments which, in fact, proceed on the ground that colored citizens are so inferior and degraded that they cannot be allowed to sit in public coaches occupied by white citizens? That, as all will admit, is the real meaning of such legislation as was enacted in Louisiana.

The sure guaranty of the peace and security of each race is the clear, distinct, unconditional recognition by our governments, national and state, of every right that inheres in civil freedom, and of the equality before the law of all citizens of the United States, without regard to race. . . .

COMMENTS AND QUESTIONS

1.   Today we know *Plessy* was wrongly decided, but how was it wrongly decided? What is the error in the Court's analysis?

2.   How does *Plessy* distinguish *Strauder*? What is the difference between the discrimination involved in these two cases?

3.   The Court refers to acts of Congress providing for the segregation of students by race in the District of Columbia. Indeed, it was the same Congress that proposed the Fourteenth Amendment to the states that required segregation of the D.C. schools. What, if anything, does that tell us about the

Equal Protection Clause? About originalism as a method of constitutional interpretation?

4. Why does Justice Harlan reach a different conclusion from the Court? Where does he differ from the Court's opinion?

5. *Plessy* inaugurated the concept of "separate but equal" as a basis for upholding racial segregation. That judicial approval of segregation plus the effective disenfranchisement of black voters in the South during the same period led to the creation of the National Association for the Advancement of Colored People (NAACP) in 1910, dedicated to promoting the equality of rights and the eradication of caste and race prejudice among the citizens of the United States. Early on it utilized the courts to try to break down segregation through its Legal Defense Fund affiliate. Its initial strategy was to bring cases challenging whether the facilities provided were indeed equal, a strategy that was increasingly successful. In 1938 the Supreme Court held that Missouri, by not allowing blacks to attend the state law school and not providing any equivalent law school for blacks violated the Equal Protection Clause. *State of Missouri ex rel. Gaines v. Canada*, 305 U.S. 337 (1938). In 1948 a similar case was successful against Oklahoma, *Sipuel v. Board of Regents*, 332 U.S. 631 (1948), and in 1950 a similar suit against Texas was also successful, *Sweatt v. Painter*, 339 U.S. 629 (1950). At this point the NAACP Legal Defense Fund faced a strategic decision. Should it continue to bring suits against states for failing to provide equal facilities, or should it attack *Plessy* and the doctrine of Separate but Equal itself? The decision was not an easy one. *Plessy* was long established precedent that the Court had continued to enforce, even if the Court and the national mood (at least outside the South) no longer supported its underlying principle that segregation of the races was appropriate. For example, in 1948 President Truman by executive order eliminated segregation by race in the armed forces. The decision to challenge Separate but Equal head-on was championed by Thurgood Marshall, the NAACP's General Counsel, who later became the first African-American Justice of the Supreme Court. The result of that decision follows.

BROWN V. BOARD OF EDUCATION

United States Supreme Court, 1954.
347 U.S. 483, 74 S.Ct. 686.

CHIEF JUSTICE WARREN delivered the opinion of the Court.

These cases come to us from the States of Kansas, South Carolina, Virginia, and Delaware. . . .

In each of the cases, minors of the Negro race, through their legal representatives, seek the aid of the courts in obtaining admission to the public schools of their community on a nonsegregated basis. In each instance, they have been denied admission to schools attended by white children under laws requiring or permitting segregation according to race. This segregation was alleged to deprive the plaintiffs of the equal protection of the laws under the Fourteenth Amendment. In each of the cases other than the Delaware case, a three-judge federal district court denied relief to the plaintiffs on the so-called 'separate but equal' doctrine announced by this Court in *Plessy v. Ferguson*. Under that doctrine, equality of treatment is accorded when the races are provided substantially equal facilities, even though these facilities be separate. In the Delaware case, the Supreme Court of Delaware adhered to that doctrine, but ordered that the plaintiffs be admitted to the white schools because of their superiority to the Negro schools.

The plaintiffs contend that segregated public schools are not "equal" and cannot be made "equal," and that hence they are deprived of the equal protection of the laws. Because of the obvious importance of the question presented, the Court took jurisdiction. Argument was heard in the 1952 Term, and reargument was heard this Term on certain questions propounded by the Court.

Reargument was largely devoted to the circumstances surrounding the adoption of the Fourteenth Amendment in 1868. . . . This discussion and our own investigation convince us that, although these sources cast some light, it is not enough to resolve the problem with which we are faced. At best, they are inconclusive. The most avid proponents of the post-War Amendments undoubtedly intended them to remove all legal distinctions among "all persons born or naturalized in the United States." Their opponents, just as certainly, were antagonistic to both the letter and the spirit of the Amendments and wished them to have the most limited effect. What others in Congress and the state legislatures had in mind cannot be determined with any degree of certainty.

An additional reason for the inconclusive nature of the Amendment's history, with respect to segregated schools, is the status of public education at that time. In the South, the movement toward free common schools, supported by general taxation, had not yet taken hold. Education of white children was largely in the hands of private groups. Education of Negroes was almost nonexistent, and practically all of the race were illiterate. In fact, any education of Negroes was forbidden by law in some states. . . . It is true that public school education at the time of the Amendment had advanced further in the North, but the effect of the Amendment on Northern States was generally ignored in the congressional debates. Even in the North, the conditions of public education did not approximate those existing today. The curriculum was usually rudimentary; ungraded schools were common in rural areas; the school term was but three months a year in many states; and compulsory school attendance was virtually unknown. As a consequence, it is not surprising that there should be so little in the history of the Fourteenth Amendment relating to its intended effect on public education.

In the first cases in this Court construing the Fourteenth Amendment, decided shortly after its adoption, the Court interpreted it as proscribing all state-imposed discriminations against the Negro race. The doctrine of "separate but equal" did not make its appearance in this court until 1896 in the case of *Plessy v. Ferguson*, involving not education but transportation. American courts have since labored with the doctrine for over half a century. In this Court, there have been six cases involving the "separate but equal" doctrine in the field of public education. . . . In none of these cases was it necessary to re-examine the doctrine to grant relief to the Negro plaintiff.

In the instant cases, that question is directly presented. Here, unlike *Sweatt v. Painter*, there are findings below that the Negro and white schools involved have been equalized, or are being equalized, with respect to buildings, curricula, qualifications and salaries of teachers, and other "tangible" factors. Our decision, therefore, cannot turn on merely a comparison of these tangible factors in the Negro and white schools involved in each of the cases. We must look instead to the effect of segregation itself on public education.

In approaching this problem, we cannot turn the clock back to 1868 when the Amendment was adopted, or even to 1896 when *Plessy v. Ferguson* was written. We must consider public education in the light of its full development and its present place in American life throughout the Nation. Only in this way can it be determined if segregation in public schools deprives these plaintiffs of the equal protection of the laws.

Today, education is perhaps the most important function of state and local governments. Compulsory school attendance laws and the great expenditures for education both demonstrate our recognition of the importance of education to our democratic society. It is required in the performance of our most basic public responsibilities, even service in the armed forces. It is the very foundation of good citizenship. Today it is a principal instrument in awakening the child to cultural values, in preparing him for later professional training, and in helping him to adjust normally to his environment. In these days, it is doubtful that any child may reasonably be expected to succeed in life if he is denied the opportunity of an education. Such an opportunity, where the state has undertaken to provide it, is a right which must be made available to all on equal terms.

We come then to the question presented: Does segregation of children in public schools solely on the basis of race, even though the physical facilities and other "tangible" factors may be equal, deprive the children of the minority group of equal educational opportunities? We believe that it does.

In *Sweatt v. Painter*, in finding that a segregated law school for Negroes could not provide them equal educational opportunities, this Court relied in large part on "those qualities which are incapable of objective measurement but which make for greatness in a law school." . . . Such considerations apply with added force to children in grade and high schools.

To separate them from others of similar age and qualifications solely because of their race generates a feeling of inferiority as to their status in the community that may affect their hearts and minds in a way unlikely ever to be undone. The effect of this separation on their educational opportunities was well stated by a finding in the Kansas case by a court which nevertheless felt compelled to rule against the Negro plaintiffs:

> Segregation of white and colored children in public schools has a detrimental effect upon the colored children. The impact is greater when it has the sanction of the law; for the policy of separating the races is usually interpreted as denoting the inferiority of the negro group. A sense of inferiority affects the motivation of a child to learn. Segregation with the sanction of law, therefore, has a tendency to (retard) the educational and mental development of Negro children and to deprive them of some of the benefits they would receive in a racial(ly) integrated school system.

Whatever may have been the extent of psychological knowledge at the time of *Plessy v. Ferguson*, this finding is amply supported by modern authority.[11] Any language in *Plessy v. Ferguson* contrary to this finding is rejected.

We conclude that in the field of public education the doctrine of "separate but equal" has no place. Separate educational facilities are inherently unequal. Therefore, we hold that the plaintiffs and others similarly situated for whom the actions have been brought are, by reason of the segregation complained of, deprived of the equal protection of the laws guaranteed by the Fourteenth Amendment. . . .

COMMENTS AND QUESTIONS

1. *Brown* is unanimous, but its outcome was more in doubt than the final resolution suggests. After its initial argument in 1953, the first tentative votes by the justices appeared to be 5–4 in favor of upholding *Plessy* on the basis of precedent. Nevertheless, the case was set for reargument in the next term, in which the Court asked for briefing in particular on the history of the Equal Protection Clause as it related to racial segregation in schools. Before reargument, however, Chief Justice Vinson, a conservative southerner who favored upholding *Plessy*, died, and President Eisenhower appointed Earl Warren, a former Republican governor of California who had supported Eisenhower's nomination for President, to replace Vinson. From his public

---

[11] K.B. Clark, Effect of Prejudice and Discrimination on Personality Development (Midcentury White House Conference on Children and Youth, 1950); Witmer and Kotinsky, Personality in the Making (1952), c. VI; Deutscher and Chein, The Psychological Effects of Enforced Segregation: A Survey of Social Science Opinion, 26 J.Psychol. 259 (1948); Chein, What are the Psychological Effects of Segregation Under Conditions of Equal Facilities?, 3 Int. J. Opinion and Attitude Res. 229 (1949); Brameld, Educational Costs, in Discrimination and National Welfare (MacIver, ed., 1949), 44–48; Frazier, The Negro in the United States (1949), 674–681. And see generally Myrdal, An American Dilemma (1944).

background as a Republican governor and attorney general of California, who had supported the internment of Japanese during World War II, no one would have guessed that Warren would be a champion of minority rights. It is said that President Eisenhower later said that appointing Earl Warren Chief Justice was his greatest mistake. On the other hand, some believe it was his greatest accomplishment, if albeit unintentional. In any case, Warren strongly supported elimination of segregation and felt it was imperative that the Court speak with one voice on this issue, doing all in his power to bring it about.

2.   It is often assumed that *Brown* overruled *Plessy*. Is that accurate? What does *Brown* say about segregation in railroad cars? Does the analysis of *Brown* with respect to education apply to segregation in other circumstances? The first cases in the Supreme Court following *Brown* involved segregation of public beaches, municipal golf courses, municipal buses, and public parks. What does *Brown*'s analysis say about segregation in these circumstances? Nevertheless, in each the Court rejected racial segregation without opinion, sometimes simply by citing *Brown*. What does this suggest?

3.   Again, the history of the Fourteenth Amendment is as clear as history can be that those who proposed it to the states and those who ratified it did not intend for it to ban racial segregation. If this history is accurate, does this suggest *Brown* was wrong? If not, what does this say about originalism as an interpretive method? It is an interesting factoid that of the nine justices on the Court deciding *Brown*, only one (Sherman Minton) had previously been a judge before being appointed to the Supreme Court. Compare that to today when only one of the justices (Elena Kagan) was *not* an appellate judge when appointed to the Supreme Court. Some believe that this difference explains a lot about the differences between the Court then and now. Why might those different backgrounds result in different methodologies of judging?

4.   A companion case to *Brown* was *Bolling v. Sharpe*, 347 U.S. 497 (1954), which involved a challenge to schools segregated in the District of Columbia pursuant to laws dating back to at least 1866, the year Congress proposed the Fourteenth Amendment to the states. The Fourteenth Amendment, including its Equal Protection Clause, the basis for *Brown*, only applies to the states, however, not the federal government. The Court, therefore, had a bit of a problem. In a very short opinion, the Court concluded: "In view of our decision that the Constitution prohibits the states from maintaining racially segregated public schools, it would be unthinkable that the same Constitution would impose a lesser duty on the Federal Government. We hold that racial segregation in the public schools of the District of Columbia is a denial of the due process of law guaranteed by the Fifth Amendment to the Constitution." It is difficult to square this conclusion with the text or history of the Fifth Amendment. Indeed, if the Due Process Clause was thought to include an equal protection component, there would have been no need in the Fourteenth Amendment to include the Equal Protection Clause in addition to its Due Process Clause. Nevertheless, ever since *Bolling*, this conclusion that the Due Process Clause of the Fifth Amendment contains an equal protection component has been black letter law resulting in identical applications of the

Equal Protection Clause to both the federal and state governments, with one exception: the treatment of alienage. Moreover, only Justice Thomas has suggested any problem with this conclusion.

5.   Having found that racial segregation in public schools was unconstitutional, the Court was faced with the proper remedy. In *Brown*, it set the case for reargument as to remedy. The Court was aware that its decision in *Brown* would be met with great hostility throughout the South where segregation by law was still intact, and not just in the school systems. In *Brown v. Board of Education (II)*, 349 U.S. 294 (1955), the Court tried to mediate the forced end of a deep cultural and legal tradition by relying first on local school authorities to implement the decision in light of local conditions, with federal courts overseeing the transition through the use of equitable remedies. Moreover, while requiring "a prompt and reasonable start toward full compliance" with *Brown I*, the Court recognized that "additional time [might be] necessary to carry out the ruling in an effective manner." It concluded with the expression that segregation should be ended "with all deliberate speed."

6.   The response of the South was massive resistance, ranging from stonewalling to bombing. In 1964, ten years after *Brown*, when still only one black child in a hundred in the South attended an integrated school, Congress passed the Civil Rights Act, two portions of which dealt with school desegregation. Perhaps the most potent part was Title VI, which withheld federal financial assistance from any racially discriminatory program. The case below is an example of what a relatively progressive school district might have provided.

GREEN V. COUNTY SCHOOL BOARD OF NEW KENT COUNTY

United States Supreme Court, 1968.
391 U.S. 430, 88 S.Ct. 1689.

MR. JUSTICE BRENNAN delivered the opinion of the Court.

The question for decision is whether, under all the circumstances here, respondent School Board's adoption of a "freedom-of-choice" plan which allows a pupil to choose his own public school constitutes adequate compliance with the Board's responsibility "to achieve a system of determining admission to the public schools on a non-racial basis."

Petitioners brought this action in March 1965 seeking injunctive relief against respondent's continued maintenance of an alleged racially segregated school system. New Kent County is a rural county in Eastern Virginia. About one-half of its population of some 4,500 are Negroes. There is no residential segregation in the county; persons of both races reside throughout. [T]he District Court found that the "school system serves approximately 1,300 pupils, of which 740 are Negro and 550 are White. The School Board operates one white combined elementary and high school (New Kent), and one Negro combined elementary and high school (George W. Watkins). There are no attendance zones. Each school serves the entire county." The record indicates that 21 school buses—11 serving the Watkins school and 10 serving the New Kent school—travel overlapping routes throughout the county to transport pupils to and from the two schools.

The segregated system was initially established and maintained under the compulsion of Virginia constitutional and statutory provisions mandating racial segregation in public education.... The respondent School Board continued the segregated operation of the system after the *Brown* decisions.... However on August 2, 1965, five months after the suit was brought, respondent School Board, in order to remain eligible for federal financial aid, adopted a "freedom-of-choice" plan for desegregating the schools. Under that plan, each pupil, except those entering the first and eighth grades, may annually choose between the New Kent and Watkins schools and pupils not making a choice are assigned to the school previously attended; first and eighth grade pupils must affirmatively choose a school. [T]he District Court approved the "freedom-of-choice.".... The Court of Appeals for the Fourth Circuit, en banc, affirmed....

It is against this background that 13 years after *Brown II* commanded the abolition of dual systems we must measure the

William Brennan

President Eisenhower appointed Brennan to the Supreme Court in 1956. At the time Brennan was serving on the New Jersey Supreme Court, and political advisors to Eisenhower believed appointing a Catholic Democrat from the Northeast would help Eisenhower's reelection campaign. Brennan was an eager ally for Chief Justice Warren's activist view of the judiciary to protect individual rights, and he served as its prime mover after Warren left the Court and until 1990 when he retired for reasons of ill health.

effectiveness of respondent School Board's "freedom-of-choice" plan to achieve that end. The School Board contends that it has fully discharged its obligation by adopting a plan by which every student, regardless of race, may "freely" choose the school he will attend.... In the context of the state-imposed segregated pattern of long standing, the fact that in 1965 the Board opened the doors of the former "white" school to Negro children and of the "Negro" school to white children merely begins, not ends, our inquiry whether the Board has taken steps adequate to abolish its dual, segregated system.... School boards such as the respondent then operating state-compelled dual systems were ... clearly charged with the affirmative duty to take whatever steps might be necessary to convert to a unitary system in which racial discrimination would be eliminated root and branch.

The New Kent School Board's "freedom-of-choice" plan cannot be accepted as a sufficient step to "effectuate a transition" to a unitary system.

In three years of operation not a single white child has chosen to attend Watkins school and although 115 Negro children enrolled in New Kent school in 1967 (up from 35 in 1965 and 111 in 1966) 85% of the Negro children in the system still attend the all-Negro Watkins school. In other words, the school system remains a dual system. Rather than further the dismantling of the dual system, the plan has operated simply to burden children and their parents with a responsibility which *Brown II* placed squarely on the School Board. The Board must be required to formulate a new plan and, in light of other courses which appear open to the Board, such as zoning, fashion steps which promise realistically to convert promptly to a system without a "white" school and a "Negro" school, but just schools. . . .

COMMENTS AND QUESTIONS

1.   Why is the school board's freedom of choice plan not acceptable? The school board is no longer maintaining a *de jure* (by law) racially segregated school system. If the black students do not choose to go to the previously "white" school, why should they be required to? Or, if white students do not choose to go to the previously "Negro" school, why should they be required to? What exactly is the Supreme Court requiring?

2.   Lower courts adopted orders that imposed mathematical targets for racial balance in individual schools and required school busing in many cases in order to achieve those targets. Challenges to these orders resulted in the Supreme Court's decision in *Swann v. Charlotte-Mecklenburg Board of Education*, 402 U.S. 1 (1971), which upheld race conscious remedies, including numerical targets and busing.

3.   In the North there had not been the legal institution of segregation in schools or elsewhere well before *Brown*. Nevertheless, inner city schools could be overwhelmingly populated by minorities, largely as a result of a policy of neighborhood schools and racially-identifiable neighborhoods. Where this *de facto* segregation of schools was not the result of racial discrimination by the school system, it was not unconstitutional. However, when it could be shown that the school system had sited schools intentionally to keep white schools white and black schools black, this was unconstitutional. *Keyes v. School District*, 413 U.S. 189 (1973).

4.   The trigger for remedial measures in *Green* and other cases was the fact that the school district had engaged in unconstitutional discrimination. In the suburbs in the North and newly developing in the South, however, there may not have been unconstitutional discrimination, if only because the school districts did not exist at the time of *Brown*. Nevertheless, with white flight to the suburbs, in part to avoid desegregation in the cities, the traditional remedy of busing students to achieve racially balanced schools would require inter-district busing between the inner city school district and the suburban school districts. In *Milliken v. Bradley*, 418 U.S. 717 (1974), however, the Court called a halt to such remedies unless the suburban districts could be found to have

also engaged in unconstitutional discrimination. The district court in Kansas City, faced with an inner city school district that was 68% black and 25 schools in the district with greater than 90% black students, established a plan to create magnet schools in the city that would voluntarily entice students from other districts that were overwhelmingly white to attend the inner city schools and help to break down those schools' racial identity. The Supreme Court, however, found this remedy inappropriate by a 5–4 vote. *See Missouri v. Jenkins*, 515 U.S. 70 (1995). Absent interdistrict discrimination, it said, the court's remedial powers could not extend even to entice out-of-district students. "In effect, the District Court has devised a remedy to accomplish indirectly what it admittedly lacks the remedial authority to mandate directly: the interdistrict transfer of students."

5. As the *Jenkins* case reflects, forty years after *Brown* lower courts were still involved in overseeing school desegregation cases. As a simplistic matter, the goal in these cases was to establish a racial composition in these schools that would have existed but for the unconstitutional discrimination. Life is more complicated, however, and as they say, you can't put the genie back in the bottle. That is, desegregating schools had its own effect on residential choices, and residential choices also tended to reflect economic status. In short, the poor tended to be located in one area, and the poor tended to be disproportionately minority. Consequently, many school districts, like Kansas City, struggled with mixed success in establishing truly integrated schools. The question arose then as to what was required finally to end judicial orders providing judicial oversight of schools. In *Freeman v. Pitts*, 503 U.S. 467 (1992), the Court said:

> That there was racial imbalance in student attendance zones was not tantamount to a showing that the school district was in noncompliance with the decree or with its duties under the law. Racial balance is not to be achieved for its own sake. It is to be pursued when racial imbalance has been caused by a constitutional violation. Once the racial imbalance due to the *de jure* violation has been remedied, the school district is under no duty to remedy imbalance that is caused by demographic factors. If the unlawful *de jure* policy of a school system has been the cause of the racial imbalance in student attendance, that condition must be remedied. The school district bears the burden of showing that any current imbalance is not traceable, in a proximate way, to the prior violation. . . .
>
> Where resegregation is a product not of state action but of private choices, it does not have constitutional implications. It is beyond the authority and beyond the practical ability of the federal courts to try to counteract these kinds of continuous and massive demographic shifts. . . . As the *de jure* violation becomes more remote in time and these demographic changes intervene, it becomes less likely that a current racial imbalance in a school district is a vestige of the prior *de jure* system. The causal link between current

conditions and the prior violation is even more attenuated if the school district has demonstrated its good faith.

6. Studies suggest that the integration of schools has regressed since 1988. A 2007 study showed that a typical black student attended a school that was only 30% white; a typical Latino student attended a school that was only 27% white; and a typical white student attended a school that was 77% white. *See* Gary Orfield & Chungmei Lee, *Historic Reversals, Accelerating Resegregation, and the Need for New Integration Strategies* (2007). A 2022 study reported that 46% of white students attended a school that was 75% or more white, while 59% of black students and 60% of Hispanic students attended a school that was over 75% students of color. RACIAL/ETHNIC ENROLLMENT IN PUBLIC SCHOOLS, National Center for Education Statistics, https://nces.ed.gov/programs/coe/indicator/cge/racial-ethnic-enrollment.

7. Racial discrimination was not limited to school segregation, of course. As indicated earlier, states imposed separation of the races from *Plessy*'s railroad cars to city buses, from city parks to swimming pools. *Brown* effectively made all of them unconstitutional. Nor was all racial discrimination aimed at blacks. Asian-Americans had long been subject to discriminatory laws in the West, and the Japanese attack on Pearl Harbor on December 7, 1941, precipitated federal action against Japanese-Americans on the West Coast. First, there was a curfew order directed against Japanese-Americans. Second, there was an order, enforced by a federal statute, excluding Japanese-Americans from designated areas on the West Coast. Finally, there was a statute authorizing the detention of Japanese-Americans in relocation centers away from the West Coast. The first two were explicitly upheld by the Supreme Court in *Hirabayashi v. United States*, 320 U.S. 81 (1943), and *Korematsu v. United States*, 323 U.S. 214 (1944), respectively. In both cases, the Court deferred to the military authorities' decision at the time immediately after Pearl Harbor that there was an imminent grave danger because of possible sabotage and espionage by Japanese-American sympathizers. In the latter case the Court stated that curtailing the civil rights of a single racial group is "immediately suspect" and must be subject to "the most rigid scrutiny." In hindsight we can say today that the Court's scrutiny was not very rigid and its deference to the military authorities was not warranted, especially because they affirmatively misled the Court as to the facts. In the third case, *Ex parte Endo*, 323 U.S. 283 (1944), the Court avoided the constitutional issues by finding that the executive order and statute that impliedly authorized the detention in relocation centers did not authorize the continued detention of concededly loyal Japanese-Americans who posed no threat of sabotage or espionage. Two weeks later the exclusion order was rescinded and persons were allowed to leave the centers.

8. There are numerous federal laws that provide special rules relating to Native Americans. There has been a recurring question whether these laws discriminate on the basis of race. The Supreme Court, however, has long held that classifications based on whether someone is a member of an Indian tribe is a political classification rather than a racial classification. *See, e.g., Morton*

v. Mancari, 417 U.S. 535 (1974). On the other hand, the Court held that a state law that allowed only "native Hawaiians" to vote for trustees for Office of Hawaiian Affairs involved a racial classification, because it was based on ancestry, rather than membership in a political entity. *Rice v. Cayetano*, 528 U.S. 495 (2000). As this book is being written, there is a case before the Supreme Court involving a law applying to Indians that may raise this issue again. *Brackeen v. Haaland.*

2. WHEN IS DISCRIMINATION *RACIAL* DISCRIMINATION?

When the law on its face discriminates on the basis of race, as was the case in the South with respect to segregation, it is clear that what is involved is *racial* discrimination. However, as the following case makes clear, racial discrimination can take place even under facially neutral laws.

YICK WO V. HOPKINS
United States Supreme Court, 1886.
118 U.S. 356, 6 S.Ct. 1064.

JUSTICE MATHEWS delivered the opinion of the Court.

[San Francisco ordinances prohibited the operation of a laundry except in a brick or stone building, presumably because laundries then utilized open fires to heat the water used in washing, and such a requirement reduced the likelihood of the building catching on fire. However, the ordinances provided that laundries in wooden buildings could be specially permitted by the approval of the Board of Supervisors. Applications for such a permit were made by 280 different persons. Two hundred of the applicants were Chinese, and all of their applications were denied. Of the 80 non-Chinese applicants, all but one were granted. Yick Wo was criminally prosecuted for operating a laundry in a wooden building without a permit. After noting that the ordinances did not provide any standards governing when a permit should be issued, such that it could be granted or denied on the most arbitrary of grounds, the Court went on.]

In the present cases, we are not obliged to reason from the probable to the actual, and pass upon the validity of the ordinances complained of, as tried merely by the opportunities which their terms afford, of unequal and unjust discrimination in their administration; for the cases present the ordinances in actual operation, and the facts shown establish an administration directed so exclusively against a particular class of persons as to warrant and require the conclusion that, whatever may have been the intent of the ordinances as adopted, they are applied by the public authorities charged with their administration, and thus representing the state itself, with a mind so unequal and oppressive as to amount to a practical denial by the state of that equal protection of the laws which is secured to the petitioners, as to all other persons, by the broad and benign provisions of the fourteenth amendment to the constitution of the United States. Though the law itself be fair on its face, and impartial in appearance, yet, if it is applied and administered by public authority with an evil eye and an unequal hand, so as practically to make unjust and illegal discriminations between persons in similar circumstances, material to their rights, the denial of equal justice is still within the prohibition of the constitution. . . .

The present cases, as shown by the facts disclosed in the record, are within this class. It appears that both petitioners have complied with every requisite deemed by the law, or by the public officers charged with its administration, necessary for the protection of neighboring property from fire, or as a precaution against injury to the public health. No reason whatever . . . is assigned why they should not be permitted to carry on, in the accustomed manner, their harmless and useful occupation, on which they depend for a livelihood; and while this consent of the supervisors is withheld from them, and from 200 others who have also petitioned, all of whom happen to be Chinese subjects, 80 others, not Chinese subjects, are permitted to carry on the same business under similar conditions. The fact of this discrimination is admitted. No reason for it is shown, and the conclusion cannot be resisted that no reason for it exists except hostility to the race and nationality to which the petitioners belong, and which, in the eye of the law, is not justified. The discrimination is therefore illegal, and the public administration which enforces it is a denial of the equal protection of the laws, and a violation of the fourteenth amendment of the constitution. The imprisonment of the petitioners is therefore illegal, and they must be discharged.

WASHINGTON V. DAVIS
United States Supreme Court, 1976.
426 U.S. 229, 96 S.Ct. 2040.

JUSTICE WHITE delivered the opinion of the Court.

This case involves the validity of a qualifying test administered to applicants for positions as police officers in the District of Columbia Metropolitan Police Department. . . .

This action began on April 10, 1970, when two Negro police officers filed suit against the then Commissioner of the District of Columbia, the Chief of the District's Metropolitan Police Department, and the Commissioners of the United States Civil Service Commission [alleging] that the Department's recruiting procedures discriminated on the basis of race against black applicants by a series of practices including, but not limited to, a written personnel test which excluded a disproportionately high number of Negro applicants. [The plaintiffs] filed a motion for partial summary judgment . . . seeking a declaration that the test administered to those applying to become police officers is "unlawfully discriminatory and

thereby in violation of the due process clause of the Fifth Amendment . . . ."
. . .

According to the findings and conclusions of the District Court, to be accepted by the Department and to enter an intensive 17-week training program, the police recruit was required to satisfy certain physical and character standards, to be a high school graduate or its equivalent, and to receive a grade of at least 40 out of 80 on "Test 21," which is "an examination that is used generally throughout the federal service," which "was developed by the Civil Service Commission, not the Police Department," and which was "designed to test verbal ability, vocabulary, reading and comprehension."

The validity of Test 21 was the sole issue before the court on the motions for summary judgment. The District Court noted that there was no claim of "an intentional discrimination or purposeful discriminatory acts" but only a claim that Test 21 bore no relationship to job performance and "has a highly discriminatory impact in screening out black candidates." [Plaintiffs'] evidence, the District Court said, warranted three conclusions: "(a) The number of black police officers, while substantial, is not proportionate to the population mix of the city. (b) A higher percentage of blacks fail the Test than whites. (c) The Test has not been validated to establish its reliability for measuring subsequent job performance." [T]he court nevertheless concluded that on the undisputed facts [plaintiffs] were not entitled to relief. The District Court relied on several factors. Since August 1969, 44% of new police force recruits had been black; that figure also represented the proportion of blacks on the total force and was roughly equivalent to 20- to 29-year-old blacks in the 50-mile radius in which the recruiting efforts of the Police Department had been concentrated. It was undisputed that the Department had systematically and affirmatively sought to enroll black officers many of whom passed the test but failed to report for duty. The District Court rejected the assertion that Test 21 was culturally slanted to favor whites and was "satisfied that the undisputable facts prove the test to be reasonably and directly related to the requirements of the police recruit training program and that it is neither so designed nor operates (Sic) to discriminate against otherwise qualified blacks." . . .

Having lost . . . in the District Court, [plaintiffs] brought the case to the Court of Appeals claiming that their summary judgment motion . . . should have been granted. The tendered constitutional issue was whether the use of Test 21 invidiously discriminated against Negroes and hence denied them due process of law contrary to the commands of the Fifth Amendment. The Court of Appeals, addressing that issue, announced that it would be guided by . . . a case involving the interpretation and application of Title VII of the Civil Rights Act of 1964, and held that the statutory standards elucidated in that case were to govern the due process question tendered in this one. The court went on to declare that lack of discriminatory intent in designing and administering Test 21 was irrelevant; the critical fact was rather that a far greater proportion of blacks four times as many failed the test than did whites. This disproportionate impact, standing alone and without regard to whether it indicated a discriminatory purpose, was held sufficient to establish a constitutional violation, absent proof by petitioners that the test was an adequate measure of job performance in addition to being an indicator of probable success in the training program, a burden which the court ruled petitioners had failed to discharge. That the Department had made substantial efforts to recruit blacks was held beside the point and the fact that the racial distribution of recent hirings and of the Department itself might be roughly equivalent to the racial makeup of the surrounding community, broadly conceived, was put aside as a "comparison (not) material to this appeal. . . .

Because the Court of Appeals erroneously applied the legal standards applicable to Title VII cases in resolving the constitutional issue before it, we reverse its judgment in [plaintiffs]' favor.

As the Court of Appeals understood Title VII, employees or applicants proceeding under it need not concern themselves with the employer's possibly discriminatory purpose but instead may focus solely on the racially differential impact of the challenged hiring or promotion practices. This is not the constitutional rule. We have never held that the constitutional standard for adjudicating claims of invidious racial discrimination is identical to the standards applicable under Title VII, and we decline to do so today.

The central purpose of the Equal Protection Clause of the Fourteenth Amendment is the prevention of official conduct discriminating on the basis of race. It is also true that the Due Process Clause of the Fifth Amendment contains an equal protection component prohibiting the United States from invidiously discriminating between individuals or groups. *Bolling v. Sharpe*. But our cases have not embraced the proposition that a law or other official act, without regard to whether it reflects a racially discriminatory purpose, is unconstitutional solely because it has a racially disproportionate impact. . . .

Almost 100 years ago, *Strauder v. West Virginia* established that the exclusion of Negroes from grand and petit juries in criminal proceedings violated the Equal Protection Clause, but the fact that a particular jury or a series of juries does not statistically reflect the racial composition of the community does not in itself make out an invidious discrimination forbidden by the Clause. . . .

The school desegregation cases have also adhered to the basic equal protection principle that the invidious quality of a law claimed to be racially discriminatory must ultimately be traced to a racially discriminatory purpose. That there are both predominantly black and predominantly white schools in a community is not alone violative of the Equal Protection Clause. The essential element of De jure segregation is "a current condition of segregation resulting from intentional state action. The differentiating factor between De jure segregation and so-called De facto segregation . . . is Purpose or Intent to segregate.". . .

This is not to say that the necessary discriminatory racial purpose must be express or appear on the face of the statute, or that a law's disproportionate impact is irrelevant in cases involving Constitution-based claims of racial discrimination. A statute, otherwise neutral on its face, must not be applied so as invidiously to discriminate on the basis of race. *Yick Wo v. Hopkins.* It is also clear from the cases dealing with racial discrimination in the selection of juries that the systematic exclusion of Negroes is itself such an "unequal application of the law . . . as to show intentional discrimination.". . .

Necessarily, an invidious discriminatory purpose may often be inferred from the totality of the relevant facts, including the fact, if it is true, that the law bears more heavily on one race than another. It is also not infrequently true that the discriminatory impact in the jury cases for example, the total or seriously disproportionate exclusion of Negroes from jury venires may for all practical purposes demonstrate unconstitutionality because in various circumstances the discrimination is very difficult to explain on nonracial grounds. Nevertheless, we have not held that a law, neutral on its face and serving ends otherwise within the power of government to pursue, is invalid under the Equal Protection Clause simply because it may affect a greater proportion of one race than of another. Disproportionate impact is not irrelevant, but it is not the sole touchstone of an invidious racial discrimination forbidden by the Constitution. Standing alone, it does not trigger the rule that racial classifications are to be subjected to the strictest scrutiny and are justifiable only by the weightiest of considerations. . . .

Nor on the facts of the case before us would the disproportionate impact of Test 21 warrant the conclusion that it is a purposeful device to discriminate against Negroes and hence an infringement of the constitutional rights of [plaintiffs] as well as other black applicants. As we have said, the test is neutral on its face and rationally may be said to serve a purpose the Government is constitutionally empowered to pursue. Even agreeing with the District Court that the differential racial effect of Test 21 called for further inquiry, we think the District Court correctly held that the affirmative efforts of the Metropolitan Police Department to recruit black officers, the changing racial composition of the recruit classes and of the force in general, and the relationship of the test to the training program negated any inference that the Department discriminated on the basis of race or that "a police officer qualifies on the color of his skin rather than ability." . . .

A rule that a statute designed to serve neutral ends is nevertheless invalid, absent compelling justification, if in practice it benefits or burdens one race more than another would be far-reaching and would raise serious questions about, and perhaps invalidate, a whole range of tax, welfare, public service, regulatory, and licensing statutes that may be more burdensome to the poor and to the average black than to the more affluent white. . . .

MR. JUSTICE STEVENS, concurring.

[T]he requirement of purposeful discrimination is a common thread running through the cases summarized in [the Court's opinion]. . . .

Frequently the most probative evidence of intent will be objective evidence of what actually happened rather than evidence describing the subjective state of mind of the actor. For normally the actor is presumed to have intended the natural consequences of his deeds. This is particularly true in the case of governmental action which is frequently the product of compromise, of collective decisionmaking, and of mixed motivation. It is unrealistic, on the one hand, to require the victim of alleged discrimination to uncover the actual subjective intent of the decisionmaker or, conversely, to invalidate otherwise legitimate action simply because an improper motive affected the deliberation of a participant in the decisional process. . . .

My point in making this observation is to suggest that the line between discriminatory purpose and discriminatory impact is not nearly as bright, and perhaps not quite as critical, as the reader of the Court's opinion might assume. I agree, of course, that a constitutional issue does not arise every time some disproportionate impact is shown. On the other hand, when the disproportion is as dramatic as in . . . *Yick Wo v. Hopkins*, it really does not matter whether the standard is phrased in terms of purpose or effect. . . .

My agreement with the conclusion reached in . . . the Court's opinion rests on a ground narrower than the Court describes. I do not rely at all on the evidence of good-faith efforts to recruit black police officers. In my judgment, neither those efforts nor the subjective good faith of the District administration, would save Test 21 if it were otherwise invalid.

There are two reasons why I am convinced that the challenge to Test 21 is insufficient. First, the test serves the neutral and legitimate purpose of requiring all applicants to meet a uniform minimum standard of literacy. Reading ability is manifestly relevant to the police function, there is no evidence that the required passing grade was set at an arbitrarily high level, and there is sufficient disparity among high schools and high school graduates to justify the use of a separate uniform test. Second, the same test is used throughout the federal service. The applicants for employment in the District of Columbia Police Department represent such a small fraction of the total number of persons who have taken the test that their experience is of minimal probative value in assessing the neutrality of the test itself. That evidence, without more, is not sufficient to overcome the presumption that a test which is this widely used by the Federal Government is in fact neutral in its effect as well as its "purposes," as that term is used in constitutional adjudication. . . .

COMMENTS AND QUESTIONS

1.   What's the difference between *Yick Wo* and *Washington v. Davis?* In the first a facially neutral law with discriminatory impacts is found to involve racial discrimination. In the second it is not. Does *Washington v. Davis* overrule *Yick Wo*, or are they distinguishable and consistent?

2.   The "rule" of *Washington v. Davis* is well settled today, but before the Court's decision several circuits had ruled as the D.C. Circuit had in this case— holding that intentional discrimination based on race was unnecessary to make out an equal protection claim, at least in the employment context. As the Court notes, it had earlier interpreted Title VII of the 1964 Civil Rights Act, which prohibits discrimination on the basis of race (and sex) in employment, as only requiring a showing of disparate impact in order to shift the burden to the employer to justify the complained of action. At the time of *Washington v. Davis*, Title VII did not apply to the federal government (and therefore the District of Columbia). Today, it does.

3.   What's the difference between Justice Stevens and the Court? Why does Justice Stevens think that Test 21 is "valid"? It was conceded that the test had not been "validated," meaning it had not been shown actually to test accurately what was needed for the job.

4.   Does racial discrimination have to be the sole basis for a government action in order to trigger strict scrutiny? No. In *Arlington Heights v. Metropolitan Housing Development Corporation*, 429 U.S. 252 (1977), the Court made clear that if racial discrimination is "a motivating factor," that is sufficient.

5.   *Washington v. Davis* provides the underlying reason why *de facto* segregation, whether of schools, employment, or housing, does not run afoul of the Constitution. If government action does not have a purpose or intent to discriminate on the basis of race, then the action does not involve racial discrimination. *De facto* residential segregation is usually due either to economic factors or racial discrimination by private actors, for example, landlords with respect to whom they will rent and banks with respect to whom they will make mortgages. *De facto* school segregation usually is the result of *de facto* residential segregation. And private discrimination is not subject to the Equal Protection Clause.

3. AFFIRMATIVE ACTION

Recall that *Green v. County School Board of New Kent County* said that entities that violated the Equal Protection Clause had a constitutional duty to right the wrong their violation created. Also recall that *Swann v. Charlotte-Mecklenburg Board of Education* said that when righting that wrong, the entity could use race-conscious methods, such as school assignments and busing on the basis of race to achieve integration. The question then became: what race conscious measures may an entity take if it had *not* engaged in unconstitutional discrimination but wished to overcome the societal impacts that separated the races?

REGENTS OF UNIV. OF CALIFORNIA V. BAKKE

United States Supreme Court, 1978.
438 U.S. 265, 98 S.Ct. 2733.

MR. JUSTICE POWELL announced the judgment of the Court.

Lewis Powell

President Nixon appointed Justice Powell to the Court in 1972, on the same day he appointed William Rehnquist. A southerner and partner at a large corporate law firm in Richmond, Virginia, he was expected to be another reliable conservative vote on the Court. While generally that was true, he tended toward moderation and compromise, often providing the swing vote in a case or taking a middle position between the liberals and conservatives, as in *Bakke*. He retired in 1988 and was replaced by Justice Anthony Kennedy.

This case presents a challenge to the special admissions program of the petitioner, the Medical School of the University of California at Davis, which is designed to assure the admission of a specified number of students from certain minority groups. The Superior Court of California sustained respondent's challenge, holding that petitioner's program violated the California Constitution, Title VI of the Civil Rights Act of 1964, and the Equal Protection Clause of the Fourteenth Amendment.... The Supreme Court of California affirmed those portions of the trial court's judgment declaring the special admissions program unlawful and enjoining petitioner from considering the race of any applicant....

For the reasons stated in the following opinion, I believe that so much of the judgment of the California court as holds petitioner's special admissions program unlawful and directs that respondent be admitted to the Medical School must be affirmed. For the reasons expressed in a separate opinion, my Brothers THE CHIEF JUSTICE, Mr. Justice STEWART, Mr. Justice REHNQUIST and Mr. Justice STEVENS concur in this judgment.

I also conclude for the reasons stated in the following opinion that the portion of the court's judgment enjoining petitioner from according any consideration to race in its admissions process must be reversed. For reasons expressed in separate opinions, my Brothers Mr. Justice BRENNAN, Mr. Justice WHITE, Mr. Justice MARSHALL, and Mr. Justice BLACKMUN concur in this judgment.

I*

The Medical School of the University of California at Davis opened in 1968. . . . No admissions program for disadvantaged or minority students existed when the school opened, and the first class contained three Asians but no blacks, no Mexican-Americans, and no American Indians. Over the next two years, the faculty devised a special admissions program to increase the representation of "disadvantaged" students in each Medical School class. The special program consisted of a separate admissions system operating in coordination with the regular admissions process. . . .

The special admissions program operated with a separate committee. . . . The applications . . . were rated by the special committee in a fashion similar to that used by the general admissions committee, except that special candidates did not have to meet the 2.5 grade point average cutoff applied to regular applicants. . . . The special committee [recommended] special applicants until a number prescribed by faculty vote were admitted. [W]hen the class size [was] 100, the prescribed number of special admissions [was] 16.

[T]he special program [over a four-year period] resulted in the admission of 21 black students, 30 Mexican-Americans, and 12 Asians, for a total of 63 minority students. Over the same period, the regular admissions program produced 1 black, 6 Mexican-Americans, and 37 Asians, for a total of 44 minority students. Although disadvantaged whites applied to the special program in large numbers, none received an offer of admission through that process. . . .

Allan Bakke is a white male who applied to the Davis Medical School in both 1973 and 1974. In both years Bakke's application was considered under the general admissions program, [but] Bakke was rejected. . . .

Applicants admitted under the special program . . . had benchmark scores significantly lower than many students, including Bakke, rejected under the general admissions program. . . .

II

In this Court the parties neither briefed nor argued the applicability of Title VI of the Civil Rights Act of 1964. Rather, as had the California

---

* Mr. Justice BRENNAN, Mr. Justice WHITE, Mr. Justice MARSHALL, and Mr. Justice BLACKMUN join Parts I and V-C of this opinion. Mr. Justice WHITE also joins Part III-A of this opinion.

court, they focused exclusively upon the validity of the special admissions program under the Equal Protection Clause. Because it was possible, however, that a decision on Title VI might obviate resort to constitutional interpretation, we requested supplementary briefing on the statutory issue. . . .

The language of [Title VI], like that of the Equal Protection Clause, is majestic in its sweep: "No person in the United States shall, on the ground of race, color, or national origin, be excluded from participation in, be denied the benefits of, or be subjected to discrimination under any program or activity receiving Federal financial assistance.". . .

In view of the clear legislative intent, Title VI must be held to proscribe only those racial classifications that would violate the Equal Protection Clause or the Fifth Amendment.

III

A

The parties . . . disagree as to the level of judicial scrutiny to be applied to the special admissions program. Petitioner argues that the court below erred in applying strict scrutiny, as this inexact term has been applied in our cases. That level of review, petitioner asserts, should be reserved for classifications that disadvantage "discrete and insular minorities." *See United States v. Carolene Products Co.* Respondent, on the other hand, contends that the California court correctly rejected the notion that the degree of judicial scrutiny accorded a particular racial or ethnic classification hinges upon membership in a discrete and insular minority. . . .

En route to this crucial battle over the scope of judicial review, the parties fight a sharp preliminary action over the proper characterization of the special admissions program. Petitioner prefers to view it as establishing a "goal" of minority representation in the Medical School. Respondent, echoing the courts below, labels it a racial quota.

This semantic distinction is beside the point: The special admissions program is undeniably a classification based on race and ethnic background. To the extent that there existed a pool of at least minimally qualified minority applicants to fill the 16 special admissions seats, white applicants could compete only for 84 seats in the entering class, rather than the 100 open to minority applicants. Whether this limitation is described as a quota or a goal, it is a line drawn on the basis of race and ethnic status.

The guarantees of the Fourteenth Amendment extend to all persons. Its language is explicit: "No State shall . . . deny to any person within its jurisdiction the equal protection of the laws." It is settled beyond question that the "rights created by the first section of the Fourteenth Amendment are, by its terms, guaranteed to the individual. The rights established are personal rights." The guarantee of equal protection cannot mean one thing when applied to one individual and something else when applied to a person of another color. If both are not accorded the same protection, then it is not equal. . . .

"[A]ll legal restrictions which curtail the civil rights of a single racial group are immediately suspect. That is not to say that all such restrictions are unconstitutional. It is to say that courts must subject them to the most rigid scrutiny." *Korematsu.*

The Court has never questioned the validity of those pronouncements. Racial and ethnic distinctions of any sort are inherently suspect and thus call for the most exacting judicial examination. . . .

Petitioner urges us to adopt for the first time a more restrictive view of the Equal Protection Clause and hold that discrimination against members of the white "majority" cannot be suspect if its purpose can be characterized as "benign." The clock of our liberties, however, cannot be turned back to 1868. It is far too late to argue that the guarantee of equal protection to *all* persons permits the recognition of special wards entitled to a degree of protection greater than that accorded others. . . .

Petitioner contends that on several occasions this Court has approved preferential classifications without applying the most exacting scrutiny. Most of the cases upon which petitioner relies are drawn from three areas: school desegregation, employment discrimination, and sex discrimination. Each of the cases cited presented a situation materially different from the facts of this case.

The school desegregation cases are inapposite. Each involved remedies for clearly determined constitutional violations. *E. g., Swann v. Charlotte-Mecklenburg Board of Education; Green v. County School Board.* Racial classifications thus were designed as remedies for the vindication of constitutional entitlement. Moreover, the scope of the remedies was not permitted to exceed the extent of the violations. Here, there was no judicial determination of constitutional violation as a predicate for the formulation of a remedial classification. . . .

IV

We have held that in "order to justify the use of a suspect classification, a State must show that its purpose or interest is both constitutionally permissible and substantial, and that its use of the classification is 'necessary . . . to the accomplishment' of its purpose or the safeguarding of its interest." *Loving v. Virginia.* The special admissions program purports to serve the purposes of: (i) "reducing the historic deficit of traditionally disfavored minorities in medical schools and in the medical profession"; (ii) countering the effects of societal discrimination; (iii) increasing the number of physicians who will practice in communities currently underserved; and (iv) obtaining the educational benefits that flow from an ethnically diverse student body. It is necessary to decide which, if any, of these purposes is substantial enough to support the use of a suspect classification.

If petitioner's purpose is to assure within its student body some specified percentage of a particular group merely because of its race or ethnic origin, such a preferential purpose must be rejected not as insubstantial but as facially invalid. Preferring members of any one group for no reason other than race or ethnic origin is discrimination for its own sake. This the Constitution forbids.

The State certainly has a legitimate and substantial interest in ameliorating, or eliminating where feasible, the disabling effects of identified discrimination. The line of school desegregation cases, commencing with *Brown*, attests to the importance of this state goal and the commitment of the judiciary to affirm all lawful means toward its attainment. In the school cases, the States were required by court order to redress the wrongs worked by specific instances of racial discrimination. That goal was far more focused than the remedying of the effects of "societal discrimination," an amorphous concept of injury that may be ageless in its reach into the past. . . .

Hence, the purpose of helping certain groups whom the faculty of the Davis Medical School perceived as victims of "societal discrimination" does not justify a classification that imposes disadvantages upon persons like respondent, who bear no responsibility for whatever harm the beneficiaries of the special admissions program are thought to have suffered. To hold otherwise would be to convert a remedy heretofore reserved for violations of legal rights into a privilege that all institutions throughout the Nation could grant at their pleasure to whatever groups are perceived as victims of societal discrimination. That is a step we have never approved.

Petitioner identifies, as another purpose of its program, improving the delivery of health-care services to communities currently underserved. It may be assumed that in some situations a State's interest in facilitating the health care of its citizens is sufficiently compelling to support the use of a suspect classification. But there is virtually no evidence in the record indicating that petitioner's special admissions program is either needed or geared to promote that goal. . . . Nevertheless, there are more precise and reliable ways to identify applicants who are genuinely interested in the medical problems of minorities than by race. An applicant of whatever race who has demonstrated his concern for disadvantaged minorities in the past and who declares that practice in such a community is his primary professional goal would be more likely to contribute to alleviation of the medical shortage than one who is chosen entirely on the basis of race and disadvantage. In short, there is no empirical data to demonstrate that any one race is more selflessly socially oriented or by contrast that another is more selfishly acquisitive.". . .

The fourth goal asserted by petitioner is the attainment of a diverse student body. This clearly is a constitutionally permissible goal for an institution of higher education. Academic freedom, though not a specifically enumerated constitutional right, long has been viewed as a special concern of the First Amendment. The freedom of a university to make its own judgments as to education includes the selection of its student body. . . .

The atmosphere of "speculation, experiment and creation"—so essential to the quality of higher education—is widely believed to be promoted by a diverse student body. . . .

Ethnic diversity, however, is only one element in a range of factors a university properly may consider in attaining the goal of a heterogeneous student body. Although a university must have wide discretion in making the sensitive judgments as to who should be admitted, constitutional limitations protecting individual rights may not be disregarded. Respondent urges—and the courts below have held—that petitioner's dual admissions program is a racial classification that impermissibly infringes his rights under the Fourteenth Amendment. As the interest of diversity is compelling in the context of a university's admissions program, the question remains whether the program's racial classification is necessary to promote this interest.

V

A

It may be assumed that the reservation of a specified number of seats in each class for individuals from the preferred ethnic groups would contribute to the attainment of considerable ethnic diversity in the student body. But petitioner's argument that this is the only effective means of serving the interest of diversity is seriously flawed. In a most fundamental sense the argument misconceives the nature of the state interest that would justify consideration of race or ethnic background. It is not an interest in simple ethnic diversity, in which a specified percentage of the student body is in effect guaranteed to be members of selected ethnic groups, with the remaining percentage an undifferentiated aggregation of students. The diversity that furthers a compelling state interest encompasses a far broader array of qualifications and characteristics of which racial or ethnic origin is but a single though important element. Petitioner's special admissions program, focused *solely* on ethnic diversity, would hinder rather than further attainment of genuine diversity. . . .

The experience of other university admissions programs, which take race into account in achieving the educational diversity valued by the First Amendment, demonstrates that the assignment of a fixed number of places to a minority group is not a necessary means toward that end. An illuminating example is found in the Harvard College program:

"In recent years Harvard College has expanded the concept of diversity to include students from disadvantaged economic, racial and ethnic groups. Harvard College now recruits not only Californians or Louisianans but also blacks and Chicanos and other minority students. . . .

"In practice, this new definition of diversity has meant that race has been a factor in some admission decisions. When the Committee on Admissions reviews the large middle group of applicants who are 'admissible' and deemed capable of doing good work in their courses, the race of an applicant may tip the balance in his favor just as geographic origin or a life spent on a farm may tip the balance in other candidates' cases. A farm boy from Idaho can bring something to Harvard College that a Bostonian cannot offer. Similarly, a black student can usually bring something that a white person cannot offer.

"In Harvard College admissions the Committee has not set target-quotas for the number of blacks, or of musicians, football players, physicists or Californians to be admitted in a given year. . . . But that awareness [of the necessity of including more than a token number of black students] does not mean that the Committee sets a minimum number of blacks or of people from west of the Mississippi who are to be admitted.

In such an admissions program, race or ethnic background may be deemed a "plus" in a particular applicant's file, yet it does not insulate the individual from comparison with all other candidates for the available seats. The file of a particular black applicant may be examined for his potential contribution to diversity without the factor of race being decisive when compared, for example, with that of an applicant identified as an Italian-American if the latter is thought to exhibit qualities more likely to promote beneficial educational pluralism. Such qualities could include exceptional personal talents, unique work or service experience, leadership potential, maturity, demonstrated compassion, a history of overcoming disadvantage, ability to communicate with the poor, or other qualifications deemed important. In short, an admissions program operated in this way is flexible enough to consider all pertinent elements of diversity in light of the particular qualifications of each applicant, and to place them on the same footing for consideration, although not necessarily according them the same weight. Indeed, the weight attributed to a particular quality may vary from year to year depending upon the "mix" both of the student body and the applicants for the incoming class.

This kind of program treats each applicant as an individual in the admissions process. The applicant who loses out on the last available seat to another candidate receiving a "plus" on the basis of ethnic background will not have been foreclosed from all consideration for that seat simply because he was not the right color or had the wrong surname. It would mean only that his combined qualifications, which may have included similar nonobjective factors, did not outweigh those of the other applicant.

His qualifications would have been weighed fairly and competitively, and he would have no basis to complain of unequal treatment under the Fourteenth Amendment. . . .

B

In summary, it is evident that the Davis special admissions program involves the use of an explicit racial classification never before countenanced by this Court. It tells applicants who are not Negro, Asian, or Chicano that they are totally excluded from a specific percentage of the seats in an entering class. No matter how strong their qualifications, quantitative and extracurricular, including their own potential for contribution to educational diversity, they are never afforded the chance to compete with applicants from the preferred groups for the special admissions seats. At the same time, the preferred applicants have the opportunity to compete for every seat in the class.

The fatal flaw in petitioner's preferential program is its disregard of individual rights as guaranteed by the Fourteenth Amendment. Such rights are not absolute. But when a State's distribution of benefits or imposition of burdens hinges on ancestry or the color of a person's skin, that individual is entitled to a demonstration that the challenged classification is necessary to promote a substantial state interest. Petitioner has failed to carry this burden. For this reason, that portion of the California court's judgment holding petitioner's special admissions program invalid under the Fourteenth Amendment must be affirmed.

C

In enjoining petitioner from ever considering the race of any applicant, however, the courts below failed to recognize that the State has a substantial interest that legitimately may be served by a properly devised admissions program involving the competitive consideration of race and ethnic origin. For this reason, so much of the California court's judgment as enjoins petitioner from any consideration of the race of any applicant must be reversed. . . .

Opinion of MR. JUSTICE BRENNAN, MR. JUSTICE WHITE, MR. JUSTICE MARSHALL, and MR. JUSTICE BLACKMUN, concurring in the judgment in part and dissenting in part.

[W]e agree with Mr. Justice POWELL that, as applied to the case before us, Title VI goes no further in prohibiting the use of race than the Equal Protection Clause of the Fourteenth Amendment itself. We also agree that the effect of the California Supreme Court's affirmance of the judgment of the Superior Court of California would be to prohibit the University from establishing in the future affirmative-action programs that take race into account. Since we conclude that the affirmative admissions program at the Davis Medical School is constitutional, we would reverse the judgment below in all respects. Mr. Justice POWELL agrees that some uses of race in university admissions are permissible and, therefore, he joins with us to make five votes reversing the judgment below insofar as it prohibits the University from establishing race-conscious programs in the future. . . .

[C]laims that law must be "color-blind" or that the datum of race is no longer relevant to public policy must be seen as aspiration rather than as description of reality. This is not to denigrate aspiration; for reality rebukes us that race has too often been used by those who would stigmatize and oppress minorities. Yet we cannot—and, as we shall demonstrate, need not under our Constitution or Title VI, which merely extends the constraints of the Fourteenth Amendment to private parties who receive federal funds—let color blindness become myopia which masks the reality that many "created equal" have been treated within our lifetimes as inferior both by the law and by their fellow citizens. . . .

In our view, Title VI prohibits only those uses of racial criteria that would violate the Fourteenth Amendment if employed by a State or its agencies; it does not bar the preferential treatment of racial minorities as a means of remedying past societal discrimination to the extent that such action is consistent with the Fourteenth Amendment. The legislative history of Title VI, administrative regulations interpreting the statute, subsequent congressional and executive action, and the prior decisions of this Court compel this conclusion. None of these sources lends support to the proposition that Congress intended to bar all race-conscious efforts to extend the benefits of federally financed programs to minorities who have been historically excluded from the full benefits of American life. . . .

We turn, therefore, to our analysis of the Equal Protection Clause of the Fourteenth Amendment.

[O]ur cases have always implied that an "overriding statutory purpose," could be found that would justify racial classifications. . . . We conclude, therefore, that racial classifications are not *per se* invalid under the Fourteenth Amendment. Accordingly, we turn to the problem of articulating what our role should be in reviewing state action that expressly classifies by race.

[U]nquestionably we have held that a government practice or statute which restricts "fundamental rights" or which contains "suspect classifications" is to be subjected to "strict scrutiny" and can be justified only if it furthers a compelling government purpose and, even then, only if no less restrictive alternative is available. But no fundamental right is involved here. Nor do whites as a class have any of the "traditional indicia of suspectness: the class is not saddled with such disabilities, or subjected to such a history of purposeful unequal treatment, or relegated to such a position of political powerlessness as to command extraordinary protection from the majoritarian political process."

[N]or has anyone suggested that the University's purposes contravene the cardinal principle that racial classifications that stigmatize—because they are drawn on the presumption that one race is inferior to another or because they put the weight of government behind racial hatred and separatism—are invalid without more.

On the other hand, the fact that this case does not fit neatly into our prior analytic framework for race cases does not mean that it should be analyzed by applying the very loose rational-basis standard of review that is the very least that is always applied in equal protection cases.... Instead, a number of considerations ... lead us to conclude that racial classifications designed to further remedial purposes " 'must serve important governmental objectives and must be substantially related to achievement of those objectives.' "

Davis's articulated purpose of remedying the effects of past societal discrimination is, under our cases, sufficiently important to justify the use of race-conscious admissions programs where there is a sound basis for concluding that minority underrepresentation is substantial and chronic, and that the handicap of past discrimination is impeding access of minorities to the Medical School....

[T]he requirement of a judicial determination of a constitutional or statutory violation as a predicate for race-conscious remedial actions would be self-defeating. Such a requirement would severely undermine efforts to achieve voluntary compliance with the requirements of law. And our society and jurisprudence have always stressed the value of voluntary efforts to further the objectives of the law. Judicial intervention is a last resort to achieve cessation of illegal conduct or the remedying of its effects rather than a prerequisite to action.

Properly construed, therefore, our prior cases unequivocally show that a state government may adopt race-conscious programs if the purpose of such programs is to remove the disparate racial impact its actions might otherwise have and if there is reason to believe that the disparate impact is itself the product of past discrimination, whether its own or that of society at large. There is no question that Davis's program is valid under this test....

The second prong of our test—whether the Davis program stigmatizes any discrete group or individual and whether race is reasonably used in light of the program's objectives—is clearly satisfied by the Davis program.

It is not even claimed that Davis's program in any way operates to stigmatize or single out any discrete and insular, or even any identifiable, nonminority group. Nor will harm comparable to that imposed upon racial minorities by exclusion or separation on grounds of race be the likely result of the program. It does not, for example, establish an exclusive preserve for minority students apart from and exclusive of whites. Rather, its purpose is to overcome the effects of segregation by bringing the races together. True, whites are excluded from participation in the special admissions program, but this fact only operates to reduce the number of whites to be admitted in the regular admissions program in order to permit admission of a reasonable percentage—less than their proportion of the California population—of otherwise underrepresented qualified minority applicants.

Nor was Bakke in any sense stamped as inferior by the Medical School's rejection of him. Indeed, it is conceded by all that he satisfied those criteria regarded by the school as generally relevant to academic performance better than most of the minority members who were admitted. Moreover, there is absolutely no basis for concluding that Bakke's rejection as a result of Davis's use of racial preference will affect him throughout his life in the same way as the segregation of the Negro schoolchildren in *Brown I* would have affected them. Unlike discrimination against racial minorities, the use of racial preferences for remedial purposes does not inflict a pervasive injury upon individual whites in the sense that wherever they go or whatever they do there is a significant likelihood that they will be treated as second-class citizens because of their color. This distinction does not mean that the exclusion of a white resulting from the preferential use of race is not sufficiently serious to require justification; but it does mean that the injury inflicted by such a policy is not distinguishable from disadvantages caused by a wide range of government actions, none of which has ever been thought impermissible for that reason alone.

Finally, Davis's special admissions program cannot be said to violate the Constitution simply because it has set aside a predetermined number of places for qualified minority applicants rather than using minority status as a positive factor to be considered in evaluating the applications of disadvantaged minority applicants. For purposes of constitutional adjudication, there is no difference between the two approaches. In any admissions program which accords special consideration to disadvantaged racial minorities, a determination of the degree of preference to be given is unavoidable, and any given preference that results in the exclusion of a white candidate is no more or less constitutionally acceptable than a program such as that at Davis. Furthermore, the extent of the preference inevitably depends on how many minority applicants the particular school is seeking to admit in any particular year so long as the number of qualified minority applicants exceeds that number. There is no sensible, and certainly no constitutional, distinction between, for example, adding a set number of points to the admissions rating of disadvantaged minority applicants as an expression of the preference with the expectation that this will result in the admission of an approximately determined number of qualified minority applicants and setting a fixed number of places for such applicants as was done here.

The "Harvard" program, as those employing it readily concede, openly and successfully employs a racial criterion for the purpose of ensuring that some of the scarce places in institutions of higher education are allocated to disadvantaged minority students. That the Harvard approach does not also make public the extent of the preference and the precise workings of the system while the Davis program employs a specific, openly stated number, does not condemn the latter plan for purposes of Fourteenth Amendment adjudication. It may be that the Harvard plan is more acceptable to the public than is the Davis "quota." If it is, any State, including California, is free to adopt it in preference to a less acceptable alternative, just as it is generally free, as far as the Constitution is concerned, to abjure granting any racial preferences in its admissions program. But there is no basis for preferring a particular preference program simply because in achieving the same goals that the Davis Medical School is pursuing, it proceeds in a manner that is not immediately apparent to the public.

MR. JUSTICE MARSHALL.

I agree with the judgment of the Court only insofar as it permits a university to consider the race of an applicant in making admissions decisions. I do not agree that petitioner's admissions program violates the Constitution. For it must be remembered that, during most of the past 200 years, the Constitution as interpreted by this Court did not prohibit the most ingenious and pervasive forms of discrimination against the Negro. Now, when a State acts to remedy the effects of that legacy of discrimination, I cannot believe that this same Constitution stands as a barrier.

The position of the Negro today in America is the tragic but inevitable consequence of centuries of unequal treatment. Measured by any benchmark of comfort or achievement, meaningful equality remains a distant dream for the Negro.

A Negro child today has a life expectancy which is shorter by more than five years than that of a white child. The Negro child's mother is over three times more likely to die of complications in childbirth, and the infant mortality rate for Negroes is nearly twice that for whites. The median income of the Negro family is only 60% that of the median of a white family, and the percentage of Negroes who live in families with incomes below the poverty line is nearly four times greater than that of whites.

When the Negro child reaches working age, he finds that America offers him significantly less than it offers his white counterpart. For Negro adults, the unemployment rate is twice that of whites, and the unemployment rate for Negro teenagers is nearly three times that of white teenagers. A Negro male who completes four years of college can expect a median annual income of merely $110 more than a white male who has only a high school diploma. Although Negroes represent 11.5% of the population, they are only 1.2% of the lawyers, and judges, 2% of the physicians, 2.3% of the dentists, 1.1% of the engineers and 2.6% of the college and university professors.

The relationship between those figures and the history of unequal treatment afforded to the Negro cannot be denied. At every point from birth to death the impact of the past is reflected in the still disfavored position of the Negro.

In light of the sorry history of discrimination and its devastating impact on the lives of Negroes, bringing the Negro into the mainstream of American life should be a state interest of the highest order. To fail to do so is to ensure that America will forever remain a divided society.

I do not believe that the Fourteenth Amendment requires us to accept that fate. Neither its history nor our past cases lend any support to the conclusion that a university may not remedy the cumulative effects of society's discrimination by giving consideration to race in an effort to increase the number and percentage of Negro doctors. . . .

It is plain that the Fourteenth Amendment was not intended to prohibit measures designed to remedy the effects of the Nation's past treatment of Negroes. The Congress that passed the Fourteenth Amendment is the same Congress that passed the 1866 Freedmen's Bureau Act, an Act that provided many of its benefits only to Negroes.

While I applaud the judgment of the Court that a university may consider race in its admissions process, it is more than a little ironic that, after several hundred years of class-based discrimination against Negroes, the Court is unwilling to hold that a class-based remedy for that discrimination is permissible. In declining to so hold, today's judgment ignores the fact that for several hundred years Negroes have been discriminated against, not as individuals, but rather solely because of the color of their skins. It is unnecessary in 20th-century America to have individual Negroes demonstrate that they have been victims of racial discrimination; the racism of our society has been so pervasive that none, regardless of wealth or position, has managed to escape its impact. The experience of Negroes in America has been different in kind, not just in degree, from that of other ethnic groups. It is not merely the history of slavery alone but also that a whole people were marked as inferior by the law. And that mark has endured. The dream of America as the great melting pot has not been realized for the Negro; because of his skin color he never even made it into the pot.

These differences in the experience of the Negro make it difficult for me to accept that Negroes cannot be afforded greater protection under the Fourteenth Amendment where it is necessary to remedy the effects of past discrimination. . . .

MR. JUSTICE STEVENS, with whom THE CHIEF JUSTICE, MR. JUSTICE STEWART, and MR. JUSTICE REHNQUIST join, concurring in the judgment in part and dissenting in part.

[B]oth petitioner and respondent have asked us to determine the legality of the University's special admissions program by reference to the Constitution. Our settled practice, however, is to avoid the decision of a constitutional issue if a case can be fairly decided on a statutory ground.

Section 601 of the Civil Rights Act of 1964 provides:

> "No person in the United States shall, on the ground of race, color, or national origin, be excluded from participation in, be denied the benefits of, or be subjected to discrimination under any program or activity receiving Federal financial assistance."

The University, through its special admissions policy, excluded Bakke from participation in its program of medical education because of his race. The University also acknowledges that it was, and still is, receiving federal financial assistance. The plain language of the statute therefore requires affirmance of the judgment below. A different result cannot be justified unless that language misstates the actual intent of the Congress that enacted the statute or the statute is not enforceable in a private action. Neither conclusion is warranted. . . .

COMMENTS AND QUESTIONS

1. *Bakke* is one of those strange cases in which a lone justice gets to decide the outcome of the case. No one agrees with Justice Powell's analysis, but his conclusion that Bakke was unlawfully denied admission to the Davis medical school is joined by Chief Justice Burger and Justices Stevens, Stewart, and Rehnquist, while Justice Powell's conclusion that race may be considered in admissions under a program like Harvard's is agreed to by Justices Brennan, Marshall, Blackmun, and White. Over time, virtually all of Justice Powell's analysis was adopted by the Court. Specifically, his use of "strict scrutiny" analysis of affirmative action plans became the Court's rule nine years later; his conclusion that the protections of Title VI were identical to the protections of the Equal Protection Clause likewise became the Court's opinion; his conclusion that attacking the effects of past societal discrimination was not a compelling government interest was adopted by the full Court, his determination that diversity in education was a compelling government interest was also adopted by the Court; and his approval of the Harvard Plan as a necessary means to achieve that interest was likewise followed.

2. Are you convinced that courts should use "strict scrutiny" to assess the constitutionality of racial considerations unquestionably used for the purpose of aiding members of a race long discriminated against? If so, why? Do members of the majority race need the protection of courts when the majoritarian political process results in voluntarily giving members of minority races certain benefits? If you are not convinced "strict scrutiny" is

appropriate for affirmative action programs, why not? In words used by the current Chief Justice, why is it not the way to stop discrimination on the basis of race to stop discriminating on the basis of race? If you liked Justice Harlan's dissent in *Plessy*, how would it apply to affirmative action that discriminates to benefit minority races?

3.   The lack of unanimity on the Court with respect to Davis's affirmative action program was reproduced in virtually all the subsequent affirmative action cases. Two years later, in *Fullilove v. Klutznick*, 448 U.S. 448 (1980), the Court upheld a federal law providing a 10% set aside of federal funds for minority-owned business enterprises on public works construction projects. There was no majority opinion. The plurality opinion for three justices did not include any specific test for assessing affirmative action plans, but it held that Congress had a sufficient basis to adopt this program pursuant to its powers under the Constitution because to retain the traditional method of awarding contracts for public works construction projects would perpetuate the effects of prior discrimination. Three justices concurred in the judgment but adhered to their opinion in *Bakke* that the test to judge affirmative action plans was not strict scrutiny but a lesser intermediate scrutiny requiring an important (as opposed to compelling) governmental interest and a substantial (as opposed to necessary) relationship between the means used and the interest to be achieved. Three justices dissented, with two specifically calling for a complete end to any racial classification, whether classified as benign or invidious.

Nine years later, however, the Court overturned a similar set aside for public works established by the city of Richmond, Virginia. In *Richmond v. J.A. Croson Co.*, 488 U.S. 469 (1989), the majority opinion rejected the idea that overcoming past societal discrimination is a compelling government interest. Moreover, it held that there was no evidence of racial discrimination in the Richmond construction industry (the city that was the former capital of the Confederacy that fought to preserve slavery!?). Finally, it held that, even if there had been such evidence, a quota system was not narrowly tailored to curing that problem. Five justices, albeit in separate opinions, embraced "strict scrutiny" as the proper test for affirmative action plans. Four justices distinguished *Fullilove*, because it was a federal plan and the Equal Protection Clause might place less restrictions on Congress's attempts to deal with historical discrimination. Nevertheless, six years later, in *Adarand Constructors, Inc. v. Pena*, 515 U.S. 200 (1995), the Court rejected this distinction, saying any racial classification, state or federal, is subject to strict scrutiny and effectively overruled *Fullilove* by a 5–4 vote.

Affirmative action to maintain integration of teachers in public schools was struck down in *Wygant v. Jackson Board of Education*, 476 U.S. 267 (1986). There the school district provided that when teachers were laid off, layoffs under the seniority system (last hired, first fired) could not reduce the percentage of minority teachers. This was challenged, and the Court held this plan unconstitutional. There was no majority opinion, but the three justice plurality opinion applied strict scrutiny and rejected the goal of providing minority role models in order to overcome societal discrimination as a compelling government interest. Two justices separately concurred in the judgment. Four justices dissented.

Thirty-five years after *Bakke* was decided, the Court finally confirmed Justice Powell's belief that diversity in higher education was a compelling state interest. However, in two cases, the Court applied his strict scrutiny test to uphold one school's affirmative action plan and to strike down another's. In *Grutter v. Bollinger*, 539 U.S. 306 (2003), the Court upheld the University of Michigan Law School's affirmative action program which like the Harvard Plan involved individual consideration of each applicant, but which ensured that a "critical mass" of minority students were admitted. The decision was extremely close, 5–4, with Justice O'Connor, the author of the Court's opinion, clearly reflecting her reluctance, stating that it had been 25 years since *Bakke*, and "we expect that 25 years from now, the use of racial preferences will no longer be necessary to further the [compelling] interest [of racial diversity in higher education.]" The four dissenting justices viewed the "critical mass" the school required as a barely disguised quota, which would not be allowed, because it would not be narrowly tailored to achieve the desired diversity. In a companion case, *Gratz v. Bollinger*, 539 U.S. 244 (2003), the Court by a 6–3 margin (the four dissenters in *Grutter* plus Justice O'Connor, the author of *Grutter*, and Justice Breyer) struck down the affirmative action program of the University of Michigan's undergraduate institution. There, largely because of the number of applicants, the school had used numerical criteria rather than individualized consideration to compare the applicants. Points were awarded on the basis of high school GPA, standardized test scores, as well as a number of other criteria, including whether the applicant was a member of an underrepresented racial or ethnic minority. The points awarded to members of such underrepresented groups amounted to 20% of the total needed for guaranteed admission, whereas the points awarded for leadership, service, personal achievement, and geographic diversity were capped at much lower levels. This, the Court concluded, did not meet the requirement for individualized consideration that the Court in *Grutter* and Justice Powell in *Bakke* had found critical.

Four years after *Grutter* and *Gratz*, in *Parents Involved in Community Schools v. Seattle School District*, 551 U.S. 701 (2007), the Court, in another pair of companion cases, decided by a 5–4 margin that attempts by school districts to maintain integrated schools notwithstanding changing residential patterns or other demographic factors were unconstitutional. In one case, the Seattle school district established a freedom of choice plan that allowed students to choose which high school to attend, but if a particular school was oversubscribed, the school used "tie-breakers" to decide which students would get their first choice. The first tie-breaker allowed students to attend the same school as a sibling already enrolled there. The second tie-breaker depended on the racial make-up of the school and the student's race. If the school was not within 10% of the district average of 41% white and 59% non-white, then the student who would move the school toward the average would be admitted before one who would not. The Seattle school district never operated segregated schools and never was subject to court-ordered desegregation.

Jefferson County Public Schools operate the schools in Louisville, Kentucky. Jefferson County was subject to court-ordered desegregation from 1975 to 2000, at which time the order was dissolved. Thereafter, in order to retain the integration achieved pursuant to the court order, Jefferson County adopted its voluntary student assignment plan. That plan allowed students at all grade levels to request reassignment to other schools within the district, but the request could be denied because of lack of space or because assigning the student to the requested school would put the school out of compliance with the district's requirement that no school have less than 15% black students and no school more than 50% black students.

The Court found that neither of these plans survived strict scrutiny. First, the Court rejected the defense of the plans based on *Grutter*, because, the Court said, *Grutter*'s approval of diversity in education as a compelling government interest did not approve of diversity solely in terms of race. That is, "[t]he diversity interest was not focused on race alone but encompassed 'all factors that may contribute to student body diversity.'" In the two school plans, however, the only diversity involved in the plans was strictly racial, and the Court noted that even the racial diversity was limited to white and non-white in Seattle and black and "other" in Jefferson County. Second, the Court rejected the defense of the plans as aimed at the "educational and broader socialization benefits [that] flow from a racially diverse learning environment." Without deciding whether these benefits indeed existed, or if they did, whether they constituted a compelling state interest, the Court said that the plans were not narrowly tailored to achieve those ends. "In design and operation, the plans are directed only to racial balance, pure and simple, an objective this Court has repeatedly condemned as illegitimate." Because both plans were tied to the specific racial demographics of the two districts, rather than to "any pedagogic concept of the level of diversity needed to obtain the asserted educational benefits," they were not narrowly tailored to achieve the claimed interest.

Over the course of years from *Brown*, the Court has recognized only two compelling state interests justifying the use of race in school admissions or assignments: first, the need of a government entity to remedy the effects of its past intentional discrimination; and second, albeit reluctantly by a 5–4 margin, the need to obtain diversity in higher education, a diversity not limited to racial diversity. The former interest was held to justify race conscious school assignments aimed at achieving a numerical goal that reflected the community's racial composition. The latter interest, however, was much more constrained in both its means and its goals.

In 2013, the Court again addressed the issue of an affirmative action plan in higher education. Prior to *Grutter*, the Fifth Circuit had held the University of Texas's affirmative action plan unconstitutional. To replace it, the state adopted its Top Ten Percent Law, a "race neutral" plan under which anyone who graduated in the top 10% of their Texas high school class would be admitted to the university. While race neutral by its terms, in effect it resulted in a substantial number of minorities being admitted, ironically because of the number of high schools in Texas that were effectively, if not legally, segregated. After *Grutter*, the university sought to further diversity by applying to those who were not admitted under the Top Ten Percent Law an admission system that in part took account of race. In *Fisher v. University of Texas Austin*, 570 U.S. 297 (2013)(*Fisher* I), the Court held 7–1 that the new plan did not survive "the demanding burden of strict scrutiny." Justices Scalia and Thomas concurred but noted they would overrule *Grutter*.

Three years later the case was back. *Fisher v. University of Texas Austin*, 579 U.S. 365 (2016)(*Fisher II*). The university had re-tooled its justification for taking account of race, and so re-justified, the Court by a 4–3 margin upheld the program. Justice Scalia's seat was vacant, and Justice Kagan was recused because she had participated in an earlier iteration of the case while Solicitor General of the United States. In *Fisher I*, the Court (and in *Fisher II* the dissent) stressed the importance of exhausting race neutral measures before any race conscious measures could be employed.

As this edition is being written, the Supreme Court has granted certiorari and has heard oral argument in two cases involving university affirmative action plans. In *Students for Fair Admissions Inc. v. President & Fellows of Harvard College*, the Harvard Plan, originally used as a model by Justice Powell in *Bakke*, is being challenged as a violation of Title VI of the Civil Rights Act, and in *Students for Fair Admissions v. University of North Carolina*, UNC's affirmative action plan is being challenged as a violation of the Equal Protection Clause. In both cases, the Court granted certiorari with respect to whether *Grutter* should be overruled. We know Justice Thomas's view, and we can guess how Justices Kagan, Sotomayor, and Jackson will vote. We also know that the Chief Justice prefers to narrow precedent rather than overrule it. But what do we think will be position of Justices Alito, Kavanaugh, and Barrett? Stay tuned.

4. Virtually all law schools today utilize some form of the affirmative action system used by the University of Michigan and approved in *Grutter*. If the Supreme Court were to overrule *Grutter*, do you think law schools would voluntarily dismantle the system they have been using for years, absent a court order or enforcement action brought by the Department of Education under Title VI of the Civil Rights Act? In other words, would they act like the South acted after *Brown v. Board of Education*.

5. A recent book, Classified: The Untold Story of Racial Classification in America (2022), by David Bernstein, a professor at the Antonin Scalia Law School of George Mason University, attacks the classifications that usually are used in affirmative action programs. For example, why should Afghans be treated as "white" but Pakistanis as "Asian"? What do persons from India have in common with persons from Japan to both be considered the same race for purposes of "diversity." Why should persons from Barcelona and persons from Tijuana, Mexico, be considered the same race or ethnicity?

PROBLEM

Certain psychological studies support the idea that some members of racial minorities learn best in an environment in which they are not minorities. Noting that there are a number of private historically black colleges that have an overwhelmingly black student body, although they do not discriminate against others who may apply, the state of Z is contemplating establishing the option in its inner cities of an all-black K–12 learning path, where all the teachers and students would be of the same race. No one would be required to (work in) or attend these schools; they would be open only to those who chose to attend. But they would not be open to members of other racial groups. Would this be constitutional?

---

4. VOTING

Despite the 15th Amendment's prohibition on denying the right to vote on the basis of race, Southern states after Reconstruction erected various barriers to voting that effectively denied that right to African-Americans. For example, in the South at the time, the only real electoral contest involved the Democratic primary, because in reaction to Lincoln and the Civil War, the Republican party was viewed as the devil. Consequently, states passed laws, *see Nixon v. Herndon*, 273 U.S. 536 (1927), or took other measures, *see Nixon v. Condon*, 286 U.S. 73 (1932), designed to keep African-Americans from voting in the Democratic primaries. These laws and state actions were declared unconstitutional. The Democratic parties in the Southern states then continued to discriminate against African-Americans without support from the state and defended their actions on the basis that it was only discrimination by a private group, not the state. The Court rejected this defense in a number of cases, ultimately in *Terry v. Adams*, 345 U.S. 461 (1953), holding that it was state action to allow actions in primary elections that would be forbidden in public elections.

Other techniques were also used: especially poll taxes and literacy tests. The former were made unconstitutional in federal elections by the 24th Amendment and in state and local elections by the Supreme Court in *Harper v. Virginia State Board of Elections*, 383 U.S. 663 (1966). The Court, however, first in *Guinn v. United States*, 238 U.S. 347 (1915), and later in *Lassiter v. Northampton County Election Board*, 360 U.S. 45 (1959), found that literacy tests did not violate the constitution absent strong evidence of an intent to use the test to discriminate on the basis of race. That such tests had a disparate impact was not sufficient to impugn their validity, because the Court believed that the ability to read and write had a direct relationship to intelligent voting. Nevertheless, the federal 1965 Voting Rights Act effectively banned the use of literacy tests in states where less than half the eligible voters in the state were registered to vote, and amendments to that Act in 1970 banned literacy tests outright.

The 1965 Act did more than merely prohibit certain state activities that had the effect of discriminating against African-Americans' voting rights; Sections 4 and 5 of the Act also created a regime whereby those states and localities in which there was an established history of discrimination could not make changes to their electoral systems without the approval of the Attorney General of the United States. In the recent past, this resulted in blocking voter ID laws in these states. Its most frequent use, however, involved changes to electoral districts. As a result of the Supreme Court's "one person/one vote" decision, districts around the nation generally have to be reapportioned every ten years (as a result of the decennial census required by Article I, Sec. 2, cl. 3 of the Constitution). These reapportionments in the affected states and localities had to be approved by the Attorney General. The Government interpreted Section 5 to require reapportionments to reflect and to maintain the position of racial minorities with respect to their effective exercise of the electoral franchise. This, in effect, meant that some districts should have non-white majorities in order for non-whites to compete effectively in elections, rather than gerrymander the districts so that non-whites would never constitute a large enough voting base to elect a non-white representative.

Although the Act, and Sections 4 and 5 in particular, were upheld in the face of a constitutional challenge in 1966, *see South Carolina v. Katzenbach*, 383 U.S. 301 (1966), in 2013 the Supreme Court found Section 4 unconstitutional by a vote of 5–4. *See Shelby County v. Holder*, 570 U.S. 529 (2013). Section 4 was that portion of the Act that identified which states and localities were subject to the Section 5 "preclearance" procedure. The covered states and localities had been identified in 1965 on the basis of their past discrimination against African-Americans by means of keeping them from voting or minimizing the effect of their voting through racial gerrymandering. The coverage formula and the preclearance requirement originally were to sunset in five years, but they were reauthorized several times, most recently in 2006 for an additional 25 years, but the coverage formula remained based on the original, forty year-old data. The Court described Section 5's preclearance requirements as "extraordinary measures," because of their effect on state sovereignty. They could be justified only by the particular circumstances existing at the time of enactment—the identified racial discrimination in voting that existed at the time in those states. Today, however, the Court said, circumstances had changed. The identified states have about the same level of minority voter registration as other states, and minority voter turnout in the covered states either exceeds or is the same as in non-covered states. The Court was not convinced that this was due only to the continued presence of the preclearance procedures. Consequently, the extraordinary measures of Section 5 were no longer justified with respect to the states and localities identified in Section 4.

Section 2 of the Act, which prohibits the denying or abridging of the right of any citizen to vote on account of race or color, continues in full effect, but it is difficult to prove after the fact that a particular state or local action has this effect or purpose. Under Sections 4 and 5, the covered states and localities had to convince the Attorney General that their changes would not have this effect or purpose. The difficulty of proving violations under Section 2 was later reflected in the Supreme Court's 5–4 decision in *Abbott v. Perez*, 138 S.Ct. 2305 (2018), which reversed the lower court's findings of Section 2 violations in one congressional and seven state districts in Texas, as well as in *Brnovich v. Democratic Nat'l Comm.*, 141 S.Ct. 2321 (2021), which also reversed a lower court's findings of Section 2 violations.

C. GENDER

Certainly no one in 1868 imagined that the Equal Protection Clause required equal protection of women. Indeed, in 1872, a woman challenging the refusal of the state of Illinois to allow her to be a lawyer did not even raise an equal protection claim, and her challenge under the Privileges and Immunities Clauses of both the 14th Amendment and Article IV was rejected out of hand. *See Bradwell v. People of State of Illinois*, 83 U.S. 130 (1872). Apparently the first case in the Supreme Court involving sexual discrimination that raised an equal protection claim was *Goesaert v. Cleary*, 335 U.S. 464, in 1948, where the Court upheld a law that prohibited women from being bartenders unless they were the wife or daughter of the owner. The Court found it obvious that the state could bar all women from being bartenders, "[since] bartending by women may, in the allowable legislative judgment, give rise to moral and social problems against which it may devise preventive measures." As late as 1961, the Court upheld the automatic exclusion of women from jury pools because "Despite the enlightened emancipation of women from the restrictions and protections of bygone years, and their entry into many parts of community life formerly considered to be reserved to men, woman is still regarded as the center of home and family life." *Hoyt v. State of Fla.*, 368 U.S. 57, 61 (1961). Consequently, the state could exempt women as a class from jury duty so as not to interfere with these important responsibilities.

This all changed in 1971, when the Court found unconstitutional a state practice of preferring men over women when appointing administrators of estates. *Reed v. Reed*, 404 U.S. 71 (1971). Although the opinion characterized its analysis as determining whether there was a "rational relationship" between the sexual discrimination and the legitimate state objective (avoiding administrative costs of having to determine the relative competences of competing applicants), in fact its analysis seemed to require much more than the traditional rational relationship analysis under the Equal Protection Clause would have required. The nature of the scrutiny to be applied to sex discrimination remained an open question. In *Frontiero v. Richardson*, 411 U.S. 677 (1973), the Court overturned a federal law that provided a dependency allowance to male members of the military, but female members could only obtain a dependency allowance upon a certification that their husbands were dependent upon them. In other words, the statute presumed that wives were dependent upon husbands and presumed that husbands were not dependent upon wives. There was, however, no majority opinion. The plurality would have treated sex as a "suspect classification" requiring "strict scrutiny" of any classification based upon sex. Three other justices did not think such scrutiny was required in this case because the law would fail under the rationality test of *Reed*.

In 1976 the Court settled on its current level of scrutiny in the unlikely case of an 18-year-old male and a beer retailer challenging the Oklahoma law prohibiting the sale of 3.2% beer to men under the age of 21, but allowing the sale to women 18 years of age or older.

CRAIG V. BOREN

United States Supreme Court, 1976.
429 U.S. 190, 97 S.Ct. 451.

JUSTICE BRENNAN delivered the opinion of the Court.

[T]he question to be decided is whether such a gender-based differential constitutes a denial to males 18–20 years of age of the equal protection of the laws in violation of the Fourteenth Amendment. . . .

Before 1972, Oklahoma defined the commencement of civil majority at age 18 for females and age 21 for males. . . . In 1972, 18 . . . was established as the age of majority for males and females in civil matters, except that . . . the 3.2% beer statute w[as] simultaneously codified to create an exception to the gender-free rule.

[T]o withstand constitutional challenge, previous cases establish that classifications by gender must serve important governmental objectives and must be substantially related to achievement of those objectives. Thus, in *Reed*, the objectives of "reducing the workload on probate courts," and "avoiding intrafamily controversy were deemed of insufficient importance to sustain use of an overt gender criterion in the appointment of administrators of intestate decedents' estates. Decisions following *Reed* similarly have rejected administrative ease and convenience as sufficiently important objectives to justify gender-based classifications.

Reed v. Reed has also provided the underpinning for decisions that have invalidated statutes employing gender as an inaccurate proxy for other, more germane bases of classification. Hence, "archaic and overbroad" generalizations concerning the financial position of servicewomen and working women could not justify use of a gender line in determining eligibility for certain governmental entitlements. Similarly, increasingly outdated misconceptions concerning the role of females in the home rather than in the "marketplace and world of ideas" were rejected as loose-fitting characterizations incapable of supporting state statutory schemes that were premised upon their accuracy. . . . We turn then to the question whether, under *Reed*, the difference between males and females with respect to the purchase of 3.2% beer warrants the differential in age drawn by the Oklahoma statute. We conclude that it does not.

The District Court recognized that *Reed v. Reed* was controlling. In applying the teachings of that case, the court found the requisite important governmental objective in the traffic-safety goal proffered by the Oklahoma Attorney General. It then concluded that the statistics introduced by the appellees established that the gender-based distinction was substantially related to achievement of that goal.

We accept for purposes of discussion the District Court's identification of the objective underlying [the 3.2% beer rule] as the enhancement of traffic safety.[7] Clearly, the protection of public health and safety represents an important function of state and local governments. However, appellees' statistics in our view cannot support the conclusion that the gender-based distinction closely serves to achieve that objective and therefore the distinction cannot under Reed withstand equal protection challenge.

The appellees introduced a variety of statistical surveys. First, an analysis of arrest statistics for 1973 demonstrated that 18–20-year-old male arrests for "driving under the influence" and "drunkenness" substantially exceeded female arrests for that same age period.[8] Similarly, youths aged 17–21 were found to be overrepresented among those killed or injured in traffic accidents, with males again numerically exceeding females in this regard. Third, a random roadside survey in Oklahoma City revealed that young males were more inclined to drive and drink beer than were their female counterparts. . . . Finally, statistical evidence gathered in other jurisdictions, particularly Minnesota and Michigan, was offered to corroborate Oklahoma's experience by indicating the pervasiveness of youthful participation in motor vehicle accidents following the imbibing of alcohol. Conceding that "the case is not free from doubt," the District Court nonetheless concluded that this statistical showing substantiated "a

---

[7]   That this was the true purpose is not at all self-evident. . . . [T]he attorney for Oklahoma, while proposing traffic safety as a legitimate rationale for the 3.2% beer law, candidly acknowledged at oral argument that he is unable to assert that traffic safety is "indeed the reason" for the gender line.

[8]   The disparities in 18–20-year-old male-female arrests were substantial for both categories of offenses: 427 versus 24 for driving under the influence of alcohol, and 966 versus 102 for drunkenness. . . .

rational basis for the legislative judgment underlying the challenged classification."

Even were this statistical evidence accepted as accurate, it nevertheless offers only a weak answer to the equal protection question presented here. The most focused and relevant of the statistical surveys, arrests of 18–20-year-olds for alcohol-related driving offenses, exemplifies the ultimate unpersuasiveness of this evidentiary record. Viewed in terms of the correlation between sex and the actual activity that Oklahoma seeks to regulate—driving while under the influence of alcohol—the statistics broadly establish that .18% of females and 2% of males in that age group were arrested for that offense. While such a disparity is not trivial in a statistical sense, it hardly can form the basis for employment of a gender line as a classifying device. Certainly if maleness is to serve as a proxy for drinking and driving, a correlation of 2% must be considered an unduly tenuous "fit." Indeed, prior cases have consistently rejected the use of sex as a decisionmaking factor even though the statutes in question certainly rested on far more predictive empirical relationships than this.[13]

[T]here is no reason to belabor this line of analysis. It is unrealistic to expect either members of the judiciary or state officials to be well versed in the rigors of experimental or statistical technique. But this merely illustrates that proving broad sociological propositions by statistics is a dubious business, and one that inevitably is in tension with the normative philosophy that underlies the Equal Protection Clause. Suffice to say that the showing offered by the appellees does not satisfy us that sex represents a legitimate, accurate proxy for the regulation of drinking and driving. In fact, when it is further recognized that Oklahoma's statute prohibits only the selling of 3.2% beer to young males and not their drinking the beverage once acquired (even after purchase by their 18–20-year-old female companions), the relationship between gender and traffic safety becomes far too tenuous to satisfy *Reed*'s requirement that the gender-based difference be substantially related to achievement of the statutory objective.

[Concurring opinions by JUSTICES POWELL, STEVENS, and BLACKMUN, an opinion concurring in the judgment by JUSTICE STEWART, and a dissenting opinion by CHIEF JUSTICE BURGER are omitted.]

MR. JUSTICE REHNQUIST, dissenting.

The Court's disposition of this case is objectionable on two grounds. First is its conclusion that men challenging a gender-based statute which

---

[13] For example, we can conjecture that in *Reed*, Idaho's apparent premise that women lacked experience in formal business matters (particularly compared to men) would have proved to be accurate in substantially more than 2% of all cases. And in . . . *Frontiero*, we expressly found appellees' empirical defense of mandatory dependency tests for men but not women to be unsatisfactory, even though we recognized that husbands are still far less likely to be dependent on their wives than vice versa.

treats them less favorably than women may invoke a more stringent standard of judicial review than pertains to most other types of classifications. Second is the Court's enunciation of this standard, without citation to any source, as being that "classifications by gender must serve important governmental objectives and must be substantially related to achievement of those objectives." The only redeeming feature of the Court's opinion, to my mind, is that it apparently signals a retreat by those who joined the plurality opinion in *Frontiero v. Richardson* from their view that sex is a "suspect" classification for purposes of equal protection analysis. I think the Oklahoma statute challenged here need pass only the "rational basis" equal protection analysis expounded in cases such *Williamson v. Lee Optical Co.*, and I believe that it is constitutional under that analysis. . . .

[T]he Court's application here of an elevated or "intermediate" level scrutiny, like that invoked in cases dealing with discrimination against females, raises the question of why the statute here should be treated any differently from countless legislative classifications unrelated to sex which have been upheld under a minimum rationality standard. Most obviously unavailable to support any kind of special scrutiny in this case, is a history or pattern of past discrimination, such as was relied on by the plurality in *Frontiero* to support its invocation of strict scrutiny. There is no suggestion in the Court's opinion that males in this age group are in any way peculiarly disadvantaged, subject to systematic discriminatory treatment, or otherwise in need of special solicitude from the courts. . . .

COMMENTS AND QUESTIONS

1.   What is the level of scrutiny that a majority has settled on? The Court's opinion cites *Reed* as controlling, but the *Reed* Court characterized its opinion as using the rational relationship test, which requires neither an *important* government interest nor a *substantial* relationship of the classification to the interest, both of which findings the Court in *Craig* said were necessary to uphold a classification based on gender. As a result, Justice Rehnquist's characterization of the scrutiny for gender discrimination as "intermediate" has stuck.

2.   Note that Justice Rehnquist says that this heightened form of scrutiny is not warranted when the discrimination is against men, who have not historically been discriminated against. But Justice Rehnquist took the position that racial affirmative action called for strict scrutiny even when the discrimination was against whites. Is this inconsistent, or is there a principled basis for the distinction? Even if men have not historically been discriminated against, might some laws discriminating against men, such as in *Craig*, actually reflect stereotypical gender roles as much as a law discriminating against women? In *Craig*, the age differential applicable to the sale of 3.2% beer was the same as the historical differential for the age of majority, which itself reflected the view that women would marry at a younger age than men, because women needed neither schooling nor training in order to raise a family.

3.   The history of the Court's treatment of gender discrimination after *Craig* is uneven. In some cases, the intermediate, heightened scrutiny resulted in findings of unconstitutional discrimination. For example, in *Mississippi University for Women v. Hogan*, 458 U.S. 718 (1982), the Court, in an opinion by the then recently appointed Justice O'Connor, found the exclusion of men from the state nursing school unconstitutional. A number of sex-based distinctions in the Social Security laws were also found unconstitutional. *See, e.g., Califano v. Goldfarb*, 430 U.S. 199 (1977)(survivors' benefits automatically paid to a widow but survivors' benefits paid to a widower only if he had been receiving at least half of his support from his wife). In *Orr v. Orr*, 440 U.S. 268 (1979), the Court struck down an Alabama law that imposed alimony obligations on a husband but not on a wife. At the same time, the Court upheld an Alabama regulation barring women from being correctional officers in a male prison, *Dothard v. Rawlinson*, 433 U.S. 321 (1977), and a California law that made it a crime for a man to have sex with a woman under 18 (even if the man was under 18) but not a crime for a woman to have sex with a man under 18, *Michael M. v. Superior Court*, 450 U.S. 464 (1981). And the exemption of women from the requirement to register for the draft was found constitutional in *Rostker v. Goldberg*, 453 U.S. 57 (1981).

4.   Unlike race, there are significant biological differences between men and women that may well be relevant for legal purposes in some circumstances. The difficulty is discerning when those biological differences matter. In *Michael M.*, for instance, the Court relied to some extent on the fact that the consequences of unwanted pregnancy fall harder on a woman than a man, so that it was unnecessary to criminalize women having sex with men under 18.

5.   Coincident with *Reed*, Congress proposed the Equal Rights Amendment to the states in 1972. Its one operative provision simply stated that "equality of rights under the law shall not be denied or abridged by the United States or by any state on account of sex." In its first year, 22 of the necessary 38 states had ratified the amendment, but the momentum slowed and by 1975 only twelve more had ratified it. Conservative political elements argued that ratification would require unisex bathrooms, the drafting of women into the armed forces, and approval of same-sex marriages. As a result, within the seven year period set for ratification, the amendment received only 35 state ratifications, three short of the number necessary. Congress responded by extending the ratification period until 1982, but no other state ratified the amendment, and the proposed amendment then lapsed.

6.   This history raises a couple of questions. First, what would the Equal Rights Amendment have accomplished that has not been accomplished under the Equal Protection Clause? Second, were the conservative political elements correct in arguing that the amendment would require unisex bathrooms (in public facilities), registering women for the draft, and allowance of same sex marriages?

7.   Political developments and social mores in subsequent years eliminated almost all gender based discrimination, reducing the importance

and frequency of litigation. However, the following case highlights some interesting aspects of eliminating gender discrimination.

UNITED STATES V. VIRGINIA

United States Supreme Court, 1996.
518 U.S. 515, 116 S.Ct. 2264.

JUSTICE GINSBURG delivered the opinion of the Court.

Ruth Bader Ginsburg

President Clinton appointed Justice Ginsburg to the court in 1993. Prior to her appointment she had served on the D.C. Circuit since 1980. She began her career as a law professor, becoming the first tenured female law professor at Columbia Law School. Later, she became General Counsel of the ACLU and led the ACLU's Women's Rights Project, arguing and winning several cases before the Supreme Court. Physically diminutive and seemingly frail, Justice Ginsburg battled back from three bouts of cancer but finally succumbed in 2020, enabling President Trump to appoint Justice Barrett to her seat.

Virginia's public institutions of higher learning include an incomparable military college, Virginia Military Institute (VMI). The United States maintains that the Constitution's equal protection guarantee precludes Virginia from reserving exclusively to men the unique educational opportunities VMI affords. We agree.

Founded in 1839, VMI is today the sole single-sex school among Virginia's 15 public institutions of higher learning. VMI's distinctive mission is to produce "citizen-soldiers," men prepared for leadership in civilian life and in military service. VMI pursues this mission through pervasive training of a kind not available anywhere else in Virginia. Assigning prime place to character development, VMI uses an "adversative method" modeled on English public schools and once characteristic of military instruction. VMI constantly endeavors to instill physical and mental discipline in its cadets and impart to them a strong moral code. . . .

VMI has notably succeeded in its mission to produce leaders; among its alumni are military generals, Members of Congress, and business executives. The school's alumni overwhelmingly perceive that their VMI training helped them to realize their personal goals. VMI's endowment reflects the loyalty of its graduates; VMI has the largest per-student endowment of all public undergraduate institutions in the Nation.

Neither the goal of producing citizen-soldiers nor VMI's implementing methodology is inherently unsuitable to women. And the school's impressive record in producing leaders has made admission desirable to some women. Nevertheless, Virginia has elected to preserve exclusively for men the advantages and opportunities a VMI education affords. . . . VMI produces its "citizen-soldiers" through "an adversative, or doubting, model of education" which features "[p]hysical rigor, mental stress, absolute equality of treatment, absence of privacy, minute regulation of behavior, and indoctrination in desirable values." . . .

VMI cadets live in spartan barracks where surveillance is constant and privacy nonexistent; they wear uniforms, eat together in the mess hall, and regularly participate in drills. Entering students are incessantly exposed to the rat line, "an extreme form of the adversative model," comparable in intensity to Marine Corps boot camp. Tormenting and punishing, the rat line bonds new cadets to their fellow sufferers and, when they have completed the 7-month experience, to their former tormentors. . . .

In 1990, prompted by a complaint filed with the Attorney General by a female high-school student seeking admission to VMI, the United States sued the Commonwealth of Virginia and VMI, alleging that VMI's exclusively male admission policy violated the Equal Protection Clause of the Fourteenth Amendment. . . .

In the two years preceding the lawsuit, . . . VMI had received inquiries from 347 women, but had responded to none of them. [W]ith recruitment, VMI could "achieve at least 10% female enrollment"—"a sufficient 'critical mass' to provide the female cadets with a positive educational experience." And it was also established that "some women are capable of all of the individual activities required of VMI cadets." . . .

The District Court ruled in favor of VMI, however, and rejected the equal protection challenge pressed by the United States.

The Court of Appeals for the Fourth Circuit disagreed and vacated the District Court's judgment. . . .

The parties agreed that "some women can meet the physical standards now imposed on men," and the court was satisfied that "neither the goal of producing citizen soldiers nor VMI's implementing methodology is inherently unsuitable to women." The Court of Appeals, however, accepted the District Court's finding that "at least these three aspects of VMI's program—physical training, the absence of privacy, and the adversative approach—would be materially affected by coeducation." Remanding the case, the appeals court assigned to Virginia, in the first instance, responsibility for selecting a remedial course. . . .

In response to the Fourth Circuit's ruling, Virginia proposed a parallel program for women: Virginia Women's Institute for Leadership (VWIL). The 4-year, state-sponsored undergraduate program would be located at Mary Baldwin College, a private liberal arts school for women, and would be open, initially, to about 25 to 30 students. Although VWIL would share

VMI's mission-to produce "citizen-soldiers"—the VWIL program would differ, as does Mary Baldwin College, from VMI in academic offerings, methods of education, and financial resources.

The average combined SAT score of entrants at Mary Baldwin is about 100 points lower than the score for VMI freshmen. Mary Baldwin's faculty holds "significantly fewer Ph.D.'s than the faculty at VMI," and receives significantly lower salaries. While VMI offers degrees in liberal arts, the sciences, and engineering, Mary Baldwin, at the time of trial, offered only bachelor of arts degrees. . . .

Experts in educating women at the college level composed the Task Force charged with designing the VWIL program; Task Force members were drawn from Mary Baldwin's own faculty and staff. Training its attention on methods of instruction appropriate for "most women," the Task Force determined that a military model would be "wholly inappropriate" for VWIL.

VWIL students would participate in ROTC programs and a newly established, "largely ceremonial" Virginia Corps of Cadets, but the VWIL House would not have a military format and VWIL would not require its students to eat meals together or to wear uniforms during the schoolday. In lieu of VMI's adversative method, the VWIL Task Force favored "a cooperative method which reinforces self-esteem." In addition to the standard bachelor of arts program offered at Mary Baldwin, VWIL students would take courses in leadership, complete an off-campus leadership externship, participate in community service projects, and assist in arranging a speaker series.

Virginia represented that it will provide equal financial support for in-state VWIL students and VMI cadets, and the VMI Foundation agreed to supply a $5.4625 million endowment for the VWIL program. Mary Baldwin's own endowment is about $19 million; VMI's is $131 million. Mary Baldwin will add $35 million to its endowment based on future commitments; VMI will add $220 million. . . .

Virginia returned to the District Court seeking approval of its proposed remedial plan, and the court decided the plan met the requirements of the Equal Protection Clause. . . . A divided Court of Appeals affirmed the District Court's judgment. . . . [T]he adversative method vital to a VMI education "has never been tolerated in a sexually heterogeneous environment." The method itself "was not designed to exclude women," the court noted, but women could not be accommodated in the VMI program, the court believed, for female participation in VMI's adversative training "would destroy . . . any sense of decency that still permeates the relationship between the sexes.". . .

The cross-petitions in this suit present two ultimate issues. First, does Virginia's exclusion of women from the educational opportunities provided by VMI—extraordinary opportunities for military training and civilian leadership development—deny to women capable of all of the individual activities required of VMI cadets the equal protection of the laws guaranteed by the Fourteenth Amendment? Second, if VMI's "unique" situation—as Virginia's sole single-sex public institution of higher education—offends the Constitution's equal protection principle, what is the remedial requirement? We note, once again, the core instruction of this Court's pathmarking decision . . . in . . . *Mississippi Univ. for Women*: Parties who seek to defend gender-based government action must demonstrate an "exceedingly persuasive justification" for that action.

Today's skeptical scrutiny of official action denying rights or opportunities based on sex responds to volumes of history. . . .

Without equating gender classifications, for all purposes, to classifications based on race or national origin, the Court, in post-*Reed* decisions, has carefully inspected official action that closes a door or denies opportunity to women (or to men). To summarize the Court's current directions for cases of official classification based on gender: Focusing on the differential treatment for denial of opportunity for which relief is sought, the reviewing court must determine whether the proffered justification is "exceedingly persuasive." The burden of justification is demanding and it rests entirely on the State. The State must show "at least that the [challenged] classification serves 'important governmental objectives and that the discriminatory means employed' are 'substantially related to the achievement of those objectives.' " The justification must be genuine, not hypothesized or invented post hoc in response to litigation. And it must not rely on overbroad generalizations about the different talents, capacities, or preferences of males and females. . . .

Measuring the record in this case against the review standard just described, we conclude that Virginia has shown no "exceedingly persuasive justification" for excluding all women from the citizen-soldier training afforded by VMI. . . .

Virginia . . . asserts two justifications in defense of VMI's exclusion of women. First, the Commonwealth contends, "single-sex education provides important educational benefits," and the option of single-sex education contributes to "diversity in educational approaches." Second, the Commonwealth argues, "the unique VMI method of character development and leadership training," the school's adversative approach, would have to be modified were VMI to admit women. We consider these two justifications in turn.

Single-sex education affords pedagogical benefits to at least some students, Virginia emphasizes, and that reality is uncontested in this litigation. Similarly, it is not disputed that diversity among public educational institutions can serve the public good. But Virginia has not shown that VMI was established, or has been maintained, with a view to diversifying, by its categorical exclusion of women, educational opportunities within the Commonwealth. . . .

Neither recent nor distant history bears out Virginia's alleged pursuit of diversity through single-sex educational options. . . .In sum, we find no persuasive evidence in this record that VMI's male-only admission policy "is in furtherance of a state policy of 'diversity.' " . . . A purpose genuinely to advance an array of educational options, as the Court of Appeals recognized, is not served by VMI's historic and constant plan—a plan to "affor[d] a unique educational benefit only to males." However "liberally" this plan serves the Commonwealth's sons, it makes no provision whatever for her daughters. That is not equal protection.

Virginia next argues that VMI's adversative method of training provides educational benefits that cannot be made available, unmodified, to women. Alterations to accommodate women would necessarily be "radical," so "drastic," Virginia asserts, as to transform, indeed "destroy," VMI's program. Neither sex would be favored by the transformation, Virginia maintains: Men would be deprived of the unique opportunity currently available to them; women would not gain that opportunity because their participation would "eliminat[e] the very aspects of [the] program that distinguish [VMI] from . . . other institutions of higher education in Virginia."

The District Court forecast from expert witness testimony, and the Court of Appeals accepted, that coeducation would materially affect "at least these three aspects of VMI's program—physical training, the absence of privacy, and the adversative approach." And it is uncontested that women's admission would require accommodations, primarily in arranging housing assignments and physical training programs for female cadets. It is also undisputed, however, that "the VMI methodology could be used to educate women." . . .

In support of its initial judgment for Virginia, a judgment rejecting all equal protection objections presented by the United States, the District Court made "findings" on "gender-based developmental differences." These "findings" restate the opinions of Virginia's expert witnesses, opinions about typically male or typically female "tendencies." For example, "[m]ales tend to need an atmosphere of adversativeness," while "[f]emales tend to thrive in a cooperative atmosphere." "I'm not saying that some women don't do well under [the] adversative model," VMI's expert on educational institutions testified, "undoubtedly there are some [women] who do"; but educational experiences must be designed "around the rule," this expert maintained, and not "around the exception."

The United States does not challenge any expert witness estimation on average capacities or preferences of men and women. Instead, the United States emphasizes that time and again since this Court's turning point decision in *Reed v. Reed*, we have cautioned reviewing courts to take a "hard look" at generalizations or "tendencies" of the kind pressed by Virginia, and relied upon by the District Court. State actors controlling gates to opportunity, we have instructed, may not exclude qualified individuals based on "fixed notions concerning the roles and abilities of males and females."

It may be assumed, for purposes of this decision, that most women would not choose VMI's adversative method. [I]t is also probable that "many men would not want to be educated in such an environment." (On that point, even our dissenting colleague might agree.) Education, to be sure, is not a "one size fits all" business. The issue, however, is not whether "women—or men—should be forced to attend VMI"; rather, the question is whether the Commonwealth can constitutionally deny to women who have the will and capacity, the training and attendant opportunities that VMI uniquely affords.

The notion that admission of women would downgrade VMI's stature, destroy the adversative system and, with it, even the school, is a judgment hardly proved, a prediction hardly different from other "self-fulfilling prophec[ies]," once routinely used to deny rights or opportunities. . . .

Women's successful entry into the federal military academies, and their participation in the Nation's military forces, indicate that Virginia's fears for the future of VMI may not be solidly grounded. The Commonwealth's justification for excluding all women from "citizen-soldier" training for which some are qualified, in any event, cannot rank as "exceedingly persuasive," as we have explained and applied that standard. . . .

In the second phase of the litigation, Virginia presented its remedial plan—maintain VMI as a male-only college and create VWIL as a separate program for women. . . . The United States challenges this "remedial" [plan] as pervasively misguided.

A remedial decree, this Court has said, must closely fit the constitutional violation; it must be shaped to place persons unconstitutionally denied an opportunity or advantage in "the position they would have occupied in the absence of [discrimination]." The constitutional violation in this suit is the categorical exclusion of women from an extraordinary educational opportunity afforded men. A proper remedy for an unconstitutional exclusion, we have explained, aims to "eliminate [so far as possible] the discriminatory effects of the past" and to "bar like discrimination in the future."

Virginia chose not to eliminate, but to leave untouched, VMI's exclusionary policy. For women only, however, Virginia proposed a separate program, different in kind from VMI and unequal in tangible and intangible facilities. . . . Virginia described VWIL as a "parallel program," and asserted that VWIL shares VMI's mission of producing "citizen-soldiers" and VMI's goals of providing "education, military training, mental and physical discipline, character . . . and leadership development." . . . A comparison of the programs said to be "parallel" informs our answer. . . . [As described earlier, the VWIL program is in many ways not parallel to the VMI program and in no case is it equal to it.]

In contrast to the generalizations about women on which Virginia rests, we note again these dispositive realities: VMI's "implementing methodology" is not "inherently unsuitable to women"; "some women . . . do well under [the] adversative model"; "some women, at least, would want to attend [VMI] if they had the opportunity; "some women are capable of all of the individual activities required of VMI cadets" and "can meet the physical standards [VMI] now impose[s] on men. It is on behalf of these women that the United States has instituted this suit, and it is for them that a remedy must be crafted, a remedy that will end their exclusion from a state-supplied educational opportunity for which they are fit, a decree that will "bar like discrimination in the future." . . .

JUSTICE THOMAS took no part in the consideration or decision of these cases.

CHIEF JUSTICE REHNQUIST, concurring in the judgment.

The Court holds first that Virginia violates the Equal Protection Clause by maintaining the Virginia Military Institute's (VMI's) all-male admissions policy, and second that establishing the Virginia Women's Institute for Leadership (VWIL) program does not remedy that violation. While I agree with these conclusions, I disagree with the Court's analysis and so I write separately.

Two decades ago in *Craig v. Boren*, we announced that "[t]o withstand constitutional challenge, . . . classifications by gender must serve important governmental objectives and must be substantially related to achievement of those objectives." We have adhered to that standard of scrutiny ever since. While the majority adheres to this test today, it also says that the Commonwealth must demonstrate an " 'exceedingly persuasive justification' " to support a gender-based classification. It is unfortunate that the Court thereby introduces an element of uncertainty respecting the appropriate test.

While terms like "important governmental objective" and "substantially related" are hardly models of precision, they have more content and specificity than does the phrase "exceedingly persuasive justification." That phrase is best confined, as it was first used, as an observation on the difficulty of meeting the applicable test, not as a formulation of the test itself. . . .

Our cases dealing with gender discrimination also require that the proffered purpose for the challenged law be the actual purpose. It is on this ground that the Court rejects the first of two justifications Virginia offers for VMI's single-sex admissions policy, namely, the goal of diversity among its public educational institutions. While I ultimately agree that the Commonwealth has not carried the day with this justification, I disagree with the Court's method of analyzing the issue. . .

Before this Court, Virginia has sought to justify VMI's single-sex admissions policy primarily on the basis that diversity in education is desirable, and that while most of the public institutions of higher learning in the Commonwealth are coeducational, there should also be room for single-sex institutions. I agree with the Court that there is scant evidence in the record that this was the real reason that Virginia decided to maintain VMI as men only. But, unlike the majority, I would consider only evidence that postdates our decision in *Hogan*, and would draw no negative inferences from the Commonwealth's actions before that time. I think that after *Hogan*, the Commonwealth was entitled to reconsider its policy with respect to VMI, and not to have earlier justifications, or lack thereof, held against it. . . .

Virginia offers a second justification for the single-sex admissions policy: maintenance of the adversative method. I agree with the Court that this justification does not serve an important governmental objective. A State does not have substantial interest in the adversative methodology unless it is pedagogically beneficial. While considerable evidence shows that a single-sex education is pedagogically beneficial for some students, and hence a State may have a valid interest in promoting that methodology, there is no similar evidence in the record that an adversative method is pedagogically beneficial or is any more likely to produce character traits than other methodologies.

The Court defines the constitutional violation in these cases as "the categorical exclusion of women from an extraordinary educational opportunity afforded to men." By defining the violation in this way, and by emphasizing that a remedy for a constitutional violation must place the victims of discrimination in " 'the position they would have occupied in the absence of [discrimination],' " the Court necessarily implies that the only adequate remedy would be the admission of women to the all-male institution. As the foregoing discussion suggests, I would not define the violation in this way; it is not the "exclusion of women" that violates the Equal Protection Clause, but the maintenance of an all-men school without providing any-much less a comparable-institution for women.

Accordingly, the remedy should not necessarily require either the admission of women to VMI or the creation of a VMI clone for women. An adequate remedy in my opinion might be a demonstration by Virginia that its interest in educating men in a single-sex environment is matched by its interest in educating women in a single-sex institution. To demonstrate such, the Commonwealth does not need to create two institutions with the same number of faculty Ph.D.'s, similar SAT scores, or comparable athletic fields. Nor would it necessarily require that the women's institution offer the same curriculum as the men's; one could be strong in computer science, the other could be strong in liberal arts. It would be a sufficient remedy, I think, if the two institutions offered the same quality of education and were of the same overall caliber. . . .

In the end, the women's institution Virginia proposes, VWIL, fails as a remedy, because it is distinctly inferior to the existing men's institution and will continue to be for the foreseeable future. VWIL simply is not, in any sense, the institution that VMI is. In particular, VWIL is a program appended to a private college, not a self-standing institution; and VWIL is substantially underfunded as compared to VMI. I therefore ultimately agree with the Court that Virginia has not provided an adequate remedy.

JUSTICE SCALIA, dissenting.

Today the Court shuts down an institution that has served the people of the Commonwealth of Virginia with pride and distinction for over a century and a half. To achieve that desired result, it rejects (contrary to our established practice) the factual findings of two courts below, sweeps aside the precedents of this Court, and ignores the history of our people. As to facts: It explicitly rejects the finding that there exist "gender-based developmental differences" supporting Virginia's restriction of the "adversative" method to only a men's institution, and the finding that the all-male composition of the Virginia Military Institute (VMI) is essential to that institution's character. As to precedent: It drastically revises our established standards for reviewing sex-based classifications. And as to history: It counts for nothing the long tradition, enduring down to the present, of men's military colleges supported by both States and the Federal Government.

Much of the Court's opinion is devoted to deprecating the closed-mindedness of our forebears with regard to women's education, and even with regard to the treatment of women in areas that have nothing to do with education. Closed-minded they were—as every age is, including our own, with regard to matters it cannot guess, because it simply does not consider them debatable. The virtue of a democratic system with a First Amendment is that it readily enables the people, over time, to be persuaded that what they took for granted is not so, and to change their laws accordingly. That system is destroyed if the smug assurances of each age are removed from the democratic process and written into the Constitution. So to counterbalance the Court's criticism of our ancestors, let me say a word in their praise: They left us free to change. The same cannot be said of this most illiberal Court, which has embarked on a course of inscribing one after another of the current preferences of the society (and in some cases only the counter-majoritarian preferences of the society's law-trained elite) into our Basic Law. Today it enshrines the notion that no substantial educational value is to be served by an all-men's military academy—so that the decision by the people of Virginia to maintain such an institution denies equal protection to women who cannot attend that institution but can attend others. Since it is entirely clear that the Constitution of the United States—the old one—takes no sides in this educational debate, I dissent.

I shall devote most of my analysis to evaluating the Court's opinion on the basis of our current equal protection jurisprudence, which regards this Court as free to evaluate everything under the sun by applying one of three tests: "rational basis" scrutiny, intermediate scrutiny, or strict scrutiny. . . .

I have no problem with a system of abstract tests such as rational basis, intermediate, and strict scrutiny (though I think we can do better than applying strict scrutiny and intermediate scrutiny whenever we feel like it). Such formulas are essential to evaluating whether the new restrictions that a changing society constantly imposes upon private conduct comport with that "equal protection" our society has always accorded in the past. But in my view the function of this Court is to preserve our society's values regarding (among other things) equal protection, not to revise them; to prevent backsliding from the degree of restriction the Constitution imposed upon democratic government, not to prescribe, on our own authority, progressively higher degrees. For that reason it is my view that, whatever abstract tests we may choose to devise, they cannot supersede—and indeed ought to be crafted so as to reflect—those constant and unbroken national traditions that embody the people's understanding of ambiguous constitutional texts. More specifically, it is my view that "when a practice not expressly prohibited by the text of the Bill of Rights bears the endorsement of a long tradition of open, widespread, and unchallenged use that dates back to the beginning of the Republic, we have no proper basis for striking it down." The same applies, *mutatis mutandis*, to a practice asserted to be in violation of the post-Civil War Fourteenth Amendment.

The all-male constitution of VMI comes squarely within such a governing tradition. Founded by the Commonwealth of Virginia in 1839 and continuously maintained by it since, VMI has always admitted only men. And in that regard it has not been unusual. For almost all of VMI's more than a century and a half of existence, its single-sex status reflected the uniform practice for government-supported military colleges. [A]ll the federal military colleges—West Point, the Naval Academy at Annapolis, and even the Air Force Academy, which was not established until 1954— admitted only males for most of their history. Their admission of women in 1976 (upon which the Court today relies) came not by court decree, but because the people, through their elected representatives, decreed a change. In other words, the tradition of having government-funded military schools for men is as well rooted in the traditions of this country as the tradition of sending only men into military combat. The people may decide to change the one tradition, like the other, through democratic processes; but the assertion that either tradition has been unconstitutional through the centuries is not law, but politics-smuggled-into-law. . . .

To reject the Court's disposition today, however, it is not necessary to accept my view that the Court's made-up tests cannot displace longstanding national traditions as the primary determinant of what the Constitution means. It is only necessary to apply honestly the test the Court has been applying to sex-based classifications for the past two decades. It is well settled, as Justice O'CONNOR stated some time ago for a unanimous Court, that we evaluate a statutory classification based on sex under a standard that lies "[b]etween th[e] extremes of rational basis review and strict scrutiny." We have denominated this standard "intermediate scrutiny" and under it have inquired whether the statutory classification is "substantially related to an important governmental objective." . . .

Although the Court in two places recites th[is] test, . . . the Court never answers the question presented in anything resembling that form. When it engages in analysis, the Court instead prefers the phrase "exceedingly persuasive justification" from *Hogan*. The Court's nine invocations of that phrase and even its fanciful description of that imponderable as "the core instruction" of the Court's decision[ ] in . . . *Hogan* would be unobjectionable if the Court acknowledged that whether a "justification" is "exceedingly persuasive" must be assessed by asking "[whether] the classification serves important governmental objectives and [whether] the discriminatory means employed are substantially related to the achievement of those objectives." Instead, however, the Court proceeds to interpret "exceedingly persuasive justification" in a fashion that contradicts the reasoning of *Hogan* and our other precedents. . . .

Only the amorphous "exceedingly persuasive justification" phrase, and not the standard elaboration of intermediate scrutiny, can be made to yield this conclusion that VMI's single-sex composition is unconstitutional because there exist several women (or, one would have to conclude under the Court's reasoning, a single woman) willing and able to undertake VMI's program. Intermediate scrutiny has never required a least-restrictive-means analysis, but only a "substantial relation" between the classification and the state interests that it serves. . . .

COMMENTS AND QUESTIONS

1.   The *VMI* case raises two questions—is the exclusion of women from VMI a violation of the Equal Protection Clause, and, if so, can the creation of a "parallel" women's-only college cure that violation? Is it a fair criticism of the Court's opinion that it uses an "exceedingly persuasive justification" test rather than an "intermediate scrutiny" test to answer the first question? What is the difference between these two tests?

2.　What is the reason the Court rejects Virginia's claimed important interest in providing diversity among public educational institutions? Why does it reject Virginia's claimed important interest in the pedagogical benefits of single-sex education?

3.　Did Virginia's proposed solution of creating the VWIL remind you of the "separate but equal" doctrine with respect to racial segregation? If not, why not? Why did the Court dismiss Virginia's claim that admitting women would destroy the "adversative" system? Do you agree with the Court or Virginia?

4.　Do you think Chief Justice Rehnquist's differences from the majority merited a separate opinion? What exactly did he disagree with?

5.　Justice Scalia presents two separate approaches to the problem, either of which, he says, leads to a different conclusion than the Court's. Would not his first approach eliminate from the Equal Protection Clause any restriction on gender discrimination, because it is clear that in 1868 and for long thereafter the allowance of such discrimination was one of our "constant and unbroken national traditions that embody the people's understanding of ambiguous constitutional texts." Might not the same even be said for racial segregation?

6.　A theme running through the Court's opinion is that traditional notions of women's abilities and interests cannot be used to exclude women not fitting those notions from equal opportunities with men. Why is it then that the Court concedes that there must be changes to housing arrangements and physical training programs, if not aspects of the adversative approach? What if VMI admitted women but treated them exactly the same as men—same uniform, same haircut, same barracks, same bathrooms, same physical training requirements, same rat line—would this drive women away, returning VMI to an all male school as a practical matter? If so, would it still be in violation of the Equal Protection Clause?

7.　In answering that question, recall *Washington v. Davis*, in which the Court said that in order to trigger application of strict scrutiny the government actor must intend to discriminate on the basis of race; mere disparate impact, while perhaps evidence of intent, does not itself trigger the heightened scrutiny. The Court reached the same conclusion with respect to the trigger for intermediate scrutiny applicable to gender discrimination. In *Personnel Administrator v. Feeney*, 442 U.S. 256 (1979), the Court upheld Massachusetts's veteran preference for state civil service positions despite its greatly disproportionate adverse effect on women. The Court determined that the state had not adopted it for gender related reasons, and therefore tested it under the rational relationship test, which it easily passed as a measure to make up for the sacrifice veterans had made for their country.

8.　In *Sessions v. Morales*, 137 S.Ct. 1678 (2017), the Court in an opinion by Justice Ginsburg reiterated *VMI*'s rule that legislation that differentiates on the basis of gender requires an "exceedingly persuasive justification" and that the defender of such legislation must show "at least that the [challenged] classification serves important governmental objectives and that the discriminatory means employed are substantially related to the achievement of those objectives." Utilizing this test, the Court found that different standards between unwed citizen mothers and unwed citizen fathers for continuous presence in the United States in order to transmit citizenship to their children born abroad violated equal protection. Rather than serving an important government interest, the distinction favoring mothers reflected only the traditional stereotype that the mother was the child's natural and sole guardian. The more difficult question for the Court was what the remedy should be—which of the two requirements (the father's or the mother's) should be enjoined as violating the Constitution? The Court acknowledged that normally in Equal Protection cases the Court extends the protection denied to the plaintiff by the statute, rather than striking down the more liberal requirement. Nevertheless, it said that "[h]ow equality is accomplished . . . is a matter on which the Constitution is silent," and the answer should turn on the legislature's intent. Here, the main rule was the stricter requirement applicable to unwed citizen fathers, while the more liberal requirement was expressly an exception to that general rule. Moreover, making the more liberal requirement the rule for unwed citizen fathers would create irrational inconsistencies with other provisions governing the citizenship of children born abroad to a married couple, one of whom was a citizen. Consequently, the Court held that the stricter requirement applicable to unwed citizen fathers should prospectively apply to unwed citizen mothers.

Under the Court's remedial holding the plaintiff did not get any relief—he was denied citizenship because his father had not satisfied the requirement for continuous presence in the United States. In light of this, Justice Thomas, joined by Justice Alito, concurred in the judgment but not the opinion of the Court, finding that the plaintiff had lacked standing to bring the case in the first place, making it unnecessary to address the constitutional issues. The majority did not address this argument.

9.   In a Title VII case, the Supreme Court found that employment actions based on gender stereotyping—failure to act according to expectations defined by gender—constituted sex discrimination. *See Price Waterhouse v. Hopkins*, 490 U.S. 228 (1989). Would the same analysis be used to determine if discrimination on the basis of gender stereotyping was a violation of equal protection?

PROBLEM

A woman enters a "Ladies Room" in a local courthouse only to find a man there coming out of a stall. She flees the rest room and quickly finds a court officer who arrests the man. At a court hearing, the man defends on the ground that providing for separate rest rooms for men and women is equivalent to providing separate rest rooms for whites and blacks, as had been the case in the South before *Brown v. Board of Ed.* and therefore a violation of equal protection. He also submits evidence that the men's room

> at the time had a sign "temporarily closed for cleaning." How
> should a court rule?

D. DISCRIMINATION AGAINST OTHER GROUPS

The federal and state governments have, of course, discriminated against persons on bases other than race and gender. In assessing the constitutionality of targeting these different groups, a recurring question is what level of scrutiny should be afforded to that discrimination. As we have seen, if courts use strict or intermediate scrutiny, the discriminatory law has a heavy burden to establish its constitutionality. On the other hand, if the discrimination is subject only to traditional rational relationship review, the challenger has the heavy burden to show that the discrimination is totally irrational.

1. ALIENAGE

Until 1948 the Court routinely upheld state laws discriminating against aliens, and it was not until 1971 that the Court, harking back to the footnote in *Carolene Products*, concluded that "aliens as a class are a prime example of a discrete and insular minority," and therefore "classifications based on alienage [are] inherently suspect and subject to close judicial scrutiny." Consequently, state laws denying lawfully admitted aliens welfare benefits violated the Equal Protection Clause. *Graham v. Richardson*, 403 U.S. 365 (1971). Cases followed that struck down state laws banning aliens from the state civil service and barring them from admission to the bar. *Sugarman v. Dougall*, 413 U.S. 634 (1973); *In re Griffiths*, 413 U.S. 717 (1973).

Later, however, in a series of highly divided decisions, with the conservatives carrying the day by a 5–4 vote in each case, the Court created an exception to the rule that alienage classifications should receive strict scrutiny. This exception is known as the *governmental functions exception*. Building on dictum in *Sugarman* that a state could require citizenship as a qualification for a government office "in an appropriately defined class of positions," the Court concluded that states could require citizenship for jobs that involve important government functions, functions that fulfill "a most fundamental obligation of government to its constituency." Electoral offices would seem to fit this category, but the Court extended the exception to government jobs that involve a high degree of discretion in the creation, interpretation, or administration of state laws. This test sounds restrictive, but the Court's application suggests otherwise. In *Foley v. Connelie*, 435 U.S. 291 (1978), the Court upheld New York's exclusion of aliens from the state police force. In *Ambach v. Norwick*, 441 U.S. 68 (1979), the Court upheld New York's refusal to employ lawfully admitted aliens as elementary or secondary school teachers. And *Cabell v. Chavez-Salido*, 454 U.S. 432 (1982), upheld California's prohibition on aliens being employed in any position having the powers of a peace officer as applied to a probation officer. Where the governmental functions exception applies, the appropriate test is the rational relationship test rather than strict scrutiny.

In *Mathews v. Diaz*, 426 U.S. 67 (1976), the Court created another exception to the strict scrutiny test as applied to aliens. There the issue was the constitutionality of a federal statute, a provision of the Medicare law that denied benefits to aliens unless they were admitted to permanent residence and had in fact resided for at least five years in the United States. The Court, recognizing Congress's plenary powers over immigration and naturalization, concluded that Congress necessarily had to draw lines between citizens and aliens. Rather than put the burden on the government to defend those lines, the Court held that the burden was on the person challenging the line drawn to show that it is "totally irrational." In short, if the alienage classification is in federal law, then the appropriate test is rational relationship.

In all of the above cases, the alienage classification was challenged by lawfully admitted aliens, and the cases did not suggest that the protection afforded lawfully admitted aliens would apply to persons not lawfully present.

2. ILLEGITIMACY

Illegitimacy or bastardy is the status of a child born out of wedlock, that is, to people who are not married to each other. Historically, because sex outside of marriage was a sin condemned by religions and illegal under the law, an unmarried woman having a child suffered great stigma. Whether to create a disincentive to such procreation by punishing the children or to protect the fathers responsible, inheritance and child support laws generally did not protect illegitimate children. In most states, only when a father officially acknowledged an illegitimate child as his, was he liable for support or was the child entitled to inheritance in intestacy.

In 1968 the Supreme Court first overturned a state law creating a disability for illegitimates. In *Levy v. Louisiana*, 391 U.S. 68 (1968), five illegitimate children sued a doctor for the wrongful death of their mother, but Louisiana law only allowed legitimate children to bring such actions. The Supreme Court held the law unconstitutional, saying that the children's illegitimacy had no relation to the nature of the law they were trying to utilize. Louisiana's workers compensation law contained a similar disqualification for illegitimate children of a worker killed in the course of his employment. In *Weber v. Aetna Casualty & Surety Co.*, 406 U.S. 164 (1972), the Court likewise struck this disqualification, saying

> The status of illegitimacy has expressed through the ages society's condemnation of irresponsible liaisons beyond the bonds of marriage. But visiting this condemnation on the head of an infant is illogical and unjust. Moreover, imposing disabilities on the

illegitimate child is contrary to the basic concept of our system that legal burdens should bear some relationship to individual responsibility or wrongdoing. Obviously, no child is responsible for his birth and penalizing the illegitimate child is an ineffectual— as well as an unjust—way of deterring the parent. Courts are powerless to prevent the social opprobrium suffered by these hapless children, but the Equal Protection Clause does enable us to strike down discriminatory laws relating to status of birth where—as in this case—the classification is justified by no legitimate state interest, compelling or otherwise.

In subsequent years, however, both the level of scrutiny and the outcomes seemed to vary. For example, in *Mathews v. Lucas*, 427 U.S. 495 (1976), the Court by a 6–3 margin, explicitly using rational basis review, upheld a provision of the Social Security Act that denied Social Security survivor benefits to certain illegitimate children. The provision required children to be dependent upon the deceased wage earner, but certain children were presumed dependent and did not have to show actual dependency. These children were all legitimate children and those illegitimate children who under state law could inherit intestate, who were acknowledged in writing, or who had received court ordered child support. Other illegitimate children were not denied survivor benefits outright, but they had to prove they were actually dependent on the deceased wage earner. Although this law's requirement for showing actual dependency only applied to illegitimate children, the fact that some other illegitimate children did not have to make individual proof suggested that the classification was not on the basis of illegitimacy *per se* but was simply a "reasonable empirical judgment[ ] . . . consistent with a design to qualify entitlement to benefits upon a child's dependency." The dissent was not convinced that the classification was not the "product of a tradition of thinking of illegitimates as less deserving persons than legitimates."

Similarly, in *Fiallo v. Bell*, 430 U.S. 787 (1977), using a rational basis test, the Court upheld a provision of the Immigration and Nationalization Act that granted a special immigration preference to alien children of U.S. citizen parents, but defined "child" to include the illegitimate child of a U.S. citizen mother but not of a U.S. citizen father.

In *Clark v. Jeter*, 486 U.S. 456 (1988), however, the Court, without acknowledging what tests it had used in earlier cases, unanimously stated that the test for assessing classifications based on legitimacy was intermediate scrutiny and proceeded to strike down a state law that required child support actions to be brought within six years of the child's birth. The state's justification—the desire to avoid stale claims when proof would be difficult—clearly would have satisfied the rational basis test, but here the Court found social pressures might stop an unmarried mother from bringing a claim in a timely fashion and "increasingly sophisticated tests for genetic markers permit the exclusion of 99% of those who might be accused of paternity" regardless of when the claim was brought.

Nevertheless, some lower courts have reverted to the rational basis test when the classification is made in the context of immigration law, citing back to *Fiallo. See, e.g., Johnson v. Whitehead*, 647 F.3d 120 (4th Cir. 2011), *cert. denied*, 565 U.S. 1111 (2012).

Finally, in *Nguyen v. INS*, 533 U.S. 53 (2001), the Court upheld a provision of the Immigration and Naturalization Act that created requirements for birthright citizenship for illegitimate children of American citizen fathers that were different and more difficult than those applicable to the illegitimate children of American citizen mothers, and also more difficult than the requirements for obtaining birthright citizenship by the legitimate children of either American citizen fathers or mothers. In this case, however, the sole claim was that the law discriminated on the basis of sex, not illegitimacy. Nevertheless, applying intermediate scrutiny, the Court by a 5–4 vote concluded that treating citizen mothers and fathers differently substantially related to two important government objectives: the importance of assuring that a biological parent-child relationship exists and the importance of ensuring that the child and the citizen parent have some demonstrated opportunity or potential to develop not just a legal relationship, but one that consists of the real, everyday ties that provide a connection between child and citizen parent and, in turn, the United States. The Court dismissed the sophistication of DNA testing to satisfy the first objective, ignoring its reliance on it in *Clark v. Jeter.*

Perhaps, from both the alienage and illegitimacy cases, we can discern, whatever test is used, a significant deference to Congress in the lines that it draws in the field of immigration and naturalization.

3. INTELLECTUAL DISABILITY

CLEBURNE V. CLEBURNE LIVING CENTER

United States Supreme Court, 1985.
473 U.S. 432, 105 S.Ct. 3249.

JUSTICE WHITE delivered the opinion of the Court.

A Texas city denied a special use permit for the operation of a group home for the mentally retarded, acting pursuant to a municipal zoning ordinance requiring permits for such homes. The Court of Appeals for the Fifth Circuit held that mental retardation is a "quasi-suspect" classification and that the ordinance violated the Equal Protection Clause because it did not substantially further an important governmental purpose. We hold that a lesser standard of scrutiny is appropriate, but conclude that under that standard the ordinance is invalid as applied in this case.

In July 1980, respondent Jan Hannah purchased a building at 201 Featherston Street in the city of Cleburne, Texas, with the intention of leasing it to Cleburne Living Center, Inc. (CLC), for the operation of a group home for the mentally retarded. . . .

The city informed CLC that a special use permit would be required for the operation of a group home at the site, and CLC accordingly submitted a permit application. In response to a subsequent inquiry from CLC, the city explained that under the zoning regulations applicable to the site, a special use permit, renewable annually, was required for the construction of "[h]ospitals for the insane or feeble-minded, or alcoholic [*sic*] or drug addicts, or penal or correctional institutions." The city had determined that the proposed group home should be classified as a "hospital for the feebleminded." After holding a public hearing on CLC's application, the City Council voted 3 to 1 to deny a special use permit.

CLC then filed suit in Federal District Court against the city and a number of its officials, alleging, *inter alia,* that the zoning ordinance was invalid on its face and as applied because it discriminated against the mentally retarded in violation of the equal protection rights of CLC and its potential residents. The District Court found that "[i]f the potential residents of the Featherston Street home were not mentally retarded, but the home was the same in all other respects, its use would be permitted under the city's zoning ordinance," and that the City Counsel's decision "was motivated primarily by the fact that the residents of the home would be persons who are mentally retarded." Even so, the District Court held the ordinance and its application constitutional. Concluding that . . . mental retardation was neither a suspect nor a quasi-suspect classification, the court employed the minimum level of judicial scrutiny applicable to equal protection claims. The court deemed the ordinance, as written and applied, to be rationally related to the city's legitimate interests in "the legal responsibility of CLC and its residents, . . . the safety and fears of residents in the adjoining neighborhood," and the number of people to be housed in the home.

The Court of Appeals for the Fifth Circuit reversed, determining that mental retardation was a quasi-suspect classification and that it should assess the validity of the ordinance under intermediate-level scrutiny. Because mental retardation was in fact relevant to many legislative actions, strict scrutiny was not appropriate. But in light of the history of "unfair and often grotesque mistreatment" of the retarded, discrimination against them was "likely to reflect deep-seated prejudice." In addition, the mentally retarded lacked political power, and their condition was immutable. The court considered heightened scrutiny to be particularly appropriate in this case, because the city's ordinance withheld a benefit which, although not fundamental, was very important to the mentally retarded. Without group homes, the court stated, the retarded could never hope to integrate themselves into the community. Applying the test that it considered appropriate, the court held that the ordinance was invalid on its face [and as applied] because it did not substantially further any important governmental interests. . . .

The Equal Protection Clause of the Fourteenth Amendment commands that no State shall "deny to any person within its jurisdiction the equal protection of the laws," which is essentially a direction that all persons similarly situated should be treated alike. . . . The general rule is that legislation is presumed to be valid and will be sustained if the classification drawn by the statute is rationally related to a legitimate state interest. When social or economic legislation is at issue, the Equal Protection Clause allows the States wide latitude, and the Constitution presumes that even improvident decisions will eventually be rectified by the democratic processes.

The general rule gives way, however, when a statute classifies by race, alienage, or national origin. These factors are so seldom relevant to the achievement of any legitimate state interest that laws grounded in such considerations are deemed to reflect prejudice and antipathy—a view that those in the burdened class are not as worthy or deserving as others. For these reasons and because such discrimination is unlikely to be soon rectified by legislative means, these laws are subjected to strict scrutiny and will be sustained only if they are suitably tailored to serve a compelling state interest.

Legislative classifications based on gender also call for a heightened standard of review. That factor generally provides no sensible ground for differential treatment. "[W]hat differentiates sex from such nonsuspect statuses as intelligence or physical disability . . . is that the sex characteristic frequently bears no relation to ability to perform or contribute to society." Rather than resting on meaningful considerations, statutes distributing benefits and burdens between the sexes in different ways very likely reflect outmoded notions of the relative capabilities of men and women. A gender classification fails unless it is substantially related to a sufficiently important governmental interest. . . .

We have declined, however, to extend heightened review to differential treatment based on age. . . . *Massachusetts Board of Retirement v. Murgia*, 427 U.S. 307 (1976). The lesson of *Murgia* is that where individuals in the group affected by a law have distinguishing characteristics relevant to interests the State has the authority to implement, the courts have been very reluctant, as they should be in our federal system and with our respect for the separation of powers, to closely scrutinize legislative choices as to whether, how, and to what extent those interests should be pursued. In such cases, the Equal Protection Clause requires only a rational means to serve a legitimate end.

Against this background, we conclude for several reasons that the Court of Appeals erred in holding mental retardation a quasi-suspect classification calling for a more exacting standard of judicial review than is normally accorded economic and social legislation. First, it is undeniable, and it is not argued otherwise here, that those who are mentally retarded have a reduced ability to cope with and function in the everyday world. . . . They are thus different, immutably so, in relevant respects, and the States' interest in dealing with and providing for them is plainly a legitimate one. How this large and diversified group is to be treated under the law is a difficult and often a technical matter, very much a task for legislators guided by qualified professionals and not by the perhaps ill-informed opinions of the judiciary. Heightened scrutiny inevitably involves substantive judgments about legislative decisions, and we doubt that the predicate for such judicial oversight is present where the classification deals with mental retardation.

Second, the distinctive legislative response, both national and state, to the plight of those who are mentally retarded demonstrates not only that they have unique problems, but also that the lawmakers have been addressing their difficulties in a manner that belies a continuing antipathy or prejudice and a corresponding need for more intrusive oversight by the judiciary. Thus, the Federal Government has not only outlawed discrimination against the mentally retarded in federally funded programs, but it has also provided the retarded with the right to receive "appropriate treatment, services, and habilitation" in a setting that is "least restrictive of [their] personal liberty." In addition, the Government has conditioned federal education funds on a State's assurance that retarded children will enjoy an education that, "to the maximum extent appropriate," is integrated with that of nonmentally retarded children. . . . The State of Texas has similarly enacted legislation that acknowledges the special status of the mentally retarded by conferring certain rights upon them, such as "the right to live in the least restrictive setting appropriate to [their] individual needs and abilities," including "the right to live . . . in a group home."

Third, the legislative response, which could hardly have occurred and survived without public support, negates any claim that the mentally retarded are politically powerless in the sense that they have no ability to attract the attention of the lawmakers. Any minority can be said to be powerless to assert direct control over the legislature, but if that were a criterion for higher level scrutiny by the courts, much economic and social legislation would now be suspect.

Fourth, if the large and amorphous class of the mentally retarded were deemed quasi-suspect for the reasons given by the Court of Appeals, it would be difficult to find a principled way to distinguish a variety of other groups who have perhaps immutable disabilities setting them off from others, who cannot themselves mandate the desired legislative responses, and who can claim some degree of prejudice from at least part of the public at large. One need mention in this respect only the aging, the disabled, the mentally ill, and the infirm. We are reluctant to set out on that course, and we decline to do so.

Doubtless, there have been and there will continue to be instances of discrimination against the retarded that are in fact invidious, and that are properly subject to judicial correction under constitutional norms. But the appropriate method of reaching such instances is not to create a new quasi-suspect classification and subject all governmental action based on that classification to more searching evaluation. Rather, we should look to the likelihood that governmental action premised on a particular classification is valid as a general matter, not merely to the specifics of the case before us. Because mental retardation is a characteristic that the government may legitimately take into account in a wide range of decisions, and because both State and Federal Governments have recently committed themselves to assisting the retarded, we will not presume that any given legislative action, even one that disadvantages retarded individuals, is rooted in considerations that the Constitution will not tolerate.

Our refusal to recognize the retarded as a quasi-suspect class does not leave them entirely unprotected from invidious discrimination. To withstand equal protection review, legislation that distinguishes between the mentally retarded and others must be rationally related to a legitimate governmental purpose. This standard, we believe, affords government the latitude necessary both to pursue policies designed to assist the retarded in realizing their full potential, and to freely and efficiently engage in activities that burden the retarded in what is essentially an incidental manner. The State may not rely on a classification whose relationship to an asserted goal is so attenuated as to render the distinction arbitrary or irrational. Furthermore, some objectives—such as "a bare . . . desire to harm a politically unpopular group,"—are not legitimate state interests. . . .

We turn to the issue of the validity of the zoning ordinance insofar as it requires a special use permit for homes for the mentally retarded. We inquire first whether requiring a special use permit for the Featherston home in the circumstances here deprives respondents of the equal protection of the laws. . . . The constitutional issue is clearly posed. The city does not require a special use permit in an R-3 zone for apartment houses, multiple dwellings, boarding and lodging houses, fraternity or sorority houses, dormitories, apartment hotels, hospitals, sanitariums, nursing homes for convalescents or the aged (other than for the insane or feebleminded or alcoholics or drug addicts), private clubs or fraternal orders, and other specified uses. It does, however, insist on a special permit for the Featherston home, and it does so, as the District Court found, because it would be a facility for the mentally retarded. May the city require the permit for this facility when other care and multiple-dwelling facilities are freely permitted?

It is true, as already pointed out, that the mentally retarded as a group are indeed different from others not sharing their misfortune, and in this respect they may be different from those who would occupy other facilities that would be permitted in an R-3 zone without a special permit. But this difference is largely irrelevant unless the Featherston home and those who would occupy it would threaten legitimate interests of the city in a way that other permitted uses such as boarding houses and hospitals would not. Because in our view the record does not reveal any rational basis for believing that the Featherston home would pose any special threat to the city's legitimate interests, we affirm the judgment below insofar as it holds the ordinance invalid as applied in this case.

The District Court found that the City Council's insistence on the permit rested on several factors. First, the Council was concerned with the negative attitude of the majority of property owners located within 200 feet of the Featherston facility, as well as with the fears of elderly residents of the neighborhood. But mere negative attitudes, or fear, unsubstantiated by factors which are properly cognizable in a zoning proceeding, are not permissible bases for treating a home for the mentally retarded differently from apartment houses, multiple dwellings, and the like. It is plain that the electorate as a whole, whether by referendum or otherwise, could not order city action violative of the Equal Protection Clause, and the City may not avoid the strictures of that Clause by deferring to the wishes or objections of some fraction of the body politic. "Private biases may be outside the reach of the law, but the law cannot, directly or indirectly, give them effect."

Second, the Council had two objections to the location of the facility. It was concerned that the facility was across the street from a junior high school, and it feared that the students might harass the occupants of the Featherston home. But the school itself is attended by about 30 mentally retarded students, and denying a permit based on such vague, undifferentiated fears is again permitting some portion of the community to validate what would otherwise be an equal protection violation. The other objection to the home's location was that it was located on "a five hundred year flood plain." This concern with the possibility of a flood, however, can hardly be based on a distinction between the Featherston home and, for example, nursing homes, homes for convalescents or the aged, or sanitariums or hospitals, any of which could be located on the Featherston site without obtaining a special use permit. The same may be said of another concern of the Council—doubts about the legal responsibility for actions which the mentally retarded might take. If there is no concern about legal responsibility with respect to other uses that would be permitted in the area, such as boarding and fraternity houses, it is difficult to believe that the groups of mildly or moderately mentally retarded individuals who would live at 201 Featherston would present any different or special hazard. . . .

The short of it is that requiring the permit in this case appears to us to rest on an irrational prejudice against the mentally retarded, including those who would occupy the Featherston facility and who would live under the closely supervised and highly regulated conditions expressly provided for by state and federal law.

The judgment of the Court of Appeals is affirmed insofar as it invalidates the zoning ordinance as applied to the Featherston home. . . .

JUSTICE STEVENS, with whom THE CHIEF JUSTICE joins, concurring.

The Court of Appeals disposed of this case as if a critical question to be decided were which of three clearly defined standards of equal protection review should be applied to a legislative classification discriminating against the mentally retarded. In fact, our cases have not delineated three- or even one or two-such well-defined standards. Rather, our cases reflect a continuum of judgmental responses to differing classifications which have been explained in opinions by terms ranging from "strict scrutiny" at one extreme to "rational basis" at the other. I have never been persuaded that these so-called "standards" adequately explain the decisional process. Cases involving classifications based on alienage, illegal residency, illegitimacy, gender, age, or—as in this case—mental retardation, do not fit well into sharply defined classifications.

I am inclined to believe that what has become known as the [tiered] analysis of equal protection claims does not describe a completely logical method of deciding cases, but rather is a method the Court has employed to explain decisions that actually apply a single standard in a reasonably consistent fashion. In my own approach to these cases, I have always asked myself whether I could find a "rational basis" for the classification at issue. The term "rational," of course, includes a requirement that an impartial lawmaker could logically believe that the classification would serve a legitimate public purpose that transcends the harm to the members of the disadvantaged class. Thus, the word "rational"—for me at least—includes elements of legitimacy and neutrality that must always characterize the performance of the sovereign's duty to govern impartially.

The rational-basis test, properly understood, adequately explains why a law that deprives a person of the right to vote because his skin has a different pigmentation than that of other voters violates the Equal Protection Clause. It would be utterly irrational to limit the franchise on the basis of height or weight; it is equally invalid to limit it on the basis of skin color. None of these attributes has any bearing at all on the citizen's willingness or ability to exercise that civil right. We do not need to apply a special standard, or to apply "strict scrutiny," or even "heightened scrutiny," to decide such cases.

In every equal protection case, we have to ask certain basic questions. What class is harmed by the legislation, and has it been subjected to a "tradition of disfavor" by our laws?[6] What is the public purpose that is being served by the law? What is the characteristic of the disadvantaged class that justifies the disparate treatment? In most cases the answer to these questions will tell us whether the statute has a "rational basis." The answers will result in the virtually automatic invalidation of racial classifications and in the validation of most economic classifications, but they will provide differing results in cases involving classifications based on alienage, gender, or illegitimacy. But that is not because we apply an "intermediate standard of review" in these cases; rather it is because the characteristics of these groups are sometimes relevant and sometimes irrelevant to a valid public purpose, or, more specifically, to the purpose that the challenged laws purportedly intended to serve.

Every law that places the mentally retarded in a special class is not presumptively irrational. The differences between mentally retarded persons and those with greater mental capacity are obviously relevant to certain legislative decisions. An impartial lawmaker—indeed, even a member of a class of persons defined as mentally retarded—could rationally vote in favor of a law providing funds for special education and special treatment for the mentally retarded. A mentally retarded person could also recognize that he is a member of a class that might need special supervision in some situations, both to protect himself and to protect others. Restrictions on his right to drive cars or to operate hazardous equipment might well seem rational even though they deprived him of employment opportunities and the kind of freedom of travel enjoyed by other citizens. . . .

The record convinces me that this permit was required because of the irrational fears of neighboring property owners, rather than for the protection of the mentally retarded persons who would reside in respondent's home. . . .

Accordingly, I join the opinion of the Court.

---

[6] The Court must be especially vigilant in evaluating the rationality of any classification involving a group that has been subjected to a "tradition of disfavor [for] a traditional classification is more likely to be used without pausing to consider its justification than is a newly created classification. Habit, rather than analysis, makes it seem acceptable and natural to distinguish between male and female, alien and citizen, legitimate and illegitimate; for too much of our history there was the same inertia in distinguishing between black and white. But that sort of stereotyped reaction may have no rational relationship-other than pure prejudicial discrimination-to the stated purpose for which the classification is being made."

JUSTICE MARSHALL, with whom JUSTICE BRENNAN and JUSTICE BLACKMUN join, concurring in the judgment in part and dissenting in part.

The Court holds that all retarded individuals cannot be grouped together as the "feebleminded" and deemed presumptively unfit to live in a community. Underlying this holding is the principle that mental retardation *per se* cannot be a proxy for depriving retarded people of their rights and interests without regard to variations in individual ability. With this holding and principle I agree. The Equal Protection Clause requires attention to the capacities and needs of retarded people as individuals.

I cannot agree, however, with the way in which the Court reaches its result or with the narrow, as-applied remedy it provides for the city of Cleburne's equal protection violation. The Court holds the ordinance invalid on rational-basis grounds and disclaims that anything special, in the form of heightened scrutiny, is taking place. Yet Cleburne's ordinance surely would be valid under the traditional rational-basis test applicable to economic and commercial regulation. In my view, it is important to articulate, as the Court does not, the facts and principles that justify subjecting this zoning ordinance to the searching review—the heightened scrutiny—that actually leads to its invalidation. Moreover, in invalidating Cleburne's exclusion of the "feebleminded" only as applied to respondents, rather than on its face, the Court radically departs from our equal protection precedents. Because I dissent from this novel and truncated remedy, and because I cannot accept the Court's disclaimer that no "more exacting standard" than ordinary rational-basis review is being applied, I write separately. . . .

[T]he Court's heightened-scrutiny discussion is even more puzzling given that Cleburne's ordinance is invalidated only after being subjected to precisely the sort of probing inquiry associated with heightened scrutiny. To be sure, the Court does not label its handiwork heightened scrutiny, and perhaps the method employed must hereafter be called "second order" rational-basis review rather than "heightened scrutiny." But however labeled, the rational basis test invoked today is most assuredly not the rational-basis test of *Williamson v. Lee Optical of Oklahoma, Inc.* . . . . The "record" is said not to support the ordinance's classifications, but under the traditional standard we do not sift through the record to determine whether policy decisions are squarely supported by a firm factual foundation. Finally, the Court further finds it "difficult to believe" that the retarded present different or special hazards inapplicable to other groups. In normal circumstances, the burden is not on the legislature to convince the Court that the lines it has drawn are sensible; legislation is presumptively constitutional, and a State "is not required to resort to close distinctions or to maintain a precise, scientific uniformity with reference" to its goals.

I share the Court's criticisms of the overly broad lines that Cleburne's zoning ordinance has drawn. But if the ordinance is to be invalidated for its imprecise classifications, it must be pursuant to more powerful scrutiny than the minimal rational-basis test used to review classifications affecting only economic and commercial matters. The same imprecision in a similar ordinance that required opticians but not optometrists to be licensed to practice, *see Williamson v. Lee Optical of Oklahoma, Inc.,* or that excluded new but not old businesses from parts of a community, *see New Orleans v. Dukes,* would hardly be fatal to the statutory scheme.

The refusal to acknowledge that something more than minimum rationality review is at work here is, in my view, unfortunate in at least two respects. The suggestion that the traditional rational-basis test allows this sort of searching inquiry creates precedent for this Court and lower courts to subject economic and commercial classifications to similar and searching "ordinary" rational-basis review-a small and regrettable step back toward the days of *Lochner v. New York.* Moreover, by failing to articulate the factors that justify today's "second order" rational-basis review, the Court provides no principled foundation for determining when more searching inquiry is to be invoked. Lower courts are thus left in the dark on this important question, and this Court remains unaccountable for its decisions employing, or refusing to employ, particularly searching scrutiny. Candor requires me to acknowledge the particular factors that justify invalidating Cleburne's zoning ordinance under the careful scrutiny it today receives.

I have long believed the level of scrutiny employed in an equal protection case should vary with "the constitutional and societal importance of the interest adversely affected and the recognized invidiousness of the basis upon which the particular classification is drawn." When a zoning ordinance works to exclude the retarded from all residential districts in a community, these two considerations require that the ordinance be convincingly justified as substantially furthering legitimate and important purposes.

First, the interest of the retarded in establishing group homes is substantial. . . . For retarded adults, this right means living together in group homes, for as deinstitutionalization has progressed, group homes have become the primary means by which retarded adults can enter life in the community. . . .

Second, the mentally retarded have been subject to a "lengthy and tragic history," of segregation and discrimination that can only be called grotesque. . . .

In light of the importance of the interest at stake and the history of discrimination the retarded have suffered, the Equal Protection Clause requires us to do more than review the distinctions drawn by Cleburne's zoning ordinance as if they appeared in a taxing statute or in economic or commercial legislation. The searching scrutiny I would give to restrictions on the ability of the retarded to establish community group homes leads me to conclude that Cleburne's vague generalizations for classifying the "feeble-minded" with drug addicts, alcoholics, and the insane, and excluding them where the elderly, the ill, the boarder, and the transient are allowed, are not substantial or important enough to overcome the suspicion that the ordinance rests on impermissible assumptions or outmoded and perhaps invidious stereotypes. . . .

For the retarded, just as for Negroes and women, much has changed in recent years, but much remains the same; out-dated statutes are still on the books, and irrational fears or ignorance, traceable to the prolonged social and cultural isolation of the retarded, continue to stymie recognition of the dignity and individuality of retarded people. Heightened judicial scrutiny of action appearing to impose unnecessary barriers to the retarded is required in light of increasing recognition that such barriers are inconsistent with evolving principles of equality embedded in the Fourteenth Amendment.

COMMENTS AND QUESTIONS

1. How do you react to Justice White's explanation as to why classifications based on mental retardation should not receive heightened scrutiny? Consider how his analysis would apply to classifications based on race or sex. After all, by 1985 (the date of *Cleburne*), there were many laws addressing discrimination based on race or sex, but the Court continued to apply heightened scrutiny to such classifications.

2. Do you agree with Justice Stevens that really there is one form of scrutiny—rational relationship—but that its application simply yields different outcomes because of the underlying facts in each given case? Do you think it would promote more consistent outcomes to use such an approach? More accurate outcomes?

3. Justice Marshall's opinion is notable for telling it like it is—the Court's opinion is not the "rational basis" test as the Court had previously described and applied it. Marshall calls it "second order rational-basis review"; this author prefers "rational basis review with a bite" to distinguish it from the toothless rational basis review normally applied with respect to social and economic regulation. Can we discern an underlying principle (or principles) for when this heightened rational basis review should be used?

4. Marshall appears to agree with Justice Stevens that segregating levels of judicial scrutiny into three distinct categories—strict, intermediate, and rational basis—is wrong. How does his preferred approach differ from Justice Stevens'?

5. Edited from Justice Marshall's opinion is his history of discrimination against the intellectually disabled up to the then-present day. Those interested in that history should consult the full opinion.

6. Notwithstanding *Cleburne*'s heightened rational basis review regarding a law adversely affecting the intellectually disabled, in a later case the Court applied the more traditional rational basis review to a law that allowed the involuntary commitment of the intellectually disabled on different and less strict grounds than the mentally ill. The Court, in an opinion by Justice Kennedy, held by a 5–4 vote that the differential treatment met rational basis review because it was "reasonably conceivable" that violent behavior by the intellectually disabled was more easily predicted than such behavior by the mentally ill and because the treatment afforded the involuntarily committed mentally ill was more invasive and therefore should occur only under stricter standards. *See Heller v. Doe by Doe*, 509 U.S. 312 (1993).

4. SEXUAL ORIENTATION

In 1972 two gay activists in Minnesota attempted to obtain a marriage license. When it was denied because they were of the same sex, they challenged the denial as a violation of their First, Eighth, Ninth, and Fourteenth Amendment rights. In claiming a denial of equal protection, however, they asserted they were subject to sex discrimination, not discrimination on the basis of their sexual orientation. The case went to the Minnesota Supreme Court, which denied their claim. They then appealed to the United States Supreme Court. Without opinion the Supreme Court dismissed the appeal for want of a substantial federal question. *Baker v. Nelson*, 409 U.S. 810 (1972). Because such a dismissal is technically considered a decision on the merits, as opposed to a refusal to hear the case at all, that decision bound lower courts.

It was fourteen years later in *Bowers v. Hardwick*, 478 U.S. 186 (1986), considered earlier under substantive due process and the right of privacy, that the Court next addressed gay issues, but not with any better results from the perspective of the gay community. Rather it was *Romer v. Evans*, 517 U.S. 620 (1996), ten years after *Bowers* that marked a turning point. There, Colorado by referendum had amended the state constitution to prohibit the state government and any city or local government from enacting any law to ban discrimination on the basis of sexual orientation. The Supreme Court in an opinion by Justice Kennedy held that the constitutional amendment violated the Equal Protection Clause of the Fourteenth Amendment. Chief Justice Rehnquist and Justices Scalia and Thomas dissented. By its terms the opinion uses the rational relationship test and holds that the amendment "lacks a rational relationship to legitimate state interests." However, much like *Cleburne*, the opinion faults the defenders of the amendment for failure to supply a legitimate state interest furthered by the law, rather than placing the burden on the opponents to negative any possible legitimate state interest the amendment might further. And like Justice White in *Cleburne*, Justice Kennedy does not admit he is using anything other than normal rational relationship scrutiny. Nevertheless, he suggests that the amendment raises the "inevitable inference that the disadvantage imposed is born of animosity toward the class of persons affected. '[I]f the constitutional conception of 'equal protection of the laws' means anything, it must at the very least mean that a bare . . . desire to harm a politically unpopular group cannot constitute a *legitimate* governmental interest.' " Recall the Court's similar statement in *Cleburne*.

In *Lawrence v. Texas*, 539 U.S. 558 (2003), also considered earlier under substantive due process and the right of privacy, the Court struck down Texas's law banning homosexual sodomy but not on equal protection grounds. Justice O'Connor, however, concurred in the judgment because she believed that the law violated the equal protection rights of homosexuals. She analyzed the law under rational basis review, but citing *Cleburne* and *Romer*, she said:

> We have consistently held, however, that some objectives, such as "a bare . . . desire to harm a politically unpopular group," are not legitimate state interests. When a law exhibits such a desire to harm a politically unpopular group, we have applied a more searching form of rational basis review to strike down such laws under the Equal Protection Clause. . . . The statute at issue here makes sodomy a crime only if a person "engages in deviate sexual intercourse with another individual of the same sex." Sodomy between opposite-sex partners, however, is not a crime in Texas. That is, Texas treats the same conduct differently based solely on the participants. Those harmed by this law are people who have a same-sex sexual orientation and thus are more likely to engage in behavior prohibited. . . .
>
> Texas attempts to justify its law, and the effects of the law, by arguing that the statute satisfies rational basis review because it furthers the legitimate governmental interest of the promotion of morality. . . . Moral disapproval of this group, like a bare desire to harm the group, is an interest that is insufficient to satisfy rational basis review under the Equal Protection Clause. Indeed, we have never held that moral disapproval, without any other asserted state interest, is a sufficient rationale under the Equal Protection Clause to justify a law that discriminates among groups of persons. Moral disapproval of a group cannot be a legitimate governmental interest under the Equal Protection Clause because legal classifications must not be "drawn for the purpose of disadvantaging the group burdened by the law."

Cases challenging bans on same-sex marriage routinely raised both due process and equal protection claims, and beginning in about 2012 most of the lower courts found the bans unconstitutional under either substantive due process, using strict scrutiny, *see, e.g., Kitchen v. Herbert,*

755 F.3d 1193 (10th Cir. 2014); equal protection, using either the heightened rational relationship test of *Romer* and *Cleburne* in light of the historical animus directed at gays and lesbians, *see, e.g., Baskin v. Bogan*, 766 F.3d 648 (7th Cir. 2014) or strict scrutiny; or both, *see, e.g., Bostic v. Schaefer*, 760 F.3d 352 (4th Cir. 2014). The Supreme Court, of course, decided the issue in *Obergefell v. Hodges*, considered in the last chapter, under an amalgamation of due process and equal protection.

Today, an increasing issue is the treatment of transgender persons, and as always the question is what level of scrutiny should be applied to laws or government practices that harm them. At least three circuits have used the heightened, intermediate scrutiny applied to sex discrimination to discrimination against transgender persons. *See, e.g., Grimm v. Gloucester County School Board*, 972 F.3d 586 (4th Cir. 2020); *Glenn v. Brumby*, 663 F.3d 1312 (11th Cir. 2011); *Smith v. City of Salem*, 378 F.3d 566 (6th Cir.2004). The Supreme Court has yet to hear a constitutional case involving discrimination against transgender persons, but in *Bostock v. Clayton County*, 140 S.Ct. 1731 (2020), the Court concluded by a 6–3 vote that Title VII of the Civil Rights Act of 1964, banning discrimination in employment on the basis of sex (as well as other things), banned discrimination against homosexuals and transgender persons. Many were surprised that the Court's opinion was written by Justice Gorsuch, but his analysis purported to be that of a simple strict textualist. As he wrote, if a man is fired because he is sexually attracted to a man, while a woman would not be fired for being sexually attracted to a man, they are being treated differently on the basis of their sex. Similarly, "take an employer who fires a transgender person who was identified as a male at birth but who now identifies as a female. If the employer retains an otherwise identical employee who was identified as female at birth, the employer intentionally penalizes a person identified as male at birth for traits or actions that it tolerates in an employee identified as female at birth." The question necessarily arises now, whether the Court would use the same analysis for a constitutional challenge. That is, would governmental discrimination on the basis of sexual orientation or sexual identity be viewed as discrimination based on sex, for which there is ample Supreme Court precedent applying a heightened scrutiny, or would it be viewed as sui generis, subject possibly to a rational basis test or the heightened rational basis test used in *Romer v. Evans*?

PROBLEM

Some states have passed laws requiring persons to use the restrooms identified for the sex that is on their birth certificates, which would effectively prohibit transgender persons from using the restroom of the sex they identify as. Do these laws violate the Equal Protection Clause?

5. AGE AND POVERTY

Minimum age requirements and mandatory retirements both discriminate on the basis of age, but the Court has never found such requirements to merit any form of heightened scrutiny. In *Massachusetts Board of Retirement v. Murgia*, 427 U.S. 307 (1976), in the course of upholding Massachusetts's mandatory retirement age for state troopers at age 50, the Court explained that, while the elderly have been subject to discrimination, unlike gender and race, old age is not a characteristic which one is born with. Rather, it is a stage of life that everyone will experience.

At the height of the activist Warren Court there was dicta in cases suggesting that classifications based on poverty would be subject to searching scrutiny, but later in the one case in which the then-Burger Court actually addressed a law that explicitly treated low income persons differently, it was not willing to provide heightened scrutiny, and it upheld the classification. *See James v. Valtierra*, 402 U.S. 137 (1971)(upholding requirement of local referendum before a low-income housing project could be built).

E. DISCRIMINATION AGAINST THE EXERCISE OF FUNDAMENTAL RIGHTS

Up to this point in our consideration of equal protection, the focus has been on discrimination against some identified group of people, whether opticians, African-Americans, women, gays, or the aged. Discrimination against some groups results in some form of heightened scrutiny, while discrimination against others does not. The Warren Court, however, created a new category when heightened scrutiny—indeed, strict scrutiny—should apply: when government creates a category that interferes with the exercise of a fundamental right. Here, as we saw regarding substantive due process involving unenumerated rights, one major issue is what constitutes a fundamental right. Moreover, adding additional confusion, sometimes these "fundamental right" cases are analyzed under equal protection and sometimes under substantive due process without apparent distinctions. For example, *Eisenstadt v. Baird*, discussed earlier as an extension of *Griswold v. Connecticut*'s right to use contraceptives to the right of unmarried persons to have access to contraceptives, was actually decided under the rubric of equal protection— it was a denial of equal protection to treat unmarried persons differently from married persons with respect to a fundamental right to be able to use contraceptives. But, *Carey v. Population Services, International*, also discussed earlier as extending *Griswold* and *Eisenstadt* to persons under 16, was decided as a substantive due process case—denying a fundamental right without showing a close relationship to a significant state interest.

1. THE RIGHT TO VOTE

As important as voting is to a democratic polity, nowhere in the Constitution is there an enumerated "right to vote." While there are amendments that limit the ability of states to *deny* the vote for various reasons, the Constitution generally leaves the question of who may vote in federal elections up to the states. "Electors" (*i.e.*, voters) for Senators and Members of the House of Representatives shall be those people who can vote in state elections for "the most numerous branch of the state legislature," typically the state house of representatives or state legislative assembly, as opposed to the state senate. Article I, Sec. 2, cl. 1; Amendment XVII, cl 1. "Electors" for the President are to be appointed by each state "in such manner as the Legislature thereof may direct." Article II, Sec. 1, cl. 2. And nothing is said about qualifications for voting in state and local elections, other than prohibiting disqualification based upon race, sex, or the age of anyone eighteen years or older.

During the Warren Court's tenure, however, the Court proclaimed a fundamental right to vote as an unenumerated right in the Constitution, such that its denial would be viewed under strict scrutiny.

The development began with *Baker v. Carr* in 1962, in which the Court held that a challenge to the inequitable apportionment of state legislators presented a justiciable question, but there the Court did not reach the merits to hold that such an apportionment would indeed violate the Constitution. The next year the Court held that the so-called "county unit system" of counting votes in Georgia's Democratic primary violated the Equal Protection Clause. *Gray v. Sanders*, 372 U.S. 368 (1963). Whereas *Baker* had involved legislative districting, *Gray* involved the actual methodology of vote counting that resulted in rural counties having more votes to cast for a candidate than their populations suggested. The Court concluded:

> How then can one person be given twice or 10 times the voting power of another person in a statewide election merely because he lives in a rural area or because he lives in the smallest rural county? Once the geographical unit for which a representative is to be chosen is designated, all who participate in the election are to have an equal vote—whatever their race, whatever their sex, whatever their occupation, whatever their income, and wherever their home may be in that geographical unit. This is required by the Equal Protection Clause of the Fourteenth Amendment. . . . The conception of political equality from the Declaration of Independence, to Lincoln's Gettysburg Address, to the Fifteenth, Seventeenth, and Nineteenth Amendments can mean only one thing—one person, one vote.

The following year the Court reached the merits on the question of apportioning legislative districts in the following case.

REYNOLDS V. SIMS

United States Supreme Court, 1964.
377 U.S. 533, 84 S.Ct. 1362.

MR. CHIEF JUSTICE WARREN delivered the opinion of the Court.

[O]n August 26, 1961, [r]esidents, taxpayers and voters of Jefferson County, Alabama, filed a complaint in the United States District Court for the Middle District of Alabama, in their own behalf and on behalf of all similarly situated Alabama voters, challenging the apportionment of the Alabama Legislature. . . . The complaint alleged a deprivation of rights under the Alabama Constitution and under the Equal Protection Clause of the Fourteenth Amendment. . . .

Plaintiffs below alleged that the last apportionment of the Alabama Legislature was based on the 1900 federal census, despite the requirement of the State Constitution that the legislature be reapportioned decennially. They asserted that, since the population growth in the State from 1900 to 1960 had been uneven, Jefferson and other counties were now victims of serious discrimination with respect to the allocation of legislative representation. As a result of the failure of the legislature to reapportion itself, plaintiffs asserted, they were denied "equal suffrage in free and equal elections * * * and the equal protection of the laws" in violation of the Alabama Constitution and the Fourteenth Amendment to the Federal Constitution. . . .

On July 21, 1962, the District Court held that the inequality of the existing representation in the Alabama Legislature violated the Equal Protection Clause of the Fourteenth Amendment, a finding which the Court noted had been "generally conceded" by the parties to the litigation, since population growth and shifts had converted the 1901 scheme, as perpetuated some 60 years later, into an invidiously discriminatory plan completely lacking in rationality. Under the existing provisions, applying 1960 census figures, only 25.1% of the State's total population resided in districts represented by a majority of the members of the Senate, and only 25.7% lived in counties which could elect a majority of the members of the House of Representatives. Population-variance ratios of up to about 41-to-1 existed in the Senate, and up to about 16-to-1 in the House. Bullock County, with a population of only 13,462, and Henry County, with a population of only 15,286, each were allocated two seats in the Alabama House, whereas Mobile County, with a population of 314,301, was given only three seats, and Jefferson County, with 634,864 people, had only seven representatives. With respect to senatorial apportionment, since the pertinent Alabama constitutional provisions had been consistently construed as prohibiting the giving of more than one Senate seat to any one county, Jefferson County, with over 600,000 people, was given only one senator, as was Lowndes County, with a 1960 population of only 15,417, and Wilcox County, with only 18,739 people. . . .

Undeniably the Constitution of the United States protects the right of all qualified citizens to vote, in state as well as in federal elections. A consistent line of decisions by this Court in cases involving attempts to deny or restrict the right of suffrage has made this indelibly clear. It has been repeatedly recognized that all qualified voters have a constitutionally protected right to vote and to have their votes counted. . . . The right to vote can neither be denied outright, nor destroyed by alteration of ballots, nor diluted by ballot-box stuffing. . . . Racially based gerrymandering and the conducting of white primaries, both of which result in denying to some citizens their right to vote, have been held to be constitutionally impermissible. And history has seen a continuing expansion of the scope of the right of suffrage in this country. The right to vote freely for the candidate of one's choice is of the essence of a democratic society, and any restrictions on that right strike at the heart of representative government. And the right of suffrage can be denied by a debasement or dilution of the weight of a citizen's vote just as effectively as by wholly prohibiting the free exercise of the franchise. . . .

Undoubtedly, the right of suffrage is a fundamental matter in a free and democratic society. Especially since the right to exercise the franchise in a free and unimpaired manner is preservative of other basic civil and political rights, any alleged infringement of the right of citizens to vote must be carefully and meticulously scrutinized. . . .

Legislators represent people, not trees or acres. Legislators are elected by voters, not farms or cities or economic interests. As long as ours is a representative form of government, and our legislatures are those instruments of government elected directly by and directly representative of the people, the right to elect legislators in a free and unimpaired fashion is a bedrock of our political system. It could hardly be gainsaid that a constitutional claim had been asserted by an allegation that certain otherwise qualified voters had been entirely prohibited from voting for members of their state legislature. And, if a State should provide that the votes of citizens in one part of the State should be given two times, or five times, or 10 times the weight of votes of citizens in another part of the State, it could hardly be contended that the right to vote of those residing in the disfavored areas had not been effectively diluted. It would appear extraordinary to suggest that a State could be constitutionally permitted to enact a law providing that certain of the State's voters could vote two, five, or 10 times for their legislative representatives, while voters living elsewhere could vote only once. And it is inconceivable that a state law to the effect that, in counting votes for legislators, the votes of citizens in one part of the State would be multiplied by two, five, or 10, while the votes of persons in another area would be counted only at face value, could be constitutionally sustainable. Of course, the effect of state legislative districting schemes which give the same number of representatives to unequal numbers of constituents is identical. Overweighting and overvaluation of the votes of those living here has the certain effect of dilution and undervaluation of the votes of those living there. The resulting discrimination against those individual voters living in disfavored areas is easily demonstrable mathematically. Their right to vote is simply not the same right to vote as that of those living in a favored part of the State. Two, five, or 10 of them must vote before the effect of their voting is equivalent to that of their favored neighbor. Weighting the votes of citizens differently, by any method or means, merely because of where they happen to reside, hardly seems justifiable. . . .

Logically, in a society ostensibly grounded on representative government, it would seem reasonable that a majority of the people of a State could elect a majority of that State's legislators. . . . Since legislatures are responsible for enacting laws by which all citizens are to be governed, they should be bodies which are collectively responsive to the popular will. And the concept of equal protection has been traditionally viewed as requiring the uniform treatment of persons standing in the same relation to the governmental action questioned or challenged. With respect to the allocation of legislative representation, all voters, as citizens of a State, stand in the same relation regardless of where they live. Any suggested criteria for the differentiation of citizens are insufficient to justify any discrimination, as to the weight of their votes, unless relevant to the permissible purposes of legislative apportionment. Since the achieving of fair and effective representation for all citizens is concededly the basic aim of legislative apportionment, we conclude that the Equal Protection Clause guarantees the opportunity for equal participation by all voters in the election of state legislators. Diluting the weight of votes because of place of residence impairs basic constitutional rights under the Fourteenth Amendment just as much as invidious discriminations based upon factors such as race. . . .

We hold that, as a basic constitutional standard, the Equal Protection Clause requires that the seats in both houses of a bicameral state legislature must be apportioned on a population basis. Simply stated, an individual's right to vote for state legislators is unconstitutionally impaired when its weight is in a substantial fashion diluted when compared with votes of citizens living on other parts of the State. . . .

[Alabama proposed a plan that] at least superficially resembles the scheme of legislative representation followed in the Federal Congress. Under this plan, each of Alabama's 67 counties is allotted one senator, and no counties are given more than one Senate seat. Arguably, this is analogous to the allocation of two Senate seats, in the Federal Congress, to each of the 50 States, regardless of population. Seats in the Alabama House, under the proposed constitutional amendment, are distributed by giving each of the 67 counties at least one, with the remaining 39 seats being allotted among the more populous counties on a population basis. This scheme, at least at first glance, appears to resemble that prescribed for the Federal House of Representatives, where the 435 seats are distributed among the States on a population basis, although each State, regardless of its population, is given at least one Congressman. . . .

Much has been written . . . about the applicability of the so-called federal analogy to state legislative apportionment arrangements. After considering the matter, the court below concluded that no conceivable analogy could be drawn between the federal scheme and the apportionment of seats in the Alabama Legislature under the proposed [plan]. We agree with the District Court, and find the federal analogy inapposite and irrelevant to state legislative districting schemes. . . .

The system of representation in the two Houses of the Federal Congress is one ingrained in our Constitution, as part of the law of the land. It is one conceived out of compromise and concession indispensable to the establishment of our federal republic. Arising from unique historical circumstances, it is based on the consideration that in establishing our type of federalism a group of formerly independent States bound themselves together under one national government. . . . [A]t the time of the inception of the system of representation in the Federal Congress, a compromise between the larger and smaller States on this matter averted a deadlock in the Constitutional Convention which had threatened to abort the birth of our Nation. . . .

Political subdivisions of States—counties, cities, or whatever—never were and never have been considered as sovereign entities. Rather, they have been traditionally regarded as subordinate governmental instrumentalities created by the State to assist in the carrying out of state governmental functions. . . . The relationship of the States to the Federal Government could hardly be less analogous. . . .

Since we find the so-called federal analogy inapposite to a consideration of the constitutional validity of state legislative apportionment schemes, we necessarily hold that the Equal Protection Clause requires both houses of a state legislature to be apportioned on a population basis. . . .

MR. JUSTICE CLARK, concurring in the affirmance. [opinion omitted]

MR. JUSTICE STEWART concurring in the judgment [opinion omitted]

MR. JUSTICE HARLAN, dissenting.

In these cases the Court holds that seats in the legislatures of six States are apportioned in ways that violate the Federal Constitution.

Under the Court's ruling it is bound to follow that the legislatures in all but a few of the other 44 States will meet the same fate. These decisions, with . . . *Gray v. Sanders*, . . . have the effect of placing basic aspects of state political systems under the pervasive overlordship of the federal judiciary. Once again, I must register my protest.

Today's holding is that the Equal Protection Clause of the Fourteenth Amendment requires every State to structure its legislature so that all the members of each house represent substantially the same number of people; other factors may be given play only to the extent that they do not significantly encroach on this basic "population" principle. Whatever may be thought of this holding as a piece of political ideology—and even on that score the political history and practices of this country from its earliest beginnings leave wide room for debate—I think it demonstrable that the Fourteenth Amendment does not impose this political tenet on the States or authorize this Court to do so.

The Court's constitutional discussion . . . is remarkable . . . for its failure to address itself at all to the Fourteenth Amendment as a whole or to the legislative history of the Amendment pertinent to the matter at hand. Stripped of aphorisms, the Court's argument boils down to the assertion that appellees' right to vote has been invidiously "debased" or "diluted" by systems of apportionment which entitle them to vote for fewer legislators than other voters, an assertion which is tied to the Equal Protection Clause only by the constitutionally frail tautology that "equal" means "equal."

Had the Court paused to probe more deeply into the matter, it would have found that the Equal Protection Clause was never intended to inhibit the States in choosing any democratic method they pleased for the apportionment of their legislatures. This is shown by the language of the Fourteenth Amendment taken as a whole, by the understanding of those who proposed and ratified it, and by the political practices of the States at the time the Amendment was adopted. It is confirmed by numerous state and congressional actions since the adoption of the Fourteenth Amendment, and by the common understanding of the Amendment as evidenced by subsequent constitutional amendments and decisions of this Court before *Baker v. Carr* made an abrupt break with the past in 1962.

The failure of the Court to consider any of these matters cannot be excused or explained by any concept of "developing" constitutionalism. It is meaningless to speak of constitutional "development" when both the language and history of the controlling provisions of the Constitution are wholly ignored. Since it can, I think, be shown beyond doubt that state legislative apportionments, as such, are wholly free of constitutional limitations, save such as may be imposed by the Republican Form of Government Clause (Const., Art. IV, s 4), the Court's action now bringing them within the purview of the Fourteenth Amendment amounts to nothing less than an exercise of the amending power by this Court.

So far as the Federal Constitution is concerned, the complaints in these cases should all have been dismissed below for failure to state a cause of action, because what has been alleged or proved shows no violation of any constitutional right. . . .

A. *The Language of the Fourteenth Amendment.*

The Court relies exclusively on that portion of § 1 of the Fourteenth Amendment which provides that no State shall "deny to any person within its jurisdiction the equal protection of the laws," and disregards entirely the significance of § 2. . . . Whatever one might take to be the application of these cases of the Equal Protection Clause if it stood alone, I am unable to understand the Court's utter disregard of the second section which expressly recognizes the States' power to deny "or in any way" abridge the right of their inhabitants to vote for "the members of the (State) Legislature," and its express provision of a remedy for such denial or abridgment. The comprehensive scope of the second section and its particular reference to the state legislatures preclude the suggestion that the first section was intended to have the result reached by the Court today. If indeed the words of the Fourteenth Amendment speak for themselves, as the majority's disregard of history seems to imply, they speak as clearly as may be against the construction which the majority puts on them. But we are not limited to the language of the Amendment itself.

B. *Proposal and Ratification of the Amendment.*

The history of the adoption of the Fourteenth Amendment provides conclusive evidence that neither those who proposed nor those who ratified the Amendment believed that the Equal Protection Clause limited the power of the States to apportion their legislatures as they saw fit. Moreover, the history demonstrate that the intention to leave this power undisturbed was deliberate and was widely believed to be essential to the adoption of the Amendment. [The extensive history is omitted.]

The facts recited above show beyond any possible doubt:

(1) that Congress, with full awareness of and attention to the possibility that the States would not afford full equality in voting rights to all their citizens, nevertheless deliberately chose not to interfere with the States' plenary power in this regard when it proposed the Fourteenth Amendment;

(2) that Congress did not include in the Fourteenth Amendment restrictions on the States' power to control voting rights because it believed that if such restrictions were included, the Amendment would not be adopted; and

(3) that at least a substantial majority, if not all, of the States which ratified the Fourteenth Amendment did not consider that in so doing, they were accepting limitations on their freedom, never before questioned, to regulate voting rights as they chose.

Even if one were to accept the majority's belief that it is proper entirely to disregard the unmistakable implications of the second section of the Amendment in construing the first section, one is confounded by its disregard of all this history. There is here none of the difficulty which may attend the application of basic principles to situations not contemplated or understood when the principles were framed. The problems which concern the Court now were problems when the Amendment was adopted. By the deliberate choice of those responsible for the Amendment, it left those problems untouched.

C.   After 1868.

The years following 1868, far from indicating a developing awareness of the applicability of the Fourteenth Amendment to problems of apportionment, demonstrate precisely the reverse: that the States retained and exercised the power independently to apportion their legislatures. . . .

D.   Today.

Since the Court now invalidates the legislative apportionments in six States, and has so far upheld the apportionment in none, it is scarcely necessary to comment on the situation in the States today, which is of course, as fully contrary to the Court's decision as is the record of every prior period in this Nation's history. As of 1961, the Constitutions of all but 11 States, roughly 20% of the total, recognized bases of apportionment other than geographic spread of population, and to some extent favored sparsely populated areas by a variety of devices, ranging from straight area representation or guaranteed minimum area representation to complicated schemes of the kind exemplified by the provisions of New York's Constitution of 1894, still in effect until struck down by the Court today. . . .

E.   Other Factors.

In this summary of what the majority ignores, note should be taken of the Fifteenth and Nineteenth Amendments. The former prohibited the States from denying or abridging the right to vote "on account of race, color, or previous condition of servitude." The latter, certified as part of the Constitution in 1920, added sex to the prohibited classifications. . . .

If constitutional amendment was the only means by which all men and, later, women, could be guaranteed the right to vote at all, even for federal officers, how can it be that the far less obvious right to a particular kind of apportionment of state legislatures . . . can be conferred by judicial construction of the Fourteenth Amendment? Yet, unless one takes the highly implausible view that the Fourteenth Amendment controls methods of apportionment but leaves the right to vote itself unprotected, the conclusion is inescapable that the Court has, for purposes of these cases, relegated the Fifteenth and Nineteenth Amendments to the same limbo of constitutional anachronisms to which the second section of the Fourteenth Amendment has been assigned. . . .

The Court's elaboration of its new "constitutional" doctrine indicates how far—and how unwisely—it has strayed from the appropriate bounds of its authority. The consequence of today's decision is that in all but the handful of States which may already satisfy the new requirements the local District Court or, it may be, the state courts, are given blanket authority and the constitutional duty to supervise apportionment of the State Legislatures. It is difficult to imagine a more intolerable and inappropriate interference by the judiciary with the independent legislatures of the States. . . .

Finally, these decisions give support to a current mistaken view of the Constitution and the constitutional function of this Court. This view, in a nutshell, is that every major social ill in this country can find its cure in some constitutional "principle," and that this Court should "take the lead" in promoting reform when other branches of government fail to act. The Constitution is not a panacea for every blot upon the public welfare, nor should this Court, ordained as a judicial body, be thought of as a general haven for reform movements. The Constitution is an instrument of government, fundamental to which is the premise that in a diffusion of governmental authority lies the greatest promise that this Nation will realize liberty for all its citizens. This Court, limited in function in accordance with that premise, does not serve its high purpose when it exceeds its authority, even to satisfy justified impatience with the slow workings of the political process. For when, in the name of constitutional interpretation, the Court adds something to the Constitution that was deliberately excluded from it, the Court in reality substitutes its view of what should be so for the amending process. . . .

COMMENTS AND QUESTIONS

1.   What suffices to satisfy the one person-one vote requirement is often unclear. Most recently, in *Evenwel v. Abbott*, 578 U.S. 54 (2016), the Court summarized the state of the law as follows:

> States must draw congressional districts with populations as close to perfect equality as possible. But, when drawing state and local legislative districts, jurisdictions are permitted to deviate somewhat from perfect population equality to accommodate traditional districting objectives, among them, preserving the integrity of political subdivisions, maintaining communities of interest, and creating geographic compactness. Where the maximum population

deviation between the largest and smallest district is less than 10%, the Court has held, a state or local legislative map presumptively complies with the one-person, one-vote rule. Maximum deviations above 10% are presumptively impermissible.

In *Evenwel*, it faced a new question: what is the correct population base when comparing different districts—the total population of the different districts or the registered voter or voter eligible population of the different districts? In *Evenwel*, the state used total population and the deviation between districts was below 10%. However, if one measured those districts by their voter eligible populations, the deviation would have reached 40% between some districts. Some voters challenged the use of total population, saying the correct metric should be the voter eligible population. The Supreme Court rejected the challenge. It found that history, precedent, and practice demonstrated that it is plainly permissible for jurisdictions to measure equalization by the total population of state and local legislative districts. In this way, the voters in each district have the power to elect a representative who represents the same number of constituents as all other representatives. The Court did not decide, however, whether using voter eligible populations might also be permissible, but it was clearly not required.

HARPER v. VIRGINIA STATE BOARD OF ELECTIONS

United States Supreme Court, 1966.
383 U.S. 663, 86 S.Ct. 1079.

JUSTICE DOUGLAS delivered the opinion of the Court.

These are suits by Virginia residents to have declared unconstitutional Virginia's poll tax.

While the right to vote in federal elections is conferred by Art. I, § 2, of the Constitution, the right to vote in state elections is nowhere expressly mentioned. [However,] once the franchise is granted to the electorate, lines may not be drawn which are inconsistent with the Equal Protection Clause of the Fourteenth Amendment. . . .

We conclude that a State violates the Equal Protection Clause of the Fourteenth Amendment whenever it makes the affluence of the voter or payment of any fee an electoral standard. Voter qualifications have no relation to wealth nor to paying or not paying this or any other tax. Our cases demonstrate that the Equal Protection Clause of the Fourteenth Amendment restrains the States from fixing voter qualifications which invidiously discriminate. . . .

Long ago in *Yick Wo v. Hopkins*, the Court referred to "the political franchise of voting" as a "fundamental political right, because preservative of all rights." Recently in *Reynolds v. Sims*, 377 U.S. 533 (1964) [mandating the one person/one vote requirement], we said, "Undoubtedly, the right of suffrage is a fundamental matter in a free and democratic society. Especially since the right to exercise the franchise in a free and unimpaired manner is preservative of other basic civil and political rights, any alleged infringement of the right of citizens to vote must be carefully and meticulously scrutinized." . . .

We say the same whether the citizen, otherwise qualified to vote, has $1.50 in his pocket or nothing at all, pays the fee or fails to pay it. The principle that denies the State the right to dilute a citizen's vote on account of his economic status or other such factors by analogy bars a system which excludes those unable to pay a fee to vote or who fail to pay.

[T]o introduce wealth or payment of a fee as a measure of a voter's qualifications is to introduce a capricious or irrelevant factor. The degree of the discrimination is irrelevant. In this context—that is, as a condition of obtaining a ballot—the requirement of fee paying causes an "invidious" discrimination that runs afoul of the Equal Protection Clause.

We agree, of course, with Mr. Justice Holmes that the Due Process Clause of the Fourteenth Amendment "does not enact Mr. Herbert Spencer's Social Statics." Likewise, the Equal Protection Clause is not shackled to the political theory of a particular era. In determining what lines are unconstitutionally discriminatory, we have never been confined to historic notions of equality, any more than we have restricted due process to a fixed catalogue of what was at a given time deemed to be the limits of fundamental rights. Notions of what constitutes equal treatment for purposes of the Equal Protection Clause do change. This Court in 1896 held that laws providing for separate public facilities for white and Negro citizens did not deprive the latter of the equal protection and treatment that the Fourteenth Amendment commands. Seven of the eight Justices then sitting subscribed to the Court's opinion, thus joining in expressions of what constituted unequal and discriminatory treatment that sound strange to a contemporary ear. . . .

We have long been mindful that where fundamental rights and liberties are asserted under the Equal Protection Clause, classifications which might invade or restrain them must be closely scrutinized and carefully confined.

Those principles apply here. For to repeat, wealth or fee paying has, in our view, no relation to voting qualifications; the right to vote is too precious, too fundamental to be so burdened or conditioned.

MR. JUSTICE BLACK, dissenting.

In *Breedlove v. Suttles*, 302 U.S. 277, decided December 6, 1937, a few weeks after I took my seat as a member of this Court, we unanimously upheld the right of the State of Georgia to make payment of its state poll tax a prerequisite to voting in state elections. We rejected at that time contentions that the state law violated the Equal Protection Clause of the Fourteenth Amendment because it put an unequal burden on different groups of people according to their age, sex, and ability to pay. . . .

Believing at that time that the Court had properly respected the limitation of its power under the Equal Protection Clause and was right in rejecting the equal protection argument, I joined the Court's judgment and opinion. Later, I joined the Court's judgment in *Butler v. Thompson*, 341 U.S. 937 (1951), upholding, over the dissent of Mr. Justice Douglas, the Virginia state poll tax law challenged here against the same equal protection challenges. Since the *Breedlove* and *Butler* cases were decided the Federal Constitution has not been amended in the only way it could constitutionally have been, that is, as provided in Article V of the Constitution. I would adhere to the holding of those cases. The Court, however, overrules *Breedlove* in part, but its opinion reveals that it does so not by using its limited power to interpret the original meaning of the Equal Protection Clause, but by giving that clause a new meaning which it believes represents a better governmental policy. From this action I dissent.

It should be pointed out at once that the Court's decision is to no extent based on a finding that the Virginia law as written or as applied is being used as a device or mechanism to deny Negro citizens of Virginia the right to vote on account of their color. Apparently the Court agrees with the District Court below and with my Brothers HARLAN and STEWART that this record would not support any finding that the Virginia poll tax law the Court invalidates has any such effect. If the record could support a finding that the law as written or applied has such an effect, the law would of course be unconstitutional as a violation of the Fourteenth and Fifteenth Amendments. . . . What the Court does hold is that the Equal Protection Clause necessarily bars all States from making payment of a state tax, any tax, a prerequisite to voting.

I think the interpretation that this Court gave the Equal Protection Clause in *Breedlove* was correct. The mere fact that a law results in treating some groups differently from others does not, of course, automatically amount to a violation of the Equal Protection Clause. . . . Voting laws are no exception to this principle. All voting laws treat some persons differently from others in some respects. Some bar a person from voting who is under 21 years of age; others bar those under 18. Some bar convicted felons or the insane, and some have attached a freehold or other property qualification for voting. The *Breedlove* case upheld a poll tax which was imposed on men but was not equally imposed on women and minors, and the Court today does not overrule that part of *Breedlove* which approved those discriminatory provisions. And in *Lassiter v. Northampton Election Board*, 360 U.S. 45 (1959), this Court held that state laws which disqualified the illiterate from voting did not violate the Equal Protection Clause. From these cases and all the others decided by this Court interpreting the Equal Protection Clause it is clear that some discriminatory voting qualifications can be imposed without violating the Equal Protection Clause.

A study of our cases shows that this Court has refused to use the general language of the Equal Protection Clause as though it provided a handy instrument to strike down state laws which the Court feels are based on bad governmental policy. The equal protection cases carefully analyzed boil down to the principle that distinctions drawn and even discriminations imposed by state laws do not violate the Equal Protection Clause so long as these distinctions and discriminations are not "irrational," "irrelevant," "unreasonable," "arbitrary," or "invidious." These vague and indefinite terms do not, of course, provide a precise formula or an automatic mechanism for deciding cases arising under the Equal Protection Clause. The restrictive connotations of these terms, however . . ., are a plain recognition of the fact that under a proper interpretation of the Equal Protection Clause States are to have the broadest kind of leeway in areas where they have a general constitutional competence to act. In view of the purpose of the terms to restrain the courts from a wholesale invalidation of state laws under the Equal Protection Clause it would be difficult to say that the poll tax requirement is "irrational" or "arbitrary" or works "invidious discriminations." State poll tax legislation can "reasonably," "rationally" and without an "invidious" or evil purpose to injure anyone be found to rest on a number of state policies including (1) the State's desire to collect its revenue, and (2) its belief that voters who pay a poll tax will be interested in furthering the State's welfare when they vote. Certainly it is rational to believe that people may be more likely to pay taxes if payment is a prerequisite to voting. And if history can be a factor in determining the "rationality" of discrimination in a state law . . ., then whatever may be our personal opinion, history is on the side of "rationality" of the State's poll tax policy. Property qualifications existed in the Colonies and were continued by many States after the Constitution was adopted. Although I join the Court in disliking the policy of the poll tax, this is not in my judgment a justifiable reason for holding this poll tax law unconstitutional. Such a holding on my part would, in my judgment, be an exercise of power which the Constitution does not confer upon me. . . .

The Court's justification for consulting its own notions rather than following the original meaning of the Constitution, as I would, apparently is based on the belief of the majority of the Court that for this Court to be bound by the original meaning of the Constitution is an intolerable and debilitating evil; . . . that to save the country from the original Constitution the Court must have constant power to renew it and keep it abreast of this Court's more enlightening theories of what is best for our society. [W]hen a "political theory" embodied in our Constitution becomes outdated, it seems to me that a majority of the nine members of this Court are not only without constitutional power but are far less qualified to choose a new constitutional political theory than the people of this country proceeding in the manner provided by Article V.

MR. JUSTICE HARLAN, whom MR. JUSTICE STEWART joins, dissenting.

The final demise of state poll taxes, already totally proscribed by the Twenty-Fourth Amendment with respect to federal elections and abolished by the States themselves in all but four States with respect to state elections, is perhaps in itself not of great moment. But that fact that the coup de grace has been administered by this Court instead of being left to the affected States or to the federal political process should be a matter of continuing concern to all interested in maintaining the proper role of this tribunal under our scheme of government. . . .

The Equal Protection Clause prevents States from arbitrarily treating people differently under their laws. Whether any such differing treatment is to be deemed arbitrary depends on whether or not it reflects an appropriate differentiating classification among those affected; the clause has never been thought to require equal treatment of all persons despite differing circumstances. The test evolved by this Court for determining whether an asserted justifying classification exists is whether such a classification can be deemed to be founded on some rational and otherwise constitutionally permissible state policy. . . .

But today in holding unconstitutional state poll taxes and property qualifications for voting . . ., the Court reverts to the highly subjective judicial approach manifested by *Reynolds*. In substance the Court's analysis of the equal protection issue goes no further than to say that the electoral franchise is "precious" and "fundamental," and to conclude that "(t)o introduce wealth or payment of a fee as a measure of a voter's qualifications is to introduce a capricious or irrelevant factor." These are of course captivating phrases, but they are wholly inadequate to satisfy the standard governing adjudication of the equal protection issue: Is there a rational basis for Virginia's poll tax as a voting qualification? I think the answer to that question is undoubtedly yes.

Property qualifications and poll taxes have been a traditional part of our political structure. . . . Over the years these and other restrictions were gradually lifted, primarily because popular theories of political representation had changed. Often restrictions were lifted only after wide public debate. The issue of woman suffrage, for example, raised question of family relationships, of participation in public affairs, of the very nature of the type of society in which Americans wished to live; eventually a consensus was reached, which culminated in the Nineteenth Amendment no more than 45 years ago.

Similarly with property qualifications, it is only by fiat that it can be said, especially in the context of American history, that there can be no rational debate as to their advisability. . . .

Property and poll-tax qualifications, very simply, are not in accord with current egalitarian notions of how a modern democracy should be organized. It is of course entirely fitting that legislatures should modify the law to reflect such changes in popular attitudes. However, it is all wrong, in my view, for the Court to adopt the political doctrines popularly accepted at a particular moment of our history and to declare all others to be irrational and invidious, barring them from the range of choice by reasonably minded people acting through the political process. . . .

COMMENTS AND QUESTIONS

1. As one can see from the dissent in *Harper*, the idea that the Equal Protection Clause protects an equal right to vote is a relatively modern conception, arising like so many other rights found during the heyday of the Warren Court. The Court never did abolish literacy tests, so that its decision in *Lassiter* still stands, but Congress in the 1965 Voting Rights Act made them illegal, and the Court upheld this prohibition in light of Congress's findings that such tests had been used to deny African-Americans the ability to vote. *See South Carolina v. Katzenbach*, 383 U.S. 301 (1966).

2. A number of cases followed *Harper* with like results. In *Kramer v. Union Free School Dist.*, 395 U.S. 621 (1969), the Court struck down New York's law that restricted voters in school district elections to those who were parents of children in the schools or who were owners of or renters in taxable real property. Applying strict scrutiny, the Court found the state's claimed interest in having persons primarily interested or affected by school district decisions be those who chose the district's leaders was not narrowly tailored. Its voting restriction would still allow some people who were uninterested in the schools to have a vote while denying some who were interested from voting. In the same year, the Court found a property ownership requirement for voting in a local municipal utility bond issuance election to be unconstitutional. *See Cipriano v. Houma*, 395 U.S. 701 (1969). Here, indeed, the requirement seemed tenuous, because the bonds would be paid out of the utility's revenues, not property taxes, but the next year the Court also struck down a requirement that voters be property owners in an election on general obligation bonds paid largely through property taxes. *See Phoenix v. Kolodziejski*, 399 U.S. 204 (1970). The routine application of strict scrutiny appears to have ended with *Salyer Land Co. v. Tulare Lake Basin Water Storage Dist.*, 410 U.S. 719 (1973), in which the Court in an opinion by Justice Rehnquist, over the dissents of three justices, held that voters in a special purpose water storage district could be limited to landowners in the district and whose votes would be proportioned according to the assessed valuation of their land. The Court did not use strict scrutiny in light of the district's "special limited purpose and of the disproportionate effect of its activities on landowners as a group." In *Burdick v. Takushi*, 504 U.S. 428 (1992), the Court upheld Hawaii's prohibition on write-in voting. The Court said it was an erroneous assumption that a law imposing any burden on the right to vote must be subjected to strict scrutiny. Rather, a court "must weigh the character and magnitude of the asserted injury to the [voting] rights . . . against the precise interests put forward by the State as justifications for the burden imposed by its rule, taking into consideration the extent to which those interests make it necessary to burden the plaintiff's rights." Thus, if the law imposes "severe restrictions" on the

voting right, then the scrutiny becomes strict, but when the law only imposes "reasonable, nondiscriminatory restrictions," the State's "important regulatory interests are generally sufficient" to justify the restrictions.

3.   Today one of the major issues with respect to voting rights and equal protection is the imposition of voter ID laws. These laws, purportedly to address possible voter fraud at the polls, require specified forms of identification in order for a person to cast a vote at the polls. An early challenge to an Indiana law that had been passed on a straight party-line vote was unsuccessful, but the Court could not muster a majority opinion, although the plurality and concurring opinion both cited *Burdick*'s methodology for assessing restrictions on voters' right. *See Crawford v. Marion County Election Bd.*, 553 U.S. 181 (2008). Lower courts have subsequently been struggling with the issue, and the Supreme Court has yet to resolve it.

4.   In addition to the numerous cases involving a right to vote, there is also a substantial body of law relating to access to the ballot. The Court has said that restrictions on access to the ballot:

> burden two distinct and fundamental rights, "the right of individuals to associate for the advancement of political beliefs, and the right of qualified voters, regardless of their political persuasion to cast their votes effectively." The freedom to associate as a political party, a right we have recognized as fundamental, has diminished practical value if the party can be kept off the ballot. Access restrictions also implicate the right to vote because absent recourse to referendums, "voters can assert their preferences only through candidates or parties or both." By limiting the choices available to voters, the State impairs the voters' ability to express their political preferences.

Ill. State Bd. of Elections v. Socialist Workers Party, 440 U.S. 173, 184 (1979). Consequently, the Court said that a "State must establish that its classification is necessary to serve a compelling interest." *Id.* In other words, the classification is subject to strict scrutiny. At the same time, the Court has recognized that states have a legitimate (and presumably compelling) interest in limiting the number of candidates on a ballot in order to avoid confusion. Where the classification was totally illogical (as in *Ill. State Bd.*, where it took more signatures to get on the local Chicago ballot than on the statewide Illinois ballot) or where the classification was based on an illegitimate interest (as in *Williams v. Rhodes*, 393 U.S. 23 (1968), where the purpose of the law was to restrict the ballot to the two major parties), a decision that the classification failed strict scrutiny was easy. However, the inevitable line drawing involved in establishing who has demonstrated enough support to justify being listed on the ballot has resulted in the same lessened strictness of scrutiny reflected in *Burdick* above with respect to voting rights.

5.   Over the past twenty-five years, there have been a number of cases claiming that partisan gerrymandering of electoral districts violates the Constitution and in particular the Equal Protection Clause. The Supreme Court rejected all of the claims but struggled with attempting to determine the

limits, if any, the Constitution sets on the gerrymandering of voters along partisan lines. Historically, the Court has said that it is not unconstitutional to consider partisan effects in drawing districts, but that it might be unconstitutional if the partisan effects are too great. The difficulty was in creating a "clear, manageable, and politically neutral" test for determining how great would be too great. The case of *Rucho v. Common Cause*, 139 S.Ct. 2484 (2019)(considered earlier in Chapter 2 regarding the Political Question Doctrine), ended (at least until a different majority makes up the Court) this struggle. In *Rucho*, the Court by a 5–4 vote held that the issue was a non-justiciable political question because there was no judicially discoverable and manageable standard for answering that question. Thus, the Court did not resolve when gerrymanders would be unconstitutional and left the problem to Congress and the states to address.

6.   Finally, there is *Bush v. Gore*, 531 U.S. 98 (2000), the case that decided the 2000 Presidential election. There seven justices concluded that the recount ordered by the Florida Supreme Court would violate Equal Protection, because votes from one locality in Florida could be counted in a different manner than votes in another locality. While such differences are widespread in ordinary elections, the Court distinguished them by saying this was "the special instance of a statewide recount under the authority of a single state judicial officer. Our consideration is limited to the present circumstances. . . ." The Court went on to say that it was not questioning "whether local entities, in the exercise of their expertise, may develop different systems for implementing elections. Instead, we are presented with a situation where a state court with the power to assure uniformity has ordered a statewide recount with minimal procedural safeguards." *Bush v. Gore* has been criticized from a number of perspectives, not the least of which is the failure to explain why a state, which has the power to assure uniformity in elections throughout the state but instead leaves it to local jurisdictions to determine how to count votes, is different from the statewide recount ordered by the Florida Supreme Court which left to the local jurisdictions how to make the recount. In any case, *Bush v. Gore* has not had much traction in subsequent voting cases.

2.   EQUAL ACCESS TO THE COURTS

Over the entrance to the Supreme Court is the phrase, "Equal Justice Under Law." One might argue today that those who cannot afford a highly successful, private defense attorney and must rely on a public defender to defend them in a criminal case do not receive equal justice under law as a matter of fact. Whatever the truth of that argument, there was a time within the memory of those still living when the inability to hire a lawyer to defend you in a criminal case meant you did not have a lawyer to defend you at all. It was not until 1938 that the Court held that the Sixth Amendment required appointment of counsel for indigents in federal criminal trials. *Johnson v. Zerbst*, 304 U.S. 458 (1938). And it was not until 1963 that the Court incorporated this right to apply to the states through the Fourteenth Amendment. *Gideon v. Wainwright*, 372 U.S. 335 (1963).

Interestingly, even before *Gideon*, the Court had held that a state could not condition the appeal of a criminal conviction on the defendant providing the trial transcript to the appellate court. *Griffin v. Illinois*, 351 U.S. 12 (1956). While the Court recognized that there was no constitutional right to appellate review at all, to provide review only to those who could afford to pay for a transcript would deny equal protection. Despite the Court's recognition of the lack of a constitutional right of appeal, the Court clearly saw the ability to receive appellate review as a very important interest. After all, no one would suggest that a state may not condition riding the public bus on paying a fare or requiring those who drive on a public toll road to pay a toll. Burdening the poor by a requirement that persons pay for certain state-provided goods or services does not usually constitute an equal protection violation.

A companion case to *Gideon* extended *Griffin* to require appointed counsel for indigent defendants' "first appeal, granted as a matter of right to rich and poor alike, from a criminal conviction." *Douglas v. California*, 372 U.S. 353 (1963). Seizing on the quoted language, the Court in *Ross v. Moffitt*, 417 U.S. 600 (1974) retrenched and held that there was no equal protection violation when the state did not provide appointed counsel in discretionary appeals following initial appeals as of right.

But what about access to the courts in civil cases? In 1971 the Court held that welfare recipients could not be denied access to the courts in order to seek a divorce because they could not afford the court fees. *Boddie v. Connecticut*, 401 U.S. 371 (1971). Two years later, however, in *United States v. Kras*, 409 U.S. 434 (1973), the Court found no equivalent right in persons denied the ability to file for bankruptcy because they could not afford the filing fees. And later in the same year the Court said that persons seeking to appeal a welfare decision reducing their benefits could be denied the ability to appeal if they could not pay the $25 filing fee. *Ortwein v. Schwab*, 410 U.S. 656 (1973). Nevertheless, in *Little v. Streeter*, 452 U.S. 1 (1981), the Court found that the state had to provide a blood test to a defendant in a paternity action who was unable to afford it himself in order to disprove his paternity. Finally, much later, the Court held that a person appealing an order terminating parental rights could not be denied that appeal on the grounds that she could not afford to pay for the preparation of the record for appeal. *MLB v. SLJ*, 519 U.S. 102 (1996).

There does seem to be a thread that runs through these decisions. First, the issue in each case is whether denying someone access to the courts because of an inability to pay is unconstitutional. While this is often framed as whether there is a fundamental right of access to the courts, normally a fundamental right cannot be conditioned on payment of money even by those who can afford it. Recall the poll tax case. The poll tax is unconstitutional even with respect to rich people. With respect to access to the courts, however, those who can afford it must pay the requisite fees to obtain a divorce, fight the termination of parental rights, or defend against a paternity action. Rather the right of access to the courts found in these cases hinges on why the person needs the access to the courts. Where the reason is one which itself involves a fundamental right or interest, such as not having your parental rights taken away, the Court finds access to the courts necessary, even if one cannot afford it. On the other hand, where the reason is one that simply goes to one's pecuniary interest, there is no such necessity. In these cases, the government can require payment of a fee for the benefit of a judicial proceeding, just as it might for the use of buses, subways, libraries, and public golf courses.

3.   A RIGHT TO TRAVEL

SHAPIRO V. THOMPSON
United States Supreme Court, 1969.
394 U.S. 618, 89 S.Ct. 1322.

MR. JUSTICE BRENNAN delivered the opinion of the Court.

[This case involves appeals from decisions] holding unconstitutional a State or District of Columbia statutory provision which denies welfare assistance to residents of the State or District who have not resided within their jurisdictions for at least one year immediately preceding their applications for such assistance. We affirm the judgments. . . .

[In each of the cases, a mother moved from one state to another or to the District of Columbia and within a year of her move filed for welfare benefits in her new residence. In each case her application was denied on the basis of a state or D.C. law that required her to be a resident in the state or D.C. for one year before she would be eligible for welfare benefits.]

There is no dispute that the effect of the waiting-period requirement in each case is to create two classes of needy resident families indistinguishable from each other except that one is composed of residents who have resided a year or more, and the second of residents who have resided less than a year, in the jurisdiction. On the basis of this sole difference the first class is granted and the second class is denied welfare aid upon which may depend the ability of the families to obtain the very means to subsist—food, shelter, and other necessities of life. In each case, the District Court found that appellees met the test for residence in their jurisdictions, as well as all other eligibility requirements except the requirement of residence for a full year prior to their applications. [A]ppellees' central contention is that the statutory prohibition of benefits to residents of less than a year creates a classification which constitutes an invidious discrimination denying them equal protection of the laws. We agree. The interests which appellants assert are promoted by the classification either may not constitutionally be promoted by government or are not compelling governmental interests.

Primarily, appellants justify the waiting-period requirement as a protective device to preserve the fiscal integrity of state public assistance programs. It is asserted that people who require welfare assistance during their first year of residence in a State are likely to become continuing burdens on state welfare programs. Therefore, the argument runs, if such people can be deterred from entering the jurisdiction by denying them welfare benefits during the first year, state programs to assist long-time residents will not be impaired by a substantial influx of indigent newcomers.

There is weighty evidence that exclusion from the jurisdiction of the poor who need or may need relief was the specific objective of these provisions. [W]e do not doubt that the one-year waiting period device is well suited to discourage the influx of poor families in need of assistance. An indigent who desires to migrate, resettle, find a new job, and start a new life will doubtless hesitate if he knows that he must risk making the move without the possibility of falling back on state welfare assistance during his first year of residence, when his need may be most acute. But the purpose of inhibiting migration by needy persons into the State is constitutionally impermissible.

This Court long ago recognized that the nature of our Federal Union and our constitutional concepts of personal liberty unite to require that all citizens be free to travel throughout the length and breadth of our land uninhibited by statutes, rules, or regulations which unreasonably burden or restrict this movement. . . .

We have no occasion to ascribe the source of this right to travel interstate to a particular constitutional provision.[8] It suffices that, as Mr. Justice Stewart said for the Court in *United States v. Guest*, 383 U.S. 745, 757–758 (1966):

> The constitutional right to travel from one State to another * * * occupies a position fundamental to the concept of our Federal Union. It is a right that has been firmly established and repeatedly recognized.

> * * * (The) right finds no explicit mention in the Constitution. The reason, it has been suggested, is that a right so elementary was conceived from the beginning to be a necessary concomitant

---

[8] In Corfield v. Coryell, 6 Fed.Cas. pp. 546, 552 (No. 3230)(C.C.E.D.Pa.1825), Paul v. Virginia, 8 Wall. (75 U.S.) 168, 180 (1869), and Ward v. Maryland, 12 Wall. (79 U.S.) 418, 430 (1871), the right to travel interstate was grounded upon the Privileges and Immunities Clause of Art. IV, s 2. In Edwards v. California, 314 U.S. 160, 181, 183–185 (1941)(Douglas and Jackson, JJ., concurring), and Twining v. New Jersey, 211 U.S. 78 (1908), reliance was placed on the Privileges and Immunities Clause of the Fourteenth Amendment. In Edwards v. California, *supra*, and the Passenger Cases, 7 How. 283 (1849), a Commerce Clause approach was employed. *See also* Kent v. Dulles, 357 U.S. 116, 125 (1958); Aptheker v. Secretary of State, 378 U.S. 500, 505—506 (1964); Zemel v. Rusk, 381 U.S. 1, 14 (1965), where the freedom of Americans to travel outside the country was grounded upon the Due Process Clause of the Fifth Amendment.

of the stronger Union the Constitution created. In any event, freedom to travel throughout the United States has long been recognized as a basic right under the Constitution.

Thus, the purpose of deterring the in-migration of indigents cannot serve as justification for the classification created by the one-year waiting period, since that purpose is constitutionally impermissible. . . .

Alternatively, appellants argue that even if it is impermissible for a State to attempt to deter the entry of all indigents, the challenged classification may be justified as a permissible state attempt to discourage those indigents who would enter the State solely to obtain larger benefits. . . .

[However], a State may no more try to fence out those indigents who seek higher welfare benefits than it may try to fence out indigents generally. Implicit in any such distinction is the notion that indigents who enter a State with the hope of securing higher welfare benefits are somehow less deserving than indigents who do not take this consideration into account. But we do not perceive why a mother who is seeking to make a new life for herself and her children should be regarded as less deserving because she considers, among others factors, the level of a State's public assistance. Surely such a mother is no less deserving than a mother who moves into a particular State in order to take advantage of its better educational facilities.

Appellants argue further that the challenged classification may be sustained as an attempt to distinguish between new and old residents on the basis of the contribution they have made to the community through the payment of taxes. We have difficulty seeing how long-term residents who qualify for welfare are making a greater present contribution to the State in taxes than indigent residents who have recently arrived. If the argument is based on contributions made in the past by the long-term residents, there is some question, as a factual matter. . . . But we need not rest on the particular facts of these cases. Appellants' reasoning would logically permit the State to bar new residents from schools, parks, and libraries or deprive them of police and fire protection. Indeed it would permit the State to apportion all benefits and services according to the past tax contributions of its citizens. The Equal Protection Clause prohibits such an apportionment of state services.

We recognize that a State has a valid interest in preserving the fiscal integrity of its programs. It may legitimately attempt to limit its expenditures, whether for public assistance, public education, or any other program. But a State may not accomplish such a purpose by invidious distinctions between classes of its citizens. It could not, for example, reduce expenditures for education by barring indigent children from its schools. Similarly, in the cases before us, appellants must do more than show that denying welfare benefits to new residents saves money. The saving of welfare costs cannot justify an otherwise invidious classification.

In sum, neither deterrence of indigents from migrating to the State nor limitation of welfare benefits to those regarded as contributing to the State is a constitutionally permissible state objective.

Appellants next advance as justification certain administrative and related governmental objectives allegedly served by the waiting-period requirement. They argue that the requirement (1) facilitates the planning of the welfare budget; (2) provides an objective test of residency; (3) minimizes the opportunity for recipients fraudulently to receive payments from more than one jurisdiction; and (4) encourages early entry of new residents into the labor force.

At the outset, we reject appellants' argument that a mere showing of a rational relationship between the waiting period and these four admittedly permissible state objectives will suffice to justify the classification. [I]n moving from State to State or to the District of Columbia appellees were exercising a constitutional right, and any classification which serves to penalize the exercise of that right, unless shown to be necessary to promote a compelling governmental interest, is unconstitutional.

The argument that the waiting-period requirement facilitates budget predictability is wholly unfounded. The records in all three cases are utterly devoid of evidence that either State or the District of Columbia in fact uses the one-year requirement as a means to predict the number of people who will require assistance in the budget year. . . .

The argument that the waiting period serves as an administratively efficient rule of thumb for determining residency similarly will not withstand scrutiny. The residence requirement and the one-year waiting-period requirement are distinct and independent prerequisites for assistance under these three statutes, and the facts relevant to the determination of each are directly examined by the welfare authorities. . . .

Similarly, there is no need for a State to use the one-year waiting period as a safeguard against fraudulent receipt of benefits; for less drastic means are available, and are employed, to minimize that hazard. Of course, a State has a valid interest in preventing fraud by any applicant, whether a newcomer or a long-time resident. It is not denied, however, that the investigations now conducted entail inquiries into facts relevant to that subject. . . .

Pennsylvania suggests that the one-year waiting period is justified as a means of encouraging new residents to join the labor force promptly. But this logic would also require a similar waiting period for long-term residents of the State. A state purpose to encourage employment provides no rational basis for imposing a one-year waiting-period restriction on new residents only.

We conclude therefore that appellants in these cases do not use and have no need to use the one-year requirement for the governmental purposes suggested. Thus, even under traditional equal protection tests a classification of welfare applicants according to whether they have lived in the State for one year would seem irrational and unconstitutional. But, of course, the traditional criteria do not apply in these cases. Since the classification here touches on the fundamental right of interstate movement, its constitutionality must be judged by the stricter standard of whether it promotes a compelling state interest. Under this standard, the waiting-period requirement clearly violates the Equal Protection Clause.[21]

The waiting-period requirement in the District of Columbia Code . . . is also unconstitutional even though it was adopted by Congress as an exercise of federal power. In terms of federal power, the discrimination created by the one-year requirement violates the Due Process Clause of the Fifth Amendment. . . . For the reasons we have stated in invalidating the Pennsylvania and Connecticut provisions, the District of Columbia provision is also invalid—the Due Process Clause of the Fifth Amendment prohibits Congress from denying public assistance to poor persons otherwise eligible solely on the ground that they have not been residents of the District of Columbia for one year at the time their applications are filed.

MR. JUSTICE STEWART, concurring. [Opinion omitted]

MR. CHIEF JUSTICE WARREN, with whom MR. JUSTICE BLACK joins, dissenting.

In my opinion the issue before us can be simply stated: May Congress, acting under one of its enumerated powers, impose minimal nationwide residence requirements or authorize the States to do so? Since I believe that Congress does have this power and has constitutionally exercised it in these cases, I must dissent. . . .

Congress has imposed a residence requirement in the District of Columbia and authorized the States to impose similar requirements. . . . Appellees insist that a congressionally mandated residence requirement would violate their right to travel. The import of their contention is that Congress, even under its "plenary" power to control interstate commerce, is constitutionally prohibited from imposing residence requirements. I reach a contrary conclusion for I am convinced that the extent of the burden

---

[21] We imply no view of the validity of waiting-period or residence requirements determining eligibility to vote, eligibility for tuition-free education, to obtain a license to practice a profession, to hunt or fish, and so forth. Such requirements may promote compelling state interests on the one hand, or, on the other, may not be penalties upon the exercise of the constitutional right of interstate travel.

on interstate travel when compared with the justification for its imposition requires the Court to uphold this exertion of federal power. . . .

The Court's decision reveals only the top of the iceberg. Lurking beneath are the multitude of situations in which States have imposed residence requirements including eligibility to vote, to engage in certain professions or occupations or to attend a state-supported university. Although the Court takes pains to avoid acknowledging the ramifications of its decision, its implications cannot be ignored. I dissent.

MR. JUSTICE HARLAN, dissenting.

The Court today holds unconstitutional Connecticut, Pennsylvania, and District of Columbia statutes which restrict certain kinds of welfare benefits to persons who have lived within the jurisdiction for at least one year immediately preceding their applications. The Court has accomplished this result by an expansion of the comparatively new constitutional doctrine that some state statutes will be deemed to deny equal protection of the laws unless justified by a "compelling" governmental interest, and by holding that the Fifth Amendment's Due Process Clause imposes a similar limitation on federal enactments. . . .

The "compelling interest" doctrine, which today is articulated more explicitly than ever before, constitutes an increasingly significant exception to the long established rule that a statute does not deny equal protection if it is rationally related to a legitimate governmental objective. The "compelling interest" doctrine has two branches. The branch which requires that classifications based upon "suspect" criteria be supported by a compelling interest apparently had its genesis in cases involving racial classifications, which have . . . been regarded as inherently "suspect."

[I] think that this branch of the "compelling interest" doctrine is sound when applied to racial classifications, for historically the Equal Protection Clause was largely a product of the desire to eradicate legal distinctions founded upon race. . . .

The second branch of the "compelling interest" principle is . . . more troublesome. For it has been held that a statutory classification is subject to the "compelling interest" test if the result of the classification may be to affect a "fundamental right," regardless of the basis of the classification. . . . It has reappeared today in the Court's cryptic suggestion that the "compelling interest" test is applicable merely because the result of the classification may be to deny the appellees "food, shelter, and other necessities of life," as well as in the Court's statement that "(s)ince the classification here touches on the fundamental right of interstate movement, its constitutionality must be judged by the stricter standard of whether it promotes a compelling state interest."

I think this branch of the "compelling interest" doctrine particularly unfortunate and unnecessary. It is unfortunate because it creates an exception which threatens to swallow the standard equal protection rule. Virtually every state statute affects important rights. This Court has repeatedly held, for example, that the traditional equal protection standard is applicable to statutory classifications affecting such fundamental matters as the right to pursue a particular occupation, the right to receive greater or smaller wages, or to work more or less hours, and the right to inherit property. Rights such as these are in principle indistinguishable from those involved here, and to extend the "compelling interest" rule to all cases in which such rights are affected would go far toward making this Court a "super-legislature."

[I] conclude with the following observations. Today's decision, it seems to me, reflects to an unusual degree the current notion that this Court possesses a peculiar wisdom all its own whose capacity to lead this Nation out of its present troubles is contained only by the limits of judicial ingenuity in contriving new constitutional principles to meet each problem as it arises. For anyone who, like myself, believes that it is an essential function of this Court to maintain the constitutional divisions between state and federal authority and among the three branches of the Federal Government, today's decision is a step in the wrong direction. . . .

COMMENTS AND QUESTIONS

1. The Court reached the same conclusion regarding a county requirement that a person be a resident of the county for at least one year as a condition of receiving free county medical care. *Memorial Hosp. v. Maricopa County*, 415 U.S. 250 (1974). The Court analogized *Shapiro*'s denial of the basic necessities of life with medical care. "Governmental privileges or benefits necessary to basic sustenance have often been viewed as being of greater constitutional significance than less essential forms of governmental entitlements." *Id.*, at 259.

2. Again, a one-year residency in a state was an unconstitutional condition on the right to vote. *Dunn v. Blumstein*, 405 U.S. 330 (1972). The Court acknowledged that the state could assure that a person was indeed a bona fide resident, but that was not the issue in the case and the period involved was longer than required to protect against fraud. In *Marston v. Lewis*, 410 U.S. 679 (1973)(per curiam), the next year, the Court upheld a 50-day durational residency requirement.

3. In each of these cases, the Court recognizes that the state can require the person to be a resident of the state, so what does it take to be a resident? Generally, the test for residency is that one be in the state with a present intention to remain in the state indefinitely and to abandon his or her prior residence. Precisely because this test is so subjective, states typically wish persons to evidence their intent by, for example, obtaining the state's driver's license or registering their car in the state. Moreover, as the cases demonstrate, for various purposes states have established specific periods of time as evidence of an intent to remain.

4.   In two areas the Court has allowed for an extended durational residency requirement. First, the Court upheld a one-year residency requirement in order to qualify for in-state tuition at a state university. *Starns v. Malkerson*, 326 F.Supp. 234 (D. Minn. 1970), *aff'd mem.*, 401 U.S. 441 (1971). The lower court distinguished *Shapiro* because imposing higher tuition on recent arrivals to the state did not impose the same hardships or burdens as depriving a person of the essentials of life. The Supreme Court did not render an opinion, but in a later case it did say that a permanent bar from obtaining in-state status would be impermissible. *Vlandis v. Kline*, 412 U.S. 441 (1973). Second, it upheld a one-year residency requirement for a petitioner for divorce (if the respondent was not a resident of the state). *Sosna v. Iowa*, 419 U.S. 393 (1975). The Court's explanation was a bit muddled. It said the requirement merely delayed access to the courts, but of course in *Shapiro* the requirement merely delayed welfare payments. In addition, the Court said that the state's interest was not just administrative convenience or saving money; it was "in avoiding officious intermeddling in matters in which another State has a paramount interest and in minimizing the susceptibility of its own decrees to collateral attack." What this language recognizes is that if the respondent is not a citizen of the state, which must be the case for the petitioner's one-year residency requirement to apply, there is another state and its interests are also involved in the ultimate divorce decree. Accordingly, it is not inappropriate to require the one person claiming state residency to have more than an ephemeral relationship to the state.

5.   Although *Sosna* reflected the then growing tendency to rein back on the Warren Court's extension of fundamental rights doctrine, with four appointees of President Nixon contributing to the six person majority, the Court in subsequent years utilized other tools to limit states' ability to punish late-comers to a state. In *Zobel v. Williams*, 457 U.S. 55 (1982), the State of Alaska found itself newly wealthy as a result of discovery of oil on state-owned lands. Rather than having to tax its residents, it was able to pay them dividends. Alaska decided to pay one dividend unit for each year of residency in Alaska since its statehood, meaning that long-time residents received much more than new residents. The Court found that this violated the Equal Protection Clause, but it declined to apply heightened scrutiny under the *Shapiro* line of cases. Rather, it said that the Alaska law failed the minimum rationality test, primarily because Alaska's main justification for the differential payments was to reward citizens for past contributions. The Court said this was simply not a legitimate state objective, citing *Shapiro*. Two state statutes that granted benefits to veterans on the basis that they had been state residents in the past were similarly held to violate equal protection by attempting to reward past citizenship. *See Attorney General of New York v. Soto-Lopez*, 476 U. S. 898 (1986); *Hooper v. Bernalillo County Assessor*, 472 U.S. 612 (1985). Finally, in *Saenz v. Roe*, 526 U.S. 489 (1999), California tried to avoid the precedent of *Shapiro* by requiring a one-year residency requirement in order to obtain California level welfare benefits but granting to the person whatever welfare benefits they would have received in their prior state. Because this scheme did not burden the person's interstate travel, the

Court conceded this case was not governed by *Shapiro*. Nonetheless, as discussed earlier following the *Slaughterhouse Cases*, the Court invalidated the requirement relying upon the Fourteenth Amendment's Privileges and Immunities Clause. The only case to give effect to that clause.

4. EDUCATION

While many modern constitutions list access to education as a fundamental right, the Supreme Court has never accepted such a claim. In *San Antonio Ind. School Dist. v. Rodriguez*, 411 U.S. 1 (1973), persons living in one school district challenged the Texas system of school funding largely through a local tax base that resulted in some districts having significantly less money than others. The plaintiffs asked the Court to use strict scrutiny in evaluating the system because they claimed that education was a fundamental right "because it is essential to the effective exercise of First Amendment freedoms and to intelligent utilization of the right to vote." While noting that the case did not involve the total deprivation of education, but only differences in spending levels, the Court rejected the idea that there is a fundamental right to education in the Constitution. Consequently, the state's system only had to satisfy the traditional standard of minimum rationality, which it did. Similarly, in *Martinez v. Bynum*, 461 U.S. 321 (1983), the Court rejected a challenge to a Texas law that authorized school districts to deny tuition-free education to children who live apart from their parents and are in the school district for the primary purpose of attending that district's schools. And in *Kadrmas v. Dickinson Public Schools*, 487 U.S. 450 (1988), the Court upheld a South Dakota law allowing school boards to charge students a fee for using a school bus against a claim that the fee effectively prevented the student from being able to attend school.

The one exception to these cases was *Plyler v. Doe*, 457 U.S. 202 (1982). In that case Texas law only extended the right to a free public education to children who were either citizens or lawfully admitted aliens. Children who were illegal aliens challenged their exclusion. The Court rejected any claim that the children were a suspect class or that education was a fundamental right. Nevertheless, the law

> impose[d] a lifetime hardship on a discrete class of children not accountable for their disabling status. The stigma of illiteracy will mark them for the rest of their lives. By denying these children a basic education, we deny them the ability to live within the structure of our civic institutions, and foreclose any realistic possibility that they will contribute in even the smallest way to the progress of our Nation. In determining the rationality of [the law], we may appropriately take into account its costs to the Nation and to the innocent children who are its victims. In light of these countervailing costs, the discrimination contained in [the

law] can hardly be considered rational unless it furthers some substantial goal of the State.

Using this heightened scrutiny, the Court by a 5–4 vote overturned the denial of the free public education to these children.

CHAPTER 9

THE FIRST AMENDMENT—
FREEDOM OF SPEECH

■ ■ ■

The First Amendment provides that "Congress shall make no law . . . abridging the freedom of speech, or of the press. . . ." Despite the seemingly absolute language of "no law abridging the freedom of speech, or of the press," in the first decade of the nation Congress passed the Alien and Sedition Acts, which among other things made it a crime to "write, print, utter, or publish . . . any false, scandalous and malicious writing" against the government. Several prosecutions were successfully brought against newspapers and editors that criticized the then Adams administration. Today, we assume such laws would be unconstitutional. *See New York Times Co. v. Sullivan*, 376 U.S. 254, 276 (1964). Nevertheless, the Supreme Court did not find any law to abridge the freedom of speech or of the press until the 1930s, and there continue to be various laws that restrict speech or the press which do not appear to raise First Amendment problems—such as laws banning false advertising, criminalizing perjury, penalizing slander, prohibiting threats, and outlawing obscenity. In short, the plain text of the Amendment cannot mean that it is unconstitutional to make any law restricting speech. But if it does not mean that, what does it mean?

The text says that Congress shall make no law abridging "the freedom of speech," so the question might be: what is "the freedom of speech" that cannot be abridged. There are at least two possible answers to this. First, it might refer to the freedom of speech that persons enjoyed in their states at the time. This freedom was protected by common law or state constitutions or statutes. Under the First Amendment, Congress and the new national government could not limit the freedom of speech persons enjoyed under these state laws. Nevertheless, the state freedom of speech was not absolute; state laws imposed various restrictions on speech. Where the state restricted speech, so could the federal government. The other possible answer is that "the freedom of speech" might refer to a natural or God-given right. The Founding Fathers, as products of the Enlightenment, for the most part believed in natural rights or their religious equivalent— God-given rights. These rights might to one extent or another be reflected in common law or state bills of rights, but the "freedom" referred to was one that derived from nature or God, not the law. Under this interpretation, it was this freedom that Congress could not abridge.

These two answers are not mutually exclusive. Undoubtedly, many believed that their states' protection of free speech accorded with the natural or God-given right. In any case, today the scope of the freedom of speech cannot be derived from the text itself. One could attempt to discern what speech states protected in 1791 or what speech rights persons in 1791 believed were natural or God-given rights. As you will see, some current members of the Supreme Court believe this is the appropriate way to assess the meaning of the First Amendment. However, almost all of the Supreme Court cases interpreting the First Amendment, and particularly the Free Speech Clause, do not attempt such an analysis. Rather, the Court has judged in particular cases whether a law abridges some current notion of what should be considered "the freedom of speech." Or stated another way, courts must determine for themselves what speech should be protected.

By characterizing freedom of speech as a "fundamental right," one might give strict scrutiny to laws restricting speech, as has been done with the unenumerated fundamental rights protected under Due Process or Equal Protection, and this is a good default position for analyzing free speech cases. However, the Supreme Court has in case law over the years developed various tests applicable to particular free speech issues that take the place of a generalized strict scrutiny analysis. The sections that follow illustrate those tests.

A. INCITEMENT

SCHENCK V. UNITED STATES

United States Supreme Court, 1919.
249 U.S. 47, 39 S.Ct. 247.

MR. JUSTICE HOLMES delivered the opinion of the Court.

[Schenck and Baer were convicted of conspiracy to violate the Espionage Act of 1917 by attempting to cause insubordination in the military and naval forces of the United States and by obstructing the recruiting and enlistment service of the United States, when the United States was at war with the German Empire. The evidence was that they conspired to have printed and circulated to men who had been drafted for military service a document intended to cause such insubordination and obstruction. The front side of the document] recited the first section of the Thirteenth Amendment, said that the idea embodied in it was violated by the conscription act and that a conscript is little better than a convict. In

Charles Schenck

impassioned language it intimated that
conscription was despotism in its worst form and
a monstrous wrong against humanity in the
interest of Wall Street's chosen few. It said, "Do
not submit to intimidation," but in form at least
confined itself to peaceful measures such as a
petition for the repeal of the act. The other . . .
side of the sheet was headed "Assert Your
Rights." It stated reasons for alleging that any
one violated the Constitution when he refused to
recognize "your right to assert your opposition to
the draft," and went on, "If you do not assert and
support your rights, you are helping to deny or
disparage rights which it is the solemn duty of

Elizabeth Baer

all citizens and residents of the United States to retain." It described the
arguments on the other side as coming from cunning politicians and a
mercenary capitalist press, and even silent consent to the conscription law
as helping to support an infamous conspiracy. It denied the power to send
our citizens away to foreign shores to shoot up the people of other lands,
and added that words could not express the condemnation such cold-
blooded ruthlessness deserves, &c., &c., winding up, "You must do your
share to maintain, support and uphold the rights of the people of this
country." Of course, the document would not have been sent unless it had
been intended to have some effect, and we do not see what effect it could be
expected to have upon persons subject to the draft except to influence them
to obstruct the carrying of it out. The defendants do not deny that the jury
might find against them on this point.

But it is said, suppose that that was the tendency of this circular, it is
protected by the First Amendment to the Constitution. . . . It well may be
that the prohibition of laws abridging the freedom of speech is not confined
to previous restraints, although to prevent them may have been the main
purpose. . . . We admit that in many places and in ordinary times the
defendants in saying all that was said in the circular would have been
within their constitutional rights. But the character of every act depends
upon the circumstances in which it is done. The most stringent protection
of free speech would not protect a man in falsely shouting fire in a theatre
and causing a panic. . . . The question in every case is whether the words
used are used in such circumstances and are of such a nature as to create
a clear and present danger that they will bring about the substantive evils
that Congress has a right to prevent. It is a question of proximity and
degree. When a nation is at war many things that might be said in time of
peace are such a hindrance to its effort that their utterance will not be
endured so long as men fight and that no Court could regard them as
protected by any constitutional right. It seems to be admitted that if an
actual obstruction of the recruiting service were proved, liability for words

that produced that effect might be enforced. . . . If the act, (speaking, or circulating a paper,) its tendency and the intent with which it is done are the same, we perceive no ground for saying that success alone warrants making the act a crime. . . .

COMMENTS AND QUESTIONS

1.   The Court acknowledges that the freedom of speech is not confined to bans on prior restraints, although that may have been its main purpose. Prior restraints come in two forms—prior censorship or licensing and injunctions against publication. Historically in England there were laws requiring a license before any material could be printed and before any book could be imported or sold. While the principal purpose of the law may have been to raise revenue, because there was a fee for the license, it was also used to control the content of some written materials that were deemed subversive. Although these laws were eliminated before our independence, there is some evidence to support the idea that they were the motivating force behind the First Amendment's protection of speech and press. In *Near v. Minnesota*, 283 U.S. 697 (1931), the Court analogized the historical licensing laws with a state statute authorizing an injunction against newspapers from publishing malicious and scandalous matters. Believing that "subsequent punishment for abuses as may exist is the appropriate remedy," the Court held that prior restraints would only be allowed "in exceptional circumstances," such as the prevention of the publication of the sailing dates of troop transports in time of war. *See also New York Times Co. v. United States*, 403 U.S. 713 (1971)(refusing to issue an injunction to stop publication by the New York Times of the so-called Pentagon Papers, an internal military study of the Vietnam War's origin classified Top Secret). Today, prior licensing in the form of permits are commonly required for the use of public resources (like streets and parks) for demonstrations, parades, or protests, and the Court has placed strict limits on such licensing to assure that it is not used to thwart public expression. *See Cox v. New Hampshire*, 312 U.S. 569 (1941)(upholding a permit requirement for a parade on a public street because it had to be issued in a timely manner and only addressed the time, place, and manner of the parade, not whatever theme or message it was to convey). *Compare Collin v. Smith*, 578 F.2d 1197, *cert. denied*, 439 U.S. 916 (1978)(overturning local ordinance requiring a permit for a parade by the American Nazi Party and banning the wearing of military-style uniforms and the dissemination of material that incited racial or religious hatred).

2.   *Schenck* is famous both for Justice Holmes's "Clear and Present Danger" test and for his analogy to falsely shouting fire in a theater. From the facts provided, which are all the Court used to decide the case, do you think that Schenck and Baer's one-page, double-sided paper created a clear and present danger to the enlistment service of the United States? As to falsely shouting fire in a crowded theater, what if the shouter honestly believed there was a fire, and he hoped to save lives by announcing it? Could he still be held liable?

3. The speakers in *Schenck* are advocating the violation of the law. Why should advocacy of violating the law ever be protected? In a functioning democracy, one can call for the change of laws believed to be wrong or unjust. Why should advocating illegal conduct not be able to be punished generally, not just when it would cause a clear and present danger of the conduct occurring?

4. In the same year as *Schenck*, Justice Holmes also wrote for a unanimous Court upholding the conviction of the Presidential candidate of the Socialist Party on the same grounds. *Debs v. United States*, 249 U.S. 211 (1919). In fact, Debs had been careful not to say that persons should violate the law, but he had expressed sympathy and admiration for those who were in prison for obstructing the draft and that, along with his admission that he opposed all war, was considered sufficient evidence of obstructing the enlistment service. Justice Holmes concluded his opinion by stating that it was enough if Debs's words "had as their natural tendency and reasonably probable effect to obstruct the recruiting service" and if he "had the specific intent to do so in his mind."

5. It should be noted that the Espionage Act did not by its terms restrict speech; it simply criminalized obstruction of the recruitment service, which might be done by physically blocking entrances or by destroying government files. Here, however, the obstruction was through speech, which, at least if persuasive, might have the intended result.

6. Justice Holmes was a wounded veteran of the Civil War and a Boston Brahmin. Do you think that affected his views of the Socialist opponents of World War I? If you think so, consider the following case. In 1917, three years after World War I began but only the first year of American participation, Russian revolutionaries overthrew the Tsarist regime. In October of that year, the Bolsheviks (Communists) overthrew the democratic provisional government of Russia and undertook to make peace with (*i.e.*, surrender to) Germany. The combination of the triumph of the Communists and the possible loss of an eastern front in the war against Germany led the allies (primarily France, Great Britain, and the United States) to send troops to Russia in July, 1918, in the hopes of overturning the new Communist government in favor of a government that would keep at war against Germany. American communists opposed this American invasion of Russia.

ABRAMS V. UNITED STATES

United States Supreme Court, 1919.
250 U.S. 616, 40 S.Ct. 17.

MR. JUSTICE CLARKE delivered the opinion of the Court.

[The defendants were convicted of conspiring to violate provisions of the Espionage Act of 1917] by printing, writing and distributing in the city of New York many copies of a leaflet or circular, printed in the English language, and of another printed in the Yiddish language. . . .

All of the five defendants were born in Russia. They were intelligent, had considerable schooling, and at the time they were arrested they had lived in the United States terms varying from five to ten years, but none of them had applied for naturalization. Four of them testified as witnesses in their own behalf, and of these three frankly avowed that they were "rebels," "revolutionists," "anarchists," that they did not believe in government in any form, and they declared that they had no interest whatever in the government of the United States. The fourth defendant testified that he was a "Socialist" and believed in "a proper kind of government, not capitalistic," but in his classification the government of the United States was "capitalistic."

It was admitted on the trial that the defendants had united to print and distribute the described circulars and that 5,000 of them had been printed and distributed about the 22d day of August, 1918. The group had a meeting place in New York City, in rooms rented by defendant Abrams, under an assumed name, and there the subject of printing the circulars was discussed about two weeks before the defendants were arrested. The defendant Abrams, although not a printer, on July 27, 1918, purchased the printing outfit with which the circulars were printed, and installed it in a basement room where the work was done at night. The circulars were distributed, some by throwing them from a window of a building where one of the defendants was employed and others secretly, in New York City.

The defendants pleaded "not guilty," and the case of the government consisted in showing the facts we have stated, and in introducing in evidence copies of the two printed circulars attached to the indictment, a sheet entitled "Revolutionists Unite for Action," written by the defendant Lipman, and found on him when he was arrested, and another paper, found at the headquarters of the group, and for which Abrams assumed responsibility.

[O]n the record thus described it is argued, somewhat faintly, that the acts charged against the defendants were not unlawful because within the protection of that freedom of speech and of the press which is guaranteed by the First Amendment to the Constitution of the United States. . . .

This contention is sufficiently discussed and is definitely negatived in *Schenck v. United States.* . . .

The claim chiefly elaborated upon by the defendants in the oral argument and in their brief is that there is no substantial evidence in the record to support the judgment upon the verdict of guilty and that the motion of the defendants for an instructed verdict in their favor was erroneously denied. A question of law is thus presented, which calls for an examination of the record, not for the purpose of weighing conflicting testimony, but only to determine whether there was some evidence, competent and substantial, before the jury, fairly tending to sustain the verdict. . . .

The first of the two articles attached to the indictment is conspicuously headed, "The Hypocrisy of the United States and her Allies." After denouncing President Wilson as a hypocrite and a coward because troops were sent into Russia, it proceeds to assail our government in general, saying:

> His [the President's] shameful, cowardly silence about the intervention in Russia reveals the hypocrisy of the plutocratic gang in Washington and vicinity. He [the President] is too much of a coward to come out openly and say: 'We capitalistic nations cannot afford to have a proletarian republic in Russia.' The Russian Revolution cries: Workers of the World! Awake! Rise! Put down your enemy and mine! Yes friends, there is only one enemy of the workers of the world and that is CAPITALISM. Awake! Awake, you Workers of the World! REVOLUTIONISTS.

This is clearly an appeal to the "workers" of this country to arise and put down by force the government of the United States which they characterize as their "hypocritical," "cowardly" and "capitalistic" enemy. . . .

The second of the articles was printed in the Yiddish language and in the translation [states:]

> Workers-Wake Up. Workers, Russian emigrants, you who had the least belief in the honesty of *our* government, must now throw away all confidence, must spit in the face the false, hypocritic, military propaganda which has fooled you so relentlessly, calling forth your sympathy, your help, to the prosecution of the war. With the money which you have loaned, or are going to loan them, they will make bullets not only for the Germans, but also for the Workers Soviets of Russia. *Workers in the ammunition factories, you are producing bullets, bayonets, cannon, to murder not only the Germans, but also your dearest, best, who are in Russia and are fighting for freedom.* America and her Allies have betrayed [the Workers]. Their robberish aims are clear to all men. The destruction of the Russian Revolution, that is the politics of the march to Russia. *Workers, our reply to the barbaric intervention has to be a general strike! An open challenge* only will let the government know that not only the Russian Worker fights for freedom, but also *here in America lives the spirit of Revolution.* 'Do not let the government scare you with their wild punishment in prisons, hanging and shooting. We must not and will not betray the splendid fighters of Russia. *Workers, up to fight.* Woe unto those who will be in the way of progress. Let solidarity live!

It is signed, "The Rebels."

The purpose of this obviously was to persuade the persons to whom it was addressed to turn a deaf ear to patriotic appeals in behalf of the government of the United States, and to cease to render it assistance in the prosecution of the war. It will not do to say, as is now argued, that the only intent of these defendants was to prevent injury to the Russian cause. Men must be held to have intended, and to be accountable for, the effects which their acts were likely to produce. Even if their primary purpose and intent was to aid the cause of the Russian Revolution, the plan of action which they adopted necessarily involved, before it could be realized, defeat of the war program of the United States, for the obvious effect of this appeal, if it should become effective, as they hoped it might, would be to persuade persons of character such as those whom they regarded themselves as addressing, not to aid government loans and not to work in ammunition factories, where their work would produce "bullets, bayonets, cannon" and other munitions of war, the use of which would cause the "murder" of Germans and Russians.

This is not an attempt to bring about a change of administration by candid discussion, for no matter what may have incited the outbreak on the part of the defendant anarchists, the manifest purpose of such a publication was to create an attempt to defeat the war plans of the government of the United States, by bringing upon the country the paralysis of a general strike, thereby arresting the production of all munitions and other things essential to the conduct of the war. . . .

These excerpts sufficiently show, that while the immediate occasion for this particular outbreak of lawlessness, on the part of the defendant alien anarchists, may have been resentment caused by our government sending troops into Russia as a strategic operation against the Germans on the eastern battle front, yet the plain purpose of their propaganda was to excite, at the supreme crisis of the war, disaffection, sedition, riots, and, as they hoped, revolution, in this country for the purpose of embarrassing and if possible defeating the military plans of the government in Europe. [T]he language of these circulars was obviously intended to provoke and to encourage resistance to the United States in the war, as the third count runs, and, the defendants, in terms, plainly urged and advocated a resort to a general strike of workers in ammunition factories for the purpose of curtailing the production of ordnance and munitions necessary and essential to the prosecution of the war as is charged in the fourth count. Thus it is clear not only that some evidence but that much persuasive evidence was before the jury tending to prove that the defendants were guilty as charged. . . .

MR. JUSTICE HOLMES, dissenting.

[I] never have seen any reason to doubt that the questions of law that alone were before this Court in the Cases of *Schenck* and *Debs* were rightly decided. I do not doubt for a moment that by the same reasoning that would justify punishing persuasion to murder, the United States constitutionally may punish speech that produces or is intended to produce a clear and imminent danger that it will bring about forthwith certain substantive evils that the United States constitutionally may seek to prevent. The power undoubtedly is greater in time of war than in time of peace because war opens dangers that do not exist at other times.

But as against dangers peculiar to war, as against others, the principle of the right to free speech is always the same. It is only the present danger of immediate evil or an intent to bring it about that warrants Congress in setting a limit to the expression of opinion where private rights are not concerned. Congress certainly cannot forbid all effort to change the mind of the country. Now nobody can suppose that the surreptitious publishing of a silly leaflet by an unknown man, without more, would present any immediate danger that its opinions would hinder the success of the government arms or have any appreciable tendency to do so. . . .

I do not see how anyone can find the intent required by the statute in any of the defendant's words. The second leaflet is the only one that affords even a foundation for the charge, and there, without invoking the hatred of German militarism expressed in the former one, it is evident from the beginning to the end that the only object of the paper is to help Russia and stop American intervention there against the popular government—not to impede the United States in the war that it was carrying on. . . .

In this case sentences of twenty years imprisonment have been imposed for the publishing of two leaflets that I believe the defendants had as much right to publish as the Government has to publish the Constitution of the United States now vainly invoked by them. Even if I am technically wrong and enough can be squeezed from these poor and puny anonymities to turn the color of legal litmus paper; I will add, even if what I think the necessary intent were shown; the most nominal punishment seems to me all that possibly could be inflicted, unless the defendants are to be made to suffer not for what the indictment alleges but for the creed that they avow—a creed that I believe to be the creed of ignorance and immaturity when honestly held, as I see no reason to doubt that it was held here but which, although made the subject of examination at the trial, no one has a right even to consider in dealing with the charges before the Court.

Persecution for the expression of opinions seems to me perfectly logical. If you have no doubt of your premises or your power and want a certain result with all your heart you naturally express your wishes in law and sweep away all opposition. To allow opposition by speech seems to indicate that you think the speech impotent, as when a man says that he has squared the circle, or that you do not care whole heartedly for the result, or that you doubt either your power or your premises. But when men have realized that time has upset many fighting faiths, they may come to believe even more than they believe the very foundations of their own conduct that the ultimate good desired is better reached by free trade in ideas—that the best test of truth is the power of the thought to get itself accepted in the competition of the market, and that truth is the only ground upon which their wishes safely can be carried out. That at any rate is the theory of our Constitution. It is an experiment, as all life is an experiment. Every year if not every day we have to wager our salvation upon some prophecy based upon imperfect knowledge. While that experiment is part of our system I think that we should be eternally vigilant against attempts to check the expression of opinions that we loathe and believe to be fraught with death, unless they so imminently threaten immediate interference with the lawful and pressing purposes of the law that an immediate check is required to save the country. I wholly disagree with the argument of the Government that the First Amendment left the common law as to seditious libel in force. History seems to me against the notion. I had conceived that the United States through many years had shown its repentance for the Sedition Act of 1798, by repaying fines that it imposed. Only the emergency that makes it immediately dangerous to leave the correction of evil counsels to time warrants making any exception to the sweeping command, "Congress shall make no law abridging the freedom of speech." Of course I am speaking only of expressions of opinion and exhortations, which were all that were uttered here, but I regret that I cannot put into more impressive words my belief that in their conviction upon this indictment the defendants were deprived of their rights under the Constitution of the United States.

MR. JUSTICE BRANDEIS concurs with the foregoing opinion.

COMMENTS AND QUESTIONS

1.   The Court's opinion dismisses the defendants' First Amendment claims with a one sentence citation to *Schenck*. The body of the opinion purports to address the claim that as a matter of law the evidence did not support the verdict, in particular because the statute required an intent to hinder the war effort. Justice Holmes expresses doubt that the evidence reflects such an intent. What do you think? However, the bulk of Justice Holmes's opinion addresses the First Amendment. How does he distinguish *Schenck* and *Debs*, whose correctness he reaffirms?

2.   Justice Holmes's dissent is famous for his invocation of the First Amendment as protecting a marketplace of ideas, where good ideas will win out over bad ideas if given a chance. Is this a good analogy? Do we not allow government regulation of the commercial marketplace precisely because of the damage that bad products may cause before they are found to be bad?

3.   Justice Holmes's dissent makes only a dimly veiled allusion to the possibility that the defendants' convictions (and affirmances on appeal) were the product of prejudice against their politics, if not their religion and lack of citizenship. Note that Justice Brandeis, the first Jewish justice, whose

appointment was highly controversial precisely because he was Jewish, joined Justice Holmes in dissent.

4. The history of the First Amendment's protection of speech over the next forty years reflects the same lack of protection for speech found in *Schenck* and *Abrams*. Indeed, one might say it took a step backward. After the Bolshevik revolution in Russia, there was a fear throughout the industrialized world that the revolution would spread. In the United States, radical leftists employed the rhetoric already seen in the *Abrams* pamphlets, but there were also physical acts. In April, 1919 there was a plot involving 36 letter bombs, each containing a stick of dynamite, sent to government officials and leading private figures, including the Attorney General of the United States, Justice Oliver Wendell Holmes, J.P. Morgan, and John D. Rockefeller. In June bombs were exploded simultaneously in eight cities, one of which destroyed the house of the Attorney General, A. Mitchell Palmer. In 1920 a bomb was set off on Wall Street that killed 38 and injured 141. The Federal government responded with a Sedition Act and the so-called Palmer Raids, named after the Attorney General, that targeted alien activists for deportation. Many states passed sedition laws. These followed two different models. One involved "criminal anarchy" laws, which criminalized the "advocacy, advising or teaching the duty, necessity or propriety of overthrowing or overturning organized government by force or violence." The other involved "criminal syndicalism" laws, which criminalized the organizing or membership in any group organized for the purpose of advocating any crime as a means of accomplishing a change in industrial ownership or effecting any political change. In *Gitlow v. New York*, 268 U.S. 652 (1925), the Court upheld over the dissents of Justices Holmes and Brandeis the first type of law. In *Whitney v. California*, 274 U.S. 357 (1927), it upheld the second type. In *Whitney*, Justice Brandeis joined by Justice Holmes concurred in the judgment affirming the convictions, but disagreed with the Court that mere membership in an organization "formed to advocate the desirability of a proletarian revolution by mass action at some date necessarily far in the future" was not protected by the First Amendment.

5. Unlike *Schenck*, *Debs*, and *Abrams*, these cases involved statutes that punished speech per se, teaching or advocating the desirability of criminal action to achieve political or social ends. The Court reasoned from Justice Holmes's "Clear and Present Danger" analysis in *Schenck*, saying that the state legislatures had determined that such speech was a clear and present danger, and that the Court could not say that the states were in error in this determination. Thus, the Court had gone from *its* determination of a clear and present danger in a particular case justifying suppression of speech to allowing legislatures to make a generic determination that would justify such suppression.

6. The "Red Scare" that occurred in the United States after the Bolshevik revolution in 1917 returned after World War II, when the Soviet Union took over eastern Europe and exploded an atomic bomb at least in part as a result of secrets stolen by espionage activities in the United States under the cover of the Communist Party, U.S.A. China, the world's most populous

nation, had "gone" Communist. In 1950, Communist North Korea invaded South Korea. A principal tool to use against American Communists was the Smith Act, which made unlawful the knowing advocacy of the desirability of overthrowing the government of the United States by force or violence. In *Dennis v. United States*, 341 U.S. 494 (1951), the Court upheld the Act, again interpreting the "clear and present danger" test. However, the Court seemed to disown *Gitlow* and *Whitney*, distinguishing them from the situation here. In the earlier cases, there had been no super-power underwriting the anarchists, but here the nation was involved in a life-or-death struggle with the Soviet Union, so that the actual threat posed by communists was much more significant than the threat posed by the anarchists after World War I. Justices Black and Douglas dissented.

7.   *Dennis*, however, was the last of its kind. Subsequent cases under the Smith Act interpreted it narrowly. *See Yates v. United States*, 354 U.S. 298 (1957); *Scales v. United States*, 367 U.S. 203 (1961); *Noto v. United States*, 367 U.S. 290 (1961). By the time of the Vietnam "war," speech equivalent to that in *Schenck*, *Debs*, and *Abrams* was viewed as protected by the First Amendment. The following case states the current "test."

BRANDENBURG V. OHIO

United States Supreme Court, 1969.
395 U.S. 444, 89 S.Ct. 1827.

PER CURIAM.

The appellant, a leader of a Ku Klux Klan group, was convicted under the Ohio Criminal Syndicalism statute for "advocat(ing) * * * the duty, necessity, or propriety of crime, sabotage, violence, or unlawful methods of

 terrorism as a means of accomplishing industrial or political reform" and for "voluntarily assembl(ing) with any society, group, or assemblage of persons formed to teach or advocate the doctrines of criminal syndicalism." [T]he appellant challenged the constitutionality of the criminal syndicalism statute under the First and Fourteenth Amendments to the United States Constitution. . . .

The record shows that a man, identified at trial as the appellant, telephoned an announcer-reporter on the staff of a Cincinnati television station and invited him to come to a Ku Klux Klan "rally" to be held at a farm in Hamilton County. With the cooperation of the organizers, the reporter and a cameraman attended the meeting and filmed the events. Portions of the films were later broadcast on the local station and on a national network. . . .

One film showed 12 hooded figures, some of whom carried firearms. They were gathered around a large wooden cross, which they burned. No one was present other than the participants and the newsmen who made the film. Most of the words uttered during the scene were incomprehensible when the film was projected, but scattered phrases could be understood that were derogatory of Negroes and, in one instance, of Jews.[1] Another scene on the same film showed the appellant, in Klan regalia, making a speech. The speech, in full, was as follows:

> This is an organizers' meeting. We have had quite a few members here today which are—we have hundreds, hundreds of members throughout the State of Ohio. I can quote from a newspaper clipping from the Columbus, Ohio Dispatch, five weeks ago Sunday morning. The Klan has more members in the State of Ohio than does any other organization. We're not a revengent organization, but if our President, our Congress, our Supreme Court, continues to suppress the white, Caucasian race, it's possible that there might have to be some revengeance taken.

> We are marching on Congress July the Fourth, four hundred thousand strong. From there we are dividing into two groups, one group to march on St. Augustine, Florida, the other group to march into Mississippi. Thank you.

The second film showed six hooded figures one of whom, later identified as the appellant, repeated a speech very similar to that recorded on the first film. The reference to the possibility of "revengeance" was omitted, and one sentence was added: "Personally, I believe the nigger should be returned to Africa, the Jew returned to Israel." Though some of the figures in the films carried weapons, the speaker did not.

The Ohio Criminal Syndicalism Statute was enacted in 1919. From 1917 to 1920, identical or quite similar laws were adopted by 20 States and two territories. In 1927, this Court sustained the constitutionality of California's Criminal Syndicalism Act, the text of which is quite similar to that of the laws of Ohio. *Whitney v. California.* The Court upheld the statute on the ground that, without more, "advocating" violent means to effect political and economic change involves such danger to the security of the State that the State may outlaw it. But *Whitney* has been thoroughly discredited by later decisions. *See Dennis v. United States.* These later decisions have fashioned the principle that the constitutional guarantees of free speech and free press do not permit a State to forbid or proscribe advocacy of the use of force or of law violation except where such advocacy

---

[1] The significant portions that could be understood were: "How far is the nigger going to—yeah." "This is what we are going to do to the niggers." "A dirty nigger." "Send the Jews back to Israel." "Let's give them back to the dark garden." "Save America." "Let's go back to constitutional betterment." "Bury the niggers." "We intend to do our part." "Give us our state rights." "Freedom for the whites." "Nigger will have to fight for every inch he gets from now on."

is directed to inciting or producing imminent lawless action and is likely to incite or produce such action. As we said in *Noto v. United States*, "the mere abstract teaching * * * of the moral propriety or even moral necessity for a resort to force and violence, is not the same as preparing a group for violent action and steeling it to such action." A statute which fails to draw this distinction impermissibly intrudes upon the freedoms guaranteed by the First and Fourteenth Amendments. It sweeps within its condemnation speech which our Constitution has immunized from governmental control.

Measured by this test, Ohio's Criminal Syndicalism Act cannot be sustained. . . .

Accordingly, we are here confronted with a statute which, by its own words and as applied, purports to punish mere advocacy and to forbid, on pain of criminal punishment, assembly with others merely to advocate the described type of action. Such a statute falls within the condemnation of the First and Fourteenth Amendments. The contrary teaching of *Whitney v. California* cannot be supported, and that decision is therefore overruled.

MR. JUSTICE BLACK, concurring. [opinion omitted]

MR. JUSTICE DOUGLAS, concurring. [opinion omitted]

COMMENTS AND QUESTIONS

1. The Court overturns the convictions under the Ohio Criminal Syndicalism Statute because the law does not require the necessary showing the Court says the First Amendment demands. The Court does not say whether under a proper statute the speech here could be prohibited. Do you think it could be? Should be? How do you think this speech might affect an African-American family living in Hamilton County?

2. Can you find the "rule" in *Brandenburg*? Is it really different than "clear and present danger," or is the real difference the way the test is applied? Consider the following more recent case.

HOLDER V. HUMANITARIAN LAW PROJECT
United States Supreme Court, 2010.
561 U.S. 1, 130 S.Ct. 2705.

CHIEF JUSTICE ROBERTS delivered the opinion of the Court.

Congress has prohibited the provision of "material support or resources" to certain foreign organizations that engage in terrorist activity. That prohibition is based on a finding that the specified organizations "are so tainted by their criminal conduct that any contribution to such an organization facilitates that conduct." The plaintiffs in this litigation seek to provide support to two such organizations. Plaintiffs claim that they seek to facilitate only the lawful, nonviolent purposes of those groups, and that applying the material-support law to prevent them from doing so violates the Constitution. In particular, they claim that the statute . . . infringes their rights to freedom of speech and association, in violation of the First Amendment. We conclude that the material-support statute is constitutional as applied to the particular activities plaintiffs have told us they wish to pursue. We do not, however, address the resolution of more difficult cases that may arise under the statute in the future.

This litigation concerns 18 U.S.C. § 2339B, which makes it a federal crime to "knowingly provid[e] material support or resources to a foreign terrorist organization." Congress has . . . defined ["material support"] as follows:

> [T]he term "material support or resources" means any property, tangible or intangible, or service, including currency or monetary instruments or financial securities, financial services, lodging, training, expert advice or assistance, safehouses, false documentation or identification, communications equipment, facilities, weapons, lethal substances, explosives, personnel (1 or more individuals who may be or include oneself), and transportation, except medicine or religious materials.

[I]n 1997, the Secretary of State designated 30 groups as foreign terrorist organizations. Two of those groups are the Kurdistan Workers' Party (also known as the Partiya Karkeran Kurdistan, or PKK) and the Liberation Tigers of Tamil Eelam (LTTE). The PKK is an organization founded in 1974 with the aim of establishing an independent Kurdish state in southeastern Turkey. The LTTE is an organization founded in 1976 for the purpose of creating an independent Tamil state in Sri Lanka. . . .

Plaintiffs in this litigation are two U.S. citizens and six domestic organizations. . . . In 1998, plaintiffs filed suit in federal court challenging the constitutionality of the material-support statute. Plaintiffs claimed that they wished to provide support for the humanitarian and political activities of the PKK and the LTTE in the form of monetary contributions, other tangible aid, legal training, and political advocacy, but that they could not do so for fear of prosecution. . . .

As relevant here, plaintiffs claimed that the material-support statute was unconstitutional [because] it violated their freedom of speech and freedom of association under the First Amendment, because it criminalized their provision of material support to the PKK and the LTTE, without requiring the Government to prove that plaintiffs had a specific intent to further the unlawful ends of those organizations. . . .

Congress[, however] amended § 2339B and the definition of "material support or resources" [to clarify that] the mental state necessary to violate § 2339B, requir[es] knowledge of the foreign group's designation as a terrorist organization or the group's commission of terrorist acts. . . .

Finally, the [amendment] clarified the scope of the term "personnel" by providing:

> No person may be prosecuted under [§ 2339B] . . . unless that person has knowingly provided, attempted to provide, or conspired to provide a foreign terrorist organization with 1 or more individuals (who may be or include himself) to work under that terrorist organization's direction or control or to organize, manage, supervise, or otherwise direct the operation of that organization. Individuals who act entirely independently of the foreign terrorist organization to advance its goals or objectives shall not be considered to be working under the foreign terrorist organization's direction and control. . . .

We [now] consider whether the material-support statute, as applied to plaintiffs, violates the freedom of speech guaranteed by the First Amendment. Both plaintiffs and the Government take extreme positions on this question. Plaintiffs claim that Congress has banned their "pure political speech." It has not. Under the material-support statute, plaintiffs may say anything they wish on any topic. They may speak and write freely about the PKK and LTTE, the governments of Turkey and Sri Lanka, human rights, and international law. They may advocate before the United Nations. As the Government states: "The statute does not prohibit independent advocacy or expression of any kind." [C]ongress has not, therefore, sought to suppress ideas or opinions in the form of "pure political speech." Rather, Congress has prohibited "material support," which most often does not take the form of speech at all. And when it does, the statute is carefully drawn to cover only a narrow category of speech to, under the direction of, or in coordination with foreign groups that the speaker knows to be terrorist organizations.

For its part, the Government takes the foregoing too far, claiming that the only thing truly at issue in this litigation is conduct, not speech. Section 2339B is directed at the fact of plaintiffs' interaction with the PKK and LTTE, the Government contends, and only incidentally burdens their expression. . . . The Government is wrong that the only thing actually at issue in this litigation is conduct. . . . Plaintiffs want to speak to the PKK and the LTTE, and whether they may do so under § 2339B depends on what they say. If plaintiffs' speech to those groups imparts a "specific skill" or communicates advice derived from "specialized knowledge"—for example, training on the use of international law or advice on petitioning the United Nations—then it is barred. On the other hand, plaintiffs' speech is not barred if it imparts only general or unspecialized knowledge. . . .

The First Amendment issue before us is more refined than either plaintiffs or the Government would have it. It is not whether the Government may prohibit pure political speech, or may prohibit material support in the form of conduct. It is instead whether the Government may prohibit what plaintiffs want to do—provide material support to the PKK and LTTE in the form of speech.

Everyone agrees that the Government's interest in combating terrorism is an urgent objective of the highest order. Plaintiffs' complaint is that the ban on material support, applied to what they wish to do, is not "necessary to further that interest." The objective of combating terrorism does not justify prohibiting their speech, plaintiffs argue, because their support will advance only the legitimate activities of the designated terrorist organizations, not their terrorism.

Whether foreign terrorist organizations meaningfully segregate support of their legitimate activities from support of terrorism is an empirical question. When it enacted § 2339B in 1996, Congress made specific findings regarding the serious threat posed by international terrorism. One of those findings explicitly rejects plaintiffs' contention that their support would not further the terrorist activities of the PKK and LTTE: "[F]oreign organizations that engage in terrorist activity are so tainted by their criminal conduct that *any contribution to such an organization* facilitates that conduct." § 301(a)(7)(emphasis added).

Plaintiffs argue that the reference to "any contribution" in this finding meant only monetary support. There is no reason to read the finding to be so limited, particularly because Congress expressly prohibited so much more than monetary support in § 2339B. Congress's use of the term "contribution" is best read to reflect a determination that any form of material support furnished "to" a foreign terrorist organization should be barred, which is precisely what the material-support statute does. Indeed, when Congress enacted § 2339B, Congress simultaneously removed an exception that had existed in § 2339A(a)(1994 ed.) for the provision of material support in the form of "humanitarian assistance to persons not directly involved in" terrorist activity. That repeal demonstrates that Congress considered and rejected the view that ostensibly peaceful aid would have no harmful effects.

We are convinced that Congress was justified in rejecting that view. The PKK and the LTTE are deadly groups. . . . It is not difficult to conclude as Congress did that the "tain[t]" of such violent activities is so great that working in coordination with or at the command of the PKK and LTTE serves to legitimize and further their terrorist means.

Material support meant to "promot[e] peaceable, lawful conduct," can further terrorism by foreign groups in multiple ways. "Material support" is a valuable resource by definition. Such support frees up other resources within the organization that may be put to violent ends. It also importantly helps lend legitimacy to foreign terrorist groups—legitimacy that makes it easier for those groups to persist, to recruit members, and to raise funds—all of which facilitate more terrorist attacks. . . .

The dissent argues that there is "no natural stopping place" for the proposition that aiding a foreign terrorist organization's lawful activity promotes the terrorist organization as a whole. But Congress has settled on just such a natural stopping place: The statute reaches only material support coordinated with or under the direction of a designated foreign terrorist organization. Independent advocacy that might be viewed as promoting the group's legitimacy is not covered.[6]

Providing foreign terrorist groups with material support in any form also furthers terrorism by straining the United States' relationships with its allies and undermining cooperative efforts between nations to prevent terrorist attacks. We see no reason to question Congress's finding that "international cooperation is required for an effective response to terrorism. . . ." The material-support statute furthers this international effort by prohibiting aid for foreign terrorist groups that harm the United States' partners abroad. . . .

In analyzing whether it is possible in practice to distinguish material support for a foreign terrorist group's violent activities and its nonviolent activities, we do not rely exclusively on our own inferences drawn from the record evidence. We have before us an affidavit stating the Executive Branch's conclusion on that question. The State Department informs us that "[t]he experience and analysis of the U.S. government agencies charged with combating terrorism strongly suppor[t]" Congress's finding that all contributions to foreign terrorist organizations further their terrorism. . . .

That evaluation of the facts by the Executive, like Congress's assessment, is entitled to deference. This litigation implicates sensitive and weighty interests of national security and foreign affairs. . . .

Our precedents, old and new, make clear that concerns of national security and foreign relations do not warrant abdication of the judicial role. We do not defer to the Government's reading of the First Amendment, even when such interests are at stake. We are one with the dissent that the Government's "authority and expertise in these matters do not automatically trump the Court's own obligation to secure the protection that the Constitution grants to individuals." But when it comes to collecting evidence and drawing factual inferences in this area, "the lack of competence on the part of the courts is marked" and respect for the Government's conclusions is appropriate.

One reason for that respect is that national security and foreign policy concerns arise in connection with efforts to confront evolving threats in an

---

[6] The dissent also contends that the particular sort of material support plaintiffs seek to provide cannot be diverted to terrorist activities, in the same direct way as funds or goods. This contention misses the point. Both common sense and the evidence submitted by the Government make clear that material support of a terrorist group's lawful activities facilitates the group's ability to attract "funds," "financing," and "goods" that will further its terrorist acts.

area where information can be difficult to obtain and the impact of certain conduct difficult to assess. . . . In this context, conclusions must often be based on informed judgment rather than concrete evidence, and that reality affects what we may reasonably insist on from the Government. The material-support statute is, on its face, a preventive measure—it criminalizes not terrorist attacks themselves, but aid that makes the attacks more likely to occur. The Government, when seeking to prevent imminent harms in the context of international affairs and national security, is not required to conclusively link all the pieces in the puzzle before we grant weight to its empirical conclusions. . . .

We also find it significant that Congress has been conscious of its own responsibility to consider how its actions may implicate constitutional concerns. First, § 2339B only applies to designated foreign terrorist organizations. There is, and always has been, a limited number of those organizations designated by the Executive Branch, and any groups so designated may seek judicial review of the designation. Second, in response to the lower courts' holdings in this litigation, Congress added clarity to the statute by providing narrowing definitions of the terms "training," "personnel," and "expert advice or assistance," as well as an explanation of the knowledge required to violate § 2339B. Third, in effectuating its stated intent not to abridge First Amendment rights, Congress has also displayed a careful balancing of interests in creating limited exceptions to the ban on material support. The definition of material support, for example, excludes medicine and religious materials. . . . Finally, and most importantly, Congress has avoided any restriction on independent advocacy, or indeed any activities not directed to, coordinated with, or controlled by foreign terrorist groups. . . .

In responding to the foregoing, the dissent fails to address the real dangers at stake. It instead considers only the possible benefits of plaintiffs' proposed activities in the abstract. The dissent seems unwilling to entertain the prospect that training and advising a designated foreign terrorist organization on how to take advantage of international entities might benefit that organization in a way that facilitates its terrorist activities. In the dissent's world, such training is all to the good. Congress and the Executive, however, have concluded that we live in a different world: one in which the designated foreign terrorist organizations "are so tainted by their criminal conduct that any contribution to such an organization facilitates that conduct." . . .

All this is not to say that any future applications of the material-support statute to speech or advocacy will survive First Amendment scrutiny. It is also not to say that any other statute relating to speech and terrorism would satisfy the First Amendment. In particular, we in no way suggest that a regulation of independent speech would pass constitutional muster, even if the Government were to show that such speech benefits foreign terrorist organizations. We also do not suggest that Congress could extend the same prohibition on material support at issue here to domestic organizations. We simply hold that, in prohibiting the particular forms of support that plaintiffs seek to provide to foreign terrorist groups, § 2339B does not violate the freedom of speech. . . .

JUSTICE BREYER, with whom JUSTICES GINSBURG and SOTOMAYOR join, dissenting.

[I] cannot agree with the Court's conclusion that the Constitution permits the Government to prosecute the plaintiffs criminally for engaging in coordinated teaching and advocacy furthering the designated organizations' lawful political objectives. . . .

In my view, the Government has not made the strong showing necessary to justify under the First Amendment the criminal prosecution of those who engage in these activities. All the activities involve the communication and advocacy of political ideas and lawful means of achieving political ends. Even the subjects the plaintiffs wish to teach— using international law to resolve disputes peacefully or petitioning the United Nations, for instance—concern political speech. We cannot avoid the constitutional significance of these facts on the basis that some of this speech takes place outside the United States and is directed at foreign governments, for the activities also involve advocacy in *this* country directed to *our* government and *its* policies. The plaintiffs, for example, wish to write and distribute publications and to speak before the United States Congress.

That this speech and association for political purposes is the *kind* of activity to which the First Amendment ordinarily offers its strongest protection is elementary.

Although in the Court's view the statute applies only where the PKK helps to coordinate a defendant's activities, the simple fact of "coordination" alone cannot readily remove protection that the First Amendment would otherwise grant. That amendment, after all, also protects the freedom of association. "Coordination" with a political group, like membership, involves association.

"Coordination" with a group that engages in unlawful activity also does not deprive the plaintiffs of the First Amendment's protection under any traditional "categorical" exception to its protection. The plaintiffs do not propose to solicit a crime. They will not engage in fraud or defamation or circulate obscenity. And the First Amendment protects advocacy even of *unlawful* action so long as that advocacy is not "directed to inciting or producing *imminent lawless action* and . . . *likely to incite or produce* such action." *Brandenburg v. Ohio.* Here the plaintiffs seek to advocate peaceful, *lawful* action to secure *political* ends; and they seek to teach others how to do the same. No one contends that the plaintiffs' speech to these organizations can be prohibited as incitement under *Brandenburg*.

Moreover, the Court has previously held that a person who associates with a group that uses unlawful means to achieve its ends does not thereby necessarily forfeit the First Amendment's protection for freedom of association. *See Scales v. United States*. Rather, the Court has pointed out in respect to associating with a group advocating overthrow of the Government through force and violence: "If the persons assembling have committed crimes elsewhere . . ., they may be prosecuted for their . . . violation of valid laws. But it is a different matter when the State, instead of prosecuting them for such offenses, seizes upon mere participation in a peaceable assembly and a lawful public discussion as the basis for a criminal charge." . . .

[W]here, as here, a statute applies criminal penalties and at least arguably does so on the basis of content-based distinctions, I should think we would scrutinize the statute and justifications "strictly"—to determine whether the prohibition is justified by a "compelling" need that cannot be "less restrictively" accommodated.

But, even if we assume for argument's sake that "strict scrutiny" does not apply, . . . I doubt that the statute, as the Government would interpret it, can survive any reasonably applicable First Amendment standard.

The Government does identify a compelling countervailing interest, namely, the interest in protecting the security of the United States and its nationals from the threats that foreign terrorist organizations pose by denying those organizations financial and other fungible resources. I do not dispute the importance of this interest. But I do dispute whether the interest can justify the statute's criminal prohibition. To put the matter more specifically, precisely how does application of the statute to the protected activities before us *help achieve* that important security-related end?

The Government makes two efforts to answer this question. *First,* the Government says that the plaintiffs' support for these organizations is "fungible" in the same sense as other forms of banned support. Being fungible, the plaintiffs' support could, for example, free up other resources, which the organization might put to terrorist ends.

The proposition that the two very different kinds of "support" are "fungible," however, is not *obviously* true. There is no *obvious* way in which undertaking advocacy for political change through peaceful means or teaching the PKK and LTTE, say, how to petition the United Nations for political change is fungible with other resources that might be put to more sinister ends in the way that donations of money, food, or computer training are fungible. It is far from obvious that these advocacy activities can themselves be redirected, or will free other resources that can be directed, towards terrorist ends. . . .

Second, the Government says that the plaintiffs' proposed activities will "bolste[r] a terrorist organization's efficacy and strength in a community" and "undermin[e] this nation's efforts to *delegitimize and weaken* those groups." In the Court's view, too, the Constitution permits application of the statute to activities of the kind at issue in part because those activities could provide a group that engages in terrorism with "legitimacy." The Court suggests that, armed with this greater "legitimacy," these organizations will more readily be able to obtain material support of the kinds Congress plainly intended to ban—money, arms, lodging, and the like.

Yet the Government does not claim that the statute forbids *any* speech "legitimating" a terrorist group. Rather, it reads the statute as permitting (1) membership in terrorist organizations, (2) "peaceably assembling with members of the PKK and LTTE for lawful discussion," or (3) "independent advocacy" on behalf of these organizations. The Court, too, emphasizes that activities not "*coordinated with*" the terrorist groups are not banned. And it argues that speaking, writing, and teaching aimed at furthering a terrorist organization's peaceful political ends could "mak[e] it easier for those groups to persist, to recruit members, and to raise funds."

But this "legitimacy" justification cannot by itself warrant suppression of political speech, advocacy, and association. Speech, association, and related activities on behalf of a group will often, perhaps always, help to legitimate that group. Thus, were the law to accept a "legitimating" effect, in and of itself and without qualification, as providing sufficient grounds for imposing such a ban, the First Amendment battle would be lost in untold instances where it should be won. Once one accepts this argument, there is no natural stopping place. The argument applies as strongly to "independent" as to "coordinated" advocacy. That fact is reflected in part in the Government's claim that the ban here, so supported, prohibits a lawyer hired by a designated group from filing on behalf of that group an *amicus* brief before the United Nations or even before this Court. . . .

Regardless, the "legitimacy" justification itself is inconsistent with critically important First Amendment case law. Consider the cases involving the protection the First Amendment offered those who joined the Communist Party intending only to further its peaceful activities. In those cases, this Court took account of congressional findings that the Communist Party not only advocated theoretically but also sought to put into practice the overthrow of our Government through force and violence. The Court had previously accepted Congress's determinations that the American Communist Party was a "Communist action organization" which (1) acted under the "control, direction, and discipline" of the world Communist movement, a movement that sought to employ "espionage, sabotage, terrorism, and any other means deemed necessary, to establish a Communist totalitarian dictatorship," and (2) "endeavor[ed]" to bring about "the overthrow of existing governments by . . . force if necessary."

Nonetheless, the Court held that the First Amendment protected an American's right to belong to that party—despite whatever "legitimating" effect membership might have had—as long as the person did not share the party's unlawful purposes. As I have pointed out, those cases draw further support from other cases permitting pure advocacy of even the most unlawful activity—as long as that advocacy is not "directed to inciting or producing imminent lawless action and . . . likely to incite or produce such action." *Brandenburg*. The Government's "legitimating" theory would seem to apply to these cases with equal justifying force; and, if recognized, it would have led this Court to conclusions other than those it reached.

Nor can the Government overcome these considerations simply by narrowing the covered activities to those that involve *coordinated,* rather than *independent,* advocacy. Conversations, discussions, or logistical arrangements might well prove necessary to carry out the speech-related activities here at issue (just as conversations and discussions are a necessary part of *membership* in any organization). The Government does not distinguish this kind of "coordination" from any other. I am not aware of any form of words that might be used to describe "coordination" that would not, at a minimum, seriously chill not only the kind of activities the plaintiffs raise before us, but also the "independent advocacy" the Government purports to permit. And, as for the Government's willingness to distinguish *independent* advocacy from *coordinated* advocacy, the former is *more* likely, not *less* likely, to confer legitimacy than the latter. Thus, other things being equal, the distinction "coordination" makes is arbitrary in respect to furthering the statute's purposes. And a rule of law that finds the "legitimacy" argument adequate in respect to the latter would have a hard time distinguishing a statute that sought to attack the former. . . .

Throughout, the majority emphasizes that it would defer strongly to Congress's "informed judgment." But here, there is no evidence that Congress has made such a judgment regarding the specific activities at issue in these cases. In any event, "whenever the fundamental rights of free speech and assembly are alleged to have been invaded, it must remain open [for judicial determination] whether there actually did exist at the time a clear danger; whether the danger, if any, was imminent; and whether the evil apprehended was one so substantial as to justify the stringent restriction interposed by the legislature." *Whitney* (Brandeis, J., concurring). In such circumstances, the "judicial function commands analysis of whether the specific conduct charged falls within the reach of the statute and if so whether the legislation is consonant with the Constitution." Hence, a legislative declaration "does not preclude enquiry into the question whether, at the time and under the circumstances, the conditions existed which are essential to validity under the Federal Constitution." *Whitney.* . . .

COMMENTS AND QUESTIONS

1.   The majority does not relate the prohibition in 2339B to any of the cases above, but the dissent does. Do you think the cases relating to advocacy of unlawful action—the subject of *Schenck, Debs, Gitlow,* and *Whitney* are relevant? Here plaintiffs are not seeking to advocate unlawful action, but they are seeking to provide support in the form of teaching about lawful actions to organizations that do engage in unlawful action.

2.   Note that the statute prohibits providing "material support" to terrorist organizations, but it also includes certain speech within the concept of material support. Is this more like the criminal syndicalism or criminal anarchy laws, or is it more like the Espionage Act's prohibition on obstructing the recruitment service, the former which criminalized certain speech *per se* but the latter which criminalized acts intended to achieve a prohibited end, acts which might include speech?

3.   Is the Court's deference to the findings of Congress and the Executive reminiscent of the Court's deference to legislatures in *Gitlow* and *Whitney* and to Congress in *Dennis*? Or is it distinguishable?

4.   Should *Brandenburg*'s test be the appropriate test in cases like this? Is there something fundamentally different between a group of rednecks meeting in a field threatening to return African-Americans to Africa and Jews to Israel and coordination with an acknowledged terrorist organization with thousands of victims, even when that coordination involves only attempting to help them achieve their aims peacefully, rather than through violence?

5.   The Government maintains that the statute does and constitutionally can prohibit a lawyer hired by a designated group from filing on behalf of that group an *amicus* brief before the United Nations or even before the Supreme Court. Yet, the Government provides a means for a designated group to appeal to the courts a determination that it is a terrorist organization. Would the lawyer representing a group appealing such a determination be liable under this Act, at least if the appeal failed?

PROBLEM

Protesters repeatedly disrupt a candidate's campaign rallies. The candidate, frustrated by these disruptions, calls out to his supporters in the crowd: "The next time somebody interrupts me, knock the crap out of them, would you? Seriously. OK? Just knock the hell—I promise you, I will pay for the legal fees." Indeed, some supporters respond and beat up some protesters. The supporters are arrested for assault. Would it be constitutional to arrest the candidate as well as an accessory to the assaults?

B. INDIRECT INCITEMENT

Schenck and *Brandenburg* at least have in common that the defendant is charged with attempting to incite persons to do something illegal. What if the speaker does not intend to incite persons to do something illegal, but the effect of the person's speech is still likely to result in unlawful action?

CHAPLINSKY V. NEW HAMPSHIRE

United States Supreme Court, 1942.
315 U.S. 568, 62 S.Ct. 766.

MR. JUSTICE MURPHY delivered the opinion of the Court.

Appellant, a member of the sect known as Jehovah's Witnesses, was convicted in the municipal court of Rochester, New Hampshire, for violation of Chapter 378, Section 2, of the Public Laws of New Hampshire: "No person shall address any offensive, derisive or annoying word to any other person who is lawfully in any street or other public place, nor call him by any offensive or derisive name, nor make any noise or exclamation in his presence and hearing with intent to deride, offend or annoy him, or to prevent him from pursuing his lawful business or occupation."

The complaint charged that appellant "with force and arms, in a certain public place in said city of Rochester, to wit, on the public sidewalk on the easterly side of Wakefield Street, near unto the entrance of the City Hall, did unlawfully repeat, the words following, addressed to the complainant, that is to say, 'You are a God damned racketeer' and 'a damned Fascist and the whole government of Rochester are Fascists or agents of Fascists' the same being offensive, derisive and annoying words and names."

[B]y motions and exceptions, appellant raised the questions that the statute was invalid under the Fourteenth Amendment of the Constitution of the United States in that it placed an unreasonable restraint on freedom of speech, freedom of the press, and freedom of worship, and because it was vague and indefinite. These contentions were overruled and the case comes here on appeal.

There is no substantial dispute over the facts. Chaplinsky was distributing the literature of his sect on the streets of Rochester on a busy Saturday afternoon. Members of the local citizenry complained to the City Marshal, Bowering, that Chaplinsky was denouncing all religion as a "racket." Bowering told them that Chaplinsky was lawfully engaged, and then warned Chaplinsky that the crowd was getting restless. Some time later a disturbance occurred and the traffic officer on duty at the busy intersection started with Chaplinsky for the police station, but did not inform him that he was under arrest or that he was going to be arrested. On the way they encountered Marshal Bowering who had been advised that a riot was under way and was therefore hurrying to the scene.

Bowering repeated his earlier warning to Chaplinsky who then addressed to Bowering the words set forth in the complaint. . . .

Appellant admitted that he said the words charged in the complaint with the exception of the name of the Deity. . . .

It is now clear that freedom of speech and freedom of the press, which are protected by the First Amendment from infringement by Congress, are among the fundamental personal rights and liberties which are protected by the Fourteenth Amendment from invasion by state action. . . .

Allowing the broadest scope to the language and purpose of the Fourteenth Amendment, it is well understood that the right of free speech is not absolute at all times and under all circumstances. There are certain well-defined and narrowly limited classes of speech, the prevention and punishment of which have never been thought to raise any Constitutional problem. These include the lewd and obscene, the profane, the libelous, and the insulting or "fighting" words—those which by their very utterance inflict injury or tend to incite an immediate breach of the peace. It has been well observed that such utterances are no essential part of any exposition of ideas, and are of such slight social value as a step to truth that any benefit that may be derived from them is clearly outweighed by the social interest in order and morality. Resort to epithets or personal abuse is not in any proper sense communication of information or opinion safeguarded by the Constitution, and its punishment as a criminal act would raise no question under that instrument.

The state statute here challenged comes to us authoritatively construed by the highest court of New Hampshire. . . . On the authority of its earlier decisions, the state court declared that the statute's purpose was to preserve the public peace, no words being forbidden except such as have a direct tendency to cause acts of violence by the person to whom, individually, the remark is addressed. It was further said: "The word 'offensive' is not to be defined in terms of what a particular addressee thinks. * * * The test is what men of common intelligence would understand would be words likely to cause an average addressee to fight. * * * The English language has a number of words and expressions which by general consent are 'fighting words' when said without a disarming smile. * * * Such words, as ordinary men know, are likely to cause a fight. So are threatening, profane or obscene revilings. Derisive and annoying words can be taken as coming within the purview of the statute as heretofore interpreted only when they have this characteristic of plainly tending to excite the addressee to a breach of the peace. * * * The statute, as construed, does no more than prohibit the face-to-face words plainly likely to cause a breach of the peace by the addressee, words whose speaking constitute a breach of the peace by the speaker—including 'classical fighting words', words in current use less 'classical' but equally likely to cause violence, and other disorderly words, including profanity, obscenity and threats."

We are unable to say that the limited scope of the statute as thus construed contravenes the constitutional right of free expression. It is a statute narrowly drawn and limited to define and punish specific conduct lying within the domain of state power, the use in a public place of words likely to cause a breach of the peace.

Nor can we say that the application of the statute to the facts disclosed by the record substantially or unreasonably impinges upon the privilege of free speech. Argument is unnecessary to demonstrate that the appellations "damn racketeer" and "damn Fascist" are epithets likely to provoke the average person to retaliation, and thereby cause a breach of the peace. . . .

COMMENTS AND QUESTIONS

1. *Chaplinsky* is still good law today for its statement of the "fighting words" doctrine—that speech is not protected by the First Amendment if a person of ordinary understanding would expect it to lead to immediate violence if made face-to-face to a person. *Chaplinsky*'s application of the doctrine, however, is probably not good law. In subsequent cases courts have established a stricter standard of what are fighting words when addressed to police officers, because they have received training about how to react to verbal abuse. Consequently, cases have said that various profanities (*e.g.*, "fuck you," "asshole," and "son-of-a-bitch") and a raised middle finger did not constitute fighting words, although the courts are split on "mother fucker."

2. *Chaplinsky* refers to categories of speech the restriction of which have never raised a constitutional problem—the lewd and obscene, the profane, the libelous—but, as we shall see, the lewd and profane now are protected, obscenity has been narrowly defined, and not all libel is unprotected today. Thus, *Chaplinsky* today is generally not good law, even if its "fighting words" exception remains.

FEINER V. NEW YORK

United States Supreme Court, 1951.
340 U.S. 315, 71 S.Ct. 303.

MR. CHIEF JUSTICE VINSON delivered the opinion of the Court.

Petitioner was convicted of the offense of disorderly conduct . . . and was sentenced to thirty days in the county penitentiary. [T]he case is here on certiorari, petitioner having claimed that the conviction is in violation of his right of free speech under the Fourteenth Amendment. . . .

Irving Feiner

On the evening of March 8, 1949, petitioner Irving Feiner was addressing an open-air meeting at the corner of South McBride and Harrison Streets in the City of Syracuse. At approximately 6:30 p.m., the police received a telephone complaint concerning the meeting, and two officers were detailed to investigate. One of these officers went to the scene immediately, the other arriving some twelve minutes later. They found a crowd of about seventy-five or eighty people, both Negro and white, filling the sidewalk and spreading out into the street. Petitioner, standing on a large wooden box on the sidewalk, was addressing the crowd through a loud-speaker system attached to an automobile. Although the purpose of his speech was to urge his listeners to attend a meeting to be held that night in the Syracuse Hotel, in its course he was making derogatory remarks concerning President Truman, the American Legion, the Mayor of Syracuse, and other local political officials.

The police officers made no effort to interfere with petitioner's speech, but were first concerned with the effect of the crowd on both pedestrian and vehicular traffic. They observed the situation from the opposite side of the street, noting that some pedestrians were forced to walk in the street to avoid the crowd. Since traffic was passing at the time, the officers attempted to get the people listening to petitioner back on the sidewalk. The crowd was restless and there was some pushing, shoving and milling around. One of the officers telephoned the police station from a nearby store, and then both policemen crossed the street and mingled with the crowd without any intention of arresting the speaker.

At this time, petitioner was speaking in a "loud, high-pitched voice." He gave the impression that he was endeavoring to arouse the Negro people against the whites, urging that they rise up in arms and fight for equal rights. The statements before such a mixed audience "stirred up a little excitement." Some of the onlookers made remarks to the police about their inability to handle the crowd and at least one threatened violence if the police did not act. There were others who appeared to be favoring petitioner's arguments. Because of the feeling that existed in the crowd both for and against the speaker, the officers finally "stepped in to prevent it from resulting in a fight." One of the officers approached the petitioner, not for the purpose of arresting him, but to get him to break up the crowd.

He asked petitioner to get down off the box, but the latter refused to accede to his request and continued talking. The officer waited for a minute and then demanded that he cease talking. Although the officer had thus twice requested petitioner to stop over the course of several minutes, petitioner not only ignored him but continued talking. During all this time, the crowd was pressing closer around petitioner and the officer. Finally, the officer told petitioner he was under arrest and ordered him to get down from the box, reaching up to grab him. . . . Petitioner had been speaking for over a half hour.

[W]e are not faced here with blind condonation by a state court of arbitrary police action. . . . The trial judge heard testimony supporting and contradicting the judgment of the police officers that a clear danger of disorder was threatened. After weighing this contradictory evidence, the trial judge reached the conclusion that the police officers were justified in taking action to prevent a breach of the peace. . . . The courts below recognized petitioner's right to hold a street meeting at this locality, to make use of loud-speaking equipment in giving his speech, and to make derogatory remarks concerning public officials and the American Legion. They found that the officers in making the arrest were motivated solely by a proper concern for the preservation of order and protection of the general welfare, and that there was no evidence which could lend color to a claim that the acts of the police were a cover for suppression of petitioner's views and opinions.[2] Petitioner was thus neither arrested nor convicted for the making or the content of his speech. Rather, it was the reaction which it actually engendered.

[W]hen clear and present danger of riot, disorder, interference with traffic upon the public streets, or other immediate threat to public safety, peace, or order, appears, the power of the State to prevent or punish is obvious. . . . This Court respects, as it must, the interest of the community in maintaining peace and order on its streets. We cannot say that the preservation of that interest here encroaches on the constitutional rights of this petitioner.

We are well aware that the ordinary murmurings and objections of a hostile audience cannot be allowed to silence a speaker, and are also mindful of the possible danger of giving overzealous police officials complete discretion to break up otherwise lawful public meetings. . . . But we are not faced here with such a situation. . . . The findings of the state courts as to the existing situation and the imminence of greater disorder

---

[2] The New York Court of Appeals said: "An imminent danger of a breach of the peace, of a disturbance of public order, perhaps even of riot, was threatened * * * the defendant, as indicated above, disrupted pedestrian and vehicular traffic on the sidewalk and street, and, with intent to provoke a breach of the peace and with knowledge of the consequences, so inflamed and agitated a mixed audience of sympathizers and opponents that, in the judgment of the police officers present, a clear danger of disorder and violence was threatened. Defendant then deliberately refused to accede to the reasonable request of the officer, made within the lawful scope of his authority, that the defendant desist in the interest of public welfare and safety."

coupled with petitioner's deliberate defiance of the police officers convince us that we should not reverse this conviction in the name of free speech.

MR. JUSTICE FRANKFURTER concurs in the result.

MR. JUSTICE BLACK, dissenting.

The record before us convinces me that petitioner, a young college student, has been sentenced to the penitentiary for the unpopular views he expressed on matters of public interest while lawfully making a street-corner speech in Syracuse, New York. [Justice Black then argues that the facts do not support a conclusion that violence was imminent, and his view that what really happened was that Feiner was arrested because of what he said.]

Moreover, assuming that the "facts" did indicate a critical situation, I reject the implication of the Court's opinion that the police had no obligation to protect petitioner's constitutional right to talk. The police of course have power to prevent breaches of the peace. But if, in the name of preserving order, they ever can interfere with a lawful public speaker, they first must make all reasonable efforts to protect him. Here the policemen did not even pretend to try to protect petitioner. According to the officers' testimony, the crowd was restless but there is no showing of any attempt to quiet it; pedestrians were forced to walk into the street, but there was no effort to clear a path on the sidewalk; one person threatened to assault petitioner but the officers did nothing to discourage this when even a word might have sufficed. Their duty was to protect petitioner's right to talk, even to the extent of arresting the man who threatened to interfere. Instead, they shirked that duty and acted only to suppress the right to speak. . . .

In my judgment, today's holding means that as a practical matter, minority speakers can be silenced in any city. Hereafter, despite the First and Fourteenth Amendments, the policeman's club can take heavy toll of a current administration's public critics. Criticism of public officials will be too dangerous for all but the most courageous. . . .

MR. JUSTICE DOUGLAS, with whom MR. JUSTICE MINTON concurs, dissenting.

Public assemblies and public speech occupy an important role in American life. One high function of the police is to protect these lawful gatherings so that the speakers may exercise their constitutional rights. When unpopular causes are sponsored from the public platform, there will commonly be mutterings and unrest and heckling from the crowd. When a speaker mounts a platform it is not unusual to find him resorting to exaggeration, to vilification of ideas and men, to the making of false charges. But those extravagances . . . do not justify penalizing the speaker by depriving him of the platform or by punishing him for his conduct.

A speaker may not, of course, incite a riot any more than he may incite a breach of the peace by the use of "fighting words." But this record shows no such extremes. It shows an unsympathetic audience and the threat of one man to haul the speaker from the stage. It is against that kind of threat that speakers need police protection. If they do not receive it and instead the police throw their weight on the side of those who would break up the meetings, the police become the new censors of speech. . . .

COMMENTS AND QUESTIONS

1.   *Feiner* has not fared well at the hands of commentators or in subsequent cases. Most commentators have sided with the dissenters, viewing the case as one of a "heckler's veto." That is, if the government can constitutionally silence a person who is engaged in otherwise concededly constitutionally protected speech simply because the listeners threaten the public peace, is this consistent with the First Amendment? Or, is the government required to protect the person who is engaged in protected speech from the threatened illegal conduct by others? How do you read the facts in *Feiner*? Do you think the police had an alternative? Could the two policemen on site have been able to control the crowd of 80? In fairness, both dissents have been radically shortened here, eliminating most of their characterization of the facts supporting their views.

2.   One could view *Feiner* as *Chaplinsky* writ large. That is, in *Chaplinsky* where one uses language that would cause his listener to respond in violence, one loses the constitutional protection for his speech; in *Feiner* where one engages in expression that will result in a crowd responding violently, one loses the constitutional protection. Or one might view *Feiner* as a variant of the *Brandenburg* rule: where one engages in expression that will likely result in imminent illegal action and the person is aware of this likely result and therefore is implicitly intending the natural consequences of his actions, one loses constitutional protection for the speech. In either case, what all three cases have in common is the risk of imminent violence—where more speech will not be able to counter the negative social effects of the speech-inducing violence. And this suggests that when there is an unavoidable collision between speech and imminent breach of the peace, speech must give way.

3.   In *Feiner*, implicit in the Court's decision and contested by the dissent is the conclusion that the police could not have averted the imminent violence by dealing with those who were about to breach the peace rather than with the speaker. Thus, the collision between the speech and the imminent breach of the peace was unavoidable except by silencing the speaker. That, of course, is a factual issue, and therefore one to which courts ordinarily would defer to the trial court's resolution, as the Court did in *Feiner*. In First Amendment cases, however, there is a practice of appellate courts independently determining the facts necessary to decide a First Amendment claim. For example, in *Schenck*, Justice Holmes assumed that it was the Supreme Court's responsibility to assess whether the speech there actually constituted a clear and present

danger, and it was that independent determination that led the Justices Black, Douglas, and Minton to dissent in *Feiner*.

4.   *Feiner* occurred before police had electronic communication with headquarters to call for reinforcements, so maybe it was unrealistic to think the two policemen could control the unruly crowd. Today, the ability of the police to respond effectively and quickly is improved. Consequently, the unavoidability of preventing the violence except through silencing the speaker becomes less likely.

5.   What if it is predictable that someone's speech or parade will produce substantial public discord and probable violence by persons opposed to the speech? After a large civil rights demonstration in the county had required the use of 3,000 state and local police and National Guardsmen to counter 1000 counterdemonstrators at a cost of $670,000, the county adopted an ordinance providing that a permit fee of up to $1000 could be charged toward defraying the costs of keeping public order. When this ordinance was applied to a proposed demonstration by the Ku Klux Klan, the Klan argued that it was unconstitutional. By a 5–4 vote the Court overturned the ordinance, saying that a permit fee could not be tied to a crowd's expected reaction to protected speech. *Forsyth County, Georgia v. The Nationalist Movement*, 505 U.S. 123 (1992). In the same year, the Klan proposed to march along Constitution Avenue in Washington, D.C. from the Capitol to the Washington Monument. Anticipating significant crowd response, the District government only allowed the march to extend four blocks. In *Christian Knights of Ku Klux Klan Invisible Empire v. District of Columbia*, 972 F.2d 365 (D.C. Cir. 1992), the D.C. Circuit upheld a district court's injunction against limiting the Klan's march. The full march took place, and 27 hooded Klansmen drew 1,000 counterdemonstrators who were kept at bay by 3,500 police officers. Six counterdemonstrators and eight policemen suffered injuries, but the First Amendment rights of the Klan were protected.

C. OFFENSIVE SPEECH

Some speech may be offensive but not so extreme as to engender violence on behalf of listeners or onlookers.

COHEN V. CALIFORNIA

United States Supreme Court, 1971.
403 U.S. 15, 91 S.Ct. 1780.

MR. JUSTICE HARLAN delivered the opinion of the Court.

[A]ppellant Paul Robert Cohen was convicted in the Los Angeles Municipal Court of violating that part of [the] California Penal Code which prohibits "maliciously and willfully disturb(ing) the peace or quiet of any neighborhood or person * * * by * * * offensive conduct * * *." [T]he facts upon which his conviction rests are detailed in the opinion of the Court of Appeal of California, Second Appellate District, as follows: "On April 26,

1968, the defendant was observed in the Los Angeles County Courthouse in the corridor outside of division 20 of the municipal court wearing a jacket bearing the words 'Fuck the Draft' which were plainly visible. There were women and children present in the corridor. The defendant was arrested. The defendant testified that he wore the jacket knowing that the words were on the jacket as a means of informing the public of the depth of his feelings against the Vietnam War and the draft. The defendant did not engage in, nor threaten to engage in, nor did anyone as the result of his conduct in fact commit or threaten to commit any act of violence." . . . .

The conviction quite clearly rests upon the asserted offensiveness of the words Cohen used to convey his message to the public. The only "conduct" which the State sought to punish is the fact of communication. Thus, we deal here with a conviction resting solely upon "speech." [F]urther, the State certainly lacks power to punish Cohen for the underlying content of the message the inscription conveyed. At least so long as there is no showing of an intent to incite disobedience to or disruption of the draft, Cohen could not, consistently with the First and Fourteenth Amendments, be punished for asserting the evident position on the inutility or immorality of the draft his jacket reflected.

Appellant's conviction, then, rests squarely upon his exercise of the "freedom of speech" protected from arbitrary governmental interference by the Constitution and can be justified, if at all, only as a valid regulation of the manner in which he exercised that freedom, not as a permissible prohibition on the substantive message it conveys. This does not end the inquiry, of course, for the First and Fourteenth Amendments have never been thought to give absolute protection to every individual to speak whenever or wherever he pleases or to use any form of address in any circumstances that he chooses. . . .

This Court has also held that the States are free to ban the simple use, without a demonstration of additional justifying circumstances, of so-called "fighting words," those personally abusive epithets which, when addressed to the ordinary citizen, are, as a matter of common knowledge, inherently likely to provoke violent reaction. *Chaplinsky v. New Hampshire.* While the four-letter word displayed by Cohen in relation to the draft is not uncommonly employed in a personally provocative fashion, in this instance it was clearly not "directed to the person of the hearer." No individual actually or likely to be present could reasonably have regarded the words on appellant's jacket as a direct personal insult. Nor do we have here an instance of the exercise of the State's police power to prevent a speaker from intentionally provoking a given group to hostile reaction. *Cf. Feiner v. New York.* There is, as noted above, no showing that anyone who saw Cohen was in fact violently aroused or that appellant intended such a result.

Finally, in arguments before this Court much has been made of the claim that Cohen's distasteful mode of expression was thrust upon unwilling or unsuspecting viewers, and that the State might therefore legitimately act as it did in order to protect the sensitive from otherwise unavoidable exposure to appellant's crude form of protest. Of course, the mere presumed presence of unwitting listeners or viewers does not serve automatically to justify curtailing all speech capable of giving offense. While this Court has recognized that government may properly act in many situations to prohibit intrusion into the privacy of the home of unwelcome views and ideas which cannot be totally banned from the public dialogue, we have at the same time consistently stressed that "we are often 'captives' outside the sanctuary of the home and subject to objectionable speech." The ability of government, consonant with the Constitution, to shut off discourse solely to protect others from hearing it is, in other words, dependent upon a showing that substantial privacy interests are being invaded in an essentially intolerable manner. Any broader view of this authority would effectively empower a majority to silence dissidents simply as a matter of personal predilections.

In this regard, persons confronted with Cohen's jacket were in a quite different posture than, say, those subjected to the raucous emissions of sound trucks blaring outside their residences. Those in the Los Angeles courthouse could effectively avoid further bombardment of their sensibilities simply by averting their eyes. And, while it may be that one has a more substantial claim to a recognizable privacy interest when walking through a courthouse corridor than, for example, strolling through Central Park, surely it is nothing like the interest in being free from unwanted expression in the confines of one's own home. Given the subtlety and complexity of the factors involved, if Cohen's "speech" was otherwise entitled to constitutional protection, we do not think the fact that some unwilling "listeners" in a public building may have been briefly exposed to it can serve to justify this breach of the peace conviction where, as here, there was no evidence that persons powerless to avoid appellant's conduct did in fact object to it, and where that portion of the statute upon which Cohen's conviction rests evinces no concern, either on its face or as construed by the California courts, with the special plight of the captive auditor, but, instead, indiscriminately sweeps within its prohibitions all "offensive conduct" that disturbs "any neighborhood or person."

Against this background, the issue flushed by this case stands out in bold relief. It is whether California can excise, as "offensive conduct," one particular scurrilous epithet from the public discourse, either upon the theory of the court below that its use is inherently likely to cause violent reaction or upon a more general assertion that the States, acting as guardians of public morality, may properly remove this offensive word from the public vocabulary.

The rationale of the California court is plainly untenable. At most it reflects an "undifferentiated fear or apprehension of disturbance (which) is not enough to overcome the right to freedom of expression."

[A]dmittedly, it is not so obvious that the First and Fourteenth Amendments must be taken to disable the States from punishing public utterance of this unseemly expletive in order to maintain what they regard as a suitable level of discourse within the body politic. We think, however, that examination and reflection will reveal the shortcomings of a contrary viewpoint.

At the outset, we cannot overemphasize that, in our judgment, most situations where the State has a justifiable interest in regulating speech will fall within one or more of the various established exceptions, discussed above but not applicable here, to the usual rule that governmental bodies may not prescribe the form or content of individual expression. Equally important to our conclusion is the constitutional backdrop against which our decision must be made. The constitutional right of free expression is powerful medicine in a society as diverse and populous as ours. It is designed and intended to remove governmental restraints from the arena of public discussion, putting the decision as to what views shall be voiced largely into the hands of each of us, in the hope that use of such freedom will ultimately produce a more capable citizenry and more perfect polity and in the belief that no other approach would comport with the premise of individual dignity and choice upon which our political system rests.

To many, the immediate consequence of this freedom may often appear to be only verbal tumult, discord, and even offensive utterance. These are, however, within established limits, in truth necessary side effects of the broader enduring values which the process of open debate permits us to achieve. That the air may at times seem filled with verbal cacophony is, in this sense not a sign of weakness but of strength. . . .

Against this perception of the constitutional policies involved, we discern certain more particularized considerations that peculiarly call for reversal of this conviction. First, the principle contended for by the State seems inherently boundless. How is one to distinguish this from any other offensive word? Surely the State has no right to cleanse public debate to the point where it is grammatically palatable to the most squeamish among us. Yet no readily ascertainable general principle exists for stopping short of that result were we to affirm the judgment below. For, while the particular four-letter word being litigated here is perhaps more distasteful than most others of its genre, it is nevertheless often true that one man's vulgarity is another's lyric. Indeed, we think it is largely because governmental officials cannot make principled distinctions in this area that the Constitution leaves matters of taste and style so largely to the individual.

Additionally, we cannot overlook the fact, because it is well illustrated by the episode involved here, that much linguistic expression serves a dual communicative function: it conveys not only ideas capable of relatively precise, detached explication, but otherwise inexpressible emotions as well. In fact, words are often chosen as much for their emotive as their cognitive force. We cannot sanction the view that the Constitution, while solicitous of the cognitive content of individual speech has little or no regard for that emotive function which practically speaking, may often be the more important element of the overall message sought to be communicated. . . .

Finally, and in the same vein, we cannot indulge the facile assumption that one can forbid particular words without also running a substantial risk of suppressing ideas in the process. Indeed, governments might soon seize upon the censorship of particular words as a convenient guise for banning the expression of unpopular views. We have been able, as noted above, to discern little social benefit that might result from running the risk of opening the door to such grave results.

It is, in sum, our judgment that, absent a more particularized and compelling reason for its actions, the State may not, consistently with the First and Fourteenth Amendments, make the simple public display here involved of this single four-letter expletive a criminal offense. Because that is the only arguably sustainable rationale for the conviction here at issue, the judgment below must be reversed.

MR. JUSTICE BLACKMUN, with whom THE CHIEF JUSTICE and MR. JUSTICE BLACK join.

I dissent. . . .

Cohen's absurd and immature antic, in my view, was mainly conduct and little speech. . . . Further, the case appears to me to be well within the sphere of *Chaplinsky v. New Hampshire*, where Mr. Justice Murphy, a known champion of First Amendment freedoms, wrote for a unanimous bench. As a consequence, this Court's agonizing over First Amendment values seem misplaced and unnecessary.

MR. JUSTICE WHITE concurs in . . . MR. JUSTICE BLACKMUN's dissenting opinion [on other grounds].

COMMENTS AND QUESTIONS

1.   Everyone agrees that Mr. Cohen could have had the expression "End the Draft" on his jacket without problem. Some supporters of the war in Vietnam might have been offended, especially if Mr. Cohen had had long hair and looked like a "hippie," but no one imagines that such offense would justify government suppression of the words. Thus, it is clear that it is the particular word "fuck" that triggers the statutory prohibition. *Chaplinsky* stated that "There are certain well-defined and narrowly limited classes of speech, the prevention and punishment of which have never been thought to raise any

Constitutional problem. These include the lewd and obscene, the profane, the libelous, and the insulting or "fighting" words. . . ." And *Cohen* cites *Chaplinsky* favorably regarding fighting words. Does *Cohen* overrule *Chaplinsky* with respect to profanity?

2.   The Court says that unwilling or unsuspecting viewers could simply avert their eyes but would that really cure the problem of having been exposed to this expression? Today, perhaps, this particular word has lost some of its ability to shock. What about a jacket today with the words: "No More Nigger Presidents," or "No Cunt for President"? Most of us would be horribly shocked and offended. Would simply averting our eyes cure the problem? Is there anything in *Cohen* that would suggest a way to distinguish it?

3.   *Cohen* is notable today for the proposition that offensive speech is still protected speech and for the idea that the First Amendment protects not only the content or idea involved but also the way the message is conveyed. There are, however, limits on the way the message may be conveyed.

4.   Simon Tam, lead singer of the Asian-American rock group "The Slants," sought federal trademark registration of the mark "THE SLANTS." This term, however, is a derogatory term for Asian persons, so the Patent and Trademark Office (PTO) denied the application under a Lanham Act provision prohibiting the registration of trademarks that may "disparage . . . or bring . . . into contemp[t] or disrepute" any "persons, living or dead." Arguing that by using that term he wished to "reclaim" the term and drain its denigrating force, Tam challenged this denial as a violation of his First Amendment right to freedom of speech. In *Matal v. Tam*, 137 S.Ct. 1744 (2017), all the Justices agreed that the statute was unconstitutional, but they could not agree on why. They first addressed various government arguments that would either eliminate any First Amendment protection or result in highly permissive rational-basis review of trademark regulation. All the Justices agreed that by granting trademark protection to a mark, the mark did not become government speech; the mark remains private speech. Justice Alito, joined by the Chief Justice and Justices Thomas and Breyer, also concluded that neither was a trademark the equivalent of government-subsidized speech, where the government can have more control over the content of the speech, nor did it fall within a supposed "government program" doctrine, a new doctrine invented by the government for this case. Even if it did, Justice Alito found the provision to constitute viewpoint-based discrimination, which would damn the provision in any case. These justices went on to ask whether a trademark was "commercial speech," governed by a less strict First Amendment standard. They said they need not decide that question, because the statute failed even the less strict test for commercial speech, because it was not "narrowly drawn" to drive out trademarks that support invidious discrimination. "The clause reaches any trademark that disparages *any person, group, or institution*. It applies to trademarks like the following: 'Down with racists,' 'Down with sexists,' 'Down with homophobes.' It is not an anti-discrimination clause; it is a happy-talk clause. In this way, it goes much further than is necessary to serve the interest asserted." In dicta, Justice Alito wrote: "Speech that

demeans on the basis of race, ethnicity, gender, religion, age, disability, or any other similar ground is hateful; but the proudest boast of our free speech jurisprudence is that we protect the freedom to express the thought that we hate." Justice Kennedy, joined by Justices Ginsburg, Sotomayor, and Kagan, took a different approach. He focused on the fact that the law involved viewpoint discrimination, "an 'egregious form of content discrimination,' which is 'presumptively unconstitutional.' " Justice Kennedy explained: "At its most basic, the test for viewpoint discrimination is whether—within the relevant subject category—the government has singled out a subset of messages for disfavor based on the views expressed. In the instant case, the disparagement clause the Government now seeks to implement and enforce identifies the relevant subject as 'persons, living or dead, institutions, beliefs, or national symbols.' Within that category, an applicant may register a positive or benign mark but not a derogatory one. The law thus reflects the Government's disapproval of a subset of messages it finds offensive. This is the essence of viewpoint discrimination." Because the statute involved viewpoint discrimination, it was irrelevant whether the speech was commercial speech or not, because viewpoint discrimination is always subject to heightened scrutiny. Although Justice Thomas concurred in Justice Alito's constitutional analysis, he wrote separately to restate his belief "that when the government seeks to restrict truthful speech in order to suppress the ideas it conveys, strict scrutiny is appropriate, whether or not the speech in question may be characterized as 'commercial.' " Justice Gorsuch took no part in the decision, so the constitutional analysis split 4–4.

A similar issue arose when a person was denied trademark registration for his clothing line under the name FUCT. The denial was based on a provision that prohibited the registration of "immoral[ ] or scandalous" material. Again the Court held the provision unconstitutional, *Iancu v. Brunetti*, 139 S.Ct. 2294 (2019), although the opinion for the Court was joined by four separate opinions. Justice Kagan, writing for the Court, characterized *Tam* as reflecting agreement that the provision there involved viewpoint discrimination, and if a trademark registration bar is viewpoint-based, it violates the First Amendment. She went on to find that the "immoral or scandalous" bar was likewise viewpoint-based discrimination, giving as examples a number of past registration denials under this provision. The Chief Justice and Justices Breyer and Sotomayor concurred with the Court that the ban on "immoral" trademark registrations involved viewpoint discrimination and was unconstitutional. Each, however, opined that the ban on "scandalous" trademark registrations, interpreted to mean only the most vulgar, profane, or obscene words or images, would not involve viewpoint discrimination. It would involve content discrimination, but Justices Sotomayor and Breyer expressed the view that it should not be subject to strict scrutiny, because the inability to *register* a trademark involves only the denial of some ancillary benefits beyond those that are enjoyed under common law from simple use of a trademark by a person. They likened this situation to the limited public forum where content-based discrimination is acceptable if it is reasonable. And here they believed the bar would be reasonable.

PROBLEM

A public university has a policy that prohibits "harassment of all kinds," and defines harassment as "when a person engages in conduct that has the purpose or effect of creating an intimidating, hostile, or offensive working, campus living, athletic or academic environment." Could a public university constitutionally penalize a student who wore on campus a T-shirt with a Nazi style swastika? Could a city punish him under a statute banning the public display of scandalous signs or language?

D. EXPRESSIVE CONDUCT

During the Vietnam War, four persons who opposed the war, including a Jesuit priest, went to a Selective Service (draft) office after notifying the media that there was going to be a demonstration there. At the office the protestors proceeded to pour blood over the draft files in front of the cameras and were promptly arrested, tried, and convicted of destruction of government property and interference with the selective service system. *See United States v. Eberhardt*, 417 F.2d 1009 (4th Cir. 1969). It was clear that they did not really believe their destruction of a few records would in any meaningful way impede the war effort or the draft system; what they did believe was that their action would dramatically communicate their belief that the war was immoral and illegal and hopefully would lead others to oppose the war as well. In other words, they were trying to communicate an idea in a particularly dramatic way. However, no one, including the protestors, believed that their action was protected by the First Amendment, any more than spray painting anti-war slogans on government buildings would be protected. The communication of an idea does not privilege the destruction or damage of someone else's property in order to communicate that idea.

UNITED STATES V. O'BRIEN
United States Supreme Court, 1968.
391 U.S. 367, 88 S.Ct. 1673.

MR. CHIEF JUSTICE WARREN delivered the opinion of the Court.

On the morning of March 31, 1966, David Paul O'Brien and three companions burned their Selective Service registration certificates on the steps of the South Boston Courthouse.... For this act, O'Brien was indicted, tried, convicted, and sentenced in the United States District Court for the District of Massachusetts. He did not contest the fact that he had burned the certificate. He stated in argument to the jury that he burned the certificate publicly to influence others to adopt his antiwar beliefs, as he put it, "so that other people would reevaluate their positions with

Selective Service, with the armed forces, and reevaluate their place in the culture of today, to hopefully consider my position." The indictment upon

which he was tried charged that he "willfully and knowingly did multilate, destroy, and change by burning * * * (his) Registration Certificate (Selective Service System Form No. 2); in violation of Section 462(b)[(3)] of the Universal Military Training and Service Act of 1948. Section 462(b)(3) . . . was amended by Congress in 1965 (adding the words italicized below), so that at the time O'Brien burned his certificate an offense was committed by any person "who forges, alters, *knowingly destroys, knowingly mutilates*, or in any manner changes any such certificate * * *."

In the District Court, O'Brien argued that the 1965 Amendment prohibiting the knowing destruction or mutilation of certificates was unconstitutional because it was enacted to abridge free speech, and because it served no legitimate legislative purpose.... On appeal, the Court of Appeals for the First Circuit held the 1965 Amendment unconstitutional as a law abridging freedom of speech. At the time the Amendment was enacted, a regulation of the Selective Service System required registrants to keep their registration certificates in their "personal possession at all times." Willful violations of regulations promulgated pursuant to the Universal Military Training and Service Act were made criminal by statute. The Court of Appeals, therefore, was of the opinion that conduct punishable under the 1965 Amendment was already punishable under the nonpossession regulation, and consequently that the Amendment served no valid purpose; further, that in light of the prior regulation, the Amendment must have been "directed at public as distinguished from private destruction." On this basis, the court concluded that the 1965 Amendment ran afoul of the First Amendment by singling out persons engaged in protests for special treatment....

We hold that the 1965 Amendment is constitutional both as enacted and as applied.

When a male reaches the age of 18, he is required by the Universal Military Training and Service Act to register with a local draft board. He is assigned a Selective Service number, and within five days he is issued a registration certificate. Subsequently, and based on a questionnaire completed by the registrant, he is assigned a classification denoting his eligibility for induction, and "(a)s soon as practicable" thereafter he is issued a Notice of Classification. This initial classification is not necessarily permanent, and if in the interim before induction the registrant's status changes in some relevant way, he may be reclassified. After such a reclassification, the local board "as soon as practicable" issues to the registrant a new Notice of Classification.

Both the registration and classification certificates are small white cards, approximately 2 by 3 inches. The registration certificate specifies the name of the registrant, the date of registration, and the number and address of the local board with which he is registered. Also inscribed upon it are the date and place of the registrant's birth, his residence at registration, his physical description, his signature, and his Selective Service number. The Selective Service number itself indicates his State of registration, his local board, his year of birth, and his chronological position in the local board's classification record.

The classification certificate shows the registrant's name, Selective Service number, signature, and eligibility classification. It specifies whether he was so classified by his local board, an appeal board, or the President. It contains the address of his local board and the date the certificate was mailed.

Both the registration and classification certificates bear notices that the registrant must notify his local board in writing of every change in address, physical condition, and occupational, marital, family, dependency, and military status, and of any other fact which might change his classification. Both also contain a notice that the registrant's Selective Service number should appear on all communications to his local board.

Congress demonstrated its concern that certificates issued by the Selective Service System might be abused well before the 1965 Amendment here challenged. The 1948 Act itself prohibited many different abuses involving "any registration certificate, * * * or any other certificate issued pursuant to or prescribed by the provisions of this title, or rules or regulations promulgated hereunder * * *." [I]n addition, as previously mentioned, regulations of the Selective Service System required registrants to keep both their registration and classification certificates in their personal possession at all times. . . .

By the 1965 Amendment, Congress added to § 12(b)(3) of the 1948 Act the provision here at issue, subjecting to criminal liability not only one who "forges, alters, or in any manner changes" but also one who "knowingly destroys (or) knowingly mutilates" a certificate. We note at the outset that the 1965 Amendment plainly does not abridge free speech on its face, and we do not understand O'Brien to argue otherwise. Amended § 12(b)(3) on its face deals with conduct having no connection with speech. It prohibits the knowing destruction of certificates issued by the Selective Service System, and there is nothing necessarily expressive about such conduct. The Amendment does not distinguish between public and private destruction, and it does not punish only destruction engaged in for the purpose of expressing views. A law prohibiting destruction of Selective

Service certificates no more abridges free speech on its face than a motor vehicle law prohibiting the destruction of drivers' licenses, or a tax law prohibiting the destruction of books and records.

O'Brien nonetheless argues that the 1965 Amendment is unconstitutional in its application to him, and is unconstitutional as enacted because what he calls the "purpose" of Congress was "to suppress freedom of speech." We consider these arguments separately.

O'Brien first argues that the 1965 Amendment is unconstitutional as applied to him because his act of burning his registration certificate was protected "symbolic speech" within the First Amendment. His argument is that the freedom of expression which the First Amendment guarantees includes all modes of "communication of ideas by conduct," and that his conduct is within this definition because he did it in "demonstration against the war and against the draft."

We cannot accept the view that an apparently limitless variety of conduct can be labeled "speech" whenever the person engaging in the conduct intends thereby to express an idea. However, even on the assumption that the alleged communicative element in O'Brien's conduct is sufficient to bring into play the First Amendment, it does not necessarily follow that the destruction of a registration certificate is constitutionally protected activity. This Court has held that when "speech" and "nonspeech" elements are combined in the same course of conduct, a sufficiently important governmental interest in regulating the nonspeech element can justify incidental limitations on First Amendment freedoms. To characterize the quality of the governmental interest which must appear, the Court has employed a variety of descriptive terms: compelling; substantial; subordinating; paramount; cogent; strong. Whatever imprecision inheres in these terms, we think it clear that a government regulation is sufficiently justified if it is within the constitutional power of the Government; if it furthers an important or substantial governmental interest; if the governmental interest is unrelated to the suppression of free expression; and if the incidental restriction on alleged First Amendment freedoms is no greater than is essential to the furtherance of that interest. We find that the 1965 Amendment to § 12(b)(3) of the Universal Military Training and Service Act meets all of these requirements, and consequently that O'Brien can be constitutionally convicted for violating it.

The constitutional power of Congress to raise and support armies and to make all laws necessary and proper to that end is broad and sweeping. . . . Pursuant to this power, Congress may establish a system of registration for individuals liable for training and service, and may require such individuals within reason to cooperate in the registration system. The issuance of certificates indicating the registration and eligibility classification of individuals is a legitimate and substantial administrative aid in the functioning of this system. And legislation to insure the continuing availability of issued certificates serves a legitimate and substantial purpose in the system's administration.

O'Brien's argument to the contrary is necessarily premised upon his unrealistic characterization of Selective Service certificates. He essentially adopts the position that such certificates are so many pieces of paper designed to notify registrants of their registration or classification, to be retained or tossed in the wastebasket according to the convenience or taste of the registrant. Once the registrant has received notification, according to this view, there is no reason for him to retain the certificates. O'Brien notes that most of the information on a registration certificate serves no notification purpose at all; the registrant hardly needs to be told his address and physical characteristics. We agree that the registration certificate contains much information of which the registrant needs no notification. This circumstance, however, does not lead to the conclusion that the certificate serves no purpose, but that, like the classification certificate, it serves purposes in addition to initial notification. Many of these purposes would be defeated by the certificates' destruction or mutilation. Among these are:

1. The registration certificate serves as proof that the individual described thereon has registered for the draft. The classification certificate shows the eligibility classification of a named but undescribed individual. Voluntarily displaying the two certificates is an easy and painless way for a young man to dispel a question as to whether he might be delinquent in his Selective Service obligations. Correspondingly, the availability of the certificates for such display relieves the Selective Service System of the administrative burden it would otherwise have in verifying the registration and classification of all suspected delinquents. Further, since both certificates are in the nature of 'receipts' attesting that the registrant has done what the law requires, it is in the interest of the just and efficient administration of the system that they be continually available, in the event, for example, of a mix-up in the registrant's file. Additionally, in a time of national crisis, reasonable availability to each registrant of the two small cards assures a rapid and uncomplicated means for determining his fitness for immediate induction, no matter how distant in our mobile society he may be from his local board.

2. The information supplied on the certificates facilitates communication between registrants and local boards, simplifying the system and benefiting all concerned. To begin with, each certificate bears the address of the registrant's local board, an item unlikely to be committed to memory. Further, each card bears the registrant's Selective Service number, and a registrant who has his number readily available so that he can communicate

it to his local board when he supplies or requests information can make simpler the board's task in locating his file. Finally, a registrant's inquiry, particularly through a local board other than his own, concerning his eligibility status is frequently answerable simply on the basis of his classification certificate; whereas, if the certificate were not reasonably available and the registrant were uncertain of his classification, the task of answering his questions would be considerably complicated.

3. Both certificates carry continual reminders that the registrant must notify his local board of any change of address, and other specified changes in his status. The smooth functioning of the system requires that local boards be continually aware of the status and whereabouts of registrants, and the destruction of certificates deprives the system of a potentially useful notice device.

4. The regulatory scheme involving Selective Service certificates includes clearly valid prohibitions against the alteration, forgery, or similar deceptive misuse of certificates. The destruction or mutilation of certificates obviously increases the difficulty of detecting and tracing abuses such as these. Further, a mutilated certificate might itself be used for deceptive purposes.

The many functions performed by Selective Service certificates establish beyond doubt that Congress has a legitimate and substantial interest in preventing their wanton and unrestrained destruction and assuring their continuing availability by punishing people who knowingly and wilfully destroy or mutilate them. And we are unpersuaded that the pre-existence of the nonpossession regulations in any way negates this interest. . . .

We think it apparent that the continuing availability to each registrant of his Selective Service certificates substantially furthers the smooth and proper functioning of the system that Congress has established to raise armies. We think it also apparent that the Nation has a vital interest in having a system for raising armies that functions with maximum efficiency and is capable of easily and quickly responding to continually changing circumstances. For these reasons, the Government has a substantial interest in assuring the continuing availability of issued Selective Service certificates.

It is equally clear that the 1965 Amendment specifically protects this substantial governmental interest. We perceive no alternative means that would more precisely and narrowly assure the continuing availability of issued Selective Service certificates than a law which prohibits their wilful mutilation or destruction. The 1965 Amendment prohibits such conduct and does nothing more. In other words, both the governmental interest and the operation of the 1965 Amendment are limited to the noncommunicative aspect of O'Brien's conduct. The governmental interest and the scope of the 1965 Amendment are limited to preventing harm to the smooth and efficient functioning of the Selective Service System. When O'Brien deliberately rendered unavailable his registration certificate, he wilfully frustrated this governmental interest. For this noncommunicative impact of his conduct, and for nothing else, he was convicted.

The case at bar is therefore unlike one where the alleged governmental interest in regulating conduct arises in some measure because the communication allegedly integral to the conduct is itself thought to be harmful. In *Stromberg v. People of State of California*, 283 U.S. 359 (1931), for example, this Court struck down a statutory phrase which punished people who expressed their "opposition to organized government" by displaying "any flag, badge, banner, or device." Since the statute there was aimed at suppressing communication it could not be sustained as a regulation of noncommunicative conduct.

In conclusion, we find that because of the Government's substantial interest in assuring the continuing availability of issued Selective Service certificates, because amended § 462(b) is an appropriately narrow means of protecting this interest and condemns only the independent noncommunicative impact of conduct within its reach, and because the noncommunicative impact of O'Brien's act of burning his registration certificate frustrated the Government's interest, a sufficient governmental interest has been shown to justify O'Brien's conviction.

O'Brien finally argues that the 1965 Amendment is unconstitutional as enacted because what he calls the "purpose" of Congress was "to suppress freedom of speech." We reject this argument because under settled principles the purpose of Congress, as O'Brien uses that term, is not a basis for declaring this legislation unconstitutional.

It is a familiar principle of constitutional law that this Court will not strike down an otherwise constitutional statute on the basis of an alleged illicit legislative motive. As the Court long ago stated: "The decisions of this court from the beginning lend no support whatever to the assumption that the judiciary may restrain the exercise of lawful power on the assumption that a wrongful purpose or motive has caused the power to be exerted."

[I]nquiries into congressional motives or purposes are a hazardous matter. When the issue is simply the interpretation of legislation, the Court will look to statements by legislators for guidance as to the purpose of the legislature. . . . It is entirely a different matter when we are asked to void a statute that is, under well-settled criteria, constitutional on its face, on the basis of what fewer than a handful of Congressmen said about it. What motivates one legislator to make a speech about a statute is not necessarily what motivates scores of others to enact it, and the stakes are sufficiently high for us to eschew guesswork. We decline to void essentially on the ground that it is unwise legislation which Congress had the undoubted power to enact and which could be reenacted in its exact form if the same or another legislator made a "wiser" speech about it. . . .

We think it not amiss, in passing, to comment upon O'Brien's legislative-purpose argument. There was little floor debate on this legislation in either House. Only Senator Thurmond commented on its substantive features in the Senate. After his brief statement, and without any additional substantive comments, the bill passed the Senate. In the House debate only two Congressmen addressed themselves to the Amendment—Congressmen Rivers and Bray. The bill was passed after their statements without any further debate by a vote of 393 to 1. It is principally on the basis of the statements by these three Congressmen that O'Brien makes his congressional-"purpose" argument. We note that if we were to examine legislative purpose in the instant case, we would be obliged to consider not only these statements but also the more authoritative reports of the Senate and House Armed Services Committees. . . . While both reports make clear a concern with the "defiant" destruction of so-called "draft cards" and with "open" encouragement to others to destroy their cards, both reports also indicate that this concern stemmed from an apprehension that unrestrained destruction of cards would disrupt the smooth functioning of the Selective Service System.

MR. JUSTICE MARSHALL took no part in the consideration or decision of these cases.

APPENDIX TO OPINION OF THE COURT.

PORTIONS OF THE REPORTS OF THE COMMITTEES ON ARMED SERVICES OF THE SENATE AND HOUSE EXPLAINING THE 1965 AMENDMENT.

The "Explanation of the Bill" in the Senate Report is as follows:

Section 12(b)(3) of the Universal Military Training and Service Act of 1951, as amended, provides, among other things, that a person who forges, alters, or changes a draft registration certificate is subject to a fine of not more than $10,000 or imprisonment of not more than 5 years, or both. There is no explicit prohibition in this section against the knowing destruction or mutilation of such cards.

The committee has taken notice of the defiant destruction and mutilation of draft cards by dissident persons who disapprove of national policy. If allowed to continue unchecked this contumacious conduct represents a potential threat to the exercise of the power to raise and support armies. . . .

And the House Report explained:

Section 12(b)(3) of the Universal Military Training and Service Act of 1951, as amended, provides that a person who forges, alters, or in any manner changes his draft registration card, or any notation duly and validly inscribed thereon, will be subject to a fine of $10,000 or imprisonment of not more than 5 years. H.R. 10306 would amend this provision to make it apply also to those persons who knowingly destroy or knowingly mutilate a draft registration card.

The House Committee on Armed Services is fully aware of, and shares in, the deep concern expressed throughout the Nation over the increasing incidences in which individuals and large groups of individuals openly defy and encourage others to defy the authority of their Government by destroying or mutilating their draft cards.

While the present provisions of the Criminal Code with respect to the destruction of Government property may appear broad enough to cover all acts having to do with the mistreatment of draft cards in the possession of individuals, the committee feels that in the present critical situation of the country, the acts of destroying or mutilating these cards are offenses which pose such a grave threat to the security of the Nation that no question whatsoever should be left as to the intention of the Congress that such wanton and irresponsible acts should be punished. . . .

MR. JUSTICE HARLAN, concurring.

The crux of the Court's opinion, which I join, is of course its general statement, ante, at 1679, that:

> a government regulation is sufficiently justified if it is within the constitutional power of the Government; if it furthers an important or substantial governmental interest; if the governmental interest is unrelated to the suppression of free expression; and if the incidental restriction on alleged First Amendment freedoms is no greater than is essential to the furtherance of that interest.

I wish to make explicit my understanding that this passage does not foreclose consideration of First Amendment claims in those rare instances when an 'incidental' restriction upon expression, imposed by a regulation which furthers an "important or substantial" governmental interest and satisfies the Court's other criteria, in practice has the effect of entirely preventing a "speaker" from reaching a significant audience with whom he could not otherwise lawfully communicate. This is not such a case, since O'Brien manifestly could have conveyed his message in many ways other than by burning his draft card.

MR. JUSTICE DOUGLAS, dissenting. [opinion omitted. Justice Douglas called for rehearing to address whether the draft was constitutional in the absence of a declared war.]

COMMENTS AND QUESTIONS

1. While *O'Brien* ends up being not very protective of expressive conduct, it does establish a test that if applied with a bit more scrutiny can be protective. Can you find the test?

2. The Court states that "It is a familiar principle of constitutional law that this Court will not strike down an otherwise constitutional statute on the basis of an alleged illicit legislative motive." Recall, however, that the "intent" of the lawmaker to discriminate on the basis of race is critical to whether strict scrutiny should be applied. Is "intent" different from "motive"? Of course, courts usually look to objective criteria to discern intent, such as either the language of the law or the effect of the law, and presumably that could have been attempted here by showing that the *only* persons prosecuted under this statute were persons who publicly burned their draft cards. Nevertheless, should articulated reasons given by congressional leaders be ignored? Here, the only comments in the House on the proposed legislation came not from just any congressmen but from the Chair and ranking minority member of the House Armed Services Committee, which reported the bill. The Chair stated:

> The purpose of the bill is clear.... It is a straightforward clear answer to those who would make a mockery of our efforts in South Vietnam by engaging in the mass destruction of draft cards.... If it can be proved that a person knowingly destroyed or mutilated his draft card, then under the committee proposal, he can be sent to prison, where he belongs. This is the least we can do for our men in South Vietnam fighting to preserve freedom, while a vocal minority in this country thumb their noses at their own Government.

The ranking minority member of the committee said:

> The need of this legislation is clear. Beatniks and so-called "campus-cults" have been publicly burning their draft cards to demonstrate their contempt for the United States and our resistance to Communist takeovers. Such actions have been suggested and led by college professors—professors supported by taxpayers' money.... These so-called "student" mobs at home and abroad make demands and threats; they hurl rocks and ink bottles at American buildings; they publicly mutilate or burn their draft cards; they even desecrate the American flag. Chanting and screaming vile epithets, these mobs of so-called "students" and Communist "stooges" attempt to create fear and destroy self-confidence in our country and its citizens and to downgrade the United States in the eyes of the world. Such organized "student" groups in the United States have sent congratulations and money to Ho Chi Minh and have made anonymous and insulting calls to families of our servicemen killed in Vietnam. This proposed legislation to make it illegal to knowingly destroy or mutilate a draft card is only one step in bringing some legal control over those who would destroy American freedom. This legislation, if passed, will be of some assistance to our country if the officers and courts charged

with the enforcement of the law will have the energy, courage, and guts to make use of it. . . .

In the Senate, the only comment on the bill was made by the Chair of the Senate Armed Services Committee, which reported the bill. He said:

> Mr. President, recently the public and officials of our country have been appalled by reports of mass public burnings of draft registration cards. It is not fitting for our country to permit such conduct while our people are giving their lives in combat with the enemy. * * * Recent incidents of mass destruction of draft cards constitute open defiance of the warmaking powers of the Government and have demonstrated an urgent need for this legislation. Such conduct as public burnings of draft cards and public pleas for persons to refuse to register for their draft should not and must not be tolerated by a society whose sons, brothers, and husbands are giving their lives in defense of freedom and countrymen against Communist aggression

Can the Court really say with a straight face that it cannot discern an intent to stifle free expression from this? Is Chief Justice Warren, the author of *Brown v. Board of Education*, acting like Justice Brown, the author of *Plessy*, who could find no basis for believing the segregation placed any badge of inferiority on the colored race?

3.   Note the concurrence of Justice Harlan, the author of *Cohen v. California*, in which he concludes that restricting O'Brien from burning his draft card was constitutional because "O'Brien manifestly could have conveyed his message in many ways other than by burning his draft card." Is that not the very argument Justice Harlan rejected with respect to Cohen, that he could have expressed his opposition to the draft in a more acceptable way?

TEXAS V. JOHNSON
United States Supreme Court, 1989.
491 U.S. 397, 109 S.Ct. 2533.

JUSTICE BRENNAN delivered the opinion of the Court.

After publicly burning an American flag as a means of political protest, Gregory Lee Johnson was convicted of desecrating a flag in violation of Texas law. This case presents the question whether his conviction is consistent with the First Amendment. We hold that it is not.

While the Republican National Convention was taking place in Dallas in 1984, respondent Johnson participated in a political demonstration dubbed the "Republican War Chest Tour." [T]he purpose of this event was to protest the policies of the Reagan administration and of certain Dallas-based corporations. The demonstrators marched through the Dallas streets, chanting political slogans and stopping at several corporate locations to stage "die-ins" intended to dramatize the consequences of nuclear war. On several occasions they spray-painted the walls of buildings and overturned potted plants, but Johnson himself took no part in such activities. He did, however, accept an American flag handed to him by a fellow protestor who had taken it from a flagpole outside one of the targeted buildings.

The demonstration ended in front of Dallas City Hall, where Johnson unfurled the American flag, doused it with kerosene, and set it on fire. While the flag burned, the protestors chanted: "America, the red, white, and blue, we spit on you." [N]o one was physically injured or threatened with injury, though several witnesses testified that they had been seriously offended by the flag burning.

Of the approximately 100 demonstrators, Johnson alone was charged with a crime. The only criminal offense with which he was charged was the desecration of a venerated object in violation of Tex. Penal Code Ann. § 42.09(a)(3)(1989). After a trial, he was convicted, sentenced to one year in prison, and fined $2,000.

Johnson was convicted of flag desecration for burning the flag rather than for uttering insulting words. This fact somewhat complicates our consideration of his conviction under the First Amendment. We must first determine whether Johnson's burning of the flag constituted expressive conduct, permitting him to invoke the First Amendment in challenging his conviction. If his conduct was expressive, we next decide whether the State's regulation is related to the suppression of free expression. *See, e.g., United States v. O'Brien.* If the State's regulation is not related to expression, then the less stringent standard we announced in *United States v. O'Brien* for regulations of noncommunicative conduct controls. If it is, then we are outside of *O'Brien*'s test, and we must ask whether this interest justifies Johnson's conviction under a more demanding standard. A third possibility is that the State's asserted interest is simply not implicated on these facts, and in that event the interest drops out of the picture.

The First Amendment literally forbids the abridgment only of "speech," but we have long recognized that its protection does not end at the spoken or written word. While we have rejected "the view that an apparently limitless variety of conduct can be labeled "speech" whenever the person engaging in the conduct intends thereby to express an idea," we have acknowledged that conduct may be "sufficiently imbued with elements of communication to fall within the scope of the First and Fourteenth Amendments."

In deciding whether particular conduct possesses sufficient communicative elements to bring the First Amendment into play, we have asked whether "[a]n intent to convey a particularized message was present, and [whether] the likelihood was great that the message would be understood by those who viewed it." Hence, we have recognized the expressive nature of students' wearing of black armbands to protest American military involvement in Vietnam, *Tinker v. Des Moines Independent Community School Dist.,* 393 U.S. 503 (1969); of a sit-in by blacks in a "whites only" area to protest segregation, *Brown v. Louisiana,* 383 U.S. 131 (1966); of the wearing of American military uniforms in a dramatic presentation criticizing American involvement in Vietnam, *Schacht v. United States,* 398 U.S. 58 (1970); and of picketing about a wide variety of causes.

Especially pertinent to this case are our decisions recognizing the communicative nature of conduct relating to flags. Attaching a peace sign to the flag; refusing to salute the flag; and displaying a red flag, we have held, all may find shelter under the First Amendment. That we have had little difficulty identifying an expressive element in conduct relating to flags should not be surprising. The very purpose of a national flag is to serve as a symbol of our country. . . .

Pregnant with expressive content, the flag as readily signifies this Nation as does the combination of letters found in "America."

[T]he State of Texas conceded for purposes of its oral argument in this case that Johnson's conduct was expressive conduct. . . . Johnson burned an American flag as part—indeed, as the culmination—of a political demonstration that coincided with the convening of the Republican Party and its renomination of Ronald Reagan for President. The expressive, overtly political nature of this conduct was both intentional and overwhelmingly apparent. . . . Johnson's burning of the flag was conduct "sufficiently imbued with elements of communication" to implicate the First Amendment.

The government generally has a freer hand in restricting expressive conduct than it has in restricting the written or spoken word. It may not, however, proscribe particular conduct *because* it has expressive elements. . . . A law *directed at* the communicative nature of conduct must, like a law directed at speech itself, be justified by the substantial showing of need that the First Amendment requires. . . . It is, in short, not simply the verbal or nonverbal nature of the expression, but the governmental interest at stake, that helps to determine whether a restriction on that expression is valid.

Thus, although we have recognized that where " 'speech' and 'nonspeech' elements are combined in the same course of conduct, a sufficiently important governmental interest in regulating the nonspeech element can justify incidental limitations on First Amendment freedoms," we have limited the applicability of *O'Brien's* relatively lenient standard to those cases in which "the governmental interest is unrelated to the suppression of free expression." [W]e have highlighted the requirement that the governmental interest in question be unconnected to expression in order to come under *O'Brien*'s less demanding rule.

In order to decide whether *O'Brien*'s test applies here, therefore, we must decide whether Texas has asserted an interest in support of Johnson's conviction that is unrelated to the suppression of expression. If we find that an interest asserted by the State is simply not implicated on the facts before us, we need not ask whether *O'Brien*'s test applies. The State offers two separate interests to justify this conviction: preventing breaches of the peace and preserving the flag as a symbol of nationhood and national unity. We hold that the first interest is not implicated on this record and that the second is related to the suppression of expression.

Texas claims that its interest in preventing breaches of the peace justifies Johnson's conviction for flag desecration. However, no disturbance of the peace actually occurred or threatened to occur because of Johnson's burning of the flag. . . . The only evidence offered by the State at trial to show the reaction to Johnson's actions was the testimony of several persons who had been seriously offended by the flag burning.

The State's position, therefore, amounts to a claim that an audience that takes serious offense at particular expression is necessarily likely to disturb the peace and that the expression may be prohibited on this basis. Our precedents do not countenance such a presumption. . . .

Nor does Johnson's expressive conduct fall within that small class of "fighting words" that are "likely to provoke the average person to retaliation, and thereby cause a breach of the peace." No reasonable onlooker would have regarded Johnson's generalized expression of dissatisfaction with the policies of the Federal Government as a direct personal insult or an invitation to exchange fisticuffs.

We thus conclude that the State's interest in maintaining order is not implicated on these facts. . . .

The State also asserts an interest in preserving the flag as a symbol of nationhood and national unity. . . . We are . . . persuaded that this interest is related to expression in the case of Johnson's burning of the flag. The State, apparently, is concerned that such conduct will lead people to believe either that the flag does not stand for nationhood and national unity, but instead reflects other, less positive concepts, or that the concepts reflected in the flag do not in fact exist, that is, that we do not enjoy unity as a Nation. These concerns blossom only when a person's treatment of the flag communicates some message, and thus are related "to the suppression of free expression" within the meaning of *O'Brien*. We are thus outside of *O'Brien*'s test altogether.

It remains to consider whether the State's interest in preserving the flag as a symbol of nationhood and national unity justifies Johnson's conviction.

"We are confronted with a case of prosecution for the expression of an idea through activity," and "[a]ccordingly, we must examine with particular care the interests advanced by [petitioner] to support its prosecution." Johnson was not, we add, prosecuted for the expression of just any idea; he was prosecuted for his expression of dissatisfaction with the policies of this country, expression situated at the core of our First Amendment values.

Moreover, Johnson was prosecuted because he knew that his politically charged expression would cause "serious offense." If he had burned the flag as a means of disposing of it because it was dirty or torn, he would not have been convicted of flag desecration under this Texas law: federal law designates burning as the preferred means of disposing of a flag "when it is in such condition that it is no longer a fitting emblem for display," and Texas has no quarrel with this means of disposal. The Texas law is thus not aimed at protecting the physical integrity of the flag in all circumstances, but is designed instead to protect it only against impairments that would cause serious offense to others.

Whether Johnson's treatment of the flag violated Texas law thus depended on the likely communicative impact of his expressive conduct. . . .

[J]ohnson's political expression was restricted because of the content of the message he conveyed. We must therefore subject the State's asserted interest in preserving the special symbolic character of the flag to "the most exacting scrutiny."

Texas argues that its interest in preserving the flag as a symbol of nationhood and national unity survives this close analysis. Quoting extensively from the writings of this Court chronicling the flag's historic and symbolic role in our society, the State emphasizes the "special place" reserved for the flag in our Nation. [T]he State's claim is that it has an interest in preserving the flag as a symbol of *nationhood* and *national unity*, a symbol with a determinate range of meanings. According to Texas, if one physically treats the flag in a way that would tend to cast doubt on either the idea that nationhood and national unity are the flag's referents or that national unity actually exists, the message conveyed thereby is a harmful one and therefore may be prohibited.

If there is a bedrock principle underlying the First Amendment, it is that the government may not prohibit the expression of an idea simply because society finds the idea itself offensive or disagreeable.

We have not recognized an exception to this principle even where our flag has been involved. In *Street v. New York,* 394 U.S. 576 (1969), we held that a State may not criminally punish a person for uttering words critical of the flag. . . . Nor may the government, we have held, compel conduct that would evince respect for the flag. . . .

In short, nothing in our precedents suggests that a State may foster its own view of the flag by prohibiting expressive conduct relating to it. To bring its argument outside our precedents, Texas attempts to convince us that even if its interest in preserving the flag's symbolic role does not allow it to prohibit words or some expressive conduct critical of the flag, it does permit it to forbid the outright destruction of the flag. The State's argument cannot depend here on the distinction between written or spoken words and nonverbal conduct. That distinction, we have shown, is of no moment where the nonverbal conduct is expressive, as it is here, and where the regulation of that conduct is related to expression, as it is here. . . .

It is not the State's ends, but its means, to which we object. It cannot be gainsaid that there is a special place reserved for the flag in this Nation, and thus we do not doubt that the government has a legitimate interest in making efforts to "preserv[e] the national flag as an unalloyed symbol of our country." We reject the suggestion, urged at oral argument by counsel for Johnson, that the government lacks "any state interest whatsoever" in regulating the manner in which the flag may be displayed. Congress has, for example, enacted precatory regulations describing the proper treatment of the flag, and we cast no doubt on the legitimacy of its interest in making such recommendations. To say that the government has an interest in encouraging proper treatment of the flag, however, is not to say that it may criminally punish a person for burning a flag as a means of political protest. . . .

We are fortified in today's conclusion by our conviction that forbidding criminal punishment for conduct such as Johnson's will not endanger the special role played by our flag or the feelings it inspires. . . .

We are tempted to say, in fact, that the flag's deservedly cherished place in our community will be strengthened, not weakened, by our holding today. Our decision is a reaffirmation of the principles of freedom and inclusiveness that the flag best reflects, and of the conviction that our toleration of criticism such as Johnson's is a sign and source of our strength. Indeed, one of the proudest images of our flag, the one immortalized in our own national anthem, is of the bombardment it survived at Fort McHenry. It is the Nation's resilience, not its rigidity, that Texas sees reflected in the flag—and it is that resilience that we reassert today.

The way to preserve the flag's special role is not to punish those who feel differently about these matters. It is to persuade them that they are wrong. . . . We do not consecrate the flag by punishing its desecration, for in doing so we dilute the freedom that this cherished emblem represents.

JUSTICE KENNEDY, concurring.

I write not to qualify the words Justice BRENNAN chooses so well, for he says with power all that is necessary to explain our ruling. I join his opinion without reservation, but with a keen sense that this case, like others before us from time to time, exacts its personal toll. This prompts me to add to our pages these few remarks.

The case before us illustrates better than most that the judicial power is often difficult in its exercise. We cannot here ask another Branch to share responsibility, as when the argument is made that a statute is flawed or incomplete. For we are presented with a clear and simple statute to be judged against a pure command of the Constitution. The outcome can be laid at no door but ours.

The hard fact is that sometimes we must make decisions we do not like. We make them because they are right, right in the sense that the law and the Constitution, as we see them, compel the result. And so great is our commitment to the process that, except in the rare case, we do not pause to express distaste for the result, perhaps for fear of undermining a valued principle that dictates the decision. This is one of those rare cases. . . .

CHIEF JUSTICE REHNQUIST, with whom JUSTICE WHITE and JUSTICE O'CONNOR join, dissenting.

In holding this Texas statute unconstitutional, the Court ignores Justice Holmes's familiar aphorism that "a page of history is worth a volume of logic." For more than 200 years, the American flag has occupied a unique position as the symbol of our Nation, a uniqueness that justifies a governmental prohibition against flag burning in the way respondent Johnson did here. . . .

The flag symbolizes the Nation in peace as well as in war. It signifies our national presence on battleships, airplanes, military installations, and public buildings from the United States Capitol to the thousands of county courthouses and city halls throughout the country. Two flags are prominently placed in our courtroom. Countless flags are placed by the graves of loved ones each year on what was first called Decoration Day, and is now called Memorial Day. The flag is traditionally placed on the casket of deceased members of the Armed Forces, and it is later given to the deceased's family. Congress has provided that the flag be flown at half-staff upon the death of the President, Vice President, and other government officials "as a mark of respect to their memory." The flag identifies United States merchant ships, and "[t]he laws of the Union protect our commerce wherever the flag of the country may float."

No other American symbol has been as universally honored as the flag. In 1931, Congress declared "The Star-Spangled Banner" to be our national anthem. In 1949, Congress declared June 14th to be Flag Day. In 1987, John Philip Sousa's "The Stars and Stripes Forever" was designated as the national march. Congress has also established "The Pledge of Allegiance to the Flag" and the manner of its deliverance. The flag has appeared as the principal symbol on approximately 33 United States postal stamps and in the design of at least 43 more, more times than any other symbol.

Both Congress and the States have enacted numerous laws regulating misuse of the American flag. Until 1967, Congress left the regulation of misuse of the flag up to the States. Now, however, 18 U.S.C. § 700(a) provides that: "Whoever knowingly casts contempt upon any flag of the United States by publicly mutilating, defacing, defiling, burning, or trampling upon it shall be fined not more than $1,000 or imprisoned for not more than one year, or both."

The American flag, then, throughout more than 200 years of our history, has come to be the visible symbol embodying our Nation. It does not represent the views of any particular political party, and it does not represent any particular political philosophy. The flag is not simply another "idea" or "point of view" competing for recognition in the marketplace of ideas. Millions and millions of Americans regard it with an almost mystical reverence regardless of what sort of social, political, or philosophical beliefs they may have. I cannot agree that the First Amendment invalidates the Act of Congress, and the laws of 48 of the 50 States, which make criminal the public burning of the flag. . . .

But the Court insists that the Texas statute prohibiting the public burning of the American flag infringes on respondent Johnson's freedom of expression. Such freedom, of course, is not absolute. *See Schenck v. United States.* In *Chaplinsky v. New Hampshire,* a unanimous Court said:

> [T]here are certain well-defined and narrowly limited classes of speech, the prevention and punishment of which have never been thought to raise any Constitutional problem. These include the lewd and obscene, the profane, the libelous, and the insulting or "fighting" words—those which by their very utterance inflict injury or tend to incite an immediate breach of the peace. It has been well observed that such utterances are no essential part of any exposition of ideas, and are of such slight social value as a step to truth that any benefit that may be derived from them is clearly outweighed by the social interest in order and morality.

The Court upheld Chaplinsky's conviction under a state statute that made it unlawful to "address any offensive, derisive or annoying word to any person who is lawfully in any street or other public place." Chaplinsky had told a local marshal, "You are a God damned racketeer and a damned Fascist and the whole government of Rochester are Fascists or agents of Fascists."

Here it may equally well be said that the public burning of the American flag by Johnson was no essential part of any exposition of ideas, and at the same time it had a tendency to incite a breach of the peace. Johnson was free to make any verbal denunciation of the flag that he wished; indeed, he was free to burn the flag in private. He could publicly burn other symbols of the Government or effigies of political leaders. . . .

The Court could not, and did not, say that Chaplinsky's utterances were not expressive phrases—they clearly and succinctly conveyed an extremely low opinion of the addressee. The same may be said of Johnson's public burning of the flag in this case; it obviously did convey Johnson's bitter dislike of his country. But his act, like Chaplinsky's provocative words, conveyed nothing that could not have been conveyed and was not conveyed just as forcefully in a dozen different ways. As with "fighting words," so with flag burning, for purposes of the First Amendment. . . .

The result of the Texas statute is obviously to deny one in Johnson's frame of mind one of many means of "symbolic speech." Far from being a case of "one picture being worth a thousand words," flag burning is the equivalent of an inarticulate grunt or roar that, it seems fair to say, is most likely to be indulged in not to express any particular idea, but to antagonize others. . . . The Texas statute deprived Johnson of only one rather inarticulate symbolic form of protest—a form of protest that was profoundly offensive to many—and left him with a full panoply of other symbols and every conceivable form of verbal expression to express his deep disapproval of national policy. Thus, in no way can it be said that Texas is punishing him because his hearers—or any other group of people—were profoundly opposed to the message that he sought to convey. Such opposition is no proper basis for restricting speech or expression under the First Amendment. It was Johnson's use of this particular symbol, and not the idea that he sought to convey by it or by his many other expressions, for which he was punished. . . .

The Court decides that the American flag is just another symbol, about which not only must opinions pro and con be tolerated, but for which the most minimal public respect may not be enjoined. The government may conscript men into the Armed Forces where they must fight and perhaps die for the flag, but the government may not prohibit the public burning of the banner under which they fight. I would uphold the Texas statute as applied in this case.

JUSTICE STEVENS, dissenting.

As the Court analyzes this case, it presents the question whether the State of Texas, or indeed the Federal Government, has the power to prohibit the public desecration of the American flag. The question is unique. In my judgment rules that apply to a host of other symbols, such as state flags, armbands, or various privately promoted emblems of political or commercial identity, are not necessarily controlling. Even if flag burning could be considered just another species of symbolic speech under the logical application of the rules that the Court has developed in its interpretation of the First Amendment in other contexts, this case has an intangible dimension that makes those rules inapplicable.

A country's flag is a symbol of more than "nationhood and national unity." It also signifies the ideas that characterize the society that has chosen that emblem as well as the special history that has animated the growth and power of those ideas. . . .

So it is with the American flag. It is more than a proud symbol of the courage, the determination, and the gifts of nature that transformed 13 fledgling Colonies into a world power. It is a symbol of freedom, of equal opportunity, of religious tolerance, and of good will for other peoples who share our aspirations. The symbol carries its message to dissidents both at home and abroad who may have no interest at all in our national unity or survival.

The value of the flag as a symbol cannot be measured. Even so, I have no doubt that the interest in preserving that value for the future is both significant and legitimate. Conceivably that value will be enhanced by the Court's conclusion that our national commitment to free expression is so strong that even the United States as ultimate guarantor of that freedom is without power to prohibit the desecration of its unique symbol. But I am unpersuaded. The creation of a federal right to post bulletin boards and graffiti on the Washington Monument might enlarge the market for free expression, but at a cost I would not pay. Similarly, in my considered judgment, sanctioning the public desecration of the flag will tarnish its value—both for those who cherish the ideas for which it waves and for those who desire to don the robes of martyrdom by burning it. That tarnish is not justified by the trivial burden on free expression occasioned by requiring that an available, alternative mode of expression—including uttering words critical of the flag—be employed. . . .

The Court is therefore quite wrong in blandly asserting that respondent "was prosecuted for his expression of dissatisfaction with the policies of this country, expression situated at the core of our First Amendment values." Respondent was prosecuted because of the method he chose to express his dissatisfaction with those policies. Had he chosen to spray-paint—or perhaps convey with a motion picture projector—his message of dissatisfaction on the facade of the Lincoln Memorial, there would be no question about the power of the Government to prohibit his means of expression. The prohibition would be supported by the legitimate interest in preserving the quality of an important national asset. Though the asset at stake in this case is intangible, given its unique value, the same interest supports a prohibition on the desecration of the American flag.

COMMENTS AND QUESTIONS

1.   *Texas v. Johnson* is a close case with an interesting line-up of justices. Normally "liberal" Justice Stevens joins the conservatives, arguing that government can criminalize the desecration of the flag, while normally "conservative" Justice Scalia joins the liberals to find desecration of the flag

constitutionally protected. Justice Kennedy, setting the stage for later developments, in one of his early cases is the swing vote on the side of liberty.

2.   Why is burning a United States flag, which was stolen (!), protected, but burning a draft card is not? Is burning a flag the same as posting graffiti on the Washington Monument? Of course not, so why does Justice Stevens use that hypothetical? His later hypothetical of using a motion picture projector to project a message on the Lincoln Memorial is more interesting. Why would it be clear that the government could stop that?

3.   *Texas v. Johnson* provoked substantial public outrage, and Congress immediately undertook to propose an amendment to the First Amendment to allow punishment for desecration of the flag. Although undoubtedly many congresspersons felt some reluctance to amend the First Amendment, the public pressure of the moment made it difficult to oppose the proposal. At that point, a number of highly regarded, liberal constitutional law scholars suggested that they had crafted statutory language that would pass the *O'Brien* test. Liberal congresspersons seized on this as an alternative to amending the First Amendment, so Congress passed and the President signed the Flag Protection Act of 1989. Immediately, flags were burned in protest of the Act, and after district courts found the Act unconstitutional under *Texas v. Johnson*, the Court granted an immediate appeal as provided for in the Act. Whereas the Texas statute had only proscribed flag burning that the actor knew would seriously offend onlookers, the new federal Act was said only to protect the physical integrity of the flag. In *United States v. Eichman*, 496 U.S. 310 (1990), the Court was not convinced. The prohibitions on mutilating, defacing, and defiling all "unmistakably connote[ ] disrespectful treatment of the flag and suggest[ ] a focus on those acts likely to damage the flag's symbolic value." Accordingly, the Act was as directed at expression as much as the Texas law. Again, the vote was 5–4 with the same line-up as in *Texas v. Johnson*. The passage of time, however, had spent the passion engendered by the former case, and the movement for amending the First Amendment fizzled out.

4.   Note the dissent's argument that Johnson could have made his point without burning the flag, that he could have expressed his views in an alternative and clearly protected manner. Did not *Cohen* answer that argument?

5.   In *Masterpiece Cakeshop, Ltd. v. Colorado Civil Rights Comm'n*, 138 S.Ct. 1719 (2018), a baker who refused to create a wedding cake to celebrate a same-sex wedding was found by the state agency to have discriminated on the basis of sexual orientation in violation of the state anti-discrimination law. The Supreme Court set aside that decision on the basis that the decision reflected a hostility toward religion in violation of the baker's First Amendment right to the free exercise of his religion. The baker had also argued that the decision violated his First Amendment right to freedom of speech, because it compelled him to express a view he did not have—that a same-sex wedding was something to be celebrated. The Court did not reach that question, but Justice Thomas (joined by Justice Gorsuch) in concurrence agreed with the baker that his cake would be expressive conduct, such that it would violate his rights to

be forced to express a view he did not agree with. Justice Ginsburg (joined by Justice Sotomayor) disagreed. She argued that in order for conduct to be considered protected expressive conduct the Court's precedents require that a reasonable observer would perceive the conduct to be communicative. She did not believe that a reasonable observer of a wedding cake at a same-sex wedding would view the wedding cake as expressing the views of the baker of the cake. This issue continues to arise with respect to various purveyors of goods and services for weddings objecting to being forced to provide those goods or services. Do you think that custom wedding cakes, wedding photographs, and flower arrangements for weddings constitute First Amendment protected speech by bakers, photographers, and flower arrangers? As this is being written, the Supreme Court is considering this issue in *303 Creative LLC v. Elenis* involving a wedding web page designer.

PROBLEM

A college student protesting the United States support of Israel burns a flag outside the United States Court in New York City, while holding a sign that says Support Palestine, Not Israel! He is promptly arrested a New York City policeman and charged with violating a city ordinance banning open fires in the city without a permit. Does he have a First Amendment defense?

E. OBSCENITY AND PORNOGRAPHY

Recall *Chaplinsky*'s statement that there were "certain well-defined and narrowly limited classes of speech, the prevention and punishment of which have never been thought to raise any Constitutional problem. These include the lewd and obscene, the profane, the libelous, and the insulting or 'fighting' words. . . . It has been well observed that such utterances are no essential part of any exposition of ideas, and are of such slight social value as a step to truth that any benefit that may be derived from them is clearly outweighed by the social interest in order and morality." We have already seen profanity reach protected status in *Cohen*, and we will see that most libel receives some protection as well. Obscenity, however, is not protected.

Historically, something was obscene if it had the tendency to deprave or corrupt its readers by inciting lascivious thoughts or arousing lustful desires. In *Roth v. United States*, 354 U.S. 476 (1957), Justice Brennan in his first constitutional law opinion on the Supreme Court upheld both the federal and California obscenity laws, concluding that obscenity was simply not protected speech under the First Amendment. Nevertheless, to assure that regulation of this unprotected speech did not spill over to protected speech, the Court fashioned a slightly restrictive definition of obscenity: "whether to the average person, applying contemporary community standards, the dominant theme of the material taken as a whole appeals to prurient interest." Then came the 60's. The definition became stricter: "three elements must coalesce: it must be established that (a) the dominant theme of the material taken as a whole appeals to a prurient interest in sex; (b) the material is patently offensive because it affronts contemporary community standards relating to the description or representation of sexual matters; and (c) the material is utterly without redeeming social value." *A Book named "John Cleland's Memoirs of a Woman of Pleasure" v. Massachusetts*, 383 U.S. 413, 418 (1966)(otherwise known as *Fanny Hill*). And three years later the Court held that the First Amendment prohibited the criminalization of the possession of obscene materials in one's home. *Stanley v. Georgia*, 394 U.S. 557 (1969). Some believed the moment had come for the Court to protect "obscene" material, but in two cases decided the same day the Court retreated.

PARIS ADULT THEATRE I V. SLATON
United States Supreme Court, 1973.
413 U.S. 49, 93 S.Ct. 2628.

MR. CHIEF JUSTICE BURGER delivered the opinion of the Court.

Petitioners are two Atlanta, Georgia, movie theaters and their owners and managers, operating in the style of "adult" theaters. On December 28, 1970, respondents, the local state district attorney and the solicitor for the local state trial court, filed civil complaints in that court alleging that petitioners were exhibiting to the public for paid admission two allegedly obscene films. The two films in question . . . depict sexual conduct characterized by the Georgia Supreme Court as "hard core pornography" leaving "little to the imagination."

[T]his Court has consistently held that obscene material is not protected by the First Amendment as a limitation on the state police power by virtue of the Fourteenth Amendment.

[W]e categorically disapprove the theory, apparently adopted by the trial judge, that obscene, pornographic films acquire constitutional immunity from state regulation simply because they are exhibited for consenting adults only. This holding was properly rejected by the Georgia Supreme Court. Although we have often pointedly recognized the high importance of the state interest in regulating the exposure of obscene materials to juveniles and unconsenting adults, this Court has never declared these to be the only legitimate state interests permitting regulation of obscene material. The States have a long-recognized legitimate interest in regulating the use of obscene material in local commerce and in all places of public accommodation, as long as these regulations do not run afoul of specific constitutional prohibitions.

In particular, we hold that there are legitimate state interests at stake in stemming the tide of commercialized obscenity, even assuming it is feasible to enforce effective safeguards against exposure to juveniles and to passersby. [T]hese include the interest of the public in the quality of life and the total community environment, the tone of commerce in the great city centers, and, possibly, the public safety itself. The Hill-Link Minority Report of the Commission on Obscenity and Pornography indicates that there is at least an arguable correlation between obscene material and crime. Quite apart from sex crimes, however, there remains one problem of large proportions aptly described by Professor Bickel:

> It concerns the tone of the society, the mode, or to use terms that have perhaps greater currency, the style and quality of life, now and in the future. A man may be entitled to read an obscene book in his room, or expose himself indecently there . . . . We should protect his privacy. But if he demands a right to obtain the books and pictures he wants in the market, and to foregather in public places—discreet, if you will, but accessible to all—with others who share his tastes, then to grant him his right is to affect the world about the rest of us, and to impinge on other privacies. Even supposing that each of us can, if he wishes, effectively avert the eye and stop the ear (which, in truth, we cannot), what is commonly read and seen and heard and done intrudes upon us all, want it or not.

As Mr. Chief Justice Warren stated, there is a "right of the Nation and of the States to maintain a decent society . . . ."

But, it is argued, there are no scientific data which conclusively demonstrate that exposure to obscene material adversely affects men and women or their society. It is urged on behalf of the petitioners that, absent such a demonstration, and kind of state regulation is "impermissible." We reject this argument. It is not for us to resolve empirical uncertainties underlying state legislation, save in the exceptional case where that legislation plainly impinges upon rights protected by the Constitution itself. . . . Although there is no conclusive proof of a connection between antisocial behavior and obscene material, the legislature of Georgia could quite reasonably determine that such a connection does or might exist. In deciding *Roth*, this Court implicitly accepted that a legislature could legitimately act on such a conclusion to protect "the social interest in order and morality."

From the beginning of civilized societies, legislators and judges have acted on various unprovable assumptions. Such assumptions underlie much lawful state regulation of commercial and business affairs. On the basis of these assumptions both Congress and state legislatures have, for example, drastically restricted associational rights by adopting antitrust laws, and have strictly regulated public expression by issuers of and dealers in securities, profit sharing "coupons," and "trading stamps," commanding what they must and must not publish and announce.

Understandably those who entertain an absolutist view of the First Amendment find it uncomfortable to explain why rights of association, speech, and press should be severely restrained in the marketplace of goods and money, but not in the marketplace of pornography.

If we accept the unprovable assumption that a complete education requires the reading of certain books, and the well nigh universal belief that good books, plays, and art lift the spirit, improve the mind, enrich the human personality, and develop character, can we then say that a state legislature may not act on the corollary assumption that commerce in obscene books, or public exhibitions focused on obscene conduct, have a tendency to exert a corrupting and debasing impact leading to antisocial behavior?

It is also argued that the State has no legitimate interest in "control (of) the moral content of a person's thoughts," and we need not quarrel with this. But we reject the claim that the State of Georgia is here attempting to control the minds or thoughts of those who patronize theaters. Preventing unlimited display or distribution of obscene material, which by definition lacks any serious literary, artistic, political, or scientific value as communication is distinct from a control of reason and the intellect. . . .

Finally, petitioners argue that conduct which directly involves "consenting adults" only has, for that sole reason, a special claim to constitutional protection. Our Constitution establishes a broad range of conditions on the exercise of power by the States, but for us to say that our Constitution incorporates the proposition that conduct involving consenting adults only is always beyond state regulation is a step we are unable to take. Commercial exploitation of depictions, descriptions, or exhibitions of obscene conduct on commercial premises open to the adult public falls within a State's broad power to regulate commerce and protect the public environment. The issue in this context goes beyond whether someone, or even the majority, considers the conduct depicted as "wrong" or "sinful." The States have the power to make a morally neutral judgment that public exhibition of obscene material, or commerce in such material, has a tendency to injure the community as a whole, to endanger the public safety, or to jeopardize in Mr. Chief Justice Warren's words, the States' "right . . . to maintain a decent society."

To summarize, we have today reaffirmed the basic holding of *Roth v. United States*, that obscene material has no protection under the First Amendment. We have directed our holdings, not at thoughts or speech, but at depiction and description of specifically defined sexual conduct that States may regulate within limits designed to prevent infringement of First Amendment rights. . . .

MR. JUSTICE DOUGLAS, dissenting.

My Brother BRENNAN is to be commended for seeking a new path through the thicket which the Court entered when it undertook to sustain the constitutionality of obscenity laws and to place limits on their application. I have expressed on numerous occasions my disagreement with the basic decision that held that "obscenity" was not protected by the First Amendment. I disagreed also with the definitions that evolved. Art and literature reflect tastes; and tastes, like musical appreciation, are hardly reducible to precise definitions. That is one reason I have always felt that "obscenity" was not an exception to the First Amendment. For matters of taste, like matters of belief, turn on the idiosyncrasies of individuals. They are too personal to define and too emotional and vague to apply. . . .

The other reason I could not bring myself to conclude that "obscenity" was not covered by the First Amendment was that prior to the adoption of our Constitution and Bill of Rights the Colonies had no law excluding "obscenity" from the regime of freedom of expression and press that then existed. I could find no such laws; and more important, our leading colonial expert, Julius Goebel, could find none. So I became convinced that the creation of the "obscenity" exception to the First Amendment was a legislative and judicial tour de force; that if we were to have such a regime of censorship and punishment, it should be done by constitutional amendment.

People are, of course, offended by many offerings made by merchants in this area. They are also offended by political pronouncements, sociological themes, and by stories of official misconduct. The list of activities and publications and pronouncements that offend someone is endless. . . . Life in this crowded modern technological world creates many offensive statements and many offensive deeds. There is no protection against offensive ideas, only against offensive conduct. . . .

I am sure I would find offensive most of the books and movies charged with being obscene. But in a life that has not been short, I have yet to be trapped into seeing or reading something that would offend me. I never read or see the materials coming to the Court under charges of "obscenity," because I have thought the First Amendment made it unconstitutional for me to act as a censor. I see ads in bookstores and neon lights over theaters that resemble bait for those who seek vicarious exhilaration. As a parent or a priest or as a teacher I would have no compunction in edging my children or wards away from the books and movies that did no more than excite man's base instincts. But I never supposed that government was permitted to sit in judgment on one's tastes or beliefs—save as they involved action within the reach of the police power of government. . . .

MR. JUSTICE BRENNAN, with whom MR. JUSTICE STEWART and MR. JUSTICE MARSHALL join, dissenting.

This case requires the Court to confront once again the vexing problem of reconciling state efforts to suppress sexually oriented expression with the protections of the First Amendment, as applied to the States through the Fourteenth Amendment. No other aspect of the First Amendment has, in recent years, demanded so substantial a commitment of our time, generated such disharmony of views, and remained so resistant to the formulation of stable and manageable standards. I am convinced that the approach initiated 16 years ago in *Roth v. United States*, and culminating in the Court's decision today, cannot bring stability to this area of the law without jeopardizing fundamental First Amendment values, and I have concluded that the time has come to make a significant departure from that approach.

[O]ur experience with the *Roth* approach has certainly taught us that the outright suppression of obscenity cannot be reconciled with the fundamental principles of the First and Fourteenth Amendments. For we have failed to formulate a standard that sharply distinguishes protected from unprotected speech, and . . . offers only the most obscure guidance to legislation, adjudication by other courts, and primary conduct. . . . It comes as no surprise that judicial attempts to follow our lead conscientiously have often ended in hopeless confusion. . . .

Our experience since *Roth* requires us not only to abandon the effort to pick out obscene material on a case-by-case basis, but also to reconsider a fundamental postulate of *Roth*: that there exists a definable class of sexually oriented expression that may be totally suppressed by the Federal and State Governments. Assuming that such a class of expression does in fact exist, I am forced to conclude that the concept of "obscenity" cannot be defined with sufficient specificity and clarity to provide fair notice to persons who create and distribute sexually oriented materials, to prevent substantial erosion of protected speech as a byproduct of the attempt to suppress unprotected speech, and to avoid very costly institutional harms. Given these inevitable side effects of state efforts to suppress what is assumed to be unprotected speech, we must scrutinize with care the state interest that is asserted to justify the suppression. For in the absence of some very substantial interest in suppressing such speech, we can hardly condone the ill effects that seem to flow inevitably from the effort. . . .

In *Stanley* we pointed out that "(t)here appears to be little empirical basis for" the assertion that "exposure to obscene materials may lead to deviant sexual behavior or crimes of sexual violence."[26] In any event, we

---

[26] Indeed, since *Stanley* was decided, the President's Commission on Obscenity and Pornography has concluded: "In sum, empirical research designed to clarify the question has found no evidence to date that exposure to explicit sexual materials plays a significant role in the causation of delinquent or criminal behavior among youth or adults. The Commission cannot conclude that exposure to erotic materials is a factor in the causation of sex crime or sex delinquency." Report of the Commission on Obscenity and Pornography 27 (1970)(footnote omitted). To the contrary, the Commission found that "(o)n the positive side, explicit sexual materials are sought as a source of entertainment and information by substantial numbers of

added that "if the State is only concerned about printed or filmed materials inducing antisocial conduct, we believe that in the context of private consumption of ideas and information we should adhere to the view that '(a)mong free men, the deterrents ordinarily to be applied to prevent crime are education and punishment for violations of the law . . . .' "

Even a legitimate, sharply focused state concern for the morality of the community cannot . . . justify an assault on the protections of the First Amendment. Where the state interest in regulation of morality is vague and ill defined, interference with the guarantees of the First Amendment is even more difficult to justify.

In short, while I cannot say that the interests of the State—apart from the question of juveniles and unconsenting adults—are trivial or nonexistent, I am compelled to conclude that these interests cannot justify the substantial damage to constitutional rights and to this Nation's judicial machinery that inevitably results from state efforts to bar the distribution even of unprotected material to consenting adults. I would hold, therefore, that at least in the absence of distribution to juveniles or obtrusive exposure to unconsenting adults, the First and Fourteenth Amendments prohibit the State and Federal Governments from attempting wholly to suppress sexually oriented materials on the basis of their allegedly "obscene" contents. . . .

COMMENTS AND QUESTIONS

1.   A companion case to *Paris Adult Theatre, Miller v. California*, 413 U.S. 15 (1973), set out to define with some specificity what constituted, unprotected obscene speech. Its definition is known as the *"Miller* test."

State statutes designed to regulate obscene materials must be carefully limited. As a result, we now confine the permissible scope of such regulation to works which depict or describe sexual conduct. That conduct must be specifically defined by the applicable state law, as written or authoritatively construed. A state offense must also be limited to works which, taken as a whole, appeal to the prurient interest in sex, which portray sexual conduct in a patently offensive way, and which, taken as a whole, do not have serious literary, artistic, political, or scientific value.

The basic guidelines for the trier of fact must be: (a) whether "the average person, applying contemporary community standards" would find that the work, taken as a whole, appeals to the prurient interest; (b) whether the work depicts or describes, in a patently offensive way, sexual conduct specifically defined by the applicable state law; and (c) whether the work, taken as a whole, lacks serious literary, artistic, political, or scientific value.

American adults. At times, these materials also appear to serve to increase and facilitate constructive communication about sexual matters within marriage."

While not greatly different from the standard announced in the *Fanny Hill* case, the *Miller* test specified that the depiction had to be of actual sexual conduct defined in state law; nudity *per se* would not qualify. At the same time the *Miller* test changed the final part of the standard from "utterly without" literary, artistic, political, or scientific value to lacking "serious" literary, artistic, political, or scientific value.

2.   A subsequent case clarified that when "the average person" applies "contemporary community standards," a "juror is entitled to draw on his own knowledge of the views of the average person in the community or vicinage from which he comes for making the required determination" as to whether the work appeals to the prurient interest or depicts the sexual conduct in a patently offensive way. *Hamling v. United States*, 418 U.S. 87 (1974). On the other hand, the determination as to whether a work has serious value is not to be made on the basis of an average person in the community, but on the basis of a "reasonable person," purportedly an objective, nationwide standard. *See Pope v. Illinois*, 481 U.S. 497 (1987).

3.   The Court's opinion in *Paris Adult Theatre* spends a lot of time affirming the arguably rational basis for banning obscene speech even with respect to consenting adults. Of course, if obscenity is simply outside any protection of the First Amendment, then no heightened scrutiny is called for, and an "any rational relationship" test might be appropriate. What is missing from *Paris Adult Theatre*, however, is any justification for why obscenity is unprotected speech in the first place—other than the fact that that had always been the case. The arguments for the rationality of prohibiting obscenity could arguably be used to justify creating an exception for obscenity from First Amendment protection. As such, however, they are notably weak, lacking any of the hallmarks of imminent harm that have otherwise justified exceptions from First Amendment protection. Some commentators have tried to fill the gap. First, it is probably true that accepting obscenity (as opposed to banning it) has effects on society at large, even on those who do not partake in it. However, the same can be said of accepting profanity and blasphemy, which *Cohen* protects. Second, it is said that obscenity simply has no redeeming social value. Such a conclusion, though, would seem to be exactly what the First Amendment intended to preclude legislatures from making. And is it true? One study had persons watch pornographic movies and asked them whether they were offended by what they saw. The persons said they were. They were also asked whether they learned anything, and the answer was yes, they learned a lot. Third, some have argued that obscenity is different from other speech because it does not appeal to the mind or intellect. Rather it is intended only to have a physical effect. But is that what distinguishes it from humor (intended to provoke the physical effect of laughter, which releases endorphins, the feel-good brain chemicals), tear jerkers, or action movies (intended to provoke an adrenalin rush), or is it that the particular physical effect produced by obscenity is disfavored as immoral? Ultimately, obscenity is apparently enjoyed by many as a form of pleasurable entertainment with no more concern for literary, artistic, political, or scientific value than is provided by watching professional sports. Fourth, feminist authors have suggested obscenity should

be banned because of its effect on women. The effect is not limited to those involved in the production of obscenity; it also extends to women who might suffer at the hands of men who partake of the obscenity. No doubt obscenity and the pornography trade in particular can have these effects, but the same can be said for unquestionably protected activities.

4.   If obscenity is not protected by the First Amendment and is criminalized by almost every state and the federal government, why is it that it is so readily available on the internet and in every "adult" book store and video arcade?

NEW YORK V. FERBER

United States Supreme Court, 1982.
458 U.S. 747, 102 S.Ct. 3348.

JUSTICE WHITE delivered the opinion of the Court.

At issue in this case is the constitutionality of a New York criminal statute which prohibits persons from knowingly promoting sexual performances by children under the age of 16 by distributing material which depicts such performances.

In recent years, the exploitive use of children in the production of pornography has become a serious national problem. The Federal Government and 47 States have sought to combat the problem with statutes specifically directed at the production of child pornography. At least half of such statutes do not require that the materials produced be legally obscene. Thirty-five States and the United States Congress have also passed legislation prohibiting the distribution of such materials; 20 States prohibit the distribution of material depicting children engaged in sexual conduct without requiring that the material be legally obscene.

New York is one of the 20. In 1977, the New York Legislature enacted Article 263 of its Penal Law. Section 263.05 criminalizes as a class C felony the use of a child in a sexual performance:

> A person is guilty of the use of a child in a sexual performance if knowing the character and content thereof he employs, authorizes or induces a child less than sixteen years of age to engage in a sexual performance or being a parent, legal guardian or custodian of such child, he consents to the participation by such child in a sexual performance.

A "[s]exual performance" is defined as "any performance or part thereof which includes sexual conduct by a child less than sixteen years of age."

"Sexual conduct" is in turn defined in § 263.00(3):

> "Sexual conduct" means actual or simulated sexual intercourse, deviate sexual intercourse, sexual bestiality,

masturbation, sado-masochistic abuse, or lewd exhibition of the genitals.

A performance is defined as "any play, motion picture, photograph or dance" or "any other visual representation exhibited before an audience."

At issue in this case is § 263.15, defining a class D felony:

> A person is guilty of promoting a sexual performance by a child when, knowing the character and content thereof, he produces, directs or promotes any performance which includes sexual conduct by a child less than sixteen years of age.

To "promote" is also defined:

> "Promote" means to procure, manufacture, issue, sell, give, provide, lend, mail, deliver, transfer, transmute, publish, distribute, circulate, disseminate, present, exhibit or advertise, or to offer or agree to do the same.

This case arose when Paul Ferber, the proprietor of a Manhattan bookstore specializing in sexually oriented products, sold two films to an undercover police officer. The films are devoted almost exclusively to depicting young boys masturbating. Ferber was indicted on . . . two counts of violating § 263.15, the two New York laws controlling dissemination of child pornography. After a jury trial, Ferber was . . . found guilty of the two counts under § 263.15, which did not require proof that the films were obscene. . . . [The New York Court of Appeals reversed, holding that only *obscene* child pornography could be made criminal.]

In *Chaplinsky v. New Hampshire*, the Court laid the foundation for the excision of obscenity from the realm of constitutionally protected expression. . . .

Embracing this judgment, the Court squarely held in *Roth v. United States* that "obscenity is not within the area of constitutionally protected speech or press." [R]*oth* was followed by 15 years during which this Court struggled with "the intractable obscenity problem." [T]hroughout this period, we recognized "the inherent dangers of undertaking to regulate any form of expression." Consequently, our difficulty was not only to assure that statutes designed to regulate obscene materials sufficiently defined what was prohibited, but also to devise substantive limits on what fell within the permissible scope of regulation. In *Miller v. California*, a majority of the Court agreed that a "state offense must also be limited to works which, taken as a whole, appeal to the prurient interest in sex, which portray sexual conduct in a patently offensive way, and which, taken as a whole, do not have serious literary, artistic, political, or scientific value."

[T]he *Miller* standard, like its predecessors, was an accommodation between the State's interests in protecting the "sensibilities of unwilling recipients" from exposure to pornographic material and the dangers of censorship inherent in unabashedly content-based laws. Like obscenity statutes, laws directed at the dissemination of child pornography run the risk of suppressing protected expression by allowing the hand of the censor to become unduly heavy. For the following reasons, however, we are persuaded that the States are entitled to greater leeway in the regulation of pornographic depictions of children.

First. It is evident beyond the need for elaboration that a State's interest in "safeguarding the physical and psychological well-being of a minor" is "compelling." . . . Accordingly, we have sustained legislation aimed at protecting the physical and emotional well-being of youth even when the laws have operated in the sensitive area of constitutionally protected rights. . . .

The prevention of sexual exploitation and abuse of children constitutes a government objective of surpassing importance. . . . Suffice it to say that virtually all of the States and the United States have passed legislation proscribing the production of or otherwise combating "child pornography." The legislative judgment, as well as the judgment found in the relevant literature, is that the use of children as subjects of pornographic materials is harmful to the physiological, emotional, and mental health of the child. That judgment, we think, easily passes muster under the First Amendment.

Second. The distribution of photographs and films depicting sexual activity by juveniles is intrinsically related to the sexual abuse of children in at least two ways. First, the materials produced are a permanent record of the children's participation and the harm to the child is exacerbated by their circulation. Second, the distribution network for child pornography must be closed if the production of material which requires the sexual exploitation of children is to be effectively controlled. Indeed, there is no serious contention that the legislature was unjustified in believing that it is difficult, if not impossible, to halt the exploitation of children by pursuing only those who produce the photographs and movies. While the production of pornographic materials is a low-profile, clandestine industry, the need to market the resulting products requires a visible apparatus of distribution. The most expeditious if not the only practical method of law enforcement may be to dry up the market for this material by imposing severe criminal penalties on persons selling, advertising, or otherwise promoting the product. Thirty-five States and Congress have concluded that restraints on the distribution of pornographic materials are required in order to effectively combat the problem, and there is a body of literature and testimony to support these legislative conclusions.

Respondent does not contend that the State is unjustified in pursuing those who distribute child pornography. Rather, he argues that it is enough for the State to prohibit the distribution of materials that are legally obscene under the *Miller* test. While some States may find that this approach properly accommodates its interests, it does not follow that the First Amendment prohibits a State from going further. The *Miller* standard, like all general definitions of what may be banned as obscene, does not reflect the State's particular and more compelling interest in prosecuting those who promote the sexual exploitation of children. Thus, the question under the *Miller* test of whether a work, taken as a whole, appeals to the prurient interest of the average person bears no connection to the issue of whether a child has been physically or psychologically harmed in the production of the work. Similarly, a sexually explicit depiction need not be "patently offensive" in order to have required the sexual exploitation of a child for its production. In addition, a work which, taken on the whole, contains serious literary, artistic, political, or scientific value may nevertheless embody the hardest core of child pornography. "It is irrelevant to the child [who has been abused] whether or not the material . . . has a literary, artistic, political or social value." We therefore cannot conclude that the *Miller* standard is a satisfactory solution to the child pornography problem.

Third. The advertising and selling of child pornography provide an economic motive for and are thus an integral part of the production of such materials, an activity illegal throughout the Nation. . . . We note that were the statutes outlawing the employment of children in these films and photographs fully effective, and the constitutionality of these laws has not been questioned, the First Amendment implications would be no greater than that presented by laws against distribution: enforceable production laws would leave no child pornography to be marketed.

Fourth. The value of permitting live performances and photographic reproductions of children engaged in lewd sexual conduct is exceedingly modest, if not *de minimis*. We consider it unlikely that visual depictions of children performing sexual acts or lewdly exhibiting their genitals would often constitute an important and necessary part of a literary performance or scientific or educational work. As a state judge in this case observed, if it were necessary for literary or artistic value, a person over the statutory age who perhaps looked younger could be utilized. Simulation outside of the prohibition of the statute could provide another alternative. Nor is there any question here of censoring a particular literary theme or portrayal of sexual activity. The First Amendment interest is limited to that of rendering the portrayal somewhat more "realistic" by utilizing or photographing children.

Fifth. Recognizing and classifying child pornography as a category of material outside the protection of the First Amendment is not, incompatible with our earlier decisions. [I]t is not rare that a content-based classification of speech has been accepted because it may be appropriately generalized that within the confines of the given classification, the evil to be restricted so overwhelmingly outweighs the expressive interests, if any, at stake, that no process of case-by-case adjudication is required. When a definable class of material, such as that covered by § 263.15, bears so heavily and pervasively on the welfare of children engaged in its production, we think the balance of competing interests is clearly struck and that it is permissible to consider these materials as without the protection of the First Amendment.

There are, of course, limits on the category of child pornography which, like obscenity, is unprotected by the First Amendment. As with all legislation in this sensitive area, the conduct to be prohibited must be adequately defined by the applicable state law, as written or authoritatively construed. Here the nature of the harm to be combated requires that the state offense be limited to works that *visually* depict sexual conduct by children below a specified age. The category of "sexual conduct" proscribed must also be suitably limited and described. . . .

Section 263.15's prohibition [meets this test]. The forbidden acts to be depicted are listed with sufficient precision and represent the kind of conduct that, if it were the theme of a work, could render it legally obscene: "actual or simulated sexual intercourse, deviate sexual intercourse, sexual bestiality, masturbation, sado-masochistic abuse, or lewd exhibition of the genitals." The term "lewd exhibition of the genitals" is not unknown in this area and, indeed, was given in *Miller* as an example of a permissible regulation. A performance is defined only to include live or visual depictions: "any play, motion picture, photograph or dance . . . [or] other visual representation exhibited before an audience." . . .

It remains to address the claim that the New York statute is unconstitutionally overbroad because it would forbid the distribution of material with serious literary, scientific, or educational value or material which does not threaten the harms sought to be combated by the State. Respondent prevailed on that ground below, and it is to that issue that we now turn. . . .

The traditional rule is that a person to whom a statute may constitutionally be applied may not challenge that statute on the ground that it may conceivably be applied unconstitutionally to others in situations not before the Court. . . . What has come to be known as the First Amendment overbreadth doctrine is one of the few exceptions to this principle and must be justified by "weighty countervailing policies." The doctrine is predicated on the sensitive nature of protected expression: "persons whose expression is constitutionally protected may well refrain from exercising their rights for fear of criminal sanctions by a statute susceptible of application to protected expression." It is for this reason that we have allowed persons to attack overly broad statutes even though the conduct of the person making the attack is clearly unprotected and could be proscribed by a law drawn with the requisite specificity.

The scope of the First Amendment overbreadth doctrine, like most exceptions to established principles, must be carefully tied to the circumstances in which facial invalidation of a statute is truly warranted. Because of the wide-reaching effects of striking down a statute on its face at the request of one whose own conduct may be punished despite the First Amendment, we have recognized that the overbreadth doctrine is "strong medicine" and have employed it with hesitation, and then "only as a last resort." We have, in consequence, insisted that the overbreadth involved be "substantial" before the statute involved will be invalidated on its face. . . .

The premise that a law should not be invalidated for overbreadth unless it reaches a substantial number of impermissible applications is hardly novel. On most occasions involving facial invalidation, the Court has stressed the embracing sweep of the statute over protected expression. . . . "We have never held that a statute should be held invalid on its face merely because it is possible to conceive of a single impermissible application, and in that sense a requirement of substantial overbreadth is already implicit in the doctrine." . . .

Applying these principles, we hold that § 263.15 is not substantially overbroad. We consider this the paradigmatic case of a state statute whose legitimate reach dwarfs its arguably impermissible applications. . . . While the reach of the statute is directed at the hard core of child pornography, the Court of Appeals was understandably concerned that some protected expression, ranging from medical textbooks to pictorials in the National Geographic would fall prey to the statute. How often, if ever, it may be necessary to employ children to engage in conduct clearly within the reach of § 263.15 in order to produce educational, medical, or artistic works cannot be known with certainty. Yet we seriously doubt, and it has not been suggested, that these arguably impermissible applications of the statute amount to more than a tiny fraction of the materials within the statute's reach. Nor will we assume that the New York courts will widen the possibly invalid reach of the statute by giving an expansive construction to the proscription on "lewd exhibition[s] of the genitals." Under these circumstances, § 263.15 is "not substantially overbroad and . . . whatever overbreadth may exist should be cured through case-by-case analysis of the fact situations to which its sanctions, assertedly, may not be applied." . . .

JUSTICE BLACKMUN concurs in the result.

JUSTICE O'CONNOR, concurring. [omitted]

JUSTICE BRENNAN, with whom JUSTICE MARSHALL joins, concurring in the judgment.

I agree with much of what is said in the Court's opinion. . . . I also agree with the Court that the "tiny fraction" of material of serious artistic, scientific, or educational value that could conceivably fall within the reach of the statute is insufficient to justify striking the statute on the grounds of overbreadth.

But in my view application of § 263.15 or any similar statute to depictions of children that in themselves do have serious literary, artistic, scientific, or medical value, would violate the First Amendment. As the Court recognizes, the limited classes of speech, the suppression of which does not raise serious First Amendment concerns, have two attributes. They are of exceedingly "slight social value," and the State has a compelling interest in their regulation. The First Amendment value of depictions of children that are in themselves serious contributions to art, literature, or science, is, by definition, simply not "*de minimis.*" At the same time, the State's interest in suppression of such materials is likely to be far less compelling. For the Court's assumption of harm to the child resulting from the "permanent record" and "circulation" of the child's "participation," lacks much of its force where the depiction is a serious contribution to art or science. The production of materials of serious value is not the "low-profile, clandestine industry" that according to the Court produces purely pornographic materials. In short, it is inconceivable how a depiction of a child that is itself a serious contribution to the world of art or literature or science can be deemed "material outside the protection of the First Amendment."

JUSTICE STEVENS, concurring in the judgment.

Two propositions seem perfectly clear to me. First, the specific conduct that gave rise to this criminal prosecution is not protected by the Federal Constitution; second, the state statute that respondent violated prohibits some conduct that is protected by the First Amendment. The critical question, then, is whether this respondent, to whom the statute may be applied without violating the Constitution, may challenge the statute on the ground that it conceivably may be applied unconstitutionally to others in situations not before the Court. I agree with the Court's answer to this question but not with its method of analyzing the issue. . . .

The Court's holding that this respondent may not challenge New York's statute as overbroad follows its discussion of the contours of the category of nonobscene child pornography that New York may legitimately prohibit. Having defined that category in an abstract setting, the Court makes the empirical judgment that the arguably impermissible application of the New York statute amounts to only a "tiny fraction of the materials within the statute's reach." Even assuming that the Court's empirical analysis is sound, I believe a more conservative approach to the issue would adequately vindicate the State's interest in protecting its children and cause less harm to the federal interest in free expression.

A hypothetical example will illustrate my concern. Assume that the operator of a New York motion picture theater specializing in the exhibition of foreign feature films is offered a full-length movie containing one scene that is plainly lewd if viewed in isolation but that nevertheless is part of a serious work of art. If the child actor resided abroad, New York's interest in protecting its young from sexual exploitation would be far less compelling than in the case before us. The federal interest in free expression would, however, be just as strong as if an adult actor had been used. There are at least three different ways to deal with the statute's potential application to that sort of case.

First, at one extreme and as the Court appears to hold, the First Amendment inquiry might be limited to determining whether the offensive scene, viewed in isolation, is lewd. When the constitutional protection is narrowed in this drastic fashion, the Court is probably safe in concluding that only a tiny fraction of the materials covered by the New York statute is protected. And with respect to my hypothetical exhibitor of foreign films, he need have no uncertainty about the permissible application of the statute; for the one lewd scene would deprive the entire film of any constitutional protection.

Second, at the other extreme and as the New York Court of Appeals correctly perceived, the application of this Court's cases requiring that an obscenity determination be based on the artistic value of a production taken as a whole would afford the exhibitor constitutional protection and result in a holding that the statute is invalid because of its overbreadth. Under that approach, the rationale for invalidating the entire statute is premised on the concern that the exhibitor's understanding about its potential reach could cause him to engage in self-censorship. This Court's approach today substitutes broad, unambiguous, state-imposed censorship for the self-censorship that an overbroad statute might produce.

Third, as an intermediate position, I would refuse to apply overbreadth analysis for reasons unrelated to any prediction concerning the relative number of protected communications that the statute may prohibit. Specifically, I would postpone decision of my hypothetical case until it actually arises. Advocates of a liberal use of overbreadth analysis could object to such postponement on the ground that it creates the risk that the exhibitor's uncertainty may produce self-censorship. But that risk obviously interferes less with the interest in free expression than does an abstract, advance ruling that the film is simply unprotected whenever it contains a lewd scene, no matter how brief. . . .

Moreover, it is probably safe to assume that the category of speech that is covered by the New York statute generally is of a lower quality than most other types of communication. On a number of occasions, I have expressed the view that the First Amendment affords some forms of speech more protection from governmental regulation than other forms of speech. Today the Court accepts this view, putting the category of speech described in the New York statute in its rightful place near the bottom of this hierarchy. Although I disagree with the Court's position that such speech is totally without First Amendment protection, I agree that generally marginal speech does not warrant the extraordinary protection afforded by the overbreadth doctrine.

COMMENTS AND QUESTIONS

1.   One might be surprised that child pornography is not by definition obscene, but the laws of several states, including New York's in *Ferber*, prohibited child pornography without the *Miller* specification that it not have any serious literary, artistic, political, or scientific value. Of course, most child pornography could be prosecuted under the state's obscenity statutes as well, because it undoubtedly would satisfy all of the *Miller* test. Prosecutions under obscenity statutes, however, are much more expensive because they require expert testimony, often opposed by expert testimony by the defense, as to the literary, artistic, political, or scientific value of the material.

2.   Note the fundamentally different justification for child pornography's exception from First Amendment protection compared to obscenity's. Rather than the absence of any redeeming social value and its negative effect on the morals of those viewing it, the justification for exempting child pornography from the First Amendment is the effect on the children involved in the making the pornography. As a result, written descriptions of sexual activities with children, actual depictions of adults who look like children, or computer-created pictures of children engaged in sexual activities, although they may have the same effect on the reader/observer, are not "child pornography" within the meaning of *Ferber*. The Supreme Court confirmed this in *Ashcroft v. Free Speech Coalition*, 535 U.S. 234 (2002), which held that the Child Pornography Prevention Act of 1996 was unconstitutional in its criminalization of virtual child pornography created through computer simulation.

3.   The premise behind the Court's decision in *Ferber* is that New York can pass a law to protect the welfare of children. That is obvious as to New York children, but why does New York have an interest in protecting the children in California, much less in Thailand? Nevertheless, the Court does not seem concerned about where the child pornography comes from or what the policy is of that state or nation. Could New York make it illegal to sell shoes in New York that had been produced from child labor in Vietnam? In fact, who is a "child"? New York, the federal government, and sixteen states define a child as someone under 16, but four states define it as under 17, and sixteen states define it as someone under 18.

4.   The retreat from *Stanley* signaled by *Paris Adult Theatre* and *Miller* was extended in *Osborne v. Ohio*, 495 U.S. 103 (1990). There, Osborne was prosecuted for the possession of child pornography in his home, and he argued that this violated the First Amendment just as the prohibition on the possession of obscenity in one's home was found unconstitutional in *Stanley*. The Court rejected his argument, saying: "[i]n *Stanley*, Georgia primarily sought to proscribe the private possession of obscenity because it was concerned that obscenity would poison the minds of its viewers. . . . The difference here is obvious: The State does not rely on a paternalistic interest in

regulating Osborne's mind. Rather, Ohio has enacted [its law] in order to protect the victims of child pornography; it hopes to destroy a market for the exploitative use of children."

5.   *Ferber* contains a good discussion of the important and unique First Amendment doctrine of "overbreadth." Normally, as the Court states, one cannot argue that a statute would be unconstitutional as applied to someone else, when it would be constitutional to apply it to the person raising the claim. Essentially, this rule is based on the law of standing, because a court decision that the law would be unconstitutional in other circumstances would not redress or avoid the litigant's injury. However, because the mere existence of the law might inhibit others, who would be protected, from exercising their First Amendment rights, the Court has created the overbreadth doctrine to allow even the unprotected party to raise the unconstitutionality of a law that might be unconstitutional as to others. *Ferber* reflects the modern, relatively restrictive, approach to this doctrine that requires the law to be "substantially overbroad" before one can invoke this doctrine. The overbreadth doctrine should be distinguished from unconstitutional vagueness. The vagueness doctrine arises from Due Process, not the First Amendment, and is intended to ensure that, before someone can be penalized, the law is clear as to what is prohibited. In the free speech area, the vagueness doctrine is aggressively applied, again to assure that protected speech is not chilled, but like other claims, the person making the vagueness claim must be in the position of someone for whom the meaning of the law might have been unclear. It is not a basis for avoiding the general rule that one cannot raise a claim on behalf of someone not before the court.

F. FALSE SPEECH

Whether one thinks that the values of the First Amendment are to protect the marketplace of ideas, to further democratic self-governance, or to enable self-actualization and individual autonomy through self-expression, there does not, at least at first glance, seem to be much value in protecting speech that is demonstrably false. Indeed, in *Chaplinsky* the Court listed libel as one of the classes of speech the punishment of which was never thought to raise a constitutional question. Well, not until 1964.

NEW YORK TIMES V. SULLIVAN

United States Supreme Court, 1964.
376 U.S. 254, 84 S.Ct. 710.

JUSTICE BRENNAN delivered the opinion of the Court.

We are required in this case to determine for the first time the extent to which the constitutional protections for speech and press limit a State's power to award damages in a libel action brought by a public official against critics of his official conduct.

Respondent L. B. Sullivan is one of the three elected Commissioners of the City of Montgomery, Alabama[, and his duties include] supervision of the Police Department. . . . He brought this civil libel action against the four individual petitioners, who are Negroes and Alabama clergymen, and against petitioner the New York Times Company, a New York corporation which publishes the New York Times, a daily newspaper. A jury in the Circuit Court of Montgomery County awarded him damages of $500,000, the full amount claimed, against all the petitioners. . . .

Respondent's complaint alleged that he had been libeled by statements in a full-page advertisement that was carried in the New York Times on March 29, 1960. Entitled "Heed Their Rising Voices," the advertisement began by stating that "As the whole world knows by now, thousands of Southern Negro students are engaged in widespread non-violent demonstrations in positive affirmation of the right to live in human dignity as guaranteed by the U.S. Constitution and the Bill of Rights." It went on to charge that "in their efforts to uphold these guarantees, they are being met by an unprecedented wave of terror by those who would deny and negate that document which the whole world looks upon as setting the pattern for modern freedom. * * *" Succeeding paragraphs purported to illustrate the "wave of terror" by describing certain alleged events. The text concluded with an appeal for funds for three purposes: support of the student movement, "the struggle for the right-to-vote," and the legal defense of Dr. Martin Luther King, Jr., leader of the movement, against a perjury indictment then pending in Montgomery.

[T]he advertisement was signed at the bottom of the page by the 'Committee to Defend Martin Luther King and the Struggle for Freedom in the South,' and the officers of the Committee were listed.

Of the 10 paragraphs of text in the advertisement, the third and a portion of the sixth were the basis of respondent's claim of libel. They read as follows:

> In Montgomery, Alabama, after students sang "My Country, 'Tis of Thee" on the State Capitol steps, their leaders were expelled from school, and truckloads of police armed with shotguns and tear-gas ringed the Alabama State College Campus. When the entire student body protested to state authorities by refusing to re-register, their dining hall was padlocked in an attempt to starve them into submission.

> Again and again the Southern violators have answered Dr. King's peaceful protests with intimidation and violence. They have bombed his home almost killing his wife and child. They have assaulted his person. They have arrested him seven times-for "speeding," "loitering" and similar "offenses." And now they have charged him with "perjury"—a felony under which they could imprison him for ten years. * * *

Although neither of these statements mentions respondent by name, he contended that the word "police" in the third paragraph referred to him as the Montgomery Commissioner who supervised the Police Department, so that he was being accused of "ringing" the campus with police. He further claimed that the paragraph would be read as imputing to the police, and hence to him, the padlocking of the dining hall in order to starve the students into submission. As to the sixth paragraph, he contended that since arrests are ordinarily made by the police, the statement "They have arrested (Dr. King) seven times" would be read as referring to him; he further contended that the "They" who did the arresting would be equated with the "They" who committed the other described acts and with the "Southern violators." Thus, he argued, the paragraph would be read as accusing the Montgomery police, and hence him, of answering Dr. King's protests with "intimidation and violence," bombing his home, assaulting his person, and charging him with perjury. Respondent and six other Montgomery residents testified that they read some or all of the statements as referring to him in his capacity as Commissioner.

It is uncontroverted that some of the statements contained in the two paragraphs were not accurate descriptions of events which occurred in Montgomery. Although Negro students staged a demonstration on the State Capital steps, they sang the National Anthem and not "My Country, 'Tis of Thee." [N]ot the entire student body, but most of it, had protested the expulsion, not by refusing to register, but by boycotting classes on a single day; virtually all the students did register for the ensuing semester. The campus dining hall was not padlocked on any occasion, and the only students who may have been barred from eating there were the few who had neither signed a preregistration application nor requested temporary meal tickets. Although the police were deployed near the campus in large numbers on three occasions, they did not at any time "ring" the campus, and they were not called to the campus in connection with the demonstration on the State Capitol steps, as the third paragraph implied. Dr. King had not been arrested seven times, but only four; and although he claimed to have been assaulted some years earlier in connection with his arrest for loitering outside a courtroom, one of the officers who made the arrest denied that there was such an assault.

On the premise that the charges in the sixth paragraph could be read as referring to him, respondent was allowed to prove that he had not participated in the events described. Although Dr. King's home had in fact been bombed twice when his wife and child were there, both of these occasions antedated respondent's tenure as Commissioner, and the police were not only not implicated in the bombings, but had made every effort to apprehend those who were. Three of Dr. King's four arrests took place before respondent became Commissioner. Although Dr. King had in fact been indicted (he was subsequently acquitted) on two counts of perjury, each of which carried a possible five-year sentence, respondent had nothing to do with procuring the indictment.

Respondent made no effort to prove that he suffered actual pecuniary loss as a result of the alleged libel.[3] One of his witnesses, a former employer, testified that if he had believed the statements, he doubted whether he "would want to be associated with anybody who would be a party to such things that are stated in that ad," and that he would not re-employ respondent if he believed "that he allowed the Police Department to do the things that the paper say he did." But neither this witness nor any of the others testified that he had actually believed the statements in their supposed reference to respondent.

The cost of the advertisement was approximately $4800, and it was published by the Times upon an order from a New York advertising agency acting for the signatory Committee. The agency submitted the advertisement with a letter from A. Philip Randolph, Chairman of the Committee, certifying that the persons whose names appeared on the advertisement had given their permission. . . .

The trial judge submitted the case to the jury under instructions that the statements in the advertisement were "libelous per se" and were not privileged, so that petitioners might be held liable if the jury found that they had published the advertisement and that the statements were made "of and concerning" respondent. The jury was instructed that, because the statements were libelous per se, "the law * * * implies legal injury from the bare fact of publication itself," "falsity and malice are presumed," "general damages need not be alleged or proved but are presumed," and "punitive damages may be awarded by the jury even though the amount of actual damages is neither found nor shown." An award of punitive damages—as distinguished from "general" damages, which are compensatory in nature—apparently requires proof of actual malice under Alabama law, and the judge charged that "mere negligence or carelessness is not evidence of actual malice or malice in fact, and does not justify an award of exemplary or punitive damages." [T]he judge rejected petitioners' contention that his rulings abridged the freedoms of speech and of the press that are guaranteed by the First and Fourteenth Amendments.

In affirming the judgment, the Supreme Court of Alabama sustained the trial judge's rulings and instructions in all respects. . . . It rejected petitioners' constitutional contentions with the brief statements that "The First Amendment of the U.S. Constitution does not protect libelous publications" and "The Fourteenth Amendment is directed against State action and not private action."

---

[3]   Approximately 394 copies of the edition of the Times containing the advertisement were circulated in Alabama. Of these, about 35 copies were distributed in Montgomery County. The total circulation of the Times for that day was approximately 650,000 copies.

Because of the importance of the constitutional issues involved, we granted the separate petitions for certiorari of the individual petitioners and of the Times. We reverse the judgment. We hold that the rule of law applied by the Alabama courts is constitutionally deficient for failure to provide the safeguards for freedom of speech and of the press that are required by the First and Fourteenth Amendments in a libel action brought by a public official against critics of his official conduct. We further hold that under the proper safeguards the evidence presented in this case is constitutionally insufficient to support the judgment for respondent.

We may dispose at the outset of two grounds asserted to insulate the judgment of the Alabama courts from constitutional scrutiny. The first is the proposition relied on by the State Supreme Court—that the Fourteenth Amendment is directed against State action and not private action. That proposition has no application to this case. Although this is a civil lawsuit between private parties, the Alabama courts have applied a state rule of law which petitioners claim to impose invalid restrictions on their constitutional freedoms of speech and press. It matters not that that law has been applied in a civil action and that it is common law only, though supplemented by statute. The test is not the form in which state power has been applied but, whatever the form, whether such power has in fact been exercised.

The second contention is that the constitutional guarantees of freedom of speech and of the press are inapplicable here, at least so far as the Times is concerned, because the allegedly libelous statements were published as part of a paid, "commercial" advertisement. . . .

The publication here was not a "commercial" advertisement. . . . It communicated information, expressed opinion, recited grievances, protested claimed abuses, and sought financial support on behalf of a movement whose existence and objectives are matters of the highest public interest and concern. That the Times was paid for publishing the advertisement is as immaterial in this connection as is the fact that newspapers and books are sold. Any other conclusion would discourage newspapers from carrying "editorial advertisements" of this type, and so might shut off an important outlet for the promulgation of information and ideas by persons who do not themselves have access to publishing facilities—who wish to exercise their freedom of speech even though they are not members of the press. . . . To avoid placing such a handicap upon the freedoms of expression, we hold that if the allegedly libelous statements would otherwise be constitutionally protected from the present judgment, they do not forfeit that protection because they were published in the form of a paid advertisement. . . .

Respondent relies heavily, as did the Alabama courts, on statements of this Court to the effect that the Constitution does not protect libelous publications. Those statements do not foreclose our inquiry here. None of the cases sustained the use of libel laws to impose sanctions upon expression critical of the official conduct of public officials. . . . Like insurrection, contempt, advocacy of unlawful acts, breach of the peace, obscenity, solicitation of legal business, and the various other formulae for the repression of expression that have been challenged in this Court, libel can claim no talismanic immunity from constitutional limitations. It must be measured by standards that satisfy the First Amendment.

The general proposition that freedom of expression upon public questions is secured by the First Amendment has long been settled by our decisions. . . .

Thus we consider this case against the background of a profound national commitment to the principle that debate on public issues should be uninhibited, robust, and wide-open, and that it may well include vehement, caustic, and sometimes unpleasantly sharp attacks on government and public officials. The present advertisement, as an expression of grievance and protest on one of the major public issues of our time, would seem clearly to qualify for the constitutional protection. The question is whether it forfeits that protection by the falsity of some of its factual statements and by its alleged defamation of respondent.

Authoritative interpretations of the First Amendment guarantees have consistently refused to recognize an exception for any test of truth— whether administered by judges, juries, or administrative officials—and especially one that puts the burden of proving truth on the speaker. The constitutional protection does not turn upon "the truth, popularity, or social utility of the ideas and beliefs which are offered." [T]hat erroneous statement is inevitable in free debate, and that it must be protected if the freedoms of expression are to have the "breathing space" that they "need * * * to survive.". . .

Injury to official reputation error affords no more warrant for repressing speech that would otherwise be free than does factual error. Where judicial officers are involved, this Court has held that concern for the dignity and reputation of the courts does not justify the punishment as criminal contempt of criticism of the judge or his decision. This is true even though the utterance contains "half-truths" and "misinformation." If judges are to be treated as "men of fortitude, able to thrive in a hardy climate," surely the same must be true of other government officials, such as elected city commissioners. Criticism of their official conduct does not lose its constitutional protection merely because it is effective criticism and hence diminishes their official reputations.

If neither factual error nor defamatory content suffices to remove the constitutional shield from criticism of official conduct, the combination of the two elements is no less inadequate. This is the lesson to be drawn from the great controversy over the Sedition Act of 1798. . . . That statute made it a crime, punishable by a $5,000 fine and five years in prison, "if any person shall write, print, utter or publish * * * any false, scandalous and malicious writing or writings against the government of the United States, or either house of the Congress * * *, or the President * * *, with intent to defame * * * or to bring them, or either of them, into contempt or disrepute; or to excite against them, or either or any of them, the hatred of the good people of the United States." The Act allowed the defendant the defense of truth, and provided that the jury were to be judges both of the law and the facts. Despite these qualifications, the Act was vigorously condemned as unconstitutional in an attack joined in by Jefferson and Madison. . . .

Although the Sedition Act was never tested in this Court, the attack upon its validity has carried the day in the court of history. Fines levied in its prosecution were repaid by Act of Congress on the ground that it was unconstitutional. The invalidity of the Act has also been assumed by Justices of this Court. *See* Holmes, J., dissenting and joined by Brandeis, J., in *Abrams v. United States*; Jackson, J., dissenting in *Beauharnais v. Illinois*, 343 U.S. 250; Douglas, The Right of the People (1958). These views reflect a broad consensus that the Act, because of the restraint it imposed upon criticism of government and public officials, was inconsistent with the First Amendment. . . .

The judgment awarded in this case—without the need for any proof of actual pecuniary loss—was one thousand times greater than the maximum fine provided by the Alabama criminal statute, and one hundred times greater than that provided by the Sedition Act. And since there is no double-jeopardy limitation applicable to civil lawsuits, this is not the only judgment that may be awarded against petitioners for the same publication.[18] Whether or not a newspaper can survive a succession of such judgments, the pall of fear and timidity imposed upon those who would give voice to public criticism is an atmosphere in which the First Amendment freedoms cannot survive.

The state rule of law is not saved by its allowance of the defense of truth. A defense for erroneous statements honestly made is no less essential here than was the requirement of proof of guilty knowledge which, we held indispensable to a valid conviction of a bookseller for possessing obscene writings for sale. . . .

A rule compelling the critic of official conduct to guarantee the truth of all his factual assertions—and to do so on pain of libel judgments virtually unlimited in amount—leads to a . . . "self-censorship." Allowance of the defense of truth, with the burden of proving it on the defendant, does not mean that only false speech will be deterred.[19] . . . Under such a rule,

---

[18] The Times states that four other libel suits based on the advertisement have been filed against it by others who have served as Montgomery City Commissioners and by the Governor of Alabama; that another $500,000 verdict has been awarded in the only one of these cases that has yet gone to trial; and that the damages sought in the other three total $2,000,000.

[19] Even a false statement may be deemed to make a valuable contribution to public debate, since it brings about 'the clearer perception and livelier impression of truth, produced by its

would-be critics of official conduct may be deterred from voicing their criticism, even though it is believed to be true and even though it is in fact true, because of doubt whether it can be proved in court or fear of the expense of having to do so. . . . The rule thus dampens the vigor and limits the variety of public debate. It is inconsistent with the First and Fourteenth Amendments.

The constitutional guarantees require, we think, a federal rule that prohibits a public official from recovering damages for a defamatory falsehood relating to his official conduct unless he proves that the statement was made with "actual malice"—that is, with knowledge that it was false or with reckless disregard of whether it was false or not.

We conclude that such a privilege is required by the First and Fourteenth Amendments.

We hold today that the Constitution delimits a State's power to award damages for libel in actions brought by public officials against critics of their official conduct. Since this is such an action,[23] the rule requiring proof of actual malice is applicable.

[S]ince respondent may seek a new trial, we deem that considerations of effective judicial administration require us to review the evidence in the present record to determine whether it could constitutionally support a judgment for respondent. This Court's duty is not limited to the elaboration of constitutional principles; we must also in proper cases review the evidence to make certain that those principles have been constitutionally applied. . . . We must "make an independent examination of the whole record," so as to assure ourselves that the judgment does not constitute a forbidden intrusion on the field of free expression.

Applying these standards, we consider that the proof presented to show actual malice lacks the convincing clarity which the constitutional standard demands, and hence that it would not constitutionally sustain the judgment for respondent under the proper rule of law. . . .

We also think the evidence was constitutionally defective in another respect: it was incapable of supporting the jury's finding that the allegedly libelous statements were made "of and concerning" respondent. . . . There was no reference to respondent in the advertisement, either by name or official position. . . . [There was no] basis for the belief that respondent himself was attacked in the advertisement beyond the bare fact that he was in overall charge of the Police Department and thus bore official responsibility for police conduct. . . . This reliance on the bare fact of

collision with error.' Mill, On Liberty (Oxford: Blackwell, 1947), at 15; see also Milton, Areopagitica, in Prose Works (Yale, 1959), Vol. II, at 561.

   [23] We have no occasion here to determine how far down into the lower ranks of government employees the "public official" designation would extend for purposes of this rule, or otherwise to specify categories of persons who would or would not be included. Nor need we here determine the boundaries of the "official conduct" concept. . . .

respondent's official position was made explicit by the Supreme Court of Alabama. That court . . . based its ruling on the proposition that:

> We think it common knowledge that the average person knows that municipal agents, such as police and firemen, and others, are under the control and direction of the city governing body, and more particularly under the direction and control of a single commissioner. In measuring the performance or deficiencies of such groups, praise or criticism is usually attached to the official in complete control of the body.

This proposition has disquieting implications for criticism of governmental conduct. . . . Raising as it does the possibility that a good-faith critic of government will be penalized for his criticism, the proposition relied on by the Alabama courts strikes at the very center of the constitutionally protected area of free expression. We hold that such a proposition may not constitutionally be utilized to establish that an otherwise impersonal attack on governmental operations was a libel of an official responsible for those operations.

The judgment of the Supreme Court of Alabama is reversed and the case is remanded to that court for further proceedings not inconsistent with this opinion.

MR. JUSTICE BLACK, with whom MR. JUSTICE DOUGLAS joins (concurring). [opinion omitted]

MR. JUSTICE GOLDBERG, with whom MR. JUSTICE DOUGLAS joins (concurring in the result).

[I]n my view, the First and Fourteenth Amendments to the Constitution afford to the citizen and to the press an absolute, unconditional privilege to criticize official conduct despite the harm which may flow from excesses and abuses. . . . It may be urged that deliberately and maliciously false statements have no conceivable value as free speech. That argument, however, is not responsive to the real issue presented by this case, which is whether that freedom of speech which all agree is constitutionally protected can be effectively safeguarded by a rule allowing the imposition of liability upon a jury's evaluation of the speaker's state of mind. If individual citizens may be held liable in damages for strong words, which a jury finds false and maliciously motivated, there can be little doubt that public debate and advocacy will be constrained. . . .

This is not to say that the Constitution protects defamatory statements directed against the private conduct of a public official or private citizen. Freedom of press and of speech insures that government will respond to the will of the people and that changes may be obtained by peaceful means. Purely private defendant has little to do with the political ends of a self-governing society. The imposition of liability for private defamation does not abridge the freedom of public speech or any other freedom protected by the First Amendment.

The conclusion that the Constitution affords the citizen and the press an absolute privilege for criticism of official conduct does not leave the public official without defenses against unsubstantiated opinions or deliberate misstatements. "Under our system of government, counterargument and education are the weapons available to expose these matters, not abridgment * * * of free speech * * *."

The public official certainly has equal if not greater access than most private citizens to media of communication. In any event, despite the possibility that some excesses and abuses may go unremedied, we must recognize that "the people of this nation have ordained in the light of history, that, in spite of the probability of excesses and abuses, (certain) liberties are, in the long view, essential to enlightened opinion and right conduct on the part of the citizens of a democracy."

COMMENTS AND QUESTIONS

1. Although the Court may be correct that none of its precedents involved a libel action by a public official against someone who criticized him, it is still fair to say that no case had ever held libel to be constitutionally protected. Moreover, Alabama's libel law is a good example of historical, common-law libel, in which truth is a defense and certain imputations were deemed "libelous per se" because of their natural tendency to harm one's reputation. Nevertheless, for almost 200 years the American press had not only survived but flourished while engaged in both legitimate muckraking and yellow journalism. Accordingly, *New York Times* was a truly revolutionary decision, and it was unanimous, with the concurring justices indicating they would have been even more protective of speech. While *New York Times* is a First Amendment case, the fact that it arose out of a concerted attempt to frustrate the civil rights movement may well explain its outcome. Its impact, of course, has been much broader.

2. The Court's condemnation of the Sedition Act of 1798 is certainly the modern view, but the Court's evidence of its rejection is slim and unconventional. That is, it cites Jefferson and Madison's criticism of the Act, but as opponents of the Act and leaders of the political party at which it was aimed, their expressions of its constitutionality might be somewhat suspect. Similarly, the fact that a subsequent Congress, captured by the party that opposed the Act, repaid the fines levied on the party's members who were prosecuted under the Act says little about the constitutionality of the law. The Court also notes that Supreme Court justices have assumed it was unconstitutional, but the only sources cited are dissenting opinions and a book. In short, today the idea that certain criticism of the government could be made criminal seems fundamentally at odds with the First Amendment, but general acceptance of protection of such speech is a relatively modern development.

3.　Under the Court's new standard, libel of a public official relating to his official conduct loses its First Amendment protection only when committed with "actual malice," defined as made with knowledge that the statement was false or with a reckless disregard for the truth. In other words, negligent (*i.e.*, unreasonable) false statements that harm an official's reputation are protected. The concurring justices would have protected even intentionally false statements. And it is worth noting that the protection afforded by *New York Times* is not limited to the media; it is a right enjoyed by all persons.

4.　Footnote 23 of the opinion left a number of questions unanswered. The concept of a public official seems to extend quite far down the chain. For example, in *Rosenblatt v. Baer*, 383 U.S. 75 (1966), the Court applied the term to a supervisor of a publicly owned ski resort, because he could "appear to the public to [have] substantial responsibility for or control over the conduct of government affairs." And while *New York Times* expressed the protection as one involving libel of a "public official," it was soon extended to "public figures" "involved in issues in which the public has a justified and important interest." *Curtis Publishing Co. v. Butts*, 388 U.S. 130 (1967). What constitutes a "public figure" is not exactly clear. Those who voluntarily thrust themselves into the public view, *e.g.*, celebrities, apparently are, but mere public interest in a particular person because of her wealth or status apparently is not. *See Time, Inc. v. Firestone*, 424 U.S. 448 (1976)(extramarital sexual activities of the very wealthy did not involve a public controversy even though the public might have been very curious about them). Nevertheless, even an alleged rape victim may be considered a public figure if the alleged rape and the prosecution become highly publicized and controversial as to whether justice was being done. *See Street v. National Broadcasting Co.*, 645 F.2d 1227 (6th Cir. 1981), *cert. granted*, 454 U.S. 815, *cert. dismissed*, 454 U.S. 1095. The Court has distinguished between persons who are public figures for all purposes because of their pervasive fame or notoriety and those persons who are public figures with respect to a particular controversy. It is also not clear when a statement about a public official "relates to his official conduct," although the Court has said that "anything which might touch on an official's fitness for office" would qualify. *Garrison v. Louisiana*, 379 U.S. 64 (1964). Similarly, it is not clear when a statement about a public figure involves "issues in which the public has a justified and important interest."

5.　In *Gertz v. Robert Welch, Inc.*, 418 U.S. 323 (1974), the Court addressed a situation in which a person who was not a public figure for any purpose was defamed with respect to a public controversy in which he was tangentially involved. Weighing the relative interests of a need for a robust press addressing issues of public concern and of individuals to be able to protect their good names, the Court concluded that the protections of *New York Times* were not appropriate. Nevertheless, the Court said that the First Amendment required that liability could not be imposed without a showing of falsity as a result of fault (*i.e.*, negligence, rather than "actual malice" in *New York Times* or strict liability as under the common law). Moreover, punitive damages could not be awarded without a showing of "actual malice." And later, in *Dun & Bradstreet, Inc. v. Greenmoss Builders, Inc.*, 472 U.S. 749 (1985), a split Court made clear that when the libel does not involve either a public figure or a matter of public concern, the First Amendment does not restrict state libel laws.

6. In footnote 19 in *New York Times*, the Court suggests that even false statements may have positive social value. In *Gertz*, however, the Court categorically states "there is no constitutional value in false statements of fact. Neither the intentional lie nor the careless error materially advances society's interest in 'uninhibited, robust, and wide-open' debate on public issues." It then goes on to explain that because of the inevitability of occasional error, the "First Amendment requires that we protect some falsehood in order to protect speech that matters."

7. Ohio has a law that criminalizes making "a false statement concerning the voting record of a candidate or public official," or posting, publishing, circulating, distributing, or otherwise disseminating "a false statement concerning a candidate, either knowing the same to be false or with reckless disregard of whether it was false or not." The Susan B. Anthony List (SBA) is a pro-life advocacy organization, and prior to the 2010 congressional election it made a press release stating that the incumbent Congressman had "voted for a health care bill that includes taxpayer-funded abortion." The Congressman filed a complaint with the Ohio Elections Commission, which found probable cause that SBA had violated the statute, and SBA filed suit in federal court arguing that the statute was unconstitutional. Although the Congressman's complaint was withdrawn when he lost the election, the federal suit continued challenging the statute on its face. The Sixth Circuit found that SBA lacked standing, but the Supreme Court unanimously reversed, remanding the case to be considered on its merits. *Susan B. Anthony List v. Driehaus*, 573 U.S. 149 (2014). How do you think the lower court should rule? On remand, the district court found both statutory provisions unconstitutional as not narrowly tailored to achieving the compelling government interest of maintaining the integrity of elections, and the Sixth Circuit affirmed.

HUSTLER MAGAZINE V. FALWELL

United States Supreme Court, 1988.
485 U.S. 46, 108 S.Ct. 876.

CHIEF JUSTICE REHNQUIST delivered the opinion of the Court.

Petitioner Hustler Magazine, Inc., is a magazine of nationwide circulation. Respondent Jerry Falwell, a nationally known minister who has been active as a commentator on politics and public affairs, sued petitioner and its publisher, petitioner Larry Flynt, to recover damages for . . . intentional infliction of emotional distress. . . . The jury found . . . for respondent on the claim for intentional infliction of emotional distress and awarded damages. We now consider whether this award is consistent with the First and Fourteenth Amendments of the United States Constitution.

The inside front cover of the November 1983 issue of Hustler Magazine featured a "parody" of an advertisement for Campari Liqueur that contained the name and picture of respondent and was entitled "Jerry Falwell talks about his first time." This parody was modeled after actual Campari ads that included interviews with various celebrities about their "first times." Although it was apparent by the end of each interview that this meant the first time they sampled Campari, the ads clearly played on the sexual double entendre of the general subject of "first times." Copying the form and layout of these Campari ads, Hustler's editors chose respondent as the featured celebrity and drafted an alleged "interview" with him in which he states that his "first time" was during a drunken incestuous rendezvous with his mother in an outhouse. The Hustler parody portrays respondent and his mother as drunk and immoral, and suggests that respondent is a hypocrite who preaches only when he is drunk. In small print at the bottom of the page, the ad contains the disclaimer, "ad parody—not to be taken seriously." The magazine's table of contents also lists the ad as "Fiction; Ad and Personality Parody."

[T]his case presents us with a novel question involving First Amendment limitations upon a State's authority to protect its citizens from the intentional infliction of emotional distress. We must decide whether a public figure may recover damages for emotional harm caused by the publication of an ad parody offensive to him, and doubtless gross and repugnant in the eyes of most. Respondent would have us find that a State's interest in protecting public figures from emotional distress is sufficient to deny First Amendment protection to speech that is patently offensive and is intended to inflict emotional injury, even when that speech could not reasonably have been interpreted as stating actual facts about the public figure involved. This we decline to do.

At the heart of the First Amendment is the recognition of the fundamental importance of the free flow of ideas and opinions on matters of public interest and concern. . . .

The sort of robust political debate encouraged by the First Amendment is bound to produce speech that is critical of those who hold public office or those public figures who are "intimately involved in the resolution of important public questions or, by reason of their fame, shape events in areas of concern to society at large." . . .

Of course, this does not mean that *any* speech about a public figure is immune from sanction in the form of damages. Since *New York Times Co. v. Sullivan,* we have consistently ruled that a public figure may hold a speaker liable for the damage to reputation caused by publication of a defamatory falsehood, but only if the statement was made "with knowledge that it was false or with reckless disregard of whether it was false or not." False statements of fact are particularly valueless; they interfere with the truth-seeking function of the marketplace of ideas, and they cause damage to an individual's reputation that cannot easily be repaired by counterspeech, however persuasive or effective. But even though falsehoods have little value in and of themselves, they are "nevertheless inevitable in free debate," and a rule that would impose strict liability on a publisher for false factual assertions would have an undoubted "chilling" effect on speech relating to public figures that does have constitutional value. . . . This breathing space is provided by a constitutional rule that allows public figures to recover for libel or defamation only when they can prove *both* that the statement was false and that the statement was made with the requisite level of culpability.

Respondent argues, however, that a different standard should apply in this case because here the State seeks to prevent not reputational damage, but the severe emotional distress suffered by the person who is the subject of an offensive publication. In respondent's view, and in the view of the Court of Appeals, so long as the utterance was intended to inflict emotional distress, was outrageous, and did in fact inflict serious emotional distress, it is of no constitutional import whether the statement was a fact or an opinion, or whether it was true or false. It is the intent to cause injury that is the gravamen of the tort, and the State's interest in preventing emotional harm simply outweighs whatever interest a speaker may have in speech of this type.

Generally speaking the law does not regard the intent to inflict emotional distress as one which should receive much solicitude, and it is quite understandable that most if not all jurisdictions have chosen to make it civilly culpable where the conduct in question is sufficiently "outrageous." But in the world of debate about public affairs, many things done with motives that are less than admirable are protected by the First Amendment. . . .

Thus while such a bad motive may be deemed controlling for purposes of tort liability in other areas of the law, we think the First Amendment prohibits such a result in the area of public debate about public figures.

Were we to hold otherwise, there can be little doubt that political cartoonists and satirists would be subjected to damages awards without any showing that their work falsely defamed its subject. Webster's defines a caricature as "the deliberately distorted picturing or imitating of a person, literary style, etc. by exaggerating features or mannerisms for satirical effect." Webster's New Unabridged Twentieth Century Dictionary of the English Language 275 (2d ed. 1979). The appeal of the political cartoon or caricature is often based on exploitation of unfortunate physical traits or politically embarrassing events—an exploitation often calculated to injure the feelings of the subject of the portrayal. The art of the cartoonist is often not reasoned or evenhanded, but slashing and one-sided. . . .

Several famous examples of this type of intentionally injurious speech were drawn by Thomas Nast, probably the greatest American cartoonist to date, who was associated for many years during the post-Civil War era with Harper's Weekly. In the pages of that publication Nast conducted a graphic vendetta against William M. "Boss" Tweed and his corrupt associates in New York City's "Tweed Ring."

[D]espite their sometimes caustic nature, from the early cartoon portraying George Washington as an ass down to the present day, graphic depictions and satirical cartoons have played a prominent role in public and political debate. Nast's castigation of the Tweed Ring, Walt McDougall's characterization of Presidential candidate James G. Blaine's banquet with the millionaires at Delmonico's as "The Royal Feast of Belshazzar," and numerous other efforts have undoubtedly had an effect on the course and outcome of contemporaneous debate. Lincoln's tall, gangling posture, Teddy Roosevelt's glasses and teeth, and Franklin D. Roosevelt's jutting jaw and cigarette holder have been memorialized by political cartoons with an effect that could not have been obtained by the photographer or the portrait artist. From the viewpoint of history it is clear that our political discourse would have been considerably poorer without them.

Respondent contends, however, that the caricature in question here was so "outrageous" as to distinguish it from more traditional political cartoons. There is no doubt that the caricature of respondent and his mother published in Hustler is at best a distant cousin of the political cartoons described above, and a rather poor relation at that. If it were possible by laying down a principled standard to separate the one from the other, public discourse would probably suffer little or no harm. But we doubt that there is any such standard, and we are quite sure that the pejorative description "outrageous" does not supply one. "Outrageousness" in the area of political and social discourse has an inherent subjectiveness about it which would allow a jury to impose liability on the basis of the jurors' tastes or views, or perhaps on the basis of their dislike of a particular expression. . . .

We conclude that public figures and public officials may not recover for the tort of intentional infliction of emotional distress by reason of publications such as the one here at issue without showing in addition that the publication contains a false statement of fact which was made with "actual malice," *i.e.,* with knowledge that the statement was false or with reckless disregard as to whether or not it was true. This is not merely a "blind application" of the *New York Times* standard, it reflects our considered judgment that such a standard is necessary to give adequate "breathing space" to the freedoms protected by the First Amendment.

Here it is clear that respondent Falwell is a "public figure" for purposes of First Amendment law. The jury found against respondent on his libel claim when it decided that the Hustler ad parody could not "reasonably be understood as describing actual facts about [respondent] or actual events in which [he] participated." The Court of Appeals interpreted the jury's finding to be that the ad parody "was not reasonably believable," and in accordance with our custom we accept this finding. Respondent is thus relegated to his claim for damages awarded by the jury for the intentional infliction of emotional distress by "outrageous" conduct. But for reasons heretofore stated this claim cannot, consistently with the First Amendment, form a basis for the award of damages when the conduct in question is the publication of a caricature such as the ad parody involved here.

JUSTICE KENNEDY took no part in the consideration or decision of this case.

JUSTICE WHITE, concurring in the judgment.

As I see it, the decision in *New York Times Co. v. Sullivan* has little to do with this case, for here the jury found that the ad contained no assertion of fact. But I agree with the Court that the judgment below, which penalized the publication of the parody, cannot be squared with the First Amendment.

COMMENTS AND QUESTIONS

1.   The Court says that a public figure cannot recover in a claim for emotional distress "without showing . . . that the publication contains a false statement of fact which was made with 'actual malice.' " Did not Hustler's ad parody state a false fact with knowledge that it was false? Why is it then that Falwell loses?

2.   Perhaps the public figure can be parodied, but is the inclusion of false and disgusting statements about the figure's family fair game too? None of the examples given by the Court involve a parody or cartoon of a public figure's family member. At the time of the publication Falwell's mother was deceased, but if she had been alive, could she have sued successfully for intentional infliction of emotional distress?

3.   In *New York Times* intentional false statements were not protected, but in *Hustler* they were. Why?

UNITED STATES V. ALVAREZ
United States Supreme Court, 2012.
567 U.S. 709, 132 S.Ct. 2537.

JUSTICE KENNEDY announced the judgment of the Court and delivered an opinion, in which THE CHIEF JUSTICE, JUSTICE GINSBURG, and JUSTICE SOTOMAYOR join.

Lying was his habit. Xavier Alvarez, the respondent here, lied when he said that he played hockey for the Detroit Red Wings and that he once married a starlet from Mexico. But when he lied in announcing he held the Congressional Medal of Honor, respondent ventured onto new ground; for that lie violates a federal criminal statute, the Stolen Valor Act of 2005.

In 2007, respondent attended his first public meeting as a board member of the Three Valley Water District Board. The board is a governmental entity with headquarters in Claremont, California. He introduced himself as follows: "I'm a retired marine of 25 years. I retired in the year 2001. Back in 1987, I was awarded the Congressional Medal of Honor. I got wounded many times by the same guy." None of this was true. For all the record shows, respondent's statements were but a pathetic attempt to gain respect that eluded him. The statements do not seem to have been made to secure employment or financial benefits or admission to privileges reserved for those who had earned the Medal. . . . Here the statement that the speaker held the Medal was an intended, undoubted lie.

Xavier Alvarez

It is right and proper that Congress, over a century ago, established an award so the Nation can hold in its highest respect and esteem those who, in the course of carrying out the "supreme and noble duty of contributing to the defense of the rights and honor of the nation," have acted with extraordinary honor. . . .

The Government contends the criminal prohibition is a proper means to further its purpose in creating and awarding the Medal. When content-based speech regulation is in question, however, exacting scrutiny is required. Statutes suppressing or restricting speech must be judged by the sometimes inconvenient principles of the First Amendment. By this measure, the statutory provisions under which respondent was convicted must be held invalid, and his conviction must be set aside.

Respondent's claim to hold the Congressional Medal of Honor was false. There is no room to argue about interpretation or shades of meaning. On this premise, respondent violated § 704(b); and, because the lie concerned the Congressional Medal of Honor, he was subject to an enhanced penalty under subsection (c). Those statutory provisions are as follows:

(b) FALSE CLAIMS ABOUT RECEIPT OF MILITARY DECORATIONS OR MEDALS.—Whoever falsely represents himself or herself, verbally or in writing, to have been awarded any decoration or medal authorized by Congress for the Armed Forces of the United States . . . shall be fined under this title, imprisoned not more than six months, or both.

(c) ENHANCED PENALTY FOR OFFENSES INVOLVING CONGRESSIONAL MEDAL OF HONOR.—

(1) IN GENERAL.—If a decoration or medal involved in an offense under subsection (a) or (b) is a Congressional Medal of Honor, in lieu of the punishment provided in that subsection, the offender shall be fined under this title, imprisoned not more than 1 year, or both.

Respondent challenges the statute as a content-based suppression of pure speech, speech not falling within any of the few categories of expression where content-based regulation is permissible. The Government defends the statute as necessary to preserve the integrity and purpose of the Medal, an integrity and purpose it contends are compromised and frustrated by the false statements the statute prohibits. It argues that false statements "have no First Amendment value in themselves," and thus "are protected only to the extent needed to avoid chilling fully protected speech." Although the statute covers respondent's speech, the Government argues that it leaves breathing room for protected speech, for example speech which might criticize the idea of the Medal or the importance of the military. The Government's arguments cannot suffice to save the statute.

"[A]s a general matter, the First Amendment means that government has no power to restrict expression because of its message, its ideas, its subject matter, or its content." As a result, the Constitution "demands that content-based restrictions on speech be presumed invalid . . . and that the Government bear the burden of showing their constitutionality."

In light of the substantial and expansive threats to free expression posed by content-based restrictions, this Court has rejected as "startling and dangerous" a "free-floating test for First Amendment coverage . . . [based on] an ad hoc balancing of relative social costs and benefits." Instead, content-based restrictions on speech have been permitted, as a general matter, only when confined to the few " 'historic and traditional categories [of expression] long familiar to the bar,' " Among these categories are advocacy intended, and likely, to incite imminent lawless action, *see Brandenburg v. Ohio*; obscenity, *see, e.g., Miller v. California*; defamation, *see, e.g., New York Times Co. v. Sullivan; Gertz v. Robert Welch, Inc.*; speech integral to criminal conduct, *see, e.g., Giboney v. Empire Storage & Ice Co.*, 336 U.S. 490 (1949); so-called "fighting words," *see Chaplinsky v. New Hampshire*, 315 U.S. 568; child pornography, *see New York v. Ferber*; fraud, *see Virginia Bd. of Pharmacy v. Virginia Citizens Consumer Council, Inc.*, 425 U.S. 748 (1976); true threats, *see Watts v. United States*, 394 U.S. 705; and speech presenting some grave and imminent threat the government has the power to prevent, *see Near v. Minnesota ex rel. Olson*, 283 U.S. 697 (1931), although a restriction under the last category is most difficult to sustain, *see New York Times Co. v. United States*, 403 U.S. 713 (1971). These categories have a historical foundation in the Court's free speech tradition. The vast realm of free speech and thought always protected in our tradition can still thrive, and even be furthered, by adherence to those categories and rules.

Absent from those few categories where the law allows content-based regulation of speech is any general exception to the First Amendment for false statements. This comports with the common understanding that some false statements are inevitable if there is to be an open and vigorous expression of views in public and private conversation, expression the First Amendment seeks to guarantee.

The Government disagrees with this proposition. It cites language from some of this Court's precedents to support its contention that false statements have no value and hence no First Amendment protection. These isolated statements in some earlier decisions do not support the Government's submission that false statements, as a general rule, are beyond constitutional protection. That conclusion would take the quoted language far from its proper context. For instance, the Court has stated "[f]alse statements of fact are particularly valueless [because] they interfere with the truth-seeking function of the marketplace of ideas," *Hustler Magazine, Inc. v. Falwell* (1988), and that false statements "are not protected by the First Amendment in the same manner as truthful statements," *Brown v. Hartlage,* 456 U.S. 45 (1982). *See also, e.g., Virginia Bd. of Pharmacy, supra* ("Untruthful speech, commercial or otherwise, has never been protected for its own sake"); *Herbert v. Lando,* 441 U.S. 153 (1979)("Spreading false information in and of itself carries no First Amendment credentials"); *Gertz, supra* ("[T]here is no constitutional value in false statements of fact"); *Garrison v. Louisiana,* 379 U.S. 64 (1964)("[T]he knowingly false statement and the false statement made with reckless disregard of the truth, do not enjoy constitutional protection").

These quotations all derive from cases discussing defamation, fraud, or some other legally cognizable harm associated with a false statement, such as an invasion of privacy or the costs of vexatious litigation. In those decisions the falsity of the speech at issue was not irrelevant to our analysis, but neither was it determinative. The Court has never endorsed the categorical rule the Government advances: that false statements receive no First Amendment protection. Our prior decisions have not confronted a measure, like the Stolen Valor Act, that targets falsity and nothing more. . . .

The Government thus seeks to use this principle for a new purpose. It seeks to convert a rule that limits liability even in defamation cases where the law permits recovery for tortious wrongs into a rule that expands liability in a different, far greater realm of discourse and expression. That inverts the rationale for the exception. The requirements of a knowing falsehood or reckless disregard for the truth as the condition for recovery in certain defamation cases exists to allow more speech, not less. A rule designed to tolerate certain speech ought not blossom to become a rationale for a rule restricting it.

The Government then gives three examples of regulations on false speech that courts generally have found permissible: first, the criminal prohibition of a false statement made to a Government official, 18 U.S.C. § 1001; second, laws punishing perjury; and third, prohibitions on the false representation that one is speaking as a Government official or on behalf of the Government, *see, e.g.,* § 912; § 709. These restrictions, however, do not establish a principle that all proscriptions of false statements are exempt from exacting First Amendment scrutiny.

The federal statute prohibiting false statements to Government officials . . . does not lead to the broader proposition that false statements are unprotected when made to any person, at any time, in any context.

The same point can be made about what the Court has confirmed is the "unquestioned constitutionality of perjury statutes." [I]t is not simply because perjured statements are false that they lack First Amendment protection. Perjured testimony "is at war with justice" because it can cause a court to render a "judgment not resting on truth."

Statutes that prohibit falsely representing that one is speaking on behalf of the Government, or that prohibit impersonating a Government officer, also protect the integrity of Government processes, quite apart from merely restricting false speech. . . . The same can be said for prohibitions on the unauthorized use of the names of federal agencies such as the Federal Bureau of Investigation in a manner calculated to convey that the communication is approved, or using words such as "Federal" or "United States" in the collection of private debts in order to convey that the communication has official authorization. These examples, to the extent that they implicate fraud or speech integral to criminal conduct, are inapplicable here. . . .

The probable, and adverse, effect of the Act on freedom of expression illustrates, in a fundamental way, the reasons for the Law's distrust of content-based speech prohibitions.

The Act by its plain terms applies to a false statement made at any time, in any place, to any person. It can be assumed that it would not apply to, say, a theatrical performance. Still, the sweeping, quite unprecedented reach of the statute puts it in conflict with the First Amendment. Here the lie was made in a public meeting, but the statute would apply with equal force to personal, whispered conversations within a home. The statute seeks to control and suppress all false statements on this one subject in almost limitless times and settings. And it does so entirely without regard to whether the lie was made for the purpose of material gain.

Permitting the government to decree this speech to be a criminal offense, whether shouted from the rooftops or made in a barely audible whisper, would endorse government authority to compile a list of subjects about which false statements are punishable. That governmental power has no clear limiting principle. . . . Were this law to be sustained, there could be an endless list of subjects the National Government or the States could single out. Where false claims are made to effect a fraud or secure moneys or other valuable considerations, say offers of employment, it is well established that the Government may restrict speech without affronting the First Amendment. But the Stolen Valor Act is not so limited in its reach. Were the Court to hold that the interest in truthful discourse alone is sufficient to sustain a ban on speech, absent any evidence that the speech was used to gain a material advantage, it would give government a broad censorial power unprecedented in this Court's cases or in our constitutional tradition. The mere potential for the exercise of that power casts a chill, a chill the First Amendment cannot permit if free speech, thought, and discourse are to remain a foundation of our freedom.

The previous discussion suffices to show that the Act conflicts with free speech principles. But even when examined within its own narrow sphere of operation, the Act cannot survive. In assessing content-based restrictions on protected speech, the Court has not adopted a free-wheeling approach, but rather has applied the "most exacting scrutiny." Although the objectives the Government seeks to further by the statute are not without significance, the Court must, and now does, find the Act does not satisfy exacting scrutiny.

The Government is correct when it states military medals "serve the important public function of recognizing and expressing gratitude for acts of heroism and sacrifice in military service," and also " 'foste[r] morale, mission accomplishment and esprit de corps' among service members." . . .

These interests are related to the integrity of the military honors system in general, and the Congressional Medal of Honor in particular. Although millions have served with brave resolve, the Medal, which is the highest military award for valor against an enemy force, has been given just 3,476 times.

But to recite the Government's compelling interests is not to end the matter. The First Amendment requires that the Government's chosen restriction on the speech at issue be "actually necessary" to achieve its interest. There must be a direct causal link between the restriction imposed and the injury to be prevented. The link between the Government's interest in protecting the integrity of the military honors system and the Act's restriction on the false claims of liars like respondent has not been shown. Although appearing to concede that "an isolated misrepresentation by itself would not tarnish the meaning of military honors," the Government asserts it is "common sense that false representations have the tendency to dilute the value and meaning of military awards." It must be acknowledged that when a pretender claims the Medal to be his own, the lie might harm the

Government by demeaning the high purpose of the award, diminishing the honor it confirms, and creating the appearance that the Medal is awarded more often than is true. Furthermore, the lie may offend the true holders of the Medal. From one perspective it insults their bravery and high principles when falsehood puts them in the unworthy company of a pretender.

Yet these interests do not satisfy the Government's heavy burden when it seeks to regulate protected speech. The Government points to no evidence to support its claim that the public's general perception of military awards is diluted by false claims such as those made by Alvarez. . . .

The lack of a causal link between the Government's stated interest and the Act is not the only way in which the Act is not actually necessary to achieve the Government's stated interest. The Government has not shown, and cannot show, why counterspeech would not suffice to achieve its interest. The facts of this case indicate that the dynamics of free speech, of counterspeech, of refutation, can overcome the lie. Respondent lied at a public meeting. Even before the FBI began investigating him for his false statements "Alvarez was perceived as a phony." Once the lie was made public, he was ridiculed online, his actions were reported in the press, and a fellow board member called for his resignation. There is good reason to believe that a similar fate would befall other false claimants. . . .

The remedy for speech that is false is speech that is true. This is the ordinary course in a free society. The response to the unreasoned is the rational; to the uninformed, the enlightened; to the straightout lie, the simple truth. . . . The First Amendment itself ensures the right to respond to speech we do not like, and for good reason. Freedom of speech and thought flows not from the beneficence of the state but from the inalienable rights of the person. And suppression of speech by the government can make exposure of falsity more difficult, not less so. Society has the right and civic duty to engage in open, dynamic, rational discourse. These ends are not well served when the government seeks to orchestrate public discussion through content-based mandates. . . .

In addition, when the Government seeks to regulate protected speech, the restriction must be the "least restrictive means among available, effective alternatives." There is, however, at least one less speech-restrictive means by which the Government could likely protect the integrity of the military awards system. A Government-created database could list Congressional Medal of Honor winners. Were a database accessible through the Internet, it would be easy to verify and expose false claims. . . .

The Government may have responses to some of these criticisms, but there has been no clear showing of the necessity of the statute, the necessity required by exacting scrutiny.

JUSTICE BREYER, with whom JUSTICE KAGAN joins, concurring in the judgment.

I agree with the plurality that the Stolen Valor Act of 2005 violates the First Amendment. But I do not rest my conclusion upon a strict categorical analysis. Rather, I base that conclusion upon the fact that the statute works First Amendment harm, while the Government can achieve its legitimate objectives in less restrictive ways.

In determining whether a statute violates the First Amendment, this Court has often found it appropriate to examine the fit between statutory ends and means. In doing so, it has examined speech-related harms, justifications, and potential alternatives. In particular, it has taken account of the seriousness of the speech-related harm the provision will likely cause, the nature and importance of the provision's countervailing objectives, the extent to which the provision will tend to achieve those objectives, and whether there are other, less restrictive ways of doing so. Ultimately the Court has had to determine whether the statute works speech-related harm that is out of proportion to its justifications.

Sometimes the Court has referred to this approach as "intermediate scrutiny," sometimes as "proportionality" review, sometimes as an examination of "fit," and sometimes it has avoided the application of any label at all.

Regardless of the label, some such approach is necessary if the First Amendment is to offer proper protection in the many instances in which a statute adversely affects constitutionally protected interests but warrants neither near-automatic condemnation (as "strict scrutiny" implies) nor near-automatic approval (as is implicit in "rational basis" review). I have used the term "proportionality" to describe this approach. But in this case, the Court's term "intermediate scrutiny" describes what I think we should do.

As the dissent points out, "there are broad areas in which any attempt by the state to penalize purportedly false speech would present a grave and unacceptable danger of suppressing truthful speech." Laws restricting false statements about philosophy, religion, history, the social sciences, the arts, and the like raise such concerns, and in many contexts have called for strict scrutiny. But this case does not involve such a law. The dangers of suppressing valuable ideas are lower where, as here, the regulations concern false statements about easily verifiable facts that do not concern such subject matter. Such false factual statements are less likely than are true factual statements to make a valuable contribution to the marketplace of ideas. And the government often has good reasons to prohibit such false speech. But its regulation can nonetheless threaten speech-related harms. Those circumstances lead me to apply what the Court has termed "intermediate scrutiny" here.

[I] must concede, as the Government points out, that this Court has frequently said or implied that false factual statements enjoy little First Amendment protection.

But these judicial statements cannot be read to mean "no protection at all." False factual statements can serve useful human objectives, for example: in social contexts, where they may prevent embarrassment, protect privacy, shield a person from prejudice, provide the sick with comfort, or preserve a child's innocence; in public contexts, where they may stop a panic or otherwise preserve calm in the face of danger; and even in technical, philosophical, and scientific contexts, where (as Socrates's methods suggest) examination of a false statement (even if made deliberately to mislead) can promote a form of thought that ultimately helps realize the truth. . . .

Further, the pervasiveness of false statements, made for better or for worse motives, made thoughtlessly or deliberately, made with or without accompanying harm, provides a weapon to a government broadly empowered to prosecute falsity without more. And those who are unpopular may fear that the government will use that weapon selectively, say by prosecuting a pacifist who supports his cause by (falsely) claiming to have been a war hero, while ignoring members of other political groups who might make similar false claims.

I also must concede that many statutes and common-law doctrines make the utterance of certain kinds of false statements unlawful. Those prohibitions, however, tend to be narrower than the statute before us, in that they limit the scope of their application, sometimes by requiring proof of specific harm to identifiable victims; sometimes by specifying that the lies be made in contexts in which a tangible harm to others is especially likely to occur; and sometimes by limiting the prohibited lies to those that are particularly likely to produce harm.

[F]ew statutes, if any, simply prohibit without limitation the telling of a lie, even a lie about one particular matter. Instead, in virtually all these instances limitations of context, requirements of proof of injury, and the like, narrow the statute to a subset of lies where specific harm is more likely to occur. The limitations help to make certain that the statute does not allow its threat of liability or criminal punishment to roam at large, discouraging or forbidding the telling of the lie in contexts where harm is unlikely or the need for the prohibition is small.

The statute before us lacks any such limiting features. It may be construed to prohibit only knowing and intentional acts of deception about readily verifiable facts within the personal knowledge of the speaker, thus reducing the risk that valuable speech is chilled. But it still ranges very broadly. And that breadth means that it creates a significant risk of First Amendment harm. As written, it applies in family, social, or other private contexts, where lies will often cause little harm. It also applies in political contexts, where although such lies are more likely to cause harm, the risk of censorious selectivity by prosecutors is also high. Further, given the potential haziness of individual memory along with the large number of military awards covered (ranging from medals for rifle marksmanship to the Congressional Medal of Honor), there remains a risk of chilling that is not completely eliminated by *mens rea* requirements; a speaker might still be worried about being *prosecuted* for a careless false statement, even if he does not have the intent required to render him liable. And so the prohibition may be applied where it should not be applied, for example, to bar stool braggadocio or, in the political arena, subtly but selectively to speakers that the Government does not like. These considerations lead me to believe that the statute as written risks significant First Amendment harm.

Like both the plurality and the dissent, I believe the statute nonetheless has substantial justification. It seeks to protect the interests of those who have sacrificed their health and life for their country. The statute serves this interest by seeking to preserve intact the country's recognition of that sacrifice in the form of military honors. To permit those who have not earned those honors to claim otherwise dilutes the value of the awards. Indeed, the Nation cannot fully honor those who have sacrificed so much for their country's honor unless those who claim to have received its military awards tell the truth. Thus, the statute risks harming protected interests but only in order to achieve a substantial countervailing objective.

We must therefore ask whether it is possible substantially to achieve the Government's objective in less burdensome ways. In my view, the answer to this question is "yes." . . . As is indicated by the limitations on the scope of the many other kinds of statutes regulating false factual speech, it should be possible significantly to diminish or eliminate these remaining risks by enacting a similar but more finely tailored statute. For example, not all military awards are alike. Congress might determine that some warrant greater protection than others. And a more finely tailored statute might, as other kinds of statutes prohibiting false factual statements have done, insist upon a showing that the false statement caused specific harm or at least was material, or focus its coverage on lies most likely to be harmful or on contexts where such lies are most likely to cause harm.

I recognize that in some contexts, particularly political contexts, such a narrowing will not always be easy to achieve. In the political arena a false statement is more likely to make a behavioral difference (say, by leading the listeners to vote for the speaker) but at the same time criminal prosecution is particularly dangerous (say, by radically changing a potential election result) and consequently can more easily result in censorship of speakers and their ideas. Thus, the statute may have to be significantly narrowed in its applications. Some lower courts have upheld the constitutionality of roughly comparable but narrowly tailored statutes in political contexts. Without expressing any view on the validity of those cases, I would also note, like the plurality, that in this area more accurate information will normally counteract the lie. And an accurate, publicly available register of military awards, easily obtainable by political opponents, may well adequately protect the integrity of an award against those who would falsely claim to have earned it. And so it is likely that a more narrowly tailored statute combined with such information-disseminating devices will effectively serve Congress's end.

The Government has provided no convincing explanation as to why a more finely tailored statute would not work.

JUSTICE ALITO, with whom JUSTICE SCALIA and JUSTICE THOMAS join, dissenting.

Only the bravest of the brave are awarded the Congressional Medal of Honor, but the Court today holds that every American has a constitutional right to claim to have received this singular award. The Court strikes down the Stolen Valor Act of 2005, which was enacted to stem an epidemic of false claims about military decorations. These lies, Congress reasonably concluded, were undermining our country's system of military honors and inflicting real harm on actual medal recipients and their families.

Building on earlier efforts to protect the military awards system, Congress responded to this problem by crafting a narrow statute that presents no threat to the freedom of speech. The statute reaches only knowingly false statements about hard facts directly within a speaker's personal knowledge. These lies have no value in and of themselves, and proscribing them does not chill any valuable speech.

By holding that the First Amendment nevertheless shields these lies, the Court breaks sharply from a long line of cases recognizing that the right to free speech does not protect false factual statements that inflict real harm and serve no legitimate interest. I would adhere to that principle and would thus uphold the constitutionality of this valuable law.

The Stolen Valor Act makes it a misdemeanor to "falsely represen[t]" oneself as having been awarded a medal, decoration, or badge for service in the Armed Forces of the United States. Properly construed, this statute is limited in five significant respects. First, the Act applies to only a narrow category of false representations about objective facts that can almost always be proved or disproved with near certainty. Second, the Act concerns facts that are squarely within the speaker's personal knowledge. Third, as the Government maintains, and both the plurality and the concurrence seemingly accept, a conviction under the Act requires proof beyond a reasonable doubt that the speaker actually knew that the representation was false. Fourth, the Act applies only to statements that could reasonably be interpreted as communicating actual facts; it does not reach dramatic performances, satire, parody, hyperbole, or the like. Finally, the Act is strictly viewpoint neutral. The false statements proscribed by the Act are highly unlikely to be tied to any particular political or ideological message. In the rare cases where that is not so, the Act applies equally to all false statements, whether they tend to disparage or commend the Government, the military, or the system of military honors. . . .

[C]ongress long ago made it a federal offense for anyone to wear, manufacture, or sell certain military decorations without authorization. Although this Court has never opined on the constitutionality of that particular provision, we have said that § 702, which makes it a crime to wear a United States military uniform without authorization, is "a valid statute on its face."

Congress passed the Stolen Valor Act in response to a proliferation of false claims concerning the receipt of military awards. For example, in a single year, *more than 600* Virginia residents falsely claimed to have won the Medal of Honor. An investigation of the 333 people listed in the online edition of Who's Who as having received a top military award revealed that fully a third of the claims could not be substantiated. When the Library of Congress compiled oral histories for its Veterans History Project, 24 of the 49 individuals who identified themselves as Medal of Honor recipients had not actually received that award. The same was true of 32 individuals who claimed to have been awarded the Distinguished Service Cross and 14 who claimed to have won the Navy Cross. Notorious cases brought to Congress's attention included the case of a judge who falsely claimed to have been awarded *two* Medals of Honor and displayed counterfeit medals in his courtroom; a television network's military consultant who falsely claimed that he had received the Silver Star; and a former judge advocate in the Marine Corps who lied about receiving the Bronze Star and a Purple Heart.

As Congress recognized, the lies proscribed by the Stolen Valor Act inflict substantial harm. In many instances, the harm is tangible in nature: Individuals often falsely represent themselves as award recipients in order to obtain financial or other material rewards, such as lucrative contracts and government benefits. . . . In other cases, the harm is less tangible, but nonetheless significant. The lies proscribed by the Stolen Valor Act tend to debase the distinctive honor of military awards. . . .

It is well recognized in trademark law that the proliferation of cheap imitations of luxury goods blurs the " 'signal' given out by the purchasers of the originals." In much the same way, the proliferation of false claims about military awards blurs the signal given out by the actual awards by making them seem more common than they really are, and this diluting effect harms the military by hampering its efforts to foster morale and esprit de corps. . . .

The plurality and the concurrence . . . suggest that Congress could protect the system of military honors by enacting a narrower statute. The plurality recommends a law that would apply only to lies that are intended to "secure moneys or other valuable considerations." In a similar vein, the concurrence comments that "a more finely tailored statute might . . . insist upon a showing that the false statement caused specific harm." But much damage is caused, both to real award recipients and to the system of military honors, by false statements that are not linked to any financial or other tangible reward. Unless even a small financial loss—say, a dollar given to a homeless man falsely claiming to be a decorated veteran—is more important in the eyes of the First Amendment than the damage caused to the very integrity of the military awards system, there is no basis for distinguishing between the Stolen Valor Act and the alternative statutes that the plurality and concurrence appear willing to sustain.

Time and again, this Court has recognized that as a general matter false factual statements possess no intrinsic First Amendment value.

Consistent with this recognition, many kinds of false factual statements have long been proscribed without " 'rais[ing] any Constitutional problem.' " Laws prohibiting fraud, perjury, and defamation, for example, were in existence when the First Amendment was adopted, and their constitutionality is now beyond question.

We have also described as falling outside the First Amendment's protective shield certain false factual statements that were neither illegal nor tortious at the time of the Amendment's adoption. . . .

All told, there are more than 100 federal criminal statutes that punish false statements made in connection with areas of federal agency concern.

These examples amply demonstrate that false statements of fact merit no First Amendment protection in their own right. It is true, as Justice BREYER notes, that many in our society either approve or condone certain discrete categories of false statements, including false statements made to prevent harm to innocent victims and so-called "white lies." But respondent's false claim to have received the Medal of Honor did not fall into any of these categories. His lie did not "prevent embarrassment, protect privacy, shield a person from prejudice, provide the sick with comfort, or preserve a child's innocence." Nor did his lie "stop a panic or otherwise preserve calm in the face of danger" or further philosophical or scientific debate. Respondent's claim, like all those covered by the Stolen Valor Act, served no valid purpose. . . .

While we have repeatedly endorsed the principle that false statements of fact do not merit First Amendment protection for their own sake, we have recognized that it is sometimes necessary to "exten[d] a measure of strategic protection" to these statements in order to ensure sufficient " 'breathing space' " for protected speech. . . .

[I]n stark contrast to hypothetical laws prohibiting false statements about history, science, and similar matters, the Stolen Valor Act presents no risk at all that valuable speech will be suppressed. The speech punished by the Act is not only verifiably false and entirely lacking in intrinsic value, but it also fails to serve any instrumental purpose that the First Amendment might protect. Tellingly, when asked at oral argument what truthful speech the Stolen Valor Act might chill, even respondent's counsel conceded that the answer is none.

Neither of the two opinions endorsed by Justices in the majority claims that the false statements covered by the Stolen Valor Act possess either intrinsic or instrumental value. Instead, those opinions appear to be based on the distinct concern that the Act suffers from overbreadth. But to strike down a statute on the basis that it is overbroad, it is necessary to show that the statute's "overbreadth [is] *substantial,* not only in an absolute sense, but also relative to [its] plainly legitimate sweep." The plurality and the concurrence do not even attempt to make this showing. . . .

COMMENTS AND QUESTIONS

1.   The dissent suggests that the other justices are really arguing that the Act is overbroad, because it penalizes some lies about receiving a medal that would be meaningless at best. And, if that is so, then the dissent is certainly correct that the overbreadth must be substantial. Do you think the Stolen Valor Act is substantially overbroad; that is, that it penalizes a substantial amount of speech that should be protected?

2.   In *New York Times* and *Hustler* the protection of false speech was deemed necessary to provide breathing room for speech concerning public figures and public issues, the life-blood of a functioning democracy. Why is the false speech in *Alvarez* protected?

3.   The harm caused by the false speech prohibited by the Stolen Valor Act really is different from the harm caused by fraud, perjury, and defamation. The latter types of false speech all create specific and immediate harm, while the harm caused by the former is more diffuse—"debas[ing] the distinctive honor of military awards." Does that difference in harm justify a distinction in the protection of the speech involved?

4.   Can Congress draft a new Stolen Valor Act that would pass constitutional muster?

PROBLEM

A state publishes a voters guide before each election. Candidates may include in the guide a statement as to why persons should vote for them. The law provides, however, that a candidate who includes in his or her statement a false statement of fact, knowing it to be false, is guilty of a misdemeanor. A candidate includes in his statement that he had been awarded the Congressional Medal of Honor. When it was discovered after the election, which he won, that the statement was false, he was tried and convicted. He appeals on the ground that the law is unconstitutional. Should he win?

G. COMMERCIAL SPEECH

Although commercial speech was not mentioned in *Chaplinsky* as one of those "classes of speech, the prevention and punishment of which have never been thought to raise any Constitutional problem," it might well have been included, for no one had at the time thought that the First Amendment limited government regulations of advertising. Indeed, in the same year as *Chaplinsky*, the Court stated flatly that "the Constitution imposes no . . . restraint on government as respects purely commercial advertising." *Valentine v. Chrestensen*, 316 U.S. 52 (1942). And, in a 1949 case involving a city ban on advertising on any motor vehicle except for identifying the owner of the vehicle, no one thought to raise any First Amendment claim, raising instead equal protection and due process claims, which lost. *See Railway Express Agency, Inc. v. New York*, 336 U.S. 106 (1949).

Just as the Civil Rights Movement was an important impetus behind *New York Times v. Sullivan*, the Abortion Rights Movement was the origin of protection for commercial speech. In *Bigelow v. Virginia*, 421 U.S. 809 (1975), the Court set aside a Virginia law making it a crime to advertise the availability of an abortion, although abortions were by then protected under *Roe v. Wade*. The Court noted that the "advertisement" in question "did more than simply propose a commercial transaction. It contained factual material of clear 'public interest.' Portions of its message, most prominently the lines, 'Abortions are now legal in New York. There are no residency requirements,' involve the exercise of the freedom of communicating information and disseminating opinion." The opinion concluded: "we need not decide in this case the precise extent to which the First Amendment permits regulation of advertising that is related to activities the State may legitimately regulate or even prohibit." How do you think *Bigelow* would come out today?

While *Bigelow* could have been limited to its particular circumstances, in the next year the Court struck down another Virginia law, but one involving an activity that a state might legitimately regulate.

VIRGINIA STATE BOARD OF PHARMACY V. VIRGINIA CITIZENS CONSUMER COUNCIL, INC.

United States Supreme Court, 1976.
425 U.S. 748, 96 S.Ct. 1817.

MR. JUSTICE BLACKMUN delivered the opinion of the Court.

The plaintiff-appellees in this case attack, as violative of the First and Fourteenth Amendments, [the Virginia law that] provides that a pharmacist licensed in Virginia is guilty of unprofessional conduct if he "(3) publishes, advertises or promotes, directly or indirectly, in any manner whatsoever, any amount price, fee, premium, discount, rebate or credit terms . . . for any drugs which may be dispensed only by prescription."

[I]nasmuch as only a licensed pharmacist may dispense prescription drugs in Virginia, advertising or other affirmative dissemination of prescription drug price information is effectively forbidden in the State.

[T]he appellants contend that the advertisement of prescription drug prices is outside the protection of the First Amendment because it is "commercial speech." There can be no question that in past decisions the Court has given some indication that commercial speech is unprotected. . . . Last Term, in *Bigelow v. Virginia*, the notion of unprotected "commercial speech" all but passed from the scene. . . .

Some fragment of hope for the continuing validity of a "commercial speech" exception arguably might have persisted because of the subject matter of the advertisement in *Bigelow*. . . .

Here, in contrast, the question whether there is a First Amendment exception for "commercial speech" is squarely before us. Our pharmacist does not wish to editorialize on any subject, cultural, philosophical, or political. He does not wish to report any particularly newsworthy fact, or to make generalized observations even about commercial matters. The "idea" he wishes to communicate is simply this: "I will sell you the X prescription drug at the Y price." Our question, then, is whether this communication is wholly outside the protection of the First Amendment.

We begin with several propositions that already are settled or beyond serious dispute. It is clear, for example, that speech does not lose its First Amendment protection because money is spent to project it, as in a paid advertisement of one form or another. *New York Times Co. v. Sullivan*. Speech likewise is protected even though it is carried in a form that is "sold" for profit. . . .

Our question is whether speech which does "no more than propose a commercial transaction," is so removed from any "exposition of ideas," *Chaplinsky v. New Hampshire*, and from " 'truth, science, morality, and arts in general, in its diffusion of liberal sentiments on the administration of Government,' " *Roth v. United States*, that it lacks all protection. Our answer is that it is not.

Focusing first on the individual parties to the transaction that is proposed in the commercial advertisement, we may assume that the advertiser's interest is a purely economic one. That hardly disqualifies him from protection under the First Amendment. The interests of the contestants in a labor dispute are primarily economic, but it has long been settled that both the employee and the employer are protected by the First Amendment when they express themselves on the merits of the dispute in order to influence its outcome. . . .

As to the particular consumer's interest in the free flow of commercial information, that interest may be as keen, if not keener by far, than his interest in the day's most urgent political debate. Appellee' case in this respect is a convincing one. Those whom the suppression of prescription drug price information hits the hardest are the poor, the sick, and particularly the aged. A disproportionate amount of their income tends to be spent on prescription drugs; yet they are the least able to learn, by shopping from pharmacist to pharmacist, where their scarce dollars are best spent. When drug prices vary as strikingly as they do, information as to who is charging what becomes more than a convenience. It could mean the alleviation of physical pain or the enjoyment of basic necessities.

Generalizing, society also may have a strong interest in the free flow of commercial information. Even an individual advertisement, though entirely "commercial," may be of general public interest. The facts of decided cases furnish illustrations: advertisements stating that referral services for legal abortions are available, *Bigelow v. Virginia*; that a manufacturer of artificial furs promotes his product as an alternative to the extinction by his competitors of fur-bearing mammals; and that a domestic producer advertises his product as an alternative to imports that tend to deprive American residents of their jobs. Obviously, not all commercial messages contain the same or even a very great public interest element. There are few to which such an element, however, could not be added. Our pharmacist, for example, could cast himself as a commentator on store-to-store disparities in drug prices, giving his own and those of a competitor as proof. We see little point in requiring him to do so, and little difference if he does not.

Moreover, there is another consideration that suggests that no line between publicly "interesting" or "important" commercial advertising and the opposite kind could ever be drawn. Advertising, however tasteless and excessive it sometimes may seem, is nonetheless dissemination of information as to who is producing and selling what product, for what reason, and at what price. So long as we preserve a predominantly free enterprise economy, the allocation of our resources in large measure will be made through numerous private economic decisions. It is a matter of public interest that those decisions, in the aggregate, be intelligent and well informed. To this end, the free flow of commercial information is indispensable. . . .

Arrayed against these substantial individual and societal interests are a number of justifications for the advertising ban. These have to do principally with maintaining a high degree of professionalism on the part of licensed pharmacists. Indisputably, the State has a strong interest in maintaining that professionalism. It is exercised in a number of ways for the consumer's benefit. There is the clinical skill involved in the compounding of drugs. . . . The expertise of the pharmacist may supplement that of the prescribing physician, if the latter has not specified the amount to be dispensed or the directions that are to appear on the label. The pharmacist, a specialist in the potencies and dangers of drugs, may even be consulted by the physician as to what to prescribe. He may know of a particular antagonism between the prescribed drug and another that the customer is or might be taking, or with an allergy the customer may suffer. . . . Some pharmacists, concededly not a large number, "monitor" the health problems and drug consumptions of customers who come to them repeatedly. A pharmacist who has a continuous relationship with his customer is in the best position, of course, to exert professional skill for the customer's protection.

Price advertising, it is argued, will place in jeopardy the pharmacist's expertise and, with it, the customer's health. It is claimed that the aggressive price competition that will result from unlimited advertising will make it impossible for the pharmacist to supply professional services in the compounding, handling, and dispensing of prescription drugs. Such services are time consuming and expensive; if competitors who economize by eliminating them are permitted to advertise their resulting lower prices, the more painstaking and conscientious pharmacist will be forced either to follow suit or to go out of business. It is also claimed that prices might not necessarily fall as a result of advertising. If one pharmacist advertises, others must, and the resulting expense will inflate the cost of drugs. It is further claimed that advertising will lead people to shop for their prescription drugs among the various pharmacists who offer the lowest prices, and the loss of stable pharmacist-customer relationships will make individual attention and certainly the practice of monitoring impossible. Finally, it is argued that damage will be done to the professional image of the pharmacist. This image, that of a skilled and specialized craftsman, attracts talent to the profession and reinforces the better habits of those who are in it. Price advertising, it is said, will reduce the pharmacist's status to that of a mere retailer.

The strength of these proffered justifications is greatly undermined by the fact that high professional standards, to a substantial extent, are guaranteed by the close regulation to which pharmacists in Virginia are subject. And this case concerns the retail sale by the pharmacist more than it does his professional standards. Surely, any pharmacist guilty of professional dereliction that actually endangers his customer will promptly lose his license. At the same time, we cannot discount the Board's justifications entirely. . . .

The challenge now made, however, is based on the First Amendment. This casts the Board's justifications in a different light, for on close inspection it is seen that the State's protectiveness of its citizens rests in large measure on the advantages of their being kept in ignorance. The advertising ban does not directly affect professional standards one way or the other. It affects them only through the reactions it is assumed people will have to the free flow of drug price information. There is no claim that the advertising ban in any way prevents the cutting of corners by the pharmacist who is so inclined. That pharmacist is likely to cut corners in any event. The only effect the advertising ban has on him is to insulate him from price competition and to open the way for him to make a substantial, and perhaps even excessive, profit in addition to providing an inferior service. The more painstaking pharmacist is also protected but, again, it is a protection based in large part on public ignorance.

It appears to be feared that if the pharmacist who wishes to provide low cost, and assertedly low quality, services is permitted to advertise, he will be taken up on his offer by too many unwitting customers. They will choose the low-cost, low-quality service and drive the "professional" pharmacist out of business. They will respond only to costly and excessive advertising, and end up paying the price. They will go from one pharmacist to another, following the discount, and destroy the pharmacist-customer relationship. They will lose respect for the profession because it advertises. All this is not in their best interests, and all this can be avoided if they are not permitted to know who is charging what.

There is, of course, an alternative to this highly paternalistic approach. That alternative is to assume that this information is not in itself harmful, that people will perceive their own best interests if only they are well enough informed, and that the best means to that end is to open the channels of communication rather than to close them. If they are truly open, nothing prevents the "professional" pharmacist from marketing his own assertedly superior product, and contrasting it with that of the low-cost, high-volume prescription drug retailer. But the choice among these alternative approaches is not ours to make or the Virginia General Assembly's. It is precisely this kind of choice, between the dangers of suppressing information, and the dangers of its misuse if it is freely available, that the First Amendment makes for us. Virginia is free to require whatever professional standards it wishes of its pharmacists; it may subsidize them or protect them from competition in other ways. But it may not do so by keeping the public in ignorance of the entirely lawful terms that competing pharmacists are offering. In this sense, the justifications Virginia has offered for suppressing the flow of prescription drug price information, far from persuading us that the flow is not protected by the First Amendment, have reinforced our view that it is. We so hold.

In concluding that commercial speech, like other varieties, is protected, we of course do not hold that it can never be regulated in any way. Some forms of commercial speech regulation are surely permissible. We mention a few only to make clear that they are not before us and therefore are not foreclosed by this case. . . .

[T]here [is no] claim that prescription drug price advertisements are forbidden because they are false or misleading in any way. Untruthful speech, commercial or otherwise, has never been protected for its own sake. Obviously, much commercial speech is not provably false, or even wholly false, but only deceptive or misleading. We foresee no obstacle to a State's dealing effectively with this problem.[24] The First Amendment, as we construe it today does not prohibit the State from insuring that the stream of commercial information flow cleanly as well as freely.

Attributes such as these, the greater objectivity and hardiness of commercial speech, may make it less necessary to tolerate inaccurate statements for fear of silencing the speaker. They may also make it appropriate to require that a commercial message appear in such a form, or include such additional information, warnings, and disclaimers, as are necessary to prevent its being deceptive.

Also, there is no claim that the transactions proposed in the forbidden advertisements are themselves illegal in any way. . . .

What is at issue is whether a State may completely suppress the dissemination of concededly truthful information about entirely lawful activity, fearful of that information's effect upon its disseminators and its recipients. Reserving other questions,[25] we conclude that the answer to this one is in the negative.

---

[24] In concluding that commercial speech enjoys First Amendment protection, we have not held that it is wholly undifferentiable from other forms. There are commonsense differences between speech that does "no more than propose a commercial transaction" and other varieties. Even if the differences do not justify the conclusion that commercial speech is valueless, and thus subject to complete suppression by the State, they nonetheless suggest that a different degree of protection is necessary to insure that the flow of truthful and legitimate commercial information is unimpaired. The truth of commercial speech, for example, may be more easily verifiable by its disseminator than, let us say, news reporting or political commentary, in that ordinarily the advertiser seeks to disseminate information about a specific product or service that he himself provides and presumably knows more about than anyone else. Also, commercial speech may be more durable than other kinds. Since advertising is the sine qua non of commercial profits, there is little likelihood of its being chilled by proper regulation and forgone entirely.

[25] We stress that we have considered in this case the regulation of commercial advertising by pharmacists. Although we express no opinion as to other professions, the distinctions, historical and functional, between professions, may require consideration of quite different factors. Physicians and lawyers, for example, do not dispense standardized products; they render

MR. JUSTICE STEVENS took no part in the consideration or decision of this case.

MR. CHIEF JUSTICE BURGER, concurring.

The Court notes that roughly 95% of all prescriptions are filled with dosage units already prepared by the manufacturer and sold to the pharmacy in that form. These are the drugs that have a market large enough to make their preparation profitable to the manufacturer; for the same reason, they are the drugs that it is profitable for the pharmacist to advertise. In dispensing these *prepackaged* items, the pharmacist performs largely a packaging rather than a compounding function of former times. Our decision today, therefore, deals largely with the State's power to prohibit pharmacists from advertising the retail price of *prepackaged drugs*. As the Court notes quite different factors would govern were we faced with a law regulating or even prohibiting advertising by the traditional learned professions of medicine or law. . . . Attorneys and physicians are engaged primarily in providing services in which professional judgment is a large component, a matter very different from the retail Sale of labeled drugs already prepared by others. . . .

MR. JUSTICE STEWART, concurring. [opinion omitted]

MR. JUSTICE REHNQUIST, dissenting.

The logical consequences of the Court's decision in this case, a decision which elevates commercial intercourse between a seller hawking his wares and a buyer seeking to strike a bargain to the same plane as has been previously reserved for the free marketplace of ideas, are far reaching indeed. Under the Court's opinion the way will be open not only for dissemination of price information but for active promotion of prescription drugs, liquor, cigarettes, and other products the use of which it has previously been thought desirable to discourage. Now, however, such promotion is protected by the First Amendment so long as it is not misleading or does not promote an illegal product or enterprise. In coming to this conclusion, the Court has overruled a legislative determination that such advertising should not be allowed. . . .

In the final footnote the opinion tosses a bone to the traditionalists in the legal and medical professions by suggesting that because they sell services rather than drugs the holding of this case is not automatically applicable to advertising in those professions. But if the sole limitation on permissible state proscription of advertising is that it may not be false or misleading, surely the difference between pharmacists' advertising and lawyers' and doctors' advertising can be only one of degree and not of kind. I cannot distinguish between the public's right to know the price of drugs

---

professional services of almost infinite variety and nature, with the consequent enhanced possibility for confusion and deception if they were to undertake certain kinds of advertising.

and its right to know the price of title searches or physical examinations or other professional services for which standardized fees are charged. . . .

In the case of "our" hypothetical pharmacist, he may now presumably advertise not only the prices of prescription drugs, but may attempt to energetically promote their sale so long as he does so truthfully. Quite consistently with Virginia law requiring prescription drugs to be available only through a physician, "our" pharmacist might run any of the following representative advertisements in a local newspaper:

"Pain getting you down? Insist that your physician prescribe Demerol. You pay a little more than for aspirin, but you get a lot more relief."

"Can't shake the flu? Get a prescription for Tetracycline from your doctor today."

"Don't spend another sleepless night. Ask your doctor to prescribe Seconal without delay."

Unless the State can show that these advertisements are either actually untruthful or misleading, it presumably is not free to restrict in any way commercial efforts on the part of those who profit from the sale of prescription drugs to put them in the widest possible circulation. But such a line simply makes no allowance whatever for what appears to have been a considered legislative judgment in most States that while prescription drugs are a necessary and vital part of medical care and treatment, there are sufficient dangers attending their widespread use that they simply may not be promoted in the same manner as hair creams, deodorants, and toothpaste. The very real dangers that general advertising for such drugs might create in terms of encouraging, even though not sanctioning, illicit use of them by individuals for whom they have not been prescribed, or by generating patient pressure upon physicians to prescribe them, are simply not dealt with in the Court's opinion. If prescription drugs may be advertised, they may be advertised on television during family viewing time. Nothing we know about the acquisitive instincts of those who inhabit every business and profession to a greater or lesser extent gives any reason to think that such persons will not do everything they can to generate demand for these products in much the same manner and to much the same degree as demand for other commodities has been generated. . . .

COMMENTS AND QUESTIONS

1. Virginia is worried that price competition between pharmacists will have a number of negative consequences for the people of Virginia. It does have an alternative not mentioned by the Court to avoid such competition besides a ban on advertising prices. That would be for the state to set the prices itself. States traditionally have and still do set or approve the prices sold for some goods or services. Of course, that would be more difficult for the state, requiring a continuing administrative apparatus. If the state concededly can by law

eliminate price competition altogether, why should it not be able to take the lesser step of simply limiting the advertising of price? Why is the cheaper and easier interference with the free market more objectionable than the greater and more expensive interference?

2.   Justice Rehnquist in dissent warns that to allow price competition between pharmacists will lead to lawyers and doctors advertising prices. Despite the Court's footnote suggesting a distinction between pharmacists and lawyers and doctors, Justice Rehnquist's prediction was accurate. Indeed, over the years the Court has struck down virtually all state restrictions on attorney advertising. *See Bates v. State Bar of Arizona*, 433 U.S. 350 (1977)(price advertising); *In re R.M.J.*, 455 U.S. 191 (1982)(advertising areas of practice and courts admitted to; mailing announcements of opening an office); *Zauderer v. Office of Disciplinary Counsel*, 471 U.S. 626 (1985)(newspaper advertising for representation in Dalkon Shield cases, including a statement that no fee would be charged if there was no recovery); *Shapero v. Kentucky Bar Ass'n*, 486 U.S. 466 (1988)(direct mail targeting of persons known to need legal service of a particular kind); *Peel v. Attorney Registration and Disciplinary Comm'n of Ill.*, 496 U.S. 91 (1990)(stationery letterhead stating attorney was "certified" as a civil trial specialist by National Board of Trial Advocacy). *But see Ohralik v. Ohio State Bar Ass'n*, 436 U.S. 447 (1978)(upholding attorney suspension for personally soliciting business from a person in the hospital after an accident); *Florida Bar v. Went For It, Inc.*, 515 U.S. 618 (1995)(upholding bar rule prohibiting direct mail solicitation for personal injury clients within 30 days of an accident).

3.   In *Virginia Pharmacy* the Court suggests that false and misleading advertising is not protected by the First Amendment. False and misleading campaign promises by candidates for office, however, presumably are protected by the First Amendment. Moreover, the Court has held that advertising for an illegal transaction is not protected speech, *see, e.g., Pittsburgh Press Co. v. Pittsburgh Human Relations Comm'n*, 413 U.S. 376 (1973)(upholding city ordinance prohibiting advertising for jobs in gender designated columns). But, again, non-commercial speech suggesting a person violate the law is protected unless it meets the *Brandenburg* test. Thus, it is clear the Court is distinguishing commercial speech from "core speech." The following case was the Court's attempt to establish a "test" for commercial speech.

CENTRAL HUDSON GAS V. PUBLIC SERVICE COMM'N

United States Supreme Court, 1980.
447 U.S. 557, 100 S.Ct. 2343.

MR. JUSTICE POWELL delivered the opinion of the Court.

This case presents the question whether a regulation of the Public Service Commission of the State of New York violates the First and Fourteenth Amendments because it completely bans promotional advertising by an electrical utility.

[The Commission adopted a] Policy Statement [that] divided advertising expenses "into two broad categories: promotional—advertising intended to stimulate the purchase of utility services—and institutional and informational, a broad category inclusive of all advertising not clearly intended to promote sales." The Commission declared all promotional advertising contrary to the national policy of conserving energy. . . .

When it rejected requests for rehearing on the Policy Statement, the Commission supplemented its rationale for the advertising ban. The agency observed that additional electricity probably would be more expensive to produce than existing output. . . . The state agency also thought that promotional advertising would give "misleading signals" to the public by appearing to encourage energy consumption at a time when conservation is needed. . . .

The Commission's order restricts only commercial speech, that is, expression related solely to the economic interests of the speaker and its audience. The First Amendment, as applied to the States through the Fourteenth Amendment, protects commercial speech from unwarranted governmental regulation. Commercial expression not only serves the economic interest of the speaker, but also assists consumers and furthers the societal interest in the fullest possible dissemination of information. . . .

Nevertheless, our decisions have recognized "the 'commonsense' distinction between speech proposing a commercial transaction, which occurs in an area traditionally subject to government regulation, and other varieties of speech." The Constitution therefore accords a lesser protection to commercial speech than to other constitutionally guaranteed expression. The protection available for particular commercial expression turns on the nature both of the expression and of the governmental interests served by its regulation.

The First Amendment's concern for commercial speech is based on the informational function of advertising. Consequently, there can be no constitutional objection to the suppression of commercial messages that do not accurately inform the public about lawful activity. The government may ban forms of communication more likely to deceive the public than to inform it, or commercial speech related to illegal activity.[6]

If the communication is neither misleading nor related to unlawful activity, the government's power is more circumscribed. The State must assert a substantial interest to be achieved by restrictions on commercial speech. Moreover, the regulatory technique must be in proportion to that

---

[6]   In most other contexts, the First Amendment prohibits regulation based on the content of the message. Two features of commercial speech permit regulation of its content. First, commercial speakers have extensive knowledge of both the market and their products. Thus, they are well situated to evaluate the accuracy of their messages and the lawfulness of the underlying activity. In addition, commercial speech, the offspring of economic self-interest, is a hardy breed of expression that is not "particularly susceptible to being crushed by overbroad regulation."

interest. The limitation on expression must be designed carefully to achieve the State's goal. Compliance with this requirement may be measured by two criteria. First, the restriction must directly advance the state interest involved; the regulation may not be sustained if it provides only ineffective or remote support for the government's purpose. Second, if the governmental interest could be served as well by a more limited restriction on commercial speech, the excessive restrictions cannot survive. . . .

We now apply this four-step analysis for commercial speech to the Commission's arguments in support of its ban on promotional advertising.

The Commission does not claim that the expression at issue either is inaccurate or relates to unlawful activity. . . .

The Commission offers two state interests as justifications for the ban on promotional advertising. The first concerns energy conservation. Any increase in demand for electricity . . . means greater consumption of energy. The Commission argues, and the New York court agreed, that the State's interest in conserving energy is sufficient to support suppression of advertising designed to increase consumption of electricity. In view of our country's dependence on energy resources beyond our control, no one can doubt the importance of energy conservation. Plainly, therefore, the state interest asserted is substantial. . . .

Next, we focus on the relationship between the State's interests and the advertising ban. [T]he State's interest in energy conservation is directly advanced by the Commission order at issue here. There is an immediate connection between advertising and demand for electricity. Central Hudson would not contest the advertising ban unless it believed that promotion would increase its sales. Thus, we find a direct link between the state interest in conservation and the Commission's order.

We come finally to the critical inquiry in this case: whether the Commission's complete suppression of speech ordinarily protected by the First Amendment is no more extensive than necessary to further the State's interest in energy conservation. The Commission's order reaches all promotional advertising, regardless of the impact of the touted service on overall energy use. But the energy conservation rationale, as important as it is, cannot justify suppressing information about electric devices or services that would cause no net increase in total energy use. In addition, no showing has been made that a more limited restriction on the content of promotional advertising would not serve adequately the State's interests.

Appellant insists that but for the ban, it would advertise products and services that use energy efficiently. These include the "heat pump," which both parties acknowledge to be a major improvement in electric heating, and the use of electric heat as a "backup" to solar and other heat sources. [I]n the absence of authoritative findings to the contrary, we must credit as within the realm of possibility the claim that electric heat can be an efficient alternative in some circumstances.

The Commission's order prevents appellant from promoting electric services that would reduce energy use by diverting demand from less efficient sources, or that would consume roughly the same amount of energy as do alternative sources. In neither situation would the utility's advertising endanger conservation or mislead the public. To the extent that the Commission's order suppresses speech that in no way impairs the State's interest in energy conservation, the Commission's order violates the First and Fourteenth Amendments and must be invalidated.

The Commission also has not demonstrated that its interest in conservation cannot be protected adequately by more limited regulation of appellant's commercial expression. To further its policy of conservation, the Commission could attempt to restrict the format and content of Central Hudson's advertising. It might, for example, require that the advertisements include information about the relative efficiency and expense of the offered service, both under current conditions and for the foreseeable future.[13] In the absence of a showing that more limited speech regulation would be ineffective, we cannot approve the complete suppression of Central Hudson's advertising. . . .

MR. JUSTICE BRENNAN, concurring in the judgment. [opinion omitted]

MR. JUSTICE BLACKMUN, with whom MR. JUSTICE BRENNAN joins, concurring in the judgment.

I agree with the Court that the Public Service Commission's ban on promotional advertising of electricity by public utilities is inconsistent with the First and Fourteenth Amendments. I concur only in the Court's judgment, however, because I believe the test now evolved and applied by the Court is not consistent with our prior cases and does not provide adequate protection for truthful, nonmisleading, noncoercive commercial speech.

The Court asserts that "a four-part analysis has developed" from our decisions concerning commercial speech. Under this four-part test a restraint on commercial "communication [that] is neither misleading nor related to unlawful activity" is subject to an intermediate level of scrutiny, and suppression is permitted whenever it "directly advances" a "substantial" governmental interest and is "not more extensive than is necessary to serve that interest." I agree with the Court that this level of intermediate scrutiny is appropriate for a restraint on commercial speech designed to protect consumers from misleading or coercive speech, or a

---

[13] The Commission also might consider a system of previewing advertising campaigns to insure that they will not defeat conservation policy. It has instituted such a program for approving "informational" advertising under the Policy Statement challenged in this case. We have observed that commercial speech is such a sturdy brand of expression that traditional prior restraint doctrine may not apply to it.

regulation related to the time, place, or manner of commercial speech. I do not agree, however, that the Court's four-part test is the proper one to be applied when a State seeks to suppress information about a product in order to manipulate a private economic decision that the State cannot or has not regulated or outlawed directly.

Since the Court, without citing empirical data or other authority, finds a "direct link" between advertising and energy consumption, it leaves open the possibility that the State may suppress advertising of electricity in order to lessen demand for electricity. I, of course, agree with the Court that, in today's world, energy conservation is a goal of paramount national and local importance. I disagree with the Court, however, when it says that suppression of speech may be a permissible means to achieve that goal. . . .

The Court recognizes that we have never held that commercial speech may be suppressed in order to further the State's interest in discouraging purchases of the underlying product that is advertised. Permissible restraints on commercial speech have been limited to measures designed to protect consumers from fraudulent, misleading, or coercive sales techniques. Those designed to deprive consumers of information about products or services that are legally offered for sale consistently have been invalidated.

I seriously doubt whether suppression of information concerning the availability and price of a legally offered product is ever a permissible way for the State to "dampen" demand for or use of the product. Even though "commercial" speech is involved, such a regulatory measure strikes at the heart of the First Amendment. This is because it is a covert attempt by the State to manipulate the choices of its citizens, not by persuasion or direct regulation, but by depriving the public of the information needed to make a free choice. . . .

It appears that the Court would permit the State to ban all direct advertising of air conditioning, assuming that a more limited restriction on such advertising would not effectively deter the public from cooling its homes. In my view, our cases do not support this type of suppression. If a governmental unit believes that use or overuse of air conditioning is a serious problem, it must attack that problem directly, by prohibiting air conditioning or regulating thermostat levels. . . .

MR. JUSTICE STEVENS, with whom MR. JUSTICE BRENNAN joins, concurring in the judgment. [opinion omitted]

MR. JUSTICE REHNQUIST, dissenting.

The Court today invalidates an order issued by the New York Public Service Commission designed to promote a policy that has been declared to be of critical national concern. The order was issued by the Commission in 1973 in response to the Mideastern oil embargo crisis. It prohibits electric corporations "from *promoting* the use of electricity through the use of advertising, subsidy payments . . ., or employee incentives."

[T]he Court's asserted justification for invalidating the New York law is the public interest discerned by the Court to underlie the First Amendment in the free flow of commercial information. Prior to this Court's recent decision in *Virginia Pharmacy Board v. Virginia Citizens Consumer Council,* however, commercial speech was afforded no protection under the First Amendment whatsoever. Given what seems to me full recognition of the holding of *Virginia Pharmacy Board* that commercial speech is entitled to some degree of First Amendment protection, I think the Court is nonetheless incorrect in invalidating the carefully considered state ban on promotional advertising in light of pressing national and state energy needs.

The Court's analysis in my view is wrong in several respects. [I] think that the Court errs here in failing to recognize that the state law is most accurately viewed as an economic regulation and that the speech involved (if it falls within the scope of the First Amendment at all) occupies a significantly more subordinate position in the hierarchy of First Amendment values than the Court gives it today. Finally, the Court in reaching its decision improperly substitutes its own judgment for that of the State in deciding how a proper ban on promotional advertising should be drafted. With regard to this latter point, the Court adopts as its final part of a four-part test a "no more extensive than necessary" analysis that will unduly impair a state legislature's ability to adopt legislation reasonably designed to promote interests that have always been rightly thought to be of great importance to the State. . . .

COMMENTS AND QUESTIONS

1. A case subsequent to *Central Hudson* clarified (or altered, depending on your perspective) the fourth prong of the *Central Hudson* test: whether the restriction is "no more extensive than necessary to further the state's interest." In *Board of Trustees, State Univ. of New York v. Fox*, 492 U.S. 469 (1989), the Court said the word "necessary" did not mean that the state had to use the least restrictive alternative.

> What our decisions require is a "fit" between the legislature's ends and the means chosen to accomplish those ends—a fit that is not necessarily perfect, but reasonable; that represents not necessarily the single best disposition but one whose scope is "in proportion to the interest served"; that employs not necessarily the least restrictive means but, as we have put it in the other contexts discussed above, a means narrowly tailored to achieve the desired objective. Within those bounds we leave it to governmental decisionmakers to judge what manner of regulation may best be employed.

Do you think that is the test that the Court used in *Central Hudson*?

2.   Justice Blackmun's opinion concurring in the judgment suggests that if the state wants to reduce the purchases of new air conditioners, it should do it directly, which would not raise First Amendment issues; it should not limit advertisements promoting the purchase of air conditioners, which does. Do you think Central Hudson, consumers, or the sellers of air conditioners would think that a preferable situation to the promotional advertising ban?

3.   The cases thus far all involved regulation of advertising of at least arguably socially beneficial goods or services, but what if the restriction on advertising involved the so-called vices: alcohol, cigarettes, and gambling? The first cases seemed to apply *Central Hudson*'s test with a light touch. *See Posadas de Puerto Rico Assocs. v. Tourism Co. of Puerto Rico*, 478 U.S. 328 (1986)(upholding Puerto Rico's ban on advertising casino gambling in Puerto Rico, although such gambling is both legal and advertised outside Puerto Rico to draw tourists); *United States v. Edge Broadcasting Co.*, 509 U.S. 418 (1993)(upholding federal statute making it unlawful to broadcast lottery advertisements from stations licensed in states that do not allow lotteries, even though most of the station's listeners were in a state that conducted lotteries). But then came the following case.

RUBIN v. COORS BREWING CO.
United States Supreme Court, 1995.
514 U.S. 476, 115 S.Ct. 1585.

JUSTICE THOMAS delivered the opinion of the Court.

Respondent brews beer. In 1987, respondent applied to the Bureau of Alcohol, Tobacco and Firearms (BATF), an agency of the Department of the Treasury, for approval of proposed labels and advertisements that disclosed the alcohol content of its beer. BATF rejected the application on the ground that [§ 205(e)(2) of] the Federal Alcohol Administration Act (FAAA or Act) prohibited disclosure of the alcohol content of beer on labels or in advertising. Respondent then filed suit in the District Court for the District of Colorado seeking a declaratory judgment that the relevant provisions of the Act violated the First Amendment. . . . The Government took the position that the ban was necessary to suppress the threat of "strength wars" among brewers, who, without the regulation, would seek to compete in the marketplace based on the potency of their beer.

[B]oth parties agree that the information on beer labels constitutes commercial speech. . . . *Central Hudson* identified several factors that courts should consider in determining whether a regulation of commercial speech survives First Amendment scrutiny: "For commercial speech to come within [the First Amendment], it at least must concern lawful activity and not be misleading. Next, we ask whether the asserted governmental interest is substantial. If both inquiries yield positive answers, we must determine whether the regulation directly advances the governmental interest asserted, and whether it is not more extensive than is necessary to serve that interest."

We now apply *Central Hudson*'s test to § 205(e)(2).[2]

Both the lower courts and the parties agree that respondent seeks to disclose only truthful, verifiable, and nonmisleading factual information about alcohol content on its beer labels. Thus, our analysis focuses on the substantiality of the interest behind § 205(e)(2) and on whether the labeling ban bears an acceptable fit with the Government's goal. A careful consideration of these factors indicates that § 205(e)(2) violates the First Amendment's protection of commercial speech.

The Government identifies [an interest] it considers sufficiently "substantial" to justify § 205(e)(2)'s labeling ban. [T]he Government contends that § 205(e)(2) advances Congress's goal of curbing "strength wars" by beer brewers who might seek to compete for customers on the basis of alcohol content. According to the Government, the FAAA's restriction prevents a particular type of beer drinker—one who selects a beverage because of its high potency—from choosing beers solely for their alcohol content. In the Government's view, restricting disclosure of information regarding a particular product characteristic will decrease the extent to which consumers will select the product on the basis of that characteristic. . . .

[T]he Government here has a significant interest in protecting the health, safety, and welfare of its citizens by preventing brewers from competing on the basis of alcohol strength, which could lead to greater alcoholism and its attendant social costs. Both panels of the Court of Appeals that heard this case concluded that the goal of suppressing strength wars constituted a substantial interest, and we cannot say that their conclusion is erroneous. We have no reason to think that strength wars, if they were to occur, would not produce the type of social harm that the Government hopes to prevent.

---

[2] The Government argues that *Central Hudson* imposes too strict a standard for reviewing § 205(e)(2), and urges us to adopt instead a far more deferential approach to restrictions on commercial speech concerning alcohol. Relying on *United States v. Edge Broadcasting Co.* and *Posadas de Puerto Rico Associates v. Tourism Co. of P.R.*, the Government suggests that legislatures have broader latitude to regulate speech that promotes socially harmful activities, such as alcohol consumption, than they have to regulate other types of speech. Although *Edge Broadcasting* and *Posadas* involved the advertising of gambling activities, the Government argues that we also have applied this principle to speech concerning alcohol.

Neither *Edge Broadcasting* nor *Posadas* compels us to craft an exception to the *Central Hudson* standard, for in both of those cases we applied the *Central Hudson* analysis. Indeed, *Edge Broadcasting* specifically avoided reaching the argument the Government makes here because the Court found that the regulation in question passed muster under *Central Hudson*. To be sure, *Posadas* did state that the Puerto Rico Government could ban promotional advertising of casino gambling because it could have prohibited gambling altogether. But the Court reached this argument only *after* it already had found that the state regulation survived the *Central Hudson* test. . . .

[T]he remaining *Central Hudson* factors require that a valid restriction on commercial speech directly advance the governmental interest and be no more extensive than necessary to serve that interest. We have said that "[t]he last two steps of the *Central Hudson* analysis basically involve a consideration of the 'fit' between the legislature's ends and the means chosen to accomplish those ends." The Tenth Circuit found that § 205(e)(2) failed to advance the interest in suppressing strength wars sufficiently to justify the ban. We agree.

[T]he Government carries the burden of showing that the challenged regulation advances the Government's interest "in a direct and material way." That burden "is not satisfied by mere speculation or conjecture; rather, a governmental body seeking to sustain a restriction on commercial speech must demonstrate that the harms it recites are real and that its restriction will in fact alleviate them to a material degree.". . .

The Government attempts to meet its burden by pointing to current developments in the consumer market. It claims that beer producers are already competing and advertising on the basis of alcohol strength in the "malt liquor" segment of the beer market. The Government attempts to show that this competition threatens to spread to the rest of the market by directing our attention to respondent's motives in bringing this litigation. Respondent allegedly suffers from consumer misperceptions that its beers contain less alcohol than other brands. According to the Government, once respondent gains relief from § 205(e)(2), it will use its labels to overcome this handicap.

Under the Government's theory, § 205(e)(2) suppresses the threat of such competition by preventing consumers from choosing beers on the basis of alcohol content. It is assuredly a matter of "common sense," that a restriction on the advertising of a product characteristic will decrease the extent to which consumers select a product on the basis of that trait. In addition to common sense, the Government urges us to turn to history as a guide. According to the Government, at the time Congress enacted the FAAA, the use of labels displaying alcohol content had helped produce a strength war. Section 205(e)(2) allegedly relieved competitive pressures to market beer on the basis of alcohol content, resulting over the long term in beers with lower alcohol levels.

We conclude that § 205(e)(2) cannot directly and materially advance its asserted interest because of the overall irrationality of the Government's regulatory scheme. While the laws governing labeling prohibit the disclosure of alcohol content unless required by state law, federal regulations apply a contrary policy to beer advertising. Like § 205(e)(2), these restrictions prohibit statements of alcohol content in advertising, but, unlike § 205(e)(2), they apply only in States that affirmatively prohibit such advertisements. As only 18 States at best prohibit disclosure of content in advertisements, brewers remain free to disclose alcohol content in advertisements, but not on labels, in much of the country. The failure to prohibit the disclosure of alcohol content in advertising, which would seem to constitute a more influential weapon in any strength war than labels, makes no rational sense if the Government's true aim is to suppress strength wars.

Other provisions of the FAAA and its regulations similarly undermine § 205(e)(2)'s efforts to prevent strength wars. While § 205(e)(2) bans the disclosure of alcohol content on beer labels, it allows the exact opposite in the case of wines and spirits. Thus, distilled spirits may contain statements of alcohol content, and such disclosures are required for wines with more than 14 percent alcohol. If combating strength wars were the goal, we would assume that Congress would regulate disclosure of alcohol content for the strongest beverages as well as for the weakest ones. Further, the Government permits brewers to signal high alcohol content through use of the term "malt liquor." Although the Secretary has proscribed the use of various colorful terms suggesting high alcohol levels, manufacturers still can distinguish a class of stronger malt beverages by identifying them as malt liquors. One would think that if the Government sought to suppress strength wars by prohibiting numerical disclosures of alcohol content, it also would preclude brewers from indicating higher alcohol beverages by using descriptive terms.

Even if § 205(e)(2) did meet [*Central Hudson*'s third prong], it would still not survive First Amendment scrutiny because the Government's regulation of speech is not sufficiently tailored to its goal. The Government argues that a sufficient "fit" exists here because the labeling ban applies to only one product characteristic and because the ban does not prohibit all disclosures of alcohol content—it applies only to those involving labeling and advertising. In response, respondent suggests several alternatives, such as directly limiting the alcohol content of beers, prohibiting marketing efforts emphasizing high alcohol strength (which is apparently the policy in some other western nations), or limiting the labeling ban only to malt liquors, which is the segment of the market that allegedly is threatened with a strength war. We agree that the availability of these options, all of which could advance the Government's asserted interest in a manner less intrusive to respondent's First Amendment rights, indicates that § 205(e)(2) is more extensive than necessary.

JUSTICE STEVENS, concurring in the judgment.

Although I agree with the Court's persuasive demonstration that this statute does not serve the Government's purported interest in preventing "strength wars," I write separately because I am convinced that the constitutional infirmity in the statute is more patent than the Court's opinion indicates. Instead of relying on the formulaic approach announced in *Central Hudson Gas & Elec. Corp. v. Public Serv. Comm'n of N.Y.,* I believe the Court should ask whether the justification for allowing more regulation of commercial speech than other speech has any application to this unusual statute.

In my opinion the "commercial speech doctrine" is unsuited to this case, because the Federal Alcohol Administration Act (FAAA) neither prevents misleading speech nor protects consumers from the dangers of incomplete information. A truthful statement about the alcohol content of malt beverages would receive full First Amendment protection in any other context; without some justification tailored to the special character of commercial speech, the Government should not be able to suppress the same truthful speech merely because it happens to appear on the label of a product for sale.

[I] am willing to assume that an interest in avoiding the harmful consequences of so-called "strength wars" would justify disclosure requirements explaining the risks and predictable harms associated with the consumption of alcoholic beverages. Such a measure could be justified as a means to ensure that consumers are not led, by incomplete or inaccurate information, to purchase products they would not purchase if they knew the truth about them. I see no basis, however, for upholding a prohibition against the dissemination of truthful, nonmisleading information about an alcoholic beverage merely because the message is propounded in a commercial context.

[W]hatever standard is applied, I find no merit whatsoever in the Government's assertion that an interest in restraining competition among brewers to satisfy consumer demand for stronger beverages justifies a statutory abridgment of truthful speech. Any "interest" in restricting the flow of accurate information because of the perceived danger of that knowledge is anathema to the First Amendment; more speech and a better informed citizenry are among the central goals of the Free Speech Clause. Accordingly, the Constitution is most skeptical of supposed state interests that seek to keep people in the dark for what the government believes to be their own good. One of the vagaries of the "commercial speech" doctrine in its current form is that the Court sometimes takes such paternalistic motives seriously.

In my opinion, the Government's asserted interest, that consumers should be misled or uninformed for their own protection, does not suffice to justify restrictions on protected speech in *any* context, whether under "exacting scrutiny" or some other standard. If Congress is concerned about the potential for increases in the alcohol content of malt beverages, it may, of course, take other steps to combat the problem without running afoul of the First Amendment—for example, Congress may limit directly the alcoholic content of malt beverages. But Congress may not seek to accomplish the same purpose through a policy of consumer ignorance, at the expense of the free-speech rights of the sellers and purchasers. If varying alcohol strengths are lawful, I see no reason why brewers may not advise customers that their beverages are stronger—or weaker—than competing products.

COMMENTS AND QUESTIONS

1.   The Court unanimously overturns the federal law, with eight of the nine justices finding that it fails both the third and fourth prongs of the *Central Hudson* test. Nevertheless, those eight justices seem to suggest that a more tailored, consistent approach to restricting the labeling and advertisement of alcohol content of alcoholic beverages would pass muster. Only Justice Stevens would flatly ban any such restrictions, relying instead on government-mandated disclosure requirements—more speech—to counter any bad effects from advertising alcohol content. Only a year later, however, Justice Thomas, the author of *Rubin*, wrote a separate concurrence in a case overturning a state's ban on advertising liquor prices. In that opinion he stated that attempts by a state to reduce demand for a lawful product or service by restricting advertising was *per se* unconstitutional under the First Amendment. *See 44 Liquormart, Inc. v. Rhode Island*, 517 U.S. 484 (1996)(Thomas, J., concurring in part and concurring in the judgment). In the same case, four other justices said that if the state could achieve the same goal through direct regulation as it was attempting to further through an advertising restriction, then the restriction fails *Central Hudson*'s fourth prong, because there would be a less speech restrictive alternative—direct regulation. *Id.* (Stevens, J., joined by Justices Kennedy, Souter, and Ginsburg).

2.   A government mandate requiring people to express something raises its own problems, as you will see later in this chapter. However, generally the Court has said that if a government regulation simply requires a commercial speaker to disclose "purely factual and uncontroversial information," courts will apply a more permissive standard of review than under *Central Hudson*. *Zauderer v. Office of Disciplinary Counsel of Supreme Court of Ohio*, 471 U.S. 626 (1985). Because that kind of regulation normally has only a "minimal" effect on First Amendment interests, it normally need only be "reasonably related to the State's interest in preventing deception of consumers."

LORILLARD TOBACCO CO. V. REILLY

United States Supreme Court, 2001.
533 U.S. 525, 121 S.Ct. 2404.

JUSTICE O'CONNOR delivered the opinion of the Court.

In January 1999, the Attorney General of Massachusetts promulgated comprehensive regulations governing the advertising and sale of cigarettes, smokeless tobacco, and cigars. Petitioners, a group of cigarette, smokeless tobacco, and cigar manufacturers and retailers, filed suit in Federal District Court claiming that the regulations violate federal law and the United States Constitution. . . . The first question presented for our review is whether certain cigarette advertising regulations are pre-empted by the Federal Cigarette Labeling and Advertising Act (FCLAA). The second question presented is whether certain regulations governing the advertising and sale of tobacco products violate the First Amendment. . . .

The cigarette, [cigar, little cigar,] and smokeless tobacco regulations being challenged before this Court provide: [that it is unlawful to engage in outdoor advertising of these products, including advertising from within a retail establishment that is directed toward or visible from the outside of the establishment, in any location that is within a 1,000 foot radius of any public playground, playground area in a public park, elementary school or secondary school, or to make any point-of-sale advertising of these products any portion of which is placed lower than five feet from the floor of any retail establishment which is located within a one thousand foot radius of any public playground, playground area in a public park, elementary school or secondary school, and which is not an adult-only retail establishment.]

Before reaching the First Amendment issues, we must decide to what extent federal law pre-empts the Attorney General's regulations. [The Court concluded that the FCLAA preempted all advertising restrictions applicable to cigarettes.]

By its terms, the FCLAA's pre-emption provision only applies to cigarettes. Accordingly, we must evaluate the smokeless tobacco and cigar petitioners' First Amendment challenges to the State's outdoor and point-of-sale advertising regulations. . . .

For over 25 years, the Court has recognized that commercial speech does not fall outside the purview of the First Amendment. Instead, the Court has afforded commercial speech a measure of First Amendment protection " 'commensurate' " with its position in relation to other constitutionally guaranteed expression. In recognition of the "distinction between speech proposing a commercial transaction, which occurs in an area traditionally subject to government regulation, and other varieties of speech," we developed a framework for analyzing regulations of commercial speech. . . . The analysis contains four elements: "At the outset, we must determine whether the expression is protected by the First Amendment. For commercial speech to come within that provision, it at least must concern lawful activity and not be misleading. Next, we ask whether the asserted governmental interest is substantial. If both inquiries yield positive answers, we must determine whether the regulation directly advances the governmental interest asserted, and whether it is not more extensive than is necessary to serve that interest." *Central Hudson.*

Petitioners urge us to reject the *Central Hudson* analysis and apply strict scrutiny. . . . Admittedly, several Members of the Court have expressed doubts about the *Central Hudson* analysis and whether it should apply in particular cases. But here . . . we see "no need to break new ground. *Central Hudson,* as applied in our more recent commercial speech cases, provides an adequate basis for decision."

Only the last two steps of *Central Hudson's* four-part analysis are at issue here. The Attorney General has assumed for purposes of summary judgment that petitioners' speech is entitled to First Amendment protection. With respect to the second step, none of the petitioners contests the importance of the State's interest in preventing the use of tobacco products by minors.

The third step of *Central Hudson* concerns the relationship between the harm that underlies the State's interest and the means identified by the State to advance that interest. It requires that "the speech restriction directly and materially advanc[e] the asserted governmental interest. 'This burden is not satisfied by mere speculation or conjecture; rather, a governmental body seeking to sustain a restriction on commercial speech must demonstrate that the harms it recites are real and that its restriction will in fact alleviate them to a material degree.' "

We do not, however, require that "empirical data come . . . accompanied by a surfeit of background information . . . . [W]e have permitted litigants to justify speech restrictions by reference to studies and anecdotes pertaining to different locales altogether, or even, in a case applying strict scrutiny, to justify restrictions based solely on history, consensus, and 'simple common sense.' "

The last step of the *Central Hudson* analysis "complements" the third step, "asking whether the speech restriction is not more extensive than necessary to serve the interests that support it." We have made it clear that "the least restrictive means" is not the standard; instead, the case law requires a reasonable " 'fit between the legislature's ends and the means chosen to accomplish those ends, . . . a means narrowly tailored to achieve the desired objective.' " Focusing on the third and fourth steps of the *Central Hudson* analysis, we first address the outdoor advertising and point-of-sale advertising regulations for smokeless tobacco and cigars. . . .

The smokeless tobacco and cigar petitioners contend that the Attorney General's regulations do not satisfy *Central Hudson's* third step. They . . . contend that the Attorney General cannot prove that advertising has a causal link to tobacco use such that limiting advertising will materially alleviate any problem of underage use of their products.

In previous cases, we have acknowledged the theory that product advertising stimulates demand for products, while suppressed advertising may have the opposite effect. The Attorney General cites numerous studies to support this theory in the case of tobacco products. . . .

Our review of the record reveals that the Attorney General has provided ample documentation of the problem with underage use of smokeless tobacco and cigars. In addition, we disagree with petitioners' claim that there is no evidence that preventing targeted campaigns and limiting youth exposure to advertising will decrease underage use of smokeless tobacco and cigars. . . .

Whatever the strength of the Attorney General's evidence to justify the outdoor advertising regulations, however, we conclude that the regulations do not satisfy the fourth step of the *Central Hudson* analysis. The final step of the *Central Hudson* analysis, the "critical inquiry in this case," requires a reasonable fit between the means and ends of the regulatory scheme. The Attorney General's regulations do not meet this standard. The broad sweep of the regulations indicates that the Attorney General did not "carefully calculat[e] the costs and benefits associated with the burden on speech imposed" by the regulations.

The outdoor advertising regulations prohibit any smokeless tobacco or cigar advertising within 1,000 feet of schools or playgrounds. In the District Court, petitioners maintained that this prohibition would prevent advertising in 87% to 91% of Boston, Worcester, and Springfield, Massachusetts. The 87% to 91% figure appears to include not only the effect of the regulations, but also the limitations imposed by other generally applicable zoning restrictions. The Attorney General disputed petitioners' figures but "concede[d] that the reach of the regulations is substantial." Thus, the Court of Appeals concluded that the regulations prohibit advertising in a substantial portion of the major metropolitan areas of Massachusetts.

The substantial geographical reach of the Attorney General's outdoor advertising regulations is compounded by other factors. "Outdoor" advertising includes not only advertising located outside an establishment, but also advertising inside a store if that advertising is visible from outside the store. . . .

In some geographical areas, these regulations would constitute nearly a complete ban on the communication of truthful information about smokeless tobacco and cigars to adult consumers. The breadth and scope of the regulations, and the process by which the Attorney General adopted the regulations, do not demonstrate a careful calculation of the speech interests involved.

First, the Attorney General did not seem to consider the impact of the 1,000-foot restriction on commercial speech in major metropolitan areas. . . . The degree to which speech is suppressed—or alternative avenues for speech remain available—under a particular regulatory scheme tends to be case specific. And a case specific analysis makes sense, for although a State or locality may have common interests and concerns about underage smoking and the effects of tobacco advertisements, the impact of a restriction on speech will undoubtedly vary from place to place. . . . [T]he effect of the Attorney General's speech regulations will vary based on whether a locale is rural, suburban, or urban. The uniformly broad sweep of the geographical limitation demonstrates a lack of tailoring.

In addition, the range of communications restricted seems unduly broad. [A] ban on all signs of any size seems ill suited to target the problem of highly visible billboards, as opposed to smaller signs. To the extent that studies have identified particular advertising and promotion practices that appeal to youth, tailoring would involve targeting those practices while permitting others. As crafted, the regulations make no distinction among practices on this basis. . . .

The State's interest in preventing underage tobacco use is substantial, and even compelling, but it is no less true that the sale and use of tobacco products by adults is a legal activity. We must consider that tobacco retailers and manufacturers have an interest in conveying truthful information about their products to adults, and adults have a corresponding interest in receiving truthful information about tobacco products. In a case involving indecent speech on the Internet we explained that "the governmental interest in protecting children from harmful materials . . . does not justify an unnecessarily broad suppression of speech addressed to adults." As the State protects children from tobacco advertisements, tobacco manufacturers and retailers and their adult consumers still have a protected interest in communication.

In some instances, Massachusetts's outdoor advertising regulations would impose particularly onerous burdens on speech. . . . If some retailers have relatively small advertising budgets, and use few avenues of communication, then the Attorney General's outdoor advertising regulations potentially place a greater, not lesser, burden on those retailers' speech.

In addition, a retailer in Massachusetts may have no means of communicating to passersby on the street that it sells tobacco products because alternative forms of advertisement, like newspapers, do not allow that retailer to propose an instant transaction in the way that onsite advertising does. The ban on any indoor advertising that is visible from the outside also presents problems in establishments like convenience stores, which have unique security concerns that counsel in favor of full visibility of the store from the outside. It is these sorts of considerations that the Attorney General failed to incorporate into the regulatory scheme.

We conclude that the Attorney General has failed to show that the outdoor advertising regulations for smokeless tobacco and cigars are not more extensive than necessary to advance the State's substantial interest in preventing underage tobacco use. . . .

Massachusetts has also restricted indoor, point-of-sale advertising for smokeless tobacco and cigars. Advertising cannot be "placed lower than five feet from the floor of any retail establishment which is located within a one thousand foot radius of" any school or playground. . . .

We conclude that the point-of-sale advertising regulations fail both the third and fourth steps of the *Central Hudson* analysis. A regulation cannot be sustained if it " 'provides only ineffective or remote support for the government's purpose,' " or if there is "little chance" that the restriction will advance the State's goal. As outlined above, the State's goal is to prevent minors from using tobacco products and to curb demand for that activity by limiting youth exposure to advertising. The 5-foot rule does not seem to advance that goal. Not all children are less than 5 feet tall, and those who are certainly have the ability to look up and take in their surroundings. . . .

JUSTICE KENNEDY, with whom JUSTICE SCALIA joins, concurring in part and concurring in the judgment.

The obvious overbreadth of the outdoor advertising restrictions suffices to invalidate them under the fourth part of the test in *Central Hudson*. As a result, in my view, there is no need to consider whether the restrictions satisfy the third part of the test, a proposition about which there is considerable doubt. Neither are we required to consider whether *Central Hudson* should be retained in the face of the substantial objections that can be made to it. My continuing concerns that the test gives insufficient protection to truthful, nonmisleading commercial speech require me to refrain from expressing agreement with the Court's application of the third part of *Central Hudson*.

JUSTICE THOMAS, concurring in part and concurring in the judgment.

I join the opinion of the Court (with the exception of [the discussion of *Central Hudson*'s third step with respect to the outdoor advertising]) because I agree that the Massachusetts cigarette advertising regulations are pre-empted by the FCLAA. I also agree with the Court's disposition of the First Amendment challenges to the other regulations at issue here, and I share the Court's view that the regulations fail even the intermediate scrutiny of *Central Hudson*. At the same time, I continue to believe that when the government seeks to restrict truthful speech in order to suppress the ideas it conveys, strict scrutiny is appropriate, whether or not the speech in question may be characterized as "commercial." I would subject all of the advertising restrictions to strict scrutiny and would hold that they violate the First Amendment. . . .

Respondents have identified no principle of law or logic that would preclude the imposition of restrictions on fast food and alcohol advertising similar to those they seek to impose on tobacco advertising. In effect, they seek a "vice" exception to the First Amendment. No such exception exists. If it did, it would have almost no limit, for "any product that poses some threat to public health or public morals might reasonably be characterized by a state legislature as relating to 'vice activity.' " That is why "a 'vice' label that is unaccompanied by a corresponding prohibition against the commercial behavior at issue fails to provide a principled justification for the regulation of commercial speech about that activity."

No legislature has ever sought to restrict speech about an activity it regarded as harmless and inoffensive. Calls for limits on expression always are made when the specter of some threatened harm is looming. The identity of the harm may vary. People will be inspired by totalitarian dogmas and subvert the Republic. They will be inflamed by racial demagoguery and embrace hatred and bigotry. Or they will be enticed by cigarette advertisements and choose to smoke, risking disease. It is therefore no answer for the State to say that the makers of cigarettes are doing harm: perhaps they are. But in that respect they are no different from the purveyors of other harmful products, or the advocates of harmful ideas. When the State seeks to silence them, they are all entitled to the protection of the First Amendment.

JUSTICE SOUTER, concurring in part and dissenting in part.

I join . . . the Court's opinion [except for its conclusion on preemption and its discussion of the failure of the outdoor advertising ban to meet the fourth step in *Central Hudson*.] I join . . . the opinion of Justice STEVENS [regarding preemption] concurring in part, concurring in the judgment in part, and dissenting in part. I respectfully dissent from . . . the opinion of the Court regarding the failure of the outdoor advertising ban to meet the fourth step in *Central Hudson*], and like Justice STEVENS would remand for trial on the constitutionality of the 1,000-foot limit.

JUSTICE STEVENS, with whom JUSTICE GINSBURG and JUSTICE BREYER join, and with whom JUSTICE SOUTER joins as to [the preemption issue], concurring in part, concurring in the judgment in part, and dissenting in part.

This suit presents two separate sets of issues. The first—involving pre-emption—is straightforward. The second—involving the First Amendment—is more complex. Because I strongly disagree with the Court's conclusion that the FCLAA precludes States and localities from regulating the location of cigarette advertising, I dissent from [those parts of the Court's opinion dealing with preemption]. On the First Amendment questions, I agree with the Court both that the outdoor advertising restrictions imposed by Massachusetts serve legitimate and important state interests and that the record does not indicate that the measures were properly tailored to serve those interests. Because the present record does not enable us to adjudicate the merits of those claims on summary judgment, I would vacate the decision upholding those restrictions and remand for trial on the constitutionality of the outdoor advertising regulations. Finally, because I do not believe that . . . the point-of-sale advertising restrictions . . . implicate significant First Amendment concerns, I would uphold them in their entirety.

[I] would . . . uphold the regulation limiting tobacco advertising in certain retail establishments to the space five feet or more above the floor. When viewed in isolation, this provision appears to target speech. Further, to the extent that it does target speech it may well run into constitutional problems, as the connection between the ends the statute purports to serve and the means it has chosen are dubious. Nonetheless, I am ultimately persuaded that the provision is unobjectionable because it is little more than an adjunct to . . . sales practice restrictions. As the Commonwealth of Massachusetts can properly legislate the placement of products and the nature of displays in its convenience stores, I would not draw a distinction between such restrictions and height restrictions on related product advertising. I would accord the Commonwealth some latitude in imposing restrictions that can have only the slightest impact on the ability of adults to purchase a poisonous product and may save some children from taking the first step on the road to addiction.

COMMENTS AND QUESTIONS

1.   Massachusetts defended its advertising restrictions on the basis of protecting children, which the Court agreed was an important, if not compelling government interest. But, consistent with decisions in other areas besides commercial speech, the Court held that one cannot justify keeping otherwise lawful speech from adults in order to protect children. Because the outdoor advertising restriction effectively banned *any* outside advertising of cigars, little cigars, and smokeless tobacco in large parts of the state, this was not narrowly tailored to keeping it from children but allowing it to adults.

2.   What if Massachusetts had said that its purpose was also to keep the advertising from adults because health studies all show these products are unhealthy? Is not protecting the public health a substantial state interest?

3.   Justices Thomas, Kennedy, and Scalia call for elimination of the *Central Hudson* test as insufficiently protective of truthful, nonmisleading commercial speech. While Justices Kennedy and Scalia are no longer on the Court, their replacements, Justices Gorsuch and Kavanaugh, have in other contexts indicated a very strong protection of the freedom of speech. Moreover, Justice Alito replaced Justice O'Connor, and Justice Alito has likewise reflected a very strong protection of the freedom of speech, albeit not of false speech. Is *Central Hudson* ripe for demise?

4.   Several states have decriminalized the sale and use of marijuana; some legislators have called for the decriminalization of other drugs as well. Some have also called for the regulation, rather than the criminalization, of prostitution. If this were done, would this mean that there would be a First Amendment right to advertise "truthful, nonmisleading" availability and pricing of drugs and prostitution? Could that conclusion be avoided by retaining a $1 criminal fine for selling drugs or sex and simply not enforcing the criminal law? After all, the Court has never backed off from saying there

is no constitutional right to advertise an illegal transaction. Does this make any sense?

PROBLEMS

1. A state that has legalized recreational marijuana nevertheless prohibits its advertisement in public places where children might be present. The sale, possession, and use of marijuana is, however, still illegal under federal law. Is the advertising ban constitutional?

2. Nevada allows prostitution in counties (other than those including Reno and Las Vegas) that approve it by referendum. Nevertheless, the state prohibits the advertising of prostitution by any means throughout the state. A prostitute in a county where prostitution is lawful challenges the advertising restriction. How should the court rule?

H. MONEY AS SPEECH

Government regulation of election financing goes back to the beginning of the last century. First Amendment concerns with restrictions on such financing are more recent, as is most First Amendment law for that matter. The following, seminal case arose out of the Federal Election Campaign Act of 1971, which arose out of issues from the 1968 presidential election.

BUCKLEY V. VALEO

United States Supreme Court, 1976.
424 U.S. 1, 96 S.Ct. 612.

PER CURIAM.

These appeals present constitutional challenges to the key provisions of the Federal Election Campaign Act of 1971 (Act). . . . The statutes at issue summarized in broad terms, contain the following provisions: (a) individual political contributions are limited to $1,000 to any single candidate per election, with an overall annual limitation of $25,000 by any contributor; independent expenditures by individuals and groups "relative to a clearly identified candidate" are limited to $1,000 a year; campaign spending by candidates for various federal offices and spending for national conventions by political parties are subject to prescribed limits; (b) contributions and expenditures above certain threshold levels must be reported and publicly disclosed; (c) a system for public funding of Presidential campaign activities is established by Subtitle H of the Internal Revenue Code; and (d) a Federal Election Commission is established to administer and enforce the legislation. . . .

I.   CONTRIBUTION AND EXPENDITURE LIMITATIONS

The intricate statutory scheme adopted by Congress to regulate federal election campaigns includes restrictions on political contributions and expenditures that apply broadly to all phases of and all participants in the election process. The major contribution and expenditure limitations in the Act prohibit individuals from contributing more than $25,000 in a single year or more than $1,000 to any single candidate for an election campaign and from spending more than $1,000 a year "relative to a clearly identified candidate." Other provisions restrict a candidate's use of personal and family resources in his campaign and limit the overall amount that can be spent by a candidate in campaigning for federal office. . . .

The Act's contribution and expenditure limitations operate in an area of the most fundamental First Amendment activities. Discussion of public issues and debate on the qualifications of candidates are integral to the operation of the system of government established by our Constitution. The First Amendment affords the broadest protection to such political expression in order "to assure (the) unfettered interchange of ideas for the bringing about of political and social changes desired by the people." . . .

It is with these principles in mind that we consider the primary contentions of the parties with respect to the Act's limitations upon the giving and spending of money in political campaigns. Those conflicting contentions could not more sharply define the basic issues before us. Appellees contend that what the Act regulates is conduct, and that its effect on speech and association is incidental at most. Appellants respond that contributions and expenditures are at the very core of political speech, and that the Act's limitations thus constitute restraints on First Amendment liberty that are both gross and direct. . . .

We cannot share the view that the present Act's contribution and expenditure limitations are comparable to the restrictions on conduct upheld in *O'Brien*. The expenditure of money simply cannot be equated with such conduct as destruction of a draft card. Some forms of communication made possible by the giving and spending of money involve speech alone, some involve conduct primarily, and some involve a combination of the two. Yet this Court has never suggested that the dependence of a communication on the expenditure of money operates itself to introduce a nonspeech element or to reduce the exacting scrutiny required by the First Amendment. . . .

Even if the categorization of the expenditure of money as conduct were accepted, the limitations challenged here would not meet the *O'Brien* test because the governmental interests advanced in support of the Act involve "suppressing communication." The interests served by the Act include restricting the voices of people and interest groups who have money to spend and reducing the overall scope of federal election campaigns.

Although the Act does not focus on the ideas expressed by persons or groups subject to its regulations, it is aimed in part at equalizing the relative ability of all voters to affect electoral outcomes by placing a ceiling on expenditures for political expression by citizens and groups. Unlike *O'Brien*, where the Selective Service System's administrative interest in the preservation of draft cards was wholly unrelated to their use as a means of communication, it is beyond dispute that the interest in regulating the alleged "conduct" of giving or spending money "arises in some measure because the communication allegedly integral to the conduct is itself thought to be harmful." . . .

A restriction on the amount of money a person or group can spend on political communication during a campaign necessarily reduces the quantity of expression by restricting the number of issues discussed, the depth of their exploration, and the size of the audience reached. This is because virtually every means of communicating ideas in today's mass society requires the expenditure of money. The distribution of the humblest handbill or leaflet entails printing, paper, and circulation costs. Speeches and rallies generally necessitate hiring a hall and publicizing the event. The electorate's increasing dependence on television, radio, and other mass media for news and information has made these expensive modes of communication indispensable instruments of effective political speech.

The expenditure limitations contained in the Act represent substantial rather than merely theoretical restraints on the quantity and diversity of political speech. The $1,000 ceiling on spending "relative to a clearly identified candidate" would appear to exclude all citizens and groups except candidates, political parties, and the institutional press from any significant use of the most effective modes of communication. . . .

By contrast with a limitation upon expenditures for political expression, a limitation upon the amount that any one person or group may contribute to a candidate or political committee entails only a marginal restriction upon the contributor's ability to engage in free communication. A contribution serves as a general expression of support for the candidate and his views, but does not communicate the underlying basis for the support. The quantity of communication by the contributor does not increase perceptibly with the size of his contribution, since the expression rests solely on the undifferentiated, symbolic act of contributing. At most, the size of the contribution provides a very rough index of the intensity of the contributor's support for the candidate. A limitation on the amount of money a person may give to a candidate or campaign organization thus involves little direct restraint on his political communication, for it permits the symbolic expression of support evidenced by a contribution but does not in any way infringe the contributor's freedom to discuss candidates and issues. . . .

Given the important role of contributions in financing political campaigns, contribution restrictions could have a severe impact on political dialogue if the limitations prevented candidates and political committees from amassing the resources necessary for effective advocacy. There is no indication, however, that the contribution limitations imposed by the Act would have any dramatic adverse effect on the funding of campaigns and political associations. The overall effect of the Act's contribution ceilings is merely to require candidates and political committees to raise funds from a greater number of persons and to compel people who would otherwise contribute amounts greater than the statutory limits to expend such funds on direct political expression, rather than to reduce the total amount of money potentially available to promote political expression.

The Act's contribution and expenditure limitations also impinge on protected associational freedoms. Making a contribution, like joining a political party, serves to affiliate a person with a candidate. In addition, it enables like-minded persons to pool their resources in furtherance of common political goals. The Act's contribution ceilings thus limit one important means of associating with a candidate or committee, but leave the contributor free to become a member of any political association and to assist personally in the association's efforts on behalf of candidates. And the Act's contribution limitations permit associations and candidates to aggregate large sums of money to promote effective advocacy. By contrast, the Act's $1,000 limitation on independent expenditures "relative to a clearly identified candidate" precludes most associations from effectively amplifying the voice of their adherents, the original basis for the recognition of First Amendment protection of the freedom of association. . . .

In sum, although the Act's contribution and expenditure limitations both implicate fundamental First Amendment interests, its expenditure ceilings impose significantly more severe restrictions on protected freedoms of political expression and association than do its limitations on financial contributions.

[T]he primary First Amendment problem raised by the Act's contribution limitations is their restriction of one aspect of the contributor's freedom of political association. . . . In view of the fundamental nature of the right to associate, governmental "action which may have the effect of curtailing the freedom to associate is subject to the closest scrutiny." Yet, it is clear that "(n)either the right to associate nor the right to participate in political activities is absolute." Even a " 'significant interference' with protected rights of political association" may be sustained if the State demonstrates a sufficiently important interest and employs means closely drawn to avoid unnecessary abridgment of associational freedoms.

[A]ccording to the parties and amici, the primary interest served by the limitations and, indeed, by the Act as a whole, is the prevention of corruption and the appearance of corruption spawned by the real or imagined coercive influence of large financial contributions on candidates' positions and on their actions if elected to office. . . .

It is unnecessary to look beyond the Act's primary purpose to limit the actuality and appearance of corruption resulting from large individual financial contributions in order to find a constitutionally sufficient justification for the $1,000 contribution limitation. . . . To the extent that large contributions are given to secure a political quid pro quo from current and potential office holders, the integrity of our system of representative democracy is undermined. Although the scope of such pernicious practices can never be reliably ascertained, the deeply disturbing examples surfacing after the 1972 election demonstrate that the problem is not an illusory one.

Of almost equal concern as the danger of actual quid pro quo arrangements is the impact of the appearance of corruption stemming from public awareness of the opportunities for abuse inherent in a regime of large individual financial contributions. [C]ongress could legitimately conclude that the avoidance of the appearance of improper influence "is also critical . . . if confidence in the system of representative Government is not to be eroded to a disastrous extent."

[T]he Act's $1,000 contribution limitation focuses precisely on the problem of large campaign contributions the narrow aspect of political association where the actuality and potential for corruption have been identified while leaving persons free to engage in independent political expression, to associate actively through volunteering their services, and to assist to a limited but nonetheless substantial extent in supporting candidates and committees with financial resources. . . .

We find that, under the rigorous standard of review established by our prior decisions, the weighty interests served by restricting the size of financial contributions to political candidates are sufficient to justify the limited effect upon First Amendment freedoms caused by the $1,000 contribution ceiling. . . .

In addition to the $1,000 limitation on the nonexempt contributions that an individual may make to a particular candidate for any single election, the Act contains an overall $25,000 limitation on total contributions by an individual during any calendar year. A contribution made in connection with an election is considered, for purposes of this subsection, to be made in the year the election is held. Although the constitutionality of this provision was drawn into question by appellants, it has not been separately addressed at length by the parties. The overall $25,000 ceiling does impose an ultimate restriction upon the number of candidates and committees with which an individual may associate himself by means of financial support. But this quite modest restraint upon protected political activity serves to prevent evasion of the $1,000 contribution limitation by a person who might otherwise contribute massive amounts of money to a particular candidate through the use of unearmarked contributions to political committees likely to contribute to that candidate, or huge contributions to the candidate's political party. The limited, additional restriction on associational freedom imposed by the overall ceiling is thus no more than a corollary of the basic individual contribution limitation that we have found to be constitutionally valid.

The Act's expenditure ceilings impose direct and substantial restraints on the quantity of political speech. The most drastic of the limitations restricts individuals and groups to an expenditure of $1,000 "relative to a clearly identified candidate during a calendar year." Other expenditure ceilings limit spending by candidates, their campaigns, and political parties in connection with election campaigns. It is clear that a primary effect of these expenditure limitations is to restrict the quantity of campaign speech by individuals, groups, and candidates. The restrictions, while neutral as to the ideas expressed, limit political expression "at the core of our electoral process and of the First Amendment freedoms."

Section 608(e)(1) provides that "(n)o person may make any expenditure . . . relative to a clearly identified candidate during a calendar year which, when added to all other expenditures made by such person during the year advocating the election or defeat of such candidate, exceeds $1,000." The plain effect of § 608(e)(1) is to prohibit all individuals, who are neither candidates nor owners of institutional press facilities, and all groups, except political parties and campaign organizations, from voicing their views "relative to a clearly identified candidate" through means that entail aggregate expenditures of more than $1,000 during a calendar year. The provision, for example, would make it a federal criminal offense for a person or association to place a single one-quarter page advertisement "relative to a clearly identified candidate" in a major metropolitan newspaper.

[W]e turn then to the basic First Amendment question whether § 608(e)(1) . . . impermissibly burdens the constitutional right of free expression. . . .

The discussion [earlier] explains why the Act's expenditure limitations impose far greater restraints on the freedom of speech and association than do its contribution limitations. The markedly greater burden on basic freedoms caused by § 608(e)(1) thus cannot be sustained simply by invoking the interest in maximizing the effectiveness of the less intrusive contribution limitations. Rather, the constitutionality of § 608(e)(1) turns on whether the governmental interests advanced in its support satisfy the exacting scrutiny applicable to limitations on core First Amendment rights of political expression.

We find that the governmental interest in preventing corruption and the appearance of corruption is inadequate to justify § 608(e)(1)'s ceiling on independent expenditures. First, assuming, arguendo, that large independent expenditures pose the same dangers of actual or apparent quid pro quo arrangements as do large contributions, § 608(e)(1) does not provide an answer that sufficiently relates to the elimination of those dangers. Unlike the contribution limitations' total ban on the giving of large amounts of money to candidates, § 608(e)(1) prevents only some large expenditures. So long as persons and groups eschew expenditures that in express terms advocate the election or defeat of a clearly identified candidate, they are free to spend as much as they want to promote the candidate and his views. The exacting interpretation of the statutory language necessary to avoid unconstitutional vagueness thus undermines the limitation's effectiveness as a loophole-closing provision by facilitating circumvention by those seeking to exert improper influence upon a candidate or office-holder. It would naively underestimate the ingenuity and resourcefulness of persons and groups desiring to buy influence to believe that they would have much difficulty devising expenditures that skirted the restriction on express advocacy of election or defeat but nevertheless benefited the candidate's campaign. Yet no substantial societal interest would be served by a loophole-closing provision designed to check corruption that permitted unscrupulous persons and organizations to expend unlimited sums of money in order to obtain improper influence over candidates for elective office.

Second, quite apart from the shortcomings of § 608(e)(1) in preventing any abuses generated by large independent expenditures, the independent advocacy restricted by the provision does not presently appear to pose dangers of real or apparent corruption comparable to those identified with large campaign contributions. The parties defending § 608(e)(1) contend that it is necessary to prevent would-be contributors from avoiding the contribution limitations by the simple expedient of paying directly for media advertisements or for other portions of the candidate's campaign activities. They argue that expenditures controlled by or coordinated with the candidate and his campaign might well have virtually the same value to the candidate as a contribution and would pose similar dangers of abuse. Yet such controlled or coordinated expenditures are treated as contributions rather than expenditures under the Act. . . . By contrast, § 608(e)(1) limits expenditures for express advocacy of candidates made totally independently of the candidate and his campaign. Unlike contributions, such independent expenditures may well provide little assistance to the candidate's campaign and indeed may prove counterproductive. The absence of prearrangement and coordination of an expenditure with the candidate or his agent not only undermines the value of the expenditure to the candidate, but also alleviates the danger that expenditures will be given as a quid pro quo for improper commitments from the candidate. Rather than preventing circumvention of the contribution limitations, § 608(e)(1) severely restricts all independent advocacy despite its substantially diminished potential for abuse.

While the independent expenditure ceiling thus fails to serve any substantial governmental interest in stemming the reality or appearance of corruption in the electoral process, it heavily burdens core First Amendment expression. For the First Amendment right to " 'speak one's mind . . . on all public institutions' " includes the right to engage in " 'vigorous advocacy' no less than 'abstract discussion.' " Advocacy of the election or defeat of candidates for federal office is no less entitled to protection under the First Amendment than the discussion of political policy generally or advocacy of the passage or defeat of legislation.

It is argued, however, that the ancillary governmental interest in equalizing the relative ability of individuals and groups to influence the outcome of elections serves to justify the limitation on express advocacy of the election or defeat of candidates imposed by § 608(e)(1)'s expenditure ceiling. But the concept that government may restrict the speech of some elements of our society in order to enhance the relative voice of others is wholly foreign to the First Amendment. . . . The First Amendment's protection against governmental abridgment of free expression cannot properly be made to depend on a person's financial ability to engage in public discussion.

For the reasons stated, we conclude that § 608(e)(1)'s independent expenditure limitation is unconstitutional under the First Amendment. . . .

MR. JUSTICE STEVENS took no part in the consideration or decision of these cases.

MR. CHIEF JUSTICE BURGER, concurring in part and dissenting in part.

[I] agree fully with that part of the Court's opinion that holds unconstitutional the limitations the Act puts on campaign expenditures. . . . Yet when it approves similarly stringent limitations on contributions, the Court ignores the reasons it finds so persuasive in the context of expenditures. For me contributions and expenditures are two sides of the same First Amendment coin. . . .

The Court attempts to separate the two communicative aspects of political contributions the "moral" support that the gift itself conveys, which the Court suggests is the same whether the gift is $10 or $10,000, and the fact that money translates into communication. The Court dismisses the effect of the limitations on the second aspect of contributions: "(T)he transformation of contributions into political debate involves speech by someone other than the contributor." On this premise that contribution limitations restrict only the speech of "someone other than the contributor" rests the Court's justification for treating contributions differently from expenditures. . . .

The Court's attempt to distinguish the communication inherent in political contributions from the speech aspects of political expenditures simply "will not wash." We do little but engage in word games unless we recognize that people, candidates, and contributors spend money on political activity because they wish to communicate ideas, and their constitutional interest in doing so is precisely the same whether they or someone else utters the words. . . .

MR. JUSTICE WHITE, concurring in part and dissenting in part.

[T]he disclosure requirements and the limitations on contributions and expenditures are challenged as invalid abridgments of the right of free speech protected by the First Amendment. I would reject these challenges. I agree with the Court's . . . judgment upholding the limitations on contributions. I dissent, however, from the Court's view that the expenditure limitations violate the First Amendment.

Concededly, neither the limitations on contributions nor those on expenditures directly or indirectly purport to control the content of political speech by candidates or by their supporters or detractors. What the Act regulates is giving and spending money, acts that have First Amendment significance not because they are themselves communicative with respect to the qualifications of the candidate, but because money may be used to defray the expenses of speaking or otherwise communicating about the merits or demerits of federal candidates for election. The act of giving money to political candidates, however, may have illegal or other undesirable consequences: it may be used to secure the express or tacit understanding that the giver will enjoy political favor if the candidate is elected. Both Congress and this Court's cases have recognized this as a mortal danger against which effective preventive and curative steps must be taken.

Since the contribution and expenditure limitations are neutral as to the content of speech and are not motivated by fear of the consequences of the political speech of particular candidates or of political speech in general, this case depends on whether the nonspeech interests of the Federal Government in regulating the use of money in political campaigns are sufficiently urgent to justify the incidental effects that the limitations visit upon the First Amendment interests of candidates and their supporters.

Despite its seeming struggle with the standard by which to judge this case, this is essentially the question the Court asks and answers in the affirmative with respect to the limitations on contributions which individuals and political committees are permitted to make to federal candidates. In the interest of preventing undue influence that large contributors would have or that the public might think they would have, the Court upholds the provision that an individual may not give to a candidate, or spend on his behalf if requested or authorized by the candidate to do so, more than $1,000 in any one election. This limitation is valid although it imposes a low ceiling on what individuals may deem to be their most effective means of supporting or speaking on behalf of the candidate i. e., financial support given directly to the candidate. The Court thus accepts the congressional judgment that the evils of unlimited contributions are sufficiently threatening to warrant restriction regardless of the impact of the limits on the contributor's opportunity for effective speech and in turn on the total volume of the candidate's political communications by reason of his inability to accept large sums from those willing to give.

The congressional judgment, which I would also accept, was that other steps must be taken to counter the corrosive effects of money in federal election campaigns. One of these steps is § 608(e), which, aside from those funds that are given to the candidate or spent at his request or with his approval or cooperation limits what a contributor may independently spend in support or denigration of one running for federal office. Congress was plainly of the view that these expenditures also have corruptive potential; but the Court strikes down the provision, strangely enough claiming more insight as to what may improperly influence candidates than is possessed by the majority of Congress that passed this bill and the President who signed it. Those supporting the bill undeniably included many seasoned professionals who have been deeply involved in elective processes and who have viewed them at close range over many years.

It would make little sense to me, and apparently made none to Congress, to limit the amounts an individual may give to a candidate or spend with his approval but fail to limit the amounts that could be spent on his behalf. Yet the Court permits the former while striking down the latter limitation. . . .

In sustaining the contribution limits, the Court recognizes the importance of avoiding public misapprehension about a candidate's reliance on large contributions. It ignores that consideration in invalidating § 608(e). In like fashion, it says that Congress was entitled to determine that the criminal provisions against bribery and corruption, together with the disclosure provisions, would not in themselves be adequate to combat the evil and that limits on contributions should be provided. Here, the Court rejects the identical kind of judgment made by Congress as to the need for and utility of expenditure limits. I would not do so.

The Court also rejects Congress's judgment manifested in § 608(c) that the federal interest in limiting total campaign expenditures by individual candidates justifies the incidental effect on their opportunity for effective political speech. I disagree both with the Court's assessment of the impact on speech and with its narrow view of the values the limitations will serve. . . .

In the first place, expenditure ceilings reinforce the contribution limits and help eradicate the hazard of corruption. . . . Without limits on total expenditures, campaign costs will inevitably and endlessly escalate. . . . It should be added that many successful candidates will also be saved from large, overhanging campaign debts which must be paid off with money raised while holding public office and at a time when they are already preparing or thinking about the next campaign. The danger to the public interest in such situations is self-evident.

[I] also disagree with the Court's judgment that § 608(a), which limits the amount of money that a candidate or his family may spend on his campaign, violates the Constitution. Although it is true that this provision does not promote any interest in preventing the corruption of candidates, the provision does, nevertheless, serve salutary purposes related to the integrity of federal campaigns. By limiting the importance of personal wealth, § 608(a) helps to assure that only individuals with a modicum of support from others will be viable candidates. This in turn would tend to discourage any notion that the outcome of elections is primarily a function of money. Similarly, § 608(a) tends to equalize access to the political arena, encouraging the less wealthy, unable to bankroll their own campaigns, to run for political office. . . .

MR. JUSTICE MARSHALL, concurring in part and dissenting in part.

I join in all of the Court's opinion except [the part] which deals with . . . the amount a candidate may spend from his personal funds, or family funds under his control, in connection with his campaigns during any calendar year. . . .

The Court views "(t)he ancillary interest in equalizing the relative financial resources of candidates" as the relevant rationale for § 608(a), and deems that interest insufficient to justify § 608(a). In my view the interest is more precisely the interest in promoting the reality and appearance of equal access to the political arena. Our ballot-access decisions serve as a reminder of the importance of the general interest in promoting equal access among potential candidates. . . .

One of the points on which all Members of the Court agree is that money is essential for effective communication in a political campaign. It would appear to follow that the candidate with a substantial personal fortune at his disposal is off to a significant "headstart." Of course, the less wealthy candidate can potentially overcome the disparity in resources through contributions from others. But ability to generate contributions may itself depend upon a showing of a financial base for the campaign or some demonstration of pre-existing support, which in turn is facilitated by expenditures of substantial personal sums. Thus the wealthy candidate's immediate access to a substantial personal fortune may give him an initial advantage that his less wealthy opponent can never overcome. And even if the advantage can be overcome, the perception that personal wealth wins elections may not only discourage potential candidates without significant personal wealth from entering the political arena, but also undermine public confidence in the integrity of the electoral process. . . .

MR. JUSTICE BLACKMUN, concurring in part and dissenting in part.

I am not persuaded that the Court makes, or indeed is able to make, a principled constitutional distinction between the contribution limitations, on the one hand, and the expenditure limitations on the other, that are involved here. I therefore do not join the Court's opinion [on expenditure limitations]. . . .

MR. JUSTICE REHNQUIST, concurring in part and dissenting in part.

I concur in [the Court's opinion regarding restrictions on contributions and expenditures]. . . .

COMMENTS AND QUESTIONS

1. The Court distinguishes between contributions and expenditures with respect to the nature of their expressive interests, concluding that expenditures involve a greater expressive interest. What is it that the Court says a contribution "expresses"? Do you agree with the Court as to what a contributor intends to express through the contribution?

2. Ultimately, are you convinced by the Court's distinctions between contributions and expenditures? If not, would you prefer both to be constitutionally protected here or both constitutionally subject to the statute?

3. The penultimate paragraph in the Court's opinion reflects a second proffered justification for limiting expenditures and contributions—equalizing the relative ability of individuals and *groups* to influence elections—but the Court rejects it out of hand. What do you think?

CITIZENS UNITED V. FEDERAL ELECTION COMMISSION
United States Supreme Court, 2010.
558 U.S. 310, 130 S.Ct. 876.

JUSTICE KENNEDY delivered the opinion of the Court.

Federal law prohibits corporations and unions from using their general treasury funds to make independent expenditures for speech defined as an "electioneering communication" or for speech expressly advocating the election or defeat of a candidate. 2 U.S.C. § 441b. Limits on electioneering communications were upheld in *McConnell v. Federal Election Comm'n,* 540 U.S. 93 (2003). The holding of *McConnell* rested to a large extent on an earlier case, *Austin v. Michigan Chamber of Commerce,* 494 U.S. 652 (1990). *Austin* had held that political speech may be banned based on the speaker's corporate identity.

In this case we are asked to reconsider *Austin* and, in effect, *McConnell.* It has been noted that "*Austin* was a significant departure from ancient First Amendment principles," *Federal Election Comm'n v. Wisconsin Right to Life, Inc.,* 551 U.S. 449 (2007)(*WRTL*)(SCALIA, J., concurring in part and concurring in judgment). We agree with that conclusion and hold that *stare decisis* does not compel the continued acceptance of *Austin*. The Government may regulate corporate political speech through disclaimer and disclosure requirements, but it may not suppress that speech altogether. We turn to the case now before us.

Citizens United is a nonprofit corporation. . . . Citizens United has an annual budget of about $12 million. Most of its funds are from donations by individuals; but, in addition, it accepts a small portion of its funds from for-profit corporations. . . .

Before the Bipartisan Campaign Reform Act of 2002 (BCRA), federal law prohibited—and still does prohibit—corporations and unions from using general treasury funds to make direct contributions to candidates or independent expenditures that expressly advocate the election or defeat of a candidate, through any form of media, in connection with certain qualified federal elections. 2 U.S.C. § 441b. BCRA § 203 amended § 441b to prohibit any "electioneering communication" as well. 2 U.S.C. § 441b(b)(2). An electioneering communication is defined as "any broadcast, cable, or satellite communication" that "refers to a clearly identified candidate for Federal office" and is made within 30 days of a primary or 60 days of a general election. . . . Corporations and unions are barred from using their general treasury funds for express advocacy or electioneering communications. They may establish, however, a "separate segregated fund" (known as a political action committee, or PAC) for these purposes. U.S.C. § 441b(b)(2). The moneys received by the segregated fund are limited to donations from stockholders and employees of the corporation or, in the case of unions, members of the union. . . .

The law before us is an outright ban, backed by criminal sanctions. Section 441b makes it a felony for all corporations—including nonprofit advocacy corporations—either to expressly advocate the election or defeat of candidates or to broadcast electioneering communications within 30 days of a primary election and 60 days of a general election. Thus, the following acts would all be felonies under § 441b: The Sierra Club runs an ad, within the crucial phase of 60 days before the general election, that exhorts the public to disapprove of a Congressman who favors logging in national forests; the National Rifle Association publishes a book urging the public to vote for the challenger because the incumbent U.S. Senator supports a handgun ban; and the American Civil Liberties Union creates a Web site telling the public to vote for a Presidential candidate in light of that candidate's defense of free speech. These prohibitions are classic examples of censorship. . . .

Section 441b's prohibition on corporate independent expenditures is thus a ban on speech. As a "restriction on the amount of money a person or group can spend on political communication during a campaign," that statute "necessarily reduces the quantity of expression by restricting the number of issues discussed, the depth of their exploration, and the size of the audience reached." *Buckley v. Valeo.* Were the Court to uphold these restrictions, the Government could repress speech by silencing certain voices at any of the various points in the speech process. . . . Its purpose and effect are to silence entities whose voices the Government deems to be suspect.

Speech is an essential mechanism of democracy, for it is the means to hold officials accountable to the people. The right of citizens to inquire, to hear, to speak, and to use information to reach consensus is a precondition to enlightened self-government and a necessary means to protect it. . . .

For these reasons, political speech must prevail against laws that would suppress it, whether by design or inadvertence. Laws that burden political speech are "subject to strict scrutiny," which requires the Government to prove that the restriction "furthers a compelling interest and is narrowly tailored to achieve that interest." While it might be maintained that political speech simply cannot be banned or restricted as a categorical matter, the quoted language . . . provides a sufficient framework for protecting the relevant First Amendment interests in this case. We shall employ it here.

Premised on mistrust of governmental power, the First Amendment stands against attempts to disfavor certain subjects or viewpoints. Prohibited, too, are restrictions distinguishing among different speakers, allowing speech by some but not others. As instruments to censor, these categories are interrelated: Speech restrictions based on the identity of the speaker are all too often simply a means to control content.

Quite apart from the purpose or effect of regulating content, moreover, the Government may commit a constitutional wrong when by law it identifies certain preferred speakers. By taking the right to speak from some and giving it to others, the Government deprives the disadvantaged person or class of the right to use speech to strive to establish worth, standing, and respect for the speaker's voice. The Government may not by these means deprive the public of the right and privilege to determine for itself what speech and speakers are worthy of consideration. The First Amendment protects speech and speaker, and the ideas that flow from each. . . .

We find no basis for the proposition that, in the context of political speech, the Government may impose restrictions on certain disfavored speakers. Both history and logic lead us to this conclusion.

The Court has recognized that First Amendment protection extends to corporations.

This protection has been extended by explicit holdings to the context of political speech. Under the rationale of these precedents, political speech does not lose First Amendment protection "simply because its source is a corporation." Corporations and other associations, like individuals, contribute to the discussion, debate, and the dissemination of information and ideas that the First Amendment seeks to foster. The Court has thus rejected the argument that political speech of corporations or other associations should be treated differently under the First Amendment simply because such associations are not "natural persons."

At least since the latter part of the 19th century, the laws of some States and of the United States imposed a ban on corporate direct contributions to candidates. Yet not until 1947 did Congress first prohibit independent expenditures by corporations and labor unions in § 304 of the Labor Management Relations Act 1947. In passing this Act Congress overrode the veto of President Truman, who warned that the expenditure ban was a "dangerous intrusion on free speech." . . .

[I]n *Buckley,* the Court addressed various challenges to the Federal Election Campaign Act of 1971 (FECA). . . .

Before addressing the constitutionality of § 608(e)'s independent expenditure ban, *Buckley* first upheld § 608(b), FECA's limits on direct contributions to candidates. The *Buckley* Court recognized a "sufficiently important" governmental interest in "the prevention of corruption and the appearance of corruption." This followed from the Court's concern that large contributions could be given "to secure a political *quid pro quo.*"

The *Buckley* Court explained that the potential for *quid pro quo* corruption distinguished direct contributions to candidates from independent expenditures. . . . *Buckley* invalidated § 608(e)'s restrictions on independent expenditures, with only one Justice dissenting.

Buckley did not consider § 610's separate ban on corporate and union independent expenditures. . . . The expenditure ban invalidated in *Buckley*, § 608(e), applied to corporations and unions, and some of the prevailing plaintiffs in *Buckley* were corporations.

Notwithstanding this precedent, Congress recodified § 610's corporate and union expenditure ban at 2 U.S.C. § 441b four months after *Buckley* was decided. Section 441b is the independent expenditure restriction challenged here.

Less than two years after *Buckley, First Nat. Bank of Boston v. Bellotti*, 435 U.S. 765 (1978), reaffirmed the First Amendment principle that the Government cannot restrict political speech based on the speaker's corporate identity. *Bellotti* could not have been clearer when it struck down a state-law prohibition on corporate independent expenditures related to referenda issues. . . .

It is important to note that the reasoning and holding of *Bellotti* did not rest on the existence of a viewpoint-discriminatory statute. It rested on the principle that the Government lacks the power to ban corporations from speaking.

Bellotti did not address the constitutionality of the State's ban on corporate independent expenditures to support candidates. In our view, however, that restriction would have been unconstitutional under *Bellotti*'s central principle: that the First Amendment does not allow political speech restrictions based on a speaker's corporate identity.

Thus the law stood until *Austin*. *Austin* "uph[eld] a direct restriction on the independent expenditure of funds for political speech for the first time in [this Court's] history." (KENNEDY, J., dissenting). There, the Michigan Chamber of Commerce sought to use general treasury funds to run a newspaper ad supporting a specific candidate. Michigan law, however, prohibited corporate independent expenditures that supported or opposed any candidate for state office. A violation of the law was punishable as a felony. The Court sustained the speech prohibition.

To bypass *Buckley* and *Bellotti,* the *Austin* Court identified a new governmental interest in limiting political speech: an antidistortion interest. *Austin* found a compelling governmental interest in preventing "the corrosive and distorting effects of immense aggregations of wealth that are accumulated with the help of the corporate form and that have little or no correlation to the public's support for the corporation's political ideas."

The Court is thus confronted with conflicting lines of precedent: a pre-*Austin* line that forbids restrictions on political speech based on the speaker's corporate identity and a post-*Austin* line that permits them. No case before *Austin* had held that Congress could prohibit independent expenditures for political speech based on the speaker's corporate identity. . . .

In its defense of the corporate-speech restrictions in § 441b, the Government notes the antidistortion rationale on which *Austin* and its progeny rest in part, yet it all but abandons reliance upon it. It argues instead that two other compelling interests support *Austin*'s holding that corporate expenditure restrictions are constitutional: an anticorruption interest and a shareholder-protection interest. We consider the three points in turn.

As for *Austin*'s antidistortion rationale, the Government does little to defend it. And with good reason, for the rationale cannot support § 441b.

If the First Amendment has any force, it prohibits Congress from fining or jailing citizens, or associations of citizens, for simply engaging in political speech. If the antidistortion rationale were to be accepted, however, it would permit Government to ban political speech simply because the speaker is an association that has taken on the corporate form. The Government contends that *Austin* permits it to ban corporate expenditures for almost all forms of communication stemming from a corporation. If *Austin* were correct, the Government could prohibit a corporation from expressing political views in media beyond those presented here, such as by printing books. . . .

Political speech is "indispensable to decisionmaking in a democracy, and this is no less true because the speech comes from a corporation rather than an individual." *Bellotti*. This protection for speech is inconsistent with *Austin*'s antidistortion rationale. *Austin* sought to defend the antidistortion rationale as a means to prevent corporations from obtaining " 'an unfair advantage in the political marketplace' " by using " 'resources amassed in the economic marketplace.' " But *Buckley* rejected the premise that the Government has an interest "in equalizing the relative ability of individuals and groups to influence the outcome of elections." *Buckley* was specific in stating that "the skyrocketing cost of political campaigns" could not sustain the governmental prohibition. . . .

Either as support for its antidistortion rationale or as a further argument, the *Austin* majority undertook to distinguish wealthy individuals from corporations on the ground that "[s]tate law grants corporations special advantages—such as limited liability, perpetual life, and favorable treatment of the accumulation and distribution of assets." This does not suffice, however, to allow laws prohibiting speech. "It is rudimentary that the State cannot exact as the price of those special advantages the forfeiture of First Amendment rights."(SCALIA, J., dissenting).

It is irrelevant for purposes of the First Amendment that corporate funds may "have little or no correlation to the public's support for the corporation's political ideas." All speakers, including individuals and the media, use money amassed from the economic marketplace to fund their speech. The First Amendment protects the resulting speech, even if it was enabled by economic transactions with persons or entities who disagree with the speaker's ideas.

Austin's antidistortion rationale would produce the dangerous, and unacceptable, consequence that Congress could ban political speech of media corporations. Media corporations are now exempt from § 441b's ban on corporate expenditures. Yet media corporations accumulate wealth with the help of the corporate form, the largest media corporations have "immense aggregations of wealth," and the views expressed by media corporations often "have little or no correlation to the public's support" for those views. Thus, under the Government's reasoning, wealthy media corporations could have their voices diminished to put them on par with other media entities. There is no precedent for permitting this under the First Amendment.

The media exemption discloses further difficulties with the law now under consideration. There is no precedent supporting laws that attempt to distinguish between corporations which are deemed to be exempt as media corporations and those which are not. "We have consistently rejected the proposition that the institutional press has any constitutional privilege beyond that of other speakers." With the advent of the Internet and the decline of print and broadcast media, moreover, the line between the media and others who wish to comment on political and social issues becomes far more blurred. . . .

Austin interferes with the "open marketplace" of ideas protected by the First Amendment. It permits the Government to ban the political speech of millions of associations of citizens. Most of these are small corporations without large amounts of wealth. This fact belies the Government's argument that the statute is justified on the ground that it prevents the "distorting effects of immense aggregations of wealth." It is not even aimed at amassed wealth. . . .

What we have said also shows the invalidity of other arguments made by the Government. For the most part relinquishing the antidistortion rationale, the Government falls back on the argument that corporate political speech can be banned in order to prevent corruption or its appearance. In *Buckley,* the Court found this interest "sufficiently important" to allow limits on contributions but did not extend that reasoning to expenditure limits. When *Buckley* examined an expenditure ban, it found "that the governmental interest in preventing corruption and the appearance of corruption [was] inadequate to justify [the ban] on independent expenditures." . . .

When *Buckley* identified a sufficiently important governmental interest in preventing corruption or the appearance of corruption, that interest was limited to *quid pro quo* corruption. The fact that speakers may have influence over or access to elected officials does not mean that these officials are corrupt:

> "Favoritism and influence are not . . . avoidable in representative politics. It is in the nature of an elected representative to favor certain policies, and, by necessary corollary, to favor the voters and contributors who support those policies. It is well understood that a substantial and legitimate reason, if not the only reason, to cast a vote for, or to make a contribution to, one candidate over another is that the candidate will respond by producing those political outcomes the supporter favors. Democracy is premised on responsiveness."

[T]he appearance of influence or access, furthermore, will not cause the electorate to lose faith in our democracy. By definition, an independent expenditure is political speech presented to the electorate that is not coordinated with a candidate. The fact that a corporation, or any other speaker, is willing to spend money to try to persuade voters presupposes that the people have the ultimate influence over elected officials. This is inconsistent with any suggestion that the electorate will refuse " 'to take part in democratic governance'" because of additional political speech made by a corporation or any other speaker. . . .

The *McConnell* record was "over 100,000 pages" long, yet it "does not have any direct examples of votes being exchanged for . . . expenditures." This confirms *Buckley*'s reasoning that independent expenditures do not lead to, or create the appearance of, *quid pro quo* corruption. In fact, there is only scant evidence that independent expenditures even ingratiate. Ingratiation and access, in any event, are not corruption. . . . If elected officials succumb to improper influences from independent expenditures; if they surrender their best judgment; and if they put expediency before principle, then surely there is cause for concern. We must give weight to attempts by Congress to seek to dispel either the appearance or the reality of these influences. The remedies enacted by law, however, must comply with the First Amendment; and, it is our law and our tradition that more speech, not less, is the governing rule. An outright ban on corporate political speech during the critical preelection period is not a permissible remedy. Here Congress has created categorical bans on speech that are asymmetrical to preventing *quid pro quo* corruption. . . .

[W]e need not reach the question whether the Government has a compelling interest in preventing foreign individuals or associations from influencing our Nation's political process. Cf. 2 U.S.C. § 441e (contribution and expenditure ban applied to "foreign national[s]"). . . .

Due consideration leads to this conclusion: *Austin* should be and now is overruled. We return to the principle established in *Buckley* and *Bellotti* that the Government may not suppress political speech on the basis of the speaker's corporate identity. No sufficient governmental interest justifies limits on the political speech of nonprofit or for-profit corporations.

Austin is overruled, so it provides no basis for allowing the Government to limit corporate independent expenditures. As the Government appears to concede, overruling *Austin* "effectively invalidate[s] not only BCRA Section 203, but also 2 U.S.C. 441b's prohibition on the use of corporate treasury funds for express advocacy." Section 441b's restrictions on corporate independent expenditures are therefore invalid and cannot be applied to *Hillary*.

Given our conclusion we are further required to overrule the part of *McConnell* that upheld BCRA § 203's extension of § 441b's restrictions on corporate independent expenditures. . . . This part of *McConnell* is now overruled.

Citizens United next challenges BCRA's disclaimer and disclosure provisions. . . . [The Court upheld these provisions.]

CHIEF JUSTICE ROBERTS, with whom JUSTICE ALITO joins, concurring. [omitted]

JUSTICE SCALIA, with whom JUSTICE ALITO joins, and with whom JUSTICE THOMAS joins in part, concurring. [omitted]

JUSTICE STEVENS, with whom JUSTICE GINSBURG, JUSTICE BREYER, and JUSTICE SOTOMAYOR join, concurring in part and dissenting in part.

The real issue in this case concerns how, not if, the appellant may finance its electioneering. Citizens United is a wealthy nonprofit corporation that runs a political action committee (PAC) with millions of dollars in assets. Under the Bipartisan Campaign Reform Act of 2002 (BCRA), it could have used those assets to televise and promote *Hillary: The Movie* wherever and whenever it wanted to. It also could have spent unrestricted sums to broadcast *Hillary* at any time other than the 30 days before the last primary election. Neither Citizens United's nor any other corporation's speech has been "banned." All that the parties dispute is whether Citizens United had a right to use the funds in its general treasury to pay for broadcasts during the 30-day period. The notion that the First Amendment dictates an affirmative answer to that question is, in my judgment, profoundly misguided. Even more misguided is the notion that the Court must rewrite the law relating to campaign expenditures by *for-profit* corporations and unions to decide this case.

The basic premise underlying the Court's ruling is its iteration, and constant reiteration, of the proposition that the First Amendment bars regulatory distinctions based on a speaker's identity, including its "identity" as a corporation. While that glittering generality has rhetorical appeal, it is not a correct statement of the law. . . . The conceit that corporations must be treated identically to natural persons in the political sphere is not only inaccurate but also inadequate to justify the Court's disposition of this case.

In the context of election to public office, the distinction between corporate and human speakers is significant. Although they make enormous contributions to our society, corporations are not actually members of it. They cannot vote or run for office. Because they may be managed and controlled by nonresidents, their interests may conflict in fundamental respects with the interests of eligible voters. The financial resources, legal structure, and instrumental orientation of corporations raise legitimate concerns about their role in the electoral process. Our lawmakers have a compelling constitutional basis, if not also a democratic duty, to take measures designed to guard against the potentially deleterious effects of corporate spending in local and national races.

The majority's approach to corporate electioneering marks a dramatic break from our past. Congress has placed special limitations on campaign spending by corporations ever since the passage of the Tillman Act in 1907. We have unanimously concluded that this "reflects a permissible assessment of the dangers posed by those entities to the electoral process., and have accepted the "legislative judgment that the special characteristics of the corporate structure require particularly careful regulation." The Court today rejects a century of history when it treats the distinction between corporate and individual campaign spending as an invidious novelty born of *Austin v. Michigan Chamber of Commerce.* . . .

Pervading the Court's analysis is the ominous image of a "categorical ba[n]" on corporate speech. . . . This characterization is highly misleading, and needs to be corrected.

In fact it already has been. Our cases have repeatedly pointed out that, "[c]ontrary to the [majority's] critical assumptions," the statutes upheld in *Austin* and *McConnell* do "not impose an *absolute* ban on all forms of corporate political spending." For starters, both statutes provide exemptions for PACs, separate segregated funds established by a corporation for political purposes. "The ability to form and administer separate segregated funds," we observed in *McConnell,* "has provided corporations and unions with a constitutionally sufficient opportunity to engage in express advocacy. That has been this Court's unanimous view."

[T]he laws upheld in *Austin* and *McConnell* leave open many additional avenues for corporations' political speech. Consider the statutory provision we are ostensibly evaluating in this case, BCRA § 203. It has no application to genuine issue advertising—a category of corporate speech Congress found to be far more substantial than election-related advertising—or to Internet, telephone, and print advocacy. Like numerous statutes, it exempts media companies' news stories, commentaries, and editorials from its electioneering restrictions, in recognition of the unique role played by the institutional press in sustaining public debate. . . .

At the time Citizens United brought this lawsuit, the only types of speech that could be regulated under § 203 were: (1) broadcast, cable, or satellite communications; (2) capable of reaching at least 50,000 persons in the relevant electorate; (3) made within 30 days of a primary or 60 days of a general federal election; (4) by a labor union or . . . nonmedia corporation; (5) paid for with general treasury funds; and (6) "susceptible of no reasonable interpretation other than as an appeal to vote for or against a specific candidate." The category of communications meeting all of these criteria is not trivial, but the notion that corporate political speech has been "suppress[ed] . . . altogether," that corporations have been "exclu[ded] . . . from the general public dialogue," is nonsense. . . .

The second pillar of the Court's opinion is its assertion that "the Government cannot restrict political speech based on the speaker's . . . identity." The case on which it relies for this proposition is *First Nat. Bank of Boston v. Bellotti.* . . .

The Government routinely places special restrictions on the speech rights of students, prisoners, members of the Armed Forces, foreigners, and its own employees. When such restrictions are justified by a legitimate governmental interest, they do not necessarily raise constitutional problems. In contrast to the blanket rule that the majority espouses, our cases recognize that the Government's interests may be more or less compelling with respect to different classes of speakers, and that the constitutional rights of certain categories of speakers, in certain contexts, " 'are not automatically coextensive with the rights' " that are normally accorded to members of our society. . . .

In short, the Court dramatically overstates its critique of identity-based distinctions, without ever explaining why corporate identity demands the same treatment as individual identity. Only the most wooden approach to the First Amendment could justify the unprecedented line it seeks to draw. . . .

The case on which the majority places [most weight] is *Bellotti,* claiming it "could not have been clearer" that *Bellotti*'s holding forbade distinctions between corporate and individual expenditures like the one at issue here. The Court's reliance is odd. The only thing about *Bellotti* that could not be clearer is that it declined to adopt the majority's position. *Bellotti* ruled, in an explicit limitation on the scope of its holding, that "our consideration of a corporation's right to speak on issues of general public interest implies no comparable right in the quite different context of participation in a political campaign for election to public office." *Bellotti,* in other words, did not touch the question presented in *Austin* and *McConnell,* and the opinion squarely disavowed the proposition for which the majority cites it.

The majority attempts to explain away the distinction *Bellotti* drew— between general corporate speech and campaign speech intended to promote or prevent the election of specific candidates for office—as inconsistent with the rest of the opinion and with *Buckley.* Yet the basis for this distinction is perfectly coherent: The anticorruption interests that animate regulations of corporate participation in candidate elections, the "importance" of which "has never been doubted," do not apply equally to regulations of corporate participation in referenda. A referendum cannot owe a political debt to a corporation, seek to curry favor with a corporation, or fear the corporation's retaliation. . . .

Undergirding the majority's approach to the merits is the claim that the only "sufficiently important governmental interest in preventing corruption or the appearance of corruption" is one that is "limited to *quid pro quo* corruption." This is the same "crabbed view of corruption" that was espoused by Justice KENNEDY in *McConnell* and squarely rejected by the Court in that case. While it is true that we have not always spoken about corruption in a clear or consistent voice, the approach taken by the majority cannot be right, in my judgment. It disregards our constitutional history and the fundamental demands of a democratic society.

On numerous occasions we have recognized Congress's legitimate interest in preventing the money that is spent on elections from exerting an " 'undue influence on an officeholder's judgment' " and from creating " 'the appearance of such influence,' " beyond the sphere of *quid pro quo* relationships. Corruption can take many forms. Bribery may be the paradigm case. But the difference between selling a vote and selling access is a matter of degree, not kind. And selling access is not qualitatively different from giving special preference to those who spent money on one's behalf. Corruption operates along a spectrum, and the majority's apparent belief that *quid pro quo* arrangements can be neatly demarcated from other improper influences does not accord with the theory or reality of politics. It certainly does not accord with the record Congress developed in passing BCRA, a record that stands as a remarkable testament to the energy and ingenuity with which corporations, unions, lobbyists, and politicians may go about scratching each other's backs—and which amply supported Congress's determination to target a limited set of especially destructive practices. . . .

Unlike the majority's myopic focus on *quid pro quo* scenarios and the free-floating "First Amendment principles" on which it rests so much weight, this broader understanding of corruption has deep roots in the Nation's history. "During debates on the earliest [campaign finance] reform acts, the terms 'corruption' and 'undue influence' were used nearly interchangeably."

[I]t has likewise never been doubted that "[o]f almost equal concern as the danger of actual *quid pro quo* arrangements is the impact of the appearance of corruption." Congress may "legitimately conclude that the avoidance of the appearance of improper influence is also critical . . . if confidence in the system of representative Government is not to be eroded to a disastrous extent." A democracy cannot function effectively when its constituent members believe laws are being bought and sold. . . .

Just as the majority gives short shrift to the general societal interests at stake in campaign finance regulation, it also overlooks the distinctive considerations raised by the regulation of *corporate* expenditures. The majority fails to appreciate that *Austin*'s antidistortion rationale is itself an anticorruption rationale, tied to the special concerns raised by corporations. Understood properly, "antidistortion" is simply a variant on the classic governmental interest in protecting against improper influences on officeholders that debilitate the democratic process. It is manifestly not just an " 'equalizing' " ideal in disguise. . . .

The fact that corporations are different from human beings might seem to need no elaboration, except that the majority opinion almost completely elides it. *Austin* set forth some of the basic differences. Unlike natural persons, corporations have "limited liability" for their owners and managers, "perpetual life," separation of ownership and control, "and favorable treatment of the accumulation and distribution of assets . . . that enhance their ability to attract capital and to deploy their resources in ways that maximize the return on their shareholders' investments." Unlike voters in U.S. elections, corporations may be foreign controlled. . . .

It might also be added that corporations have no consciences, no beliefs, no feelings, no thoughts, no desires. Corporations help structure and facilitate the activities of human beings, to be sure, and their "personhood" often serves as a useful legal fiction. But they are not themselves members of "We the People" by whom and for whom our Constitution was established. . . .

Austin recognized that there are substantial reasons why a legislature might conclude that unregulated general treasury expenditures will give corporations "unfai[r] influence" in the electoral process and distort public debate in ways that undermine rather than advance the interests of listeners. The legal structure of corporations allows them to amass and deploy financial resources on a scale few natural persons can match. . . . Consequently, when corporations grab up the prime broadcasting slots on the eve of an election, they can flood the market with advocacy that bears "little or no correlation" to the ideas of natural persons or to any broader notion of the public good. The opinions of real people may be marginalized. "The expenditure restrictions of [2 U.S.C.] § 441b are thus meant to ensure that competition among actors in the political arena is truly competition among ideas." . . .

JUSTICE THOMAS, concurring in part and dissenting in part. [Justice Thomas dissented only from the Court's opinion upholding the disclaimer and disclosure provisions. His opinion is omitted.]

COMMENTS AND QUESTIONS

1.   This decision resulted in the much reported public rebuke President Obama made in his State of the Union address directed at the members of the Supreme Court seated before him. The President said, among other things, that the decision "reversed a century of law." Do you think that is an accurate statement? He went on to say that the decision opened the "floodgates for . . . foreign corporations to spend without limit in our elections." At which point Justice Alito apparently mouthed the words "not true." Despite the disclaimer in the opinion regarding expenditures by foreign corporations, how could one distinguish them under the Court's explanation why corporations' political speech cannot be limited?

2.   Note that, while the case before the Supreme Court involved a discrete attempt by a non-profit corporation to show a particular documentary movie within 30 days of a primary election, the Court issues an opinion holding unconstitutional any limitation on corporate or union expenditures in support of a candidate. Is this an activist court?

3. If corporations and unions could use political action committees (PACs) without limit, did § 441(b)'s ban on direct expenditures really accomplish much? Justice Stevens suggests, as part of his argument to uphold the limitations on direct expenditures, that the availability of PACS to corporations means § 441(b) really does not restrict much corporate speech. But, if this is so, does it not also mean that the invalidated restriction would have little effect in achieving its goals? During the next election, try to note how many ads are made by corporations, as opposed to PACs. Read the fine print in the ad. Surprisingly few in the last election were by corporations.

4. If the New York Times is protected by the First Amendment and should be able to editorialize as to whom it supports, why should Citizens United be prohibited? After all, the New York Times Company has annual revenues of over $2 billion compared to Citizens United's puny $12 million. And how are elections made more democratic by denying a Mom-and-Pop corporation from spending funds to campaign for someone but allowing the Koch brothers and Sheldon Adelson (who according BusinessWeek had donated $30 million to elect Republican candidates in one election) on the one side and George Soros (who allegedly spent over $25 million in support of Democratic candidates in one election) on the other to spend without limit? In other words, is it "corporate" expenditures that pose a problem, or just expenditures by those who have very large amounts of money available to spend?

5. The Court presents a very limited concept of "corruption" in the political context, saying that it is limited to *quid pro quo* corruption.* It rejects the idea that special influence and access to a legislator resulting from large expenditures in support of the legislator's campaign could constitute the appearance of corruption. Its suggestion that a person only makes an expenditure on behalf of a candidate because the person supports the policies held by the legislator, rather than making the expenditures to influence the candidate to support the policies of the spender, seems a bit naïve.

6. In *McCutchen v. Federal Election Commission*, 572 U.S. 185 (2014), the Court extended its protection of money as speech in elections. The Federal Elections Campaign Act (FECA), as amended by the Bipartisan Campaign Reform Act of 2002, in addition to restricting the amount a person may contribute to a particular candidate or committee, also restricts how much money a person may contribute to all candidates or committees—the aggregate limits. Chief Justice Roberts wrote for the plurality that the aggregate limits violate the First Amendment. *Buckley* had upheld the aggregate limits in the original FECA almost as an afterthought, inasmuch as no party had specifically challenged them. Reiterating that the only justifications for contribution limits is avoiding *quid pro quo* corruption or the appearance of such corruption, the Chief Justice subjected the limits to close scrutiny and found no adequate justification for the limits. Inasmuch as each individual

---

* Quid pro quo corruption means in essence a bribe or implicit bribe—contributing money to a candidate with the expectation or understanding that the candidate, if elected, will act to further the donor's interests because of the contribution.

contribution would have to be within the statute's limits, which the statute presumes is not enough to raise corruption concerns, it was difficult to see how there would be any greater likelihood of corruption simply because more candidates could receive this amount from the same person. Justice Thomas concurred in the judgment, saying that he would overrule *Buckley* altogether, rather than distinguish it, and bar any limitation on contributions. Justice Breyer dissented, joined by Justices Kagan, Sotomayor, and Ginsburg. He first took issue with the plurality's narrow conception of corruption and its rejection of corruption as including contributions to obtain "influence over or access to" elected officials or political parties, although this limited conception had already been announced in *Citizens United*. He also indicated his belief, discounted by the plurality, that absent the aggregate limits the political parties could find ways to channel money from one candidate to another, so that one candidate could receive much more from a particular donor than the donor could directly give the candidate, thereby making *quid pro quo* corruption possible.

I. PLACES THAT MATTER

1. OF PUBLIC FORUMS

Once upon a time public parks, streets, and sidewalks were considered the property of the city or the state, and the owners of property could exclude persons or limit speech thereon at will. In 1939, however, in *Hague v. CIO*, 307 U.S. 496, 515–516 (1939), Justice Roberts (no relation to the current Chief Justice) wrote a concurring opinion that included the following:

> Wherever the title of streets and parks may rest, they have immemorially been held in trust for the use of the public and, time out of mind, have been used for purposes of assembly, communicating thoughts between citizens, and discussing public questions. Such use of the streets and public places has, from ancient times, been a part of the privileges, immunities, rights, and liberties of citizens. The privilege of a citizen of the United States to use the streets and parks for communication of views on national questions may be regulated in the interest of all; it is not absolute, but relative, and must be exercised in subordination to the general comfort and convenience, and in consonance with peace and good order; but it must not, in the guise of regulation, be abridged or denied.

And by 1951, this language had become the starting point for an analysis of the limits of government regulation of speech in these public places. *See Kunz v. People of the State of New York*, 340 U.S. 290 (1951).

As Justice Roberts recognized, while persons have a right to use the streets and parks for purposes of assembly and communication, it is not an absolute right. Cities typically responded by requiring permits in order to use these public places for speech. If these permits vested in the permitting authority discretion whether or not to grant the permit, the Court has routinely found the permit requirement unconstitutional. *See, e.g., Staub v. Baxley*, 355 U.S. 313 (1958)(ordinance banning solicitation of membership in a dues-paying organization without a permit); *Kunz, supra* (requiring permit before holding public worship meetings on the streets); *Cantwell v. State of Connecticut*, 310 U.S. 296 (1940)(license required for soliciting money for religious causes). If, however, the permit requirements were adequately designed to minimize discretion and assure timely consideration, then they could pass muster.

COX v. NEW HAMPSHIRE
United States Supreme Court, 1941.
312 U.S. 569, 61 S.Ct. 762.

MR. CHIEF JUSTICE HUGHES delivered the opinion of the Court.

Appellants are five "Jehovah's Witnesses" who, with sixty-three others of the same persuasion, were convicted in the municipal court of Manchester, New Hampshire, for violation of a state statute prohibiting a "parade or procession" upon a public street without a special license.

By motions and exceptions, appellants raised the questions that the statute was invalid under the Fourteenth Amendment of the Constitution of the United States in that it deprived appellants of their rights of freedom of worship, freedom of speech and press, and freedom of assembly, vested unreasonable and unlimited arbitrary and discriminatory powers in the licensing authority, and was vague and indefinite. These contentions were overruled and the case comes here on appeal. The statutory prohibition is as follows: "No theatrical or dramatic representation shall be performed or exhibited, and no parade or procession upon any public street or way, and no open-air public meeting upon any ground abutting thereon, shall be permitted, unless a special license therefor shall first be obtained from the selectmen of the town, or from a licensing committee for cities hereinafter provided for."

The facts, which are conceded by the appellants to be established by the evidence, are these: The sixty-eight defendants and twenty other persons met at a hall in the City of Manchester on the evening of Saturday, July 8, 1939, "for the purpose of engaging in an information march." The company was divided into four or five groups, each with about fifteen to twenty persons. Each group then proceeded to a different part of the business district of the city and there "would line up in single-file formation and then proceed to march along the sidewalk, 'single-file,' that is, following one another." Each of the defendants carried a small staff with a sign reading "Religion is a Snare and a Racket" and on the reverse "Serve God and Christ the King." [T]he marchers also handed out printed leaflets announcing a meeting to be held at a later time in the hall from which they had started, where a talk on government would be given to the public free of charge. Defendants did not apply for a permit and none was issued.

[T]he recital of facts which prefaced the opinion of the state court thus summarizes the effect of the march: "Manchester had a population of over 75,000 in 1930, and there was testimony that on Saturday nights in an hour's time 26,000 persons passed one of the intersections where the defendants marched. The marchers interfered with the normal sidewalk travel, but no technical breach of the peace occurred. The march was a prearranged affair, and no permit for it was sought, although the defendants understood that under the statute one was required."

[T]he sole charge against appellants was that they were "taking part in a parade or procession" on public streets without a permit as the statute required. . . .

Civil liberties, as guaranteed by the Constitution, imply the existence of an organized society maintaining public order without which liberty itself would be lost in the excesses of unrestrained abuses. The authority of a municipality to impose regulations in order to assure the safety and convenience of the people in the use of public highways has never been regarded as inconsistent with civil liberties but rather as one of the means of safeguarding the good order upon which they ultimately depend. The control of travel on the streets of cities is the most familiar illustration of this recognition of social need. Where a restriction of the use of highways in that relation is designed to promote the public convenience in the interest of all, it cannot be disregarded by the attempted exercise of some civil right which in other circumstances would be entitled to protection. One would not be justified in ignoring the familiar red traffic light because he thought it his religious duty to disobey the municipal command or sought by that means to direct public attention to an announcement of his opinions. As regulation of the use of the streets for parades and processions is a traditional exercise of control by local government, the question in a particular case is whether that control is exerted so as not to deny or unwarrantedly abridge the right of assembly and the opportunities for the communication of thought and the discussion of public questions immemorially associated with resort to public places.

In the instant case, we are aided by the opinion of the Supreme Court of the State which construed the statute and defined the limitations of the authority conferred for the granting of licenses for parades and processions. [R]ecognizing the importance of the civil liberties invoked by appellants, the court thought it significant that the statute prescribed "no measures for controlling or suppressing the publication on the highways of facts and opinions, either by speech or by writing"; that communication "by the distribution of literature or by the display of placards and signs" was in no respect regulated by the statute; that the regulation with respect to parades and processions was applicable only "to organized formations of persons using the highways"; and that "the defendants separately or collectively in groups not constituting a parade or procession," were "under no contemplation of the act." In this light, the court thought that interference with liberty of speech and writing seemed slight; that the distribution of pamphlets and folders by the groups "traveling in unorganized fashion" would have had as large a circulation, and that "signs carried by members of the groups not in marching formation would have been as conspicuous, as published by them while in parade or procession."

It was with this view of the limited objective of the statute that the state court considered and defined the duty of the licensing authority and the rights of the appellants to a license for their parade, with regard only to considerations of time, place and manner so as to conserve the public convenience. The obvious advantage of requiring application for a permit was noted as giving the public authorities notice in advance so as to afford opportunity for proper policing. And the court further observed that, in fixing time and place, the license served "to prevent confusion by overlapping parades or processions, to secure convenient use of the streets by other travelers, and to minimize the risk of disorder." But the court held that the licensing board was not vested with arbitrary power or an unfettered discretion; that its discretion must be exercised with "uniformity of method of treatment upon the facts of each application, free from improper or inappropriate considerations and from unfair discrimination"; that a "systematic, consistent and just order of treatment, with reference to the convenience of public use of the highways, is the statutory mandate." The defendants, said the court, "had a right, under the act, to a license to march when, where and as they did, if after a required investigation it was found that the convenience of the public in the use of the streets would not thereby be unduly disturbed, upon such conditions or changes in time, place and manner as would avoid disturbance."

If a municipality has authority to control the use of its public streets for parades or processions, as it undoubtedly has, it cannot be denied authority to give consideration, without unfair discrimination, to time, place and manner in relation to the other proper uses of the streets. We find it impossible to say that the limited authority conferred by the licensing provisions of the statute in question as thus construed by the state court contravened any constitutional right.

[T]here is no evidence that the statute has been administered otherwise than in the fair and non-discriminatory manner which the state court has construed it to require. . . .

COMMENTS AND QUESTIONS

1.   *Cox* reflects modern law with its characterization of acceptable restrictions as being only "time, place, and manner" restrictions. It also reflects modern doctrine in accepting state courts' restrictive interpretations of state

(and city) laws in order to save their constitutionality. *See, e.g., Boos v. Barry,* 485 U.S. 312 (1988)(allowing the court of appeals narrowing construction of a D.C. provision to keep it from being unconstitutionally overbroad or vague).

2.   In a portion of the opinion edited out, the Court also upheld a fee for the special license ranging between a nominal amount and $300, saying

> The [New Hampshire] court construed the Act as requiring "a reasonable fixing of the amount of the fee." "The charge," said the court, "for a circus parade or a celebration procession of length, each drawing crowds of observers, would take into account the greater public expense of policing the spectacle, compared with the slight expense of a less expansive and attractive parade or procession, to which the charge would be adjusted." The fee was held to be "not a revenue tax, but one to meet the expense incident to the administration of the act and to the maintenance of public order in the matter licensed." There is nothing contrary to the Constitution in the charge of a fee limited to the purpose stated.

Recall, however, the *Forsyth County* case, discussed in a note after *Feiner*. There the Supreme Court held the fee unconstitutional because it was set in light of the expected reaction of the onlookers. Is there a difference between setting a higher fee because a circus parade will draw lots of spectators and because a demonstration by a highly unpopular group will draw numerous objecting onlookers?

3.   *Cox* involves speech in a traditional public forum—the streets, parks, and sidewalks of a city—where the public has a right to engage in speech activities. But not all streets and sidewalks necessarily qualify as a public forum. In *Greer v. Spock,* 424 U.S. 828 (1976), the Court held that the streets on a military base were not a public forum, and in *United States v. Kokinda,* 497 U.S. 720 (1990), the Court found that the sidewalk that provided access to a post office and was entirely on Postal Service property was not a public forum.

4.   Even in a public forum, the right to speak does not include the right to establish a permanent monument. In *Pleasant Grove City v. Summum,* 555 U.S. 1125 (2009), a group wanted to erect in a city park a permanent monument containing the Seven Aphorisms of Summum, to add to the eleven privately donated monuments, including a monument containing the Ten Commandments, that were already present. The city refused to allow the monument, and the Court unanimously upheld that decision, deciding that the city's allowance of a permanent monument in a public park was in its nature government speech, not private speech, so public forum principles were simply out of place.

HEFFRON V. INTERNATIONAL SOC. FOR KRISHNA CONSCIOUSNESS, INC.

United States Supreme Court, 1981.
452 U.S. 640, 101 S.Ct. 2559.

JUSTICE WHITE delivered the opinion of the Court.

The question presented for review is whether a State, consistent with the First and Fourteenth Amendments, may require a religious organization desiring to distribute and sell religious literature and to solicit donations at a state fair to conduct those activities only at an assigned location within the fairgrounds even though application of the rule limits the religious practices of the organization.

Each year, the Minnesota Agricultural Society (Society), a public corporation organized under the laws of Minnesota, operates a State Fair on a 125-acre state-owned tract located in St. Paul, Minn.... The Fair is a major public event and attracts visitors from all over Minnesota as well as from other parts of the country. During the past five years, the average total attendance for the 12-day

Minnesota State Fair
(Minnesota State Fair photograph courtesy of Tony Webster from Minneapolis, Minnesota.)

Fair has been 1,320,000 persons. The average daily attendance on weekdays has been 115,000 persons and on Saturdays and Sundays 160,000.

The Society is authorized to make all "bylaws, ordinances, and rules, not inconsistent with law, which it may deem necessary or proper for the government of the fairgrounds...." Under this authority, the Society promulgated Minnesota State Fair Rule 6.05 which provides in relevant part that: "[s]ale or distribution of any merchandise, including printed or written material except under license issued [by] the Society and/or from a duly-licensed location shall be a misdemeanor."

As Rule 6.05 is construed and applied by the Society, "all persons, groups or firms which desire to sell, exhibit or distribute materials during the annual State Fair must do so only from fixed locations on the fairgrounds." Although the Rule does not prevent organizational representatives from walking about the fairgrounds and communicating the organization's views with fair patrons in face-to-face discussions, it does require that any exhibitor conduct its sales, distribution, and fund solicitation operations from a booth rented from the Society. Space in the fairgrounds is rented to all comers in a nondiscriminatory fashion on a first-come, first-served basis with the rental charge based on the size and location of the booth. The Rule applies alike to nonprofit, charitable, and commercial enterprises.

One day prior to the opening of the 1977 Minnesota State Fair, respondents International Society for Krishna Consciousness, Inc. (ISKCON), an international religious society espousing the views of the Krishna religion, . . . filed suit against numerous state officials seeking a declaration that Rule 6.05, both on its face and as applied, violated respondents' rights under the First Amendment. . . . Specifically, ISKCON asserted that the Rule would suppress the practice of Sankirtan, one of its religious rituals, which enjoins its members to go into public places to distribute or sell religious literature and to solicit donations for the support of the Krishna religion.

[T]he State does not dispute that the oral and written dissemination of the Krishnas' religious views and doctrines is protected by the First Amendment. Nor does it claim that this protection is lost because the written materials sought to be distributed are sold rather than given away or because contributions or gifts are solicited in the course of propagating the faith. . . .

It is also common ground, however, that the First Amendment does not guarantee the right to communicate one's views at all times and places or in any manner that may be desired. [T]he activities of ISKCON, like those of others protected by the First Amendment, are subject to reasonable time, place, and manner restrictions. "We have often approved restrictions of that kind provided that they are justified without reference to the content of the regulated speech, that they serve a significant governmental interest, and that in doing so they leave open ample alternative channels for communication of the information." The issue here, as it was below, is whether Rule 6.05 is a permissible restriction on the place and manner of communicating the views of the Krishna religion, more specifically, whether the Society may require the members of ISKCON who desire to practice Sankirtan at the State Fair to confine their distribution, sales, and solicitation activities to a fixed location.

A major criterion for a valid time, place and manner restriction is that the restriction "may not be based upon either the content or subject matter of speech." Rule 6.05 qualifies in this respect, since . . . the Rule applies evenhandedly to all who wish to distribute and sell written materials or to solicit funds. No person or organization, whether commercial or charitable, is permitted to engage in such activities except from a booth rented for those purposes.

Nor does Rule 6.05 suffer from the more covert forms of discrimination that may result when arbitrary discretion is vested in some governmental authority. The method of allocating space is a straightforward first-come, first-served system. The Rule is not open to the kind of arbitrary application that this Court has condemned as inherently inconsistent with a valid time, place, and manner regulation because such discretion has the potential for becoming a means of suppressing a particular point of view.

A valid time, place, and manner regulation must also "serve a significant governmental interest." Here, the principal justification asserted by the State in support of Rule 6.05 is the need to maintain the orderly movement of the crowd given the large number of exhibitors and persons attending the Fair.[13]

The fairgrounds comprise a relatively small area of 125 acres, the bulk of which is covered by permanent buildings, temporary structures, parking lots, and connecting thoroughfares. There were some 1,400 exhibitors and concessionaires renting space for the 1977 and 1978 Fairs, chiefly in permanent and temporary buildings. The Fair is designed to exhibit to the public an enormous variety of goods, services, entertainment, and other matters of interest. This is accomplished by confining individual exhibitors to fixed locations, with the public moving to and among the booths or other attractions, using streets and open spaces provided for that purpose. Because the Fair attracts large crowds, it is apparent that the State's interest in the orderly movement and control of such an assembly of persons is a substantial consideration.

As a general matter, it is clear that a State's interest in protecting the "safety and convenience" of persons using a public forum is a valid governmental objective. Furthermore, consideration of a forum's special attributes is relevant to the constitutionality of a regulation since the significance of the governmental interest must be assessed in light of the characteristic nature and function of the particular forum involved. This observation bears particular import in the present case since respondents make a number of analogies between the fairgrounds and city streets which have "immemorially been held in trust for the use of the public and . . . have been used for purposes of assembly, communicating thoughts between citizens, and discussing public questions." But it is clear that there are significant differences between a street and the fairgrounds. A street is continually open, often uncongested, and constitutes not only a necessary conduit in the daily affairs of a locality's citizens, but also a place where people may enjoy the open air or the company of friends and neighbors in a relaxed environment. The Minnesota Fair, as described above, is a

---

[13] Petitioners assert two other state interests in support of the Rule. First, petitioners claim that the Rule forwards the State's valid interest in protecting its citizens from fraudulent solicitations, deceptive or false speech, and undue annoyance. Petitioners also forward the State's interest in protecting the fairgoers from being harassed or otherwise bothered, on the grounds that they are a captive audience. In light of our holding that the Rule is justified solely in terms of the State's interest in managing the flow of the crowd, we do not reach whether these other two purposes are constitutionally sufficient to support the imposition of the Rule.

temporary event attracting great numbers of visitors who come to the event for a short period to see and experience the host of exhibits and attractions at the Fair. The flow of the crowd and demands of safety are more pressing in the context of the Fair. As such, any comparisons to public streets are necessarily inexact.

[T]he justification for the Rule should not be measured by the disorder that would result from granting an exemption solely to ISKCON. That organization and its ritual of Sankirtan have no special claim to First Amendment protection as compared to that of other religions who also distribute literature and solicit funds. None of our cases suggest that the inclusion of peripatetic solicitation as part of a church ritual entitles church members to solicitation rights in a public forum superior to those of members of other religious groups that raise money but do not purport to ritualize the process. Nor for present purposes do religious organizations enjoy rights to communicate, distribute, and solicit on the fairgrounds superior to those of other organizations having social, political, or other ideological messages to proselytize. These nonreligious organizations seeking support for their activities are entitled to rights equal to those of religious groups to enter a public forum and spread their views, whether by soliciting funds or by distributing literature. . . .

Given these considerations, we hold that the State's interest in confining distribution, selling, and fund solicitation activities to fixed locations is sufficient to satisfy the requirement that a place or manner restriction must serve a substantial state interest. . . .

For similar reasons, we cannot agree with the Minnesota Supreme Court that Rule 6.05 is an unnecessary regulation because the State could avoid the threat to its interest posed by ISKCON by less restrictive means, such as penalizing disorder or disruption, limiting the number of solicitors, or putting more narrowly drawn restrictions on the location and movement of ISKCON's representatives. [T]he inquiry must involve not only ISKCON, but also all other organizations that would be entitled to distribute, sell, or solicit if the booth rule may not be enforced with respect to ISKCON. Looked at in this way, it is quite improbable that the alternative means suggested by the Minnesota Supreme Court would deal adequately with the problems posed by the much larger number of distributors and solicitors that would be present on the fairgrounds if the judgment below were affirmed.

For Rule 6.05 to be valid as a place and manner restriction, it must also be sufficiently clear that alternative forums for the expression of respondents' protected speech exist despite the effects of the Rule. Rule 6.05 is not vulnerable on this ground. First, the Rule does not prevent ISKCON from practicing Sankirtan anywhere outside the fairgrounds. More importantly, the Rule has not been shown to deny access within the forum in question. Here, the Rule does not exclude ISKCON from the fairgrounds, nor does it deny that organization the right to conduct any desired activity at some point within the forum. Its members may mingle with the crowd and orally propagate their views. The organization may also arrange for a booth and distribute and sell literature and solicit funds from that location on the fairgrounds itself. The Minnesota State Fair is a limited public forum in that it exists to provide a means for a great number of exhibitors temporarily to present their products or views, be they commercial, religious, or political, to a large number of people in an efficient fashion. Considering the limited functions of the Fair and the combined area within which it operates, we are unwilling to say that Rule 6.05 does not provide ISKCON and other organizations with an adequate means to sell and solicit on the fairgrounds. . . .

JUSTICE BRENNAN, with whom JUSTICE MARSHALL and JUSTICE STEVENS join, concurring in part and dissenting in part.

As the Court recognizes, the issue in this case is whether Minnesota State Fair Rule 6.05 constitutes a reasonable time, place, and manner restriction on respondents' exercise of protected First Amendment rights. In deciding this issue, the Court considers whether the regulation serves a significant governmental interest and whether that interest can be served by a less intrusive restriction. The Court errs, however, in failing to apply its analysis separately to each of the protected First Amendment activities restricted by Rule 6.05. Thus, the Court fails to recognize that some of the State's restrictions may be reasonable while others may not.

Rule 6.05 restricts three types of protected First Amendment activity: distribution of literature, sale of literature, and solicitation of funds. No individual or group is permitted to engage in these activities at the Minnesota State Fair except from preassigned, rented booth locations. . . .

The State advances three justifications for its booth Rule. The justification relied upon by the Court today is the State's interest in maintaining the orderly movement of the crowds at the fair. The second justification . . . is the State's interest in protecting its fairgoers from fraudulent, deceptive, and misleading solicitation practices. The third justification, based on the "captive audience" doctrine, is the State's interest in protecting its fairgoers from annoyance and harassment.

I quite agree with the Court that the State has a significant interest in maintaining crowd control on its fairgrounds. I also have no doubt that the State has a significant interest in protecting its fairgoers from fraudulent or deceptive solicitation practices. Indeed, because I believe on this record that this latter interest is substantially furthered by a Rule that restricts sales and solicitation activities to fixed booth locations, where the State will have the greatest opportunity to police and prevent possible deceptive practices, I would hold that Rule 6.05's restriction on those particular forms of First Amendment expression is justified as an antifraud measure. Accordingly, I join the judgment of the Court insofar as it upholds

Rule 6.05's restriction on sales and solicitations. However, because I believe that the booth Rule is an overly intrusive means of achieving the State's interest in crowd control, and because I cannot accept the validity of the State's third asserted justification, I dissent from the Court's approval of Rule 6.05's restriction on the distribution of literature.

[N]o restrictions are placed on any fairgoer's right to speak at any time, at any place, or to any person. Thus, if on a given day 5,000 members of ISKCON came to the fair and paid their admission fees, all 5,000 would be permitted to wander throughout the fairgrounds, delivering speeches to whomever they wanted, about whatever they wanted. Moreover, because this right does not rest on Sankirtan or any other religious principle, it can be exercised by every political candidate, partisan advocate, and common citizen who has paid the price of admission. All share the identical right to move peripatetically and speak freely throughout the fairgrounds.

Because of Rule 6.05, however, as soon as a proselytizing member of ISKCON hands out a free copy of the Bhagavad-Gita to an interested listener, or a political candidate distributes his campaign brochure to a potential voter, he becomes subject to arrest and removal from the fairgrounds. This constitutes a significant restriction on First Amendment rights. By prohibiting distribution of literature outside the booths, the fair officials sharply limit the number of fairgoers to whom the proselytizers and candidates can communicate their messages. Only if a fairgoer affirmatively seeks out such information by approaching a booth does Rule 6.05 fully permit potential communicators to exercise their First Amendment rights.

In support of the crowd control justification, petitioners contend that if fairgoers are permitted to distribute literature, large crowds will gather, blocking traffic lanes and causing safety problems. . . .

But petitioners have failed to provide any support for these assertions. They have made no showing that relaxation of the booth Rule would create additional disorder in a fair that is already characterized by the robust and unrestrained participation of hundreds of thousands of wandering fairgoers. If fairgoers can make speeches, engage in face-to-face proselytizing, and buttonhole prospective supporters, they can surely distribute literature to members of their audience without significantly adding to the State's asserted crowd control problem. The record is devoid of any evidence that the 125-acre fairgrounds could not accommodate peripatetic distributors of literature just as easily as it now accommodates peripatetic speechmakers and proselytizers.

Relying on a general, speculative fear of disorder, the State of Minnesota has placed a significant restriction on respondents' ability to exercise core First Amendment rights. This restriction is not narrowly drawn to advance the State's interests, and for that reason is unconstitutional. . . .

Because I believe that the State could have drafted a more narrowly drawn restriction on the right to distribute literature without undermining its interest in maintaining crowd control on the fairgrounds, I would affirm that part of the judgment below that strikes down Rule 6.05 as it applies to distribution of literature.

JUSTICE BLACKMUN, concurring in part and dissenting in part. [opinion omitted]

COMMENTS AND QUESTIONS

1.   This case is a good example of the Court's application of Time, Place, and Manner restrictions to a particular situation. First, it determines if the restriction is content neutral. If so, it then asks whether the restriction directly serves a "significant" public interest, *i.e.*, less than a compelling government interest, and, if so, if there are adequate alternative avenues for expression. Courts and commentators have analogized the test for Time, Place, and Manner restrictions and the *O'Brien* test applied to expressive conduct, *see, e.g., Clark v. Community for Creative Non-Violence*, 468 U.S. 288 (1984)(prohibition on sleeping in the parks in the District of Columbia upheld as a valid Time, Place, and Manner restriction with respect to a demonstration regarding homelessness in the nation's capital that desired to have the homeless sleep in tents across the street from the White House). Inasmuch as both look to see whether the restriction is intended to limit expression, directly furthers a significant government interest, and leaves open other alternative means of expression, they are quite similar.

2.   In *Heffron*, Justice Brennan's dissent applies the same test as the majority, but it applies it a bit more strictly, finding the restriction on handing out literature not narrowly enough tailored to serve the legitimate government interests. Just as the *O'Brien* test is relatively lax after determining that the purpose of the law is not to restrict expression, the Time, Place, and Manner test is usually relatively lax after determining that the restriction is content neutral. For instance, in the *Clark v. Community for Creative Non-Violence* case in the previous note, the claim was that the restriction on sleeping was not necessary and did not further the government's interest in preserving the parks for the enjoyment of all when the Park Service granted the permit to erect tents in the park and allowed people to be in the tents for a 24-hour period, but prohibited them from sleeping in the tents. They could pretend to be asleep, but they could not actually sleep. The distinction sounds silly when phrased that way, but the Court with only two dissenters found the restriction reasonable, saying it was not for judges to decide "how much protection of park lands is wise and how that level of conservation is to be attained." In other words, while both the *O'Brien* test and the Time, Place, and Manner test implicitly have some sort of narrow tailoring requirement, in practice that requirement is ordinarily not given full effect.

3.   The state claimed that one of the purposes for requiring booths and not to allow solicitation at large in the fair was a concern for the fair patrons

being a "captive audience." While the Court did not reach this issue in this case, it has recognized that First Amendment protections do not always embrace "offensive speech that is so intrusive that the unwilling audience cannot avoid it." *Hill v. Colorado*, 530 U.S. 703, 716 (2000). For example, in *Hill*, the Court upheld restrictions on demonstrations within 100 feet of a health care facility (*e.g.*, abortion provider), noting that persons seeking an abortion could not avoid the unwanted communication and confrontation that might result in potential psychological trauma. In *Frisby v. Schultz*, 487 U.S. 474 (1988), the Court upheld a restriction on demonstrations targeted at a particular personal residence, because the person residing in the home was "a captive[,] figuratively, and perhaps literally, trapped within the home." An exception that perhaps proves the rule occurred in *McCullen v. Coakley*, 573 U.S. 464 (2014). There, a Massachusetts law made it a crime to knowingly be on a public way or sidewalk within 35 feet of an entrance or driveway to any facility during business hours where abortions were performed, other than a hospital, with exceptions for persons entering or leaving such facility, employees of such facility acting within the scope of their employment, law enforcement, ambulance, firefighting, construction, utilities, public works and other municipal agents acting within the scope of their employment, persons using the public sidewalk or street right-of-way adjacent to such facility solely for the purpose of reaching a destination other than such facility. This restricted abortion protesters outside of abortion clinics, but it also restricted those who wanted not to protest against abortions but to communicate personally with those seeking abortions about alternatives and help in pursuing those alternatives. The Court found the law to be a content-neutral time, place, and manner restriction in a public forum, but concluded that the restriction was not narrowly tailored, because it "burden[ed] substantially more speech than is necessary to further the government's legitimate interests." The law already prohibited deliberate obstruction of entrances to the facilities, and Massachusetts could pass a law making it a crime to obstruct, intimidate, or interfere with persons seeking abortion services. While the Court's judgment was unanimous, four justices concurred only in the result. Justice Scalia, writing for himself and Justices Kennedy and Thomas, disagreed that the law was content neutral, believing that a blanket prohibition on the use of streets and sidewalks where speech on only one politically controversial topic is likely to occur—and where that speech can most effectively be communicated—is content based notwithstanding its facial neutrality. Justice Alito went further, believing the law to be viewpoint based, inasmuch as it allowed employees of the clinic in the area, where they could speak in favor of abortion.

4.   In *Heffron*, the Court assumes that the state fair is a public forum, but different types of public property might be treated differently.

PERRY EDUCATION ASSN. v. PERRY LOCAL EDUCATORS' ASSN.

United States Supreme Court, 1983.
460 U.S. 37, 103 S.Ct. 948.

JUSTICE WHITE delivered the opinion of the Court.

Perry Education Association is the duly elected exclusive bargaining representative for the teachers of the Metropolitan School District of Perry Township, Ind. A collective-bargaining agreement with the Board of Education provided that Perry Education Association, but no other union, would have access to the interschool mail system and teacher mailboxes in the Perry Township schools. The issue in this case is whether the denial of similar access to the Perry Local Educators' Association, a rival teacher group, violates the First and Fourteenth Amendments.

The Metropolitan School District of Perry Township, Ind., operates a public school system of 13 separate schools. Each school building contains a set of mailboxes for the teachers. Interschool delivery by school employees permits messages to be delivered rapidly to teachers in the district. The primary function of this internal mail system is to transmit official messages among the teachers and between the teachers and the school administration. In addition, teachers use the system to send personal messages and individual school building principals have allowed delivery of messages from various private organizations.[2]

[P]LEA and two of its members filed this action . . . against PEA and individual members of the Perry Township School Board. Plaintiffs contended that PEA's preferential access to the internal mail system violates the First Amendment and the Equal Protection Clause of the Fourteenth Amendment. . . .

The primary question presented is whether the First Amendment, applicable to the states by virtue of the Fourteenth Amendment, is violated when a union that has been elected by public school teachers as their exclusive bargaining representative is granted access to certain means of communication, while such access is denied to a rival union. There is no question that constitutional interests are implicated by denying PLEA use of the interschool mail system. . . .

In places which by long tradition or by government fiat have been devoted to assembly and debate, the rights of the state to limit expressive activity are sharply circumscribed. At one end of the spectrum are streets and parks which "have immemorially been held in trust for the use of the public, and, time out of mind, have been used for purposes of assembly,

---

[2] Local parochial schools, church groups, YMCAs, and Cub Scout units have used the system. The record does not indicate whether any requests for use have been denied, nor does it reveal whether permission must separately be sought for every message that a group wishes delivered to the teachers.

communicating thoughts between citizens, and discussing public questions." *Hague v. CIO.* In these quintessential public forums, the government may not prohibit all communicative activity. For the state to enforce a content-based exclusion it must show that its regulation is necessary to serve a compelling state interest and that it is narrowly drawn to achieve that end. The state may also enforce regulations of the time, place, and manner of expression which are content-neutral, are narrowly tailored to serve a significant government interest, and leave open ample alternative channels of communication.

A second category consists of public property which the state has opened for use by the public as a place for expressive activity. The Constitution forbids a state to enforce certain exclusions from a forum generally open to the public even if it was not required to create the forum in the first place. *Widmar v. Vincent,* 454 U.S. 263 (1981)(university meeting facilities); *City of Madison Joint School District v. Wisconsin Public Employment Relations Comm'n,* 429 U.S. 167 (1976)(school board meeting); *Southeastern Promotions, Ltd. v. Conrad,* 420 U.S. 546 (1975)(municipal theater).[7] Although a state is not required to indefinitely retain the open character of the facility, as long as it does so it is bound by the same standards as apply in a traditional public forum. Reasonable time, place and manner regulations are permissible, and a content-based prohibition must be narrowly drawn to effectuate a compelling state interest.

Public property which is not by tradition or designation a forum for public communication is governed by different standards. We have recognized that the "First Amendment does not guarantee access to property simply because it is owned or controlled by the government." In addition to time, place, and manner regulations, the state may reserve the forum for its intended purposes, communicative or otherwise, as long as the regulation on speech is reasonable and not an effort to suppress expression merely because public officials oppose the speaker's view. As we have stated on several occasions, "the State, no less than a private owner of property, has power to preserve the property under its control for the use to which it is lawfully dedicated."

The school mail facilities at issue here fall within this third category. The Court of Appeals recognized that Perry School District's interschool mail system is not a traditional public forum. . . . On this point the parties agree. Nor do the parties dispute that . . . the "normal and intended function [of the school mail facilities] is to facilitate internal communication of school related matters to teachers." The internal mail system, at least by policy, is not held open to the general public. It is instead

---

[7]   A public forum may be created for a limited purpose such as use by certain groups, *e.g.,* *Widmar v. Vincent* (student groups), or for the discussion of certain subjects, *e.g., City of Madison Joint School District v. Wisconsin Public Employment Relations Comm'n* (school board business).

PLEA's position that the school mail facilities have become a "limited public forum" from which it may not be excluded because of the periodic use of the system by private non-school connected groups, and PLEA's own unrestricted access to the system prior to PEA's certification as exclusive representative.

Neither of these arguments is persuasive. The use of the internal school mail by groups not affiliated with the schools is no doubt a relevant consideration. If by policy or by practice the Perry School District has opened its mail system for indiscriminate use by the general public, then PLEA could justifiably argue a public forum has been created. This, however, is not the case. As the case comes before us, there is no indication in the record that the school mailboxes and interschool delivery system are open for use by the general public. Permission to use the system to communicate with teachers must be secured from the individual building principal. There is no court finding or evidence in the record which demonstrates that this permission has been granted as a matter of course to all who seek to distribute material. We can only conclude that the schools do allow some outside organizations such as the YMCA, Cub Scouts, and other civic and church organizations to use the facilities. This type of selective access does not transform government property into a public forum. . . .

Moreover, even if we assume that by granting access to the Cub Scouts, YMCAs, and parochial schools, the school district has created a "limited" public forum, the constitutional right of access would in any event extend only to other entities of similar character. While the school mail facilities thus might be a forum generally open for use by the Girl Scouts, the local boys' club and other organizations that engage in activities of interest and educational relevance to students, they would not as a consequence be open to an organization such as PLEA, which is concerned with the terms and conditions of teacher employment. . . .

Because the school mail system is not a public forum, the School District had no "constitutional obligation per se to let any organization use the school mail boxes." In the Court of Appeals' view, however, the access policy adopted by the Perry schools favors a particular viewpoint, that of the PEA, on labor relations, and consequently must be strictly scrutinized regardless of whether a public forum is involved. There is, however, no indication that the school board intended to discourage one viewpoint and advance another. We believe it is more accurate to characterize the access policy as based on the *status* of the respective unions rather than their views. Implicit in the concept of the nonpublic forum is the right to make distinctions in access on the basis of subject matter and speaker identity. These distinctions may be impermissible in a public forum but are inherent and inescapable in the process of limiting a nonpublic forum to activities compatible with the intended purpose of the property. The touchstone for evaluating these distinctions is whether they are reasonable in light of the purpose which the forum at issue serves.

The differential access provided PEA and PLEA is reasonable because it is wholly consistent with the district's legitimate interest in "preserv[ing] the property . . . for the use to which it is lawfully dedicated." Use of school mail facilities enables PEA to perform effectively its obligations as exclusive representative of *all* Perry Township teachers. Conversely, PLEA does not have any official responsibility in connection with the school district and need not be entitled to the same rights of access to school mailboxes. . . .

Finally, the reasonableness of the limitations on PLEA's access to the school mail system is also supported by the substantial alternative channels that remain open for union-teacher communication to take place. These means range from bulletin boards to meeting facilities to the United States mail. During election periods, PLEA is assured of equal access to all modes of communication. There is no showing here that PLEA's ability to communicate with teachers is seriously impinged by the restricted access to the internal mail system. The variety and type of alternative modes of access present here compare favorably with those in other non-public forum cases where we have upheld restrictions on access. . . .

JUSTICE BRENNAN, with whom JUSTICE MARSHALL, JUSTICE POWELL, and JUSTICE STEVENS join, dissenting.

The Court today holds that an incumbent teachers' union may negotiate a collective bargaining agreement with a school board that grants the incumbent access to teachers' mailboxes and to the interschool mail system and denies such access to a rival union. Because the exclusive access provision in the collective bargaining agreement amounts to viewpoint discrimination that infringes the respondents' First Amendment rights and fails to advance any substantial state interest, I dissent.

The Court properly acknowledges that teachers have protected First Amendment rights within the school context. . . .

[B]ased on a finding that the interschool mail system is not a "public forum," the Court states that the respondents have no right of access to the system, and that the school board is free "to make distinctions in access on the basis of subject matter and speaker identity," if the distinctions are "reasonable in light of the purpose which the forum at issue serves." According to the Court, the petitioner's status as the exclusive bargaining representative provides a reasonable basis for the exclusive access policy.

[I]n focusing on the public forum issue, the Court disregards the First Amendment's central proscription against censorship, in the form of viewpoint discrimination, in any forum, public or nonpublic.

The First Amendment's prohibition against government discrimination among viewpoints on particular issues falling within the realm of protected speech has been noted extensively in the opinions of this Court. . . .

There is another line of cases, closely related to those implicating the prohibition against viewpoint discrimination, that have addressed the First Amendment principle of subject matter, or content, neutrality. Generally, the concept of content neutrality prohibits the government from choosing the subjects that are appropriate for public discussion. . . .

We have invoked the prohibition against content discrimination to invalidate government restrictions on access to public forums. We also have relied on this prohibition to strike down restrictions on access to a limited public forum. Finally, we have applied the doctrine of content neutrality to government regulation of protected speech in cases in which no restriction of access to public property was involved.

Admittedly, this Court has not always required content neutrality in restrictions on access to government property. . . . These cases provide some support for the notion that the government is permitted to exclude certain subjects from discussion in nonpublic forums. They provide no support, however, for the notion that government, once it has opened up government property for discussion of specific subjects, may discriminate among viewpoints on those topics.

Once the government permits discussion of certain subject matter, it may not impose restrictions that discriminate among viewpoints on those subjects whether a nonpublic forum is involved or not.

Against this background, it is clear that the Court's approach to this case is flawed. By focusing on whether the interschool mail system is a public forum, the Court disregards the independent First Amendment protection afforded by the prohibition against viewpoint discrimination. This case does not involve a claim of an absolute right of access to the forum to discuss any subject whatever. If it did, public forum analysis might be relevant. This case involves a claim of equal access to discuss a subject that the board has approved for discussion in the forum. In essence, the respondents are not asserting a right of access at all; they are asserting a right to be free from discrimination. The critical inquiry, therefore, is whether the board's grant of exclusive access to the petitioner amounts to prohibited viewpoint discrimination.

[T]he Court responds to the allegation of viewpoint discrimination by suggesting that there is no indication that the board intended to discriminate and that the exclusive access policy is based on the parties' status rather than on their views. In this case, . . . the intent to discriminate can be inferred from the effect of the policy, which is to deny an effective channel of communication to the respondents, and from other facts in the case. . . .

Addressing the question of viewpoint discrimination directly, free of the Court's irrelevant public forum analysis, it is clear that the exclusive access policy discriminates on the basis of viewpoint. The Court of Appeals found that "the access policy adopted by the Perry schools, in form a speaker restriction, favors a particular viewpoint on labor relations in the Perry schools . . .: the teachers inevitably will receive from [the petitioner] self-laudatory descriptions of its activities on their behalf and will be denied the critical perspective offered by [the respondents]." This assessment of the effect of the policy is eminently reasonable. Moreover, certain other factors strongly suggest that the policy discriminates among viewpoints.

On a practical level, the only reason for the petitioner to seek an exclusive access policy is to deny its rivals access to an effective channel of communication. No other group is explicitly denied access to the mail system. In fact, as the Court points out, many other groups have been granted access to the system. Apparently, access is denied to the respondents because of the likelihood of their expressing points of view different from the petitioner's on a range of subjects. The very argument the petitioner advances in support of the policy, the need to preserve labor peace, also indicates that the access policy is not viewpoint-neutral.

In short, the exclusive access policy discriminates against the respondents based on their viewpoint. The board has agreed to amplify the speech of the petitioner, while repressing the speech of the respondents based on the respondents' point of view. This sort of discrimination amounts to censorship and infringes the First Amendment rights of the respondents. In this light, the policy can survive only if the petitioner can justify it. [Justice Brennan then applied strict scrutiny and concluded that the exclusion of PEA did not further a compelling government interest.]

COMMENTS AND QUESTIONS

1.   *Perry* distinguishes between three different sorts of public spaces: the traditional public forum, the designated (sometimes called "limited") public forum, and the non-public (confusingly also sometimes called "limited") forum. The rules governing the traditional public forum are set by the Time, Place, and Manner test. The designated public forum, once designated, is governed by the same rules and test, with one major caveat reflected in the Court's footnote 7: in designating the space as a public forum, the government may decide the identity of those for whom the space is designated as a forum or the subject matter for which the space is designated as a forum. How else was it that the Court decided that the PLEA was not a similar entity to the YMCA, Cub Scouts, and other civic and church organizations? Although the Court's initial conclusion was that the mailboxes were a non-public forum, it went on

to say that, even if the mailboxes constituted a limited public forum, PLEA's exclusion was constitutional. In a non-public forum, reasonable government regulations are constitutional if they are viewpoint neutral.

2. The Court holds that the denial of access to PLEA is not viewpoint discrimination. The dissent believes it is. Or is it content discrimination (which is permissible in non-public forums)? It might be said that distinguishing between the communication of a union with respect to its members' employment in the school and the communication of a union to non-members that it wishes to have as members is a difference in content, not in viewpoint. What do you think?

3. Usually, distinguishing between content discrimination and viewpoint discrimination is simple. A ban on political advertising on city buses is content discrimination. The ban treats all political viewpoints equally. Were it to ban Republican or Democratic ads, it would be viewpoint discrimination. However, cases do not always provide simple problems, as the *Perry* case demonstrates. In *Christian Legal Society Chapter of the University of California, Hastings College of the Law v. Martinez*, 561 U.S. 661 (2010), Hastings Law School required all student groups wishing to receive school support to abide by the school's anti-discrimination policy, meaning that students could not be excluded from a group because of the student's beliefs or sexual orientation. The Christian Legal Society objected to this requirement, because it was inconsistent with its bylaws, requiring members to profess faith in Jesus Christ and to abjure homosexual activity. The Court found that the school's student group program was a "limited public forum," by which it meant a non-public forum, so that regulations that were reasonable and not viewpoint discriminatory were permissible. By a 5–4 vote the Court held that the anti-discrimination policy's application to the student groups was not viewpoint discrimination. Because the anti-discrimination policy applied equally to all groups without respect to any group's viewpoint, the majority found the policy viewpoint neutral. To the dissent, however, the anti-discrimination policy itself discriminated on the basis of viewpoint by denying student group status to those whose beliefs required adherence to the idea that homosexuality is sinful and that Jesus Christ is the savior. Who do you think was right?

4. The difficulty in distinguishing between the different types of forums is further illustrated in the next case.

INTERNATIONAL SOCIETY FOR KRISHNA CONSCIOUSNESS, INC. [ISKCON] v. LEE

United States Supreme Court, 1992.
505 U.S. 672, 112 S.Ct. 2701.

LEE v. ISKCON

United States Supreme Court, 1992.
505 U.S. 830, 112 S.Ct. 2709.

[These two cases arose out of attempts by ISKCON to perform its ritual known as *sankirtan*, consisting of going into public places, disseminating religious literature and soliciting funds to support the religion, in the airport terminals operated by the Port Authority of New York and New Jersey, a government entity. The Port Authority had adopted a regulation forbidding the solicitation of money or distribution of literature within the terminals. The court below had upheld the regulation with respect to the solicitation of money but had found the ban on distribution of literature unconstitutional under the First Amendment. Both sides sought and were granted certiorari. The Supreme Court in *ISKCON v. Lee* affirmed the court below and upheld the ban on solicitation, but in *Lee v. ISKCON* the Court, without a majority opinion, also affirmed the court below and struck down the ban on the distribution of literature.]

CHIEF JUSTICE REHNQUIST delivered the opinion of the Court [in *ISKCON v. Lee*].

In this case we consider whether an airport terminal operated by a public authority is a public forum and whether a regulation prohibiting solicitation in the interior of an airport terminal violates the First Amendment. . . .

The Port Authority owns and operates three major airports in the greater New York City area: John F. Kennedy International Airport (Kennedy), La Guardia Airport (La Guardia), and Newark International Airport (Newark). . . .

The terminals are generally accessible to the general public and contain various commercial establishments such as restaurants, snack stands, bars, newsstands, and stores of various types. Virtually all who visit the terminals do so for purposes related to air travel. These visitors principally include passengers, those meeting or seeing off passengers, flight crews, and terminal employees.

The Port Authority has adopted a regulation forbidding within the terminals the repetitive solicitation of money or distribution of literature. . . .

The regulation governs only the terminals; the Port Authority permits solicitation and distribution on the sidewalks outside the terminal buildings. The regulation effectively prohibits ISKCON from performing *sankirtan* in the terminals. As a result, ISKCON brought suit seeking declaratory and injunctive relief under 42 U.S.C. § 1983, alleging that the regulation worked to deprive its members of rights guaranteed under the First Amendment. . . .[3]

It is uncontested that the solicitation at issue in this case is a form of speech protected under the First Amendment. But it is also well settled that the government need not permit all forms of speech on property that it owns and controls. Where the government is acting as a proprietor, managing its internal operations, rather than acting as lawmaker with the power to regulate or license, its action will not be subjected to the heightened review to which its actions as a lawmaker may be subject. Thus, we have upheld a ban on political advertisements in city-operated transit vehicles, *Lehman v. Shaker Heights,* 418 U.S. 298 (1974), even though the city permitted other types of advertising on those vehicles. Similarly, we have permitted a school district to limit access to an internal mail system used to communicate with teachers employed by the district. *Perry Ed. Assn. v. Perry Local Educators' Assn.*

These cases reflect, either implicitly or explicitly, a "forum based" approach for assessing restrictions that the government seeks to place on the use of its property. Under this approach, regulation of speech on government property that has traditionally been available for public expression is subject to the highest scrutiny. Such regulations survive only if they are narrowly drawn to achieve a compelling state interest. The second category of public property is the designated public forum, whether of a limited or unlimited character—property that the State has opened for expressive activity by part or all of the public. Regulation of such property is subject to the same limitations as that governing a traditional public forum. Finally, there is all remaining public property. Limitations on expressive activity conducted on this last category of property must survive only a much more limited review. The challenged regulation need only be reasonable, as long as the regulation is not an effort to suppress the speaker's activity due to disagreement with the speaker's view.

The parties do not disagree that this is the proper framework. Rather, they disagree whether the airport terminals are public fora or nonpublic fora. They also disagree whether the regulation survives the "reasonableness" review governing nonpublic fora, should that prove the appropriate category. [W]e conclude that the terminals are nonpublic fora and that the regulation reasonably limits solicitation.

[O]ur recent cases provide additional guidance on the characteristics of a public forum. [We have] noted that a traditional public forum is property that has as "a principal purpose . . . the free exchange of ideas."

---

[3] We deal here only with petitioners' claim regarding the permissibility of solicitation. Respondent's cross-petition concerning the leafletting ban is disposed of in the companion case, *Lee v. International Society for Krishna Consciousness, Inc.*

Moreover, consistent with the notion that the government—like other property owners—"has power to preserve the property under its control for the use to which it is lawfully dedicated," the government does not create a public forum by inaction. Nor is a public forum created "whenever members of the public are permitted freely to visit a place owned or operated by the Government." The decision to create a public forum must instead be made "by intentionally opening a nontraditional forum for public discourse." Finally, we have recognized that the location of property also has bearing because separation from acknowledged public areas may serve to indicate that the separated property is a special enclave, subject to greater restriction.

These precedents foreclose the conclusion that airport terminals are public fora. Reflecting the general growth of the air travel industry, airport terminals have only recently achieved their contemporary size and character. But given the lateness with which the modern air terminal has made its appearance, it hardly qualifies for the description of having "immemorially . . . time out of mind" been held in the public trust and used for purposes of expressive activity. Moreover, even within the rather short history of air transport, it is only "[i]n recent years [that] it has become a common practice for various religious and non-profit organizations to use commercial airports as a forum for the distribution of literature, the solicitation of funds, the proselytizing of new members, and other similar activities." Thus, the tradition of airport activity does not demonstrate that airports have historically been made available for speech activity. . . . In short, there can be no argument that society's time-tested judgment, expressed through acquiescence in a continuing practice, has resolved the issue in petitioners' favor. . . .

[A]irports are commercial establishments funded by users fees and designed to make a regulated profit, and where nearly all who visit do so for some travel related purpose. As commercial enterprises, airports must provide services attractive to the marketplace. In light of this, it cannot fairly be said that an airport terminal has as a principal purpose promoting "the free exchange of ideas." To the contrary, the record demonstrates that Port Authority management considers the purpose of the terminals to be the facilitation of passenger air travel, not the promotion of expression. . . .

[A]lthough many airports have expanded their function beyond merely contributing to efficient air travel, few have included among their purposes the designation of a forum for solicitation and distribution activities. Thus, we think that neither by tradition nor purpose can the terminals be described as satisfying the standards we have previously set out for identifying a public forum.

The restrictions here challenged, therefore, need only satisfy a requirement of reasonableness. The restriction " 'need only be *reasonable;* it need not be the most reasonable or the only reasonable limitation.' " We have no doubt that under this standard the prohibition on solicitation passes muster.

We have on many prior occasions noted the disruptive effect that solicitation may have on business. "Solicitation requires action by those who would respond: The individual solicited must decide whether or not to contribute (which itself might involve reading the solicitor's literature or hearing his pitch), and then, having decided to do so, reach for a wallet, search it for money, write a check, or produce a credit card." Passengers who wish to avoid the solicitor may have to alter their paths, slowing both themselves and those around them. The result is that the normal flow of traffic is impeded. This is especially so in an airport, where "[a]ir travelers, who are often weighted down by cumbersome baggage . . . may be hurrying to catch a plane or to arrange ground transportation." Delays may be particularly costly in this setting, as a flight missed by only a few minutes can result in hours worth of subsequent inconvenience.

In addition, face-to-face solicitation presents risks of duress that are an appropriate target of regulation. The skillful, and unprincipled, solicitor can target the most vulnerable, including those accompanying children or those suffering physical impairment and who cannot easily avoid the solicitation. The unsavory solicitor can also commit fraud through concealment of his affiliation or through deliberate efforts to shortchange those who agree to purchase. Compounding this problem is the fact that, in an airport, the targets of such activity frequently are on tight schedules. This in turn makes such visitors unlikely to stop and formally complain to airport authorities. As a result, the airport faces considerable difficulty in achieving its legitimate interest in monitoring solicitation activity to assure that travelers are not interfered with unduly.

The Port Authority has concluded that its interest in monitoring the activities can best be accomplished by limiting solicitation and distribution to the sidewalk areas outside the terminals. This sidewalk area is frequented by an overwhelming percentage of airport users. Thus the resulting access of those who would solicit the general public is quite complete. In turn we think it would be odd to conclude that the Port Authority's terminal regulation is unreasonable despite the Port Authority having otherwise assured access to an area universally traveled.

The inconveniences to passengers and the burdens on Port Authority officials flowing from solicitation activity may seem small, but viewed against the fact that "pedestrian congestion is one of the greatest problems facing the three terminals," the Port Authority could reasonably worry that even such incremental effects would prove quite disruptive. . . . As a result, we conclude that the solicitation ban is reasonable.

JUSTICE O'CONNOR, concurring in *ISKCON v. Lee* and concurring in the judgment in *Lee v. ISKCON*.

In the decision below, the Court of Appeals upheld a ban on solicitation of funds within the airport terminals operated by the Port Authority of New York and New Jersey, but struck down a ban on the repetitive distribution of printed or written material within the terminals. I would affirm both parts of that judgment.

I concur in the Court's opinion in [*ISKCON v. Lee*] and agree that publicly owned airports are not public fora. . . .

For these reasons, the Port Authority's restrictions on solicitation and leafletting within the airport terminals do not qualify for the strict scrutiny that applies to restriction of speech in public fora. That airports are not public fora, however, does not mean that the government can restrict speech in whatever way it likes. [We] have consistently stated that restrictions on speech in nonpublic fora are valid only if they are "reasonable" and "not an effort to suppress expression merely because public officials oppose the speaker's view." The determination that airports are not public fora thus only begins our inquiry.

"The reasonableness of the Government's restriction [on speech in a nonpublic forum] must be assessed in light of the purpose of the forum and all the surrounding circumstances." " '[C]onsideration of a forum's special attributes is relevant to the constitutionality of a regulation since the significance of the governmental interest must be assessed in light of the characteristic nature and function of the particular forum involved.' " In this case, the "special attributes" and "surrounding circumstances" of the airports operated by the Port Authority are determinative. Not only has the Port Authority chosen *not* to limit access to the airports under its control, it has created a huge complex open to travelers and nontravelers alike. The airports house restaurants, cafeterias, snack bars, coffee shops, cocktail lounges, post offices, banks, telegraph offices, clothing shops, drug stores, food stores, nurseries, barber shops, currency exchanges, art exhibits, commercial advertising displays, bookstores, newsstands, dental offices, and private clubs. . . .

We have said that a restriction on speech in a nonpublic forum is "reasonable" when it is "consistent with the [government's] legitimate interest in 'preserv[ing] the property . . . for the use to which it is lawfully dedicated.' " Ordinarily, this inquiry is relatively straightforward, because we have almost always been confronted with cases where the fora at issue were discrete, single-purpose facilities. The Port Authority urges that this case is no different and contends that it, too, has dedicated its airports to a single purpose—facilitating air travel—and that the speech it seeks to prohibit is not consistent with that purpose. But the wide range of activities promoted by the Port Authority is no more directly related to facilitating air travel than are the types of activities in which the International Society for Krishna Consciousness, Inc. (ISKCON), wishes to engage. In my view, the Port Authority is operating a shopping mall as well as an airport. The reasonableness inquiry, therefore, is not whether the restrictions on speech are "consistent with . . . preserving the property" for air travel, but whether they are reasonably related to maintaining the multipurpose environment that the Port Authority has deliberately created.

Applying that standard, I agree with the Court in [*ISKCON v. Lee*] that the ban on solicitation is reasonable. Face-to-face solicitation is incompatible with the airport's functioning in a way that the other, permitted activities are not. We have previously observed that "[s]olicitation impedes the normal flow of traffic [because it] requires action by those who would respond: The individual solicited must decide whether or not to contribute (which itself might involve reading the solicitor's literature or hearing his pitch), and then, having decided to do so, reach for a wallet, search it for money, write a check, or produce a credit card. . . . As residents of metropolitan areas know from daily experience, confrontation by a person asking for money disrupts passage and is more intrusive and intimidating than an encounter with a person giving out information.". . .

In my view, however, the regulation banning leafletting . . . cannot be upheld as reasonable on this record. I therefore concur in the judgment in *Lee v. ISKCON* striking down that prohibition. While the difficulties posed by solicitation in a nonpublic forum are sufficiently obvious that its regulation may "rin[g] of common-sense," the same is not necessarily true of leafletting. To the contrary, we have expressly noted that leafletting does not entail the same kinds of problems presented by face-to-face solicitation. Specifically, "[o]ne need not ponder the contents of a leaflet or pamphlet in order mechanically to take it out of someone's hand. . . . 'The distribution of literature does not require that the recipient stop in order to receive the message the speaker wishes to convey; instead the recipient is free to read the message at a later time.' " With the possible exception of avoiding litter, it is difficult to point to any problems intrinsic to the act of leafletting that would make it naturally incompatible with a large, multipurpose forum such as those at issue here. . . .

Of course, it is still open for the Port Authority to promulgate regulations of the time, place, and manner of leafletting which are "content-neutral, are narrowly tailored to serve a significant government interest, and leave open ample alternative channels of communication." For example, during the many years that this litigation has been in progress, the Port Authority has not banned *sankirtan* completely from JFK International Airport, but has restricted it to a relatively uncongested part of the airport terminals, the same part that houses the airport chapel. In my view, that regulation meets the standards we have applied to time, place, and manner restrictions of protected expression.

JUSTICE KENNEDY, with whom JUSTICE BLACKMUN, JUSTICE STEVENS, and JUSTICE SOUTER join as to Part I, concurring in the judgments.

While I concur in the judgments affirming in these cases, my analysis differs in substantial respects from that of the Court. In my view the airport corridors and shopping areas outside of the passenger security zones, areas operated by the Port Authority, are public forums, and speech in those places is entitled to protection against all government regulation inconsistent with public forum principles. The Port Authority's blanket prohibition on the distribution or sale of literature cannot meet those stringent standards, and I agree it is invalid under the First and Fourteenth Amendments. The Port Authority's rule disallowing in-person solicitation of money for immediate payment, however, is in my view a narrow and valid regulation of the time, place, and manner of protected speech in this forum, or else is a valid regulation of the nonspeech element of expressive conduct. I would sustain the Port Authority's ban on solicitation and receipt of funds.

I

An earlier opinion expressed my concern that "[i]f our public forum jurisprudence is to retain vitality, we must recognize that certain objective characteristics of Government property and its customary use by the public may control" the status of the property. These cases before us do not heed that principle. Our public forum doctrine ought not to be a jurisprudence of categories rather than ideas or convert what was once an analysis protective of expression into one which grants the government authority to restrict speech by fiat. I believe that the Court's public forum analysis in these cases is inconsistent with the values underlying the Speech and Press Clauses of the First Amendment. . . .

The Court today holds that traditional public forums are limited to public property which have as " 'a principal purpose . . . the free exchange of ideas,' "; and that this purpose must be evidenced by a long-standing historical practice of permitting speech. The Court also holds that designated forums consist of property which the government intends to open for public discourse. All other types of property are, in the Court's view, nonpublic forums (in other words, not public forums), and government-imposed restrictions of speech in these places will be upheld so long as reasonable and viewpoint neutral. Under this categorical view the application of public forum analysis to airport terminals seems easy. Airports are of course public spaces of recent vintage, and so there can be no time-honored tradition associated with airports of permitting free speech. And because governments have often attempted to restrict speech within airports, it follows *a fortiori* under the Court's analysis that they cannot be so-called "designated" forums. So, the Court concludes, airports must be nonpublic forums, subject to minimal First Amendment protection.

This analysis is flawed at its very beginning. . . . The Court's error lies in its conclusion that the public forum status of public property depends on the government's defined purpose for the property, or on an explicit decision by the government to dedicate the property to expressive activity. In my view, the inquiry must be an objective one, based on the actual, physical characteristics and uses of the property. . . .

The First Amendment is a limitation on government, not a grant of power. Its design is to prevent the government from controlling speech. Yet under the Court's view the authority of the government to control speech on its property is paramount, for in almost all cases the critical step in the Court's analysis is a classification of the property that turns on the government's own definition or decision, unconstrained by an independent duty to respect the speech its citizens can voice there. The Court acknowledges as much, by reintroducing today into our First Amendment law a strict doctrinal line between the proprietary and regulatory functions of government which I thought had been abandoned long ago.

The Court's approach is contrary to the underlying purposes of the public forum doctrine. . . . Public places are of necessity the locus for discussion of public issues, as well as protest against arbitrary government action. At the heart of our jurisprudence lies the principle that in a free nation citizens must have the right to gather and speak with other persons in public places. The recognition that certain government-owned property is a public forum provides open notice to citizens that their freedoms may be exercised there without fear of a censorial government, adding tangible reinforcement to the idea that we are a free people.

A fundamental tenet of our Constitution is that the government is subject to constraints which private persons are not. The public forum doctrine vindicates that principle by recognizing limits on the government's control over speech activities on property suitable for free expression. The doctrine focuses on the physical characteristics of the property because government ownership is the source of its purported authority to regulate speech. . . .

The Court's analysis rests on an inaccurate view of history. The notion that traditional public forums are properties that have public discourse as their principal purpose is a most doubtful fiction. The types of property that we have recognized as the quintessential public forums are streets, parks, and sidewalks. It would seem apparent that the principal purpose of streets and sidewalks, like airports, is to facilitate transportation, not public discourse, and we have recognized as much. Similarly, the purpose for the creation of public parks may be as much for beauty and open space as for discourse. Thus under the Court's analysis, even the quintessential public forums would appear to lack the necessary elements of what the Court defines as a public forum.

The effect of the Court's narrow view of the first category of public forums is compounded by its description of the second purported category, the so-called "designated" forum. The requirements for such a designation are so stringent that I cannot be certain whether the category has any content left at all. In any event, it seems evident that under the Court's analysis today few, if any, types of property other than those already recognized as public forums will be accorded that status.

[I]n my view the policies underlying the [public forum] doctrine cannot be given effect unless we recognize that open, public spaces and thoroughfares that are suitable for discourse may be public forums, whatever their historical pedigree and without concern for a precise classification of the property. . . . Without this recognition our forum doctrine retains no relevance in times of fast-changing technology and increasing insularity. In a country where most citizens travel by automobile, and parks all too often become locales for crime rather than social intercourse, our failure to recognize the possibility that new types of government property may be appropriate forums for speech will lead to a serious curtailment of our expressive activity.

One of the places left in our mobile society that is suitable for discourse is a metropolitan airport. It is of particular importance to recognize that such spaces are public forums because in these days an airport is one of the few government-owned spaces where many persons have extensive contact with other members of the public. Given that private spaces of similar character are not subject to the dictates of the First Amendment, it is critical that we preserve these areas for protected speech. In my view, our public forum doctrine must recognize this reality, and allow the creation of public forums that do not fit within the narrow tradition of streets, sidewalks, and parks. . . .

[U]nder the proper circumstances I would accord public forum status to other forms of property, regardless of their ancient or contemporary origins and whether or not they fit within a narrow historic tradition. If the objective, physical characteristics of the property at issue and the actual public access and uses that have been permitted by the government indicate that expressive activity would be appropriate and compatible with those uses, the property is a public forum. The most important considerations in this analysis are whether the property shares physical similarities with more traditional public forums, whether the government has permitted or acquiesced in broad public access to the property, and whether expressive activity would tend to interfere in a significant way with the uses to which the government has as a factual matter dedicated the property. In conducting the last inquiry, courts must consider the consistency of those uses with expressive activities in general, rather than the specific sort of speech at issue in the case before it; otherwise the analysis would be one not of classification but rather of case-by-case balancing, and would provide little guidance to the State regarding its discretion to regulate speech. Courts must also consider the availability of reasonable time, place, and manner restrictions in undertaking this compatibility analysis. The possibility of some theoretical inconsistency between expressive activities and the property's uses should not bar a finding of a public forum, if those inconsistencies can be avoided through simple and permitted regulations. . . .

Under this analysis, it is evident that the public spaces of the Port Authority's airports are public forums. First, the District Court made detailed findings regarding the physical similarities between the Port Authority's airports and public streets. . . .

Second, the airport areas involved here are open to the public without restriction. . . . Of course, airport operators retain authority to restrict public access when necessary, for instance to respond to special security concerns. But if the Port Authority allows the uses and open access to airports that is shown on this record, it cannot argue that some vestigial power to change its practices bars the conclusion that its airports are public forums, any more than the power to bulldoze a park bars a finding that a public forum exists so long as the open use does.

Third, and perhaps most important, it is apparent from the record, and from the recent history of airports, that when adequate time, place, and manner regulations are in place, expressive activity is quite compatible with the uses of major airports. . . . The Authority makes no showing that any real impediments to the smooth functioning of the airports cannot be cured with reasonable time, place, and manner regulations. In fact, the history of the Authority's own airports, as well as other major airports in this country, leaves little doubt that such a solution is quite feasible. The Authority has for many years permitted expressive activities by petitioners and others, without any apparent interference with its ability to meet its transportation purposes. . . .

The danger of allowing the government to suppress speech is shown in the cases now before us. A grant of plenary power allows the government to tilt the dialog heard by the public, to exclude many, more marginal, voices. The first challenged Port Authority regulation establishes a flat prohibition on "[t]he sale or distribution of flyers, brochures, pamphlets, books or any other printed or written material," if conducted within the airport terminal, "in a continuous or repetitive manner." We have long recognized that the right to distribute flyers and literature lies at the heart of the liberties guaranteed by the Speech and Press Clauses of the First Amendment. See, *e.g., Schneider v. State (Town of Irvington)*, 308 U.S. 147 (1939); *Murdock v. Pennsylvania,* 319 U.S. 105 (1943). The Port Authority's rule, which prohibits almost all such activity, is among the most restrictive possible of those liberties. The regulation is in fact so broad and restrictive of speech, Justice O'CONNOR finds it void even under the standards applicable to government regulations in nonpublic forums. I have no difficulty deciding the regulation cannot survive the far more stringent rules applicable to regulations in public forums. The regulation is not drawn in narrow terms, and it does not leave open ample alternative channels for communication. The Port Authority's concerns with the problem of congestion can be addressed through narrow restrictions on the time and place of expressive activity. I would strike down the regulation as an unconstitutional restriction of speech.

II

It is my view, however, that the Port Authority's ban on the "solicitation and receipt of funds" within its airport terminals should be upheld under the standards applicable to speech regulations in public forums. The regulation may be upheld as either a reasonable time, place, and manner restriction, or as a regulation directed at the nonspeech element of expressive conduct. The two standards have considerable overlap in a case like this one.

It is well settled that "even in a public forum the government may impose reasonable restrictions on the time, place, or manner of protected speech, provided the restrictions 'are justified without reference to the content of the regulated speech, that they are narrowly tailored to serve a significant governmental interest, and that they leave open ample alternative channels for communication of the information.' " We have held further that the government in appropriate circumstances may regulate conduct, even if the conduct has an expressive component. And in several recent cases we have recognized that the standards for assessing time, place, and manner restrictions are little, if any, different from the standards applicable to regulations of conduct with an expressive component. The confluence of the two tests is well demonstrated by a case like this, where the government regulation at issue can be described with equal accuracy as a regulation of the manner of expression, or as a regulation of conduct with an expressive component.

I am in full agreement with the statement of the Court that solicitation is a form of protected speech. If the Port Authority's solicitation regulation prohibited all speech that requested the contribution of funds, I would conclude that it was a direct, content-based restriction of speech in clear violation of the First Amendment. The Authority's regulation does not prohibit all solicitation, however; it prohibits the "solicitation and receipt of funds." I do not understand this regulation to prohibit all speech that solicits funds. It reaches only personal solicitations for immediate payment of money. Otherwise, the "receipt of funds" phrase would be written out of the provision. The regulation does not cover, for example, the distribution of preaddressed envelopes along with a plea to contribute money to the distributor or his organization. As I understand the restriction, it is directed only at the physical exchange of money, which is an element of conduct interwoven with otherwise expressive solicitation. In other words, the regulation permits expression that solicits funds, but limits the manner of that expression to forms other than the immediate receipt of money.

So viewed, I believe the Port Authority's rule survives our test for speech restrictions in the public forum. In-person solicitation of funds, when combined with immediate receipt of that money, creates a risk of fraud and duress that is well recognized, and that is different in kind from other forms of expression or conduct. Travelers who are unfamiliar with the airport, perhaps even unfamiliar with this country, its customs, and its language, are an easy prey for the money solicitor. I agree in full with the Court's discussion of these dangers. . . .

Because the Port Authority's solicitation ban is directed at these abusive practices and not at any particular message, idea, or form of speech, the regulation is a content-neutral rule serving a significant government interest. . . .

To survive scrutiny, the regulation must be drawn in narrow terms to accomplish its end and leave open ample alternative channels for communication. Regarding the former requirement, we have held that to be narrowly tailored a regulation need not be the least restrictive or least intrusive means of achieving an end. The regulation must be reasonable, and must not burden substantially more speech than necessary. Under this standard the solicitation ban survives with ease, because it prohibits only solicitation of money for immediate receipt. The regulation does not burden any broader category of speech or expressive conduct than is the source of the evil sought to be avoided. . . .

I have little difficulty in deciding that the Port Authority has left open ample alternative channels for the communication of the message which is an aspect of solicitation. [T]he Authority's rule does not prohibit all solicitation of funds: It restricts only the manner of the solicitation, or the conduct associated with solicitation, to prohibit immediate receipt of the solicited money. Requests for money continue to be permitted, and in the course of requesting money solicitors may explain their cause, or the purposes of their organization, without violating the regulation. It is only if the solicitor accepts immediate payment that a violation occurs. . . .

JUSTICE SOUTER, with whom JUSTICE BLACKMUN and JUSTICE STEVENS join, concurring in [*Lee v. ISKCON*] and dissenting in *ISKCON v. Lee*.

I join in Part I of Justice KENNEDY's opinion and the judgment of affirmance in [*Lee v. ISKCON*]. I agree with Justice KENNEDY's view of the rule that should determine what is a public forum and with his conclusion that the public areas of the airports at issue here qualify as such. . . .

From the Court's conclusion in [*ISKCON v. Lee*], however, sustaining the total ban on solicitation of money for immediate payment, I respectfully dissent. "We have held the solicitation of money by charities to be fully protected as the dissemination of ideas. . . .

Even if I assume, *arguendo,* that the ban on the petitioners' activity at issue here is both content neutral and merely a restriction on the manner of communication, the regulation must be struck down for its failure to satisfy the requirements of narrow tailoring to further a significant state interest and availability of "ample alternative channels for communication."

As Justice KENNEDY's opinion indicates, respondent comes closest to justifying the restriction as one furthering the government's interest in preventing coercion and fraud.* The claim to be preventing coercion is weak to start with. While a solicitor can be insistent, a pedestrian on the street or airport concourse can simply walk away or walk on. . . . Since there is here no evidence of any type of coercive conduct, over and above the merely importunate character of the open and public solicitation, that might justify a ban, the regulation cannot be sustained to avoid coercion.

As for fraud, our cases do not provide government with plenary authority to ban solicitation just because it could be fraudulent. . . . The evidence of fraudulent conduct here is virtually nonexistent. It consists of one affidavit describing eight complaints, none of them substantiated, "involving some form of fraud, deception, or larceny" over an entire 11-year period between 1975 and 1986, during which the regulation at issue here was, by agreement, not enforced. [T]here has not been a single claim of fraud or misrepresentation since 1981. . . .

Even assuming a governmental interest adequate to justify some regulation, the present ban would fall when subjected to the requirement of narrow tailoring. . . .

Finally, I do not think the Port Authority's solicitation ban leaves open the "ample" channels of communication required of a valid content-neutral time, place, and manner restriction. A distribution of preaddressed envelopes is unlikely to be much of an alternative. The practical reality of the regulation, which this Court can never ignore, is that it shuts off a uniquely powerful avenue of communication for organizations like the International Society for Krishna Consciousness, and may, in effect, completely prohibit unpopular and poorly funded groups from receiving funds in response to protected solicitation.

---

*   Respondent also attempts to justify his regulation on the alternative basis of "interference with air travelers," referring in particular to problems of "annoyance" and "congestion." The First Amendment inevitably requires people to put up with annoyance and uninvited persuasion. Indeed, in such cases we need to scrutinize restrictions on speech with special care. In their degree of congestion, most of the public spaces of these airports are probably more comparable to public streets than to the fairground as we described it in *Heffron v. International Soc. for Krishna Consciousness, Inc.* Consequently, the congestion argument, which was held there to justify a regulation confining solicitation to a fixed location, should have less force here. Be that as it may, the conclusion of a majority of the Court today that the Constitution forbids the ban on the sale, as well as the distribution, of leaflets puts to rest respondent's argument that congestion justifies a total ban on solicitation. While there may, of course, be congested locations where solicitation could severely compromise the efficient flow of pedestrians, the proper response would be to tailor the restrictions to those choke points.

COMMENTS AND QUESTIONS

1.   The vote is 6–3 with a majority opinion to uphold the ban on solicitation and 5–4 with no majority opinion to strike the ban on leafleting. Can you see where the votes are and what the bases for the various opinions are? What is the "law" to be derived from this case? What does the case say about whether modern equivalents of a traditional public forum may be treated like a traditional public forum?

2.   There was a time when the Court was willing to analogize certain privately owned places with the public streets, parks, and sidewalks. Originally, in *Marsh v. Alabama*, 326 U.S. 501 (1946), the Court held that the streets and sidewalks of a "company town"* were a public forum. Next, in *Amalgamated Food Employees v. Logan Valley Plaza*, 391 U.S. 308 (1968), the Court held that the privately owned streets, sidewalks, and parking areas at a shopping mall were like the streets and sidewalks of the company town and hence were a public forum from which labor picketers could not be excluded. However, in *Lloyd Corp. v. Tanner*, 407 U.S. 551 (1972), the Court by a 5–4 vote distinguished *Logan Valley* on the basis that there the labor picketers' target was a business at the mall, whereas in *Lloyd* the activity was leafleting against the war in Vietnam, which had no relationship to the mall's activities. Consequently, the mall could constitutionally exclude the anti-war leafletters. Finally, in *Hudgens v. NLRB*, 424 U.S. 507 (1976), the Court characterized *Lloyd* as effectively overruling *Logan Valley* and concluded that private property could not be considered a public forum.

3.   In *Walker v. Sons of Confederate Veterans*, 576 U.S. 200 (2015), the question was how to treat specialty license plates issued by Texas upon request by private persons and approved by the Texas Board of Motor Vehicles. The Sons of Confederate Veterans proposed a specialty plate with a Confederate battle flag, but the Board denied approval. The Court by a 5–4 vote held that license plate designs, specialty or otherwise, are government speech, not private speech. As such, government is not required to be viewpoint neutral. Although the designs of specialty plates are proposed by private persons, the state by approving them adopts them as its own. The five-member majority was an unusual constellation—the four "liberal" members of the Court and Justice Thomas. Justice Alito authored the dissent that argued the speech was private speech, not government speech. In his view, the state had created a limited public forum by offering to allow persons to create specialty plates for a fee. He found it ludicrous to say that the state had adopted the messages contained on more than 350 specialty plates, messages which included among other things the logos for Remax, Dr. Pepper, Mighty Fine Burgers, and 37 out-of-state universities (to see them all, go to txdmv.gov/motorists/license-plates/

---

* A company town used to be relatively common in the United States. It consisted of an entire town where all the land and buildings were owned by a particular company, and where the company provided what would normally be public services, such as water and sewer service and road building and repair. Typically, it was inhabited exclusively by workers for the company, who, again typically, could live nowhere else. They do not exist anymore.

specialty-license-plates). As a limited public forum, the state would not be allowed to discriminate on the basis of viewpoint.

4.   In *Reed v. Town of Gilbert*, 576 U.S. 155 (2015), the Good News Community Church, not having a building of its own, wished to advertise the time and place of their Sunday services, because they were held in a variety of different locations. It typically deployed signs early on Saturday and removed them around midday on Sunday. However, this violated the town's sign ordinance that prohibited temporary signs intended to direct persons to a "qualifying event" more than 12 hours before the event and more than one hour after the event. Church services fell within the category of qualifying events. Other types of signs, such as ideological and political signs were not subject to such strict requirements. The Court unanimously found the sign ordinance unconstitutional, but the Court split 6–3 on the proper analysis. The majority in an opinion by Justice Thomas found that the ordinance was not content neutral; that is, it discriminated on the basis of content. Accordingly, the Court used strict scrutiny to assess its constitutionality, and it found that, even assuming there were compelling government interests, the ordinance was "hopelessly underinclusive." Justice Kagan, writing for herself and Justices Breyer and Ginsburg, conceded that the ordinance was content based, but she believed that strict scrutiny was not the proper test. She noted that not all protected speech that is regulated on the basis of content is subject to strict scrutiny, notably commercial speech and speech assessed under the secondary effects doctrine (the next section of this book). She argued that content-based restrictions are suspect for two reasons—they may interfere with the free marketplace of ideas, or they may reflect government hostility or favoritism toward the underlying message. Neither was suggested to be present here. Moreover, applying strict scrutiny to all municipal sign ordinances could wreak havoc with such unobjectionable laws as those banning illuminated signs in residential neighborhoods unless they identify the address of a home. She also noted that the federal Highway Beautification Act limits signs along interstate highways unless they direct travelers to "scenic and historic attractions" or advertise free coffee. She concluded that, inasmuch as the ordinance in this case would fail "strict scrutiny, intermediate scrutiny, or even the laugh test,"* it was unnecessary to require the use of strict scrutiny.

5.   North Carolina law made it a felony for a registered sex offender "to access a commercial social networking Web site where the sex offender knows that the site permits minor children to become members or to create or maintain personal Web pages." In *Packingham v. North Carolina*, 137 S.Ct. 1730 (2017), the Court found the law unconstitutional. Packingham was a registered sex offender but maintained a Facebook page. Justice Kennedy, writing for the Court, began by asserting that cyberspace is one of the most important places for the exchange of views, apparently analogizing it to a public forum. Intermediate scrutiny was appropriate, he said, because the law

---

*   As a matter of absolute trivia, the term "laugh test" had been used three times before Justice Kagan's use in *Town of Gilbert*: twice by Justice Scalia and once by Justice Rehnquist, and never in a majority opinion.

was assumed to be content neutral. Nevertheless, to survive intermediate scrutiny, a law must be "narrowly tailored to serve a significant governmental interest." But this law, he said, "enacts a prohibition unprecedented in the scope of First Amendment speech it burdens." Moreover, the state failed to show that the law was necessary to keep convicted sex offenders away from vulnerable victims. The Court did make clear, however, that the opinion should not be interpreted as barring a State from enacting more specific laws than the one at issue. Specifically, the Court said: "it can be assumed that the First Amendment permits a State to enact specific, narrowly tailored laws that prohibit a sex offender from engaging in conduct that often presages a sexual crime, like contacting a minor or using a website to gather information about a minor." Justice Alito, joined by the Chief Justice and Justice Thomas, concurred in the judgment but not the opinion because of its "undisciplined dicta," in particular the equating of the internet with public streets and parks. This would suggest, he said, that government would be unable to ban sex offenders from any web site, even those specifically tailored to children or to teen dating sites. Here, he agreed that the law cast too wide a net with respect to prohibited sites. Recall that it was Justice Kennedy who concluded in the *ISKCON* cases that an airport terminal (outside of the security area) could be likened to a public forum, but he was in a minority there.

2. OF ZONING AND SECONDARY EFFECTS

YOUNG V. AMERICAN MINI THEATRES, INC.

United States Supreme Court, 1976.
427 U.S. 50, 96 S.Ct. 2440.

MR. JUSTICE STEVENS delivered the opinion of the Court.[*]

Zoning ordinances adopted by the city of Detroit differentiate between motion picture theaters which exhibit sexually explicit "adult" movies and those which do not. The principal question presented by this case is whether that statutory classification is unconstitutional because it is based on the content of communication protected by the First Amendment.

Effective November 2, 1972, Detroit adopted the ordinances challenged in this litigation. Instead of concentrating "adult" theaters in limited zones, these ordinances require that such theaters be dispersed.

---

[*] Part III of this opinion is joined by only THE CHIEF JUSTICE, Mr. Justice WHITE, and Mr. Justice REHNQUIST.

Specifically, an adult theater may not be located within 1,000 feet of any two other "regulated uses" or within 500 feet of a residential area. The term "regulated uses" includes 10 different kinds of establishments in addition to adult theaters.[3]

The classification of a theater as "adult" is expressly predicated on the character of the motion pictures which it exhibits. If the theater is used to present "material distinguished or characterized by an emphasis on matter depicting, describing or relating to 'Specified Sexual Activities' or 'Specified Anatomical Areas,' "[4] it is an adult establishment.

[I]n the opinion of urban planners and real estate experts who supported the ordinances, the location of several such businesses in the same neighborhood tends to attract an undesirable quantity and quality of transients, adversely affects property values, causes an increase in crime, especially prostitution, and encourages residents and businesses to move elsewhere.

Respondents are the operators of two adult motion picture theaters. . . . The respondents brought two separate actions against appropriate city officials, seeking a declaratory judgment that the ordinances were unconstitutional and an injunction against their enforcement. . . .

[R]espondents contend (1) that the ordinances are so vague that they violate the Due Process Clause of the Fourteenth Amendment; (2) that they are invalid under the First Amendment as prior restraints on protected communication; and (3) that the classification of theaters on the basis of the content of their exhibitions violates the Equal Protection Clause of the Fourteenth Amendment. We consider their arguments in that order.

I

[The Court found the ordinance not unconstitutionally vague.]

II

[T]he ordinances are not challenged on the ground that they impose a limit on the total number of adult theaters which may operate in the city of Detroit. There is no claim that distributors or exhibitors of adult films are denied access to the market or, conversely, that the viewing public is

---

[3] In addition to adult motion picture theaters and "mini" theaters, which contain less than 50 seats, the regulated uses include adult bookstores; cabarets (group "D"); establishments for the sale of beer or intoxicating liquor for consumption on the premises; hotels or motels; pawnshops; pool or billiard halls; public lodging houses; secondhand stores; shoeshine parlors; and taxi dance halls.

[4] These terms are defined as follows: "For the purpose of this Section, 'Specified Sexual Activities' is defined as: 1. Human Genitals in a state of sexual stimulation or arousal; 2. Acts of human masturbation, sexual intercourse or sodomy; 3. Fondling or other erotic touching of human genitals, pubic region, buttock or female breast. And 'Specified Anatomical Areas' is defined as: 1. Less than completely and opaquely covered: (a) human genitals, pubic region, (b) buttock, and (c) female breast below a point immediately above the top of the areola; and 2. Human male genitals in a discernibly turgid state, even if completely and opaquely covered."

unable to satisfy its appetite for sexually explicit fare. Viewed as an entity, the market for this commodity is essentially unrestrained.

It is true, however, that adult films may only be exhibited commercially in licensed theaters. But that is also true of all motion pictures. The city's general zoning laws require all motion picture theaters to satisfy certain locational as well as other requirements; we have no doubt that the municipality may control the location of theaters as well as the location of other commercial establishments, either by confining them to certain specified commercial zones or by requiring that they be dispersed throughout the city. The mere fact that the commercial exploitation of material protected by the First Amendment is subject to zoning and other licensing requirements is not a sufficient reason for invalidating these ordinances.

Putting to one side for the moment the fact that adult motion picture theaters must satisfy a locational restriction not applicable to other theaters, we are also persuaded that the 1,000-foot restriction does not, in itself, create an impermissible restraint on protected communication. The city's interest in planning and regulating the use of property for commercial purposes is clearly adequate to support that kind of restriction applicable to all theaters within the city limits. In short, apart from the fact that the ordinances treat adult theaters differently from other theaters and the fact that the classification is predicated on the content of material shown in the respective theaters, the regulation of the place where such films may be exhibited does not offend the First Amendment. We turn, therefore, to the question whether the classification is consistent with the Equal Protection Clause.

III

[A] remark attributed to Voltaire characterizes our zealous adherence to the principle that the government may not tell the citizen what he may or may not say. Referring to a suggestion that the violent overthrow of tyranny might be legitimate, he said: "I disapprove of what you say, but I will defend to the death your right to say it." The essence of that comment has been repeated time after time in our decisions invalidating attempts by the government to impose selective controls upon the dissemination of ideas.

[E]ven though we recognize that the First Amendment will not tolerate the total suppression of erotic materials that have some arguably artistic value, it is manifest that society's interest in protecting this type of expression is of a wholly different, and lesser, magnitude than the interest in untrammeled political debate that inspired Voltaire's immortal comment. Whether political oratory or philosophical discussion moves us to applaud or to despise what is said, every schoolchild can understand why our duty to defend the right to speak remains the same. But few of us would march our sons and daughters off to war to preserve the citizen's right to see "Specified Sexual Activities" exhibited in the theaters of our choice. Even though the First Amendment protects communication in this area from total suppression, we hold that the State may legitimately use the content of these materials as the basis for placing them in a different classification from other motion pictures.

The remaining question is whether the line drawn by these ordinances is justified by the city's interest in preserving the character of its neighborhoods. . . . The record disclosed a factual basis for the Common Council's conclusion that this kind of restriction will have the desired effect.[34] It is not our function to appraise the wisdom of its decision to require adult theaters to be separated rather than concentrated in the same areas. In either event, the city's interest in attempting to preserve the quality of urban life is one that must be accorded high respect. Moreover, the city must be allowed a reasonable opportunity to experiment with solutions to admittedly serious problems.

Since what is ultimately at stake is nothing more than a limitation on the place where adult films may be exhibited,[35] even though the determination of whether a particular film fits that characterization turns on the nature of its content, we conclude that the city's interest in the present and future character of its neighborhoods adequately supports its classification of motion pictures. We hold that the zoning ordinances requiring that adult motion picture theaters not be located within 1,000 feet of two other regulated uses does not violate the Equal Protection Clause of the Fourteenth Amendment. . . .

MR. JUSTICE POWELL, concurring in the judgment and portions of the opinion.

Although I agree with much of what is said in the Court's opinion, and concur in Parts I and II, my approach to the resolution of this case is sufficiently different to prompt me to write separately.[1] I view the case as presenting an example of innovative land-use regulation, implicating First Amendment concerns only incidentally and to a limited extent.

One-half century ago this Court broadly sustained the power of local municipalities to utilize the then relatively novel concept of land-use

---

[34] The Common Council's determination was that a concentration of "adult" movie theaters causes the area to deteriorate and become a focus of crime, effects which are not attributable to theaters showing other types of films. It is this secondary effect which these zoning ordinances attempt to avoid, not the dissemination of "offensive" speech. . . .

[35] The situation would be quite different if the ordinance had the effect of suppressing, or greatly restricting access to, lawful speech. Here, however, the District Court specifically found that "(t)he Ordinances do not affect the operation of existing establishments but only the location of new ones. There are myriad locations in the City of Detroit which must be over 1000 feet from existing regulated establishments. This burden on First Amendment rights is slight." . . .

[1] I do not think we need reach, nor am I inclined to agree with, the holding in Part III (and supporting discussion) that nonobscene, erotic materials may be treated differently under First Amendment principles from other forms of protected expression. . . .

regulation in order to meet effectively the increasing encroachments of urbanization upon the quality of life of their citizens. . . .

Against this background of precedent, it is clear beyond question that the Detroit Common Council had broad regulatory power to deal with the problem that prompted enactment of the Anti-Skid Row Ordinance. As the Court notes, the Council was motivated by its perception that the "regulated uses," when concentrated, worked a "deleterious effect upon the adjacent areas" and could "contribute to the blighting or downgrading of the surrounding neighborhood." The purpose of preventing the deterioration of commercial neighborhoods was certainly within the concept of the public welfare that defines the limits of the police power. Respondents apparently concede the legitimacy of the ordinance as passed in 1962, but challenge the amendments 10 years later that brought within its provisions adult theaters as well as adult bookstores and "topless" cabarets. Those amendments resulted directly from the Common Council's determination that the recent proliferation of these establishments and their tendency to cluster in certain parts of the city would have the adverse effect upon the surrounding areas that the ordinance was aimed at preventing.

Respondents' attack on the amended ordinance, insofar as it affects them, can be stated simply. [T]hey argue that the 1972 amendments abridge First Amendment rights by restricting the places at which an adult theater may locate on the basis of nothing more substantial than unproved fears and apprehensions about the effects of such a business upon the surrounding area. And, even if Detroit's interest in preventing the deterioration of business areas is sufficient to justify the impact upon freedom of expression, the ordinance is nevertheless invalid because it impermissibly discriminates between types of theaters solely on the basis of their content.

I reject respondents' argument for the following reasons.

This is the first case in this Court in which the interests in free expression protected by the First and Fourteenth Amendments have been implicated by a municipality's commercial zoning ordinances. Respondents would have us mechanically apply the doctrines developed in other contexts. But this situation is not analogous to cases involving expression in public forums or to those involving individual expression or, indeed, to any other prior case. The unique situation presented by this ordinance calls, as cases in this area so often do, for a careful inquiry into the competing concerns of the State and the interests protected by the guarantee of free expression.

Because a substantial burden rests upon the State when it would limit in any way First Amendment rights, it is necessary to identify with specificity the nature of the infringement in each case. The primary concern of the free speech guarantee is that there be full opportunity for expression in all of its varied forms to convey a desired message. Vital to this concern is the corollary that there be full opportunity for everyone to receive the message. Motion pictures, the medium of expression involved here, are fully within the protection of the First Amendment. . . .

In this case, there is no indication that the application of the Anti-Skid Row Ordinance to adult theaters has the effect of suppressing production of or, to any significant degree, restricting access to adult movies. The [Respondents] concededly will not be able to exhibit adult movies at [their] present location[s]. The constraints of the ordinance with respect to location may indeed create economic loss for some who are engaged in this business. But in this respect they are affected no differently from any other commercial enterprise that suffers economic detriment as a result of land-use regulation. . . .

The inquiry for First Amendment purposes is not concerned with economic impact; rather, it looks only to the effect of this ordinance upon freedom of expression. This prompts essentially two inquiries: (i) Does the ordinance impose any content limitation on the creators of adult movies or their ability to make them available to whom they desire, and (ii) does it restrict in any significant way the viewing of these movies by those who desire to see them? On the record in this case, these inquiries must be answered in the negative. At most the impact of the ordinance on these interests is incidental and minimal. Detroit has silenced no message, has invoked no censorship, and has imposed no limitation upon those who wish to view them. The ordinance is addressed only to the places at which this type of expression may be presented, a restriction that does not interfere with content. Nor is there any significant overall curtailment of adult movie presentations, or the opportunity for a message reach an audience. On the basis of the District Court's finding, it appears that if a sufficient market exists to support them the number of adult movie theaters in Detroit will remain approximately the same, free to purvey the same message. To be sure some prospective patrons may be inconvenienced by this dispersal. But other patrons, depending upon where they live or work, may find it more convenient to view an adult movie when adult theaters are not concentrated in a particular section of the city.

In these circumstances, it is appropriate to analyze the permissibility of Detroit's action under the four-part test of *United States v. O'Brien.* Under that test, a governmental regulation is sufficiently justified, despite its incidental impact upon First Amendment interests, "if it is within the constitutional power of the Government; if it furthers an important or substantial governmental interest; if the governmental interest is unrelated to the suppression of free expression; and if the incidental restriction on . . . First Amendment freedoms is no greater than is essential to the furtherance of that interest." . . .

There is, as noted earlier, no question that the ordinance was within the power of the Detroit Common Council to enact. Nor is there doubt that the interests furthered by this ordinance are both important and substantial. Without stable neighborhoods, both residential and commercial, large sections of a modern city quickly can deteriorate into an urban jungle with tragic consequences to social, environmental, and economic values. . . .

The third and fourth tests of O'Brien also are met on this record. It is clear both from the chronology and from the facts that Detroit has not embarked on an effort to suppress free expression. [I]t is not seriously challenged that the governmental interest prompting the inclusion in the ordinance of adult establishments was wholly unrelated to any suppression of free expression. Nor is there reason to question that the degree of incidental encroachment upon such expression was the minimum necessary to further the purpose of the ordinance. The evidence presented to the Common Council indicated that the urban deterioration was threatened, not by the concentration of *all* movie theaters with other "regulated uses," but only by a concentration of those that elected to specialize in adult movies. The case would present a different situation had Detroit brought within the ordinance types of theaters that had not been shown to contribute to the deterioration of surrounding areas. . . .

The Detroit zoning ordinance . . . affects expression only incidentally and in furtherance of governmental interests wholly unrelated to the regulation of expression. At least as applied to respondents, it does not offend the First Amendment. Although courts must be alert to the possibility of direct rather than incidental effect of zoning on expression, and especially to the possibility of using the power to zone as a pretext for suppressing expression, it is clear that this is not such a case.

MR. JUSTICE STEWART, with whom MR. JUSTICE BRENNAN, MR. JUSTICE MARSHALL, and MR. JUSTICE BLACKMUN join, dissenting.

The Court today holds that the First and Fourteenth Amendments do not prevent the city of Detroit from using a system of prior restraints and criminal sanctions to enforce content-based restrictions on the geographic location of motion picture theaters that exhibit nonobscene but sexually oriented films. I dissent from this drastic departure from established principles of First Amendment law.

This case does not involve a simple zoning ordinance, or a content-neutral time, place, and manner restriction, or a regulation of obscene expression or other speech that is entitled to less than the full protection of the First Amendment. The kind of expression at issue here is no doubt objectionable to some, but that fact does not diminish its protected status any more than did the particular content of the "offensive" expression in [any number of other cases in which we found the government restriction unconstitutional.]

What this case does involve is the constitutional permissibility of selective interference with protected speech whose content is thought to produce distasteful effects. It is elementary that a prime function of the First Amendment is to guard against just such interference. By refusing to invalidate Detroit's ordinance the Court rides roughshod over cardinal principles of First Amendment law, which require that time, place, and manner regulations that affect protected expression be content neutral except in the limited context of a captive or juvenile audience. In place of these principles the Court invokes a concept wholly alien to the First Amendment. Since "few of us would march our sons and daughters off to war to preserve the citizen's right to see 'Specified Sexual Activities' exhibited in the theaters of our choice," the Court implies that these films are not entitled to the full protection of the Constitution. This stands "Voltaire's immortal comment" on its head. For if the guarantees of the First Amendment were reserved for expression that more than a "few of us" would take up arms to defend, then the right of free expression would be defined and circumscribed by current popular opinion. The guarantees of the Bill of Rights were designed to protect against precisely such majoritarian limitations on individual liberty. . . .

MR. JUSTICE BLACKMUN, with whom MR. JUSTICE BRENNAN, MR. JUSTICE STEWART, and MR. JUSTICE MARSHALL join, dissenting. [opinion, which joined JUSTICE STEWART's opinion and also found the ordinance unconstitutionally vague, omitted]

COMMENTS AND QUESTIONS

1.   Five members of the Court conclude that the ordinance is not unconstitutionally vague and that zoning theaters generally, like other commercial enterprises, does not violate the First Amendment. There is no majority opinion, however, regarding the special classification of adult theaters. Because the classification of the adult theaters turns on the content of the films they show, one might have expected the Court to apply strict scrutiny, as it normally does when government regulates on the basis of the content of speech. The plurality opinion, written by Justice Stevens, however, treats the issue as a question of Equal Protection and concludes that the interest of the city in preserving and protecting its neighborhoods outweighs the interests of those who wish to show "specified sexual activities" at the location of their choosing. In reaching this conclusion, Justice Stevens uses a novel approach to First Amendment questions, treating some speech as protected from being prohibited but allowing it to be regulated on a reasonable basis. This recognition of what some have called "second tier speech," speech not deserving full First Amendment protection, has never been embraced by a majority of the Court as a basis for decision, although undoubtedly it may in some way affect how they feel about a case.

2.   Justice Powell's opinion has been the one that has carried the day, although subsequent cases take some liberties with his opinion. For Justice

Powell, while the adult theaters are classified and zoned on the basis of the content of the films, the city is not zoning them because the city disapproves of the content. Rather, it is simply that there is an established correlation between the decay of neighborhoods, with its associated increase in crime, and the concentration of adult businesses. The city cares about the neighborhood decay and increased crime, which is a "secondary effect" of the concentration of the adult businesses. This had also been alluded to by Justice Stevens in his footnote 34. Thus, according to Justice Powell, when the city zones on the basis of secondary effects associated with particular speech content, rather than on the content itself, the *O'Brien* test can be brought to play. Under that test, again according to Justice Powell, the zoning in *American Mini Theatres* is narrowly tailored because it does not actually reduce the availability of films showing "specified sexual activities" in the city. Recall the similarity between the *O'Brien* test and the Time, Place, and Manner test.

3.   The first case following *American Mini Theatres* involved a city zoning provision that effectively banned all live, nude entertainment in the commercial area of the city. *See Schad v. Mount Ephraim*, 452 U.S. 61 (1981). The Court overturned the ban, distinguishing *American Mini Theatres* on the grounds that in *Schad* the effect was a total prohibition, thereby eliminating the availability of the "speech," and there was no showing, as there had been in *American Mini Theatres*, that there were adverse secondary effects associated with the presence of the live, nude entertainment. In *Renton v. Playtime Theatres, Inc.*, 475 U.S. 41 (1986), where the city had zoned adult theaters to concentrate them, rather than disperse them as in *American Mini Theatres*, the Court found that the primary aim of the zoning was to address the possible secondary effects that might be associated with adult theaters, not the content of the films shown, so that the Court could apply a Time, Place, and Manner test to the ordinance. There was evidence, however, that a motivation for the ordinance was dislike of the content of the films, and the city had neither made any studies nor provided any evidence of adverse secondary effects associated with the dispersed adult theaters. The Court responded that so long as dealing with secondary effects was a "primary aim," that was sufficient, and it would not delve into the motivations of individual members of the city council (who had expressed distaste for adult films). Moreover, the city was entitled to rely on the experience of other cities, such as Seattle just to its north, and was not required to do particularized studies. Applying the Time, Place, and Manner test, the Court found the ordinance constitutional, although it appeared that its practical effect would be to diminish substantially, if not eliminate, the availability of adult films in the city due to the high cost of land in the only places adult theaters could locate under the ordinance. The *Renton* approach of not scrutinizing very strictly a claimed secondary effects rationale for zoning has been broadly adopted by the lower courts and subsequent Supreme Court decisions. *See, e.g., City of Los Angeles v. Alameda Books, Inc.*, 535 U.S. 425 (2002); *City of Erie v. Pap's A.M.*, 529 U.S. 277 (2000); *Barnes v. Glen Theatre, Inc.*, 501 U.S. 560 (1991).

J. THE FREEDOM NOT TO SPEAK

Does the freedom of speech include a freedom not to speak? In *Minersville School District v. Gobitis*, 310 U.S. 586 (1940), the Supreme Court upheld the constitutionality of a local school district's requirement that all students begin the school day with a salute to the flag and recitation of the Pledge of Allegiance. This requirement had been challenged by Jehovah's Witnesses on the grounds that it violated their freedom of religion, because their religion prohibits them from making such pledges to earthly institutions or symbols. As a result, the state of West Virginia made such a requirement for all schools in its state, which resulted in the following case.

WEST VIRGINIA STATE BOARD OF EDUCATION V. BARNETTE

United States Supreme Court, 1943.
319 U.S. 624, 63 S.Ct. 1178.

MR. JUSTICE JACKSON delivered the opinion of the Court.

The [West Virginia] Board of Education on January 9, 1942, adopted a resolution . . . ordering that the salute to the flag become "a regular part of the program of activities in the public schools," that all teachers and pupils "shall be required to participate in the salute honoring the Nation represented by the Flag; provided, however, that refusal to salute the Flag be regarded as an Act of insubordination, and shall be dealt with accordingly."

[W]hat is now required is the "stiff-arm" salute, the saluter to keep the right hand raised with palm turned up while the following is repeated: "I pledge allegiance to the Flag of the United States of America and to the Republic for which it stands; one Nation, indivisible, with liberty and justice for all."

[A]ppellees . . . brought suit in the United States District Court for themselves and others similarly situated asking its injunction to restrain enforcement of these laws and regulations against Jehovah's Witnesses. . . .

Children of this faith have been expelled from school and are threatened with exclusion for no other cause. Officials threaten to send them to reformatories maintained for criminally inclined juveniles. Parents of such children have been prosecuted and are threatened with prosecutions for causing delinquency.

This case calls upon us to reconsider a precedent decision. . . . Before turning to the *Gobitis* case, however, it is desirable to notice certain characteristics by which this controversy is distinguished.

The freedom asserted by these appellees does not bring them into collision with rights asserted by any other individual. It is such conflicts which most frequently require intervention of the State to determine where the rights of one end and those of another begin. But the refusal of these persons to participate in the ceremony does not interfere with or deny rights of others to do so. Nor is there any question in this case that their behavior is peaceable and orderly. The sole conflict is between authority and rights of the individual. The State asserts power to condition access to public education on making a prescribed sign and profession and at the same time to coerce attendance by punishing both parent and child. The latter stand on a right of self-determination in matters that touch individual opinion and personal attitude. . . .

There is no doubt that, in connection with the pledges, the flag salute is a form of utterance. Symbolism is a primitive but effective way of communicating ideas. The use of an emblem or flag to symbolize some system, idea, institution, or personality, is a short cut from mind to mind. Causes and nations, political parties, lodges and ecclesiastical groups seek to knit the loyalty of their followings to a flag or banner, a color or design. The State announces rank, function, and authority through crowns and maces, uniforms and black robes; the church speaks through the Cross, the Crucifix, the altar and shrine, and clerical raiment. Symbols of State often convey political ideas just as religious symbols come to convey theological ones. Associated with many of these symbols are appropriate gestures of acceptance or respect: a salute, a bowed or bared head, a bended knee. A person gets from a symbol the meaning he puts into it, and what is one man's comfort and inspiration is another's jest and scorn.

Over a decade ago Chief Justice Hughes led this Court in holding that the display of a red flag as a symbol of opposition by peaceful and legal means to organized government was protected by the free speech guaranties of the Constitution. Here it is the State that employs a flag as a symbol of adherence to government as presently organized. It requires the individual to communicate by word and sign his acceptance of the political ideas it thus bespeaks. Objection to this form of communication when coerced is an old one, well known to the framers of the Bill of Rights.[13]

It is also to be noted that the compulsory flag salute and pledge requires affirmation of a belief and an attitude of mind. It is not clear whether the regulation contemplates that pupils forego any contrary convictions of their own and become unwilling converts to the prescribed ceremony or whether it will be acceptable if they simulate assent by words without belief and by a gesture barren of meaning. . . . To sustain the compulsory flag salute we are required to say that a Bill of Rights which guards the individual's right to speak his own mind, left it open to public authorities to compel him to utter what is not in his mind.

Whether the First Amendment to the Constitution will permit officials to order observance of ritual of this nature does not depend upon whether as a voluntary exercise we would think it to be good, bad or merely innocuous. Any credo of nationalism is likely to include what some disapprove or to omit what others think essential, and to give off different overtones as it takes on different accents or interpretations. . . .

Nor does the issue as we see it turn on one's possession of particular religious views or the sincerity with which they are held. While religion supplies appellees' motive for enduring the discomforts of making the issue in this case, many citizens who do not share these religious views hold such a compulsory rite to infringe constitutional liberty of the individual. It is not necessary to inquire whether non-conformist beliefs will exempt from the duty to salute unless we first find power to make the salute a legal duty. . . .

Government of limited power need not be anemic government. Assurance that rights are secure tends to diminish fear and jealousy of strong government, and by making us feel safe to live under it makes for its better support. Without promise of a limiting Bill of Rights it is doubtful if our Constitution could have mustered enough strength to enable its ratification. To enforce those rights today is not to choose weak government over strong government. It is only to adhere as a means of strength to individual freedom of mind in preference to officially disciplined uniformity for which history indicates a disappointing and disastrous end. . . .

[T]he very heart of the *Gobitis* opinion [is where] it reasons that "National unity is the basis of national security," that the authorities have "the right to select appropriate means for its attainment," and hence reaches the conclusion that such compulsory measures toward "national

---

[13] Early Christians were frequently persecuted for their refusal to participate in ceremonies before the statue of the emperor or other symbol of imperial authority. The story of William Tell's sentence to shoot an apple off his son's head for refusal to salute a bailiff's hat is an ancient one. The Quakers, William Penn included, suffered punishment rather than uncover their heads in deference to any civil authority. [The Court does not mention it, but at the same time as this case, Jehovah's Witnesses were being placed in concentration camps in Nazi Germany for refusal to pledge allegiance to the Führer, Adolf Hitler.]

unity" are constitutional. Upon the verity of this assumption depends our answer in this case.

National unity as an end which officials may foster by persuasion and example is not in question. The problem is whether under our Constitution compulsion as here employed is a permissible means for its achievement.

Struggles to coerce uniformity of sentiment in support of some end thought essential to their time and country have been waged by many good as well as by evil men. Nationalism is a relatively recent phenomenon but at other times and places the ends have been racial or territorial security, support of a dynasty or regime, and particular plans for saving souls. As first and moderate methods to attain unity have failed, those bent on its accomplishment must resort to an ever-increasing severity. As governmental pressure toward unity becomes greater, so strife becomes more bitter as to whose unity it shall be. Probably no deeper division of our people could proceed from any provocation than from finding it necessary to choose what doctrine and whose program public educational officials shall compel youth to unite in embracing. Ultimate futility of such attempts to compel coherence is the lesson of every such effort from the Roman drive to stamp out Christianity as a disturber of its pagan unity, the Inquisition, as a means to religious and dynastic unity, the Siberian exiles as a means to Russian unity, down to the fast failing efforts of our present totalitarian enemies. Those who begin coercive elimination of dissent soon find themselves exterminating dissenters. Compulsory unification of opinion achieves only the unanimity of the graveyard.

It seems trite but necessary to say that the First Amendment to our Constitution was designed to avoid these ends by avoiding these beginnings. There is no mysticism in the American concept of the State or of the nature or origin of its authority. We set up government by consent of the governed, and the Bill of Rights denies those in power any legal opportunity to coerce that consent. Authority here is to be controlled by public opinion, not public opinion by authority.

The case is made difficult not because the principles of its decision are obscure but because the flag involved is our own. Nevertheless, we apply the limitations of the Constitution with no fear that freedom to be intellectually and spiritually diverse or even contrary will disintegrate the social organization. To believe that patriotism will not flourish if patriotic ceremonies are voluntary and spontaneous instead of a compulsory routine is to make an unflattering estimate of the appeal of our institutions to free minds. We can have intellectual individualism and the rich cultural diversities that we owe to exceptional minds only at the price of occasional eccentricity and abnormal attitudes. When they are so harmless to others or to the State as those we deal with here, the price is not too great. But freedom to differ is not limited to things that do not matter much. That would be a mere shadow of freedom. The test of its substance is the right to differ as to things that touch the heart of the existing order.

If there is any fixed star in our constitutional constellation, it is that no official, high or petty, can prescribe what shall be orthodox in politics, nationalism, religion, or other matters of opinion or force citizens to confess by word or act their faith therein. If there are any circumstances which permit an exception, they do not now occur to us.

We think the action of the local authorities in compelling the flag salute and pledge transcends constitutional limitations on their power and invades the sphere of intellect and spirit which it is the purpose of the First Amendment to our Constitution to reserve from all official control.

The decision of this Court in *Minersville School District v. Gobitis* [is] overruled, and the judgment enjoining enforcement of the West Virginia Regulation is affirmed.

MR. JUSTICE ROBERTS and MR. JUSTICE REED adhere to the views expressed by the Court in *Minersville School District v. Gobitis* and are of the opinion that the judgment below should be reversed.

MR. JUSTICE BLACK and MR. JUSTICE DOUGLAS, concurring. [opinion omitted]

MR. JUSTICE MURPHY, concurring. [opinion omitted]

MR. JUSTICE FRANKFURTER, dissenting.

One who belongs to the most vilified and persecuted minority in history is not likely to be insensible to the freedoms guaranteed by our Constitution. Were my purely personal attitude relevant I should whole-heartedly associate myself with the general libertarian views in the Court's opinion, representing as they do the thought and action of a lifetime. But as judges we are neither Jew nor Gentile, neither Catholic nor agnostic. We owe equal attachment to the Constitution and are equally bound by our judicial obligations whether we derive our citizenship from the earliest or the latest immigrants to these shores. As a member of this Court I am not justified in writing my private notions of policy into the Constitution, no matter how deeply I may cherish them or how mischievous I may deem their disregard. The duty of a judge who must decide which of two claims before the Court shall prevail, that of a State to enact and enforce laws within its general competence or that of an individual to refuse obedience because of the demands of his conscience, is not that of the ordinary person. It can never be emphasized too much that one's own opinion about the wisdom or evil of a law should be excluded altogether when one is doing one's duty on the bench. The only opinion of our own even looking in that direction that is material is our opinion whether legislators could in reason have enacted such a law. In the light of all the circumstances, including the history of this question in this Court, it would require more daring than I possess to deny that reasonable legislators could have taken the action which is before us for review. Most unwillingly, therefore, I must differ from my brethren with regard to legislation like this. I cannot bring my mind to believe that the "liberty" secured by the Due Process Clause gives this Court authority to deny to the State of West Virginia the attainment of that which we all recognize as a legitimate legislative end, namely, the promotion of good citizenship, by employment of the means here chosen.

[O]f course patriotism cannot be enforced by the flag salute. But neither can the liberal spirit be enforced by judicial invalidation of illiberal legislation. Our constant preoccupation with the constitutionality of legislation rather than with its wisdom tends to preoccupation of the American mind with a false value. The tendency of focusing attention on constitutionality is to make constitutionality synonymous with wisdom, to regard a law as all right if it is constitutional. Such an attitude is a great enemy of liberalism. Particularly in legislation affecting freedom of thought and freedom of speech much which should offend a free-spirited society is constitutional. Reliance for the most precious interests of civilization, therefore, must be found outside of their vindication in courts of law. Only a persistent positive translation of the faith of a free society into the convictions and habits and actions of a community is the ultimate reliance against unabated temptations to fetter the human spirit.

COMMENTS AND QUESTIONS

1.   *Barnette* is an extraordinary case. What had been an 8–1 decision in *Gobitis* is overruled by a vote of 6–3 a mere three years later, and it occurs in the midst of wartime, when national patriotic feelings run highest. Moreover, rather than carve an exception for the Jehovah's Witnesses, because of their religious beliefs, the Court simply finds it beyond government's power, as circumscribed by the First Amendment, to require anyone to affirm a belief the person does not wish to affirm. The strength of this doctrine is exemplified by the later case of *Wooley v. Maynard*, 430 U.S. 705 (1977), in which the Court held that New Hampshire could not punish Maynard for placing tape over the state motto, Live Free or Die, on his license plate, which motto he objected to on moral and religious grounds.

2.   Note the salute in the picture and as described by the Court. It is identical to the Nazi salute in Germany at the time, except that the palm is turned up, rather than down. Also note the absence of "under God" in the Pledge of Allegiance. That language was added in 1954 to distinguish the United States from "godless communism."

3.   *Barnette*, however, does not preclude the government from requiring persons to speak against their will in various situations. For example, in the commercial speech area, courts have frequently upheld requirements to disclose information on labels or in advertising in order to adequately advise potential purchasers as to what they are purchasing. *See, e.g., New York State Restaurant Ass'n. v. New York City Bd. of Health*, 556 F.3d 114 (2d Cir.

2009)(upholding city's requirement that chain restaurants display the calorie counts of their food). In the political realm, the Court has continued to approve of mandatory disclosure requirements of campaign financing. *See, e.g., Citizens United v. Federal Election Commission*, 558 U.S. 310 (2010). *See also John Doe No. 1 v. Reed*, 561 U.S. 186 (2010)(upholding a state public records law providing for disclosure of referendum petitions containing the names and addresses of signatories). When television was available only from broadcast stations, the Court upheld requirements that mandated certain coverage by broadcast stations. *See Red Lion Broadcasting Co. v. FCC*, 395 U.S. 367 (1969). Also, recall that the Constitution requires all officers of the United States and state governments to swear or affirm to support the Constitution. This oath, as well as the President's oath under Article II, involves a promise of what the person will *do*, not what the person will believe. In addition, we all can be compelled to speak pursuant to a subpoena.

4.   On the other hand, there are circumstances where the government cannot compel even factual speech. For example, newspapers cannot be required to publish responses by those they criticize. *See Miami Herald Pub. Co. v. Tornillo*, 418 U.S. 241 (1974). While professional fundraisers may be required to disclose their financial dealings to the government, they cannot be forced to disclose to potential donors the percentage of charitable contributions collected during the previous twelve months that were actually turned over to charity. *See Riley v. National Federation of the Blind*, 487 U.S. 781 (1988). Similarly, in *McIntyre v. Ohio Elections Comm'n*, 514 U.S. 334 (1995), the Court held it unconstitutional for the state to ban anonymous political campaign literature.

NATIONAL INSTITUTE OF FAMILY LIFE ADVOCATES V. BECERRA

United States Supreme Court, 2018.
138 S.Ct. 2361.

JUSTICE THOMAS delivered the opinion of the Court.

The California Reproductive Freedom, Accountability, Comprehensive Care, and Transparency Act (FACT Act) requires clinics that primarily serve pregnant women to provide certain notices. Licensed clinics must notify women that California provides free or low-cost services, including abortions, and give them a phone number to call. Unlicensed clinics must notify women that California has not licensed the clinics to provide medical services. The question in this case is whether these notice requirements violate the First Amendment.

The California State Legislature enacted the FACT Act to regulate crisis pregnancy centers. Crisis pregnancy centers are "pro-life (largely Christian belief-based) organizations that offer a limited range of free pregnancy options, counseling, and other services to individuals that visit a center." "[U]nfortunately," the author of the FACT Act stated, "there are nearly 200 licensed and unlicensed" crisis pregnancy centers in California.

These centers "aim to discourage and prevent women from seeking abortions." The author of the FACT Act observed that crisis pregnancy centers "are commonly affiliated with, or run by organizations whose stated goal" is to oppose abortion—including "the National Institute of Family and Life Advocates," one of the petitioners here. To address this perceived problem, the FACT Act imposes two notice requirements on facilities that provide pregnancy-related services—one for licensed facilities and one for unlicensed facilities.

The first notice requirement applies to "licensed covered facilit[ies]." To fall under the definition of "licensed covered facility," a clinic must be a licensed primary care or specialty clinic or qualify as an intermittent clinic under California law. A licensed covered facility also must have the "primary purpose" of "providing family planning or pregnancy-related services." . . .

The FACT Act exempts several categories of clinics that would otherwise qualify as licensed covered facilities. Clinics operated by the United States or a federal agency are excluded, as are clinics that are "enrolled as a Medi-Cal provider" and participate in "the Family Planning, Access, Care, and Treatment Program" (Family PACT program). . . .

If a clinic is a licensed covered facility, the FACT Act requires it to disseminate a government-drafted notice on site. The notice states that "California has public programs that provide immediate free or low-cost access to comprehensive family planning services (including all FDA-approved methods of contraception), prenatal care, and abortion for eligible women. To determine whether you qualify, contact the county social services office at [insert the telephone number]." This notice must be posted in the waiting room, printed and distributed to all clients, or provided digitally at check-in. The notice must be in English and any additional languages identified by state law. In some counties, that means the notice must be spelled out in 13 different languages.

The stated purpose of the FACT Act, including its licensed notice requirement, is to "ensure that California residents make their personal reproductive health care decisions knowing their rights and the health care services available to them." The Legislature posited that "thousands of women remain unaware of the public programs available to provide them with contraception, health education and counseling, family planning, prenatal care, abortion, or delivery." Citing the "time sensitive" nature of pregnancy-related decisions, the Legislature concluded that requiring licensed facilities to inform patients themselves would be "[t]he most effective" way to convey this information.

The second notice requirement in the FACT Act applies to "unlicensed covered facilit[ies]." To fall under the definition of "unlicensed covered facility," a facility must not be licensed by the State, not have a licensed medical provider on staff or under contract, and have the "primary purpose" of "providing pregnancy-related services." . . .

Unlicensed covered facilities must provide a government-drafted notice stating that "[t]his facility is not licensed as a medical facility by the State of California and has no licensed medical provider who provides or directly supervises the provision of services." This notice must be provided on site and in all advertising materials. Onsite, the notice must be posted "conspicuously" at the entrance of the facility and in at least one waiting area. It must be "at least 8.5 inches by 11 inches and written in no less than 48-point type." In advertisements, the notice must be in the same size or larger font than the surrounding text, or otherwise set off in a way that draws attention to it. Like the licensed notice, the unlicensed notice must be in English and any additional languages specified by state law. Its stated purpose is to ensure "that pregnant women in California know when they are getting medical care from licensed professionals."

After the Governor of California signed the FACT Act, petitioners—a licensed pregnancy center, an unlicensed pregnancy center, and an organization composed of crisis pregnancy centers—filed this suit. Petitioners alleged that the licensed and unlicensed notices abridge the freedom of speech protected by the First Amendment. The District Court denied their motion for a preliminary injunction. The Court of Appeals for the Ninth Circuit affirmed. We granted certiorari to review the Ninth Circuit's decision. We reverse with respect to both notice requirements.

We first address the licensed notice.

The First Amendment, applicable to the States through the Fourteenth Amendment, prohibits laws that abridge the freedom of speech. When enforcing this prohibition, our precedents distinguish between content-based and content-neutral regulations of speech. Content-based regulations "target speech based on its communicative content." As a general matter, such laws "are presumptively unconstitutional and may be justified only if the government proves that they are narrowly tailored to serve compelling state interests." This stringent standard reflects the fundamental principle that governments have " 'no power to restrict expression because of its message, its ideas, its subject matter, or its content.' "

The licensed notice is a content-based regulation of speech. By compelling individuals to speak a particular message, such notices "alte[r] the content of [their] speech." *Riley v. National Federation of Blind of N. C., Inc.* Here, for example, licensed clinics must provide a government-drafted script about the availability of state-sponsored services, as well as contact information for how to obtain them. One of those services is abortion—the very practice that petitioners are devoted to opposing. By requiring petitioners to inform women how they can obtain state-subsidized abortions—at the same time petitioners try to dissuade women from choosing that option—the licensed notice plainly "alters the content" of petitioners' speech.

Although the licensed notice is content based, the Ninth Circuit did not apply strict scrutiny because it concluded that the notice regulates "professional speech." . . .

But this Court has not recognized "professional speech" as a separate category of speech. Speech is not unprotected merely because it is uttered by "professionals." . . . This Court's precedents do not permit governments to impose content-based restrictions on speech without " 'persuasive evidence . . . of a long (if heretofore unrecognized) tradition' " to that effect.

This Court's precedents do not recognize such a tradition for a category called "professional speech." This Court has afforded less protection for professional speech in two circumstances—neither of which turned on the fact that professionals were speaking. First, our precedents have applied more deferential review to some laws that require professionals to disclose factual, noncontroversial information in their "commercial speech." See, e.g., *Zauderer v. Office of Disciplinary Counsel of Supreme Court of Ohio*; *Ohralik v. Ohio State Bar Assn.* Second, under our precedents, States may regulate professional conduct, even though that conduct incidentally involves speech. See, e.g., *Planned Parenthood of Southeastern Pa. v. Casey* (opinion of O'Connor, Kennedy, and Souter, JJ.). But neither line of precedents is implicated here.

This Court's precedents have applied a lower level of scrutiny to laws that compel disclosures in certain contexts. In *Zauderer*, for example, this Court upheld a rule requiring lawyers who advertised their services on a contingency-fee basis to disclose that clients might be required to pay some fees and costs. Noting that the disclosure requirement governed only "commercial advertising" and required the disclosure of "purely factual and uncontroversial information about the terms under which . . . services will be available," the Court explained that such requirements should be upheld unless they are "unjustified or unduly burdensome."

The *Zauderer* standard does not apply here. Most obviously, the licensed notice is not limited to "purely factual and uncontroversial information about the terms under which . . . services will be available." The notice in no way relates to the services that licensed clinics provide. Instead, it requires these clinics to disclose information about state-sponsored services—including abortion, anything but an "uncontroversial" topic. Accordingly, *Zauderer* has no application here.

In addition to disclosure requirements under *Zauderer*, this Court has upheld regulations of professional conduct that incidentally burden speech. "[T]he First Amendment does not prevent restrictions directed at commerce or conduct from imposing incidental burdens on speech," and professionals are no exception to this rule. . . . While drawing the line between speech and conduct can be difficult, this Court's precedents have long drawn it. . . .

In *Planned Parenthood of Southeastern Pa. v. Casey*, for example, this Court upheld a law requiring physicians to obtain informed consent before they could perform an abortion. Pennsylvania law required physicians to inform their patients of "the nature of the procedure, the health risks of the abortion and childbirth, and the 'probable gestational age of the unborn child.'" The law also required physicians to inform patients of the availability of printed materials from the State, which provided information about the child and various forms of assistance.

The joint opinion in *Casey* rejected a free-speech challenge to this informed-consent requirement. It described the Pennsylvania law as "a requirement that a doctor give a woman certain information as part of obtaining her consent to an abortion," which "for constitutional purposes, [was] no different from a requirement that a doctor give certain specific information about any medical procedure." The joint opinion explained that the law regulated speech only "as part of the practice of medicine, subject to reasonable licensing and regulation by the State." Indeed, the requirement that a doctor obtain informed consent to perform an operation is "firmly entrenched in American tort law."

The licensed notice at issue here is not an informed-consent requirement or any other regulation of professional conduct. . . . Tellingly, many facilities that provide the exact same services as covered facilities—such as general practice clinics—are not required to provide the licensed notice. The licensed notice regulates speech as speech.

Outside of the two contexts discussed above—disclosures under *Zauderer* and professional conduct—this Court's precedents have long protected the First Amendment rights of professionals. . . .

The dangers associated with content-based regulations of speech are also present in the context of professional speech. As with other kinds of speech, regulating the content of professionals' speech "pose[s] the inherent risk that the Government seeks not to advance a legitimate regulatory goal, but to suppress unpopular ideas or information." Take medicine, for example. "Doctors help patients make deeply personal decisions, and their candor is crucial." Throughout history, governments have "manipulat[ed] the content of doctor-patient discourse" to increase state power and suppress minorities. . . .

Further, when the government polices the content of professional speech, it can fail to "'preserve an uninhibited marketplace of ideas in which truth will ultimately prevail.'" Professionals might have a host of good-faith disagreements, both with each other and with the government, on many topics in their respective fields. Doctors and nurses might disagree about the ethics of assisted suicide or the benefits of medical marijuana; lawyers and marriage counselors might disagree about the prudence of prenuptial agreements or the wisdom of divorce; bankers and accountants might disagree about the amount of money that should be devoted to savings or the benefits of tax reform. . . .

In sum, neither California nor the Ninth Circuit has identified a persuasive reason for treating professional speech as a unique category that is exempt from ordinary First Amendment principles. We do not foreclose the possibility that some such reason exists. We need not do so because the licensed notice cannot survive even intermediate scrutiny. California asserts a single interest to justify the licensed notice: providing low-income women with information about state-sponsored services. Assuming that this is a substantial state interest, the licensed notice is not sufficiently drawn to achieve it.

If California's goal is to educate low-income women about the services it provides, then the licensed notice is "wildly underinclusive." The notice applies only to clinics that have a "primary purpose" of "providing family planning or pregnancy-related services.". . . Other clinics that have another primary purpose, or that provide only one category of those services, also serve low-income women and could educate them about the State's services. According to the legislative record, California has "nearly 1,000 community clinics"—including "federally designated community health centers, migrant health centers, rural health centers, and frontier health centers"—that "serv[e] more than 5.6 million patients . . . annually through over 17 million patient encounters." But most of those clinics are excluded from the licensed notice requirement without explanation. Such "[u]nderinclusiveness raises serious doubts about whether the government is in fact pursuing the interest it invokes, rather than disfavoring a particular speaker or viewpoint."

The FACT Act also excludes, without explanation, federal clinics and Family PACT providers from the licensed-notice requirement. California notes that those clinics can enroll women in California's programs themselves, but California's stated interest is informing women that these services exist in the first place. California has identified no evidence that the exempted clinics are more likely to provide this information than the covered clinics. . . .

Further, California could inform low-income women about its services "without burdening a speaker with unwanted speech." Most obviously, it could inform the women itself with a public-information campaign. California could even post the information on public property near crisis pregnancy centers. California argues that it has already tried an advertising campaign, and that many women who are eligible for publicly-funded healthcare have not enrolled. But California has identified no evidence to that effect. . . .

In short, petitioners are likely to succeed on the merits of their challenge to the licensed notice. Contrary to the suggestion in the dissent, we do not question the legality of health and safety warnings long considered permissible, or purely factual and uncontroversial disclosures about commercial products.

We next address the unlicensed notice. The parties dispute whether the unlicensed notice is subject to deferential review under *Zauderer*. We need not decide whether the *Zauderer* standard applies to the unlicensed notice. Even under *Zauderer*, a disclosure requirement cannot be "unjustified or unduly burdensome." Our precedents require disclosures to remedy a harm that is "potentially real not purely hypothetical," and to extend "no broader than reasonably necessary." Otherwise, they risk "chilling" protected speech." Importantly, California has the burden to prove that the unlicensed notice is neither unjustified nor unduly burdensome. It has not met its burden.

We need not decide what type of state interest is sufficient to sustain a disclosure requirement like the unlicensed notice. California has not demonstrated any justification for the unlicensed notice that is more than "purely hypothetical." The only justification that the California Legislature put forward was ensuring that "pregnant women in California know when they are getting medical care from licensed professionals." At oral argument, however, California denied that the justification for the FACT Act was that women "go into [crisis pregnancy centers] and they don't realize what they are." Indeed, California points to nothing suggesting that pregnant women do not already know that the covered facilities are staffed by unlicensed medical professionals. The services that trigger the unlicensed notice—such as having "volunteers who collect health information from clients," "advertis[ing] . . . pregnancy options counseling," and offering over-the-counter "pregnancy testing," § 123471(b)—do not require a medical license. And California already makes it a crime for individuals without a medical license to practice medicine. At this preliminary stage of the litigation, we agree that petitioners are likely to prevail on the question whether California has proved a justification for the unlicensed notice.

Even if California had presented a nonhypothetical justification for the unlicensed notice, the FACT Act unduly burdens protected speech. The unlicensed notice imposes a government-scripted, speaker-based disclosure requirement that is wholly disconnected from California's informational interest. It requires covered facilities to post California's precise notice, no matter what the facilities say on site or in their advertisements. And it covers a curiously narrow subset of speakers. While the licensed notice applies to facilities that provide "family planning" services and "contraception or contraceptive methods," the California Legislature dropped these triggering conditions for the unlicensed notice. The unlicensed notice applies only to facilities that primarily provide "pregnancy-related" services. Thus, a facility that advertises and provides pregnancy tests is covered by the unlicensed notice, but a facility across the street that advertises and provides nonprescription contraceptives is excluded—even though the latter is no less likely to make women think it is licensed. This Court's precedents are deeply skeptical of laws that "distinguis[h] among different speakers, allowing speech by some but not others." Speaker-based laws run the risk that "the State has left unburdened those speakers whose messages are in accord with its own views."

The application of the unlicensed notice to advertisements demonstrates just how burdensome it is. The notice applies to all "print and digital advertising materials" by an unlicensed covered facility. These materials must include a government-drafted statement that "[t]his facility is not licensed as a medical facility by the State of California and has no licensed medical provider who provides or directly supervises the provision of services." An unlicensed facility must call attention to the notice, instead of its own message, by some method such as larger text or contrasting type or color. This scripted language must be posted in English and as many other languages as California chooses to require. As California conceded at oral argument, a billboard for an unlicensed facility that says "Choose Life" would have to surround that two-word statement with a 29-word statement from the government, in as many as 13 different languages. In this way, the unlicensed notice drowns out the facility's own message. More likely, the "detail required" by the unlicensed notice "effectively rules out" the possibility of having such a billboard in the first place.

For all these reasons, the unlicensed notice does not satisfy *Zauderer*, assuming that standard applies. California has offered no justification that the notice plausibly furthers. It targets speakers, not speech, and imposes an unduly burdensome disclosure requirement that will chill their protected speech. Taking all these circumstances together, we conclude that the unlicensed notice is unjustified and unduly burdensome under *Zauderer*. We express no view on the legality of a similar disclosure requirement that is better supported or less burdensome.

We hold that petitioners are likely to succeed on the merits of their claim that the FACT Act violates the First Amendment. We reverse the judgment of the Court of Appeals and remand the case for further proceedings consistent with this opinion.

JUSTICE KENNEDY, with whom THE CHIEF JUSTICE, JUSTICE ALITO, and JUSTICE GORSUCH join, concurring.

I join the Court's opinion in all respects.

This separate writing seeks to underscore that the apparent viewpoint discrimination here is a matter of serious constitutional concern. . . .

It does appear that viewpoint discrimination is inherent in the design and structure of this Act. This law is a paradigmatic example of the serious threat presented when government seeks to impose its own message in the place of individual speech, thought, and expression. For here the State requires primarily pro-life pregnancy centers to promote the State's own preferred message advertising abortions. This compels individuals to contradict their most deeply held beliefs, beliefs grounded in basic philosophical, ethical, or religious precepts, or all of these. And the history of the Act's passage and its underinclusive application suggest a real possibility that these individuals were targeted because of their beliefs. . . .

JUSTICE BREYER, with whom JUSTICE GINSBURG, JUSTICE SOTOMAYOR, and JUSTICE KAGAN join, dissenting.

The petitioners ask us to consider whether two sections of a California statute violate the First Amendment. . . . In my view both statutory sections are likely constitutional, and I dissent from the Court's contrary conclusions. . . .

Before turning to the specific law before us, I focus upon the general interpretation of the First Amendment that the majority says it applies. It applies heightened scrutiny to the Act because the Act, in its view, is "content based." "By compelling individuals to speak a particular message," it adds, "such notices 'alte[r] the content of [their] speech.' " "As a general matter," the majority concludes, such laws are "presumptively unconstitutional" and are subject to "stringent" review. . . .

This constitutional approach threatens to create serious problems. . . . Virtually every disclosure law could be considered "content based," for virtually every disclosure law requires individuals "to speak a particular message." Thus, the majority's view, if taken literally, could radically change prior law, perhaps placing much securities law or consumer protection law at constitutional risk, depending on how broadly its exceptions are interpreted.

Many ordinary disclosure laws would fall outside the majority's exceptions for disclosures related to the professional's own services or conduct. These include numerous commonly found disclosure requirements relating to the medical profession (requiring hospitals to tell parents about child seat belts)(requiring hospitals to ask incoming patients if they would like the facility to give their family information about patients' rights and responsibilities)(requiring hospitals to tell parents of newborns about pertussis disease and the available vaccine). These also include numerous disclosure requirements found in other areas (requiring signs by elevators showing stair locations)(requiring property owners to inform tenants about garbage disposal procedures).

The majority, . . . perhaps recognizing this problem, adds a general disclaimer. It says that it does not "question the legality of health and safety warnings long considered permissible, or purely factual and uncontroversial disclosures about commercial products." But this generally phrased disclaimer would seem more likely to invite litigation than to provide needed limitation and clarification. The majority, for example, does not explain why the Act here, which is justified in part by health and safety considerations, does not fall within its "health" category. [See] *Planned Parenthood of Southeastern Pa. v. Casey* (joint opinion of O'Connor, Kennedy, and Souter, JJ.)(reasoning that disclosures related to fetal development and childbirth are related to the health of a woman seeking an abortion). . . .

Precedent does not require a test such as the majority's. Rather, in saying the Act is not a longstanding health and safety law, the Court substitutes its own approach—without a defining standard—for an approach that was reasonably clear. Historically, the Court has been wary of claims that regulation of business activity, particularly health-related activity, violates the Constitution. . . .

The Court has taken this same respectful approach to economic and social legislation when a First Amendment claim like the claim present here is at issue. . . .

The Court, in justification, refers to widely accepted First Amendment goals, such as the need to protect the Nation from laws that " 'suppress unpopular ideas or information' " or inhibit the " 'marketplace of ideas in which truth will ultimately prevail.' " I, too, value this role that the First Amendment plays—in an appropriate case. But here, the majority enunciates a general test that reaches far beyond the area where this Court has examined laws closely in the service of those goals. . . .

Still, what about this specific case? The disclosure at issue here concerns speech related to abortion. It involves health, differing moral values, and differing points of view. Thus, rather than set forth broad, new, First Amendment principles, I believe that we should focus more directly upon precedent more closely related to the case at hand. This Court has more than once considered disclosure laws relating to reproductive health. . . .

In *Planned Parenthood of Southeastern Pa. v. Casey*, the Court . . . considered a state law that required doctors to provide information to a woman deciding whether to proceed with an abortion. . . .

The joint opinion specifically discussed the First Amendment, the constitutional provision now directly before us. It concluded that the statute did not violate the First Amendment. It wrote:

> "All that is left of petitioners' argument is an asserted First Amendment right of a physician not to provide information about the risks of abortion, and childbirth, in a manner mandated by the State. To be sure, the physician's First Amendment rights not to

speak are implicated, but only as part of the practice of medicine, subject to reasonable licensing and regulation by the State. We see no constitutional infirmity in the requirement that the physician provide the information mandated by the State here."

Thus, the Court considered the State's statutory requirements, including the requirement that the doctor must inform his patient about where she could learn how to have the newborn child adopted (if carried to term) and how she could find related financial assistance. To repeat the point, the Court then held that the State's requirements did not violate either the Constitution's protection of free speech or its protection of a woman's right to choose to have an abortion.

Taking *Casey* as controlling, [i]f a State can lawfully require a doctor to tell a woman seeking an abortion about adoption services, why should it not be able, as here, to require a medical counselor to tell a woman seeking prenatal care or other reproductive healthcare about childbirth and abortion services? As the question suggests, there is no convincing reason to distinguish between information about adoption and information about abortion in this context. After all, the rule of law embodies evenhandedness, and "what is sauce for the goose is normally sauce for the gander."

The majority tries to distinguish *Casey* as concerning a regulation of professional conduct that only incidentally burdened speech. *Casey*, in its view, applies only when obtaining "informed consent" to a medical procedure is directly at issue. . . .

The majority contends that the disclosure here is unrelated to a "medical procedure," unlike that in *Casey*, and so the State has no reason to inform a woman about alternatives to childbirth (or, presumably, the health risks of childbirth). Really? No one doubts that choosing an abortion is a medical procedure that involves certain health risks. But the same is true of carrying a child to term and giving birth. That is why prenatal care often involves testing for anemia, infections, measles, chicken pox, genetic disorders, diabetes, pneumonia, urinary tract infections, preeclampsia, and hosts of other medical conditions. Childbirth itself, directly or through pain management, risks harms of various kinds, some connected with caesarean or surgery-related deliveries, some related to more ordinary methods of delivery. Indeed, nationwide "childbirth is 14 times more likely than abortion to result in" the woman's death. Health considerations do not favor disclosure of alternatives and risks associated with the latter but not those associated with the former.

In any case, informed consent principles apply more broadly than only to discrete "medical procedures." Prescription drug labels warn patients of risks even though taking prescription drugs may not be considered a "medical procedure."

The majority also finds it "[t]ellin[g]" that general practice clinics—*i.e.*, paid clinics—are not required to provide the licensed notice. But the lack-of-information problem that the statute seeks to ameliorate is a problem that the State explains is commonly found among low-income women. . . . Nor is it surprising that those with low income, whatever they choose in respect to pregnancy, might find information about financial assistance particularly useful. There is "nothing inherently suspect" about this distinction, which is not "based on the content of [the advocacy] each group offers," but upon the patients the group generally serves and the needs of that population.

Separately, finding no First Amendment infirmity in the licensed notice is consistent with earlier Court rulings. For instance, in *Zauderer* we upheld a requirement that attorneys disclose in their advertisements that clients might be liable for significant litigation costs even if their lawsuits were unsuccessful. . . . The majority concludes that *Zauderer* does not apply because the disclosure "in no way relates to the services that licensed clinics provide." But information about state resources for family planning, prenatal care, and abortion is related to the services that licensed clinics provide. These clinics provide counseling about contraception (which is a family-planning service), ultrasounds or pregnancy testing (which is prenatal care), or abortion. The required disclosure is related to the clinic's services because it provides information about state resources for the very same services. A patient who knows that she can receive free prenatal care from the State may well prefer to forgo the prenatal care offered at one of the clinics here. And for those interested in family planning and abortion services, information about such alternatives is relevant information to patients offered prenatal care, just as *Casey* considered information about adoption to be relevant to the abortion decision.

Regardless, *Zauderer* is not so limited. *Zauderer* turned on the "material differences between disclosure requirements and outright prohibitions on speech." A disclosure requirement does not prevent speakers "from conveying information to the public," but "only require[s] them to provide somewhat more information than they might otherwise be inclined to present." Where a State's requirement to speak "purely factual and uncontroversial information" does not attempt "to 'prescribe what shall be orthodox in politics, nationalism, religion, or other matters of opinion or force citizens to confess by word or act their faith therein,' " it does not warrant heightened scrutiny.

In *Zauderer*, the Court emphasized the reason that the First Amendment protects commercial speech at all: "the value to consumers of the information such speech provides." For that reason, a professional's "constitutionally protected interest in not providing any particular factual information in his advertising is minimal." . . .

Accordingly, the majority's reliance on cases that prohibit rather than require speech is misplaced. I agree that " 'in the fields of medicine and public heath, . . . information can save lives,' " but the licensed disclosure serves that informational interest by requiring clinics to notify patients of the availability of state resources for family planning services, prenatal care, and abortion, which . . . is truthful and nonmisleading information. Abortion is a controversial topic and a source of normative debate, but the availability of state resources is not a normative statement or a fact of debatable truth. The disclosure includes information about resources available should a woman seek to continue her pregnancy or terminate it, and it expresses no official preference for one choice over the other. Similarly, the majority highlights an interest that often underlies our decisions in respect to speech prohibitions—the marketplace of ideas. But that marketplace is fostered, not hindered, by providing information to patients to enable them to make fully informed medical decisions in respect to their pregnancies.

Of course, one might take the majority's decision to mean that speech about abortion is special, that it involves in this case not only professional medical matters, but also views based on deeply held religious and moral beliefs about the nature of the practice. . . . But assuming that is so, the law's insistence upon treating like cases alike should lead us to reject the petitioners' arguments that I have discussed. . . . [A] Constitution that allows States to insist that medical providers tell women about the possibility of adoption should also allow States similarly to insist that medical providers tell women about the possibility of abortion.

[T]he petitioners [also] argue that it unconstitutionally discriminates on the basis of viewpoint because it primarily covers facilities with supporters, organizers, and employees who are likely to hold strong pro-life views. They contend that the statute does not cover facilities likely to hold neutral or pro-choice views, because it exempts facilities that enroll patients in publicly funded programs that include abortion. In doing so, they say, the statute unnecessarily imposes a disproportionate burden upon facilities with pro-life views, the very facilities most likely to find the statute's references to abortion morally abhorrent.

[B]ut the key question is whether these exempt clinics are significantly more likely than are the pro-life clinics to tell or to have told their pregnant patients about the existence of these programs—in the absence of any statutory compulsion. If so, it may make sense—in terms of the statute's informational objective—to exempt them, namely if there is no need to cover them.

The second statutory provision covers pregnancy-related facilities that provide women with certain medical-type services (such as obstetric ultrasounds or sonograms, pregnancy diagnosis, counseling about pregnancy options, or prenatal care), are not licensed as medical facilities by the State, and do not have a licensed medical provider on site. The statute says that such a facility must disclose that it is not "licensed as a medical facility." And it must make this disclosure in a posted notice and in advertising.

The majority does not question that the State's interest (ensuring that "pregnant women in California know when they are getting medical care from licensed professionals") is the type of informational interest that *Zauderer* encompasses. Nor could it. In *Riley*, the Court noted that the First Amendment would permit a requirement for "professional fundraisers to disclose their professional status"—nearly identical to the unlicensed disclosure at issue here. Such informational interests have long justified regulations in the medical context.

Nevertheless, the majority concludes that the State's interest is "purely hypothetical" because unlicensed clinics provide innocuous services that do not require a medical license. To do so, it applies a searching standard of review based on our precedents that deal with speech restrictions, not disclosures. This approach is incompatible with *Zauderer* (upholding attorney disclosure requirements where "reasonably related to the State's interest").

There is no basis for finding the State's interest "hypothetical." The legislature heard that information-related delays in qualified healthcare negatively affect women seeking to terminate their pregnancies as well as women carrying their pregnancies to term, with delays in qualified prenatal care causing life-long health problems for infants. Even without such testimony, it is "self-evident" that patients might think they are receiving qualified medical care when they enter facilities that collect health information, perform obstetric ultrasounds or sonograms, diagnose pregnancy, and provide counseling about pregnancy options or other prenatal care. The State's conclusion to that effect is certainly reasonable.

The majority also suggests that the Act applies too broadly, namely, to all unlicensed facilities "no matter what the facilities say on site or in their advertisements." But the Court has long held that a law is not unreasonable merely because it is overinclusive. For instance, in *Semler* the Court upheld as reasonable a state law that prohibited licensed dentists from advertising that their skills were superior to those of other dentists. A dentist complained that he was, in fact, better than other dentists. Yet the Court held that "[i]n framing its policy, the legislature was not bound to provide for determinations of the relative proficiency of particular practitioners." To the contrary, "[t]he legislature was entitled to consider the general effects of the practices which it described, and if these effects were injurious in facilitating unwarranted and misleading claims, to counteract them by a general rule, even though in particular instances there might be no actual deception or misstatement."

Relatedly, the majority suggests that the Act is suspect because it covers some speakers but not others. . . . There is no cause for such concern here. The Act does not, on its face, distinguish between facilities that favor pro-life and those that favor pro-choice points of view. Nor is there any convincing evidence before us or in the courts below that discrimination was the purpose or the effect of the statute. Notably, California does not single out pregnancy-related facilities for this type of disclosure requirement. See, e.g., Cal. Bus. & Prof.Code Ann. § 2053.6 (West 2012)(unlicensed providers of alternative health services must disclose that "he or she is not a licensed physician" and "the services to be provided are not licensed by the state"). And it is unremarkable that the State excluded the provision of family planning and contraceptive services as triggering conditions. After all, the State was seeking to ensure that "pregnant women in California know when they are getting medical care from licensed professionals," and pregnant women generally do not need contraceptive services.

Finally, the majority concludes that the Act is overly burdensome. But these and similar claims are claims that the statute could be applied unconstitutionally, not that it is unconstitutional on its face. And it will be open to the petitioners to make these claims if and when the State threatens to enforce the statute in this way. . . . For instance, the majority highlights that the statute requires facilities to write their "medical license" disclaimers in 13 languages. As I understand the Act, it would require disclosure in no more than two languages—English and Spanish—in the vast majority of California's 58 counties. The exception is Los Angeles County, where, given the large number of different-language speaking groups, expression in many languages may prove necessary to communicate the message to those whom that message will help. Whether the requirement of 13 different languages goes too far and is unnecessarily burdensome in light of the need to secure the statutory objectives is a matter that concerns Los Angeles County alone, and it is a proper subject for a Los Angeles-based as applied challenge in light of whatever facts a plaintiff finds relevant. At most, such facts might show a need for fewer languages, not invalidation of the statute.

COMMENTS AND QUESTIONS

1. In *Planned Parenthood of Southeastern Pennsylvania v. Casey*, the 1992 case that reaffirmed the essence of *Roe v. Wade*, the Court upheld the state requirement that before a person could receive an abortion a doctor would have to provide information concerning alternatives to abortion, the gestational age of the fetus, and opportunities for adoption. How is the information the licensed pro-life centers are required to post about the availability of state programs providing free or low-cost family planning services, prenatal care, and abortion distinguishable?

2.   What is controversial about the information required to be provided by the licensed pro-life centers? Is it not simply factual information? If it is controversial, why wasn't the information required to be provided by doctors in *Casey* also controversial?

3.   What is the objection by non-licensed pro-life centers to having to inform people that they do not have licensed medical providers? Do you think that many persons would assume that persons performing ultra-sounds, reading ultra-sound results, and diagnosing pregnancy might be licensed medical providers or at least supervised by such persons? After all, even nurse practitioners and RNs are licensed medical providers.

4.   Is this case really all about what the author of the FACT Act said in explaining the bill in the California legislature? If the law really was intended to promote abortion over other options that would be a problem. Is that what the legislator was intending, or was he intending that women should simply know they have alternatives when being counseled not to have an abortion? How much should what a legislator says be used to attack the validity of a law formally justified on other grounds? Recall what key legislators said with regard to the bill criminalizing the burning of draft cards and the Court's response.

5.   *Masterpiece Cakeshop, Ltd. v. Colorado Civil Rts Comm'n*, 138 S.Ct. 1719 (2018), discussed earlier under Expressive Conduct, involved the Colorado baker who would not bake a custom wedding cake for a same-sex wedding. Although the baker raised both Free Speech and Free Exercise claims in his challenge to the finding of liability for violating the state's antidiscrimination law, the Court only addressed the Free Exercise claim, finding for the baker. Justice Thomas, joined by Justice Gorsuch, would have reached the Free Speech claim and would also have ruled in the baker's favor on that basis. In their view, the case was like *Hurley v. Irish-American Gay, Lesbian and Bisexual Group of Boston*, 515 U.S. 557 (1995), which held that the state antidiscrimination law could not force the St. Patrick's Day Parade organizers to allow a group espousing gay pride to participate in the parade. The unanimous Court there found that this would be compelling a person to express a view they did not agree with in violation of the First Amendment's Free Speech Clause. Similarly, to require a baker to make a cake celebrating an activity inconsistent with the views of the baker would compel him to express a view he did not agree with. Because the Court's decision on Free Exercise was narrowly based, and because the Free Speech issue is arising with frequency in the lower courts, the Supreme Court will have to address the Free Speech claim in the not distant future. *See, e.g., Telescope Media Group v. Lucero*, 939 F.3d 740 (8th Cir. 2019)(state antidiscrimination law cannot force wedding video photographers to create wedding videos of a same-sex wedding); *State v. Arlene's Flowers, Inc.*, 193 Wash.2d 469 (2019), petition for *cert. denied* (2021). (Free Speech Clause did not shield a flower arranger from liability under the state antidiscrimination law for refusing to provide flowers for a same-sex wedding); *303 Creative, LLC v. Elenis*, 6 F.4th 1160 (10th Cir. 2021), *cert. granted* (2022)(Neither Free Speech Clause nor Free Exercise

Clause shielded a web page designer for weddings from the Colorado anti-discrimination law).

6.   If money can be speech when it is used to enable speech, can the government require a person to provide money, if the money will be used to support speech the person does not agree with? In *Abood v. Detroit Bd. of Ed.*, 431 U.S. 209 (1977), the Court held that the mandatory union dues of public school teachers could not be used to support an ideological or political cause the member might oppose. Similarly, bar dues required of lawyers could not be used for political purposes. *See Keller v. State Bar of Cal.*, 496 U.S. 1 (1990). *Abood*, however, found no constitutional infirmity in requiring non-members of a union, to whom the union was statutorily required to provide equal representation, to pay that portion of union dues dedicated to representational, as opposed to ideological or political, costs. That conclusion was overruled in *Janus v. AFSCME*, 138 S.Ct. 2448 (2018), where the Court by a 5–4 vote held that representation by public employee unions necessarily involved political considerations, such as whether to pay teachers higher salaries or to have smaller class sizes. Consequently, to require non-members of a public employee union to pay for representational costs they disagreed with would be to force them to support political speech they did not agree with.

In the context of mandatory student fees in support of extracurricular student groups, some of whose speech might be opposed by some required to pay the fee, the Court decided that so long as the student groups were funded on a viewpoint neutral basis the assessment was constitutional. *See Board of Regents of the University of Wisconsin System v. Southworth*, 529 U.S. 217 (2000). The Court seemed to view this assessment as funding "dynamic discussions of philosophical, religious, scientific, social, and political subjects in their extracurricular campus life" as part of its educational goals, rather than funding particular viewpoints.

A seemingly recurring issue has been government-mandated payments by agricultural producers into a fund for advertising the agricultural product. The three cases that have come before the Supreme Court reached three different conclusions. The first, *Glickman v. Wileman Brothers & Elliott, Inc.*, 521 U.S. 457 (1997), upheld the assessment because it involved commodities in which the government had effectively eliminated the free market and had instead instituted a government-organized collective of which the producer-funded advertising was but a part. It did not involve funding political or ideological speech the producer might disagree with. The second, *United States v. United Foods, Inc.*, 533 U.S. 405 (2001), struck down an assessment on mushroom growers used to fund advertising of mushrooms. It distinguished *Glickman* on the basis that here there was no government-organized collective; it was simply assessing people to pay for mushroom advertising, which the Court said constituted impermissible government-mandated support of speech to which the producers were opposed. The last, *Johanns v. Livestock Marketing Assn.*, 544 U.S. 550 (2005), took an entirely different approach. It held that the speech involved—advertising beef products—was government speech, not the speech of third parties to which the plaintiffs were opposed. People have no First

Amendment right to object to government speech and no First Amendment right to object to paying for government speech to which they are opposed. The one caveat was that the government speech—here beef advertising—could not indicate that these beef producers were responsible for or approved of the advertising. The Court noted that this argument had not been made in the earlier two cases, suggesting that if it had, those cases would have been decided on the same basis.

PROBLEM

A commercial photographer who specializes in wedding photos refuses to perform his services for same-sex or inter-racial weddings. His state law classifies his occupation as a public accommodation and prohibits discrimination on the basis of race or sexual orientation. Is the law constitutional as applied to the photographer?

K. THE FREEDOM OF ASSOCIATION

The First Amendment does not address in terms a freedom of association, although it speaks of a freedom peaceably to assemble. Nevertheless, whether founded on the freedom of speech or the freedom of assembly, the Court has since the beginning of the modern era recognized a freedom of association protected by the First Amendment.

ROBERTS V. UNITED STATES JAYCEES

United States Supreme Court, 1984.
468 U.S. 609, 104 S.Ct. 3244.

JUSTICE BRENNAN delivered the opinion of the Court.

This case requires us to address a conflict between a State's efforts to eliminate gender-based discrimination against its citizens and the constitutional freedom of association asserted by members of a private organization.

The United States Jaycees (Jaycees), founded in 1920 as the Junior Chamber of Commerce, is a nonprofit membership corporation. . . . The objective of the Jaycees, as set out in its bylaws, is to pursue

> such educational and charitable purposes as will promote and foster the growth and development of young men's civic organizations in the United States, designed to inculcate in the individual membership of such organization a spirit of genuine Americanism and civic interest, and as a supplementary education institution to provide them with opportunity for personal development and achievement and an avenue for intelligent participation by young men in the affairs of their

community, state and nation, and to develop true friendship and understanding among young men of all nations.

The organization's bylaws establish seven classes of membership, including individual or regular members, associate individual members, and local chapters. Regular membership is limited to young men between the ages of 18 and 35, while associate membership is available to individuals or groups ineligible for regular membership, principally women and older men. An associate member, whose dues are somewhat lower than those charged regular members, may not vote, hold local or national office, or participate in certain leadership training and awards programs. . . . At the time of trial in August 1981, the Jaycees had approximately 295,000 members in 7,400 local chapters affiliated with 51 state organizations. There were at that time about 11,915 associate members. The national organization's executive vice president estimated at trial that women associate members make up about two percent of the Jaycees' total membership. . . .

[C]harges of discrimination [against the national organization were filed] with the Minnesota Department of Human Rights. The complaints alleged that the exclusion of women from full membership required by the national organization's bylaws violated the Minnesota Human Rights Act (Act), which provides in part: "It is an unfair discriminatory practice: To deny any person the full and equal enjoyment of the goods, services, facilities, privileges, advantages, and accommodations of a place of public accommodation because of race, color, creed, religion, disability, national origin or sex."

The term "place of public accommodation" is defined in the Act [in a way as to include the Jaycees.]

Our decisions have referred to constitutionally protected "freedom of association" in two distinct senses. In one line of decisions, the Court has concluded that choices to enter into and maintain certain intimate human relationships must be secured against undue intrusion by the State because of the role of such relationships in safeguarding the individual freedom that is central to our constitutional scheme. In this respect, freedom of association receives protection as a fundamental element of personal liberty. In another set of decisions, the Court has recognized a right to associate for the purpose of engaging in those activities protected by the First Amendment—speech, assembly, petition for the redress of grievances, and the exercise of religion. The Constitution guarantees freedom of association of this kind as an indispensable means of preserving other individual liberties. . . .

The Court has long recognized that, because the Bill of Rights is designed to secure individual liberty, it must afford the formation and preservation of certain kinds of highly personal relationships a substantial measure of sanctuary from unjustified interference by the State. . . . [T]he constitutional shelter afforded such relationships reflects the realization that individuals draw much of their emotional enrichment from close ties with others. Protecting these relationships from unwarranted state interference therefore safeguards the ability independently to define one's identity that is central to any concept of liberty.

The personal affiliations that exemplify these considerations, and that therefore suggest some relevant limitations on the relationships that might be entitled to this sort of constitutional protection, are those that attend the creation and sustenance of a family—marriage, childbirth, the raising and education of children, and cohabitation with one's relatives. Family relationships, by their nature, involve deep attachments and commitments to the necessarily few other individuals with whom one shares not only a special community of thoughts, experiences, and beliefs but also distinctively personal aspects of one's life. Among other things, therefore, they are distinguished by such attributes as relative smallness, a high degree of selectivity in decisions to begin and maintain the affiliation, and seclusion from others in critical aspects of the relationship. . . . Conversely, an association lacking these qualities—such as a large business enterprise—seems remote from the concerns giving rise to this constitutional protection. . . . [Thus, the Jaycees do not qualify for protection under this strand of associational freedom.]

We turn therefore to consider the extent to which application of the Minnesota statute to compel the Jaycees to accept women infringes the group's freedom of expressive association.

An individual's freedom to speak, to worship, and to petition the government for the redress of grievances could not be vigorously protected from interference by the State unless a correlative freedom to engage in group effort toward those ends were not also guaranteed. . . . Consequently, we have long understood as implicit in the right to engage in activities protected by the First Amendment a corresponding right to associate with others in pursuit of a wide variety of political, social, economic, educational, religious, and cultural ends. In view of the various protected activities in which the Jaycees engages, that right is plainly implicated in this case.

Government actions that may unconstitutionally infringe upon this freedom can take a number of forms. Among other things, government may seek to impose penalties or withhold benefits from individuals because of their membership in a disfavored group, *e.g.*, *Healy v. James*, 408 U.S. 169 (1972) [denial to local chapter of Students for a Democratic Society of recognition as an official student group]; it may attempt to require disclosure of the fact of membership in a group seeking anonymity, *e.g.*, *Brown v. Socialist Workers' 74 Campaign Committee*, 459 U.S. 87 (1982) [the First Amendment prohibits a state from compelling disclosure by minor political parties that would subject those persons identified to the reasonable probability of threats, harassment, or reprisals]; and it may try to interfere with the internal organization or affairs of the group, *e.g.*, *Cousins v. Wigoda*, 419 U.S. 477 (1975) [state court could not order seating of particular delegates to a national political convention]. By requiring the Jaycees to admit women as full voting members, the Minnesota Act works an infringement of the last type. There can be no clearer example of an intrusion into the internal structure or affairs of an association than a regulation that forces the group to accept members it does not desire. Such a regulation may impair the ability of the original members to express only those views that brought them together. Freedom of association therefore plainly presupposes a freedom not to associate.

The right to associate for expressive purposes is not, however, absolute. Infringements on that right may be justified by regulations adopted to serve compelling state interests, unrelated to the suppression of ideas, that cannot be achieved through means significantly less restrictive of associational freedoms. We are persuaded that Minnesota's compelling interest in eradicating discrimination against its female citizens justifies the impact that application of the statute to the Jaycees may have on the male members' associational freedoms.

On its face, the Minnesota Act does not aim at the suppression of speech, does not distinguish between prohibited and permitted activity on the basis of viewpoint, and does not license enforcement authorities to administer the statute on the basis of such constitutionally impermissible criteria. Nor does the Jaycees contend that the Act has been applied in this case for the purpose of hampering the organization's ability to express its views. Instead, as the Minnesota Supreme Court explained, the Act reflects the State's strong historical commitment to eliminating discrimination and assuring its citizens equal access to publicly available goods and services. That goal, which is unrelated to the suppression of expression, plainly serves compelling state interests of the highest order. . . .

[I]n explaining its conclusion that the Jaycees local chapters are "place[s] of public accommodations" within the meaning of the Act, the Minnesota court noted the various commercial programs and benefits offered to members and stated that "[l]eadership skills are 'goods,' [and] business contacts and employment promotions are 'privileges' and 'advantages'. . . ." Assuring women equal access to such goods, privileges, and advantages clearly furthers compelling state interests.

In applying the Act to the Jaycees, the State has advanced those interests through the least restrictive means of achieving its ends. Indeed, the Jaycees has failed to demonstrate that the Act imposes any serious burdens on the male members' freedom of expressive association. To be sure, as the Court of Appeals noted, a "not insubstantial part" of the Jaycees' activities constitutes protected expression on political, economic, cultural, and social affairs. . . . There is, however, no basis in the record for concluding that admission of women as full voting members will impede the organization's ability to engage in these protected activities or to disseminate its preferred views. The Act requires no change in the Jaycees' creed of promoting the interests of young men, and it imposes no restrictions on the organization's ability to exclude individuals with ideologies or philosophies different from those of its existing members. Moreover, the Jaycees already invites women to share the group's views and philosophy and to participate in much of its training and community activities. Accordingly, any claim that admission of women as full voting members will impair a symbolic message conveyed by the very fact that women are not permitted to vote is attenuated at best.

While acknowledging that "the specific content of most of the resolutions adopted over the years by the Jaycees has nothing to do with sex," the Court of Appeals nonetheless entertained the hypothesis that women members might have a different view or agenda with respect to these matters so that, if they are allowed to vote, "some change in the Jaycees' philosophical cast can reasonably be expected." . . . In claiming that women might have a different attitude about such issues as the federal budget, school prayer, voting rights, and foreign relations, or that the organization's public positions would have a different effect if the group were not "a purely young men's association," the Jaycees relies solely on unsupported generalizations about the relative interests and perspectives of men and women. Although such generalizations may or may not have a statistical basis in fact with respect to particular positions adopted by the Jaycees, we have repeatedly condemned legal decisionmaking that relies uncritically on such assumptions. In the absence of a showing far more substantial than that attempted by the Jaycees, we decline to indulge in the sexual stereotyping that underlies appellee's contention that, by allowing women to vote, application of the Minnesota Act will change the content or impact of the organization's speech.

In any event, even if enforcement of the Act causes some incidental abridgment of the Jaycees' protected speech, that effect is no greater than is necessary to accomplish the State's legitimate purposes. As we have explained, acts of invidious discrimination in the distribution of publicly available goods, services, and other advantages cause unique evils that government has a compelling interest to prevent—wholly apart from the point of view such conduct may transmit. Accordingly, like violence or other types of potentially expressive activities that produce special harms distinct from their communicative impact, such practices are entitled to no constitutional protection. In prohibiting such practices, the Minnesota Act therefore "responds precisely to the substantive problem which legitimately concerns" the State and abridges no more speech or associational freedom than is necessary to accomplish that purpose. . . .

JUSTICE REHNQUIST concurs in the judgment.

THE CHIEF JUSTICE and JUSTICE BLACKMUN took no part in the decision of this case.

JUSTICE O'CONNOR, concurring in part and concurring in the judgment.

[I] agree with the Court that the Jaycees cannot claim a right of association deriving from this Court's cases concerning "marriage, procreation, contraception, family relationships, and child rearing and education." . . .

[I] agree with the Court that application of the Minnesota law to the Jaycees does not contravene the First Amendment, but I reach that conclusion for reasons distinct from those offered by the Court. I believe the Court has adopted a test that unadvisedly casts doubt on the power of States to pursue the profoundly important goal of ensuring nondiscriminatory access to commercial opportunities in our society. At the same time, the Court has adopted an approach to the general problem presented by this case that accords insufficient protection to expressive associations and places inappropriate burdens on groups claiming the protection of the First Amendment.

The Court analyzes Minnesota's attempt to regulate the Jaycees' membership using a test that I find both overprotective of activities undeserving of constitutional shelter and underprotective of important First Amendment concerns. The Court declares that the Jaycees' right of association depends on the organization's making a "substantial" showing that the admission of unwelcome members "will change the message communicated by the group's speech." I am not sure what showing the Court thinks would satisfy its requirement of proof of a membership-message connection, but whatever it means, the focus on such a connection is objectionable.

Imposing such a requirement, especially in the context of the balancing-of-interests test articulated by the Court, raises the possibility that certain commercial associations, by engaging occasionally in certain kinds of expressive activities, might improperly gain protection for discrimination. The Court's focus raises other problems as well. How are we to analyze the First Amendment associational claims of an organization that invokes its right, settled by the Court in *NAACP v. Alabama ex rel. Patterson*, 357 U.S. 449 (1958), to protect the privacy of its membership? And would the Court's analysis of this case be different if, for example, the Jaycees membership had a steady history of opposing public issues thought (by the Court) to be favored by women? It might seem easy to conclude, in the latter case, that the admission of women to the Jaycees' ranks would affect the content of the organization's message, but I do not believe that should change the outcome of this case. Whether an association is or is not constitutionally protected in the selection of its membership should not depend on what the association says or why its members say it.

The Court's readiness to inquire into the connection between membership and message reveals a more fundamental flaw in its analysis. The Court pursues this inquiry as part of its mechanical application of a "compelling interest" test, under which the Court weighs the interests of the State of Minnesota in ending gender discrimination against the Jaycees' First Amendment right of association. The Court entirely neglects to establish at the threshold that the Jaycees is an association whose activities or purposes should engage the strong protections that the First Amendment extends to expressive associations.

On the one hand, an association engaged exclusively in protected expression enjoys First Amendment protection of both the content of its message and the choice of its members. Protection of the message itself is judged by the same standards as protection of speech by an individual. Protection of the association's right to define its membership derives from the recognition that the formation of an expressive association is the creation of a voice, and the selection of members is the definition of that voice. A ban on specific group voices on public affairs violates the most basic guarantee of the First Amendment—that citizens, not the government, control the content of public discussion.

On the other hand, there is only minimal constitutional protection of the freedom of commercial association. There are, of course, some constitutional protections of commercial speech—speech intended and used to promote a commercial transaction with the speaker. But the State is free to impose any rational regulation on the commercial transaction itself. The Constitution does not guarantee a right to choose employees, customers, suppliers, or those with whom one engages in simple commercial transactions, without restraint from the State. A shopkeeper has no constitutional right to deal only with persons of one sex. . . .

Many associations cannot readily be described as purely expressive or purely commercial. No association is likely ever to be exclusively engaged in expressive activities, if only because it will collect dues from its members or purchase printing materials or rent lecture halls or serve coffee and cakes at its meetings. And innumerable commercial associations also engage in some incidental protected speech or advocacy. The standard for deciding just how much of an association's involvement in commercial activity is enough to suspend the association's First Amendment right to control its membership cannot, therefore, be articulated with simple precision. Clearly the standard must accept the reality that even the most expressive of associations is likely to touch, in some way or other, matters of commerce. The standard must nevertheless give substance to the ideal of complete protection for purely expressive association, even while it readily permits state regulation of commercial affairs.

In my view, an association should be characterized as commercial, and therefore subject to rationally related state regulation of its membership and other associational activities, when, and only when, the association's activities are not predominantly of the type protected by the First Amendment. It is only when the association is predominantly engaged in protected expression that state regulation of its membership will necessarily affect, change, dilute, or silence one collective voice that would otherwise be heard. An association must choose its market. Once it enters the marketplace of commerce in any substantial degree it loses the complete control over its membership that it would otherwise enjoy if it confined its affairs to the marketplace of ideas.

Determining whether an association's activity is predominantly protected expression will often be difficult, if only because a broad range of activities can be expressive. It is easy enough to identify expressive words or conduct that are strident, contentious, or divisive, but protected expression may also take the form of quiet persuasion, inculcation of traditional values, instruction of the young, and community service. The purposes of an association, and the purposes of its members in adhering to it, are doubtless relevant in determining whether the association is primarily engaged in protected expression. Lawyering to advance social goals may be speech, but ordinary commercial law practice is not. A group boycott or refusal to deal for political purposes may be speech, though a similar boycott for purposes of maintaining a cartel is not. Even the training of outdoor survival skills or participation in community service might become expressive when the activity is intended to develop good morals, reverence, patriotism, and a desire for self-improvement.[1]

In summary, this Court's case law recognizes radically different constitutional protections for expressive and nonexpressive associations. The First Amendment is offended by direct state control of the membership of a private organization engaged exclusively in protected expressive activity, but no First Amendment interest stands in the way of a State's rational regulation of economic transactions by or within a commercial association. The proper approach to analysis of First Amendment claims of associational freedom is, therefore, to distinguish nonexpressive from expressive associations and to recognize that the former lack the full constitutional protections possessed by the latter.

Minnesota's attempt to regulate the membership of the Jaycees chapters operating in that State presents a relatively easy case for application of the expressive-commercial dichotomy. Both the Minnesota Supreme Court and the United States District Court, which expressly

---

[1] See, *e.g.*, Girl Scouts of the U.S.A., You Make the Difference (1980); W. Hillcourt, The Official Boy Scout Handbook (1979); P. Fussell, The Boy Scout Handbook and Other Observations 7–8 (1982)("The Official Boy Scout Handbook, for all its focus on Axmanship, Backpacking, Cooking, First Aid, Flowers, Hiking, Map and Compass, Semaphore, Trees, and Weather, is another book about goodness. No home, and certainly no government office, should be without a copy").

adopted the state court's findings, made findings of fact concerning the commercial nature of the Jaycees' activities. . . .

The "not insubstantial" volume of protected Jaycees activity found by the Court of Appeals is simply not enough to preclude state regulation of the Jaycees' commercial activities. . . .

For these reasons, I agree with the Court that the Jaycees' First Amendment challenge to the application of Minnesota's public accommodations law is meritless.

COMMENTS AND QUESTIONS

1.   The Court says that the Minnesota law will not require any change in "the Jaycees' creed of promoting the interests of *young men*," but later it says there is no basis, other than discredited stereotypes, for believing that including women as voting members "will change the content or impact of the organization's speech." Does that make sense? Do you think the women who become voting members are going to support promoting the interests only of young men? The Court also says that the Minnesota law would not prevent the Jaycees from excluding "individuals with ideologies or philosophies different from those of its existing members." Does that mean it can exclude women who do not believe that the organization should be devoted to young *men*'s interests and not women's interests? Of course, the Court goes on to say that even if the Minnesota law did have some "incidental abridgement" of the Jaycees' speech, it would not matter because the state's interest in eliminating invidious discrimination outweighs the Jaycees' interest.

2.   How does Justice O'Connor's analysis differ from the Court's? Does she, by classifying the Jaycees as an entity primarily engaged in commercial activities, essentially eliminate it from having a First Amendment right of expressive association? What do you think about her examples of organizations with such a right, like the Girl Scouts and the Boy Scouts?

BOY SCOUTS OF AMERICA V. DALE

United States Supreme Court, 2000.
530 U.S. 640, 120 S.Ct. 2446.

CHIEF JUSTICE REHNQUIST delivered the opinion of the Court.

Petitioners are the Boy Scouts of America. . . . The Boy Scouts is a private, not-for-profit organization engaged in instilling its system of values in young people. The Boy Scouts asserts that homosexual conduct is inconsistent with the values it seeks to instill. Respondent is James Dale, a former Eagle Scout whose adult membership in the Boy Scouts was revoked when the Boy Scouts learned that he is an avowed homosexual and gay rights activist. The New Jersey Supreme Court held that New Jersey's public accommodations law requires that the Boy Scouts readmit Dale. This case presents the question whether applying New Jersey's public accommodations law in this way violates the Boy Scouts' First Amendment right of expressive association. We hold that it does.

James Dale entered Scouting in 1978 at the age of eight. . . . By all accounts, Dale was an exemplary Scout. In 1988, he achieved the rank of Eagle Scout, one of Scouting's highest honors.

Dale applied for adult membership in the Boy Scouts in 1989. The Boy Scouts approved his application for the position of assistant scoutmaster of Troop 73. [While at college Dale came out and] eventually became the copresident of the Rutgers University Lesbian/Gay Alliance. . . . A newspaper . . . interviewed Dale about his advocacy of homosexual teenagers' need for gay role models. In early July 1990, the newspaper published the interview and Dale's photograph over a caption identifying him as the copresident of the Lesbian/Gay Alliance.

Later that month, Dale received a letter from [a Boy Scouts executive], James Kay, revoking his adult membership[, stating] that the Boy Scouts "specifically forbid membership to homosexuals."

In 1992, Dale filed a complaint against the Boy Scouts [alleging] that the Boy Scouts had violated New Jersey's public accommodations statute . . . by revoking Dale's membership based solely on his sexual orientation. New Jersey's public accommodations statute prohibits, among other things, discrimination on the basis of sexual orientation in places of public accommodation. . . .

In *Roberts v. United States Jaycees,* we observed that "implicit in the right to engage in activities protected by the First Amendment" is "a corresponding right to associate with others in pursuit of a wide variety of political, social, economic, educational, religious, and cultural ends." This right is crucial in preventing the majority from imposing its views on groups that would rather express other, perhaps unpopular, ideas. Government actions that may unconstitutionally burden this freedom may take many forms, one of which is "intrusion into the internal structure or affairs of an association" like a "regulation that forces the group to accept members it does not desire." *Id.* Forcing a group to accept certain members may impair the ability of the group to express those views, and only those views, that it intends to express. Thus, "[f]reedom of association . . . plainly presupposes a freedom not to associate."

The forced inclusion of an unwanted person in a group infringes the group's freedom of expressive association if the presence of that person affects in a significant way the group's ability to advocate public or private viewpoints. But the freedom of expressive association, like many freedoms, is not absolute. We have held that the freedom could be overridden "by regulations adopted to serve compelling state interests, unrelated to the suppression of ideas, that cannot be achieved through means significantly less restrictive of associational freedoms." *Roberts.*

To determine whether a group is protected by the First Amendment's expressive associational right, we must determine whether the group engages in "expressive association." The First Amendment's protection of expressive association is not reserved for advocacy groups. But to come within its ambit, a group must engage in some form of expression, whether it be public or private.

Because this is a First Amendment case where the ultimate conclusions of law are virtually inseparable from findings of fact, we are obligated to independently review the factual record to ensure that the state court's judgment does not unlawfully intrude on free expression. The record reveals the following. The Boy Scouts is a private, nonprofit organization. According to its mission statement: "It is the mission of the Boy Scouts of America to serve others by helping to instill values in young people and, in other ways, to prepare them to make ethical choices over their lifetime in achieving their full potential." [The Scout Oath includes among the values it seeks to promote the duty to keep oneself "physically strong, mentally awake, and morally straight." In addition, the Scout Law includes among its requirements the need to be "clean."]

Thus, the general mission of the Boy Scouts is clear: "[T]o instill values in young people." The Boy Scouts seeks to instill these values by having its adult leaders spend time with the youth members, instructing and engaging them in activities like camping, archery, and fishing. During the time spent with the youth members, the scoutmasters and assistant scoutmasters inculcate them with the Boy Scouts' values—both expressly and by example. It seems indisputable that an association that seeks to transmit such a system of values engages in expressive activity. See *Roberts* (O'CONNOR, J., concurring).

Given that the Boy Scouts engages in expressive activity, we must determine whether the forced inclusion of Dale as an assistant scoutmaster would significantly affect the Boy Scouts' ability to advocate public or private viewpoints. This inquiry necessarily requires us first to explore, to a limited extent, the nature of the Boy Scouts' view of homosexuality.

The values the Boy Scouts seeks to instill are "based on" those listed in the Scout Oath and Law. The Boy Scouts explains that the Scout Oath and Law provide "a positive moral code for living; they are a list of 'do's' rather than 'don'ts.' " The Boy Scouts asserts that homosexual conduct is inconsistent with the values embodied in the Scout Oath and Law, particularly with the values represented by the terms "morally straight" and "clean."

Obviously, the Scout Oath and Law do not expressly mention sexuality or sexual orientation. And the terms "morally straight" and "clean" are by no means self-defining. Different people would attribute to those terms very different meanings. For example, some people may believe that engaging in homosexual conduct is not at odds with being "morally straight" and "clean." And others may believe that engaging in homosexual conduct is contrary to being "morally straight" and "clean." The Boy Scouts says it falls within the latter category.

[I]t is not the role of the courts to reject a group's expressed values because they disagree with those values or find them internally inconsistent.

The Boy Scouts asserts that it "teach[es] that homosexual conduct is not morally straight," and that it does "not want to promote homosexual conduct as a legitimate form of behavior." We accept the Boy Scouts' assertion. . . .

We must then determine whether Dale's presence as an assistant scoutmaster would significantly burden the Boy Scouts' desire to not "promote homosexual conduct as a legitimate form of behavior." As we give deference to an association's assertions regarding the nature of its expression, we must also give deference to an association's view of what would impair its expression. . . . Dale was the copresident of a gay and lesbian organization at college and remains a gay rights activist. Dale's presence in the Boy Scouts would, at the very least, force the organization to send a message, both to the youth members and the world, that the Boy Scouts accepts homosexual conduct as a legitimate form of behavior. . . .

The New Jersey Supreme Court determined that the Boy Scouts' ability to disseminate its message was not significantly affected by the forced inclusion of Dale as an assistant scoutmaster because of the following findings: "Boy Scout members do not associate for the purpose of disseminating the belief that homosexuality is immoral; Boy Scouts discourages its leaders from disseminating *any* views on sexual issues; and Boy Scouts includes sponsors and members who subscribe to different views in respect of homosexuality."

We disagree with the New Jersey Supreme Court's conclusion drawn from these findings.

First, associations do not have to associate for the "purpose" of disseminating a certain message in order to be entitled to the protections of the First Amendment. An association must merely engage in expressive activity that could be impaired in order to be entitled to protection. . . .

Second, even if the Boy Scouts discourages Scout leaders from disseminating views on sexual issues—a fact that the Boy Scouts disputes with contrary evidence—the First Amendment protects the Boy Scouts' method of expression. If the Boy Scouts wishes Scout leaders to avoid questions of sexuality and teach only by example, this fact does not negate the sincerity of its belief discussed above.

Third, the First Amendment simply does not require that every member of a group agree on every issue in order for the group's policy to be "expressive association." The Boy Scouts takes an official position with respect to homosexual conduct, and that is sufficient for First Amendment purposes. In this same vein, Dale makes much of the claim that the Boy Scouts does not revoke the membership of heterosexual Scout leaders that openly disagree with the Boy Scouts' policy on sexual orientation. But if this is true, it is irrelevant. The presence of an avowed homosexual and gay rights activist in an assistant scoutmaster's uniform sends a distinctly different message from the presence of a heterosexual assistant scoutmaster who is on record as disagreeing with Boy Scouts policy. The Boy Scouts has a First Amendment right to choose to send one message but not the other. The fact that the organization does not trumpet its views from the housetops, or that it tolerates dissent within its ranks, does not mean that its views receive no First Amendment protection.

Having determined that the Boy Scouts is an expressive association and that the forced inclusion of Dale would significantly affect its expression, we inquire whether the application of New Jersey's public accommodations law to require that the Boy Scouts accept Dale as an assistant scoutmaster runs afoul of the Scouts' freedom of expressive association. We conclude that it does. . . .

We recognized in cases such as *Roberts* that States have a compelling interest in eliminating discrimination against women in public accommodations. But . . . we went on to conclude that the enforcement of these statutes would not materially interfere with the ideas that the organization sought to express. . . .

We thereupon concluded in each of these cases that the organizations' First Amendment rights were not violated by the application of the States' public accommodations laws. . . .

We are not, as we must not be, guided by our views of whether the Boy Scouts' teachings with respect to homosexual conduct are right or wrong; public or judicial disapproval of a tenet of an organization's expression does not justify the State's effort to compel the organization to accept members where such acceptance would derogate from the organization's expressive message.

JUSTICE STEVENS, with whom JUSTICE SOUTER, JUSTICE GINSBURG, and JUSTICE BREYER join, dissenting.

[T]he majority holds that New Jersey's law violates BSA's right to associate and its right to free speech. But that law does not "impos[e] any serious burdens" on BSA's "collective effort on behalf of [its] shared goals," *Roberts v. United States Jaycees*, nor does it force BSA to communicate any message that it does not wish to endorse. New Jersey's law, therefore, abridges no constitutional right of BSA. . . .

In this case, BSA contends that it teaches the young boys who are Scouts that homosexuality is immoral. Consequently, it argues, it would violate its right to associate to force it to admit homosexuals as members, as doing so would be at odds with its own shared goals and values. This contention, quite plainly, requires us to look at what, exactly, are the values that BSA actually teaches. . . .

To bolster its claim that its shared goals include teaching that homosexuality is wrong, BSA directs our attention to two terms appearing in the Scout Oath and Law. The first is the phrase "morally straight," which appears in the Oath ("On my honor I will do my best . . . To keep myself . . . morally straight"); the second term is the word "clean," which appears in a list of 12 characteristics together constituting the Scout Law.

[Justice Stevens then quotes from the Boy Scout Handbook's explanations of these terms and points out that none of the explanations say anything about sexual matters, much less homosexuality.]

BSA's published guidance on that topic underscores this point. Scouts, for example, are directed to receive their sex education at home or in school, but not from the organization. . . . To be sure, Scouts are not forbidden from asking their Scoutmaster about issues of a sexual nature, but Scoutmasters are, literally, the last person Scouts are encouraged to ask: "If you have questions about growing up, about relationships, sex, or making good decisions, ask. Talk with your parents, religious leaders, teachers, or Scoutmaster." . . .

The Court seeks to fill the void by pointing to a statement of "policies and procedures relating to homosexuality and Scouting," signed by BSA's President and Chief Scout Executive in 1978 and addressed to the members of the Executive Committee of the national organization. The letter says that the BSA does "not believe that homosexuality and leadership in Scouting are appropriate." . . .

Four aspects of the 1978 policy statement are relevant to the proper disposition of this case. First, at most this letter simply adopts an exclusionary membership policy. But simply adopting such a policy has never been considered sufficient, by itself, to prevail on a right to associate claim.

Second, the 1978 policy was never publicly expressed. . . . It was an internal memorandum, never circulated beyond the few members of BSA's Executive Committee. It remained, in effect, a secret Boy Scouts policy. Far from claiming any intent to express an idea that would be burdened by the presence of homosexuals, BSA's *public* posture—to the world and to the Scouts themselves—remained what it had always been: one of tolerance, welcoming all classes of boys and young men. . . .

Third, it is apparent that the draftsmen of the policy statement foresaw the possibility that laws against discrimination might one day be amended to protect homosexuals from employment discrimination. Their statement clearly provided that, in the event such a law conflicted with their policy, a Scout's duty to be "obedient" and "obe[y] the laws.". . .

Fourth, the 1978 statement simply says that homosexuality is not "appropriate." It makes no effort to connect that statement to a shared goal or expressive activity of the Boy Scouts. Whatever values BSA seeks to instill in Scouts, the idea that homosexuality is not "appropriate" appears entirely unconnected to, and is mentioned nowhere in, the myriad of publicly declared values and creeds of the BSA. That idea does not appear to be among any of the principles actually taught to Scouts. Rather, the 1978 policy appears to be no more than a private statement of a few BSA executives that the organization wishes to exclude gays—and that wish has nothing to do with any expression BSA actually engages in. . . .

BSA's claim finds no support in our cases. We have recognized "a right to associate for the purpose of engaging in those activities protected by the First Amendment—speech, assembly, petition for the redress of grievances, and the exercise of religion." *Roberts*. And we have acknowledged that "when the State interferes with individuals' selection of those with whom they wish to join in a common endeavor, freedom of association . . . may be implicated." *Ibid.* But "[t]he right to associate for expressive purposes is not . . . absolute"; rather, "the nature and degree of constitutional protection afforded freedom of association may vary depending on the extent to which . . . the constitutionally protected liberty is at stake in a given case.". . . For example, we have routinely and easily rejected assertions of this right by expressive organizations with discriminatory membership policies, such as private schools, law firms, and labor organizations. In fact, until today, we have never once found a claimed right to associate in the selection of members to prevail in the face of a State's antidiscrimination law. To the contrary, we have squarely held that a State's antidiscrimination law does not violate a group's right to associate simply because the law conflicts with that group's exclusionary membership policy. . . .

Several principles are made perfectly clear by *Jaycees*. . . . First, to prevail on a claim of expressive association in the face of a State's antidiscrimination law, it is not enough simply to engage in *some kind* of expressive activity. [T]he Jaycees . . . engaged in expressive activity protected by the First Amendment, yet that fact was not dispositive. Second, it is not enough to adopt an openly avowed exclusionary membership policy. [T]he Jaycees . . . did that as well. Third, it is not sufficient merely to articulate *some* connection between the group's expressive activities and its exclusionary policy. . . .

Rather, in *Jaycees,* we asked whether Minnesota's Human Rights Law requiring the admission of women "impose[d] any *serious burdens*" on the group's "collective effort on behalf of [its] *shared goals*." Notwithstanding the group's obvious publicly stated exclusionary policy, we did not view the inclusion of women as a "serious burden" on the Jaycees' ability to engage in the protected speech of its choice. . . . The relevant question is whether the mere inclusion of the person at issue would "impose any serious burden," "affect in any significant way," or be "a substantial restraint upon" the organization's "shared goals," "basic goals," or "collective effort to foster beliefs." . . .

The evidence before this Court makes it exceptionally clear that BSA has, at most, simply adopted an exclusionary membership policy and has no shared goal of disapproving of homosexuality. BSA's mission statement and federal charter say nothing on the matter; its official membership policy is silent; its Scout Oath and Law—and accompanying definitions— are devoid of any view on the topic; its guidance for Scouts and Scoutmasters on sexuality declare that such matters are "not construed to be Scouting's proper area," but are the province of a Scout's parents and pastor; and BSA's posture respecting religion tolerates a wide variety of views on the issue of homosexuality. Moreover, there is simply no evidence that BSA otherwise teaches anything in this area, or that it instructs Scouts on matters involving homosexuality in ways not conveyed in the Boy Scout or Scoutmaster Handbooks. In short, Boy Scouts of America is simply silent on homosexuality. There is no shared goal or collective effort to foster a belief about homosexuality at all—let alone one that is significantly burdened by admitting homosexuals.

As in *Jaycees,* there is "no basis in the record for concluding that admission of [homosexuals] will impede the [Boy Scouts'] ability to engage in [its] protected activities or to disseminate its preferred views" and New Jersey's law "requires no change in [BSA's] creed.". . .

JUSTICE SOUTER, with whom JUSTICE GINSBURG and JUSTICE BREYER join, dissenting. [opinion omitted]

COMMENTS AND QUESTIONS

1.   Is *Dale* consistent with *Jaycees*? Recall that *Jaycees* was a unanimous decision by the seven participating justices, but that then-Justice Rehnquist concurred in the judgment without opinion. Does having an openly gay, gay activist in a "leadership" position "materially interfere" with the message the Boy Scouts were trying to express? Did having females as full voting members, when they were already allowed to be associate members, "materially interfere" with the message the Jaycees were trying to express? There is a difference, is there not, between excluding women because the group's interest is limited to promoting young men in business and excluding homosexuals because the group believes that homosexual conduct is morally wrong and should be condemned?

2.   What do you make of Justice Stevens's argument that opposition to homosexual conduct has never been the subject of the Boy Scouts' expression? Rather, the Boy Scouts have simply excluded homosexuals. That is, the Boy

Scouts may disapprove of homosexuality, but it has never been part of their "expression." What do you think of the Chief Justice's response?

3.   Both the Court and Justice Stevens, in portions of their opinions that have been edited out, cited *Hurley v. Irish-American Gay, Lesbian and Bisexual Group of Boston*, 515 U.S. 557 (1995), in support of their positions. In *Hurley*, a gay group wishing to show pride in being both Irish and gay sought to participate in the annual Boston St. Patrick's Day parade, an event conducted by a private group, the South Boston Allied War Veterans Council. The Council, however, would not allow them to participate. This was deemed a violation of the state's public accommodation law, which prohibits discrimination on the basis of sexual orientation, but the Supreme Court unanimously held that to mandate inclusion of a pro-gay message in the parade would violate the Council's right not to be compelled to convey a message it did not agree with. The Court in *Dale* found *Hurley* on point because that case held that requiring a group to include a message it did not agree with violated the First Amendment. Justice Stevens, who with the other dissenters had joined the opinion in *Hurley*, found *Hurley* totally distinguishable, because a parade is inherently expressive and inclusion of a group with a banner stating support of gay pride would be viewed as part of the expression of the parade organizers. In other words, to require the parade organizers to include the gay group would have forced them to convey a message they disapproved of. In *Dale*, however, the Boy Scouts were only being told not to exclude a person from membership; they were not being forced to convey any message at all. Interestingly, in *Hurley*, it was conceded that the parade organizers would not exclude gay persons from the parade simply because they were gay. It was precisely the message the group wished to convey that resulted in their exclusion.

4.   The Court has said that it utilizes strict scrutiny to assess freedom of association cases, but in *Dale* the Court concluded that the law was unconstitutional simply because it materially interfered with the message the Boy Scouts were attempting to convey. It did not take the step of asking whether there was a compelling government interest and whether the law was narrowly tailored to achieving that compelling government interest. Instead, it distinguished *Jaycees* on the ground that the Court there found that the law did not seriously interfere with any message the Jaycees were trying to express. In *Jaycees*, however, that conclusion was offered in support of the idea that the law was narrowly tailored, not as *sine qua non* for a constitutional restriction on an association's message. Consider the "undue burden" test adopted in *Planned Parenthood v. Casey*. Is the Court in *Dale* suggesting a similar test with respect to the right of expressional association; that is, if there is an undue burden on the right of expressional association, then it is unconstitutional?

5.   The above cases all involved government actions that allegedly interfered with the message the organization wished to express by requiring the organization to include persons inconsistent with that message. The Court in *Roberts* explained, however, that the First Amendment also protects a

freedom of association from government actions that can harm the organization in different ways, as the following recent case demonstrates.

AMERICANS FOR PROSPERITY FOUNDATION V. BONTA

United States Supreme Court, 2021.
141 S.Ct. 2373.

CHIEF JUSTICE ROBERTS delivered the opinion of the Court, except as to Part II-B-1.

To solicit contributions in California, charitable organizations must disclose to the state Attorney General's Office the identities of their major donors. The State contends that having this information on hand makes it easier to police misconduct by charities. We must decide whether California's disclosure requirement violates the First Amendment right to free association.

The California Attorney General's Office is responsible for statewide law enforcement, including the supervision and regulation of charitable fundraising. Under state law, the Attorney General is authorized to "establish and maintain a register" of charitable organizations and to obtain "whatever information, copies of instruments, reports, and records are needed for the establishment and maintenance of the register." In order to operate and raise funds in California, charities generally must register with the Attorney General and renew their registrations annually.

California law empowers the Attorney General to make rules and regulations regarding the registration and renewal process. Pursuant to this regulatory authority, the Attorney General requires charities renewing their registrations to file copies of their Internal Revenue Service Form 990, along with any attachments and schedules. Form 990 contains information regarding tax-exempt organizations' mission, leadership, and finances. Schedule B to Form 990—the document that gives rise to the present dispute—requires organizations to disclose the names and addresses of donors who have contributed more than $5,000 in a particular tax year (or, in some cases, who have given more than 2 percent of an organization's total contributions).

The petitioners are tax-exempt charities that solicit contributions in California and are subject to the Attorney General's registration and renewal requirements. Americans for Prosperity Foundation is a public charity that is "devoted to education and training about the principles of a free and open society, including free markets, civil liberties, immigration reform, and constitutionally limited government." Thomas More Law Center is a public interest law firm whose "mission is to protect religious freedom, free speech, family values, and the sanctity of human life." Since 2001, each petitioner has renewed its registration and has filed a copy of its Form 990 with the Attorney General. Out of concern for their donors' anonymity, however, the petitioners have declined to file their Schedule Bs . . . with the State.

[W]hen they continued to resist disclosing their contributors' identities, the Attorney General threatened to suspend their registrations and fine their directors and officers.

The petitioners each responded by filing suit in the Central District of California. In their complaints, they alleged that the Attorney General had violated their First Amendment rights and the rights of their donors. The petitioners alleged that disclosure of their Schedule Bs would make their donors less likely to contribute and would subject them to the risk of reprisals. Both organizations challenged the disclosure requirement on its face and as applied to them.

* * *

II

A

The First Amendment prohibits government from "abridging the freedom of speech, or of the press; or the right of the people peaceably to assemble, and to petition the Government for a redress of grievances." This Court has "long understood as implicit in the right to engage in activities protected by the First Amendment a corresponding right to associate with others." . . . Government infringement of this freedom "can take a number of forms." We have held, for example, that the freedom of association may be violated where a group is required to take in members it does not want, where individuals are punished for their political affiliation, see *Elrod v. Burns*, 427 U.S. 347 (1976)(plurality opinion), or where members of an organization are denied benefits based on the organization's message, see *Healy v. James*, 408 U.S. 169 (1972).

We have also noted that "[i]t is hardly a novel perception that compelled disclosure of affiliation with groups engaged in advocacy may constitute as effective a restraint on freedom of association as [other] forms of governmental action." *NAACP v. Alabama ex rel. Patterson*, 357 U.S. 449 (1958). *NAACP* v. *Alabama* involved this chilling effect in its starkest form. The NAACP opened an Alabama office that supported racial integration in higher education and public transportation. In response, NAACP members were threatened with economic reprisals and violence. As part of an effort to oust the organization from the State, the Alabama Attorney General sought the group's membership lists. We held that the First Amendment prohibited such compelled disclosure. We explained that "[e]ffective advocacy of both public and private points of view, particularly controversial ones, is undeniably enhanced by group association," and we noted "the vital relationship between freedom to associate and privacy in one's associations." Because NAACP members faced a risk of reprisals if their affiliation with the organization became known—and because

Alabama had demonstrated no offsetting interest "sufficient to justify the deterrent effect" of disclosure—we concluded that the State's demand violated the First Amendment.

B

1

NAACP v. *Alabama* did not phrase in precise terms the standard of review that applies to First Amendment challenges to compelled disclosure. We have since settled on a standard referred to as "exacting scrutiny." *Buckley* v. *Valeo*, 424 U.S. 1 (1976)(*per curiam*). Under that standard, there must be "a substantial relation between the disclosure requirement and a sufficiently important governmental interest." "To withstand this scrutiny, the strength of the governmental interest must reflect the seriousness of the actual burden on First Amendment rights." Such scrutiny, we have held, is appropriate given the "deterrent effect on the exercise of First Amendment rights" that arises as an "inevitable result of the government's conduct in requiring disclosure."

The Law Center (but not the Foundation) argues that we should apply strict scrutiny, not exacting scrutiny. Under strict scrutiny, the government must adopt "the least restrictive means of achieving a compelling state interest," rather than a means substantially related to a sufficiently important interest. The Law Center contends that only strict scrutiny adequately protects the associational rights of charities. . . .

It is true that we first enunciated the exacting scrutiny standard in a campaign finance case. [But] as we explained in *NAACP* v. *Alabama*, "it is immaterial" to the level of scrutiny "whether the beliefs sought to be advanced by association pertain to political, economic, religious or cultural matters." Regardless of the type of association, compelled disclosure requirements are reviewed under exacting scrutiny.

2

The Law Center (now joined by the Foundation) argues in the alternative that even if exacting scrutiny applies, such review incorporates a least restrictive means test similar to the one imposed by strict scrutiny. The United States and the Attorney General respond that exacting scrutiny demands no additional tailoring beyond the "substantial relation" requirement noted above. We think that the answer lies between those two positions. While exacting scrutiny does not require that disclosure regimes be the least restrictive means of achieving their ends, it does require that they be narrowly tailored to the government's asserted interest.

The need for narrow tailoring was set forth early in our compelled disclosure cases. In *Shelton* v. *Tucker*, we considered an Arkansas statute that required teachers to disclose every organization to which they belonged or contributed. We acknowledged the importance of "the right of a State to investigate the competence and fitness of those whom it hires to teach in its schools." . . . But we nevertheless held that the Arkansas statute was invalid because even a "legitimate and substantial" governmental interest "cannot be pursued by means that broadly stifle fundamental personal liberties when the end can be more narrowly achieved."

Shelton stands for the proposition that a substantial relation to an important interest is not enough to save a disclosure regime that is insufficiently tailored. This requirement makes sense. Narrow tailoring is crucial where First Amendment activity is chilled—even if indirectly— "[b]ecause First Amendment freedoms need breathing space to survive."

[A] substantial relation is necessary but not sufficient to ensure that the government adequately considers the potential for First Amendment harms before requiring that organizations reveal sensitive information about their members and supporters. Where exacting scrutiny applies, the challenged requirement must be narrowly tailored to the interest it promotes, even if it is not the least restrictive means of achieving that end. . . .

III

[F]or the reasons below, we conclude that California's blanket demand for Schedule Bs is facially unconstitutional.

As explained, exacting scrutiny requires that there be "a substantial relation between the disclosure requirement and a sufficiently important governmental interest," and that the disclosure requirement be narrowly tailored to the interest it promotes. . . . [P]roperly applied, the narrow tailoring requirement is not satisfied by the disclosure regime [here].

We do not doubt that California has an important interest in preventing wrongdoing by charitable organizations. . . .

There is a dramatic mismatch, however, between the interest that the Attorney General seeks to promote and the disclosure regime that he has implemented in service of that end. Recall that 60,000 charities renew their registrations each year, and nearly all are required to file a Schedule B. Each Schedule B, in turn, contains information about a charity's top donors—a small handful of individuals in some cases, but hundreds in others. This information includes donors' names and the total contributions they have made to the charity, as well as their addresses.

Given the amount and sensitivity of this information harvested by the State, one would expect Schedule B collection to form an integral part of California's fraud detection efforts. It does not. To the contrary, the record amply supports the District Court's finding that there was not "a single, concrete instance in which pre-investigation collection of a Schedule B did anything to advance the Attorney General's investigative, regulatory or enforcement efforts." . . . And even if the State relied on up-front collection in some cases, its showing falls far short of satisfying the means-end fit that exacting scrutiny requires. California is not free to enforce *any* disclosure regime that furthers its interests. It must instead demonstrate its need for universal production in light of any less intrusive alternatives. . . .

[T]he Attorney General tries to downplay the burden on donors, arguing that "there is no basis on which to conclude that California's requirement results in any broad-based chill." He emphasizes that "California's Schedule B requirement is confidential," and he suggests that certain donors—like those who give to noncontroversial charities—are unlikely to be deterred from contributing. He also contends that disclosure to his office imposes no added burdens on donors because tax-exempt charities already provide their Schedule Bs to the IRS.

We are unpersuaded. Our cases have said that disclosure requirements can chill association "[e]ven if there [is] no disclosure to the general public." In *Shelton*, for example, we noted the "constant and heavy" pressure teachers would experience simply by disclosing their associational ties to their schools. Exacting scrutiny is triggered by "state action which *may* have the effect of curtailing the freedom to associate," and by the "*possible* deterrent effect" of disclosure. While assurances of confidentiality may reduce the burden of disclosure to the State, they do not eliminate it.*

It is irrelevant, moreover, that some donors might not mind—or might even prefer—the disclosure of their identities to the State. . . . The petitioners here, for example, introduced evidence that they and their supporters have been subjected to bomb threats, protests, stalking, and physical violence. Such risks are heightened in the 21st century and seem to grow with each passing year, as "anyone with access to a computer [can] compile a wealth of information about" anyone else, including such sensitive details as a person's home address or the school attended by his children.

The gravity of the privacy concerns in this context is further underscored by the filings of hundreds of organizations as *amici curiae* in support of the petitioners. Far from representing uniquely sensitive causes, these organizations span the ideological spectrum, and indeed the full range of human endeavors: from the American Civil Liberties Union to the Proposition 8 Legal Defense Fund; from the Council on American-Islamic

---

* Here the State's assurances of confidentiality are not worth much. The dissent acknowledges that the Foundation and Law Center "have unquestionably provided evidence that their donors face a reasonable probability of threats, harassment, and reprisals if their affiliations are made public," but it concludes that the petitioners have no cause for concern because the Attorney General "has implemented security measures to ensure that Schedule B information remains confidential." The District Court—whose findings, again, we review only for clear error—disagreed. After two full bench trials, the court found that the Attorney General's promise of confidentiality "rings hollow," and that "[d]onors and potential donors would be reasonably justified in a fear of disclosure."

Relations to the Zionist Organization of America; from Feeding America—Eastern Wisconsin to PBS Reno. The deterrent effect feared by these organizations is real and pervasive, even if their concerns are not shared by every single charity operating or raising funds in California. . . .

Finally, California's demand for Schedule Bs cannot be saved by the fact that donor information is already disclosed to the IRS as a condition of federal tax-exempt status. For one thing, each governmental demand for disclosure brings with it an additional risk of chill. For another, revenue collection efforts and conferral of tax-exempt status may raise issues not presented by California's disclosure requirement, which can prevent charities from operating in the State altogether.

We are left to conclude that the Attorney General's disclosure requirement imposes a widespread burden on donors' associational rights. And this burden cannot be justified on the ground that the regime is narrowly tailored to investigating charitable wrongdoing, or that the State's interest in administrative convenience is sufficiently important. We therefore hold that the up-front collection of Schedule Bs is facially unconstitutional, because it fails exacting scrutiny in "a substantial number of its applications . . . judged in relation to [its] plainly legitimate sweep." . . .

JUSTICE THOMAS, concurring in Parts I, II-A, II-B-2, and III-A, and concurring in the judgment. [omitted]

JUSTICE ALITO, with whom JUSTICE GORSUCH joins, concurring in Parts I, II-A, II-B-2, and III, and concurring in the judgment. [omitted]

JUSTICE SOTOMAYOR, with whom JUSTICE BREYER and JUSTICE KAGAN join, dissenting.

Although this Court is protective of First Amendment rights, it typically requires that plaintiffs demonstrate an actual First Amendment burden before demanding that a law be narrowly tailored to the government's interests, never mind striking the law down in its entirety. Not so today. Today, the Court holds that reporting and disclosure requirements must be narrowly tailored even if a plaintiff demonstrates no burden at all. The same scrutiny the Court applied when NAACP members in the Jim Crow South did not want to disclose their membership for fear of reprisals and violence now applies equally in the case of donors only too happy to publicize their names across the websites and walls of the organizations they support. . . .

[C]alifornia regulations expressly require that Schedule Bs remain confidential, and the attorney general's office has implemented enhanced

Sonia Sotomayor

In 2009 President Obama appointed Justice Sotomayor to the Supreme Court, the first Hispanic member of the Court. Raised by a single mother in the Bronx, Justice Sotomayor was *summa cum laude* from Princeton and an editor of the Yale Law Journal. After serving as an Assistant District Attorney in New York, she entered private practice doing commercial litigation. President George H. W. Bush appointed her to Southern District of New York in 1992, and President Bill Clinton appointed her to the Second Circuit in 1998. On the Supreme Court, she has consistently been part of the liberal wing, especially aligning with Justice Ginsburg. Justice Sotomayor is the only member of the Court with experience as a trial judge.

protocols to ensure confidentiality.[1] California relies on Schedule Bs to investigate fraud and other malfeasance. . . .

Given the indeterminacy of how disclosure requirements will impact associational rights, this Court requires plaintiffs to demonstrate that a requirement is likely to expose their supporters to concrete repercussions in order to establish an actual burden. It then applies a level of means-end tailoring proportional to that burden. . . .

Today, the Court abandons the requirement that plaintiffs demonstrate that they are chilled, much less that they are reasonably chilled. Instead, it presumes (contrary to the evidence, precedent, and common sense) that all disclosure requirements impose associational burdens. . . .

A reasonable assessment of the burdens imposed by disclosure should begin by determining whether those burdens even exist. If a disclosure requirement imposes no burdens at all, then of course there are no "unnecessary" burdens. Likewise, if a disclosure requirement imposes no burden for the Court to remedy, there is no need for it to be closely scrutinized. By forgoing the requirement that plaintiffs adduce evidence of tangible burdens, such as increased vulnerability to harassment or reprisals, the Court gives itself license to substitute its own policy preferences for those of politically accountable actors.

All this would be less troubling if the Court still required means-end tailoring commensurate to the actual burden imposed. It does not. Instead,

---

[1]   Schedule Bs are kept in a confidential database used only by the Charitable Trusts Section and inaccessible to others in California's attorney general's office. Employees who fail to safeguard confidential information are subject to discipline. In light of previous security breaches disclosed in this litigation, the attorney general's office instituted a series of measures to ensure that Schedule B information remains confidential. The office has adopted a system of text searching forms before they are uploaded onto the Internet to ensure that none contain Schedule B information. The office now also runs automated scans of publicly accessible government databases to identify and remove any documents containing Schedule B information that may be inadvertently uploaded.

it adopts a new rule that every reporting or disclosure requirement be narrowly tailored.

Disclosure requirements burden associational rights only indirectly and only in certain contexts. For that reason, this Court has never necessarily demanded such requirements to be narrowly tailored. Rather, it has reserved such automatic tailoring for state action that "directly and immediately affects associational rights." When it comes to reporting and disclosure requirements, the Court has instead employed a more flexible approach, which it has named "exacting scrutiny."

Exacting scrutiny requires two things: first, there must be " 'a "substantial relation" between the disclosure requirement and a "sufficiently important" government interest,' " and second, " 'the strength of the governmental interest must reflect the seriousness of the actual burden on First Amendment rights.' " Exacting scrutiny thus incorporates a degree of flexibility into the means-end analysis. The more serious the burden on First Amendment rights, the more compelling the government's interest must be, and the tighter must be the fit between that interest and the government's means of pursuing it. By contrast, a less substantial interest and looser fit will suffice where the burden on First Amendment rights is weaker (or nonexistent). In other words, to decide how closely tailored a disclosure requirement must be, courts must ask an antecedent question: How much does the disclosure requirement actually burden the freedom to associate?

This approach reflects the longstanding principle that the requisite level of scrutiny should be commensurate to the burden a government action actually imposes on First Amendment rights.

The Court now departs from this nuanced approach in favor of a "one size fits all" test. Regardless of whether there is any risk of public disclosure, and no matter if the burdens on associational rights are slight, heavy, or nonexistent, disclosure regimes must always be narrowly tailored. . . .

Under a First Amendment analysis that is faithful to this Court's precedents, California's Schedule B requirement is constitutional. Begin with the burden it imposes on associational rights. Petitioners have unquestionably provided evidence that their donors face a reasonable probability of threats, harassment, and reprisals if their affiliations are made public. California's Schedule B regulation, however, is a nonpublic reporting requirement, and California has implemented security measures to ensure that Schedule B information remains confidential.

Nor have petitioners shown that their donors, or any organization's donors, will face threats, harassment, or reprisals if their names remain in the hands of a few California state officials. . . . If California's reporting requirement imposes any burden at all, it is at most a very slight one.

Given the modesty of the First Amendment burden, California may justify its Schedule B requirement with a correspondingly modest showing that the means achieve its ends. California easily meets this standard. . . .

The Schedule B reporting requirement is properly tailored to further California's efforts to police charitable fraud. . . .

As a former [state official involved in investigating claims of charitable fraud] described it, Schedule B combined with the rest of Form 990 provides "[a] roadmap to the rest of the investigation that follows." Indeed, having Schedule Bs on hand is important to attorneys' decisions regarding whether to advance an investigation at all. One of the first things an auditor or lawyer does upon receiving a complaint is review the entire Form 990, including Schedule B. One Section leader testified that she used Schedule Bs "[a]ll the time" for this purpose.

In sum, the evidence shows that California's confidential reporting requirement imposes trivial burdens on petitioners' associational rights and plays a meaningful role in Section attorneys' ability to identify and prosecute charities engaged in malfeasance. That is more than enough to satisfy the First Amendment here. . . .

In a final coup de grâce, the Court concludes that California's reporting requirement is unconstitutional not just as applied to petitioners, but on its very face. "In the First Amendment context," such broad relief requires proof that the requirement is unconstitutional in " 'a substantial number of . . . applications . . ., judged in relation to the statute's plainly legitimate sweep.' " The Court points to not a single piece of record evidence showing that California's reporting requirement will chill "a substantial number" of top donors from giving to their charities of choice. Yet it strikes the requirement down in every application. . . .

COMMENTS AND QUESTIONS

1.   After this case, is it constitutional for the IRS to require Schedule B to be filed by charitable organizations claiming tax exempt status? What is different between what the IRS does with information and what California did?

2.   *Americans for Prosperity* mentions disclosure issues in campaign finance laws. Those portions of the campaign finance cases in this book have been edited out. In all of the campaign finance disclosure cases the Court upheld the disclosure requirement using the so-called exacting scrutiny test.

PROBLEM

The Ku Klux Klan is a membership organization. Its membership requirements include: be a native-born White American, non-Jewish citizen; be a believer of the Lord God, the Creator of all; accept Jesus Christ as the Son of God and your personal Savior; believe in the teachings of the Holy Bible; believe in the United States Constitution as it was originally written; and believe in the preservation and advancement of the White Race. It describes itself as a white man's organization, exalting the Caucasian Race and teaching the doctrine of White Supremacy. Under the state of Z's public accommodation law, the KKK qualifies as a public accommodation because it solicits membership from the public at large, like the Boy Scouts and Jaycees. Moreover, the state's public accommodation law prohibits discrimination on the basis of race. Are the KKK's membership requirements constitutionally protected against the state's public accommodation law?

L. FREEDOM OF SPEECH IN SCHOOLS

The Court has long distinguished the speech rights of those in K–12 schools from those in higher education, recognizing a greater freedom for those in higher education. We have already seen in *West Virginia State Bd. of Education v. Barnette* (the flag salute case) that students in school do not lose all their rights at the schoolhouse door, as the following case also makes clear.

TINKER V. DES MOINES INDEPENDENT SCHOOL DIST.

United States Supreme Court, 1969.
393 U.S. 503, 89 S.Ct. 733.

MR. JUSTICE FORTAS delivered the opinion of the Court.

[I]n December 1965, a group of adults and students in Des Moines held a meeting. . . . The group determined to publicize their objections to the hostilities in Vietnam and their support for a truce by wearing black armbands during the holiday season and by fasting on December 16 and New Year's Eve. Petitioners and their parents had previously engaged in similar activities, and they decided to participate in the program.

The principals of the Des Moines schools became aware of the plan to wear armbands. On December 14, 1965, they met and adopted a policy that any student wearing an armband to school would be asked to remove it, and if he refused he would be suspended until he returned without the armband. . . .

On December 16, Mary Beth [Tinker] and Christopher [Eckhardt] wore black armbands to their schools. John Tinker wore his armband the next day. They were all sent home and suspended from school until they would come back without their armbands. They did not return to school until after the planned period for wearing armbands had expired—that is, until after New Year's Day. . . .

[T]he wearing of an armband for the purpose of expressing certain views is the type of symbolic act that is within the Free Speech Clause of the First Amendment. As we shall discuss, the wearing of armbands in the circumstances of this case was entirely divorced from actually or potentially disruptive conduct by those participating in it. It was closely akin to "pure speech" which, we have repeatedly held, is entitled to comprehensive protection under the First Amendment.

First Amendment rights, applied in light of the special characteristics of the school environment, are available to teachers and students. It can hardly be argued that either students or teachers shed their constitutional rights to freedom of speech or expression at the schoolhouse gate. . . .

On the other hand, the Court has repeatedly emphasized the need for affirming the comprehensive authority of the States and of school officials, consistent with fundamental constitutional safeguards, to prescribe and control conduct in the schools. Our problem lies in the area where students in the exercise of First Amendment rights collide with the rules of the school authorities.

The problem posed by the present case does not relate to regulation of the length of skirts or the type of clothing, to hair style, or deportment. It does not concern aggressive, disruptive action or even group demonstrations. Our problem involves direct, primary First Amendment rights akin to "pure speech."

The school officials banned and sought to punish petitioners for a silent, passive expression of opinion, unaccompanied by any disorder or disturbance on the part of petitioners. There is here no evidence whatever of petitioners' interference, actual or nascent, with the schools' work or of collision with the rights of other students to be secure and to be let alone. Accordingly, this case does not concern speech or action that intrudes upon the work of the schools or the rights of other students.

Only a few of the 18,000 students in the school system wore the black armbands. Only five students were suspended for wearing them. There is no indication that the work of the schools or any class was disrupted. Outside the classrooms, a few students made hostile remarks to the children wearing armbands, but there were no threats or acts of violence on school premises.

The District Court concluded that the action of the school authorities was reasonable because it was based upon their fear of a disturbance from the wearing of the armbands. But, in our system, undifferentiated fear or apprehension of disturbance is not enough to overcome the right to freedom of expression. . . .

In order for the State in the person of school officials to justify prohibition of a particular expression of opinion, it must be able to show that its action was caused by something more than a mere desire to avoid the discomfort and unpleasantness that always accompany an unpopular viewpoint. Certainly where there is no finding and no showing that engaging in the forbidden conduct would "materially and substantially interfere with the requirements of appropriate discipline in the operation of the school," the prohibition cannot be sustained.

In the present case, the District Court made no such finding, and our independent examination of the record fails to yield evidence that the school authorities had reason to anticipate that the wearing of the armbands would substantially interfere with the work of the school or impinge upon the rights of other students. Even an official memorandum prepared after the suspension that listed the reasons for the ban on wearing the armbands made no reference to the anticipation of such disruption.[3]

On the contrary, the action of the school authorities appears to have been based upon an urgent wish to avoid the controversy which might result from the expression, even by the silent symbol of armbands, of opposition to this Nation's part in the conflagration in Vietnam.[4] . . .

It is also relevant that the school authorities did not purport to prohibit the wearing of all symbols of political or controversial significance. The record shows that students in some of the schools wore buttons relating to national political campaigns, and some even wore the Iron Cross, traditionally a symbol of Nazism. The order prohibiting the wearing of armbands did not extend to these. Instead, a particular symbol—black armbands worn to exhibit opposition to this Nation's involvement in Vietnam—was singled out for prohibition. Clearly, the prohibition of expression of one particular opinion, at least without evidence that it is necessary to avoid material and substantial interference with schoolwork or discipline, is not constitutionally permissible. . . .

[This] principle . . . is not confined to the supervised and ordained discussion which takes place in the classroom. The principal use to which

---

[3]   The only suggestions of fear of disorder in the report are these: "A former student of one of our high schools was killed in Viet Nam. Some of his friends are still in school and it was felt that if any kind of a demonstration existed, it might evolve into something which would be difficult to control." "Students at one of the high schools were heard to say they would wear arm bands of other colors if the black bands prevailed." Moreover, the testimony of school authorities at trial indicates that it was not fear of disruption that motivated the regulation prohibiting the armbands; and regulation was directed against "the principle of the demonstration" itself. School authorities simply felt that "the schools are no place for demonstrations," and if the students "didn't like the way our elected officials were handling things, it should be handled with the ballot box and not in the halls of our public schools."

[4]   The District Court found that the school authorities, in prohibiting black armbands, were influenced by the fact that "(t)he Viet Nam war and the involvement of the United States therein has been the subject of a major controversy for some time. When the arm band regulation involved herein was promulgated, debate over the Viet Nam war had become vehement in many localities. A protest march against the war had been recently held in Washington, D.C. A wave of draft card burning incidents protesting the war had swept the country. At that time two highly publicized draft card burning cases were pending in this Court. Both individuals supporting the war and those opposing it were quite vocal in expressing their views."

the schools are dedicated is to accommodate students during prescribed hours for the purpose of certain types of activities. Among those activities is personal intercommunication among the students. This is not only an inevitable part of the process of attending school; it is also an important part of the educational process. A student's rights, therefore, do not embrace merely the classroom hours. When he is in the cafeteria, or on the playing field, or on the campus during the authorized hours, he may express his opinions, even on controversial subjects like the conflict in Vietnam, if he does so without "materially and substantially interfer(ing) with the requirements of appropriate discipline in the operation of the school" and without colliding with the rights of others. But conduct by the student, in class or out of it, which for any reason—whether it stems from time, place, or type of behavior—materially disrupts classwork or involves substantial disorder or invasion of the rights of others is, of course, not immunized by the constitutional guarantee of freedom of speech. . . .

As we have discussed, the record does not demonstrate any facts which might reasonably have led school authorities to forecast substantial disruption of or material interference with school activities, and no disturbances or disorders on the school premises in fact occurred. . . . They caused discussion outside of the classrooms, but no interference with work and no disorder. In the circumstances, our Constitution does not permit officials of the State to deny their form of expression. . . .

MR. JUSTICE STEWART, concurring. [opinion omitted]

MR. JUSTICE WHITE, concurring. [opinion omitted]

MR. JUSTICE BLACK, dissenting.

[O]rdered to refrain from wearing the armbands in school by the elected school officials and the teachers vested with state authority to do so, apparently only seven out of the school system's 18,000 pupils deliberately refused to obey the order. One defying pupil was Paul Tinker, 8 years old, who was in the second grade; another, Hope Tinker, was 11 years old and in the fifth grade; a third member of the Tinker family was 13, in the eighth grade; and a fourth member of the same family was John Tinker, 15 years old, an 11th grade high school pupil. Their father, a Methodist minister without a church, is paid a salary by the American Friends Service Committee. Another student who defied the school order and insisted on wearing an armband in school was Christopher Eckhardt, an 11th grade pupil and a petitioner in this case. His mother is an official in the Women's International League for Peace and Freedom.

As I read the Court's opinion it relies upon the following grounds for holding unconstitutional the judgment of the Des Moines school officials and the two courts below. First, the Court concludes that the wearing of armbands is "symbolic speech" which is "akin to 'pure speech' " and therefore protected by the First and Fourteenth Amendments. Secondly, the Court decides that the public schools are an appropriate place to exercise "symbolic speech" as long as normal school functions are not "unreasonably" disrupted. Finally, the Court arrogates to itself, rather than to the State's elected officials charged with running the schools, the decision as to which school disciplinary regulations are "reasonable."

Assuming that the Court is correct in holding that the conduct of wearing armbands for the purpose of conveying political ideas is protected by the First Amendment, the crucial remaining questions are whether students and teachers may use the schools at their whim as a platform for the exercise of free speech—"symbolic" or "pure"—and whether the courts will allocate to themselves the function of deciding how the pupils' school day will be spent. While I have always believed that under the First and Fourteenth Amendments neither the State nor the Federal Government has any authority to regulate or censor the content of speech, I have never believed that any person has a right to give speeches or engage in demonstrations where he pleased and when he pleases. This Court has already rejected such a notion. . . .

While the record does not show that any of these armband students shouted, used profane language, or were violent in any manner, detailed testimony by some of them shows their armbands caused comments, warnings by other students, the poking of fun at them, and a warning by an older football player that other, nonprotesting students had better let them alone. There is also evidence that a teacher of mathematics had his lesson period practically "wrecked" chiefly by disputes with Mary Beth Tinker, who wore her armband for her "demonstration." Even a casual reading of the record shows that this armband did divert students' minds from their regular lessons, and that talk, comments, etc., made John Tinker "self-conscious" in attending school with his armband. While the absence of obscene remarks or boisterous and loud disorder perhaps justifies the Court's statement that the few armband students did not actually "disrupt" the classwork, I think the record overwhelmingly shows that the armbands did exactly what the elected school officials and principals foresaw they would, that is, took the students' minds off their classwork and diverted them to thoughts about the highly emotional subject of the Vietnam war. . . .

MR. JUSTICE HARLAN, dissenting.

I certainly agree that state public school authorities in the discharge of their responsibilities are not wholly exempt from the requirements of the Fourteenth Amendment respecting the freedoms of expression and association. At the same time I am reluctant to believe that there is any disagreement between the majority and myself on the proposition that school officials should be accorded the widest authority in maintaining discipline and good order in their institutions. To translate that proposition into a workable constitutional rule, I would, in cases like this, cast upon those complaining the burden of showing that a particular school measure was motivated by other than legitimate school concerns—for example, a desire to prohibit the expression of an unpopular point of view, while permitting expression of the dominant opinion.

Finding nothing in this record which impugns the good faith of respondents in promulgating the armband regulation, I would affirm the judgment below.

COMMENTS AND QUESTIONS

1.   One year after *O'Brien* we see the Court firmly embrace symbolic speech as fully protected, at least when the government prohibition relates to the expressive elements of the conduct, which was undeniably present here.

2.   What do you make of the different characterizations of the facts between the Court's opinion and Justice Black's dissent? Justice Black notes that only seven of the school district's 18,000 students wore the armbands, so it is perhaps not surprising that there was little reaction. Justice Black implies that but for the school's ban on the armbands there might have been many more students wearing them, and therefore greater disruption might have been anticipated. How much disruption, or anticipated disruption, is necessary under the Court's opinion before the school may ban armbands or their equivalent?

3.   What is Justice Black's point in stressing that some of the students were too young to have had any idea what they were protesting and that their parents were activist peace advocates? Presumably those parents should have been very happy to have their children suspended and threatened with punishment, inasmuch as it resulted in substantial publicity for their cause and a Supreme Court decision to boot.

BETHEL SCHOOL DIST. NO. 403 V. FRASER

United States Supreme Court, 1986.
478 U.S. 675, 106 S.Ct. 3159.

CHIEF JUSTICE BURGER delivered the opinion of the Court.

[O]n April 26, 1983, respondent Matthew N. Fraser, a student at Bethel High School in Pierce County, Washington, delivered a speech nominating a fellow student for student elective office. Approximately 600 high school students, many of whom were 14-year-olds, attended the assembly. Students were required to attend the assembly or to report to the study hall. The assembly was part of a school-sponsored educational program in self-government. Students who elected not to attend the assembly were required to report to study hall. During the entire speech, Fraser referred to his candidate in terms of an elaborate, graphic, and explicit sexual metaphor. . . .

During Fraser's delivery of the speech, a school counselor observed the reaction of students to the speech. Some students hooted and yelled; some by gestures graphically simulated the sexual activities pointedly alluded to in respondent's speech. Other students appeared to be bewildered and embarrassed by the speech. One teacher reported that on the day following the speech, she found it necessary to forgo a portion of the scheduled class lesson in order to discuss the speech with the class.

A Bethel High School disciplinary rule prohibiting the use of obscene language in the school provides: "Conduct which materially and substantially interferes with the educational process is prohibited, including the use of obscene, profane language or gestures."

The morning after the assembly, the Assistant Principal called Fraser into her office and notified him that the school considered his speech to have been a violation of this rule. Fraser was presented with copies of five letters submitted by teachers, describing his conduct at the assembly; he was given a chance to explain his conduct, and he admitted to having given the speech described and that he deliberately used sexual innuendo in the speech. Fraser was then informed that he would be suspended for three days, and that his name would be removed from the list of candidates for graduation speaker at the school's commencement exercises.

Respondent, by his father as guardian ad litem, then brought this action in the United States District Court for the Western District of Washington. Respondent alleged a violation of his First Amendment right to freedom of speech. . . . The District Court held that the school's sanctions violated respondent's right to freedom of speech under the First Amendment to the United States Constitution. . . .

The Court of Appeals for the Ninth Circuit affirmed the judgment of the District Court, holding that respondent's speech was indistinguishable from the protest armband in *Tinker v. Des Moines Independent Community School Dist.*

We granted certiorari. We reverse.

This Court acknowledged in *Tinker v. Des Moines Independent Community School Dist.* that students do not "shed their constitutional rights to freedom of speech or expression at the schoolhouse gate." The Court of Appeals read that case as precluding any discipline of Fraser for indecent speech and lewd conduct in the school assembly. That court appears to have proceeded on the theory that the use of lewd and obscene speech in order to make what the speaker considered to be a point in a nominating speech for a fellow student was essentially the same as the wearing of an armband in *Tinker* as a form of protest or the expression of a political position.

The marked distinction between the political "message" of the armbands in *Tinker* and the sexual content of respondent's speech in this case seems to have been given little weight by the Court of Appeals. In upholding the students' right to engage in a nondisruptive, passive expression of a political viewpoint in *Tinker,* this Court was careful to note that the case did "not concern speech or action that intrudes upon the work of the schools or the rights of other students."

It is against this background that we turn to consider the level of First Amendment protection accorded to Fraser's utterances and actions before an official high school assembly attended by 600 students.

The role and purpose of the American public school system were well described by two historians, who stated: "[P]ublic education must prepare pupils for citizenship in the Republic. . . . It must inculcate the habits and manners of civility as values in themselves conducive to happiness and as indispensable to the practice of self-government in the community and the nation.". . .

These fundamental values of "habits and manners of civility" essential to a democratic society must, of course, include tolerance of divergent political and religious views, even when the views expressed may be unpopular. . . . The undoubted freedom to advocate unpopular and controversial views in schools and classrooms must be balanced against the society's countervailing interest in teaching students the boundaries of socially appropriate behavior. Even the most heated political discourse in a democratic society requires consideration for the personal sensibilities of the other participants and audiences.

In our Nation's legislative halls, where some of the most vigorous political debates in our society are carried on, there are rules prohibiting the use of expressions offensive to other participants in the debate. . . . Can it be that what is proscribed in the halls of Congress is beyond the reach of school officials to regulate?

The First Amendment guarantees wide freedom in matters of adult public discourse. A sharply divided Court upheld the right to express an antidraft viewpoint in a public place, albeit in terms highly offensive to most citizens. *See Cohen v. California.* It does not follow, however, that simply because the use of an offensive form of expression may not be prohibited to adults making what the speaker considers a political point, the same latitude must be permitted to children in a public school. . . . As cogently expressed by Judge Newman, "the First Amendment gives a high school student the classroom right to wear Tinker's armband, but not Cohen's jacket."

[T]he determination of what manner of speech in the classroom or in school assembly is inappropriate properly rests with the school board.

[T]he schools, as instruments of the state, may determine that the essential lessons of civil, mature conduct cannot be conveyed in a school that tolerates lewd, indecent, or offensive speech and conduct such as that indulged in by this confused boy.

The pervasive sexual innuendo in Fraser's speech was plainly offensive to both teachers and students—indeed to any mature person. By glorifying male sexuality, and in its verbal content, the speech was acutely insulting to teenage girl students. The speech could well be seriously damaging to its less mature audience, many of whom were only 14 years old and on the threshold of awareness of human sexuality. Some students were reported as bewildered by the speech and the reaction of mimicry it provoked. . . .

We hold that petitioner School District acted entirely within its permissible authority in imposing sanctions upon Fraser in response to his offensively lewd and indecent speech. Unlike the sanctions imposed on the students wearing armbands in *Tinker,* the penalties imposed in this case were unrelated to any political viewpoint. The First Amendment does not prevent the school officials from determining that to permit a vulgar and lewd speech such as respondent's would undermine the school's basic educational mission. A high school assembly or classroom is no place for a sexually explicit monologue directed towards an unsuspecting audience of teenage students. Accordingly, it was perfectly appropriate for the school to disassociate itself to make the point to the pupils that vulgar speech and lewd conduct is wholly inconsistent with the "fundamental values" of public school education. . . .

JUSTICE BLACKMUN concurs in the result.

JUSTICE BRENNAN, concurring in the judgment.

Respondent gave the following speech at a high school assembly in support of a candidate for student government office: " 'I know a man who is firm—he's firm in his pants, he's firm in his shirt, his character is firm—but most . . . of all, his belief in you, the students of Bethel, is firm. Jeff Kuhlman is a man who takes his point and pounds it in. If necessary, he'll take an issue and nail it to the wall. He doesn't attack things in spurts—he drives hard, pushing and pushing until finally—he succeeds. Jeff is a man who will go to the very end—even the climax, for each and every one of you. So vote for Jeff for A.S.B. vice-president—he'll never come between you and the best our high school can be."

The Court, referring to these remarks as "obscene," "vulgar," "lewd," and "offensively lewd," concludes that school officials properly punished respondent for uttering the speech. Having read the full text of respondent's remarks, I find it difficult to believe that it is the same speech the Court describes.[2] To my mind, the most that can be said about

---

2   The Court speculates that the speech was "insulting" to female students, and "seriously damaging" to 14-year-olds, so that school officials could legitimately suppress such expression in order to protect these groups. There is no evidence in the record that any students, male or female, found the speech "insulting." And while it was not unreasonable for school officials to conclude

respondent's speech—and all that need be said—is that in light of the discretion school officials have to teach high school students how to conduct civil and effective public discourse, and to prevent disruption of school educational activities, it was not unconstitutional for school officials to conclude, under the circumstances of this case, that respondent's remarks exceeded permissible limits. . . .

JUSTICE MARSHALL, dissenting.

I agree with the principles that Justice BRENNAN sets out in his opinion concurring in the judgment. I dissent from the Court's decision, however, because in my view the School District failed to demonstrate that respondent's remarks were indeed disruptive. The District Court and Court of Appeals conscientiously applied *Tinker v. Des Moines Independent Community School Dist.* and concluded that the School District had not demonstrated any disruption of the educational process. I recognize that the school administration must be given wide latitude to determine what forms of conduct are inconsistent with the school's educational mission; nevertheless, where speech is involved, we may not unquestioningly accept a teacher's or administrator's assertion that certain pure speech interfered with education. Here the School District, despite a clear opportunity to do so, failed to bring in evidence sufficient to convince either of the two lower courts that education at Bethel School was disrupted by respondent's speech. I therefore see no reason to disturb the Court of Appeals' judgment.

JUSTICE STEVENS, dissenting. [opinion omitted] [While agreeing that the school could prohibit Fraser's remarks, he dissented from upholding the sanctions imposed, because in Justice Stevens's view Fraser did not have adequate notice that his speech was prohibited.]

COMMENTS AND QUESTIONS

1.   Don't worry about Matthew Fraser; although he was disqualified from being a graduation speaker, he was admitted to UC Berkeley, later became Program Director of the Stanford Debate Society, and currently is the founder and CEO of Education Unlimited, an academic summer camp located in Berkeley, California.

2.   The offending speech was made in the context of campaign speeches for student government as part of the school's program in teaching students about self-government. The students apparently received a very educational lesson—if government has the power to censor campaign speeches it does not

---

that respondent's remarks were inappropriate for a school-sponsored assembly, the language respondent used does not even approach the sexually explicit speech regulated in *Ginsberg v. New York*, 390 U.S. 629 (1968), or the indecent speech banned in *FCC v. Pacifica Foundation*, 438 U.S. 726 (1978). Indeed, to my mind, respondent's speech was no more "obscene," "lewd," or "sexually explicit" than the bulk of programs currently appearing on prime time television or in the local cinema. Thus, I disagree with the Court's suggestion that school officials could punish respondent's speech out of a need to protect younger students.

like, it will. Usually we expect to learn this lesson from events in other countries.

3.   While the Chief Justice's opinion may appear somewhat "over the top," eight of the nine justices agreed with the conclusion that the school could prohibit such speech consistent with the First Amendment, recognizing that schools can regulate what occurs as part of their programs. That is, while the Chief Justice's opinion stresses the claimed adverse consequences of the speech, to distinguish it from the armbands in *Tinker*, it is not clear that any particular disruption was even necessary for the Court to reach its conclusion.

4.   This deference to school officials has continued. For example, in *Hazelwood School Dist. v. Kuhlmeier*, 484 U.S. 260 (1988), the Court upheld the decision of a high school principal to delete an article on teen pregnancy from the school newspaper because he thought it "inappropriate." The Court broadly affirmed the ability of a school to exercise "editorial control over the style and content of student speech in school-sponsored expressive activities so long as their actions are reasonably related to legitimate pedagogical concerns." It distinguished *Tinker* as involving student speech, not school-sponsored speech. It characterized *Fraser* as resting on the inappropriateness of the speech, not its tendency to disrupt school programs. More recently, in *Morse v. Frederick*, 551 U.S. 393 (2007), the Court upheld the suspension of a student for displaying a banner that read "BONG HiTS 4 JESUS" during a school-sponsored outing to view the carrying of the Olympic torch through the town. The Court accepted at face value the school's belief that the banner promoted drug use in violation of the school's anti-drug policy.

5.   Lower courts have struggled with the ability of schools to discipline students for off-campus publications or for material the students have published on the internet or sent in emails. *See* generally Mickey Lee Jett, *The Reach of the Schoolhouse Gate: The Fate Of Tinker in the Age of Digital Social Media*, 61 Cath. U. L. Rev. 895 (2012).

MAHANOY AREA SCHOOL DISTRICT V. B. L.

United States Supreme Court, 2021.
141 S.Ct. 2038.

JUSTICE BREYER delivered the opinion of the Court.

[B.] L. (who, together with her parents, is a respondent in this case) was a student at Mahanoy Area High School, a public school in Mahanoy City, Pennsylvania. At the end of her freshman year, B. L. tried out for a position on the school's varsity cheerleading squad. . . . She did not make the varsity cheerleading team. . . , but she was offered a spot on the cheerleading squad's junior varsity team. B. L. did not accept the coach's decision with good grace, particularly because the squad coaches had placed an entering freshman on the varsity team.

That weekend, B. L. and a friend visited the Cocoa Hut, a local convenience store. There, B. L. used her smartphone to post two photos on

Snapchat, a social media application that allows users to post photos and videos that disappear after a set period of time. B. L. posted the images to her Snapchat "story," a feature of the application that allows any person in the user's "friend" group (B. L. had about 250 "friends") to view the images for a 24 hour period.

The first image B. L. posted showed B. L. and a friend with middle fingers raised; it bore the caption: "Fuck school fuck softball fuck cheer fuck everything." The second image was blank but for a caption, which read: "Love how me and [another student] get told we need a year of jv before we make varsity but tha[t] doesn't matter to anyone else?" The caption also contained an upside-down smiley-face emoji.

B. L.'s Snapchat "friends" included other Mahanoy Area High School students, some of whom also belonged to the cheerleading squad. At least one of them, using a separate cellphone, took pictures of B. L.'s posts and shared them with other members of the cheerleading squad. One of the students who received these photos showed them to her mother (who was a cheerleading squad coach), and the images spread. That week, several cheerleaders and other students approached the cheerleading coaches "visibly upset" about B. L.'s posts. Questions about the posts persisted during an Algebra class taught by one of the two coaches.

After discussing the matter with the school principal, the coaches decided that because the posts used profanity in connection with a school extracurricular activity, they violated team and school rules. As a result, the coaches suspended B. L. from the junior varsity cheerleading squad for the upcoming year. B. L.'s subsequent apologies did not move school officials. The school's athletic director, principal, superintendent, and school board, all affirmed B. L.'s suspension from the team. In response, B. L., together with her parents, filed this lawsuit in Federal District Court.

The District Court found in B. L.'s favor. . . . On appeal, a panel of the Third Circuit affirmed the District Court's conclusion. . . .

The school district filed a petition for certiorari in this Court, asking us to decide "[w]hether [*Tinker*], which holds that public school officials may regulate speech that would materially and substantially disrupt the work and discipline of the school, applies to student speech that occurs off campus." We granted the petition.

We have made clear that students do not "shed their constitutional rights to freedom of speech or expression," even "at the school house gate." But we have also made clear that courts must apply the First Amendment "in light of the special characteristics of the school environment." One such characteristic, which we have stressed, is the fact that schools at times stand *in loco parentis*, *i.e.*, in the place of parents.

This Court has previously outlined three specific categories of student speech that schools may regulate in certain circumstances: (1) "indecent," "lewd," or "vulgar" speech uttered during a school assembly on school grounds, (2) speech, uttered during a class trip, that promotes "illegal drug use," and (3) speech that others may reasonably perceive as "bear[ing] the imprimatur of the school," such as that appearing in a school-sponsored newspaper.

Finally, in *Tinker*, we said schools have a special interest in regulating speech that "materially disrupts classwork or involves substantial disorder or invasion of the rights of others." These special characteristics call for special leeway when schools regulate speech that occurs under its supervision.

[W]e do not believe the special characteristics that give schools additional license to regulate student speech always disappear when a school regulates speech that takes place off campus. The school's regulatory interests remain significant in some off-campus circumstances. The parties' briefs, and those of *amici*, list several types of off-campus behavior that may call for school regulation. These include serious or severe bullying or harassment targeting particular individuals; threats aimed at teachers or other students; the failure to follow rules concerning lessons, the writing of papers, the use of computers, or participation in other online school activities; and breaches of school security devices, including material maintained within school computers.

Even B. L. herself and the *amici* supporting her would redefine the off-campus/on-campus distinction, treating as on campus: all times when the school is responsible for the student; the school's immediate surroundings; travel en route to and from the school; all speech taking place over school laptops or on a school's website; speech taking place during remote learning; activities taken for school credit; and communications to school e-mail accounts or phones. And it may be that speech related to extracurricular activities, such as team sports, would also receive special treatment under B. L.'s proposed rule.

We are uncertain as to the length or content of any such list of appropriate exceptions or carveouts to [a rule that would entirely] deny the off-campus applicability of *Tinker's* highly general statement about the nature of a school's special interests. Particularly given the advent of computer-based learning, we hesitate to determine precisely which of many school-related off-campus activities belong on such a list. Neither do we now know how such a list might vary, depending upon a student's age, the nature of the school's off-campus activity, or the impact upon the school itself. Thus, we do not now set forth a broad, highly general First Amendment rule stating just what counts as "off campus" speech and whether or how ordinary First Amendment standards must give way off campus to a school's special need to prevent, *e.g.*, substantial disruption of learning-related activities or the protection of those who make up a school community.

We can, however, mention three features of off-campus speech that often, even if not always, distinguish schools' efforts to regulate that speech from their efforts to regulate on-campus speech. Those features diminish the strength of the unique educational characteristics that might call for special First Amendment leeway.

First, a school, in relation to off-campus speech, will rarely stand *in loco parentis*. The doctrine of *in loco parentis* treats school administrators as standing in the place of students' parents under circumstances where the children's actual parents cannot protect, guide, and discipline them. Geographically speaking, off-campus speech will normally fall within the zone of parental, rather than school-related, responsibility.

Second, from the student speaker's perspective, regulations of off-campus speech, when coupled with regulations of on-campus speech, include all the speech a student utters during the full 24-hour day. That means courts must be more skeptical of a school's efforts to regulate off-campus speech, for doing so may mean the student cannot engage in that kind of speech at all. When it comes to political or religious speech that occurs outside school or a school program or activity, the school will have a heavy burden to justify intervention.

Third, the school itself has an interest in protecting a student's unpopular expression, especially when the expression takes place off campus. America's public schools are the nurseries of democracy. Our representative democracy only works if we protect the "marketplace of ideas." This free exchange facilitates an informed public opinion, which, when transmitted to lawmakers, helps produce laws that reflect the People's will. That protection must include the protection of unpopular ideas, for popular ideas have less need for protection. . . .

Given the many different kinds of off-campus speech, the different potential school-related and circumstance-specific justifications, and the differing extent to which those justifications may call for First Amendment leeway, we can, as a general matter, say little more than this: Taken together, these three features of much off-campus speech mean that the leeway the First Amendment grants to schools in light of their special characteristics is diminished. We leave for future cases to decide where, when, and how these features mean the speaker's off-campus location will make the critical difference. This case can, however, provide one example.

Consider B. L.'s speech. Putting aside the vulgar language, the listener would hear criticism, of the team, the team's coaches, and the school—in a word or two, criticism of the rules of a community of which B. L. forms a part. This criticism did not involve features that would place it outside the First Amendment's ordinary protection. B. L.'s posts, while crude, did not amount to fighting words. And while B. L. used vulgarity, her speech was not obscene as this Court has understood that term. To the contrary, B. L.

uttered the kind of pure speech to which, were she an adult, the First Amendment would provide strong protection.

Consider too when, where, and how B. L. spoke. Her posts appeared outside of school hours from a location outside the school. She did not identify the school in her posts or target any member of the school community with vulgar or abusive language. B. L. also transmitted her speech through a personal cellphone, to an audience consisting of her private circle of Snapchat friends. These features of her speech, while risking transmission to the school itself, nonetheless (for reasons we have just explained, *supra*) diminish the school's interest in punishing B. L.'s utterance.

But what about the school's interest, here primarily an interest in prohibiting students from using vulgar language to criticize a school team or its coaches—at least when that criticism might well be transmitted to other students, team members, coaches, and faculty? We can break that general interest into three parts.

First, we consider the school's interest in teaching good manners and consequently in punishing the use of vulgar language aimed at part of the school community. The strength of this anti-vulgarity interest is weakened considerably by the fact that B. L. spoke outside the school on her own time.

B. L. spoke under circumstances where the school did not stand *in loco parentis*. And there is no reason to believe B. L.'s parents had delegated to school officials their own control of B. L.'s behavior at the Cocoa Hut. Moreover, the vulgarity in B. L.'s posts encompassed a message, an expression of B. L.'s irritation with, and criticism of, the school and cheerleading communities. Further, the school has presented no evidence of any general effort to prevent students from using vulgarity outside the classroom. Together, these facts convince us that the school's interest in teaching good manners is not sufficient, in this case, to overcome B. L.'s interest in free expression.

Second, the school argues that it was trying to prevent disruption, if not within the classroom, then within the bounds of a school-sponsored extracurricular activity. But we can find no evidence in the record of the sort of "substantial disruption" of a school activity or a threatened harm to the rights of others that might justify the school's action. Rather, the record shows that discussion of the matter took, at most, 5 to 10 minutes of an Algebra class "for just a couple of days" and that some members of the cheerleading team were "upset" about the content of B. L.'s Snapchats. But when one of B. L.'s coaches was asked directly if she had "any reason to think that this particular incident would disrupt class or school activities other than the fact that kids kept asking ... about it," she responded simply, "No." As we said in *Tinker*, "for the State in the person of school officials to justify prohibition of a particular expression of opinion, it must be able to show that its action was caused by something more than a mere desire to avoid the discomfort and unpleasantness that always accompany an unpopular viewpoint." The alleged disturbance here does not meet *Tinker's* demanding standard.

Third, the school presented some evidence that expresses (at least indirectly) a concern for team morale. One of the coaches testified that the school decided to suspend B. L., not because of any specific negative impact upon a particular member of the school community, but "based on the fact that there was negativity put out there that could impact students in the school." There is little else, however, that suggests any serious decline in team morale—to the point where it could create a substantial interference in, or disruption of, the school's efforts to maintain team cohesion. As we have previously said, simple "undifferentiated fear or apprehension . . . is not enough to overcome the right to freedom of expression."

It might be tempting to dismiss B. L.'s words as unworthy of the robust First Amendment protections discussed herein. But sometimes it is necessary to protect the superfluous in order to preserve the necessary. "We cannot lose sight of the fact that, in what otherwise might seem a trifling and annoying instance of individual distasteful abuse of a privilege, these fundamental societal values are truly implicated." *Cohen.*

* * *

[T]he school violated B. L.'s First Amendment rights. The judgment of the Third Circuit is therefore affirmed.

JUSTICE ALITO, with whom JUSTICE GORSUCH joins, concurring.

I join the opinion of the Court but write separately to explain my understanding of the Court's decision and the framework within which I think cases like this should be analyzed. This is the first case in which we have considered the constitutionality of a public school's attempt to regulate true off-premises student speech, and therefore it is important that our opinion not be misunderstood. . . .

I start with this threshold question: Why does the First Amendment ever allow the free-speech rights of public school students to be restricted to a greater extent than the rights of other juveniles who do not attend a public school? [W]hen a public school regulates student speech, it acts as an arm of the State in which it is located. Suppose that B. L. had been enrolled in a private school and did exactly what she did in this case—send out vulgar and derogatory messages that focused on her school's cheerleading squad. The Commonwealth of Pennsylvania would have had no legal basis to punish her and almost certainly would not have even tried. So why should her status as a public school student give the Commonwealth any greater authority to punish her speech?

Our cases involving the regulation of student speech have not directly addressed this question. All those cases involved either in-school speech or speech that was tantamount to in-school speech. And in those cases, the Court appeared to take it for granted that "the special characteristics of the school environment" justified special rules.

Why the Court took this for granted is not hard to imagine. As a practical matter, it is impossible to see how a school could function if administrators and teachers could not regulate on-premises student speech, including by imposing content-based restrictions in the classroom. . . .

Because no school could operate effectively if teachers and administrators lacked the authority to regulate in-school speech in these ways, the Court may have felt no need to specify the source of this authority or to explain how the special rules applicable to in-school student speech fit into our broader framework of free-speech case law. But when a public school regulates what students say or write when they are not on school grounds and are not participating in a school program, the school has the obligation to answer the question with which I began: Why should enrollment in a public school result in the diminution of a student's free-speech rights?

The only plausible answer that comes readily to mind is consent, either express or implied. The theory must be that by enrolling a child in a public school, parents consent on behalf of the child to the relinquishment of some of the child's free-speech rights. . . .

When it comes to children, courts in this country have analyzed the issue of consent by adapting the common-law doctrine of *in loco parentis*. Under the common law, as Blackstone explained, "[a father could] delegate part of his parental authority . . . to the tutor or schoolmaster of his child; who is then *in loco parentis*, and has *such a portion of the power of the parent* committed to his charge, [namely,] that of restraint and correction, *as may be necessary to answer the purposes for which he is employed.*" . . .

If *in loco parentis* is transplanted from Blackstone's England to the 21st century United States, what it amounts to is simply a doctrine of inferred parental consent to a public school's exercise of a degree of authority that is commensurate with the task that the parents ask the school to perform. . . .

So how much authority to regulate speech do parents implicitly delegate when they enroll a child at a public school? The answer must be that parents are treated as having relinquished the measure of authority that the schools must be able to exercise in order to carry out their state-mandated educational mission, as well as the authority to perform any other functions to which parents expressly or implicitly agree—for example, by giving permission for a child to participate in an extracurricular activity or to go on a school trip.

I have already explained what this delegated authority means with respect to student speech during standard classroom instruction. And it is reasonable to infer that this authority extends to periods when students are in school but are not in class, for example, when they are walking in a hall, eating lunch, congregating outside before the school day starts, or waiting for a bus after school. During the entire school day, a school must have the authority to protect everyone on its premises, and therefore schools must be able to prohibit threatening and harassing speech. An effective instructional atmosphere could not be maintained in a school, and good teachers would be hard to recruit and retain, if students were free to abuse or disrespect them. And the school has a duty to protect students while in school because their parents are unable to do that during those hours. But even when students are on school premises during regular school hours, they are not stripped of their free-speech rights. *Tinker* teaches that expression that does not interfere with a class (such as by straying from the topic, interrupting the teacher or other students, etc.) cannot be suppressed unless it "involves substantial disorder or invasion of the rights of others."

A public school's regulation of off-premises student speech is a different matter. While the decision to enroll a student in a public school may be regarded as conferring the authority to regulate *some* off-premises speech (a subject I address below), enrollment cannot be treated as a complete transfer of parental authority over a student's speech. In our society, parents, not the State, have the primary authority and duty to raise, educate, and form the character of their children. . . .

The degree to which enrollment in a public school can be regarded as a delegation of authority over off-campus speech depends on the nature of the speech and the circumstances under which it occurs. I will not attempt to provide a complete taxonomy of off-premises speech, but relevant lower court cases tend to fall into a few basic groups. And with respect to speech in each of these groups, the question that courts must ask is whether parents who enroll their children in a public school can reasonably be understood to have delegated to the school the authority to regulate the speech in question.

One category of off-premises student speech falls easily within the scope of the authority that parents implicitly or explicitly provide. This category includes speech that takes place during or as part of what amounts to a temporal or spatial extension of the regular school program, *e.g.,* online instruction at home, assigned essays or other homework, and transportation to and from school. Also included are statements made during other school activities in which students participate with their parents' consent, such as school trips, school sports and other extracurricular activities that may take place after regular school hours or off school premises, and after-school programs for students who would otherwise be without adult supervision during that time. . . .

At the other end of the spectrum, there is a category of speech that is almost always beyond the regulatory authority of a public school. This is student speech that is not expressly and specifically directed at the school, school administrators, teachers, or fellow students and that addresses matters of public concern, including sensitive subjects like politics, religion, and social relations. Speech on such matters lies at the heart of the First Amendment's protection, and the connection between student speech in this category and the ability of a public school to carry out its instructional program is tenuous.

If a school tried to regulate such speech, the most that it could claim is that offensive off-premises speech on important matters may cause controversy and recriminations among students and may thus disrupt instruction and good order on school premises. But it is a "bedrock principle" that speech may not be suppressed simply because it expresses ideas that are "offensive or disagreeable." It is unreasonable to infer that parents who send a child to a public school thereby authorize the school to take away such a critical right. . . .

This is true even if the student's off-premises speech on a matter of public concern is intemperate and crude. When a student engages in oral or written communication of this nature, the student is subject to whatever restraints the student's parents impose, but the student enjoys the same First Amendment protection against government regulation as all other members of the public. . . .

Between these two extremes (*i.e.*, off-premises speech that is tantamount to on-campus speech and general statements made off premises on matters of public concern) lie the categories of off-premises student speech that appear to have given rise to the most litigation. A survey of lower court cases reveals several prominent categories. I will mention some of those categories, but like the Court, I do not attempt to set out the test to be used in judging the constitutionality of a public school's efforts to regulate such speech.

One group of cases involves perceived threats to school administrators, teachers, other staff members, or students. Laws that apply to everyone prohibit defined categories of threats, but schools have claimed that their duties demand broader authority.

Another common category involves speech that criticizes or derides school administrators, teachers, or other staff members. Schools may assert that parents who send their children to a public school implicitly authorize the school to demand that the child exhibit the respect that is required for orderly and effective instruction, but parents surely do not relinquish their children's ability to complain in an appropriate manner about wrongdoing, dereliction, or even plain incompetence.

Perhaps the most difficult category involves criticism or hurtful remarks about other students. Bullying and severe harassment are serious (and age-old) problems, but these concepts are not easy to define with the precision required for a regulation of speech.

The present case does not fall into any of these categories. . . .

JUSTICE THOMAS, dissenting. [omitted. Justice Thomas believes that historically, as reflected in some state cases, schools could punish students for off-campus speech such as was involved here, and because "the majority does not attempt to explain why we should not apply this historical rule and does not attempt to tether its approach to anything stable," he respectfully dissented.]

COMMENTS AND QUESTIONS

1.   Does *Mahanoy* give any real guidance for the hard cases? Is *in loco parentis* analysis really the best way to approach the school's authority?

2.   If B. L. had been a student at a private school, the school clearly could have suspended her from the cheerleading squad for a year for what she did. Why should a public school have less authority over its students? It is exercising no sovereign power over her, such as a fine or imprisonment.

3.   Is Justice Alito's idea that parental consent is what justifies school control of on campus discipline accurate? Parents do not voluntarily consent to their children being in school; school attendance is mandatory.

4.   Do you ever wonder at the fact that the Supreme Court of the United States (not to mention the Third Circuit and District Court) devotes its attention to whether or not a high school sophomore may be suspended from a junior varsity cheerleading squad?

PROBLEM

A high school student is upset by the Diversity, Equity, and Inclusion policy of his high school. Together with some friends, he organizes a group, which they call UnWoke!. They meet outside of school, where they discuss their grievances with the DEI policy. In addition, the student writes a letter to the local paper alleging that he is being taught that, by virtue of his race, color, national origin, or sex, he bears responsibility for, or should be discriminated against or receive adverse treatment because of, actions committed in the past by other members of his same race, color, national origin, or sex. Finally, the group decides that they should wear white arm bands to school as a silent protest against the DEI policy. What, if anything, can the school do about this?

M. FREEDOM OF SPEECH IN THE GOVERNMENT WORKPLACE

If you are a government employee, what free speech rights do you give up by reason of your employment? If you choose to work for the Central Intelligence Agency, you must agree "not to publish . . . any information or material relating to the Agency, its activities or intelligence activities generally, either during or after the term of your employment . . . without specific prior approval by the Agency." This smacks of a prior restraint, but the Court upheld the validity of this contract in *Snepp v. United States*, 444 U.S. 507 (1980). If you are an employee of an executive agency in the federal government, you are forbidden from engaging in plainly identifiable acts of political management and political campaigning, such as organizing a political party or club; actively participating in fund-raising activities for a partisan candidate or political party; becoming a partisan candidate for, or campaigning for, an elective public office; actively managing the campaign of a partisan candidate for public office; initiating or circulating a partisan nominating petition or soliciting votes for a partisan candidate for public office; or serving as a delegate, alternate, or proxy to a political party convention. And this is constitutional. *See U.S. Civil Service Commission v. National Ass'n of Letter Carriers, AFL-CIO*, 413 U.S. 548 (1973). These are relatively bright lines, but consider the following.

GARCETTI V. CEBALLOS

United States Supreme Court, 2006.
547 U.S. 410, 126 S.Ct. 1951.

JUSTICE KENNEDY delivered the opinion of the Court.

[T]he question presented by the instant case is whether the First Amendment protects a government employee from discipline based on speech made pursuant to the employee's official duties.

Respondent Richard Ceballos has been employed since 1989 as a deputy district attorney for the Los Angeles County District Attorney's Office. . . . In February 2000, a defense attorney contacted Ceballos about a pending criminal case. The defense attorney said there were inaccuracies in an affidavit used to obtain a critical search warrant. The attorney informed Ceballos that he had filed a motion to . . . challenge the warrant, but he also wanted Ceballos to review the case. . . .

After examining the affidavit and visiting the location it described, Ceballos determined the affidavit contained serious misrepresentations. . . .

Ceballos spoke on the telephone to the warrant affiant, a deputy sheriff from the Los Angeles County Sheriff's Department, but he did not receive a satisfactory explanation for the perceived inaccuracies. He relayed his findings to his supervisors, petitioners Carol Najera and Frank

Sundstedt, and followed up by preparing a disposition memorandum. The memo explained Ceballos's concerns and recommended dismissal of the case. On March 2, 2000, Ceballos submitted the memo to Sundstedt for his review. . . .

Based on Ceballos's statements, a meeting was held to discuss the affidavit. Attendees included Ceballos, Sundstedt, and Najera, as well as the warrant affiant and other employees from the sheriff's department. The meeting allegedly became heated, with one lieutenant sharply criticizing Ceballos for his handling of the case.

Despite Ceballos's concerns, Sundstedt decided to proceed with the prosecution, pending disposition of the defense motion to [challenge the warrant]. The trial court held a hearing on the motion. Ceballos was called by the defense and recounted his observations about the affidavit, but the trial court rejected the challenge to the warrant.

Ceballos claims that in the aftermath of these events he was subjected to a series of retaliatory employment actions. [C]eballos sued [alleging] petitioners violated the First and Fourteenth Amendments by retaliating against him based on his memo of March 2.

Petitioners responded that no retaliatory actions were taken against Ceballos and that all the actions of which he complained were explained by legitimate reasons such as staffing needs. They further contended that, in any event, Ceballos's memo was not protected speech under the First Amendment. . . .

As the Court's decisions have noted, for many years "the unchallenged dogma was that a public employee had no right to object to conditions placed upon the terms of employment—including those which restricted the exercise of constitutional rights." That dogma has been qualified in important respects. The Court has made clear that public employees do not surrender all their First Amendment rights by reason of their employment. Rather, the First Amendment protects a public employee's right, in certain circumstances, to speak as a citizen addressing matters of public concern.

Pickering v. Board of Ed. of Township High School Dist. 205, Will Cty., 391 U.S. 563 (1968) provides a useful starting point in explaining the Court's doctrine. There the relevant speech was a teacher's letter to a local newspaper addressing issues including the funding policies of his school board. "The problem in any case," the Court stated, "is to arrive at a balance between the interests of the teacher, as a citizen, in commenting upon matters of public concern and the interest of the State, as an employer, in promoting the efficiency of the public services it performs through its employees." The Court found the teacher's speech "neither [was] shown nor can be presumed to have in any way either impeded the teacher's proper performance of his daily duties in the classroom or to have interfered with the regular operation of the schools generally." Thus, the Court concluded that "the interest of the school administration in limiting teachers' opportunities to contribute to public debate is not significantly greater than its interest in limiting a similar contribution by any member of the general public."

Pickering and the cases decided in its wake identify two inquiries to guide interpretation of the constitutional protections accorded to public employee speech. The first requires determining whether the employee spoke as a citizen on a matter of public concern. If the answer is no, the employee has no First Amendment cause of action based on his or her employer's reaction to the speech. If the answer is yes, then the possibility of a First Amendment claim arises. The question becomes whether the relevant government entity had an adequate justification for treating the employee differently from any other member of the general public. This consideration reflects the importance of the relationship between the speaker's expressions and employment. A government entity has broader discretion to restrict speech when it acts in its role as employer, but the restrictions it imposes must be directed at speech that has some potential to affect the entity's operations.

To be sure, conducting these inquiries sometimes has proved difficult. . . . The Court's overarching objectives, though, are evident.

When a citizen enters government service, the citizen by necessity must accept certain limitations on his or her freedom. Government employers, like private employers, need a significant degree of control over their employees' words and actions; without it, there would be little chance for the efficient provision of public services. Public employees, moreover, often occupy trusted positions in society. When they speak out, they can express views that contravene governmental policies or impair the proper performance of governmental functions.

At the same time, the Court has recognized that a citizen who works for the government is nonetheless a citizen. The First Amendment limits the ability of a public employer to leverage the employment relationship to restrict, incidentally or intentionally, the liberties employees enjoy in their capacities as private citizens. So long as employees are speaking as citizens about matters of public concern, they must face only those speech restrictions that are necessary for their employers to operate efficiently and effectively. . . .

With these principles in mind we turn to the instant case. Respondent Ceballos believed the affidavit used to obtain a search warrant contained serious misrepresentations. He conveyed his opinion and recommendation in a memo to his supervisor. That Ceballos expressed his views inside his office, rather than publicly, is not dispositive. Employees in some cases may receive First Amendment protection for expressions made at work. . . .

The memo concerned the subject matter of Ceballos's employment, but this, too, is nondispositive. The First Amendment protects some expressions related to the speaker's job. As the Court noted in *Pickering:* "Teachers are, as a class, the members of a community most likely to have informed and definite opinions as to how funds allotted to the operation of the schools should be spent. Accordingly, it is essential that they be able to speak out freely on such questions without fear of retaliatory dismissal." The same is true of many other categories of public employees.

The controlling factor in Ceballos's case is that his expressions were made pursuant to his duties as a calendar deputy. That consideration—the fact that Ceballos spoke as a prosecutor fulfilling a responsibility to advise his supervisor about how best to proceed with a pending case— distinguishes Ceballos's case from those in which the First Amendment provides protection against discipline. We hold that when public employees make statements pursuant to their official duties, the employees are not speaking as citizens for First Amendment purposes, and the Constitution does not insulate their communications from employer discipline.

Ceballos wrote his disposition memo because that is part of what he, as a calendar deputy, was employed to do. It is immaterial whether he experienced some personal gratification from writing the memo; his First Amendment rights do not depend on his job satisfaction. The significant point is that the memo was written pursuant to Ceballos's official duties. Restricting speech that owes its existence to a public employee's professional responsibilities does not infringe any liberties the employee might have enjoyed as a private citizen. It simply reflects the exercise of employer control over what the employer itself has commissioned or created. Contrast, for example, the expressions made by the speaker in *Pickering,* whose letter to the newspaper had no official significance and bore similarities to letters submitted by numerous citizens every day. . . .

Refusing to recognize First Amendment claims based on government employees' work product does not prevent them from participating in public debate. The employees retain the prospect of constitutional protection for their contributions to the civic discourse. This prospect of protection, however, does not invest them with a right to perform their jobs however they see fit.

Our holding likewise is supported by the emphasis of our precedents on affording government employers sufficient discretion to manage their operations. Employers have heightened interests in controlling speech made by an employee in his or her professional capacity. Official communications have official consequences, creating a need for substantive consistency and clarity. Supervisors must ensure that their employees' official communications are accurate, demonstrate sound judgment, and promote the employer's mission. . . . If Ceballos's superiors thought his memo was inflammatory or misguided, they had the authority to take proper corrective action. . . .

Proper application of our precedents thus leads to the conclusion that the First Amendment does not prohibit managerial discipline based on an employee's expressions made pursuant to official responsibilities. Because Ceballos's memo falls into this category, his allegation of unconstitutional retaliation must fail.

[T]here is some argument that expression related to academic scholarship or classroom instruction implicates additional constitutional interests that are not fully accounted for by this Court's customary employee-speech jurisprudence. We need not, and for that reason do not, decide whether the analysis we conduct today would apply in the same manner to a case involving speech related to scholarship or teaching. . . .

JUSTICE STEVENS, dissenting. [omitted]

JUSTICE SOUTER, with whom JUSTICE STEVENS and JUSTICE GINSBURG join, dissenting.

The Court holds that "when public employees make statements pursuant to their official duties, the employees are not speaking as citizens for First Amendment purposes, and the Constitution does not insulate their communications from employer discipline." I respectfully dissent. I agree with the majority that a government employer has substantial interests in effectuating its chosen policy and objectives, and in demanding competence, honesty, and judgment from employees who speak for it in doing their work. But I would hold that private and public interests in addressing official wrongdoing and threats to health and safety can outweigh the government's stake in the efficient implementation of policy, and when they do public employees who speak on these matters in the course of their duties should be eligible to claim First Amendment protection.

Open speech by a private citizen on a matter of public importance lies at the heart of expression subject to protection by the First Amendment. At the other extreme, a statement by a government employee complaining about nothing beyond treatment under personnel rules raises no greater claim to constitutional protection against retaliatory response than the remarks of a private employee. In between these points lies a public employee's speech unwelcome to the government but on a significant public issue. Such an employee speaking as a citizen, that is, with a citizen's interest, is protected from reprisal unless the statements are too damaging to the government's capacity to conduct public business to be justified by any individual or public benefit thought to flow from the statements. Entitlement to protection is thus not absolute.

This significant, albeit qualified, protection of public employees who irritate the government is understood to flow from the First Amendment, in part, because a government paycheck does nothing to eliminate the value to an individual of speaking on public matters, and there is no good reason for categorically discounting a speaker's interest in commenting on a matter of public concern just because the government employs him. Still, the First Amendment safeguard rests on something more, being the value to the public of receiving the opinions and information that a public employee may disclose. . . .

The reason that protection of employee speech is qualified is that it can distract co-workers and supervisors from their tasks at hand and thwart the implementation of legitimate policy, the risks of which grow greater the closer the employee's speech gets to commenting on his own workplace and responsibilities. It is one thing for an office clerk to say there is waste in government and quite another to charge that his own department pays full-time salaries to part-time workers. Even so, we have regarded eligibility for protection by *Pickering* balancing as the proper approach when an employee speaks critically about the administration of his own government employer. . . .

As all agree, the qualified speech protection embodied in *Pickering* balancing resolves the tension between individual and public interests in the speech, on the one hand, and the government's interest in operating efficiently without distraction or embarrassment by talkative or headline-grabbing employees. The need for a balance hardly disappears when an employee speaks on matters his job requires him to address; rather, it seems obvious that the individual and public value of such speech is no less, and may well be greater, when the employee speaks pursuant to his duties in addressing a subject he knows intimately for the very reason that it falls within his duties. . . .

Nor is there any reason to raise the counterintuitive question whether the public interest in hearing informed employees evaporates when they speak as required on some subject at the core of their jobs. . . . This is not a whit less true when an employee's job duties require him to speak about such things: when, for example, a public auditor speaks on his discovery of embezzlement of public funds, when a building inspector makes an obligatory report of an attempt to bribe him, or when a law enforcement officer expressly balks at a superior's order to violate constitutional rights he is sworn to protect. (The majority, however, places all these speakers beyond the reach of First Amendment protection against retaliation.)

Nothing, then, accountable on the individual and public side of the *Pickering* balance changes when an employee speaks "pursuant" to public duties. On the side of the government employer, however, something is different, and to this extent, I agree with the majority of the Court. The majority is rightly concerned that the employee who speaks out on matters subject to comment in doing his own work has the greater leverage to create office uproars and fracture the government's authority to set policy to be carried out coherently through the ranks.... Up to a point, then, the majority makes good points: government needs civility in the workplace, consistency in policy, and honesty and competence in public service.

But why do the majority's concerns, which we all share, require categorical exclusion of First Amendment protection against any official retaliation for things said on the job? Is it not possible to respect the unchallenged individual and public interests in the speech through a *Pickering* balance . . .? This is, to be sure, a matter of judgment, but the judgment has to account for the undoubted value of speech to those, and by those, whose specific public job responsibilities bring them face to face with wrongdoing and incompetence in government, who refuse to avert their eyes and shut their mouths. And it has to account for the need actually to disrupt government if its officials are corrupt or dangerously incompetent. . . .

Two reasons in particular make me think an adjustment using the basic *Pickering* balancing scheme is perfectly feasible here. First, the extent of the government's legitimate authority over subjects of speech required by a public job can be recognized in advance by setting in effect a minimum heft for comments with any claim to outweigh it. Thus, the risks to the government are great enough for us to hold from the outset that an employee commenting on subjects in the course of duties should not prevail on balance unless he speaks on a matter of unusual importance and satisfies high standards of responsibility in the way he does it. The examples I have already given indicate the eligible subject matter, and it is fair to say that only comment on official dishonesty, deliberately unconstitutional action, other serious wrongdoing, or threats to health and safety can weigh out in an employee's favor. If promulgation of this standard should fail to discourage meritless actions . . . before they get filed, the standard itself would sift them out at the summary-judgment stage.[*]

My second reason for adapting *Pickering* to the circumstances at hand is the experience in Circuits that have recognized claims like Ceballos's here. First Amendment protection less circumscribed than what I would recognize has been available in the Ninth Circuit for over 17 years, and neither there nor in other Circuits that accept claims like this one has there been a debilitating flood of litigation. . . .

JUSTICE BREYER, dissenting.

I write separately to explain why I cannot fully accept either the Court's or Justice SOUTER's answer to the question presented. . . .

The majority [holds] that "when public employees make statements pursuant to their official duties, the employees are not speaking as citizens for First Amendment purposes, and the Constitution does not insulate

---

[*]   Summary judgment would, of course, only follow discovery. [author's note]

their communications from employer discipline." In a word, the majority says, "never." That word, in my view, is too absolute.

Like the majority, I understand the need to "affor[d] government employers sufficient discretion to manage their operations.". . . Nonetheless, there may well be circumstances with special demand for constitutional protection of the speech at issue, where governmental justifications may be limited, and where administrable standards seem readily available—to the point where the majority's fears of department management by lawsuit are misplaced. In such an instance, I believe that courts should apply the *Pickering* standard, even though the government employee speaks upon matters of public concern in the course of his ordinary duties.

This is such a case. . . . The facts present two special circumstances that together justify First Amendment review.

First, the speech at issue is professional speech—the speech of a lawyer. Such speech is subject to independent regulation by canons of the profession. Those canons provide an obligation to speak in certain instances. . . .

Second, the Constitution itself here imposes speech obligations upon the government's professional employee. A prosecutor has a constitutional obligation to learn of, to preserve, and to communicate with the defense about exculpatory and impeachment evidence in the government's possession. . . .

While I agree with much of Justice SOUTER's analysis, I believe that the constitutional standard he enunciates fails to give sufficient weight to the serious managerial and administrative concerns that the majority describes. The standard would instruct courts to apply *Pickering* balancing in all cases, but says that the government should prevail unless the employee (1) "speaks on a matter of unusual importance," and (2) "satisfies high standards of responsibility in the way he does it."

There are, however, far too many issues of public concern, even if defined as "matters of unusual importance," for the screen to screen out very much. . . .

The underlying problem with this breadth of coverage is that the standard . . . does not avoid the judicial need to *undertake the balance* in the first place. And this form of judicial activity—the ability of a dissatisfied employee to file a complaint, engage in discovery, and insist that the court undertake a balancing of interests—itself may interfere unreasonably with both the managerial function (the ability of the employer to control the way in which an employee performs his basic job) and with the use of other grievance-resolution mechanisms, such as arbitration, civil service review boards, and whistle-blower remedies, for which employees and employers may have bargained or which legislatures may have enacted.

At the same time, the list of categories substantially overlaps areas where the law already provides nonconstitutional protection through whistle-blower statutes and the like. That overlap diminishes the need for a constitutional forum and also means that adoption of the test would authorize Federal Constitution-based legal actions that threaten to upset the legislatively struck (or administratively struck) balance that those statutes (or administrative procedures) embody.

I conclude that the First Amendment sometimes does authorize judicial actions based upon a government employee's speech that both (1) involves a matter of public concern and also (2) takes place in the course of ordinary job-related duties. But it does so only in the presence of augmented need for constitutional protection and diminished risk of undue judicial interference with governmental management of the public's affairs. In my view, these conditions are met in this case and *Pickering* balancing is consequently appropriate.

COMMENTS AND QUESTIONS

1.   The Court gives a good summary of the two-step approach of *Pickering* balancing: first, is the speech about a matter of public concern, and, if so, then does the public interest in hearing that speech outweigh the substantial government interests in being able to control its employees, or, stated differently, does the government employer have a sufficient reason to treat the employee differently than a member of the public. The first part of the test is relatively straightforward, although there can always be doubts in particular cases whether a matter is of public concern. It is the second part that is more fuzzy, like most balancing tests.

2.   In *Garcetti* the Court opts for a bright line rule rather than a balancing approach favored by the several dissenters. And while the Court splits along its liberal/conservative lines, with Justice Kennedy again being the swing vote, it perhaps is more illuminating to characterize the split as between the justices who favor bright lines and the justices who favor balancing and considering all the factors.

3.   What's the difference between the approaches of Justice Souter and Justice Breyer?

4.   In *Garcetti*, the Court held that a memorandum prepared in the course of an employee's work was not protected by the First Amendment. In *Lane v. Franks*, 573 U.S. 228 (2014), the employee claimed First Amendment protection for testimony he gave in a criminal case pursuant to a subpoena. The lower courts, relying on *Garcetti*, had held it unprotected because what he testified about involved information he had gained in the course of his government employment. The Court unanimously reversed. *Garcetti* was distinguishable, it said, because the memorandum there was itself work

product of his employment; here, he did not provide the testimony as part of his work, but as a citizen. That his testimony related to his work did not change this. *Garcetti* itself had recognized that a government employee does not lose First Amendment protection for his speech merely because it concerns his employment or relates to something he learned through his employment.

5.   In *Kennedy v. Bremerton School District*, 142 S.Ct. 2407 (2022), a school district fired a football coach because after a football game he would go to the center of the 50-yard line, kneel, and quietly pray. The school district justified this on the grounds that a reasonable observer would perceive the district's allowance of this conduct to constitute its endorsement of religion in violation of the Establishment Clause. The coach challenged his firing under both the Free Speech Clause and Free Exercise Clause of the First Amendment. The Court's analysis of the Free Exercise and Establishment Clause issues are in the next chapter, but it analyzed his Free Speech Claim under the *Pickering* test. Interestingly, no one disputed that the coach's prayer satisfied the first hurdle under *Pickering*—that the speech constituted a matter of public concern—nor did anyone mention that his speech was private, not to any other person, although the Court did drop a footnote (and Justice Thomas noted in concurrence) to the effect that the Free Exercise Clause may sometimes demand a different analysis at the first step of the *Pickering-Garcetti* framework. Because the school district's sole justification for the firing was the need to avoid an Establishment Clause violation, which the Court found would not have been caused by the coach's prayers, the Court held that the district failed to satisfy the balancing test in the second step of *Pickering*.

PROBLEM

A state university has a sexual harassment policy that prohibits:

speech or physical conduct of a sexual nature when such speech or conduct

(a)   unreasonably interferes with an individual's work or academic performance or

(b)   creates an intimidating or hostile working or academic environment.

In assessing whether speech or conduct has the effect described in (a) or (b), it will be viewed through the eyes of a reasonable person in the position of the victim. Conduct or speech occurring off campus can lead to a violation of this policy.

A political science professor maintains on his own personal website studio-quality photographs of young women (but not children) posed in the nude and bound by ropes, chains, or leather straps. The site describes itself as dedicated to the depiction of the idealized woman, one that is beautiful, vulnerable, and dominated, as reflected in the site's photographs. Some female students who are enrolled in the professor's classes have learned about this website and have complained to the University President, saying that the website and discussion about it in the student body have created a hostile and offensive academic environment for them, which interferes with their academic performance. In particular, they feel uncomfortable taking any of the classes taught by this professor. The President would like to order the professor to discontinue the web site or to fire him if he refuses. If the photos are not obscene, is he constitutionally protected from having to discontinue the site or be fired?

N. FREEDOM OF SPEECH WHEN GOVERNMENT IS THE PATRON

In *South Dakota v. Dole* and *National Federation of Independent Business v. Sebelius,* the Court addressed the power of Congress to attach conditions to government funding to states in light of the Tenth Amendment. The question here is the power of government to attach conditions to government funding of persons in light of the First Amendment.

RUST V. SULLIVAN

United States Supreme Court, 1991.
500 U.S. 173, 111 S.Ct. 1759.

CHIEF JUSTICE REHNQUIST delivered the opinion of the Court.

These cases concern a facial challenge to Department of Health and Human Services (HHS) regulations which limit the ability of Title X fund recipients to engage in abortion-related activities.

In 1970, Congress enacted Title X of the Public Health Service Act (Act), which provides federal funding for family-planning services. The Act authorizes the Secretary to "make grants to and enter into contracts with public or nonprofit private entities to assist in the establishment and operation of voluntary family planning projects which shall offer a broad range of acceptable and effective family planning methods and services." Grants and contracts under Title X must "be made in accordance with such regulations as the Secretary may promulgate." Section 1008 of the Act, however, provides that "[n]one of the funds appropriated under this subchapter shall be used in programs where abortion is a method of family planning." That restriction was intended to ensure that Title X funds would "be used only to support preventive family planning services, population research, infertility services, and other related medical, informational, and educational activities." H.R.Conf.Rep. No. 91–1667.

In 1988, the Secretary promulgated new regulations [that limit Title X services] to "preconceptional counseling, education, and general reproductive health care," and expressly exclude "pregnancy care (including obstetric or prenatal care).". . .

The regulations attach three principal conditions on the grant of federal funds for Title X projects. First, the regulations specify that a "Title X project may not provide counseling concerning the use of abortion as a method of family planning or provide referral for abortion as a method of family planning." . . . Title X projects must refer every pregnant client "for appropriate prenatal and/or social services by furnishing a list of available providers that promote the welfare of mother and unborn child." The list may not be used indirectly to encourage or promote abortion, "such as by weighing the list of referrals in favor of health care providers which perform abortions, by including on the list of referral providers health care providers whose principal business is the provision of abortions, by excluding available providers who do not provide abortions, or by 'steering' clients to providers who offer abortion as a method of family planning." The Title X project is expressly prohibited from referring a pregnant woman to an abortion provider, even upon specific request. One permissible response to such an inquiry is that "the project does not consider abortion an appropriate method of family planning and therefore does not counsel or refer for abortion."

Second, the regulations broadly prohibit a Title X project from engaging in activities that "encourage, promote or advocate abortion as a method of family planning." Forbidden activities include lobbying for legislation that would increase the availability of abortion as a method of family planning, developing or disseminating materials advocating abortion as a method of family planning, providing speakers to promote abortion as a method of family planning, using legal action to make abortion available in any way as a method of family planning, and paying dues to any group that advocates abortion as a method of family planning as a substantial part of its activities.

Third, the regulations require that Title X projects be organized so that they are "physically and financially separate" from prohibited abortion activities. To be deemed physically and financially separate, "a Title X project must have an objective integrity and independence from prohibited activities. Mere bookkeeping separation of Title X funds from other monies is not sufficient." The regulations provide a list of nonexclusive factors for the Secretary to consider in conducting a case-by-case determination of objective integrity and independence, such as the existence of separate accounting records and separate personnel, and the degree of physical separation of the project from facilities for prohibited activities.

Petitioners are Title X grantees and doctors who supervise Title X funds suing on behalf of themselves and their patients. Respondent is the

Secretary of HHS. . . . Petitioners challenged the regulations on the grounds that they . . . violate the First and Fifth Amendment rights of Title X clients and the First Amendment rights of Title X health providers. . . .

We begin by pointing out the posture of the cases before us. Petitioners are challenging the *facial* validity of the regulations. Thus, we are concerned only with the question whether, on their face, the regulations are both authorized by the Act and can be construed in such a manner that they can be applied to a set of individuals without infringing upon constitutionally protected rights. Petitioners face a heavy burden in seeking to have the regulations invalidated as facially unconstitutional. "A facial challenge to a legislative Act is, of course, the most difficult challenge to mount successfully, since the challenger must establish that no set of circumstances exists under which the Act would be valid. The fact that [the regulations] might operate unconstitutionally under some conceivable set of circumstances is insufficient to render [them] wholly invalid." . . .

Petitioners contend that the regulations violate the First Amendment by impermissibly discriminating based on viewpoint because they prohibit "all discussion about abortion as a lawful option—including counseling, referral, and the provision of neutral and accurate information about ending a pregnancy—while compelling the clinic or counselor to provide information that promotes continuing a pregnancy to term." They assert that the regulations violate the "free speech rights of private health care organizations that receive Title X funds, of their staff, and of their patients" by impermissibly imposing "viewpoint-discriminatory conditions on government subsidies" and thus "penaliz[e] speech funded with non-Title X monies." Because "Title X continues to fund speech ancillary to pregnancy testing in a manner that is not evenhanded with respect to views and information about abortion, it invidiously discriminates on the basis of viewpoint." [P]etitioners also assert that while the Government may place certain conditions on the receipt of federal subsidies, it may not "discriminate invidiously in its subsidies in such a way as to 'ai[m] at the suppression of dangerous ideas.'"

There is no question but that the statutory prohibition contained in § 1008 is constitutional. In *Maher v. Roe,* 432 U.S. 464 (1977), we upheld a state welfare regulation under which Medicaid recipients received payments for services related to childbirth, but not for nontherapeutic abortions. The Court rejected the claim that this unequal subsidization worked a violation of the Constitution. We held that the government may "make a value judgment favoring childbirth over abortion, and . . . implement that judgment by the allocation of public funds." Here the Government is exercising the authority it possesses under *Maher* . . . to subsidize family planning services which will lead to conception and childbirth, and declining to "promote or encourage abortion." The Government can, without violating the Constitution, selectively fund a program to encourage certain activities it believes to be in the public interest, without at the same time funding an alternative program which seeks to deal with the problem in another way. In so doing, the Government has not discriminated on the basis of viewpoint; it has merely chosen to fund one activity to the exclusion of the other. "[A] legislature's decision not to subsidize the exercise of a fundamental right does not infringe the right.". . . .

To hold that the Government unconstitutionally discriminates on the basis of viewpoint when it chooses to fund a program dedicated to advance certain permissible goals, because the program in advancing those goals necessarily discourages alternative goals, would render numerous Government programs constitutionally suspect. When Congress established a National Endowment for Democracy to encourage other countries to adopt democratic principles, it was not constitutionally required to fund a program to encourage competing lines of political philosophy such as communism and fascism. . . .

Petitioners contend that the restrictions on the subsidization of abortion-related speech contained in the regulations are impermissible because they condition the receipt of a benefit, in these cases Title X funding, on the relinquishment of a constitutional right, the right to engage in abortion advocacy and counseling. [P]etitioners argue that "even though the government may deny [a] . . . benefit for any number of reasons, there are some reasons upon which the government may not rely. It may not deny a benefit to a person on a basis that infringes his constitutionally protected interests—especially, his interest in freedom of speech."

Petitioners' reliance on these cases is unavailing, however, because here the Government is not denying a benefit to anyone, but is instead simply insisting that public funds be spent for the purposes for which they were authorized. The Secretary's regulations do not force the Title X grantee to give up abortion-related speech; they merely require that the grantee keep such activities separate and distinct from Title X activities. Title X expressly distinguishes between a Title X *grantee* and a Title X *project*. The grantee, which normally is a health-care organization, may receive funds from a variety of sources for a variety of purposes. The grantee receives Title X funds, however, for the specific and limited purpose of establishing and operating a Title X project. The regulations govern the scope of the Title X *project's* activities, and leave the grantee unfettered in its other activities. The Title X *grantee* can continue to perform abortions, provide abortion-related services, and engage in abortion advocacy; it simply is required to conduct those activities through programs that are separate and independent from the project that receives Title X funds. . . .

JUSTICE BLACKMUN, with whom JUSTICE MARSHALL joins, with whom JUSTICE STEVENS joins. . . .

[U]ntil today, the Court never has upheld viewpoint-based suppression of speech simply because that suppression was a condition upon the acceptance of public funds. Whatever may be the Government's power to condition the receipt of its largess upon the relinquishment of constitutional rights, it surely does not extend to a condition that suppresses the recipient's cherished freedom of speech based solely upon the content or viewpoint of that speech. This rule is a sound one, for, as the Court often has noted: " 'A regulation of speech that is motivated by nothing more than a desire to curtail expression of a particular point of view on controversial issues of general interest is the purest example of a "law . . . abridging the freedom of speech, or of the press." ' "

It cannot seriously be disputed that the counseling and referral provisions at issue in the present cases constitute content-based regulation of speech. Title X grantees may provide counseling and referral regarding any of a wide range of family planning and other topics, save abortion.

The regulations are also clearly viewpoint based. While suppressing speech favorable to abortion with one hand, the Secretary compels antiabortion speech with the other. . . .

The regulations pertaining to "advocacy" are even more explicitly viewpoint based. These provide: "A Title X project may not *encourage, promote or advocate* abortion as a method of family planning." They explain: "This requirement prohibits actions to *assist* women to obtain abortions or *increase* the availability or accessibility of abortion for family planning purposes." The regulations do not, however, proscribe or even regulate anti-abortion advocacy. These are clearly restrictions aimed at the suppression of "dangerous ideas."

Remarkably, the majority concludes that "the Government has not discriminated on the basis of viewpoint; it has merely chosen to fund one activity to the exclusion of the other." By refusing to fund those family-planning projects that advocate abortion *because* they advocate abortion, the Government plainly has targeted a particular viewpoint. The majority's reliance on the fact that the regulations pertain solely to funding decisions simply begs the question. Clearly, there are some bases upon which government may not rest its decision to fund or not to fund. For example, the Members of the majority surely would agree that government may not base its decision to support an activity upon considerations of race. As demonstrated above, our cases make clear that ideological viewpoint is a similarly repugnant ground upon which to base funding decisions. . . .

In the cases at bar, the speaker's interest in the communication is both clear and vital. In addressing the family-planning needs of their clients, the physicians and counselors who staff Title X projects seek to provide them with the full range of information and options regarding their health and reproductive freedom. Indeed, the legitimate expectations of the patient and the ethical responsibilities of the medical profession demand no less. "The patient's right of self-decision can be effectively exercised only if the patient possesses enough information to enable an intelligent choice. . . . The physician has an ethical obligation to help the patient make choices from among the therapeutic alternatives consistent with good medical practice." When a client becomes pregnant, the full range of therapeutic alternatives includes the abortion option, and Title X counselors' interest in providing this information is compelling. . . .

Finally, it is of no small significance that the speech the Secretary would suppress is truthful information regarding constitutionally protected conduct of vital importance to the listener. One can imagine no legitimate governmental interest that might be served by suppressing such information. . . .

In view of the inevitable effect of the regulations, the majority's conclusion that "[t]he difficulty that a woman encounters when a Title X project does not provide abortion counseling or referral leaves her in no different position than she would have been if the Government had not enacted Title X," is insensitive and contrary to common human experience. Both the purpose and result of the challenged regulations are to deny women the ability voluntarily to decide their procreative destiny. For these women, the Government will have obliterated the freedom to choose as surely as if it had banned abortions outright. The denial of this freedom is not a consequence of poverty but of the Government's ill-intentioned distortion of information it has chosen to provide. . . .

JUSTICE O'CONNOR, dissenting. [Justice O'Connor would interpret the statute not to authorize the regulations in question, so as to avoid the constitutional question.]

COMMENTS AND QUESTIONS

1.   Government can spend its money to promote what it believes is good policy and to oppose what it thinks is bad policy. As the Court says, funding an institute for democracy does not require the government to fund competing views of government. In that sense, government speech does not have to be viewpoint neutral.

2.   The real question in this case is whether the conditions imposed on recipients of Title X funding force them to limit their independent speech. The Court says it does not; it only limits what they can say under the program. The dissent suggests otherwise. What do you think?

3.   An earlier case, *Federal Communications Commission v. League of Women Voters of California*, 468 U.S. 364 (1984), involved a condition imposed on noncommercial educational broadcasting stations receiving Corporation for Public Broadcasting grants that prohibited them from editorializing. The Court by a 5–4 vote found the condition unconstitutional. It noted that the condition did not prohibit the use of just the grant money for editorializing, but

it prohibited the station from editorializing even with money raised from different sources.

RUMSFELD V. FORUM FOR ACADEMIC AND INSTITUTIONAL RIGHTS, INC.

United States Supreme Court, 2006.
547 U.S. 47, 126 S.Ct. 1297.

CHIEF JUSTICE ROBERTS delivered the opinion of the Court.

When law schools began restricting the access of military recruiters to their students because of disagreement with the Government's policy on homosexuals in the military, Congress responded by enacting the Solomon Amendment. That provision specifies that if any part of an institution of higher education denies military recruiters access equal to that provided other recruiters, the entire institution would lose certain federal funds. The law schools responded by suing, alleging that the Solomon Amendment infringed their First Amendment freedoms of speech and association. The District Court disagreed but was reversed by a divided panel of the Court of Appeals for the Third Circuit, which ordered the District Court to enter a preliminary injunction against enforcement of the Solomon Amendment. We granted certiorari.

Respondent Forum for Academic and Institutional Rights, Inc. (FAIR), is an association of law schools and law faculties. Its declared mission is "to promote academic freedom, support educational institutions in opposing discrimination and vindicate the rights of institutions of higher education." FAIR members have adopted policies expressing their opposition to discrimination based on, among other factors, sexual orientation. They would like to restrict military recruiting on their campuses because they object to the policy Congress has adopted with respect to homosexuals in the military. The Solomon Amendment, however, forces institutions to choose between enforcing their nondiscrimination policy against military recruiters in this way and continuing to receive specified federal funding.

FAIR argued that this forced inclusion and equal treatment of military recruiters violated the law schools' First Amendment freedoms of speech and association. According to FAIR, the Solomon Amendment was unconstitutional because it forced law schools to choose between exercising their First Amendment right to decide whether to disseminate or accommodate a military recruiter's message, and ensuring the availability of federal funding for their universities.

The Constitution grants Congress the power to "provide for the common Defence," "[t]o raise and support Armies," and "[t]o provide and maintain a Navy." Congress' power in this area "is broad and sweeping," and there is no dispute in this case that it includes the authority to require campus access for military recruiters. . . .

Although Congress has broad authority to legislate on matters of military recruiting, it nonetheless chose to secure campus access for military recruiters indirectly, through its Spending Clause power. The Solomon Amendment gives universities a choice: Either allow military recruiters the same access to students afforded any other recruiter or forgo certain federal funds. Congress' decision to proceed indirectly does not reduce the deference given to Congress in the area of military affairs. Congress' choice to promote its goal by creating a funding condition deserves at least as deferential treatment as if Congress had imposed a mandate on universities.

Congress' power to regulate military recruiting under the Solomon Amendment is arguably greater because universities are free to decline the federal funds. In *Grove City College v. Bell,* 465 U.S. 555 (1984), we rejected a private college's claim that conditioning federal funds on its compliance with Title IX of the Education Amendments of 1972 violated the First Amendment. We thought this argument "warrant[ed] only brief consideration" because "Congress is free to attach reasonable and unambiguous conditions to federal financial assistance that educational institutions are not obligated to accept." We concluded that no First Amendment violation had occurred—without reviewing the substance of the First Amendment claims—because Grove City could decline the Government's funds.

Other decisions, however, recognize a limit on Congress' ability to place conditions on the receipt of funds. We recently held that " 'the government may not deny a benefit to a person on a basis that infringes his constitutionally protected . . . freedom of speech even if he has no entitlement to that benefit.' " *United States v. American Library Assn., Inc.,* 539 U.S. 194 (2003). Under this principle, known as the unconstitutional conditions doctrine, the Solomon Amendment would be unconstitutional if Congress could not directly require universities to provide military recruiters equal access to their students.

This case does not require us to determine when a condition placed on university funding goes beyond the "reasonable" choice offered in *Grove City* and becomes an unconstitutional condition. It is clear that a funding condition cannot be unconstitutional if it could be constitutionally imposed directly. Because the First Amendment would not prevent Congress from directly imposing the Solomon Amendment's access requirement, the statute does not place an unconstitutional condition on the receipt of federal funds.

The Solomon Amendment neither limits what law schools may say nor requires them to say anything. Law schools remain free under the statute to express whatever views they may have on the military's congressionally mandated employment policy, all the while retaining eligibility for federal funds. As a general matter, the Solomon Amendment regulates conduct, not speech. It affects what law schools must *do*—afford equal access to military recruiters—not what they may or may not *say*.

Nevertheless, the Third Circuit concluded that the Solomon Amendment violates law schools' freedom of speech in a number of ways. First, in assisting military recruiters, law schools provide some services, such as sending e-mails and distributing flyers, that clearly involve speech. The Court of Appeals held that in supplying these services law schools are unconstitutionally compelled to speak the Government's message. Second, military recruiters are, to some extent, speaking while they are on campus. The Court of Appeals held that, by forcing law schools to permit the military on campus to express its message, the Solomon Amendment unconstitutionally requires law schools to host or accommodate the military's speech. Third, although the Court of Appeals thought that the Solomon Amendment regulated speech, it held in the alternative that, if the statute regulates conduct, this conduct is expressive and regulating it unconstitutionally infringes law schools' right to engage in expressive conduct. We consider each issue in turn.

Some of this Court's leading First Amendment precedents have established the principle that freedom of speech prohibits the government from telling people what they must say.

The Solomon Amendment does not require any similar expression by law schools. Nonetheless, recruiting assistance provided by the schools often includes elements of speech. For example, schools may send e-mails or post notices on bulletin boards on an employer's behalf. Law schools offering such services to other recruiters must also send e-mails and post notices on behalf of the military to comply with the Solomon Amendment. As FAIR points out, these compelled statements of fact ("The U.S. Army recruiter will meet interested students in Room 123 at 11 a.m."), like compelled statements of opinion, are subject to First Amendment scrutiny.

This sort of recruiting assistance, however, is a far cry from the compelled speech in *Barnette* and *Wooley*. The Solomon Amendment, unlike the laws at issue in those cases, does not dictate the content of the speech at all, which is only "compelled" if, and to the extent, the school provides such speech for other recruiters. There is nothing in this case approaching a Government-mandated pledge or motto that the school must endorse.

The compelled speech to which the law schools point is plainly incidental to the Solomon Amendment's regulation of conduct, and "it has never been deemed an abridgment of freedom of speech or press to make a course of conduct illegal merely because the conduct was in part initiated, evidenced, or carried out by means of language, either spoken, written, or printed." Congress, for example, can prohibit employers from discriminating in hiring on the basis of race. The fact that this will require an employer to take down a sign reading "White Applicants Only" hardly means that the law should be analyzed as one regulating the employer's speech rather than conduct. Compelling a law school that sends scheduling e-mails for other recruiters to send one for a military recruiter is simply not the same as forcing a student to pledge allegiance, or forcing a Jehovah's Witness to display the motto "Live Free or Die," and it trivializes the freedom protected in *Barnette* and *Wooley* to suggest that it is.

Our compelled-speech cases are not limited to the situation in which an individual must personally speak the government's message. We have also in a number of instances limited the government's ability to force one speaker to host or accommodate another speaker's message. See *Hurley v. Irish-American Gay, Lesbian and Bisexual Group of Boston, Inc.,* 515 U.S. 557 (1995)(state law cannot require a parade to include a group whose message the parade's organizer does not wish to send). Relying on these precedents, the Third Circuit concluded that the Solomon Amendment unconstitutionally compels law schools to accommodate the military's message "[b]y requiring schools to include military recruiters in the interviews and recruiting receptions the schools arrange."

The compelled-speech violation in each of our prior cases, however, resulted from the fact that the complaining speaker's own message was affected by the speech it was forced to accommodate. The expressive nature of a parade was central to our holding in *Hurley.* . . .

In this case, accommodating the military's message does not affect the law schools' speech, because the schools are not speaking when they host interviews and recruiting receptions. A law school's recruiting services lack the expressive quality of a parade; its accommodation of a military recruiter's message is not compelled speech because the accommodation does not sufficiently interfere with any message of the school.

The schools respond that if they treat military and nonmilitary recruiters alike in order to comply with the Solomon Amendment, they could be viewed as sending the message that they see nothing wrong with the military's policies, when they do. We rejected a similar argument in *PruneYard Shopping Center v. Robins.* In that case, we upheld a state law requiring a shopping center owner to allow certain expressive activities by others on its property. We explained that there was little likelihood that the views of those engaging in the expressive activities would be identified with the owner, who remained free to disassociate himself from those views and who was "not . . . being compelled to affirm [a] belief in any governmentally prescribed position or view."

The same is true here. Nothing about recruiting suggests that law schools agree with any speech by recruiters, and nothing in the Solomon Amendment restricts what the law schools may say about the military's policies. . . .

The Solomon Amendment does not violate law schools' freedom of speech, but the First Amendment's protection extends beyond the right to speak. We have recognized a First Amendment right to associate for the purpose of speaking, which we have termed a "right of expressive association." See, *e.g., Boy Scouts of America v. Dale.* The reason we have extended First Amendment protection in this way is clear: The right to speak is often exercised most effectively by combining one's voice with the voices of others.

FAIR argues that the Solomon Amendment violates law schools' freedom of expressive association. According to FAIR, law schools' ability to express their message that discrimination on the basis of sexual orientation is wrong is significantly affected by the presence of military recruiters on campus and the schools' obligation to assist them. . . .

The Solomon Amendment, however, does not affect a law school's associational rights. To comply with the statute, law schools must allow military recruiters on campus and assist them in whatever way the school chooses to assist other employers. Law schools therefore "associate" with military recruiters in the sense that they interact with them. But recruiters are not part of the law school. Recruiters are, by definition, outsiders who come onto campus for the limited purpose of trying to hire students—not to become members of the school's expressive association. This distinction is critical. Unlike the public accommodations law in *Dale,* the Solomon Amendment does not force a law school " 'to accept members it does not desire.' "

Because Congress could require law schools to provide equal access to military recruiters without violating the schools' freedoms of speech or association, the Court of Appeals erred in holding that the Solomon Amendment likely violates the First Amendment. We therefore reverse the judgment of the Third Circuit and remand the case for further proceedings consistent with this opinion.

COMMENTS AND QUESTIONS

1.   The opinion is unanimous (although Justice Alito did not participate). Is the answer that clear to you?

2.   No one questions that the government could under Article I simply order law schools and universities to give access to military recruiters. Why not? Are there other situations in which the government can force private persons to allow government agents on their property?

3.   The Association of American Law Schools had at the time (and still has) a requirement that member schools not allow recruiters on campus who discriminate on the basis of a number of factors, including sexual orientation and age. When the Solomon Amendment was passed, given the financial impact it would have on law schools, the Association waived its requirement with respect to military recruiters' discrimination on the basis of sexual

orientation. Nobody mentioned the fact that the military also discriminates in hiring on the basis of age.

4.   In *Agency for International Development v. Alliance for Open Society International, Inc.,* 570 U.S. 205 (2013), a statute providing funding for organizations fighting HIV/AIDS abroad required that only organizations that have "a policy explicitly opposing prostitution and sex trafficking" could qualify for funding. Certain organizations objected to this requirement, because they believed their ability to fight HIV/AIDS was facilitated by interacting positively with prostitutes, and to have a policy opposing prostitution would interfere with such interaction. Chief Justice Roberts wrote for the Court. He distinguished *Rust v. Sullivan,* because here the condition was not on how the funds would be spent, but on the views of the persons receiving the funds. Moreover, it was not like *Rumsfeld v. Forum for Academic and Institutional Rights,* because there the law schools were not required to have a policy supporting military recruiters or to disavow a policy of opposing discrimination against homosexuals. Nor was this a case in which the government could independently compel an organization to have a policy opposing prostitution and sex trafficking. Rather this was the unusual case of the government conditioning funding on a person adopting a particular policy favored by the government. This made it unconstitutional.

Alas, it was a pyrrhic victory. The Court remanded this case to the courts below to implement its decision. The question arose whether the First Amendment protections that the Court found the domestic organizations enjoyed would also apply to the legally distinct foreign affiliates of these organizations through whom the organizations operated abroad. In *Agency for International Development v. Alliance for Open Society International, Inc.,* 140 S.Ct. 2082 (2020), the Court held that the foreign affiliates had no First Amendment rights. This flowed inexorably, the Court said, from the general principle that foreign persons outside the United States territory do not possess rights under the Constitution, and from the general principle of corporate law the separately incorporated organizations are separate legal entities with distinct rights and obligations. The fact that as a practical matter this meant that the domestic organizations would not be able to participate in the program, notwithstanding their First Amendment rights, because they would only be able to operate abroad through their foreign affiliates, was of no consequence to the majority. This rendered the earlier decision moot as to them.

PROBLEM

Imagine that Congress passes a law conditioning funding provided to medical schools on the medical schools not teaching how to perform abortions, on hospitals associated with medical schools not performing abortions, and on the medical schools having a policy opposing abortion. Which, if any, of these conditions would be constitutional?

CHAPTER 10

THE FIRST AMENDMENT—
FREEDOM OF RELIGION

■ ■ ■

The First Amendment contains two religion clauses. The first provides that "Congress shall make no law respecting an establishment of religion." The second prohibits Congress from "prohibiting the free exercise" of religion. The two clauses are usually viewed as complementary, that is, prohibiting government from establishing any religion helps to ensure that there will be no law prohibiting the free exercise of religion, because historically restrictions placed on religious exercise stemmed from laws passed by governments controlled by different religions. Nevertheless, sometimes the two clauses can appear to be in conflict. For example, a law banning all employment discrimination on the basis of sex would seriously interfere with at least the Catholic religion, because of its belief that only men can be priests. On the other hand, to make an exception only for religious institutions might suggest government favoritism of religion over non-religion.

This chapter begins with the Establishment Clause and its restrictions on government financial support that in some way redounds to the benefit of a religion. It proceeds to consider how the Establishment Clause may affect other government actions that in some way might constitute government "establishment" of religion. The chapter then addresses the Free Exercise Clause, and its limitations on government action that may interfere with a person's religious practices. Finally, it concludes with how to resolve apparent conflicts between the two clauses.

A. GOVERNMENT FINANCIAL SUPPORT

EVERSON V. BOARD OF EDUCATION
United States Supreme Court, 1947.
330 U.S. 1, 67 S.Ct. 504.

MR. JUSTICE BLACK delivered the opinion of the Court.

A New Jersey statute authorizes its local school districts to make rules and contracts for the transportation of children to and from schools. The appellee, a township board of education, acting pursuant to this statute authorized reimbursement to parents of money expended by them for the bus transportation of their children on regular busses operated by the public transportation system. Part of this money was for the payment of transportation of some children in the community to Catholic parochial schools. . . .

The appellant, in his capacity as a district taxpayer, filed suit in a State court challenging the right of the Board to reimburse parents of parochial school students. He contended that the statute and the resolution passed pursuant to it violated both the State and the Federal Constitutions. . . .

The New Jersey statute is challenged as a "law respecting an establishment of religion." . . . Whether this New Jersey law is one respecting the "establishment of religion" requires an understanding of the meaning of that language, particularly with respect to the imposition of taxes. Once again, therefore, it is not inappropriate briefly to review the background and environment of the period in which that constitutional language was fashioned and adopted.

A large proportion of the early settlers of this country came here from Europe to escape the bondage of laws which compelled them to support and attend government favored churches. The centuries immediately before and contemporaneous with the colonization of America had been filled with turmoil, civil strife, and persecutions, generated in large part by established sects determined to maintain their absolute political and religious supremacy. With the power of government supporting them, at various times and places, Catholics had persecuted Protestants, Protestants had persecuted Catholics, Protestant sects had persecuted other Protestant sects, Catholics of one shade of belief had persecuted Catholics of another shade of belief, and all of these had from time to time persecuted Jews. In efforts to force loyalty to whatever religious group happened to be on top and in league with the government of a particular time and place, men and women had been fined, cast in jail, cruelly tortured, and killed. Among the offenses for which these punishments had been inflicted were such things as speaking disrespectfully of the views of ministers of government-established churches, nonattendance at those churches, expressions of non-belief in their doctrines, and failure to pay taxes and tithes to support them.

These practices of the old world were transplanted to and began to thrive in the soil of the new America. The very charters granted by the English Crown to the individuals and companies designated to make the laws which would control the destinies of the colonials authorized these individuals and companies to erect religious establishments which all, whether believers or non-believers, would be required to support and attend. An exercise of this authority was accompanied by a repetition of many of the old world practices and persecutions. Catholics found themselves hounded and proscribed because of their faith; Quakers who followed their conscience went to jail; Baptists were peculiarly obnoxious to certain dominant Protestant sects; men and women of varied faiths who happened to be in a minority in a particular locality were persecuted because they steadfastly persisted in worshipping God only as their own consciences dictated. And all of these dissenters were compelled to pay tithes and taxes to support government-sponsored churches whose ministers preached inflammatory sermons designed to strengthen and consolidate the established faith by generating a burning hatred against dissenters.

These practices became so commonplace as to shock the freedom-loving colonials into a feeling of abhorrence. The imposition of taxes to pay ministers' salaries and to build and maintain churches and church property aroused their indignation. It was these feelings which found expression in the First Amendment. . . .

Prior to the adoption of the Fourteenth Amendment, the First Amendment did not apply as a restraint against the states. Most of them did soon provide similar constitutional protections for religious liberty. But some states persisted for about half a century in imposing restraints upon the free exercise of religion and in discriminating against particular religious groups. . . .

The "establishment of religion" clause of the First Amendment means at least this: Neither a state nor the Federal Government can set up a church. Neither can pass laws which aid one religion, aid all religions, or prefer one religion over another. Neither can force nor influence a person to go to or to remain away from church against his will or force him to profess a belief or disbelief in any religion. No person can be punished for entertaining or professing religious beliefs or disbeliefs, for church attendance or non-attendance. No tax in any amount, large or small, can be levied to support any religious activities or institutions, whatever they may be called, or whatever form they may adopt to teach or practice religion. Neither a state nor the Federal Government can, openly or secretly, participate in the affairs of any religious organizations or groups and vice versa. In the words of Jefferson, the clause against establishment of religion by law was intended to erect "a wall of separation between Church and State."

We must consider the New Jersey statute in accordance with the foregoing limitations imposed by the First Amendment. . . . New Jersey cannot consistently with the "establishment of religion" clause of the First Amendment contribute tax-raised funds to the support of an institution which teaches the tenets and faith of any church. On the other hand, other language of the amendment commands that New Jersey cannot hamper its citizens in the free exercise of their own religion. Consequently, it cannot exclude individual Catholics, Lutherans, Mohammedans, Baptists, Jews, Methodists, Non-believers, Presbyterians, or the members of any other faith, because of their faith, or lack of it, from receiving the benefits of public welfare legislation. While we do not mean to intimate that a state could not provide transportation only to children attending public schools, we must be careful, in protecting the citizens of New Jersey against state-established churches, to be sure that we do not inadvertently prohibit New Jersey from extending its general State law benefits to all its citizens without regard to their religious belief.

Measured by these standards, we cannot say that the First Amendment prohibits New Jersey from spending taxraised funds to pay the bus fares of parochial school pupils as a part of a general program under which it pays the fares of pupils attending public and other schools. It is undoubtedly true that children are helped to get to church schools. There is even a possibility that some of the children might not be sent to the church schools if the parents were compelled to pay their children's bus fares out of their own pockets when transportation to a public school would have been paid for by the State. The same possibility exists where the state requires a local transit company to provide reduced fares to school children including those attending parochial schools, or where a municipally owned transportation system undertakes to carry all school children free of charge. [P]arents might be reluctant to permit their children to attend schools which the state had cut off from such general government services as ordinary police and fire protection, connections for sewage disposal, public highways and sidewalks. Of course, cutting off church schools from these services, so separate and so indisputably marked off from the religious function, would make it far more difficult for the schools to operate. But such is obviously not the purpose of the First Amendment. That Amendment requires the state to be a neutral in its relations with groups of religious believers and non-believers; it does not require the state to be their adversary. State power is no more to be used so as to handicap religions, than it is to favor them. . . .

The First Amendment has erected a wall between church and state. That wall must be kept high and impregnable. We could not approve the slightest breach. New Jersey has not breached it here.

MR. JUSTICE JACKSON, dissenting.

[T]he Court concludes that this "legislation, as applied, does no more than provide a general program to help parents get their children, regardless of their religion, safely and expeditiously to and from accredited schools," and it draws a comparison between "state provisions intended to guarantee free transportation" for school children with services such as police and fire protection, and implies that we are here dealing with "laws authorizing new types of public services * * *" This hypothesis permeates the opinion. The facts will not bear that construction.

The Township of Ewing is not furnishing transportation to the children in any form; it is not operating school busses itself or contracting for their operation; and it is not performing any public service of any kind with this taxpayer's money. All school children are left to ride as ordinary paying passengers on the regular busses operated by the public transportation system. What the Township does, and what the taxpayer complains of, is at stated intervals to reimburse parents for the fares paid, provided the children attend either public schools or Catholic Church schools. This expenditure of tax funds has no possible effect on the child's safety or expedition in transit. As passengers on the public busses they travel as fast and no faster, and are as safe and no safer, since their parents are reimbursed as before. . . .

It is of no importance in this situation whether the beneficiary of this expenditure of tax-raised funds is primarily the parochial school and incidentally the pupil, or whether the aid is directly bestowed on the pupil with indirect benefits to the school. The state cannot maintain a Church and it can no more tax its citizens to furnish free carriage to those who attend a Church. The prohibition against establishment of religion cannot be circumvented by a subsidy, bonus or reimbursement of expense to individuals for receiving religious instruction and indoctrination. . . .

It seems to me that the basic fallacy in the Court's reasoning, which accounts for its failure to apply the principles it avows, is in ignoring the essentially religious test by which beneficiaries of this expenditure are selected. A policeman protects a Catholic, of course—but not because he is a Catholic; it is because he is a man and a member of our society. The fireman protects the Church school—but not because it is a Church school; it is because it is property, part of the assets of our society. Neither the fireman nor the policeman has to ask before he renders aid "Is this man or building identified with the Catholic Church." But before these school authorities draw a check to reimburse for a student's fare they must ask just that question, and if the school is a Catholic one they may render aid because it is such, while if it is of any other faith or is run for profit, the help must be withheld.* . . .

MR. JUSTICE FRANKFURTER joins in this opinion.

MR. JUSTICE RUTLEDGE, with whom MR. JUSTICE FRANKFURTER, MR. JUSTICE JACKSON and MR. JUSTICE BURTON agree, dissenting.

[T]his case forces us to determine squarely for the first time what was "an establishment of religion" in the First Amendment's conception; and by that measure to decide whether New Jersey's action violates its command. . . .

---

* Justice Jackson states that only children from Catholic schools can qualify for the reimbursement of bus fare. The town resolution, adopted pursuant to a state statute that distinguished solely between profit-making private schools and all other schools (whether public, private, or religious), in fact only provided for reimbursement for Catholic school children. Apparently, however, the only non-public schools in the town were Catholic schools. The plaintiff did not complain about the limitation to Catholic school children. In a portion of the Court's opinion that has been edited out, the opinion suggests that were there discrimination against other religions that would be a different case. [author's note]

Not simply an established church, but any law respecting an establishment of religion is forbidden. The Amendment was broadly but not loosely phrased. . . .

The Amendment's purpose was not to strike merely at the official establishment of a single sect, creed or religion, outlawing only a formal relation such as had prevailed in England and some of the colonies. Necessarily it was to uproot all such relationships. But the object was broader than separating church and state in this narrow sense. It was to create a complete and permanent separation of the spheres of religious activity and civil authority by comprehensively forbidding every form of public aid or support for religion. In proof the Amendment's wording and history unite with this Court's consistent utterances whenever attention has been fixed directly upon the question.

No provision of the Constitution is more closely tied to or given content by its generating history than the religious clause of the First Amendment. It is at once the refined product and the terse summation of that history. The history includes not only Madison's authorship and the proceedings before the First Congress, but also the long and intensive struggle for religious freedom in America, more especially in Virginia, of which the Amendment was the direct culmination. In the documents of the times, particularly of Madison, who was leader in the Virginia struggle before he became the Amendment's sponsor, but also in the writings of Jefferson and others and in the issues which engendered them is to be found irrefutable confirmation of the Amendment's sweeping content. . . .

In view of this history no further proof is needed that the Amendment forbids any appropriation, large or small, from public funds to aid or support any and all religious exercises. But if more were called for, the debates in the First Congress and this Court's consistent expressions, whenever it has touched on the matter directly, supply it. . . .

Does New Jersey's action furnish support for religion by use of the taxing power? Certainly it does, if the test remains undiluted as Jefferson and Madison made it, that money taken by taxation from one is not to be used or given to support another's religious training or belief, or indeed one's own. Today as then the furnishing of "contributions of money for the propagation of opinions which he disbelieves" is the forbidden exaction; and the prohibition is absolute for whatever measure brings that consequence and whatever amount may be sought or given to that end.

The funds used here were raised by taxation. The Court does not dispute nor could it that their use does in fact give aid and encouragement to religious instruction. It only concludes that this aid is not "support" in law. . . . Here parents pay money to send their children to parochial schools and funds raised by taxation are used to reimburse them. This not only helps the children to get to school and the parents to send them. It aids them in a substantial way to get the very thing which they are sent to the particular school to secure, namely, religious training and teaching. . . .

New Jersey's action therefore exactly fits the type of exaction and the kind of evil at which Madison and Jefferson struck. Under the test they framed it cannot be said that the cost of transportation is no part of the cost of education or of the religious instruction given. . . .

Short treatment will dispose of what remains. Whatever might be said of some other application of New Jersey's statute, the one made here has no semblance of bearing as a safety measure or, indeed, for securing expeditious conveyance. The transportation supplied is by public conveyance, subject to all the hazards and delays of the highway and the streets incurred by the public generally in going about its multifarious business.

Nor is the case comparable to one of furnishing fire or police protection, or access to public highways. These things are matters of common right, part of the general need for safety. Certainly the fire department must not stand idly by while the church burns. Nor is this reason why the state should pay the expense of transportation or other items of the cost of religious education. . . .

COMMENTS AND QUESTIONS

1.   As an initial matter, note that this is a suit by a taxpayer complaining how the town spends its tax funds. The Court does not address his standing to raise such a claim, but recall the later case of *Flast v. Cohen*, 392 U.S. 83 (1968), that allowed a taxpayer to raise Establishment Clause claims against the use of government funds. But, then, also recall that the continued validity of *Flast* hangs by a slim thread, as it has been narrowed to its facts and its doctrinal underpinnings obliterated. If taxpayers cannot raise claims against payments allegedly made in support of religion in violation of the Establishment Clause, who could?

2.   The Court alludes to the fact that at the time of the ratification of the First Amendment there were states that had "established religions." Thus, while Virginia had become strongly anti-establishment, after having originally had an established religion, the same could not be said for all the states ratifying the First Amendment. Hence the wording of the Establishment Clause prohibits Congress not just from establishing religion but also from making any law "respecting the establishment of religion," *i.e.*, disestablishing religion in the states that had an established religion. The few states that retained established religions in 1791 voluntarily disestablished them in less than 30 years. Nevertheless, it is somewhat ironic that the Establishment Clause as originally formulated created a constitutional protection for states to have an established religion if they chose to have one, but as incorporated against the states the clause now prohibits states from having an established religion, all without any clear textual basis in the Constitution for this change.

3.   Both the Court and the Rutledge dissent include extensive discussion of the history leading up to the adoption of the First Amendment's Establishment Clause, most of which has been edited out. Moreover, despite their difference ultimately as to the effect of the Establishment Clause on the particular law here, both the Court and the dissent conclude that the history suggests a strong stance against government "establishing" religion, quoting Jefferson's phrase, "a wall of separation." This historical analysis, however, has been questioned by some justices in later cases, and, as is so often the case, the truth of what was the original meaning of the Establishment Clause is hopelessly indistinct.

4.   In *Everson* the Court concludes that the policy of reimbursing bus fare for all children attending schools in the town did not constitute support for religion prohibited by the Establishment Clause. The dissent disagrees vehemently. The Court says it is the equivalent of providing fire and police protection to the church schools; the dissent disagrees. Is there a difference? What if all town buses were free, paid for by taxes levied on the inhabitants? Would it be constitutional for the children attending the parochial schools to take the town bus? How about taking the bus to church on Sunday? What if, instead, the town provided school buses to transport students to school? Could they transport children to the parochial schools?

5.   *Everson* set the tone for many of the more modern Establishment Clause cases—it involved government support that in some way redounded to the benefit of religious schools, and the Court was deeply divided. The opinions in the following case, the most recently decided case in this line, describe the uncertain path of those cases.

ZELMAN V. SIMMONS-HARRIS

United States Supreme Court, 2002.
536 U.S. 639, 122 S.Ct. 2460.

CHIEF JUSTICE REHNQUIST delivered the opinion of the Court.

The State of Ohio has established a pilot program designed to provide educational choices to families with children who reside in the Cleveland City School District. The question presented is whether this program offends the Establishment Clause of the United States Constitution. We hold that it does not.

There are more than 75,000 children enrolled in the Cleveland City School District. The majority of these children are from low-income and minority families. Few of these families enjoy the means to send their children to any school other than an inner-city public school. For more than a generation, however, Cleveland's public schools have been among the worst performing public schools in the Nation. In 1995, a Federal District Court declared a "crisis of magnitude" and placed the entire Cleveland school district under state control. Shortly thereafter, the state auditor found that Cleveland's public schools were in the midst of a "crisis that is perhaps unprecedented in the history of American education." The district had failed to meet any of the 18 state standards for minimal acceptable performance. Only 1 in 10 ninth graders could pass a basic proficiency examination, and students at all levels performed at a dismal rate compared with students in other Ohio public schools. More than two-thirds of high school students either dropped or failed out before graduation. Of those students who managed to reach their senior year, one of every four still failed to graduate. Of those students who did graduate, few could read, write, or compute at levels comparable to their counterparts in other cities.

It is against this backdrop that Ohio enacted, among other initiatives, its Pilot Project Scholarship Program. The program provides financial assistance to families in [Cleveland City School District].

The program provides two basic kinds of assistance to parents of children in a covered district. First, the program provides tuition aid for students in kindergarten through third grade, expanding each year through eighth grade, to attend a participating public or private school of their parent's choosing. Second, the program provides tutorial aid for students who choose to remain enrolled in public school.

The tuition aid portion of the program is designed to provide educational choices to parents who reside in [the] district. Any private school, whether religious or nonreligious, may participate in the program and accept program students so long as the school is located within the boundaries of [the] district and meets statewide educational standards. Participating private schools must agree not to discriminate on the basis of race, religion, or ethnic background, or to "advocate or foster unlawful behavior or teach hatred of any person or group on the basis of race, ethnicity, national origin, or religion." Any public school located in a school district adjacent to the . . . district may also participate in the program. Adjacent public schools are eligible to receive a $2,250 tuition grant for each program student accepted in addition to the full amount of per-pupil state funding attributable to each additional student. All participating schools, whether public or private, are required to accept students in accordance with rules and procedures established by the state superintendent.

Tuition aid is distributed to parents according to financial need. Families with incomes below 200% of the poverty line are given priority and are eligible to receive 90% of private school tuition up to $2,250. For these lowest income families, participating private schools may not charge a parental copayment greater than $250. For all other families, the program pays 75% of tuition costs, up to $1,875, with no copayment cap. . . . Where tuition aid is spent depends solely upon where parents who receive tuition aid choose to enroll their child. If parents choose a private school, checks are made payable to the parents who then endorse the checks over to the chosen school.

The tutorial aid portion of the program provides tutorial assistance through grants to any student in [the] district who chooses to remain in public school. Parents arrange for registered tutors to provide assistance to their children and then submit bills for those services to the State for payment. Students from low-income families receive 90% of the amount charged for such assistance up to $360. All other students receive 75% of that amount. . . .

The program has been in operation within the Cleveland City School District since the 1996–1997 school year. In the 1999–2000 school year, 56 private schools participated in the program, 46 (or 82%) of which had a religious affiliation. None of the public schools in districts adjacent to Cleveland have elected to participate. More than 3,700 students participated in the scholarship program, most of whom (96%) enrolled in religiously affiliated schools. Sixty percent of these students were from families at or below the poverty line. In the 1998–1999 school year, approximately 1,400 Cleveland public school students received tutorial aid. This number was expected to double during the 1999–2000 school year.

The program is part of a broader undertaking by the State to enhance the educational options of Cleveland's schoolchildren in response to the 1995 takeover. That undertaking includes programs governing community and magnet schools. Community schools are funded under state law but are run by their own school boards, not by local school districts. These schools enjoy academic independence to hire their own teachers and to determine their own curriculum. They can have no religious affiliation and are required to accept students by lottery. During the 1999–2000 school year, there were 10 startup community schools in the Cleveland City School District with more than 1,900 students enrolled. For each child enrolled in a community school, the school receives state funding of $4,518, twice the funding a participating program school may receive.

Magnet schools are public schools operated by a local school board that emphasize a particular subject area, teaching method, or service to students. For each student enrolled in a magnet school, the school district receives $7,746, including state funding of $4,167, the same amount received per student enrolled at a traditional public school. As of 1999, parents in Cleveland were able to choose from among 23 magnet schools, which together enrolled more than 13,000 students in kindergarten through eighth grade. These schools provide specialized teaching methods, such as Montessori, or a particularized curriculum focus, such as foreign language, computers, or the arts.

[I]n July 1999, respondents filed this action in United States District Court, seeking to enjoin the reenacted program on the ground that it violated the Establishment Clause of the United States Constitution. . . .

The Establishment Clause of the First Amendment, applied to the States through the Fourteenth Amendment, prevents a State from enacting laws that have the "purpose" or "effect" of advancing or inhibiting religion. There is no dispute that the program challenged here was enacted for the valid secular purpose of providing educational assistance to poor children in a demonstrably failing public school system. Thus, the question presented is whether the Ohio program nonetheless has the forbidden "effect" of advancing or inhibiting religion.

To answer that question, our decisions have drawn a consistent distinction between government programs that provide aid directly to religious schools, and programs of true private choice, in which government aid reaches religious schools only as a result of the genuine and independent choices of private individuals. While our jurisprudence with respect to the constitutionality of direct aid programs has "changed significantly" over the past two decades, our jurisprudence with respect to true private choice programs has remained consistent and unbroken. Three times we have confronted Establishment Clause challenges to neutral government programs that provide aid directly to a broad class of individuals, who, in turn, direct the aid to religious schools or institutions of their own choosing. Three times we have rejected such challenges.

In *Mueller v. Allen*, 463 U.S. 388 (1983), we rejected an Establishment Clause challenge to a Minnesota program authorizing tax deductions for various educational expenses, including private school tuition costs, even though the great majority of the program's beneficiaries (96%) were parents of children in religious schools. We began by focusing on the class of beneficiaries, finding that because the class included "*all* parents," including parents with "children [who] attend nonsectarian private schools or sectarian private schools," the program was "not readily subject to challenge under the Establishment Clause." Then, viewing the program as a whole, we emphasized the principle of private choice, noting that public funds were made available to religious schools "only as a result of numerous, private choices of individual parents of school-age children." This, we said, ensured that "no 'imprimatur of state approval' can be deemed to have been conferred on any particular religion, or on religion generally." We thus found it irrelevant to the constitutional inquiry that the vast majority of beneficiaries were parents of children in religious schools, saying: "We would be loath to adopt a rule grounding the constitutionality of a facially neutral law on annual reports reciting the extent to which various classes of private citizens claimed benefits under the law."

That the program was one of true private choice, with no evidence that the State deliberately skewed incentives toward religious schools, was sufficient for the program to survive scrutiny under the Establishment Clause.

In *Witters v. Washington Dept. of Servs. for Blind*, 474 U.S. 481 (1986), we used identical reasoning to reject an Establishment Clause challenge to a vocational scholarship program that provided tuition aid to a student studying at a religious institution to become a pastor. Looking at the program as a whole, we observed that "[a]ny aid . . . that ultimately flows to religious institutions does so only as a result of the genuinely independent and private choices of aid recipients." We further remarked that, as in *Mueller,* "[the] program is made available generally without regard to the sectarian-nonsectarian, or public-nonpublic nature of the institution benefited." In light of these factors, we held that the program was not inconsistent with the Establishment Clause. . . . Our holding . . . rested not on whether few or many recipients chose to expend government aid at a religious school but, rather, on whether recipients generally were empowered to direct the aid to schools or institutions of their own choosing.

Finally, in *Zobrest v. Catalina Foothills School Dist.*, 509 U.S. 1 (1993), we applied *Mueller* and *Witters* to reject an Establishment Clause challenge to a federal program that permitted sign-language interpreters to assist deaf children enrolled in religious schools. . . . Looking once again to the challenged program as a whole, we observed that the program "distributes benefits neutrally to any child qualifying as 'disabled.' " Its "primary beneficiaries," we said, were "disabled children, not sectarian schools."

We further observed that "[b]y according parents freedom to select a school of their choice, the statute ensures that a government-paid interpreter will be present in a sectarian school only as a result of the private decision of individual parents." Our focus again was on neutrality and the principle of private choice, not on the number of program beneficiaries attending religious schools. Because the program ensured that parents were the ones to select a religious school as the best learning environment for their handicapped child, the circuit between government and religion was broken, and the Establishment Clause was not implicated.

Mueller, Witters, and *Zobrest* thus make clear that where a government aid program is neutral with respect to religion, and provides assistance directly to a broad class of citizens who, in turn, direct government aid to religious schools wholly as a result of their own genuine and independent private choice, the program is not readily subject to challenge under the Establishment Clause. A program that shares these features permits government aid to reach religious institutions only by way of the deliberate choices of numerous individual recipients. The incidental advancement of a religious mission, or the perceived endorsement of a religious message, is reasonably attributable to the individual recipient, not to the government, whose role ends with the disbursement of benefits. . . . It is precisely for these reasons that we have never found a program of true private choice to offend the Establishment Clause.

We believe that the program challenged here is a program of true private choice, consistent with *Mueller, Witters,* and *Zobrest,* and thus constitutional. As was true in those cases, the Ohio program is neutral in all respects toward religion. It is part of a general and multifaceted undertaking by the State of Ohio to provide educational opportunities to the children of a failed school district. It confers educational assistance directly to a broad class of individuals defined without reference to religion, *i.e.,* any parent of a school-age child who resides in the Cleveland City School District. The program permits the participation of *all* schools within the district, religious or nonreligious. Adjacent public schools also may participate and have a financial incentive to do so. Program benefits are available to participating families on neutral terms, with no reference to religion. The only preference stated anywhere in the program is a preference for low-income families, who receive greater assistance and are given priority for admission at participating schools.

There are no "financial incentive[s]" that "ske[w]" the program toward religious schools. . . . The program here in fact creates financial *dis*incentives for religious schools. . . . Parents that choose to participate in the scholarship program and then to enroll their children in a private school (religious or nonreligious) must copay a portion of the school's tuition. Families that choose a community school, magnet school, or traditional public school pay nothing. Although such features of the program are not necessary to its constitutionality, they clearly dispel the claim that the program "creates . . . financial incentive[s] for parents to choose a sectarian school." . . .

Respondents finally claim that we should look to *Committee for Public Ed. & Religious Liberty v. Nyquist,* 413 U.S. 756 (1973), to decide these cases. We disagree for two reasons. First, the program in *Nyquist* was quite different from the program challenged here. *Nyquist* involved a New York program that gave a package of benefits exclusively to private schools and the parents of private school enrollees. Although the program was enacted for ostensibly secular purposes, we found that its "function" was "*unmistakably* to provide desired financial support for nonpublic, sectarian institutions." Its genesis, we said, was that private religious schools faced "increasingly grave fiscal problems." The program thus provided direct money grants to religious schools. It provided tax benefits "unrelated to the amount of money actually expended by any parent on tuition," ensuring a windfall to parents of children in religious schools. It similarly provided tuition reimbursements designed explicitly to "offe[r] . . . an incentive to parents to send their children to sectarian schools." Indeed, the program flatly prohibited the participation of any public school, or parent of any public school enrollee. Ohio's program shares none of these features.

Second, were there any doubt that the program challenged in *Nyquist* is far removed from the program challenged here, we expressly reserved judgment with respect to "a case involving some form of public assistance (*e.g.,* scholarships) made available generally without regard to the sectarian-nonsectarian, or public-nonpublic nature of the institution benefited." That, of course, is the very question now before us, and it has since been answered, first in *Mueller,* then in *Witters,* and again in *Zobrest.* To the extent the scope of *Nyquist* has remained an open question in light of these later decisions, we now hold that *Nyquist* does not govern neutral educational assistance programs that, like the program here, offer aid directly to a broad class of individual recipients defined without regard to religion. . . .

JUSTICE O'CONNOR, concurring.

The Court holds that Ohio's Pilot Project Scholarship Program survives respondents' Establishment Clause challenge. [A]lthough the Court takes an important step, I do not believe that today's decision . . . marks a dramatic break from the past. . . .

These cases are different from prior indirect aid cases in part because a significant portion of the funds appropriated for the voucher program reach religious schools without restrictions on the use of these funds. . . .

Although [the] $8.2 million [that flows to religious institutions under the program] is no small sum, it pales in comparison to the amount of funds that federal, state, and local governments already provide religious institutions. Religious organizations may qualify for exemptions from the federal corporate income tax, the corporate income tax in many States, and property taxes in all 50 States, and clergy qualify for a federal tax break on income used for housing expenses. In addition, the Federal Government provides individuals, corporations, trusts, and estates a tax deduction for charitable contributions to qualified religious groups. Finally, the Federal Government and certain state governments provide tax credits for educational expenses, many of which are spent on education at religious schools.

Most of these tax policies are well established, yet confer a significant relative benefit on religious institutions. The state property tax exemptions for religious institutions alone amount to very large sums annually. . . . As for the Federal Government, the tax deduction for charitable contributions reduces federal tax revenues by nearly $25 billion annually, and it is reported that over 60 percent of household charitable contributions go to religious charities. . . .

These tax exemptions, which have "much the same effect as [cash grants] . . . of the amount of tax [avoided]," are just part of the picture. Federal dollars also reach religiously affiliated organizations through public health programs such as Medicare and Medicaid, through educational programs such as the Pell Grant program and the G.I. Bill of Rights, and through childcare programs such as the Child Care and Development Block Grant Program. These programs are well-established parts of our social welfare system. . . .

A significant portion of the funds appropriated for these programs reach religiously affiliated institutions, typically without restrictions on its subsequent use. For example, it has been reported that religious hospitals, which account for 18 percent of all hospital beds nationwide, rely on Medicare funds for 36 percent of their revenue. . . .

Against this background, the support that the Cleveland voucher program provides religious institutions is neither substantial nor atypical of existing government programs. While this observation is not intended to justify the Cleveland voucher program under the Establishment Clause, it places in broader perspective alarmist claims about implications of the Cleveland program and the Court's decision in these cases.

Nor does today's decision signal a major departure from this Court's prior Establishment Clause jurisprudence. A central tool in our analysis of cases in this area has been the *Lemon* test. As originally formulated, a statute passed this test only if it had "a secular legislative purpose," if its "principal or primary effect" was one that "neither advance[d] nor inhibit [ed] religion," and if it did "not foster an excessive government entanglement with religion." *Lemon v. Kurtzman,* 403 U.S. 602 (1971). In *Agostini v. Felton,* 521 U.S. 203 (1997), we folded the entanglement inquiry into the primary effect inquiry. This made sense because both inquiries rely on the same evidence, and the degree of entanglement has implications for whether a statute advances or inhibits religion. The test today is basically the same as that set forth in *School Dist. of Abington Township v. Schempp,* 374 U.S. 203 (1963), over 40 years ago.

The Court's opinion in these cases focuses on a narrow question related to the *Lemon* test: how to apply the primary effects prong in indirect aid cases? Specifically, it clarifies the basic inquiry when trying to determine whether a program that distributes aid to beneficiaries, rather than directly to service providers, has the primary effect of advancing or inhibiting religion. . . . Courts are instructed to consider two factors: first, whether the program administers aid in a neutral fashion, without differentiation based on the religious status of beneficiaries or providers of services; second, and more importantly, whether beneficiaries of indirect aid have a genuine choice among religious and nonreligious organizations when determining the organization to which they will direct that aid. If the answer to either query is "no," the program should be struck down under the Establishment Clause. . . .

JUSTICE THOMAS, concurring. [opinion omitted] [Justice Thomas, while concurring in the Court's opinion, goes on to suggest that the Establishment Clause should have a different, and less stringent, application to state laws than to federal laws.]

JUSTICE STEVENS, dissenting.

Is a law that authorizes the use of public funds to pay for the indoctrination of thousands of grammar school children in particular religious faiths a "law respecting an establishment of religion" within the meaning of the First Amendment? In answering that question, I think we should ignore three factual matters that are discussed at length by my colleagues.

First, the severe educational crisis that confronted the Cleveland City School District when Ohio enacted its voucher program is not a matter that should affect our appraisal of its constitutionality. In the 1999–2000 school year, that program provided relief to less than five percent of the students enrolled in the district's schools. The solution to the disastrous conditions that prevented over 90 percent of the student body from meeting basic proficiency standards obviously required massive improvements unrelated to the voucher program. Of course, the emergency may have given some families a powerful motivation to leave the public school system and accept religious indoctrination that they would otherwise have avoided, but that is not a valid reason for upholding the program.

Second, the wide range of choices that have been made available to students *within the public school system* has no bearing on the question whether the State may pay the tuition for students who wish to reject public education entirely and attend private schools that will provide them with a sectarian education. The fact that the vast majority of the voucher recipients who have entirely rejected public education receive religious indoctrination at state expense does, however, support the claim that the law is one "respecting an establishment of religion." The State may choose to divide up its public schools into a dozen different options and label them magnet schools, community schools, or whatever else it decides to call them, but the State is still required to provide a public education and it is the State's decision to fund private school education over and above its traditional obligation that is at issue in these cases.

Third, the voluntary character of the private choice to prefer a parochial education over an education in the public school system seems to me quite irrelevant to the question whether the government's choice to pay for religious indoctrination is constitutionally permissible. Today, however, the Court seems to have decided that the mere fact that a family that cannot afford a private education wants its children educated in a parochial school is a sufficient justification for this use of public funds. . . .

JUSTICE SOUTER, with whom JUSTICE STEVENS, JUSTICE GINSBURG, and JUSTICE BREYER join, dissenting.

[T]he applicability of the Establishment Clause to public funding of benefits to religious schools was settled in *Everson v. Board of Ed.*, which inaugurated the modern era of establishment doctrine. The Court stated the principle in words from which there was no dissent: "No tax in any amount, large or small, can be levied to support any religious activities or institutions, whatever they may be called, or whatever form they may adopt to teach or practice religion."

The Court has never in so many words repudiated this statement, let alone, in so many words, overruled *Everson*.

Today, however, the majority holds that the Establishment Clause is not offended by Ohio's Pilot Project Scholarship Program, under which students may be eligible to receive as much as $2,250 in the form of tuition vouchers transferable to religious schools. In the city of Cleveland the overwhelming proportion of large appropriations for voucher money must be spent on religious schools if it is to be spent at all, and will be spent in amounts that cover almost all of tuition. The money will thus pay for eligible students' instruction not only in secular subjects but in religion as well, in schools that can fairly be characterized as founded to teach religious doctrine and to imbue teaching in all subjects with a religious dimension. Public tax money will pay at a systemic level for teaching the covenant with Israel and Mosaic law in Jewish schools, the primacy of the Apostle Peter and the Papacy in Catholic schools, the truth of reformed Christianity in Protestant schools, and the revelation to the Prophet in Muslim schools, to speak only of major religious groupings in the Republic. . . .

The majority's statements of Establishment Clause doctrine cannot be appreciated without some historical perspective on the Court's announced limitations on government aid to religious education, and its repeated repudiation of limits previously set. My object here is not to give any nuanced exposition of the cases, which I tried to classify in some detail in an earlier opinion, but to set out the broad doctrinal stages covered in the modern era, and to show that doctrinal bankruptcy has been reached today.

Viewed with the necessary generality, the cases can be categorized in three groups. In the period from 1947 to 1968, the basic principle of no aid to religion through school benefits was unquestioned. Thereafter for some 15 years, the Court termed its efforts as attempts to draw a line against aid that would be divertible to support the religious, as distinct from the secular, activity of an institutional beneficiary. Then, starting in 1983, concern with divertibility was gradually lost in favor of approving aid in amounts unlikely to afford substantial benefits to religious schools, when offered evenhandedly without regard to a recipient's religious character, and when channeled to a religious institution only by the genuinely free choice of some private individual. Now, the three stages are succeeded by a fourth, in which the substantial character of government aid is held to have no constitutional significance, and the espoused criteria of neutrality in offering aid, and private choice in directing it, are shown to be nothing but examples of verbal formalism.

Everson v. Board of Ed. inaugurated the modern development of Establishment Clause doctrine. . . . The majority upheld the state law . . .

[d]espite the indirect benefit to religious education, [because] the transportation was simply treated like "ordinary police and fire protection, connections for sewage disposal, public highways and sidewalks." The dissenters, however, found the benefit to religion too pronounced to survive the general principle of no establishment, no aid, and they described it as running counter to every objective served by the establishment ban: New Jersey's use of tax-raised funds forced a taxpayer to "contribut[e] to the propagation of opinions which he disbelieves in so far as . . . religions differ"; it exposed religious liberty to the threat of dependence on state money; and it had already sparked political conflicts with opponents of public funding.

The difficulty of drawing a line that preserved the basic principle of no aid was no less obvious some 20 years later in *Board of Ed. of Central School Dist. No. 1 v. Allen*, 392 U.S. 236 (1968), which upheld a New York law authorizing local school boards to lend textbooks in secular subjects to children attending religious schools, a result not self-evident from *Everson's* "general government services" rationale. The Court relied instead on the theory that the in-kind aid could only be used for secular educational purposes and found it relevant that "no funds or books are furnished [directly] to parochial schools, and the financial benefit is to parents and children, not to schools." Justice Black, who wrote *Everson*, led the dissenters. Textbooks, even when " 'secular,' realistically will in some way inevitably tend to propagate the religious views of the favored sect," he wrote. . . .

Transcending even the sharp disagreement, however, was "the consistency in the way the Justices went about deciding the case. . . . Disagreement concentrated on the true intent inferrable behind the law, the feasibility of distinguishing in fact between religious and secular teaching in church schools, and the reality or sham of lending books to pupils instead of supplying books to schools . . . . [T]he stress was on the practical significance of the actual benefits received by the schools."

Allen recognized the reality that "religious schools pursue two goals, religious instruction and secular education"; if state aid could be restricted to serve the second, it might be permissible under the Establishment Clause. But in the retrenchment that followed, the Court saw that the two educational functions were so intertwined in religious primary and secondary schools that aid to secular education could not readily be segregated, and the intrusive monitoring required to enforce the line itself raised Establishment Clause concerns about the entanglement of church and state. *See Lemon v. Kurtzman* (striking down program supplementing salaries for teachers of secular subjects in private schools). To avoid the entanglement, the Court's focus in the post-*Allen* cases was on the principle of divertibility, on discerning when ostensibly secular government aid to religious schools was susceptible to religious uses. The greater the risk of diversion to religion (and the monitoring necessary to avoid it), the less legitimate the aid scheme was under the no-aid principle. On the one hand, the Court tried to be practical, and when the aid recipients were not so "pervasively sectarian" that their secular and religious functions were inextricably intertwined, the Court generally upheld aid earmarked for secular use. [Citing to cases involving aid to universities and colleges.] But otherwise the principle of nondivertibility was enforced strictly, with its violation being presumed in most cases, even when state aid seemed secular on its face. Compare, *e.g., Levitt v. Committee for Public Ed. & Religious Liberty,* 413 U.S. 472 (1973)(striking down state program reimbursing private schools' administrative costs for teacher-prepared tests in compulsory secular subjects), with *Wolman v. Walter,* 433 U.S. 229 (1977)(upholding similar program using standardized tests); and *Meek v. Pittenger,* 421 U.S. 349 (1975)(no public funding for staff and materials for "auxiliary services" like guidance counseling and speech and hearing services), with *Wolman* (permitting state aid for diagnostic speech, hearing, and psychological testing).

The fact that the Court's suspicion of divertibility reflected a concern with the substance of the no-aid principle is apparent in its rejection of stratagems invented to dodge it. In *Committee for Public Ed. & Religious Liberty v. Nyquist,* for example, the Court struck down a New York program of tuition grants for poor parents and tax deductions for more affluent ones who sent their children to private schools. The *Nyquist* Court . . . rejected the idea that the path of state aid to religious schools might be dispositive: "far from providing a *per se* immunity from examination of the substance of the State's program, the fact that aid is disbursed to parents rather than to the schools is only one among many factors to be considered." The point was that "the effect of the aid is unmistakably to provide desired financial support for nonpublic, sectarian institutions." *Nyquist* thus held that aid to parents through tax deductions was no different from forbidden direct aid to religious schools for religious uses. The focus remained on what the public money bought when it reached the end point of its disbursement.

Like all criteria requiring judicial assessment of risk, divertibility is an invitation to argument, but the object of the arguments provoked has always been a realistic assessment of facts aimed at respecting the principle of no aid. In *Mueller v. Allen* (1983), however, that object began to fade, for *Mueller* started down the road from realism to formalism.

The aid in *Mueller* was in substance indistinguishable from that in *Nyquist,* and both were substantively difficult to distinguish from aid directly to religious schools. But the Court upheld the Minnesota tax deductions in *Mueller,* emphasizing their neutral availability for religious and secular educational expenses and the role of private choice in taking them. The Court relied on the same two principles in *Witters v. Washington*

Dept. of Servs. for Blind, approving one student's use of a vocational training subsidy for the blind at a religious college, characterizing it as aid to individuals from which religious schools could derive no "large" benefit: "the full benefits of the program [are not] limited, in large part or in whole, to students at sectarian institutions."

School Dist. of Grand Rapids v. Ball, 473 U.S. 373 (1985), overruled in part by *Agostini v. Felton,* 521 U.S. 203 (1997), clarified that the notions of evenhandedness neutrality and private choice in *Mueller* did not apply to cases involving direct aid to religious schools, which were still subject to the divertibility test. But in *Agostini,* where the substance of the aid was identical to that in *Ball,* public employees teaching remedial secular classes in private schools, the Court rejected the 30-year-old presumption of divertibility, and instead found it sufficient that the aid "supplement[ed]" but did not "supplant" existing educational services. The Court, contrary to *Ball,* viewed the aid as aid "directly to the eligible students . . . no matter where they choose to attend school."

In the 12 years between *Ball* and *Agostini,* the Court decided not only *Witters,* but two other cases emphasizing the form of neutrality and private choice over the substance of aid to religious uses, but always in circumstances where any aid to religion was isolated and insubstantial. *Zobrest v. Catalina Foothills School Dist.,* like *Witters,* involved one student's choice to spend funds from a general public program at a religious school (to pay for a sign-language interpreter). As in *Witters,* the Court reasoned that "[d]isabled children, not sectarian schools, [were] the primary beneficiaries . . .; to the extent sectarian schools benefit at all . . ., they are only incidental beneficiaries." *Rosenberger v. Rector and Visitors of Univ. of Va.,* 515 U.S. 819 (1995), like *Zobrest* and *Witters,* involved an individual and insubstantial use of neutrally available public funds for a religious purpose (to print an evangelical magazine).

To be sure, the aid in *Agostini* was systemic and arguably substantial, but, as I have said, the majority there chose to view it as a bare "supplement." And this was how the controlling opinion described the systemic aid in our most recent case, *Mitchell v. Helms,* 530 U.S. 793 (2000), as aid going merely to a "portion" of the religious schools' budgets (O'CONNOR, J., concurring in judgment). The plurality in that case did not feel so uncomfortable about jettisoning substance entirely in favor of form, finding it sufficient that the aid was neutral and that there was virtual private choice, since any aid "first passes through the hands (literally or figuratively) of numerous private citizens who are free to direct the aid elsewhere." But that was only the plurality view.

Hence it seems fair to say that it was not until today that substantiality of aid has clearly been rejected as irrelevant by a majority of this Court, just as it has not been until today that a majority, not a plurality, has held purely formal criteria to suffice for scrutinizing aid that ends up in the coffers of religious schools. . . .

Although it has taken half a century since *Everson* to reach the majority's twin standards of neutrality and free choice, the facts show that, in the majority's hands, even these criteria cannot convincingly legitimize the Ohio scheme.

Consider first the criterion of neutrality. . . .

Neutrality in this sense refers, of course, to evenhandedness in setting eligibility as between potential religious and secular recipients of public money. Thus, for example, the aid scheme in *Witters* provided an eligible recipient with a scholarship to be used at any institution within a practically unlimited universe of schools; it did not tend to provide more or less aid depending on which one the scholarship recipient chose, and there was no indication that the maximum scholarship amount would be insufficient at secular schools. Neither did any condition of Zobrest's interpreter's subsidy favor religious education.

In order to apply the neutrality test, then, it makes sense to focus on a category of aid that may be directed to religious as well as secular schools, and ask whether the scheme favors a religious direction. Here, one would ask whether the voucher provisions, allowing for as much as $2,250 toward private school tuition (or a grant to a public school in an adjacent district), were written in a way that skewed the scheme toward benefiting religious schools. . . .

[T]he majority's new use of the choice criterion, which it frames negatively as "whether Ohio is coercing parents into sending their children to religious schools," ignores the reason for having a private choice enquiry in the first place. Cases since *Mueller* have found private choice relevant under a rule that aid to religious schools can be permissible so long as it first passes through the hands of students or parents. The majority's view . . . ignores the whole point of the choice test: it is a criterion for deciding whether indirect aid to a religious school is legitimate because it passes through private hands that can spend or use the aid in a secular school. The question is whether the private hand is genuinely free to send the money in either a secular direction or a religious one. . . .

If, contrary to the majority, we ask the right question about genuine choice to use the vouchers, the answer shows that something is influencing choices in a way that aims the money in a religious direction: of 56 private schools in the district participating in the voucher program (only 53 of which accepted voucher students in 1999–2000), 46 of them are religious; 96.6% of all voucher recipients go to religious schools, only 3.4% to nonreligious ones. Unfortunately for the majority position, there is no explanation for this that suggests the religious direction results simply from free choices by parents. One answer to these statistics, for example, which would be consistent with the genuine choice claimed to be operating, might be that 96.6% of families choosing to avail themselves of vouchers choose to educate their children in schools of their own religion. This would not, in my view, render the scheme constitutional, but it would speak to the majority's choice criterion. Evidence shows, however, that almost two out of three families using vouchers to send their children to religious schools did not embrace the religion of those schools. The families made it clear they had not chosen the schools because they wished their children to be proselytized in a religion not their own, or in any religion, but because of educational opportunity.

Even so, the fact that some 2,270 students chose to apply their vouchers to schools of other religions might be consistent with true choice if the students "chose" their religious schools over a wide array of private nonreligious options, or if it could be shown generally that Ohio's program had no effect on educational choices and thus no impermissible effect of advancing religious education. But both possibilities are contrary to fact. First, even if all existing nonreligious private schools in Cleveland were willing to accept large numbers of voucher students, only a few more than the 129 currently enrolled in such schools would be able to attend, as the total enrollment at all nonreligious private schools in Cleveland for kindergarten through eighth grade is only 510 children, and there is no indication that these schools have many open seats. Second, the $2,500 cap that the program places on tuition for participating low-income pupils has the effect of curtailing the participation of nonreligious schools: "nonreligious schools with higher tuition (about $4,000) stated that they could afford to accommodate just a few voucher students." By comparison, the average tuition at participating Catholic schools in Cleveland in 1999–2000 was $1,592, almost $1,000 below the cap. . . .

Of course, the obvious fix would be to increase the value of vouchers so that existing nonreligious private and non-Catholic religious schools would be able to enroll more voucher students, and to provide incentives for educators to create new such schools given that few presently exist. . . .

There is, in any case, no way to interpret the 96.6% of current voucher money going to religious schools as reflecting a free and genuine choice by the families that apply for vouchers. The 96.6% reflects, instead, the fact that too few nonreligious school desks are available and few but religious schools can afford to accept more than a handful of voucher students. And contrary to the majority's assertion, public schools in adjacent districts hardly have a financial incentive to participate in the Ohio voucher program, and none has. For the overwhelming number of children in the voucher scheme, the only alternative to the public schools is religious. And it is entirely irrelevant that the State did not deliberately design the network of private schools for the sake of channeling money into religious institutions. The criterion is one of genuinely free choice on the part of the private individuals who choose, and a Hobson's choice is not a choice, whatever the reason for being Hobsonian.

I do not dissent merely because the majority has misapplied its own law, for even if I assumed *arguendo* that the majority's formal criteria were satisfied on the facts, today's conclusion would be profoundly at odds with the Constitution. Proof of this is clear on two levels. The first is circumstantial, in the now discarded symptom of violation, the substantial dimension of the aid. The second is direct, in the defiance of every objective supposed to be served by the bar against establishment.

The scale of the aid to religious schools approved today is unprecedented, both in the number of dollars and in the proportion of systemic school expenditure supported. Each measure has received attention in previous cases. On one hand, the sheer quantity of aid, when delivered to a class of religious primary and secondary schools, was suspect on the theory that the greater the aid, the greater its proportion to a religious school's existing expenditures, and the greater the likelihood that public money was supporting religious as well as secular instruction. . . . When neither the design nor the implementation of an aid scheme channels a series of individual students' subsidies toward religious recipients, the relevant beneficiaries for establishment purposes, the Establishment Clause is unlikely to be implicated. . . .

It is virtually superfluous to point out that every objective underlying the prohibition of religious establishment is betrayed by this scheme, but something has to be said about the enormity of the violation. I anticipated these objectives earlier in discussing *Everson,* the first being respect for freedom of conscience. Jefferson described it as the idea that no one "shall be compelled to . . . support any religious worship, place, or ministry whatsoever," and Madison thought it violated by any " 'authority which can force a citizen to contribute three pence . . . of his property for the support of any . . . establishment.' "

As for the second objective, to save religion from its own corruption, Madison wrote of the " 'experience . . . that ecclesiastical establishments, instead of maintaining the purity and efficacy of Religion, have had a contrary operation.' " In Madison's time, the manifestations were "pride and indolence in the Clergy; ignorance and servility in the laity[,] in both, superstition, bigotry and persecution"; in the 21st century, the risk is one of "corrosive secularism" to religious schools, and the specific threat is to the primacy of the schools' mission to educate the children of the faithful according to the unaltered precepts of their faith. . . .

The risk is already being realized. In Ohio, for example, a condition of receiving government money under the program is that participating religious schools may not "discriminate on the basis of . . . religion," which means the school may not give admission preferences to children who are members of the patron faith. . . . Nor is the State's religious antidiscrimination restriction limited to student admission policies: by its terms, a participating religious school may well be forbidden to choose a member of its own clergy to serve as teacher or principal over a layperson of a different religion claiming equal qualification for the job. . . .

Everson's statement is still the touchstone of sound law, even though the reality is that in the matter of educational aid the Establishment Clause has largely been read away. True, the majority has not approved vouchers for religious schools alone, or aid earmarked for religious instruction. But no scheme so clumsy will ever get before us, and in the cases that we may see, like these, the Establishment Clause is largely silenced. I do not have the option to leave it silent, and I hope that a future Court will reconsider today's dramatic departure from basic Establishment Clause principle.

JUSTICE BREYER, with whom JUSTICE STEVENS and JUSTICE SOUTER join, dissenting.

I join Justice SOUTER's opinion, and I agree substantially with Justice STEVENS. I write separately, however, to emphasize the risk that publicly financed voucher programs pose in terms of religiously based social conflict. I do so because I believe that the Establishment Clause concern for protecting the Nation's social fabric from religious conflict poses an overriding obstacle to the implementation of this well-intentioned school voucher program. . . .

[A]voiding religiously based social conflict . . . remains of great concern. As religiously diverse as America had become when the Court decided its major 20th-century Establishment Clause cases, we are exponentially more diverse today. America boasts more than 55 different religious groups and subgroups with a significant number of members. Major religions include, among others, Protestants, Catholics, Jews, Muslims, Buddhists, Hindus, and Sikhs.

Under these modern-day circumstances, how is the "equal opportunity" principle to work—without risking the "struggle of sect against sect". . .? School voucher programs finance the religious education of the young. And, if widely adopted, they may well provide billions of dollars that will do so. Why will different religions not become concerned about, and seek to influence, the criteria used to channel this money to religious schools? Why will they not want to examine the implementation of the programs that provide this money—to determine, for example, whether implementation has biased a program toward or against particular sects, or whether recipient religious schools are adequately fulfilling a program's criteria? If so, just how is the State to resolve the resulting controversies without provoking legitimate fears of the kinds of religious favoritism that, in so religiously diverse a Nation, threaten social dissension?

Consider the voucher program here at issue. That program insists that the religious school accept students of all religions. Does that criterion treat fairly groups whose religion forbids them to do so? The program also insists that no participating school "advocate or foster unlawful behavior or teach hatred of any person or group on the basis of race, ethnicity, national origin, or religion." And it requires the State to "revoke the registration of any school if, after a hearing, the superintendent determines that the school is in violation" of the program's rules. As one *amicus* argues, "it is difficult to imagine a more divisive activity" than the appointment of state officials as referees to determine whether a particular religious doctrine "teaches hatred or advocates lawlessness." . . .

In a society as religiously diverse as ours, the Court has recognized that we must rely on the Religion Clauses of the First Amendment to protect against religious strife, particularly when what is at issue is an area as central to religious belief as the shaping, through primary education, of the next generation's minds and spirits.

I concede that the Establishment Clause currently permits States to channel various forms of assistance to religious schools, for example, transportation costs for students, computers, and secular texts. States now certify the nonsectarian educational content of religious school education. Yet the consequence has not been great turmoil.

School voucher programs differ, however, in both *kind* and *degree* from aid programs upheld in the past. They differ in kind because they direct financing to a core function of the church: the teaching of religious truths to young children. For that reason the constitutional demand for "separation" is of particular constitutional concern.

Vouchers also differ in *degree*. The aid programs recently upheld by the Court involved limited amounts of aid to religion. But the majority's analysis here appears to permit a considerable shift of taxpayer dollars from public secular schools to private religious schools. That fact, combined with the use to which these dollars will be put, exacerbates the conflict problem. State aid that takes the form of peripheral secular items, with prohibitions against diversion of funds to religious teaching, holds significantly less potential for social division. . . .

I do not believe that the "parental choice" aspect of the voucher program sufficiently offsets the concerns I have mentioned. Parental choice cannot help the taxpayer who does not want to finance the religious education of children. It will not always help the parent who may see little real choice between inadequate nonsectarian public education and adequate education at a school whose religious teachings are contrary to his own. It will not satisfy religious minorities unable to participate because they are too few in number to support the creation of their own private schools. It will not satisfy groups whose religious beliefs preclude them from participating in a government-sponsored program, and who may well feel ignored as government funds primarily support the education of children in the doctrines of the dominant religions. And it does little to ameliorate the entanglement problems or the related problems of social division. Consequently, the fact that the parent may choose which school can cash the government's voucher check does not alleviate the Establishment Clause concerns associated with voucher programs. . . .

COMMENTS AND QUESTIONS

1. Is it relevant for Establishment Clause purposes that the state adopted this program because of a conceded crisis in the public education system in Cleveland? That is, imagine that a city not in the dire straits of Cleveland adopted a similar program; would its program be adjudged in any different way?

2. What is the point of Justice O'Connor's description of the various long-time government programs that provide vast amounts of money to religions? Does it undercut Justice Breyer's prediction of the likelihood of social unrest arising from voucher programs? Does it undercut Justice Souter's invocation of Jefferson and Madison's absolute principle of not requiring a taxpayer to pay even "three pence" for the support of religion? It may be worth noting that the Court in 1970, by a vote of 8–1, one of the most lop-sided of votes in an Establishment Clause case, upheld an exemption for religious property from state property tax. *Walz v. Tax Comm'n*, 397 U.S. 664 (1970). It was clearly important to the decision that every state granted such an exemption and that its historical pedigree extended back to the founding of the Republic and was granted even in states that barred any state funds from being used for religious purposes. Nevertheless, the financial benefit from those exemptions (as well as the exemptions from state and federal income taxes and the allowance of deductions from individual income for donations to religious institutions) is enormous.

3. What do you make of Justice Souter's argument that the program does not really provide a free choice between secular and sectarian private schools to parents in Cleveland because, first, there simply are not enough secular private school openings to accommodate any significant number of former public school students, and, second, that the voucher is not enough to pay the tuition at any but the parochial schools? Would parents who chose to send their children to a parochial school rather than public school, even though they were not Catholic, be happy if the Court were to invalidate the program because they did not have a "free choice"?

4. Justice O'Connor indicates her belief that the Court's decision does not represent a material change from past precedent. To defend that belief, she describes the three part test of *Lemon v. Kurtzman*, which dominated Establishment Clause analysis until recently, and applies it to the case at hand. The first part of the test asks whether the law has *a* "secular purpose." That is, is there a purpose for the law that is not religiously oriented. This part of the test is usually easily met, as it would be in this case. The second part

asks whether "the principal or primary effect" advances or inhibits religion. This is the part of the test that usually divided members of the Court over the years. The final part asks whether the law fosters "an excessive government entanglement with religion." In the earliest applications of the *Lemon* test, this seemed to include the idea that the law would result in political divisiveness, but later cases ruled that out, in favor of asking whether it would involve government in monitoring the religion's activities to assure that the government support was not used for religious purposes. As Justice O'Connor notes, the original *Lemon* test has undergone some changes over the years. After *Lynch v. Donnelly*, 465 U.S. 668 (1984), the Court, at least in some cases, substituted an "endorsement" test for the "effect" test. That is, instead of asking what was the primary effect of the government action, the Court would ask whether the effect was to endorse religion. However characterized, do you think that the "primary or principal effect" of the school voucher program was to advance religion, or that the program had the effect of endorsing religion? And in *Agostini v. Felton*, 521 U.S. 203 (1997), the Court eliminated the separate "entanglement" part of the *Lemon* test and included it within the "effect" part of the *Lemon* test. It said: "the factors we use to assess whether an entanglement is 'excessive' are similar to the factors we use to examine 'effect.' That is, to assess entanglement, we have looked to 'the character and purposes of the institutions that are benefited, the nature of the aid that the State provides, and the resulting relationship between the government and religious authority.'"

5.   Do you agree with Justice Breyer that assuring that religious schools comply with the program requirements will engender significant difficulties? Ever since *Pierce v. Society of Sisters*, 268 U.S. 510 (1925), there has been a constitutional right to send your children to a parochial school, so long as it meets the state's requirements for a secular education. Has that oversight for almost a century caused great problems?

6.   The Court in *Zelman* relies on the free choice of parents to choose where to utilize their vouchers to uphold the program. Government is not providing the support for religious institutions; individuals are. Both the Court and the dissent, however, also refer to a line of cases in which the government provided support without the intervening cut-off of parents making choices. Before 1997, direct support to a religious school or even secular support provided at a religious school faced substantial obstacles. In two cases, however, the Court provided an easier path. In *Agostini v. Felton*, the Court overruled one case and parts of another, by deciding that the place at which the support was provided was not a critical factor, and in *Mitchell v. Helms*, 530 U.S. 793 (2000), the Court overruled two more cases in which the Court had held unconstitutional the provision of secular materials directly to sectarian schools on an equal basis with other schools. In the earlier cases, the Court had feared the secular materials could be used for sectarian purposes in the religious schools (*e.g.*, maps of the Middle East for Bible study), but in *Mitchell* the presumption was reversed. Secular materials were presumed to be used for secular purposes unless the challenger proved otherwise.

7.   With whom do you agree as to whether *Zelman* is consistent with or at odds with *Everson*: the Court or Justice Souter?

PROBLEM

Imagine that a state, believing that privatizing former government functions results in both efficiencies and improvements, decides to experiment with privatizing K–12 public education, by authorizing school districts within the state to substitute paying a lump-sum tuition payment for each student in K–12 classes instead of providing schools and teachers to provide those classes. Existing public school buildings may be sold or rented to organizations meeting basic requirements for providing education for those classes. Parents of students would receive a tuition voucher for each student equal to the amount the district is currently paying for its K–12 education divided by the number of students in those classes. Parents would be able to choose where to use those vouchers among the qualifying organizations. Already existing private and charter schools would be qualifying organizations. The school district would monitor the quality of the education provided by all qualifying organizations in the same manner as it currently monitors the quality of private and charter schools that are approved to provide K–12 education.

A school district in the state uses this authorization. After a few years of transition, several new secular organizations have become qualified to provide a K–12 education, but by far the largest number of organizations, both old and new, are religiously oriented—predominantly evangelical Christian and Catholic religions. Moreover, the percentage of students attending religiously oriented schools has increased dramatically from what had existed before the privatization. Is this system constitutional?

B. GOVERNMENT ENDORSEMENT

The very day that Congress approved the First Amendment for ratification by the states it passed a resolution calling on the President to proclaim "a day of public thanksgiving and prayer, to be observed by acknowledging with grateful hearts the many and signal favors of Almighty God." And, of course, it had started that day with a prayer given by the Congressional Chaplain, a post it had created three days earlier. That history continues today. Current law directs the President to issue a proclamation "designating the first Thursday in May as a National Day of Prayer on which the people of the United States may turn to God in prayer and meditation at churches, in groups, and as individuals." 36 U.S.C. § 119. Both the House and the Senate have their own chaplains paid for out of government funds, and both bodies begin their legislative days with a prayer. The Supreme Court begins its proceedings with the call "God save the United States and this Honorable Court."

While the history of federal government endorsement of religion in these ways is not without some exceptions—Presidents Jefferson and Jackson refused to proclaim a national day of prayer—it remains quite pervasive, as reflected in the national motto adopted in 1956, "in God we trust," 36 U.S.C. § 302, which is required to be placed on coins and currency, 31 U.S.C. §§ 5112, 5114, and the phrase "under God" inserted into the pledge of allegiance in 1954. 4 U.S.C. § 4. The National Anthem, adopted in 1931, contains the statement, "And this be our motto, In God is our Trust." And while the Presidential Oath contained in the Constitution makes no reference to God, it is the common practice for the Chief Justice to prompt and the President to respond at the end of the oath, "so help me God."

Standing requirements pose substantial obstacles to judicial challenges to these practices. *See, e.g., Elk Grove Unified School Dist. v. Newdow,* 542 U.S. 1 (2004)(dismissing a challenge to "under God" in the pledge for lack of standing). In several cases not directly challenging these practices, however, members of the Court have referred to these practices as a form of ceremonial deism that is not precluded by the Establishment Clause.

This seemingly easy acceptance of such government endorsement of "God" has not been transferable into the schools. One of the first cases follows.

ENGEL V. VITALE

United States Supreme Court, 1962.
370 U.S. 421, 82 S.Ct. 1261.

MR. JUSTICE BLACK delivered the opinion of the Court.

The respondent Board of Education . . ., directed the School District's principal to cause the following prayer to be said aloud by each class in the presence of a teacher at the beginning of each school day: "Almighty God, we acknowledge our dependence upon Thee, and we beg Thy blessings upon us, our parents, our teachers and our Country."

This daily procedure was adopted on the recommendation of the State Board of Regents, a governmental agency created by the State Constitution. . . . These state officials composed the prayer which they recommended and published as a part of their "Statement on Moral and Spiritual Training in the Schools.". . .

Shortly after the practice of reciting the Regents' prayer was adopted by the School District, the parents of ten pupils brought this action in a New York State Court insisting that use of this official prayer in the public schools was contrary to the beliefs, religions, or religious practices of both themselves and their children. Among other things, these parents challenged the constitutionality of both the state law authorizing the School District to direct the use of prayer in public schools and the School District's regulation ordering the recitation of this particular prayer on the ground that these actions of official governmental agencies violate th[e Establishment Clause] of the First Amendment of the Federal Constitution. . . .

We think that by using its public school system to encourage recitation of the Regents' prayer, the State of New York has adopted a practice wholly inconsistent with the Establishment Clause. There can, of course, be no doubt that New York's program of daily classroom invocation of God's blessings as prescribed in the Regents' prayer is a religious activity. It is a solemn avowal of divine faith and supplication for the blessings of the Almighty. The nature of such a prayer has always been religious, none of the respondents has denied this and the trial court expressly so found. . . .

The petitioners contend among other things that the state laws requiring or permitting use of the Regents' prayer must be struck down as a violation of the Establishment Clause because that prayer was composed by governmental officials as a part of a governmental program to further religious beliefs. For this reason, petitioners argue, the State's use of the Regents' prayer in its public school system breaches the constitutional wall of separation between Church and State. We agree with that contention since we think that the constitutional prohibition against laws respecting an establishment of religion must at least mean that in this country it is no part of the business of government to compose official prayers for any group of the American people to recite as a part of a religious program carried on by government. . . .

There can be no doubt that New York's state prayer program officially establishes the religious beliefs embodied in the Regents' prayer. The respondents' argument to the contrary, which is largely based upon the contention that the Regents' prayer is "nondenominational" and the fact that the program, as modified and approved by state courts, does not require all pupils to recite the prayer but permits those who wish to do so to remain silent or be excused from the room, ignores the essential nature of the program's constitutional defects. Neither the fact that the prayer may be denominationally neutral nor the fact that its observance on the part of the students is voluntary can serve to free it from the limitations of the Establishment Clause, as it might from the Free Exercise Clause, of the First Amendment, both of which are operative against the States by virtue of the Fourteenth Amendment. . . . The Establishment Clause, unlike the Free Exercise Clause, does not depend upon any showing of direct governmental compulsion and is violated by the enactment of laws which establish an official religion whether those laws operate directly to coerce nonobserving individuals or not. . . .

It has been argued that to apply the Constitution in such a way as to prohibit state laws respecting an establishment of religious services in public schools is to indicate a hostility toward religion or toward prayer. Nothing, of course, could be more wrong. . . . It is neither sacrilegious nor antireligious to say that each separate government in this country should stay out of the business of writing or sanctioning official prayers and leave that purely religious function to the people themselves and to those the people choose to look to for religious guidance.[21]

MR. JUSTICE FRANKFURTER took no part in the decision of this case.

MR. JUSTICE WHITE took no part in the consideration or decision of this case.

MR. JUSTICE DOUGLAS, concurring. [opinion omitted]

MR. JUSTICE STEWART, dissenting.

A local school board in New York has provided that those pupils who wish to do so may join in a brief prayer at the beginning of each school day, acknowledging their dependence upon God and asking His blessing upon them and upon their parents, their teachers, and their country. The Court today decides that in permitting this brief non-denominational prayer the school board has violated the Constitution of the United States. I think this decision is wrong.

The Court does not hold, nor could it, that New York has interfered with the free exercise of anybody's religion. For the state courts have made clear that those who object to reciting the prayer must be entirely free of any compulsion to do so, including any "embarrassments and pressures." But the Court says that in permitting school children to say this simple prayer, the New York authorities have established "an official religion."

With all respect, I think the Court has misapplied a great constitutional principle. I cannot see how an "official religion" is established by letting those who want to say a prayer say it. On the contrary, I think that to deny the wish of these school children to join in reciting this prayer is to deny them the opportunity of sharing in the spiritual heritage of our Nation. . . .

At the opening of each day's Session of this Court we stand, while one of our officials invokes the protection of God. Since the days of John Marshall our Crier has said, "God save the United States and this Honorable Court." Both the Senate and the House of Representatives open

---

[21] There is of course nothing in the decision reached here that is inconsistent with the fact that school children and others are officially encouraged to express love for our country by reciting historical documents such as the Declaration of Independence which contain references to the Deity or by singing officially espoused anthems which include the composer's professions of faith in a Supreme Being, or with the fact that there are many manifestations in our public life of belief in God. Such patriotic or ceremonial occasions bear no true resemblance to the unquestioned religious exercise that the State of New York has sponsored in this instance.

their daily Sessions with prayer. Each of our Presidents, from George Washington to John F. Kennedy, has upon assuming his Office asked the protection and help of God.

COMMENTS AND QUESTIONS

1.   What is it about the prayer in this case that makes it unconstitutional? Is it the fact that it is a "religious activity" in the public school? Is it the fact that the prayer was composed by an organ of the state?

2.   What's the difference between beginning the school day with this prayer and what the legislatures do? Would it be unconstitutional to open a state legislature session with a prayer? In *Marsh v. Chambers*, 463 U.S. 783 (1983), the Court held that it was not. Without even a citation to *Engel v. Vitale*, the Court concluded that the unique history of two centuries of the federal and state legislatures opening their sessions with a prayer indicated that the Founders did not intend to preclude such prayers by adoption of the Establishment Clause.

3.   A year after *Engel v. Vitale,* in companion cases, the Court held unconstitutional, with only Justice Stewart dissenting, the practices of opening the school day with reading verses from the Bible or reciting the Lord's Prayer. *See School Dist. of Abington Township v. Schempp*, 374 U.S. 203 (1963). The Court again characterized these practices as religious exercises and accordingly found them a violation of the Establishment Clause, although any student could be excused upon request of a parent. In 1985 the Court was faced with an Alabama law that added the words "or voluntary prayer" to an earlier law that had required a one-minute period of silence at the beginning of the school day "for meditation." *See Wallace v. Jaffree*, 472 U.S. 38 (1985). Applying the *Lemon* test, the Court found the amendment unconstitutional because it did not have a secular purpose. However, the Court implied, and Justice O'Connor concurring expressly stated, that setting aside one-minute of silence by itself to start the school day would not be objectionable. What if a student asks her teacher, "Teacher, may I pray during that minute?" What should the teacher respond? And what does this say about the addition in 1954 of the words "under God" to the Pledge of Allegiance, which is recited daily in the classrooms of the United States. Does it matter that the legislative history indicates that the addition of "under God" was to distinguish us from "godless communism" with which we were engaged in a "cold war"?

4.   In *Lee v. Weisman*, 505 U.S. 577 (1992), the Court took a slightly different approach in holding a graduation prayer at a middle school to be unconstitutional. Although attendance at graduation was voluntary, the Court concluded that "in a fair and real sense [it was] obligatory." The Court then noted "the heightened concerns with protecting freedom of conscience from subtle coercive pressure in the elementary and secondary public schools." Justice Kennedy, writing for the Court, observed that at the ceremony there was "public as well as peer pressure" to stand or remain silent during the prayer, and such respectful consideration might be perceived as adherence. Consequently, he concluded that:

At a minimum, the Constitution guarantees that government may not coerce anyone to support or participate in religion or its exercise. [The] State's involvement in the school prayers challenged today violates these principles.

Three justices concurred but wrote separately to say that they believed the prayer sponsored by the school would violate the Establishment Clause even in the absence of any coercion. Four justices dissented, pointing out the history of non-sectarian prayers in public celebrations and denying that respectful silence occasioned by polite manners involved either coercion or implied participation in or approval of the prayer. In *Santa Fe Independent School Dist. v. Doe*, 530 U.S. 290 (2000), *Lee* was extended to a student-led prayer before a high school football game.

5.   In *Stone v. Graham*, 449 U.S. 39 (1980), the Court by a 5–4 vote held that the posting of the Ten Commandments* in public school classrooms lacked a secular purpose under the *Lemon* Test.

6.   In the famous Scopes "monkey trial," popularized by the play and movie, Inherit the Wind, a teacher was prosecuted and convicted in 1925 for violating a Tennessee law that prohibited teaching that man had evolved from the apes. On appeal, the Tennessee Supreme Court upheld the law against a claim that it violated the state's constitutional provision that "no preference shall ever be given, by law, to any religious establishment or mode of worship." Nevertheless, the sentence was overturned on a technicality, and the case was not further appealed. In 1967, Tennessee repealed its law. But Arkansas did not, and in *Epperson v. Arkansas*, 393 U.S. 97 (1968), the Supreme Court held the law unconstitutional under the Establishment Clause. The state's right to prescribe curriculum for its schools did not authorize it to ban the teaching of a scientific theory because it conflicted with some particular religious doctrine. Almost twenty years later the Court reached the same conclusion with respect to a Louisiana law that forbade the teaching of evolution in public schools unless accompanied by instruction in "creation science." *See Edwards v. Aguillard*, 482 U.S. 578 (1987). Applying the *Lemon* test, the Court held that there was no clear secular purpose for the law. The Court said:

> we need not be blind in this case to the legislature's preeminent religious purpose in enacting this statute. There is a historic and contemporaneous link between the teachings of certain religious denominations and the teaching of evolution. It was this link that concerned the Court in *Epperson v. Arkansas*. . . . These same historic and contemporaneous antagonisms between the teachings of certain religious denominations and the teaching of evolution are present in this case. The preeminent purpose of the Louisiana Legislature was clearly to advance the religious viewpoint that a supernatural being

---

*   The Ten Commandments or Mosaic Decalogue are: Thou shalt have no other gods before me. Thou shalt not make unto thee any graven images. Thou shalt not take the name of the Lord thy God in vain. Remember the sabbath day, to keep it holy. Honor thy father and thy mother. Thou shalt not kill. Thou shalt not commit adultery. Thou shalt not steal. Thou shalt not bear false witness. Thou shalt not covet.

created humankind. The term "creation science" was defined as embracing this particular religious doctrine by those responsible for the passage of the Creationism Act.

7.   While the Court has been fairly consistent in terms of strictly policing endorsement of religion within the schools, it has at the same time been vigilant in protecting religious activities on school properties from claimed Establishment Clause violations when they are privately initiated and are treated the same as non-religious activities. For example, in *Good News Club v. Milford Central School*, 533 U.S. 98 (2001), the Court held that Establishment Clause fears did not justify a school in denying the use of school facilities for worship and prayer led by a private group as part of an extracurricular program for students when those facilities were open to other groups, such as the Boy Scouts and the 4-H Club. Rather, such a denial was viewpoint discrimination violating the free speech rights of the students. Similarly, in *Shurtleff v. City of Boston*, 142 S.Ct. 1583 (2022), the Court found viewpoint discrimination in Boston's refusal to allow the flying of a "Christian" flag under the city's program allowing private groups to use one of the three flag poles on the plaza in front of city hall to fly the flag of their choosing for the duration of events sponsored by the groups.

8.   The Court has also strictly applied the Establishment Clause in cases involving actual injection of religious groups into the governmental process. For example, in *Larkin v. Grendel's Den, Inc.*, 459 U.S. 116 (1982), the Court struck down a Massachusetts statute that allowed a church to veto the placement of a liquor store within 500 feet of the church. And in *Board of Educ. of Kiryas Joel Village School Dist. v. Grumet*, 512 U.S. 687 (1994), the Court held a New York law authorizing the creation of a special school district restricted to a religious enclave violated the Establishment Clause.

9.   The Court has been less consistent with respect to government incorporation of religion in displays in public areas.

LYNCH V. DONNELLY

United States Supreme Court, 1984.
465 U.S. 668, 104 S.Ct. 1355.

THE CHIEF JUSTICE delivered the opinion of the Court.

We granted certiorari to decide whether the Establishment Clause of the First Amendment prohibits a municipality from including a crèche, or Nativity scene,* in its annual Christmas display.

---

*   A crèche or Nativity scene is a visual representation of a scene shortly after the birth of Jesus as described in the Gospels of Luke and Matthew. It depicts the stable in which Jesus was born, because there was no room in the inn, with the baby Jesus in a manger (the trough from which animals eat); his mother, Mary, and his earthly father, Joseph, beside him; and shepherds, angels, and various farm animals also in the scene. Sometimes the "three wise men" are also present with a star overhead. [author's note]

Portion of Pawtucket Display

Each year, in cooperation with the downtown retail merchants' association, the City of Pawtucket, Rhode Island, erects a Christmas display as part of its observance of the Christmas holiday season. The display is situated in a park owned by a nonprofit organization and located in the heart of the shopping district. The display is essentially like those to be found in hundreds of towns or cities across the Nation—often on public grounds—during the Christmas season. The Pawtucket display comprises many of the figures and decorations traditionally associated with Christmas, including, among other things, a Santa Claus house, reindeer pulling Santa's sleigh, candy-striped poles, a Christmas tree, carolers, cutout figures representing such characters as a clown, an elephant, and a teddy bear, hundreds of colored lights, a large banner that reads "SEASONS GREETINGS," and the crèche at issue here. All components of this display are owned by the City.

The crèche, which has been included in the display for 40 or more years, consists of the traditional figures, including the Infant Jesus, Mary and Joseph, angels, shepherds, kings, and animals, all ranging in height from 5″ to 5′. In 1973, when the present crèche was acquired, it cost the City $1365; it now is valued at $200. The erection and dismantling of the crèche costs the City about $20 per year; nominal expenses are incurred in lighting the crèche. No money has been expended on its maintenance for the past 10 years.

Respondents, Pawtucket residents . . . brought this action in the United States District Court for Rhode Island, challenging the City's inclusion of the crèche in the annual display. . . .

The Court has sometimes described the Religion Clauses as erecting a "wall" between church and state, *see, e.g., Everson v. Board of Education.* The concept of a "wall" of separation is a useful figure of speech probably deriving from views of Thomas Jefferson. The metaphor has served as a reminder that the Establishment Clause forbids an established church or anything approaching it. But the metaphor itself is not a wholly accurate description of the practical aspects of the relationship that in fact exists between church and state. . . .

The Court's interpretation of the Establishment Clause has comported with what history reveals was the contemporaneous understanding of its guarantees. . . . There is an unbroken history of official acknowledgment by all three branches of government of the role of religion in American life from at least 1789. . . .

Art galleries supported by public revenues display religious paintings of the 15th and 16th centuries, predominantly inspired by one religious faith. The National Gallery in Washington, maintained with Government support, for example, has long exhibited masterpieces with religious messages, notably the Last Supper, and paintings depicting the Birth of Christ, the Crucifixion, and the Resurrection, among many others with explicit Christian themes and messages. The very chamber in which oral arguments on this case were heard is decorated with a notable and permanent—not seasonal—symbol of religion: Moses with Ten Commandments. Congress has long provided chapels in the Capitol for religious worship and meditation. . . .

This history may help explain why the Court consistently has declined to take a rigid, absolutist view of the Establishment Clause. We have refused "to construe the Religion Clauses with a literalness that would undermine the ultimate constitutional objective *as illuminated by history.*" *Walz v. Tax Commission.* In our modern, complex society, whose traditions and constitutional underpinnings rest on and encourage diversity and pluralism in all areas, an absolutist approach in applying the Establishment Clause is simplistic and has been uniformly rejected by the Court.

Rather than mechanically invalidating all governmental conduct or statutes that confer benefits or give special recognition to religion in general or to one faith—as an absolutist approach would dictate—the Court has scrutinized challenged legislation or official conduct to determine whether, in reality, it establishes a religion or religious faith, or tends to do so. . . .

In each case, the inquiry calls for line drawing; no fixed, *per se* rule can be framed. The Establishment Clause like the Due Process Clauses is not a precise, detailed provision in a legal code capable of ready application. . . . The line between permissible relationships and those barred by the Clause can no more be straight and unwavering than due process can be defined in a single stroke or phrase or test. . . .

In the line-drawing process we have often found it useful to inquire whether the challenged law or conduct has a secular purpose, whether its principal or primary effect is to advance or inhibit religion, and whether it creates an excessive entanglement of government with religion. *Lemon v. Kurtzman.* But, we have repeatedly emphasized our unwillingness to be confined to any single test or criterion in this sensitive area. In [some] cases, the Court did not even apply the *Lemon* "test." We did not, for example, consider that analysis relevant in *Marsh.* . . .

In this case, the focus of our inquiry must be on the crèche in the context of the Christmas season. See, *e.g., Stone v. Graham; Abington School District v. Schempp, supra.* In *Stone,* for example, we invalidated a state statute requiring the posting of a copy of the Ten Commandments on public classroom walls. But the Court carefully pointed out that the Commandments were posted purely as a religious admonition, not "integrated into the school curriculum, where the Bible may constitutionally be used in an appropriate study of history, civilization, ethics, comparative religion, or the like." Similarly, in *Abington,* although the Court struck down the practices in two States requiring daily Bible readings in public schools, it specifically noted that nothing in the Court's holding was intended to "indicat[e] that such study of the Bible or of religion, when presented objectively as part of a secular program of education, may not be effected consistently with the First Amendment." Focus exclusively on the religious component of any activity would inevitably lead to its invalidation under the Establishment Clause.

The Court has invalidated legislation or governmental action on the ground that a secular purpose was lacking, but only when it has concluded there was no question that the statute or activity was motivated wholly by religious considerations. . . .

The District Court inferred from the religious nature of the crèche that the City has no secular purpose for the display. In so doing, it rejected the City's claim that its reasons for including the crèche are essentially the same as its reasons for sponsoring the display as a whole. The District Court plainly erred by focusing almost exclusively on the crèche. When viewed in the proper context of the Christmas Holiday season, it is apparent that, on this record, there is insufficient evidence to establish that the inclusion of the crèche is a purposeful or surreptitious effort to express some kind of subtle governmental advocacy of a particular religious message. In a pluralistic society a variety of motives and purposes are implicated. The City, like the Congresses and Presidents, however, has principally taken note of a significant historical religious event long celebrated in the Western World. The crèche in the display depicts the historical origins of this traditional event long recognized as a National Holiday.

The narrow question is whether there is a secular purpose for Pawtucket's display of the crèche. The display is sponsored by the City to celebrate the Holiday and to depict the origins of that Holiday. These are legitimate secular purposes. The District Court's inference, drawn from the religious nature of the crèche, that the City has no secular purpose was, on this record, clearly erroneous.[6]

The District Court found that the primary effect of including the crèche is to confer a substantial and impermissible benefit on religion in general and on the Christian faith in particular. Comparisons of the relative benefits to religion of different forms of governmental support are elusive and difficult to make. But to conclude that the primary effect of including the crèche is to advance religion in violation of the Establishment Clause would require that we view it as more beneficial to and more an endorsement of religion, for example, than expenditure of large sums of public money for textbooks supplied throughout the country to students attending church-sponsored schools, expenditure of public funds for transportation of students to church-sponsored schools, federal grants for college buildings of church-sponsored institutions of higher education combining secular and religious education, noncategorical grants to church-sponsored colleges and universities, and the tax exemptions for church properties sanctioned in *Walz*. It would also require that we view it as more of an endorsement of religion than the Sunday Closing Laws upheld in *McGowan v. Maryland,* 366 U.S. 420 (1961), . . . and the legislative prayers upheld in *Marsh*.

We are unable to discern a greater aid to religion deriving from inclusion of the crèche than from these benefits and endorsements previously held not violative of the Establishment Clause. . . .

The dissent asserts some observers may perceive that the City has aligned itself with the Christian faith by including a Christian symbol in its display and that this serves to advance religion. We can assume, *arguendo,* that the display advances religion in a sense; but our precedents plainly contemplate that on occasion some advancement of religion will result from governmental action. The Court has made it abundantly clear, however, that "not every law that confers an 'indirect,' 'remote,' or 'incidental' benefit upon [religion] is, for that reason alone, constitutionally invalid." Here, whatever benefit to one faith or religion or to all religions, is indirect, remote and incidental; display of the crèche is no more an advancement or endorsement of religion than the Congressional and Executive recognition of the origins of the Holiday itself as "Christ's Mass,"

---

[6]   The City contends that the purposes of the display are "exclusively secular." We hold only that Pawtucket has a secular purpose for its display, which is all that *Lemon* requires. . . .

or the exhibition of literally hundreds of religious paintings in governmentally supported museums.

The District Court found that there had been no administrative entanglement between religion and state resulting from the City's ownership and use of the crèche. But it went on to hold that some political divisiveness was engendered by this litigation. Coupled with its finding of an impermissible sectarian purpose and effect, this persuaded the court that there was "excessive entanglement." . . .

The Court of Appeals correctly observed that this Court has not held that political divisiveness alone can serve to invalidate otherwise permissible conduct. And we decline to so hold today. . . . In any event, apart from this litigation there is no evidence of political friction or divisiveness over the crèche in the 40-year history of Pawtucket's Christmas celebration. . . .

We are satisfied that the City has a secular purpose for including the crèche, that the City has not impermissibly advanced religion, and that including the crèche does not create excessive entanglement between religion and government. . . .

JUSTICE O'CONNOR, concurring.

I concur in the opinion of the Court. I write separately to suggest a clarification of our Establishment Clause doctrine. . . .

The Establishment Clause prohibits government from making adherence to a religion relevant in any way to a person's standing in the political community. Government can run afoul of that prohibition in two principal ways. One is excessive entanglement with religious institutions, which may interfere with the independence of the institutions, give the institutions access to government or governmental powers not fully shared by nonadherents of the religion, and foster the creation of political constituencies defined along religious lines. The second and more direct infringement is government endorsement or disapproval of religion. Endorsement sends a message to nonadherents that they are outsiders, not full members of the political community, and an accompanying message to adherents that they are insiders, favored members of the political community. Disapproval sends the opposite message.

Our prior cases have used the three-part test articulated in *Lemon v. Kurtzman* as a guide to detecting these two forms of unconstitutional government action. It has never been entirely clear, however, how the three parts of the test relate to the principles enshrined in the Establishment Clause. Focusing on institutional entanglement and on endorsement or disapproval of religion clarifies the *Lemon* test as an analytical device. . . .

Although several of our cases have discussed political divisiveness under the entanglement prong of *Lemon,* we have never relied on divisiveness as an independent ground for holding a government practice unconstitutional. Guessing the potential for political divisiveness inherent in a government practice is simply too speculative an enterprise, in part because the existence of the litigation, as this case illustrates, itself may affect the political response to the government practice. Political divisiveness is admittedly an evil addressed by the Establishment Clause. Its existence may be evidence that institutional entanglement is excessive or that a government practice is perceived as an endorsement of religion. But the constitutional inquiry should focus ultimately on the character of the government activity that might cause such divisiveness, not on the divisiveness itself. The entanglement prong of the *Lemon* test is properly limited to institutional entanglement.

The central issue in this case is whether Pawtucket has endorsed Christianity by its display of the crèche. To answer that question, we must examine both what Pawtucket intended to communicate in displaying the crèche and what message the City's display actually conveyed. The purpose and effect prongs of the *Lemon* test represent these two aspects of the meaning of the City's action.

The meaning of a statement to its audience depends both on the intention of the speaker and on the "objective" meaning of the statement in the community. . . .

The purpose prong of the *Lemon* test asks whether government's actual purpose is to endorse or disapprove of religion. The effect prong asks whether, irrespective of government's actual purpose, the practice under review in fact conveys a message of endorsement or disapproval. An affirmative answer to either question should render the challenged practice invalid.

The purpose prong of the *Lemon* test requires that a government activity have a secular purpose. . . . The proper inquiry under the purpose prong of *Lemon,* I submit, is whether the government intends to convey a message of endorsement or disapproval of religion.

Applying that formulation to this case, I would find that Pawtucket did not intend to convey any message of endorsement of Christianity or disapproval of nonChristian religions. The evident purpose of including the crèche in the larger display was not promotion of the religious content of the crèche but celebration of the public holiday through its traditional symbols. Celebration of public holidays, which have cultural significance even if they also have religious aspects, is a legitimate secular purpose. . . .

Focusing on the evil of government endorsement or disapproval of religion makes clear that the effect prong of the *Lemon* test is properly interpreted not to require invalidation of a government practice merely because it in fact causes, even as a primary effect, advancement or inhibition of religion. The law[ ] upheld in *Walz v. Tax Commission* . . . had such effects, but [it] did not violate the Establishment Clause. What is crucial is that a government practice not have the effect of communicating a message of government endorsement or disapproval of religion. It is only practices having that effect, whether intentionally or unintentionally, that make religion relevant, in reality or public perception, to status in the political community.

Pawtucket's display of its crèche, I believe, does not communicate a message that the government intends to endorse the Christian beliefs represented by the crèche. Although the religious and indeed sectarian significance of the crèche, as the district court found, is not neutralized by the setting, the overall holiday setting changes what viewers may fairly understand to be the purpose of the display—as a typical museum setting, though not neutralizing the religious content of a religious painting, negates any message of endorsement of that content. The display celebrates a public holiday, and no one contends that declaration of that holiday is understood to be an endorsement of religion. The holiday itself has very strong secular components and traditions. Government celebration of the holiday, which is extremely common, generally is not understood to endorse the religious content of the holiday, just as government celebration of Thanksgiving is not so understood. The crèche is a traditional symbol of the holiday that is very commonly displayed along with purely secular symbols, as it was in Pawtucket.

These features combine to make the government's display of the crèche in this particular physical setting no more an endorsement of religion than such governmental "acknowledgments" of religion as legislative prayers of the type approved in *Marsh v. Chambers*, government declaration of Thanksgiving as a public holiday, printing of "In God We Trust" on coins, and opening court sessions with "God save the United States and this honorable court." Those government acknowledgments of religion serve, in the only ways reasonably possible in our culture, the legitimate secular purposes of solemnizing public occasions, expressing confidence in the future, and encouraging the recognition of what is worthy of appreciation in society. For that reason, and because of their history and ubiquity, those practices are not understood as conveying government approval of particular religious beliefs. The display of the crèche likewise serves a secular purpose—celebration of a public holiday with traditional symbols. It cannot fairly be understood to convey a message of government endorsement of religion. . . . For these reasons, I conclude that Pawtucket's display of the crèche does not have the effect of communicating endorsement of Christianity.

JUSTICE BRENNAN, with whom JUSTICE MARSHALL, JUSTICE BLACKMUN and JUSTICE STEVENS join, dissenting.

The principles announced in the compact phrases of the Religion Clauses have . . . proven difficult to apply. Faced with that uncertainty, the

Court properly looks for guidance to the settled test announced in *Lemon v. Kurtzman* for assessing whether a challenged governmental practice involves an impermissible step toward the establishment of religion. Applying that test to this case, the Court reaches an essentially narrow result which turns largely upon the particular holiday context in which the City of Pawtucket's nativity scene appeared. The Court's decision implicitly leaves open questions concerning the constitutionality of the public display on public property of a crèche standing alone, or the public display of other distinctively religious symbols such as a cross. Despite the narrow contours of the Court's opinion, our precedents in my view compel the holding that Pawtucket's inclusion of a life-sized display depicting the biblical description of the birth of Christ as part of its annual Christmas celebration is unconstitutional. . . .

Applying the three-part [*Lemon*] test to Pawtucket's crèche, I am persuaded that the City's inclusion of the crèche in its Christmas display simply does not reflect a "clearly secular purpose." . . . In the present case, the City claims that its purposes were exclusively secular. Pawtucket sought, according to this view, only to participate in the celebration of a national holiday and to attract people to the downtown area in order to promote pre-Christmas retail sales and to help engender the spirit of goodwill and neighborliness commonly associated with the Christmas season.

Despite these assertions, two compelling aspects of this case indicate that our generally prudent "reluctance to attribute unconstitutional motives" to a governmental body should be overcome. First, . . . all of Pawtucket's "valid secular objectives can be readily accomplished by other means." Plainly, the City's interest in celebrating the holiday and in promoting both retail sales and goodwill are fully served by the elaborate display of Santa Claus, reindeer, and wishing wells that are already a part of Pawtucket's annual Christmas display. . . . The inclusion of a distinctively religious element like the crèche, however, demonstrates that a narrower sectarian purpose lay behind the decision to include a nativity scene. . . .

The "primary effect" of including a nativity scene in the City's display is, as the District Court found, to place the government's imprimatur of approval on the particular religious beliefs exemplified by the crèche. Those who believe in the message of the nativity receive the unique and exclusive benefit of public recognition and approval of their views. . . . The effect on minority religious groups, as well as on those who may reject all religion, is to convey the message that their views are not similarly worthy of public recognition nor entitled to public support. It was precisely this sort of religious chauvinism that the Establishment Clause was intended forever to prohibit. . . .

The Court advances two principal arguments to support its conclusion that the Pawtucket crèche satisfies the *Lemon* test. Neither is persuasive.

First. The Court, by focusing on the holiday "context" in which the nativity scene appeared, seeks to explain away the clear religious import of the crèche and the findings of the District Court that most observers understood the crèche as both a symbol of Christian beliefs and a symbol of the City's support for those beliefs. . . . The effect of the crèche, of course, must be gauged not only by its inherent religious significance but also by the overall setting in which it appears. But it blinks reality to claim, as the Court does, that by including such a distinctively religious object as the crèche in its Christmas display, Pawtucket has done no more than make use of a "traditional" symbol of the holiday, and has thereby purged the crèche of its religious content and conferred only an "incidental and indirect" benefit on religion. . . .

Finally, and most importantly, even in the context of Pawtucket's seasonal celebration, the crèche retains a specifically Christian religious meaning. I refuse to accept the notion implicit in today's decision that non-Christians would find that the religious content of the crèche is eliminated by the fact that it appears as part of the City's otherwise secular celebration of the Christmas holiday. . . . To be so excluded on religious grounds by one's elected government is an insult and an injury that, until today, could not be countenanced by the Establishment Clause.

Second. The Court also attempts to justify the crèche by entertaining a beguilingly simple, yet faulty syllogism. The Court begins by noting that government may recognize Christmas day as a public holiday; the Court then asserts that the crèche is nothing more than a traditional element of Christmas celebrations; and it concludes that the inclusion of a crèche as part of a government's annual Christmas celebration is constitutionally permissible. The Court apparently believes that once it finds that the designation of Christmas as a public holiday is constitutionally acceptable, it is then free to conclude that virtually every form of governmental association with the celebration of the holiday is also constitutional. The vice of this dangerously superficial argument is that it overlooks the fact that the Christmas holiday in our national culture contains both secular and sectarian elements. To say that government may recognize the holiday's traditional, secular elements of giftgiving, public festivities and community spirit, does not mean that government may indiscriminately embrace the distinctively sectarian aspects of the holiday. . . .

When government decides to recognize Christmas day as a public holiday, it does no more than accommodate the calendar of public activities to the plain fact that many Americans will expect on that day to spend time visiting with their families, attending religious services, and perhaps enjoying some respite from pre-holiday activities. . . . If public officials go further and participate in the *secular* celebration of Christmas—by, for example, decorating public places with such secular images as wreaths, garlands or Santa Claus figures—they move closer to the limits of their constitutional power but nevertheless remain within the boundaries set by the Establishment Clause. But when those officials participate in or appear to endorse the distinctively religious elements of this otherwise secular event, they encroach upon First Amendment freedoms. . . .

[T]he Court has never comprehensively addressed the extent to which government may acknowledge religion by, for example, incorporating religious references into public ceremonies and proclamations, and I do not presume to offer a comprehensive approach. Nevertheless, it appears from our prior decisions that at least three principles—tracing the narrow channels which government acknowledgments must follow to satisfy the Establishment Clause—may be identified. First, although the government may not be compelled to do so by the Free Exercise Clause, it may, consistently with the Establishment Clause, act to accommodate to some extent the opportunities of individuals to practice their religion. . . .

Second, our cases recognize that while a particular governmental practice may have derived from religious motivations and retain certain religious connotations, it is nonetheless permissible for the government to pursue the practice when it is continued today solely for secular reasons. As this Court noted with reference to Sunday Closing Laws in *McGowan v. Maryland,* the mere fact that a governmental practice coincides to some extent with certain religious beliefs does not render it unconstitutional. Thanksgiving Day, in my view, fits easily within this principle, for despite its religious antecedents, the current practice of celebrating Thanksgiving is unquestionably secular and patriotic. . . .

Finally, we have noted that government cannot be completely prohibited from recognizing in its public actions the religious beliefs and practices of the American people as an aspect of our national history and culture. While I remain uncertain about these questions, I would suggest that such practices as the designation of "In God We Trust" as our national motto, or the references to God contained in the Pledge of Allegiance can best be understood . . . as a form a "ceremonial deism," protected from Establishment Clause scrutiny chiefly because they have lost through rote repetition any significant religious content. Moreover, these references are uniquely suited to serve such wholly secular purposes as solemnizing public occasions, or inspiring commitment to meet some national challenge in a manner that simply could not be fully served in our culture if government were limited to purely non-religious phrases. The practices by which the government has long acknowledged religion are therefore probably necessary to serve certain secular functions, and that necessity, coupled with their long history, gives those practices an essentially secular meaning. . . .

JUSTICE BLACKMUN, with whom JUSTICE STEVENS joins, dissenting. [opinion omitted]

COMMENTS AND QUESTIONS

1.   Justice O'Connor's concurrence, with its modification of the *Lemon* test, had more influence than Chief Justice Burger's opinion for the Court. His opinion, which suggested that any effect advancing religion that was less than the effect resulting from past decisions would not be unconstitutional, has not been followed. Justice O'Connor's concept of focusing on the intent of the lawmaker and the perception of the viewer with respect to endorsing religion instead has been reflected in some later cases. Even this tweak of the *Lemon* test, however, has not necessarily driven all the subsequent cases.

2.   What do you think the viewers of the Pawtucket display perceived when they viewed the Santa Claus house, reindeer pulling Santa's sleigh, candy-striped poles, a Christmas tree, carolers, cutout figures representing such characters as a clown, an elephant, and a teddy bear, hundreds of colored lights, a large banner that read "SEASONS GREETINGS," *and* a nativity scene? Was the nativity scene's religious message lost in the noise? Or did the viewers perceive it as the message that a divine Savior was brought into the world and that the purpose of this miraculous birth was to illuminate a path toward salvation and redemption? Or should we be asking "which viewers"? Ironically, could it be that non-Christians might view it as more religious than Christians?

3.   It may also be ironic that the lawsuit (and lower courts' injunctions to remove the crèche) created more political divisiveness on religious grounds than the display had occasioned over its 40-year history.

4.   The opinions of both the Court and the dissent mention *McGowan v. Maryland*, 366 U.S. 420 (1961), in which the Court rejected Establishment Clause claims against Sunday closing laws. From the founding of the nation until late in the last century, it was common practice for states to prohibit the sale of goods or the employment of labor on Sundays, with certain exceptions for what were believed essential services. The Court acknowledged that the original motivation for these laws was to set aside the Sabbath for religious observance. However, beginning in the 19th Century the motivation for the laws turned more to assuring that workers would have at least one day a week off, and it was important that it be the same day for everyone, so as to create "one day which all members of the family and community have the opportunity to spend and enjoy together, a day on which there exists relative quiet and disassociation from the everyday intensity of commercial activities, a day on which people may visit friends and relatives who are not available during working days." Because most people preferred the one day to be Sunday, that was the day the state chose to prohibit commercial activities. The fact that this also accommodated many, if not most, persons' religious needs did not make it unconstitutional.

5.   A few years after *Lynch*, the Court was faced with another case involving Christmas displays, including one with a crèche. Since 1981 the County courthouse in downtown Pittsburgh had contained a Nativity scene at the foot of the grand staircase inside the main entrance. The scene was not accompanied by other secular symbols of Christmas, and the scene itself was donated and erected by the Holy Name Society, a Roman Catholic Group. By a 5–4 margin, using Justice O'Connor's "endorsement" analysis from *Lynch*, the Court found this display to violate the Establishment Clause. *Allegheny County v. ACLU*, 492 U.S. 573 (1989). The Court distinguished *Lynch* on the grounds that here the crèche stood alone and therefore nothing detracted from its religious message. Justice Kennedy wrote the dissent rejecting the "endorsement" test, arguing instead that the correct test was whether the government coerced anyone to support or participate in any religion or gave direct benefits to religion "in such a degree that it in fact 'establishes a [state] religion. . . .' [A]ccommodation or passive acknowledgment of existing symbols does not violate the Establishment Clause unless it benefits religion in a way more direct and substantial than practices that are accepted in our national heritage." The same case also involved a display at the City-County Building a block away. Here the city had for years erected a 45-foot Christmas tree outside the main entrance to the building, decorated with lights and ornaments. Since 1982 it had also included beside the tree an 18-foot Chanukah menorah* owned by a local Jewish religious group, and in the year in question the mayor had placed at the foot of the tree a sign bearing the mayor's name and entitled "Salute to Liberty." Beneath the title, the sign stated: "During this holiday season, the city of Pittsburgh salutes liberty. Let these festive lights remind us that we are the keepers of the flame of liberty and our legacy of freedom." The Court by a 6–3 margin, but without a majority opinion, held that the display of the menorah did not violate the Establishment Clause. The six justices reaching this conclusion included the four dissenters with respect to the crèche and two of the justices who had found the crèche unconstitutional. Justice Blackmun, one of those two, argued that both Christmas and Chanukah were secular as well as religious holidays, and that the tree and the menorah were not exclusively religious symbols, so that here they could be viewed as celebrating the two secular holidays. Justice O'Connor, the other of the two justices who had found the crèche unconstitutional, disagreed with Justice Blackmun's characterization of the holidays as secular or of the menorah as having a secular dimension. Instead she concluded that the joint display of the tree and the menorah accompanied by the sign did not suggest endorsement of religion but "conveyed a message of pluralism and freedom of belief during the holiday season." The dissenters, who had been with the majority regarding the

---

*   Chanukah is an eight-day Jewish religious and cultural holiday celebrating the rededication of the Temple of Jerusalem after its recapture in the course of a political rebellion against the Greek colonists in 125 B.C. The Temple housed a seven-branch menorah (candlestick), which was to be kept burning continuously, but there was only enough oil to last for one day. According to the Talmud, the oil miraculously lasted for eight days (the length of time it took to obtain additional oil). To celebrate and publicly proclaim this miracle, the Talmud prescribes that it is a mitzvah (*i.e.*, a religious deed or commandment) for Jews during the eight days of Chanukah to light one of the candles on a menorah on each of the days of the holiday.

crèche, believed that displaying clearly religious symbols on public property, even to promote pluralism, violated the Establishment Clause.

6. In *Capitol Square Review Board v. Pinette*, 515 U.S. 753 (1995), the Ku Klux Klan sought permission to erect a large cross on a public square adjacent to the Ohio Statehouse during a 14-day period immediately preceding Christmas. Although the square was conceded to be a public forum, the permission was denied on the basis that to allow the cross's erection in a public square would violate the Establishment Clause. Although seven justices agreed that the denial was not justified, there was no agreement among the six separate opinions as to the reason. There was agreement that because this was a public forum, and because the denial of permission was based on the content of the speech, the proper analysis was strict scrutiny under the Free Speech Clause of the First Amendment. Moreover, there was agreement that avoiding a violation of the Establishment Clause would constitute a compelling government interest. There agreement ended. Justice Scalia wrote for a plurality including Chief Justice Rehnquist and Justices Kennedy and Thomas to the effect that the "endorsement" test was wrongheaded and that as a flat rule private religious speech in a public forum could not violate the Establishment Clause. Justice O'Connor concurred in the result and, joined by Justices Souter and Breyer, utilized the "endorsement" test to conclude that a reasonable observer would not perceive the cross in the public square, which had been used for other private displays, to be government endorsement of religion, especially because the Klan indicated its willingness to have a small sign identifying the cross as privately sponsored. Justices Stevens and Ginsburg dissented, also using the "endorsement" test, but they disagreed that a reasonable observer would not perceive this as government endorsement of religion, even with the disclaimer sign. In short, four justices rejected the use of the "endorsement" test in favor of a bright-line test, while five justices utilized that test but disagreed over the result it produced.

7. Justice O'Connor's concurrence in *Lynch* refers to *Marsh v. Chambers*, in which the Court upheld a state's practice of opening its legislative sessions with a prayer given by a chaplain employed by the legislature. While she refers to that case as allowing government to "acknowledge" religion, rather than to endorse religion, the main thrust of the case was the fact that such prayers to open legislative sessions had been the historical practice since the first Congress (and the Congress that proposed the First Amendment to the states opened its session with a prayer). To suggest that such a practice violated the Establishment Clause in light of that history simply would not stand. In *Town of Greece, NY v. Galloway*, 572 U.S. 565 (2014), the same issue arose except it was a town council that opened its sessions with a prayer given by a local clergyman. The Court by a 5–4 margin held that *Marsh* governed. The dissent did not take issue with *Marsh* but instead distinguished it from the case at hand on the grounds that a town council meeting involves the public in a way that the beginning of state or federal legislative session does not. That is, the public may observe legislative sessions, but they do not participate in it. Town council meetings, however, involve the public addressing and being addressed by the council members;

members of the public are active participants in the meeting. Consequently, their discomfort at the opening prayer, which they felt excluded them, affected their very participation in the meeting. The Court did not find this level of discomfort to be coercive, and there was no indication of an intent to exclude. Perhaps the most notable aspect of the opinion was the Court's rejection of any constitutional requirement that the prayers be non-denominational or, if denominational, rotated among spiritual leaders reflecting the various denominations in the community. Absent any showing of an intent to proselytize or exclude any particular religion, denominational prayers would still be constitutional because that had been the historical practice back to the founding. Also notable was the Court's view that the Establishment Clause must be interpreted generally "by reference to historical practices and understandings," rather than by any particular test, such as the *Lemon* test or its variants.

8.   The debate over continued use of the *Lemon* test and the "endorsement test" continued in two companion cases, *McCreary County v. ACLU of Kentucky*, 545 U.S. 844 (2005), and *Van Orden v. Perry*, 545 U.S. 677 (2005), decided the same day. In *McCreary County* two Kentucky counties put up in their respective courthouses large, gold-framed copies of the Ten Commandments. In one of the counties there was a ceremony at which a church pastor said the Commandments were a creed of ethics. The ACLU of Kentucky sued in federal court to enjoin these displays as violative of the Establishment Clause of the First Amendment. Before the court could rule, the counties doubled down by adding to the display eight additional documents having a religious theme or excerpted to highlight a religious element. The district court entered a preliminary injunction requiring the immediate removal of the displays. The counties complied but then installed yet another display—nine framed documents of equal size, one of them setting out the Ten Commandments explicitly identified as the "King James Version" at Exodus 20:3-17. The other documents were the Magna Carta, the Declaration of Independence, the Bill of Rights, the lyrics of the Star Spangled Banner, the Mayflower Compact, the National Motto, the Preamble to the Kentucky Constitution,* and a picture of Lady Justice. The ACLU moved enjoin this display, and the district court granted that motion. Before the Supreme Court, the counties made no effort to defend the clearly religious purpose of the first two displays but claimed that the purpose of the third display was only to "educate the citizens of the county regarding some of the documents that played a significant role in the foundation of our system of law and government." A majority of the Court was not convinced, saying "[n]o reasonable observer could swallow the claim that the Counties had cast off the objective so unmistakable in the earlier displays." The opinion for the Court relied on *Lemon*'s first requirement that there must be a secular purpose for the government action; Justice O'Connor concurred in that opinion but said that the government's purpose here was relevant because it conveyed a

---

  *   "We, the people of the Commonwealth of Kentucky, grateful to Almighty God for the civil, political and religious liberties we enjoy, and invoking the continuance of these blessings, do ordain and establish this Constitution."

message of endorsement. Four justices dissented, arguing among other things that the *Lemon* test should be abandoned.

Van Orden also involved a display of the Ten Commandments on government property. Here, however, they were engraved on a 6-foot high and 3-foot wide monument located on the grounds of the Texas State Capitol, a 22-acre site containing 16 other monuments and 21 historical markers. In addition to the text of the Ten Commandments, the monument depicted an eagle grasping the American flag, an eye inside of a pyramid, and two small tablets with what appears to be an ancient script carved above the text of the Ten Commandments. Below the text are two Stars of David and the superimposed Greek letters X and P, which represent Christ. The bottom of the monument indicates that the monument was "PRESENTED TO THE PEOPLE AND YOUTH OF TEXAS BY THE FRATERNAL ORDER OF EAGLES OF TEXAS 1961." This time the Court upheld the constitutionality of the monument by a 5–4 vote, although there was no majority opinion. Chief Justice Rehnquist wrote the plurality decision, joined by the other dissenters in *McCreary*. He rejected the use of the *Lemon* test. He then noted the various places the Ten Commandments appear in the Nation's Capital:

> We need only look within our own Courtroom. Since 1935, Moses has stood, holding two tablets that reveal portions of the Ten Commandments written in Hebrew, among other lawgivers in the south frieze. Representations of the Ten Commandments adorn the metal gates lining the north and south sides of the Courtroom as well as the doors leading into the Courtroom. Moses also sits on the exterior east facade of the building holding the Ten Commandments tablets.

> Similar acknowledgments can be seen throughout a visitor's tour of our Nation's Capital. For example, a large statue of Moses holding the Ten Commandments, alongside a statue of the Apostle Paul, has overlooked the rotunda of the Library of Congress' Jefferson Building since 1897. And the Jefferson Building's Great Reading Room contains a sculpture of a woman beside the Ten Commandments with a quote above her from the Old Testament. A medallion with two tablets depicting the Ten Commandments decorates the floor of the National Archives. Inside the Department of Justice, a statue entitled "The Spirit of Law" has two tablets representing the Ten Commandments lying at its feet. In front of the Ronald Reagan Building is another sculpture that includes a depiction of the Ten Commandments. So too a 24-foot-tall sculpture, depicting, among other things, the Ten Commandments and a cross, stands outside the federal courthouse that houses both the Court of Appeals and the District Court for the District of Columbia. Moses is also prominently featured in the Chamber of the United States House of Representatives.

He concluded that, while the Ten Commandments have religious significance, they also have historical significance, and depictions reflecting that historical significance do not run afoul of the Establishment Clause "simply [by] having religious content or promoting a message consistent with a religious doctrine." The case engendered seven different opinions. Perhaps the most striking opinion was Justice Breyer's concurrence in the judgment. He distinguished the Ten Commandments in the classroom, given the impressionability of the young, and in the courtroom in *McCreary*, because of the particular history of that display. Here, he saw the monument as primarily involved in conveying a moral and historical message, rather than a religious one, and this, he thought, was most importantly confirmed by its presence on the grounds for 40 years without a complaint. The four dissenters relied upon *Lemon* in one form or another to argue the monument was unconstitutional.

9.   The display of the Ten Commandments in *Van Orden* was followed by a 32-foot tall Latin cross in the center of a busy intersection in Bladensburg, Maryland, honoring local servicemen who perished in World War I. In *American Legion v. American Humanist Ass'n*, 139 S.Ct. 2067 (2019), the Court reached a similar conclusion as in *Van Orden,* looking to the history and tradition of the use of the cross as a symbol for honoring war dead, with only Justices Ginsburg and Sotomayor dissenting. Notable, however, were the seven separate opinions. Between them they seemingly sounded the death knell for the *Lemon* test. Justices Kavanaugh, Gorsuch, and Thomas explicitly called for it to be overruled. Justice Alito, joined by the Chief Justice and Justice Breyer, said that it was not appropriate in cases involving the use of words or symbols with religious associations for ceremonial, celebratory, or commemorative purposes. Only Justice Kagan offered any defense of it, saying that while a "rigid application of [its] test does not solve every Establishment Clause problem[,] I think that test's focus on purposes and effects is crucial in evaluating government action in this sphere."

Justice Thomas continued his radical originalism by suggesting that the Establishment Clause should not be incorporated against the states under the Fourteenth Amendment.

Justice Gorsuch, joined by Justice Thomas, introduced yet a new argument with respect to challenges to government displays under the Establishment Clause—a denial of standing. He denied that an "offended observer" has suffered a discrete, concrete injury sufficient to allow standing. Rather, he characterized it as a generalized grievance. Could such an approach be limited to Establishment Clause cases? A significant number of environmental law cases rely on the offended observer to qualify for standing.

KENNEDY V. BREMERTON SCHOOL DISTRICT
United States Supreme Court, 2022.
142 S.Ct. 2407.

[A school employee, who lost his job as a high school football coach after he knelt at midfield after games to offer a quiet personal prayer, brought an action against the school district, alleging violations of his rights under the First Amendment's Free Speech and Free Exercise

Clauses. The school district defended on the grounds that the coach's actions would be perceived by a reasonable observer as the school district endorsing religion, thus creating an Establishment Clause violation. Consequently, it argued that it was justified in restricting the coach's speech and exercise of religion in order to avoid violating the Establishment Clause. The Supreme Court held that the coach's speech and prayer were protected under the Free Exercise and Free Speech Clauses, because the coach's prayers did not cause an Establishment of Religion on the part of the school district. Below is the portion of the Court's opinion regarding the Establishment Clause.]

JUSTICE GORSUCH delivered the opinion of the Court.

Joseph Kennedy lost his job as a high school football coach because he knelt at midfield after games to offer a quiet prayer of thanks. Mr. Kennedy prayed during a period when school employees were free to speak with a friend, call for a reservation at a restaurant, check email, or attend to other personal matters. He offered his prayers quietly while his students were otherwise occupied. Still, the Bremerton School District disciplined him anyway. It did so because it thought anything less could lead a reasonable observer to conclude (mistakenly) that it endorsed Mr. Kennedy's religious beliefs. That reasoning was misguided. Both the Free Exercise and Free Speech Clauses of the First Amendment protect expressions like Mr. Kennedy's. Nor does a proper understanding of the Amendment's Establishment Clause require the government to single out private religious speech for special disfavor. The Constitution and the best of our traditions counsel mutual respect and tolerance, not censorship and suppression, for religious and nonreligious views alike.

Like many other football players and coaches across the country, Mr. Kennedy made it a practice to give "thanks through prayer on the playing field" at the conclusion of each game. Mr. Kennedy offered his

Neil Gorsuch

After clerking for Justice Anthony Kennedy, Gorsuch joined a D.C. law firm where he litigated on behalf of corporate clients. In 2005 he worked in the Bush Justice Department as Deputy Associate Attorney General. This led to his appointment to the Tenth Circuit in 2006. There he established himself as a relatively extreme proponent of textualism in statutory interpretation and originalism in interpreting the United States Constitution. President Trump appointed him to the Supreme Court in 2017 to fill the seat vacated by Justice Scalia's death. Democrats, angered by the Republicans' refusal to consider President Obama's nominee to replace Justice Scalia, generally opposed the Gorsuch nomination. On the Supreme Court, Justice Gorsuch has been a consistent conservative and has aligned with Justice Thomas on issues where previously Justice Thomas was alone.

prayers after the players and coaches had shaken hands, by taking a knee at the 50-yard line and praying "quiet[ly]" for "approximately 30 seconds."

Initially, Mr. Kennedy prayed on his own. But over time, some players asked whether they could pray alongside him. Mr. Kennedy responded by saying, " 'This is a free country. You can do what you want.' " The number of players who joined Mr. Kennedy eventually grew to include most of the team, at least after some games. Sometimes team members invited opposing players to join. Other times Mr. Kennedy still prayed alone. Eventually, Mr. Kennedy began incorporating short motivational speeches with his prayer when others were present. Separately, the team at times engaged in pregame or postgame prayers in the locker room. It seems this practice was a "school tradition" that predated Mr. Kennedy's tenure. Mr. Kennedy explained that he "never told any student that it was important they participate in any religious activity." In particular, he "never pressured or encouraged any student to join" his postgame midfield prayers.

[After becoming aware of these practices,] the superintendent sent Mr. Kennedy a letter. In it, the superintendent identified "two problematic practices" in which Mr. Kennedy had engaged. First, Mr. Kennedy had provided "inspirational talk[s]" that included "overtly religious references" likely constituting "prayer" with the students "at midfield following the completion of . . . game[s]." Second, he had led "students and coaching staff in a prayer" in the locker-room tradition that "predated [his] involvement with the program."

The District instructed Mr. Kennedy to avoid any motivational "talks with students" that "include[d] religious expression, including prayer," and to avoid "suggest[ing], encourag[ing] (or discourag[ing]), or supervis[ing]" any prayers of students, which students remained free to "engage in." The District also explained that any religious activity on Mr. Kennedy's part must be "nondemonstrative (i.e., not outwardly discernible as religious activity)" if "students are also engaged in religious conduct" in order to "avoid the perception of endorsement."

After receiving the District's letter, Mr. Kennedy ended the tradition, predating him, of offering locker-room prayers. He also ended his practice of incorporating religious references or prayer into his postgame motivational talks to his team on the field. Mr. Kennedy further felt pressured to abandon his practice of saying his own quiet, on-field postgame prayer.

On October 14, through counsel, Mr. Kennedy sent a letter to school officials informing them that, because of his "sincerely-held religious beliefs," he felt "compelled" to offer a "post-game personal prayer" of thanks at midfield. He asked the District to allow him to continue that "private religious expression" alone. Consistent with the District's policy, Mr. Kennedy explained that he "neither requests, encourages, nor discourages students from participating in" these prayers. Mr. Kennedy emphasized that he sought only the opportunity to "wai[t] until the game is over and the players have left the field and then wal[k] to mid-field to say a short, private, personal prayer." He "told everybody" that it would be acceptable to him to pray "when the kids went away from [him]." He later clarified that this meant he was even willing to say his "prayer while the players were walking to the locker room" or "bus," and then catch up with his team. However, Mr. Kennedy objected to the logical implication of the District's letter, which he understood as banning him "from bowing his head" in the vicinity of students, and as requiring him to "flee the scene if students voluntarily [came] to the same area" where he was praying.

[I]nstead of accommodating Mr. Kennedy's request to offer a brief prayer on the field while students were busy with other activities— whether heading to the locker room, boarding the bus, or perhaps singing the school fight song—the District issued an ultimatum. It forbade Mr. Kennedy from engaging in "any overt actions" that could "appea[r] to a reasonable observer to endorse . . . prayer . . . while he is on duty as a District-paid coach." The District did so because it judged that anything less would lead it to violate the Establishment Clause.

After receiving this letter, Mr. Kennedy offered a brief prayer following the October 16 game. When he bowed his head at midfield after the game, "most [Bremerton] players were . . . engaged in the traditional singing of the school fight song to the audience." Though Mr. Kennedy was alone when he began to pray, players from the other team and members of the community joined him before he finished his prayer. This event spurred media coverage of Mr. Kennedy's dilemma and a public response from the District.

On October 23, shortly before that evening's game, the District wrote Mr. Kennedy again. It expressed "appreciation" for his "efforts to comply" with the District's directives, including avoiding "on-the-job prayer with players in the . . . football program, both in the locker room prior to games as well as on the field immediately following games." The letter also admitted that, during Mr. Kennedy's recent October 16 postgame prayer, his students were otherwise engaged and not praying with him, and that his prayer was "fleeting." Still, the District explained that a "reasonable observer" could think government endorsement of religion had occurred when a "District employee, on the field only by virtue of his employment with the District, still on duty" engaged in "overtly religious conduct." The District thus made clear that the only option it would offer Mr. Kennedy was to allow him to pray after a game in a "private location" behind closed doors and "not observable to students or the public."

After the October 23 game ended, Mr. Kennedy knelt at the 50-yard line, where "no one joined him," and bowed his head for a "brief, quiet prayer." The superintendent informed the District's board that this prayer "moved closer to what we want," but nevertheless remained "unconstitutional." After the final relevant football game on October 26, Mr. Kennedy again knelt alone to offer a brief prayer as the players engaged in postgame traditions. While he was praying, other adults gathered around him on the field. Later, Mr. Kennedy rejoined his players for a postgame talk, after they had finished singing the school fight song.

Shortly after the October 26 game, the District placed Mr. Kennedy on paid administrative leave and prohibited him from "participat[ing], in any capacity, in . . . football program activities."

[T]he District argues that its suspension of Mr. Kennedy was essential to avoid a violation of the Establishment Clause. On its account, Mr. Kennedy's prayers might have been protected by the Free Exercise and Free Speech Clauses. But his rights were in "direct tension" with the competing demands of the Establishment Clause. To resolve that clash, the District reasoned, Mr. Kennedy's rights had to "yield."

But how could that be? It is true that this Court and others often refer to the "Establishment Clause," the "Free Exercise Clause," and the "Free Speech Clause" as separate units. But the three Clauses appear in the same sentence of the same Amendment. A natural reading of that sentence would seem to suggest the Clauses have "complementary" purposes, not warring ones where one Clause is always sure to prevail over the others.

The District arrived at a different understanding this way. It began with the premise that the Establishment Clause is offended whenever a "reasonable observer" could conclude that the government has "endorse[d]" religion. The District then took the view that a "reasonable observer" could think it "endorsed Kennedy's religious activity by not stopping the practice. Because a reasonable observer could (mistakenly) infer that by allowing the prayer the District endorsed Mr. Kennedy's message, the District felt it had to act, even if that meant suppressing otherwise protected First Amendment activities.

To defend its approach, the District relied on *Lemon* and its progeny. And, to be sure, in *Lemon* this Court attempted a "grand unified theory" for assessing Establishment Clause claims. That approach called for an examination of a law's purposes, effects, and potential for entanglement with religion. In time, the approach also came to involve estimations about whether a "reasonable observer" would consider the government's challenged action an "endorsement" of religion.

What the District and the Ninth Circuit overlooked, however, is that the "shortcomings" associated with this "ambitiou[s]," abstract, and ahistorical approach to the Establishment Clause became so "apparent" that this Court long ago abandoned *Lemon* and its endorsement test offshoot. The Court has explained that these tests "invited chaos" in lower courts, led to "differing results" in materially identical cases, and created a "minefield" for legislators. This Court has since made plain, too, that the Establishment Clause does not include anything like a "modified heckler's veto, in which . . . religious activity can be proscribed" based on " 'perceptions' " or " 'discomfort.' " An Establishment Clause violation does not automatically follow whenever a public school or other government entity "fail[s] to censor" private religious speech. Nor does the Clause "compel the government to purge from the public sphere" anything an objective observer could reasonably infer endorses or "partakes of the religious." In fact, just this Term the Court unanimously rejected a city's attempt to censor religious speech based on *Lemon* and the endorsement test. See *Shurtleff*.

In place of *Lemon* and the endorsement test, this Court has instructed that the Establishment Clause must be interpreted by " 'reference to historical practices and understandings.' " *American Legion,.* " '[T]he line' " that courts and governments "must draw between the permissible and the impermissible" has to " 'accor[d] with history and faithfully reflec[t] the understanding of the Founding Fathers.' " *School Dist. of Abington Township* v. *Schempp.* An analysis focused on original meaning and history, this Court has stressed, has long represented the rule rather than some " 'exception' " within the "Court's Establishment Clause jurisprudence." See *American Legion*; *McGowan* v. *Maryland*, 366 U. S. 420, 437–440 (1961)(analyzing Sunday closing laws by looking to their "place . . . in the First Amendment's history"); *Walz* v. *Tax Comm'n of City of New York*, 397 U. S. 664, 680 (1970)(analyzing the "history and uninterrupted practice" of church tax exemptions).

Perhaps sensing that the primary theory it pursued below rests on a mistaken understanding of the Establishment Clause, the District offers a backup argument in this Court. It still contends that its Establishment Clause concerns trump Mr. Kennedy's free exercise and free speech rights. But the District now seeks to supply different reasoning for that result. Now, it says, it was justified in suppressing Mr. Kennedy's religious activity because otherwise it would have been guilty of coercing students to pray. And, the District says, coercing worship amounts to an Establishment Clause violation on anyone's account of the Clause's original meaning.

As it turns out, however, there is a pretty obvious reason why the Ninth Circuit did not adopt this theory in proceedings below: The evidence cannot sustain it. To be sure, this Court has long held that government may not, consistent with a historically sensitive understanding of the Establishment Clause, "make a religious observance compulsory." *Zorach* v. *Clauson*, 343 U. S. 306, 314 (1952). Government "may not coerce anyone to attend church," nor may it force citizens to engage in "a formal religious exercise," *Lee* v. *Weisman*, 505 U. S. 577, 589 (1992). No doubt, too, coercion along these lines was among the foremost hallmarks of religious establishments the framers sought to prohibit when they adopted the First Amendment. Members of this Court have sometimes disagreed on what exactly qualifies as impermissible coercion in light of the original meaning of the Establishment Clause. Compare *Lee*, 505 U. S., at 593, with *id.*, at 640–641 (Scalia, J., dissenting). But in this case Mr. Kennedy's private religious exercise did not come close to crossing any line one might imagine separating protected private expression from impermissible government coercion.

Begin with the District's own contemporaneous description of the facts. In its correspondence with Mr. Kennedy, the District never raised coercion concerns. To the contrary, the District conceded in a public 2015 document that there was "no evidence that students [were] directly coerced to pray with Kennedy." This is consistent with Mr. Kennedy's account too. He has repeatedly stated that he "never coerced, required, or asked any student to pray," and that he never "told any student that it was important that they participate in any religious activity."

Consider, too, the actual requests Mr. Kennedy made. The District did not discipline Mr. Kennedy for engaging in prayer while presenting locker-room speeches to students. That tradition predated Mr. Kennedy at the school. And he willingly ended it, as the District has acknowledged. He also willingly ended his practice of postgame religious talks with his team. The only prayer Mr. Kennedy sought to continue was the kind he had "started out doing" at the beginning of his tenure—the prayer he gave alone. He made clear that he could pray "while the kids were doing the fight song" and "take a knee by [him]self and give thanks and continue on." Mr. Kennedy even considered it "acceptable" to say his "prayer while the players were walking to the locker room" or "bus," and then catch up with his team.(proposing the team leave the field for the prayer). In short, Mr. Kennedy did not seek to direct any prayers to students or require anyone else to participate. His plan was to wait to pray until athletes were occupied, and he "told everybody" that's what he wished "to do." It was for three prayers of this sort alone in October 2015 that the District suspended him.

Naturally, Mr. Kennedy's proposal to pray quietly by himself on the field would have meant some people would have seen his religious exercise. Those close at hand might have heard him too. But learning how to tolerate speech or prayer of all kinds is "part of learning how to live in a pluralistic society," a trait of character essential to "a tolerant citizenry." This Court has long recognized as well that "secondary school students are mature enough . . . to understand that a school does not endorse," let alone coerce them to participate in, "speech that it merely permits on a nondiscriminatory basis." Of course, some will take offense to certain forms of speech or prayer they are sure to encounter in a society where those activities enjoy such robust constitutional protection. But "[o]ffense . . . does not equate to coercion."

The District responds that, as a coach, Mr. Kennedy "wielded enormous authority and influence over the students," and students might have felt compelled to pray alongside him. To support this argument, the District submits that, after Mr. Kennedy's suspension, a few parents told District employees that their sons had "participated in the team prayers only because they did not wish to separate themselves from the team."

This reply fails too. Not only does the District rely on hearsay to advance it. For all we can tell, the concerns the District says it heard from parents were occasioned by the locker-room prayers that predated Mr. Kennedy's tenure or his postgame religious talks, all of which he discontinued at the District's request. There is no indication in the record that anyone expressed any coercion concerns to the District about the quiet, postgame prayers that Mr. Kennedy asked to continue and that led to his suspension. Nor is there any record evidence that students felt pressured to participate in these prayers. To the contrary, and as we have seen, not a single Bremerton student joined Mr. Kennedy's quiet prayers following the three October 2015 games for which he was disciplined. On October 16, those students who joined Mr. Kennedy were " 'from the opposing team,' " and thus could not have "reasonably fear[ed]" that he would decrease their "playing time" or destroy their "opportunities" if they did not "participate," As for the other two relevant games, "no one joined" Mr. Kennedy on October 23. And only a few members of the public participated on October 26.

The absence of evidence of coercion in this record leaves the District to its final redoubt. Here, the District suggests that *any* visible religious conduct by a teacher or coach should be deemed—without more and as a matter of law—impermissibly coercive on students. In essence, the District asks us to adopt the view that the only acceptable government role models for students are those who eschew any visible religious expression. If the argument sounds familiar, it should. Really, it is just another way of repackaging the District's earlier submission that government may script everything a teacher or coach says in the workplace. The only added twist here is the District's suggestion not only that it *may* prohibit teachers from engaging in any demonstrative religious activity, but that it *must* do so in order to conform to the Constitution.

Such a rule would be a sure sign that our Establishment Clause jurisprudence had gone off the rails. In the name of protecting religious liberty, the District would have us suppress it. Rather than respect the First Amendment's double protection for religious expression, it would have us preference secular activity. Not only could schools fire teachers for praying quietly over their lunch, for wearing a yarmulke to school, or for offering a midday prayer during a break before practice. Under the

District's rule, a school would be *required* to do so. It is a rule that would defy this Court's traditional understanding that permitting private speech is not the same thing as coercing others to participate in it. It is a rule, too, that would undermine a long constitutional tradition under which learning how to tolerate diverse expressive activities has always been "part of learning how to live in a pluralistic society." We are aware of no historically sound understanding of the Establishment Clause that begins to "mak[e] it necessary for government to be hostile to religion" in this way.

[T]his case looks very different from those in which this Court has found prayer involving public school students to be problematically coercive. In *Lee*, this Court held that school officials violated the Establishment Clause by "including [a] clerical membe[r]" who publicly recited prayers "as part of [an] official school graduation ceremony" because the school had "in every practical sense compelled attendance and participation in" a "religious exercise." In *Santa Fe Independent School Dist.* v. *Doe*, the Court held that a school district violated the Establishment Clause by broadcasting a prayer "over the public address system" before each football game. The Court observed that, while students generally were not required to attend games, attendance *was* required for "cheerleaders, members of the band, and, of course, the team members themselves." None of that is true here. The prayers for which Mr. Kennedy was disciplined were not publicly broadcast or recited to a captive audience. Students were not required or expected to participate. And, in fact, none of Mr. Kennedy's students did participate in any of the three October 2015 prayers that resulted in Mr. Kennedy's discipline.

JUSTICE THOMAS, concurring. [omitted]

JUSTICE ALITO, concurring. [omitted]

JUSTICE SOTOMAYOR, with whom JUSTICE BREYER and JUSTICE KAGAN join, dissenting.

This case is about whether a public school must permit a school official to kneel, bow his head, and say a prayer at the center of a school event. The Constitution does not authorize, let alone require, public schools to embrace this conduct. Since *Engel* v. *Vitale*, this Court consistently has recognized that school officials leading prayer is constitutionally impermissible. Official-led prayer strikes at the core of our constitutional protections for the religious liberty of students and their parents, as embodied in both the Establishment Clause and the Free Exercise Clause of the First Amendment.

The Court now charts a different path, yet again paying almost exclusive attention to the Free Exercise Clause's protection for individual religious exercise while giving short shrift to the Establishment Clause's prohibition on state establishment of religion. To the degree the Court portrays petitioner Joseph Kennedy's prayers as private and quiet, it misconstrues the facts. The record reveals that Kennedy had a longstanding practice of conducting demonstrative prayers on the 50-yard line of the football field. Kennedy consistently invited others to join his prayers and for years led student athletes in prayer at the same time and location. The Court ignores this history. The Court also ignores the severe disruption to school events caused by Kennedy's conduct, viewing it as irrelevant because the Bremerton School District (District) stated that it was suspending Kennedy to avoid it being viewed as endorsing religion. Under the Court's analysis, presumably this would be a different case if the District had cited Kennedy's repeated disruptions of school programming and violations of school policy regarding public access to the field as grounds for suspending him. As the District did not articulate those grounds, the Court assesses only the District's Establishment Clause concerns. It errs by assessing them divorced from the context and history of Kennedy's prayer practice.

Today's decision goes beyond merely misreading the record. The Court overrules *Lemon* v. *Kurtzman*, 403 U. S. 602 (1971), and calls into question decades of subsequent precedents that it deems "offshoot[s]" of that decision. In the process, the Court rejects longstanding concerns surrounding government endorsement of religion and replaces the standard for reviewing such questions with a new "history and tradition" test. In addition, while the Court reaffirms that the Establishment Clause prohibits the government from coercing participation in religious exercise, it applies a nearly toothless version of the coercion analysis, failing to acknowledge the unique pressures faced by students when participating in school-sponsored activities. This decision does a disservice to schools and the young citizens they serve, as well as to our Nation's longstanding commitment to the separation of church and state. I respectfully dissent.

The Establishment Clause prohibits States from adopting laws "respecting an establishment of religion." The First Amendment's next Clause prohibits the government from making any law "prohibiting the free exercise thereof." Taken together, these two Clauses (the Religion Clauses) express the view, foundational to our constitutional system, "that religious beliefs and religious expression are too precious to be either proscribed or prescribed by the State. Instead, "preservation and transmission of religious beliefs and worship is a responsibility and a choice committed to the private sphere," which has the "freedom to pursue that mission."

The Establishment Clause protects this freedom by "command[ing] a separation of church and state. At its core, this means forbidding "sponsorship, financial support, and active involvement of the sovereign in religious activity." *Walz* v. *Tax Comm'n of City of New York*, 397 U. S. 664, 668 (1970). In the context of public schools, it means that a State cannot use "its public school system to aid any or all religious faiths or sects in the dissemination of their doctrines and ideals."

Indeed, "[t]he Court has been particularly vigilant in monitoring compliance with the Establishment Clause in elementary and secondary schools." The reasons motivating this vigilance inhere in the nature of schools themselves and the young people they serve. Two are relevant here.

First, government neutrality toward religion is particularly important in the public school context given the role public schools play in our society. " 'The public school is at once the symbol of our democracy and the most pervasive means for promoting our common destiny,' " meaning that " '[i]n no activity of the State is it more vital to keep out divisive forces than in its schools.' "Families "entrust public schools with the education of their children . . . on the understanding that the classroom will not purposely be used to advance religious views that may conflict with the private beliefs of the student and his or her family." Accordingly, the Establishment Clause "proscribes public schools from 'conveying or attempting to convey a message that religion or a particular religious belief is favored or preferred' " or otherwise endorsing religious beliefs.

Second, schools face a higher risk of unconstitutionally "coerc[ing] . . . support or participat[ion] in religion or its exercise" than other government entities. The State exercises that great authority over children, who are uniquely susceptible to "subtle coercive pressure." Cf. *Town of Greece* v. *Galloway*, 572 U. S. 565, 590 (2014)(plurality opinion)("[M]ature adults," unlike children, may not be " 'readily susceptible to religious indoctrination or peer pressure' "). Children are particularly vulnerable to coercion because of their "emulation of teachers as role models" and "susceptibility to peer pressure." Accordingly, this Court has emphasized that "the State may not, consistent with the Establishment Clause, place primary and secondary school children" in the dilemma of choosing between "participating, with all that implies, or protesting" a religious exercise in a public school.

Given the twin Establishment Clause concerns of endorsement and coercion, it is unsurprising that the Court has consistently held integrating prayer into public school activities to be unconstitutional, including when student participation is not a formal requirement or prayer is silent. The Court also has held that incorporating a nondenominational general benediction into a graduation ceremony is unconstitutional. Finally, this Court has held that including prayers in student football games is unconstitutional, even when delivered by students rather than staff and even when students themselves initiated the prayer.

Under these precedents, the Establishment Clause violation at hand is clear. This Court has held that a "[s]tate officia[l] direct[ing] the performance of a formal religious exercise" as a part of the "ceremon[y]" of a school event "conflicts with settled rules pertaining to prayer exercises for students." Kennedy was on the job as a school official "on government property" when he incorporated a public, demonstrative prayer into "government-sponsored school-related events" as a regularly scheduled feature of those events.

Kennedy's tradition of a 50-yard line prayer thus strikes at the heart of the Establishment Clause's concerns about endorsement. For students and community members at the game, Coach Kennedy was the face and the voice of the District during football games. The timing and location Kennedy selected for his prayers were "clothed in the traditional indicia of school sporting events." Kennedy spoke from the playing field, which was accessible only to students and school employees, not to the general public. Although the football game itself had ended, the football game events had not; Kennedy himself acknowledged that his responsibilities continued until the players went home. Kennedy's postgame responsibilities were what placed Kennedy on the 50-yard line in the first place; that was, after all, where he met the opposing team to shake hands after the game. Permitting a school coach to lead students and others he invited onto the field in prayer at a predictable time after each game could only be viewed as a postgame tradition occurring "with the approval of the school administration."

Kennedy's prayer practice also implicated the coercion concerns at the center of this Court's Establishment Clause jurisprudence. This Court has previously recognized a heightened potential for coercion where school officials are involved, as their "effort[s] to monitor prayer will be perceived by the students as inducing a participation they might otherwise reject." The reasons for fearing this pressure are self-evident. This Court has recognized that students face immense social pressure. Students look up to their teachers and coaches as role models and seek their approval. Students also depend on this approval for tangible benefits. Players recognize that gaining the coach's approval may pay dividends small and large, from extra playing time to a stronger letter of recommendation to additional support in college athletic recruiting. In addition to these pressures to please their coaches, this Court has recognized that players face "immense social pressure" from their peers in the "extracurricular event that is American high school football." *Santa Fe*, 530 U. S., at 311.

The record before the Court bears this out. The District Court found, in the evidentiary record, that some students reported joining Kennedy's prayer because they felt social pressure to follow their coach and teammates. Kennedy told the District that he began his prayers alone and that players followed each other over time until a majority of the team joined him, an evolution showing coercive pressure at work.

For decades, the Court has recognized that, in determining whether a school has violated the Establishment Clause, "one of the relevant questions is whether an objective observer, acquainted with the text, legislative history, and implementation of the [practice], would perceive it as a state endorsement of prayer in public schools." The Court now says for the first time that endorsement simply does not matter, and completely repudiates the test established in *Lemon*. Both of these moves are erroneous and, despite the Court's assurances, novel.

To put it plainly, the purposes and effects of a government action matter in evaluating whether that action violates the Establishment Clause, as numerous precedents beyond *Lemon* instruct in the particular context of public schools. Neither the critiques of *Lemon* as setting out a dispositive test for all seasons nor the fact that the Court has not referred to *Lemon* in all situations support this Court's decision to dismiss that precedent entirely, particularly in the school context.

Upon overruling one "grand unified theory," the Court introduces another: It holds that courts must interpret whether an Establishment Clause violation has occurred mainly "by 'reference to historical practices and understandings.'" Here again, the Court professes that nothing has changed. In fact, while the Court has long referred to historical practice as one element of the analysis in specific Establishment Clause cases, the Court has never announced this as a general test or exclusive focus.

The Court reserves any meaningful explanation of its history-and-tradition test for another day, content for now to disguise it as established law and move on. It should not escape notice, however, that the effects of the majority's new rule could be profound. The problems with elevating history and tradition over purpose and precedent are well documented. See *Dobbs* (Breyer, Sotomayor, and Kagan, JJ., dissenting)(explaining that the Framers "defined rights in general terms to permit future evolution in their scope and meaning"); *New York State Rifle & Pistol Assn., Inc.* v. *Bruen*, (Breyer, J., dissenting)(explaining the pitfalls of a "near-exclusive reliance on history" and offering examples of when this Court has "misread" history in the past).

For now, it suffices to say that the Court's history-and-tradition test offers essentially no guidance for school administrators.

COMMENTS AND QUESTIONS

1.   It is clear now that *Lemon* and its "endorsement" alternatives are dead. Lower courts now can freely ignore those tests in favor of the new test. What is the new test?

2.   In the *American Legion* case discussed in the comment preceding this case, Justice Kavanaugh in concurrence attempted to describe the "overarching principles" governing Establishment Clause questions. "If the challenged government practice is not coercive *and* if it (i) is rooted history and tradition; or (ii) treats religious people, organizations, speech, or activity equally to comparable secular people, organizations, speech, or activity; or (iii) represents a permissible legislative accommodation or exemption from a

generally applicable law, then there ordinarily is no Establishment Clause violation." That may be *his* test.

PROBLEM

After Thanksgiving a public elementary school erects in its foyer a conical evergreen tree to celebrate the winter season, which is officially denominated a "winter holiday tree." Students are invited to place ornaments they bring from home on the tree. As a result the tree is covered with miniature balls, five-pointed stars, angels, snowmen, reindeer, Santa Clauses, sleighs, bunnies, creches, antique automobiles, and plastic icicles. Virtually everyone in the school, adults and children, refers to the tree as a "Christmas tree." The parents of a Jewish first-grader are upset, because their child is disturbed and unhappy because he does not want to participate in this activity, and his non-participation has been noted and remarked upon by his peers. Moreover, he is disturbed to have to see the tree each day in the central entrance of the school. The parents come to you to assess their legal options.

C. FREE EXERCISE

The first case to raise a Free Exercise issue was *Reynolds v. United States*, 98 U.S. 145 (1878), which involved the prosecution of a Mormon for violating the federal law against bigamy in the territories. He raised a defense that the law was unconstitutional as applied to him because his polygamy was pursuant to a duty of his religion. The Court rejected his defense on the grounds that the original meaning of the free exercise of religion could not have included the practice of polygamy. Moreover, the Court noted that:

> Laws are made for the government of actions, and while they cannot interfere with mere religious belief and opinions, they may with practices. Suppose one believed that human sacrifices were a necessary part of religious worship, would it be seriously contended that the civil government under which he lived could not interfere to prevent a sacrifice?

In the 1940s there were a number of cases brought in which the religious practice involved proselytizing, and the Court's analysis was a mix of Free Speech and Free Exercise, usually finding in favor of protecting the speech. *See, e.g., Cantwell v. Connecticut*, 310 U.S. 296 (1940). It was not until 1963 that the Court first found conduct protected by the Free Exercise Clause alone.

In that case, *Sherbert v. Verner*, 374 U.S. 398 (1963), a Seventh Day Adventist was fired from her job for refusing to work on Saturday, the Sabbath Day of her faith. Unable to find other employment because of the same refusal, she applied for unemployment compensation, which was denied on the ground that she had, without good cause, failed to find suitable alternative employment. The Court made two major determinations. First, it found that the Free Exercise Clause was implicated not only by laws that proscribed some religious conduct but also by laws that denied a government benefit because of action mandated by a person's religious belief. By putting substantial pressure on an adherent to modify his behavior, the law burdened the free exercise of religion. Second, it held that such burdens were subject to strict scrutiny, requiring a compelling government interest that could not be otherwise achieved. The dissent argued that such a rule created a constitutional requirement for an exception to any otherwise unobjectionable, generally applicable rule that incidentally burdened some religion's beliefs or practices.

Sherbert was followed by two other unemployment compensation cases, *Thomas v. Review Board*, 450 U.S. 707 (1981), involving a Jehovah's Witness who was fired for refusing to work on fabricating tank turrets, because his religion would not allow him to work on armaments, and *Hobbie v. Unemployment Appeals Comm'n*, 480 U.S. 136 (1987), which was identical to *Sherbert* except that the employee came by her religion after having the job, rather than already being a member of the religion and being assigned to a new job, as in *Sherbert* and *Thomas*. In both cases, the Court reaffirmed *Sherbert* and found the denial of unemployment benefits unconstitutional for failing to satisfy strict scrutiny.

Despite this line of cases, with one exception, every other case raising Free Exercise claims was unsuccessful. In *Bowen v. Roy*, 476 U.S. 693 (1986), for example, Native American parents refused to obtain a Social Security number for their 2-year-old daughter, a condition of receiving welfare benefits, because under their religious beliefs it would "rob [her] spirit." The Court held that no exception need be made for her. Similarly, in *United States v. Lee*, 455 U.S. 252 (1982), an Old Order Amish employer refused to pay Social Security taxes because it was inconsistent with his religion's belief that families should take care of their own elderly. The Court found no basis in the Free Exercise Clause for requiring an exemption. *See also Braunfeld v. Brown*, 366 U.S. 599 (1961)(Sunday Closing Laws do not infringe the Free Exercise rights of those whose religion forbids them from working on Saturdays); *Jimmy Swaggart Ministries v. Board of Equalization*, 493 U.S. 378 (1990)(Free Exercise Clause did not prohibit the imposition of a sales tax on the sale of religious materials on the same basis as any other materials); *Bob Jones Univ. v. United States*, 461 U.S. 574 (1983)(IRS denial of tax exempt status to private school that discriminated on the basis of race because of sincerely held religious views did not violate the Free Exercise Clause); *Susan and Tony Alamo Foundation v. Sec. of Labor*, 47 U.S. 290 (1985)(Free Exercise Clause did not excuse failure to pay minimum wages to employees contrary to the beliefs of the religion); *Lyng v. Northwest Indian Cemetery Protective*

Ass'n, 485 U.S. 439 (1988)(building a road in a national forest did not violate the Free Exercise rights of Native Americans for whom the area was sacred); *Goldman v. Weinberger*, 475 U.S. 503 (1986)(Free Exercise Clause did not require an exception from military dress regulations for the wearing of yarmulkes); *O'Lone v. Estate of Shabazz*, 482 U.S. 342 (1987)(Free Exercise Clause did not require prison to excuse inmates from work requirements in order to attend worship services).

The one exception was *Wisconsin v. Yoder*, 406 U.S. 205 (1972). There Old Order Amish parents were prosecuted for violating the state's compulsory school attendance law, because they kept their 14- and 15-year-old children at home. Their defense was that further education conflicted with the Amish values and the Amish way of life; they view secondary school education as an impermissible exposure of their children to a "worldly" influence in conflict with their beliefs. High school tends to emphasize intellectual and scientific accomplishments, self-distinction, competitiveness, worldly success, and social life with other students. Amish society emphasizes informal learning-through-doing; a life of "goodness," rather than a life of intellect; wisdom, rather than technical knowledge; community welfare, rather than competition; and separation from, rather than integration with, contemporary worldly society. The Court held that the Free Exercise Clause required an exemption for the Amish in this circumstance.

The following case addressed these seemingly inconsistent results.

EMPLOYMENT DIVISION V. SMITH

United States Supreme Court, 1990.
494 U.S. 872, 110 S.Ct. 1595.

JUSTICE SCALIA delivered the opinion of the Court.

[Respondents Smith and Black were fired by a private drug rehabilitation organization because they ingested peyote, a hallucinogenic drug, for sacramental purposes at a ceremony of their Native American Church. Their applications for unemployment compensation were denied by the state of Oregon under a state law disqualifying employees discharged for work-related "misconduct." The state courts, using the analysis in *Sherbert v. Verner* held this was a violation of the applicants' First Amendment rights. The Supreme Court, however, held that *Sherbert* was not applicable when the underlying conduct for which the employee was fired was itself criminal activity. The Court, therefore, vacated the state court's judgment and remanded for a determination whether there was an exception in the state's controlled substance law, which made it a felony to possess peyote, when peyote was used for sacramental purposes. The Oregon Supreme Court held there was no such exception in the state law but then held that the state law violated the Free Exercise Clause.]

This case requires us to decide whether the Free Exercise Clause of the First Amendment permits the State of Oregon to include religiously inspired peyote use within the reach of its general criminal prohibition on use of that drug, and thus permits the State to deny unemployment benefits to persons dismissed from their jobs because of such religiously inspired use.

Oregon law prohibits the knowing or intentional possession of a "controlled substance" unless the substance has been prescribed by a medical practitioner. . . . Persons who violate this provision by possessing a controlled substance listed on Schedule I are "guilty of a Class B felony." As compiled by the State Board of Pharmacy, Schedule I contains the drug peyote, a hallucinogen derived from the plant *Lophophora williamsii Lemaire.*

Respondents Alfred Smith and Galen Black (hereinafter respondents) were fired from their jobs with a private drug rehabilitation organization because they ingested peyote for sacramental purposes at a ceremony of the Native American Church, of which both are members. When respondents applied to petitioner Employment Division (hereinafter petitioner) for unemployment compensation, they were determined to be ineligible for benefits because they had been discharged for work-related "misconduct."

Respondents' claim for relief rests on our decisions in *Sherbert v. Verner, Thomas v. Review Bd. of Indiana Employment Security Div.,* and *Hobbie v. Unemployment Appeals Comm'n of Florida,* in which we held that a State could not condition the availability of unemployment insurance on an individual's willingness to forgo conduct required by his religion. [H]owever, the conduct at issue in those cases was not prohibited by law. . . .

The Free Exercise Clause of the First Amendment, which has been made applicable to the States by incorporation into the Fourteenth Amendment provides that "Congress shall make no law respecting an establishment of religion, or *prohibiting the free exercise thereof. . . .*" . . .

But the "exercise of religion" often involves not only belief and profession but the performance of (or abstention from) physical acts: assembling with others for a worship service, participating in sacramental use of bread and wine, proselytizing, abstaining from certain foods or certain modes of transportation. It would be true, we think (though no case of ours has involved the point), that a State would be "prohibiting the free exercise [of religion]" if it sought to ban such acts or abstentions only when they are engaged in for religious reasons, or only because of the religious belief that they display. It would doubtless be unconstitutional, for example, to ban the casting of "statues that are to be used for worship purposes," or to prohibit bowing down before a golden calf.

Respondents in the present case, however, seek to carry the meaning of "prohibiting the free exercise [of religion]" one large step further. They contend that their religious motivation for using peyote places them beyond the reach of a criminal law that is not specifically directed at their religious practice, and that is concededly constitutional as applied to those who use the drug for other reasons. They assert, in other words, that "prohibiting the free exercise [of religion]" includes requiring any individual to observe a generally applicable law that requires (or forbids) the performance of an act that his religious belief forbids (or requires). As a textual matter, we do not think the words must be given that meaning. It is no more necessary to regard the collection of a general tax, for example, as "prohibiting the free exercise [of religion]" by those citizens who believe support of organized government to be sinful, than it is to regard the same tax as "abridging the freedom . . . of the press" of those publishing companies that must pay the tax as a condition of staying in business. It is a permissible reading of the text, in the one case as in the other, to say that if prohibiting the exercise of religion (or burdening the activity of printing) is not the object of the tax but merely the incidental effect of a generally applicable and otherwise valid provision, the First Amendment has not been offended.

Our decisions reveal that the latter reading is the correct one. We have never held that an individual's religious beliefs excuse him from compliance with an otherwise valid law prohibiting conduct that the State is free to regulate. On the contrary, the record of more than a century of our free exercise jurisprudence contradicts that proposition. . . . We first had occasion to assert that principle in *Reynolds v. United States,* where we rejected the claim that criminal laws against polygamy could not be constitutionally applied to those whose religion commanded the practice. . . . Subsequent decisions have consistently held that the right of free exercise does not relieve an individual of the obligation to comply with a "valid and neutral law of general applicability on the ground that the law proscribes (or prescribes) conduct that his religion prescribes (or proscribes)." . . .

The only decisions in which we have held that the First Amendment bars application of a neutral, generally applicable law to religiously motivated action have involved not the Free Exercise Clause alone, but the Free Exercise Clause in conjunction with other constitutional protections, such as freedom of speech and of the press, *see Cantwell v. Connecticut* (invalidating a licensing system for religious and charitable solicitations under which the administrator had discretion to deny a license to any cause he deemed nonreligious); *Wisconsin v. Yoder* (invalidating compulsory school-attendance laws as applied to Amish parents who refused on religious grounds to send their children to school).[1]

---

[1]   Yoder said that "the Court's holding in *Pierce v. Society of Sisters* stands as a charter of the rights of parents to direct the religious upbringing of their children. And, when the interests

The present case does not present such a hybrid situation, but a free exercise claim unconnected with any communicative activity or parental right. Respondents urge us to hold, quite simply, that when otherwise prohibitable conduct is accompanied by religious convictions, not only the convictions but the conduct itself must be free from governmental regulation. We have never held that, and decline to do so now. There being no contention that Oregon's drug law represents an attempt to regulate religious beliefs, the communication of religious beliefs, or the raising of one's children in those beliefs, the rule to which we have adhered ever since *Reynolds* plainly controls. . . .

Respondents argue that even though exemption from generally applicable criminal laws need not automatically be extended to religiously motivated actors, at least the claim for a religious exemption must be evaluated under the balancing test set forth in *Sherbert v. Verner*. Under the *Sherbert* test, governmental actions that substantially burden a religious practice must be justified by a compelling governmental interest. Applying that test we have, on three occasions, invalidated state unemployment compensation rules that conditioned the availability of benefits upon an applicant's willingness to work under conditions forbidden by his religion. We have never invalidated any governmental action on the basis of the *Sherbert* test except the denial of unemployment compensation. Although we have sometimes purported to apply the *Sherbert* test in contexts other than that, we have always found the test satisfied. . . .

Even if we were inclined to breathe into *Sherbert* some life beyond the unemployment compensation field, we would not apply it to require exemptions from a generally applicable criminal law. The *Sherbert* test, it must be recalled, was developed in a context that lent itself to individualized governmental assessment of the reasons for the relevant conduct. [O]ur decisions in the unemployment cases stand for the proposition that where the State has in place a system of individual exemptions, it may not refuse to extend that system to cases of "religious hardship" without compelling reason.

[A]lthough, as noted earlier, we have sometimes used the *Sherbert* test to analyze free exercise challenges to such laws, we have never applied the test to invalidate one. We conclude today that the sounder approach, and the approach in accord with the vast majority of our precedents, is to hold the test inapplicable to such challenges. . . . To make an individual's obligation to obey such a law contingent upon the law's coincidence with his religious beliefs, except where the State's interest is "compelling"—

---

of parenthood are combined with a free exercise claim of the nature revealed by this record, more than merely a 'reasonable relation to some purpose within the competency of the State' is required to sustain the validity of the State's requirement under the First Amendment."

permitting him, by virtue of his beliefs, "to become a law unto himself,"—contradicts both constitutional tradition and common sense. . . .[3]

Values that are protected against government interference through enshrinement in the Bill of Rights are not thereby banished from the political process. Just as a society that believes in the negative protection accorded to the press by the First Amendment is likely to enact laws that affirmatively foster the dissemination of the printed word, so also a society that believes in the negative protection accorded to religious belief can be expected to be solicitous of that value in its legislation as well. It is therefore not surprising that a number of States have made an exception to their drug laws for sacramental peyote use. But to say that a nondiscriminatory religious-practice exemption is permitted, or even that it is desirable, is not to say that it is constitutionally required, and that the appropriate occasions for its creation can be discerned by the courts. It may fairly be said that leaving accommodation to the political process will place at a relative disadvantage those religious practices that are not widely engaged in; but that unavoidable consequence of democratic government must be preferred to a system in which each conscience is a law unto itself or in which judges weigh the social importance of all laws against the centrality of all religious beliefs.

JUSTICE O'CONNOR, with whom JUSTICE BRENNAN, JUSTICE MARSHALL, and JUSTICE BLACKMUN join as to Parts I and II, concurring in the judgment.[*]

Although I agree with the result the Court reaches in this case, I cannot join its opinion. In my view, today's holding dramatically departs from well-settled First Amendment jurisprudence, appears unnecessary to resolve the question presented, and is incompatible with our Nation's fundamental commitment to individual religious liberty.

I

[omitted]

---

[3]   Justice O'CONNOR suggests that . . . all laws burdening religious practices should be subject to compelling-interest scrutiny because "the First Amendment unequivocally makes freedom of religion, like freedom from race discrimination and freedom of speech, a 'constitutional nor[m],' not an 'anomaly.'" But this comparison with other fields supports, rather than undermines, the conclusion we draw today. Just as we subject to the most exacting scrutiny laws that make classifications based on race, or on the content of speech, so too we strictly scrutinize governmental classifications based on religion. But we have held that race-neutral laws that have the effect of disproportionately disadvantaging a particular racial group do not thereby become subject to compelling-interest analysis under the Equal Protection Clause, and we have held that generally applicable laws unconcerned with regulating speech that have the effect of interfering with speech do not thereby become subject to compelling-interest analysis under the First Amendment. Our conclusion that generally applicable, religion-neutral laws that have the effect of burdening a particular religious practice need not be justified by a compelling governmental interest is the only approach compatible with these precedents.

[*]   Although Justice BRENNAN, Justice MARSHALL, and Justice BLACKMUN join Parts I and II of this opinion, they do not concur in the judgment.

II

The Court today extracts from our long history of free exercise precedents the single categorical rule that "if prohibiting the exercise of religion . . . is . . . merely the incidental effect of a generally applicable and otherwise valid provision, the First Amendment has not been offended." Indeed, the Court holds that where the law is a generally applicable criminal prohibition, our usual free exercise jurisprudence does not even apply. . . .

The Court today . . . interprets the [Free Exercise] Clause to permit the government to prohibit, without justification, conduct mandated by an individual's religious beliefs, so long as that prohibition is generally applicable. But a law that prohibits certain conduct—conduct that happens to be an act of worship for someone—manifestly does prohibit that person's free exercise of his religion. A person who is barred from engaging in religiously motivated conduct is barred from freely exercising his religion. . . . It is difficult to deny that a law that prohibits religiously motivated conduct, even if the law is generally applicable, does not at least implicate First Amendment concerns.

The Court responds that generally applicable laws are "one large step" removed from laws aimed at specific religious practices. The First Amendment, however, does not distinguish between laws that are generally applicable and laws that target particular religious practices. Indeed, few States would be so naive as to enact a law directly prohibiting or burdening a religious practice as such. Our free exercise cases have all concerned generally applicable laws that had the effect of significantly burdening a religious practice. If the First Amendment is to have any vitality, it ought not be construed to cover only the extreme and hypothetical situation in which a State directly targets a religious practice. . . .

To say that a person's right to free exercise has been burdened, of course, does not mean that he has an absolute right to engage in the conduct. Under our established First Amendment jurisprudence, we have recognized that the freedom to act, unlike the freedom to believe, cannot be absolute. Instead, we have respected both the First Amendment's express textual mandate and the governmental interest in regulation of conduct by requiring the government to justify any substantial burden on religiously motivated conduct by a compelling state interest and by means narrowly tailored to achieve that interest. . . .

The Court endeavors to escape from our decisions in *Cantwell* and *Yoder* by labeling them "hybrid" decisions, but there is no denying that both cases expressly relied on the Free Exercise Clause, and that we have consistently regarded those cases as part of the mainstream of our free exercise jurisprudence. Moreover, in each of the other cases cited by the Court to support its categorical rule, we rejected the particular constitutional claims before us only after carefully weighing the competing interests. That we rejected the free exercise claims in those cases hardly calls into question the applicability of First Amendment doctrine in the first place. Indeed, it is surely unusual to judge the vitality of a constitutional doctrine by looking to the win-loss record of the plaintiffs who happen to come before us. . . .

Once it has been shown that a government regulation or criminal prohibition burdens the free exercise of religion, we have consistently asked the government to demonstrate that unbending application of its regulation to the religious objector "is essential to accomplish an overriding governmental interest," or represents "the least restrictive means of achieving some compelling state interest." To me, the sounder approach— the approach more consistent with our role as judges to decide each case on its individual merits—is to apply this test in each case to determine whether the burden on the specific plaintiffs before us is constitutionally significant and whether the particular criminal interest asserted by the State before us is compelling. Even if, as an empirical matter, a government's criminal laws might usually serve a compelling interest in health, safety, or public order, the First Amendment at least requires a case-by-case determination of the question, sensitive to the facts of each particular claim. . . .

III

The Court's holding today not only misreads settled First Amendment precedent; it appears to be unnecessary to this case. I would reach the same result applying our established free exercise jurisprudence.

There is no dispute that Oregon's criminal prohibition of peyote places a severe burden on the ability of respondents to freely exercise their religion. Peyote is a sacrament of the Native American Church and is regarded as vital to respondents' ability to practice their religion. . . .

There is also no dispute that Oregon has a significant interest in enforcing laws that control the possession and use of controlled substances by its citizens. . . . [R]espondents do not seriously dispute that Oregon has a compelling interest in prohibiting the possession of peyote by its citizens.

Thus, the critical question in this case is whether exempting respondents from the State's general criminal prohibition "will unduly interfere with fulfillment of the governmental interest." Although the question is close, I would conclude that uniform application of Oregon's criminal prohibition is "essential to accomplish" its overriding interest in preventing the physical harm caused by the use of a Schedule I controlled substance. Oregon's criminal prohibition represents that State's judgment that the possession and use of controlled substances, even by only one person, is inherently harmful and dangerous. Because the health effects caused by the use of controlled substances exist regardless of the motivation of the user, the use of such substances, even for religious purposes, violates the very purpose of the laws that prohibit them. Moreover, in view of the societal interest in preventing trafficking in controlled substances, uniform application of the criminal prohibition at issue is essential to the effectiveness of Oregon's stated interest in preventing any possession of peyote.

For these reasons, I believe that granting a selective exemption in this case would seriously impair Oregon's compelling interest in prohibiting possession of peyote by its citizens. Under such circumstances, the Free Exercise Clause does not require the State to accommodate respondents' religiously motivated conduct. . . .

Accordingly, I concur in the judgment of the Court.

JUSTICE BLACKMUN, with whom JUSTICE BRENNAN and JUSTICE MARSHALL join, dissenting.

[I]n weighing the clear interest of respondents Smith and Black (hereinafter respondents) in the free exercise of their religion against Oregon's asserted interest in enforcing its drug laws, it is important to articulate in precise terms the state interest involved. It is not the State's broad interest in fighting the critical "war on drugs" that must be weighed against respondents' claim, but the State's narrow interest in refusing to make an exception for the religious, ceremonial use of peyote. . . .

The State's interest in enforcing its prohibition, in order to be sufficiently compelling to outweigh a free exercise claim, cannot be merely abstract or symbolic. The State cannot plausibly assert that unbending application of a criminal prohibition is essential to fulfill any compelling interest, if it does not, in fact, attempt to enforce that prohibition. In this case, the State actually has not evinced any concrete interest in enforcing its drug laws against religious users of peyote. Oregon has never sought to prosecute respondents, and does not claim that it has made significant enforcement efforts against other religious users of peyote. The State's asserted interest thus amounts only to the symbolic preservation of an unenforced prohibition. . . .

The State proclaims an interest in protecting the health and safety of its citizens from the dangers of unlawful drugs. It offers, however, no evidence that the religious use of peyote has ever harmed anyone. . . .

The fact that peyote is classified as a Schedule I controlled substance does not, by itself, show that any and all uses of peyote, in any circumstance, are inherently harmful and dangerous. The Federal Government, which created the classifications of unlawful drugs from which Oregon's drug laws are derived, apparently does not find peyote so dangerous as to preclude an exemption for religious use. . . .

The carefully circumscribed ritual context in which respondents used peyote is far removed from the irresponsible and unrestricted recreational use of unlawful drugs.[6] . . .

For these reasons, I conclude that Oregon's interest in enforcing its drug laws against religious use of peyote is not sufficiently compelling to outweigh respondents' right to the free exercise of their religion. Since the State could not constitutionally enforce its criminal prohibition against respondents, the interests underlying the State's drug laws cannot justify its denial of unemployment benefits. . . . The State of Oregon cannot, consistently with the Free Exercise Clause, deny respondents unemployment benefits.

COMMENTS AND QUESTIONS

1.   The Court, per Justice Scalia, cuts the Gordian knot of previous Free Exercise analysis by substituting a bright-line rule for the previous balancing involved in applying the so-called, but not really, strict scrutiny test. As you can see, it was a narrow victory on the Court, but interestingly it led to a political backlash. In response to *Smith*, Congress passed the Religious Freedom Restoration Act (RFRA), which prohibited federal, state, and local governments from substantially burdening a person's exercise of religion unless the government action is the least restrictive means to achieve a compelling government interest. In other words, Congress legislated the strict scrutiny test which the Court had said was not constitutionally required. In *City of Boerne v. Flores*, 521 U.S. 507 (1997), however, the Supreme Court held that it was beyond Congress's power to enact this law as to states and localities, but RFRA remains in effect as to the federal government. *See Gonzales v. O Centro Espirita Beneficente Uniao do Vegetal*, 546 U.S. 418 (2006). Congress responded to *City of Boerne* by passing the Religious Land Use and Institutionalized Persons Act (RLUIPA) pursuant to its Spending Clause and Commerce Clause powers. RLUIPA imposes a strict scrutiny requirement for any substantial burden on the exercise of religion either through local land use rules, such as zoning, or as to prisoners in state prisons or local jails. The courts have applied RFRA and RLUIPA according to their terms, that is, applying real strict scrutiny to the government restrictions. *See, e.g., Burwell v. Hobby Lobby Stores, Inc.*, 573 U.S. 682 (2014)(finding under RFRA that a requirement that employers provide health care insurance covering certain contraceptive methods could not be applied to a closely-held for-profit corporation whose owners had a religious objection to such contraceptive methods); *Holt v. Hobbs*, 574 U.S. 352 (2015)(finding that a prison prohibition on inmate beards violated RLUIPA with respect to an inmate whose religion required a beard of at least ½ inch).

---

[6]   In this respect, respondents' use of peyote seems closely analogous to the sacramental use of wine by the Roman Catholic Church. During Prohibition, the Federal Government exempted such use of wine from its general ban on possession and use of alcohol. . . .

2.   Justice O'Connor writes to preserve the strict scrutiny standard, but she concludes that the Oregon law criminalizing peyote with respect to its use by members of the Native American Church meets that test. What do you think? Is her application of strict scrutiny consistent with how strict scrutiny has been applied in racial discrimination cases under the Equal Protection Clause or content discrimination under the Free Speech Clause?

3.   Everyone on the Court agreed that courts should not be in the business of assessing the validity of any given religion, although some lower courts have engaged in such an assessment to determine if something is a sham religion invoked only to obtain privileges not available to others. *See, e.g., Theriault v. Silber,* 453 F.Supp. 254 (W.D. Tex. 1978)(prisoner created the Church of the New Song of which he was the high priest and invoked his Free Exercise rights to demand steak and wine for a holy dinner). Also, everyone on the Court agreed that courts can assess the sincerity of the person's religious beliefs.

CHURCH OF THE LUKUMI BABALU AYE, INC. v. CITY OF HIALEAH

United States Supreme Court, 1993.
508 U.S. 520, 113 S.Ct. 2217.

JUSTICE KENNEDY delivered the opinion of the Court, except as to Part II-A-2.*

I

This case involves practices of the Santeria religion, which originated in the 19th century. When hundreds of thousands of members of the Yoruba people were brought as slaves from western Africa to Cuba, their traditional African religion absorbed significant elements of Roman Catholicism. The resulting syncretion, or fusion, is Santeria, "the way of the saints." . . .

The Santeria faith teaches that every individual has a destiny from God, a destiny fulfilled with the aid and energy of [spirits called] *orishas.* The basis of the Santeria religion is the nurture of a personal relation with the *orishas,* and one of the principal forms of devotion is an animal sacrifice. . . .

According to Santeria teaching, the *orishas* are powerful but not immortal. They depend for survival on the sacrifice. Sacrifices are performed at birth, marriage, and death rites, for the cure of the sick, for the initiation of new members and priests, and during an annual celebration. Animals sacrificed in Santeria rituals include chickens, pigeons, doves, ducks, guinea pigs, goats, sheep, and turtles. The animals

---

*   THE CHIEF JUSTICE, Justice SCALIA, and Justice THOMAS join all but Part II-A-2 of this opinion. Justice WHITE joins all but Part II-A of this opinion. Justice SOUTER joins only Parts I, III, and IV of this opinion.

are killed by the cutting of the carotid arteries in the neck. The sacrificed animal is cooked and eaten, except after healing and death rituals. . . .

Petitioner Church of the Lukumi Babalu Aye, Inc. (Church), is a not-for-profit corporation organized under Florida law in 1973. The Church and its congregants practice the Santeria religion. . . . In April 1987, the Church leased land in the City of Hialeah, Florida, and announced plans to establish a house of worship as well as a school, cultural center, and museum. Pichardo[, the leader of the church,] indicated that the Church's goal was to bring the practice of the Santeria faith, including its ritual of animal sacrifice, into the open. . . .

The prospect of a Santeria church in their midst was distressing to many members of the Hialeah community, and the announcement of the plans to open a Santeria church in Hialeah prompted the city council to hold an emergency public session on June 9, 1987. . . .

First, the city council adopted Resolution 87–66, which noted the "concern" expressed by residents of the city "that certain religions may propose to engage in practices which are inconsistent with public morals, peace or safety," and declared that "[t]he City reiterates its commitment to a prohibition against any and all acts of any and all religious groups which are inconsistent with public morals, peace or safety." . . .

In September 1987, the city council adopted three substantive ordinances addressing the issue of religious animal sacrifice. . . .

Following enactment of these ordinances, the Church and Pichardo filed this action. . . .

II

The Free Exercise Clause of the First Amendment, which has been applied to the States through the Fourteenth Amendment, provides that "Congress shall make no law respecting an establishment of religion, or *prohibiting the free exercise thereof. . . .*" (Emphasis added). The city does not argue that Santeria is not a "religion" within the meaning of the First Amendment. Nor could it. Although the practice of animal sacrifice may seem abhorrent to some, "religious beliefs need not be acceptable, logical, consistent, or comprehensible to others in order to merit First Amendment protection." Neither the city nor the courts below, moreover, have questioned the sincerity of petitioners' professed desire to conduct animal sacrifices for religious reasons. We must consider petitioners' First Amendment claim.

In addressing the constitutional protection for free exercise of religion, our cases establish the general proposition that a law that is neutral and of general applicability need not be justified by a compelling governmental interest even if the law has the incidental effect of burdening a particular religious practice. *Employment Div., Dept. of Human Resources of Ore. v.*

Smith. Neutrality and general applicability are interrelated, and, as becomes apparent in this case, failure to satisfy one requirement is a likely indication that the other has not been satisfied. A law failing to satisfy these requirements must be justified by a compelling governmental interest and must be narrowly tailored to advance that interest. These ordinances fail to satisfy the *Smith* requirements. We begin by discussing neutrality.

A

[A]t a minimum, the protections of the Free Exercise Clause pertain if the law at issue discriminates against some or all religious beliefs or regulates or prohibits conduct because it is undertaken for religious reasons. . . .

1

Although a law targeting religious beliefs as such is never permissible, if the object of a law is to infringe upon or restrict practices because of their religious motivation, the law is not neutral, and it is invalid unless it is justified by a compelling interest and is narrowly tailored to advance that interest. There are, of course, many ways of demonstrating that the object or purpose of a law is the suppression of religion or religious conduct. To determine the object of a law, we must begin with its text, for the minimum requirement of neutrality is that a law not discriminate on its face. A law lacks facial neutrality if it refers to a religious practice without a secular meaning discernable from the language or context. Petitioners contend that three of the ordinances fail this test of facial neutrality because they use the words "sacrifice" and "ritual," words with strong religious connotations. We agree that these words are consistent with the claim of facial discrimination, but the argument is not conclusive. The words "sacrifice" and "ritual" have a religious origin, but current use admits also of secular meanings. . . .

We reject the contention advanced by the city that our inquiry must end with the text of the laws at issue. Facial neutrality is not determinative. The Free Exercise Clause, like the Establishment Clause, extends beyond facial discrimination. . . . Official action that targets religious conduct for distinctive treatment cannot be shielded by mere compliance with the requirement of facial neutrality. The Free Exercise Clause protects against governmental hostility which is masked, as well as overt. . . .

The record in this case compels the conclusion that suppression of the central element of the Santeria worship service was the object of the ordinances. First, though use of the words "sacrifice" and "ritual" does not compel a finding of improper targeting of the Santeria religion, the choice of these words is support for our conclusion. There are further respects in which the text of the city council's enactments discloses the improper attempt to target Santeria. Resolution 87–66, adopted June 9, 1987, recited that "residents and citizens of the City of Hialeah have expressed their concern that certain religions may propose to engage in practices which are inconsistent with public morals, peace or safety," and "reiterate[d]" the city's commitment to prohibit "any and all [such] acts of any and all religious groups." No one suggests, and on this record it cannot be maintained, that city officials had in mind a religion other than Santeria. . . .

It is a necessary conclusion that almost the only conduct subject to Ordinances 87–40, 87–52, and 87–71 is the religious exercise of Santeria church members. The texts show that they were drafted in tandem to achieve this result. . . .

The legitimate governmental interests in protecting the public health and preventing cruelty to animals could be addressed by restrictions stopping far short of a flat prohibition of all Santeria sacrificial practice. If improper disposal, not the sacrifice itself, is the harm to be prevented, the city could have imposed a general regulation on the disposal of organic garbage. It did not do so. . . . Thus, these broad ordinances prohibit Santeria sacrifice even when it does not threaten the city's interest in the public health. . . .

Under similar analysis, narrower regulation would achieve the city's interest in preventing cruelty to animals. With regard to the city's interest in ensuring the adequate care of animals, regulation of conditions and treatment, regardless of why an animal is kept, is the logical response to the city's concern, not a prohibition on possession for the purpose of sacrifice. The same is true for the city's interest in prohibiting cruel methods of killing. Under federal and Florida law and Ordinance 87–40, which incorporates Florida law in this regard, killing an animal by the "simultaneous and instantaneous severance of the carotid arteries with a sharp instrument"—the method used in kosher slaughter—is approved as humane. The District Court found that, though Santeria sacrifice also results in severance of the carotid arteries, the method used during sacrifice is less reliable and therefore not humane. If the city has a real concern that other methods are less humane, however, the subject of the regulation should be the method of slaughter itself, not a religious classification that is said to bear some general relation to it.

2

In determining if the object of a law is a neutral one under the Free Exercise Clause, we can also find guidance in our equal protection cases. Here, as in equal protection cases, we may determine the city council's object from both direct and circumstantial evidence. Relevant evidence includes, among other things, the historical background of the decision under challenge, the specific series of events leading to the enactment or official policy in question, and the legislative or administrative history, including contemporaneous statements made by members of the decisionmaking body. These objective factors bear on the question of discriminatory object.

That the ordinances were enacted " 'because of,' not merely 'in spite of,' " their suppression of Santeria religious practice is revealed by the events preceding their enactment. . . . The minutes and taped excerpts of the June 9 session, both of which are in the record, evidence significant hostility exhibited by residents, members of the city council, and other city officials toward the Santeria religion and its practice of animal sacrifice. The public crowd that attended the June 9 meetings interrupted statements by council members critical of Santeria with cheers and the brief comments of Pichardo with taunts. When Councilman Martinez, a supporter of the ordinances, stated that in prerevolution Cuba "people were put in jail for practicing this religion," the audience applauded. . . . The city attorney commented that Resolution 87–66 indicated: "This community will not tolerate religious practices which are abhorrent to its citizens. . . ." Similar comments were made by the deputy city attorney. This history discloses the object of the ordinances to target animal sacrifice by Santeria worshippers because of its religious motivation.

3

In sum, the neutrality inquiry leads to one conclusion: The ordinances had as their object the suppression of religion. The pattern we have recited discloses animosity to Santeria adherents and their religious practices; the ordinances by their own terms target this religious exercise; the texts of the ordinances were gerrymandered with care to proscribe religious killings of animals but to exclude almost all secular killings; and the ordinances suppress much more religious conduct than is necessary in order to achieve the legitimate ends asserted in their defense. These ordinances are not neutral, and the court below committed clear error in failing to reach this conclusion.

B

We turn next to a second requirement of the Free Exercise Clause, the rule that laws burdening religious practice must be of general applicability. *Employment Div., Dept. of Human Resources of Ore. v. Smith.* . . .

In this case we need not define with precision the standard used to evaluate whether a prohibition is of general application, for these ordinances fall well below the minimum standard necessary to protect First Amendment rights.

Respondent claims that Ordinances 87–40, 87–52, and 87–71 advance two interests: protecting the public health and preventing cruelty to animals. The ordinances are underinclusive for those ends. They fail to prohibit nonreligious conduct that endangers these interests in a similar or greater degree than Santeria sacrifice does. The underinclusion is substantial, not inconsequential. Despite the city's proffered interest in preventing cruelty to animals, the ordinances are drafted with care to forbid few killings but those occasioned by religious sacrifice. Many types of animal deaths or kills for nonreligious reasons are either not prohibited or approved by express provision. . . .

The ordinances are also underinclusive with regard to the city's interest in public health, which is threatened by the disposal of animal carcasses in open public places and the consumption of uninspected meat. Neither interest is pursued by respondent with regard to conduct that is not motivated by religious conviction. The health risks posed by the improper disposal of animal carcasses are the same whether Santeria sacrifice or some nonreligious killing preceded it. The city does not, however, prohibit hunters from bringing their kill to their houses, nor does it regulate disposal after their activity. . . .

We conclude, in sum, that each of Hialeah's ordinances pursues the city's governmental interests only against conduct motivated by religious belief. . . .

III

A law burdening religious practice that is not neutral or not of general application must undergo the most rigorous of scrutiny. . . . The compelling interest standard that we apply once a law fails to meet the *Smith* requirements is not "water[ed] . . . down" but "really means what it says." A law that targets religious conduct for distinctive treatment or advances legitimate governmental interests only against conduct with a religious motivation will survive strict scrutiny only in rare cases. It follows from what we have already said that these ordinances cannot withstand this scrutiny.

First, even were the governmental interests compelling, the ordinances are not drawn in narrow terms to accomplish those interests. . . .

Respondent has not demonstrated, moreover, that, in the context of these ordinances, its governmental interests are compelling. Where government restricts only conduct protected by the First Amendment and fails to enact feasible measures to restrict other conduct producing substantial harm or alleged harm of the same sort, the interest given in justification of the restriction is not compelling. . . .

JUSTICE SCALIA, with whom THE CHIEF JUSTICE joins, concurring in part and concurring in the judgment.

The Court analyzes the "neutrality" and the "general applicability" of the Hialeah ordinances in separate sections (Parts II-A and II-B, respectively), and allocates various invalidating factors to one or the other of those sections. If it were necessary to make a clear distinction between the two terms, I would draw a line somewhat different from the Court's. But I think it is not necessary, and would frankly acknowledge that the terms are not only "interrelated," but substantially overlap. . . .

Because I agree with most of the invalidating factors set forth in Part II of the Court's opinion, and because it seems to me a matter of no consequence under which rubric ("neutrality," Part II-A, or "general applicability," Part II-B) each invalidating factor is discussed, I join the judgment of the Court and all of its opinion except section 2 of Part II-A.

I do not join that section because it departs from the opinion's general focus on the object of the *laws* at issue to consider the subjective motivation of the *lawmakers, i.e.,* whether the Hialeah City Council actually *intended* to disfavor the religion of Santeria. As I have noted elsewhere, it is virtually impossible to determine the singular "motive" of a collective legislative body, and this Court has a long tradition of refraining from such inquiries, *see, e.g., United States v. O'Brien.* . . .

JUSTICE SOUTER, concurring in part and concurring in the judgment. [Justice Souter's concurring opinion indicated his disapproval of *Employment Div. v. Smith* and his willingness to reconsider it in an appropriate case.]

JUSTICE BLACKMUN, with whom JUSTICE O'CONNOR joins, concurring in the judgment. [Justice Blackmun likewise took this opportunity to express his continuing disagreement with *Employment Div. v. Smith* and accordingly would find the Hialeah ordinance unconstitutional using the pre-*Smith* analysis.]

COMMENTS AND QUESTIONS

1.   The case is unanimous in outcome but generates four opinions. What is Justice Scalia's disagreement with Justice Kennedy? With whom do you agree?

2.   This case seems relatively easy, and one might wonder why the Court's opinion is as long as it is, but it is the first Supreme Court case to apply *Employment Division v. Smith* to different facts and the first case to apply strict scrutiny under the Free Exercise Clause after *Smith.* Presumably, the Court wanted to provide some direction to lower courts. What part of its direction do you think is clear?

3.   When in the midst of the Covid-19 pandemic governors issued emergency orders closing down or restricting various businesses and gatherings, some churches sued, arguing that restricting the number of people allowed to congregate during church services violated the Free Exercise Clause. Two cases seeking temporary injunctions against emergency orders were brought before the Supreme Court. In *South Bay United Pentecostal Church v. Newsom*, 140 S.Ct. 1613 (2020)(mem.), the governor of California had restricted church services, lectures, concerts, movie showings, spectator

sports, and theatrical performances to 25% of building capacity or a maximum of 100 attendees whichever was less. However, no such restriction was placed on factories, offices, supermarkets, restaurants, retail stores, pharmacies, shopping malls, pet grooming shops, bookstores, florists, hair salons, and cannabis dispensaries. A majority of the Court declined the application for injunctive relief without opinion, although the Chief Justice penned a concurrence saying that the order did not discriminate against religious exercise, because it treated like gatherings, where large numbers of people would occupy a particular area for an extended period of time. Justice Kavanaugh, joined by Justices Thomas and Gorsuch, dissented. In his view, by not allowing church services to go forward so long as they took protective measures, such as masks and social distancing, the order discriminated against religious services compared to supermarkets and restaurants who had no occupancy restrictions if they took the required protective measures.

In *Calvary Chapel Dayton Valley v. Sisolak*, 140 S.Ct. 2603 (2020)(mem.), the governor of Nevada had issued an order generally prohibiting gatherings in groups of more than fifty people in any indoor or outdoor areas. Communities of worship and faith-based organizations were allowed to conduct in-person services so long as no more than fifty people were gathered, while respecting social distancing requirements, and movie theaters were similarly limited to a maximum of fifty people. However, casinos, bowling alleys, breweries, and fitness facilities were restricted to 50% of their capacity, which could be well in excess of fifty people. A church challenged the order as an abridgement of its free exercise of religion. Again, the Supreme Court denied the application for an injunction without opinion. This time Justice Alito joined the dissenters. He wrote, joined by Justices Thomas and Kavanaugh, arguing that this was discrimination against religion. Justice Gorsuch dissented separately in a short statement:

> This is a simple case. Under the Governor's edict, a 10-screen "multiplex" may host 500 moviegoers at any time. A casino, too, may cater to hundreds at once, with perhaps six people huddled at each craps table here and a similar number gathered around every roulette wheel there. Large numbers and close quarters are fine in such places. But churches, synagogues, and mosques are banned from admitting more than 50 worshippers—no matter how large the building, how distant the individuals, how many wear face masks, no matter the precautions at all. In Nevada, it seems, it is better to be in entertainment than religion. Maybe that is nothing new. But the First Amendment prohibits such obvious discrimination against the exercise of religion. The world we inhabit today, with a pandemic upon us, poses unusual challenges. But there is no world in which the Constitution permits Nevada to favor Caesars Palace over Calvary Chapel.

Both of these cases involved an attempt to obtain an injunction from the Supreme Court pending appeal of the merits case in the courts below, which is a relatively extraordinary action by the Court, as the Chief Justice noted in his concurrence in *South Bay*. Nevertheless, the cases, especially *Calvary Chapel*, raise the question what constitutes discrimination against religion. In *Calvary Chapel*, for example, churches were treated the same as several secular activities but worse than some others. That is, churches were not discriminated against in comparison to secular activities generally. However, they were treated worse than some secular activities. Is that enough to constitute discrimination against religion?

FULTON V. CITY OF PHILADELPHIA
United States Supreme Court, 2021.
141 S.Ct. 1868.

CHIEF JUSTICE ROBERTS delivered the opinion of the Court.

Catholic Social Services is a foster care agency in Philadelphia. The City stopped referring children to CSS upon discovering that the agency would not certify same-sex couples to be foster parents due to its religious beliefs about marriage. The City will renew its foster care contract with CSS only if the agency agrees to certify same-sex couples. The question presented is whether the actions of Philadelphia violate the First Amendment. . . .

The religious views of CSS inform its work in this system. CSS believes that "marriage is a sacred bond between a man and a woman." Because the agency understands the certification of prospective foster families to be an endorsement of their relationships, it will not certify unmarried couples—regardless of their sexual orientation—or same-sex married couples. CSS does not object to certifying gay or lesbian individuals as single foster parents or to placing gay and lesbian children. No same-sex couple has ever sought certification from CSS. If one did, CSS would direct the couple to one of the more than 20 other agencies in the City, all of which currently certify same-sex couples. For over 50 years, CSS successfully contracted with the City to provide foster care services while holding to these beliefs.

But things changed in 2018. [The Philadelphia Commission on Human Relations began an inquiry, and the Department of Human Services had a meeting with the leadership of CSS, after which the Department informed CSS that it would no longer refer children to the agency. The City later explained that the refusal of CSS to certify same-sex couples violated a non-discrimination provision in its contract with the City as well as the non-discrimination requirements of the citywide Fair Practices Ordinance. The City stated that it would not enter a full foster care contract with CSS in the future unless the agency agreed to certify same-sex couples.]

CSS and three foster parents affiliated with the agency filed suit. . . . CSS sought a temporary restraining order and preliminary injunction directing the Department to continue referring children to CSS without requiring the agency to certify same-sex couples.

The District Court denied preliminary relief. It concluded that the contractual non-discrimination requirement and the Fair Practices Ordinance were neutral and generally applicable under *Employment Division, Department of Human Resources of Oregon v. Smith*, and that the free exercise claim was therefore unlikely to succeed. . . .

The Court of Appeals for the Third Circuit affirmed. . . .

CSS and the foster parents sought review. They challenged the Third Circuit's determination that the City's actions were permissible under *Smith* and also asked this Court to reconsider that precedent. . . .

The Free Exercise Clause of the First Amendment, applicable to the States under the Fourteenth Amendment, provides that "Congress shall make no law . . . prohibiting the free exercise" of religion. As an initial matter, it is plain that the City's actions have burdened CSS's religious exercise by putting it to the choice of curtailing its mission or approving relationships inconsistent with its beliefs. The City disagrees. In its view, certification reflects only that foster parents satisfy the statutory criteria, not that the agency endorses their relationships. But CSS believes that certification is tantamount to endorsement. And "religious beliefs need not be acceptable, logical, consistent, or comprehensible to others in order to merit First Amendment protection." Our task is to decide whether the burden the City has placed on the religious exercise of CSS is constitutionally permissible.

Smith held that laws incidentally burdening religion are ordinarily not subject to strict scrutiny under the Free Exercise Clause so long as they are neutral and generally applicable. CSS urges us to overrule *Smith*, and the concurrences in the judgment argue in favor of doing so. But we need not revisit that decision here. This case falls outside *Smith* because the City has burdened the religious exercise of CSS through policies that do not meet the requirement of being neutral and generally applicable. . . .

A law is not generally applicable if it "invite[s]" the government to consider the particular reasons for a person's conduct by providing " 'a mechanism for individualized exemptions.' " *Smith*. For example, in *Sherbert v. Verner*, a Seventh-day Adventist was fired because she would not work on Saturdays. Unable to find a job that would allow her to keep the Sabbath as her faith required, she applied for unemployment benefits. The State denied her application under a law prohibiting eligibility to claimants who had "failed, without good cause . . . to accept available suitable work." We held that the denial infringed her free exercise rights and could be justified only by a compelling interest.

Smith later explained that the unemployment benefits law in *Sherbert* was not generally applicable because the "good cause" standard permitted the government to grant exemptions based on the circumstances underlying each application. *Smith* went on to hold that "where the State has in place a system of individual exemptions, it may not refuse to extend that system to cases of 'religious hardship' without compelling reason."

A law also lacks general applicability if it prohibits religious conduct while permitting secular conduct that undermines the government's asserted interests in a similar way. In *Church of Lukumi Babalu Aye, Inc. v. Hialeah*, for instance, the City of Hialeah adopted several ordinances prohibiting animal sacrifice, a practice of the Santeria faith. The City claimed that the ordinances were necessary in part to protect public health, which was "threatened by the disposal of animal carcasses in open public places." But the ordinances did not regulate hunters' disposal of their kills or improper garbage disposal by restaurants, both of which posed a similar hazard. The Court concluded that this and other forms of underinclusiveness meant that the ordinances were not generally applicable.

The City initially argued that CSS's practice violated section 3.21 of its standard foster care contract. We conclude, however, that this provision is not generally applicable as required by *Smith*. The current version of section 3.21 specifies in pertinent part:

"**Rejection of Referral**. Provider shall not reject a child or family including, but not limited to, . . . prospective foster or adoptive parents, for Services based upon . . . their . . . sexual orientation . . . unless an exception is granted by the Commissioner or the Commissioner's designee, in his/her sole discretion." . . .

Like the good cause provision in *Sherbert*, section 3.21 incorporates a system of individual exemptions, made available in this case at the "sole discretion" of the Commissioner. The City has made clear that the Commissioner "has no intention of granting an exception" to CSS. But the City "may not refuse to extend that [exemption] system to cases of 'religious hardship' without compelling reason." *Smith*. [T]he inclusion of a formal system of entirely discretionary exceptions in section 3.21 renders the contractual non-discrimination requirement not generally applicable. . . .

The concurrence protests that the "Court granted certiorari to decide whether to overrule [*Smith*]," and chides the Court for seeking to "sidestep the question." But the Court also granted review to decide whether Philadelphia's actions were permissible under our precedents. CSS has demonstrated that the City's actions are subject to "the most rigorous of scrutiny" under those precedents. Because the City's actions are therefore examined under the strictest scrutiny regardless of *Smith*, we have no occasion to reconsider that decision here.

A government policy can survive strict scrutiny only if it advances "interests of the highest order" and is narrowly tailored to achieve those interests. Put another way, so long as the government can achieve its interests in a manner that does not burden religion, it must do so.

The City asserts that its non-discrimination policies serve three compelling interests: maximizing the number of foster parents, protecting the City from liability, and ensuring equal treatment of prospective foster parents and foster children. The City states these objectives at a high level of generality, but the First Amendment demands a more precise analysis. Rather than rely on "broadly formulated interests," courts must "scrutinize[ ] the asserted harm of granting specific exemptions to particular religious claimants." The question, then, is not whether the City has a compelling interest in enforcing its non-discrimination policies generally, but whether it has such an interest in denying an exception to CSS.

Once properly narrowed, the City's asserted interests are insufficient. Maximizing the number of foster families and minimizing liability are important goals, but the City fails to show that granting CSS an exception will put those goals at risk. If anything, including CSS in the program seems likely to increase, not reduce, the number of available foster parents. As for liability, the City offers only speculation that it might be sued over CSS's certification practices. Such speculation is insufficient to satisfy strict scrutiny, particularly because the authority to certify foster families is delegated to agencies by the State, not the City.

That leaves the interest of the City in the equal treatment of prospective foster parents and foster children. We do not doubt that this interest is a weighty one, for "[o]ur society has come to the recognition that gay persons and gay couples cannot be treated as social outcasts or as inferior in dignity and worth." *Masterpiece Cakeshop*. On the facts of this case, however, this interest cannot justify denying CSS an exception for its religious exercise. The creation of a system of exceptions under the contract undermines the City's contention that its non-discrimination policies can brook no departures. The City offers no compelling reason why it has a particular interest in denying an exception to CSS while making them available to others.

The judgment of the United States Court of Appeals for the Third Circuit is reversed, and the case is remanded for further proceedings consistent with this opinion.

JUSTICE BARRETT, with whom JUSTICE KAVANAUGH joins, and with whom JUSTICE BREYER joins as to all but the first paragraph, concurring.

In *Employment Div., Dept. of Human Resources of Ore. v. Smith*, 494 U.S. 872 (1990), this Court held that a neutral and generally applicable law typically does not violate the Free Exercise Clause—no matter how severely that law burdens religious exercise. Petitioners, their *amici*, scholars, and Justices of this Court have made serious arguments that *Smith* ought to be overruled. While history looms large in this debate, I find the historical record more silent than supportive on the question whether the founding generation understood the First Amendment to

Amy Coney Barrett

In 2017 President Donald Trump appointed Barrett to the U.S. Court of Appeals for the Seventh Circuit. Prior to that she had been a professor at Notre Dame Law School, a lawyer in private practice, and a law clerk for Justice Antonin Scalia. A long time member of the Federalist Society, Judge Barrett was appointed to the Supreme Court by President Trump in 2020, replacing Justice Ruth Bader Ginsburg, who had recently passed away. The Senate confirmed her, with one exception, on a strictly party line vote, 52–48. Since her appointment, she has consistently voted with the conservative wing of the Court but has avoided taking strident positions.

require religious exemptions from generally applicable laws in at least some circumstances. In my view, the textual and structural arguments against *Smith* are more compelling. As a matter of text and structure, it is difficult to see why the Free Exercise Clause—lone among the First Amendment freedoms—offers nothing more than protection from discrimination.

Yet what should replace *Smith*? The prevailing assumption seems to be that strict scrutiny would apply whenever a neutral and generally applicable law burdens religious exercise. But I am skeptical about swapping *Smith*'s categorical antidiscrimination approach for an equally categorical strict scrutiny regime, particularly when this Court's resolution of conflicts between generally applicable laws and other First Amendment rights—like speech and assembly—has been much more nuanced. There would be a number of issues to work through if *Smith* were overruled. . . .

We need not wrestle with these questions in this case, though, because the same standard applies regardless whether *Smith* stays or goes. A longstanding tenet of our free exercise jurisprudence—one that both pre-dates and survives *Smith*—is that a law burdening religious exercise must satisfy strict scrutiny if it gives government officials discretion to grant individualized exemptions. As the Court's opinion today explains, the government contract at issue provides for individualized exemptions from its nondiscrimination rule, thus triggering strict scrutiny. And all nine Justices agree that the City cannot satisfy strict scrutiny. I therefore see no reason to decide in this case whether *Smith* should be overruled, much less what should replace it. I join the Court's opinion in full.

JUSTICE ALITO, with whom JUSTICE THOMAS and JUSTICE GORSUCH join, concurring in the judgment.

This case presents an important constitutional question that urgently calls out for review: whether this Court's governing interpretation of a bedrock constitutional right, the right to the free exercise of religion, is fundamentally wrong and should be corrected.

In *Employment Div., Dept. of Human Resources of Ore. v. Smith*, the Court abruptly pushed aside nearly 30 years of precedent and held that the First Amendment's Free Exercise Clause tolerates any rule that categorically prohibits or commands specified conduct so long as it does not target religious practice. Even if a rule serves no important purpose and has a devastating effect on religious freedom, the Constitution, according to *Smith*, provides no protection. This severe holding is ripe for reexamination.

There is no question that *Smith*'s interpretation can have startling consequences. Here are a few examples. Suppose that the Volstead Act, which implemented the Prohibition Amendment, had not contained an exception for sacramental wine. The Act would have been consistent with *Smith* even though it would have prevented the celebration of a Catholic Mass anywhere in the United States. Or suppose that a State, following the example of several European countries, made it unlawful to slaughter an animal that had not first been rendered unconscious. That law would be fine under *Smith* even though it would outlaw kosher and halal slaughter. Or suppose that a jurisdiction in this country, following the recommendations of medical associations in Europe, banned the circumcision of infants. A San Francisco ballot initiative in 2010 proposed just that. A categorical ban would be allowed by *Smith* even though it would prohibit an ancient and important Jewish and Muslim practice. Or suppose that this Court or some other court enforced a rigid rule prohibiting attorneys from wearing any form of head covering in court. The rule would satisfy *Smith* even though it would prevent Orthodox Jewish men, Sikh men, and many Muslim women from appearing. Many other examples could be added. . . .

We should reconsider *Smith* without further delay. The correct interpretation of the Free Exercise Clause is a question of great importance, and *Smith*'s interpretation is hard to defend. It can't be squared with the ordinary meaning of the text of the Free Exercise Clause or with the prevalent understanding of the scope of the free-exercise right at the time of the First Amendment's adoption. It swept aside decades of established precedent, and it has not aged well. Its interpretation has been undermined by subsequent scholarship on the original meaning of the Free Exercise Clause. Contrary to what many initially expected, *Smith* has not provided a clear-cut rule that is easy to apply, and experience has disproved the *Smith* majority's fear that retention of the Court's prior free-exercise jurisprudence would lead to "anarchy."

It is high time for us to take a fresh look at what the Free Exercise Clause demands. . . .

That project must begin with the constitutional text. . . .

[W]e should begin by considering the "normal and ordinary" meaning of the text of the Free Exercise Clause: "Congress shall make no law . . .

prohibiting the free exercise [of religion]." Most of these terms and phrases—"Congress," "shall make," "no law," and "religion"—do not require discussion for present purposes, and we can therefore focus on what remains: the term "prohibiting" and the phrase "the free exercise of religion."

Those words had essentially the same meaning in 1791 as they do today. "To prohibit" meant either "[t]o forbid" or "to hinder." 2 S. Johnson, A Dictionary of the English Language (1755). The term "exercise" had both a broad primary definition ("[p]ractice" or "outward performance") and a narrower secondary one (an "[a]ct of divine worship whether publick or private"). (The Court long ago declined to give the First Amendment's reference to "exercise" this narrow reading. See, *e.g., Cantwell v. Connecticut*.) And "free," in the sense relevant here, meant "unrestrained." 1 Johnson (1755).

If we put these definitions together, the ordinary meaning of "prohibiting the free exercise of religion" was (and still is) forbidding or hindering unrestrained religious practices or worship. That straightforward understanding is a far cry from the interpretation adopted in *Smith*. It certainly does not suggest a distinction between laws that are generally applicable and laws that are targeted.

As interpreted in *Smith*, the Clause is essentially an anti-discrimination provision: It means that the Federal Government and the States cannot restrict conduct that constitutes a religious practice for some people unless it imposes the same restriction on everyone else who engages in the same conduct. *Smith* made no real attempt to square that equal-treatment interpretation with the ordinary meaning of the Free Exercise Clause's language, and it is hard to see how that could be done. . . .

While we presume that the words of the Constitution carry their ordinary and normal meaning, we cannot disregard the possibility that some of the terms in the Free Exercise Clause had a special meaning that was well understood at the time. . . .

[W]e must ask whether the Free Exercise Clause protects a right that was known at the time of adoption to have defined dimensions. But in doing so, we must keep in mind that there is a presumption that the words of the Constitution are to be interpreted in accordance with their "normal and ordinary" sense. Anyone advocating a different reading must overcome that presumption.

What was the free-exercise right understood to mean when the Bill of Rights was ratified? And in particular, was it clearly understood that the right simply required equal treatment for religious and secular conduct?

[When the First Amendment was adopted,] the right to religious liberty already had a long, rich, and complex history in this country. . . . [B]y 1789, every State except Connecticut had a constitutional provision protecting religious liberty. . . . In all of those State Constitutions, freedom of religion enjoyed broad protection, and the right "was universally said to be an unalienable right."

[T]hese state constitutional provisions provide the best evidence of the scope of the right embodied in the First Amendment.

When we look at these provisions, we see one predominant model. This model extends broad protection for religious liberty but expressly provides that the right does not protect conduct that would endanger "the public peace" or "safety." . . .

That the free-exercise right included the right to certain religious exemptions is strongly supported by the practice of the Colonies and States. When there were important clashes between generally applicable laws and the religious practices of particular groups, colonial and state legislatures were willing to grant exemptions—even when the generally applicable laws served critical state interests.

Oath exemptions are illustrative. Oath requirements were considered "indispensable" to civil society because they were thought to ensure that individuals gave truthful testimony and fulfilled commitments. Quakers and members of some other religious groups refused to take oaths, and therefore a categorical oath requirement would have resulted in the complete exclusion of these Americans from important civic activities, such as testifying in court and voting. . . . By 1789, almost all States had passed oath exemptions. . . .

Military conscription provides an even more revealing example. In the Colonies and later in the States, able-bodied men of a certain age were required to serve in the militia, but Quakers, Mennonites, and members of some other religious groups objected to militia service on religious grounds. The militia was regarded as essential to the security of the State and the preservation of freedom, but colonial governments nevertheless granted religious exemptions. . . .

In an effort to dismiss the significance of these legislative exemptions, it has been argued that they show only what the Constitution permits, not what it requires. But legislatures provided those accommodations before the concept of judicial review took hold, and their actions are therefore strong evidence of the founding era's understanding of the free-exercise right. . . .

In sum, based on the text of the Free Exercise Clause and evidence about the original understanding of the free-exercise right, the case for *Smith* fails to overcome the more natural reading of the text. Indeed, the case against *Smith* is very convincing.

That conclusion cannot end our analysis. "We will not overturn a past decision unless there are strong grounds for doing so," but at the same time, *stare decisis* is "not an inexorable command." It "is at its weakest when we interpret the Constitution because our interpretation can be altered only by constitutional amendment or by overruling our prior decisions.

In assessing whether to overrule a past decision that appears to be incorrect, we have considered a variety of factors, and four of those weigh strongly against *Smith*: its reasoning; its consistency with other decisions; the workability of the rule that it established; and developments since the decision was handed down. No relevant factor, including reliance, weighs in *Smith*'s favor. . . .

To determine whether a law provides equal treatment for secular and religious conduct, two steps are required. First, a court must identify the secular conduct with which the religious conduct is to be compared. Second, the court must determine whether the State's reasons for regulating the religious conduct apply with equal force to the secular conduct with which it is compared. . . .

Much of *Smith*'s initial appeal was likely its apparent simplicity. *Smith* seemed to offer a relatively simple and clear-cut rule that would be easy to apply. Experience has shown otherwise. . . .

Multiple factors strongly favor overruling *Smith*. Are there countervailing factors?

None is apparent. Reliance is often the strongest factor favoring the retention of a challenged precedent, but no strong reliance interests are cited in any of the numerous briefs urging us to preserve *Smith*. Indeed, the term is rarely even mentioned. . . .

Smith was wrongly decided. As long as it remains on the books, it threatens a fundamental freedom. And while precedent should not lightly be cast aside, the Court's error in *Smith* should now be corrected.

If *Smith* is overruled, what legal standard should be applied in this case? The answer that comes most readily to mind is the standard that *Smith* replaced: A law that imposes a substantial burden on religious exercise can be sustained only if it is narrowly tailored to serve a compelling government interest. . . .

For all these reasons, I would overrule *Smith* and reverse the decision below. Philadelphia's exclusion of CSS from foster care work violates the Free Exercise Clause, and CSS is therefore entitled to an injunction barring Philadelphia from taking such action.

After receiving more than 2,500 pages of briefing and after more than a half-year of post-argument cogitation, the Court has emitted a wisp of a decision that leaves religious liberty in a confused and vulnerable state. Those who count on this Court to stand up for the First Amendment have every right to be disappointed—as am I.

JUSTICE GORSUCH, with whom JUSTICE THOMAS and JUSTICE ALITO join, concurring in the judgment. [omitted. Justice Gorsuch argued that the Philadelphia requirement does not in fact trigger the exemption exception from *Smith*, because Section 3.21 does not apply to certifying organizations as foster care agencies, and other provisions of state and local law, which do not provide any exemptions, effectively prohibited the certification of CSS. Therefore, it was necessary to address the validity of *Smith*.]

COMMENTS AND QUESTIONS

1.   Justices Alito and Gorsuch separately argue that the Court went to great lengths to avoid addressing *Smith*, even though a majority of the members of the Court have at one time or another called for *Smith* to be re-examined. Presumably, Justice Barrett's concurring opinion is intended to respond to that claim. Are you convinced?

2.   Justice Alito's opinion concurring in the judgment has been radically edited here, especially by deleting examples and citations for many of his assertions. Those interested are invited to read the entire text, which, whether one agrees with it or not, is impressive in its breadth and depth. His opinion is six times longer than the Chief Justice's opinion for the Court, and one might expect it to constitute the Court's opinion in the not distant future.

3.   Historically, it was the liberal justices who called for greater protection of free exercise, because it was the minority religions, such as Jehovah's Witnesses and Seventh Day Adventists, and their members who suffered for their beliefs. Today it is primarily the conservative justices who are pushing religious freedom the strongest, but in cases involving mainstream religions such as Baptists and Catholics.

4.   If *Smith* is overruled, would religiously based polygamy become protected? How would you apply the test Justice Alito says would be in effect?

5.   Earlier under the Expressive Conduct and the Right Not to Speak sections of the First Amendment—Free Speech chapter, *Masterpiece Cakeshop, Ltd. v. Colorado Civil Rights Comm'n*, 138 S.Ct. 1719 (2018), was discussed. That case involved the Colorado baker who would not make a custom wedding cake for a same-sex wedding. Although the baker raised both Free Speech and Free Exercise objections to the decision of the state commission that found him in violation of the state antidiscrimination provision, the Court only addressed the Free Exercise claim. The court below had relied on *Smith v. Employment Division* and said that the Colorado law was a neutral, generally applicable law, so it did not raise a valid Free Exercise claim. The Supreme Court reversed and remanded, finding that the state commission had evidenced anti-religious bias in its decision finding against the baker, consequently this was a case of discrimination against a person's exercise of religion, not a *Smith v. Employment Division* case. The facts which the Court relied upon to find anti-religious bias were rather unique and unlikely to be repeated, but cases like *Masterpiece Cakeshop* are arising with some frequency, and as this chapter is being written, the Supreme Court has heard oral argument in *303 Creative v.*

Elenis. That case involves a woman who designs wedding websites, but who because of her religious beliefs will not design websites for same sex weddings. The Colorado anti-discrimination law, however, would prohibit her from denying her services with regard to same sex weddings. The designer argues that the Colorado law violates her rights under the Free Speech and Free Exercise clauses. The Court could use this opportunity to reconsider *Smith*, but the designer also argues that *Smith* is not applicable, because the Colorado law provides for exceptions for secular reasons but not religious reasons, citing *Fulton*.

HOSANNA-TABOR EVANGELICAL LUTHERAN CHURCH AND SCHOOL V. EQUAL EMPLOYMENT OPPORTUNITY COMMISSION

United States Supreme Court, 2012.
565 U.S. 171, 132 S.Ct. 694.

CHIEF JUSTICE ROBERTS delivered the opinion of the Court.

Certain employment discrimination laws authorize employees who have been wrongfully terminated to sue their employers for reinstatement and damages. The question presented is whether the Establishment and Free Exercise Clauses of the First Amendment bar such an action when the employer is a religious group and the employee is one of the group's ministers.

Petitioner Hosanna-Tabor Evangelical Lutheran Church and School is a member congregation of the Lutheran Church-Missouri Synod, the second largest Lutheran denomination in America. Hosanna-Tabor operated a small school in Redford, Michigan, offering a "Christ-centered education" to students in kindergarten through eighth grade. . . .

Respondent Cheryl Perich was first employed by Hosanna-Tabor as a lay teacher in 1999. After Perich completed her colloquy later that school year, Hosanna-Tabor asked her to become a called teacher. Perich accepted the call and received a "diploma of vocation" designating her a commissioned minister. . . .

Perich became ill in June 2004 with what was eventually diagnosed as narcolepsy. . . .

On January 30, Hosanna-Tabor held a meeting of its congregation at which school administrators stated that Perich was unlikely to be physically capable of returning to work that school year or the next. The congregation voted to offer Perich a "peaceful release" from her call, whereby the congregation would pay a portion of her health insurance premiums in exchange for her resignation as a called teacher. Perich refused to resign and produced a note from her doctor stating that she would be able to return to work on February 22. The school board urged Perich to reconsider, informing her that the school no longer had a position for her, but Perich stood by her decision not to resign. . . . Perich responded that she had spoken with an attorney and intended to assert her legal rights. . . . [B]oard chairman Scott Salo sent Perich a letter . . . advising Perich that the congregation would consider whether to rescind her call at its next meeting. As grounds for termination, the letter cited . . . the damage she had done to her "working relationship" with the school by "threatening to take legal action." The congregation voted to rescind Perich's call on April 10, and Hosanna-Tabor sent her a letter of termination the next day.

Perich filed a charge with the Equal Employment Opportunity Commission, alleging that her employment had been terminated in violation of the Americans with Disabilities Act. The ADA prohibits an employer from discriminating against a qualified individual on the basis of disability.[1]

The EEOC brought suit against Hosanna-Tabor, alleging that Perich had been fired in retaliation for threatening to file an ADA lawsuit. Perich intervened in the litigation. . . .

Hosanna-Tabor moved for summary judgment. Invoking what is known as the "ministerial exception," the Church argued that the suit was barred by the First Amendment because the claims at issue concerned the employment relationship between a religious institution and one of its ministers. According to the Church, Perich was a minister, and she had been fired for a religious reason—namely, that her threat to sue the Church violated the Synod's belief that Christians should resolve their disputes internally. . . .

Given [our] understanding of the Religion Clauses—and the absence of government employment regulation generally—it was some time before questions about government interference with a church's ability to select its own ministers came before the courts. This Court touched upon the issue indirectly, however, in the context of disputes over church property. Our decisions in that area confirm that it is impermissible for the government to contradict a church's determination of who can act as its ministers. . . .

Until today, we have not had occasion to consider whether this freedom of a religious organization to select its ministers is implicated by a suit alleging discrimination in employment. The Courts of Appeals, in contrast, have had extensive experience with this issue. Since the passage of Title VII of the Civil Rights Act of 1964, and other employment discrimination

---

[1]　The ADA itself provides religious entities with two defenses to claims of discrimination. . . . The first provides that "[t]his subchapter shall not prohibit a religious corporation, association, educational institution, or society from giving preference in employment to individuals of a particular religion to perform work connected with the carrying on by such [entity] of its activities." The second provides that "[u]nder this subchapter, a religious organization may require that all applicants and employees conform to the religious tenets of such organization." . . . The EEOC and Perich contend, and Hosanna-Tabor does not dispute, that these defenses therefore do not apply to retaliation claims.

laws, the Courts of Appeals have uniformly recognized the existence of a "ministerial exception," grounded in the First Amendment, that precludes application of such legislation to claims concerning the employment relationship between a religious institution and its ministers.

We agree that there is such a ministerial exception. The members of a religious group put their faith in the hands of their ministers. Requiring a church to accept or retain an unwanted minister, or punishing a church for failing to do so, intrudes upon more than a mere employment decision. Such action interferes with the internal governance of the church, depriving the church of control over the selection of those who will personify its beliefs. By imposing an unwanted minister, the state infringes the Free Exercise Clause, which protects a religious group's right to shape its own faith and mission through its appointments. According the state the power to determine which individuals will minister to the faithful also violates the Establishment Clause, which prohibits government involvement in such ecclesiastical decisions.

The EEOC and Perich acknowledge that employment discrimination laws would be unconstitutional as applied to religious groups in certain circumstances. They grant, for example, that it would violate the First Amendment for courts to apply such laws to compel the ordination of women by the Catholic Church or by an Orthodox Jewish seminary. According to the EEOC and Perich, religious organizations could successfully defend against employment discrimination claims in those circumstances by invoking the constitutional right to freedom of association—a right "implicit" in the First Amendment. The EEOC and Perich thus see no need—and no basis—for a special rule for ministers grounded in the Religion Clauses themselves.

We find this position untenable. The right to freedom of association is a right enjoyed by religious and secular groups alike. It follows under the EEOC's and Perich's view that the First Amendment analysis should be the same, whether the association in question is the Lutheran Church, a labor union, or a social club. That result is hard to square with the text of the First Amendment itself, which gives special solicitude to the rights of religious organizations. We cannot accept the remarkable view that the Religion Clauses have nothing to say about a religious organization's freedom to select its own ministers.

The EEOC and Perich also contend that our decision in *Employment Div., Dept. of Human Resources of Ore. v. Smith* precludes recognition of a ministerial exception. . . .

It is true that the ADA's prohibition on retaliation, like Oregon's prohibition on peyote use, is a valid and neutral law of general applicability. But a church's selection of its ministers is unlike an individual's ingestion of peyote. *Smith* involved government regulation of only outward physical acts. The present case, in contrast, concerns government interference with an internal church decision that affects the faith and mission of the church itself. The contention that *Smith* forecloses recognition of a ministerial exception rooted in the Religion Clauses has no merit.

Having concluded that there is a ministerial exception grounded in the Religion Clauses of the First Amendment, we consider whether the exception applies in this case. We hold that it does. . . .

To begin with, Hosanna-Tabor held Perich out as a minister, with a role distinct from that of most of its members. When Hosanna-Tabor extended her a call, it issued her a "diploma of vocation" according her the title "Minister of Religion, Commissioned." . . .

Perich's title as a minister reflected a significant degree of religious training followed by a formal process of commissioning. . . .

Perich held herself out as a minister of the Church by accepting the formal call to religious service, according to its terms. She did so in other ways as well. For example, she claimed a special housing allowance on her taxes that was available only to employees earning their compensation " 'in the exercise of the ministry.' ". . .

Perich's job duties reflected a role in conveying the Church's message and carrying out its mission. Hosanna-Tabor expressly charged her with "lead[ing] others toward Christian maturity" and "teach[ing] faithfully the Word of God, the Sacred Scriptures, in its truth and purity and as set forth in all the symbolical books of the Evangelical Lutheran Church." . . .

In light of these considerations—the formal title given Perich by the Church, the substance reflected in that title, her own use of that title, and the important religious functions she performed for the Church—we conclude that Perich was a minister covered by the ministerial exception. . . .

The EEOC and Perich suggest that Hosanna-Tabor's asserted religious reason for firing Perich—that she violated the Synod's commitment to internal dispute resolution—was pretextual. That suggestion misses the point of the ministerial exception. The purpose of the exception is not to safeguard a church's decision to fire a minister only when it is made for a religious reason. The exception instead ensures that the authority to select and control who will minister to the faithful—a matter "strictly ecclesiastical"—is the church's alone. . . .

JUSTICE THOMAS, concurring.

I join the Court's opinion. I write separately to note that, in my view, the Religion Clauses require civil courts to apply the ministerial exception and to defer to a religious organization's good-faith understanding of who qualifies as its minister. As the Court explains, the Religion Clauses guarantee religious organizations autonomy in matters of internal governance, including the selection of those who will minister the faith. A religious organization's right to choose its ministers would be hollow, however, if secular courts could second-guess the organization's sincere determination that a given employee is a "minister" under the organization's theological tenets. Our country's religious landscape includes organizations with different leadership structures and doctrines that influence their conceptions of ministerial status. The question whether an employee is a minister is itself religious in nature, and the answer will vary widely. Judicial attempts to fashion a civil definition of "minister" through a bright-line test or multi-factor analysis risk disadvantaging those religious groups whose beliefs, practices, and membership are outside of the "mainstream" or unpalatable to some. . . .

The Court thoroughly sets forth the facts that lead to its conclusion that Cheryl Perich was one of Hosanna-Tabor's ministers, and I agree that these facts amply demonstrate Perich's ministerial role. But the evidence demonstrates that Hosanna-Tabor sincerely considered Perich a minister. That would be sufficient for me to conclude that Perich's suit is properly barred by the ministerial exception.

JUSTICE ALITO, with whom JUSTICE KAGAN joins, concurring.

I join the Court's opinion, but I write separately to clarify my understanding of the significance of formal ordination and designation as a "minister" in determining whether an "employee" of a religious group falls within the so-called "ministerial" exception. . . . Because virtually every religion in the world is represented in the population of the United States, it would be a mistake if the term "minister" or the concept of ordination were viewed as central to the important issue of religious autonomy that is presented in cases like this one. Instead, courts should focus on the function performed by persons who work for religious bodies. . . .

The First Amendment protects the freedom of religious groups to engage in certain key religious activities, including the conducting of worship services and other religious ceremonies and rituals, as well as the critical process of communicating the faith. Accordingly, religious groups must be free to choose the personnel who are essential to the performance of these functions.

The "ministerial" exception should be tailored to this purpose. It should apply to any "employee" who leads a religious organization, conducts worship services or important religious ceremonies or rituals, or serves as a messenger or teacher of its faith. If a religious group believes that the ability of such an employee to perform these key functions has been compromised, then the constitutional guarantee of religious freedom protects the group's right to remove the employee from his or her position. . . .

COMMENTS AND QUESTIONS

1.   Note that the Court nowhere mentions strict scrutiny. Why is there not an argument that the government has a "compelling government interest" in prohibiting discrimination in employment against the disabled that can only be achieved by prohibiting it? Of course, if such a compelling government interest trumped the church school's interests here, would there be any way to exempt churches that do not allow women to be ministers from the law prohibiting sex discrimination in employment?

2.   Consider the different approaches suggested by the Court and the concurring opinions for how to determine who is a "minister." Which do you think is the best approach?

3.   Eight years later the Court was again faced with the question: who qualifies for the ministerial exception? *Our Lady of Guadalupe School v. Morrisey-Berru*, 140 S.Ct. 2049 (2020), involved two elementary school teachers at Catholic schools who challenged their termination under federal anti-discrimination laws. The Court acknowledged that these teachers did not have the title "minister" and had less religious training than the person in *Hosanna-Tabor*, but nevertheless found their terminations to be exempt from the federal law under the ministerial exception. In reaching this conclusion, Justice Alito, writing for the Court, relied on the fact that the teachers were required to "promote a Catholic School Faith Community," " 'model and promote' Catholic 'faith and morals,' " and to teach religion in their classes in accordance with Catholic theology. He noted that in *Hosanna-Tabor* the Court had not relied solely on the basis that the person was deemed a "minister" by the religious school but considered a number of factors, including that her job involved "conveying the Church's message and carrying out its mission." Justice Thomas, joined by Justice Gorsuch, reiterated his position that courts should defer to the religious entities as to whether any particular person is a "minister" for purposes of the ministerial exception. Justice Sotomayor, joined by Justice Ginsburg, dissented, arguing that the ministerial exception should be reserved for those who are religious leaders, not extended to run-of-the-mill elementary school teachers who also happen to teach religion according to set guidelines.

D. CONFLICTS BETWEEN THE CLAUSES

Employment Division v. Smith concluded that the Free Exercise Clause is not implicated when a generally applicable law incidentally burdens religious exercise. But what if government wishes to ease that incidental burden by granting an exception to the religious exercise? It is not required by the Free Exercise Clause, but does it violate the Establishment Clause? After all, such an exception intentionally benefits religion.

In *Corporation of the Presiding Bishop of the Church of Jesus Christ of the Latter-Day Saints v. Amos*, 483 U.S. 327 (1987), an employee of a gymnasium open to the public but owned and run by the LDS Church was fired because he was not a member of the Church. He brought suit under Title VII of the 1964 Civil Rights Act alleging that he was discharged in violation of the Act's prohibition against discrimination on the basis of religion. The Church defended on the ground that the Act contained an exception for religious organizations. The fired employee argued that the exception was unconstitutional under the Establishment Clause. The Court rejected the argument, saying:

> "This Court has long recognized that the government may (and sometimes must) accommodate religious practices and that it may do so without violating the Establishment Clause." It is well established, too, that "[t]he limits of permissible state accommodation to religion are by no means co-extensive with the noninterference mandated by the Free Exercise Clause." There is ample room under the Establishment Clause for "benevolent neutrality which will permit religious exercise to exist without sponsorship and without interference."

Justice Souter in his concurrence in *Lee v. Weisman* (the middle school graduation prayer case) addressed what he believed to be the limits of accommodating religious exercise without offending the Establishment Clause. "Whatever else may define the scope of accommodation permissible under the Establishment Clause, one requirement is clear: accommodation must lift a discernible burden on the free exercise of religion." This standard would approve of the line drawn in *Amos*, because to require religious institutions to comply with employment laws inconsistent with their beliefs would place a discernible burden upon them.

Amos involved accommodating religious concerns without violating the Establishment Clause, but there is also the question of when government may go further than the Establishment Clause requires without violating the Free Exercise Clause.

For example, in *Locke v. Davey*, 540 U.S. 712 (2004), a state had created a postsecondary scholarship program for gifted students, but in accord with the state constitution did not allow the scholarships to be used to obtain a degree in devotional theology. A recipient of one of the scholarships who wished to use it to obtain such a degree challenged the restriction as a violation of the Free Exercise Clause. The Court rejected the challenge.

> The Religion Clauses of the First Amendment provide: "Congress shall make no law respecting an establishment of religion, or prohibiting the free exercise thereof." These two Clauses, the Establishment Clause and the Free Exercise Clause, are frequently in tension. Yet we have long said that "there is room for play in the joints" between them. In other words, there are some state actions permitted by the Establishment Clause but not required by the Free Exercise Clause.

This case involves that "play in the joints" described above. Under our Establishment Clause precedent, the link between government funds and religious training is broken by the independent and private choice of recipients. As such, there is no doubt that the State could, consistent with the Federal Constitution, permit Promise Scholars to pursue a degree in devotional theology, *see Witters v. Washington Dept. of Servs. for Blind*, and the State does not contend otherwise. The question before us, however, is whether Washington . . . can deny them such funding without violating the Free Exercise Clause.

The Court concluded that it could, distinguishing *Church of Lukumi Babalu Aye* as effectively prohibiting the exercise of religion, whereas here the state was merely choosing not to fund a distinct category of instruction. Here, moreover, the state was merely giving effect to a stricter sense of anti-establishment than the First Amendment, by eliminating even indirect financial support for religion. Justice Scalia, joined by Justice Thomas, dissented. They viewed the creation of an exception from a generally applicable benefit limited to degrees in devotional theology to constitute discrimination against religion contrary to the teachings of *Church of Lukumi Babalu Aye*.

Consider the Court's more recent case.

TRINITY LUTHERAN CHURCH OF COLUMBIA, INC. V. COMER

United States Supreme Court, 2017.
137 S.Ct. 2012.

CHIEF JUSTICE ROBERTS delivered the opinion of the Court, except as to footnote 3.

The Missouri Department of Natural Resources offers state grants to help public and private schools, nonprofit daycare centers, and other nonprofit entities purchase rubber playground surfaces made from recycled tires. Trinity Lutheran Church applied for such a grant for its preschool and daycare center and would have received one, but for the fact that Trinity Lutheran is a church. The Department had a policy of categorically disqualifying churches and other religious organizations from receiving grants under its playground resurfacing program. The question presented is whether the Department's policy violated the rights of Trinity Lutheran under the Free Exercise Clause of the First Amendment.

The Trinity Lutheran Church Child Learning Center is a preschool and daycare center. . . . and operates . . . on church property. . . . The Center includes a playground that is equipped with the basic playground essentials: slides, swings, jungle gyms, monkey bars, and sandboxes. Almost the entire surface beneath and surrounding the play equipment is coarse pea gravel. Youngsters, of course, often fall on the playground or tumble from the equipment. And when they do, the gravel can be unforgiving.

In 2012, the Center sought to replace a large portion of the pea gravel with a pour-in-place rubber surface by participating in Missouri's Scrap Tire Program. Run by the State's Department of Natural Resources to reduce the number of used tires destined for landfills and dump sites, the program offers reimbursement grants to qualifying nonprofit organizations that purchase playground surfaces made from recycled tires. . . .

When the Center applied, the Department had a strict and express policy of denying grants to any applicant owned or controlled by a church, sect, or other religious entity. That policy, in the Department's view, was compelled by Article I, Section 7 of the Missouri Constitution, which provides:

"That no money shall ever be taken from the public treasury, directly or indirectly, in aid of any church, sect or denomination of religion, or in aid of any priest, preacher, minister or teacher thereof, as such; and that no preference shall be given to nor any discrimination made against any church, sect or creed of religion, or any form of religious faith or worship."

[I]n a letter rejecting the Center's application, the program director explained that, under Article I, Section 7 of the Missouri Constitution, the Department could not provide financial assistance directly to a church. . . .

Trinity Lutheran sued the Director of the Department in Federal District Court. The Church alleged that the Department's failure to approve the Center's application, pursuant to its policy of denying grants to religiously affiliated applicants, violates the Free Exercise Clause of the First Amendment. Trinity Lutheran sought declaratory and injunctive relief prohibiting the Department from discriminating against the Church on that basis in future grant applications.

The District Court granted the Department's motion to dismiss. . . . The Court of Appeals for the Eighth Circuit affirmed. . . . We granted certiorari, and now reverse.

The First Amendment provides, in part, that "Congress shall make no law respecting an establishment of religion, or prohibiting the free exercise thereof." The parties agree that the Establishment Clause of that Amendment does not prevent Missouri from including Trinity Lutheran in the Scrap Tire Program. That does not, however, answer the question under the Free Exercise Clause, because we have recognized that there is "play in the joints" between what the Establishment Clause permits and the Free Exercise Clause compels. *Locke v. Davey.*

The Free Exercise Clause "protect[s] religious observers against unequal treatment" and subjects to the strictest scrutiny laws that target the religious for "special disabilities" based on their "religious status."

Applying that basic principle, this Court has repeatedly confirmed that denying a generally available benefit solely on account of religious identity imposes a penalty on the free exercise of religion that can be justified only by a state interest "of the highest order."

In *Everson v. Board of Education*, for example, we upheld against an Establishment Clause challenge a New Jersey law enabling a local school district to reimburse parents for the public transportation costs of sending their children to public and private schools, including parochial schools. In the course of ruling that the Establishment Clause allowed New Jersey to extend that public benefit to all its citizens regardless of their religious belief, we explained that a State "cannot hamper its citizens in the free exercise of their own religion. Consequently, it cannot exclude individual Catholics, Lutherans, Mohammedans, Baptists, Jews, Methodists, Non-believers, Presbyterians, or the members of any other faith, because of their faith, or lack of it, from receiving the benefits of public welfare legislation."

Three decades later, in *McDaniel v. Paty*, 435 U.S. 618 (1978), the Court struck down under the Free Exercise Clause a Tennessee statute disqualifying ministers from serving as delegates to the State's constitutional convention. Writing for the plurality, Chief Justice Burger acknowledged that Tennessee had disqualified ministers from serving as legislators since the adoption of its first Constitution in 1796, and that a number of early States had also disqualified ministers from legislative office. This historical tradition, however, did not change the fact that the statute discriminated against McDaniel by denying him a benefit solely because of his "status as a 'minister.' "....

In recent years, when this Court has rejected free exercise challenges, the laws in question have been neutral and generally applicable without regard to religion. We have been careful to distinguish such laws from those that single out the religious for disfavored treatment.... [I]n *Church of Lukumi Babalu Aye, Inc. v. Hialeah*, we struck down three facially neutral city ordinances that outlawed certain forms of animal slaughter. Members of the Santeria religion challenged the ordinances under the Free Exercise Clause, alleging that despite their facial neutrality, the ordinances had a discriminatory purpose easy to ferret out: prohibiting sacrificial rituals integral to Santeria but distasteful to local residents. We agreed. Before explaining why the challenged ordinances were not, in fact, neutral or generally applicable, the Court recounted the fundamentals of our free exercise jurisprudence. A law, we said, may not discriminate against "some or all religious beliefs." Nor may a law regulate or outlaw conduct because it is religiously motivated. And, citing *McDaniel* and *Employment Division v. Smith*, we restated the now-familiar refrain: The Free Exercise Clause protects against laws that " 'impose[ ] special disabilities on the basis of ... religious status.' "

The Department's policy expressly discriminates against otherwise eligible recipients by disqualifying them from a public benefit solely because of their religious character. If the cases just described make one thing clear, it is that such a policy imposes a penalty on the free exercise of religion that triggers the most exacting scrutiny. . . .

The Department contends that merely declining to extend funds to Trinity Lutheran does not prohibit the Church from engaging in any religious conduct or otherwise exercising its religious rights. In this sense, says the Department, its policy is unlike the ordinances struck down in *Lukumi*, which outlawed rituals central to Santeria. Here the Department has simply declined to allocate to Trinity Lutheran a subsidy the State had no obligation to provide in the first place. That decision does not meaningfully burden the Church's free exercise rights. And absent any such burden, the argument continues, the Department is free to heed the State's antiestablishment objection to providing funds directly to a church.

It is true the Department has not criminalized the way Trinity Lutheran worships or told the Church that it cannot subscribe to a certain view of the Gospel. But, as the Department itself acknowledges, the Free Exercise Clause protects against "indirect coercion or penalties on the free exercise of religion, not just outright prohibitions." . . .

The Department attempts to get out from under the weight of our precedents by arguing that the free exercise question in this case is instead controlled by our decision in *Locke v. Davey*. It is not. In *Locke*, the State of Washington created a scholarship program to assist high-achieving students with the costs of postsecondary education. The scholarships were paid out of the State's general fund, and eligibility was based on criteria such as an applicant's score on college admission tests and family income. While scholarship recipients were free to use the money at accredited religious and non-religious schools alike, they were not permitted to use the funds to pursue a devotional theology degree—one "devotional in nature or designed to induce religious faith." Davey was selected for a scholarship but was denied the funds when he refused to certify that he would not use them toward a devotional degree. He sued, arguing that the State's refusal to allow its scholarship money to go toward such degrees violated his free exercise rights.

This Court disagreed. It began by explaining what was not at issue. Washington's selective funding program was not comparable to the free exercise violations found in the "*Lukumi* line of cases," including those striking down laws requiring individuals to "choose between their religious beliefs and receiving a government benefit." At the outset, then, the Court made clear that *Locke* was not like the case now before us.

Washington's restriction on the use of its scholarship funds was different. According to the Court, the State had "merely chosen not to fund a distinct category of instruction." Davey was not denied a scholarship because of who he was; he was denied a scholarship because of what he proposed to do—use the funds to prepare for the ministry. Here there is no question that Trinity Lutheran was denied a grant simply because of what it is—a church.

The Court in *Locke* also stated that Washington's choice was in keeping with the State's antiestablishment interest in not using taxpayer funds to pay for the training of clergy; in fact, the Court could "think of few areas in which a State's antiestablishment interests come more into play." The claimant in *Locke* sought funding for an "essentially religious endeavor . . . akin to a religious calling as well as an academic pursuit," and opposition to such funding "to support church leaders" lay at the historic core of the Religion Clauses. Here nothing of the sort can be said about a program to use recycled tires to resurface playgrounds.

Relying on *Locke*, the Department nonetheless emphasizes Missouri's similar constitutional tradition of not furnishing taxpayer money directly to churches. But *Locke* took account of Washington's antiestablishment interest only after determining, as noted, that the scholarship program did not "require students to choose between their religious beliefs and receiving a government benefit." . . . In this case, there is no dispute that Trinity Lutheran is put to the choice between being a church and receiving a government benefit. The rule is simple: No churches need apply.[3] . . .

Under [the strict scrutiny] standard, only a state interest "of the highest order" can justify the Department's discriminatory policy. Yet the Department offers nothing more than Missouri's policy preference for skating as far as possible from religious establishment concerns. In the face of the clear infringement on free exercise before us, that interest cannot qualify as compelling. . . .

The State has pursued its preferred policy to the point of expressly denying a qualified religious entity a public benefit solely because of its religious character. Under our precedents, that goes too far. The Department's policy violates the Free Exercise Clause.

JUSTICE THOMAS, with whom JUSTICE GORSUCH joins, concurring in part. [omitted]

JUSTICE GORSUCH, with whom JUSTICE THOMAS joins, concurring in part.

Missouri's law bars Trinity Lutheran from participating in a public benefits program only because it is a church. I agree this violates the First Amendment and I am pleased to join nearly all of the Court's opinion. I offer only two modest qualifications.

---

[3] This case involves express discrimination based on religious identity with respect to playground resurfacing. We do not address religious uses of funding or other forms of discrimination.

First, the Court leaves open the possibility a useful distinction might be drawn between laws that discriminate on the basis of religious status and religious use. Respectfully, I harbor doubts about the stability of such a line. Does a religious man say grace before dinner? Or does a man begin his meal in a religious manner? Is it a religious group that built the playground? Or did a group build the playground so it might be used to advance a religious mission? The distinction blurs in much the same way the line between acts and omissions can blur when stared at too long, leaving us to ask (for example) whether the man who drowns by awaiting the incoming tide does so by act (coming upon the sea) or omission (allowing the sea to come upon him). Often enough the same facts can be described both ways.

Neither do I see why the First Amendment's Free Exercise Clause should care. After all, that Clause guarantees the free exercise of religion, not just the right to inward belief (or status). . . . I don't see why it should matter whether we describe that benefit, say, as closed to Lutherans (status) or closed to people who do Lutheran things (use). It is free exercise either way.

For these reasons, reliance on the status-use distinction does not suffice for me to distinguish *Locke v. Davey*. In that case, this Court upheld a funding restriction barring a student from using a scholarship to pursue a degree in devotional theology. But can it really matter whether the restriction in *Locke* was phrased in terms of use instead of status (for was it a student who wanted a vocational degree in religion? or was it a religious student who wanted the necessary education for his chosen vocation?). If that case can be correct and distinguished, it seems it might be only because of the opinion's claim of a long tradition against the use of public funds for training of the clergy, a tradition the Court correctly explains has no analogue here.

Second and for similar reasons, I am unable to join the footnoted observation, that "[t]his case involves express discrimination based on religious identity with respect to playground resurfacing." Of course the footnote is entirely correct, but I worry that some might mistakenly read it to suggest that only "playground resurfacing" cases, or only those with some association with children's safety or health, or perhaps some other social good we find sufficiently worthy, are governed by the legal rules recounted in and faithfully applied by the Court's opinion. . . .

JUSTICE BREYER, concurring in the judgment.

I agree with much of what the Court says and with its result. But I find relevant, and would emphasize, the particular nature of the "public benefit" here at issue.

The Court stated in *Everson* that "cutting off church schools from" such "general government services as ordinary police and fire protection . . . is obviously not the purpose of the First Amendment." Here, the State would cut Trinity Lutheran off from participation in a general program designed to secure or to improve the health and safety of children. I see no significant difference. . . . We need not go further. Public benefits come in many shapes and sizes. I would leave the application of the Free Exercise Clause to other kinds of public benefits for another day.

JUSTICE SOTOMAYOR, with whom JUSTICE GINSBURG joins, dissenting.

To hear the Court tell it, this is a simple case about recycling tires to resurface a playground. The stakes are higher. This case is about nothing less than the relationship between religious institutions and the civil government—that is, between church and state. The Court today profoundly changes that relationship by holding, for the first time, that the Constitution requires the government to provide public funds directly to a church. Its decision slights both our precedents and our history, and its reasoning weakens this country's longstanding commitment to a separation of church and state beneficial to both.

Founded in 1922, Trinity Lutheran Church (Church) "operates . . . for the express purpose of carrying out the commission of . . . Jesus Christ as directed to His church on earth." The Church uses "preaching, teaching, worship, witness, service, and fellowship according to the Word of God" to carry out its mission "to 'make disciples.' " The Church's religious beliefs include its desire to "associat[e] with the [Trinity Church Child] Learning Center." Located on Church property, the Learning Center provides daycare and preschool for about "90 children ages two to kindergarten."

The Learning Center serves as "a ministry of the Church and incorporates daily religion and developmentally appropriate activities into . . . [its] program." In this way, "[t]hrough the Learning Center, the Church teaches a Christian world view to children of members of the Church, as well as children of non-member residents" of the area. These activities represent the Church's "sincere religious belief . . . to use [the Learning Center] to teach the Gospel to children of its members, as well to bring the Gospel message to non-members."

The Learning Center's facilities include a playground, the unlikely source of this dispute. The Church provides the playground and other "safe, clean, and attractive" facilities "in conjunction with an education program structured to allow a child to grow spiritually, physically, socially, and cognitively." . . .

Properly understood then, this is a case about whether Missouri can decline to fund improvements to the facilities the Church uses to practice and spread its religious views. . . . [Justice Ginsburg goes on to interpret previous Establishment Clause cases as preventing the funding involved here.]

Even assuming the absence of an Establishment Clause violation and proceeding on the Court's preferred front—the Free Exercise Clause—the Court errs. It claims that the government may not draw lines based on an entity's religious "status." But we have repeatedly said that it can. When confronted with government action that draws such a line, we have carefully considered whether the interests embodied in the Religion Clauses justify that line. The question here is thus whether those interests support the line drawn in Missouri's Article I, § 7, separating the State's treasury from those of houses of worship. They unquestionably do.

Even in the absence of a violation of one of the Religion Clauses, the interaction of government and religion can raise concerns that sound in both Clauses. For that reason, the government may sometimes act to accommodate those concerns, even when not required to do so by the Free Exercise Clause, without violating the Establishment Clause. And the government may sometimes act to accommodate those concerns, even when not required to do so by the Establishment Clause, without violating the Free Exercise Clause. "[T]here is room for play in the joints productive of a benevolent neutrality which will permit religious exercise to exist without sponsorship and without interference." *Locke*. This space between the two Clauses gives government some room to recognize the unique status of religious entities and to single them out on that basis for exclusion from otherwise generally applicable laws. . . .

[Consequently], this Court has held that the government may sometimes close off certain government aid programs to religious entities. The State need not, for example, fund the training of a religious group's leaders, those "who will preach their beliefs, teach their faith, and carry out their mission." It may instead avoid the historic "antiestablishment interests" raised by the use of "taxpayer funds to support church leaders."

When reviewing a law that, like this one, singles out religious entities for exclusion from its reach, we thus have not myopically focused on the fact that a law singles out religious entities, but on the reasons that it does so.

Missouri has decided that the unique status of houses of worship requires a special rule when it comes to public funds. . . . Missouri's decision, which has deep roots in our Nation's history, reflects a reasonable and constitutional judgment.

This Court has consistently looked to history for guidance when applying the Constitution's Religion Clauses. Those Clauses guard against a return to the past, and so that past properly informs their meaning. This case is no different. . . .

The use of public funds to support core religious institutions can safely be described as a hallmark of the States' early experiences with religious establishment. Every state establishment saw laws passed to raise public funds and direct them toward houses of worship and ministers. And as the States all disestablished, one by one, they all undid those laws. . . .

In *Locke*, this Court expressed an understanding of, and respect for, this history. . . . The Court could "think of few areas in which a State's antiestablishment interests come more into play" than the "procuring [of] taxpayer funds to support church leaders."

The same is true of this case, about directing taxpayer funds to houses of worship. Like the use of public dollars for ministers at issue in *Locke*, turning over public funds to houses of worship implicates serious antiestablishment and free exercise interests. . . . A state can reasonably use status as a "house of worship" as a stand-in for "religious activities." Inside a house of worship, dividing the religious from the secular would require intrusive line-drawing by government, and monitoring those lines would entangle government with the house of worship's activities. And so while not every activity a house of worship undertakes will be inseparably linked to religious activity, "the likelihood that many are makes a categorical rule a suitable means to avoid chilling the exercise of religion." . . . If there is any " 'room for play in the joints' between" the Religion Clauses, it is here.

As was true in *Locke*, a prophylactic rule against the use of public funds for houses of worship is a permissible accommodation of these weighty interests. The rule has a historical pedigree identical to that of the provision in *Locke*. Almost all of the States that ratified the Religion Clauses operated under this rule. Seven had placed this rule in their State Constitutions. Three enforced it by statute or in practice. Only one had not yet embraced the rule. Today, thirty-eight States have a counterpart to Missouri's Article I, § 7. The provisions, as a general matter, date back to or before these States' original Constitutions. That so many States have for so long drawn a line that prohibits public funding for houses of worship, based on principles rooted in this Nation's understanding of how best to foster religious liberty, supports the conclusion that public funding of houses of worship "is of a different ilk." . . .

COMMENTS AND QUESTIONS

1.   Justices Gorsuch and Thomas, although they concur in the Court's opinion, indicate that they have difficulty distinguishing this case from *Locke* and suggest that *Locke* was wrongly decided. Justices Sotomayor and Ginsburg also have difficulty distinguishing between this case and *Locke*, but they believe this case is wrongly decided. Chief Justice Roberts, joined by Justices Kennedy, Alito, and Kagan, distinguish *Locke* as involving the religious use of the funds—to fund a degree in devotional theology—as opposed to the religious status in the present case. Justice Breyer, although he writes that he agrees "with much of what the Court says and with its result," does not join the Court's opinion. Rather, he "would emphasize, the particular nature of the 'public

benefit' here at issue"—the grant for purchase of a rubber playground surface. He "would leave the application of the Free Exercise Clause to other kinds of public benefits for another day."

2.   Justice Sotomayor, joined by Justice Ginsburg in dissent, would find an Establishment Clause violation in the provision of funds for resurfacing the playground with rubber. Their explanation for that conclusion is edited from the case, but on the basis of your past reading, what do you think?

3.   *Espinoza v. Montana Department of Revenue*, 140 S.Ct. 2246 (2020) was a case raising *Trinity Lutheran* issues, but with a twist. It was also a case that engendered six separate opinions in addition to the opinion of the Court. Montana established a program that grants tax credits up to $150 to those who donate to organizations that award scholarships for private school tuition. As a practical matter, this meant parents could "donate" $150 to a private school to cover part of their child's tuition and have that $150 returned to them by the state as a tax credit, effectively lowering the tuition by $150. However, because the Montana constitution bars government aid to any school controlled by any church or religion, the state department of revenue adopted a rule, known as the no-aid provision, prohibiting the use of these scholarships at religious schools. This was challenged by parents in state court as discriminating on the basis of the religious school they had chosen. The Montana Supreme Court, however, held that the law itself was unconstitutional as providing financial aid to all schools, whether or not they were religious, and there was no authority under state law for the department's rule prohibiting such aid to religious schools. Consequently, the court held the entire statute unconstitutional, and tax credits could not be given for scholarships at any schools, religious or not. The United States Supreme Court granted certiorari to determine "whether the Free Exercise Clause precluded the Montana Supreme Court from applying Montana's no-aid provision to bar religious schools from the scholarship program." Because that was not actually what the Montana Supreme Court had done, the Court in its opinion recast the question as whether the Montana constitutional provision prohibiting the scholarship program in religious schools was consistent with the Federal Constitution. The Court found the case governed by *Trinity Lutheran*. As in *Trinity Lutheran*, the Montana constitution disqualified "other eligible recipients . . . from a public benefit 'solely because of their religious character.' " This triggers strict scrutiny, which the Montana constitution's provision failed. Again, as in *Trinity Lutheran*, the state's interest in separating church and state beyond the protections afforded in the Federal Constitution was not compelling. This was discrimination on the basis of religion, violating the Free Exercise Clause. *Locke* was distinguished in the same way it was in *Trinity Lutheran*. Justice Thomas, joined by Justice Gorsuch, concurred but wrote to reiterate his view that the Establishment Clause only limits the federal government, not the states. Thus, a state cannot claim that its infringement of the free exercise of religion is mandated by the Establishment Clause. Justice Alito also concurred but wrote to suggest that the original intent of the Montana constitution's provision was anti-Catholic, like the similar provisions adopted at the same time in other state

constitutions. Justice Gorsuch also wrote a separate concurring opinion. He would extend strict scrutiny not only to no-aid provisions that are based on the religious identity of the recipient but also to provisions that are based on religious exercise. Justice Ginsburg, joined by Justice Kagan, argued that the Montana Supreme Court's declaration that the entire scholarship program was unconstitutional under the Montana constitution meant that there no longer was any discrimination against religious schools (or the parents who would send their children to them), because non-religious private schools would be in the same situation. Justice Sotomayor, writing separately, made the same argument. The Court responded to this argument by pointing out that the Montana Supreme Court had reached its decision by reliance on the Montana constitution's no-aid provision, which itself was unconstitutional. And if that constitution's no-aid provision was unconstitutional, then the scholarship program as contained in the statute remained valid and in existence. Justice Breyer, joined by Justice Kagan in part, saw this case as more analogous to *Locke* than *Trinity Lutheran* and therefore allowable under the Free Exercise Clause. Moreover, he inferred that the Court was backing away from the "play in the joints" that *Locke* permitted. That perception seemed to bear fruit in the following case.

CARSON V. MAKIN

United States Supreme Court, 2022.
142 S.Ct. 1987.

CHIEF JUSTICE ROBERTS delivered the opinion of the Court.

Maine has enacted a program of tuition assistance for parents who live in school districts that do not operate a secondary school of their own. Under the program, parents designate the secondary school they would like their child to attend—public or private—and the school district transmits payments to that school to help defray the costs of tuition. Most private schools are eligible to receive the payments, so long as they are "nonsectarian." The question presented is whether this restriction violates the Free Exercise Clause of the First Amendment.

Maine's Constitution provides that the State's legislature shall "require . . . the several towns to make suitable provision, at their own expense, for the support and maintenance of public schools." In accordance with that command, the legislature has required that every school-age child in Maine "shall be provided an opportunity to receive the benefits of a free public education," and that the required schools be operated by "the legislative and governing bodies of local school administrative units," But Maine is the most rural State in the Union, and for many school districts the realities of remote geography and low population density make those commands difficult to heed. Indeed, of Maine's 260 school administrative units (SAUs), fewer than half operate a public secondary school of their own.

Maine has sought to deal with this problem in part by creating a program of tuition assistance for families that reside in such areas. Under that program, if an SAU neither operates its own public secondary school nor contracts with a particular public or private school for the education of its school-age children, the SAU must "pay the tuition . . . at the public school or the approved private school of the parent's choice at which the student is accepted." Parents who wish to take advantage of this benefit first select the school they wish their child to attend. If they select a private school that has been "approved" by the Maine Department of Education, the parents' SAU "shall pay the tuition" at the chosen school up to a specified maximum rate.

Prior to 1981, parents could direct the tuition assistance payments to religious schools. Indeed, in the 1979–1980 school year, over 200 Maine students opted to attend such schools through the tuition assistance program. In 1981, however, Maine imposed a new requirement that any school receiving tuition assistance payments must be "a nonsectarian school in accordance with the First Amendment of the United States Constitution." That provision was enacted in response to an opinion by the Maine attorney general taking the position that public funding of private religious schools violated the Establishment Clause of the First Amendment. We subsequently held, however, that a benefit program under which private citizens "direct government aid to religious schools wholly as a result of their own genuine and independent private choice" does not offend the Establishment Clause. *Zelman v. Simmons-Harris*, 536 U.S. 639 (2002). Following our decision in *Zelman*, the Maine Legislature considered a proposed bill to repeal the "nonsectarian" requirement, but rejected it.

The "nonsectarian" requirement for participation in Maine's tuition assistance program remains in effect today. The Department has stated that, in administering this requirement, it "considers a sectarian school to be one that is associated with a particular faith or belief system and which, in addition to teaching academic subjects, promotes the faith or belief system with which it is associated and/or presents the material taught through the lens of this faith." "The Department's focus is on what the school teaches through its curriculum and related activities, and how the material is presented." "[A]ffiliation or association with a church or religious institution is one potential indicator of a sectarian school," but "it is not dispositive."

This case concerns two families that live in SAUs that neither maintain their own secondary schools nor contract with any nearby secondary school. [One family has children who attend high school at Bangor Christian Schools (BCS); the other has children who attend Temple Academy.]

BCS and Temple Academy are both accredited by the New England Association of Schools and Colleges (NEASC), and the Department considers each school a "private school approved for attendance purposes" under the State's compulsory attendance requirement. Yet because neither school qualifies as "nonsectarian," neither is eligible to receive tuition payments under Maine's tuition assistance program. Absent the "nonsectarian" requirement, the Carsons and the Nelsons would have asked their respective SAUs to pay the tuition to send their children to BCS and Temple Academy, respectively.

The Free Exercise Clause of the First Amendment protects against "indirect coercion or penalties on the free exercise of religion, not just outright prohibitions." In particular, we have repeatedly held that a State violates the Free Exercise Clause when it excludes religious observers from otherwise available public benefits. See Sherbert v. Verner ("It is too late in the day to doubt that the liberties of religion and expression may be infringed by the denial of or placing of conditions upon a benefit or privilege."); see also *Everson v. Board of Ed. of Ewing* (a State "cannot exclude" individuals *because of their faith, or lack of it*, from receiving the benefits of public welfare legislation").

We have recently applied these principles in the context of two state efforts to withhold otherwise available public benefits from religious organizations. In *Trinity Lutheran Church of Columbia, Inc.* v. *Comer*, we considered a Missouri program that offered grants to qualifying nonprofit organizations that installed cushioning playground surfaces made from recycled rubber tires. The Missouri Department of Natural Resources maintained an express policy of denying such grants to any applicant owned or controlled by a church, sect, or other religious entity. We deemed it "unremarkable in light of our prior decisions" to conclude that the Free Exercise Clause did not permit Missouri to "expressly discriminate[ ] against otherwise eligible recipients by disqualifying them from a public benefit solely because of their religious character."

Two Terms ago, in *Espinoza*, we reached the same conclusion as to a Montana program that provided tax credits to donors who sponsored scholarships for private school tuition. The Montana Supreme Court held that the program, to the extent it included religious schools, violated a provision of the Montana Constitution that barred government aid to any school controlled in whole or in part by a church, sect, or denomination. As a result of that holding, the State terminated the scholarship program, preventing the petitioners from accessing scholarship funds they otherwise would have used to fund their children's educations at religious schools. We again held that the Free Exercise Clause forbade the State's action. The application of the Montana Constitution's no-aid provision, we explained, required strict scrutiny because it "bar[red] religious schools from public benefits solely because of the religious character of the schools." "A State need not subsidize private education," we concluded, "[b]ut once a State decides to do so, it cannot disqualify some private schools solely because they are religious."

The "unremarkable" principles applied in *Trinity Lutheran* and *Espinoza* suffice to resolve this case. Maine offers its citizens a benefit: tuition assistance payments for any family whose school district does not provide a public secondary school. Just like the wide range of nonprofit organizations eligible to receive playground resurfacing grants in *Trinity Lutheran*, a wide range of private schools are eligible to receive Maine tuition assistance payments here. And like the daycare center in *Trinity Lutheran*, BCS and Temple Academy are disqualified from this generally available benefit "solely because of their religious character. By "condition[ing] the availability of benefits" in that manner, Maine's tuition assistance program—like the program in *Trinity Lutheran*—"effectively penalizes the free exercise" of religion.

Our recent decision in *Espinoza* applied these basic principles in the context of religious education that we consider today. There, as here, we considered a state benefit program under which public funds flowed to support tuition payments at private schools. And there, as here, that program specifically carved out private religious schools from those eligible to receive such funds. While the wording of the Montana and Maine provisions is different, their effect is the same: to "disqualify some private schools" from funding "solely because they are religious." A law that operates in that manner, we held in *Espinoza*, must be subjected to "the strictest scrutiny."

To satisfy strict scrutiny, government action "must advance 'interests of the highest order' and must be narrowly tailored in pursuit of those interests." "A law that targets religious conduct for distinctive treatment . . . will survive strict scrutiny only in rare cases." This is not one of them.

As noted, a neutral benefit program in which public funds flow to religious organizations through the independent choices of private benefit recipients does not offend the Establishment Clause. Maine's decision to continue excluding religious schools from its tuition assistance program after *Zelman* thus promotes stricter separation of church and state than the Federal Constitution requires. But as we explained in both *Trinity Lutheran* and *Espinoza*, such an "interest in separating church and state 'more fiercely' than the Federal Constitution . . . 'cannot qualify as compelling' in the face of the infringement of free exercise."

[Maine attempts] to distinguish this case from *Trinity Lutheran* and *Espinoza* on the ground that the funding restrictions in those cases were "solely status-based religious discrimination," while the challenged provision here "imposes a use-based restriction." [In *Espinoza*, w]e explained, however, that the strict scrutiny triggered by status-based discrimination could not be avoided by arguing that "one of its goals or effects [was] preventing religious organizations from putting aid to religious *uses.*" And we noted that nothing in our analysis was "meant to suggest that we agree[d] with [Montana] that some lesser degree of scrutiny applies to discrimination against religious uses of government aid."

Maine's argument, however—along with Justice BREYER's dissent—is premised on precisely such a distinction. That premise, however, misreads our precedents. In *Trinity Lutheran* and *Espinoza*, we held that the Free Exercise Clause forbids discrimination on the basis of religious status. But those decisions never suggested that use-based discrimination is any less offensive to the Free Exercise Clause. This case illustrates why. "[E]ducating young people in their faith, inculcating its teachings, and training them to live their faith are responsibilities that lie at the very core of the mission of a private religious school."

Any attempt to give effect to such a distinction by scrutinizing whether and how a religious school pursues its educational mission would also raise serious concerns about state entanglement with religion and denominational favoritism. That suggests that any status-use distinction lacks a meaningful application not only in theory, but in practice as well. In short, the prohibition on status-based discrimination under the Free Exercise Clause is not a permission to engage in use-based discrimination.

Maine and the dissents invoke *Locke v. Davey* in support of the argument that the State may preclude parents from designating a religious school to receive tuition assistance payments. In that case, Washington had established a scholarship fund to assist academically gifted students with postsecondary education expenses. But the program excluded one particular use of the scholarship funds: the "essentially religious endeavor" of pursuing a degree designed to "train[ ] a minister to lead a congregation." We upheld that restriction against a free exercise challenge, reasoning that the State had "merely chosen not to fund a distinct category of instruction."

Our opinions in *Trinity Lutheran* and *Espinoza*, however, have already explained why *Locke* can be of no help to Maine here. Both precedents emphasized, as did *Locke* itself, that the funding in *Locke* was intended to be used "to prepare for the ministry." Funds could be and were used for theology courses; only pursuing a "vocational religious" *degree* was excluded.

Locke's reasoning expressly turned on what it identified as the "historic and substantial state interest" against using "taxpayer funds to support church leaders." But as we explained at length in *Espinoza*, "it is clear that there is no 'historic and substantial' tradition against aiding [private religious] schools comparable to the tradition against state-supported clergy invoked by *Locke*." *Locke* cannot be read beyond its narrow focus on vocational religious degrees to generally authorize the State to exclude religious persons from the enjoyment of public benefits on the basis of their anticipated religious use of the benefits.

JUSTICE BREYER, with whom JUSTICE KAGAN joins, and with whom JUSTICE SOTOMAYOR joins except as to Part I-B, dissenting.

[Justice Breyer reiterated his views from *Espinoza* that there should be "play in the joints" between the religion clauses as recognized in *Locke v. Davey*, so that a state can take a stricter view of establishing religion than the federal constitution. Here, as he had predicted in *Espinoza*, he found the Court virtually eliminating that play. Moreover, he took issue with the Court's claim that it was following precedent, because in no earlier case where the Court had said the public benefit could not be withheld did the benefit involve funds going for the purpose of religious education.]

Maine wishes to provide children within the State with a secular, public education. This wish embodies, in significant part, the constitutional need to avoid spending public money to support what is essentially the teaching and practice of religion. That need is reinforced by the fact that we are today a Nation of more than 330 million people who ascribe to over 100 different religions. In that context, state neutrality with respect to religion is particularly important. The Religion Clauses give Maine the right to honor that neutrality by choosing not to fund religious schools as part of its public school tuition program. I believe the majority is wrong to hold the contrary. And with respect, I dissent.

JUSTICE SOTOMAYOR, dissenting.

This Court continues to dismantle the wall of separation between church and state that the Framers fought to build. I write separately to add three points. [Justice Sotomayor first takes issue with the path the Court took over the past several years both with regard to the federal Establishment Clause and the limited freedom of states to be stricter in their establishment law.]

From a practical perspective, today's decision directs the State of Maine (and, by extension, its taxpaying citizens) to subsidize institutions that undisputedly engage in religious instruction. In addition, while purporting to protect against discrimination of one kind, the Court requires Maine to fund what many of its citizens believe to be discrimination of other kinds. See *ante,* at ___ (BREYER, J., dissenting)(summarizing Bangor Christian Schools' and Temple Academy's policies denying enrollment to students based on gender identity, sexual orientation, and religion). The upshot is that Maine must choose between giving subsidies to its residents or refraining from financing religious teaching and practices.

The Court's analysis does leave some options open to Maine. For example, under state law, school administrative units (SAUs) that cannot feasibly operate their own schools may contract directly with a public school in another SAU, or with an approved private school, to educate their students. I do not understand today's decision to mandate that SAUs contract directly with schools that teach religion, which would go beyond

Zelman's private-choice doctrine and blatantly violate the Establishment Clause. Nonetheless, it is irrational for this Court to hold that the Free Exercise Clause bars Maine from giving money to parents to fund the only type of education the State may provide consistent with the Establishment Clause: a religiously neutral one. Nothing in the Constitution requires today's result.

COMMENTS AND QUESTIONS

1.   What can Maine do now to avoid having to pay tuition at sectarian schools?

2.   Is it true that Maine will have to pay tuition at schools that discriminate on the basis of gender identity, sexual orientation, or religion? Isn't there a simple solution to that problem?

PROBLEM

To reduce the use of fossil fuels that contribute to greenhouse gases and climate change, Congress passes a law providing grants to "public buildings" for the purpose of installing solar panels to generate electricity for the building. Although the statutory definition of "public building" clearly would otherwise encompass churches, synagogues, mosques, and similar places of worship, the statute specifically disqualifies any house of worship from receiving these grants. Is this constitutional?

APPENDIX A

THE CONSTITUTION OF THE UNITED STATES

■ ■ ■

PREAMBLE

We the People of the United States, in Order to form a more perfect Union, establish Justice, insure domestic Tranquility, provide for the common defence, promote the general Welfare, and secure the Blessings of Liberty to ourselves and our Posterity, do ordain and establish this Constitution for the United States of America.

ARTICLE I

Section 1.   All legislative Powers herein granted shall be vested in a Congress of the United States, which shall consist of a Senate and House of Representatives.

Section 2.   [1] The House of Representatives shall be composed of Members chosen every second Year by the People of the several States, and the Electors in each State shall have the Qualifications requisite for Electors of the most numerous Branch of the State Legislature.

[2] No Person shall be a Representative who shall not have attained to the Age of twenty five Years, and been seven Years a Citizen of the United States, and who shall not, when elected, be an Inhabitant of that State in which he shall be chosen.

[3] Representatives and direct Taxes shall be apportioned among the several States which may be included within this Union, according to their respective Numbers, which shall be determined by adding to the whole Number of free Persons, including those bound to Service for a Term of Years, and excluding Indians not taxed, three fifths of all other Persons. The actual Enumeration shall be made within three Years after the first Meeting of the Congress of the United States, and within every subsequent Term of ten Years, in such Manner as they shall by Law direct. The Number of Representatives shall not exceed one for every thirty Thousand, but each State shall have at Least one Representative; and until such enumeration shall be made, the State of New Hampshire shall be entitled to chuse three, Massachusetts eight, Rhode Island and Providence Plantations one, Connecticut five, New York six, New Jersey four,

Pennsylvania eight, Delaware one, Maryland six, Virginia ten, North Carolina five, South Carolina five, and Georgia three.

[4] When vacancies happen in the Representation from any State, the Executive Authority thereof shall issue Writs of Election to fill such Vacancies.

[5] The House of Representatives shall chuse their Speaker and other Officers; and shall have the sole Power of Impeachment.

Section 3.   [1] The Senate of the United States shall be composed of two Senators from each State, chosen by the Legislature thereof, for six Years; and each Senator shall have one Vote.

[2] Immediately after they shall be assembled in Consequence of the first Election, they shall be divided as equally as may be into three Classes. The Seats of the Senators of the first Class shall be vacated at the Expiration of the Second Year, of the second Class at the Expiration of the fourth Year, and of the third Class at the Expiration of the sixth Year, so that one third may be chosen every second Year; and if Vacancies happen by Resignation, or otherwise, during the Recess of the Legislature of any State, the Executive thereof may make temporary Appointments until the next Meeting of the Legislature, which shall then fill such Vacancies.

[3] No Person shall be a Senator who shall not have attained to the Age of thirty Years, and been nine Years a Citizen of the United States, and who shall not, when elected, by an Inhabitant of that State for which he shall be chosen.

[4] The Vice President of the United States shall be President of the Senate, but shall have no Vote, unless they be equally divided.

[5] The Senate shall chuse their other Officers, and also a President pro tempore, in the Absence of the Vice President, or when he shall exercise the Office of President of the United States.

[6] The Senate shall have the sole Power to try all Impeachments. When sitting for that Purpose, they shall be on Oath or Affirmation. When the President of the United States is tried, the Chief Justice shall preside: And no Person shall be convicted without the Concurrence of two thirds of the Members present.

[7] Judgment in Cases of Impeachment shall not extend further than to removal from Office, and disqualification to hold and enjoy any Office of honor, Trust, or Profit under the United States: but the Party convicted shall nevertheless be liable and subject to Indictment, Trial, Judgment, and Punishment, according to Law.

Section 4.   [1] The Times, Places and Manner of holding Elections for Senators and Representatives, shall be prescribed in each State by the

Legislature thereof; but the Congress may at any time by Law make or alter such Regulations, except as to the Places of chusing Senators.

[2]   The Congress shall assemble at least once in every Year, and such Meeting shall be on the first Monday in December, unless they shall by Law appoint a different Day.

Section 5.   [1]   Each House shall be the Judge of the Elections, Returns, and Qualifications of its own Members, and a Majority of each shall constitute a Quorum to do Business; but a smaller Number may adjourn from day to day, and may be authorized to compel the Attendance of absent Members, in such Manner, and under such Penalties as each House may provide.

[2]   Each House may determine the Rules of its Proceedings, punish its Members for disorderly Behavior, and, with the Concurrence of two thirds, expel a Member.

[3]   Each House shall keep a Journal of its Proceedings, and from time to time publish the same, excepting such Parts as may in their Judgment require Secrecy; and the Yeas and Nays of the Members of either House on any question shall, at the Desire of one fifth of those Present, be entered on the Journal.

[4]   Neither House, during the Session of Congress, shall without the Consent of the other, adjourn for more than three days, nor to any other Place than that in which the two Houses shall be sitting.

Section 6.   [1]   The Senators and Representatives shall receive a Compensation for their Services, to be ascertained by Law, and paid out of the Treasury of the United States. They shall in all Cases, except Treason, Felony and Breach of the Peace, be privileged from Arrest during their Attendance at the Session of their respective Houses, and in going to and returning from the same; and for any Speech or Debate in either House, they shall not be questioned in any other Place.

[2]   No Senator or Representative shall, during the Time for which he was elected, be appointed to any civil Office under the Authority of the United States, which shall have been created, or the Emoluments whereof shall have been increased during such time; and no Person holding any Office under the United States, shall be a Member of either House during his Continuance in Office.

Section 7.   [1]   All Bills for raising Revenue shall originate in the House of Representatives; but the Senate may propose or concur with Amendments as on other Bills.

[2]   Every Bill which shall have passed the House of Representatives and the Senate, shall, before it become a Law, be presented to the President of the United States; If he approve he shall sign it, but if not he shall return

it, with his Objections to the House in which it shall have originated, who shall enter the Objections at large on their Journal, and proceed to reconsider it. If after such Reconsideration two thirds of that House shall agree to pass the Bill, it shall be sent together with the Objections, to the other House, by which it shall likewise be reconsidered, and if approved by two thirds of that House, it shall become a Law. But in all such Cases the Votes of both Houses shall be determined by yeas and Nays, and the Names of the Persons voting for and against the Bill shall be entered on the Journal of each House respectively. If any Bill shall not be returned by the President within ten Days (Sundays excepted) after it shall have been presented to him, the Same shall be a Law, in like Manner as if he had signed it, unless the Congress by their Adjournment prevent its Return in which Case it shall not be a Law.

[3]   Every Order, Resolution, or Vote, to Which the Concurrence of the Senate and House of Representatives may be necessary (except on a question of Adjournment) shall be presented to the President of the United States; and before the Same shall take Effect, shall be approved by him, or being disapproved by him, shall be repassed by two thirds of the Senate and House of Representatives, according to the Rules and Limitations prescribed in the Case of a Bill.

Section 8.   [1]   The Congress shall have Power To lay and collect Taxes, Duties, Imposts and Excises, to pay the Debts and provide for the common Defence and general Welfare of the United States; but all Duties, Imposts and Excises shall be uniform throughout the United States;

[2]   To borrow money on the credit of the United States;

[3]   To regulate Commerce with foreign Nations, and among the several States, and with the Indian Tribes;

[4]   To establish an uniform Rule of Naturalization, and uniform Laws on the subject of Bankruptcies throughout the United States;

[5]   To coin Money, regulate the Value thereof, and of foreign Coin, and fix the Standard of Weights and Measures;

[6]   To provide for the Punishment of counterfeiting the Securities and current Coin of the United States;

[7]   To Establish Post Offices and Post Roads;

[8]   To promote the Progress of Science and useful Arts, by securing for limited Times to Authors and Inventors the exclusive Right to their respective Writings and Discoveries;

[9]   To constitute Tribunals inferior to the supreme Court;

[10] To define and punish Piracies and Felonies committed on the high Seas, and Offenses against the Law of Nations;

[11] To declare War, grant Letters of Marque and Reprisal, and make Rules concerning Captures on Land and Water;

[12] To raise and support Armies, but no Appropriation of Money to that Use shall be for a longer Term than two Years;

[13] To provide and maintain a Navy;

[14] To make Rules for the Government and Regulation of the land and naval Forces;

[15] To provide for calling forth the Militia to execute the Laws of the Union, suppress Insurrections and repel Invasions;

[16] To provide for organizing, arming, and disciplining, the Militia, and for governing such Part of them as may be employed in the Service of the United States, reserving to the States respectively, the Appointment of the Officers, and the Authority of training the Militia according to the discipline prescribed by Congress;

[17] To exercise exclusive Legislation in all Cases whatsoever, over such District (not exceeding ten Miles square) as may, by Cession of particular States, and the Acceptance of Congress, become the Seat of the Government of the United States, and to exercise like Authority over all Places purchased by the Consent of the Legislature of the State in which the Same shall be, for the Erection of Forts, Magazines, Arsenals, dock-Yards, and other needful Buildings;—And

[18] To make all Laws which shall be necessary and proper for carrying into Execution the foregoing Powers, and all other Powers vested by this Constitution in the Government of the United States, or in any Department or Officer thereof.

Section 9.   [1] The Migration or Importation of Such Persons as any of the States now existing shall think proper to admit, shall not be prohibited by the Congress prior to the Year one thousand eight hundred and eight, but a Tax or duty may be imposed on such Importation, not exceeding ten dollars for each Person.

[2] The privilege of the Writ of Habeas Corpus shall not be suspended, unless when in Cases of Rebellion or Invasion the public Safety may require it.

[3] No Bill of Attainder or ex post facto Law shall be passed.

[4] No Capitation, or other direct, Tax shall be laid, unless in Proportion to the Census or Enumeration herein before directed to be taken.

[5] No Tax or Duty shall be laid on Articles exported from any State.

[6] No Preference shall be given by any Regulation of Commerce or Revenue to the Ports of one State over those of another: nor shall Vessels

bound to, or from, one State be obliged to enter, clear, or pay Duties in another.

[7]   No money shall be drawn from the Treasury, but in Consequence of Appropriations made by Law; and a regular Statement and Account of the Receipts and Expenditures of all public Money shall be published from time to time.

[8]   No Title of Nobility shall be granted by the United States: And no Person holding any Office of Profit or Trust under them, shall, without the Consent of the Congress, accept of any present, Emolument, Office, or Title, of any kind whatever, from any King, Prince, or foreign State.

Section 10.   [1]   No State shall enter into any Treaty, Alliance, or Confederation; grant Letters of Marque and Reprisal; coin Money; emit Bills of Credit; make any Thing but gold and silver Coin a Tender in Payment of Debts; pass any Bill of Attainder, ex post facto Law, or Law impairing the Obligation of Contracts, or grant any Title of Nobility.

[2]   No State shall, without the Consent of the Congress, lay any Imposts or Duties on Imports or Exports, except what may be absolutely necessary for executing it's inspection Laws: and the net Produce of all Duties and Imposts, laid by any State on Imports or Exports, shall be for the Use of the Treasury of the United States; and all such Laws shall be subject to the Revision and Controul of the Congress.

[3]   No State shall, without the Consent of Congress, lay any Duty of Tonnage, keep Troops, or Ships of War in time of Peace, enter into any Agreement or Compact with another State, or with a foreign Power, or engage in War, unless actually invaded, or in such imminent Danger as will not admit of delay.

ARTICLE II

Section 1.   [1]   The executive Power shall be vested in a President of the United States of America. He shall hold his Office during the Term of four Years, and, together with the Vice President, chosen for the same Term, be elected, as follows:

[2]   Each State shall appoint, in such Manner as the Legislature thereof may direct, a Number of Electors, equal to the whole Number of Senators and Representatives to which the State may be entitled in the Congress; but no Senator or Representative, or Person holding an Office of Trust or Profit under the United States, shall be appointed an Elector.

[3]   The Electors shall meet in their respective States, and vote by Ballot for two Persons, of whom one at least shall not be an Inhabitant of the same State with themselves. And they shall make a List of all the Persons voted for, and of the Number of Votes for each; which List they shall sign and certify, and transmit sealed to the Seat of the Government

of the United States, directed to the President of the Senate. The President of the Senate shall, in the Presence of the Senate and House of Representatives, open all the Certificates, and the Votes shall then be counted. The Person having the greatest Number of Votes shall be the President, if such Number be a Majority of the whole Number of Electors appointed; and if there be more than one who have such Majority, and have an equal Number of Votes, then the House of Representatives shall immediately chuse by Ballot one of them for President; and if no Person have a Majority, then from the five highest on the List the said House shall in like Manner chuse the President. But in chusing the President, the Votes shall be taken by States the Representation from each State having one Vote; A quorum for this Purpose shall consist of a Member or Members from two thirds of the States, and a Majority of all the States shall be necessary to a Choice. In every Case, after the Choice of the President, the Person having the greater Number of Votes of the Electors shall be the Vice President. But if there should remain two or more who have equal Votes, the Senate shall chuse from them by Ballot the Vice President.

[4]   The Congress may determine the Time of chusing the Electors, and the Day on which they shall give their Votes; which Day shall be the same throughout the United States.

[5]   No person except a natural born Citizen, or a Citizen of the United States, at the time of the Adoption of this Constitution, shall be eligible to the Office of President; neither shall any Person be eligible to that Office who shall not have attained to the Age of thirty five Years, and been fourteen Years a Resident within the United States.

[6]   In case of the removal of the President from Office, or of his Death, Resignation or Inability to discharge the Powers and Duties of the said Office, the Same shall devolve on the Vice President, and the Congress may by Law provide for the Case of Removal, Death, Resignation or Inability, both of the President and Vice President, declaring what Officer shall then act as President, and such Officer shall act accordingly, until the Disability be removed, or a President shall be elected.

[7]   The President shall, at stated Times, receive for his Services, a Compensation, which shall neither be increased nor diminished during the Period for which he shall have been elected, and he shall not receive within that Period any other Emolument from the United States, or any of them.

[8]   Before he enter on the Execution of his Office, he shall take the following Oath or Affirmation: "I do solemnly swear (or affirm) that I will faithfully execute the Office of President of the United States, and will to the best of my Ability, preserve, protect and defend the Constitution of the United States."

Section 2.   [1]   The President shall be Commander in Chief of the Army and Navy of the United States, and of the militia of the several

States, when called into the actual Service of the United States; he may require the Opinion, in writing, of the principal Officer in each of the Executive Departments, upon any Subject relating to the Duties of their respective Offices, and he shall have Power to grant Reprieves and Pardons for Offenses against the United States, except in Cases of Impeachment.

[2] He shall have Power, by and with the Advice and Consent of the Senate to make Treaties, provided two thirds of the Senators present concur; and he shall nominate, and by and with the Advice and Consent of the Senate, shall appoint Ambassadors, other public Ministers and Consuls, Judges of the supreme Court, and all other Officers of the United States, whose Appointments are not herein otherwise provided for, and which shall be established by Law; but the Congress may by Law vest the Appointment of such inferior Officers, as they think proper, in the President alone, in the Courts of Law, or in the Heads of Departments.

[3] The President shall have Power to fill up all Vacancies that may happen during the Recess of the Senate, by granting Commissions which shall expire at the End of their next Session.

Section 3. He shall from time to time give to the Congress Information of the State of the Union, and recommend to their Consideration such Measures as he shall judge necessary and expedient; he may, on extraordinary Occasions, convene both Houses, or either of them, and in Case of Disagreement between them, with Respect to the Time of Adjournment, he may adjourn them to such Time as he shall think proper; he shall receive Ambassadors and other public Ministers; he shall take Care that the Laws be faithfully executed, and shall Commission all the Officers of the United States.

Section 4. The President, Vice President and all civil Officers of the United States, shall be removed from Office on Impeachment for, and Conviction of, Treason, Bribery, or other high Crimes and Misdemeanors.

ARTICLE III

Section 1. The judicial Power of the United States, shall be vested in one supreme Court, and in such inferior Courts as the Congress may from time to time ordain and establish. The Judges, both of the supreme and inferior Courts, shall hold their Offices during good Behaviour, and shall, at stated Times, receive for their Services a Compensation, which shall not be diminished during their Continuance in Office.

Section 2. [1] The judicial Power shall extend to all Cases, in Law and Equity, arising under this Constitution, the Laws of the United States, and Treaties made, or which shall be made, under their Authority;—to all Cases affecting Ambassadors, other public Ministers and Consuls;—to all Cases of admiralty and maritime Jurisdiction;—to Controversies to which the United States shall be a Party;—to Controversies between two or more States;—between a State and Citizens of another State;—between Citizens of different States;—between Citizens of the same State claiming Lands under the Grants of different States, and between a State, or the Citizens thereof, and foreign States, Citizens or Subjects.

[2] In all Cases affecting Ambassadors, other public Ministers and Consuls, and those in which a State shall be a Party, the supreme Court shall have original Jurisdiction. In all the other Cases before mentioned, the supreme Court shall have appellate Jurisdiction, both as to Law and Fact, with such Exceptions, and under such Regulations as the Congress shall make.

[3] The trial of all Crimes, except in Cases of Impeachment, shall be by Jury; and such Trial shall be held in the State where the said Crimes shall have been committed; but when not committed within any State, the Trial shall be at such Place or Places as the Congress may by Law have directed.

Section 3.   [1] Treason against the United States, shall consist only in levying War against them, or, in adhering to their Enemies, giving them Aid and Comfort. No Person shall be convicted of Treason unless on the Testimony of two Witnesses to the same overt Act, or on Confession in open Court.

[2] The Congress shall have Power to declare the Punishment of Treason, but no Attainder of Treason shall work Corruption of Blood, or Forfeiture except during the Life of the Person attainted.

ARTICLE IV

Section 1.   Full Faith and Credit shall be given in each State to the public Acts, Records, and judicial Proceedings of every other State. And the Congress may by general Laws prescribe the Manner in which such Acts, Records and Proceedings shall be proved, and the Effect thereof.

Section 2.   [1] The Citizens of each State shall be entitled to all Privileges and Immunities of Citizens in the several States.

[2] A Person charged in any State with Treason, Felony, or other Crime, who shall flee from Justice, and be found in another State, shall on demand of the executive Authority of the State from which he fled, be delivered up, to be removed to the State having Jurisdiction of the Crime.

[3] No Person held to Service or Labour in one State, under the Laws thereof, escaping into another, shall, in Consequence of any Law or Regulation therein, be discharged from such Service or Labour, but shall be delivered up on Claim of the Party to whom such Service or Labour may be due.

Section 3.   [1] New States may be admitted by the Congress into this Union; but no new State shall be formed or erected within the Jurisdiction of any other State; nor any State be formed by the Junction of two or more States, or Parts of States, without the Consent of the Legislatures of the States concerned as well as of the Congress.

[2] The Congress shall have Power to dispose of and make all needful Rules and Regulations respecting the Territory or other Property belonging to the United States; and nothing in this Constitution shall be so construed as to Prejudice any Claims of the United States, or of any particular State.

Section 4.   The United States shall guarantee to every State in this Union a Republican Form of Government, and shall protect each of them against Invasion; and on Application of the Legislature, or of the Executive (when the Legislature cannot be convened) against domestic Violence.

ARTICLE V

The Congress, whenever two thirds of both Houses shall deem it necessary, shall propose Amendments to this Constitution, or, on the Application of the Legislatures of two thirds of the several States, shall call a Convention for proposing Amendments, which, in either Case, shall be valid to all Intents and Purposes, as part of this Constitution, when ratified by the Legislatures of three fourths of the several States, or by Conventions in three fourths thereof, as the one or the other Mode of Ratification may be proposed by the Congress; Provided that no Amendment which may be made prior to the Year One thousand eight hundred and eight shall in any Manner affect the first and fourth Clauses in the Ninth Section of the first Article; and that no State, without its Consent, shall be deprived of its equal Suffrage in the Senate.

ARTICLE VI

[1] All Debts contracted and Engagements entered into, before the Adoption of this Constitution shall be as valid against the United States under this Constitution, as under the Confederation.

[2] This Constitution, and the Laws of the United States which shall be made in Pursuance thereof; and all Treaties made, or which shall be made, under the Authority of the United States, shall be the supreme Law of the Land; and the Judges in every State shall be bound thereby, any Thing in the Constitution or Laws of any State to the Contrary notwithstanding.

[3] The Senators and Representatives before mentioned, and the Members of the several State Legislatures, and all executive and judicial Officers, both of the United States and of the several States, shall be bound by Oath or Affirmation, to support this Constitution; but no religious Test

shall ever be required as a Qualification to any Office or public Trust under the United States.

ARTICLE VII

The Ratification of the Conventions of nine States shall be sufficient for the Establishment of this Constitution between the States so ratifying the Same.

AMENDMENTS OF THE CONSTITUTION OF THE UNITED STATES OF AMERICA

AMENDMENT I [1791]

Congress shall make no law respecting an establishment of religion, or prohibiting the free exercise thereof; or abridging the freedom of speech, or of the press; or the right of the people peaceably to assemble, and to petition the Government for a redress of grievances.

AMENDMENT II [1791]

A well regulated Militia, being necessary to the security of a free State, the right of the people to keep and bear Arms, shall not be infringed.

AMENDMENT III [1791]

No Soldier shall, in time of peace be quartered in any house, without the consent of the Owner, nor in time of war, but in a manner to be prescribed by law.

AMENDMENT IV [1791]

The right of the people to be secure in their persons, houses, papers, and effects, against unreasonable searches and seizures, shall not be violated, and no Warrants shall issue, but upon probable cause, supported by Oath or affirmation and particularly describing the place to be searched, and the persons or things to be seized.

AMENDMENT V [1791]

No person shall be held to answer for a capital, or otherwise infamous crime, unless on a presentment or indictment of a Grand Jury, except in cases arising in the land or naval forces, or in the Militia, when in actual service in time of War or public danger; nor shall any person be subject for the same offence to be twice put in jeopardy of life or limb; nor shall be compelled in any criminal case to be a witness against himself, nor be deprived of life, liberty, or property, without due process of law; nor shall private property be taken for public use, without just compensation.

AMENDMENT VI [1791]

In all criminal prosecutions, the accused shall enjoy the right to a speedy and public trial, by an impartial jury of the State and district wherein the crime shall have been committed, which district shall have been previously ascertained by law, and to be informed of the nature and cause of the accusation; to be confronted with the witnesses against him; to have compulsory process for obtaining witnesses in his favor, and to have the Assistance of Counsel for his defence.

AMENDMENT VII [1791]

In Suits at common law, where the value in controversy shall exceed twenty dollars, the right of trial by jury shall be preserved, and no fact tried by jury, shall be otherwise re-examined in any Court of the United States, than according to the rules of the common law.

AMENDMENT VIII [1791]

Excessive bail shall not be required, nor excessive fines imposed, nor cruel and unusual punishments inflicted.

AMENDMENT IX [1791]

The enumeration in the Constitution, of certain rights, shall not be construed to deny or disparage others retained by the people.

AMENDMENT X [1791]

The powers not delegated to the United States by the Constitution, nor prohibited by it to the States, are reserved to the States respectively, or to the people.

AMENDMENT XI [1798]

The Judicial power of the United States shall not be construed to extend to any suit in law or equity, commenced or prosecuted against one of the United States by Citizens of another State, or by Citizens or Subjects of any Foreign State.

AMENDMENT XII [1804]

The Electors shall meet in their respective states and vote by ballot for President and Vice-President, one of whom, at least, shall not be an inhabitant of the same state with themselves; they shall name in their ballots the person voted for as President, and in distinct ballots the person voted for as Vice-President, and they shall make distinct lists of all persons voted for as President, and of all persons voted for as Vice-President, and of the number of votes for each, which lists they shall sign and certify, and transmit sealed to the seat of the government of the United States, directed to the President of the Senate;—The President of the Senate shall, in the presence of the Senate and House of Representatives, open all the certificates and the votes shall then be counted;—The person having the greatest number of votes for President, shall be the President, if such number be a majority of the whole number of Electors appointed; and if no person have such majority, then from the persons having the highest numbers not exceeding three on the list of those voted for as President, the House of Representatives shall choose immediately, by ballot, the President. But in choosing the President, the votes shall be taken by states, the representation from each state having one vote; a quorum for this purpose shall consist of a member or members from two-thirds of the states, and a majority of all the states shall be necessary to a choice. And if the House of Representatives shall not choose a President whenever the right of choice shall devolve upon them before the fourth day of March next following, then the Vice-President shall act as President, as in the case of the death or other constitutional disability of the President.—The person having the greatest number of votes as Vice-President, shall be the Vice-President, if such number be a majority of the whole number of Electors appointed, and if no person have a majority, then from the two highest numbers on the list, the Senate shall choose the Vice-President; a quorum for the purpose shall consist of two-thirds of the whole number of Senators, and a majority of the whole number shall be necessary to a choice. But no person constitutionally ineligible to the office of President shall be eligible to that of Vice-President of the United States.

AMENDMENT XIII [1865]

Section 1.   Neither slavery nor involuntary servitude, except as a punishment for crime whereof the party shall have been duly convicted, shall exist within the United States, or any place subject to their jurisdiction.

Section 2.   Congress shall have power to enforce this article by appropriate legislation.

AMENDMENT XIV [1868]

Section 1.   All persons born or naturalized in the United States, and subject to the jurisdiction thereof, are citizens of the United States and of the State wherein they reside. No State shall make or enforce any law which shall abridge the privileges or immunities of citizens of the United States; nor shall any State deprive any person of life, liberty, or property, without due process of law; nor deny to any person within its jurisdiction the equal protection of the laws.

Section 2.   Representatives shall be apportioned among the several States according to their respective numbers, counting the whole number of persons in each State, excluding Indians not taxed. But when the right to vote at any election for the choice of electors for President and Vice President of the United States, Representatives in Congress, the Executive and Judicial officers of a State, or the members of the Legislature thereof, is denied to any of the male inhabitants of such State, being twenty-one years of age, and citizens of the United States, or in any way abridged, except for participation in rebellion, or other crime, the basis of representation therein shall be reduced in the proportion which the number of such male citizens shall bear to the whole number of male citizens twenty-one years of age in such State.

Section 3.   No person shall be a Senator or Representative in Congress, or elector of President and Vice President, or hold any office, civil or military, under the United States, or under any State, who having previously taken an oath, as a member of Congress, or as an officer of the United States, or as a member of any State legislature, or as an executive or judicial officer of any State, to support the Constitution of the United States, shall have engaged in insurrection or rebellion against the same, or given aid or comfort to the enemies thereof. But Congress may by a vote of two-thirds of each House, remove such disability.

Section 4.   The validity of the public debt of the United States, authorized by law, including debts incurred for payment of pensions and bounties for services in suppressing insurrection or rebellion, shall not be questioned. But neither the United States nor any State shall assume or pay any debt or obligation incurred in aid of insurrection or rebellion against the United States, or any claim for the loss or emancipation of any slave; but all such debts, obligations and claims shall be held illegal and void.

Section 5.   The Congress shall have power to enforce, by appropriate legislation, the provisions of this article.

AMENDMENT XV [1870]

Section 1.   The right of citizens of the United States to vote shall not be denied or abridged by the United States or by any State on account of race, color, or previous condition of servitude.

Section 2.   The Congress shall have power to enforce this article by appropriate legislation.

AMENDMENT XVI [1913]

The Congress shall have power to lay and collect taxes on incomes, from whatever source derived, without apportionment among the several States, and without regard to any census or enumeration.

AMENDMENT XVII [1913]

[1] The Senate of the United States shall be composed of two Senators from each State, elected by the people thereof, for six years; and each Senator shall have one vote. The electors in each State shall have the qualifications requisite for electors of the most numerous branch of the State legislatures.

[2] When vacancies happen in the representation of any State in the Senate, the executive authority of such State shall issue writs of election to fill such vacancies: Provided, That the legislature of any State may empower the executive thereof to make temporary appointments until the people fill the vacancies by election as the legislature may direct.

[3] This amendment shall not be so construed as to affect the election or term of any Senator chosen before it becomes valid as part of the Constitution.

AMENDMENT XVIII [1919]

Section 1.   After one year from the ratification of this article the manufacture, sale, or transportation of intoxicating liquors within, the importation thereof into, or the exportation thereof from the United States and all territory subject to the jurisdiction thereof for beverage purposes is hereby prohibited.

Section 2.   The Congress and the several States shall have concurrent power to enforce this article by appropriate legislation.

Section 3.   This article shall be inoperative unless it shall have been ratified as an amendment to the Constitution by the legislatures of the several States, as provided in the Constitution, within seven years from the date of the submission hereof to the States by the Congress.

AMENDMENT XIX [1920]

[1] The right of citizens of the United States to vote shall not be denied or abridged by the United States or by any State on account of sex.

[2] Congress shall have power to enforce this article by appropriate legislation.

AMENDMENT XX [1933]

Section 1.   The terms of the President and Vice President shall end at noon on the 20th day of January, and the terms of Senators and Representatives at noon on the 3d day of January, of the years in which such terms would have ended if this article had not been ratified; and the terms of their successors shall then begin.

Section 2.   The Congress shall assemble at least once in every year, and such meeting shall begin at noon on the 3d day of January, unless they shall by law appoint a different day.

Section 3.   If, at the time fixed for the beginning of the term of the President, the President elect shall have died, the Vice President elect shall become President. If the President shall not have been chosen before the time fixed for the beginning of his term, or if the President elect shall have failed to qualify, then the Vice President elect shall act as President until a President shall have qualified; and the Congress may by law provide for the case wherein neither a President elect nor a Vice President elect shall have qualified, declaring who shall then act as President, or the manner in which one who is to act shall be selected, and such person shall act accordingly until a President or Vice President shall have qualified.

Section 4.   The Congress may by law provide for the case of the death of any of the persons from whom the House of Representatives may choose a President whenever the right of choice shall have devolved upon them, and for the case of the death of any of the persons from whom the Senate may choose a Vice President whenever the right of choice shall have devolved upon them.

Section 5.   Sections 1 and 2 shall take effect on the 15th day of October following the ratification of this article.

Section 6.   This article shall be inoperative unless it shall have been ratified as an amendment to the Constitution by the legislatures of three-fourths of the several States within seven years from the date of its submission.

AMENDMENT XXI [1933]

Section 1.   The eighteenth article of amendment to the Constitution of the United States is hereby repealed.

Section 2.   The transportation or importation into any State, Territory, or possession of the United States for delivery or use therein of intoxicating liquors, in violation of the laws thereof, is hereby prohibited.

Section 3.   This article shall be inoperative unless it shall have been ratified as an amendment to the Constitution by conventions in the several

States, as provided in the Constitution, within seven years from the date of the submission hereof to the States by the Congress.

AMENDMENT XXII [1951]

Section 1.   No person shall be elected to the office of the President more than twice, and no person who has held the office of President, or acted as President, for more than two years of a term to which some other person was elected President shall be elected to the office of President more than once. But this Article shall not apply to any person holding the office of President when this Article was proposed by the Congress, and shall not prevent any person who may be holding the office of President, or acting as President, during the term within which this Article becomes operative from holding the office of President or acting as President during the remainder of such term.

Section 2.   This article shall be inoperative unless it shall have been ratified as an amendment to the Constitution by the legislatures of three-fourths of the several States within seven years from the date of its submission to the States by the Congress.

AMENDMENT XXIII [1961]

Section 1.   The District constituting the seat of Government of the United States shall appoint in such manner as the Congress may direct: A number of electors of President and Vice President equal to the whole number of Senators and Representatives in Congress to which the District would be entitled if it were a State, but in no event more than the least populous state; they shall be in addition to those appointed by the states, but they shall be considered, for the purposes of the election of President and Vice President, to be electors appointed by a state; and they shall meet in the District and perform such duties as provided by the twelfth article of amendment.

Section 2.   The Congress shall have power to enforce this article by appropriate legislation.

AMENDMENT XXIV [1964]

Section 1.   The right of citizens of the United States to vote in any primary or other election for President or Vice President, for electors for President or Vice President, or for Senator or Representative in Congress, shall not be denied or abridged by the United States or any State by reason of failure to pay any poll tax or other tax.

Section 2.   The Congress shall have power to enforce this article by appropriate legislation.

AMENDMENT XXV [1967]

Section 1.   In case of the removal of the President from office or of his death or resignation, the Vice President shall become President.

Section 2.   Whenever there is a vacancy in the office of the Vice President, the President shall nominate a Vice President who shall take office upon confirmation by a majority vote of both Houses of Congress.

Section 3.   Whenever the President transmits to the President pro tempore of the Senate and the Speaker of the House of Representatives his written declaration that he is unable to discharge the powers and duties of his office, and until he transmits to them a written declaration to the contrary, such powers and duties shall be discharged by the Vice President as Acting President.

Section 4.   Whenever the Vice President and a majority of either the principal officers of the executive departments or of such other body as Congress may by law provide, transmit to the President pro tempore of the Senate and the Speaker of the House of Representatives their written declaration that the President is unable to discharge the powers and duties of his office, the Vice President shall immediately assume the powers and duties of the office as Acting President. Thereafter, when the President transmits to the President pro tempore of the Senate and the Speaker of the House of Representatives his written declaration that no inability exists, he shall resume the powers and duties of his office unless the Vice President and a majority of either the principal officers of the executive department or of such other body as Congress may by law provide, transmit within four days to the President pro tempore of the Senate and the Speaker of the House of Representatives their written declaration that the President is unable to discharge the powers and duties of his office. Thereupon Congress shall decide the issue, assembling within forty-eight hours for that purpose if not in session. If the Congress, within twenty-one days after receipt of the latter written declaration, or, if Congress is not in session, within twenty-one days after Congress is required to assemble, determines by two-thirds vote of both Houses that the President is unable to discharge the powers and duties of his office, the Vice President shall continue to discharge the same as Acting President; otherwise, the President shall resume the powers and duties of his office.

AMENDMENT XXVI [1971]

Section 1.   The right of citizens of the United States, who are eighteen years of age or older, to vote shall not be denied or abridged by the United States or by any State on account of age.

Section 2.   The Congress shall have power to enforce this article by appropriate legislation.

AMENDMENT XXVII [1992]

No law, varying compensation for the services of Senators and Representatives, shall take effect, until an election of Representatives shall have intervened.

APPENDIX B

TABLE OF U.S. SUPREME COURT JUSTICES

■ ■ ■

Chief Justices

Name	State Appointment from	Appointed by President	Judicial Oath Taken	Date Service Terminated
Jay, John	New York	Washington	(a) October 19, 1789	June 29, 1795
Rutledge, John	South Carolina	Washington	August 12, 1795	December 15, 1795
Ellsworth, Oliver	Connecticut	Washington	March 8, 1796	December 15, 1800
Marshall, John	Virginia	Adams, John	February 4, 1801	July 6, 1835
Taney, Roger Brooke	Maryland	Jackson	March 28, 1836	October 12, 1864
Chase, Salmon Portland	Ohio	Lincoln	December 15, 1864	May 7, 1873
Waite, Morrison Remick	Ohio	Grant	March 4, 1874	March 23, 1888
Fuller, Melville Weston	Illinois	Cleveland	October 8, 1888	July 4, 1910
White, Edward Douglass	Louisiana	Taft	December 19, 1910	May 19, 1921
Taft, William Howard	Connecticut	Harding	July 11, 1921	February 3, 1930
Hughes, Charles Evans	New York	Hoover	February 24, 1930	June 30, 1941
Stone, Harlan Fiske	New York	Roosevelt, F.	July 3, 1941	April 22, 1946
Vinson, Fred Moore	Kentucky	Truman	June 24, 1946	September 8, 1953
Warren, Earl	California	Eisenhower	October 5, 1953	June 23, 1969
Burger, Warren Earl	Virginia	Nixon	June 23, 1969	September 26, 1986
Rehnquist, William H.	Virginia	Reagan	September 26, 1986	September 3, 2005
Roberts, John G., Jr.	Maryland	Bush, G.W.	September 29, 2005	

Associate Justices

Name	State Appointment from	Appointed by President	Judicial Oath Taken	Date Service Terminated
Rutledge, John	South Carolina	Washington	(a) February 15, 1790	March 5, 1791
Cushing, William	Massachusetts	Washington	(c) February 2, 1790	September 13, 1810
Wilson, James	Pennsylvania	Washington	(b) October 5, 1789	August 21, 1798
Blair, John	Virginia	Washington	(c) February 2, 1790	October 25, 1795
Iredell, James	North Carolina	Washington	(b) May 12, 1790	October 20, 1799
Johnson, Thomas	Maryland	Washington	(a) August 6, 1792	January 16, 1793
Paterson, William	New Jersey	Washington	(a) March 11, 1793	September 9, 1806
Chase, Samuel	Maryland	Washington	February 4, 1796	June 19, 1811
Washington, Bushrod	Virginia	Adams, John	(c) February 4, 1799	November 26, 1829
Moore, Alfred	North Carolina	Adams, John	(a) April 21, 1800	January 26, 1804
Johnson, William	South Carolina	Jefferson	May 7, 1804	August 4, 1834
Livingston, Henry Brockholst	New York	Jefferson	January 20, 1807	March 18, 1823
Todd, Thomas	Kentucky	Jefferson	(a) May 4, 1807	February 7, 1826
Duvall, Gabriel	Maryland	Madison	(a) November 23, 1811	January 14, 1835
Story, Joseph	Massachusetts	Madison	(c) February 3, 1812	September 10, 1845
Thompson, Smith	New York	Monroe	(b) September 1, 1823	December 18, 1843
Trimble, Robert	Kentucky	Adams, J. Q.	(a) June 16, 1826	August 25, 1828
McLean, John	Ohio	Jackson	(c) January 11, 1830	April 4, 1861
Baldwin, Henry	Pennsylvania	Jackson	January 18, 1830	April 21, 1844
Wayne, James Moore	Georgia	Jackson	January 14, 1835	July 5, 1867
Barbour, Philip Pendleton	Virginia	Jackson	May 12, 1836	February 25, 1841
Catron, John	Tennessee	Jackson	May 1, 1837	May 30, 1865
McKinley, John	Alabama	Van Buren	(c) January 9, 1838	July 19, 1852
Daniel, Peter Vivian	Virginia	Van Buren	(c) January 10, 1842	May 31, 1860
Nelson, Samuel	New York	Tyler	February 27, 1845	November 28, 1872
Woodbury, Levi	New Hampshire	Polk	(b) September 23, 1845	September 4, 1851
Grier, Robert Cooper	Pennsylvania	Polk	August 10, 1846	January 31, 1870
Curtis, Benjamin Robbins	Massachusetts	Fillmore	(b) October 10, 1851	September 30, 1857

Associate Justices

Name	State Appointment from	Appointed by President	Judicial Oath Taken	Date Service Terminated
Campbell, John Archibald	Alabama	Pierce	(c) April 11, 1853	April 30, 1861
Clifford, Nathan	Maine	Buchanan	January 21, 1858	July 25, 1881
Swayne, Noah Haynes	Ohio	Lincoln	January 27, 1862	January 24, 1881
Miller, Samuel Freeman	Iowa	Lincoln	July 21, 1862	October 13, 1890
Davis, David	Illinois	Lincoln	December 10, 1862	March 4, 1877
Field, Stephen Johnson	California	Lincoln	May 20, 1863	December 1, 1897
Strong, William	Pennsylvania	Grant	March 14, 1870	December 14, 1880
Bradley, Joseph P.	New Jersey	Grant	March 23, 1870	January 22, 1892
Hunt, Ward	New York	Grant	January 9, 1873	January 27, 1882
Harlan, John Marshall	Kentucky	Hayes	December 10 1877	October 14, 1911
Woods, William Burnham	Georgia	Hayes	January 5, 1881	May 14, 1887
Matthews, Stanley	Ohio	Garfield	May 17, 1881	March 22, 1889
Gray, Horace	Massachusetts	Arthur	January 9, 1882	September 15, 1902
Blatchford, Samuel	New York	Arthur	April 3, 1882	July 7, 1893
Lamar, Lucius Quintus C.	Mississippi	Cleveland	January 18, 1888	January 23, 1893
Brewer, David Josiah	Kansas	Harrison	January 6, 1890	March 28, 1910
Brown, Henry Billings	Michigan	Harrison	January 5, 1891	May 28, 1906
Shiras, George, Jr.	Pennsylvania	Harrison	October 10, 1892	February 23, 1903
Jackson, Howell Edmunds	Tennessee	Harrison	March 4, 1893	August 8, 1895
White, Edward Douglass	Louisiana	Cleveland	March 12, 1894	December 18, 1910*
Peckham, Rufus Wheeler	New York	Cleveland	January 6, 1896	October 24, 1909
McKenna, Joseph	California	McKinley	January 26, 1898	January 5, 1925
Holmes, Oliver Wendell	Massachusetts	Roosevelt, T.	December 8, 1902	January 12, 1932
Day, William Rufus	Ohio	Roosevelt, T.	March 2, 1903	November 13, 1922
Moody, William Henry	Massachusetts	Roosevelt, T.	December 17, 1906	November 20, 1910

---

*   Elevated

Associate Justices

Name	State Appointment from	Appointed by President	Judicial Oath Taken	Date Service Terminated
Lurton, Horace Harmon	Tennessee	Taft	January 3, 1910	July 12, 1914
Hughes, Charles Evans	New York	Taft	October 10, 1910	June 10, 1916
Van Devanter, Willis	Wyoming	Taft	January 3, 1911	June 2, 1937
Lamar, Joseph Rucker	Georgia	Taft	January 3, 1911	January 2, 1916
Pitney, Mahlon	New Jersey	Taft	March 18, 1912	December 31, 1922
McReynolds, James Clark	Tennessee	Wilson	October 12, 1914	January 31, 1941
Brandeis, Louis Dembitz	Massachusetts	Wilson	June 5,1916	February 13, 1939
Clarke, John Hessin	Ohio	Wilson	October 9, 1916	September 18, 1922
Sutherland, George	Utah	Harding	October 2, 1922	January 17, 1938
Butler, Pierce	Minnesota	Harding	January 2, 1923	November 16, 1939
Sanford, Edward Terry	Tennessee	Harding	February 19, 1923	March 8, 1930
Stone, Harlan Fiske	New York	Coolidge	March 2, 1925	July 2, 1941*
Roberts, Owen Josephus	Pennsylvania	Hoover	June 2, 1930	July 31, 1945
Cardozo, Benjamin Nathan	New York	Hoover	March 14, 1932	July 9, 1938
Black, Hugo Lafayette	Alabama	Roosevelt, F.	August 19, 1937	September 17, 1971
Reed, Stanley Forman	Kentucky	Roosevelt, F.	January 31, 1938	February 25, 1957
Frankfurter, Felix	Massachusetts	Roosevelt, F.	January 30, 1939	August 28, 1962
Douglas, William Orville	Connecticut	Roosevelt, F.	April 17, 1939	November 12, 1975
Murphy, Frank	Michigan	Roosevelt, F.	February 5, 1940	July 19, 1949
Byrnes, James Francis	South Carolina	Roosevelt, F.	July 8, 1941	October 3, 1942
Jackson, Robert Houghwout	New York	Roosevelt, F.	July 11, 1941	October 9, 1954
Rutledge, Wiley Blount	Iowa	Roosevelt, F.	February 15, 1943	September 10, 1949
Burton, Harold Hitz	Ohio	Truman	October 1, 1945	October 13, 1958
Clark, Tom Campbell	Texas	Truman	August 24, 1949	June 12, 1967
Minton, Sherman	Indiana	Truman	October 12, 1949	October 15, 1956
Harlan, John Marshall	New York	Eisenhower	March 28, 1955	September 23, 1971

*   Elevated

Associate Justices

Name	State Appointment from	Appointed by President	Judicial Oath Taken	Date Service Terminated
Brennan, William J., Jr.	New Jersey	Eisenhower	October 16, 1956	July 20, 1990
Whittaker, Charles Evans	Missouri	Eisenhower	March 25, 1957	March 31, 1962
Stewart, Potter	Ohio	Eisenhower	October 14, 1958	July 3, 1981
White, Byron Raymond	Colorado	Kennedy	April 16, 1962	June 28, 1993
Goldberg, Arthur Joseph	Illinois	Kennedy	October 1, 1962	July 25, 1965
Fortas, Abe	Tennessee	Johnson, L.	October 4, 1965	May 14, 1969
Marshall, Thurgood	New York	Johnson, L.	October 2, 1967	October 1, 1991
Blackmun, Harry A.	Minnesota	Nixon	June 9, 1970	August 3, 1994
Powell, Lewis F., Jr.	Virginia	Nixon	January 7, 1972	June 26, 1987
Rehnquist, William H.	Arizona	Nixon	January 7, 1972	September 26, 1986*
Stevens, John Paul	Illinois	Ford	December 19, 1975	June 29, 2010
O'Connor, Sandra Day	Arizona	Reagan	September 25, 1981	January 31, 2006
Scalia, Antonin	Virginia	Reagan	September 26, 1986	February 13, 2016
Kennedy, Anthony M.	California	Reagan	February 18, 1988	July 31, 2018
Souter, David H.	New Hampshire	Bush, G.H.W.	October 9, 1990	June 29, 2009
Thomas, Clarence	Georgia	Bush, G.H.W.	October 23, 1991	
Ginsburg, Ruth Bader	New York	Clinton	August 10, 1993	September 18, 2020
Breyer, Stephen G.	Massachusetts	Clinton	August 3, 1994	June 30, 2022
Alito, Samuel A., Jr.	New Jersey	Bush, G.W.	January 31, 2006	
Sotomayor, Sonia	New York	Obama	August 8, 2009	
Kagan, Elena	Massachusetts	Obama	August 7, 2010	
Gorsuch, Neil M.	Colorado	Trump	April 10, 2017	
Kavanaugh, Brett M.	Maryland	Trump	October 6, 2018	
Barrett, Amy Coney	Indiana	Trump	October 27, 2020	
Jackson, Ketanji Onyika Brown	District of Columbia	Biden	June 30, 2022	

---

* Elevated

Notes: The acceptance of the appointment and commission by the appointee, as evidenced by the taking of the prescribed oaths, is here implied; otherwise the individual is not carried on this list of the Members of the Court. Examples: Robert Hanson Harrison is not carried, as a letter from President Washington of February 9, 1790 states Harrison declined to serve. Neither is Edwin M. Stanton who died before he could take the necessary steps toward becoming a Member of the Court. Chief Justice Rutledge is included because he took his oaths, presided over the August Term of 1795, and his name appears on two opinions of the Court for that Term.

The date a Member of the Court took his/her Judicial oath (the Judiciary Act provided "That the Justices of the Supreme Court, and the district judges, before they proceed to execute the duties of their respective offices, shall take the following oath . . . ") is here used as the date of the beginning of his/her service, for until that oath is taken he/she is not vested with the prerogatives of the office. The dates given in this column are for the oaths taken following the receipt of the commissions. Dates without small-letter references are taken from the Minutes of the Court or from the original oath which are in the Curator's collection. The small letter (a) denotes the date is from the Minutes of some other court; (b) from some other unquestionable authority; (c) from authority that is questionable, and better authority would be appreciated.

Source: Website of the Supreme Court of the United States, www. supremecourt.gov/about/members_text.aspx.

INDEX

References are to Pages
